ZIZHI TONGJIAN

WARRING STATES AND QIN

BY SIMA GUANG

VOLUME 1 TO 8 403-207 BCE

TRANSLATED BY

JOSEPH P. YAP

WITH ANNOTATIONS AND TRANSLATION OF YANG KUAN'S

TEXTUAL RESEARCH ON THE WARRING STATES

2016

The Seven States and Zhou

Chu	楚
Hann	韓
Qi	齊
Qin	秦
Wei	魏
Yan	燕
Zhao	趙
Zhou	周

Ethnic Tribes and Minor States

Dong-Hu	東胡
Ba	巴
Lin-Hu	林胡
Min-Yue	閩越
Shu	蜀
Xiongnu	匈奴
Yue	越
Yueshi	月氏
Loufan	樓煩
Qiang	羌
Yelang	夜郎
Luo-Yue	駱越
Yang	揚
Shan-Rong	山戎
Sushen	肅慎

Cities

1.	Ying	郢
2.	Yiyang	宜陽
3.	Zheng	鄭
4.	Daliang	大梁
5.	Chen	陳
6.	Shouchun	壽春
7.	Anyi	安邑
8.	Handan	邯鄲
9.	Pingyang	平陽
10.	Xianyang	咸陽
11.	Yong	雍
12.	Jingyang	涇陽
13.	Yueyang	櫟陽
14.	Qufu	曲阜
15.	Linzi	臨淄
16.	Ji	薊
17.	Jinyang	晉陽
18.	Luoyang	洛陽

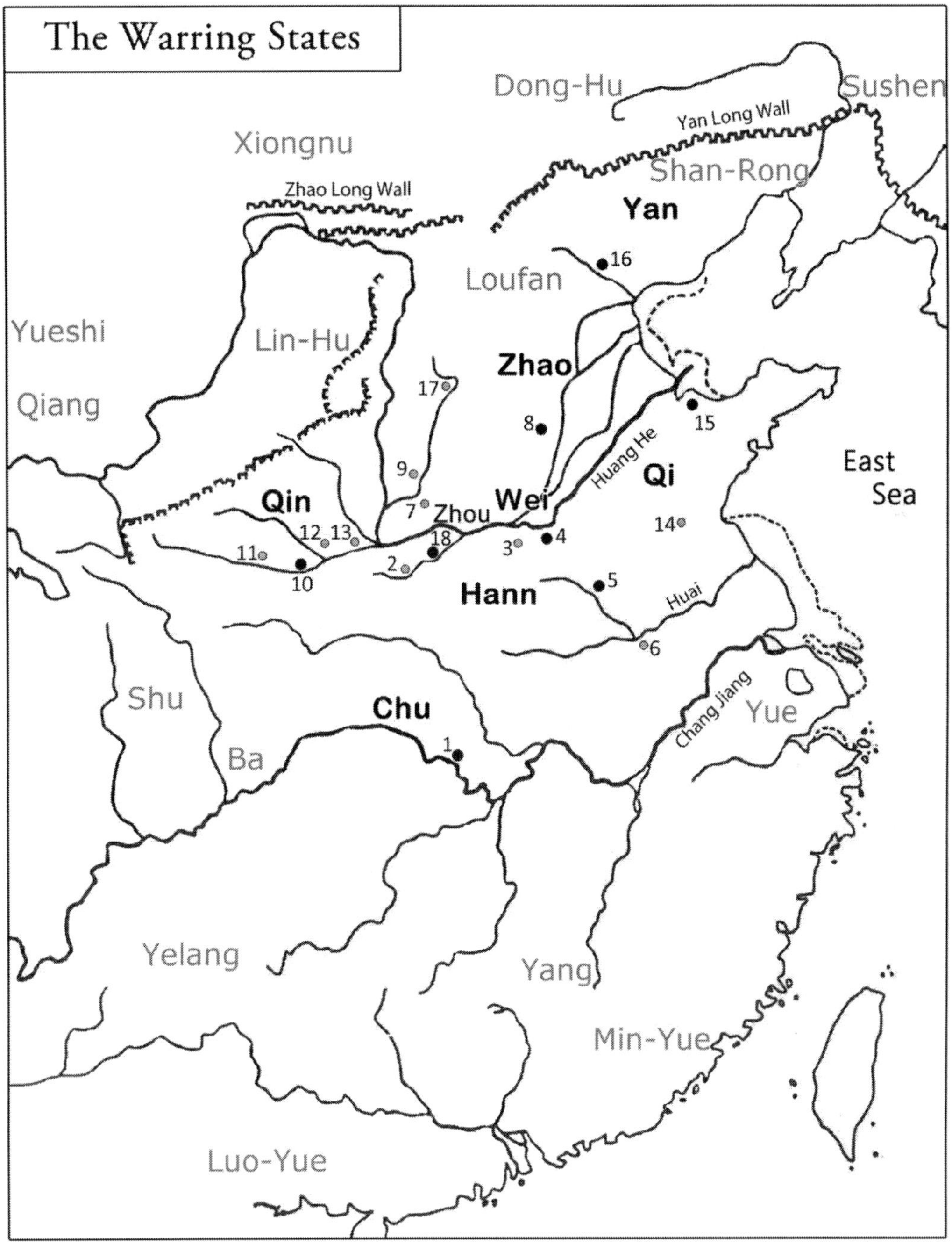

The Warring States

First published by CreateSpace
May 2016.

ISBN-13: 978-1533086938

ISBN-10: 1533086931

LCCN: 2016908788

Contents

Acknowledgements

I published my first book, the *Wars with the Xiongnu* in 2009. Ever since its publication, I noticed how inadequate it was. I had intended to re-write the entire book. However, I realized that it would serve little purpose; I then decided to rewrite the chapters I translated from *Zizhi tongjian* in entirety, reasoning that I had skipped many thorny, nonetheless, critical passages, which I found difficult to comprehend let alone translating when I was working on the *Wars*. Little did I realize it would take me four years to come up with a draft for the first eight volumes of *Zizhi tongjian*. The first draft was initially completed in spring of 2015.

I am greatly indebted to John E. Hills, the author of the *Through the Jade Gate to Rome* and his wife Jo Hill, who offered to edit my first draft. They had provided me with invaluable information on how a proper historical text should be written. After I completed my first draft in spring of 2015, I sent Volume One to Professor Michael Nylan of UC Berkley, who with her immense experience and expertise made a number of critical comments - on my translation, the sources, and annotations - in one single paragraph. In the meantime, Li Ho Cheung, a classmate from fifty years back sent me a chapter on 'Translating Texts in Chinese History and Philosophy' by Professor Nylan. The article shed a different perspective of how translation work should be done. Being an amateur and untaught historian, I had little conception of the complicities of translation. I had indeed underrated the importance of subtleties and intricacies of translation. Having spent many sleepless nights in April of 2015 after reading the Professor's email, I resorted to going back to the drawing board to rewrite the entire work from original sources, which had taken me almost eight months in the process. I am hence greatly indebted to Professor Nylan invaluable comments and inputs, although our communication was limited to the single email exchange. The revised work, I hope could be considered more acceptable by the academia, particularly coming from an amateur with little or no academic background in history.

I owe special thanks to Simon Johnston, who spent hours to do the proofreading and formatting of my final draft and especially grateful to him for preparing the computer graphics of the front cover of the book based on the imagery and elements I envisaged. I also have to thank him for doing the map. As Mr. Johnston is not literate in Chinese, he merely proofread the translated parts of the work; I am responsible for all the mistakes.

Translator's notes

The author principally based the translation of this book on Li Zongtong's *Zizhi tongjian jinzhu*. The book does not tender any translation of the classical text into modern Chinese, except it has a copious amount of annotations, elucidations of terms and research data. The other source the author draws from is Chen Liankang's translation from the classical text to the contemporary Chinese. The often-obscured meanings of classical Chinese writing, in many instances due to its laconic nature, are subjected to disparate interpretations and much scholarly debates. Furthermore, language and usages of words and phrases evolved with time, when *Zizhi tongjian* was committed in writing it was twelve centuries removed from the time of Sima Qian, almost another millennia has since lapsed from the time of Sima Guang; one can appreciate the expansive interval of time in between. Language is a living creature; it evolves and changes over time. Understandably, many changes have transpired in the interim, and the past could be as distant as a foreign country.[1] For this reason, it was by no means easy to comprehend some of the words or terms in use, despite centuries of textual studies by outstanding scholars. The author has to rely heavily on interpretations proffered by scholars.

Because of the length of the work, the author has not expended sufficient effort to make comparisons between different interpretations by various scholars in depth. In many instances, he discards the commonly held interpretations and presents his own elucidations; while it might not be considered veracious by the academia; in many instances, he attempts to interpret from the perspectives of the circumstances, rather than taking the face values of the word or phrase used.[2] The translation of the text to contemporary Chinese by Bo Yang is much easier to follow; however, his work is encumbered with inaccuracies and superfluous derivatives.[3] Notwithstanding these shortcomings, his work is invaluable on a number of counts: the dates he appends for the lords and kings are invaluable for researchers, besides his inputs on place-names are also helpful, his notes on antecedents and anecdotes are particularly useful, and the author has drawn extensive from the information he presented. Rao Zongyi's *Zizhi tongjian* has a detailed chapter on the background of the creating of the work by Sima Guang, and the author uses his materials in the preparation of the introduction.

Zizhi tongjian jinzhu 資治通鑒今註, annotated by Li, Zongtong 李宗侗, Xia, Deyi 夏德儀 et al., Vol 1, Commercial Press, 臺灣商務印書局, Taiwan, 2011.

Zizhi tongjian 資治通鑒, Chen Liankang 陳連康 ed. et al., Xian chubanshe 西安出版社, China, 2002. 6th edition.

Zizhi tongjian Bo Yang Edition 資治通鑒 柏楊版, translated by Bo Yang 柏楊, 6th edition, Yuanliu chuban gongshi 遠流出版公司, Taiwan, 1986.

---

1 David Lowenthal, 'The Past Is a Foreign Country." – quoted from M. Nylan's article 'Translating Texts in Chinese History and Philosophy.'

2 Whether the words or phrases have fallen out of current usage or textual errors due to passage of time, some of them do not yield any intelligible meaning; or perhaps attributed to the author's insubstantial erudition.

3 Bo Yang 柏楊 single-handedly translated the entire *ZZTJ* of 294 volumes, to the contemporary text in ten years during the 1980's; it was an amazing feat.

Zizhi tongjian 資治通鑒, Rao Zongyi 饒宗頤 ed; Zhonghua shuju 中華書局, 2013, Hong Kong.

Traditional versus Simplified Characters

While many would disagree with the author's choice of using the traditional over the simplified characters in the footnotes as well as citing the sources and quotations in the footnotes, however, he contends that the original text was written in the traditional characters, he sees no need to excuse himself for adhering to the traditional texts. Furthermore, he takes the liberty of translating the simplified names of the authors and names of the references into the traditional characters in order to make the work consistent. The convention used for Chinese personal names, place names and titles are Romanized by using *pinyin.* Alternative *pinyin* are used to differentiate homophones. The author has included an extensive Chinese characters of personal names and place names in the footnotes for easy reference, in fact, in most instances they are repeated on every page. He makes no apologies for the repetition as he sees it as a convenient tool for making reference.[4]

For convenience of reading, the author has avoided including Chinese characters in the translated body text, except for the section on Warring States reference books by Yang Kuan, and a number of the appendices.

Antecedents – Using the Past to Allude to the Present

Chinese ministers and literati over the centuries routinely refer or cite historical antecedents or anecdotes to accentuate a certain subject when they were reprimanding or counselling the sovereign or their superiors. For the uninitiated and novice to Chinese literature, these backgrounds information are more than baffling; worse still, these antecedents in history are dispersed in various literary sources. Unless one is well versed in Chinese history, the reader is simply bewildered by the contents. The author has thus included an extensive amount of explanatory summaries in the footnotes. Po Yang's annotation in his translation is a great help in enlightening the readers on some of the historical incidents. The author wishes to stress that not all the antecedents were historical facts while most might carry a kernel of truth; many were contrived by latter-day scholars to paraphrase an ideal epoch or an incident of the past. While the author does refer to their reliability on occasion, it is beyond the scope of the work to authenticate their accuracy. Imbedded in these antecedents was the substance or subject matter the speakers or ministers wished to deliver. The use of these paraphrases and antecedents had the advantage of declaiming the ministers or authors from being condemned by their overlords, should the matter subject been considered objectionable or offensive.

Warring States – Kings, Sovereigns, Lords and Heads of States

The reigning years of the sovereigns and heads of states during the turbulent years has been an enthusiastic subject of research and debate among scholars during the past two millennia. Whilst the author does not delve into it in details, apart from the translation on Yang Kuan's textual

4 The author had on numerous occasions lost track of people and place names over pages. This might not benefit non-Chinese readers greatly; students with some knowledge of Chinese might find it helpful.

research articles, it is a subject best left to the experts; nevertheless, he feels it is fitting to include a table of alternative dating by different authorities. (See Appendix 1a).

Warring States

Warring States epoch (475-221 BCE) to some historians commenced at the end of the Spring and Autumn era (770-476 BCE), *ZZTJ* commences its narratives in 403 BCE when King Wulie of Zhou enfeoffed the San-Jin lords. It leaves a gap of 72 years unaccounted. The author, hence, includes a summary of events from 500 BCE to fill in the gap that was missing. (See Appendix 2b)

Posthumous Titles

The author includes a chapter on the posthumous titles of kings and sovereigns translated from the *Yizhoushu*.[5] (Appendix 2c). The posthumous title of a sovereign lord was often, though not necessarily, a eulogized manifestation of the person's deeds or achievements during his lifetime. A translation work would be incomplete without the inclusion of such an entry. However, the titles and entries are often considerably complicated; a single title has had very different meanings. To affix a translated posthumous title for every entry in the body text would be extremely tedious and impede the flow of reading, whereas the inclusion of which in the footnote serve little purpose either, as little is known of the of deeds and achievements of the most of the fief lord. A brief glance in the chapter on posthumous title will provide an inkling of what the author means. (See Appendix 2c)

The Use of Names

One of the most confusing and complicated part in reading Chinese texts is to untangle the different names used by people. Ancient Chinese were appended with various names. To cite an example, Duke Jiang (Jiang Taigong) was also known as Lu Wang, Lu Shi, Lu Shang, Lu Shangfu, Zi Ya, Duke Wang (Tiagong Wang), Shang Fu and Shi Shangfu.[6] To complicate the issue, he was addressed differently under different circumstances, in some instances to suit the rhymes of poems or compilation of memorials or perhaps whelms of the author. Another example is Shang Yang, before entering Qin, was known as Gongsun Yang; as he came from Wei, he was also called Wei Yang. Later, when he was enfeoffed by Qin at Shang the text addressed him as Lord Shang; hence, he was also addressed as Shang Yang.[7] It is often a challenge for students to follow the name changes of individuals.

Some translators are of the opinion that the place names should be transliterated in the process. The author believes it is being pedantic. Even if translations are offered, it usually provides little or no benefit to the reader. However, the author hastens to qualify by saying that the statement is perhaps far too swiping and generalized – some place names are important, as they provide us with clues to the political and geographical underpinnings of some major events, which induced paradigm shift. Some of the place names, which had certain bearings on historical events, for instance, the term *Hedong*, east of the River, or *Hexi* west of the River, and *Guannei*

5 Yizhoushu 逸周書.

6 Duke Jiang 姜太公, Lu Wang 吕望, Lu Shi 吕氏, Lu Shang 吕尚, Lu Shangfu 吕尚父, Jiang Ziya 姜子牙, Taigong Wang 太公望, Shi Shangfu 師尚父.

7 Wei Yang 衛鞅, Lord Shang 商君.

within the passes are thus translated. To offer a translation of Huai River is not an easy undertaking to be effected in a few words. The river acquired its name from the Huai-Yi barbarian tribes that settled along the river basins of the river, and the usage of the name could be traced from time immemorial.[8] Hence, it is deemed unwarranted in the translation.

China or *Zhongguo*

The nominative term for China is a relative modern conception. People of China have always called their homeland or state *Zhongguo* or *Zhongyuan*; the latter means Central Plain.[9] In the translated text of *Zizhi tongjian*, the author has used *Zhongguo* or *Zhongyuan* to denote ancient China. Suffice it necessary for the author to add that the term 'China' - *Zhongguo* is used in the translated articles of Yang Kuan.

When did China start using the term *Zhongguo*? [10] The Duke of Zhou, the regent of King Cheng of Zhou founded the capital of Zhou at Anshixian, west of Luoyang in around 1042 BCE.[11] The location is contiguous with the Luohe, and Yishui rivers; from this vantage and strategic location, one could see Taishishan, Shaoshishan Mountains and above all Songshan Mountain, the most sacred mountain where the divine was supposed to reside.[12] Songshan was where King Wu of Zhou made sacrifice offerings and made *fengchan* to Heaven and Earth after defeating King Zhou of Shang.[13] He decreed to script on a bronze tumbler - *hezun*, which states, 'I intend to settle in this realm of *Zhongguo* – Middle Realm, where I will allow my people to dwell and cultivate.'[14] The Duke of Zhou also composed an ode, 'This is, where Heaven and Earth merge,

---

8 Huai-Yi 淮夷.

9 *Zhongguo* 中國 and *Zhongyuan* 中原.

10 At the commencement of the Zhou State, the Duke of Zhou enfeoffed a myriad number of fief states, the exact number is often disputed, nevertheless, it was in excess of one thousand, as according to the *Lushi chunqiu* 呂氏春秋, 'Zhou enfeoffed over four hundred states 封國, while over eight hundred states also submitted 服國.' '周之所封四百餘, 服國八百餘.' These enfeoffed states and polities basically surrounded the Kingdom of Zhou in the centre – thus *Zhongguo* – the Middle Kingdom. Chinese people have over the span of its history, up to today, called themselves the sons of *Yan* and *Huang Yan-Huang zisun* 炎黃子孫 or *Huaren* 華人, the people of *Hua*, possibly after the Hua Mountain, the loftiest mountain in the central realm of China. Alternatively, they have called themselves, people of Qin *Qinren* 秦人, or *Hanren* 漢人, or *Tangren* 唐人 people of Tang, or even *Zhongguoren* 中國人– people of the Middle Realm in all the spoken dialects, but have never called themselves Chinese.

11 Duke of Zhou – 周公旦.
The borders of China have been exceedingly fluid and volatile during the past four millennium. The territories waxed and waned with the vicissitude of the dynasties, and there were no real clear demarcations as to where the borders of Zhongguo began and ended. The two terms *Zhongguo* and *Zhongyuan* are thus taken to mean within the realms of occupied territories of the people who called themselves the descendants of King Yan 炎帝 and Emperor Huang 黄帝. The original *Zizhi tongjian* and *Shiji* used the term *Zhangguo* to denote people living within the boundaries of the central plain of China. The origin of the terminology *Zhongguo* – Middle State, traced back to the Duke of Zhou 周公, the regent of King Cheng 周成王 (1042-1021 BCE). He founded the Zhou capital at Yanshixian 偃師縣, Xian, west of Luoyang 洛陽.

12 Luohe River 洛河, Yishui River 伊水. From this strategic location, one could see Songshan 嵩山, Taishishan 太師山 and Shaoshishan 少師山 mountains.

13 Fengchan 封禪. King Zhou of Shang 商紂王 (1075-1046 BCE).

14 '余其宅茲中國, 自之乂民' from the *hezun* 何尊 inscriptions 銘文. The *hezun* tumbler was unearthed in the village of Jia near Boaji County Shaanxi 陕西 寶雞縣 賈村 in 1963. The account

where the four seasons intersect, where wind and rain converge, and where the *yin* and *yang* phases amalgamate.'[15] The land came to be known as *Zhongtu* – Middle Earth.[16]

Indices

The author has adopted a rather unconventional approach in the presentation of the indices. The indices are in four parts. The first index is on names and subject matters. Each entry is appended with a certain year followed by a section; for instance, 403-1 - denotes the year the event appears in the text, in this case year 403, section 1. The approach has its advantages and disadvantages, advantageous in that one can easily trace when the event took place in the *ZZTJ*; however, he hastens to add, it is by no means an accurate rendering of the actual date of an event, as the event might have transpired years before and it is only mentioned in passing. This form of indexing offers research students to make comparisons with different textual sources. However, it has a clear disadvantage, in that if a passage or section is particularly lengthy, it will take quite an effort to locate the name of a person, particularly an obscured person, whereas the citing of an event is far easier to follow. (Making a reference to the footnotes would be helpful.) Part II of the indexing is related to the sovereigns, kings, lords, and nobles of the various states; they are organized in chronological order, and in sequence of succession. Part III of the index is the index of major events in chronological order of each of the seven states, (in fact, more than seven if we are to include the minor states of Zhou, Lu, Wey, Zheng, Jin and Song). Readers are able to appreciate the sequence of events of a particular state by making a cursory study of the index. Finally, Index IV is an abridged summary of major events to each volume of the text.

Others

The terms of *bo, shu, zhong, meng,* and *ji* are thorny issues in translation.[17] To the Chinese, the terms of *bo* and *shu* are easily understood. When one comes across someone who he has never met and who happens to be more senior, he simply addresses him as *bo* – elder uncle more senior in age, or *shu* – younger uncle who is younger than one's father or someone older than oneself. The response is spontaneous. However, the word *bo* also carries the meaning as the head of state or a clan; and its usage is fairly loose and ubiquitous; and Chinese people simply take it for granted. The use of the other terms, of *zhong, ji, meng* are more formal in appending to names or title of certain individuals.

---

corresponds with the information in the *Yizhoushu* 逸周書 Duyijie 度邑解, and the *SJ* 史記, Zhou benji 周本紀, which stated that King Wu had intended to establish his capital near the conference of Luo and Yi rivers; it was left to Duke of Zhou to fulfill his will.

15 '天地之所合也, 四時之所交也, 風雨之所會也, 陰陽之所合也.' From the *Zhou Li* 周立, Diguan – dasitu 地官大司徒.

16 The area was then called *Zhongtu* 中土– Middle-earth – the cultural and political centre of the Kingdom of Zhou and many dynasties after. It came to be known as *Zhongguo* 中國.

17 *Bo* 伯 is a designation given to the eldest son of a family, *zhong* 仲 is the second son of a family, *shu* 叔 was the third and *ji* 季 being the youngest son of a family. When there are more sons than four, all the others younger than the second are addressed as *shu*. If a family happened to have five sons, the last son was also addressed as *shao* 少. *Meng* 孟 was also used to denote the eldest son of a family. However, it is not used in conjunction with *bo*, and the term is less commonly used than the term *bo*.

In the translation of *Zhizhi tongjian* Trilogy, the author will attempt to translate the book from Volume 1 to Volume 68, a meagre attempt on the 294 Volumes. It is hoped that other scholars could carry on the effort of translating the book in its entirety into English.

Introduction

Preface

Sima Guang (1019-1086 CE), the editor and compiler of the *Zizhi tongjian*, was a native of Xiaxian County in Shaanzhou Province.[18] (See footnotes for a list of Song emperors during the time of Sima Guang.)[19] His father was the magistrate of Guangzhou Province when he was born.[20] Hence; he was given the name Guang. At an early age of seven, he was by then studying the *Zuoshi zhuan* and had widely read other historical texts and ancient literature.[21] In 1038 CE, at the age of eighteen, he earned a first place honour of *jinshi* title at the imperial civil-service examination,[22] which admitted him to take on civic administration duties at the Song court. Subsequently, he was appointed as a civil servant working through numerous senior appointments, and, finally, he was promoted to the position as the Chief of the Ministry of Supervision, *yushi zhongcheng*,[23] (i.e. chancellor in charge of prosecution).

In 1066 CE during the 3rd year of *Zhiping* of Emperor Yingzong, Sima Guang completed his compilation of the *Warring States and Qin in Eight Volumes*, which he named the *History in a Continuum, Tongzhi*, and presented the text to the emperor.[24] Yingzong highly commended the work, finding the text exceptionally helpful in the administration of his court; he named it the *Comprehensive Mirror for Aid in Government*, or the *Compendium for Good Governance*.[25] He decreed that Sima Guang should continue with his effort.

During the reign of Emperor Shenzong of Song (1067-1085 CE), Wang Anshi, a brilliant Song scholar, was summoned to court to implement a series of major reforms to the state, which was

---

18 Sima Guang (1019-1086 CE) 司馬光, his polite name was Junshi, 字君實, Xiaxian Shaanzhou Province 陝州 夏縣.

19 List of Song emperors during Sima Guang's time.
- Emperor Zhenzong of Song 宋真宗 Zhao Heng 趙恒 (r. 997-1022 CE).
- Emperor Renzong of Song 宋仁宗 Zhao Zhen 趙禎 (r. 1022-1063 CE).
- Emperor Yingzong of Song 宋英宗 Zhao Shu 趙曙 (r. 1063-1067 CE).
- Emperor Shenzong of Song 宋神宗 Zhao Xu 趙頊 (r. 1067-1085 CE).
- Emperor Zhezong of Song 宋哲宗 Zhao Xu 趙煦 (r. 1085-1100 CE).

20 Guangzhou Province 光州 – Huangchuanxian Henan 河南 潢川縣.

21 The *Zuoshi zhuan or Zuoshi chunqiu* 左氏春秋 is also known as the *Chronicle of Zuo* or the *Commentary of Zuo*. (The text chronicles historical events of the Spring and Autumn era and the early years of the Warring States, covering the period between 722-468 BCE).

22 *Jishi jiadi* 進士甲第. He was 18 year old by Chinese reckoning. (i.e. 17 by 'Western' reckoning.)

23 The Censorate, *yushitai* 御史台 or *duchayuan* 都察院 was a senior imperial supervisory agency, first established during the Qin Dynasty (221-207 BCE). The Minister of Supervisory, *yushi zhongcheng* 御史中丞 was the most senior position in the Censorate, *yushitai* 御史台. (N.B. The translation of these titles are based on the author's understanding of the functions of government officers at the time of Song.)

24 3rd year of *Zhiping* of Emperor Yingzong 宋英宗 治平三年, 1066 CE.
The Warring States and Qin in Eight Volume, which he named the *Tongzhi* 通志 (*General History*), are in fact the first eight volumes of the *Zizhi tongjian*.

25 The *Comprehensive Mirror to Aid in Government* or the *Compendium for Good Governance* is the generally accepted translations of the title; perhaps 'The *Mirror for Good Governance*' is just as succinct and appropriate.

beset by rampant corruption.[26] The conformists at court were adamantly opposed to the proposed reforms set forth by Wang Anshi. Sima Guang, heading the conformists, maintained that the established doctrines and rites for governance instituted by the ancestors of a state were inalterable. Nevertheless, Shenzong was determined to carry out reforms to the state. Sima Guang was promoted to the position of assistant minister of the Privy Council – *shumi*.[27] Realizing he could contribute little to the court, he resigned from his position and retired to the Western Capital, *Xijing* (Luoyang), where he continued with his earlier work and devoted the next 15 years to the compilation and editing of his historical chronicle, the *Zizhi tongjian*.[28] The monumental work was finally completed in 1084 CE, the 7th year of Yuanfeng.[29]

Emperor Shenzong died in 1085 CE and was succeeded by Zhezong; the court was presided over by the Empress Dowager Gao *taihou* as regent, as the new emperor was only nine years old. The reforms undertaken by Wang Anshi on two separate occasions turned out to be futile, and he resigned; the conformists returned to power. The Empress Dowager then appointed Sima Guang to assume the position as the personal attendant of the emperor - *menxia dailang* jointly as the assistant chancellor of the state – *shangshu zuopushe*.[30] Within a matter of months, he repealed the reforms and all the 'new laws' introduced by Wang Anshi.

Sima Guang was the chancellor of Northern Song a second time for eight months and died in 1086 CE; he was honoured with the posthumous title of the Duke of Wenguo.[31]

The Historical Background of the Northern Song Dynasty

What inspired Sima Guang to compile his *Zizhi tongjian* is perhaps best understood from the historical background of the Northern Song Dynasty, as it played a crucial role in the conception of the book.

In 960 CE, Commander Zhao Kuangyin (the first Emperor of Song, Taizu) of the Imperial Army of the Later Zhou revolted against the state, assisted by his younger brother Zhao Kuangyi and Zhao Pu the councillor.[32] He seized control of the Later Zhou court, the last of the Five

---

26 Wang Anshi 王安石 (1021-1086 CE) was a native of Linchuan Jiangxi 江西臨川 – (Fuzhou Jiangxi 江西 撫州). He was also a *jinshi* scholar and was known in Chinese history for his reformation of the Song court and as one of the eight greatest poets of Song; however, his well-intended reforms turned out to be far too radical and swift for the conservatives at court and the civic officers. His reforms finally failed. Song Shenzong, Zhao Xu 宋神宗 趙頊.

27 Assistant Minister of the Privy Council *shumi fushi* 樞密副使. It was an apparent promotion, whereas it was a demotion.

28 Sima Guang spent 19 years in the compilation, of which 15 years were spent in the library in Luoyang.

29 Yuanfeng 7th year, 元豐 7th year of Emperor Shenzong, Zhao Xu 宋神宗 趙頊.

30 *Menxia dailang* 門下待郎, *shangshu zuopushe* 尚書左僕射.

31 Duke of Wenguo 温國公. Unlike the time of the Warring States and Han, the dukes during the Song period were not enfeoffed with fief and land. According to Song scholar Zhang Wenqian 宋 張文潛 (1054-1114 CE), the Sima clan was the descendants of King Anping of Jin 晉安平王 Sima Fu 司馬孚 (180-272 CE), a chancellor at the Western Jin 西晉 court and enfeoffed as King Anping. King Anping was a local of Wen at Henei 温 河南 (present-day Wenxian Qinyang Henan 河南 沁陽 温縣). Hence he was enfeoffed as the Duke of Wenguo.

32 Zhao Kuangyin 趙匡胤 Song Taizu 宋太祖 (r. 960-976 CE).
Zhao Kuangyi 趙匡義, later Song Taizong 宋太宗 the second emperor of Song (r. 976-997 CE).
Zhao Pu 趙普 (922-992 CE).

Dynasties and the Ten Kingdoms that ruled China after the fall of the mighty Tang Dynasty in 907 CE, and he went on to found the Northern Song Dynasty.[33] The capital was established at Kaifeng, and he renamed it Eastern Capital, *Dongjing*.[34] The Song Emperor began his task to reunify China after more than half a century of political division. He had high aspirations; his objective was to conquer the Jingnan, Wuping, Houshu, Nanhan and Nantang states; and his ultimate goal was to reconquer the Sixteen Provinces of Yanyun under the control of Liao, a Qidan nomadic tribe from northern China that founded a vast kingdom in the northern part of China.[35] It was to take Zhao Kuangyin fifteen years to vanquish the four states; however, his ultimate ambition of reconquering the Yanyun Sixteen Provinces never materialized.

The unification of China by the Northern Song Dynasty was seen by many historians as an appeasing reaction to the social and economic unrest after the fall of the Tang Dynasty in 907 CE. China went through half a century of turmoil and fragmentation under the Five Dynasties (907-960) and Ten Kingdoms (902-979). The Middle-Kingdom (China) was literally disintegrated into numerous states governed by the military governors installed by the Imperial Tang court.[36] China sustained one of the most turbulent and tumultuous periods since the Sixteen Kingdoms (304-439 CE), the darkest era in Chinese history according to most historians. The conciliatory stance of the formation of Northern Song was therefore established on a fragile foundation. Early Song emperors were unable to muster much military support from the former military governors. Often the forces were not cohesive. They even had to draft soldiers in responding to external military threats. Politically, Song was not at all comparable to the once powerful empire during the Tang Dynasty, and the territories held were less than half that of Tang during its peak.

Qi Liang,[37] a present day historian, paints two strikingly dissimilar and contrasting pictures of the ethos of Tang and Song. He relates, "Less than sixty years separated the Tang and Song dynasties. While both dynasties belonged to the continuous cultural stream of China; however,

Northern Song, Bei Song 北宋 (960-1127 CE).

33 Hou Zhou 後周 (951-960 CE) was the last dynasty at the time of Five Dynasties and Ten Kingdoms 五代十國. (The period is broadly accepted as between 897-979 or more specifically 907-979 CE).

34 Kaifeng 開封 - 河南 開封市, Eastern Capital, *Dongjing* 東京.

35 Jingnan 荆南 also known as Nanping 南平 (924-963 CE); one of the ten kingdoms.

Houshu, Later Shu 後蜀, also known as Mengshu 孟蜀 (934-965 CE) was one of the ten kingdoms.

Nanhan, Southern Han 南漢 (917-971 CE) was one of the ten kingdoms.

Nantang, Southern Tang 南唐 (937-975 CE) was one of the ten kingdoms.

Wuping 武平 (951-963 CE).

Yanyun Sixteen Prefectures 燕雲十六州 was under the control of Liao 遼 at this stage. Zhao Kuangyin had intended to purchase the lost territories from the Liao. Lioa 遼 (916-1125 CE). Qidan 契丹.

Shi Jingtang 石敬瑭 the founder of Later Jin 後晉 (936-947 CE) appealed to Qidan for help and ceded the 16 Prefectures of Yanyuan to the latter. It was a vast area that encompassed present-day Beijing 北京, Tianjin 天津 and parts of Shanxi 山西 and Hebei 河北. The area remained in foreign control that was to last for almost two hundred years, until the reunification by the Mongol Yuan Empire.

36 Military governors 藩鎮 also known as *fangzhen* 方鎮. These Military governors were installed towards the middle era of the Tang Dynasty to bring about peace to the extensive empire. However, Tang fell because of these governors, when they became too powerful.

The term 'Ten States' 十國 *Shiguo* was a generalization. In fact, there were more than ten, including numerous minor states; however, the ten major states did not co-exist at the same time.

37 Translated from Qi Liang's 启良 (1955-) *Zhongguo wenming shi* 中國文明史 2001. Volume 2, p. 273.

there was a world of difference between the two epochs." He adds, "The two dynasties present us with very different hues and tones used in two separate paintings." He summarizes the differences, "The international eminence and stature of Tang was extensive and far-reaching, peripheral states and neighbouring tribes were overwhelmed by its might and came to the Tang court to pay homage and to offer tribute. Whereas even during the early years of the Song Dynasty, the state was impoverished, resulting in a weakened foreign policy with neighbouring states. Throughout the entire history of Song it had taken a passive stand against its equally powerful or, in some instances, less formidable neighbouring states." Qi Liang continues, "The Song State subsisted in anxiety and apprehension. The Tang people as a whole were liberal and generous, majestically imposing and passionate. They were bold, robust and unconstrained. Chivalry and heroism were the values that people pursued. On the other hand, the Song people were introverted, sensitive and rational; exquisite, delicate and refined things were considered as beautiful and gracious. Sensitive and emotional responses were often suppressed. Perhaps the people employed a more delicate and refined way to experience life. Seeking fulfilment, the people of Tang had little time for worldly and secular philosophical studies, except for Buddhism. They were not particularly interested in the meaning of being or prevailing social problems; whereas the Song people, being melancholy and sentimental, were more interested in pursuing theoretical exotica."

Learning from the bitter failures of Tang and the Five Dynasties, the early Song emperors consolidated and centralized the military power of the Imperial Court, placing great emphasis on the importance of court-appointed civic bureaucrats and administrators acquired through the annual imperial examinations. It led to a greater concentration of power in the central government.[38] The emphasis on the examination system to acquire civic officers had far-reaching effects on the cultural development of the Song Dynasty. It gave rise to more widespread appointment of commoners as bureaucrats, which encouraged pervasive education and learning among the civilians, resulting in a blossoming of literary learning and fine arts.

In 978 CE, Zhao Kuangyin finally conquered the Wu-Yue in the south. He turned his attention to the north against the Northern Han, which fell in 979 CE; he thus achieved national unification partially. However, his army suffered two disastrous defeats by the Liao at Gaolianghe River in 979 and the Qigouguan Pass in 986 CE.[39] Henceforth, Northern Song settled for a passive and defensive stance against Liao, the equally formidable neighbour situated in the north and northeast.[40]

During the earlier years of Northern Song, the rulers attempted to strengthen the feudal autocracy; civil bureaucrats replaced senior posts in various regions formerly held by military officers, and the Imperial Court appointed county grade appointments. The elite local militia were incorporated into the Imperial army, and dedicated institutions in the central government controlled local finance. The centralized power in the government at the Imperial Court was in turn distributed among many branches to ensure that none of the offices held enough power to compromise the Imperial interest. Three principal agencies: the political, military and financial, were placed under the direct control of the Imperial Court. The Court secretariat took charge of political affairs, but the chief officer, the prime minister or chancellor invested with executive power had no control over military affairs. The military branch, under the Military Council with

---

38 Recruitment of civic administrators had been in force since the time of Sui 隋 in 587 CE.

39 Gaolianghe River 高粱河 west of present-day Beijing.

Qigouguan Pass 歧購關, southwest of modern Zhuoxian County Hebei - 河北 涿縣 西南.

40 At this stage, the territories under the reign of Northern Song were perhaps less than one-third that of the Tang dynasty. Liao held a territory almost twice the size of Northern Song.

its own chancellor, was authorized to direct all military units except the Imperial Army. The third branch, the chancellor of the Treasury, was responsible for collecting national taxes and allocation of expenditures.

The imperial army was divided into three branches, each directly under the command of a marshal. Lastly, there was a censorate, [41] headed by the chancellor, grand censor, with the duty of supervising all government officials. The system proved to be effective in suppressing ambitious and aspiring local military officers from instigating separatist movements as the court contended that civic bureaucrats tended to be less ambitious than military officers in usurpation of a regime. However, the over-concentration of power in the royal house and measures adopted to curb the power of high ministers; particularly high military officers gave rise to political corruption among the ruling elites and, at the same time, weakened the military capability of the state when faced with internal and external threats.

Even during the early years of the Northern Song Dynasty class inequity was acute, which resulted in frequent uprisings and subversions by peasants, local armed forces and ethnic minorities.[42] In 993 CE, merely three decades after the founding of Northern Song, Wang Xiaobo, an impoverished civilian, led an uprising in Qingcheng (southwest of present-day Guanxian, Sichuan).[43] He articulated the desire of the masses and raised a slogan of 'equitable wealth distribution for the rich and the poor.' It was a paradigm shift from the demand for mere survival by commoners during the previous uprisings since the time of the Qin and Han dynasties. The insurgent army under Wang grew, and unrest spread rapidly. Wang Xiaobo was killed in early 994 CE, and Li Shun,[44] his brother-in-law, succeeded him as the commander and continued with the struggle. After taking Chengdu and seizing control of a vast expanse of territories south of Jiange and north of Wuxia he established a peasant regime named the Great Shu – Da-Shu.[45] However, he made the fatal mistake of underestimating the strength of the Song government. Chengdu fell to the government forces in the summer of 994 CE; Li and 30,000 men perished in action. In 995 CE, the insurgent army completely collapsed. During the entire Song Dynasty, uprising and unrest was almost incessant, which had profound effects in weakening the state.

The middle era of the Northern Song Dynasty included the reigns of emperors Zhenzong (r. 997-1022 CE), Renzong (r. 1022-1063 CE) and Yingzong (r. 1063-1067 CE); the Northern Song reached its economic peak during the reign of Renzong, after which the state began to decline, it was also a period marred by a protracted phase of political and military decline for the kingdom. Bureaucracy, including the military bureaucrats, had become even more inflated, and political corruption continued to worsen. Venal administrators, military bureaucrats, merchants, and moguls concentrated their undivided energy on intrigue and corruption; the National Treasury became depleted and the kingdom was insolvent, not surprisingly, the victims were inevitably the

---

41 Censorate, *yushitai* 御史台 *duchayuan* 都察院 was a senior supervisory agency, first established during the Qin Dynasty 秦 (221-207 BCE). The Censorate 御史台 *yushitai*, later to become *duchayuan* 都察院, was a senior supervisory agency.

42 Normally with the onset of a new dynasty, class inequality would be at its lowest.

43 Wang Xiaobo, 王小波. Qingcheng 青城 - southwest of present day Guanxian Sichuan 四川 灌縣 西南.

44 Li Shun 李順.

45 Chengdu 成都.
Jiange 劍閣 - Jiangexian Guangyaunshi Sichuan 四川 廣元市 劍閣縣 and north of Wuxia 巫峽 – the stretch of Changjiang River 長江 gorge between Chongqing City 重慶市 and Hubei 湖北.
Great Shu, Da-Shu 大蜀.

commoners. The peasants being weighed down by harsh exploitation rose up in rebellion when uprisings became larger and, even more, frequent.

Externally, nomadic and seminomadic peoples establishing their kingdoms and states in the former territories of the Tang Dynasty were threatening the national security of Song. There was the Liao Kingdom, to the north and northeast of Song, established by a Qidan tribe near the Liaohe River (present-day Inner Mongolia, Jilin, Liaoning, and Hebei.)[46] There was the expanding kingdom of Xixia founded by Dangxiang, a conglomerate of Tibetan tribes to the northwest, situated in the present Lingxia, Gansu, northern Qinghai, Inner Mongolia and the northern sector of Shaanxi.[47] These kingdoms posed serious threats to Song's national disposition. Finally yet importantly, the Jin tribes, the precursors of the Qing, to the north of the Liao Kingdom, formerly a dependent state of Liao, were also on the rise. [48]

The Northern Song, particularly the middle period and later, was marked by remarkable and accelerated cultural and technological advancements and achievements. In general, Song society was prosperous. Farming and various production technologies had greatly improved with increased productivity. Song was perhaps the most advanced and prosperous state during the medieval era in the entire world. Money, in the form of paper currency, appeared during this period. Typography and magnetic compass came into use, and gunpowder for warfare was also introduced. A large number of outstanding scholars and poets such as Su Che, Ouyang Xiu, Sima Guang, Wang Anshi and Shen Kuo emerged to contribute to the splendid and refined literary and cultural environment of the Song Dynasty.[49]

In 1004 CE the Northern Song army sounding defeated the Liao forces that violated into the Song border. When unconfirmed rumours came that the Liao army had entered the Tanzhou Province and was approaching the Eastern Capital of Dongjing, Emperor Zhenzong was so pusillanimously scared by the ominous menace of the invaders that he had intended to abandon his capital to move south of Huaihe River immediately.[50] Prime Minister Kou Zhun and other ministers at court strongly opposed the move; they proposed that the emperor should lead the battle in person.[51] Zhenzong took their advice. The Song army, greatly inspired and motivated by his presence, went on to face the enemies with some successes. Nevertheless, the emperor was inclined to settle for peace with Liao. The unfounded looming threat (as Liao lacked the strength to conquer Song), finally stalled when the Song court agreed to pay a huge annual tribute of silk and silver. The next year, even after having defeated the Liao forces, the Song emperor settled for a humiliating peace treaty, which involved an annual tribute of 100,000 taels of silver and 200,000 bolts of silk for Liao's withdrawal. In 1044, when the Liao threatened to use force again, Emperor

46 Liao Kingdom, 遼國 to the north and northeast of Song, founded by a Qidan tribe 契丹 near the Liaohe River 遼河. The river flows past Neimeng 內蒙, Jilin 吉林, Liaoning 遼寧, and Hebei 河北.

47 Xixia 西夏 Tibetan tribe – Dangxiang 黨項. The territories of Xixia included Lingxia 寧夏, northwest of Gansu 甘肅, northeastern part of Qinghai 青海, Inner Mongolia 內蒙 and northern part of Shaanxi 陝西. The eastern extreme of Xixia extended as far as Huanghe River, to the west the Jade Gate and to the south it conjoined with Xiaoguan Pass 蕭關.

48 Present-day Heilongjiang 黑龍江.

49 Su Zhe 蘇轍 (1039-1112 CE), Ouyang Xiu 歐陽修 (1007-1072 CE), Sima Guang 司馬光 (1019-1086 CE), Wang Anshi 王安石(1021-1086 CE) and Shen Kuo 沈括 (1031-1095 CE).

50 Tanzhou 潭州, present day Puyangxian County Hebei 河北 濮陽縣.
Eastern Capital, Dongjing 東京.
Huaihe River 淮河.

51 Kou Zhun 寇準 (961-1023 CE).

Renzong agreed to add 100,000 taels of silver with an equal number of bolts of silk in exchange for transitory peace at the northern border. In the meantime, between 1040 CE and 1042 CE, three battles were fought between the Northern Song and the Xixia at Yanzhou (Yan'an, Shaanxi), Haoshuichuan (Tianshuihe, east of present-day Longde County, Gansu) and Weizhou (Pingliangxian Gansu),[52] resulting in devastating defeats for the Song army. Emperor Renzong (r. 1022-1063 CE), soon after he came to power agreed to pay Xixia an annual reparation of silver and silk in exchange for peace.

Failing with his military exploits, Zhenzong (r. 968-1022 CE) turned his attention to the ideological domain to distract his people. Commoners were encouraged to venerate a syncretic faith of Buddhism, Taoism and Confucianism.[53] The measure of obscurantism proved to be more effective than the reverence of Confucius solely, and it desensitized the people.

The movement called Neo-Confucianism fused Confucian, Buddhism and Taoism principles into a syncretic creed; and offered a more popular understanding of Confucius to advance the interests of the landowners and the elites. Zhou Dunyi was an influential thinker and progenitor of the movement;[54] he advanced the notion of the 'Ultimate' *wuji*, which he said, was the essence of the universe that transcended all material things. According to him, the feudal order was a manifestation of the 'Ultimate' in a social relationship.

Between 1067 CE and 1127 CE, which included the reigns of Shenzong, Zhezong (r. 1085-1100 CE), Huizong (r. 1100-1125 CE) and Qinzong (r. 1125-1127 CE); the Northern Song continued its decline. Political strife and corruption among the bureaucrats continued unchecked at court and throughout the kingdom. The factional struggles during the latter part of the Northern Song Dynasty, a manifestation of social inequities, found the rulers in a dilemma. Aware of the looming dangers they faced, they had a genuine desire for political and social reforms and to make amends to the state but without the power to do so, perhaps due to the will and influence of the bureaucrats and elites. To make matters worse, the court was wavering and vacillating with doubt.

During the early reign of Shenzong (1067-1085 CE) two political factions developed among the high court officials. There were those who maintained that reforms were imminent and advocated the enactment of the 'New Laws' to purge some of the power held by the elites and privileged hence as to boost agricultural production and to increase revenue for the state.

52 Yanzhou 延州 - Yan'an, Shaanxi 陝西 延安.
Haoshuichuan 好水川- Tianshuihe River, east of Longde County, Gansu 甘肅 隆德縣東 甜水河.
Weizhou 渭州 - Pingliangxian Gansu 甘肅 平涼縣.

53 Confucianism was not a religion.

54 Zhou Dunyi 周敦頤 (1016-1073 CE) was the original and principal proponent of Neo-Confucianism, he advanced the notion of the 'Ultimate' 無極 *wuji* (some scholars translate it as 'Absolute'), which he said, was the essence of the universe that transcended all material matters. According to him, the feudal order was a manifestation of the 'Ultimate' in social relations. Zhou Dunyi wrote the *An Explanation of the Diagram of the Ultimate - Taiji tu shuo* 太極圖說. His philosophical thought is considered objective idealism 客觀唯心主義. Zhang Zai 張載 (1022-1077 CE), a contemporary of Zhou Dunyi held that the materialist *qi* 氣 (roughly translated as vital elements or Greek - *pneuma*) was the essence of all things in the universe. According to him, the interaction between the *yin* 陰 and the *yang* 陽 led to changes in the *qi* and in the course of changes, things were created. Proceeding from the idealist thought that man and universe were one; he believed that the people and the sovereign of a state formed an indivisible and integral whole. He held that the contradictions between the two polarities could be gradually resolved.
Between 1056 CE and 1067 CE, the literati of Northern Song developed the Jigong School founded by Wang Anshi 王安石 荆公學派, the Wengong School by Sima Guang 司馬光 温公學派, and the Shuxue School by Su Shi 蘇軾 蜀學派.

However, the conservatives were obstinately opposed to the enactment of the 'New Laws' and believed that austerity measures by cutting state expenses was the best option. They held that the 'New Laws' would bring dire consequences instead of improved production. Under the auspices of Emperor Shenzong, the reform of the 'New Laws' was implemented on two separate occasions in 1070 CE and 1074 CE. The emperor wavered when the conservatives objected to the 'New Laws', which were implemented with haste, yielding devastating and adverse consequences. Beginning in 1085 CE, the conservatives and the reformers took turns, in capturing the support of the court. It was not until the early twelfth century that the struggles between the two factions finally came to a head.

Sima Guang (1019-1086 CE) came onto the scene in the midst of this chaotic situation. He was an uncompromising conservative at the Song court, an idealist advocating fatalism, staunchly loyal to his kingdom and family, a frugal, modest, moral and honest man. He was exceptionally learned in every aspect and facet of literature, music, almanac law, astrology and mathematics. He believed that the Divine held the supreme power to dispense the differences between the noble and ignoble, the rich and poor, the gifted and benighted, and people with longevity or brief lifespan. People, he advocated, should live in complete resignation to their preordained fate. Any deviance or noncompliance from the grand design of Providence, he argued would auger ill. Stressing the importance of following the rites – *li*, he urged a strict observance of the feudal order and its hierarchic protocols.[55] His idealistic philosophical perspective can be seen in his annotations and commentaries to his *Zizhi tongjian*. (See footnotes on the moral characters of Sima Guang and Wang Anshi).[56] Initially, he did support the reform movement led by Wang Anshi, later he recanted and opposed the changes when Wang became too radical.[57] In 1071, Sima Guang resigned from his post and moved to Luoyang to start working on his *Zizhi tongjian*, with financial aids and support provided by the court.

The leading reformer Wang Anshi (1021-1086 CE), a great classic essayist, was a materialistic philosopher. He maintained that 'primordial vitality' was the quintessence of the universe, and the modus operandi of material matters was governed by natural laws. Although the universal and

---

55 Rites – *li* 禮.

56 Sima Guang and Wang Anshi were two of the very few senior ministers at the Song court who did not keep concubines in their households. The wife of Sima Guang was desperate as they did not have any offspring, and on several occasions, she had asked him to take a concubine; however, he remained faithfully devoted to his wife. Instead, he adopted his elder brother's son Sima Kang 司馬康 as his son. Sima Guang was a frugal man throughout his life. He was a senior minister of the Song Court for many years, and a chancellor for some time before 1070 CE and resumed his former position in 1086 CE, he did not even have enough money to give his wife a proper burial when she died. He had to pawn his plot of land to give her a decent burial. Emperor Song Renzong bestowed him with millions of money and silk brocade as gifts; however, he duly returned them to the treasury; he was a man of his own beliefs and practiced what he advocated. He was genuinely concerned with his country and the people as he mingled with the commoners when he accompanied his father to take on magistrate posts in the kingdom. Sometime during his tenure as a low-ranking functionary, he became acquainted with the sufferings and torments of the common people. When Sima Guang died, people in the Song capital sold their belongings to make funeral offerings; they lamented and wept as if they had lost a loved one. People hung his image in their homes and made offerings to him before they took their meals. We can see that the political difference between Wang Anshi and Sima Guang was philosophical or ideological based, rather than for personal power or financial gain, as both men were of high moral character.

57 It was when Wang Anshi introduced 青苗法 – *qingmiao fa*, a new law sanctioning government officials to lend money to civilians with interest. Sima Guang maintained that civilian moneylenders were corrupt enough, if the government officials were allowed to lend money, the situation would be even more dire.

fundamental laws could not be altered, man could take the initiative and should not resign himself to his 'fate'. He maintained that merchants with insatiable greed and avaricious bureaucrats precipitated the deplorable and poverty stricken state of the peasants through gouging, hoarding and annexing of farmlands owned by the humble masses; whereupon the rich became richer and the poor poorer. His theory of the 'New Learning' served as his theoretical basis for introducing the 'New Laws'. The impassioned struggle between the reformists and the conservatives were also extended to the academic field, and the ideology conflict was no less acute than the political struggle at court, lasting much longer.

Emperor Shenzong appointed Wang Anshi to advance reforms in earnest. The objective was to address the issues that were plaguing the state, to balance state finances and to improve the livelihood of commoners, to relevantly deploy the military forces of the state and to employ learned scholars as functional entities of the state. As Wang Anshi stated, "The purpose (of the reform) is to make improvements on political and legislative matters, increase wealth and to toughen the military strength of the state."[58] Many high hopes were pinned on Wang Anshi when he was appointed chancellor to expedite reforms to the kingdom amid much opposition from the conservatives and the elites in 1069 CE.

Wang Anshi was far too radical with his endeavours. Many of his measures did not meet the objective requirements of his time; he introduced makeshift measures rather than addressing the root causes of the problems at stake. The most devastating setback was that he was pressing the local administrators far too hard and these officers and bureaucrats, failing to keep pace with the reform, resorted to making falsifications and fabrications to counter the Court decrees. Wang Anshi intended equality, nevertheless, created an entirely conflicting and notorious reputation for himself.[59]

Wang Anshi, having failed to implement radical reforms the kingdom of Song, ended up with even more social disturbances, implemented too briskly and too late. Besides, it was implemented hastily to revert an intransigent and entrenched course made malleable by decades of ailing and failing social and political infrastructure. The wealthy magnates, elites, landlords and conservatives, bureaucrats and royalists, with much at stake, tenaciously opposed and the chancellor totally disappointed resigned from his post when his son died.

Sima Guang was recalled to court in 1086 CE, after a lapse of 16 years away from being involved at the Song court. Wang Anshi died during the 4th month of 1086 CE while Sima Guang died in the 8th month of the same year.[60]

---

58 Comments by Wang Anshi, "修吾政刑，使將吏稱，職財谷富，兵强而已." Source: The *Song huiyao jigao* 宋會要輯稿 Shihuo volume 1 of 28 食貨一之二十八.

59 Shen Kuo 沈括 (1031-1095 CE) was another reformer, also a materialist. His range as a scientist was also immense; he knew mathematics, astronomy, calendar-making, geography, cartography, astronomy, meteorology, physics, chemistry, metallurgy, weaponry, water conservancy, botany, zoology, agriculture, medicine and pharmacology. He was outstanding in proposing many original ideas. He developed his own calculation of the summation of arithmetic series to the second order, by making the sum total of circumference and height to extract the length of a curve. He also made improvements to astronomical observation instruments and calendar making. He discussed at great length the properties of the compass and found the difference between the true north and the magnetic north.

60 Cheng Hao 程顥 (1031-1095 CE) from Luoyang was a conservative theoretician. Together with his younger brother Cheng Yi 程頤 (1033-1107) they became principle exponents of Neo-Confucianism, first advocated by Zhou Dunyi. The two came to be known as the 'Cheng Brothers.' They advanced the idea of 'reason' *li* 理, as the essence of the universe, which pre-existed before anything else – the void. According to them, "there is only 'reason' under Heaven", man and all material things were just

Fifteen years later, at the time of Emperor Huizong's reign, political struggle at court between the various ideological factions had abated somewhat, but the kingdom suffered worsening venal corruption, which was raging with abandonment among the ruling class and the bureaucrats. Driven to destitution by the insufferable abuses of oppressions and exploits, the peasants rose up in rebellion *en masse*, and civic disorder became rampant. Ruthless exploitation became intolerable, especially in the south-eastern section of the country. Fang La, a rebel leader, led a peasant uprising in Qingxi in 1120 CE.[61] In three months, he and his men took control of 6 provinces and 52 counties in the present-day Zhejiang and Anhui provinces; his forces grew from one thousand men to one million in a matter of months. After establishing his peasant regime, Fang La claimed that he could topple the Song Kingdom in ten years. The rulers greatly alarmed by such a claim sent a huge contingent of forces south and defeated the rebel and his men after a bitter struggle that lasted for more than one year. In 1121 CE, Fang La was captured and put to death. However, his men carried on fighting for another year. The uprising was finally quelled, but the Song State was never quite the same as before.

At the head of his rebellious hordes, Fang La condemned the Song rulers and elites for despoiling the peasants to allow themselves to wallow in luxury and extravagance living. The aim he declared was to overthrow the Northern Song regime to improve the livelihood of the peasants. His uprising, similar to that of Wang Xiaobo, was economically based and thus had a notable historical significance. Slightly before him, there was another major peasant rebellion in the Shandong Province led by Song Jiang; the history of the uprising was made mythical in a famed

---

one, forming an inseparable whole. Different as people were in social position, they said, each must act according to his duties and thus conform to reason - *li*. His theory falls into the category of objective idealism 客觀唯心主義, according to which the broad masses must resign themselves to a life of poverty and humiliation, placing themselves at the disposal of the feudal order, and refrain from the thought of making changes.

Su Shi 蘇軾 (1036-1101 CE) was the head of another scholastic faction. In his earlier years, he advocated political reform; later he opposed the 'New Laws.' Academically he disagreed with both Wang Anshi and the Cheng Brothers. His major achievement was in literature where he took a stand against the literary style of flowery parallelisms 華麗排比 and favoured the classic form of prose. He preferred *ci* 詞 to *shi* 詩 when writing poetry. Su Shi, his father Su Xun 蘇洵, and his younger brother Su Zhe 蘇轍 (1039-1112 CE) were collectively known as the 'Three Sus' 三蘇, and were stalwarts of classic writing. Ouyang Xiu, Liu Yong 柳永 (987-1053? CE) and Zhou Bangyan 周邦彥 (1056-1121 CE), as *ci* poets, were known for their description of the delicate feelings of young men and women and their portrayal of the sentiments of parting. Su Shi, however, broke through the confines of this archetype as he developed his distinctive plain and graceful style.

Ouyang Xiu 歐陽修 (1007-1072 CE), another statesman as well as a man of letters, was the main advocate of the classic style of prose writing. Both Sima Guang and Wang Anshi were great classic essayists.

61 Fang La 方臘 (?-1121 CE) staged his uprising at Qingxi Chunanxian Zhejiang 青溪 浙江淳安縣.
Fang La adopted Manichaeism (*Moni*) prior to his uprising, spreading the religion among his followers and organized their activities around the Manichaean teachings. Impoverished people received help from the clique, and weary distant travellers were provided with food and shelter, such measures helped to promote the spread of his movement. Members were organized down to the most basic units, and some were assigned to specific tasks of organizing religious activities and administrating of funds donated by its followers. It is evident that Fang La had done charitable groundwork prior to his uprising. (Manichaeism was an offshoot of Zoroastrainism).

novel the *Shuihuzhuan,* The *Water Margin.*[62] The difference was that Song Jiang and his men surrendered to the state and went on to fight on the side of the government.

About the time when Fang La started his uprising, the Northern Song regime sent an emissary to the state of Jin to broker an allied attack against the Liao State. The Song forces consequently lost repeatedly in the ensuing battles against Liao. In 1125 CE following the resounding conquest of Liao by Jin, the newly arisen Jin Kingdom had become intractable, ignoring its former allied pledge to withdraw from captured territories after annihilating the Liao Kingdom, it had a complete *volte-face*; it turned against its former ally for an all-out assault on the already enfeebled Song Kingdom. Two years later, in 1127 CE, the Jin armies successfully took Kaifeng, the capital of Song. Emperor Huizong, decadent and dissipated while brilliantly and artistically talented in every aspect of fine arts, was forced by his ministers to abdicate the throne to his son Qin Zong two years earlier in the face of an imminent threat by the besieging Jin. On this occasion, the Jin army returned and entered the capital city; the army plundered, pilfered, raped, and took off with more than three thousand royal family members and retainers, (another version said it was 400. However the exact number cannot be verified). The captured included the deposed Emperor Huizong and Emperor Qinzong.[63] They were carried off to the far-flung Jin capital of Yilan in Heilonhjiang with the nobles trudging on foot in misery.[64] Northern Song lost almost two-fifths of its territories, and the dynasty came to a close; only 43 years after the death of Sima Guang. The Northern Song Dynasty lasted for 167 years, reigned by nine emperors.

Siam Guang, in the midst of this chaotic, moribund and degenerative period, was perhaps searching for a world order, hoping to find solutions for his sovereign to preside with wisdom. His work can best be understood in the context of the historical background of his time. It was an age of great economic abundance, of societal, cultural and philosophical progress, nevertheless an age of turmoil, of humiliation, of defeat, of incongruity, of discrepancy, of moral decay and uncertainties. He did have a hidden agenda, and his thoughts were often reflected in his commentaries and annotations to his *Zizhi tongjian.* Indeed, the commentaries and annotations make it clear that he was an ultra-conservative, believing that with the restoration of the rites *li* propounded by Confucius the world would find peace, as opposed to Wang Anshi's perspective that only through major reforms could the state survive the uncertainties. Perhaps unknown to Sima Guang, the compilation of the *Zizhi tongjian* was a harbinger of the impending collapse of the kingdom. His thesis was principally based on his understanding of Confucianism; as he believed that fate was the supreme controller that determined the difference between the elites and humble, between the rich and the poor, between the intelligent and the ignorant, and between longevity and a short life span. People should, he believed, live in complete resignation to their fate. Any noncompliance, he said, would augur ill. Stressing the importance of following Rites - *li,* he urged a strict observance of the feudal order and its hierarchic details. The beliefs held by him are scattered throughout the text in the form of his annotations and commentaries. He, nevertheless, did not prepare a separate text commenting on his personal views on the historical events that were covered in the *Zizhi tongjian.* Apart from his commentaries and

---

62 The rebel leader was Song Jiang 宋江. *The 108 Heroes from the Water Margin* 水滸傳. The fictional novel, based on some historic facts, is usually attributed to Shi Naian 施耐庵 (1296-1372 CE) and was possibly edited by Lu Guanzhong 羅貫中 (1280-1360 CE).

63 The incident came to be known as the 'Humiliation of Jingkang 靖康之耻 *Jingkang zhi chi.'* Emperor Huizong 宋徽宗 (r. 1100-1026 CE) lived in captivity for 8 years, and Emperor Qinzong 宋欽宗 (r. 1026-1027 CE) died in captivity in 1156 CE or 1161 CE?

64 Jin capital of Yilan 依蘭 in Heilongjiang 黑龍江.

annotations in the *Zizhi tongjian*, Sima Guang did not formulate any constructive measures to improve the state of affairs of the Song.

The very notion of the breakdown of *li* was a reflection on the reason Sima Guang chose 403 BCE as the beginning date of the narratives of the *Zizhi tongjian*. He held it was the year when the Rites *li* of the Zhou State broke down; the year when King Weilie of Zhou enfeoffed the three ministers of Wei, Zhao and Hann as fief lords - an emblematic breakdown of the rites. He wrote in this annotation,

> "…. Alas! The ethical code between the sovereign and his subjects had completely disintegrated at this stage; all the fiefdoms under Heaven were employing their wit to vie for supremacy. Eventually, all the sacrificial altars inaugurated by the founding fief lords installed by Zhou met their respective demise. In the meantime, the commoners agonized over their appalling fates – when innumerable number succumbed to wholesale massacre. Pitiful it was indeed! (See 403-1)."

When people are living in an age of uncertainty and chaos, they often look for signs to explain the confusion they face which they can neither comprehend nor explain. Sima Guang was perhaps searching for clues from ancient history to find law and order in the cosmos. However, he was stuck in a depressed runnel for not being able to escape from the feudal system advocated by Confucius. Sima Guang's distorted perception of history to explain away the chaos and turmoil nevertheless does not undermine the *Zizhi tongjian's* position as a monumental work of historiography on ancient Chinese history. Sima Guang, through his efforts of nineteen years, did create a shining mirror of history that we, as modern men can usefully reflect on. History is indeed a mirror that can help one contemplate the irrationality and imprudence of people. The immense significance of the *Zizhi tongjian* will become evident as we do a brief survey of its compilation and creation.

The *Zizhi tongjian* – the Book

As a historiographic text, the *Zizhi tongian* assimilated the exceptional attributes and defining qualities of the *Zuozhuan* and the *Shiji*.[65] Since its publication, it has held a very special and esteemed position among Chinese scholars and historians. Although the volume was principally supported and financed by the Song imperial court, it was organized and written by private individuals; it, therefore, deviated significantly from historical texts prepared by court officials during previous dynasties.

Jin Yufu (1887-1962 CE) remarks,[66] "Making an examination of what Sima Guang articulated personally and taking in Liu Shu's accounts,[67] the aspiration to compile the text was neither an impetuous decision nor spurred on by momentary ambition on the part of Sima Guang. When Emperor Yingzong encouraged and directed Sima Guang to continue his effort, his aspiration of preparing a historical text was finally met. One has to note that when imperial historians were compiling historical texts they had to adhere to the stringent strictures dictated by the court. Court historians reportedly laid down their brushes frequently, staring vacantly at each other for

---

65 *The Zuozhuan* 左傳 also known as *the Chunqiu zuozhuan* 春秋左傳, *The Chronicle of Zuo* or the *Commentary of Zuo, The Chinese Classics*. The *SJ* 史記.

66 Jin Yufu 金毓黻 (1887-1962 CE).

67 Liu Shu 劉恕 Daoyuan 道原 (1032-1078 CE).

long periods, chewing on the brush-ends they held, pondering on the best approach to present their narratives without encroaching on sensitive issues. However, when Sima Guang was preparing the *Zizhi tongjian* he did not have to endure such restrictions. He appointed his assistants; he was neither burdened by assertive supervisors nor had he had to tolerate deceptive peers and colleagues, as was often the case with court historians. Liu Shu, Liu Ban, and Fan Zuyu were totally dedicated to the precise causes and objectives laid down by Sima Guang.[68] These men supplemented and complemented each other; their opinions were unanimous; hence, the Chronicle was signed off by Sima Guang as the sole editor. While, some might consider the text a court historiography in view of the financial assistance; it was, in fact profoundly different from official historical texts compiled by court historians."[69]

The earlier annalistic history compiled in China was the *Zuozhuan*.[70] After the death of Confucius, Zuo Qiuming, a contemporary of Confucius at the Lu court, concerned that the students and followers of Confucius might misconstrue the intended meaning of the *Chunqiu*, collected the historical accounts from different states during the Spring and Autumn epoch and compiled the *Zuoshi Chunqiu* into an annalistic text.[71] One and a half millennia later, Sima Guang was extremely fond of the work. He resolved that he would compile an inclusive and precise historical text commencing from the Warring States to the end of the Five Dynasties – *Wudai*, adhering to the format created by Zuo Qiuming.

By the time of the Wei (220-265 CE), Jin (265-420 CE) and Nan-Bai Chao (South-North dynasties 420-589 CE), [72] the volumes of historical texts written and accumulated had become innumerable. Later, during the Song period, cultural and educational learning in China had become even more pervasive with the invention of typographic printing, and the number of books written by scholars continued to accumulate. Faced with mountains of books, a learned scholar could spend his whole lifetime reading all the books and was barely able to skim through them briefly.

Since the compilation of the *Hanshu* by Ban Gu, whether they were annalistic official histories or chronological ordered historical accounts, the chronicles were invariably divided by dynasty. There were a few exceptions, the *Nan-Bei shi* and the *Annals of the Sixteen States*, [73] were compiled chronologically; however, there had yet to be a historic text that thread through the ages and dynasties from the most ancient times. The *Shiji* stood alone at the time of Sima Guang as the only history that covered all ages. Nevertheless, it was written in the biographic style of chronology.

---

68 Liu Ban 劉攽 Gongfu 貢父 (1023-1089 CE).
Fan Zuyu 范祖禹 Chunfu 淳甫 (1041-1098 CE).

69 Jin Yufu 金毓黻. The quote is from the *Zhongguo shixue shi* 中國史學史, p. 182.

70 Confucius (551-479 BCE).
Zuo Qiuming 左丘明 (556-451 BCE?).
The Zuozhuan 左傳 the *Zuoshi chunqiu* 左氏春秋.

71 The *Nan-Bei shi* 南北史 and the *Annals of the Sixteen States* 十六國春秋.

72 Wei 魏 (220-265 CE), Jin 晉 (265-420 CE) and Nan-Bai Chao 南北朝 (420-589 CE).

73 The *Nan-Bei shi* 南北史 and the *Spring and Autumn of the Sixteen States* the *Nan-Bei shi* and the *Spring and Autumn of the Sixteen States* 十六國春秋.

The Objectives of the Book

Sima Guang maintained that literary scholars of his days were exceptionally lacking in their historic knowledge. The accepted biographical and official historic accounts were extremely difficult to follow, as the events were scattered and dispersed in different biographical entries. It was especially demanding to ascertain a complete picture of a historic event. To delve deep into an event, having not been able to grasp the causalities and aftermaths, one had to browse through scattered accounts from different entries. It was particularly challenging to establish a complete picture of a historic event. The Song scholars of the day settled for the 'Four Former Histories' – *Qian sishi*.[74] As to the history following that time, they were invariably ill informed; in fact, only very few of the most learned scholars were interested in the Tang history.

Sima Guang deliberated over the issue for a long time and was moved to say, "There have been over fifteen hundred volumes of historical text written since the time of the Spring and Autumn era - *Chunqiu*, covering the periods between the *Shiji* and the *Wudai*. Even if one spends his whole life, he could not read all the pages; even if one is to spend his lifetime delving into them, one would merely get a superficial glimpse of it all. People avoid the tedious and opt for the uncomplicated. Parts of the history will be lost forever." He resolved to compile a historic text that provided extractions of the important events. There were two discerning and essential matters for Sima Guang to overcome before he could begin with such a monumental task; he needed some learned scholars to aid him in his task, and secondly, he needed a vast library of rare books for his research. Sima Guang began his work in his forties; he prepared the historical account of his *Liniantu*.[75] It was a brief synopsis of historical events from the Warring States to end at the Five Dynasties. The manuscript was presented to Emperor Yingzong in 1064 CE. It was in five volumes, the contents of which was principally a brief summary of major historical events, illustrating the changes and transformations of Chinese history over the period. It was Sima Guang's first historical book. Based on this work, he went on to prepare the *Tongshi*, or the *Tongzhi*, which is roughly translated as the *History in a Continuum* or *Comprehensive Records*.[76] The work commenced from the 23rd year of King Weilie of Zhou (403 BCE) and ended with the annihilation of Qin.

The work essentially became the first eight chapters of the *Zizhi tongjian*. In 1066 CE, Sima Guang presented Emperor Yingzong with his *Tongshi*, as he related, "I have cursorily delved into various historical texts since my youth. The various formats of historiographic accounts are many; the volumes are countless. Even learned scholars could not possibly have an overall view of the extensive and pervasive contents, let alone the sovereign of a state, who is weighed down by ten thousand daily pressing, impending and thorny issues. It would not be easy for him to learn from the experience of the past. I am wanting in ability; however, I dare to make a bold attempt to compile a historiographic text, beginning from the Warring States era, and ending with the *Wudai* period, drawing references from official texts, as well as incorporating other available texts as exhaustively as possible. I intend to cover the vicissitudes of states, narrate the well-being and woe

---

74 '*The Four Former Histories*' – *Qian sishi* 前四史 - 史記, 漢書, 後漢書, 三國志. They are also known as the Four Histories the *Sishi* 四史.

75 The *Liniantu* 歷年圖 was compiled in seven volumes; it was part two of his composition of the *Jigulu* 稽古錄. It could be considered as the earliest draft of the *Zizhi tongjian*; however, some of the entries in *Liniantu* do not appear in the latter. Some of the year dates in *Liniantu* are erroneous. Sima Guang presented the first five volumes of this text to Emperor Yingzong in 1064 CE.

76 The *Tongshi* 通史 or the *Tongzhi* 通志 is roughly translated as the *History in a Continuum* or *Comprehensive Records*.

of the commoners; the epitomes of such events could be emulated, while the evil and despicable deeds would be guarded against, or refrained from. Incorporated in the text are all the things a sovereign of a state should know and be aware.[77] Furthermore, I intend to adopt the historiographic format used by the *Zuoshi chunqiu zhuan* to compile the work and name the book the *History in a Continuum*." He expressed his wish that Emperor Yingzong would offer patronage to the work.

Shortly after, Yingzong ordered Sima Guang to set up his workshop at Chongwenyuan College.[78] He was allowed to select his aides to continue with his effort. In 1067 CE Shenzong succeeded to the throne; Sima Guang was invited to give lectures on the *Tongzhi* to the emperor and his ministers at court on numerous occasions. The emperor was apparently impressed by the work conducted by Sima Guang; he maintained that the work offered a righteous path for good governance. Hence, he decreed the work be named the *Zizhi tongjian* or *The Comprehensive Mirror in Aid in for Governance*. The emperor then prepared a prologue to the text and ordered that it be appended as the preface upon the completion of the finished work.[79]

From our modern perspective, the annalistic chronicle is undeniably more advantageous to readers than the biographical style. Firstly, the text uses time as its reference; historical events appear more clear-cut and explicit than in the biographical style, besides Sima Guang adopted the pluralistic style of description, rendering it easier for the reader to grasp the threads of events.

In the *Shiji,* one particular event might appear in multiple places in different biographies and chronologies while in *Zizhi tongjian* it appears condensed in one specific event. For instance, some of the accounts of the Battle of Chibi (208 CE) that principally appear in the *Houhanshu, Liu Biao zhuan*; other accounts appear in the *Sanguozhi*, and, furthermore, details are scattered in the biographies of *Wei Wudi ji, Shu xianzhu zhuan, Guan Yu, Zhuge Liang, Zhang Fei, Zhao Yun, Sun Quan, Zhou Yu, Lu Su, Zhang Zhao* and *Huang Gai*.[80] Also, scraps of information are scattered throughout various other texts. To establish a full grasp of the entire incident, a reader needs to study all the previously mentioned texts. Even if a reader studied all the texts, the accounts are far too complicated and convoluted; one is often left confused by the details. The *Zizhi tongjian* helps the reader solve this convoluted and complicated problem. Sima Guang had collated all the chronicles, through insertion, splicing and interweaving to present clear-cut and vivid picture of important events; the reader is thus offered an explicit yet concise picture of the different entries, furthermore, he does not find the account boring. The *Zizhi tongjian* is thus extremely helpful to readers who wish to have a general and comprehensive grasp of important events in history.

---

77 "國家之盛衰, 繫生民之休戚, 善可為法, 惡可為戒" - is the theme of the book.

78 Chongwenyuan College 崇文院.

79 The *Mirror for Good Governance Introduction, Zizhi tongjian xuwen* 資治通鑒序文.

80 Battle of Chibi 赤壁鏖戰, 208 CE. It was the beginning of the Three Kingdoms. The Warlord Cao Cao 曹操 led five hundred thousand troops to move south after taking Jizhou 荆州. Liu Bei 劉備 allied with Sun Kuan 孫權 met the huge army at Chibi – the Red Cliff at the Changjiang River 長江. Cao Cao was soundly defeated; it hindered his ambition to conquer south of Changjiang River and led to the creation of the Three Kingdoms in 220 CE.
The *Houhanshu* Liu Biao zhuan 後漢書 劉表傳.
The *Sanguozhi* 三國志.
The biographies of Emperor Wu of Wei 魏武帝, Shu xianzhu zhuan 蜀先主傳, Guan Yu 關羽, Zhuge Liang 諸葛亮, Zhang Fei 張非, Zhao Yun 趙雲, Sun Quan 孫權, Zhou Yu 周瑜, Lu Su 魯肅, Zhang Zhao 張昭 and Huang Gai 黃蓋.

Upon publication of the *Zizhi tongjian*, the historiographical style promoted a stylistic shift and was quickly adopted by other historians, and some even hailed the work as a canonical classic.

Division of Labour During Compilation

That Sima Guang was a great historiographer, and an outstanding politician leaves us little doubt. Modern critics are of the opinion that his political stance was far too conservative, for which he has criticised by many; however, when assessing his work on the *Zizhi tongjian*, the praises and accolades are unanimous and universal by scholars, and it has been hailed as the cardinal archetype of historiography. The two submissions to the emperors by Sima Guang and an article penned by Liu Shu, his assistant offers us a glimpse of the process of the compilation. They are invaluable in helping us to understand the significance of the work.

Liu Shu in 1078 CE wrote the earliest recorded reference of the *Zizhi tongjian*,[81] some six years before the completion of the work. He recorded a conversation with Sima Guang, "Historians without exception emulated Sima Qian's technique used in his *Shiji*, [82] and their works are known as Official History – *zhengshi*. Our time is remote from antiquity, and scholars are ever more perplexed and inundated with the numerous volumes of books and texts. The perspective of the categories of historiography often restricts them. Giving preference to the style of the *History of Western Han - Xihanshu*, widely read and well-informed individuals go as far as studying the *Shiji* and the *History of Latter Han - Donghanshu*. Recent scholars are reasonably well informed on the history of the Tang Dynasty, whereas they are relatively oblivious of the history between the times of the Three Kingdoms to the Sui Dynasty (220-618 CE).[83] With the passage of time, people have become apathetic with history. It is said that the writings of Master Zhuangzi are simple and easy to master; nevertheless, the fanciful and profound words, and abstract phases are ridiculous, while they ostensibly appear to be logical. It takes little effort for people to learn the texts; it has therefore attracted all the unsophisticated scholars. The study of history is on the decline."[84] It does appear that Sima Guang ridiculed and scorned the study of religion and philosophy.

It also appears that Sima Guang notably influenced the above passage. Liu Shu acknowledged that he was a dedicated student of Master Sima (Sima Guang). Later he related another conversation with Sima Guang; it goes to reflect that the compiler had the project in mind as early as the commencement years of *Jiayou* (1056-1063 CE), during Emperor Renzong's reign.[85] Sima Guang said to Liu Shu, "It has been over a thousand years since the Spring and Autumn epoch. There are over fifteen hundred volumes of historical texts from the time of the *SJ* to the time of the *History of the Five Dynasties, Wudaishi*. A scholar studying for years could not read all the pages, spending his whole life he could not even complete a glimpse of the broadest outlines. Scholars find it boring and tedious; consigning themselves to take on easier readings, these pages of history will soon be obliterated. I intend to compile a historical text commencing from the time when King Weilie of Zhou enfeoffed the ministers of Zhao, Wei and Hann, until the end of the

81 *The Tongjian waiji* 通鑒外紀. It is said that Liu Shu had an amazing memory; once he read a book, he would never forget its contents. *Tongjian waiji* was prepared towards the later part of his life. Six hundred days before his death, he suffered a stroke and was incapacitated. He dictated the script to his son Liu Xizhong. He died shortly after the completion of the book.

82 His record related *Shiji* as *Benji* 本記, *Nianbiao* 年表, *Shu* 書, *Shijia* 史家, *Liezhuan* 列傳.

83 Three Kingdoms 三國 to Sui Dynasty 隋朝 (the period covered the time from ~220-618 CE).

84 Zhuangzi 莊子 (369-286 BCE).

85 *Jiayou* 嘉祐 (1056-1063 CE), during the reign of Emperor Renzhong 宋仁宗.

Five Dynasties. I also intend to adopt the annalistic style of *Zuozhuan* by Qiuming; I will also emulate Xun Yue's style used in the compilation of the *Hanji*,[86] a succinct and precise rendering; in the process, I will gather, collect and collate the various textual accounts available as extensively as possible."

Scrutinizing the comments, one appreciates the impetus that spurred Sima Guang in his effort. He had hoped to compose a historical text of suitable length for scholars. Almost ten years later, during the 3rd year of *Zhiping* of Emperor Song Yingzong (1066 CE), Sima Guang took on the position as the emperor's lecturer - *daijiang*.[87] He used the *Tongjian* as his lecture notes; the emperor was greatly impressed by the work. He decreed Sima Guang to prepare a new volume on *The Events Related to the Sovereigns and Their Subjects Throughout the Various Dynasties.* The emperor added, "You, Sir please identify the outstanding scholars from the imperial libraries and the court as your aides." Sima Guang recommended Liu Shu and he said, "No one is more accomplished and proficient than Liu Shu in historiography." He added, "I have studied with (Liu Shu) for several years; when it comes to difficult and thorny issues on historical events, people are often criticial of others; nevertheless, I greatly admire his stance."[88]

It would be too simplistic to suggest that Sima Guang accomplished this monumental task single-handedly, and with his personal resources.[89] When Emperor Yingzong expressed his desire to support the project by offering Sima Guang his choice of capable and outstanding scholars as his aides; however, Sima Guang declined the offer and selected Liu Shu,[90] whom he considered as the most appropriate person for the task. He then assigned Zhao Junci as his personal aide.[91] Zhao's father had just died at that stage; hence, he was not enlisted as intended. Sima Guang then engaged Liu Ban, an expert Han historian, holding the title of the superintendent of ceremonies academician - *taichang boshi*,[92] as his personal aide. Later, during the 4th year of *Xining* (1071 CE), Liu Ban was seconded to Taizhou Province as a senior aide *tongban* under the magistrate.[93] Sima Guang subsequently appointed Fan Zuyu from the County of Longshuixian in Zizi Province to replace Liu.[94] However, available information indicates that Liu Ban continued to work on the project, particularly the passages before the Sui Dynasty.[95]

Besides Liu Shu, Liu Ban principally organized and collated the two sections on Han. The two Liu were also responsible for the unabridged drafts from the time of Wei and Jin to the end of the

---

86 Xun Yue 荀悦 (148-209 CE) composer of the *Hanji* 漢紀. This is another annalistic historic text; the contents were principally drawn from the *Hanshu* 漢書.

87 Yingzong 英宗. *Daijiang* 待講.

88 Sima Guang 司馬光, the *Zizhi tongjian waijixu* 資治通鑒外紀序.

89 Yingzong pronounced that Sima Guang was to make use of the imperial libraries for his research, which included Longtuge 龍圖閣, Tianzhangge 天章閣, Zhaowenguan 昭文館, Shiguan 史館, Jixianyuan 集賢院 and Mige 密閣. He further ordered the bestowal of the old books stored at Yingdi 穎邸 to Sima Guang.

90 Liu Shu 劉恕 Daoyuan 道原.

91 Zhao Junci 趙君賜 (?).

92 Liu Ban 劉攽 Gongfu 貢父, Superintendent of Ceremonies Academician - *taichang boshi* 太常博士.

93 4th year of *Xining* 熙寧 (1071 CE), Taizhou Province Senior Aide - *tongban* 泰州通判. *Tongban* was a magistrate assistant, acting as a balance to keep the magistrate in check for the court.

94 Fan Zuyu 范祖禹 Chunfu 字純甫 (1041-1098 CE), Longshuixian in the Zizizhou Province 知資州龍水縣.

95 Quoted from Wang Shengen 王盛恩 (1959-) *Songdai guanfang shixue yanjiu* 宋代官方史學研究, pp. 276-277.

Sui period.[96] The historical materials on the Tang Dynasty were far more extensive and complicated; they were placed under the care of Fan Zuyu. As Fan did not participate in the task during the induction phase, Sima Guang instructed him on the arrangements of the compilation,[97] he wrote, "The titles of entries are appended for your reference. Please prepare your unabridged compilation commencing from the time of Gaozu (the first emperor of Tang when he revolted against Sui in 618 CE) and ending with the time of Aidi's abdication (907 CE, the last Tang emperor).[98] The events leading to the revolt by Tang Gaozu and the aftermath of Aidi's abdication are also to be included based on currently available manuscripts. Please ask your scribes not to copy your manuscripts on rough paper, use the finest *suzhi* paper, and allow a space between each event.[99] Please also include all the events before the Sui Dynasty in your compilation, which are to be appended with Gongfu's (Liu Ban) compilations, while events after the Liang Dynasty prepared by Liu Ban and you are all to be included in the extended passage.[100] Considering that the other two gentlemen (other participants) did not study these texts, you, Sir, should forego historical events after *Wude* (the regnal year of Gaozu of Tang, 618-626 CE) and before *Tianyou* (Aidi 904-907 CE); all the historical events that transpired in between would be lost and wasted. If the other two gentlemen, working on their respective periods should come across events and materials about the Tang Dynasty, they would also be presented to you to be incorporated in your extended compilation."

The letter clearly defined the headings and the methodology adopted for the preparation of the extended or unabridged draft.[101] Sima Guang attached one volume of the extended draft compiled by Gong Fu (Liu Ban) and two extended chapters by Liu Shu for Fan Zuyu's reference. It appears that the division of labour between the three men was explicit and precise. Although the three men had different responsibilities to aid Sima Guang in their respective compilations, Liu Shu nevertheless contributed most to the work. Quan Zuwang, the author of the *A study of the Tongjian Compilers,*[102] writes, "Master Wengong (Sima Guang) profoundly appreciated the talent of Daoyuan (Liu Shu); the meanings of passages were deliberated and discussed with him in detail.

---

96 Wei 魏 (220-266 CE) and Jin 晉 (265-420 CE) to the end of the Sui 隋 (581-619 CE). N.B. There was a Nan-Beichao the Southern and Northern dynasties 南北朝 in between (420-589 CE).

97 'Responding to Fan Mengde's letter.' 答范夢得書.

98 *Wude* 武德 618-626 CE (Reigning title, *nianhao* 年號) of Gaozu 唐高祖 (r. 618-626 CE). *Tianyou* 天祐, Aidi 唐哀帝 (r 904-907 CE).

99 Suzhi 素紙. The spacing was for making cut and paste purpose, as well as for annotations and comments.

100 Liang Dynasty 梁朝 (502-587 CE).

101 The compilation of the *Zizhi tongjian* was a monumental and formidable task. Sima Guang's assistants began by collecting and collating all the information and available texts in the form of drafts. Sima Guang than merged the different volumes into one complete edition. In the process, passages and events were either discarded or appended, Sima Guang then proofread it. The work drew on formal history from 17 Official Histories, and references from 300 different sources, including Informal Histories *yeshi* 野史, genealogical records *pulu* 譜録, other compilations *bieji* 別集, local gazettes *difangzhi* 地方誌 and epitaphs *beizhi* 碑志 besides the texts kept at the libraries mentioned earlier. As Sima Guang was permitted to use the Imperial Libraries, and was able to use court-archived memorials as his sources.

Fan Zuyu 范祖禹 compiled over six hundred volumes on *Tangji* 唐紀. Sima Guang edited Tang history into 81 volumes. When he found that there were discrepancies rendering certain events, he would review the discrepancies in his *kaoyi* 考異, usually employing three or four different sources for verification and authentication.

102 *Tongjian fenxiu zhuren kao* 通鑒分修諸人考. Quan Zuwang 全祖望.

Hence, although his compilation terminated during the period of Five Dynasties, in fact, Liu Shu was the assistant redactor of the entire work."

Liu Shu died in 1078 CE, six years before the book was completed. The division of responsibilities changed somewhat. Sima Kang, the adopted son of Sima Guang, said to Chao Yuezhi,[103] the Song scholar, "The fact that the *Zizhi tongjian* could be accomplished successfully was entirely due to the capable scholars assigned. You see, there was Liu Gongfu (Liu Ban) working on the compilation of events from the *Shiji, Former Han,* and *Latter Han*. Liu Daoyuan (Liu Shu) worked on the time of the Three Kingdoms *Sanguo* in seven dynasties to Sui, and Fan Zuyu (Chunfu) compiled the histories of Tang to the time of the Five Dynasties (*Wudai*).[104] The three learned scholars were maestros of the time. My father charged with great dedication, working day and night conscientiously, ignored his meals. After struggling for a long time, he succeeded in the compilation of the work; a work that is instrumental in bringing good governance during times of chaos and crisis. He succeeded in accomplishing his ambitious aspiration."

Sima Guang - the Chief Editor

Apart from the *Tongji*, which was solely compiled and edited by Sima Guang; he also was solely responsible in editing the parts after 'the Conflicts between Chu and Han'.[105] In a letter to Song Cidao, an imperial attendant, he wrote,[106] "Ever since I moved to Luoyang, I have devoted my undivided attention to the compilation of the work. So far, I have merely completed six dynasties of Jin, Song, Qi, Liang, Chen, and Sui and had them presented to His Majesty.[107] The parts on the Tang Dynasty are particularly lengthy, I was fortunate to have the help of Fan Mengde (Zuyu),[108] who categorized the various available books and volumes according to the year and month of the events, and they were then edited as draft manuscripts. The drafts were then spliced into scrolls, each four *jiang* in length (13.3 metres). I set a goal of editing one scroll in three days; when other pressing personal issues distracted me, I would press forward by speeding up. Since the autumn before last when I began the editing, I have completed two hundred scrolls, ending at the final year of *Dali* (766-779 CE Emperor Dai of Tang).[109] The later volumes are twice as voluminous; they will come to no less than six or seven hundred scrolls; it should take roughly three more

---

103 Sima Kang 司馬康 was the adopted son of Sima Guang; he was one of the sons of Sima Guang's elder brother.

Chao Yuezhi 晁説之 (1059-1129 CE).

104 Liu Gongfu 劉貢甫(父) (Liu Ban) 劉攽.

Liu Daoyuan (Liu Shu), 劉道原 劉恕.

Fan Zuyu (Chunfu) 范祖禹 純甫.

From Chao 晁説之 the *Jingyusheng jiejuan* 景迂生集卷 17 quoted from Wang Shengen's 王盛恩 the *Songdai guanfang shixue yanjiu* 宋代官方史學研究 p. 278.

105 The conflicts between Chu and Han, 楚漢之争.

106 Song Cidao 宋次道.

107 Jin 晉 (265-420 CE), Song 宋 (420-479 CE), Qi 齊 (479-502 CE), Liang 梁朝 (502-587 CE), Chen 陳 (557-589 CE), Sui 隋 (581-619 CE).

108 Fan Mengde 范夢得 Zuyu 祖禹.

109 *Dali* 大歷 (766-779 CE, Emperor Dai of Tang 唐代宗).

years to arrive at a completed draft. Besides, the entire work needs to be re-edited and abridged to several scores of scrolls."[110]

Similar to Confucius' composition of the *Chunqiu Annals*, "The students of Zixia were not sanctioned to alter one phase of the text, not even one word." [111] The preparation of the *Zizhi tongjian* was in a similar vein. Although his aides and assistants prepared the extended draft versions of the various historical accounts, the final editing was entirely expedited by Sima Guang personally. Liu Xizhong, the son of Liu Shu, wrote in his *Tongjian wenyi*, "When my father was working at the library. He was in charge of collating similar events to be compiled into the extended draft; whereas whether they would be included in the final composition or otherwise, it was entirely up to Junshi (Sima Guang.)"[112]

Hence, the drafts of the extended version were compiled by the respective participants; it was then up to Sima Guang to edit and abbreviate the entire draft composition. He was wholly responsible for the style of the manuscript, calligraphy used, examination, and validation of historical authenticity, as well as the final pruning. In the text, Sima Guang made numerous annotations and commentaries on major events under the heading of 'Your Majesty's subject annotates' – '*chen Guang yan*' allowing his viewpoint on the events permeate throughout the entire work.[113] The endeavour is quite clear; it was to prevent it from falling into the deception of prevailing practice to avoid responsibility when it came to dubious and controversial issues by chronologists, as well as a means to express his personal perspectives.

Sima Guang considered the preface written by Emperor Zhenzong his crowning personal honour. During the 4th regnal year of Ziping (1067 CE), the emperor ordered a banquet be hosted to honour a lecture on the *Zizhi tongjian*. On the 9th day of the same month, Sima Guang gave a lecture on the Chronicle at court. The emperor bestowed upon him a preface and decreed that it would be incorporated in the text upon its completion. Sima Guang prepared a memorial under the heading of, 'Expressing Gratitude to His Majesty for His Preface on the *Zizhi tongjian*.' It articulated his aspiration to compile a historical text since childhood and that he had the complete support of Emperor Yingzong.[114] He writes,

"Your subject is neither endowed nor gifted; his education is insubstantial; though he happened to be vaguely involved with various historical texts since his childhood. He attempted to compile a historical text to eliminate the weeds and excesses, medleys and miscellaneous entities, hence as to convey the essence. Your subject searched exhaustively at attributes of good governance in times of crisis hopeful that he could come up with some measures of assistance to His Majesty. With your subject's meagre attributes, the involvement has been daunting; the task being prodigious and the passage has been long. This memorial expresses your subject's modest feeling, and the work is completed just as his hair is turning grey.[115] Your subject chanced to prostrate before the former Majesty, who yearned to investigate the righteous path of antiquity, to access and collect valuable sayings and old events; thereupon your subject's insignificant aspiration was realized. His Majesty, besides bestowing gifts of paper and writing utensils also ruled that he

110 Ma Duanlin 馬端臨, the *Wenxian tongkao* 文献通考, Zhonghua shuju 中華書局, 1986, Volume 193, p. 163.

111 Bu Zixia 卜子夏, Bu Shang 卜商 (507-?).

112 Liu Xizhong 劉羲仲, the *Tongjian wenyi*, 通鑒問疑. From the *Tongjian xinlun* 通鑒新論 by Chen Guangchong 陳光崇 (1918-2009), p. 155.

113 "臣光言" This is taken after *Zuozhuan's junzi rue* 君子曰 and 太史公曰 in the *SJ* 史記.

114 'Expressing Gratitude to His Majesty for His Preface on the *Zizhi tongjian*.' 謝賜資治通鑒序表.

115 '... 功大力薄, 任重道悠, 徒懷寸心, 行將白首.'

be allowed the convenience of borrowing texts from the imperial libraries for his research and compilation."[116]

Shortly after, Emperor Yingzong died, and Shenzong succeeded to the throne. Since the work was compiled under an imperial decree, Sima Guang submitted the re-edited *Tongji* in eight volumes to the new emperor. Shenzong highly praised the work and ordered him, 'to give lectures on the work at court.' The emperor then made another preface to the work, which was to be 'appended to the chapter titles."[117] He praised the work, "...it is extensive, and it contains all the essentials, and it is concise. Nevertheless, everything of importance has been recorded with great care,' and 'it is a compendium of codices, deeper than other texts."[118] Such were the words of praise on the work. Such honour greatly enthused Sima Guang. He wrote, 'For over a thousand years, since the time of the great historians of Zhou, Nan and Dong, Sima Qian and Ban Gu of Han,[119] they have been acclaimed as the greatest compilers of historical texts. None of their works received words of praise from a sovereign nor had an emperor written a preface;[120] especially when His Majesty humbled himself, using his imperial brush to praise the work, adorning the effort; allowing it (*Zizhi tongjian*) to radiate with brilliance. Your humble subject is simple with limited talent; his ability is insignificant compared to those of the great sage historians of the past. His work is no more than the sprouting shrubs in the wilderness, nevertheless, fortuitously; it alone has been graced by His Majesty to be honoured in posterity." In fact, it was for the preface penned by Shenzong that the *Zizhi tongjian* escaped the unthinkable destiny of being condemned and torched by the Reformist clique *Xindang*, Sima Guang's opponents.

Chronological Calendar

Before the compilation of the *Zizhi tongjian*, Liu Yishou, the eminent Song astronomer (1018-1060 CE), undertook the task of determining the accuracy of the dates of events by recalibrating the calendar, which was based on the traditional lunar calendar - *xiali*.[121] The time or year used was quite unorthodox. Instead of the *tiangan* and *dizhi* conventional method of recording the year of the event, he chose another system. The year was referred to as *Zhuyong shetige* (*Perturbation tigrays*), *Sheti* is *Kangxiu* the 7th chamber of the 24-star chamber system and the date used was not *ri*, but, rather *jia, yi, zi, chou*.[122] The system is extremely convoluted; in our translation, the

---

116 Rao Zongyi 饒宗頤 *Zizhi tongjian* 資治通鑒. p. 16.

117 '序其本原, 冠於篇秩.'

118 '典刑之總會, 册牘之淵林.'

119 Dong Hu 董狐 was a court historian of Jin 晉 and Nan Shi 南史 was a court historian of Qi 齊. It was the time of Chunqiu 春秋. Hence Sima Guang refers to them as historians of the time of Zhou 周. Both historians were known for their unyielding stance of factual and truthful treatments of historic records.

120 He writes, "....周之南, 董, 漢之遷, 固, 皆推高一時, 播美千載. 未有親屈帝文, 特紆宸翰, 曲蒙獎飾, 大振輝光. 如臣樸樕小才, 固非先賢之比; 便蕃茂澤, 獨專後世之榮."

121 Liu Yishou 劉義叟 (1018-1060 CE) was an eminent Song astronomer.
Lunar calendar *xiali* 夏歷.

122 *Tiangan* 天干 and *dizhi* 地支.
Zhuyong shetige 著雍 攝提格 (*Perturbation tigrays*), *Sheti* 攝提 is *Kangxiu* 亢宿 the 7th of the 24-star chamber-system and the date used was not *ri* 日 rather *jia* 甲, *yi* 乙, *zi* 子, *chou* 丑.
Shetige 攝提格 was an ancient calendar system that was in use during the time of Zhanguo 戰國, Qin 秦 and Han 漢. The system employed the use of an imaginary star, which had the same motion

author has chosen to use the *tiangan* and *dizhi* notation, as well as the conventional Gregorian calendar.

A Historiographic Classic

From the present day perspective, the *Zizhi tongjian* was not merely an appropriate work for sovereigns or heads-of-states; it is also a suitable work for scholars or people interested in history. As Sima Guang stated, he attempted to condense the history of China of almost fourteen hundred years into a manageable and concise volume, allowing sovereigns, who were preoccupied with ten thousand difficult daily issues to read and appreciate history; using the experience of history to enrich the sovereign's wise governance. On numerous occasions in his annotations, he said that the path of good governance of a state was comprised of no more than three essential entities. First, it was the appointment of the appropriate and reputable ministers and officers, the second, was about rewarding the meritorious, and the third was concerned with chastising administrators who failed.[123] He stressed the moral characteristic of a sovereign or ruler was the quintessential entity, as he said, 'The three indispensable moral characters of a ruler are, benevolence, clear vision while remaining indomitable and valiant.' (See footnotes for the definition of the word – *wu*.) [124] Through learning historical experiences, a ruler could establish the groundwork to reign over chaos, to preside over safety in the face of the impending danger of the annihilation or the survival of a state.[125]

In 1084 CE, the 12th month of the 7th year of *yuanfeng*, the book was finally completed. The work encompassed a period from the Warring States to Five dynasties *Wudai*, covering a span of 1362 years.[126] Sima Guang wrote a description of his experience during the process of compilation, (Please see Presentation of the *Zizhi tongjian* to the Emperor, attached.)

Just as he related, "Your subject has drained all his energy and resources to accomplish this book."

---

and speed as Jupiter (*suixing* 歲星), each cycle is equal to one *zhoutian* 周天, i.e. every twelve years; whereas the astrological stars that make counter-revolutions are called *taisui* 太歲. The position of the star was thus used to determine the year of the event. When Jupiter was located at the position of *chou*, 丑 (2nd position of), *taisui* should be in the position of *rin* 寅, that particular year would be called 攝提格, abbreviated as *sheti*.

123 "曰任官, 曰信賞, 曰必罰." Chen Guangchong, the *Tongjian xinlun* 陳光崇 通鑒新論, p. 192. Sima Guang made emphasis on Gaozu of Han, Liu Bang's 漢高祖 success against Xiang Yu 項羽. See 202-IX.

124 "人君之德三, 曰仁, 曰明, 曰武."

The original word used was *wu* 武, and the proper translation should be militaristic or marshal; however, I believe it is not the meaning of Sima Guang. A translation of the word *wu* to mean valiant or indomitable is probably closer to what he meant.

125 "治亂存亡安危之本源."

126 It is generally accepted that the work was prepared between 1066-1084 CE, for a period of 19 years. However, if we are to include the time taken to prepare the *Tongzhi* 通志, the first 8 volumes, the book would have taken over twenty years. It is quite probable that he started working on the book between Jiayou (1056-1063 CE); in which case it would have taken almost 30 years to compile. As the *Tongzhi* was solely prepared by Sima Guang, it took much longer.

A Brief Study of the Narratives, and the Historiographic Philosophy of the Work

The *Zizhi tongjian* has earned high acclaim among Chinese and Asian history scholars ever since its publication. However, the claim could not be made about Western scholars and historians, as the work has not been translated into English in its entirety; though some sections of the work have been translated, and French scholars translated a much-abbreviated version of the *Tongjian gangmu* during the 18th century.[127] Hence, the work is not widely read or circulated among Western scholars.

Chinese historiographers and scholars have placed the *Zizhi tongjian* among the classics of the *Zuozhuan*, the *Shiji* and the *Hanji*, all held highly for their descriptive narratives of historical events. Nevertheless, Sima Guang took the *Zizhi tongjian* to another level; he made a breakthrough in the field of chronological historiography. While the book is a great historical text, he did not chronicle the historical events in a fluvial stream. He employed different techniques to relate and describe historical events; he brought out the background used for his narratives; bringing historiography to a new height.

Scholars have classified his techniques into four categories. 1. Outlines - He presented a particular incident with a brief outline before he delved into the subject matter. 2. Flashback - He used the technique of ruminating or flashback; it was derived from the *Zuozhuan*. He would recount and ruminate on certain incidents to bring out the event. In the translation, one notices that there are many incidents that commence with, 'previous to this,' or 'prior to this,' or 'many years before this,' or 'relating to this event.' 3. Categorization of similar events - Some of the historical events might have been too complicated to be related individually; he emulated the techniques employed by the *Zuozhuan* and the *Hanji* by listing related events under similar categories, or connecting similar events. 4. Appended narratives - Historians before Sima Guang did not relate the origin or place of birth of a historical figure. Unless one traces the origin and background of an individual through his different biographic texts, one is often left clueless as to who the individual might have been; even if one is motivated enough to search for clues, it is tedious and time-consuming. Sima Guang briefly appended in the text the place of origin of the historical figure as well his family genealogy. These addendums offer us excellent clues as to how the individual might have been related to the incident and the role he played in the event. The techniques employed were to become the historiographic archetype of latter-day historians.[128]

Having related the benefits and advantages of the style, it is also important to note that the chronological narrative does have its shortcomings and limitations. For example, the events that transpired on the rise and fall of Wei (Liang) Dynasty happened over 180 years,[129] and the wars with Xiongnu took place over several centuries; it is often difficult, therefore, to establish a complete picture of the unfolding events. Nevertheless, compared with the biographical style, it has its advantages.

127 The Manchu version of *Tongjian gangmu* 通鑒綱目 (part of *Tongjian* 通鑒) was translated into French by Joseph-Anna-Marie de Moyriac de Mailla, a Jesuit priest. The *Histoire générale de la chine, ou Annales de cet Empire; traduit du Tong-kien-kang-mou par de Mailla* was published in Paris in 1777-1783.

128 Chen Guangchong 陳光崇, the *Tongjian xinlun* 通鑒新論. pp. 152-153.
Outline 提綱法. Flashback 追敍法. Categorization of similar events 連類法. Appended narratives 带敍法.

129 Wei 魏 (Liang 梁) 403-225 BCE.

Qian Mu, the eminent Chinese historian, wrote to his student, Yan Gengwang, a master of medieval Chinese history, makes a mention of the *Zizhi tongjian*,[130] "When ancient Chinese scholars made advanced studies, they made no distinction between literature, history and philosophy. When one reads Master Wengong's (Sima Guang) *Tongjian*, he sees that he appended two entities of novels and notes.[131] These notes were related to historical events, with much profound, latent doctrines and canons. He had successfully merged the three disciplines of literature, history and philosophy....." In the letter, Qian Mu described how to appreciate the *Zizhi tongjian* and attain a higher level of learning. It leads us to conclude that it is not merely a commonplace historiography, nor simply a resource text; it is beyond both.

Errors and Inaccuracies

The *Zizhi tongjian* has been acclaimed for its style and for being religiously meticulous, the contents being vivid and distinct, the collection of facts being exhaustive, historical materials being extensive, and one can go on with all the ovation. However, the text also suffers from some shortcomings; it is sufficient for us to point out a few flaws pertaining to the period of our translation. One of the major errors was the year when the Qi state launched an attack against Yan (313 BCE). Sima Guang following the mistake made by Sima Qian by adding 10 years to King Wei of Qi while deducting 10 years from the reign of King Min of Qi to correspond with the time of Mengzi's visit to King Xuan of Qi.[132] Another example: the details of the accounts of Yue Yi's expedition against the Qi state were flawed and perhaps were fabricated by historians during late Warring States years.[133] Another perhaps less justifiable entry was that Wang Mang poisoned King Ping of Han; in fact, the event was probably fabricated by the insurgents and was unfounded. There were also the flaws of attrition of historical events; it prompted Zhu Xi of Song to remark,[134] "Master Wen had an aversion to political trickery and tactics; when he came across such passages he would delete them summarily, but one must remember such incidents might have transpired. When he had no choice but to keep the passages, he would habitually delete a few sentences; however, in so doing the text would leave a void of the essence from the original meaning. The other approach was to make annotations or commentaries." He added, "When Master Wen edited his texts, and he came upon passages conflicting with his personal perspectives he would delete all of them. There are numerous examples in his text."[135]

The work has several other inadequacies. The book is principally based on the politics of the court and military affairs; lacking are the many accounts of economics, where the records are few and far in between. There is hardly any mention of the peoples' ethos, music, arts, and religions.

---

130 Qian Mu 錢穆 (1895-1990 CE). Yan Gengwang 嚴耕望 (1916-1996 CE).

131 The two volumes are *Xin Tangshu* 新唐書 and *Jiu Tangshu* 舊唐書 in the *Zizhi tongjian.*

132 Recent historians and Yang Kuan 楊寬 made a thorough studies of the event based on the *Bamboo annals, Zhushu jinian* came up with more accurate dates. However, it is noted that the *Zhushu jinian* in its re-composite form was probably not available to Sima Guang. Details see Appendix on Yang Kuan's notes on the Warring States period.

133 Wu Yugui 吳玉貴 (1956-) compiled the *Zizhi tongjian yinian lu* 資治通鑒疑年錄, which carries a list of 888 erroneous dates that appeared in the *Zizhi tongjian.*
Yue Yi 樂毅.

134 Zhu Xi of Song 宋 朱熹 (1130-1200 CE).

135 Cen Zhongmian 岑仲勉 (1885-1961 CE) the *Tongjian Sui-Tang ji bishi zhiyi* 通鑒隋唐紀比事質疑. His *Tongjian Sui-Tang ji bishi zhiyi* lists 670 erroneous and faulty entries.

Although there are some references to the grand masters, literati and scholars during the time of the Warring States, most of them were merely mentioned or remarked in passing.[136]

Official and Unofficial History

Official history *zhengshi* are chronicles compiled by government officials; the term is also translated as 'Standard History'. On the other hand, histories not prepared by the court officials are known as *yeshi,* the 'privately compiled history' or 'unofficial history' - *baiguan.*[137] Histories compiled by the junior functionaries of the court were called the 'unofficial history' – *yeshi* a rather pejorative term.[138]

The term *zhengshi* first appeared in the *Zhengshi xiaofan* compiled by Ruan Xiaoxu, the Nan Dynasty bibliographer, whereas the first usage of the term was in the *Suishu Jingjizhi* by Wei Zheng of Tang (580-643 CE).[139] The definition came about that books like the *Shiji,* and the *Hanshu* used the formats of sovereigns' biographies *benji.*[140] Hence, they came to be known as official histories – *zhengshi.*

During the 4th year of Emperor Qianlong of Qing (1711-1799 CE), the court ordered the compilation the *Complete Library of the Four Treasuries* - the *Siku quanshu.*[141] The court decreed that the twenty-four volumes of histories from the *Shiji* to the *Mingshi* would be recognized as Official Histories. Later during the period of the Republic of China (1912-1949 CE), the government included *The History of Qing, Qingshi gao* as the 25 Official Histories of China.[142] All the 'Official Histories' belong to the biographical genre; none was in the chronological order. Hence, the *Zizhi tongjian,* being a chronological text did not find its place in the list of Official History – *zhengshi.* Some scholars refer to the *Zizhi tongjian* as *yeshi*; it is rather unfortunate and does not do the text justice.

The Contents

The *Zizhi tongjian* has 294 volumes, with roughly three million words. The text commences its account from 403 BCE, the 23rd year of King Weilie of Zhou and ends in 959 CE, Emperor Shi of Zhou Shi - *Xiande* 6th year when the emperor made an expedition against Huainan.[143] The historical text covers sixteen dynasties, [144] a total of 1,362 years. It is noted that the narrations in

---

136 There is a lengthy passage on Xun Kuang's 荀況 perception of war, see 255-11.

137 *Baiguan* 稗官野史.

138 Official history *zhengshi* 正史 *yeshi* 野史 or privately composed history.

139 Official History – *zhengshi* 正史, the term first appeared in the *Zhengshi xiaofan* 正史削繁 Ruan Xiaoxu 阮孝緒 (479-536 CE) the Nan Dynasty bibliographer. The *Suishu jingjizhi* 隋書 經籍志, attributed to Wei Zheng of Tang 唐 魏征 (580-643 CE); in fact, the book was compiled by several scores of scholars, and it took 36 years.

140 Benji 本紀.

141 Official History 正史 *zhengshi.* During the 4th year of Emperor Qianlong 清乾隆 (r. 1735 -1799 CE) when the court decreed to compile the *Siku quanshu* 四庫全書 the *Complete Library of the Four Treasuries.*

142 *The history of Qing Qingshi gao* 清史稿 to become the 25 Official Histories of China.

143 403 BCE, the 23rd year of King Weilie of Zhou 周威烈王 and ends in 959 CE, Zhou Shizong - *Xiande* 6th year 周世宗 顯德六年 when he made an expedition against Huainan 淮南.

144 The Sixteen Ji 十六紀 - 周紀 五卷; 秦紀 三卷; 漢紀 六十卷; 魏紀 十卷; 晉紀 四十卷; 宋紀 十六卷; 齊紀十卷; 梁紀二十二卷; 陳紀十卷; 隋紀 八卷; 唐紀 八十一卷; 後梁紀 六卷; 後唐紀 八卷; 後晉紀 六卷; 後漢紀 四卷; 後周紀 五卷.

the distant past were more concise and succinct while the events closer to Sima Guang's time were more precise and extensive. The 371 years between the Sui, Tang, and Wu-Dai dynasties account for about 40% of the text. It is generally accepted that the historiographic value of the Sui and Tang period is the highest; understandably, it was only several hundred years removed from the time of Sima Guang. It is also worthy to note that Sima Guang placed much emphasis on two periods of exceptional social order, that of the reigns of emperors Wen and Jing of Han, known as *Wenjing zhizhi* (180-141 BCE) and *Zhenguan zhizhi* (627-649 CE).[145] Justifiably so, as reflected by the title of the book, those were indeed two of the greatest periods of benevolent reigns in Chinese history, when the commoners were able to enjoy decades of rare peace and opulence.

The posture adopted in the *Zizhi tongjian* is fervently orthodox; one can see the influence of literati learning permeated throughout the entire text. For example, the emperors are addressed as '*shang*' – roughly translated as His Majesty, the emperors in the Han Dynasty and even Qin Shi Huang are addressed as '*shang*' and never by their name. The exception is Wang Mang, the usurper of the Han Dynasty, [146] he is addressed simply as Mang. Other examples were the periods of great division, *San-Guo* – the Three Kingdoms, Wei have annuals *ji*, while Shu and Wu kingdoms do not, during the South and North dynasties, the South Dynasty has an annals *ji*, while the North does not. The Wu-Dai, Five dynasties have annals, while the minor ten states do not have annals. There were some exceptions, whether by design or mistaken interpretation we could not tell. Zhu Xi (1130-1200 CE) had expressed dissatisfaction in that the kings of Shu-Han being the descendants of the royal bloodline of the Eastern Han Dynasty,[147] however, Sima Guang had placed Wei as the formal imperial house, and he challenged - it was like putting the cart before the horse.

There are 186 annotations and commentaries in the entire work, of which Sima Guang accounted for 102 while 84 other commentaries were made by others. There was only one entry by Sima Qian. The 'Hanji' passages have the most annotations, followed by 'Tangji'.

A Reflection of the Time

Sima Guang did not relate all the accounts that transpired in the span of history he covered. He merely selected the important events that were to influence subsequent events, and incidents that had enduring consequences.

Sima Guang, apart from his aspiration to prepare an extraordinary historical text, having been abandoned by the Song court was most likely embittered as reflected by his annotations. That he being the chancellor was discarded on the wayside, perhaps he was finding ways and means in history to vindicate his failure, or perhaps some way to justify his belief - that to deviate from tradition would cause devastating consequences. We could only guess. However, it might not be too far from the truth, as a conformist, the deviation from the traditional Confucian value was unthinkable.

It was perhaps then a product of contention between a conformist and a reformist that neither could meet the needs of their time; Wang Anshi's thesis that there was a need for reform and Sima Guang's thesis of adhering to the old paradigm. However, at the time of Song, the world

---

145 Emperors Wen and Jing of Han, known as *Wenjing zhizhi* 文景之治 (180-141 BCE) and *Zhenguan zhizhi* 貞觀之治 (627-649 CE).

146 Wang Mang 王莽.

147 Zhu Xi 朱熹 (1130-1200 CE).
Shu-Han 蜀漢.

was changing. The nomadic tribes and Western foreign powers were on the rise, against a prosperous yet enfeebled state. Even had Wang Anshi or Sima Guang been successful, the world of the Middle Kingdom would have been overwhelmed by foreign powers, as evidenced by the eventual fall of Southern Song to the Mongols. And subsequently in the course of history, for some two or three centuries (with the exception of the Ming Dynasty, which was able to hold its own for 276 years) when China could no longer impede the surge and encroachment of foreign powers and succumbed to the more powerful, socio-political evolved entities from without. Perhaps we too could learn a few things from the legacy brought to us by Sima Guang, his time and his *Zizhi tongjian.*

The *Zizhi tongjian* as a Modern Mirror for Good Governance

For the historiographic purists delving into hair-splitting details and facts, there are perhaps better options than the *Zizhi tongjian,* as Sima Guang stated, there were, at least, fifteen hundred volumes at the time of the Warring States to Wudai. The *Zizhi tongjian* stands as an invaluable historiographic tool. As it offers an abridged account of history in the making; besides it does contain some of the valuable accounts that have since been lost in the mist of time as some of the invaluable references used by Sima Guang had since been lost after the fall of the Southern Song Dynasty. Furthermore, it might take months if not years to research into an event scattered all over various texts to arrive at a cohesive whole; the *Zizhi tongjian* offers one a rather accurate and comprehensive account of historical events in some passages. For the amateur readers who do not have the time to delve into the historical details scattered over numerous books, the *Zizhi tongjian* is perhaps the best historical text available on Chinese history between the period of the Warring States and *Wudai.*

In Closing

The *Zizhi tongjian* stands with the *Spring and Autumn Annals* and the *Shiji* as the three of most important works in Chinese historiography, not merely for their contributions of the thorough research conducted at the time, but also for their philosophical approach to history. While only the *Shiji* has been accepted as formal or Official History, it does not make the *Spring and Autumn Annals* and the *Zizhi tongjian* less as historiographic classics.

The *Zizhi tongjian* is also valuable in a reflection of history at its time. While historian classicists might consider such an undertaking as purely speculative historiography, one is reminded that history is no more than the subjective perception of the historiographer, who being human could be marred by his personal biases, despite his intention of being impartial.

Preface by Zhao Xu – Emperor Shen of Song[1]

I am cognizant that illustrious men with noble character are conversant with maxims of the past and events of yore, these men use their knowledge to cultivate their moral integrity; consequently, they improve on their moral stature and scholarship with each passing day. The *Book of Documents* says,[2] "The sovereign of a state and people are to broaden their knowledge incessantly to make constructive contributions with absorption." The *Book of Odes*, the *Book of Documents* and the *Analects* have clear elucidations of successes and failures of states in the past; they chronicle the rightful path of good governance, leaving lasting legacies for future generations to reflect upon and for due admonition.[3]

The Grand Historian Sima Qian of Han gathered the manuscripts kept at the Imperial Stone Chamber and texts achieved at the Golden Cabinet;[4] based on the *Zuoshi Annals* he made studies of the *Shiben*, the *Zhanguoce*, and the *Chu-Han Annals* to authenticate the lost and obscured events.[5] Amassing the myriad number of historical texts under Heaven for elucidation and authentication, he made broad and sweeping studies of history over several thousand years and chronicled his monumental work.[6] The work commences from the time of Emperor Qianyan to the time when Emperor Wu of Han acquired a white unicorn.[7] The five-genera of chronicling he adopted - that of *ji* royal house biography, *biao* tables, *shijia* generational biography, *shu* documents, and *zhuan* biography had become a new literary archetype,[8] a criterion later historians came to espouse as established institution. The way he presented the historical events was in conformity with the formats laid down by the sages, the praises and critiques he rendered were sincere and pertinent, unbiased and critical; it is truly an exceptional historiography.

His Majesty Yingzong placed much emphasis on studying ancient texts.[9] When he could find a spare moment amidst his ten thousand taxing state chores, he would never forgo reading. He decreed to commission Sima Guang, the Imperial Historian at Longtuge, to compile a comprehensive list of deeds of past emperors and their subjects over the dynastic past.[10] The historian was authorized to use the rare texts archived at the Imperial Library at Mige for his investigation.[11] The court supplied him with aides and stationeries. The Chronicle was to commence from the reign of King Weilie of Zhou and conclude during the Five Dynasties *Wudai*.[12] Guang's decision to commence the narratives of his historiography was based on the premises

---

1 Preface by Zhao Xu 趙頊 – Emperor Shenzong of Song 宋神宗.

2 The *Book of Documents, Shujing* 書經.

3 The *Odes, Shi* 詩.
The *Book of Documents, Shu* 書經 (*Shangshu* 尚書). The *Annals, Chunqiu* 春秋.

4 Sima Qian 司馬遷.

5 The *Zuoshi guoyu* 左氏 國語. The *Shiben* 世本. The *Zhanguoce* 戰國策 (abbreviated as *ZGC* 戰國策). The *Chu-Han annals* 楚漢春秋.

6 The *Shiji* 史記 (abbreviated as *SJ* 史記).

7 Xianyuan Huangdi 軒轅黄帝 Legendary pre-historic King.
The Emperor of *Han Wudi* 漢武帝 得白麒麟, *Yuanshou* 1st year 漢武帝 元狩元年 122 BCE. The text merely mentions 'until the acquisition of a white unicorn,' it is difficult for readers to understand if it is literately translated as such.

8 *Ji* 紀. *Biao* 表. *Shijia* 世家. *Shu* 書. *Zhuan* 傳.

9 Emperor Ying of Song 宋英宗 (r. 1063-1067 CE).

10 Longtuge zhixueshi, Longtuge Liberian 龍圖閣 直學士, Sima Guang 司馬光.

11 Mige 密閣 Mi Library.

12 King Weilie of Zhou 周 威烈王, Ji Wu 姬午 38th Zhou King (403 BCE). Wudai 五代 959 CE.

that during the reign of King Weilie, the Zhou court had become so enfeebled that it was no longer in control of the kingdom; the ceremonial, political and military authorities of the state had fallen into the hands of the fief lords. When King Ping of Zhou moved his capital to the east, after that the influence of the fiefdoms of Qi, Chu, Qin, and Jin began to augment.[13] Dukes Huan and Wen became hegemons respectively;[14] they, notwithstanding, esteemed the king; however, in reality, they were carrying the reverence-slogan to command the other fief lords under Heaven to serve their personal interests. When King Weilie decreed to enfeoff the vassal ministers of Hann, Zhao, and Wei as fief lords the Zhou dynastic court had yet to meet its demise, nevertheless the protocols and decorum of the state were by then in complete ruin. The imperial historian decided to use this particular year to commence with his narratives; it accords with ancient scholars' practice of commencing chronicle with a preconceived conception. In his work, Guang records the sage lords and their sagacious subjects working together and made changes to instill benevolent governance; he archives words of wisdom for attaining munificence; he expounds the delicate balance between ethics and judiciary for respectable systems. He further examines the relationships between the divine and the corporals, and things and events that augur ominous or propitious. He makes considerations of the underpinnings of vicissitude, the aftermaths of implemented procedures, recordings of strategic manoeuvres by commanders and generals, as well as astute and prudent governance implemented by judicious administrators. He probes into the details by offering critiques on the equitable and the ineptness of decisions, recording the temporary or enduring procedures. Not only this, he makes inclusions of some of the most charming and fluent proses, the most profound expressions; and naturally he includes some of the most contentious and controversial issues. The text covers a span of sixteen dynasties edited in two hundred and ninety-four volumes. Placing a volume as such on one's desk he is blessed forthwith with profound knowledge, and he could glean the passage of time in a glance. The span of knowledge is vast and expensive, yet simplistic to the essentials, no event of importance is spared from being included; it goes without saying it has a comprehensive coverage of all important events that had transpired. It is indisputably a compendium of the dynastic decrees, of laws, and of regulations of historical past, and indeed an archive of official manuscripts.

Xunzi said,[15] "If one wishes to comprehend the accomplishments and deeds of sages look no further than the acts of latter sovereigns." Kongzi would have articulated that he could not dispute the claim that emperors Wen and Xuan of Han and Emperor Tai of Tang were exemplary rulers.[16] Indeed, there were other outstanding sovereigns: the ones with earnest affection towards their subjects and their nation, or the ones brimming with filial piety, or the ones who were adept in appointing wise and capable administers to preside at their court or the ones who were parsimonious and cautious. Needless to add that these men were all graced in varying degree by the traditional virtues and values propounded by the sage and sagacious men. Mengzi remarked, "There are only two or perhaps three events that are worth noting between King Wu and King

---

13 King Ping of Zhou 周平王 (13th) moved his capital from Gaojing 鎬京 Xian Shaanxi 陕西 西安 to the east at Luoyang 洛陽 in 770 BCE. Qi 齊, Chu 楚, Qin 秦 and Jin 晉.

14 Duke Huan of Qi 齊桓公 Jiang Shaobai 姜小白 (r. 685-643 BCE).
Duke Wen of Jin 晉文公 Ji Zhonger 姬重耳 (r. 636-628 BCE).

15 Xunzi, Xun Qing (Quang) 荀子 荀卿 (况) (313-238 BCE).

16 Emperor Wen of Han 漢文帝 Liu Huan 劉桓 (r. 180-157 BCE).
Emperor Xuan of Han 漢宣帝 Liu Xun 劉詢 (r. 74-48 BCE).
Emperor Taizong of Tang 唐太宗 Li Shimin 李世民 (r. 626-649 CE).

Cheng."[17] As for the absurd and maddening sovereigns, we could learn so much from their despotic behaviours; while the nefarious and reprehensible sovereigns do provide us issues with revelation and subjects for introspection; they are no different from the formation of ice - as a warning of approaching chill. The *Odes* says, "The Shang dynasty should make use of the demise of Xia as a mirror to reflect upon on what had transpired."

I thus decreed to name this text, the *Zizhi tongjian.* It is unambiguously my wish to name it so.[18]

Singed –Emperor Shenzong of Song.[19]

Zhiping 4th year, 10th month (1067 CE) [20] – His Majesty summoned his subjects at court to attend a banquet and to an oration of the *Zizhi tongjian* at the imperial hall. During the 9th day of the 10th month, Sima Guang, the Imperial Historian orated, for the first time, the text according to the imperial decree. His Majesty presented Sima Guang the Imperial Preface and decreed to be appended as forewords when the text was finally completed.

Senior Counsellor at the Palace.

---

17 King Wu of Zhou 周武王 Ji Fa 姬發 (r. 1046-1043 BCE).
King Cheng of Zhou 周成王 Ji Song 姬誦 (r. 1042-0121 BCE).
The quote is from *Mengzi*, "If one is to develop a conviction on the *Shujing* (*Shangshu*) he reads, it is better to go without. Between King Wu and King Cheng, I would only choose two or three events that are worth noting. A benevolent ruler is invincible under heaven. But, why did the benevolent man allow his malevolent enemies breed until the blood ran as deep as pestles?" 孟子曰, "盡信書, 則不如無書. 吾於武成, 取二三策而已矣. 仁人無敵於天下, 以至仁伐至不仁, 而何其血之流杵也!" The *Mengzi Sishu* 孟子四書 'Jinxin zhangju' 盡心章句下 (三).

18 "The Compendium Mirror in Aid for Good Governance".

19 Emperor Shenzong of Song 宋神宗 Zhao Xu 趙頊 (r. 1067-1085 CE).

20 *Zhiping* 4th year, 10th month (1067 CE) 治平四年十月.
N.B. This note was appended by Sima Guang.

Sima Guang on the Submission of His *Zizhi tongjian*

Your humble subject was commissioned by an imperial decree issued by the former Emperor to make a compilation of the deeds and events of sovereign lords and their subjects throughout the dynastic ages. The text is embellished by an Imperial Decree to name it the *Zizhi tongjian*. The work is now completed. Your subject is obtuse; his scholastic knowledge is inadequate and deficient, being inferior in every aspect to his peers, except he eagerly endeavours to make cursory studies of ancient history. Ever since he was a child until now an elderly man, he has been tireless in his pursuit of his interest in studying history. Since the time of Sima Qian and Ban Gu, the amount of historical texts that have been accumulated is myriad in number.[1] Your subject was seriously concerned that given the spare time of a commoner, garbed in plain clothes, could not perchance to have sufficient time to read them all, let alone the sovereign of a state busily attending to the ten thousand tasks on a daily basis. Your subject, hence, harboured an ambition, perhaps aspiring above his limited competency, to compile a historical text by abrogating the unnecessary dictions and entries - opting for the essence and substance, merely focusing on matters pertinent to the vicissitude of nations and on the weal and woe of the people. Your subject had intended to include the moral and respectable deeds espoused by rulers whereby the exemplary examples could be used as illuminators for the future while the evil and nefarious deeds could be used as vigilance to guard against. Your humble subject envisioned to prepare a historical text – in chronological order and to be expedited with concision and precision; nevertheless, he was wanting in his limited financial resources and had to forgo the ambition. Your subject was most fortunate to be serving the former Emperor, who was endowed with immense wisdom and perception. His Majesty had intended to make things ancient and political events of the bygone era to be the guiding principle of good governance of the future. Consequently, he decreed to commission your subject to compile a historical chronicle. Your subject was exuberant that he finally had a chance to fulfill his ultimate ambition and complied with gratitude. His only concern was that he being inadequate in scholastic profundity might fall short in the quest bestowed upon him. The former Emperor further decreed that he was authorized to nominate the staff members to aid in his work, and a dedicated office was assigned in the Chongwen Imperial Library as his workplace. He was sanctioned to have access to texts from the three imperial libraries of – the Longtuge, Tianzhangge, and Mige; in addition to the collections of rare texts at the three literate museums of Zhaowenguan, Jixianyuan, and Guoshiguan.[2]

His Majesty further bestowed to supply your subject with writing utensils and silk script-scrolls reserved for the imperial court, and with imperial fund for fruits and canapés to inspire his aides. He also assigned his inner attendants as liaisons to keep His Majesty informed of the progress. Your subject was subjected to such privilege that it has not ensued recently or since time immemorial. It was most regrettable that His Majesty should leave us before the work was completed. When Your Majesty ascended to the throne, you committed to the ambitious exploit of the former Emperor by continuing with the project. Your Majesty has specially prepared to append a preface for the work and embroidered it with a fine and fitting title. On several occasions, you decreed to hold banquets and have the text orated at the imperial hall. Though your subject is dull and fatuous, nevertheless two exceptional emperors with much conviction have exalted him, even if he were to sustain any form of chastisement or even lose his life he

---

1 Qian 遷 - Sima Qian 司馬遷 and Gu 固 - Ban Gu 班固.

2 Chongwendian 崇文殿. Longtu 龍圖. Tianzhangge 天章閣. Sanguan 三館. Mige 秘閣.

could not possibly repay the munificence that was bestowed upon him. Your subject could only repay with even more industrious effort, drudging as far as his ability could carry him. Later, Your Majesty assigned him to take on the position as the military commander of Yongxing; [3] when at that juncture he was incapacitated by illness and was incapable of taking on such weighty responsibilities, he pleaded to be reassigned to less arduous posts. Your Majesty gracefully accepted his application, and he was reassigned as the Yushitai at the Western Capital - Xijing,[4] with a dual responsibility as the Department Head of the Songshan Palace at Xijing. Overall, your subject was assigned to six different appointments; on every occasion, he was allowed to continue to assume his responsibility with his history department and staff. In the meantime, the imperial court continued to make financial arrangements for his department, while never assigning any mandates to meet deadlines or to come up with results. Since your subject was principally relieved of other mundane chores, he was able to delve all his efforts into his work. When he could not accomplish sections of his tasks in the daytime, he continued to work deep into the night.

In the text, your subject included events and facts chronicled in the authenticated historical accounts; he also drew on the unofficial histories and scripts that were made available to him. The scripts and scrolls piled in front of him like mountainous moulds. His team members and he were completely absorbed in their work of uncovering and researching on the factual historical accounts; they studied each and every single word to ensure its accuracy; attempting to uncover the most obscured and hidden meanings. The text commences from the Warring States *Zhanguo,* ending at the time of the Five Dynasties *Wudai,* spanning one thousand three hundred sixty-two years in two hundred and ninety-four volumes. An appendix is also appended using year and month as markers for ease of reference, which he named *Mulu* - Index, in thirty volumes.[5] Furthermore, another volume called *Kaoyi* – the Divergence of Evidence, [6] in thirty volumes is also appended to the text. Overall, the entire work has three hundred and fifty-four volumes. The work commenced during the years of *Zhiping* of the reign of His Majesty, Emperor Ying and it has taken all this time to accomplish the entire work.[7] During the ensuing years, the team had had their uncertainties and reservations. One cannot claim that there were no misinterpretations and inaccuracies, and he cannot discharge himself from such erroneous entries.

Your subject, Sima Guang, fills with trepidation and anxiety, making the proper etiquette of *kowtow* and *kowtow,* implore His Majesty to exonerate your humble subject that he has been absent from the imperial court for ten and five years. While your subject has been away from the court, nevertheless, day in and day out, whether awake or asleep, he is no further away from Your Majesty in thought. Your subject being ill informed and ignorant could hardly be a suitable candidate to serve at court; he has hence tried to repay Your Majesty's graciousness by working on this literate work. Though his contribution is insignificant like droplets of water or specks of dust, hopefully, they will enhance the depth of the ocean and heighten the loftiness of a mountain. Having aged, he is emaciated, and his body has withered, his eyes are blurred, merely a few teeth are left intact, his memories are short; his life-force and his essence have been vested upon the compilation of this book. His only yearning is that Your Majesty would pardon your subject for

3 Yongxingjun 永興軍.

4 District Supervisor at the Western capital - Xijing liusi yushitai 西京留司 御史台.
Chongfugong Palace 崇福宫 Xijing Songshan 西京嵩山.

5 *Mulu* 目録.

6 *Kaoyi* 考異 – Divergence of Evidence.

7 Song Yingzong 宋英宗, *Zhiping* 治平 (reigning year 1064-1067 CE).

being audaciously presumptuous for arrogating the historical texts, an offence punishable by death. Your subject harbours an aspiration that Your Majesty would spend a brief moment in between your busy schedules to leaf through a few pages of the text. It is hoped that by reading the text, Your Majesty could make reference to the past by examining the vicissitudes of our forebears, hence as to make assessments of the merits and deficiencies of the present. With which your subject hopes the court will commend the virtuous while banishing the iniquities, and reprobate the wrongs. The accounts in the text are more than adequate to help us promote and strengthen the exuberant virtues and sagacious achievements of the past. Implemented with righteous measures Your Majesty's Kingdom will enter into a new era of prosperity and affluence, matching that of the bygone splendours epoch; hoping that all your subjects living within the Four Seas will be bestowed with renewed blessings of prosperity and bliss.[8] When your subject finally passes on, he would not hence have the slightest regret in the nether world of the Nine Springs and his lifelong ambition would also be remunerated.[9]

Your humble subject submits this memorial with great trepidation. Your subject *kowtow* and *kowtow* again respectfully to Your Majesty.

Zhao Xu's decree

His Majesty hereby decrees – The work of the *Zizhi tonjian* by Sima Guang is now successfully concluded. For an extensive period, the scholarly study of history has been left by the wayside. The chronological accounts of things past have not strictly adhered to methodical disciplines, and the deliberations on historical facts could not be affirmed with certainty; how then could chronicled history be used for making amends and reprimand against iniquity and guide one's governance towards benevolence? You, Sir, with your extensive learning and comprehensive knowledge of the past and present, have made a compendium of history, commencing from late Zhou to the time of the *Wudai* dynasties. You have created a new genre of a monumental work, whether you were making accolades or reprimands, they are entirely based on your carefully researched information. Upon reading the text, I am thoroughly amazed and astounded by the breadth and depth of the work. I hereby decree to bestow upon you gifts of silver, embroidery, clothes, a jade waistband and a fine steed fully equipped with stirrups and saddle. A list of which is presented separately, please proceed to the appropriate department to accept these gifts, this is a mere gift of inspiritment. The weather has turned cold of late; please take good care of your health. You probably appreciate my good intent; there are many things I wish to relate to you, as I am preoccupied with my busy court schedules I regret I am not able to list them in detail. Date this on the 15th day.

Yuanfeng 8th year 9th month, 17th day. The Chancery issued a Memorandum for re-editing by His Majesty decree.[10]

---

8 '... 監前世之興衰, 考當今之得失, 嘉善矜惡, 取是舍非, 足以懋稽古之聖德, 躋無前之至治, 俾四海群生, 咸蒙其福.'

9 Nine Springs, *jiuquan* 九泉 – the nether world. Also known as *jiuyuan* 九淵 – it means the extremities, a quote from Liezi 列子 the Huangdi 黄帝 – on the realm of life.

10 *Yuanfeng* 8th year 9th month, 17th day. 元豐八年, 九月十七日. The Chancery 尚書省.

Yuanyou 1st year 10th-month 14th day. His Majesty decreed to have the text sent to Hangzhou for engraving and block printing.[11]

Submitted in the 7th year, the 11th month of Yuanfeng.[12]

Review Officer	HM Subject - Sima Kang
Assistant Counsel Officer	HM Subject - Fan Zhuyu
Assistant Compiler Secretary	HM Subject - Liu Shu
Assistant Editor	HM Subject - Liu Ban
Chief Editor - Member of Imperial Academy of Duanmingdian Palace and	
Attendant to the Imperial Academy	HM Subject - Sima Guang

11 Song Zhezong 宋哲宗, Zhao Xu 趙煦 (r. 1086-1100 CE). *Yuanyou* 1st year 10th month 14th day. 元祐元年,十月十四日. Hangzhou 杭州.

12 (1084 CE).
Duanmingdian Palace Bachelor and Literary Bachelor 端明殿學士 兼翰林待讀學士
Imperial Counsellor 太中大夫
Xijing Songshan Songfu Palace 提擧 西京嵩山嵩富宮.
Shangzhuhguo 上柱國.
Duke Kaiguo of Henei Prefecture with 2600 provision households. 河内郡開國公 食邑二千六百户.
Enfeoffed with 1000 households (actual) 實封一千户.
Your humble subject – Sima Guang 司馬光
Submitted during the 7th year (1084), 11th month of *Yuanfeng* 元豐.

Review Officer 檢閱文字承事	HM Subject - Sima Kang 臣司馬康
Assistant Counsel Officer 同修奉議	HM Subject - Fan Zhuyu 臣范祖禹
Assistant Compiler Secretary 同修秘書	HM Subject - Liu Shu 臣 劉恕
Assistant Editor 同修尚書屯田員外郎充集校理	HM Subject Liu Ban 臣劉攽*
Chief Editor – Member of Imperial Academy of Duanmingdian Palace Attendant to the Imperial Academy Senior Counsellor at the Palace 編集端明殿學士兼 翰林待讀學士 太中大夫	HM Subject – Sima Guang 臣司馬光

* The title of Liu Ban is not clear.

An Overview of the Warring States, the Grand Unification by Qin and Qin's Fall [1]

Note: This short conspectus of the period offers an insight into the Warring States period.

Preamble

The Spring-and-Autumn epoch was an era of unprecedented transformations in ancient China; a time when the House of Zhou continued its accelerated decline after moving its capital to Luyi in the east in 770 BCE.[2] *For almost three centuries, there were incessant conquests and annexations when the vassal lords vied for hegemony, others for subsistence, while others simply for survival. A most important social transformation took place during the middle and late era of this epoch, that of scholarship and education. Before this, education was in essence confined to the royalists and ruling elites; whereas by the middle and late Spring and Autumn era teachings, books and learnings had by then been filtered down to the commoners, they were no longer the privileges of the elite few. It was a time of thriving and flourishing teachings and learnings when the commoners and populous were able to become educated through private tuition, as epitomized by Confucius, who as a private tutor was a teacher to three thousand students. The likes of who, of which there were many, created a crucible for the burgeoning of the hundred schools of thoughts during late Spring and Autumn and the Warring States eras.*[3]

The Spring and Autumn period saw a time that underwent considerable social and political changes; the different states and polities had impending, and imminent needs to stabilize their state politically, the need to strengthen their military and financial strength for survival, for expansion or even for hegemony. There was thus an insatiable thirst for capable scholars and erudite to govern the state on behalf of the ruling elites to bring peace and tranquility, power and might, for good governance through social, economic, and political reforms. It gave rise to the class of officers, stewards - shiren, [4] *which was to bring about the great paradigm shift socially, politically and economically during the Warring States.*

The decline of the ruling aristocracy was accompanied by the rise of the ministerial families – usually unrelated to the state rulers by blood – which had established their dominance in most states by the middle of the Spring and Autumn period. Lineages practice continued to be notably stronger with the more conservative states, such as Chu, Song, Zheng and Lu.[5] *On the other hand, the more progressive state introduced reforms to their states leading to the departure from the instituted system, and these vassal states began to use alien names ministers to administer their states on their behalf.*[6] *Unwittingly they emulated the lineage tradition introduced by the Zhou Royal House and made these alien-name administers hereditary. As time progressed these elite administers became so commanding and authoritative that they usurped the thrones, committed regicide or assumed total control of the states they served. The collapse of the Jin state was an*

---

1. Qin, 秦.
   The Warring States period is generally ascribed to be between 475-221 BCE.
2. Zhou capital - Luyi 周都 雒邑.
3. Roughly from 5th century to 221 BCE.
4. Shi – 仕 or 仕人 is loosely defined as officers, warriors, stewards of the noble household or man of service.
5. Chu 楚, Song 宋, Zheng 鄭 and Lu 魯.
6. Alien name – the original term is *waixing* 外姓, meaning persons bearing a family name that is not related to a certain clan. The use of the word 'alien' does sound like extraterritorial to some readers, however, failing to find a more suitable synonym, I allow it to stay.

archetype of the ministerial families assuming the total power of the state, and in 403 BCE it was partitioned into Hann, Wei and Zhao, known as the San-Jin.

Sima Guang, the author of the Zizhi tongjian, in his first annotation on the enfeoffment of the three fief lords by the King of Zhou, laments over the breakdown of the fengjian (feudal) rites.[7] (See 403 BCE-1). *He maintains, 'It was not the San-Jin ministers who bankrupted the instituted rites; rather, the Son of Heaven brought on the collapse.' He contends that as the illegitimate act of partitioning a state by its subjects and it was legitimized by the Son of Heaven; the Zhou king was wholly accountable for its demise.*[8] *Sima Guang thus chose to commence his chronicle of Chinese history during the eventful year – the 23rd year of King Weilei of Zhou, 403 BCE, when the Son of Heaven enfeoffed the ministers of Jin.*

The Collapse of the Jin State

One important signature during the latter part of Spring and Autumn epoch and the Warring States period was that nearly all the states went through internal strife and dissension in varying degree; the disturbances were mostly initiated by the remnants of the influential feudal barons of the past or the alien name ministerial officers.[9] Surprisingly, there were only a few mentions of civic unrests.

During this period, the Jin state underwent a chaotic episode when it sustained a clamorous and restive interlude when contention and in-fighting between the ruling elites were vile. It is seen by many that Duke Xian of Jin (r. 675-651 BCE) probably instigated the source of the problem; his rule laid down the latent complications for the demise of the Jin state. To consolidate his position the duke executed princes Huanshu and Zhuangbo and their family clans.[10] The royal family clans of Jin sustained a devastating blow and were never to recover. Shortly after, it was followed by another bloodletting event. Lady Li, the favourite concubine of the duke, conspired to make her son, Xiqi the lawful successor.[11] She entrapped Heir Apparent Shensheng (?-656 BCE), forcing him to commit suicide; meanwhile banished Prince Chonger (later Duke Wen of Jin r. 636-628 BCE), Prince Yiwu and some other princes to foreign states.[12] The *Commentary of Zuo* remarks on the purge, "Ever since then, Jin did not have any royal elites at court."[13] Nineteen years later, Duke Wen of Jin after a protracted period of struggle returned to Jin and ascended to the throne. Learning from experience, he decided not to enfeoff the royal family clans as fief lords and chose alien-name subjects to serve at his court. Those men he retained were mostly his loyal supporters, who accompanied him during his years of exile from Jin. They included Hu Mao, Hu Yan, Xian

---

7 Read, Li Feng's Early China A Social and Cultural History – 'Fengjian not Feudalism.' pp. 127-132.

8 Sima Guang, "San-Jin did not bankrupt the rites; rather, the Son of Heaven brought on the destruction."
'非三晉之壞禮, 乃天子自壞也.'

9 Spring and Autumn period 春秋 (770-476 BCE).

10 Duke Xian of Jin 晉献公 (675-651 BCE) executed the princes of Huanshu 桓叔 and Zhuangbo 莊伯 family clans.

11 Lady Li, Liji 驪姬.
Xiqi 奚齊 son of Li Ji.

12 Heir Apparent Shensheng 申生 (?-656 BCE).
Prince Chonger 重耳, later Duke Wen of Jin, 晉文公 (r. 636-628 BCE).
Prince Yiwu 夷吾.

13 The *Zuozhuan, Commentray of Zuo* 左傳宣公二年, '自是晉無公族.'

Zhen, with Zhao Shuai among others.[14] With the abrogation of the entrenched royal-family inheritance now replaced by inheritance of political power by the foreign-name ministers, it foreshadowed the final demise of Jin almost two hundred and thirty years later. Whether this was the real cause of the demise of the Jin State through a novel approach to state governance is beyond the scope of this synopsis. Nevertheless, to many historians, it is believed to be the essential reason for the demise of Jin.

Duke Wen reigned between 636-628 BCE,[15] during and after his reign; the Jin State became hegemon for nearly one century at the time of Spring and Autumn epoch. However, the state was not without its internal problems. During the reign of Duke Wen, Minister Zhao Dun assumed power at the Jin court.[16] In 620 BCE Duke Ling of Jin assumed the position as the head-of-state. He was most dissatisfied with Zhao Dun, and attempted to assassinate the minister on two occasions; however the duke ended up being murdered by Zhao Chuan, the younger brother of the minister in 607 BCE.[17] Later, after the reign of Duke Dao of Jin (r. 573-558 BCE),[18] the Jin court was thoroughly corrupted, falling into perennial decline. The Jin dukes were no longer in control of the state, and the court was controlled by six hereditary family clans - the Fan, Zhonghang, Zhi, Hann, Zhao, and Wei;[19] the Dukes were nominal in name only. In 453 BCE, ministers Master Kang of Hann and Master Huan of Wei mutinied against Master Zhibo of Zhi, Zhi Yao in power while laying siege to Jinyang,[20] held by Master Xiang of Zhao. Master Zhibo was executed. Fifty years later, in 403 BCE, the Son-of-Heaven, King Weilie of Zhou officiated the enfeoffment of the San-Jin, the three ministers of Jin as fiefs lords – Hann, Zhao and Wei.[21] It marks the year when the *Zizhi tongjian* commences its chronicles. The event is known as, "The three family clans partitioned the Jin State."[22]

Meanwhile, Qi had its fair share of court discords and frictions as well. In 671 BCE, there was a revolt in the minor polity of Chen; the royal clan members turned against the head-of-state; Prince Wan of Chen absconded to Qi.[23] The Prince was appointed as a minister at the Qi court.[24] In 545 BCE, the 4th generation descendant of Tian Wan (Chen Wan), Tian Wuyu, collaborated with the Bao, Lian, Gao clans annihilated the Jiang clan that was in power;[25] although, the attempt was supported by the royal elites and the commoners. In 489 BCE Tian Huan proclaimed himself the chancellor of Qi.[26] Eight years later, Tian Huan committed regicide; he killed Duke Jian of Qi and some the Qi royal elites; he then placed Duke Ping of Qi on the throne.[27] Tian He finally

14 Hu Mao 狐毛, Hu Yan 狐偃, Xian Zhen 先軫, Zhao Shuai 趙衰.

15 Duke Wen of Jin, 晉文公.

16 Duke Ling of Jin 晉靈公 (r. 620-607 BCE).
Zhao Dun 趙盾.

17 Zhao Chuan 趙穿, the younger brother of Zhao Dun.

18 Duke Dao of Jin 晉悼公 (r. 573-558 BCE).

19 Fan 范, Zhonghang 中行, Zhi 智, Hann 韓, Zhao 趙, and Wei 魏.

20 Hann Kangzi 韓康子, Wei Huanzi 魏桓子 and Zhao Xiangzi, Zhao Wuxu 趙襄子 趙無恤.
Master Xiang of Zhi, Zhibo Yao 智襄子 智伯瑶. Siege at Jinyang 晉陽 see 403-II.

21 King Weilie of Zhou 周威烈王 (425-402 BCE), San-Jin 三晉 - Hann 韓, Zhao 趙, and Wei 魏.

22 "The three family clans partitioned the Jin State" - 三家分晉.

23 Prince Wan of Chen 陳完.

24 The words Chen 陳 and Tian 田 were synonymous.

25 Tian Wuyu 田無宇, Bao 鮑, Lian 欒, Gao 高, Qing 慶.

26 Tian Huan 田桓.

27 Duke Jian of Qi 齊簡公 (r. 484-481 BCE). Duke Ping of Qi 齊平公 (r. 480-456 BCE).

banished Duke Kang, the last Qi Duke bearing a family name of Jiang, to an island off the coast of Qi.[28] (See 391-II). Five years later, in 386 BCE Tian He proclaimed himself the head-of-state of Qi; during the same year, King An of Zhou enfeoffed him as the marquis of Qi.[29] (See 386-I). King Kang of Qi died in 379 BCE, the Qi Tian clan officially assumed power at the Qi court, formally reigned by the Jiang family clan (also known as the Lu clan) since the 11 century BCE.[30] (See 379-II) The name of the state remained.

Unrest at Qin, Chu and their Revival

Qin and Chu states had their internal dissensions as well; fortunate for them, clans of alien names did not make entry into their courts.

After the reign of Duke Mu of Qin (r. 659-621 BCE),[31] there were many incidents of intrigues and conspiracies at the Qin court with frequent usurpations and intrigues; resulting from these incidents, Qin suffered a decline. The fief lords at Zhongyuan (Middle-Plain or Huaxia) had by then deemed the fief state a non-entity.[32] About the time of 'partitioning of Jin', Qin was not even an equal of Wei, it even lost the territories west of the River (Huanghe) to Wei in 408 BCE. The status was to remain unchanged until Duke Xiao of Qin (r. 361-338 BCE) ascended to the throne.[33] Duke Xiao appointed Shang Yang to make administrative and military reforms to the state;[34] after which Qin was on the road to becoming a most powerful state during the middle era of the Warring States. (See 361-I and 359-I)

At the Chu court, when King Hui of Chu (r. 488-432 BCE) was presiding, a major rebellion broke out.[35] Baigong Sheng, the son of Crown Prince Jian,[36] raised an army against the state and proclaimed king; the revolt failed and the dissident hanged himself. King Hui resumed to the Chu throne; the kingdom became peaceful again. It was the time when the southern tribal kingdoms of Yue and Wu were locked in decades of battles for hegemony.[37] Chu was on the verge of being annihilated by Wu. Later, Yue annihilated Wu; Chu enjoyed a reprieve. When King Dao of Chu (r. 401-381 BCE) was on the throne, he appointed Wu Qi as chancellor.[38] (See 387-II) Wu Qi introduced strict and austere measures to the state, banishing the redundant officers at court while expelling the distantly related royal elites. The savings achieved by these austere measures were redirected to serve the interests of the army and warriors. Chu, as a result, managed to quell the Bai-Yue tribes to the south; to the north, it annihilated the Chen and Cai polities.[39] It also curbed the expansion of Hann, Zhao and Wei and to its west, it even made an expedition against Qin. Chu state at this stage was at its zenith.

Qi Tian He 齊田和.

28 King Kang of Qi 齊康王 (r. 404-379 BCE).

29 King An of Zhou 周安王 (r. 401-376 BCE).

30 Lu family clan 呂 or Jiang 姜.

31 Duke Mu of Qin 秦穆公 (r. 659-621 BCE).

32 Zhongyuan 中原 (Middle-Plain, Central-Plain or Huaxia) 華夏.

33 Duke Xiao of Qin, Ying Quliang 秦孝公嬴渠梁 (r. 361-338 BCE).

34 Shang Yang 商鞅, Wey Yang 衛鞅.

35 King Hui of Chu 楚惠王 (r. 488-432 BCE).

36 Baigong Sheng 白公勝, the son of Crown Prince Jian 太子建.

37 Yue 越 and Wu 吳.

38 King Dao of Chu 楚悼王 (r. 401-381 BCE). Wu Qi 吳起. (403-V footnotes)

39 Bai-Yue 百越, Chen 陳 and Cai 蔡.

The Fall of Yue and the Rise of Yan

The chronicles of the rise and fall of the kingdom of Yue, to the south of Zhongyuan, were sketchy at best. When Gou Jian was the king of Yue,[40] the state was powerful; upon his death, the kingdom eclipsed into oblivion. When Wu Jiang of Yue ascended the throne,[41] he attempted to restore its former glory; he raised an army against Chu; King Wei of Chu gave the Yue army a resounding defeat in 306 BCE, King of Yue, Wu Jiang died. Following the campaign, Chu completely annexed Yue and the former kingdom of Wu.

In the meantime, to the extreme northeast of Zhongyuan, the state of Yan was almost completely isolated from the rest of the states in the Central Realm.[42] Yan made reforms to the state and partook in the political arena in the Central Plain. In 284 BCE, the Yan General, Yue Yi, as commander led the armies of five states attacked Qi, the general annexed over 70 walled-cities, only two walled cities held out.[43] (See 284-I, II, III, IV.) In 279 BCE, Tian Dan, a junior functionary at Jimo, through sheer determination, against all odds, recovered the state of Qi. (See 279-III)

Annihilation of the Minor Polities during the Warring States

Towards the latter part of the Spring and Autumn epoch and the beginning of the Warring States, the minor fief states lost their protectorate status when the hegemons failed; many of them were either annexed or annihilated.[44] Hann annihilated the once political prominent Zheng in 375 BCE.[45] During the Warring States era, the state of Wey repeatedly lost its territories to its more powerful neighbours; [46] the status of the Duke was reduced to marquis and even later to the status of a lord. (See 346-III and 320-I). The state of Wei almost completely assumed Wey's entire domain, only the capital Puyang remained, and it became a protectorate of Wei in 254 BCE. In 252 BCE Lord Huai of Wey met an untimely death by being executed by Wei;[47] (252-I) amazingly this was the only state that remained standing until 209 BCE, well into the reign of the Qin Empire.

Song in 487 BCE annihilated the Cao Polity.[48] Chu annexed Chen (478 BCE) and Cai (447 BCE). Even the most insignificant Qi Polity (not to be confused with the Qi State), claimed to be the descendants of the ancient Xia dynasty was appropriated by Chu.[49] At the time of the commencement of the Warring States in 445 BCE, the only minor polities of significance left were Song and Lu,[50] they, nevertheless, were no more than buffer states, enclaves among the more

---

40 King of Yue 越王 Gou Jian 勾踐.

41 King of Yue 越王 Wu Jiang 無彊 (?-306 BCE).

42 Yan 燕.

43 Yan general 燕 Yue Yi 樂毅.

44 At the commencement of Zhou, there were roughly 800 to 1000 fief states, later at the ending era of Spring and Autumn, there were about 40, and towards the beginning of the Warring States, there were between 20 to 30 minor polities.

45 Zheng 鄭.

46 Wey 衛.

47 Puyang 濮陽. Lord Huai of Wey 衛懷君 (r. 282-252 BCE).

48 Cao 曹.

49 Qi 杞, descendants of Xia 夏.

50 Some scholars consider 475 BCE as the commencement year of the Warring states.

powerful warring states and neighbours, and were often exploited as battlegrounds. At the time of Duke Dao of Lu (r. 467-437 BCE),[51] the three ministers at the Lu court were so powerful that the duke was less significant than a minor Marquis.

Disintegration of Zhou

Dissensions from within principally caused the gradual weakening of the Zhou House. Almost half of its domain was lost due to annexations by foreign powers; then the king himself divided the Zhou kingdom into two – East Zhou and West Zhou,[52] (not to be confused with Eastern Zhou, 770-255 BCE). King Nan of Zhou (r. 315-256 BCE) was, in essence, a puppet;[53] the East-Zhou and West-Zhou states had their respective heads-of-state and to make the situation worse, the divided kingdom entered into perennial squabble vying for water sources for irrigation. By this stage, Zhou had completely lost the already feeble political standing it nominally held during the Spring and Autumn period. The fief lords of the various states began to call themselves kings (it started by King Hui of Wei in 334 BCE, see 334-1),[54] the Zhou King's realm was no more than a buffer state like Song and Lu, and in some instances, it became the battleground of the fief lords. The only vague memories held by the fief lords was the *Jiuding* – the Nine Tripods,[55] still held by the Imperial Zhou House and that for some time in the distant past it was a mighty kingdom ruled by a Son-of-Heaven, mandated by Heaven.

With the downfall of Zhou, the fief lords began to eye the Nine Tripods with avarice greed. King Zhuang of Chu (r. 613-591 BCE) brazenly asked King Ding of Zhou,[56] "How heavy are the tripods?" (Meaning the king was challenged the possession of the tripods.) Wang Sunman, a minister at the Zhou court, rebuked the challenge.[57] Later King Ling of Chu (r. 540-529 BCE) made a similar attempt.[58] However, Chu was beset by internal dissension; he gave up in the end.

Towards the middle era of the Warring States, King Hui of Qin (r. 356-311 BCE) employed the strategies proposed by Zhang Yi made an attempt to appropriate the Nine-Tripods to command the other fief lords.[59] In the meantime, King Qingxiang of Chu and King Xuan of Qi were also vying for the Tripods.[60] King Nan of Zhou, brokered deals between the fief lords and made them mutually constraining the others, and managed to retain the tripods.

Song 宋 and Lu 魯. There was Zhongshan 中山 however it was not an enfeoffed state by the House of Zhou.

51 Duke of Dao of Lu 魯悼公 (r. 467-437 BCE).
The Three ministers of Lu, *San-Huan* 三桓 Jisun, 季孫氏, Shusun 叔孫氏, Mengsun 孟孫氏.

52 Dong East Zhou 東周 and Xi West Zhou 西周.

53 King Nan of Zhou 周赧王 (r. 315-256 BCE).

54 King Hui of Wei 魏惠王 (r. 370-319 BCE). See Yang Kuan's 楊寬 textual research on the changing of Regnal dates by the King.

55 The Nine Cauldrons or tripods, *Jiu-ding* 九鼎.

56 King Zhuang of Chu 楚莊王 (r. 613-591 BCE).
King Ding of Zhou, 周定王 (r. 606-586 BCE).

57 Wang Sunman 王孫满 *Zuozhuan* 左傳 'Xuangong 宣公三年', '周德雖衰, 天命未改.'

58 King Ling of Chu 楚靈王 (r. 540-529 BCE). The kings in Chu had long held the title of king.

59 King Hui of Qin 秦惠王 (r. 356-311 BCE).
Zhang Yi 張儀.

60 King Qingxiang of Chu 楚頃襄王 (r. 298-263 BCE).
King Xuan of Qi 齊宣王 (r. 320-302 BCE).

New Weapons and New War Strategies

'Historical records show rarely did two years elapse without a major battle between two or more states, and there were many years that we see multiple military campaigns.'[61] New war strategies and weapons were introduced with increasing tension between the states. It was a time when iron weapons and armours were introduced, although bronze still held its position as the mainstream weaponry. The techniques employed in offence and defence were even more astute than before. From the *Mozi* 'Gongshu pian' we learned Gongshu Pan, alias Lu Ban built siege ladder *yunti* to scale up defence walls for Chu.[62] And, at one time or another, Lu Ban and Mozi simulated a battling strategy. "The king of Chu gave Gongshu Pan an audience. Mozi removed his girdle belt, using it as the defence rampart, using the bamboo slips as his weapons to defend the city. Gongshu Pan made several attacks against the walled-city; Mozi was able to repel the attacks on nine occasions. Gongshu Pan then ran out of weapons, while Mozi had sufficient reserves to continue to defend the city." Besides the troops on foot, the cavalry was becoming increasingly important in the deployment of the army. King Wuling of Zhao learned from the nomadic tribes to his north and introduced foreign attires *hufu*,[63] as well as riding skill and shooting on horseback. (See 307-III). One can conclude that the war activities during the Warring States were wars for territorial expansion and attrition – the depreciation of enemy forces and civilians when massacre and carnage were wholesale, to say the least.

At the time of Spring and Autumn, the agrarian fields were separated by runnels and raised footpaths, crisscrossing the fields vertically and horizontally, and they were ill-suited for charging chariots and cavalry.[64] Theses runnels and footpaths were eliminated at the time of the Spring and Autumn epoch. The chariots were replaced in part by cavalry and the army became more mobile. Whence defence also became more difficult; it prompted the various states to construct Long-Walls; the escalating introduction of which illustrate the prevalence of wars and battles during that period.[65]

Wei Pursued for Power and Failure

Wei was the first state to make reform at court. Marquis Wen of Wei (r. 472-396 BCE or 446-397 BCE) appointed Li Kui to introduce reform to the state (this is mentioned in *Zizhi tongjian*).[66] The minister employed capable officers and subordinates to preside over the

---

61 Quoted from Li Feng's The *Early China, A Social, and Cultural History*, p. 187.

62 The *Mozi* 墨子 'Gongshu pian 公輸篇'. Mozi (~478-381 BCE).
There is a detailed account of the topologies, military strengths and weaknesses of each state related by Su Qin 蘇秦 see 333-III; and Xunzi 荀子 has a detailed description of the military strategies adopted by different states 議兵篇, see 255-II.
Gongshu Pan 公輸盤, possibly Lu Ban 魯班 (~507-444 BCE).
Siege ladder *Yunti* 雲梯.

63 King Wuling of Zhao 趙武靈王. *Hufu* 胡服.

64 Wellfield system, *Jing-tian* 井田.

65 Some of the Long-Walls were built to defend against the incursions of the nomadic tribes from the north.

66 Marquis Wen of Wei 魏文侯 (r. 472-396 BCE).
Li Kui 李悝 (455-395 BCE) was one of the most notable philosopher and political strategists during the Warring States period. In 422 BCE he was made the Chancellor of Wei 魏 by the Marquis Wen

administration. He rewarded the meritorious while chastising the inept attendants, meanwhile putting down the nobles and elites; he valued the people who were meritorious to the state. He abrogated the centuries-old well-field system and encouraged people to develop land for cultivation. He made changes to the military organization and prepared for war. In a series of reforms and changes, the people in Wei enjoyed a period of prosperity, while the financial situation of the state also improved enormously. When it came to the reign of Marquis Wu of Wei (r. 395-370 BCE),[67] Wei was more powerful than the other fief states; as a result, the marquis eyed the prospect of becoming the overlord of Zhongyuan, the hegemon of all under Heaven. The ambition of Wei instigated a series of calamities to the warring states in Zhongyuan.

By the time of Marquis Hui of Wei (r. 369-319 BCE),[68] the power, and influence of the state had greatly augmented. During the 15th year of King Xian of Zhou (354 BCE), Wei attacked the Zhao capital, Handan, besieging the city.[69] Zhao appealed to Qi for help the next year. The king of Qi ordered Tian Ji and Sun Bin to lead an army to bring relief to Zhao.[70] Sun Bin maintained that Wei having employed all its crack troops to attack Zhao, the capital should be left a void; he commanded the Qi army to attack the Wei capital Daliang.[71] The strategy lured Wei to retreat to make a defence. Su Bin set an ambush at Guiling, defeating Pang Juan.[72] (See 353-1)

---

of Wei 魏文侯 (446-397 BCE). He went on to make reformations to Wei, his thesis of emphasis on farming production couple with Legalism had far-reaching influence on Shang Yang 商鞅 and Hann Fei 韓非; hence, it is accepted that he was the originator of Legalism. He maintained that Wei was a small state, with one-third of the land being mountainous. Hence, the land must be put to good use. A thesis that he called *jin dili zhijiao* 盡地力之教 – roughly translated as – 'Making best use of the land'; the details of his reform are now lost, generally it promoted and encouraged the farmers to increase productivity through better agrarian management and practices while making use of accumulated farming experience. Another measure he introduced was *shan pingdi* 善平糴 - a procedure of stabilizing grain prices whereby the government would buy grain at a reasonable price during a good harvest and sell it at a reasonable price during a bad one. Resulting from this measure, the prices of grain did not fluctuate greatly from year to year. Another major advancement he made was he selected capable people as ministers to serve at court, banishing the long established hereditary system held by the nobles and elites. He appointed Wu Qi 吳起 as the Prefecture Magistrate of Xihejun 西河郡 and used Ximen Bao 西門豹 as Magistrate of Yi 鄴. Ximen Bao was a most capable administrator, who went to abrogate and banished corrupted officers and bureaucrats, exploiting the commoners with superstition. However, there is only one indirect mention of this man in *Zizhi tongjian*. Wei became one of the most powerful states during the commencing years of the Warring States. Li Kui compiled the *Fajing* – 法經 - *the Book of Law*, adopted and based on the legal systems from the other six fiefdoms. The book included Bandit Law, Thief Law, Incarceration Law, Apprehension Law, Miscellaneous Law and *jufa* 具法 which was a summary or index of the entire text. When Shang Yang went for his appointment at Qin, he brought with him a copy of the text; he later used the text as his blueprint for the reformations made to Qin. The text has since been lost; however, fragments of the book are retained in the *Qinlu* 秦律 and more recent archaeology discovery of a Qin tomb with bamboo slips at Shuifudi, Yunmengxian Hubei 湖北 雲夢縣 睡虎地 in 1975 CE, has also shed some light on the contents of the book.

67 Marquis Wu of Wei 魏武侯 (r. 395-370 BCE).

68 Marquis Hui of Wei 魏惠王 (r. 370-319 BCE).

69 15th year of King Xian of Zhou 周顯王 (354 BCE), Wei attacked the Zhao capital, Handan 趙 邯鄲.

70 Tian Ji 田忌 and Sun Bin 孫臏.

71 Dalaing, Wei capital 魏都 大梁.

72 Guiling, 桂陵. Pang Juan 龐涓.

Some 13 years later, during the 27th year of King Xian of Zhou, another major battle took place in Maling;[73] Sun Bin again defeated the Wei army. In the process, Qi captured the Crown Prince of Wei, and Pang Juan died in battle. The two great battles exemplified the classical military strategies employed at the time of the Warring States. (See 353-I and 341-I). With the failure of those two great battles, Wei went on a sharp decline as it overextended its power, towards the waning years of the king the state was relegated to an inferior state among the other fief states.

Land Extension by the Powerful States

Besides the incessant wars among the powerful states to vie for land from their neighbours, they also undertook a series of campaigns against the foreign tribes *Siyi* to the four quarters.[74] Yan, Zhao, and Qin states occupied territories bordering with Dong-Hu, Xiongnu and Rong tribes.[75] At this stage, the foreign tribes that settled at the borders or in some instances within the states were mostly under the control by the three states. While the foreign tribes that had settled within the realms of Zhongyuan for centuries and perhaps millennium; they had by then intermingled with the people of Zhongyaun and were almost completely assimilated.

For the foreign tribes to survive within the realms of Zhongyuan, they adopted the rites of Huaxia – the Chinese culture and became a part of China. The state of Zhongshan was a typical example; descendants of the Di nomadic tribes from the northern part of China founded the kingdom, and it was an enclave located between the states of Zhao, Yan and Qi.[76] Politically and culturally the people emulated the customs of the Chinese. The kingdom managed to survive until 295 BCE. Hence, it is said that Zhongshan was the last of the Yi and Di that settled within Zhongyuan. (See 295-II)

Social Revolution

Resulting from sweeping political reforms, social and cultural transformations were inevitable. Regrettably, we know very little about the social reforms towards the closing years of the Spring and Autumn period; while it must be stressed that we know more about the changes that were transpiring at the closing years of the Western Zhou period (771 BCE). We only know that the agrarian farming system went through considerable changes, and privatization of land was becoming more prevalent. The duties and dues on land were hence quite different from the past. In the meantime, manufacturing and artistry also went through significant changes. Finally, after decades and centuries of unrest, the once powerful clan families had become less influential.

Kingship was still the rule of the day. By then, scholars from varying backgrounds called *shi* aided the many fief lords and kings. Wandering strategists like Su Qin and Zhang Yi came from very modest backgrounds and made their way into important positions in the more powerful states.[77] During his earlier years of lobbying, Su Qin had difficulties finding sponsors and being retained. History texts described him as being, "physically emaciated and his face carried a dark and gloomy appearance." Upon returning home, his wife refused to spin and weave for him, while his sister-in-law did not care to cook for him. (Su Qin, 333-III). While, Zhang Yi, on the other

73 Maling 馬陵.

74 *Siyi* 四夷.

75 Dong-Hu 東胡, Xiongnu 匈奴 and Rong 戎.

76 Zhongshan 中山. Di 狄.

77 Su Qin 蘇秦. Zhang Yi 張儀.

hand, while lobbying was mistaken for a thief and was badly beaten. When he returned home, he asked his wife, "Is my tongue still intact?" The wife laughed, "Yes, it is." Zhang Yi remarked, "That is good enough." (Zhang Yi - see 333-III)

The Marquises and heads-of-state all tried their utmost to retain capable scholars *shiren*. Individuals who were capable or proficient in certain skills or artisans had no difficulty to find good employment. Lord Mengchang entertained guests at his manor; while the shrewd Feng Huan provided mercantile services for the prince.[78] People who knew trivial tricks were also able to find their niches in the society; while insignificant in the main, they were cleverly utilized in time of crisis. (Tian Wen's escape from Qin - See 298-I).[79] Nevertheless, the men those princelings sponsored and kept as guests were mostly scholars; while at the same time, some were chivalrous and valiant men, like the strong man Zhu Hai, the butcher, from Daliang the capital of Wei, who befriended the city-gate keeper Hou Ying.[80] Later, Hou Ying introduced the butcher to Lord Xinling.[81] The butcher accompanied Lord Xinling to the front and killed the Wei general, Jin Bi to appropriate control of the Wei military.[82] Lord Xinling assumed control of the Wei army with a stolen tally, repelled the Qin army besieging Zhao. (For details, see 258-IV). Nie Zheng was perhaps one of the best-known assassins at the time of early Warring States.[83] The Hann ex-minister, Yan Zhongzi befriended him, and he was respectful to Nie's mother.[84] To repay the respect, Nie Zheng went to have Xia Lei,[85] an archenemy of the ex-minister, assassinated. Having been successful with the attempt, he did not want to implicate his sister; he maimed his face, spilling his entrails and died valiantly. (Details see 397-II).

Reformation by Shang Yang at Qin

At the commencement of the Warring States, all the states were engaged in radical reforms internally at some time or other, establishing strategies for external expansion. Wei perhaps was the earliest and most successful by engaging Li Kui, followed by Wu Qi and Ximen Bao (details see 403-V and footnotes).[86] Under these capable ministers, Wei became prosperous, and its army became powerful. It made extensive campaigns to erode into other states; and for some time, it was the most powerful state in Zhongyuan. When Duke Xiao of Qin ascended to the throne, he resolved to make reforms and make his state powerful. He decreed to invite capable scholars to go to Qin. Wey Yang, (Shang Yang) answered to the call. Wey Ying, Lord Shang, introduced a series of reforms, abrogating the 'well-field' system, stressing the importance of productivity in farming and sericulture, unifying the weight and measure systems and drastically changed the administrative functions of the prefecture and county. Duke Xiao made him the left chancellor. (Shang Yang's reforms - See 359-I and 350-I). Under Shang Yang, Qin became a powerful state,

---

78 Lord Mengchang 孟嘗君. Feng Huan 馮驩 was a successful merchant at the time of the Warring States.
Feng Xuan 馮諼.

79 Tian Wen 田文.

80 Zhu Hai 朱亥, a butcher from Daliang 大梁 屠夫. City-gate keeper, Hou Ying 城吏 侯嬴.

81 Sir Xinling 信陵君.

82 Wei general 魏將 Jin Bi 晉鄙.

83 Nie Zheng 聶政.

84 Hann ex-minister 韓大夫 Yan Zhongzi 嚴仲子.

85 Xia Lei 俠累.

86 Wu Qi 吳起 and Ximen Bao 西門豹.

gathering military and financial might, and was to become the most powerful state towards the middle and waning years of the Warring States; culminating in the grand unification of all under Heaven by Qin in 221 BCE.

Aftermaths of Reform

As mentioned before, Wei became the most powerful state with the reforms. Later, when Qin and other states made concerted attacks against it, it was reduced to the status of a second-grade state. At about this time, Qin made an inroad into Shu,[87] annexing the fertile land, which was sparsely populated. (See 316-1). It was a move that made Qin, even more, formidable. Zhang Yi had suggested that perhaps they should invade Hann. Sima Cuo had a different perspective;[88] he maintained that with an attack against Hann would create conflict and tension among the other fief lords and it would be most unfavourable for Qin. Whereas the kingdom of Shu, being situated to the most remote southwest of Qin was frail, if Qin were to invade the land it could be taken easily. What was, even more, compelling; it would not incite the other fief lords to unite against Qin. Sima Cuo turned out to be accurate with his assessment. It was a significant turning point (against the Yi and Di tribes) during the Warring States, and it laid the economic foundation for Qin to annihilate the six kingdoms.

Qin as a Hegemon

Upon the weakening of Wei, the states of Qin, Qi and Chu became the three most powerful states in Zhongyuan. King Hui of Qin retained capable leaders, [89] promoted Legalism and continued with its expansive to the east. In 330 BCE, the Qin general *daliangzao*, Gongsun Yang gave the Wei army a resounding defeat at Diaoyin.[90] Not much later, Wei ceded the land west of the River *Hexi* to Qin.[91] Qin henceforth used Huanghe River and Hanguguan Pass as demarcation lines to repel the various invasions by the fief lords; [92] it was a strategic topology most suited for making advances, while at the same time most favourable for making defence. In 318 BCE, the armies from Hann, Zhao, Yan, Chu and Wei formed an alliance against Qin, which gave the assailants another resounding defeat. Later, Zhang Yi lobbied at Qi and Wei breaking the pledged alliance. Qin army took advantage of the breakup defeated the Chu army and annexed Hanzhong.[93]

Qi had intended to take advantage of the internal strife in Yan to occupy the land; however, the campaign failed. In 312 BCE, king of Yan, Ji Guai abdicated the throne to his chancellor, Zi Zhi.[94] During the chancellor's tenure as the king of Yan, the political situation of the state was reduced to utter chaos; the civilians were abhorred by the despotic and corrupted reign. Qi and Zhongshan took advantage of the unrest marched into Yan, the civilians unexpectedly welcome the invaders with open arms. King Guai and Zi Zhi were killed during the ensuing unrest. Later, the

---

87 Shu 蜀.

88 Sima Cuo 司馬錯.

89 King Hui of Qin 秦惠王 (r. 337-311 BCE).

90 Qin general, *daliangzao* 秦 大良造 Gongsun Yan 公孫衍.
Diaoyin 雕陰.

91 Hexi 河西.

92 Huanghe 黃河 and Hanguguan Pass 函谷關.

93 Hanzhong 漢中.

94 King Yan, Ji Guai 燕姬噲. Yan chancellor, Zi Zhi 子之.

Qi army went on a wholesale rampage of massacre and carnage; the people of Yan rose up in arms and repelled the invaders. Qi retreated. While Qi had gained much respect in the political arena during the siege of Yan, it nevertheless had sustained devastating squander to its economic strength. While, at about the same time Qin and Chu entered into battle, Chu sustained a humiliating defeat, and had to cede its most strategic area of Hanzhong to Qin, which opened up the passage for Qin to invade Chu in the south. During the years around 311 BCE, Qin was the most powerful among the three powerful states.

Weakening of Chu

Qi, having failed in its attempt to annihilate Yan; Chu was the only state left with some power to contend against Qin, but barely. While the states in the north had engaged in years of wars and incessant battles, Chu took advantage of the confusion and invaded the Qi territories at the north of the Huaishui River. In the meanwhile, it tried to coerce Hann, Zhou, and Lu to submit to its power.[95] Qin was weary of Chu's strategic intent, lest it might acquire more new territories in the process. Hence, it made a pre-emptive strike against Chu before the conflict between Yan and Qi came to a head. In 280 BCE, Chu lost a battle to Qin, ceding areas of Shangyong and north of Hanshui River to sue for peace.[96] (See 280-1). The next year, General Bai Qi of Qin attacked Chu again, occupying Yancheng, and Xiling.[97] In 278 BCE, Bai Qi occupied the capital of Chu, Yancheng, razing the mausoleums and holy shrines of the former Chu kings to the ground; the Chu army totally collapsed; Chu had little to choose, it moved its capital to Chen, retaining the name of Yancheng, to avoid confrontation against Qin.[98] (See 278-1).

After these campaigns, Chu was no longer a threat to Qin; it was only a matter of time before Qin made the grand unification of all under Heaven.

The Way of Ruling All Under Heaven to Bring Peace

Under the threatening political under-toll and social unrests, it promoted an amazing development of scholastic, political, humanistic and philosophic schools, never seen before or after in China. The scholars propounded different treatises vying for either recognition or question the very fundamental inquiry into the existence and origin of the cosmos. It was a period flourishing with profound, bold, and revolutionary thoughts.

The *Hanshu* 'Yiwenzhi' chronicles ten schools of thoughts – Literati, Mo, Dao, Legalism, Ying-Yang, Ming, Zong-Heng, Za, Bing and Xiaoshuo.[99] While the various schools had their respective emphasis, some on politics, others on military, such as the Legalists and Horizontal and Vertical Alliance. Other schools made emphasis on moral values, such as the Literati and Mohist; whereas others stressed the importance of logic and discourses such as the Mingjia. The Daoist's

---

95 Huaishui River 淮水.

96 Shangyong 上庸 and north of Hanshui River 漢水北.

97 Bai Qi 白起.
Yancheng 鄢城 - Yichengxian Hubei 湖北 宜城縣.
Xiling 西陵 - Yichangxian Hubei 湖北 宜昌縣.

98 Capital of Chu 楚都 Yancheng 鄢城.
Chen 陳 (Henan Huaiyang 淮陽河南), retaining the name Yancheng 鄢城.

99 Literati 儒, Mo 墨, Dao 道, Legalism 法, Yin-Yang 陰陽, Ming 名, Zong-Heng 縱横, Za 雜, Bing 兵 and Xiaoshuo 小說.

highlighted on non-intervention or inactivity. Nevertheless, the central thesis of all the schools was on 'governance'; in other words, each of the schools acquired a thesis of substance to propagate debates, hence as to come up with ways and means to bring peace to all under Heaven.

Three Pieces of Influential Literary Works

The *Zhuangzi* 'Tianxia pian'[100] was based on the Daoist perspectives to make assessments and critique of the innumerable schools prevailing at that stage; it can be considered as one of the earliest philosophical literature.

Xunzi in his work, the *Xunzi* 'Feishierzi pian'[101] made critical repudiations of the various schools in existence. He came to conclude that the turmoil and unrest during the Warring States was a consequence of the different propositions propounded by the 'hundred schools' scholars. To attain ultimate social stability and peace under Heaven, he argues, 'There is only one path under Heaven - the sages should all think alike.'[102] In other words, he was an adherent of feudal governance. Delving deeper into his works, one finds that he was perplexed by his ill-conceived logic, and he took on a rather subjective view of his percept. In the end, he even used phrases such as, 'those *can-ru* worthless and pedantic literati' to portray his peers.[103]

The *Hannfeizi* 'Xianxue pian',[104] Hann Fei's stance was based on his notion of statehood; he made a critical attack on the two most influential schools, the *Ru* – Literati and *Mo* – Mohism; and extensively expounded Legalism in his works.

The Road to Grand Unification – Defeating the San-Jin

With the waning of Qi and Chu, the state of Yan became an underling state of Qin, through the effective Qin political strategy proposed by Fan Ju of 'befriending distant states, while attacking neighbouring states.' The shrewd diplomacy was buttressed by the military might of Qin. General Bai Qi was perhaps the most influential Qin general who was instrumental in overwhelming the three Jins – San-Jin – Hann, Wei and Zhao states.

During the 34th year of King Zhao of Qin (273 BCE), Bai Qi attacked the allied forces of Zhao and Wei at Huayang.[105] Mang Mao the Wei general fled the fields, three generals of Hann, Zhao and Wei were captured, some one hundred and thirty thousand soldiers lost their heads.[106] (See 273-1). It was followed by a battle with General Jia Yan of Zhao,[107] some twenty thousand Zhao soldiers were driven into the river and drowned. During the 43rd year of King Zhao (264 BCE), Bai Qi attacked Jingcheng of Hann,[108] annexing five cities, decapitated some fifty thousand

---

100 The *Zhaungzi* 'Tianxia pian 莊子 天下篇.'

101 The *Xunzi* 'Feishierzi pian 荀子 非十二子篇.'

102 *Xunzi* 荀子, "天下無二道 聖人無二心."

103 *Can-ru* 殘儒 - worthless and pedantic literati. *Ru* is also translated as Confucians; it is also loosely used to mean scholars.

104 The *Hannfeizi* 韓非子 'Xianxue pian 顯學篇'.

105 King Zhao of Qin 秦昭王 (273 BCE).
Huayang 華陽 – north of Xinzheng Henan 河南 新鄭北.

106 Wei General 魏將 Mang Mao 芒卯.

107 Zhao General 趙將 Jia Yan 賈偃.

108 Jingcheng of Hann 韓 陘城.

heads. During the 45th year, Qin attacked Yewang of Hann.[109] (see 262-II) Yewang County surrendered to Qin, the passage from Shangdang to the capital of Hann was severed.[110] Magistrate of Shangdang Prefecture appealed to Zhao, pledging to surrender to Zhao, with this move it incited Qin to attack Zhao. During the 47th year of King Zhao, Bai Qi returned to join battle with Zhao at Changping (see 260-I),[111] the Zhao soldiers were led into a ruse; over four hundred thousand surrendered soldiers were buried alive. Zhao lost its stamina and vigour; it was no longer an opposition against Qin.

In the meantime, there were also changes at the Qin court. King Zhao was wearied of the overwhelming power of Marquis Rang, the king's distaff uncle.[112] With the help of Fan Ju, the king managed to banish his uncle, [113] replacing Fan Ju as the new chancellor. Fan Ju was a narrow-minded foreign guest *keqing*; the victory at Changping made him jealous of Bai Qi, fearing that the general might take his place at the Qin court. He gave a repartee to the King, who recalled Bai Qi from the front. (273-III). Shortly after, the mighty general was discharged from his duties and was ordered by the king to take his own life.

Qin Annihilated the Zhou Kingdom

The king of Zhou was greatly alarmed by the repeated losses by the San-Jin states. West Zhou conjured up a plan for an alliance against Qin. Nevertheless, it offered Qin an excuse that it was threatening its security and had it annihilated; shortly after East Zhou was also annihilated. (See 256-II).

In 249 BCE, King Xiaolei of Chu ordered an expedition against Lu, annihilating it.[114] Lu had all along held a very close relationship with the state of Zhou, and it was also the buffer state for the kingdom. While the two events appeared to be insignificant in history, however, they were the harbinger of the demise of the six states.

Yan and San-Jin

With the repeated defeats of the three Jin states of Hann, Wei and Zhao, Yan did not come to its senses that it might also meet the fate of the Jin states. It persistently allied with Qin to make wars with the other states. When Qin ceased its campaigns against the Jin states, Yan invaded Zhao on its own. When King Xi of Yan came to the throne in 251 BCE,[115] he heard from his ministers that the young men at Zhao were almost completely obliterated during the Battle of Changping, and it could be taken easily. Some of his minister at court reprimanded against it, maintaining that the state had a long history of wars and battles, and the civilians were hardy soldiers and it could not be taken down easily. The king bent on making war decided to go his own way. (see 251-II). Zhao retained the great general, Lian Po and defeated Yan soundly while Qin was watching on the sideline with avarice. The battle between Yan and Zhao offered Qin a

---

109 Yewang 野王 - Qinyangxian Henan 河南 沁陽縣.

110 Shangdang 上黨.

111 Zhao at Changping 長平.

112 Marquis Rang 穰侯.

113 Fan Ju 范雎.

114 King Xiaolei of Chu 楚 孝烈王 (r. 262-238 BCE).

115 King Xi of Yan 燕喜王 (r. 254-222 BCE).

great opportunity to attack Zhao again, which lost 37 walled-cities. (248-1). Lord Xinling of Wei,[116] managed to rally the armed forces of several states to the rescue of Zhao by defeating Qin. Nevertheless, it was only a fleeting moment of exaltation. (257-11) and (247-1), the three Jin states were moribund.

The Final Horizontal Alliance

The only person with some courage and insight, and who was able to hold the encroachment of Qin for some time was Lord Xinling of Wei, he died in 244 BCE, having been disregarded and dismissed by his elder brother, the king of Wei. Ever since then the resistance against Qin had remiss to an all-time low. Qi, being much farther away from Zhongyuan adopted a passive diplomatic strategy and tried to stay natural while Yan continued to retain its tie with Qin. Chu was relatively stronger than the rest of the states in Zhongyuan at this stage, however, beset by the reigns of inept rulers. In 241 BCE, the allied forces of Chu, Zhao, Wei, Hann and Wey made a final and desperate ditch against Qin. (241-1), General Pang Xuan of Zhao led the armies from five states to attack Qin.[117] The armies marched as far as the Hanguguan Pass. The Qin defenders opened their gates to meet the besiegers head on; disunity set in, the allied forces disintegrated and dispersed. The last Vertical Alliance failed miserably. After this, the six states had neither the will nor the power to muster any forces to go against Qin; they sat in wait for the final onslaught by Qin, being picked off one by one.

The Seclusion of the Six States and their Final Demise

Ying Zheng, the king of Qin, ascended to the throne in 246 BCE at the age of 13.[118] For the first several years, he did not preside at the Qin court. When he came of age, it only took him ten years to annex and annihilate the six states. The most meritorious general was Wang Jian.[119] The sequence of annihilation was Hann, Zhao, Yan, Wei, Chu and Qi. Wey, being a minor polity and having submitted to Qin as a protectorate state earlier, was left untouched.

In 231 BCE, Sheng the Nanyang magistrate of Hann offered land to Qin, which appointed him as capital magistrate *neishi.* (231-1)[120] The year following, Qin sent Sheng to attack Hann; the king of Hann was captured. Qin changed the Hann territories into a prefecture, Yingchuanjun; Hann was no more.[121]

In 229 BCE, Ying Zheng ordered Wang Jian and Yang Duanhe to attack Zhao to the west and south.[122] Zhao responded by dispatching Li Mu and Sima Shang to make defence.[123] Qin appreciated that Li Mu was a seasoned warrior, employed the trick of sowing seeds of discord behind the enemy lines, Qin bribed the traitor, Guo Kai to spread rumours that Li Mu and Sima Shang were planning a revolt.[124] The king killed Li Mu and arrested Sima Shang. The next year,

---

116 Lord Xinling 信陵君 (?-243 BCE).

117 Pang Xuan 龐煖 of Zhao.

118 King of Qin 秦王 Ying Zheng 嬴政 (r. 247-210 BCE).

119 Wang Jian 王翦.

120 Nanyang magistrate of Hann *neishi* 韓内史 Sheng 勝.

121 Yingchuan 穎川郡.

122 Yang Duanhe 楊端和.

123 Li Mu 李牧 and Sima Shang 司馬尚.

124 Guo Kai 郭開.

Wang Jian gave the Zhao army a devastating defeat; the king of Zhao, Qian was captured.[125] The territories of Zhao was turned into a prefecture, Handanjun.[126] Zhao met its demise. (See 229-I and 228-I)

Ying Zheng had planned to order his army to continue its march into Yan. The prince of Yan, Ji Dan was greatly alarmed,[127] he decided to send an assassin to take the life of Ying Zheng. Jing Ke,[128] a chivalrous and strong man, was sent on the mission. The mission failed, Jing died. (228-VI and 227-I). In 227 BCE, Qin sent Wang Jian and Xin Sheng to lay siege to Yan.[129] Yan employed the men from the Rong and Dai to make a defence. (226-I) Qin captured Jicheng, the capital city of Yan.[130] King Xi of Yan escaped to Liaodong.[131] The king sent an assassin to have his crown prince, Ji Dan, murdered to sue for peace. It did not help; Qin had the king killed later. Qin turned Yan into the prefecture of Guangyang and continued to annex the prefectures founded by Yan: Shanggu, Yuyang, You Beiping, Liaoxi and Liaodong.[132] Yan expired.

In 225 BCE, Qin sent Wang Ben against Wei,[133] the king found shelter in the capital of Daliang. The Qin forces diverted the water from Huanghe River to inundate the city. After three months, the city was flooded, King Jia surrendered and was executed.[134] (See 225-I). Two prefectures were established, Dang in the eastern part of Wei and the former Song territories previously annexed by Wei was renamed Sishui Prefecture.[135]

During the same year, generals Li Xin and Meng Wu of Qin attacked Chu in the south, but the army suffered a defeat from Chu.[136] (See 225-II). The next year, Qin ordered Wang Jian to lead an armed force of six hundred thousand men to attack Qin. The Chu army was overwhelmed at a place called Qi, the Chu general; Xiang Yan took his own life.[137] In 223 BCE, generals Wang Jian and Meng Wu entered the capital of Chu, Shouchun, the king of Chu, Fuchu was captured.(see 223-I).[138] Qin then established three prefectures - Jiujiang, Hengshan and Changsha.[139] Chu was obliterated. The next year, Wang Jian led his forces east and quelled the former Yue kingdom, previously annexed by Chu. The general pacified the local tribal leaders, establishing the prefecture of Kuaiji.[140]

In 221 BCE, Wang Ben, the Qin general, after annihilating Yan, led his forces south and attacked Qi, which did not make any preparations for war. The King of Qi, Jian surrendered and

---

125 King of Zhao 趙王 Qian 遷.

126 Handan 邯鄲郡.

127 Ji Dan 姬丹.

128 Jing Ke 荆軻.

129 Xin Sheng 辛勝.

130 Jicheng 薊城, the capital city of Yan 燕都.

131 Liaodong 遼東.

132 Guangyang 廣陽郡 and continued to annex the prefectures founded by Yan: Shanggu 上谷, Yuyang 漁陽, You Beiping 右北平, Liaoxi 遼西 and Liaodong 遼東.

133 Wang Ben 王賁.

134 King Jia of Wei 魏王假.

135 Dang Prefecture 碭郡; Sishui prefecture 泗水郡.

136 Li Xin 李信 and Meng Wu 蒙武.

137 Qi 蘄. Chu General 楚將 Xiang Yan 項燕.

138 Chu capital 楚都 Shouchun 壽春. The King of Chu 楚王 Fuchu 負芻 (r. 227-223 BCE).

139 Jiujiang 九江郡, Hengshan 衡山郡 and Changsha 長沙郡.

140 Kuaiji 會稽郡.

was banished to a pine forest, where he died of hunger.[141] Qin established the prefectures of Qi and Langya. Qi was vanquished.[142] (221-I)

With the gradual fall and demise of the six states, the remnants of the six states could no longer muster up any energy to oppose Qin. Nevertheless, it was not an easy undertaking for Qin either; apart from Qi, which did not put up any resistance, the other five states did fight to their bitter ends. Furthermore, there were pockets of resistance from the remnants of the former royalists and generals who simply refused to surrender to Qin; while they had given up the hope of recovering their former states; they had chosen to die fighting. (222-V)

The only state left untouched was the state of Wey at Yewang.[143] The annihilation of the state was not addressed until the time of the Second Emperor. (209-VI)

The Grand Unification by Qin First Emperor and Reactions by the Former Forces

The unification of all under Heaven by Qin was not entirely achieved through military might. Among the seven states, Qin had the most comprehensive and encompassing internal political strategy. At the time of the Warring States, Xunzi after visiting Qin wrote in his 'Qiangguo pian',[144] "The customs of the Qin people are basically simple and unadulterated; the officers are committed to their duties while the ministers are loyal to the court. The clerical functions at court are highly efficient, it did not come as a surprise that the state has become powerful, it is a natural progression." Upon the unification, the First Emperor had intended to dissimilate the ideal to the rest of all under Heaven, using the Qin model of institution for the rest of his kingdom. He maintained that the fief lords under the feudal system were the cause of incessant wars under Heaven. Tracing back to the time when King Wu of Zhou was the Son-of-Heaven, who began to enfeoff his siblings, descendants and meritorious subjects, the situation was acceptable. However, with the passage of time, the fief lords became distant and began to fight against each other; the latter Sons-of-Heaven could not prevent those bloodsheds. Hence, the First Emperor believed the six states should be annihilated, dividing the kingdom into 36 prefectures, confiscating all the weapons and had them stored in the capital of Xianyang.[145] The weapons collected were forged into twelve colossal bronze statues. He then decreed to unify all the weights and measures, adopting a common written language, introducing a standard width rut for chariots, carriages and carts throughout his kingdom. All the rich, elites, and wealthy families were repatriated to Xianyang and placed under strict surveillance.

Li Si was an ardent adherent of the First Emperor, a man from Shangcai at Chu.[146] In his youth, he studied under Xunzi on the 'Techniques of Sovereignty'.[147] Later, he was appointed the chancellor of Qin and was instrumental in initiating the political and military strategies towards Qin's grand unification.

The established political strategies did not go down well with the literati and scholars after the unification, and the government met strong resistance. It led to the burning of books and

---

141 King of Qi, Jian 齊王建 (r. 264-221 BCE).

142 Qijun 齊郡 and Langyajun 琅琊郡.

143 Wey 衛 Yewang 野王.

144 The *Xunzi* 荀子 'Qiangguo pian Chapter 16 强國篇 第十六'. When Xunzi visited Qin, Marquis Ying 應侯 of Qin asked him what he saw in Qin, this was his response.

145 Qin capital, Xianyang - 秦都 咸陽.

146 Li Si 李斯 from Shangcai of Chu 楚上蔡.

147 Techniques of Sovereignty or Operandi of Kings and Emperor 帝王之術.

burial of *ru* – literati.[148] During the 26th year of the First Emperor (221-IV), the court academician, a man from Qi,[149] voiced his opposition to the prefecture and county system, he suggested that the kingdom should restore the feudal system of enfeoffing the princelings. The chancellor, Li Si rebuffed the suggestion and suggested to abrogate the fief system of enfeoffment. The First Emperor decreed to divide his kingdom into 36 prefectures. (221-IV) Li Si went on to suggest that the officers and commoners should not be allowed to "disparage the present by extolling the past",[150] furthermore using one's private learning to disparage the court was also proscribed. The First Emperor accepted Li Si's suggestion and decreed to burn all the historical chronicles of the former fief states, except the chronicles of Qin.[151] The *Odes – Shi* and the *Documents – Shu* kept by scholars were also ordered to be burned and destroyed, except the copies kept at the Imperial academician library. (213-II)[152] People who discussed the *Shi* and the *Shu* were put to death, while people who disparaged the present by extolling the past, met a worse fate, the entire family clan were put to death. A strict prohibition was placed on private tuition. The people who aspired to learn law and legal system of the kingdom could become understudies under the legal bureaucrats at court. The next year, two occult scholars, masters Hou and Lu made disparaging remarks about the First Emperor and absconded for their lives.[153] When the First Emperor heard of their remarks, he was furious and ordered his Judiciary Department to make an investigation into the matter. Four hundred and sixty scholars were arrested and sentenced to be buried alive. (212-III)[154]

The First Emperor did not find peace with himself sitting in state; there were numerous attempts on his life. Gao Jianli,[155] a blind musician, attempted to assassinate the First Emperor, the assassin failed and was killed. Zhang Liang,[156] a descendant of a noble family from the state of Hann, hired a strongman to assassinate the Emperor while he was on tour; the strongman hit at the wrong carriage with a mallet. Zhang Liang escaped unscathed.

The Fall of the Qin Empire

The First Emperor died during his fourth expeditionary tours to the east of his kingdom. The imperial carriage superintendent *zhongjufu*, Zhao Gao, a eunuch, conspired with Li Si to change the imperial will, decreed the death of Fu Su, the legitimate heir and General Meng Tian.[157] They placed Ying Huhai, the youngest son of the Emperor on the throne, known as the Second Emperor.[158] (210-I) The young emperor, having no experience to rule the state, wallowed in luxury with wanton abandonment, and listened only to the advice of Zhao Gao. The eunuch distorted

---

148 焚書坑儒 – to be fair, not all the scholars buried were literati, scholars from other schools of thought were also buried.

149 Court academician 博士 Chun Yuyue 淳于越.

150 "Disparage the present by extolling the past." '以古非今'.

151 The *Qin Chronicles, Qinji* 秦記.

152 The *Odes* 詩 and the *Documents* 書.

153 Master Hou 侯生 and Master Lu 盧生.

154 Kang ru 坑儒.

155 Gao Jianli 高漸離.

156 Marquis Liu 留侯 Zhang Liang 張良.

157 Horse and Carriage Superintendent 中車府 Zhao Gao 趙高.
Ying Fusu 嬴扶蘇. Meng Tian 蒙恬.

158 Qin Second Emperor 二世皇帝 Ying Huhai 嬴胡亥 (r. 209-207 BCE).

facts from truth for the Emperor, banishing all the people, who were against his personal interest. He then machinated to remove Li Si, assuming the position as the chancellor of Qin.

In 209 BCE, two junior Qin officers, Chen Sheng and Wu Guang took up arms; the Qin kingdom fell into great turmoil.[159] Zhao Gao took advantage of the confusion and forced the Second Emperor to take his own life, replacing him with Ying Ying, the son of the former crown prince.[160] Ying Ying, in turn, executed the eunuch, wiping out the three family clans of the eunuch. At this stage, the clan members of former influential fief lords also rose up in arms; among them, Xiang Yu, the grandson of Xiang Yan, the Chu general who lost the battle to Qin in 223 BCE.[161] As the fief lords and rebels gathered strength and momentum, they finally broke into the capital city of Qin; they killed King Ziying (Ying Ying) and all the royal family members. The palaces were torched, and the vast quantities of treasures were divided among the rebels. Qin finally met its demise. The Qin empire only lasted for 15 years. (213-207 BCE)

Zhao Gao persecuted both Li Si, who in part was instrumental in the grand unification of Qin and the powerful General Meng Tian, and they met their ends under most iniquitous circumstances. The demise of the two most influential people in the Qin court hastened the downfall of the state. The conflict between the military and civic officers was one of the many causes of Qin's final collapse. Notwithstanding the short reign of the Qin empire, it left lasting legacies of political, court and legal practices into Han and succeeding dynasties.

The Contest between Chu and Han

Upon the fall of Qin, Da-Chu and Han entered into an extensive period of battles and unrest that lasted for eight years. Liu Bang (Han) and Xiang Yu (Da-Chu) were brilliant political strategists that revolted against Qin.[162] The contest after the throne by Chu and Han, together with many other contenders was the first instance in Chinese history - the cycle of an era of respectable governance, followed by a period of unrest had become a paradigm of Chinese history ever since.

When the Qin government fell into frailty, the civilians, the local gentries, the former royalists and opportunists all rose up and rebelled in unison, carving out territories and proclaimed themselves king. Chen Sheng and Wu Guang were the first two peasants who mutinied against the government in Chinese history.[163] The two men came from the village of Dazexiang,[164] having missed escorting convicts to a designated location on time, an offence punishable by death; they revolted and became the champions that incited the rest of the kingdom to rise up in arms. Chen Sheng proclaimed himself king at the Chen Prefecture. He proclaimed, 'The Lords and elites are no different from us, they are men like us,' breaking the long-held dictum that the Son of Heaven was a mandate from Heaven. Chen Sheng and Wu Guang were two true peasants who rebelled against a kingdom.

The contest between Chu and Han had one significant difference with the changing of dynasties of latter days, among the supporters of Chu and Han there were the remnants of royalists from the former states. The people revolted carrying the righteous banner of restoring

---

159 Chen Sheng 陳勝 and Wu Guang 吳廣.

160 Ying Ziying 嬴子嬰 or Ying Ying 嬴嬰.

161 Xiang Ji 項籍 (Yu 羽), grandson of Xiang Yan 項燕,

162 Han Liu Bang 漢 劉邦 (256-195 BCE) and Chu Xiang Yu 楚 項羽 (r. 232-202 BCE).

163 However, it was not the first commoner uprising. The civilians rebelled against King Li of Zhou 周厲王. (r. 877-841 BCE).

164 Dazexiang 大澤鄉 - Xuxian Anhui 安徽 宿縣.

their former kingdoms, and many of those men were the royalists and generals from the defunct warring states. Xiang Yu was one of the remnants, he was the grandson of the Chu general, Xiang Yan, and he followed his uncle Xiang Liang to rise against Qin. When the uncle died in battle, he took over the commanding position of the Chu army. In 207 BCE, faced against all odds, he won a resounding victory against a much larger crack troops of Qin at Julu.[165] Later, when Qin fell he proclaimed himself the Hegemonic King of Chu and governed the nine prefectures of Liang and Chu at the lower reaches of Huanghe and Changjiang rivers.[166] Finally, after repeated losses to Liu Bang, the chivalrous quest to restore the former Chu kingdom failed and Xiang Yu ran himself through valiantly at the Wujiang River.[167] The person who finally made the conquest of all under Heaven was a rogue, a lowly functionary constable at Xishui, Liu Bang. Besides Zhang Liang, the only royalist remnant in his entourage of followers, all of Liu Bang's attendants were from lowly and peasant background. Cao Shan and Xiao He were minor functionaries, Fan Kuai was a butcher, Xiahou Ying was a horse attendant, Guan Ying was a cloth peddler; Zhou Bo sold weed baskets and at times took a part-time job as a funeral reed-pipe player.[168] The Qing scholar, Zhao Yi summing up the meritorious subjects of the founding of Han succinctly said, "Han was founded by people garbed in plain clothes."[169] At the beginning of the Han court, the ceremony and rites were simplistic to the rudimentary, when the meritorious subjects ... "were roaring drunk, each vying to gain recognition of his exploits; bellowing out vulgarly, drew their swords slashing at the pillars at the imperial hall at will."

However, that was a different chronicle, which we will take up in Volume II.

The *fengjian* (feudal system) or perhaps more appropriately the lineage system,[170] having gone through a passage of almost two millennium, that of Xia, Shang (Yin), Zhou, Spring and Autumn, the Warring States and finally Qin, came to a close. Even the Qin dynasty that had the remnants of the enfeoffed nobles were banished and toppled forever. In their stead, a civilian rose up and made himself a founding emperor of a dynasty that was to last for almost four centuries.

References

Sima Guang *Zizhi tongjian* 司馬光 資治通鑒. Volume I to VIII.

Bo Yang, 柏楊版 資治通鑒 Book 1 to 3.

---

165 Julu 巨鹿.

166 Hegemonic King of Chu 楚霸王.
Liang-Chu 梁楚 the lower reaches of Huanghe River and Changjiang River. 黄河長江下游.

167 Wujiang River 烏江.

168 Liu Bang 劉邦, Constable of Sishui 泗水亭長.
Zhang Liang 張良.
Xiao He 蕭何
Cao Shan 曹參.
Fan Kuai 樊噲 was a butcher.
Xiahou Ying 夏侯嬰 was a horse attendant 馬夫.
Guan Ying 灌嬰 was a cloth peddler 布販.
Zhou Bo 周勃 was a weed-basket peddler and played a reed pipe at funeral possessions 賣筐, 喪事吹笙手.

169 Qing scholar 清史學家 Zhao Yi 趙翼.

170 Fengjian 封建.

Lei, Haizong *Guoshi Gangyao* 雷海宗 國史綱要 pp. 28-83.

Li, Feng, *Early China, A Social and Cultural History*, 'The age of territorial states: Warring States politics and institutions (480-221 BCE)', pp 182-205.

Bai Shouyi, *An Outline History of China*. Chapter V and VI.

Burton Watson, *Records of the Grand Historian*.

Zi Ye 子夜, *Zhongguo lishi niandai jianbiao* 中國歷史年代簡表.Wenwu chubanshe 文物出版社, Sanlian shudian 三聯書店, 2003 Second Edition.

Abbreviations

SJ *Shiji wenbai duaizhao* 史記文白對照 (Sima Qian 司馬遷), edited by Wu Yun 吳雲 et al., Zhongyang minzu daxue chubanshe 中央民族大學出版社, China, 2002.

ZG LS ND JB *Zhongguo lishi niandai jianbiao* 中國歷史年代簡表. Edited by Wenwu chubanshe bianjibu 文物出版社編輯部, Joint Publishing (H.K.) Co. Ltd., 三聯書店, Hong Kong, 2003, 2nd edition.

ZGC *Zhanguoce* 戰國策 (Edited by Liu Xiang 劉向), annotations by He Wei et al. 賀偉 點校; 5th edition, Qilu shushe 齊魯書社, China, 2010.

ZGS *Zhanguoshi* 戰國史, Yang Kuan 楊寬. Shanghai Renmin chubanshe 上海人民出版社, China, 2003.

ZZTJ *Zizhi tongjian* 資治通鑒文白對照. (Sima Guang 司馬光). Edited by Chen Liankang et al. 陳連康, Xian chbanshe 西安出版社, China, 2002.

ZZTJ BY Edition, *Zizhi tongjian Bo Yang's Edition* 資治通鑒 柏楊版 (Sima Guang 司馬光). Translated by Yang B. 柏楊. 1986. 6th edition.

ZZTJ JZ *Zizhi tongjian jinzhu* 資治通鑒今註 (Sima Guang 司馬光), Edited by Li, Zongtong, et al. 李宗侗, Commercial Press, Taiwan. 2011

ZIZHI TONGJIAN

VOLUME 1 TO 8

WARRING STATES AND QIN

403-207 BCE

Zizhi tongjian Key Events and Annotations on the Warring States and Qin 403-207 BCE

Volume I. Zhou Records 周紀一 From 403 BCE to 369 BCE - 35 years p. 9

403-I	Partition of Jin by three Jin ministers	三家分晉
	(Sima Guang's annotation on the collapse of rites)	(司馬光論周王失禮)[1]
403-II	The siege of Jinyang, demise of the Zhi family clan (455 BCE)	晉陽之圍 智氏覆亡
	(Sima Guang annotates on Master Xiangzi of Zhi, Zhi Yao)	(司馬光論智襄子之敗)
403-III	Yu Rang attempted to assassinate Zhi Yao (455 BCE)	豫讓欲刺趙襄子報 智瑶之死
403-V	Marquis Wen of Wei attracted sages to his court	魏文侯重賢 廷多賢能
403-V	Wu Qi killed his wife to serve at Wei	吳起殺妻 任命於魏
402-I	King Weilie of Zhou died, succeeded by King An	周威烈王崩 子安王立
402-II	King Sheng of Chu was killed by bandits	盜殺楚聲王
398-I	Si Ziyang, Chancellor of Zheng was assassinated	鄭相駟子陽被刺殺
397-II	Yan Zhongzi hired Nie Zheng to assassinate Xia Lei, Hann chancellor	嚴仲子僱聶政 刺殺韓相俠累
396-I	Si Ziyang's clansmen killed Duke Ru of Zheng	駟子陽黨羽殺鄭繻公
391-II	Qi Tian clan ousted Duke Kang of Qi	齊田氏逐齊康公
389-II	Qi Tian clan seized power of the Qi court	齊田氏篡齊政權
387-II	Wu Qi escaped to Chu, Wu Qi carried out reforms at Chu	吳起奔楚 吳起變法
385-I	Revolt at Qin, Duke Chu of Qin was murdered	秦政變 秦出公被殺
381-I	King Dao of Chu died, Wu Qi was killed, King Su of Chu cleansed the royal household	楚悼王薨 吳起被殺 肅王屠王族
379-II	The demise of Qi Jiang clan	齊姜氏亡
375-I	King An of Zhou died, succeeded by King Xi	周安王崩 子烈王立
371-II	Hann minister Yan Shi assassinated Marquis Ai of Hann	韓大夫刺殺韓哀侯
371-III	Wei Ying vied with Gongzhong Huan for succession	魏罃 公中緩争承繼
370-IV	King Wei of Qi rewarded Jimo magistrate, boiled Ayi magistrate in a caldron for deception Qi attained prosperity and power	田因齊 奬即墨大夫 烹阿邑大夫 齊大治
369-III	King Lie of Zhou died, succeeded by King Xian	周烈王崩 弟姬扁立 是為顯王
369-III	Strife at Wei, Wei Ying killed Gongzhong Huan King Hui of Wei assumed power	魏内亂 魏惠王 殺公中緩

Volume II. Zhou Records II 周紀二 368 BCE to 321 BCE – 48 years p. 64

362-V	Topology of the Warring States Qin made reforms	戰國地形 秦發憤圖强

[1] The headings in brackets are annotations and commentaries.

361-I	Duke Xiao of Qin sought sages to make reforms	秦孝公頒布招賢令
	Gongsun Cuo on deathbed recommended Gongsun Yang	公叔痤臨終 薦公孫鞅
	Gongsun Yang responded to Qin's call	公孫鞅奔秦
359-I	Gongsun Yang made reforms to Qin	公孫鞅變法
	Gongsun Yang pledged to make reform	公孫鞅遷木立信
	(Sima Guang comments on integrity of a sovereign)	(司馬光論君王之威信)
355-I	The four treasures of Qi	齊國四寶
353-I	Pang Juan framed Sun Bin	龐涓陷害孫臏
	Laying siege to Wei to save Zhao, the Battle of Guiling	圍魏救趙 桂陵之役
353-III	Words of wisdom by Jing Yi	江乙之言
351-III	Shen Buhai appointed as Hann Chancellor	申不害為韓相
350-I	Qin moved its capital to Xianyang	秦遷都咸陽
	Gongsun Yang continued reforms at Qin	公孫鞅再變法
346-III	Duke Cheng of Wey demoted his title of Marquis	衛成公自貶為侯
341-I	Pang Juan of Wei invaded Hann	魏龐涓攻韓
	Sun Bin used *Sunzi bingfa* to rescue Hann	孫臏引孫子兵法救韓
	Pang Juan died at the Battle of Maling	龐涓命喪馬陵之役
341-II	Tian Ji, Qi general, escaped to Chu	齊將田忌奔楚
340-I	Gongsun Yang captured General Wei Ang by deceit	公孫鞅計擒魏將魏卬
	Wei sued for peace by ceding west of River- *Hexi* to Qin	魏獻河西地于秦求和
	Wei moved its capital to Daliang	魏遷都大梁
340-II	Gongsun Yang enfeoffed as Lord Shang	秦封公孫鞅商君
338-I	Duke Xiao died Gongsun Yang met his demise,	秦孝公薨
	quartered by 5 horses	公孫鞅被五馬分屍
337-I	Shen Buhai, Hann chancellor, died	申不害卒
336-II	Mengzi (Mencius) visited King Hui of Wei (Liang)	孟子見梁(魏)惠王
	(Sima Guang comments on benefits versus benevolence)	(司馬光論利益與仁義)
334-I	King Wei of Qi and King Hui of Wei proclaimed as kings	齊威王 魏惠王 互稱王
334-III	Chu annihilated the Yue Kingdom	楚亡越
333-III	Su Qin failed to impress King Hui of Qin	蘇秦晉見秦惠王 不果
	Su Qin promoted Vertical Alliance at Yan, Zhao, Hann,	蘇秦 去燕, 趙, 韓, 魏, 齊
	Wei, Qi and Chu	說縱橫
	Su Qin helped Zhang Yi to go to Qin	蘇秦佐張儀去秦
	The six states appointed Su Qin as chancellor	六國封蘇秦為相
332-I	Qin used deceit, the Vertical Alliance dissolved	秦瓦解合縱聯盟
325-I	Qin, Ying Si proclaimed king	秦嬴駟稱王
325-II	Marquis Si of Wey sought an escapee from Wei	衛嗣侯索魏逃犯
324-II	Su Qin found refuge at Qi	蘇秦投齊
321-I	Lord Jingguo, Tian Ying assumed power at Qi	靖郭君田嬰得勢于齊
	Lord Mengchang, Tian Wen, son of Lord Jingguo	孟嘗君 靖郭君之子
	(Sima Guang comments on keeping scholars)	(司馬光論養士)

321-IV	Lord Mengchang visited Chu (Sima Guang on Lord Mengchang's open-mindedness)	孟嘗君訪楚 (司馬光論 孟嘗君樂于受諫)

Volume III. Zhou Records III 周紀三 From 320 BCE to 298 BCE – 23 years p. 118

320-I	Marquis of Wey demoted his title as Sir	衛侯自貶為君
319-II	Mencius - Mengzi visited King Xiang of Wei	孟子見魏襄王
318-I	Qin defeated the five allied forces at Hangu Pass	五國聯軍 兵敗函谷關
318-II	Song Yan proclaimed as King Kang	宋偃稱康王
317-II	Su Qin assassinated by a Qi minister	齊大夫刺殺蘇秦
317-III	Zhang Yi convinced Wei to forego Vertical Alliance	張儀説魏退出合縱
316-I	Qin conquered Shu	秦征服蜀
316-II	King Kang of Song abdicated his throne to Zi Zhi	宋康王禪讓于子之
315-I	King Shenjing of Zhou died, King Nan succeeded	周慎靚王崩 子 周赧王立
314-IV	Yan in chaos, Qi general killed Zi Zhi and King Kang of Song	齊將殺子之 宋康王
313-II	Zhang Yi deceived Chu King Huai to break the Vertical Alliance	張儀騙楚懷王背盟
312-II	King Zhao of Yan resolved to avenge the defeat by Qi	燕昭王發憤圖强 報齊入侵之辱
312-I	Chu suffered a great loss against Qin	秦大敗楚軍
311-II	Zhang Yi broke the Vertical Alliance, enfeoffed as Lord Wuxin	張儀破合縱 封武信君
	King Hui of Qin died; the Allies renewed the Alliance	秦惠王薨 合縱恢復
310-I	Zhang Yi lost support, died in Wei	張儀失勢 病死魏國
	(Mengzi comments on Gongsun Yan and Zhang Yi)	(孟子論公孫衍與張儀)
	(Fayan - Yang Xiong comments on Zhang Yi and Su Qin)	(揚雄論 張儀 蘇秦)
308-II	The pledge at Xirang between the Qin king and Gan Mao	秦王與甘茂 息壤誓言
307-II	Ying Tang died lifting a tripod	秦王舉鼎 力竭而死
307-III	King Zhao introduced foreign attire, shooting on horseback	趙王厲行 胡服騎射
306-I	Gan Mao fell to defamation, escaped to Qi	甘茂栽于毀謗 奔齊
305-III	Ying Ji was young; Wei Ran presided as regent	嬴稷年少 魏冉當權
299-I	Zhao Yong abdicated the throne to Zhao He	趙王雍讓位於趙何
299-III	Chu King Huai deceived to enter Qin, hostage at Xianyang	楚懷王 被騙入秦武關
	Chu ministers placed King Qingxiang on the throne	楚立頃襄王
298-III	Lord Pingyuan had several thousand guests at his manor	平原君 食客嘗數千
	Gongsun Long – 'A Slave has Three Ears' thesis	公孫龍論, '臧三耳'

Volume IV. Zhou Records IV 周紀四 From 292 BCE -273 BCE – 25 years p. 160

296-I	King Huai of Chu died in Xianyang	楚懷王病死秦咸陽
295-II	Zhao Zhang revolted, Zhao king died of starvation at Shaqiu	趙章造反 趙王雍餓死沙丘

		秦坑殺趙降卒四十萬
259-I	A rift developed between Bai Qi and Fan Ju	白起與范雎不和
259-III	Kong Bin predicted the six states would fall within 20 years	孔斌預言 六國將亡
258-II	Lord Pingyuan went to Chu for help; Mao Sui volunteered	平原君去楚求救 毛遂自薦
258-V	Lord Xinling stole tally, killed General Jin Bi to save Zhao	信陵君盜兵符 殺晉鄙救趙
257-I	King of Qin forced the death of Bai Qi	秦王賜劍白起 白起自殺
257-II	Lord Xinling allies sounding defeated Qin	信陵君聯軍破秦軍
257-III	Lu Buwei met Ying Yiren - a piece of rare merchandise	呂不韋遇奇貨 嬴異人
256-I	Kingdom of Zhou annihilated	周王國亡

Volume VI. Qin Records 1 秦紀一 From 255 BCE to 228 BCE – 28 years p. 242

255-I	Fan Ju retired from the Qin court	范雎辭秦廷
255-II	Xunzi - Xun Kuang discussed military affairs with King of Zhao	荀子與趙王論軍事 議兵篇
251-II	Yan attacked weakened Zhao; Lian Po defeated the invader	趙弱 燕攻伐 廉頗大破燕軍
247-II	Lord Xinling returned to Wei, led 5 armies defeated Qin	信陵君返魏 領五聯軍破秦軍
247-IV	Lord Xinling discharged by Wei; died 4 years later	秦王反間 信陵君辭廷 四年後死
247-V	Ying Zheng ascended to the Qin throne	嬴政即位
245-II	Lian Po was framed and discharged	廉頗被讒罷黜
244-III	Li Mu once defeated the Xiongnu at Dai and Yanmen	李牧曾破匈奴 於代與雁門
244-IV	The barbaric tribes in and around Zhongyuan	中原周邊各蠻夷部落
242-II	Ju Xin of Yan attacked Zhao, killed by Zhao	燕將劇辛攻趙 被殺
241-I	Final South-North Alliance against Qin at Hanguguan Pass	六國聯軍最後一擊 函谷關
238-VI	Lao Ai revolted, executed	嫪毐之亂 被殺
238-VII	Lord Chunshen presented impregnated woman to Chu king	春申君獻有孕女為后
	Huang Xie died violently	黄歇慘死
	(Yang Xiong on the Four Lords of the Warring States)	(揚雄論 戰國四公子)
237-I	Ying Zheng recalled guest minister Li Si	嬴政見客卿李斯
235-I	Lu Buwei committed suicide	呂不韋自殺
	(Fayan - Yang Xiong comments on Lu Buwei)	(揚雄論 呂不韋)
234-I	Zhao General Li Mu defeated Qin forces	趙將李牧大敗秦軍
233-I	Hann Fei died in Qin	韓非身死秦國
	(Fayan - Yang Xiong comments on Hann Fei)	(法言揚雄 論韓非)

	(Sima Guang comments on Hann Fei)	(司馬光 論韓非)
230-I	Hann annihilated	韓亡
229-I	Ji Mu replaced, killed	李牧被殺
228-I	Zhao annihilated	趙亡
228-III	Zhao Jia escaped to Dai, as king of Dai	趙嘉逃代 稱代王
228-VI	Prince Dan of Yan sought revenge	燕丹子謀報仇

Volume VII. Qin Records 2 秦紀二 From 227 BCE to 209 BCE – 19 years p. 292

227-I	Jing Ke attempted to assassinate Qin Ying Zheng	荊軻刺秦王
226-I	Prince Dan of Yan executed by King of Yan	燕丹子被殺
225-I	Wei king surrendered, executed; Wei annihilated	魏王降被殺 魏亡
225-II	Wang Jian attacked Chu with 600,000 troops	王翦六十萬軍攻楚
223-I	Chu annihilated	楚亡
222-I	Yan annihilated	燕亡
	(Sima Guang comments on Prince Dan of Yan and Jing Ke)	(司馬光論燕丹子 荊軻)
222-II	King of Dai captured, end of Zhao	趙嘉被擒 趙亡
221-I	Qi surrendered without a fight, annihilated	齊投降 齊亡
	(Sima Guang on Vertical Alliance and Horizontal Coalition)	(司馬光論合縱連橫)
221-II	Qin unified All under Heaven, changed title to Emperor	秦統一天下 秦王改稱皇帝
221-III	Qin adopted Zao Yan's Five Virtues	秦用鄒衍伍德相運説
221-IV	Qin abrogated enfeoffment, divided kingdom into 36 prefectures	秦癈封侯 致三十六郡
220-I	First Emperor made tours All under Heaven	秦嬴政巡天下
219-I	First Emperor Feng-Chen at Taishan searched for immortals at the Eastern Sea	秦皇泰山封禪 東海尋仙縱
218-I	Zhang Liang attempted to assassinate the First Emperor	張良謀刺殺秦皇
214-II	Meng Tian made expeditions against the Xiongnu, recovered lands at Henan, constructed new sections of Long-Walls	蒙恬伐匈奴 收復河南 修築長城
213-II	First Emperor burned books	秦嬴政焚書
212-II	First Emperor built Afenggong, constructed Lishan Mound	秦嬴政建阿房宮 建驪山陵墓
212-III	First Emperor buried literati and scholars	秦嬴政坑儒
210-I	First Emperor died at Shaqiu	秦嬴政病死沙丘
	Zhao Gao helped Ying Huhai to usurp the throne, killed Crown Prince Fusu	趙高謀嬴胡亥篡位 殺太子扶蘇
	Ying Huhai executed Meng Tian and Meng Yi	嬴胡亥殺蒙恬蒙毅
	(Fayan - Yang Xiong comments on Meng Tian)	(揚雄法言 論蒙恬)
	(Sima Guang comments on Meng Tian)	(司馬光 論蒙恬)
209-II	Ying Huhai despotic reign	嬴胡亥苛政
209-III	Chen Sheng and Wu Guang rebelled	陳勝 吳廣反秦
209-IV	Zhang Er and Chen Yu revolted	張耳 陳餘起義

209-IV	Liu Bang revolted	劉邦起義
	Xiang Liang and Xiang Yi rose up in arms	項梁 項羽起義
	Former royalists proclaimed kings	故國貴族 各自稱王
209-VI	Wey finally was annihilated	衛國亡

Volume VIII. Qin Records 3 秦紀三 From 208 BCE to 207 BCE – 2 years p. 332

208-III	Chu generals killed Wu Guang	衆楚將殺吳廣
	Qin general, Zhang Han won a series of battles against Chu	章邯連敗叛軍
208-IV	Ying Huhai kept berating Li Si	嬴胡亥厲責李斯
208-IV	Ying Huhai became, even more, despotic	嬴胡亥苛政變本加厲
208-VII	Zhuang Jia carriage man assassinated Chen Sheng	莊賈殺陳勝
208-X	Ying Bu rebelled	英布起義
208-XI	Zhang Liang submitted to Liu Bang	張良歸附劉邦
208-XII	Liu Bang submitted to Xiang Yu	劉邦歸附項梁
	Fan Zeng suggested placing a Chu royalist on the Chu throne	范增議立楚後為王
	Mi Xin was made king of Chu	芈心當楚懷王
208-XIV	Ying Huhai to retire into the inner palace, Zhao Gao took over	趙高議嬴胡亥 退隱後宮作樂
	Zhao Gao executed Li Si	趙高殺李斯
208-XV	Xiang Liang died in battle	項梁戰死
208-XVIII	Zhang Han laid siege to Zhao Handan, Zhang Er and Zhao King besieged	章邯圍趙王 張耳於邯鄲
	Other forces came to the rescue waited	救兵囤邯鄲 按兵不動
	Song Yi made Commander General of Chu	芈心令宋義為上將軍
	Mi Xin pledged, first general to enter the Inner Pass would be made king	芈心約各將 先入關為王
	Liu Bang commanded to march west towards Xianyang	芈心令劉邦西攻關內
	Mi Xin ordered Xiang Yu to rescue Zhao	芈心令項羽北上救趙
207-III	Song Yi arrived at Anyang and waited	宋義兵至安陽 按兵不動
	Xiang Yu executed Song Yu and assumed control of Chu army	項羽殺宋義 代為將軍
207-VI	Qin made fierce attacks against Handan	秦猛攻邯鄲
207-VI	Zhang Er repeatedly appealed to Chen Yu to fight against Qin	張耳催陳餘解邯鄲之圍
	Xiang Yu crossed the River and headed north to Handan	項羽渡河 北上至邯鄲
	Xiang Yu won a bloody battle against Qin; Qin withdrew	項羽血戰秦　秦不敵退
	Zhang Er and Chen Yu fell out	張耳 陳餘反目
207-VII	Liyi Qi related Alliance incidents to Liu Bang	酈食其述 戰國合縱事故
207-VIII	Chen Hui surrendered to Liu Bang	陳恢降劉邦
207-IX	Zhang Han surrendered to Xiang Yu	章邯降項羽

207-XI	Zhao Gao assumed total control of the Qin court	趙高指鹿為馬
	Zhao Gao committed regicide; Huhai committed suicide	趙高弑君 嬴胡亥自殺
	Zhao Gao placed Ying Ying on the throne as king	趙高立嬴嬰為王
	Ying Ying executed Zhao Gao	嬴嬰殺趙高
	Liu Bang defeated Qin forces at Lantian	劉邦血戰秦于藍田

Volume I. 資治通鑒 卷第一 周紀一 403-369 BCE

The narratives of this volume commence from the 33rd year (403 BCE) of King Weilie of Zhou, ending in the 7th year of King Lie. (369 BCE).[1]

403 BCE - The three principal ministers of Jin were enfeoffed this year, the family clans of Wei, Zhao and Hann.[2] The three ministerial family clans had previously annihilated the Zhi clan and divided their land.[3]

Master Xiangzi of Zhao, Zhao Wuxu, hated Zhibo so balefully that he used his skull as his drinking vessel.[4]

Yu Rang attempted to assassinate Zhao Xiangzi to avenge the death of his master, Zhi Yao.[5]

Marquis Wen of Wei, Wei Si, was courteous to the wise and respectful of the intellectuals, he attracted many capable people to his court.[6]

Wu Qi killed his wife to earn a general position at Wei.[7] When his mother died, he did not attend to her funeral. Marquis Wen of Wei made Wu Qi a general. Wu Qi was an exemplary army commander.

397 BCE - Nie Zheng assassinated Xia Lei, the chancellor of Hann.[8]

389 BCE - The minister of Qi, Tian He, was enfeoffed as a fief lord and took over the Qi State.[9]

387 BCE - Wu Qi left Wei and headed off to serve Chu. King Dao of Chu made him the chancellor.[10] Wu Qi made reforms to Chu by instituting new legal systems and strengthening the military power. He pacified the people to the south at Bai-Yue, held off the encroachments of the San-Jin (Three Jins - Hann, Zhao and Wei); and he made expeditions

---

1 King Weilie of Zhou 周威烈王 Ji Wu 姬午 (r. 425-402 BCE) was the 20th king of Eastern Zhou. (r. - denotes the reigning period. For comparison of reigning dates of the Zhao kings, fief lords, dukes and marquises during the Warring States period from different sources, see Appendix I. Also, see Appendix II -Yang Kuan's 楊寬 textual research.) N.B. The dates in the footnotes are predominantly based on *ZG LS ND JB*.
King Lie of Zhou 周烈王 Ji Xi 姬喜 (r. 375-369 BCE).

2 San-Jin 三晉 - Wei 魏; Zhao 趙; Hann 韓.

3 Zhi family clan - 智家族.

4 Master Xiang (Xiangzi) of Zhao 趙襄子 Zhao Wuxu 趙無恤 (r. 457-425 BCE).
Zhibo 智伯.

5 Yu Rang 豫讓.
Master Xiang (Xiangzi) of Zhi 智襄子 Zhi Yao 智瑤 (? – 453 BCE).

6 Marquis Wen of Wei 魏文侯 Wei Si 魏斯 (r. ?-396 BCE) or (r. 446-397 BCE) or (r. 445-396 BCE).

7 Wu Qi 吳起 (440-381 BCE).

8 Chancellor of Hann 韓相 Xia Lei 俠累 (?-397 BCE).
Nie Zheng 聶政 (?-397 BCE).

9 Minister of Qi 齊大夫 Tian He 田和 (r. 386-384 BCE).

10 King Dao of Chu 楚悼王 (r. 401-381 BCE).

against Qin to the west.[11] The feudal lords were getting apprehensive of the strengthening of Chu; however, the royal elites and nobles at Chu were resentful of Wu Qi.

381 BCE - King Dao of Chu died; Chu nobles and aristocrats and elites took advantage of the confusion killed Wu Qi.

371 BCE - Marquis Wu of Wei, Wei Ji, died. He did not leave a will, his son Wei Ying vied for the throne with Gongzhong Huan; the state fell into complete chaos.[12]

370 BCE - King Wei of Qi was fair with merits and punishments. He enfeoffed the magistrate of Jimo for his merits and executed the magistrate of Dong'a for deception; the fiefdom entered into a period of resurgence.[13]

Volume I. Zhou Records 周紀一

---

403 BCE *Wuyin* 戊寅 Warring States 戰國

King Weilie of Zhou	周威烈王	23rd year[14]
Duke Mu of Lu	魯穆公	7th year
Duke Jian of Qin	秦簡公	12th year
Duke Ru of Zheng	鄭繻公	20th year
Duke Dao of Song	宋悼公	1st year
King Sheng of Chu	楚聲王	5th year
Duke Kang of Qi	齊康公	2nd year
Duke Lie of Jin	晉烈公	19th year
Marquis Wen of Wei	魏文侯	44th year

---

11 Bai-Yue 百越.

12 Marquis Wu of Wei 魏武侯 Wei Ji 魏擊 (r. 396-371BCE) or (r. 395-370 BCE).
Wei Ying 魏罃 (r. 396-319 BCE) or (r. 370-319 BCE). See Yang Kuan's 楊寬 textual research.
Gongzhong Huan 公中緩 was the younger brother of Wei Ying.

13 King Wei of Qi 齊威王 (r. 358-320 BCE) or (r. 356-320 BCE).
Jimo Magistrate 即墨大夫.
Dong'a Magistrate 東阿大夫.

14 Hu Sansheng 胡三省 said, "The 23rd year of King Weilie of Zhou was 78 years from the time of Spring and Autumn - Chunqiu when a unicorn was captured 春秋 獲麟七十八年 or 71 years from the time of the 'Master Xiangzi of Zhao and Zhibo' incident 趙襄子 惎 智伯七十一年 (*sic*)." It is thus said that the *ZZTJ* is a continuation of the *Zuo Zhuan* 左傳 (Chronicle of *Zuo*). *ZZTJ JZ*, Vol 1, p. 14.
N.B. The first year of Master Xiangzi of Zhao 趙襄子 was 457 BCE (18th year of Duke Chu of Jin 晉出公.)
Zhibo 智伯 died in 453 BCE (approx.). Hence, the incident should be 50 years from Master Xiang of Zhao 趙襄子 Ji 惎 Zhibo 智伯 to the time of 23rd year (403 BCE) of King Weilie of Zhou. Master Xiangzi of Zhao reigned between 457-425 BCE, the postulation made by Hu Sansheng was incorrect. Observation based on *SJ* 史記, 卷 113, Zhao shijia 趙世家, 第 13, p. 1644.

Marquis Jing of Hann	韓景侯	6th year
Marquis Lie of Zhao	趙烈侯	6th year
Duke Min of Yan	燕湣公	31st year
Duke Shen of Wey	衛慎公	12th year[15]

1. King Weilie of Zhou decreed to enfeoff Jin ministers Wei Si, Zhao Ji and Hann Qian as fief lords.[16]

---

15 King Weilie of Zhou 周威烈王 Ji Wu 姬午 (r. 425-402 BCE).

Duke Mu of Lu 魯穆公 Ji Xian 姬顯 (r. 407-376 BCE) or (r. 415-377 BCE) was the 29th sovereign of Lu.

Duke Jian of Qin 秦簡公 Ying Daozi 嬴悼子 (r. 414-400 BCE) or (r. 414-406 BCE), the 26th sovereign of Qin.

Duke Ru of Zheng 鄭繻公 Ji Dai 姬駘 (r. 422-396 BCE) the 24th ruler of Zheng.

Duke Dao of Song 宋悼公 Zi Gouyou 子購由 (r. 403-396 BCE) or (r. 403-396 BCE).

King Sheng of Chu, aka King Shengheng 楚聲王 or 聲恒王, Mi-Xiong Dang 芈熊當 (r. 407-402 BCE). Rebels killed him.

Duke Kang of Qi 齊康公 Jiang Dai 姜貸 Lu Shi 呂氏 (r. 404-379 BCE) or (r. 404-385 BCE) or (r. 404-386 BCE), was the last of the Jiang 姜 family clan. He was banished to die on an island; another account relates that it was a walled city near the sea. After him, the Tian family clan 田氏 assumed power.

Duke Lie of Jin 晉烈公 Ji Zhi 姬止 (r. 422-393 BCE) or (r. 419-393 BCE) or (r. 415-389 BCE). The once most powerful fiefdom of Jin was divided by Wei, Hann and Zhao in 403 BCE. Some texts assert that the duke died in 386 or 385 BCE.

Marquis Wen of Wei 魏文侯 Ji Si 姬斯 Wei Shi 魏氏 (r. 446-397 BCE) or (r. 445-396 BCE).

Marquis Jing of Hann 韓景侯 Hann Qian 韓虔 (r. 408-400 BCE) or (r. 409-401 BCE).

Marquis Lie of Zhao 趙烈侯 Zhao Ji 趙籍 (r. 409-400 BCE) or (r. 409-387 BCE) or (408-387 BCE).

Duke Min of Yan 燕湣公 aka Duke Min 閔公 (r. 433-403 BCE) or (r. 434-403 BCE) or (r. 438-415 BCE); was the 33rd sovereign of Yan. Another source says he was only a marquis.

Duke Shen of Wey 衛慎公 Ji Tui 姬頽 (r. 414-373 BCE).

N.B. The reigning dates of the Zhou and Qin kings are accurate during the early Warring States. However, the dates of the reigns of the rulers of the other fief states varied considerably; the most notable example is King Hui of Wei (Liang) 魏 (梁) 惠王, as he changed his regnal year, which caused considerable confusion. The inaccurate reigning dates of some of these heads of states have given historians extensive trouble in affixing accurate dates of events. They varied considerably with different texts, which were results of incomplete records and errors made at the time of chronicling and subsequent errors made by historians. During the last century, much progress on accurate dating has been made by recent archaeological discoveries and textual research. For a detailed comparison of different dates from different sources, see Appendix 1, which is a compilation from different sources.

It is also noted that the reign of a new sovereign commenced during the subsequent year of the death of the former sovereign, which was assumed as the first year of the new sovereign. This form of recording gave rise to erroneous entries at times, particularly when a sovereign of a state changed his regnal year, or when there was usurpation. (See Appendix 2 – translations of Yang Kuan's articles on the Warring States textual research.)

The *ZZTJ* uses a different form of recording the year; instead, of entries of a specific year of *nian* 年 it uses 著雍攝提格 '*zhuyongshetige*', instead of *jia, yi... and zi, chou* 甲, 乙... and 子, 丑... in the *tiangan* 天干 and *dizhi* 地支 system; this form of recording further gave rise to confusion and inconsistencies. (For more details, see the introduction on the chronological calendar.) *ZZTJ JZ*, 資治通鑒今註, Vol 1, 2011, p. 14.

16 Marquis Wen of Wei 魏文侯 Wei Si 魏斯.
Marquis Lie of Zhao 趙烈侯 Zhao Ji 趙籍.
Marquis Jing of Hann 韓景侯 Hann Qian 韓虔.
The ancestor of the Wei 魏 clan was Bi Gong Gao 畢公高 (the family name was Ji 姬), a son by a concubine of King Wen of Zhou 周文王 (~1056 BCE). Bi Gong Gao assisted King Wu of Zhou 周武王 (r. 1046-1043 BCE) in toppling the Ying (Shang) 殷商 Dynasty. He was enfeoffed at Bi 畢 and named Gao 高. Bi Wan 畢萬 served under Duke Xiangong of Jin 晉献公 (r. 676-651 BCE). *ZG LS ND JB* and was enfeoffed at Wei 魏; the family clan changed the surname to Wei. *HSS ZZTJ* vol 1. Bi Wan's son Wei Chou 魏犨 served under Duke Wen of Jin 晉文公 (r. 636-628 BCE) and participated in the Battle of Chengpu 城濮之戰 (632 BCE), a conflict between Chu 楚 and Jin 晉. Wei Shu 魏舒 became one of the chief ministers at the Jin court during the reign of Duke Qing of Jin 晉頃公 (r. 525-512 BCE). *ZZTJ JZ,* 資治通鑒今註, Vol 1, 2011, pp. 14-15.
Hu Sansheng ZZTJ Vol 1, 胡三省註 資治通鑒. 國學導航. Guoxue123.com copyright 2006. http://www.guoxue123.com/shibu/0101/01zztjhz/).
The ancestor of Zhoa 趙 was the descendant of Zuofu 造父, a legendary charioteer (the family name was Ying 嬴, same as Qin 秦 and the two clans were related). Shu Dai 叔带 (?) began to serve at the Jin court. (The 5th successor) Zhao Su 趙夙 was enfeoffed by Duke Xian of Jin 晉献公 (r. 676-651) at Geng 耿. Zhao Dun 趙盾 became a minister at the Jin court (r. 622-601 BCE). Zhao Ji 趙籍 was the 6th generation successor. (N.B. The 8th succession in 6 generations). *HSS ZZTJ* Vol 1. Zhao Su's younger brother Zhao Shuai 趙衰 served under Duke Wen of Jin 晉文公 (r. 636-628 BCE), he also participated in the Battle of Chengpu 城濮之戰 (632 BCE). Zhao Shuai's son, Zhao Dun 趙盾 became a chief minister at Duke Ling of Jin's court 晉靈公 (r. 620-607 BCE). *ZZTJ JZ,* Vol 1, 資治通鑒今註, p. 15.
The ancestor of Hann 韓 was a son of King Wu of Zhou 周武王. Master Hann Wuzi 韓武子 (~700 BCE) served at Jin 晉 and was enfeoffed at Hannyuan 韓原. The 4th generation successor Hann Jue 韓厥 became the presiding minister at the Jin court. After six generations the position was passed to Hann Qian 韓虔. *SJ* 史記 卷 115, 'Hann shijia 韓世家' 第 15, pp. 1705-1709.
Hann Qian 韓虔 was Marquis Jing of Hann 韓景侯. Previously it was believed that he was a descendant of Marquis Hann 韓侯, a son of King Wu while another account relates that he was the descendent of Quwo Huanshu 曲沃 桓叔. However, in the *Book of Jin* 晉語, Master Hann Xuanzi 韓宣子 spoke to Shu Xiang 叔向, "Since the time of Huanshu (ancestor), all the progenies had to thank you, my dear Sir, for your munificence." It is thus; we could conclude that the Hann offspring came from the branch of Quwo Huanshu. Marquis Hann 韓侯 was a different branch. Hann Jue 韓厥 became a principal minister at the Jin court during the time of Duke Dao of Jin 晉悼公 (r. 573-558 BCE), *ZZTJ JZ,* Vol 1, 資治通鑒今註, p. 15.
The three family clans were principal ministers at the Jin court, whereas when they were serving at the Zhou Court, they were junior ministers – *peichen* 陪臣. When the Zhou Court began to decline, the dukes at the Jin Court started to preside over the other fief lords as the Hegemonic leader of Huameng 晉主夏盟. At which stage they were still serving under the Zhou court, paying partial reverence, the dukes of Jin came to be addressed as Bo – Grand Duke 伯. The three ministers at the Jin court were eyeing the throne of Jin, disparaging the duke of Jin with contempt and were conspiring to usurp the sovereign throne, which was a treasonous act punishable by death under the mandate of the Zhou state. King Weilie of Zhou did not discipline nor execute them; he enfeoffed them as fief lords. The Zhou King, in fact, exalted the criminal ministers. The narratives of the *ZZTJ* commenced with this incident, articulating the importance of proper authorities (ethical code), titles, and insignias. The Jin state having been partitioned into three new political entities, the remnants of the powerful former fiefdom, once a hegemon, was reduced to a paltry and minuscule state. Jin, as a state survived until 349 BCE. *SJ* 史記, 卷 109, 'Jin shijia 晉世家' 第 9, pp. 1517-1536.
Jin capital 晉都 – Xintian 新田 Quwoxian Shanxi 山西 曲沃縣.

Sima Guang annotates:[17]

Your subject has heard that the most indispensable responsibility of a Son of Heaven is none other than espousing the instituted feudal ethical code.[18] The most important purpose of the ethical code is to sanctify the defined social status,[19] while the most defining quality of social status is no more than redressing the designated titles. What is the feudal ethical code? It is the constitution of a state. What is social status? They are the positions that differentiate a sovereign and his subjects. What are titles? They are the names and labels of the dukes, marquises, ministers, and subjects as such.

Within the immeasurable realms of the Four Seas, millions of people make abode, and yet their livelihood is completely vested in one person. There are people with incomparable strength and individuals who are exceptionally talented; they nevertheless wholly submit to the desires and decrees of the sovereign. Is it not the instituted ethical code at work? The Son of Heaven thus presides over the Three-

---

17 'Sima Guang annotates – 臣光曰' - This annotation style is taken after the *Zuo zhuan* 左傳, which were either in the form of '*junzi yue* 君子曰' or 'Confucius *yue* 孔子曰'. *ZZTJ JZ*, Vol 1, 資治通鑒今註, p. 15.

18 *Li* 禮 - feudal ethical code, or simply translated as rite.

Confucius depicted *li* 禮 'rites' as a traditional form of social conduct. He said, "When one arrives at a state (which practices proper rites), one notices the etiquettes of the people; they are gentle, honest and sincere." 孔子曰, '入其國, 其教可知也, 其為人也, 温柔敦厚.' The *Odes* says, '*Li* – is the essence of education."' 詩, '教也.' (The *Liji Jingjie* 禮記 經解)." He also said, "It is unsettling when the ethical code is lost. When the ethical code was lost at the time of Spring and Autumn - *Chunqiu*, there was chaos." '禮之失, 煩. 春秋之失, 亂.'"

Li means rites but it can also be used to refer to ceremonies or rules of conduct; in our translation, we define it as, 'the feudal ethical code.' The term has also come to be associated with proper decorum. Confucius felt that *li* should be employed to emphasize the spirit of piety and respect for others through rigidly established guidelines of conducts and ceremonies. As outlined in the *Book of Rites*, the *Liji* 禮記, *li* was meant to restore the significance of traditional forms by looking at the simplicity of the past. Confucius asserted that a standardized conduct that focused on traditional forms would be a way to alleviate the chaos of the Spring and Autumn - *Chunqiu* 春秋 period. According to him, the absolute power of *li* was thus demonstrated in the *Book of Rites*: "Of all things to which the people owe their lives the rites are the most important..." (Translated by Dawson, R. *Confucius*, The Guernsey Press, GB, 1981, p. 32). 子曰, '安上治民, 莫善於禮.' (The *Liji* 禮記 Jingjie 經解).

The idea of *li* was thus closely associated with human nature, when ethics and social order integrated *li* into the lives of the people, it was beneficial to society, as it obliged people to recognize and fulfil their responsibilities toward others. Confucius said, "Hence the proper etiquettes of making homage at court are the most defining practice between a sage sovereign and his subjects. As to the etiquettes of making tributes to the sovereign by the fief lords, it is a measure to make them pay respect to each other." 子曰, "故朝覲之禮, 所以明君之義也. 聘問之禮, 所以使諸侯相尊敬也." (The *Liji* 禮記 Jingjie 經解). As far as Confucius was concerned, the etiquettes of *li* were extended beyond a sovereign lord and his subject, to parents, kin, friends and even strangers; in other words, it was a form of social order.

19 Fen 分 – means social status or position.

Excellences *sangong*,[20] who in turn lead the feudal lords, while the feudal lords oversee the ministers, and the ministers preside over the subjects and the commoners. The nobles command the humble and deprived commoners; who in turn accept the directives imposed by the elite. The relationship between the sovereign and his subjects could be likened to one's heart and torso controlling the movements of one's limbs or liken to roots and trunk of a tree regulating the functions of leaves and branches. The subjects serve the elite as if they were limbs making protection of one's heart and torso, or like branches and leaves providing protections to the trunk and roots of a tree. A sovereign state achieves well-being and security through this reciprocal arrangement and corroboration. It is hence said that the obligatory onus of a Son of Heaven is no more important than defending the instituted ethical code.

When King Wen of Zhou made annotations to the *Book of Changes Yijing* he affixed *qian* and *kun* as the two most notable entities of the text.[21] Kongzi (Confucius) interpreted it as such,[22] "The relationship between the Divines in Heaven and the lowly corporal beings is preordained by the cosmic principle of *qian* and *kun*.[23] The elites ostensibly preside up high, while the humble position below; they are wholly integrated into their respective social niches." He emphasized that the hierarchical position of a sovereign and his subjects was unalterable like the bond between Heaven and Earth. The *Annals* wittingly suppressed the status of the fief lords while making reverence to the aristocrats, [24] even the insignificant attendants of the king were positioned above the fief lords. It is evident that the sage was meticulously attentive to the hierarchical status of the sovereign and his subjects.

---

20 Three-Excellences – *sangong* 三公.

21 King Wen of Zhou 周文王 Ji Chang 姬昌 was a pre-dynastic king of Zhou (r. ~1152~1056 BCE approx.). *SJ* 史記, 卷 22 'Zhou benji 周本紀' 第 4, p. 121.

Liu Shu 劉恕 said in his the *Zizhi tongjian waiji* 資治通鑒 外紀, "Zhou (King of Shang) imprisoned Chang (Ji Chang 姬昌 at Youli 羑里 牖里; Chang made annotations to the *Book of Changes* 易經."

"紂囚昌于羑里, 昌為易卦辭." Liu Shu 劉恕 *Zizhi tongjian waiji* 資治通鑒 外紀.

The *Book of Changes – Yijing* 易經.

Qian (*yang*), 乾 (陽) positive; *kun* (*yin*), 坤 (陰) negative – are the two fundamental and complementary cosmic forces that interact to form a dynamic entity, in which the whole is greater than the sum of the parts.

22 "天尊地卑, 乾坤定矣, 卑高以陳, 貴賤位矣." This quote is from the *Book of Changes Yi Xici* 易繫辭 上傳.

23 It is often unclear if there was only one divine 神 in Heaven or many. However, to the Chinese, the notion of *shen* 神 is ill-defined and nebulous; hence, the author chooses to use the plural for the many divines in Heaven.

24 Annals - *Spring and Autumn annals* 春秋.

Had it not for the despotic King Jie of Xia and the nefarious King Zhou of Shang being challenged by the sagacious kings of Tang and Wu;[25] with the people rallying and pledging to their cause, further fostered by the mandate from Heaven, the hierarchical positions between a sovereign, his subjects, and commoners were unalterable. A code of standard to be stalwartly upheld by death. Had Master Weizi, the elder brother of King Zhou of Shang, been made the king instead of Zhou, Cheng Tang the founding father of Shang would still be basking in the glory of the mandate from Heaven. Had Ji Zha been made the king of Wu, the blood-sacrificial rituals made to the Grand Duke, the founding father of Wu, would have endured.[26] However, the two men facing the certain expiration of their kingdoms chose not to take on the

---

25 King Jie of Xia, Xia Jie, Si Lugui 夏桀 姒履癸 was the last king of Xia 夏 (d. ~1600 BCE). He was notorious for his cruelty and tyrannical brutality. *SJ* 史記, 卷 20, 'Xia benji 夏本紀 第 2', p. 99. *SJ*. King Zhou of Shang 商紂 Zi Shouxin 子受辛 (r. ~1075~1046 BCE), was the last king of Shang, also known for his cruelty and despotic brutality. *SJ*.

King Tang of Shang 商湯 Zi Tianyi 子天乙 (r. ~1600 BCE) was the founding king of Shang. *SJ* 史記, 卷 21 'Yin benji 殷本紀' 第 3, p. 108.

King Wu of Zhou 周武王 Ji Fa 姬發 (r. 1046-1043 BCE) was the founding king of Zhou. *SJ* 史記, 卷 22 'Zhou benji 周本紀' 第 4, p. 122.

26 Ziqi 子啓 Weizi Qi 微子啓 was the elder brother of King Zhou of Shang 商(殷) 紂王. "Weizi was the eldest son of King Yi of Shang 殷帝乙, he was born of a concubine, and was the elder brother of King Zhou." *SJ* 史記, 卷 105, 'Song Weizi shijia 宋微子世家' 第 8, p. 1500.

According to the *SJ* 史記, 'Yin benji 殷本紀', "The eldest son of Di Yi was Weizi Qi. The mother of Weizi was of humble origin; hence, he did not attain the primogeniture right. The youngest son was Xin 辛 (Zhou 紂); Xin's mother was the queen, he attained the primogeniture right." *SJ* 史記, 卷 21 'Yin benji 殷本紀' 第 3, p. 111.

ZZTJ JZ, Vol 1, p. 15.

According to the *Shiji suoyin* 史記索隱 quoting from the *Lushi chunqiu* 呂氏春秋, Qi 啓 was the elder brother of King Zhou of Shang 商紂王 (r. 1075-1046 BCE), the last king of Shang. Qi's mother was not designated the *bona fide* queen of Shang (wife of King of Shang, Di Yi 商帝乙 r. 1101-1076 BCE) when Qi was born. Later when King Zhou was born, the mother was made queen; hence, Zhou inherited the inheritance right. The account in the *Taiping yulan* 太平御覽 83 quoting from the *Diwang shiji* 帝王世紀 is similar to the *Lushi chunqiu* 呂氏春秋. It is asserted here that had his elder brother Weizi been made king the Shang dynasty might not have fallen.

Wu Jizha 吳季札 Ji Zha 姬札 (576-484 BCE?) alias Prince Zha (Gongzi Zha) 公子札 was the fourth son of King Shoumeng of Wu 吳王 壽夢; he was enfeoffed at Yanling 延陵 at present day Zhoulai 州來. He was elected to succeed to his father; however he chose to become a recluse, giving up his dukedom and became a farmer at Yaoguo Mountain 舜過山. He was a man of high moral character and education, an outstanding politician and a statesman, sharing a comparable fame with Confucius his contemporary. It is asserted in the text here that had he assumed his father's throne; the Wu Kingdom might not meet its demise. Wu Tai Bo 吳太伯 was the founder of the Wu family clan. King of Wu Zhufan 吳王 諸樊 (~560 BCE) had intended to abdicate the throne to Jizha 季札, the younger brother, Jizha declined. Prince Guang 公子光 (later, King Helu 闔盧) contested the throne with King Liao 王僚 and had the latter assassinated. After the death of King Helu, the throne was passed to the son of Guang, who was known as King Wu Fuchai 吳王 夫差, the kingdom met its demise under King Fuchai in 473 BCE. *ZZTJ JZ*, Vol 1, p. 16.

SJ 史記, 卷 101, 'Wu Taibo shijia 吳太伯世家' 第 1, pp. 1395-1399.

positions, as they bore staunch conviction that they could not disparage the ethical feudal code.[27] Hence, it is said, the essential purpose of the ethical code is to differentiate and to uphold the social status.

The ethical code is to delineate the elite from the commoners; it demarcates the royal lineage from the remotely related kin and is used to make distinctions between innumerable things and issues, allowing people to deal with their daily routines. Without designated titles to address one another, it would be difficult to bring approbation; without proper insignias, it would be impossible to manifest a distinct structure. A state is regulated with appropriate titles and designations while proper insignias and icons are employed to differentiate the status of the people; under these circumstances, the interpersonal relationship could then be regulated in an orderly fashion. It is the quintessence of the ethical code. Whereas, when all pertinent designations and insignias are annulled, devoid of both entities, the ethical code cannot endure on its own.

In ancient time, when Zhongshu Yuxi was meritorious to Wey,[28] he turned down the fief land that was bestowed upon him and pleaded to be granted with a red tassel to adorn his horse.[29] Kongzi opined that he could have been awarded with even more appanage; nevertheless, his request could not be sanctioned.[30] Titles and insignias could not be bestowed summarily: it was the indispensable privilege of a sovereign. Failing to uphold this fundamental creed the political structure of a state would fail and the kingdom face moribund. The sovereign of Wey had intended to appoint Kongzi as a minister of the state; however, the sage was preoccupied with assessing appropriate status prior to his appointment, asserting that if the official titles of a state were not regulated with precision the commoners would be in bewilderment.[31]

---

27 As Son of Heaven or Head of State.

28 Zhongshu Yuxi 仲叔 于奚. According to the *Zuozhuan* 左傳, during the 2nd year of Duke Cheng of Wey 衛 成公二年 (approx. 633 BCE), Qi 齊 invaded Wey 衛; the two armies joined battle at Xinzhu 新築 - Damingxian Henan 河南 大名縣; Wey was soundingly defeated. A Wey civilian Zhongshu Yuxi rallied the local militia to go against Qi and managed to repel the invading army, and successfully rescued Sun Liangfu 孫良夫 (Sun Huanzi 孫桓子) the minister in power; Zhongshu Yuxi 于奚 was later made the chancellor of Wey.
ZZTJ BY Edition, Vol 1, p. 7.
ZZTJ JZ, Vol 1, p. 16.

29 A red tassel was an insignia for adorning the neck of a horse; it was a privilege reserved exclusively for royalties.

30 仲尼聞之曰, "惜也! 不如多與之邑. 唯名與器, 不可以假人, 君之所司也. 名以出信, 信以守器, 器以藏禮, 禮以行義, 義以生利, 利以平民, 政之大節也. 若以假人, 與人政也. 政亡, 則國家從之, 不可止也已." Quote from - The *Zuozhuan* 'King Cheng 2nd year 左傳 成公二年'.

31 Confucius on 'Official title of a state 孔子欲先正名.' The *Lunyu* 論語, Zilu pian 子路篇, 子路曰, "衛君待子而為政, 子將奚先?" 子曰, "必也正名乎!" 子路曰, "有是哉子之迂也! 奚其正?"

A red tassel was a trivial ornament. Nevertheless, Kongzi staunchly treasured and cherished it. The naming of titles of officers was also a minor issue, however he placed it above all other matters. He emphasized that the forfeiture of the symbols and titles was tantamount to allowing the ethical code to degenerate; consequently, the status of the sovereign and his subjects could not be upheld properly.

Matters of importance invariably stem from the insignificant and inconsequential, and they become increasingly significant with the passage of time. Kongzi planned with foresight; he attended to the trivial things, he was thus able to alleviate the teething problems. The mundane people are concerned with pressing issues and have to wait for things to go disconcertingly astray before they realize that amends are warranted. Attending to minor issues takes little effort at the outset, while the yields are immeasurable great, whereas, with those trying to salvage a situation that has gone astray, they could try with their utmost but to no avail. The *Book of Changes* thus relates,[32] "When one treads on frost, he knows slippery ice is about to form." The *Book of Documents* also relates, "One has to stay focused on the ten thousand minor changes that transpire every day." Both passages are addressing the same concern. Hence, the most important attribute of social status is the appropriate designation of titles.

Alas! When King Li and King You of Zhou lost their virtuous path;[33] the Zhou Dynasty was declining by the day, the instituted rite of the kingdom was in complete ruin. Subordinates displaced the elites; the fief lords attacked and assailed against each other; the ministers arrogating themselves to power at court, the ethical code had completely lost its significance.[34] In spite of these uncertainties and vagaries, the holy shrines of King Wen, and King Wu endured, and the progenies of Zhou preserved the legitimate title. Why was it so?

子曰, "野哉由也! 君子於其所不知蓋闕如也! 名不正則言不順, 言不順則事不成, 事不成則禮樂不興, 禮樂不興則刑罰不中, 刑罰不中則民無所錯手足. 故君子名之必可信也, 言之必可信也. 君子於其言, 無所苟而已矣." *ZZTJ JZ,* Vol 1, p. 16.

32 The *Book of Changes, Yijing* 易經, '坤卦初六爻文', "履霜堅冰至." *ZZTJ JZ,* Vol 1, (2011), p. 16.
The *Book of Records, Shangshu* 尚書, 'Gaotaomo 皋陶謨', "一日二日萬幾." *ZZTJ JZ,* Vol 1, (2011), p. 16.

33 King You and King Li lost their virtuous path - 幽厲失德.
King Li of Zhou, 10th king of Zhou 周厲王 姬胡 (r. 877?-841 BCE) was banished to Zhi 彘 and died in 828 BCE. *ZZTJ JZ,* Vol 1, p. 16,
ZG LS ND JB.
King You of Zhou 周幽王 Ji Gongnie 姬宮涅 (r. 781-771 BCE) was the 12th king of Zhou and was the last king of Western Zhou (Xizhou) 西周. He was licentious and excessively depraved. He was killed by the nomadic Quan-Rong 犬戎 invaders at Lishan Mountain 驪山. It was the end of Western Zhou. King Ping of Zhou 周平王 (r. 770-720 BCE) moved the capital to the East, Eastern Zhou commenced. *ZZTJ JZ,* Vol 1, p. 16.
ZG LS ND JB.

34 The original text is, ".... lost almost seven or eight out of ten of its significance."

When Duke Wen of Jin was meritorious to the Royal House of Zhou,[35] he implored King Xiang that the tunnel-burial rite could be conferred upon him.[36] The king declined his request saying, "It is the constitution of the kingdom. There has yet to be a change of dynasty; how could there be two kings on the throne?[37] My uncle,[38] if you were to consider it seriously: you would also object to it. Whereas you own a vast expanse of appanage, you can decide how to bury your remains by whatever means you choose; why are you seeking permission from me?" The duke, not daring to violate the instituted code, retracted his request.[39]

After the decline, the domain of Zhou was not larger than the Cao or Teng fiefdoms, no more populous than the Zhu or Ju polities,[40] yet amazingly, the Zhou

---

35 Duke Wen of Jin, Ji Zhonger 晉文公 姬重耳 (r. 636-628 BCE) was the 24th Duke of Jin.
King Xiang of Zhou, Ji Zheng 周襄王 姬鄭 (r. 651-619 BCE) was the 18th king of Eastern Zhou.

36 During the Zhou era, only the Son of Heaven was sanctioned with the tunnel-burial rite - *suizang* 隧葬, whereby an inclined passageway was excavated from the ground level for delivery of the casket and sarcophagus into the burial chamber; whereas the dukes and lords of the kingdom were buried by having their coffins lowered into the burial pits. *ZZTJ JZ,* Vol 1, p. 16.
In 636 BCE, Prince Ji Dai 太子姬带 the younger brother of the king, (King Xiang of Zhou 周襄王 Ji Zheng 姬鄭) had an adulterous affair with Queen Zhaishu Wei 翟叔隗, the throne was usurped; Ji Zheng was forced to go into exile at Fanyi 氾邑 - Xiangchengxian Henan 河南 襄城縣. Ji Zhonger 姬重耳, later Duke Wen of Jin 晉文公 (r. 636-628 BCE) raised an army to go to the aid of the king restoring Ji Zheng to the throne. (from the *Zuozhuan* 左傳 Duke of Xi 25th year 僖公二十五年). *ZZTJ YB Edition,* Vol1, p. 9.
ZZTJ JZ, Vol 1, p. 16.

37 The meaning of the statement is - if the king of Zhou sanctioned the burial, the duke would be recognized by the status of a king.

38 'My uncle' - *shufu* 叔父, all the family elders with the same family name were referred to as *bo* 伯 or *shu* 叔 by the Zhou royal members; in this case, the king was not addressing an uncle directly related through his father.

39 In essence, the duke still embraced some respect for the ethical code.

40 Cao Fiefdom 曹國 - Hezexian Shandong 山東 荷澤縣 was an insignificant fief state. The second son of King Wen of Zhou 周文王, Cao Shu Zhenduo 曹叔 振鐸 was enfeoffed at Taoqiu 陶丘 (Dingtao 定陶) and the fief came to be known as Cao in around 1045 BCE (?). The fiefdom lasted for 26 generations; it was finally annihilated by Duke Jing of Song 宋景公 in 487 BCE. *ZZTJ JZ,* Vol 1, p. 17.
Teng Fiefdom 滕 - Tengxian Shandong 山東 滕縣. Teng was another petty fief state at the time of Xizhou 西周, Chunqiu 春秋 and Zhanguo 戰國. *ZZTJ JZ,* Vol 1, p. 17.
The family name of Teng Fiefdom was Ji 姬. When King Wu 周武王 defeated Shang 商 in 1045 BCE, he enfeoffed his younger brother Cuoshu Xiu 錯叔綉 by a different mother at Teng. The state lasted until 326 BCE or slightly later (?); the last fief lord was Duke Wen of Teng 滕文公 (r. 326-? BCE); other texts claimed that he was Duke Yuan of Teng 滕元公 while others maintain that they were the same person; Duke Wen was his posthumous title. He lived around the time of Mengzi 孟子 (372-289 BCE), as there is a passage in Mengzi, Duke of Wen 孟子 - 滕文公. According to Zhang Zhipeng 張志鹏 the polity met its demise in 296 BCE. See 滕國新考 - Zhang Z. P. 張志鹏 滕國新考 http://www.gwz.fudan.edu.cn/SrcShow.asp?Src_ID=1428.
(N.B. Lord Menchang 孟嘗君 was later enfeoffed at Teng. see 279-VIII).

kings retained the title as the Master of All under Heaven for several hundred more years.

At that point, the fiefdoms of Jin, Qin, Qi and Chu were formidable states; they did not dismiss the king of Zhou summarily. Why was it so? Merely because the ethical code of social status was still being preserved and upheld to a certain extent.

The ministers of the Ji clan at Lu, Tian Chang of Qi, Bai Gong of Chu and Zhibo of Ji, were commanding enough to banish their fief lords and proclaimed themselves as heads of states.[41] Nevertheless, they did not resort to that. Did they lack the prowess

---

Zhu 邾 (Zou 鄒) Fiefdom - Zouxian Shandong 鄒 - 山東 鄒縣. The details of this fiefdom are obscure. All we know is that King Wu of Zhou 周武王 enfeoffed Cao Jia 曹挾 at Zhu 邾; at the time of Duke Mu of Lu 魯穆公 (r. 407-375 BCE), it changed its name to Zou 鄒 and became a protectorate of Lu 魯. The fiefdom lasted for 29 generations until it was finally annihilated by King Xuan of Chu 楚宣王 (r. 369-340 BCE). *ZZTJ JZ,* Vol 1, p. 17.

Ju 莒 Fiefdom - Juxian Shandong - 山東 莒縣. *ZZTJ JZ,* Vol 1, p. 17. The information on this fiefdom is very sketchy; its founder leader was enfeoffed at the time of King Wu of Zhou 周武王 and lasted for 30 generations, as to exactly when it was annihilated, history is silent.

41 Ji clan at Lu – 季氏之於魯 – Prince Huan of Lu, Ji You 魯桓公子 季友 (?-644 BCE) was meritorious to the court of Duke Shan of Lu 魯僖公, (the *SJ* 史記 refers to him as Duke Xi of Lu 魯釐公 r. 659-627 BCE). The descendants of Ji You, Jisun shi 季孫氏 presided at the Lu court as ministers for generations. Master Ji Ping 季平子 banished Duke Zhao of Lu 魯昭公 (r. 541-510 BCE), later Master Ji Kangzi 季康子 banished Duke Shuai of Lu 魯衰公 (r. 494-467 or 468 BCE?). Nevertheless, they did not usurp the throne of Lu. The *Zuo zhuan* 左傳 and the *SJ* 史記, 卷 103, 'Duke of Lu shijia 魯周公世家' 第 3, pp. 1439-1444.

ZZTJ JZ, Vol 1, p. 17.

Tian Chang at Qi 田常之於齊 = Tian Huan 田桓 (r. 459-450 BCE). Prince Wan of Chen 陳公子完 (706-BCE?) escaped to Qi, Duke Huan of Qi 齊桓公 (r. ?-643 BCE) made him the minister in charge of production. The ministerial position was passed on for seven generations until the time of Tian Chang 田常, who committed regicide, he assassinated Duke Jian of Qi 齊簡公 (r. 484-481 BCE). Later at the time of Tian He 田和 (r. 386-385 BCE?), the Tian family clan assumed control of the Qi court, displacing the Jiang 姜 family clan. The incident happened during the 23rd year of 周安王. Details see *Zuo zhuan* 左傳 and the *SJ* 史記, 卷 116, 'Tian Jing Zhongwan 田敬仲完世家' 第 16, pp. 1716-1717. The *SJ* 史記 referred to him as Tian Chang 田常, whereas the *Zuozhuan* 左傳 and the *Lunyu* 論語 referred to him as Chen Heng 陳恆. *ZZTJ* took after the *SJ* 史記. The two words, Tian 田 and Chen 陳 were synonymous during the time of Zhanguo 戰國. *ZZTJ JZ,* Vol 1, p. 17.

Bai Gong at Chu 白公之於楚. Bai Gong Sheng 白公勝 (526?-479 BCE) was the son of the heir apparent Jian of Chu 太子建, who in turn was the son of King Ping of Chu 楚平王 (r. 528-516 BCE). Bai Gong Sheng revolted against the state and killed General Zixi 令尹 子西 (Gongzi Shen 公子申) and Minister of War, Ziqi 司馬子期. One of his subordinates, Shi Qi 石乞 said to Bai, "You have burned the Treasury, and committed regicide. It is not a good idea, and it is not proper." Bai Gong answered, "To commit regicide is inauspicious, and having burned the Treasury to empty the reserves; what is left for me to guard against?" He committed suicide. The above is from the *Zuo zhuan* 左傳. The incident also appears in the *SJ* 史記, 卷 100, 'Chu shijia 楚世家' 第 10, p. 1573.

Master Zhibo at Jin 知 (智) 伯之於晉. (*SJ* 史記, 卷 109, 'Jin shijia 晉世家' 第 9). "Zhibo, Zhao 趙, Hann 韓 and Wei 魏 divided the lands of Fan 范 and Zhongheng 中行 and made the lands their

or was it for compassionate reasons? It was for fear of infringing upon the established ethical code, which might incite all the other fief lords Under Heaven to make expeditions against them for their treasonous act.

However, the Jin ministers were treating their sovereign with total disdain, and they partitioned the Jin state. The Son of Heaven did not even attempt to raise an army against the conspirators; instead, he enfeoffed them, raising them as equals to the other legitimate fief lords. The titular title held by the Son of Heaven was not even defended; worse, it was dismissed outright. The ethical code instituted by the founders of Zhou was lost forever.

It was suggested that perhaps the House of Zhou, having fallen into such an emaciated state, was left without other options except to comply with the demands of the three powerful Jin ministers or perhaps they were simply far too imperious with their demands. It is a great misconception. The truth is while the three ministers might be formidable; had they not harbour any concern for being impeached by other fief lords for infringing on the established ethical code they would not seek sanction from the Son of Heaven. Had they not sought the blessing from the Son of Heaven, their act would be construed as subversive and seditious. Had there been some righteous and sagacious lords like the dukes of Huan and Wen under Heaven they would most certainly rally to support the Zhou Court,[42] brandishing the ethical and righteous banners, to go against the conspirators. Now the ministers beseeched the Son of Heaven, and he lawfully sanctioned them, making them *bona fide* fief

---

counties. Duke Chu of Jin 晉出公 (r. 474-457 BCE) was incensed; he informed Qi 齊 and Lu 魯 that he intended to make an expedition against the four ministers. The four ministers were disquiet and revolted. The duke made a run for his life to Qi and died on the passage. Zhibo placed Jiao 驕 the great-grandson of Duke Zhao of Jin 晉昭公 (r. 531-526 BCE) on the throne. He was known posthumously as Duke Ai 晉哀公 (r. 456-438 BCE)." *ZZTJ JZ*, Vol 1, p. 17.

42 Duke Huan of Qi 齊桓公 Jiang Xiaobai 姜小白 (r. 685-643 BCE) was the 15th sovereign of Qi. At that stage the Zhou Kingdom 周 fell into disarray, the duke of Qi rallied the fief lords to its aid. Later the duke helped Yan 燕 to repel the barbaric tribes of Bei-Rong 北戎 in the north. He then went on to give assistance to the state of Geng 邢國 and helped Wey 衛國 to ward off the attacks by the barbaric Di tribe 狄. Later, he allied with the fiefdoms in Zhongyuan 中原 to go against Chu 楚, and finally helped settled the internal disputes at Zhou. He became one of the five most powerful hegemons at the time of Chunqiu 春秋. *SJ* 史記, 卷 102, 'Qi Taigong shijia 齊太公世家' 第 2, pp. 1411-1413.

Duke Wen of Jin 晉文公 Ji Zhonger 姬重耳 (r. 636-628 BCE) was in exile for 19 years before returning to Jin to assume the position as the head of state in 636 BCE. In 635 BCE, Prince Dai 王子带, the younger brother of King Xiang of Zhou 周襄王 revolted, the Zhou king escaped to Zheng 鄭 and appealed to Duke Wen of Jin for help. The duke led an army to go against the Prince, defeating him; and he escorted King Xiang of Zhou to return to the Zhou capital. The king enfeoffed the areas in *Henei* 河内 and Yangfan 陽樊 to Jin. The duke then became one of the five hegemons during the early years of Chunqiu 春秋. *SJ* 史記, 卷 109, 'Jin shijia 晉世家' 第 9, pp. 1524 -1529.

lords. Who could challenge them? So it is said that the Jin ministers were not the malefactors who demolished the ethical code, rather it was the Son of Heaven who bankrupted the system himself.

Alas! The ethical code between the sovereign and his subjects had completely disintegrated at this stage; all the fiefdoms under Heaven were employing their wit to vie for supremacy. Eventually, all the sacrificial altars inaugurated by the founding fief lords installed by Zhou met their respective demise. In the meantime, the commoners agonized over their appalling fates – when innumerable number succumbed to wholesale massacre. Pitiful it was indeed!

II. Prior to this, Master Xuanzi of Zhi decided to name Yao as his lawful successor.[43] Zhi Guo said,[44] "Why don't you consider Xiao?[45] Zhi Yao has five exceptional attributes except he also has one quality that is not comparable with others. He is good looking with an outstanding beard and physique. He is skilled at horse riding and arrow shooting, and he is stupendously proficient with the various combat techniques. He speaks with eloquence and writes superbly, besides he is resolute and decisive. He nevertheless suffers from one flaw; he lacks compassion. Who could endure a man with five exceptional attributes, lacking in compassion? If you make, Zhi Yao your successor the Zhi clan will face obliteration." Zhi Shen refused to listen. Zhi Guo took leave of the clan and pleaded with a grand historian to change his family name to Fu.[46]

The eldest son of Master Jianzi of Zhao was Bo Lu, and the younger was Wuxu.[47] Jian was considering appointing his successor and was hesitant. He wrote down some instructions on two

---

43 Before partitioning of Jin, there were four family clans presiding over the administrative functions of the state; besides Zhao 趙, Wei 魏 and Hann 韓 there was the Zhi 智 family clan.
In fact since the 6th century BCE the Jin state was presided by six family clans, which had control of the Jin court, known collectively as the, 'Six Ministers of Jin.' 晉國六卿. Zhao 趙氏, Hann 韓氏, Wei 魏氏, Zhi 智氏, Fan 范氏 and Zhonghang 中行氏. The *Zuozhuan* 左傳 and *SJ* 史記, 卷 109, Jin shijia 晉世家 第 9, p. 1534.
Master Xuanzi, Zhi Shen 智宣子 智申 was the clan elder of the Zhi family.
The word *zi* 子 usually means master when appended to someone's title, but it also means viscount or a minor fief-lord of a fief state. To add certain confusion to the use of the word; it was also a family name and at times, it was a given name.
Master Xiangzi 智襄子 Zhi Yao 智瑶, alias Zhibo 智伯.

44 Zhi Guo 智果 was a Zhi clan member; he changed his name to Fu 輔.

45 Zhi Xiao 智宵 was another son of Zhi Xuanzi by a concubine.

46 Grand Historian – *taishi* 太史. The grand historians at the time of Zhanguo were in charge of issuance of family and clan names. *ZZTJ JZ*, Vol 1, p. 18.
Fu 輔. Changing the family name by Zhi Guo was an act to distance his family members from the Zhi clan; if something untoward happened to the Zhi clan, his family members would not be implicated.

47 Master Jianzi of Zhao - Zhao Yang 趙簡子 趙鞅. Zhao Yang was the head of the Zhao clan.
The word *bo* 伯 was usually a designation given to the eldest son of a family, the second son was known as - *zhong* 仲 and third and fourth, etc sons were called *shu* 叔 and the youngest was called *ji* 季.

sets of bamboo slips and gave them to his sons, instructing them, "You are to learn my directives by heart." Three years later, he asked them what they had learned. Bo Lu could not relate the contents; he had even lost the slips. Jian asked Wuxu; who recited the contents fluently; and when asked for the slips Wuxu took them out from his sleeves, and presented them. Zhao Yang decided by then that Wuxu was the worthy successor he was looking for and designated him as his lawful heir.[48]

Master Jian instructed Yin Duo to preside at Jinyang.[49] Yin Duo asked, "Sir, do you want me to exact taxes from the land or to secure a refuge for an unexpected event?" Jian answered, "As a possible refuge." Yin Duo then reduced taxes for the locals. Master Jianzi instructed Zhao Wuxu, "If something untoward should happen at Jin take flight to Jinyang to find refuge.[50] Do not bear any misgiving that Yin Duo is young nor should you consider the city is far too remote. You could find refuge there."[51]

Upon the passing of Master Xiangzi of Zhi, (Zhibo) assumed the administrative duties. The Master was hosting a banquet at Nantai Terrace to entertain Master Kangzi of Hann and Master Huanzi of Wei.[52] Zhibo derided Master Kangzi and made affront of Duan Gui.[53] Zhi Guo heard of what had happened; he reproached the Master, "Your Highness, you have not made preparations

---

The words *bo* and *shu* are still in use today; bo is used to address someone more senior than oneself or the eldest brother of one's father and shu as someone younger than one's father or simply someone more senior in age than oneself; it is thus a polite way to address seniors.

Zhao Bo Lu 趙伯魯.

Master Xiangzi, Zhao Wuxu 趙襄子 趙無恤 (r. 457-425 BCE). Zhao Wuxu was the son of a concubine, who was a Di tribeswoman 翟人; hence, his position in the family clan was lowly. *SJ* 史記, 卷 113, 'Zhao shijia 趙世家' 第 13, p. 1643.

48 This account is at slight variance with *SJ* 史記, 卷 113, Zhao shijia 趙世家' 第 13, p. 1643. The latter relates, "Master Jianzi 趙簡子 spoke to his sons and considered Zhao Wuxu the most capable. The Master then told his sons, "I have hidden a prized tally at Changshan Mountain 常山. The one of you who comes back with the tally will be rewarded." The sons rode to the mountain; they returned empty-handed. When Wuxu returned, he said to his father, "I found the tally." Master Jianzi said, "Relate to me." Wuxu answered, "Changshan Mountain is near the polity of Dai, and it can be taken easily." Master Jianzi knew that Wuxu was the worthy successor he was looking for, he abrogated the succession right of Bo Lu and nominated Wuxu as his lawful successor." The *ZZTJ*'s account is based on *Hannshi waizhuan* 韓詩外傳. *ZZTJ JZ*, Vol 1, p. 18.

49 Yin Duo 尹鐸 was a descendant of Shaohao 少昊 (one of the legendary Three Emperors and Five Kings *Sanhuang Wudi* 三皇五帝); Yin Duo was a retainer of Master Jianzi of Zhao 趙簡子 (?-458 BCE), one of the presiding ministers at Jin 晉.

Yin Duo 尹鐸, *Guoyu* 國語 卷 15, Jinyu 晉語 9, p. 631.

Jinyang 晉陽 - Taiyuanxian Shanxi 山西 太原縣. Jinyang was the nascent estate of the Zhao clan.

According to Hu Sansheng 胡三省 Jinyang should be in the present day Taiyuanxian County 太原縣. *ZZTJ JZ*, Vol 1, p. 18.

50 Jin 晉 - the capital was at Quwoxian Shanxi 山西 曲沃縣.

51 Jinyang 晉陽 was 200 km from Quwo 曲沃.

52 Nantai Terrace 藍臺.

Master Kangzi of Hann 韓康子 Hann Hu 韓虎 (r. ?-424 BCE).

Master Hengzi of Wei 魏恒子 Wei Ju 魏駒 (?).

53 Duan Gui 段規 was a chancellor - *xiang* 相 of Hann.

for possible retributions; calamity will follow."[54] Zhibo answered, "I create all the calamities. If I do not bring catastrophes onto others who dares to raise them?" Zhi Guo answered, "It is not so. The *Book of Xia* says, 'A person makes many mistakes; the resentments held against him might not be discernable; however, one should be vigilant that people might loathe him furtively.'[55] A gentleman should be vigilant with trifling things; it is an assured way to avert lurking dangers. Your Highness, you have slighted the clan leader of the Hann family and insulted their chancellor at the banquet, and yet you are ill prepared for their reprisal, merely believing, 'They do not have the audacity to create trouble.' It is a very poor assumption. You see, a mosquito, an ant, a bee, or even a scorpion can bring harm to people, let alone the leader and the chancellor of a state." Zhibo refused to listen.

Zhibo demanded land from Master Kangzi. Kangzi was considering not complying; Duan Gui said to him, "Zhibo is avaricious with minor gains and is obstinate in nature. If we refuse his demand, he will make an expedition against us. We should yield as he demands. Upon arrogating the land, he will exact land from other fief lords as well; if they refuse to comply, war will be inevitable. We will spare ourselves from unnecessary dangers; in the meantime, we will wait for things to unfold." Master Kangzi said, "Good!" He asked his envoy to cede a ten-thousand-households county to Zhibo, who was in glee. He proceeded to demand land from Master Huanzi of Wei. Huanzi was about to refuse, Ren Zhang the chancellor, asked,[56] "Why are you refusing to comply?" Huanzi answered, "His demand is unfounded, and hence I am refusing to comply." Ren Zhang answered, "His demand is indeed unwarranted. The other fief lords will be alarmed by his unreasonable demands. If we yield, Zhibo will become conceited and believed that he is invincible. It will coerce the few alarmed families to ally against a common foe that slights his enemies. The Master Zhi will have little time left.[57] The *Book of Zhou* says,[58] 'Give aid to your enemy if you intend to crush him; if you intend to devour him, give him whatever he wants.' My Lord, you should comply as he demands; it will make him even more arrogant. After that, we will contrive a scheme with others sharing our common interest to bring down the Zhishi clan. Why do we have to bear the burden of rejecting his demand?" Huanzi answered, "Good." He ceded a ten-thousand-households county to Zhibo.

---

54 Zhi Guo 智國 the text does not give an account of this person; he was a minister at the Zhi court.
The expression of 'Your Highness' used was *zhu* 主, which means master; in order not to be confused with the 'Master' I have chosen to translate it as – Your Highness.

55 The *Book of Xia, Xiashu,* 夏書, "一人三失, 怨豈在明, 不見是圖." The quote is from *Xiashu,* 'Song of the Five Princes', however, this part of the *Shangshu* 尚書 was from 'Fabricated Shangshu, *Wei guowen shangsh'* 偽古文尚書. *ZZTJ JZ,* Vol 1, p. 18.
Tai Kang 太康 (~2000 BCE, 2nd king of Xia 夏) was the son of Xia Qi 夏啓, he lost his kingdom to one of his subjects Yi 羿. The five sons (princes) of Qi were banished to Chaoge 朝歌, legend has it that they composed, the 'Ballads of the Five Princes', '*Wuzi zhige* 五子之歌', lamenting over the loss of their kingdom.

56 Chancellor, *xiang* 相, Ren Zhang 任章.

57 The text uses Zhishi 智氏 = Zhibo 智伯= Master Xiang 智襄子.

58 The *Zhoushu,* the *Book of Zhou,* 周書, "將欲敗之, 必姑輔之, 將欲取之, 必姑與之." In fact, this passage is from the *Lost Book of Zhou, Yizhoushu* 逸周書 and not from the *Zhoushu* 周書 in the *Shangshu* 尚書. *ZZTJ JZ,* Vol 1, p. 19.

Zhibo then demanded Gaolang of Cai from Master Xiangzi of Zhao. Xiangzi refused to comply.[59] Zhibo was in a rage; he raised an allied army bolstered by Hann and Wei to go against Zhao. Master Xiangzi of Zhao was preparing to flee. He asked his retainer, "Where can I go?" The attendant answered, "Changzi is near,[60] and besides the city walls have recently been fortified." Xiangzi responded, "The people are exhausted from the reconstruction of the city walls. Who in their right mind would die for me?" The attendant suggested, "The granary at Handan is abundant with large reserves."[61] Xiangzi answered, "The reserves are extorted from the hard earned wealth of the local people. How can we expect them to risk their lives for me? Who will help me? I think I should go to Jinyang, the homeland of our ancestors. Yin Duo has been most munificent to the locals. I think people there will rally to my plight." He took flight to Jinyang.

The armed forces of the three families surrounded Jinyang, and dams were breached causing extensive flooding.[62] The floodwaters rose to three-plank breadth from the top of the city walls.[63] The cooking stoves in the city were waterlogged, and frogs thrived in them.[64] However, no civilian

---

59 Cai 蔡 – the capital of Cai was Gaolang 臯狼 - Lishixian Shanxi 山西 離石縣.

Gaolang of Cai 蔡 臯狼 – Hu Sansheng 胡三省 noted that Shi Zhao 史炤 said, 'The Gaolang region belonged to Cai during the time of Chunqiu 春秋, later it became a Zhao county 趙邑.' According to my understanding, at the time of Chunqiu, while Jin 晉 and Chu 楚 were vying for hegemony, it was unlikely that Jin could straddle across the Zheng 鄭 polity to make a conquest of Cai. When the three Jin fief lords partitioned Jin, Hann occupied Chenggao 成臯, at the same time it took possession of Zheng 鄭. At that time, the Cai Polity was already annihilated by Chu and the southern part of Zheng was also annexed by Chu. Had Gaolang been part of Zheng, Master Xiangzi of Zhao could not possibly have occupied the territory. The *Hanshu dilizhi* 漢書地理志 says, 'There is a Gaolang County in Xihejun 西河郡, besides there is a Lin County 藺縣. Ever since the time of Chunqiu the territories of *Xihe* in Hann had all along been part of Jin's domain 晉. The ancient scripts of Cai and Lin were very similar; it is highly probably that the two words were erroneously substituted." The deduction made by Hu Sansheng made sense, as the territory of Gaolang was not part of Cai. Shi Zhao was incorrect with his assumption. Gaolangxian is situated to the northwest of Yongningxian Shaanxi 陝西 永寧縣, and Lin 藺縣 is situated to the west of Yongning. *ZZTJ JZ*, Vol 1, p. 19.

Shi Zhao 史炤 (~1090 CE) was the composer of the *Zizhi tongjian shiwen* 資治通鑒釋文.

60 Changzi 長子 – Changzixian Shanxi 山西 長子縣.

61 Handan 邯鄲 – It was to become the capital of Zhao 趙, Handanxian Hebei 河北 邯鄲縣.

62 The dams at *Fenshui* River 汾水河.

The siege of Jinyang began in 455 BCE, the 14th year of King Zhengding of Zhou 周貞定王 (r. 468-441 BCE) and lasted until 453 BCE. The text does not relate that the siege lasted for over two years. *SJ* 史記, 卷 113, Zhao shijia 趙世家, 第 13, p. 1645.

63 Three-plank breadth (lumber) - *sanban* 三版 - six *che* 尺, about one and a half metres in total.

Ancient Chinese city walls were constructed by the *banzhu* 版築 technique, the *bentu* technique 坌土 or stamp-earth technique. Each *ban* was equivalent to two *che*, roughly 50 cm. Two wooden planks, each two *che* in width were initially laid down to form the frame for stamping. Earth was then poured into the frame, workers would then pound the mixture of earth and clay until it became rock solid. Yap, J., The *Wars With the Xiongnu*, p. 5-6.

64 The original text was *shenzao chanwa* 沈竈產鼃 - the word 鼃 is now written as *wa* 蛙, meaning frog.

Yu Yue 俞樾 (1821-1906 CE) maintains that the word *shen* 沈 was synonymous with *chen* 煁 while 爾雅釋言 defines 煁 as *wei* 烓 – i.e. a stove. Guo Pu 郭璞 (276-324 CE) says, "It is a three-notched stove, 三隅竈." The *Shuowen jiezi* 說文解字 explains, "It is a stove, a portable stove 烓行竈也." Hao Yiheng 郝懿行 (1757-1825 CE) explains, "The three notched-strove that Guo referred to

contemplated surrendering. Zhibo made an inspection tour of the waterlogged surroundings. The war chariot was steered by Master Huanzi of Wei while Master Kangzi of Hann stood guard beside Zhibo as the *cancheng*.[65] Zhibo said, "Now I understand why floodwaters could bring on the demise of a state." Huanzi elbowed Kangzi with a nudge while Kangzi trod on Huanzi's instep lightly. They came to realize that the Fenshui River could be used to flood Anyi of Wei, and the water from the Jiangshui River could be directed to inundate Pingyang of Hann.[66]

Zhi Ci said to Zhibo,[67] "Hann and Wei will mutiny." Zhibo asked, "Sir. How do you know?" Zhi Ci answered, "It is common sense. It would be quite apparent to Hann and Wei by now that if the Zhao clan is annihilated they will meet the same fate. We have agreed with the two families that we will apportion the land of Zhao after overwhelming the state. Now the city is about to fall, the floodwaters is only three-plank breadth from the top of the city walls; people in the city are reduced to cannibalism and consuming horse flesh to stay alive, and the city is about to fall in a matter of days. The two masters should be jubilant with our impending victory, yet I detect no pleasure in their expressions; instead, I sense that they are extremely apprehensive. If they are not contemplating revolt, what else could they be thinking?"

The next day, Zhibo related what Zhi Ci said to Kangzi and Huanzi. The two men said, "It must be a rumour instigated by Zhao to sow seeds of discord between us, a conspiracy to create suspicion between us hence as to slacken our assaults against Zhao. We are on the brink of partitioning the lands of Zhao, how could we be so naive as to risk ourselves for something so intangible?" The two men departed.

Zhi Ci entered and asked, "My Lord, why did you tell the two masters what your subject told you?" Zhibo said, "Sir. How do you know?" Zhi Ci said, "When your subject came across them just now they glared as they raced past him. They knew your subject saw through them." Zhibo refused to listen. Zhi Ci requested to go to the Qi state as an emissary.[68]

---

was similar to the wind-stove - *fenglu* 風爐 of today; it is shaped like a brush holder. The cooking wok or utensil is placed on top of the notches. There are three empty spaces to allow air to pass through. They come in various sized and are quite portable, and could be carried on boats and carriages. Hence they are also known as *hengzao* 行竈 – portable stove." *ZZTJ JZ*, Vol 1, pp. 19-20. N.B. The best description of a portable stove is an inverted tripod.

65 *Cancheng* 驂乘 – An ancient chariot carried three warriors; one was the general or commander; the second was the carriage driver, and third a guard holding a spear or halberd, standing guard on the right side of the carriage. The *Zuo zhuan* 左傳 refers to the position as *you* 右. *Cancheng* 驂乘 thus means right *you* 右. *ZZTJ JZ*, Vol 1, p. 20.

66 Fenshui River 汾水河. Anyi 安邑 was the capital of Wei 魏 at that stage - Xiaxian Shanxi 山西 夏縣. (In 430 BCE the capital was moved to Huanshui 洹水 – Weixian Hebei 河北 魏縣 and in 339 BCE it moved to Daliang 大梁 – Kaifengxian Henan 河南 開封). *SJ* 史記, 卷 114, 'Wei shijia 魏世家' 第 14, p. 1687. N.B. Wei was not a fief state in 430 BCE, the capital of Wei was an enfeoffed estate of the Wei clan.

Jiangshui River 絳水. Pingyang 平陽 was the capital of Hann 韓 at that stage - Lingfenxian Shanxi 山西 臨汾縣. In 376 BCE the capital was moved to Xinzheng 新鄭 when it annihilated Zheng 鄭 - Xinzheng Henan 河南 新鄭. *SJ* 史記, 卷 115, 'Hann shijia 韓世家', 第 15, p. 1706.

67 Zhi Ci 絺疵 was a court strategist at the Zhi 智 household.

68 Zhi Ci sensed an impending calamity was about to unfold; he took leave.

Master Xiangzi instructed Zhang Mengtan to steal out of the city to meet the two masters.[69] The emissary related to the two masters, "Your subject has heard that when one loses his lips, his teeth feel the chill of the cold air.[70] Now, Zhibo is leading Hann and Wei against Zhao; when Zhao falls, Hann and Wei will be next." The two masters responded, "We are mindful of that, but we are concerned lest the conspiracy might spring a leak, calamity would fall upon us." Zhang Mengtan answered, "You, Sirs, are supposed to come up with the scheme; your subject is merely a listener; what harm could it bring?" The two masters and Zhang Mengtan agreed to a clandestine alliance and arranged a date for the mutiny; after that, the emissary returned. Master Xiangzi dispatched his men to attack the sentinels guarding the floodgates in the middle of the night and then breached the dams to drain the floodwaters into Zhibo's camp. Zhibo's men tried desperately to salvage the equipment and fell into disarray. The armies under the Hann and Wei clans broke into the Zhi camp from both flanks, making fierce assaults. Master Xiangzi led his troops against the Zhi forces for a frontal attack; Zhibo's forces were completely overwhelmed. Zhibo was executed, and all the Zhi clan members were eliminated; the only person who managed to escape was Zhi Guo.[71]

Sima Guang Annotates:

The reason for the demise of Zhibo was that his prodigious aptitude prevailed over his moral character. Aptitude and moral attributes are disparate entities, but mundane people are too inadequate to discern the subtleties. When they come across a person with exceptional aptitude, they label him as being sagacious and worthy, but how wrong they are with their assessment! The defining qualifications of aptitude are intelligence, perception, determination and resolve, whereas the defining qualifications of moral character are justice, righteousness, being impartial and amiable in nature. Aptitude is one of the entities of virtue, whereas virtue is the ultimate of aptitude. It is held that the bamboo stem from Yunmeng is the sturdiest of all under Heaven,[72] however, without straightening the warps, and without attaching feather as fetching, it cannot pierce tough armour. The gold (copper) at Tangxi is known for its quality, yet without forging and buffing, it cannot be cast into lethal weapons.[73] One can only be considered as a sage if he

---

69 Zhang Mengtan 張孟談 was a strategic counsellor at the Zhao court.

70 唇亡齒寒 – the expression means that lips and teeth are closely related, an analogy meaning if one loses his lips his teeth feel the chill. Slitting the lips of criminals was a common chastisement in ancient China. The expression is from the *Zuo zhuan* 左傳 'Duke of Xi 5th year 僖公五年 宮之奇諫虞公語 Gong Zhiqi jian Yugong yu'.

71 Zhi Guo escaped as he had the prescience to change his family name to Fu 輔.

72 Yunmeng 雲夢 – was an ancient lake. Du Yi 杜預 relates, "Yunmeng was a part of Chu 楚, it straddled across the River (Changjiang 長江) from the south to the north. The *Hanshu* 漢書, dili zhi 地理志 relates, "Mengyun Lake 雲夢澤 is situated to the south of Huarongxian County 華容縣." Jianli and Shishou counties Hubei 湖北 監利 石首縣 belonged to the former Huarong County. *ZZTJ JZ* Vol 1, p. 20.

73 Tangxi 棠谿 - Suipingxian Hebei 河北 遂平縣.

possesses both exceptional aptitude and moral character; lacking both he is but an ignoramus. When the moral character of a person exceeds that of his aptitude he is a man of noble character; whereas when one's aptitude exceeds that of his moral character he is merely a lowly and humble person. If a worthy person or a man of noble character cannot be found to assume an important responsibility to serve at court one might as well appoint a lowly and humble person. Why? A person of noble character uses his wisdom and capabilities to advance virtuous deeds, whereas a lowly and contemptible person uses his wrought intelligence to engender his wicked intents. Munificence will be pervasive if one employs his capabilities to enhance benevolence, whereas, a humble and lowly person will bring on more iniquities employing his aptitude to attain his own means. An ignoramus might have the desire to carry out wicked deeds. However, he is restrained by his intelligence, and he can accomplish little. It is compared to wrestling with a new-born pup, which can be stopped with one slight move. While, with a lowly and vile individual, gifted with depravity and intelligence, he can use his skills to augment his wickedness with fearlessness; manifesting his viciousness - like a tiger being bestowed with wings. These lowly and vile individuals merely bring more calamities to humanity. People respect a person with moral character while they also admire one with exceptional intelligence. They readily accepted people with exceptional aptitude, while they distance themselves from the ones with unflinching moral integrity. An observer is often deceived by the aptitude of people while neglecting their moral character.

Since time immemorial, the treacherous ministers who fomented the subjugation of kingdoms and the prodigals were invariably gifted with exceptional intelligence but lacking in moral character; they brought on the annihilation of many a nation and the demise of many a family. Zhibo was not the only one. Hence, if the sovereign of a state or the patriarch of a family could make distinctions between aptitude and moral character, making distinction of the priorities, what worry does he hold for not employing the right people for his state or family?

The copper from Tangxi 棠谿 was noted for its fine quality. The original phrase used is '棠谿之金, 天下之利也'. To translate it as, "The gold of Tangxi is the sharpest under Heaven does not make sense."

'不砥礪' the expression here is used a verb meaning to grand and buff. The word *di* 砥 means coarse grindstone while the word *li* 礪 means fine whetstone. *ZZTJ JZ,* Vol I, p. 20.

N.B. Metal was also known as gold at the time of the Warring States, particularly the metal copper.

III. The three family clans partitioned Zhi's lands. Master Zhao Xiangzi applied varnish to Zhibo's skull, [74] using it as his drinking vessel. Yu Rang, a retainer of Zhibo decided to seek revenge for his former master. He disguised himself as a convicted inmate and sneaked into Master Xiangzi's palace, bearing a dagger and hid in the latrine. When Xiangzi was heading towards the latrine, he had a sudden change of heart and asked his attendants to carry out a search; Yu Rang was captured. The retainers had intended to execute the man, but Xiangzi said, "The Zhibo's clan is left without an heir; it is understandable that this man wants to avenge the death of his master. He is a loyal subject; I intend to avoid him." He ordered the man released. Yu Rang then applied varnish to his own body, bringing on a rash; he swallowed charcoal impairing his speech. He begged at the marketplace; even his wife could not recognize him. On one occasion, an old acquaintance saw and recognized him. The old friend was in tears, "With your abilities you could easily seek patronage under Master Zhao Xiangzi; [75] it would offer you a chance to get close to him to do whatever you want. Would it not be easier? Why do you have to torment yourself like this? It is one difficult way to make revenge." Yu Rang answered, "Had I sought shelter under him I would become his retainer; to murder one's master is a reprehensible act. I do not intend to be disloyal to the master I serve. I know the path I chose is dauntingly difficult, the reason I took this path is that I want to put the perfidious subjects under Heaven to shame." Master Xiangzi left his palace. Yu Rang concealed himself beneath a bridge where Master Xiang was passing through. When he arrived at the bridge his horse was startled, he ordered his guards to carry out a search and found Yu Rang in hiding. He executed him.[76]

Master Xiangzi had five sons of his own; he did not nominate a successor amongst them.[77] He enfeoffed Bo Lu's son at Dai; honouring him as Lord Daicheng.[78] Lord Daicheng died young; he then nominated Daicheng's son, Huan as his lawful successor.[79] Upon the

---

74 Master Xiang (Xiangzi) of Zhao, Zhao Wuxu 趙襄子 趙無恤.
Zhi Yao 智瑤.

75 The text uses Zhao Meng 趙孟, which was the other name for Zhao Xiangzi 趙襄子.

76 Yu Rang 豫讓. The *SJ* 史記, Cike liezhuan 刺客列傳 goes on to relate, "Yu Rang said, 'Your subject is told that a wise man does not try to hide the virtues of others; a loyal subject dies for righteousness. You, Sir, have spared my life previously; all the people under Heaven are singing your praise as a sage. As for what is happening today, your subject is prepared to accept his fate. However, before you execute him, please allow him to strike at your cloak as a symbol of taking revenge for his master.' Zhao Wuxu removed his cloak and gave it to the assassin. Yu Rang raised his sword and stabbed at the cloak, saying, 'I have made retribution for my master, Zhibo 智伯.' He raised his sword and ran it through himself." N.B. The cover design of this book, probably from a stone rubbing, depicts the incident. *SJ* 史記, 卷 56, Cike liezhuan 刺客列傳, 第 26, pp. 706-708.

77 Zhao Bolu 趙伯魯. The text reads, "Because of Bolu, Xiangzi did not nominate an heir." Taking the face value of the text, it does not make sense. The background of the event was because the father of Xiangzi revoked the inheritance right of Bo Lu, Xiangzi was somewhat remorseful, and he hence did not pass the throne to his sons. *SJ* 史記, 卷 113, 'Zhao shijia 趙世家' 第 13, p. 1643.

78 Dai 代 – Laiyuanxian Hebei 河北 涞源縣. *ZZTJ JZ*, Vol 1, p. 21.
Lord Daicheng 代成君.

79 Zhao Huanzi 趙桓子 was the younger brother of Xiangzi 襄子.
Master Xianzi of Zhao 趙獻子 Zhao Huan 趙浣 (r. 423-410 BCE). The spellings of Huanzi 桓 and 浣 are the same, and the two names tend to be confusing.

death of Master Xiangzi, Master Huanzi the younger brother of Xiangzi banished Zhao Huan and made himself the successor of the Zhao clan. [80] Master Huanzi died a year later. The Zhao clansmen decided, "It was not the will of Master Xiangzi to make Huanzi the successor." The clan members executed the son of Master Huanzi, reinstating Zhao Huan, known as Master Xianzi. Xianzi had a son by the name of Ji; he was known posthumously as Marquis Lie of Zhao.[81]

Wei Si, known posthumously as Marquis Wen of Wei, was the grandson of Master Huanzi of Wei.[82]

IV. Master Kangzi of Hann begot Master Wuzi, who in turn fathered Hann Qian - Marquis Jing of Hann, (the first sovereign of the Hann state).[83]

V. Marquis Wen of Wei (Wei Si) honoured Master Bu Zixia and Master Tian Zifang as his tutors; [84] whenever he chanced to pass by the residence of Master Duangan Mu he would lower his head in reverence.[85] When intellects and worthy individuals from the four quarters heard of his respect for sages and scholars, they went and gathered at his court.[86]

Marquis Wen hosted a banquet to entertain his senior officials. The Marquis and the guests were highly spirited when it rained. The Marquis ordered his retainers to prepare his carriage to ride off to a nearby suburb. His retainers asked him, "Everybody is enjoying himself at the banquet, besides it is starting to rain and where is Your Highness heading?" Marquis Wen answered, "I have an appointment with the Minister of Agriculture to go hunting today; [87] while everyone is enjoying himself, how could I break my pledge?" He rode off to tell the minister that their appointment was postponed.

Hann sought military help from Wei to make an expedition against Zhao. Marquis Wen said, "Zhao is my brotherly state; I dare not comply." Zhao also appealed to Wei for military aid to go against Hann. The Marquis gave the same response. The two marquises were infuriated by his refusal, they left. Later, when the marquises realized that they were treated equally as brotherly states, they began to make tributes to the Wei court. Ever

---

80 Zhao Wuxu 趙無恤 died in 425 BCE.
Master Hengzi of Zhao 趙恒子 Zhao Jia 趙嘉 (? -424 BCE).

81 Marquis Lie of Zhao 趙烈侯 Zhao Ji 趙籍 (r. 409-400 BCE) or (r. 409-387 BCE) or (r. 408-387 BCE).

82 Marquis Wen of Wei 魏文侯 Wei Si 魏斯 (r. 446-397 BCE) or (r. 445-396 BCE) was the grandson of Master Huanzi of Wei 魏桓子.

83 Master Wuzi of Hann 韓武子 Hann Qizhang 韓啓章 (r. ?-409 BCE).
Marquis Jing of Hann 韓景侯 Hann Qian 韓虔 (r. 408-400 BCE) or (r. 409-401 BCE).

84 Master Bu Zixia 卜子夏 (507-420 BCE), Master Tian Zifang 田子方 (?) (N.B. the word *zi* here means master or tutor.)

85 The word for etiquettes used is *shi* 式. *Shi* was the wooden banister or handrail in front of a carriage. The word is used as a verb. It means holding onto the banister, stroke gently while lowering one's head in reverence. *ZZTJ JZ,* Vol 1, p. 21.

86 Master Duangan Mu 段干木 (475-386 BCE) was a student of Zixia 子夏 (Bu Zixia 卜子夏) and was an acclaimed and honourable scholar at that stage.

87 Minister of Agriculture, *yuren* 虞人.

since then Wei became the most powerful state among the three San-Jin of Wei, Hann and Zhao, none of the other fief lords were comparable with its supremacy.

Marquis Wen sent Yue Yang on an expedition against the state of Zhongshan, which fell.[88] He then enfeoffed the annexed territories to his son Wei Ziji.[89]

Marquis Wen asked his ministers, "What kind of ruler am I?" Everyone answered, "You are a benevolent lord." Ren Zuo responded,[90] "My Lord, you annexed Zhongshan, you enfeoffed your son and not your younger brother, how could one call that benevolent?" Marquis Wen threw a tantrum; Ren Zuo excused himself and left hurriedly. Wei Si then asked Zhai Huang.[91] Zhai Huang answered, "Benevolent Lord!" Wei Si asked, "What do you mean by that?" Zhai Huang answered, "Your subject is told that if a lord is benevolent, his subjects will be straightforward and forthright. Ren Zuo was spontaneous in his candidness; your subject thus knows." The Marquis was most delighted with the response. He sent Zhai Huang to invite Ren Zuo to return to court. He descended to the lower terrace at the audience hall to bid him welcome, inviting him to be seated at the most prominent position reserved for the guest of honour.

Marquis Wen was drinking with Master Tian Zifang.[92] The Marquis noted, "The music is discordant; the chime is high on the left-side." Tian Zifang smiled. Marquis Wen asked, "Why are you smiling?" The Master answered, "Your subject is told that a sovereign of a state simply needs to attend to his music master, he does not have to be overly concerned with the premise of music.[93] Your Highness might have mastered the thesis of music; however your subject is afraid you could have become tone deaf presiding over your subordinates."[94] The Marquis responded, "Excellent point."

Wei Ziji, the son of Wei Si, chanced to come across Master Tian Zifang at the thoroughfare; he promptly dismounted from his carriage to make proper etiquettes. Zifian did not reciprocate. Ziji was in a towering rage; he asked, "Are the elites allowed to be arrogant or the humble and lowly?" Zifang answered, "Naturally, it is the humble! Do the elites dare to be arrogant? When a sovereign becomes arrogant, he loses his state; while a minister becomes conceited, he loses his family clan. When an elite lord loses his state, he is no longer held as a lord. When a minister loses his family, he is no longer treated as a minister. Modest folks, being lowly and humble, when his advice and proposition are no longer heeded, and his acts do not comply with the etiquettes stipulated; he simply slips

---

88 Yue Yang 樂羊 a general of Wei.

89 Zhongshan 中山國 – Dingxian Hebei 河北 定縣. (See footnotes below on Zhongsun 中山國). Wei Ziji 魏子擊.

90 Ren Zuo 任座 was a minister at the Wei court.

91 Zhai Huang 翟璜 was the chancellor of Wei 魏 for over thirty years.

92 Master Tian Zifang 田子方, a Wei 魏 national, was a distinguished scholar and student of Master Zigong 子貢, who was one of the 72 most prominent students of Confucius 孔子.

93 Music officer, *Yueguan* 樂官.

94 There is a play of word in the comment, '今君甚審於音, 臣恐其聾於官也.' The meaning is while you have mastered the thesis of music; your subject fears that you have lost the touch to preside over your subordinates.

on his footwear and takes leave, and continues to be lowly and humble wherever he goes." Wei Ziji promptly apologized.[95]

Marquis Wen asked Li Ke,[96] "You, sir, once remarked, 'When one is impoverished one thinks of his virtuous wife at home; when a state falls into disarray one thinks of the departed worthy ministers.' I intend to appoint either Cheng or Huang as my chancellor.[97] How are the two compared?" Li Ke responded, "A humble person is in no position to make major decisions for the state, and a distant relative of a family should not be making decisions for his kinfolk. Your subject is posted beyond the palace-gate, and he dares not make any suggestions." Marquis Wen said, "Sir, this is pertinent to our state, please don't be humble." Li Ke answered, "My Lord, you have not been attentive to the minor details. Please observe the people one befriends. Upon making a fortune, observe how he dispenses with his wealth. Take note of the people he recommends. When he was humble, did he behave wantonly and indiscriminately; and when he was impecunious did he accept ill-gotten wealth. One reaches a satisfactory conclusion by assessing the five points I just raised. Why do you need my comments?"

Marquis Wen said, "Sir, please retire and rest, I have decided who to appoint as my chancellor." Li Ke left and met Zhai Huang. Zhai Huang asked, "I am told that His Highness had summoned you to court to seek your opinion on appointing the chancellor; who did you recommend?" Li Ke said, "Wei Cheng." Zhai Huang had a complete about-face, and said, "I recommended Wu Qi as the magistrate of Hexi territories; and when His highness was troubled by the administration of Yecheng I recommended Ximen Bao.[98]

---

95 The account in the *SJ* 史記 is different, "Ziji was displeased and departed." "子籍不懌而去." *ZZTJ JZ*, Vol 1, p. 22.

96 Zhongshan General, Li Ke 中山守將 李克.

97 Cheng 成 = Wei Cheng 魏成. Huang 璜 = Zhai Huang 翟璜.

98 Xihe 西河.

Wu Qi 吳起.

The statement would make more sense when translated as, "When His Highness was concerned with the safety of Hexi territories, I recommended Wu Qi as the magistrate of Hexi territories..."

Yecheng 鄴城 - Linzhangxian Henan 河南 臨漳縣.

Wu Qi 吳起 (440-381 BCE), a Wey national 衛, was born into a wealthy family, during his earlier years he was unsuccessful in securing a government appointment when he expended all his family fortune on his quest. His neighbours and family members teased and mocked him for his failure; when he could not bear the shame any longer he murdered over 30 people for having goaded him, he then escaped from Wey. He said to his mother before leaving that he would never consider returning home unless he had become a chancellor. Later he studied literati teaching under Ceng Shen 曾申 (son of Cengzi 曾子- Ceng Cen 曾參). When Wu Qi's mother passed away, he did not return home to pay his last reverence; Ceng Shen was infuriated for his lack of filial piety and severed his teacher-student relationship. Wu Qi then turned to serve under Jisun 魯季孫氏 at the Lu fiefdom. In 412 BCE, Duke Xuan of Qi 齊宣公 (r. 455-405 BCE) launched an attack against Lu at Juxian county 莒縣 and Anyang 安陽; Duke Mu of Lu 魯穆公 (r. 415?-377? BCE) had intended to make Wu Qi his commanding general. However, Wu's wife was a Qi national, the duke was vacillating with uncertainty, Wu Qi killed his wife to show his resolve to serve the Lu state. The duke then assigned him to command the army, which gave the Qi army a resounding defeat. Someone at court spread words of malign against Wu Qi for his cruelty and his treacherous behaviour; the duke relieved him of his duties. Wu Qi exasperated left Lu to go forth to the Fiefdom of Wei 魏. Marquis

Furthermore, when he decided to make an expedition against Zhongshan, I recommended Yue Yang.[99] Upon annexing Zhongshan, he could not find a suitable general to preside at the territories, I recommended you, sir. The heir to His Highness did not have a capable tutor; I recommended Quhou Fu.[100] From what you have seen and heard; which of the above matters have I fallen short against Wei Cheng?"

Li Ke answered, "When you recommended me to His Highness, I did not believe it was your intention to make me your associate to garner for higher positions. When His Highness asked my opinion, I answered candidly. How did I know His Highness would nominate Wei Cheng? You see, Wei Cheng earns an annual emolument of one thousand *zhong* and yet he used nine-tenth of which to make many friends,[101] leaving one-tenth for himself. That was how he came across sage masters like Bu Zixia, Tian Zifang and Duangan Mu from the east.[102] His Highness honoured these three scholars as his tutors; whereas the men you recommended to His Highness are employed as minister. Sir, so how could you be compared with Wei Cheng?" Zhai Huang backed off by making repeated solemn bows to apologize and said, "Huang is a boor; I have been most impolite. Please take me as your student for the rest of my life."

Wen of Wei 魏文侯 appointed Wu Qi as a commanding general, assisting Yue Yang 樂羊 in an expedition against the Zhongshan Polity 中山國. In 409 BCE, the Marquis made him a commanding general to go against Qin 秦 and was successful in recovering all the territories previously lost to Qin. He was made the Prefecture Magistrate of *Hexi* 河西. While being the Magistrate he studied under Zixia 子夏 (a student of Confucius). He proceeded to institute what is called *wuzuzhi* 武卒制 – a recruitment procedure for vigorous warriors. The potential recruit had to be fully armoured, able to carry a 12 dan bow (not the weight, but the strength to pull the string), 50 arrows, three days of ration and capable of running a distance of 100 *li* (about 40 km) within half a day. An applicant, who qualified after such a grilling test, would be relieved of corvee and land levies. During his tenure at Wei, he led the Wei army into 76 battles, with 64 decisive wins and the rest being impasses. Wu Qi left profound influences on the military and political affairs in the states of Wei and Chu while Shang Yang 商鞅, also a Wey national, was greatly inspired by him. The *shiwu lianzuo fa* 什伍連坐法 – One being implicated for not divulging one's neighbour's criminal activities, it was introduced by Wu Qi, Shang Yang took over the practice. (*SJ* 史記, 卷 35, 'Sunzi, Wu Qi liezhuan 孫子 吳起列傳' 第五. pp. 397-399.

Ximen Bao 西門豹, a Wei 魏 national, was a statesman and waterworks specialist. He was the magistrate of the Ye county 鄴 at the times of Marquis Wen of Wei 魏文侯. He was instrumental in eradicating superstition fabricated by local officials in making human sacrifices to a fabricated river deity He Bo 河伯. He opened twelve canals for agricultural purposes; the canals are known as Ximen Bao Canals. The *ZZTJ* has only one mention of him, while historical texts the *Hannfeizi* 韓非子, the *Shiji* 史記, the *Lunheng* 論衡, the *ZGC* 戰國策, the *Huainanzi* 淮南子 and the *Shuoyuan* 說苑 all refer to this person.

99 Yue Yang 樂羊 was an outstanding general at the Wei court. The king of Zhongshan 中山 killed his son, cooked him to a stew, and presented it to the general, who drank the stew to show his resolve. Later, he laid siege to Zhongshan and gave it a resounding defeat. King Wei was nevertheless suspicious of him, maintaining he had no emotional attachment to his son. Source The *Siku quanshu* 四庫全書, *Hann Feizi* 韓非子 'Shaolin part I, 說林上'. pp. 5273.

100 Quhou Fu 屈侯鮒.

101 *Zhong* 鐘 - one *zhong* = six *hu* 斛 and four *dou* 斗; one *hu* = 10 *dou*, hence one *zhong* = 64 *dou*. One *dou* = approximately one decalitre – but may well have been differed in size during this period.

102 Bu Zixia 卜子夏, Tian Zifang 田子方 and Duangan Mu 段干木. The three scholars were collective known as 'The Three Sages of *Hedong* - East of the River' - 河東三賢.

Wu Qi, a Wei national, was seeking an official position in the state of Lu.[103] At that stage, Qi attacked Lu. The people in Lu were considering appointing him as a general; however, the wife of Wu Qi was a Qi national and the Lu court was uncertain about his fidelity. Wu Qi murdered his wife to assume the appointment, and he led the Lu forces against Qi and won a resounding victory.

Someone slandered Wu Qi by remarking to Marquis Lu, "Qi studied under Master Zhen Cen previously.[104] When his mother died, he did not return home to attend to her funeral; Zhen expunged the tutor-student relationship.[105] Wu Qi killed his wife to assume the position as your general; this man is hideously malicious and callous. Lu is a small state, once rumour spreads that we could take down one of the most powerful states it might invite the other fiefdoms to unite against us." Wu Qi feared that he might be implicated and when he heard that Marquis Wen was a sage he hastened to the state. Marquis Wen sought the opinion of Li Ke, who said, "Wu Qi is avaricious and lecherous; nevertheless, he is a brilliant general, even the celebrated Grand Marshal Sima Rangju of Qi was not his equal."[106] Marquis Wen nominated Wu Qi as his commanding general, who led an army against Qin and captured five walled-cities.

As a commander, Wu Qi wore the same clothes as the lowliest soldiers, consumed the same rations; he slept on the floor and did not set up bedsteads for himself; while marching his troops, he walked instead of riding on his horse, hauling his own rations and fodder supplies. One of the soldiers developed a boil; Wu Qi sucked the puss from the lesion with his mouth. When the mother of the soldier heard what Wu Qi had done, she cried in despair. People were curious and asked, "Your son is a lowly corporal and the general sucked the puss from his boil, why are you crying?" The mother said, "You don't understand. Years ago, Master Wu sucked out the puss of a boil for my son's father; he died valiantly going against the enemies. Now Master Wu is doing the same thing for his son. I know not where or when he will die. How could I not be sad?"

VI. Duke Min of Yan died; his son Duke Xi succeeded to his position.[107]

---

103 Wu Qi 吳起 was a Wey national 衛國人 - Puyangxian Hebei 河北 濮陽縣.
Lu 魯國 - Qufuxian Shandong 山東 曲阜縣.

104 Zhen Cen 曾參 (505-435 BCE), Master Zhenzi 曾子, with a polite name of Ziyu 子輿, was one of the seventy-two outstanding students of Confucius, he was known for his filial piety. N.B. Wu Qi lived between 440-381 BCE, if the dates were accurate, it was very unlikely that Wu Qi studied under Zhen Cen.

105 Zhen Cen maintained that he lacked filial piety.

106 Grand Marshal of Qi 齊司馬 Tian Rangju 田穰苴. Tian Rangju probably lived at the time of Duke Jing of Qi 齊景公 (r. 547-490 BCE); although there is a biography on him in *SJ* 史記, we are not sure of the time he lived. He was reputed to be one of most brilliant military generals in Chinese history. Yan Ying 晏嬰 (~ 578-500 BCE) recommended him to Duke Jing. He led the Qi army to defeat the combined forces of Yan 燕 and Jin 晉 according to the *SJ* 史記, 卷 34, 'Sima Rangju lie zhuan 司馬穰苴列傳' 第 4, pp. 392-393. (However, there was no other record of a combined force between Yan and Jin against Qi in history.)

107 Duke Min of Yan 燕湣公 (r. 434-403? BCE) or (r. 433-403 BCE) or (r. 438-415 BCE) 31st ?
According to Hu Sansheng 胡三省, "Since the time of Duke Zhao of Yan 燕召公 (Shi 奭) being enfeoffed at Northern Yan 北燕 to the time of Duke Min, it had gone through 32 generations." *ZZTJ JZ*, Vol 1, p. 22.

402 BCE *Jimao* 己卯 Warring States 戰國

King Weilie of Zhou	周威烈王	24th year
Duke Mu of Lu	魯穆公	8th year
Duke Jian of Qin	秦簡公	13th year
Duke Ru of Zheng	鄭繻公	21st year
Duke Dao of Song	宋悼公	2nd year
King Sheng of Chu	楚聲王	6th year
Duke Kang of Qi	齊康公	3rd year
Duke Lie of Jin	晉烈公	20th year
Marquis Wen of Wei	魏文侯	45th year
Marquis Jing of Hann	韓景侯	7th year
Marquis Lie of Zhao	趙烈侯	7th year
Duke of Xi Yan	燕僖公	1st year[108]
Duke of Sheng Wey	衛慎公	13th year

I. King Weilie of Zhou died, and his son succeeded him; he was known posthumously as King An.[109]

II. Outlaws murdered King Sheng of Chu; the aristocrats at Chu placed his son on the throne, he was known as King Dao of Chu.[110]

401 BCE *Gengchen* 庚辰 Warring States 戰國

King of An of Zhou	周安王	1st year
Duke Mu of Lu	魯穆公	9th year

108 Duke Xi of Yan 燕僖公 (another source says it was Marquis Xi of Yan 燕釐侯. Some sources claimed that he was Duke Houjian of Yan 燕 後簡公, his name was either Ji Dai 姬戴 or Ji Kuan 姬款 (r. 402-373 BCE) or (r. 414-370 BCE). The background of this Duke is obscured. According to the *ZZTJ* Chapter 1, 403-VI, Duke Min of Yan 燕湣公 died in 403 BCE and his son Duke Xi 僖公 ascended to the throne of the dukedom.

According to Chen Mengjia 陳夢家 Duke Min 湣公 was Duke Wen 文公, who reigned between 438-415 BCE and he was succeeded by Duke Jian 簡公 (r. 414-370 BCE). Chen Mengjia 陳夢家, *Xizhu niandako, Liguo nianbiao* 西周年代考 六國年表, 2007 edition, 中華書局, China, pp. 85-87.

109 King Weilie of Zhou, Ji Wu 周威烈王 姬午 38th.

King An of Zhou 周安王 Ji Jiao 姬驕 39th (r. 401-376 BCE).

110 King Sheng of Chu 楚聲王 aka King Shengheng 聲恒王 Mi Dang, Mi-Xiong Dang 芈當 芈熊當 (r. 407-402 BCE). Details of the death of the Chu king are lacking, except we know that Chu was in a state of turmoil during his reign.

It was formally believed that Zhou 周 enfeoffed Xiong Yi 熊繹 at Chu; however, this lacks credibility. From Xiong Yi to King Sheng of Chu, it had lasted for 30 generations. *ZZTJ JZ*, Vol 1, p. 23.

Duke Jian of Qin	秦簡公	14th year
Duke Ru of Zheng	鄭繻公	22st year
Duke Dao of Song	宋悼公	3rd year
King Dao of Chu	楚悼王	1st year[111]
Duke Kang of Qi	齊康公	4th year
Duke Lie of Jin	晉烈公	21st year
Marquis Wen of Wei	魏文侯	46th year
Marquis Jing of Hann	韓景侯	8th year
Marquis Lie of Zhao	趙烈侯	8th year
Duke Xi of Yan	燕僖公	2nd year
Duke Shen of Wey	衛慎公	14th year

1. Qin invaded Wei,[112] and marched as far as Yanggu.[113]

---

400 BCE *Xinsi* 辛巳 Warring States 戰國

King An of Zhou	周安王	2nd year
Duke Mu of Lu	魯穆公	10th year
Duke Jian of Qin	秦簡公	15th year
Duke Ru of Zheng	鄭繻公	23rd year
Duke Dao of Song	宋悼公	4th year
King Dao of Chu	楚悼王	2nd year
Duke Kang of Qi	齊康公	5th year
Duke Lie of Jin	晉烈公	22nd year
Marquis Wen of Wei	魏文侯	47th year
Marquis Jing of Hann	韓景侯	9th year

---

111 King Dao of Chu 楚悼王 Mi-Xiong Yi 芈熊疑 (r. 401-381 BCE).
N.B. Before the founding of the Qin Empire; people used both *xing* 姓 and *shi* 氏 or either; men used to use *shi* 氏 (father's surname or bestowed name) but not *xing* (mother's family name). The word *xing* 姓 has an implication of – born of a woman. Hence, some of the most significant ancient family names at that stage carried a 'woman' 女 as radical, for example, Ji 姬, Si 姒, Gui 媯, Yao 姚, Jiang 姜, Ying 嬴. It was a vestige of the matriarch society of ancient China.

112 The people of Qin 秦 had a Ying 嬴 family name. In the beginning the Qin people lived in the east of Zhongyuan 中原, later they migrated to Shanxi 山西. At the time of King Xiao of Zhou 周孝王, Feizi 非子 was enfeoffed at Qin, present day Gansu 甘肅 province. (The dates cannot be verified.) Towards the beginning of Qin, the state was enfeoffed at Qinteng Hanlongxian 漢隴縣 秦亭, which is north of Qingshuixian Gansu 甘肅 清水縣. When Duke Xiang of Qin 秦襄公 (r. 778 or 777-766 BCE) assisted Zhou to fight off the Quan-Rong 犬戎, he was enfeoffed at Fenghao 豐鎬, the domain of Qin had expanded to as far as present-day Shaanxi 陝西. *ZZTJ JZ*, Vol 1, p. 23.

113 Yanggu 陽孤 - Yanghucheng Xinjiangxian Shanxi 山西 新絳縣 陽壺城.

Marquis Lie of Zhao	趙烈侯	9th year
Duke Xi of Yan	燕僖公	3rd year
Duke Shen of Wey	衛慎公	15th year

I. Wei, Hann, and Zhao joined forces against Chu, the army advanced as far as Sangqiu.[114]

II. Zheng besieged Yangzhai of Hann.[115]

III. Marquis Jing of Hann died, his son, known posthumously as Marquis Lie, succeeded him.[116]

IV. Marquis Lie of Zhao died and was succeeded by his younger brother, known posthumously as Marquis Wu of Zhao.[117]

V. Duke Jian of Qin died and was succeeded by his son Duke Hui.[118]

---

399 BCE *Renwu* 壬午 Warring States 戰國

King An of Zhou	周安王	3rd year
Duke Mu of Lu	魯穆公	11th year
Duke Hui of Qin	秦惠公	1st year
Duke Ru of Zheng	鄭繻公	24th year
Duke Dao of Song	宋悼公	5th year
King Dao of Chu	楚悼王	3rd year
Duke Kang of Qi	齊康公	6th year
Duke Lie of Jin	晉烈公	23rd year
Marquis Wen of Wei	魏文侯	48th year
Marquis Lie of Hann	韓烈侯	1st year

---

114 Sangqiu 桑丘, the *SJ* 史記 chronicles this place as Chengqiu 乘丘 - Ziyangxian Shandong 山東 滋陽縣. *ZZTJ JZ,* Vol 1, p. 24.

115 Zheng 鄭.
Hann 韓, Yangzhai 陽翟 was the capital of Hann.
Yangzhai 陽翟 - Yuxian Henan 河南 禹縣.

116 Marquis Jing of Hann 韓景侯 Hann Qian 韓虔.
Marquis Lie of Hann 韓烈侯 Hann Qu 韓取 (r. 399-387 BCE) or (r. 400-378 BCE) or (r. 399-377 BCE).

117 Marquis Lie of Zhao 趙烈侯 Zhao Ji 趙籍 (r. 409-400 BCE) 1st.
Marquis Wu of Zhao 趙武侯 (r. 399-387 BCE) or (r. 400-387 BCE), was also known as Duke Wu of Zhao 趙武公 2nd, his name is not known.

118 Duke Jian of Qin 秦簡公 Ying Daozi 嬴悼子 (r. 414-400 BCE) or (r. 415-400 BCE) or (r. 414-406 BCE) 21st.
Duke Hui of Qin 秦惠公 (r. 399-387 BCE), was the 22nd sovereign of Qin.

Marquis Wu of Zhao	趙武侯	1st year
Duke Xi of Yan	燕僖公	4th year
Duke Shen of Wey	衛慎公	16th year

I. Prince Ding escaped to Jin.[119]

II. There was landslide at the Gaoshan Mountain; the debris impeded the flow of the River (Huanghe).[120]

---

398 BCE *Guiwei* 癸未 Warring States 戰國

King An of Zhou	周安王	4th year
Duke Mu of Lu	魯穆公	12th year
Duke Hui of Qin	秦惠公	2nd year
Duke Ru of Zheng	鄭繻公	25th year
Duke Dao of Song	宋悼公	6th year
King Dao of Chu	楚悼王	4th year
Duke Kang of Qi	齊康公	7th year
Duke Lie of Jin	晉烈公	24th year
Marquis Wen of Wei	魏文侯	49th year
Marquis Lie of Hann	韓烈侯	2nd year
Marquis Wu of Zhao	趙武侯	2nd year
Duke Xi of Yan	燕僖公	5th year
Duke Shen of Wey	衛慎公	17th year

I. Chu laid siege to Zheng. The people in Zheng executed Chancellor Si Ziyang.[121]

---

397 BCE *Jiashen* 甲申 Warring States 戰國

King An of Zhou	周安王	5th year

---

119 Zhou Prince 周王子 Ji Ding 姬定 escaped to Jin 晉 in 399 BCE. King Shenjing of Zhou 周 慎靚王, also named Ji Ding 姬定, 42nd (r. 320-315 BCE), ascended the throne in 320 BCE. It was unlikely to be the same person, as 79 years separated Prince Ding's escape and the year Ji Ding ascended to the throne; alternatively, the entry of 399 BCE was erroneous. The *ZZTJ* is the only text that mentions the prince's flight.

120 Guoshan 虢山 - Shaanxian Henan 河南 陝縣. *ZZTJ JZ* Vol 1, p. 25.

121 Zheng 鄭, the capital of Zheng was Xinzheng 新鄭 - Xinzhengxian Henan 河南 新鄭縣.
Chancellor, *xiang* 相, Master Si Ziyang 史記 駟子陽 (?-398 BCE) was a Zheng elite; he was the son of Duke Mu of Zheng, Ji Lan 鄭穆公 姬蘭, 11th. *ZZTJ JZ* Vol 1, p. 25. Other texts only relate that he was austere and determined; two years later, remnants of Sizi Yang's clique murdered Duke Ru of Zheng 鄭繻公 and made Duke Kang 鄭康公 the head-of-state. See 396-I.

Duke Mu of Lu	魯穆公	13th year
Duke Hui of Qin	秦惠公	3rd year
Duke Ru of Zheng	鄭繻公	26th year
Duke Dao of Song	宋悼公	7th year
King Dao of Chu	楚悼王	5th year
Duke Kang of Qi	齊康公	8th year
Duke Lie of Jin	晉烈公	25th year
Marquis Wen of Wei	魏文侯	50th year
Marquis Lie of Hann	韓烈侯	3rd year
Marquis Wu of Zhao	趙武侯	3rd year
Duke Xi of Yan	燕僖公	6th year
Duke Shen of Wey	衛慎公	18th year

I. There was a solar eclipse.

II. 3rd month. An assassin killed Xia Lei, the chancellor of Hann.[122] Xia Lei was estranged with Yan Zhongzi, a Puyang man.[123] Zhongzi heard that there was a chivalrous man at Zhi by the name of Nie Zheng; [124] he presented one hundred *yi* of gold to his mother as a birthday gift, pleading him to kill Xia Lei to seek revenge.[125] Nie Zheng declined the offer; he said, "My mother is old and needy; I dare not sacrifice myself." Upon the death of his mother, Zhongzi again pleaded Zheng to assassinate Xia Lei. Xia Lei was seated at his manor, which was heavily guarded. Nie Zheng charged up to the uppermost terrace in the audience hall; he stabbed at Xia Lei killing him. Nie Zheng used his knife to disfigure his face, gouged out his eyes and slit his stomach, and his entrails strewn everywhere. The Hann people hauled the remains of the assassin for display at the market, appending a

---

122 Hann chancellor, *xiang*, 韓相 Xia Lei 俠累 (?-397 BCE).
Marquis Lie of Hann 韓烈侯 (r. 399-385 BCE) vested his trust in Xia Lei 俠累; the chancellor of Hann, Yan Zhongzi 嚴仲子 (?) was estranged, feeling threatened he escaped from the fiefdom. In his wandering, he sought the help of Nie Zheng 聶政 to avenge his banishment. The passage was included in the *ZZTJ* as an illustration of chivalry; exemplifying that Nie Zheng was a man of filial piety and that he, refusing the rich gift, was grateful to Yan Zhong for being treated with exceptional respect. Another account claims that the incident happened during the time of Duke Ai of Hann 韓哀侯 (r. 376-371 BCE) or (r. 377-375 BCE) or (r.376-374 BCE) - Nie Zheng is one of the five celebrated assassins mentioned in the *SJ* 史記, 卷 56, 'Ceke liezuan 刺客列傳' 第 26, pp. 704-713. The five assassins were Cao Mo 曹沫 (?) who held Duke Huan of Qi 齊桓公 (?-643 BCE) hostage at knifepoint. Zhuan Zhu 專著 (?-515 BCE) assassinated the king of Wu, Wang Liao 吳王 王僚 with a knife hidden in a fish dish. Yu Rang 豫讓 (see 403 BCE), Nie Zheng 聶政 and Jing Ke's 荆軻 (?-227 BCE) attempted to assassinate the king of Qin, Ying Zheng 秦王 嬴政.

123 Puyang 濮陽 - Huaxian Henan 河南 滑縣.
Yan Zhongzi 嚴仲子, his polite name was Sui 遂 and was a minister at the Hann court.

124 Zhiyi 軹邑 – Jiyuanxian Henan 河南 濟源縣.
Nie Zheng 聶政.

125 *Bai yi* 百溢 - two thousand and four hundred *liang* 两. One *yi* = 24 taels, others maintain it was only 20.

warrant for the identification of the murderer. Nie An, the elder sister of Nie Zheng heard news of the assassination went to the market and identified her brother. [126] She wept over his remains, "He is Nie Zheng from Shenjing Hamlet in the County of Zhi.[127] He maimed himself, as he was afraid lest I would be implicated. I have no concern for death. How dare I cling on to life while allowing the illustrious name of my worthy brother to be hidden in obscurity?" She died beside Zheng's remains.

III. Marquis Wen of Wei died; his son Wei Ji succeeded him, he was known as Marquis Wu. N.B.[128]

---

396 BCE *Yiyou* 乙酉 Warring States 戰國

King An of Zhou	周安王	6th year
Duke Mu of Lu	魯穆公	14th year
Duke Hui of Qin	秦惠公	4th year
Duke Ru of Zheng	鄭繻公	27th year
Duke Dao of Song	宋悼公	8th year
King Dao of Chu	楚悼王	6th year
Duke Kang of Qi	齊康公	9th year
Duke Lie of Jin	晉烈公	26th year
Marquis Wu of Wei	魏武侯	1st year (See F.N.)
Marquis Lie of Hann	韓烈侯	4th year
Marquis Wu of Zhao	趙武侯	4th year
Duke Xi of Yan	燕僖公	7th year
Duke Shen of Wey	衛愼公	19th year

I. The clansmen of Master Si Ziyang, the former chancellor of Zheng, assassinated Duke Ru of Zheng, and made his younger brother Ji Yi as the head of state; he was known posthumously as Duke Kang.[129]

II. Duke Dao of Song died; his son Song Tian succeeded him, he was known posthumously as Duke Xiu.[130]

---

126 Nie An 聶荌, the elder sister of Nie Zheng.

127 Shenjing Hamlet at the county of Zhi (Zhiyi) - 軹邑 深井里.

128 Marquis Wen of Wei 魏文侯 Wei Si 魏斯 1st (r. 446-397 BCE) or (r. 445-396 BCE). Details of his reign see Yang Kuan's 楊寬 textual research.
Marquis Wu of Wei, Wei Ji 魏武侯 魏擊 2nd. It should be either 397 BCE or 396 BCE; the original text made a mistake; it is recorded as 387 BCE.

129 Zheng Chancellor 鄭相 Si Ziyang 駟子陽.
Duke Ru of Zheng 鄭繻公 Ji Yi 姬駘.
Duke Kang of Zheng 鄭康公 Ji Yi 姬乙 (r. 395-378 BCE), he died in 375 BCE.

395 BCE *Bingxu* 丙戌 Warring States 戰國

King An of Zhou	周安王	7th year
Duke Mu of Lu	魯穆公	15th year
Duke Hui of Qin	秦惠公	5th year
Duke Kang of Zheng	鄭康公	1st year
Duke Xiu of Song	宋休公	1st year
King Dao of Chu	楚悼王	7th year
Duke Kang of Qi	齊康公	10th year
Duke Lie of Jin	晉烈公	27th year
Marquis Wu of Wei	魏武侯	2nd year
Marquis Lie of Hann	韓烈侯	5th year
Marquis Wu of Zhao	趙武侯	5th year
Duke Xi of Yan	燕僖公	8th year
Duke Shen of Wey	衛慎公	20th year

There was no record this year.

394 BCE *Dinghai* 丁亥 Warring States 戰國

King An of Zhou	周安王	8th year
Duke Mu of Lu	魯穆公	16th year
Duke Hui of Qin	秦惠公	6th year
Duke Kang of Zheng	鄭康公	2nd year
Duke Xiu of Song	宋休公	2nd year
King Dao of Chu	楚悼王	8th year
Duke Kang of Qi	齊康公	11th year
Duke Lie of Jin	晉烈公	28th year
Marquis Wu of Wei	魏武侯	3rd year
Marquis Lie of Hann	韓烈侯	6th year
Marquis Wu of Zhao	趙武侯	6th year
Duke Xi of Yan	燕僖公	9th year

---

130 Duke Dao of Song 宋悼公 Song Gouyou 宋購由 31st.
The family name of Song was Zi 子. Weizi Qi 微子啟 was enfeoffed at Song, Shangqiuxian Henan 河南 商邱縣. Duke Dao of Song was the 27th generation (31 successions) since the time of Weizi. *ZZTJ JZ* Vol 1, p. 26.
Duke Xiu of Song 宋休公 Song Tian 宋田 32nd (r. 396-373 BCE?) or (r. 395- ? BCE).

Duke Shen of Wey	衛慎公	21st year

I. Qi invaded Lu; Zui was annexed.[131]

II. The people at Fushu revolted; it was returned to Hann.[132]

---

393 BCE *Wuzi* 戊子 Warring States 戰國

King An of Zhou	周安王	9th year
Duke Mu of Lu	魯穆公	17th year
Duke Hui of Qin	秦惠公	7th year
Duke Kang of Zheng	鄭康公	3rd year
Duke Xiu of Song	宋休公	3rd year
King Dao of Chu	楚悼王	9th year
Duke Kang of Qi	齊康公	12th year
Duke Lie of Jin	晉烈公	29th year
Marquis Wu of Wei	魏武侯	4th year
Marquis Lie of Hann	韓烈侯	7th year
Marquis Wu of Zhao	趙武侯	7th year
Duke Xi of Yan	燕僖公	10th year
Duke Shen of Wey	衛慎公	22nd year

I. Wei attacked Zheng.

II. Duke Lie of Jin died; his son, known posthumously as Duke Xiao, succeeded him.[133]

---

392 BCE *Jichou* 己丑 Warring States 戰國

King An of Zhou	周安王	10th year

---

131 Qi 齊 - the capital of Qi was Linzixian Shandong 山東 臨淄縣.
Qi, Duke Jiang - Taigong 姜太公 was enfeoffed at Qi 齊. From Taigong to Duke Kang 康公 the state lasted for 29 generations (32 successions). During the 11th year of Duke Kang, he was banished to an island. The Jiang family clan was annihilated while Tian Chang 田常 assumed control of the Qi state. *ZZTJ JZ,* Vol 1, p. 27. Qi came to be known as Jiang Qi 姜齊 and later Tian Qi 田齊.
Lu 魯 - Qufuxian Shandong 山東 曲阜縣.
Zui 最, place unknown.
Zhou Prince Bo Qin 伯禽 was enfeoffed at Qufu 曲阜縣. 28 generations (30 successions) separated Bo Qin and Duke Mu 魯穆公. *ZZTJ JZ,* Vol 1, p. 27.

132 Fushu 負黍 - Dengfengxian Henan 河南 登封縣. Zheng 鄭 annexed the city in 407 BCE.

133 Duke Lie of Jin 晉烈公 Ji Zhi 姬止, 38th.
Duke Xiao of Jin 晉孝公 Ji Qing 姬傾, 39th (r. 392-378 BCE) or (r. 388-369 BCE).

Duke Mu of Lu	魯穆公	18th year
Duke Hui of Qin	秦惠公	8th year
Duke Kang of Zheng	鄭康公	4th year
Duke Xiu of Song	宋休公	4th year
King Dao of Chu	楚悼王	10th year
Duke Kang of Qi	齊康公	13th year
Duke Xiao of Jin	晉孝公	1st year
Marquis Wu of Wei	魏武侯	5th year
Marquis Lie of Hann	韓烈侯	8th year
Marquis Wu of Zhao	趙武侯	8th year
Duke Xi of Yan	燕僖公	11th year
Duke Shen of Wey	衛慎公	23rd year

There was no record this year.

---

391 BCE *Gengyin* 庚寅 Warring States 戰國

King An of Zhou	周安王	11th year
Duke Mu of Lu	魯穆公	19th year
Duke Hui of Qin	秦惠公	9th year
Duke Kang of Zheng	鄭康公	5th year
Duke Xiu of Song	宋休公	5th year
King Dao of Chu	楚悼王	11th year
Duke Kang of Qi	齊康公	14th year
Duke Xiao of Jin	晉孝公	2nd year
Marquis Wu of Wei	魏武侯	6th year
Marquis of Hann	韓烈侯	9th year
Marquis Wu of Zhao	趙武侯	9th year
Duke Xi of Yan	燕僖公	12th year
Duke Shen of Wey	衛慎公	24th year

I. Qin attacked Hann at Yiyang; [134] six counties were annexed.

II. Before this, Tian Chang fathered Master Xiangzi, Pan; Pan had a son Master Zhuangzi named Bai, Bai begot Grand Duke Tian He.[135] This year, Tian He banished Duke Kang of Qi

134 Yiyang 宜陽 was the capital of Hann. Yiyang 宜陽 - Yiyangxian Henan 河南 宜陽縣. N.B. Hann later moved its capital to Xinzheng 新鄭.

135 Master Chengzi of Qi 齊成子 Tian Heng 田恒 (恆), alias Tian Chang 田常.
Master Xiangzi of Qi 齊襄子 Tian Pan 田盤 (?).

to an island in the sea.[136] The duke was given one walled-city as his provision fief; the proceeds were used to make sacrifices to his ancestors.

390 BCE *Xinmao* 辛卯 Warring States 戰國

King An of Zhou	周安王	12th year
Duke Mu of Lu	魯穆公	20th year
Duke Hui of Qin	秦惠公	10th year
Duke Kang of Zheng	鄭康公	6th year
Duke Xiu of Song	宋休公	6th year
King Dao of Chu	楚悼王	12th year
Duke Kang of Qi	齊康公	15th year
Duke Xiao of Jin	晉孝公	3rd year
Marquis Wu of Wei	魏武侯	7th year
Marquis Lie of Hann	韓烈侯	10th year
Marquis Wu of Zhao	趙武侯	10th year
Duke Xi of Yan	燕僖公	13th year
Duke Shen of Wey	衛慎公	25th year

I. Qin and Jin joined battle at the walled-city of Wucheng.[137]

II. Qi attacked Wei; Xiangyang fell to Qi.[138]

III. Lu defeated Qi forces at Pinglu.[139]

Master Zhuangzi 齊莊子 Tian Bai 田白. There was a Master Tian Dao 田悼 who was the clan leader for six years between Tian Bai and Tian He. After the death of Tian Dao, the Tian family clan split into two branches, one was headed by Tian He, the other branch headed by Tian Sun 田孫, who was executed, Tian Hui 田會 under this branch surrendered to Zhao 趙.

136 Duke Kang of Qi 齊康公 Jiang Dai 姜貸, 32nd Qi sovereign. He was sent into exile on an island or a small city at the eastern seashore.
The capital of Qi 齊, Linzi 臨淄 - Linzixian Shandong 山東 臨淄縣.

137 Jin 晉 – Jin's capital was at Quwoxian Shanxi 山西 曲沃縣.
Wucheng 武城: Hu Sansheng 胡三省 quoting Du Yu 杜預, 'There is a Wangcheng 王城 east of Fengyi Linjinxian 馮翊 臨晉縣, now called Wuxiang 武鄉.' Linjinxian 臨晉縣 is located in Dalixian Shaanxi 陝西 大荔縣. *ZZTJ JZ* Vol 1, p. 28.
It was unlikely to be Jin that entered into battle with Qin, as the state had already been carved up by the three fiefdoms of Wei, Zhao and Hann; it was more likely to be either Wei or Hann, as they were closer to Qin geographically.
Wucheng 武城 – Hengshuishi Shandong 山東 衡水市.

138 Hu Sansheng 胡三省, "The word Yang 陽 should be Ling 陵." *ZZTJ JZ* Vol 1, p. 28.
Xiangling 襄陵 - Linfenxian Shanxi 山西 臨汾縣.

139 Pinglu 平陸 - Wenshangxian Shandong 山東 汶上縣.

389 BCE *Renchen* 壬辰 Warring States 戰國

King An of Zhou	周安王	13th year
Duke Mu of Lu	魯穆公	21st year
Duke Hui of Qin	秦惠公	11th year
Duke Kang of Zheng	鄭康公	7th year
Duke Xiu of Song	宋休公	7th year
King Dao of Chu	楚悼王	13th year
Duke Kang of Qi	齊康公	16th year
Grand Duke of Qi	齊太公	24th year *Taigong*[140]
Duke Xiao of Jin	晉孝公	4th year
Marquis Wu of Wei	魏武侯	8th year
Marquis Lie of Hann	韓烈侯	11th year
Marquis Wu of Zhao	趙武侯	11th year
Duke Xi of Yan	燕僖公	14th year
Duke Shen of Wey	衛慎公	26th year

I. Qin invaded Jin.[141]

II. Tian He of Qi met Marquis Wen of Wei and the emissaries from Chu and Wey at Zuze.[142] Tian He solicited help from the attendees to make him the *de facto* fief lord of Qi. Marquis of Wen of Wei made a request on Tian He's behalf to the king of Zhou and other fief lords.[143] The king approved. (Tian He came to be known as the Grand Duke of Qi, *Taigong*).

---

388 BCE *Guisi* 癸巳 Warring States 戰國

King An of Zhou	周安王	14th year
Duke Mu of Lu	魯穆公	22nd year
Duke Hui of Qin	秦惠公	12th year
Duke Kang of Zheng	鄭康公	8th year
Duke Xiu of Song	宋休公	8th year
King Dao of Chu	楚悼王	14th year

140 Grand Duke of Qi (*Taigong*) 齊太公. The *taigong* 太公 title was given to the founder of a state or a family clan.

141 Most likely to be Wei or Hann, instead of Jin.

142 Qi minister 齊大夫 Tian He 田和, later Grand Duke of Qi (*Taigong*) 齊太公 (r. 413-388 BCE) or (r. 404-385 BCE) or (r. 386-384 BCE).
Wei 魏, Wei Si 魏斯.
Zhuoze Marsh 濁澤 - Linyingxian Henan 河南 臨潁縣.

143 King An of Zhou 周安王 Ji Jiao 姬驕.

Duke Kang of Qi	齊康公	17th year
Grand Duke of Qi	齊太公	25th year *Taigong*
Duke Xiao of Jin	晉孝公	5th year
Marquis Wu of Wei	魏武侯	9th year
Marquis Lie of Hann	韓烈侯	12th year
Marquis Wu of Zhao	趙武侯	12th year
Duke Xi of Yan	燕僖公	15th year
Duke Shen of Wey	衛慎公	27th year

I. There was no record this year.

(N.B. The Grand Duke of Qi *Taigong* died this year; his son Tian Yan succeeded him.[144] The text missed this succession, causing a series of subsequent succession errors.)

---

387 BCE *Jiawu* 甲午 Warring States 戰國

King An of Zhou	周安王	15th year
Duke Mu of Lu	魯穆公	23rd year
Duke Hui of Qin	秦惠公	13th year
Duke Kang of Zheng	鄭康公	9th year
Duke Xiu of Song	宋休公	9th year
King Dao of Chu	楚悼王	15th year
Duke Kang of Qi	齊康公	18th year
Qi Tian Yan	齊田剡	1st year
Duke Xiao of Jin	晉孝公	6th year
Marquis Wu of Wei	魏武侯	10th year
Marquis Lie of Hann	韓烈侯	13th year
Marquis of Zhao	趙武侯	13th year
Duke Xi of Yan	燕僖公	16th year
Duke Shen of Wey	衛慎公	28th year

I. Qin made an expedition against Shu and annexed Nanzheng.[145]

II. Marquis Wen of Wei died; his son Wei Ji, known posthumously as Marquis Wu of Wei, succeeded him.[146] (N.B. This record is erroneous. See 397 BCE.)

---

144 Tian Yan 田剡.

145 Shu 蜀.
Nanzheng 南鄭 - Nanzheng Shaanxi 陝西 南鄭縣.

146 Marquis Wu of Wei 魏武侯 Wei Ji 魏擊.

Marquis Wu was sailing downstream on the Xihe River; at mid-stream, he said to Wu Qi,[147] "What a splendiferous landscape! This site is simply impregnable, truly the national treasure of our Wei state." Wu Qi responded, "The safety of a state is contingent upon the moral character of the sovereign, the topology is of no consequence to the security of a sovereign state. In times of antiquity, the San-Miao tribe was protected by Lake Dongteng to its left and Pengli Lake to its right; [148] when the leader fell into a state of moral decay, King Yu annihilated it.[149] The capital of King Jie of Xia was protected by the Huanghe and Ji rivers to the left, Mount Taihua to the right; to the south, the Yique Pass shielded it, and it was protected by the Slope of Yangchang at the north.[150] Nevertheless, his reign was so corrupted and debauched that King Tang brought him down and banished him. The capital city of King Zhou of Shang was protected by Mengmen to his left; the Taihang Mountain Range to his right, Changshan Mountain to the north and Huanghe River to his south and yet he lost the virtuous path of governance, and King Wu of Zhou executed him.[151] All these instances illustrate that the strategic location of a sovereign state has the least to do with its sanctuary and safety; it is entirely dependent on the moral character of its sovereign. If a sovereign of a state fails to act responsibly and virtuously in the interests of his people, I am afraid each and every one of your trusted retinues onboard this ship might become your archenemy." Marquis Wu responded, "Excellent point."

Wei appointed Tian Wen as the new chancellor. Wu Qi was most unhappy with the arrangement; he asked Tian Wen, "Sir. Shall we discuss our contributions to the state?" Tian Wen answered, "Sure." Wu Qi asked, "I am in charge of the three armies of our state, our soldiers have no qualms dying for our country, and our enemies are intimidated by our military might. How are you compared to me?" Tian Wen answered, "I am not comparable to you, Sir." Wu Qi asked again, "I made our hundred ministers fully

---

147 Wu Qi 吳起. There is a biography on Wu Qi in the *SJ* 史記, 卷 35, 'Sunzi, Wu Qi liezhuan 孫子吳起列傳' 第 5, pp. 397-399.

148 San-Miao 三苗 was an ancient tribal clan that could be traced back as far as 21st century BCE, the legendary tribes of San-Miao migrated to Yunnan 雲南 and western parts of Hunan 湖南 from *Zhongyuan* 中原 after their defeat by King Yu of Xia 夏禹. (The ancient tribes held many independent verbal legendary accounts of their distant past until recent time. Those accounts helped us to verify the accuracy of some of the ancient texts of China written by the Pre-Qin and Han scholars, for example, the legendary accounts of the *Shanhaijing* 山海經, the *Yizhoushu* 逸周書, *Lushi chunqiu* 呂氏春秋, the *Huayanguo zhi* 華陽國志 and others.)
Lake Dongting 洞庭 - Dogtinghu 洞庭湖, Pengli 彭蠡 - Lake Poyanghu 鄱陽湖.

149 King Yu, Yu of Xia, Si Wenming 夏禹 姒文命, the first king of Xia.

150 Xia Jie, Si Lugui 夏桀 姒履癸 was the 17th and last king of Xia.
The capital of Xia 夏 was Anyi 安邑 - Xiaxian Shanxi 山西 夏縣.
East: He 河 - Huanghe River 黄河; Ji - Jishui 濟水 in Shandong 山東 (the river has since become obliterated).
West: Taihua 泰華 - Mount Huashan 華山 - Huayinxian Shaanxi 陕西 華陰縣.
South: Yique Pass 伊闕 - Luoyangxian Henan 河南 洛陽縣.
North: Yangchang 羊腸 - Yangchangban Slope 羊腸阪 – Huguanxian Shanxi 山西 壺關縣.
King Tang of Shang, Zi Tianyi 商湯 子天乙 was the 1st king of Shang.

151 King Zhou of Shang, Zi Shouxin 商紂王 子受辛.
Left: Mengmen 孟門 - Qixian Henan 河南 淇縣. Right: Taihang Mountains 太行山. North: Hengshan Mountain 恒山. South: Huanghe River 黄河.

functional, I bring benignity to our ten thousand civilians and make them settle in peace, and our treasury is full. How are you compared to me?" Tian Wen answered, "I am nowhere close to you, Sir." Wu Qi asked again, "I made defences at the Xihe River; the Qin army abandoned facing us in the east. Hann and Zhao are subservient to us, and how am I compared to you?" Tian Wen answered, "I am not comparable." Wu Qi said, "Based on the three issues I just raised you have admitted that you are nowhere comparable to me, I'd like to know why you are holding a position more senior than me?" Wen answered, "Our sovereign is young; there are powerful ministers and officers at court, besides he has not earned the trust of the civilians. At this critical juncture; do you think the position should belong to you or me?" Wu Qi silently pondered over the issues for long and answered, "It should belong to you."[152]

A long time after this, Chancellor Gongshu, whose wife was a Wei Princess, was uneasy with Wu Qi.[153] A retainer of Gongshu suggested, "It will be quite easy to dispose of Wu Qi. You see the man is far too unyielding, conceited, besides being self-assured. All you have to do is to tell His Highness that, 'Wu Qi is a worthy man. I am afraid; Wei being a small state might not be able to retain him for long. Your Highness may be able to test his loyalty by betrothing a princess to him in marriage. If he is not committed to Wei, he will take leave.' Following this you could then conspire with the princess; instructing her to insults Your Highness when you invite him to a banquet. When Qi realizes that the princess is such an unbridled individual, treating people with total contempt, he would most certainly refuse such a proposition. You plan to oust Qi would work." Gongshu acted accordingly. Wu Qi apologized to the Marquis that he could not accept the proposal. Marquis Wu of Wei began to doubt the fealty of the general. Wu Qi was fearful that he might be executed and escaped to Chu.

King Dao of Chu had long held considerable respect for the capabilities of Wu Qi; [154] he promptly appointed him as chancellor. As soon as Wu Qi took office, he introduced drastic reforms by enforcing austere disciplines and clear legal directives. Officers and Ministers without functioning capacities were dismissed outright; distantly related aristocrats on government payrolls and ration-fiefs had their privileges retracted. The funds saved were used to drill the armed forces, refining their combat capabilities. He dismissed the wandering canvassers who advocated forming alliances. Under Wu Qi, Chu quelled Bai-Yue tribes to the south.[155] To its north, Chu held back the encroachments by the San-Jin of Zhao, Hann and Wei. At the western front, its army made expeditions against Qin. The various fief lords were increasingly apprehensive of the power of Chu, whereas the Chu royal elites and ministers were grudgingly hostile against him.

---

152 It is a very unlikely account, as in 403 BCE, some 16 years ago, Wei Ji was challenging the tutor Master Tian Zifang; Wei Ji 魏擊 (r. 396-371 BCE) would be at least in his 30's by 387 BCE.

153 Wei Chancellor, Gongshu 公叔. Wei 魏 might have more than one chancellor, or, Tian Wen 田文 had at this stage passed on; or perhaps the event happened a few years before this. The chancellor was intimidated by the exceptional abilities of Wu Qi and was most apprehensive lest the general might assume his position at court.

154 King Dao of Chu 楚悼王 Mi Yi 芈疑 17th.

155 Bai-Yue 百越 – Present day Zhejiang and Fujian 浙江 福建.

III. Duke Hui of Qin died; his son Duke Chu succeeded him.[156]

IV. Marquis Wu of Zhao died. The people of Zhao reinstated Prince Zhang the son of Marquis Lie to the throne; he was known posthumously as Marquis Jing.[157]

V. Marquis Lie of Hann died; his son Marquis Wen took over the marquisate.[158]

---

386 BCE *Yiwei* 乙未 Warring States 戰國

King An of Zhou	周安王	16th year
Duke Mu of Lu	魯穆公	24th year
Duke Chu of Qin	秦出公	1st year[159]
Duke Kang of Zheng	鄭康公	10th year
Duke Xiu of Song	宋休公	10th year
King Dao of Chu	楚悼王	16th year
Duke Kang of Qi	齊康公	19th year
Qi Tian Yan	齊田剡	2nd year
Duke Xiao of Jin	晉孝公	7th year
Marquis Wu of Wei	魏武侯	11th year
Marquis Wen of Hann	韓文侯	1st year[160]
Marquis Jing of Zhao	趙敬侯	1st year
Duke Xi of Yan	燕僖公	17th year
Duke Shen of Wey	衛慎公	29th year

I. The king of Zhou decreed to raise Tian He the minister of Qi to the statue of fief lord of Qi.[161] (N.B. This is an erroneous entry as Tian He was already made the fief lord of Qi in 389 BCE.)

II. Prince Chao, a royal family member from Zhao revolted against the state. The prince failed and made a run for his life to Wei, which helped him to lay siege against Handan; the attempt failed.[162]

---

156 Duke Hui of Qin 秦惠公 was the 22nd sovereign of Qin.
Duke Chu of Qin 秦出公 23rd. (r. 386-385 BCE).

157 Marquis Wu of Zhao 趙武侯 2nd.
Marquis Jing 趙敬侯 Zhao Zhang 趙章 3rd (r. 386-375 BCE).

158 Marquis Lie of Hann 韓烈侯 Hann Qu 韓取, 2nd.
Marquis Wen of Hann 韓文侯 3rd (r. 386?-377 BCE?).

159 Duke Chu of Qin 秦出公.

160 Marquis Wen of Hann 韓文侯.

161 King An of Zhou 周安王 Ji Jiao 姬驕.

162 Zhao prince (*gongzi*) 趙公子 Zhao Chao 趙朝.
Handan 邯鄲 – Handanxian Hebei 河北 邯鄲縣.

385 BCE *Bingshen* 丙申 Warring States 戰國

King An of Zhou	周安王	17th year
Duke Mu of Lu	魯穆公	25th year
Duke Chu of Qin	秦出公	2nd year
Duke Kang of Zheng	鄭康公	11th year
Duke Xiu of Song	宋休公	11th year
King Dao of Chu	楚悼王	17th year
Duke Kang of Qi	齊康公	20th year
Qi Tian Yan	齊田剡	3rd year
Duke Xiao of Jin	晉孝公	8th year
Marquis Wu of Wei	魏武侯	12th year
Marquis Wen of Hann	韓文侯	2nd year
Marquis Jing of Zhao	趙敬侯	2nd year
Duke Xi of Yan	燕僖公	18th year
Duke Shen of Wey	衛慎公	30th year

I. A military colonel of Qin instigated a coup against the state; [163] he hailed the return of an elite nobleman Duke Xian in exile west of the River *Hexi* and placed him on the throne.[164] Chuzi of Qin and his mother were captured and drowned in a river.[165]

II. Qi attacked Lu.

III. Hann attacked Zheng and annexed the city of Yangcheng. Hann then made assaults against Song; Duke Xiu of Hann was captured.[166]

IV. The Grand Duke of Qi *Taigong* died; his son Tian Wu, known posthumously as Duke Huan, succeeded him.[167] (N.B. Tian Wu was the grandson of Tian He. The text is mistaken here.)

---

163 Qin Military Colonel, *shuzhang* 庶長. (Details see Appendix 2b - Titles)

164 Hexi 河西 - Middle section of Gansu 甘肅.
Duke Xian of Qin 秦獻公 Ying Shixi 嬴師隰.
In 415 BCE, the 20th sovereign of Qin, Duke Ling of Qin 秦靈公, Ying Su 嬴肅 died; Ying Su's uncle, Ying Daozi 嬴悼子 usurped the dukedom, succeeding him as the 21st sovereign, known as Duke Jian 秦簡公. Ying Shixi 嬴師隰 the son of Ying Su escaped to *Hexi* 河西. In 400 BCE, Dao died and was succeed by his son Duke Hui 秦惠公 as the 22nd sovereign; Hui died in 387 BCE. Duke Chu of Qin 秦出公 succeeded to the throne, two years later he was captured and drowned in a river, he was only a few years old. *SJ* 史記, 卷 23, 'Qin benji 秦本紀' 第 5, pp. 162.

165 Qin Chuzi 出子 was the sovereign of Qin.

166 Yangcheng 陽城 - Goachengxian Dengfengxian Henan 河南 登封縣 告城縣.
Song 宋. Duke Xiu of Song 宋休公 Song Tian 宋田.

384 BCE *Dingyou* 丁酉 Warring States 戰國

King An of Zhou	周安王	18th year
Duke Mu of Lu	魯穆公	26th year
Duke Xian of Qin	秦獻公	1st year
Duke Kang of Zheng	鄭康公	12th year
Duke Xiu of Song	宋休公	12th year
King Dao of Chu	楚悼王	18th year
Duke Kang of Qi	齊康公	21st year
Qi Tian Yan	齊田剡	4th year
Duke Xiao of Jin	晉孝公	9th year
Marquis Wu of Wei	魏武侯	13th year
Marquis Wen of Hann	韓文侯	3rd year
Marquis Jing of Zhao	趙敬侯	3rd year
Duke Xi of Yan	燕僖公	19th year
Duke Shen of Wey	衛慎公	31st year

There was no record this year.

383 BCE *Wuxu* 戊戌 Warring States 戰國

King An of Zhou	周安王	19th year
Duke Mu of Lu	魯穆公	27th year
Duke Xian of Qin	秦獻公	2nd year
Duke Kang of Zheng	鄭康公	13th year
Duke Xiu of Song	宋休公	13th year
King Dao of Chu	楚悼王	19th year
Duke Kang of Qi	齊康公	22nd year
Qi Tian Yan	齊田剡	5th year
Duke Xiao of Jin	晉孝公	10th year
Marquis Wu of Wei	魏武侯	14th year
Marquis Wen of Hann	韓文侯	4th year
Marquis Jing of Zhao	趙敬侯	4th year
Duke Xi of Yan Xi	燕僖公	20th year

[167] Grand Duke of Qi (*Taigong*) 齊太公 Tian He 田和.
Duke Huan of Qi 齊桓公 Tian Wu 田午 (r. 377-359 BCE) or (r.375-357 BCE) or (r. 374-357 BCE).

Duke Shen of Wey	衛愼公	32nd year

1. Wei defeated the Zhao army at Tutai.[168]

---

382 BCE *Jihai* 已亥 Warring States 戰國

King An of Zhou	周安王	20th year
Duke Mu of Lu	魯穆公	28th year
Duke Xian of Qin	秦獻公	3rd year
Duke Kang of Zheng	鄭康公	14th year
Duke Xiu of Song	宋休公	14th year
King Dao of Chu	楚悼王	20th year
Duke Kang of Qi	齊康公	23rd year
Qi Tian Yan	齊田剡	6th year
Duke Xiao of Jin	晉孝公	11th year
Marquis of Wei	魏武侯	15th year
Marquis Wen of Hann	韓文侯	5th year
Marquis Jing of Zhao	趙敬侯	5th year
Duke Xi of Yan	燕僖公	21st year
Duke Shen of Wey	衛愼公	33rd year

1. There was a total solar eclipse.[169]

---

381 BCE *Gengzi* 庚子 Warring States 戰國

King An of Zhou	周安王	21st year
Duke Mu of Lu	魯穆公	29th year
Duke Xiang of Qin	秦獻公	4th year
Duke Kang of Zheng	鄭康公	15th year
Duke Xiu of Song	宋休公	15th year
King Dao of Chu	楚悼王	21st year
Duke Kang of Qi	齊康公	24th year
Qi Tian Yan	齊田剡	7th year
Duke Xiao of Jin	晉孝公	12th year
Marquis Wu of Wei	魏武侯	16th year
Marquis of Hann	韓文侯	6th year

168 Tutai 兔台 - place unknown.

169 The text uses the word *ji* 既 for eclipse; a total eclipse is known as *ji*.

Marquis Jing of Zhao	趙敬侯	6th year
Duke Xi of Yan	燕僖公	22nd year
Duke Shen of Wey	衛慎公	34th year

I. King Dao of Chu died.[170] The royal family clans, nobles, and ministers took advantage of the confusion and attacked Wu Qi. Qi escaped to the funeral hall, prostrating himself against the remains of the deceased king. The rebels shot him with arrows, which also found their marks on the remains of the king. After the interment of the king, King Su acceded to the marquis position.[171] He promptly decreed to execute all the mutineers; over seventy family clans were implicated.

---

380 BCE *Xinchou* 辛丑 Warring States 戰國

King An of Zhou	周安王	22nd year
Duke Mu of Lu	魯穆公	30th year
Duke Xian of Qin	秦獻公	5th year
Duke Kang of Zheng	鄭康公	16th year
Duke Xiu of Song	宋休公	16th year
King Su of Chu	楚肅王	1st year
Duke Kang of Qi	齊康公	25th year
Qi Tian Yan	齊田剡	8th year
Duke Xiao of Jin	晉孝公	13th year
Marquis Wu of Wei	魏武侯	17th year
Marquis Wen of Hann	韓文侯	7th year
Marquis of Zhao	趙敬侯	7th year
Duke Xi of Yan	燕僖公	23rd year
Duke Shen of Wey	衛慎公	35th year

I. Qi attacked Yan, and Sangqiu was annexed.[172]

II. Wei, Hann, Zhao formed an alliance against Qi; the forces penetrated as far as Sangqiu.

---

379 BCE *Renyin* 壬寅 Warring States 戰國

King An of Zhou	周安王	23rd year

170 King Dao of Chu 楚悼王 Mi Yi 芈疑.

171 King Su of Chu 楚肅王 Mi-Xiong Zang 芈熊臧 18th (r. 380-370 BCE) or (380-370 BCE) or (381-370 BCE).

172 Sangqiu 桑丘 - Xushuixian Hebei 河北 徐水縣.

Duke Mu of Lu	魯穆公	31th year
Duke Xian of Qin	秦獻公	6th year
Duke Kang of Zheng	鄭康公	17th year
Duke Xiu of Song	宋休公	17th year
King Su of Chu	楚肅王	2nd year
Duke Kang of Qi	齊康公	26th year
Qi Tian Yan	齊田剡	9th year
Duke Xiao of Jin	晉孝公	14th year
Marquis of Wei	魏武侯	18th year
Marquis Wen of Hann	韓文侯	8th year
Marquis Jing of Zhao	趙敬侯	8th year
Duke Xi of Yan	燕僖公	24th year
Duke Shen of Wey	衛愼公	36th year

I. Zhao raid Wey; [173] the campaign failed.

II. Duke Kang of Qi passed away; he did not leave an heir. The Tian clan took over the Qi state.[174]

III. Duke Huan of Qi also died; his son Yinqi, known posthumously as King Wei succeeded him.[175]

---

378 BCE *Guimao* 癸卯 Warring States 戰國

King An of Zhou	周安王	24th year
Duke Mu of Lu	魯穆公	32nd year
Duke Xian of Qin	秦獻公	7th year
Duke Kang of Zheng	鄭康公	18th year
Duke Xiu of Song	宋休公	18th year
King Su of Chu	楚肅王	3rd year
Qi Tian Yan	齊田剡	10th year
Duke Xiao of Jin	晉孝公	15th year

---

173 Wey 衛 - Puyangxian Hebei 河北 濮陽縣.

174 The Jiang royal house as the sovereign of Qi ended with the death of Duke Kang.
Duke Kang of Qi 齊康公 Jiang Dai 姜貸 32nd. Qi fiefdom reigned by the Jiang clan 姜氏 lasted from 1046 BCE? to 379 BCE.

175 Duke Huan of Qi 齊恒公 Tian Wu 田午.
King Wei of Qi 齊威王 Tian Yinqi 田因齊 (r. 358-320 BCE) or (r. 356-321 BCE) or (r. 356-319 BCE).
N.B. The text is mistaken here, as Tian Wu did not succeed to the marquisate until 377 BCE or 375 BCE.

Marquis Wu of Wei	魏武侯	19th year
Marquis Wen of Hann	韓文侯	9th year
Marquis Jing of Zhao	趙敬侯	9th year
Duke Xi of Yan	燕僖公	25th year
Duke Shen of Wey	衛慎公	37th year

I. The Di tribe defeated the Wei army near at Kuai River.[176]

II. The allied forces of Wei, Hann and Zhao attacked Qi; the armies marched as far as Lingqiu.[177]

III. Duke Xiao of Jin died; his son Jujiu, succeeded to the marquis position, and was known posthumously as Duke Jing.[178]

---

377 BCE *Jiachen* 甲辰 Warring States 戰國

King An of Zhou	周安王	25th year
Duke Mu of Lu	魯穆公	33rd year
Duke Xian of Qin	秦獻公	8th year
Duke Kang of Zheng	鄭康公	19th year
Duke Xiu of Song	宋休公	19th year
King Su of Chu	楚肅王	4th year
Duke Huan of Qi	齊桓公	1st year[179]
Duke Jing of Jin	晉靖公	1st year
Marquis Wu of Wei	魏武侯	20th year
Marquis Wen of Hann	韓文侯	10th year
Marquis Jing of Zhao	趙敬侯	10th year
Duke Xi of Yan	燕僖公	26th year
Duke Shen of Wey	衛慎公	38th year

I. Shu made an expedition against Chu; Zifang was annexed.[180]

II. Zisi recommended Gou Bian to the Marquis of Wey.[181] Zisi said, "He is capable of commanding five hundred chariots into battle." Wey Tui responded, "I am fully cognisant of his

---

176 The Di 狄 tribes settled in the northern part of Shanxi province 山西.
Kuaishan 澮山 - Yichengxian Shanxi 山西 翼城縣.

177 Qi 齊. Lingqiu 靈丘 - Gaotangxian Shandong 山東 高唐縣.

178 Duke Xiao of Jin 晉孝公 Ji Qing 姬傾 (r. 392-378 BCE).
Duke Jing of Jin 晉靖公 Ji Jujiu 姬俱酒 (r. 377-376 BCE?) died in 349 BCE and was the last ruler of Jin.

179 Duke Huan of Qi 齊桓公 (r. 377-359 BCE) or (r. 375-357 BCE) or (r. 374-357 BCE).

180 Zifang 兹方 - Fengjiexian Sichuan 四川 奉節縣.

181 Wey 衛.

skill. But I have my reservations when Bian was a tax collector he pocketed two eggs from a commoner; hence, I will not retain him." Zisi answered, "When it comes to appointing officers, a sage Lord should assume the stance of an expert wood craftsman choosing suitable timber for his crafts: that is to take advantage of the strong points while ignoring the minor shortcomings. A catalpa log with a girth so wide it takes several men to circumvent it, a gifted craftsman would not abandon it as it has some minor flaws of a few feet. Now, Your Highness, your state is engaged in perennial wars; you are in dire need of capable and chivalrous men. However, you are rejecting a most capable general who can defend your cities for two eggs. This absurd reasoning should never be known to our neighbouring states." The Marquis apologized, "I accept your recommendation."

Whenever the Marquis of Wey made an erroneous decision, the ministers at court invariably maintained unanimously that his decision was resolutely correct. Zisi said to Gonqiu Yizi,[182] "According to my observation of Wey, your sovereign does not exhibit the proper comportment of a sovereign, and his subjects do not behave like subjects." Yizi responded, "Why do you say that?" Zisi answered, "When a sovereign of a state is opinionated, his subjects will not proffer their opinions. Even had an issue been handled fittingly, while not taking in the opinions of others - it tantamount to rejecting the opinions of others. To make matter worse, the subjects at court all subscribe to erroneous judgments, promoting iniquitous routine. It is the epitome of befuddlement if one does not attempt to seek the truth, merely craving for praises. Simply paying lip service in expressing loyalty, without due concern for truth, is perhaps the loftiest of all sycophantism. With befuddled sovereign and fawning subjects presiding over the commoners, they will not condone it. When the practice persists, a state is no longer a state."

Zisi said to the Marquis of Wey, "Your Highness's state will face dire consequences." Wey Tui asked, "Why?" Kong Ji answered, "There are reasons. Your Highness is opinionated, your ministers are afraid to proffer correct opinions; furthermore, your ministers are also prejudiced, and the commoners dread offering suggestions. Your Highness and your ministers wholly believe that you are wise, and your subjects and commoners do not have the audacity to suggest amends. People who praise and consent to your views are met with bliss and good fortune, while others making suggestions for improvements are considered as noncompliant, bringing on adversities onto themselves. How could good governance be expedited among your people? The *Book of Odes* says, 'If everyone thinks he is a sage, who could tell the difference between a male and a female crow?'[183] Perhaps this is a most appropriate statement for you and your subjects."

III. Duke Mu of Lu died, his son took over the dukedom, he was known posthumously as Duke Gong of Lu.[184]

Kong Ji 孔伋, alias Zisi 子思 (483-402 BCE) was the grandson of Confucius. This event probably happened many years before this as Zisi died in 402 BCE.

Marquis Shen of Wey, Wey Tui 衛愼公 衛頹.

Gou Bian 苟變 was to become an outstanding general of Wey.

182 Gongqiu Yizi 公丘懿子 was a minister at the Wey court.

183 The *Book of Odes, Shijing* 詩經, Xiaoya, Qifu zhishi, zhengyue 小雅, 祈父之什, 正月, "具曰予聖, 誰知烏之雌雄?"

184 Duke Mu of Lu, Ji Xian 魯穆公 姬顯.

Duke Gong of Lu, Ji Fen 魯共公 姬奮 (r. 376-355 BCE), or (r. 375-353 BCE).

IV. Marquis Wen of Hann died; his son Marquis Ai succeeded him.[185]

---

376 BCE *Yisi* 乙巳 Warring States 戰國

King An of Zhou	周安王	26th year
Duke Gong of Lu	魯共公	1st year
Duke Xian of Qin	秦獻公	9th year
Duke Kang of Zheng	鄭康公	20th year
Duke Xiu of Song	宋休公	20th year
King Su of Chu	楚肅王	5th year
Duke Huan of Qi	齊桓公	2nd year
Duke Jing of Jin	晉靖公	2nd year
Marquis Wu of Wei	魏武侯	21st year
Marquis Ai of Hann	韓哀侯	1st year
Marquis Jing of Zhao	趙敬侯	11th year
Duke Xi of Yan	燕僖公	27th year
Duke Shen of Wey	衛慎公	39th year

I. The King of Zhou died; his son acceded to the throne, he was known posthumously as King Lie.[186]

II. Wei, Hann, and Zhao collaborated; they disposed Duke Jing of Jin, reducing him to the status of a commoner, and went on to partition the Jin territories.[187]

---

375 BCE *Bingwu* 丙午 Warring States 戰國

King Lie of Zhou	周烈王	1st year
Duke Gong of Lu	魯共公	2nd year
Duke Xian of Qin	秦獻公	10th year
Duke Kang of Zheng	鄭康公	21st year
Duke Xiu of Song	宋休公	21st year

---

185 Marquis Wen of Hann 韓文侯 3rd.
Marquis Ai of Hann 韓哀侯 4th (r. 376-371 BCE) or (r. 377-375 BCE) or (r. 376-374 BCE).

186 King An of Zhou 周安王 Ji Jiao 姬驕.
King Lie of Zhou 周烈王 Ji Xi 姬喜 (r. 375-369 BCE).

187 Duke Jing of Jin 晉靖公 Ji Jujiu 姬俱酒.
Xintian 新田 - Quwoxian Shanxi 山西 曲沃縣.
The land owned by the duke was insignificant at this stage; after this, the fiefdom of Jin was completely subjugated. Jin 晉 lasted from 1046 to 376 BCE. *SJ* 史記, 卷 109, Jin shijia 晉世家 第 9, p. 1536.

King Su of Chu	楚肅王	6th year
Duke Huan of Qi	齊桓公	3rd year
Marquis Wu of Wei	魏武侯	22nd year
Marquis Ai of Hann	韓哀侯	2nd year
Marquis Jing of Zhao	趙敬侯	12th year
Duke Xi of Yan	燕僖公	28th year
Duke Shen of Wey	衛慎公	40th year

I. There was a solar eclipse.

II. Hann annihilated Zheng. Hann moved its capital to Zheng.[188]

III. Marquis Jing of Zhao died; his son Zhong, succeeded to the marquisate; he was known posthumously as Marquis Cheng.[189]

---

374 BCE *Dingwei* 丁未 Warring States 戰國

King Lie of Zhou	周烈王	2nd year
Duke Gong of Lu	魯共公	3rd year
Duke Xian of Qin	秦獻公	11th year
Duke Xiu of Song	宋休公	22nd year
King Su of Chu	楚肅王	7th year
Duke Huan of Qi	齊桓公	4th year
Marquis Wu of Wei	魏武侯	23rd year
Marquis Ai of Hann	韓哀侯	3rd year
Marquis Cheng of Zhao	趙成侯	1st year
Duke Xi of Yan	燕僖公	29th year
Duke Shen of Wey	衛慎公	41st year

There was no record this year.

---

373 BCE *Wushen* 戊申 Warring States 戰國

King Lie of Zhou	周烈王	3rd year

188 The capital was moved to Xinzheng 新鄭 from Yangzhai 陽翟.
Xinzheng 新鄭 - Xinzhengxian Henan 河南 新鄭縣.
Zheng 鄭 (806-375 BCE) the state lasted for 432 years.
Yangzhai 陽翟 - Yuxian Henan 河南 禹縣.

189 Marquis Jing of Zhao 趙敬侯 Zhao Zhang 趙章 3rd.
Marquis Cheng of Zhao 趙成侯 Zhao Zhong 趙種 4th (r. 374-350 BCE) or (r. 373-350 BCE).

Duke Gong of Lu	魯共公	4th year
Duke Xian of Qin	秦獻公	12th year
Duke Xiu of Song	宋休公	23rd year
King Su of Chu	楚肅王	8th year
Duke Huan of Qi	齊桓公	5th year
Marquis Wu of Wei	魏武侯	24th year
Marquis Ai of Hann	韓哀侯	4th year
Marquis Cheng of Zhao	趙成侯	2nd year
Duke Xi of Yan	燕僖公	30th year
Duke Shen of Wey	衛慎公	42nd year

I. Yan defeated the army of Qi at Linhu.[190]

II. Lu attacked Qi; the Yangguan Pass was annexed.[191]

III. Wei attacked Qi; the army advanced as far as Boling.[192]

IV. Duke Xi of Yan died; his son, Duke Huan succeeded him.[193]

V. Duke Xiu of Song died; his son Pi succeeded him, he was known posthumously as Duke Pi.[194]

VI. Duke Shen of Wey died; his son Xun succeeded to the dukedom; he was known posthumously as Duke Sheng.[195]

---

372 BCE *Jiyou* 己酉 Warring States 戰國

King Lie of Zhou	周烈王	4th year
Duke Gong of Lu	魯共公	5th year
Duke Xian of Qin	秦獻公	13th year
Duke Pi of Song	宋辟公	1st year
King Su of Chu	楚肅王	9th year
Duke Huan of Qi	齊桓公	6th year
Marquis Wu of Wei	魏武侯	25th year

190 Linhu 林狐 the location is not clear, probably Yanshanxian Hebei 河北 鹽山縣.

191 Yangguan Pass 陽關 - Taianxian Shandong 山東 泰安縣.

192 Boling 博陵 - Bopingxian Shandong 山東 博平縣.

193 Duke Xi of Yan 燕僖公 35th.
Duke Huan of Yan 燕恒公.

194 Duke Xiu of Song 宋休公 Song Tian 宋田.
Duke Pi of Song 宋辟公 Song Pibing 宋辟兵 (r. 372-370 BCE) was the 35th Sovereign of Song.

195 Duke Shen of Wey 衛慎公 Wey Tui 衛頹.
Duke Sheng of Wey 衛聲公 Wey Xun 衛訓 (r. 372-362 BCE).

Marquis Ai of Hann	韓哀侯	5th year
Marquis Cheng of Zhao	趙成侯	3rd year
Duke Huan of Yan	燕桓公	1st year
Duke Sheng of Wey	衛聲公	1st year

I. Zhao attacked Wey and annexed seventy-three cities and villages adjacent to the Wey capital Bi.[196]

II. Wei defeated the Zhao forces at Beilin.[197]

---

371 BCE *Gengxu* 庚戌 Warring States 戰國

King Lie of Zhou	周烈王	5th year
Duke Gong of Lu	魯共公	6th year
Duke Xian of Qin	秦獻公	14th year
Duke Pi of Song	宋辟公	2nd year
King Su of Chu	楚肅王	10th year
Duke Huan of Qi	齊桓公	7th year
Marquis Qu of Wei	魏武侯	26th year
Marquis Ai of Hann	韓哀侯	6th year
Marquis Cheng of Zhao	趙成侯	4th year
Duke Huan of Yan	燕桓公	2nd year
Duke Sheng of Wey	衛聲公	2nd year

I. Wei made an expedition against Chu; Luyang fell to Wei.[198]

II. Yan Sui of Hann committed regicide; he assassinated Marquis Ai of Hann.[199] The nobles nominated the Marquis's son to succeed to the marquisate; he was known posthumously as Marquis Yi.[200] Before this, Marquis Ai appointed Hann Gui as his chancellor, [201] although he trusted Yan Zhu more than the chancellor. The two men hated each other balefully. Yan Sui hired an assassin to murder Hann Gui at court. To avoid the assassin Hann Gui dodged behind the

196 Wey capital *bi* 衛都鄙 – *bi* 鄙 means surrounding counties. Diqiu 帝丘 - Puyangxian Hebei 河北 濮陽縣.

197 Beilin 北藺 (漢藺) - Lishixian Shanxi 山西 離石縣.

198 Luyang 魯陽 - Lushanxian Henan 河南 魯山縣.

199 Hann Minister 韓大夫 Yan Sui 嚴遂.
Marquis Ai of Hann 韓哀侯, 4th Hann sovereign.

200 Marquis Yi of Hann 韓懿侯 Hann Ruoshan 韓若山.

201 Hann Gui 韓廆.

Marquis. The Marquis clasped hold of the chancellor shielding him; the assassin stabbed at the chancellor; Hann Gui and Marquis Ai died.[202]

III. Marquis Wu of Wei died; he did not designate an heir; his son Ying and Gongzhong Huan vied for succession; the fiefdom fell into chaos.[203]

---

370 BCE *Xinhai* 辛亥 Warring States 戰國

King Lie of Zhou	周烈王	6th year
Duke Gong of Lu	魯共公	7th year
Duke Xiang of Qin	秦獻公	15th year
Duke Pi of Song	宋辟公	3rd year
King Su of Chu	楚肅王	11th year
Duke Huan of Qi	齊桓公	8th year
King Hui of Wei	魏惠王	1st year[204]
Marquis Yi of Hann	韓懿侯	1st year[205]
Marquis Cheng of Zhao	趙成侯	5th year
Duke Huan of Yan	燕桓公	3rd year
Duke Sheng of Wey	衛聲公	3rd year

I. King Wei of Qi arrived at the capital of Luoyang to pay homage to King Lie of Zhou.[206] At this time, the kingdom of Zhou was a feeble and paltry state; the fiefdoms and dukedoms no longer pay homage at court. Qi was the only fiefdom to make a homage, the fiefs lords from All under Heaven considered his move most sagacious.[207]

II. Zhao invaded Qi; the army marched as far as Juan.[208]

III. Wei defeated the forces of Zhao at Huai.[209]

---

202 The *ZGC* 戰國策 relates the assassinations of Nie Zheng 聶政 and Aihou 哀侯 as one incident; whereas the *SJ* 史記 relates them as two separate incidents. The accounts in the *ZZTJ* 資治通鑑 are based on the *SJ* 史記.

203 Marquis Wu of Wei 魏武侯 Wei Ji 魏擊.
Wei Ying 魏罃.
Gongzhong Huan 公中緩 Wei Huan 魏緩, the *SJ* 史記 refers to him as 公中緩.

204 Marquis Hui of Wei 魏惠侯 alias 魏惠王; the Marquis changed his title to king, *wang* 王 in 334 BCE (he reigned between 370-319 BCE). See Appendix II, Yang Kuan's 楊寬 textual research.

205 Marquis Yi of Hann 韓懿侯 (r. 370-359 BCE) or according to the *Bamboo annals, Zhushu jinian* 竹書紀年 it was (r. 374-363 BCE).

206 Qi Tian Yinqi 齊 田因.
Luoyang 洛陽.
King Xi of Zhou 周烈王 Ji Xi 姬喜.

207 It appears to be an erroneous entry, as Duke Huan of Qi, the 3rd sovereign of Qi (Tian), was still presiding as the head-of-state.

208 Juancheng 鄄城 - Puxian Shangdong 山東 濮縣.

IV. King Wei of Qi summoned the District Magistrate of Jimo to the capital.[210] He said to the Magistrate, "Ever since you took office at Jimo, I have been receiving disparaging reports against you almost daily. When I dispatched my attendants to make investigations at Jimo, I was told that you were busily cultivating wastelands for agrarian use, and the people are blissful with prosperity. The officers under you are dedicated; the eastern sector of our state is consequently peaceful. As far as I am concerned, the reason you did not receive a more commendable treatment is because you do not seek favours from my attendants." He enfeoffed ten thousand households to the magistrate as his fief. The king then summoned the Magistrate from the District of A (Dong'a) to the capital.[211] He said to him, "Ever since I posted you to the District of A, the accolades and praises for your performance have been incessant by the day. When I sent someone to observe, he found that the fields at your county have withered; the people are poverty-stricken. Previously when Zhao launched an assault against Juan, [212] you did not dispatch an armed force to its rescue. When Wey took Xueling, you were oblivious to what was happening.[213] I have thus concluded that handsome bribes bought all the praises to heap upon you by my aides." On the same day, the king decreed to have the A District magistrate and the ministers that had repeatedly sung praises boiled to stew. The ministers and officers at court were stunned by what had transpired and began to make changes to their work ethics, taking on their tasks and duties earnestly. The state of Qi enjoyed a spell of sound governance and became a powerful state.[214]

V. King Su of Chu died. The king did not leave an heir; his younger brother took over the throne, he was known as King Xuan.[215] VI. Duke Pi of Song died; his son Ticheng succeeded him to the dukedom.[216]

---

369 BCE *Renzi* 壬子 Warring States 戰國

King Lie of Zhou	周烈王	7th year
Duke Gong of Lu	魯共公	8th year
Duke Xian of Qin	秦獻公	16th year
Song Ticheng	宋剔成	1st year[217]
King Xuan of Chu	楚宣王	1st year

---

209 Huaixian 懷縣 - Wuzhixian Henan 河南 武陟縣.

210 Tian Yinqi 田因齊 was the 1st Tian marquis as the head of state of Qi (r. 358-320 BCE) or (r. 356-321 BCE) or (r. 356-320 BCE).
District magistrate of Jimo 即墨大夫.
Linzi 臨淄 - Linzixian Shandong 山東 臨淄縣.

211 A 阿 - A'yi 阿邑 (Dong'a 東阿) - Yangguxian Shandong 山東 陽穀縣.

212 Juancheng 鄄城 - Puxian Shandong 山東 濮縣.

213 Xueling 薛陵 - Yangguxian Shandong 山東 陽穀縣.

214 N.B. Tian Yinqi took over the marquisates in 358 or 356 BCE; hence, this incident is incorrectly appended.

215 King Su of Chu 楚肅王 Mi Zang 芈臧, the 18th sovereign of Chu.
King Xuan of Chu 楚宣王 Mi Liangfu 芈良夫 was the 19th sovereign of Chu (r. 369-340 BCE).

216 Duke Pi of Song 宋辟公 Song Pibing 宋辟兵 was the 33rd sovereign of Song.

217 Song Ticheng 宋剔成 34th (r. 369-329 BCE).

Duke Huan of Qi	齊桓公	9th year
King Hui of Wei	魏惠王	2nd year
Marquis Yi of Hann	韓懿侯	2nd year
Marquis Cheng of Zhao	趙成侯	6th year
Duke Huan of Yan	燕桓公	4th year
Duke Sheng of Wey	衛聲公	4th year

I. There was a solar eclipse.

II. The king died; his younger brother acceded to the throne, he was known posthumously as King Xian.[218]

III. Wang Cuo, a minister at the Wei court, escaped to Hann.[219] Gongsun Qi suggested to Marquis Yi of Hann,[220] "Wei is in chaos. It can be taken easily." Marquis Yi of Hann allied with Marquis Cheng of Zhao; the two armies marched against Wei. At the Zhuoze Marsh, the Wei army was given a resounding thrashing, the allies then laid siege to the capital of Wei.[221] Marquis Cheng suggested, "We should execute Wei Ying and elect Gongzhong Huan as the new Marquis, [222] having ceded some territories between us, we will retreat. It is best for our mutual interest." Marquis Yi said, "No, it will not do. If we were to execute Wei Ying we would be branded as despots, if we ceded their territories, we could earn a reputation for being rapacious. It is a better idea if we partition it into two separate states. Upon being partitioned, it will not be more significant than the states of Song and Wey. After that, we will be relieved of the recurrent pressure exerted upon us by Wei." Marquis Cheng refused to listen. Marquis Yi was enraged; he marched off with his army in the middle of the night. Marquis Cheng of Zhao also marched off to leave. Wei Ying killed Gongzhong Huan and made himself the new marquis; he was King Hui of Wei.

Sima Qian annotates:

King Hui of Wei managed to escape from his predicament unscathed, with his state intact, for a simple reason - the strategies between Hann and Zhao were in variance. Had the two states agreed to either one of the arrangements proposed,

---

218 King Lie of Zhou 周烈王 Ji Xi 姬喜.
King Xian of Zhou 顯王 Ji Bian 姬扁 (r. 368-321 BCE).

219 The internal strife in the Wei state went unabated for three years.
Wei minister, *dafu* 魏國大夫 Wang Cuo 王錯.

220 Gongsun Qi 公孫頎.
Marquis Yi of Hann 韓懿侯 Hann Ruoshan 韓若山.

221 Zhao 趙, Zhao Zhong 趙種 the sovereign of Zhao.
Zhuoze 濁澤 - Jiexian Shanxi 山西 解縣. (The word *ze* 澤 can also be interpreted as a lake.)
Anyi 安邑 - Xiaxian Shanxi 山西 夏縣.

222 Wei Ying 魏罃. King Hui of Wei (Liang) 魏惠王, 梁惠王 (r. 370-319 BCE) or (r. 369-318 BCE). The passage is erroneously appended; it should be 370 BCE when he took over the throne.
Gongzhong Huan 公中緩.

Wei would have been partitioned. It is thus said, "If a soveeign does not leave a will for inherence his state can be vanquished easily.

Volume II. 資治通鑒 卷第二 周紀二 368-321 BCE

The narratives of this volume commence from the first year of King Xian of Zhou, in 368 BCE and end in his 48th year in 321 BCE.[1]

361-359 BCE - Duke Xiao of Qin succeeded to the throne,[2] he was humiliated by the treatment of his state by the other fief lords, and he decided to invite capable people from all over to carry out reforms. Wey Yang responded to his call and made critical changes to Qin,[3] which became the most powerful states.

355 BCE - King Wei of Qi and King Hui of Wei discussed their respective perspectives of national treasuries.[4]

353 BCE - Wei invaded Zhao, the capital city Handan was placed under siege; the army of Qi marched off to the rescue of Zhao; Tian Ji was made the commanding general, and Sun Bin as the strategist. Instead of heading towards Zhao, the Qi army laid siege to Wei, forcing it to retreat from Zhao; the retreating forces were soundly defeated at Guiling.[5]

351 BCE - Shen Buhai was made the chancellor of Hann, and he made reforms to the state;[6] it gathered strength.

341 BCE - Wei attacked Hann, Qi sent Sun Bin to march to the rescue. Sun Bin employed a ruse and defeated Pang Juan at the Maling Gorge; the crown prince of Wei, Shen, was captured; General Pang Juan committed suicide.[7]

340 BCE - Wey Yang led the Qin forces against the Wei army, which was defeated; the king of Wei sued for peace by ceding the areas west of the River *Hexi*.[8]

340 BCE - Wei abandoned its capital at Anyi and moved to Daliang to avoid confrontation with Qin.[9]

340 BCE - Qin enfeoffed Wei Yang with fifteen counties and gave him the title of Lord Shang.[10]

---

1 King Xian of Zhou 周顯王.

2 Duke Xiao of Qin 秦孝公.

3 Wey Yang 衛鞅, alias Gongsun Yang 公孫鞅, Lord Shang Yang 商鞅.

4 King Wei of Qi 齊威王.
King Hui of Wei 魏惠王.

5 Tian Ji 田忌 was the Commanding General of Qi 齊.
Sun Bin 孫臏 was the Strategic Consultant.
Guiling 桂陵.

6 Shen Buhai 申不害 - the Chancellor of Hann 韓.

7 Maling 馬陵.
Crown Prince, Shen of Wei 魏太子 Wei Shen 魏申.
General Pang Juan 龐涓.

8 Wey Yang 衛鞅.
Wei 魏, West of the River - *Hexi* 河西.

9 Wei 魏 moved its capital from Anyi 安邑 to Daliang 大梁.

338 BCE - King Xiao of Qin died, the nobles and elites at Qin took revenge on Wey Yang, and five charging carriages dismembered him.

334 BCE - Chu defeated Yue, annexing the territories that belonged to the defunct kingdom of Wu, [11] the kingdom of Yue became a protectorate of Chu.

333 BCE - Su Qin and Zhang Yi promoted their concepts of forming the South-North Vertical Alliance and East-West Horizontal Coalition.[12]

321 BCE - Lord Mengchang of Qi hosted several thousands of guests at his manor.[13]

Volume II. Zhou Records II 周紀二

---

368 BCE *Guichou* 癸丑 Warring States 戰國

King Xian of Zhou	周顯王	1st year[14]
Duke Gong of Lu	魯共公	9th year
Duke Xian of Qin	秦獻公	17th year
Song Ticheng	宋剔成	2nd year
King Xuan of Chu	楚宣王	2nd year
Duke Huan of Qi	齊桓公	10th year
King Hui of Wei	魏惠王	3rd year
Marquis Yi of Hann	韓懿侯	3rd year
Marquis Cheng of Zhao	趙成侯	7th year
Duke Huan of Yan	燕桓公	5th year
Duke Sheng of Wey	衛聲公	5th year

I. Qi attacked Wei and annexed Guanjin.[15]

II. Zhao invaded Qi, and occupied the Long-Wall.[16]

---

10 Lord Shang 商君.

11 Yue 越, Kingdom of Wu 吳.

12 Su Qin 蘇秦, Zhang Yi 張儀.
Vertical Alliance 合縱 and Horizontal Coalition 連橫.

13 Lord Mengchang of Qi 齊 孟嘗君.

14 King Xian of Zhou 周顯王 Ji Bian 姬扁 (r. 368-321 BCE), 23rd King of Zhou.

15. Guanjin 觀津 - Guanchengxian Shandong 山東 觀城縣.

16. Qi Long-Wall 齊長城. The Qi Long-Wall was built along the bank of Huanghe River; it commenced at Changqingxian 山東 長清縣 then extended south along the River and at Taishan Mountain 泰山 it turned southeast. The Long-Wall in this Qi section extended for several hundred *li* and at the southeast of Linyixian 臨沂縣, the Wall reached the sea. The Long-Wall referred here was probably a walled city along the Long-Wall. *ZZTJ JZ*, Vol 1, p. 44.

367 BCE *Jiayin* 甲寅 Warring States 戰國

King Xian of Zhou	周顯王	2nd year
Duke Gong of Lu	魯共公	10th year
Duke Xian of Qin	秦獻公	18th year
Song Ticheng	宋剔成	3rd year
King Xuan of Chu	楚宣王	3rd year
Duke Huan of Qi	齊桓公	11th year
King Hui of Wei	魏惠王	4th year
Marquis Yi of Hann	韓懿侯	4th year
Marquis Cheng of Zhao	趙成侯	8th year
Duke of Huan of Yan	燕桓公	6th year
Duke Sheng of Wey	衛聲公	6th year

There was no record this year.

366 BCE *Yimao* 乙卯 Warring States 戰國

King Xian of Zhou	周顯王	3rd year
Duke Gong of Lu	魯共公	11th year
Duke Xian of Qin	秦獻公	19th year
Song Ticheng	宋剔成	4th year
King Xuan of Chu	楚宣王	4th year
Duke Huan of Qi	齊桓公	12th year

The phrase of 'The Great Wall of China' is a modern terminology conceived by Western scholars. Chinese have always referred to the Wall as the Long-Wall 長城. Throughout this translation, I have adhered to the conventional term of Long-Wall. Before building of the Long-Wall, fief states during the time of Xia 夏 and Shang 商 built walled cities (polities or *guo* 國) to define the territories they held. The word *guo* 國, a derivative of oracle script, suggests that within the boundaries of the four walls called *wei* - 囗 there is a territory - *yu* 或 owned by a certain fief lord or state. Textual records of building walled cities could be traced as far back as a stanza in the *Book of Odes, Shijing Xiaoya chuju* 詩經 小雅 出車 as it relates, "....The chariots are thundering like war-drums, banners and standards fluttering in the midst. The Son of Heaven decreed to construct walled-forts to defence our north. The majestic General Nan Zhong overwhelmed the invading Xian-Yun at Xiang ...." Nan Zhong was a minister/general at King Wen of Zhou's 周文王 court (r. 1096?-1047 BCE), the king commanded him to take up the defence at Shuofang 朔方, north of the Zhou capital Haocheng 鎬城, notably in the northern regions of Shaanxi 陝西, Gansu 甘肅 and Ningxia 寧夏. 詩經 小雅 鹿鳴之什 出車, "...出車彭彭, 旂旐央央, 天子命我, 城彼朔方, 赫赫南仲, 玁狁于襄...." Yap, J., (2009), *Wars with the Xiongnu*, Bloomington: Author-House, pp. 5-6.
Recent archaeological discoveries show that wall building in China traced back to late Neolithic time.

King Hui of Wei	魏惠王	5th year
Marquis Yi of Hann	韓懿侯	5th year
Marquis Cheng of Zhao	趙成侯	9th year
Duke Huan of Yan	燕桓公	7th year
Duke Sheng of Wey	衛聲公	7th year

I. Wei and Hann met at Zhaiyang.[17]

II. Qin defeated the allied forces of Wei and Hann at Luoyang.[18]

---

365 BCE *Bingchen* 丙辰 Warring States 戰國

King Xian of Zhou	周顯王	4th year
Duke Gong of Lu	魯共公	12th year
Duke Xian of Qin	秦獻公	20th year
Song Ticheng	宋剔成	5th year
King Xuan of Chu	楚宣王	5th year
Duke Huan of Qi	齊桓公	13th year
King Hui of Wei	魏惠王	6th year
Marquis Yi of Hann	韓懿侯	6th year
Marquis Cheng of Zhao	趙成侯	10th year
Duke of Huan of Yan	燕桓公	8th year
Duke of Sheng Wey	衛聲公	8th year

I. Wei made an expedition against Song.[19]

---

364 BCE *Dingsi* 丁巳 Warring States 戰國

King Xian of Zhou	周顯王	5th year
Duke Gong of Lu	魯共公	13th year
Duke Xian of Qin	秦獻公	21st year
Song Ticheng	宋剔成	6th year

---

17 Zhaiyang 宅陽 - Yingyang Henan 河南 滎陽縣.

18 Luoyang 洛陽 – The Luoyang referred here means the general areas north of Luoshui River 洛水. Present day – Dengcheng, Xiayang, Luochuan counties in Shaanxi 陝西 澄城 郃陽 洛川地區, this is not to be confused with Luoyang 洛陽 in Henan 河南. *ZZTJ JZ*, Vol 1, p. 44.

19 Song 宋 - Shangqiuxian Henan 河南 商丘縣.
N.B. The sovereign of Song, Lord Song Tijun 宋剔君, Dai Ticheng 戴剔成, did not have a posthumous title as he died in exile. Duke Huan of Song 宋桓公 was wantonly depraved; Lord Song Tijun 宋剔君 usurped the throne. *SJ* 史記, 卷 108, 'Song Weizi shijia 宋微子世家' 第 8, p. 1506.

King Xuan of Chu	楚宣王	6th year
Duke of Qi	齊桓公	14th year
King of Wei	魏惠王	7th year
Marquis of Hann	韓懿侯	7th year
Marquis of Zhao	趙成侯	11th year
Duke Huan of Yan	燕桓公	9th year
Duke of Wey	衛聲公	9th year

1. Duke Xian of Qin defeated the allied San-Jin forces of Hann, Wei, and Zhao at Shimen;[20] some sixty thousand soldiers were decapitated. The king Zhou bestowed an official trapping called *fufu zhifu* upon the duke.[21]

---

363 BCE *Wuwu* 戊午 Warring States 戰國

King Xian of Zhou	周顯王	6th year
Duke Gong of Lu	魯共公	14th year
Duke Xian of Qin	秦獻公	22nd year
Song Ticheng	宋剔成	7th year
King Xuan of Chu	楚宣王	7th year
Duke Huan of Qi	齊桓公	15th year
King Hui of Wei	魏惠王	8th year
Marquis Yi of Hann	韓懿侯	8th year
Marquis Cheng of Zhao	趙成侯	12th year
Duke Huan of Yan	燕桓公	10th year
Duke Sheng of Wey	衛聲公	10th year

There was no record this year.

---

20 Duke Xian of Qin 秦獻公 Ying Shixi 嬴師隰.

Shimen 石門 - Sanyuanxian Shaanxi 陝西 三原縣. N.B. The battle took place within the territories of Qin; it implied that the allied forces were the invaders.

It was unlikely that the San-Jin 三晉 could take on Qin in unison. According to the *SJ* 史記 'Qin benji 秦本紀', during the 21st year of Duke Xian of Qin 秦獻公 (King Xian of Zhou 5th year), "(Qin) joined battle with Jin at Shimen 石門." At this stage, the three fief lords had already partitioned Jin. It is suspected that when Sima Guang was compiling the *ZZTJ*, he could not positively identify which of the states battled with Qin. Hence, he generalized it as San-Jin. *ZZTJ JZ*, Vol 1, p. 45.

21 King Xian of Zhou 周顯王 Ji Bian 姬扁.

The official trapping 黻黼之服 *fufu zhifu*. The official trapping was embroidered with white, black and green floral motifs, and was also adorned with halberd designs and with two 'e' shaped patterns - back to back. The text does not explain why the Son of Heaven bestowed him with an official trapping. *ZZTJ JZ*, Vol 1, p. 45.

362 BCE *Jiwei* 己未 Warring States 戰國

King Xian of Zhou	周顯王	7th year
Duke Gong of Lu	魯共公	15th year
Duke Xiang of Qin	秦獻公	23rd year
Song Ticheng	宋剔成	8th year
King Xuan of Chu	楚宣王	8th year
Duke Huan of Qi	齊桓公	16th year
King Hui of Wei	魏惠王	9th year
Marquis Yi of Hann	韓懿侯	9th year
Marquis Cheng of Zhao	趙成侯	13th year
Duke Huan of Yan	燕桓公	11th year
Duke Sheng of Wey	衛聲公	11th year

I. Wei defeated the combined forces of Hann and Zhao near the Huishui River.[22]

II. Qin and Wei joined battle at Shaoliang; the Wei forces were completely overwhelmed; the Commanding General Gongsun Cuo was captured.[23]

III. Duke Sheng of Wey died; his son succeeded the dukedom, he was known posthumously as Marquis Cheng.[24]

IV. Duke Huan of Yan died, his son Duke Wen succeeded him.[25]

V. Duke Xian of Qin died; his son succeeded to the dukedom, he was known posthumously as Duke Xiao. Duke Xiao was twenty-one years old.[26]

At this time, to the east beyond the River and the Mountain, there were six powerful states: Qi, Hann, Zhao, Wei, Yan and Chu, whereas there were more than ten minor polities between Huai River and Sishui River.[27] Chu and Wei adjoined borders with Qin. Wei built sections to the Long-Walls from

---

22 Huishui River 澮水 - the river flowed past Yichengxian Shanxi 山西 翼城縣. It is difficult to identify the exact location without providing a place name. *ZZTJ JZ*, Vol 1, p. 46.

23 Shaoliang 少梁 – south of Hannchengxian Shaanxi 陝西 韓城縣.
Gongsun Cuo 公孫痤, also known as Gongsun Cuo 公孫痤. (See 361-I)

24 Duke Sheng of Wey 衛聲公 Wey Xun 衛訓, 42nd.
Marquis Cheng of Wey 成侯 Wey Su 衛速, 43rd (r. 361-333 BCE) or (r. 361-343 BCE).

25 Duke Huan of Yan 燕桓公, 36th.
Duke Wen of Yan 燕文公, 37th (r. 361-333 BCE) or (r. 362-333 BCE).

26 Duke Xian of Qin 秦獻公 Ying Shixi 嬴師隰, 24th.
Duke Xiao of Qin 秦孝公 Ying Quliang 嬴渠梁, 25th (361-338 BCE).

27 He 河 - Huanghe 黄河.
N.B. *He* – the word *he* 河 used by itself was an exclusive abbreviation of Huanghe – the Yellow River, no other river was to bear the honour of *he*, while the word *jiang* 江 – an abbreviation of Changjiang was not exclusively used to denote Changjiang.
The Mountain was Xiaoshan 崤山 – Henan 河南 (see author's notes below).

Zheng along the north bank of Luohe River through to the Shangjun Prefecture.[28] Extending from the area of Hanzhong Chu occupied Ba and Qianzhong in the south.[29] The feudal lords regarded Qin no different from the Yi or Di barbaric tribes and excluded it from attending the meetings and alliances in Zhongguo.[30] Duke Xiao of Qin was determined to make rectifications and reforms to strengthen his state.[31]

---

361 BCE *Gengshen* 庚申 Warring States 戰國

King Xian of Zhou	周顯王	8th year
Duke Gong of Lu	魯共公	16th year
Duke Xiao of Qin	秦孝公	1st year
Song Ticheng	宋剔成	9th year

Huaihe River 淮河.
Sishui River 泗水.
The larger polities in this region at this stage were – Zhongshan 中山, Song 宋, Lu 魯, Teng 滕, Xue 薛, Zuo 鄒 (Xiaozhu 小邾), Ju 莒, Wey 衛, Huaiyi 淮夷 and Hua 滑. *ZZTJ JZ*, Vol 1, p. 46.
N.B. *ZZTJ JZ*, Vol 1, p. 46 – It is noted that the 'shan 山 – Mountain' referred to is Taihangshan 太行山; and most authorities have referred to it as Taihangshan. However, the author contends that It is an erroneous assumption, as the Taihangshan Mountain range is situated between Shanxi 山西 and Hebei 河北; and it is more likely to be Xiaoshan 崤山. The Xiaoshan is a mountain range that runs from the west to the east in the westernmost part of Henan. North of Xiaoshan was the ancient Pass of Hangu 函谷關 (present day Lingbao 靈寶縣). Huanghe River after circumventing the grand Ordos Loop flows south and at Fenglingdu 風陵渡 it turns east and continues to flow east; Fenglingdu is only about 50 km northeast of Lingbao. The text states that east of the He (River) and Mountain there were six powerful states. Hence, this author maintains that the 'Mountain' referred to in the text was the Xiaoshan mountain range in Henan 河南. Furthermore, there were only two states east of Taihang Mountain, that of Qi and Yan. *Zhonghua Renmin gongheguo fensheng dituji* 中華人民共和國分省地圖集 地圖出版社, China, 1974, pp. 河北 13-4, 山西 17-18 and 河南 p. 69.

28 The Long-Walls were built to prevent the incursions by Qin.
Zhengxian 鄭縣 - *Huaxian Shaanxi* 陝西 華縣.
Luoshui River 洛水. N.B. This is the North Luo River, as there are two Luoshui rivers; the north Luoshui is north of Weihe River 渭河 and the other one is situated to the south of Weihe. They are two separate river systems and are not connected. *Zhonghua Renmin gongheguo fensheng dituji* 中華人民共和國分省地圖集, *Ditu chubanshe* 地圖出版社, China, 1974, 河南 洛河, pp. 69-70, 陝西 洛河 pp. 93-94.
Shangjun Prefecture 上郡 - Suidexian Shaanxi 陝西 綏德縣.

29 Hanzhong 漢中 - Nanzhengxian Shaanxi 陝西 南鄭縣.
Bacheng 巴城 - Chongqing City 重慶市.
Qianzhong 黔中 - Yuanlingxian Hunan 湖南 沅陵縣.

30 Yi 夷, Di 翟 (狄) both terms are generic names of the nomadic tribes to the north and west of Zhongyuan 中原. The word Di 翟 is pronounced as *zhai* when used as a family name.
The term '*Zhongguo* 中國' used in the text refers to the fief states that were situated in Zhongyuan 中原, the heartland of China. Qin was situated to the westernmost of *Zhongyuan* and was not considered one of the civilized states at the time of early Zhanguo 戰國.

31 Duke Xiao of Qin 秦孝公.

King Xuan of Chu	楚宣王	9th year
Duke Huan of Qi	齊桓公	17th year
King Hui of Wei	魏惠王	10th year
Marquis Yi of Hann	韓懿侯	10th year
Marquis Cheng of Zhao	趙成侯	14th year
Duke Wen of Yan	燕文公	1st year
Marquis Cheng of Wey	衛成侯	1st year

1. Duke Xiao issued a decree to his subjects, "Our former sovereign Duke Mu promoted virtues and made great military exploits, he made immense progress in the region between Qishan Mountain and Yongshui River.[32] To the east, he quelled the unrests in Jin;[33] he redefined our border at the Huanghe River;[34] to the west, he subjugated the Rong and Di barbaric tribes,[35] and our realm expanded by one thousand *li*. The Son-of-Heaven made him a grand duke, all the fief lords came forth to honour him, and he had laid down the splendid foundation of our state. Regrettably, he was succeeded by Dukes Li, Zao and Jian, and the turbulent period under Chuzi followed.[36] During which stage, our state fell into internal strife; the dukes neglected our foreign

---

32 Duke Xiao of Qin 秦孝公 Ying Quliang 嬴渠梁 (r. 361-338 BCE).
Duke Mu of Qin 秦穆公 Ying Renhao 嬴任好 9th (r. 659-621 BCE).
Duke Mu annihilated 14 states, expanded Qin by over 1000 *li*; he was named as one of the hegemons during the Chunqiu era 春秋.
Qishan Mountain 岐山 - Qishanxian Shaanxi 陝西 岐山縣.
Yongshui River 雍水 - Fengxiangxian Shaanxi 陝西 鳳翔縣.

33 Duke Mu 秦穆公 married the daughter of Duke Xian of Jin 晉獻公. When Duke Xian died, his son Xiqi 奚齊 (r. 651 BCE) ascended to the throne. Minister of Jin, Li Ke 里克 executed Xiqi after a few days, Zhuozi 卓子 the elder brother of Xiqi, was then placed on the throne; Li Ke again executed him (r. 651 BCE). Duke Mu of Qin sent Yiwu 夷吾, the son of Duke Xian, to return to Jin accompanied by Qin's army; Yiwu ascended to the throne, he was Duke Hui of Jin 晉惠公 (r. 650-637 BCE). Upon Hui's death, his son Yu 圉 ascended to the throne, known as Duke Huai 懷公 (r. 637 BCE). The duke was despotic, Duke Mu of Qin then sent 重耳 the son of Duke Xian to return to Jin, he was Duke Wen of Jin 晉文公 (r. 636-628 BCE). The unrest at Jin came to a head. *ZZTJ JZ*, Vol 1, p. 48; and *SJ* 史記, 卷 23, 'Qin benji 秦本紀' 第 5, pp. 157-160.

34 He redefined the border with Jin.

35 西霸戎翟 Duke Mu made an expedition to Qin's west, and he took 12 polities; Qin became the hegemon of Western Rong Xirong 西戎. *ZZTJ JZ* Vol 1, p. 48.

36 Duke Li of Qin 秦厲公, 17th (r. 476-443 BCE). *ZG LS ND JB.*
Duke Zao of Qin 秦躁公, 18th (r. 442-429 BCE). *ZG LS ND JB.*
Duke Jian of Qin 秦簡公, 21st (r. 414-400 BCE). *ZG LS ND JB.*
Duke Chu (Chuzi) of Qin 秦出子, 23rd (r. 386-385 BCE). *ZG LS ND JB.*
Duke Ligong 厲共公 or Duke Li 厲公 (r. 476-443 BCE) was the 10th generation grandson of Duke Mu 穆公 (r. 659-621 BCE), he was on the throne for 34 years. He made an expedition against Yiqu 義渠, annexed Dali 大荔 and attacked Buning 不寧. Duke Zao 躁公 (r. 442-429 BCE) was the son of Duke Li 厲共公; he was on the throne for 14 years. Under him, Nanzheng 南鄭 revolted and Yiqu 義渠 invaded Qin 秦. Duke Jian 簡公 (r. 414-400 BCE) was the son of Duke Huai 懷公 (r. 428-425 BCE), the younger brother of Duke Zao 躁公. When Duke Zao died, his younger brother Duke Huai succeeded. When Duke Huai died, his grandson Duke Ling 靈公 (r. 424-415 BCE)

policies. The San-Jin states of Hann, Zhao and Wei invaded and occupied areas west of the river *Hexi* that belonged to our forebears.[37] It was intensely humiliating. When Duke Xian succeeded to the throne, he pacified the borders and moved the capital to Yueyang.[38] He had intended to make an expedition to the east, hopeful that he would regain the lost territories of Duke Mu; [39] in the meanwhile, he restored the political stance of the former Duke. It brings a pang of pain to my heart whenever I reflect upon the former king's aspiration.[40] Now, I decree to solicit a wise person among my guests and ministers gifted with exceptional strategies to enhance the power of Qin. I intend to designate him as senior minister at my court and impart upon him fief estates as rewards."

Gongsun Yang of Wey heard of the proclamation travelled west to Qin.[41]

Gongsun Yang was a grandson of a Wey ducal (a son by a concubine).[42] He was fond of learning legal disciplines and regulations and served as a functionary under Chancellor Gongshu Cuo of Wei. [43] Cuo appreciated his aptitudes and was about to recommend him to the king of Wei,[44] however, he took ill.

---

succeeded him. After the death of Duke Ling, his son Duke Xian 獻公 did not succeed to the throne, it was passed to Duke Jian 簡公. Qin Chuzi 秦出子 (r. 386-385 BCE) was the grandson of Duke Jian. When Duke Jian died, his son Duke Hui 惠公 succeeded him. Chuzi succeeded Duke Hui. Minister Zhao 黽庶長 killed Chuzi and returned the throne to Duke Xian 獻公 (r. 384-362 BCE). *ZZTJ JZ,* Vol 1, p. 49. Dates are from *ZG LS ND JB.*

(N.B. This Chuzi is not to be confused with another Qin Chuzi 秦出子 who reigned between 703 and 698 BCE.)

37 *Hexi* 河西地 – the area west of Huanghe River 黄河. The area north of Huaxian Shaanxi 陕西 華縣 to Hanncheng 韓城 was referred to as Jin's *Hexi* River–West area 晉 河西. It was an area heavily contested between Qin and Jin 晉. *ZZTJ JZ,* Vol 1, p. 49.

38 Yueyang 櫟陽 - 70 km northeast of Lintongxian Shaanxi 陝西 臨潼縣.

39 During the reign of Duke Mu, Qin's territories extended to Huanghe to the east and encompassed area as far east as Yishixian 猗氏縣 in Shanxi 山西. *ZZTJ JZ,* Vol 1, p. 49.

40 Duke Xian died before he could carry out his aspiration.

41 Wey 衛.

42 Wey Yang 衛鞅, Gongsun Yang 公孫鞅, alias Shang Yang 商鞅 (395-338 BCE). The text says, "衛之庶孫也", which means he was the grandson of a concubine of a Wey noble.

"商君者, 衛之諸庶孽公子也, 名鞅, 姓公孫氏, 其祖本姬姓也." *SJ* 史記, 卷 38, 'Shangjun liezhuan 商君列傳' 第 8, p. 441.

According to Liu Yuanfu 劉原夫, a Song scholar, "His (Shang Yang) father was a Wey noble with a title of prince 公子; his grandfather was head of state, known as Gongsun 公孫." At that stage, the sovereign of Wey was Duke Sheng 衛聲公, (r. 382-372 BCE), son of Duke Shen 衛慎公 (r. 414-383 BCE), it does not appear that he was the grandson of Duke Sheng; he was probably from a minor royal family household. Yang B., *ZZTJ B.Y. Edition,* Vol 1, p 103.

43 *Xingming zhixue* 刑名之學 - Legalism, criminal law.

Wey Yang was from Wey 衛 and was serving at Wei 魏.

Gongshu Cuo 公叔痤, this was the same Wei general who was captured by Zhao in 362 the year before this, except he was called Gongsun Cuo 公孫痤.

Zhongshuzi 中庶子 was the title of a junior attendant.

44 King Hui of Wei 魏惠王 Wei Ying 魏罃. N.B. At this stage, Wei Ying had yet to proclaim himself king. However the text refers to him as king; hence, this incident probably happened a few years before 361 BCE. Yang B., *ZZTJ B.Y. Edition.* p. 103.

King Hui of Wei paid Gongshu Cuo a visit; he asked, "Sir if something untoward might happen with your illness, who I should seek advice to take care of our holy shrine?"[45] Gongshu responded, "My junior assistant *zhongshuzi* Wey Yang is most capable; while he might still be quite young. Nevertheless, he has exceptional capabilities. Your Highness might consider entrusting your kingdom to him." The king was dumbfounded. Gongshu added, "If Your Highness can't use the man you have to dispatch him immediately, do not even allow him to leave our kingdom." The king agreed that he would attend to it and left. Gongshu Cuo summoned Wei Yang to his side and apologized, "I have to serve the interest of our king before looking after your interest. I recommended His Highness to employ you. I also told him to execute you if he could not use you. Now, run for your life." Gongsun Yang answered, "His Highness did not heed your advice to employ your subject; do you expect him to listen to your suggestion of executing him?" He stayed.

Upon departing from the chancellor's manor the king said to his aides, "Gongshu is critically ill, how sad! He asked me to engage Gongsun Yang to attend to my national affairs, and then he told me to have him executed. Did he not contradict himself?"

When Wey Yang arrived at Qin, he arranged through a trusted minion *bichen* Jing Jian to have an audience with Duke Xiao, [46] to whom he presented strategies to make reforms to make Qin a powerful state and to strengthen its military might. The duke was delighted and discussed with him on the national affairs.

---

360 BCE *Xinyou* 辛酉 Warring States 戰國

King Xian of Zhou	周顯王	9th year
Duke Gong of Lu	魯共公	17th year
Duke Xiao of Qin	秦孝公	2nd year
Song Ticheng	宋剔成	10th year
King Xuan of Chu	楚宣王	10th year
Duke Huan of Qi	齊桓公	18th year
King Hui of Wei	魏惠王	11th year
Marquis Yi of Hann	韓懿侯	11th year
Marquis Cheng of Zhao	趙成侯	15th year
Duke Wen of Yan	燕文公	2nd year
Marquis Cheng of Wey	衛成侯	2nd year

There were no records this year.

---

45 Meaning – 'to administer the state'.

46 *Bichen* – minion 嬖臣 Jing Jian 景監.

359 BCE *Renxu* 壬戌 Warring States 戰國

King Xian of Zhou	周顯王	10th year
Duke Gong of Lu	魯共公	18th year
Duke Xiao of Qin	秦孝公	3rd year
Song Ticheng	宋剔成	11th year
King Xuan of Chu	楚宣王	11th year
Duke Huan of Qi	齊桓公	19th year
King Hui of Wei	魏惠王	12th year
Marquis Yi of Hann	韓懿侯	12th year
Marquis Cheng of Zhao	趙成侯	16th year
Duke Wen of Yan	燕文公	3rd year
Marquis Cheng of Wey	衛成侯	3rd year

1. Wey Yang made plans to reform the state; [47] the people of Qin were unhappy with the proposed changes. Yang said to Duke Xiao of Qin, "One seeks not the opinions of the commoners

47 *Ying Quliang* 嬴渠梁.

Historians have considered the reformation at Qin by Shang Yang's 商鞅 a most significant event during the Warring States epoch. The *ZZTJ* is somewhat brief in its accounts of Shang Yang's reform. There were two instances of major reforms; the first took place in 356 BCE and the second in 350 BCE. Having secured the trust of Duke Xiao, Ying Quliang 秦孝公嬴渠梁, Shang Yang proceeded to make drastic reforms to Qin administrative institutions. He rewarded those meritorious in farming and battle. The purpose was to strengthen the rule of the monarchy. Land ownership was revoked. He promoted farm production by carrying out a policy of elevating the importance of agrarian activities while denouncing the significance of commerce, as he considered merchants and traders non-productive entities of a state, as merchants and traders were becoming increasingly powerful and influential during the latter part of the Warring States. Finally, he decreed that land could not be traded freely. Measures were adopted to ensure maximum utilization of the labour force for agricultural production. Families with two or more males living in the same household were required to pay twice as much tax as a household with a single male. Families harvesting more grain or producing more silk were exempt from corvée while merchants and the indolent were condemned to slavery along with their wives and children. He went on to abolish the customary privileges of the aristocrats and introduced twenty ranks of honour based on merit and contributions to the state. (For a listing of the 20 ranks see appendix 2b - Titles). Social hierarchy was clearly defined, and a person with particular rank was entitled to an appropriate amount of properties, estates, retainers, concubines and wearing certain trappings. Nobles who did not distinguish themselves on the battlefield would have their names removed from the royal roster while those who distinguished themselves were rewarded accordingly. To enforce an autocratic political system he grouped all villages and towns of the state into 30 to 40 prefectures - *jun* 郡 to be governed by magistrates and their deputies, supported by military commanders. These officers were appointed or de-commissioned by the sovereign himself. He then divided the households into groups of ten; each household was responsible for keeping watch over the behaviour of their immediate neighbours. Those failing to report an unlawful act by their neighbours were chopped in half at the waist. Furthermore, for those who complied they were rewarded as if they had cut down an enemy in battle. Shang Yang also standardized weights and measurements for Qin. Yang K. 楊寬, *ZGS*, 戰國史, pp. 200-212.

Zhao Y. 趙毅 and Zhao Y. F. 趙軼峰, *Zhongguo gudai shi* 中國古代史, (2002), China, Gaodeng jiaoyu chuban she, 高等教育出版社, China, pp. 199-200.

when making preliminary decisions; one can only share with them the fruits of success. A person endowed with exceptional virtue does not subscribe to mundane reckonings and an individual destined to achieve exceptional exploits does not seek the opinions of the masses. That is why only the sages were capable of making their kingdoms powerful, as they were not bound by rigid conventions." Gan Long said,[48] "I disagree. Governance with established regulations promotes peace and accord as the officers and functionaries are acquainted with them." Wey Yang said, "Mundane people are contented with routines, whereas scholars are constrained by their pedantic erudition. These men are more than adequate to administer conventional practices; however, one ought not to consult them on decisions beyond established practices. A sage makes radical changes to instituted practices while the ill-informed people proscribe them. The wise makes changes to the ethical codes of *li,* while the unworthy clings on doggedly to conventional practices." The duke said, "Excellent." He made Wey Yang the Left Colonel *zuoshuzhang* and decreed to make reforms to his state.[49]

The people of the state were reorganized into units of ten-household called *shi* or five-household called *wu.* Each household was to keep close surveillance on the other households within each unit. Informants on wrongdoers were rewarded no differently than the soldiers who cut off enemy heads at the front. People who concealed unlawful activities were treated as deserters. Soldiers were rewarded according to their merits. People who fought amongst themselves were punished according to the seriousness of their charges. Civilians were encouraged to work industriously at their occupations. Farmers who produced more grains and clothes than their allotment were exempted from paying taxes and serving corvee. Merchants who made earnings through trading, indolent individuals and people fell into impoverishment had their wives incarcerated and sold into slavery. The elites not meritorious in battle were hence eliminated from the elite roster. The status of the enfeoffed marquises and ministers were organized by their rankings, and by their seniority, they were assigned with proportional fief-land, manors, number of attendants, concubines and trappings. People who made meritorious contributions to the state were rewarded with honour accordingly, whereas even with the elites and wealthy families who did not contribute to the state were slighted and could not attain prominence.

When the proposed reforms were written and yet to be decreed, Wey Yang was concerned that the people might not accede to it. He erected a three *jiang* pole at the south gate of the capital city and invited civilians to move the pole to the north gate, declaring that the person would be rewarded with ten units of gold.[50] The civilians found the proposition most

---

The reform of Shang Yang lasted for more than twenty-one years; it greatly enhanced the position of Qin. The kingdom started off as a meagre and paltry state to the northwest of *Zhongguo* was to become a powerful kingdom after Shang Yang's death. The reform is considered a cornerstone in Qin's final push for hegemony in *Zhongguo* one hundred and thirty years later. The Qin state principally adopted the measures Shang Yang introduced until the founding of the Qin Empire.

Zhou G.C. 周谷城 *Zhongguo tongshi* 中國通史, (2001) 22nd edition. Shangmu 商務印書館, China, pp. 148-151.

Wang S.L 王士立 and Sun K. Q. 孫開秦 (ed.), *Zhongguo gudai shi* (Vol 1), 中國古代史 上册 (2001), pp. 138-141.

48 Gan Long 甘龍 was a senior minister at the Qin court.

49 Left Colonel, *zuoshuzhang* 左庶長. There were twenty grades of enfeoffment at Qin, *zuoshuzhang* was the 10th grade. *ZZTJ JZ,* Vol 1, p. 52. See Appendix 2b.

50 The capital of Qin 秦 was Yueyang 櫟陽 at this stage.

preposterous; no one dared to move it. He hence said, "A person who can move the pole will be rewarded by fifty units of gold." Someone moved the pole to the north gate and was rewarded accordingly with fifty units of gold. He then decreed to set the reform in motion.

The decree was enforced for one year, thousands of Qin civilians converged at the capital city, protesting on the inconvenience of the reforms. At this time, the crown prince breached the instituted state law.[51] Wey Yang said, "Failure to comply with government law invariably comes from the elites. The prince is the heir of the throne, and he cannot be chastised. His tutor Gongzi Qian will be punished, and his teacher Gongsun Jia is to have his face tattooed."[52] From the day after, the people of Qin abide by the new edict. It was enforced for ten years, the people within the dukedom became law abiding citizens, there were no petty thieves or bandits in the mountainous areas; even if people dropped something on the wayside, no one would pick it up to take possession. The civilians devotedly went against their enemies, while losing all interests to fight among themselves. The countryside became peaceful and prosperous. A group of Qin people who initially complained about the deficiencies came forth to claim that the new law was most favourable. Wey Yang said, "These people are obstructing the law and order of the country, and should be punished." They were banished to the wilderness in the frontier. Since then, no one even dared to discuss politics.

Sima Guang annotates:

Credibility is the most invaluable asset of a sovereign. People safeguard a state, and the people are protected by the credibility of their sovereign. Lacking credibility a sovereign cannot make his people amenable, without the support of the people a sovereign cannot uphold his state. Hence, in ancient times, a sage Lord did not deceive the world; a hegemonic Lord did not take advantage of his neighbours. A sage Lord did not deceive its people; an honourable patriarch did not deceive his kinsmen. A worthless sovereign acted contrarily, he deceived his neighbours, he deceived his subjects; he swindled his siblings and misled his father and offspring. The elites under him did not trust their subordinates while the subordinates distrust their overlords, being totally at odds with each other, leading the state to fail and expire. The minor gains he appropriated from his exploits could not mend the wounds they caused. The seized rewards were hardly adequate to cover the losses. What a sad state. In ancient times, Duke Huan of Qi did not disclaim the pledge he made with Cao Mo. Duke Wen of Jin did not take advantage of seizing Yuan; Marquis Wen of Wei did not neglect the hunting engagement with his agriculture minister, and Duke Xiao of Qin was not misery with the pledge when the log was relocated.[53]

Shijin 十金 = 10 units = two hundred and forty *liang* or taels of gold. During the times of the Warring States and Qin, one *liang* 両 was 15.8 gm.

51 Heir Apparent, *taizi*, Ying Si 太子 嬴駟.

52 The Tutor, Gongzi Qian 公子虔, met the chastisement of *rhinokopia* 劓刑, *yixing* penalty with his nose slit. Teacher Gongsun Jia 公孫賈 was punished by having his face tattooed *Qingxing* 黥刑.

53 Duke Huan of Qi 齊桓公 Jiang Xiaobai 姜小白 (r. 685-643 BCE), 16th Duke of Qi (see 403 BCE - footnotes 13).

The four sovereigns might not be faultless in every way; nevertheless, the approach adopted by Lord Shang was perhaps the most contemptible. On the other hand, it was the time of social turmoil and war; it was a time when people Under Heaven used deceit to attain their ends. Even then, the Lord did not nonchalantly dismiss his conviction of certitude to prevail over the subjects. The attribute of credibility is, even more, indispensable with a sovereign who presides within the Four Seas.

II. Marquis Yi of Hann died; his son Marquis Zhao succeeded him.[54]

III. See footnotes.[55]

---

358 BCE *Guihai* 癸亥 Warring States 戰國

King Xuan of Zhou	周顯王	11th year
Duke Gong of Lu	魯共公	19th year
Duke Xiao of Qin	秦孝公	4th year
Song Ticheng	宋剔成	12th year
King Xuan of Chu	楚宣王	12th year
King Wei of Qi	齊威王	1st year

Cao Mo 曹沫. In 681 BCE, Duke Huan of Qi 齊桓公 invaded Lu 魯 defeating the fiefdom; Duke Zhuang of Lu 魯莊公 sued for peace by ceding Suiyi County 遂邑 to Qi. Duke Huan accepted the offer and the two heads of state met at Ke 柯 to settle the capitulation of Lu. Lu General Cao Mo 曹沫 rushed forth with a dagger to threaten the life of the Qi sovereign, demanding the return of the Lu territory; Duke Huan having no choice, agreed to the demand. Upon removal of the threatening dagger by the general, Duke Huan recanted and wanted to execute Cao Mo. Guan Zhong 管仲, the chancellor of Qi, disputed it, as he felt it would be unwise to lose the trust of all the other fief lords by recanting a pledge made by a sovereign. The duke returned the county as pledged to Lu. *ZZTJ JZ*, Vol 1 p. 52 and *SJ* 史記, 卷 56, 'Cike liezhuan 刺客列傳' 第 26, p.p. 704-705.

Duke Wen of Jin 晉文公 Ji Zhonger 姬重耳 (r. 637-628 BCE). Duke Wen was laying siege to the walled city of Yuancheng 原城; he vowed to his generals that if the city were not taken in three days, he would withdraw. Three days later, there was no sign of surrendering on the part of the people in the city. Duke Wen ordered his troops to withdraw when his retainers returned with the news that the city had intended to surrender, and his advisors suggested that they should take the city. Duke Wen rejected the proposal saying, "I might have captured a city; however people would have lost faith in me for not living up to my pledge." He withdrew from the siege. The people of Yuancheng chased after him for thirty *li* and surrendered the city to Jin, and it became part of Jin territories. *ZZTJ JZ*, Vol 1, p.p. 52-53.

The sovereign of Wei, Marquis Wen of Wei 魏文侯 Wei Si 魏斯 (See 403 BCE - V.)

Ying Quliang 嬴渠梁 (see 357 - I).

54 Marquis Yi of Hann 韓懿侯 Hann Ruoshan 韓若山 5th.

Marquis Zhao of Hann 韓昭侯. 6th (r. 358-333 BCE) or (r. 362-333 BCE).

55 The text missed the death of Duke Huan of Qi, Tian Wu 田午; his son Tian Yinqi 田因齊 succeeded him.

Duke Huan of Qi 齊桓公 Tian Wu 田午 died, his son King Wei of Qi 齊威王 Tian Yinqi 田因齊, succeeded him 4th (r. 356-320 BCE). *ZG LS ND JB.* This Duke Huan is not to be confused with Duke Huan Jiang Xiaobai 姜小白 (r. 685-643 BCE).

King Hui of Wei	魏惠王	13th year
Marquis Zhao of Hann	韓昭侯	1st year
Marquis Cheng of Zhao	趙成侯	17th year
Duke Wen of Yan	燕文公	4th year
Marquis Cheng of Wey	衛成侯	4th year

1. Qin defeated the Hann army at the Xishan Mountains.[56]

---

357 BCE *Jiazi* 甲子 Warring States 戰國

King Xian of Zhou	周顯王	12th year
Duke Gong of Lu	魯共公	20th year
Duke Xiao of Qin	秦孝公	5th year
Song Ticheng	宋剔成	13th year
King Xuan of Chu	楚宣王	13th year
King Wei of Qi	齊威王	2nd year
King Hui of Wei	魏惠王	14th year
Marquis Zhao of Hann	韓昭侯	2nd year
Marquis Cheng of Zhao	趙成侯	18th year
Duke Wen of Yan	燕文公	5th year
Marquis Cheng of Wey	衛成侯	5th year

1. Wei and Hann met at Hao.[57]

---

356 BCE *Yichou* 乙丑 Warring States 戰國

King Xian of Zhou	周顯王	13th year
Duke Gong of Lu	魯共公	21st year
Duke Xiao of Qin	秦孝公	6th year
Song Ticheng	宋剔成	14th year
King Xuan of Chu	楚宣王	14th year
King Wei of Qi	齊威王	3rd year

---

56 The naming of geographic locations of ancient *Zhongguo* 中國 is often quite confusing. The area west of Taihangshan 太行山 was called Shanxi 山西; it means west of the Mountains. The area west of Huanghe River 黄河 at Shaanxi 陕西 was called Hexi 河西 - west of the River, or Xihe 西河. There is a Xiongershan Mountain range 熊耳山 in Yiyangxian Henan 河南 宜陽縣; areas west of the mountain range was also called Xishan 西山, the area at this stage belonged to Hann 韓; hence, Xishan is not to be confused with Shanxi. *ZZTJ JZ,* Vol 1, p. 53.

57 Hao 鄗 - Haocheng 鄗城 - Boxiangxian Hebei 河北 柏鄉縣.

King Hui of Wei	魏惠王	15th year
Marquis Zhao of Hann	韓昭侯	3rd year
Marquis Cheng of Zhao	趙成侯	19th year
Duke Wen of Yan	燕文公	6th year
Marquis Cheng of Wey	衛成侯	6th year

I. Zhao and Yan met at A County.[58]

II. Zhao, Qi and Song met at Pinglu.[59]

---

355 BCE *Bingyin* 丙寅 Warring States 戰國

King Xian of Zhou	周顯王	14th year
Duke Gong of Lu	魯共公	22nd year
Duke Xiao of Qin	秦孝公	7th year
Song Ticheng	宋剔成	15th year
King Xuan of Chu	楚宣王	15th year
King Wei of Qi	齊威王	4th year
King Hui of Wei	魏惠王	16th year
Marquis Zhao of Hann	韓昭侯	4th year
Marquis Cheng of Zhao	趙成侯	20th year
Duke Wen of Yan	燕文公	7th year
Marquis Cheng of Wey	衛成侯	7th year

I. King Wei of Qi and King Hui of Wei met and were hunting at the outskirts.[60] King Hui asked, "What national treasures does your kingdom possess?" King Wei answered, "None." King Hui said, "While our kingdom might be small, we own ten pearls over one inch *cun* in diameter; [61] they glow so bright that they light up twelve carriages, fore-and-aft. Qi kingdom is a large state; don't you possess any treasure similar?" King Wei answered, "My notion of national treasure is totally at variance with yours, Your Highness. Among my senior officers, I have a Master Tanzi, who presides over the security of our southern border; the people of Chu do not have the nerve to provoke our kingdom; [62] twelve minor fiefdoms near the Sishui River region come to my court to pay tributes.[63] I have another Master Panzi, he is garrisoned at Gaotang; the people at Zhao ceased their

58 A county 阿 - Yangguxian Shandong 山東 陽穀縣.

59 Pinglu 平陸 - Wenshangxian Shandong 山東 汶上縣.

60 King Wei of Qi 齊威王 Tian Yinqi 田因齊.
King of Wei 魏王 Wei Ying 魏罃.

61 One *cun* 寸 ~ 2cm.

62 Master Tanzi 檀子.

63 Sishui River 泗水. 泗上十二諸侯皆來朝, the 12 minor fiefdoms were the ones mentioned in 362 BCE. (See footnotes 362-V.)

fishing activities in our east at the Huanghe River.[64] I have another Master Qian Fu, he presides at the Xuzhou Province; the Yan people pray and make sacrificial offerings at the North-gate as an alternative while Zhao people burn incense at the West-gate; [65] overall, some seven thousand households came to settle in my kingdom. I have yet another minister Zhong Shou, [66] who is in charge of security; he guards against thieves and bandits and allows our people live in peace, and honesty prevails all over my entire kingdom. Those four ministers shine for one thousand *li*, let alone twelve carriages." King Hui was embarrassed.

II. Duke Xiao of Qin and King Hui of Wei met at Duping.[67]

III. Duke Gong of Lu died; Mao his son succeeded to the dukedom, he was known posthumously as Duke Kang.[68]

---

354 BCE *Dingmao* 丁卯 Warring States 戰國

King Xian of Zhou	周顯王	15th year
Duke Kang of Lu	魯康公	1st year
Duke Xiao of Qin	秦孝公	8th year
Song Ticheng	宋剔成	16th year
King Xuan of Chu	楚宣王	16th year
King Wei of Qi	齊威王	5th year
King Hui of Wei	魏惠王	17th year

---

64 Master Tian Pan 田盼, also known as Panzi 盼子, was a military general of Qi 齊; he participated in the battle of Maling 馬陵 and was a veteran general. Upon the retirement of Sun Bin 孫臏 and the fleeing of Tian Ji 田忌, Tian Pan became the most notable general of Qi. In 325 BCE, he led an army forming an alliance with Gongsun Yan 公孫衍 of Wei 魏 to face against the combined forces from Zhao 趙 and Hann 韓; the latter were given a resounding defeat; as a result, Qi annexed Pingyi County 平邑. *ZGC* 戰國策, Qice 齊策 1, King Wei of Chu Won Battle at Xuzhou 楚威王戰勝於徐州, p. 89; Qice 齊策 6, The Incident at Pushang 濮上之事, p. 143; Weice 魏策 2, Xishou Tian Pan rallied the support of Qi and Wei to attack Zhao 犀首田盼欲得齊魏之兵以伐趙, p. 256.
Gaotang 高唐 - Yuchengxian Shandong 山東 禹城縣.

65 Master Qian Fu 黔夫.
Xuzhou 徐州 - Tengxian Shandong 山東 滕縣.
Yan 燕; Northgate - Beimen 北門; Zhao 趙, Westgate - Ximen 西門. It means that the Yan people avoided making sacrifices to their ancestors at the South gate, they made sacrifices at the North-gate instead; while the Zhao people dared not make sacrifices at the East-gate and made them at the West-gate instead. *ZZTJ JZ*, p. 55.

66 Zhong Shou 種首.

67 Duke Xiao of Qin 秦孝公 Ying Quliang 嬴渠梁.
King Hui of Wei 魏惠王 Wei Ying 魏罃.
Duping 杜平 - Dengchengxian Shaanxi 陝西 澄城縣.

68 Duke Gong of Lu 魯共公 Ji Fen 姬奮.
Duke Kang of Lu 魯康公 Ji Mao 姬毛 (r. 354-346 BCE) or (r. 352-344 BCE).

Marquis Zhao of Hann	韓昭侯	5th year
Marquis Cheng of Zhao	趙成侯	21st year
Duke Wen of Yan	燕文公	8th year
Marquis Cheng of Wey	衛成侯	8th year

1. Qin defeated the forces of Wei at Yuanli; the army decapitated seven thousand heads and went on to occupy Shaoliang.[69]

11. King Hui of Wei made an expedition against Zhao; Handan was besieged.[70] The king of Chu commanded Jing She to go to the aid of Zhao.[71]

---

353 BCE *Wuchen* 戊辰 Warring States 戰國

King Xian of Zhou	周顯王	16th year
Duke Kang of Lu	魯康公	2nd year
Duke Xiao of Qin	秦孝公	9th year
Song Ticheng	宋剔成	17th year
King Xuan of Chu	楚宣王	17th year
Duke Wei of Qi	齊威王	6th year
King Hui of Wei	魏惠王	18th year
Marquis Zhao of Hann	韓昭侯	6th year
Marquis Cheng of Zhao	趙成侯	22nd year
Duke Wen of Yan	燕文公	9th year
Marquis Cheng of Wey	衛成侯	9th year

1. King Wei of Qi instructed Tian Ji the commanding general to lead an army to give relief to Zhao.[72]

Before this, Sun Bin and Pang Juan studied military disciplines. Pang Juan was appointed as general at Wei. Resenting the fact that his military expertise was inferior to Sun Bin, he invited Bin to Wei. When Sun Bin arrived, the Wei court indicted him by law and had his kneecaps hacked off by *bin* and his face tattooed by the *qing* penalties; hence as to disable and decommission him for life.[73] A Qi envoy was visiting Wei; Sun Bin met the envoy secretly as a convict and persuaded him

---

69 Yuanli 元里 - Dengchengxian Shaanxi 陝西 澄城縣.
Shaoliang 少梁 - Hannchengxian Shaanxi 陝西 韓城縣.

70 King Hui of Wei 魏惠王 Wei Ying 魏罃 3rd.
Zhao 趙 capital, Handan 邯鄲 - Handanxian Hebei 河北 邯鄲縣.

71 King Xuan of Chu 楚宣王 Mi Liangfu 羋良夫.

72 Commanding General, Tian Ji 田忌.

73 *Binxing* 臏刑; *qingxing* 黥刑.
It was hoped with these measures the other states would not consider retaining Sun Bin as an officer having been labelled a criminal.

to help him escape. The envoy concealed him in his carriage and smuggled him to Qi. Tian Ji received him as a guest of honour and introduced him to King Wei. The king quizzed him on military matters and appointed him as his tutor.

At this stage, King Wei of Qi was planning to bring relief to Zhao; he wanted to make Sun Bin the commanding general. Sun Bin nevertheless declined, as he maintained that he being crippled by criminal castigation could hardly earn the trust of the army. The king then made Tian Ji the commander and Sun his counselling officer. Sunzi concealed himself in a military carriage covertly giving out instructions and strategies.

Tian Ji planned to march to Zhao's relief immediately. Sunzi said, "One must not resort to using force to stop a dispute between two men in a fight. The mediator is best to avoid being involved physically. It is sensible to assess the situation, take advantage of the weak spot, and the conflict can be resolved easily. The Liang and Zhao armies are now engaged in pitched battles; [74] it is obvious Wei would have mobilised all their elite troops to the front leaving their capital vulnerable, defended only by their frail and emancipated soldiers. Sir, you might as well march speedily against the capital of Wei, while en route place our army at the strategic passes; attack them where they are weak. Thus deployed, the Wei army will have to abandon the siege against Zhao to return and defend its capital. With such a move, we will bring relief to Zhao and at the same time inflict severe damages on Wei." Tian Ji accepted Sun's strategy.

10th month. Handan, the capital of Zhao, surrendered to Wei.[75] Wei forces retreated, it joined battle with Qi at Guiling; [76] the Wei army was resoundingly beaten.

II. Hann made an expedition against Eastern Zhou, annexing Lingguan and Linqiu.[77]

The story of Sun Bin 孫臏 and Pang Juan 龐涓 was slightly more intricate. According to the *SJ* 史記, Pang Juan perfidiously branded Sun with an indictment of treason, and Sun was sentenced to death. Pang then treacherously pretended to beg the king for his life; he then cajoled Sun Bin to write down a military text composed by their Grand Master Gui Guzi 鬼谷子. When Sun was diligently preoccupied with writing down the scripts, he discovered that his fellow student had betrayed him; pretending he had gone completely pixilated, he managed to stay alive. The word *bin* was a penalty by cutting off the kneecaps of the convict. Sun came to be known as Sun Bin; which was not his real name and was more likely to be a given name after his chastisement. Sun Bin's book on war strategies was lost for more than 2,000 years and was rediscovered in 1972 when his book written on bamboo slips was unearthed in a *Han* dynasty period tomb. Previous to 1972, fragments of the *Sun Bin's Art of War* 孫臏兵法 were only known through quotations from other ancient texts. The *Sun Bin's Art of War* is not to be confused with the *Sunzi, the Art of War, Sunzi bingfa* 孫子兵法. *Sun Bin* was a descendant of Sunzi; the two men were separated by over a century. Yap J., *Wars with the Xiongnu,* Bloomington: Author-House (2009), p. 9.

74 Daliang 大梁 – the capital of Wei 魏.
It was the incident of the proverb, 'Laying siege to Wei to bring relief to Zhao' - 圍魏救趙.

75 Handan 邯鄲 - Handanxian Hebei 河北 邯鄲縣.

76 Guiling 桂陵 - 10km northeast of Hezexian Shandong 山東 荷澤縣.

77 Lingguan 陵觀, Linqiu 廩丘 the exact locations of both places are unknown today, but they should be somewhere near Gongxian Henan 河南 鞏縣.
Zhou 周 was reduced to the status of a small state by the time of Warring States. It only had control of seven small walled cities. Wangcheng 王城 - Jinguwei village, Luoyangxian Henan 河南 洛陽縣 金谷園; Luoyang 洛陽 - Luoyangxian 洛陽縣; Gucheng 穀城 - Xinanxian Henan 河南 新

III. Chu elected Zhao Xixu as the new chancellor. Jiang Yi spoke to the king of Chu,[78] "A man was exceedingly fond of his dog; the dog urinated in the family's water well. A neighbour saw what had happened and intended to inform the owner. The dog hunkered down at the threshold and bit the neighbour. Zhao Xixu has always tried to frustrate your subject to see Your Highness, just like the dog hunkering down at the threshold. When someone praises others, Your Highness would say, 'Now, this is a gentleman.' Moreover, you choose to be close to the man. Whereas when someone points out the faults of others, you would say, 'This is a vile character.' You choose to distance him. Whereas there are sons out there who commit patricide, and subjects who commit regicide, My Lord, you are oblivious to them. Why? Your Highness is only interested in people making praises of others, and you detest people uncovering the malicious deeds of others." The king said, "You are right. I will listen to both sides in the future."

352 BCE *Jisi* 己巳 Warring States 戰國

King Xian of Zhou	周顯王	17th year
Duke Kang of Lu	魯康公	3rd year
Duke Xiao of Qin	秦孝公	10th year
Song Ticheng	宋剔成	18th year
King Xuan of Chu	楚宣王	18th year
Duke Wei of Qi	齊威王	7th year
King Hui of Wei	魏惠王	19th year
Marquis Zhao of Hann	韓昭侯	7th year
Marquis Cheng of Zhao	趙成侯	23rd year
Duke Wen of Yan	燕文公	10th year
Marquis Cheng of Wey	衛成侯	10th year

I. The army commander *daliangzao* of Qin led an army to go against Wei.[79]

安縣; Pingyin 平陰 - Mengjinxian Henan 河南 孟津縣; Yanshi 偃師 - Yanshixian Henan 河南 偃師縣; Gongxian 鞏縣 - Gongxian Henan 河南 鞏縣 and Goushi 緱氏 - Goushizhen Village Yanshixian Henan 河南 偃師縣 緱氏鎮.

In 439 BCE, King Kao of Zhou 周考王 Ji Huai 姬槐 enfeoffed his younger brother Ji Jie 姬揭 at Gongxian; thus further reduced the territories of the already petty Zhou State. The Ji Jie sovereign was known as East Zhou 東周, but he did not hold a title as king and was initially known as *jun* 君 – a Lord later as Duke – gong 公. Duke Hui of East Zhou, the 3rd 東周 惠公, enfeoffed his son Ji Ban 姬班 at Yanshi 偃師, which later came to be known as West Zhou - Xihou 西周. Yang B. *ZZTJ B. Y. Edition*, 柏陽 資治通鑒, (1986 6th ed), pp. 121-122.

The area invaded by Hann 韓 was the Gongxian county 鞏縣.

78 King Xuan of Chu 楚宣王 Mi Liangfu 羋良夫, 19th.

Zhao Xixu 昭奚恤; Jiang Yi 江乙.

79 Army Commander *daliangzao* 大良造 Gongsun Yang 公孫鞅. *Daliangzao* was the 16th of the 20 grades of enfeoffment at Qin. *Daliangzao* was also known as *dashangzao* 大上造. See Appendix 2b.

II. The fief lords under Heaven formed an allied army and had Xiangling of Wei completely surrounded.[80]

351 BCE *Gengwu* 庚午 Warring States 戰國

King Xian of Zhou	周顯王	18th year
Duke Kang of Lu	魯康公	4th year
Duke Xiao of Qin	秦孝公	11th year
Song Ticheng	宋剔成	19th year
King Xuan of Chu	楚宣王	19th year
Duke Wei of Qi	齊威王	8th year
King Hui of Wei	魏惠王	20th year
Marquis Zhao of Hann	韓昭侯	8th year
Marquis Cheng of Zhao	趙成侯	24th year
Duke Wen of Yan	燕文公	11th year
Marquis Cheng of Wey	衛成侯	11th year

I. Wey Yang of Qin led the Qin army besieged Guyang of Wei; it was annexed.[81]

II. Wei returned Handan to Zhao; Wei and Zhao formed an alliance at the bank of Zhangshui River.[82]

III. Marquis Zhao of Hann nominated Shen Buhai as chancellor.[83]

Shen Buhai was a junior functionary from Zheng; he studied Huanglao and Legalism.[84] He introduced himself to Marquis Zhao of Hann, who appointed him as his chancellor. Within the state, he made reforms to the law and improved civic erudition, while adopted a peaceful and amiable policy with other fief states. Within a period of fifteen years, until his death, Hann was reign by good governance and was a powerful state militarily.

There was an occasion when Shen Buhai recommended his elder cousin to take on a position as an officer at court. Marquis Zhao rejected the request; Shen Buhai was resentful. Marquis Zhao said, "Sir, I used what I learned from you to rule my state. Do you want me to abide by your request and discard the practices you taught me? Alternatively, do you want me to adhere to your teachings and disregard your request? Sir, you have taught me to promote the meritorious, to be attentive to the gradation of contribution. Now, you are asking me for a personal favour. Which of

80 Xiangling 襄陵 - Linfenxian Shanxi 山西 臨汾縣.

81 Guyang 固陽 - Guyangxian Neimeng 内蒙 固陽縣.

82 Zhangshui River 漳水 - Yecheng 鄴城縣 at Changzixian Shanxi 山西 長子縣.

83 Duke Zhao of Hann 韓昭侯.
Shen Buhai 申不害 was from the defunct state of Zheng 鄭. Also known as Shenzi 申子. He was a proponent of the Technique *shu* 術派 branch of the *fajia* Legalism 法家. *SJ* 史記, 卷 33, 'Laozi, Hann Fei liezhuan 老子韓非列傳' 第 3, p. 385.

84 Huanglao 黄老 - Lao was Laozi 老子 and Huang 黄 was Huangdi 黄帝. Legalism 法家.

the alternatives should I adhere to?" Shen Buhai promptly left where he was seated and begged for pardon, "Your Highness, you are truly a sage."

Marquis Zhao of Hann had a pair of worn trousers, and he ordered his retainers to have them kept in storage. The retainer said, "Your Highness is not a charitable person, instead of giving the pair of trousers to your attendants, you have them stored." Marquis Zhao answered, "I have heard that a sage lord treasures every move he makes. A frown is saved for an occasion when he is displeased; whereas a smile is retained for an occasion when he is happy. A pair of worn trousers is no different from a frown or a smile; I am preserving them for someone who is worthy."

---

350 BCE *Xinwei* 辛未 Warring States 戰國

King Xian of Zhou	周顯王	19th year
Duke Kang of Lu	魯康公	5th year
Duke Xiao of Qin	秦孝公	12th year
Song Ticheng	宋剔成	20th year
King Xuan of Chu	楚宣王	20th year
Duke Wei of Qi	齊威王	9th year
King Hui of Wei	魏惠王	21st year
Marquis Zhao of Hann	韓昭侯	9th year
Marquis Cheng of Zhao	趙成侯	25th year
Duke Wen of Yan	燕文公	12th year
Marquis Cheng of Wey	衛成侯	12th year

1. Shang Yang of Qin constructed watchtowers and palaces at Xianyang, [85] having completed the constructions Qin moved its capital to the new site.

Shang Yang issued an order that parents and siblings were strictly forbidden to share the same living quarters.[86] The larger villages and hamlets were reorganized to become counties; each county was presided by a prefect, assisted by a secretary.[87] After the reorganization, there were thirty-one counties to the state of Qin. The grid-farming system was hence abrogated; furthermore, he demolished the crisscrossing pathways in the fields; and proceeded to standardise the volume, weight and length gauges of *dou, tong, quan, heng, jiang* and *chi*.[88]

---

85 Gongsun Yang 公孫鞅.
Xianyang 咸陽 - Northwest of Changan 長安, present-day Xi'an, Shaanxi 陝西 西安.

86 Northern China is extremely cold in the winter months. To keep warm during the night, people used to sleep on the mud cooking stoves (or *kang* 炕), with divans placed on top of the stoves; all the family members shared one bed.

87 County - *xian* 縣, County Prefect, *xianzhang* 縣長; Secretary, *cheng* 丞.

88 The various fiefdoms were using different measurement and weight systems at this stage.
Dou 斗 was a volume measurement that was about 2 litres.

II. The Qin and Wei armies joined battle at Tong.[89]

III. Marquis Cheng of Zhao died; one of his sons Zhao Xie challenged the crown prince for succession; Zhao Xie failed and escaped to Hann.[90]

---

349 BCE *Renshen* 壬申 Warring States 戰國

King Xian of Zhou	周顯王	20th year
Duke Kang of Lu	魯康公	6th year
Duke Xiao of Qin	秦孝公	13th year
Song Ticheng	宋剔成	21st year
King Xuan of Chu	楚宣王	21st year
Duke Wei of Qi	齊威王	10th year
King Hui of Wei	魏惠王	22nd year
Marquis Zhao of Hann	韓昭侯	10th year
Marquis Su of Zhao	趙肅侯	1st year
Duke Wen of Yan	燕文公	13th year
Marquis of Wey	衛成侯	13th year

There was no record this year.

---

348 BCE Guiyou 癸酉 Warring States 戰國

King Xian of Zhou	周顯王	21st year
Duke Kang of Lu	魯康公	7th year
Duke Xiao of Qin	秦孝公	14th year
Song Ticheng	宋剔成	22nd year
King Xuan of Chu	楚宣王	22nd year
Duke Wei of Qi	齊威王	11th year

Tong 桶 (*hu* 斛) - was a bucket, it probably meant *hu* 斛, a volume measurement, which was about 20 litres.

Quan 權 - a weight measure balance.

Heng 衡 - a weight apparatus.

Zhang 丈 was a length measure that was about 2.31 metres.

Chi 尺 was a length that was about 23.1 cm.

89 Wei 魏, Tong 彤 - Huaxian Shaanxi 陝西 華縣.

90 Marquis Cheng of Zhao 趙成侯 Zhao Zhong 趙種.
Zhao Xie 趙緤.
Crown Prince Zhao Yu 趙語.

King Hui of Wei	魏惠王	23rd year
Marquis Zhao of Hann	韓昭侯	11th year
Marquis Su of Zhao	趙肅侯	2nd year
Duke Wen of Yan	燕文公	14th year
Duke Cheng of Wey	衛成侯	14th year

1. Shang Yang of Qin issued a new tax law on behalf of the sovereign; it was implemented immediately.

---

347 BCE *Jiaxu* 甲戌 Warring States 戰國

King Xian of Zhou	周顯王	22nd year
Duke Kang of Lu	魯康公	8th year
Duke Xiao of Qin	秦孝公	15th year
Song Ticheng	宋剔成	23rd year
King Xuan of Chu	楚宣王	23rd year
Duke Wei of Qi	齊威王	12th year
King Hui of Wei	魏惠王	24th year
Marquis Zhao of Hann	韓昭侯	12th year
Marquis of Zhao	趙肅侯	3rd year
Duke of Yan	燕文公	15th year
Duke of Wey	衛成侯	15th year

1. Zhao Fan, a prince from Zhao led an army against Handan.[91] He died in the attempt.

---

346 BCE *Yihai* 乙亥 Warring States 戰國

King Xian of Zhou	周顯王	23rd year
Duke Kang of Lu	魯康公	9th year
Duke Xiao of Qin	秦孝公	16th year
Song Ticheng	宋剔成	24th year
King Xuan of Chu	楚宣王	24th year
Duke of Qi	齊威王	13th year
King Hui of Wei	魏惠王	25th year
Marquis Zhao of Hann	韓昭侯	13th year
Marquis Su of Zhao	趙肅侯	4th year

---

91 Zhao Fan 趙范.
Handan 邯鄲 - Handanxian Hebei 河北 邯鄲縣.

Duke Wen of Yan	燕文公	16th year
Duke Cheng of Wey	衛成侯	16th year

I. Qi executed Minister Mou.[92]

II. Duke Kang of Lu died; his son Duke Jing succeeded to the dukedom.[93]

III. Duke Cheng of Wey relegated himself to the status as a marquis;[94] and submitted to San-Jin of Zhao, Wei and Hann as their protectorate.[95]

---

345 BCE *Bingzi* 丙子 Warring States 戰國

King Xian of Zhou	周顯王	24th year
Duke Jing of Lu	魯景公	1st year
Duke Xiao of Qin	秦孝公	17th year
Song Ticheng	宋剔成	25th year
King Xuan of Chu	楚宣王	25th year
King Wei of Qi	齊威王	14th year
King Hui of Wei	魏惠王	26th year
Marquis Zhao of Hann	韓昭侯	14th year
Marquis Su of Zhao	趙肅侯	5th year
Duke Wen of Yan	燕文公	17th year
Marquis Cheng of Wey	衛成侯	17th year

There was no record this year.

---

344 BCE *Dingchou* 丁丑 Warring States 戰國

King Xian of Zhou	周顯王	25th year
Duke Jing of Lu	魯景公	2nd year
Duke Xiao of Qin	秦孝公	18th year
Song Ticheng	宋剔成	26th year
King Xuan of Chu	楚宣王	26th year
King Wei of Qi	齊威王	15th year
King Hui of Wei	魏惠王	27th year

---

92 Qi minister, *dafu* 齊大夫, Tian Mou 田牟, the identity of this person cannot be traced.

93 Duke Kang of Lu 魯康公 Ji Mao 姬毛; Duke Jing of Lu 魯景公 Ji Yan 姬偃.

94 Duke Cheng of Wey - We have been using the marquis title since the 1st year of his reign in 361 BCE, he was a duke before 346 BCE.

95 Duke Cheng of Wei 衛成公 Wey Ao 衛遨.

Marquis Zhao of Hann	韓昭侯	15th year
Marquis Su of Zhao	趙肅侯	6th year
Duke Wen of Yan	燕文公	18th year
Marquis Cheng of Wey	衛成侯	18th year

1. The fief lords met at the Zhou capital of Luoyang.

---

343 BCE *Wuyin* 戊寅 Warring States 戰國

King Xian of Zhou	周顯王	26th year
Duke Jing of Lu	魯景公	3rd year
Duke Xiao of Qin	秦孝公	19th year
Song Ticheng	宋剔成	27th year
King Xuan of Chu	楚宣王	27th year
King Wei of Qi	齊威王	16th year
King Hui of Wei	魏惠王	28th year
Marquis Zhao of Hann	韓昭侯	16th year
Marquis Su of Zhao	趙肅侯	7th year
Duke Wen of Yan	燕文公	19th year
Marquis Cheng of Wey	衛成侯	19th year

1. The king of Zhou enfeoffed the duke of Qin as Bo.[96] The sovereigns from various fief states went to Qin to express well wishing. Duke Xiao of Qin ordered his son Ying Shaoguan to lead an army and the head-of-states to meet at Fengze Lake to pay homage to the king of Zhou.

---

342 BCE *Jimao* 己卯 Warring States 戰國

King Xian of Zhou	周顯王	27th year
Duke Jing of Lu	魯景公	4th year
Duke Xiao of Qin	秦孝公	20th year
Song Ticheng	宋剔成	28th year
King Xuan of Chu	楚宣王	28th year

96 King Xian of Zhou 周顯王 Ji Bian 姬扁.
Bo 伯.
Duke Xiao of Qin 秦孝公 Ying Quliang 嬴渠梁.
Ying Shaoquan 嬴少官.
Fengze Lake 逢澤, according to the *Dilizhi* 地理志 the Lake was north of Yingyangxian Henan 河南 滎陽縣.

King Wei of Qi	齊威王	17th year
King Hui of Wei	魏惠王	29th year
Marquis Zhao of Hann	韓昭侯	17th year
Marquis Su of Zhao	趙肅侯	8th year
Duke Wen of Yan	燕文公	20th year
Marquis Cheng of Wey	衛成侯	20th year

There was no record this year.

341 BCE *Gengchen* 庚辰 Warring States 戰國

King Xian of Zhou	周顯王	28th year
Duke Jing of Lu	魯景公	5th year
Duke Xiao of Qin	秦孝公	21st year
Song Ticheng	宋剔成	29th year
King Xuan of Chu	楚宣王	29th year
Duke Wei of Qi	齊威王	18th year
King Hui of Wei	魏惠王	30th year
Marquis Zhao of Hann	韓昭侯	18th year
Marquis Su of Zhao	趙肅侯	9th year
Duke Wen of Yan	燕文公	21st year
Marquis Cheng of Wey	衛成侯	21st year

1. Pang Juan of Wei made an expedition against Hann,[97] which appealed to Qi for help. King Wei of Qi summoned his ministers to deliberate on the issue. He asked, "Should we send our army post haste to help or delay?" Marquis Cheng, the chancellor, said,[98] "I do not think we should even get involved." Tian Ji said, "If we reject their appeal, Hann will fall; and Wei will annex its territories. I think we should move quickly." Sun Bin said, "There are no signs of weakening on either side. If we hasten to Hann's aid now, our forces will bear the brunt from Wei on behalf of Hann; besides, even if we win, we will have to abide by conditions meted out by Hann. We know Wei is resolved in subjugating Hann and when the Hann people realize that their kingdom is about to face subjugation they will come east to Qi to plea for help. If we wait until then before answering to their plea, we will bolster our liaison with Hann besides we will face an exhausted enemy. It is like killing two birds with one stone, garnishing the honour of winning a war and earning the fame for aiding Hann." The king said, "Excellent." The Qi court then furtively conveyed to the envoy that they were committed to going to their aid and dispatched him. With the reassurance from Qi, the Hann warriors fought valiantly but lost five consecutive battles. In desperation, Hann sent an envoy to Qi agreeing to submit to them if they came to their aid.

97 Pang Juan of Wei 魏 龐涓.
Hann 韓. Capital city Xinzheng 新鄭 - Xinzhengxian Henan 河南 新鄭縣.

98 Chancellor, Marquis Cheng 成侯 Zou Ji 鄒忌.

Qi raised an army, dispatching Tian Ji, Tian Ying and Tian Pan as the commanding generals while Sunzi took on the position as the consultative officer.[99] The army marched directly against the capital of Wei.[100] When Pang Juan heard news of the advancing army, he retreated to return. Meanwhile, Wei reacted by decreeing a general mobilization and appointed Crown Prince Wei Shen as the commander to face the encroaching Qi army.[101] Sunzi said to Tian Ji, "The warriors of San-Jin are valiant and ferocious fighters and they disdain our Qi soldiers, [102] labelling us as cowards. A competent commander takes advantage of favourable circumstances and takes the initiatives while avoiding the unfavourable conditions. Military strategy text relates,[103] 'To march a hundred *li* to pursue a swift victory a general is bound to lose while trying to march fifty *li* only half of the troops will arrive at the destination." [104] When the Qi army arrived at the Wei territories, Sunzi instructed the troops to prepare one hundred thousand pit-stoves when they made camp. The next day the number was reduced to fifty thousand and the following day only twenty thousand. Pang Juan marched for three days saw what had happened and was beside himself with glee, "I knew the Qi were cowards, more than half of their troops have dispersed after marching only three days into our territories; half of their soldiers have absconded." He ordered his elite light troops to double the speed in hot pursuit, leaving his infantry troops trailing in the rear. Sunzi predicted that the Wei troops would march past a steep defile at Maling by dusk.[105] The passage was steep, narrow and difficult to access, Sunzi thought it was a perfect location for an ambush, he ordered his men to cut off the bark of a huge tree, and on the exposed trunk he wrote, "Pang Juan dies beneath this tree." He then instructed ten thousand Qi expert crossbow archers from his ranks to hide in waiting along the trail, instructing them to fire their arrows when they see torchlights from below at dusk.

As envisaged Pang Juan arrived at the defile at dusk, when he rode past the tree he caught a glimpse of writings on an exposed tree trunk. He ordered his men to light a torch for a closer inspection. There was hardly any time for him to finish reading the scripts when salvos of arrows rained down from all directions. Wei troops dispersed in a frenzied stampede. Pang Juan knew he had lost and that he could not escape this calamity, he cut his throat, sighed before dying, "And thus, I made the idiot a legend."[106] The Qi army followed in hot pursuit of the dispersing Wei forces, routing the retreating army; Prince Shen was captured.[107]

---

99 Tian Ji 田忌.
Tian Ying 田嬰.
Tian Pan 田盼.

100 Daliang 大梁.

101 Wei Shen 魏申.

102 San-Jin 三晉 – Hann 韓, Wei 魏, Zhao 趙.

103 The *Sunzi bingfa* 孫子兵法. The text used the term *bingfa* 兵灋, which was the old variant of *bingfa* 兵法.

104 *Li* 里 - some scholars have chosen to translate *li* as a league, which varied from 3.5 to 5.556 km, a Chinese *li*, on the other hand, varied over time, was only about .4 km and not much more than this. To use league as a translation is off the mark.

105 Maling 馬陵.

106 How could he have known that he had made Sun Bin a legend? Later historians probably appended the comment.

107 Captured Crown Prince Shen 虜太子申. According to bamboo slips unearthed in a Han tomb (1972) at Yinque Shan 銀雀山漢墓竹簡, the accounts mentioned in the Battles of Guiling and Maling were at variance with the *SJ* and the *ZZTJ*. In *SJ* there is no mention of Pang Juan at the Battle of Guiling, whereas it mentions the suicide of Pang Juan 13 years later at Maling and that the Crown Prince of

11. Marquis Cheng, the chancellor of Qi was resentful of Tian Ji.[108] He sent a retainer bearing ten units of gold to ask a diviner at the market to make a divination.[109] The retainer announced, "I am from the household of Tian Ji. My general has won three consecutive battles. Please make a divination if it is auspicious to carry out another great exploit?" When the diviner was about to depart, the guards had the man arrested. Tian Ji could not vindicate himself from the charges brought against him; he led his followers to attack Linzi, [110] intending to capture Marquis Cheng but failed. Tian Ji absconded to Chu.

---

340 BCE *Xinsi* 辛巳 Warring States 戰國

King Xian of Zhou	周顯王	29th year
Duke Jing of Lu	魯景公	6th year
Duke Xiao of Qin	秦孝公	22nd year
Song Ticheng	宋剔成	30th year
King Xuan of Chu	楚宣王	30th year
King Wei of Qi	齊威王	19th year
King Hui of Wei	魏惠王	31st year
Marquis Zhao of Hann	韓昭侯	19th year
Marquis Su of Zhao	趙肅侯	10th year
Duke Wen of Yan	燕文公	22nd year
Marquis Cheng of Wey	衛成侯	22nd year

1. Wey Yang suggested to Duke Xiao of Qin, "The relationship between Qin and Wei is like the abdominal or heart ailment affecting a person. Both are vying for an opportunity to annihilate their opponent. What is the reason? Wei is situated to the west of the precipitous mountain range, and its capital city is located at Anyi; it shares its border with Qin, with the Huanghe River as the demarcation line. To the east, it holds a most advantageous position for being sheltered by the Mountain range.[111] When Wei was powerful, it marched west to invade Qin; but when it became weak, it retreated to the east to reclaim land. Auspiciously, under the sage reign of Your Highness, our Kingdom has become formidable. Wei was given a resounding defeat by Qi last year, and its dependent vassals have since transferred their loyalty. I think we should take advantage of this opportunity and advance against it. I don't think it could sustain another assault from

---

Wei, Shen, was captured. The bamboo script, the *Sun Bin bingfa qin Pang Juan* 孫臏兵法禽龐涓 mentions that Pang Juan was captured at Guiling, apparently this contradicts with *SJ* 史記 and *ZZTJ*. From available information, it appears that Pang Juan was captured at Guiling and not at Maling. Yang Kuan 楊寬, *Zhanguoshi* 戰國史 p. 24.
http://baike.baidu.com/view/911288.htm?fromtitle=%E9%93%B6%E9%9B%80%E5%B1%B1%E6%B1%89%E7%AE%80&fromid=4194818&type=syn#2_4 - (2015 Baiu).

108 Chancellor of Qi, *xiang*, Zou Ji 齊相 鄒忌.
Tian Ji 田忌.

109 Ten catties = two hundred and forty *liang* 两.

110 Linzi 臨淄 - Linzixian Shandong 山東 臨淄縣.

111 Mountain range - Xiaoshan 崤山.

Qin in its weakened state. With a successful campaign, Wei is left with one option; that is to relocate its capital farther to the east. With such an effective reposition, the territories of Qin will take possession of the potency and expediency of the Huanghe River and the Mountain. We can take advantage of the natural terrain to control the numerous fiefdoms to the east. It will be a grand exploit by a mighty king." The duke agreed to it. He ordered Wey Yang to lead an army to go against Wei.[112]

Wei responded by nominating Prince Yang to lead an army to oppose the invading Qin army.[113]

When the two armies were facing each other, Wey Yang dispatched a missive to Prince Yang. It read, "Your Highness and I were close acquaintances previously, and now we have become commanders of two enemy states. I am most reluctant to instigate this conflict. I yearn to meet you in person; we will discuss ways and means to resolve this impending battle and settle our differences through a peaceful accord. After that we will drink to our hearts content, returning to our capitals in peace, not putting the people of Qin and Wei in harm's way."

Wei Yang thought the request made sense; he went to the meeting. Having finished the drinking session, the guards hidden by Wey Yang attacked and captured Prince Yang. Taking advantage of the void the Qin forces attacked the Wei army and gave it a resounding defeat.

King Hui of Wei was in consternation; he dispatched an envoy to Qin, presenting the areas west of the River *Hexi* to sue for peace.[114] Wei had no choice but to abandon Anyi, and moved its capital city to Daliang.[115] The king of Wei sighed and said, "I regret I did not listen to Gongshu Cuo."[116]

II. Qin awarded Wey Yang with fifteen counties in the region of Shangyu and enfeoffed him as Lord Shang.[117]

III. Qi and Zhao made an expedition against Wei.

IV. King Xuan of Chu died, his son, Shang, succeeded to the throne; he was known posthumously as King Wei.[118]

---

112 The Wei State was cut into two halves by Hann at that stage. The western part of Wei was situated west of He (Huanghe) and the eastern part was further to the east. It was a strategic move by Wey Yang 衛鞅, who saw if the western part of Wei should fall to Qin, it would be much easier for Qin to make exploitation against the other Warring States.

113 Wei Yang 魏卬.

114 King Hui of Wei 魏惠王 Wei Ying 魏罃. *Hexi* 河西 was the area on the west bank of Huanghe 黄河, the eastern part of Shaanxi province 陕西.

115 Anyi 安邑 – Xiaxian Shanxi 山西 夏縣. The move to Daliang was towards the commencing years of King Hui 惠王. The *ZZTJ* took after the *SJ* 史記, which is erroneous. *ZZTJ JZ*, Vol 1, p. 65.
Daliang – Kaifengxian Henan 河南 開封縣.

116 Gongshu Cuo 公叔痤 suggested to Wei Ying 魏罃 that he should either employ Gongsun Yang or execute him immediately in 361 BCE. (see 361 BCE-I).

117 Shangyu 商於 - Zhechuanxian Henan 河南 浙川縣; Lord Shang 商君.

339 BCE *Renwu* 壬午 Warring States 戰國

King Xian of Zhou	周顯王	30th year
Duke Jing of Lu	魯景公	7th year
Duke Xiao of Qin	秦孝公	23rd year
Song Ticheng	宋剔成	31st year
King Wei of Chu	楚威王	1st year
King Wei of Qi	齊威王	20th year
King Hui of Wei	魏惠王	32nd year
Marquis Zhao of Hann	韓昭侯	20th year
Marquis Su of Zhao	趙肅侯	11th year
Duke Wen of Yan	燕文公	23rd year
Marquis Cheng of Wey	衛成侯	23rd year

There was no record this year.

338 BCE *Guiwei* 癸未 Warring States 戰國

King Xian of Zhou	周顯王	31st year
Duke Jing f Lu	魯景公	8th year
Duke Xiao of Qin	秦孝公	24th year
Song Ticheng	宋剔成	32nd year
King Wei of Chu	楚威王	2nd year
King Wei of Qi	齊威王	21st year
King Hui of Wei	魏惠王	33rd year
Marquis Zhao of Hann	韓昭侯	21st year
Marquis Su of Zhao	趙肅侯	12th year
Duke Wen of Yan	燕文公	24th year
Marquis Cheng of Wey	衛成侯	24th year

1. Duke Xiao of Qin died; he was succeeded by his son, King Huiwen.[119] The followers of Prince Qian indicted Lord Shang for scheming treason against the state and sent law enforcers to arrest him.[120] Lord Shang fled to Wei; the people of Wei refused him entry,

---

118 King Xuan of Chu 楚宣王 Mi Liangfu 羋良夫.
King Wei of Chu 楚威王 Mi Shang 羋商.

119 Duke Xiao of Qin 秦孝公 Ying Quliang 嬴渠梁, 25th.
King Hui of Qin 秦惠王 Ying Si 嬴駟 26th (r. 337-311 BCE).

120 Prince Qian 虔 was the tutor of Ying Si who endured *rhinokopia*.

returning him to Qin. Lord Yang raised his followers at Shangyu to attack the Zhengyu County.[121] The Qin loyalists dispatched an army against him, killing him. He was dismembered by horse-drawn chariots - the penalty of *julie* to serve as a warning to all;[122] all his family members were executed.

Previously, when Lord Shang was the chancellor of Qin he was known for his brutal ruthlessness in applying the law. On one occasion he was presiding over litigations at the bank of the Weishui River, the river turned crimson red from the executions. He was the chancellor of Qin for ten years and during his tenure, most of the people loathed him. Before his death, Zhao Liang paid him a visit.[123] Lord Shang asked, "Sir. Based on your observations of my governance of Qin, who do you think is more sagacious, the Five Fleece Minister – *Wugu dafu* or I?"[124] Zhao Liang answered, "When one thousand persons who acquiesce to every order they are nowhere comparable to one who dares to speak his mind to the contrary. Your subject will air his view if you give assurance not to execute him. Can you do that?" Lord Shang said, "Yes." Zhao Liang said, "The Five Fleece Minister was a lowly functionary slave from Jing.[125] Duke Mu raised him from his humble position as a cattle rancher to be above the hundred surnames as a Qin chancellor.[126] The people at Qin dared not look up to him. He was the chancellor of Qin for six or seven years; he successfully made conquest of the state of Zheng in the east, and he appointed three successive Jin lords.[127] He averted an impending calamity at Jing.[128] When he was the chancellor of Qin no matter how weary he was, he did not ride in a carriage; no matter how warm the weather was, he did not raise a canopy.[129] When he was making an inspection tour of the state, he did not ride in a carriage and did not need a large entourage of armed guards bearing spears and halberds for his protection. When the Five Fleece Minister died, men and women at Qin cried and lamented their loss, children ceased singing, and peasant women stopped chanting in chorus while shucking grains. Whereas, look at you now, sir, you are entirely dissimilar. You were introduced to the

---

121 Shangyu 商於 - Zhechuanxian Henan 河南 浙川縣.
Zhengxian 鄭縣 - Huaxian Shaanxi 陕西 華縣.

122 *Julie* 車裂 - was the chastisement of dismemberment by five-horse drawn chariots, and in the case of Wey Yang he was quartered after death. While the punishment was carried on live convicts, it was also a symbolic punishment conducted on executed prisoners, as Chinese believed that one should die with his remains intact.

123 Zhao Liang 趙良 was a Qin national and was a guest at Wey Yang's manor.

124 Baili Xi 百里奚 also known as Five-fleece Minister - *wugu dafu* 五羖大夫 was an outstanding minister at the Qin court during the time of Duke Mu of Qin 秦穆公 (r. 659-621 BCE). Baili Xi was sold as a slave to Chu 楚, the duke of Qin bought him for five sheets of male goat-fleece; hence, he came to be known as *wugu dafu. ZZTJ JZ,* Vol 1. p. 67.
Dafu – the term for minister.

125 Jing 荆 the other name for Chu 楚.

126 Ying Renhao 贏任好.

127 Expedition against Zheng 鄭 – During the 22nd year (630 BCE) of King Xiang of Zhou, Qin and Jin besieged Zheng. *ZZTJ JZ,* Vol 1, p. 67.
Jin lords 晉君.

128 Chu 楚.

129 *Anju* 安車 – canopied carriage.

duke through his trusted minion Jing Jian.[130] When you oversee the court, you intimidate and terrorize the nobles, and you have been cruel and callous with the civilians. Prince Qian stayed in his manor for eight years.[131] Then you executed Zhu Huan and employed the chastisement of the tattoo on Gongsun Jia.[132] The *Book of Odes* says,[133] 'He who wins people's support excels and rises, he who loses people's favour stumbles and collapses." Based on the above observations you apparently have not won the approval of the people. A large entourage of armed men follows your carriage with strong and powerful guards wielding spears and halberds run alongside to offer protection. You would never venture out if one of the precautions were not taken. The *Book of Documents* says, 'A person who exercises virtue prospers; he who uses force expires and falls.'[134] Based on the above, you can hardly be considered as a champion of virtues. Your situation is most precarious; it is like the morning dew that swiftly dissipates. Sir, you are wallowing in the riches at Shangyu; [135] clinging onto the power of the Qin court, while the people are festering with subdued animosity for your deeds. If something untoward happens to the king of Qin, without him defending his guests at court, the excuses to make indictments against you will not be scarce." Lord Shang did not subscribe to the assessments. Not five months had elapsed before he faced his demise.

---

337 BCE *Jiashen* 甲申 Warring States 戰國

King Xian of Zhou	周顯王	32nd year
Duke Jing of Lu	魯景公	9th year
King Hui of Qin	秦惠王	1st year
Song Ticheng	宋剔成	33rd year
King Wei of Chu	楚威王	3rd year
King Wei of Qi	齊威王	22nd year
King Hui of Wei	魏惠王	34th year
Marquis Zhao of Hann	韓昭侯	22nd year
Marquis Su of Zhao	趙肅侯	13th year
Duke Wen of Yan	燕文公	25th year
Marquis Cheng of Wey	衛成侯	25th year

1. Shen Buhai of Hann, the chancellor of Hann, died.[136]

---

130 Jing Jian 景監. It was a most reprehensible way to be introduced to the Qin court through a lowly minion.

131 Prince Qian, Ying Qian 公子虔 嬴虔.

132 Zhu Huan 祝懽.
Gongsun Jia 公孫賈 was the teacher of Ying Si 嬴駟.

133 The *Odes, Shijing* 詩經, "得人者興, 失人者崩." The current version of the *Odes* does not have this stanza or the one below. *ZZTJ JZ,* Vol 1, p. 68.

134 The *Book of Document, Shujing* 書經, "恃德者昌, 恃力者亡." *ZZTJ JZ,* Vol 1, p. 68.

135 Shangyu 商於 - Zhechuanxian Henan 河南 淅川縣.

136 Hann 韓, Shen Buhai 申不害.

336 BCE *Yiyou* 乙酉 Warring States 戰國

King Xian of Zhou	周顯王	33rd year
Duke Jing of Lu	魯景公	10th year
King Hui of Qin	秦惠王	2nd year
Song Ticheng	宋剔成	34th year
King Wei of Chu	楚威王	4th year
King Wei of Qi	齊威王	23rd year
King Hui of Wei	魏惠王	35th year
Marquis Zhao of Hann	韓昭侯	23rd year
Marquis Su of Zhao	趙肅侯	14th year
Duke Wen of Yan	燕文公	26th year
Marquis Cheng of Wey	衛成侯	26th year

I. The sacrificial shrine constructed by Song at Taiqiu collapsed.[137]

II. Meng Ke from the Zou polity paid a tribute to King Hui of Wei.[138] The king asked him, "Sir, you have travelled far from one thousand *li* away to visit us; what beneficial suggestions have you installed for my kingdom?" Mengzi answered, "Why is Your Highness always concerned with lucrative gains? To dispense benevolence and righteousness is more than adequate. When Your Highness asks, 'What benefits do you bring to my kingdom?' Your subjects at court will ask, 'What benefits do you bring to my family?' While the civilians will ask, 'What benefits do you bring me?' Once the population of a state are all feverishly pursuing after personal gains, it leads to calamity and the demise of a state. A benevolent person does not relinquish his kin; while a righteous person does not relegate his sovereign." The king responded, "You are right."

137 Taiqiu 太丘 - Yongchengxian Henan 河南 永城縣.

138 Zou 鄒 (Zhu 邾) - Zoupingxian Shandong 山東 鄒平縣. Zou was a minor polity at the time of Chunqiu 春秋 and the Warring States. The original name of the polity was Zhu 邾; it was annihilated by Chu during the middle era of the Warring States. Duke Mu of Lu 魯穆公 changed the name to Zou; the polity was located at the present day Zoupingxian Shandong 鄒平縣. *ZZTJ JZ*, Vol 1, pp. 69-70.
Mengke 孟柯 = Mendzi 孟子 = Mencius (371 or 372-289 BCE). Mengzi lived about 30 years after Kong Ji 孔伋, alias Zisi 子思 (483-402 BCE). The text relates that Mengzi studied under Zisi, "初, 孟子師子思....". *SJ* 史記 has a different account, it says, "Meng Ke was a Zou national, he studied under the student of Zi Si." "孟軻, 鄒人也, 受業子思之門人." *SJ* 史記, 卷 44, 'Mengzi, Xunqing liezhuan 孟子荀卿列傳' 第 14, p. 542.

Previously, Mengzi (Meng Ke) studied under Master Zisi and had asked his tutor what was the most significant issue in shepherding a population. Zisi answered,[139] "One must commence by teaching the people to pursue after benefits and gains." Mengzi asked again, "Shouldn't the elites instruct their people to practice benevolence and righteousness? Why talk of pursuing after benefits and gains?" Zishi responded, "Righteousness is the penultimate of all benefits and gains. If the elites do not harbour any benevolent sentiments, the commoners will be at odds with each other; and when the elites are corrupt and unethical, his dependents will be out in force deceiving each other. It would be most unfavourable and detrimental. The *Book of Changes* says, 'The meaning of gains is the aggregates of righteousness.'[140] It is also said, 'Employing gains to settle the populous is a manifestation of virtue.' Is is the veritable meaning of gains and benefits."

Sima Guang annotates:

Zisi and Mengzi held reciprocal views. Only truly sagacious people understand that the ultimate of benefit and gain are benevolent and righteous based while the people wanting in such virtues do not comprehend the subtleties. Mengzi did not raise the issue of gains and benefits with the king of Liang, whereas he emphasised the significance of benevolence and righteousness, as he was addressing an audience with a different conceptual disposition.

335 BCE *Bingsu* 丙戌 Warring States 戰國

King Xian of Zhou	周顯王	34th year
Duke Jing of Lu	魯景公	11th year
King Hui of Qin	秦惠王	3rd year
Song Ticheng	宋剔成	35th year
King Wei of Chu	楚威王	5th year
King Wei of Qi	齊威王	24th year
King Hui of Wei	魏惠王	36th year
Marquis Zhao of Hann	韓昭侯	24th year
Marquis Su of Zhao	趙肅侯	15th year
Duke Wen of Yan	燕文公	27th year

139 Kong Ji 孔伋 (483-402 BCE), with a polite name of Zisi 子思, was a Lu 魯 national, one of the most outstanding literati icons. He was the grandson of Confucius and the son of Kong Li 孔鯉. *SJ* 史記, 卷 117 'Kongzi shijia 孔子世家' 第 17, p. 1748.
Zisi worked for Duke Mu of Lu 魯穆公 (r. 415-383 BCE) for some time. Legend has it that he compiled the *Zhongyong* 中庸 one of the *Four-Books, Sishu* 四書. However, this could not be verified. The book he composed, the *Zisi zi* 子思子 has since been lost.

140 The *Book of Changes, Yijing* 易經, 上經, 第一卦 乾, annotation of 'li' 利 "利者, 義之和也."
The *Yijing* 易經, Xici part II 繫辭 下傳 第五章, "利用安身, 以崇德也."

Marquis Cheng of Wey	衛成侯	27th year

I. Qin invaded Hann; Yiyang was annexed.[141]

---

334 BCE *Dinghai* 丁亥 Warring States 戰國

King Xian of Zhou	周顯王	35th year
Duke Jing of Lu	魯景公	12th year
King Hui of Qin	秦惠王	4th year
Song Ticheng	宋剔成	36th year
King Wei of Chu	楚威王	6th year
King Wei of Qi	齊威王	25th year
King Hui of Wei	魏惠王	Houyuan 後元 1st year
Marquis Zhao of Hann	韓昭侯	25th year
Marquis Su of Zhao	趙肅侯	16th year
Duke of Yan	燕文公	28th year
Marquis Cheng of Wey	衛成侯	28th year

I. The king of Qi met the king of Wei at the Xuzhou Province. The kings honoured each other with the status of king.[142]

II. Marquis Zhao of Hann constructed a lofty gateway.[143] Qu Tijiu said,[144] "Your Highness, I don't think you should use this gate. Why? It is not the right time. By this, I do not mean using the gate at a specific time or choosing a right date according to divination. When one goes through life, he goes through the vicissitudes of life. Previously when Your Highness was enjoying affluence and success you did not construct a gate. The year before last, the king of Qin annexed your Yiyang and now your state is agonizing over a drought. Instead of trying to be frugal and prudent to bring some much-needed relief for your citizenry, you are squandering your resources during challenging times. Hence, it is not an opportune time to construct the gate."

III. The king of Yue was preparing to invade Qi.[145] The king of Qi sent his emissary to persuade the king that it would be far more rewarding had he attacked Chu instead.[146] The king of Yue then

---

141 Hann 韓. Yiyang 宜陽 - Yiyangxian Henan 河南 宜陽縣.

142 King Wei of Qi 齊威王 Tian Yinqi 田因齊.
King Hui of Wei 魏惠王 Wei Ying 魏罃. Marquis Hei changed his title this year to King – *wang* 王, also changing his regnal year to *houyuan* 後元. See translation of Yang Kuan's article for details of the confusion caused by this incident.
Xuzhou 徐州 - Tengxian Shandong 山東 滕縣.
It was a turning point in the history of the Warring States, as the sovereigns of Qi and Wei proclaimed kings, without going through the sanction of the Zhou King. It indicated the breakdown of the instituted rites and etiquettes. The two kings set examples for the other fief states to follow.

143 Marquis Zhao of Hann 韓昭侯 6th.

144 Qu Yijiu 屈宜臼 was a minister of Chu 楚; he was visiting Hann 韓 at this stage.

145 King of Yue 越王 Si Wujiang 姒無彊.

attacked Chu. The armed forces of Chu gave the invaders a resounding defeat; it followed up by annexing all the territories of the former kingdom of Wu.[147] The territories of Chu extended to Zhejiang in the east. Yue people subsequently dispersed; the remnants of the Yue royal households fell into internecine fighting; some proclaimed themselves as kings, or as lords; others led their tribes to settle in the coastal regions, in the end, they all submitted to Chu.

---

333 BCE *Wuzi* 戊子 Warring States 戰國

King Xian of Zhou	周顯王	36th year
Duke Jing of Lu	魯景公	13th year
King Hui of Qin	秦惠王	5th year
Song Ticheng	宋剔成	37th year
King Wei of Chu	楚威王	7th year
King Wei of Qi	齊威王	26th year
King Hui of Wei	魏惠王	Houyuan 2nd year
Marquis Zhao of Hann	韓昭侯	26th year
Marquis Su of Zhao	趙肅侯	17th year
Duke Wen of Yan	燕文公	29th year
Marquis Cheng of Wey	衛成侯	29th year

I. Chu made an expedition against Qi and had Xuzhou placed under siege.[148]

II. The huge gateway constructed by Hann was completed. Marquis Zhao died, his son King Xuanhui succeeded to his position.[149]

III. Some time before this, Su Qin from Luoyang proposed a grand unification scheme of All under Heaven to the king of Qin.[150] The king disregarded his proposal. Su Qin then travelled forth to Yan and proposed to Duke Wen of Yan;[151] he said, "The reason Yan has not been invaded and subjected to warfare is because Zhao is a protective buffer to your south. If Qin invades Yan, the war front is one thousand *li* from its heartland, whereas if Zhao invades Yan the battlefield is only one hundred *li*

Yue 越王 (r. 354-333 BCE). *SJ* 史記, 卷 111, 'Yuewang Gou Jian shijia 越王勾踐世家' 第 11, pp. 1605-1607.
The kingdom lasted for 164 years.

146 Tian Yinqi 田因齊.

147 King of Wu 吳王 (r. 585-473 BCE). Wu 吳 was one of the Five Hegemons during the Spring and Autumn era 春秋; Yue 越 finally annihilated it, the kingdom was situated in Yue, present-day Zhejiang 越 浙江. *SJ* 史記, 卷 101, 'Wu Taibo shijia 吳太伯世家' 第 1, pp. 1397-1398.

148 Xuzhou 徐州 - Tengxian Shandong 山東 滕縣.

149 Marquis Zhao of Hann 韓昭侯, 6th.
Marquis Wei 威侯 7th (332-326 BCE).

150 Zhou Luoyang native 周 洛陽人, Su Qin 蘇秦.
King Hui of Qin 秦惠王 Ying Si 嬴駟.

151 Duke Wen of Yan 燕文公. The strategy Su Qin proposed to Duke Wen was in variance with his original scheme he proposed to Qin.

from Zhao's territories. It is a fallacious notion to be uneasy about an invasion coming from one thousand *li* away while the least concerned with probable calamities coming from within one hundred *li*. There is yet a worse strategy than this. I would like to negotiate on your behalf, Your Highness, with Zhao for peaceful coexistence to unite as brotherly states; [152] after that Yin does not have to be overly concerned about its security." Duke Wen accepted the proposal. He financed Su Qin to arrange horses and carriages to travel to Zhao. Su Qin said to Marquis Su, "There is no state more powerful than yours east of the Mountains.[153] There is no state more feared by Qin than Zhao; nevertheless, they are hesitant in invading Zhao for one simple reason, you have Hann and Wei at your rear. If Qin invades Hann and Wei, it will be quite easy for Qin as the two states are located on a plain without the obstacles of swift rivers and lofty mountains to stem the march of its army.[154] Making a slight inroad into the two states, Qin can easily march as far as their capital cities. If Hann and Wei cannot sustain the assault, they will submit to Qin. Without the hindrance of Hann and Wei, Qin will bring calamity to Zhao. Your subject has made a study of the map of the world and concluded that the combined areas held by all the major fiefdoms are five times larger than Qin, and the military forces are ten times more numerous. If the six kingdoms are to form an alliance to face west against Qin, it will indubitably break. Whereas, there are horizontal coalition advocates who propose to the various states to cede their land to Qin to settle for peace. When Qin's objective is met, these advocates will enjoy prosperity and glory, leaving these states to suffer from the oppressive consequences coming from Qin. Moreover, these men do not have to bear or even concerned about the consequences of their deeds. They incessantly exaggerate the power of Qin; through intimidation, they coerce the fief lords to cede more land to Qin. Your Highness should seriously consider other options. As far as your subject is concerned, Your Highness, the best option is to form an alliance with Hann, Wei, Qi, Chu, Yan, and Zhao to go against Qin. The way forward is to arrange a conference with the generals and chancellors to meet near the Huanshui River; there you could make exchanges of held hostages and settle for an alliance. The pledge is, 'If Qin attacks any one of the six states, the other five will respond with an allied force for a counteroffensive; or cause disturbances to Qin or they will march to bring relief to the state. If one of the states breaks its pledge, the other five states will go against the pledge-breaker.' Once this alliance is achieved to go against Qin, it will not have the mettle to march beyond the Hangu Pass to bring more destruction to the fiefdoms east of the Mountains."[155] Marquis Su was immensely pleased with the proposal, he made Su Qin a guest of honour, showering him with rich and opulent gifts, and he then asked him to set off to persuade the other fiefdoms to participate in the alliance.[156]

---

152 The *ZGC* 戰國策 relates, "Duke Wen of Yan 燕文王 said, 'My Fiefdom is far too paltry, to my west I have the powerful state of Qin, to my south I have Zhao 趙 and Qi 齊, besides they too are powerful states to be reckoned with. You, Sir, your speech has enlightened me. If a south-north alliance could be negotiated and accomplished to bring peace and security to the Yan State 燕, I will pledge my entire nation in support of the alliance.'" *ZGC* 戰國策, 卷 29, 'Yance Su Qin 燕策 1 - 蘇秦將爲從', p. 326.

153 Marquis Su of Zhao 趙肅侯 Zhao Yu 趙語.
Shandong 山東 east of the Xiaohan Mountains 崤山.

154 Hann's capital - Xinzheng 新鄭 - Xinzhengxian Henan 河南 新鄭縣.
Daliang 大梁 - Kaifengxian Henan 河南 開封縣.

155 Hanguguan Pass 函谷關 – Lingbaoxian Henan 河南 靈寶縣.
Shandong – east of the Mountains.

156 The *ZGC* 戰國策 relates, "Zhao Yu 趙語 said, 'I am young and inexperienced, besides I have just acceded to the throne, no one has provided me with any guidance to govern my state. Sir, your

It was about this time when Sishou of Qin invaded Wei;[157] the Wei army with its forty thousand or more men was given a resounding defeat. Long Jia, the Wei general was captured, and the city of Diaoyin was annexed.[158] The Qin army was poised to march farther east. Su Qin was apprehensive that had the Qin army marched into Zhao his plan for an alliance would be in jeopardy. He reasoned that Zhang Yi was the only person who could be an envoy to go to Qin; hence, he inflamed Zhang Yi to proceed.[159]

---

pacification plan to bring peace to all the states, preventing aggressor to invade the others is a superlative idea. I wish to comply.'" He enfeoffed Su Qin as Lord Wuan 武安君, bestowed him with one hundred *anche* carriages with seats, two hundred and twenty taels - *liang* of gold coins, one hundred pure white jade pieces, and one thousand bales (*shu* 束) of embroidery. *ZGC* 戰國策, 卷 19, 'Zhao strategy 趙策 2 蘇秦從燕之趙', P. 201.

157 Qin General 秦將軍 Xishou 犀首 - Gongsun Yan 公孫衍.

158 Wei General 魏將軍 Long Jia 龍賈.

Diaoyin 雕陰 - Luxian Shaanxi 陝西 鄜縣.

159 Zhang Yi 張儀 (?-310 BCE) was a Wei national 魏人. At the time of King Hui of Wei 魏惠王 (370-319 BCE) he entered the Qin court 秦. Duke Huiwen of Qin 秦 惠文公 (r. 337-311 BCE) made him a guest Counsellor or Consultant - *keqing* 客卿. During the 10th year of Duke Huiwen 惠文 (328 BCE), the duke ordered Zhang Yi and Prince Hua 公子華 to attack Wei 魏; which capitulated and sued for peace by ceding Shangjun Prefecture 上郡. The same year Zhang Yi was made the chancellor of Qin. King Huiwen of Qin 秦惠文王 *gengyaun* 更元 2nd year, Zhang Yi and the ministers from Qi 齊, Chu 楚 and Wei 魏 met at Niesang 齧桑 (322 BCE); Zhang Yi was discharged of his duty upon returning to Qin. Next year he was made the chancellor of Wei. *Gengyuan* 更元 8th year (316 BCE), he was made chancellor of Qin again. *Gengyuan* 12th year, Zhang Yi was made the chancellor of Chu, shortly after he returned to Qin. King Huiwen of Qin died in 311 BCE and was succeeded by King Wu 秦武王; Zhang Yi and the new king had all along held differences. He finally left Qin in 310 BCE to return to Wei, according to the *Zhushu jinian* 竹書紀年 Zhang Yi died during the 5th month of 310 BCE. According to the *ZGC* 戰國策 Zhang Yi and Su Qin 蘇秦 were opposing political strategists. Sima Guang 司馬光 adopted Sima Qian's 司馬遷 *SJ Zhang Yi liezhuan's* 史記 張儀列傳 accounts and narrated them as contemporaries. *SJ* even suggested that after Su Qin successfully made a career as a guest strategist prompted Zhang Yi to serve at the Qin court and that Zhang Yi died after Su Qin; these incidents did not match historical facts. (The accounts in the *ZZTJ* are principally based on the *SJ* 史記). According to detailed textual studies by contemporary scholars, Zhang Yi lived some time before Su Qin. Strategists Gongsun Yan 公孫衍, Hui Shi 惠施 and Chen Zhen 陳軫 were his contemporaries. Su Qin became politically active after the death of Zhang Yi. The dates of the activities of Zhang Yi in the *SJ* are accurate; however, the dates of Su Qin have been pushed back by some 30 years. The *Xunzi chendao* 荀子 臣道 maintains that both men were crafty sycophants, skilful toadies at earning favours from kings. Sima Qian; on the one hand, claimed that Zhang Yi contrived the propagation of the Horizontal Coalition while he was also a commanding figure in bringing drastic power shifts. The *Hanshu* 漢書 Yiwenzhi Zhangzi 藝文志 張子 mentions that that there were ten chapters on Zhang Yi, which were lost after the Han dynasty.

Yang K. 楊寬, *Zhanguoshi* 戰國史, 'Authenticating the historical materials on hezhong 合縱連橫史料的去偽存真.' pp. 15-16. (See translation in the Appendix).

Yang K. 楊寬, *Zhanguoshi* 戰國史, pp. 348-355.

ZG LS BK QS The Zhongguo lishi baike quanshu 中國歷史百科全書. p. 354, p. 512.

Zhang Yi was a Wei national; he and Su Qin had served under Master Guigu on political strategies.[160] Su Qin maintained that he was nowhere as talented as Zhang Yi and yet the latter, having drifted through all the states at length was not appreciated for his outstanding knowledge, and was mired at Chu. Su Qin invited him to travel to Zhao; but upon his arrival, he purposely insulted him. Zhang Yi was in distress and concluded that only Qin among all the fief lords could bring calamity to Zhao. Hence, he headed to Qin. Su Qin clandestinely dispatched his retainer to accompany Zhang Yi to Qin, showering money to aid Yi as he proceeded. Zhang Yi managed to gain an audience with the king of Qin. The king was immensely pleased and made him a foreign guest advisor *keqing*.[161] At this stage, the covert retainer bid Zhang Yi farewell, he said, "My master Lord Su was most concerned that Qin might invade Zhao; as it would undermine the proposed alliance. He maintained that only you could restrain the power of Qin; hence, he asked me to prod you along intentionally. He told me to provide you with every financial support in secret. Everything has been conducted meticulously according to Lord Su's scheme." Zhang Yi said, "Oh my goodness, I fell into a ruse, and I was not even aware of it. It is quite obvious that I am inferior to Lord Su; please thank him for me. Also, please tell him as long as he is working on his scheme, Zhang Yi dares not discuss issues related to the matter."[162]

Su Qin then proposed to King Xuanhui of Hann,[163] "Hann has over nine hundred *li* of land; and Your Highness, you have several hundred thousand armed men. The finest bows, crossbows, and swords under Heaven are produced in Hann. It is said a Hann archer can use his feet to draw his crossbow to shoot over one hundred times without getting tired. The gallant Hann warriors, armed

---

160 Political Alliances – *Zongheng beihe* 縱橫捭闔 was probably the earliest form of political science, the art of making alliances and creating political discords among warring and friendly states.
Master Guiguzi 鬼谷子.

161 Guest Advisor, or Counsellor, or Consultant *keqing* 客卿.

162 The historical events of Su Qin are related in the *ZGC* 戰國策 and the *SJ* 史記. The *SJ* maintains that he was a native of Dongzhou Luoyang 東周 洛陽人. When Sima Qian 司馬遷 was composing his *SJ*, he realized that many accounts of Su Qin were unreliable. While he was especially careful in the treatment of dates and historic facts, he nevertheless did make some mistakes. Most scholars now accept that Su Qin was probably active during the time of King Zhao of Yan 燕昭王 (r. 311-279 BCE) and King Min of Qi 齊湣王 (r. 301-284 BCE). He took on a ministry position at Yan, at which stage his principle task was to create animosity between Qi and Zhao to bring relief to Yan; and to ally with Zhao, Li Dui 趙國 李兑 and the five fiefdoms for an allied front against Qin. Later he left Yan to go to Qi and was greatly respected by King Min of Qi, while he remained loyal to Yan covertly, working clandestinely on its behalf. He encouraged Qi to assault against Song 宋 shifting the attention away from Yan; Qi was caught off guarded and was defeated by Yan. The conspiracy against Qi was finally discovered; the kingdom punished him by dismemberment by the chariots. (In *ZZTJ* he was assassinated by a Qi minister see 317 BCE, 317-11). The *Hanshu* 漢書 Yiwenzhi 藝文志 mentions that there were 31 chapters on *Suzi* 蘇子; however the books were lost after the Han Dynasty. In the more recent archaeological discovery of Mawangdui Han Tomb 馬王堆 漢墓 (excavated in 1973), in one of the texts of the *Boshuben* 帛書本, there are 11 chapters of memorials submitted to the king of Yan and king of Zhao by Su Qin. These are not recorded in the *ZGC*.
Reference: the *Zhongguo lishi baike quanshu* 中國歷史百科全書, p. 354.
N.B. For more details of textual research on Su Qin and Zhang Yi see the translation of Yang Kuan's articles in Appendix 3.
Yang K. 楊寬, *Zhanguoshi* 戰國史, 'Hezhong lianheng shiliao di quwei cunzhen 合縱連橫史料的去偽存真.' pp. 15-16.

163 Marquis Wei of Hann 韓威侯 was also known as King Xuanhui 宣惠王 1st (332-312 BCE).

to the teeth, wearing sturdy protective armour, carrying crossbows and arrows, wielding sharp swords, one man alone could easily take on a hundred enemies; it is not even worth mentioning. However, Your Highness is submissive to Qin. It is obvious that Qin will demand the ceding of Yiyang and Chenggao.[164] They may demand those two counties this year, come next year they will return for more. If you comply, there will be no more land to cede, and if they refuse to accept the fact the affable relationship between the two states will be gone forever, and calamity will soon follow. We all know that land is limited at Hann; whereas the avarice greed of Qin is insatiable and unlimited. It is a disastrous strategy for peace and Qin does not need a war to take over Hann. There is a common adage, 'It's better to be the grimy beaks of a chicken, rather than the rear of an ox.'[165] With the astuteness of Your Highness, besides being backed by your valiant warriors, you have chosen to be the rear of an ox. I am ashamed of you, Your Highness." The king of Hann accepted Su Qin's suggestion.[166]

Su Qin suggested to the king of Wei, "Your Highness has a domain of one thousand *li*; ostensibly a small state, nevertheless within the realms there are numerous villages and hamlets; the agrarian farms have taken up so much acreage that there is a shortage of land for herding. The kingdom is densely populated; the cities are teeming with carriages and horses, hustling hither and thither day in and day out; people are coming and going bustling with activities, reminding one of the endless military parades of the three armies. Your subject's educated guess is your military force is no smaller than that of Chu, and I have heard that your army is made up of two hundred thousand field warriors; two hundred thousand green-turban infantries; two hundred thousand assault warriors; one hundred thousand provision labourers; six hundred chariots and five thousand warhorses. Nevertheless, you are heeding the advice of your ministers at court that you should submit to Qin. The king of Zhao sent me to pay Your Highness a visit, and to relate to you my humble scheme to form an alliance, hoping that you will give the proposal some serious considerations." The king of Wei accepted the proposal.[167]

Su Qin said to the king of Qi,[168] "Strategic passes surround Qi to its four quarters. Qi boasts of an area of two thousand *li*. You have an armed force of several hundred thousand strong, with food reserves stored in mountainous heaps. The three armed forces *sanjun* are exceptionally well trained, supported by the crack regiments from the five-family clans.[169] Upon making advances, they are swift

---

164 Yiyang 宜陽, Chenggao 成皋.

165 "It is better to be the grimy beaks of a chicken, than the rear of an ox." "寧為鷄口，無為牛後." According to annotation by Han scholars, the two phases are, "寧為鷄尸，無為牛從." The meaning of these two statements is, 'One would rather be the master of a brood of chicken than the follower of a herd of cattle.' *ZZTJ JZ*, Vol 1, p. 77.

166 According to the *ZGC* 戰國策, "The expression of Duke Zhao of Hann turned grim, holding onto his sword, he sighed and said sternly, 'I would rather die than lowering myself to submit to Qin. Please relay my message to Marquis Zhao that I wish to pledge my allegiance."

167 The *ZGC* 戰國策 relates, "Wei Ying said, 'I am so uneducated, I have never heard of such words of wisdom, now please relate to me what your sovereign (Zhao Yu 趙語) has to say, and we will comply with much delight.'"

168 King Wei of Qi 齊威王 Tian Yinqi 田因齊.

169 *Sanjun* 三軍. At the time of Zhanguo the armies were made up of *shangjun* 上軍, *zhongjun* 中軍 and *xiajun* 下軍; these were probably the representations of their level of military skills and training. *ZZTJ Yang Bo Edition*, Vol 1, p. 163.
During Western Zhou, only the Son of Heaven was allowed to have six or three regiments of armies; the fief lords were only allowed to have one.

as airborne arrows; upon entering into battle, they are ferocious like thunder claps; when they retreat, they vanish like wind and rain. Even had there been any military conscription for war, the recruits were not conscripted from beyond the Taishan Mountain, or across the Clear River, or the Bohai Sea.[170] There are seventy thousand households in the capital city of Linzi, [171] and I estimate that there are at least three young men from each household eligible for military service. Your Highness you do not have to go to remote counties for recruitment, in the city of Linzi alone there are at least two hundred and one thousand men eligible for conscription. Linzi is an opulent metropolis, and the people are affluent, the civilians are passionately engaged in cockfighting, dog racing, gambling on chess game of *liubo*, and playing football of *taju*.[172] In the main streets, the roadways are so cluttered that the spokes of carriages are crashing and ramming into others; people are rubbing shoulders as they walk down the street using their lapels as sunshades and wiping off sweat streaming down like rain. Hann and Wei are intimidated by Qin for their territorial proximity. Once a war breaks out, within ten days the two states will have reached a critical phase of survival or annihilation; and even had they won the battle they would have lost half of their armed forces; neither state could protect their frontiers. Whereas if they lost the battle against Qin, they are moribund, followed shortly by subjugation. It explains why Hann and Wei have been particularly cautious in their diplomatic policies; they find it difficult to make wars with Qin but much easier to submit to it with forbearance. Whereas if Qin invades Qi, it will have Hann and Wei at its rear. Their army has to pass the Passage of Yangjin of Wey, continuing they have to pass through the defile of Kangfu; [173] the passage is so narrow that carriages cannot wheel through in pairs and cavalry cannot ride forth in pairs. When one hundred men are garrisoned at the strategic point, even one thousand men cannot make an advance. If Qin risks a long-range expedition, it has to consider seriously what Hann and Wey could connive at its rear. Your subject has therefore concluded that Qin is merely making vacant threats against your kingdom, beating war drums without real intention of making war. It is obvious Qin could not find a suitable strategy to go against your state. You are not deliberating over their lack of alternatives, merely considering facing west to serve Qin. It is without any doubt an

---

Wujia 五家, five households - these were the elite households that controlled the Qi 齊 court at one stage – Gao 高, Guo 國, Qing 慶, Cui 崔 and Chen 陳 (Tian 田), apparently they still controlled the armies. *ZZTJ JZ*, Vol 1, p. 78.

170 Taishan Mountain 泰山, Huanghe River 黄河, Bohai Sea 渤海.

171 Linzi 臨淄 - Linzixian Shandong 山東 臨淄縣 – the capital of Qi 齊.

172 *Liubo* 六博, also known as *lubo* 陸博 or *liubo* 六簙, was a form of chess game, details of how the game was played are now lost; some claim that it was the forerunner of modern Chinese chess. A full set of the game was unearthed at the tomb of the king of Changsha at Mawangdui 長沙王 馬王堆 number 3 tomb, which was interred during the 12th year (168 BCE) of Emperor Wen of Han 漢文帝.

Zhanguoshi 戰國史, Yang K. 楊寬, p. 604.

Football,* *taju* 蹋鞠 was a game of football; the mention of which was perhaps the earliest reference in China texts. The ball was made with a leather pouch, which was stuffed with cloth fibre or feather. The rules of the game have since been lost, but it might have been played similarly to the modern football game. When Huo Qubing 霍去病 was making expeditions against the Xiongnu, he asked his retainers to clear fields for him to play *taju* – Yap, J., *Wars with the Xiongnu*, 119 BCE, p. 192. * Some would contend that it is more appropriate to translate football as soccer, nevertheless it was a ball game played by kicking a ball. It is interesting to note that the game is preserved in Japan and is played during festive time with eight participants.

Zhanguoshi 戰國史, Yang K. 楊寬. p. 647.

173 Wey 衛, Yangjin Aidao Passage 陽晉隘道 - Yunchengxian Shandong 山東 鄆城縣.

Kangfu 亢夫 - Jiningxian Shandong 山東 濟寧縣.

intrigue conjured up by your ministers to let you believe that it is the only viable solution. Now with your subject's plan, you can dismiss the notion that you have to serve Qin while attaining actual benefit of strengthening your state. Your Highness, please consider his proposal carefully."[174] The king of Qi agreed to the proposal.

Su Qin travelled southwest to Chu; he said to King Wei,[175] "Chu is a powerful state under Heaven. You have a vast domain of six thousand over *li*. Your state boasts of having one million or more armed men, one thousand war chariots, ten thousand warhorses and you have amassed food reserve to last for ten years. All these are invaluable assets for attaining hegemony. Among the states under Heaven Qin dreads Chu most. When Chu was powerful Qin became enfeebled, and when Qin became powerful Chu became weak. There is no room for a peaceful coexistence. It will be a long lasting and enduring strategy for your kingdom to consider joining the alliance to isolate Qin. Your subject will find means to make the various states east of the Mountains submit to your kingdom, paying tributes and homage to Your Highness during the four seasons of the year. Your Highness will be the head of the alliance. The other states will surrender their holy shrines to your command, and you will also be responsible for training the allied troops placed under your charge. On the other hand, if you participate in the east-west coalition proposed by Qin in a bid for peace, it, in reality, means ceding more land to service Qin. The two options are diametrically opposite and are vastly different. Your Highness, where do you stand?" The king of Chu also settled for the proposal.[176]

The heads of states nominated Su Qin as the chief of the Alliance, taking on the chancellorship of the six states in unison. Su Qin returned to Zhao in the north to report his progress; armed guards and impedimenta accompanied his carriages; he was treated no differently to the head of a state.

---

174 The *ZGC* 戰國策 relates, "Tian Yinqi 田因齊 responded, 'I am a fool. Sir, you have enlightened me with words of wisdom from the Marquis of Zhao 趙侯; I will lead my people to follow Zhao." *ZGC,* 戰國策 卷 8, 'Qice 1 齊一, 蘇秦爲趙合從說齊宣王', p. 101.

175 King Wei of Chu 楚威王.

176 According to the *ZGC* 戰國策 - The king of Chu 楚王 Mi Shang 芈商 said, "My kingdom borders with Qin 秦 in the west. Qin has already captured and occupied Ba 巴 and Shu 蜀 which were Chu counties previously; we know they have the ambition to take procession of Hanzhong 漢中 (southern parts of Shaanxi 陝西 南部) as well. Qin is a ferocious and bellicose state; no nation should even go near it. Hann 韓 and Wei 魏 are terrorized and intimidated by the might of Qin; I do not think we should place too much faith in those two states; in case if they have an about face and go over to the Qin camp, exposing our secret plan, putting us all in harm's way. I have been thinking about the issue seriously; if my kingdom were to enter into a war with Qin, chances are we might not win. Whereas discussing the issue with my officers and ministers for a strategy, they could not proffer anything useful and exceptional. I could not sleep at night; I eat my food but cannot savour its taste. I am utterly confused and disconcerted; like a banner fluttering in the wind. Sir, you have come up with this notion of forming an Alliance to ensure our independence; my kingdom will participate in the Alliance." *ZGC,* 戰國策, 卷 14, 'Chuce 楚策 1, 蘇秦爲趙合從說楚威王', p. 154.

IV. King Wei of Qi died; his son succeeded to the throne, he was known as King Xuan posthumously.[177] The new king appreciated that Marquis Cheng framed Tian Ji, he summoned him to return to the state and restored his former position. (N.B.)[178]

V. Duke Wen of Yan passed away; his son King Yi succeeded to the throne.[179]

VI. Marquis Cheng of Wey died; his son Marquis Ping succeeded his position.[180]

---

332 BCE *Jichou* 己丑 Warring States 戰國

King Xian of Zhou	周顯王	37th year
Duke Jing of Lu	魯景公	14th year
King Hui of Qin	秦惠王	6th year
Song Ticheng	宋剔成	38th year
King Wei of Chu	楚威王	8th year
King Wei of Qi	齊威王	27th year
King Wei of Wei	魏惠王	Houyuan 後元 3rd year
Marquis Wei of Hann	韓威侯	1st year
Marquis Su of Zhao	趙肅侯	18th year
King Yi of Yan	燕易王	1st year
Marquis Ping of Wey	衛平侯	1st year

I. King Hui of Qin commanded Xishou to incite Qi and Wei to go against Zhao through intrigue,[181] a move to dislodge the Alliance. Marquis Su of Zhao reprimanded Su Qin for his duplicity. Su Qin was apprehensive; he requested to go to Yan, seeking the marquis's support to make retribution against Qi for breaching the Alliance. Upon Su Qin's departure from Zhao, the Alliance broke up completely. The Zhao army broke river dams to inundate the invading Qi and Wei armies, which withdrew.

II. Wei ceded the city of Yinjin to Qin, as a prerequisite for peace; Yinjin was Huayin.

III. Qi invaded Yan, the army captured ten cities, which were returned later.

---

177 King Wei of Qi 齊威王 Tian Yinqi 田因齊, 1st.
King Xuan of Qi 齊宣王 Tian Pijiang 田辟彊 2nd (r. 319-301 BCE) or (r. 320-302 BCE).

178 Tian Yinqi did not die this year; he died in 320 BCE, the text has made an error here.

179 Duke Wen of Yan 燕文公 37th.
King Yi of Yan 燕易王 38th (r. 332-321 BCE).

180 Duke Cheng of Wey 衛成侯 Wey Su 衛速 43rd.
Marquis Ping of Wey 衛平侯 44th (r. 332-325 BCE) or (r. 342-335 BCE).

181 King Hui of Qin 秦惠王 Ying Si 嬴駟.
Xishou 犀首 = Gongsun Yan 公孫衍.
Qin indicated that they would return the seven walled cities, (including Xiangling 襄陵, southeast of Linfen 臨汾 in Shanxi 山西) previously seized from Wei 魏. It prompted Jia Yi 賈誼 (200-168 BCE) the Han scholar to remark, "Qin did not cause the demise of the six kingdoms."

331 BCE *Gengyin* 庚寅 Warring States 戰國

King Xian of Zhou	周顯王	38th year
Duke Jing of Lu	魯景公	15th year
King Hui of Qin	秦惠王	7th year
Song Ticheng	宋剔成	39th year
King Wei of Chu	楚威王	9th year
King Wei of Qi	齊威王	28th year
King Hui of Wei	魏惠王	Houyuan 後元 4th year
Marquis Wei of Hann	韓威侯	2nd year
Marquis Su of Zhao	趙肅侯	19th year
King of Yi Yan	燕易王	2nd year
Marquis Ping of Wey	衛平侯	2nd year

There was no record this year.

330 BCE *Xinmao* 辛卯 Warring States 戰國

King Xian of Zhou	周顯王	39th year
Duke Jing of Lu	魯景公	16th year
Duke Hui of Qin	秦惠王	8th year
Song Ticheng	宋剔成	40th year
King Wei of Chu	楚威王	10th year
King Wei of Qi	齊威王	29th year
King Hui of Wei	魏惠王	Houyuan 後元 5th year
Marquis of Hann	韓威侯	3rd year
Marquis Su of Zhao	趙肅侯	20th year
King of Yi Yan	燕易王	3rd year
Marquis Ping of Wey	衛平侯	3rd year

1. Qin invaded Wei; Jiao and Quwo were besieged; Wei surrendered areas west of Shaoliang and west of the River *Hexi* to Qin.[182]

---

[182] Jiaocheng 焦城 – Shaanxian Henan 河南 陜縣.
Quwo 曲沃 - Shaanxian Henan 河南 陜縣, 20 km southwest of Quwozhen 曲沃鎮.
Wei capital, Shaoliang 少梁 - Hannchengxian Shaanxi 陜西 韓城縣 and West of Huanghe *Hexi* 河西 黄河. Wei had already capitulated parts of *Hexi* to Qin before this. (see 403-1).
In 330 BCE, the Qin General *daliangzao* 大良造, Gongsun Yan 公孫衍 gave the Wei army a resounding defeat at Diaoyin 雕陰 – south of Ganquanxian Shaanxi 陜西 甘泉縣南.

329 BCE *Renchen* 壬辰 Warring States 戰國

King Xian of Zhou	周顯王	40th year
Duke Jing of Lu	魯景公	17th year
King Hui of Qin	秦惠王	9th year
Song Ticheng	宋剔成	41st year
King Wei of Chu	楚威王	11th year
King Wei of Qi	齊威王	30th year
King Hui of Wei	魏惠王	Houyuan 後元 6th year
Marquis Wei of Hann	韓威侯	4th year
Marquis Su of Zhao	趙肅侯	21st year
King Yi of Yan	燕易王	4th year
Marquis Ping of Wey	衛平侯	4th year

I. Qin invaded Wei; the army crossed the Huanghe River and occupied Fenyin and Pishi; Jiao was also annexed.[183]

II. King Wei of Chu died; his son, Huai, known posthumously as King Huai succeeded him.[184]

III. Song Yan, the younger brother of the duke of Song, revolted against the state; he attacked Ticheng; Song Ticheng escaped and sought refuge at Qi, Song Yan proclaimed as the Head of State.[185]

328 BCE *Guisi* 癸巳 Warring States 戰國

King Xian of Zhou	周顯王	41st year
Duke Jing of Lu	魯景公	18th year
Duke Hui of Qin	秦惠王	10th year
King Kang of Song	宋康王	1st year
King Huai of Chu	楚懷王	1st year
King Wei of Qi	齊威王	31st year

183 Fenyin 汾陰 - Ronghexian Shanxi 山西 榮河縣.
Pishan 皮山 - Hejinxian Shanxi 山西 河津縣.
Jiaocheng 焦城 - Shaanxian Henan 河南 陝縣.

184 King Wei of Chu 楚威王 Mi Shang 羋商, 20th.
King Huai of Chu 楚懷王 Mi Huai 羋槐, 21st (r. 328-299 BCE).

185 Song Techeng 宋剔成 34th.
Song Yan 宋偃 35th (r. 369-329 BCE).

King Hui of Wei	魏惠王	Houyuan 後元 7th year
Marquis Wei of Hann	韓威侯	5th year
Marquis Su of Zhao	趙肅侯	22nd year
King Yi of Yan	燕易王	5th year
Marquis Ping of Wey	衛平侯	5th year

I. Prince Hua of Qin, a Qin noble and Zhang Yi led an army to go against Wei at Puyang and annexed the city.[186] Zhang Yi suggested to the king of Qin to return Puyang to Wei. It was further agreed to send Prince Yao to Wei as a hostage.[187] Zhang Yi then said King Hui of Wei, "Qin is exceptional munificent with Wei, and Wei should not be discourteous towards Qin." Wei promptly ceded fifteen counties at Shangjun Prefecture to Qin.[188] Upon Zhang Yi's return to Qin, he resumed his position as Qin chancellor.

---

327 BCE *Jiawu* 甲午 Warring States 戰國

King Xian of Zhou	周顯王	42nd year
Duke Jing of Lu	魯景公	19th year
King Hui of Qin	秦惠王	11th year
King Kang of Song	宋康王	2nd year
King Huai of Chu	楚懷王	2nd year
King Wei of Qi	齊威王	32nd year
King Wei of Wei	魏惠王	Houyuan 8th year
Marquis Wei of Hann	韓威侯	6th year
Marquis Su of Zhao	趙肅侯	23rd year
King Yi of Yan	燕易王	6th year
Marquis Ping of Wey	衛平侯	6th year

I. Qin established the Yiqu County, [189] the tribal chieftain was appointed to serve at the Qin court.

II. Qin returned the cities of Jiao and Quwo to Wei.[190]

---

326 BCE *Yiwei* 乙未 Warring States 戰國

---

186 Ying Hua 贏華, Zhang Yi 張儀.
Puyang 蒲陽 - Yongjixian Shanxi 山西 永濟縣.

187 Ying Yao 贏繇, one of the members of the royal family.

188 Shangjun 上郡 – Suidexian Shaanxi 陝西 綏德縣.
King Hui of Wei 魏惠王 Wei Ying 魏罃.

189 Yiqu 義渠 was a Rong nomadic tribe 戎族 that settled at Yiquxian 義渠縣, Ningxian Gansu 甘肅 寧縣.

190 See 328 BCE.

King Xian of Zhou	周顯王	43rd year
Duke Jing of Lu	魯景公	20th year
King Hui of Qin	秦惠王	12th year
King Kang of Song	宋康王	3rd year
King Huai of Chu	楚懷王	3rd year
King Wei of Qi	齊威王	33rd year
King Hui of Wei	魏惠王	Houyuan 後元 9th year
Marquis Wei of Hann	韓威侯	7th year
Marquis Su of Zhao	趙肅侯	24th year
King Yi of Yan	燕易王	7th year
Marquis Ping of Wey	衛平侯	7th year

1. Marquis Su of Zhao died; his son took over the marquisate, known posthumously as King Wuling.[191] He appointed three senior consultants *bowenshi* to preside at his court, as well as three left inspectors *zuoshiguo* and three right inspectors *youshiguo*. He then awarded rich gifts to Fai Yi, a senior minister of his deceased father, and he increased his entitlements.

---

325 BCE *Bingshen* 丙申 Warring States 戰國

King Xian of Zhou	周顯王	44th year
Duke Jing of Lu	魯景公	21st year
King Hui of Qin	秦惠王	13th year
King Kang of Song	宋康王	4th year
King Huai of Chu	楚懷王	4th year
King Wei of Qi	齊威王	4th year
King Hui of Wei	魏惠王	Houyuan 後元 10th year
Marquis Wei of Hann	韓威侯	8th year
King Wuling of Zhao	趙武靈王	1st year
King Yi of Yan	燕易王	8th year
Marquis Ping of Wey	衛平侯	8th year

1. Summer. 4th month 4th day. Duke of Qin proclaimed king.[192]

---

191 Marquis Su of Zhao 趙肅侯 Zhao Yu 趙語.
King Wuling of Zhao 趙武靈王 Zhao Yong 趙雍 (r. 325- 299 BCE) or (r. 325-298 BCE).
Senior consultant *bowenshi* 博聞師, left inspector *zuoshiguo* 左司過, right inspector, *youshiguo* 右司過.
Fei Yi 肥義.

192 Qin sovereign, King Hui of Qin 秦惠王 Ying Si 嬴駟 1st. For convenience, we have denoted him as king during the past 13 years in the year chronicle.

II. Marquis Ping of Wey died, his son Lord Si succeeded him to the marquisate.[193] There was a Wey servitude, who escaped to Wei. The man had successfully treated the ailment of the Wei Queen, the wife of Wei Ying.[194] Lord Si offered fifty units of gold in exchange for the fugitive, but Wei refused to comply. After five protracted negotiations, Wei was still reluctant to meet the terms. Wey Si offered the city of Zuoshi in exchange.[195] The ministers at the Wey Court remonstrated against it, "Is a petty fugitive worth a city to purchase?" Lord Si responded, "This is something beyond your comprehension. When presiding over a state, one must not neglect the trifling matters; chaos will not ensue. If the law of a state cannot be enacted and chastisement cannot be meted out; even ten Zhoshi cities would be useless. If the legal system of a state could be upheld and chastisement implemented with justice, even if we were to lose ten cities it would matter little."

When the king of Wei heard of the remarks, he responded, "This is the aspiration of a sovereign, it would be inauspicious if we don't heed his concern." He ordered the fugitive returned unconditionally in a convict carriage.

---

324 BCE *Dingyou* 丁酉 Warring States 戰國

King Xian of Zhou	周顯王	45th year
Duke Jing of Lu	魯景公	22nd year
King Hui of Qin	秦惠王	1st year
King Kang of Song	宋康王	5th year
King Huai of Chu	楚懷王	5th year
King Wei of Qi	齊威王	35th year
King Hui of Wei	魏惠王	Houyuan 11th year
Marquis Wei of Hann	韓威侯	9th year
King Wuling of Zhao	趙武靈王	2nd year
King Yi of Yan	燕易王	9th year
Sir Wey Si	衛嗣君	1st year

I. Zhang Yi of Qin headed an army invaded Wei; the city of Shaan was annexed.[196]

II. Su Qin had an adulterous affair with the wife of Duke Wen of Yan, the former king. King Yi uncovered the affair. Su Qin was in a dire panic, he proposed to the king, "My presence at Yan serves little purpose in strengthening your kingdom; perhaps I could raise the political expediency

---

193 Marquis Ping of Wey 衛平侯 44th.
Lord Si of Wey 衛嗣君 45th (r. 324-283 BCE) or (r. 334-293 BCE).

194 Queen of Wei 魏后.
Wei Ying 魏罃.

195 Zuoshicheng 左氏城 – place unknown.

196 Qin Chancellor, *xiang* 秦相 Zhang Yi 張儀.
Shaan 陝 was Jiaocheng 焦城, i.e. Shaanxian 陝縣, it was returned to Wei 魏 in 327 BCE.

of Yan by going to Qi." The king accepted his proposal. Su Qin feigned an excuse that he had offended the king of Yan and escaped to Qi. King Xuan of Qi appointed him as a foreign consultant *keqing*. Su Qin persuaded the king of Qi to construct lofty towers and palaces, adding parks, and animal sanctuaries to the kingdom, to manifest the status of the Qi king. It was an effort to weaken Qi on behalf of Yan.

---

323 BCE *Wuxu* 戊戌 Warring States 戰國

King Xian of Zhou	周顯王	46th year
Duke Jing of Lu	魯景公	23rd year
King Hui of Qin	秦惠王	2nd year
King Kang of Song	宋康王	6th year
King Huai of Chu	楚懷王	6th year
King Wei of Qi	齊威王	36th year
King Hui of Wei	魏惠王	Houyuan 後元 12th year
King Xuanhui of Hann	韓宣惠王	10th year
King Wuling of Zhao	趙武靈王	3rd year
King Yi of Yan	燕易王	10th year
Sir Wei Si	衛嗣君	2nd year

I. Zhang Yi of Qin met the Qi and Chu chancellors at Niesang.[197]

II. The sovereigns of Hann and Yan also assumed the title as kings. The exception was King Wuling of Zhao.[198] He maintained, "When the essence of a kingdom is lacking, how one could proclaim king?" He retained his title as Lord of Zhao.

---

322 BCE *Jihai* 己亥 Warring States 戰國

King Xian of Zhou	周顯王	47th year
Duke Jing of Lu	魯景公	24th year
King Hui of Qin	秦惠王	3rd year
King Kang of Song	宋康王	7th year
King Huai of Chu	楚懷王	7th year
King Wei of Qi	齊威王	37th year
King Hui of Wei	魏惠王	Houyuan 後元 13th year
King Xuanhui of Hann	韓宣惠王	11th year
King Wuling of Zhao	趙武靈王	4th year

197 Qin 秦, Zhang Yi 張儀.
Niesang 齧桑 - Peixian Jiangsu 江蘇 沛縣.

198 King Wuling of Zhao 趙武靈王 Zhao Yong 趙雍. The title of king was appended later.

King Yi of Yan	燕易王	11th year
Sir Wei Si	衛嗣君	3rd year

I. Upon returning from Niesang to Qin, Zhang Yi of Qin was released of his duties as chancellor. He went to Wei and took on the position as chancellor.[199] He persuaded the king of Wei to submit to Qin, setting an example for the other fief lords to follow. The king of Wei refused to comply; Qin dispatched an army against it, occupying Quwo and Pingzhou.[200] In the meantime, the Qin court surreptitiously bestowed rich gifts upon Zhang Yi.

---

321 BCE *Gengzi* 庚子 Warring States 戰國

King Xian of Zhou	周顯王	48th year
Duke Jing of Lu	魯景公	25th year
King Hui of Qin	秦惠王	4th year
King Kang of Song	宋康王	8th year
King Huai of Chu	楚懷王	8th year
King Wei of Qi	齊威王	38th year
King Hui of Wei	魏惠王	Houyuan 後元 14th year
King Xuanhui of Hann	韓宣惠王	12th year
King Wuling of Zhao	趙武靈王	5th year
King Yi of Yan	燕易王	12th year
Sir Wey Si	衛嗣君	4th year

I. The king of Zhou died, his son Guai succeeded to the throne; he was known posthumously as King Shenjing of Zhou.[201]

II. King Yi of Yan died; his son Guai ascended to the throne.[202]

III. The king of Qi bestowed land to Tian Ying at Xue, enfeoffing him as Lord Jingguo.[203] Lord Jingguo suggested to the Qi king, "It is obligatory for the sovereign of a state to attend to the daily court session, to read and review the memorials submitted by his five ministers." The king accepted his proposal; after some time, he found it tiresome; he then appointed Lord Jingguo to attend the court sessions. Hence, Lord Jingguo assumed total control of the Qi court.

---

199 Daliang 大梁 - Kaifengxian Henan 河南 開封縣.

200 Quwo 曲沃 - Quwozhen Shaanxian Henan 河南 陝縣 曲沃鎮.

201 King Xian of Zhou 周顯王 Ji Bian 姬扁.
King Shenjing of Zhou 周 慎靚王 Ji Ding 姬定 (r. 320-315 BCE).

202 Yan Ji Guai 燕 姬噲 (r. 320-316) or (r. 320-312 BCE).

203 Xueyi 薛邑 - Tengxian Shandong 山東 滕縣.
Lord Jingguo 靖郭君 Tian Ying 田嬰.

Lord Jingguo was considering building a city at Xue, a guest reminded him, "Have you not heard of the story of a big fish living in the sea. The creature was so huge that fishnet could not ensnare it, and the fishhooks could not catch it; however as soon as it swam ashore, deprived of water, the ants took care of it. Sir, Qi is your water in the sea. You already have full control of the Qi court. Why do you need a city at Xue? If the kingdom of Qi was lost, even if you were to build impregnable walls reaching into the sky at Xue, what purpose would it serve?" Tian Ying put an end to his plan.

Lord Jingguo had forty sons; Tian Wen was born to a lowly and humble concubine. Wen was exceptionally intelligent, resourceful with brilliant schemes and ideas. He convinced Lord Jingguo to spend his riches to befriend and host scholars at his manor. Lord Jingguo made him responsible for the receptions of his guests. The guests at the Tian manor commended and praised Tian Wen, and they bid that he be appointed as the heir. Upon Lord Jingguo's death, Wen assumed the enfeoffment of Xue; naming himself Lord Mengchang.[204] He befriended fief lords, roaming scholars, fugitives, and escaped convicts. He sheltered these men, providing them with money and salaries; he even provided reliefs to their kin and families. Several thousand men came and stayed in his manor, each maintaining that Lord Mengchang was treating him like his next of kin; his fame and popularity spread throughout all under Heaven.

Sima Guang annotates:

A gentleman retains worthy scholars to service the people.[205] The *Book of Changes* says, "A sage retains capable and virtuous men, bringing bounty to the masses." The virtuous men among these scholars with high integrity were adequately accomplished to realign flawed customs, so gifted that they could bring ratifications to corrupted establishments, and so insightful that they could discern the slightest uneasiness with prescience. Their fortitude was so compelling that they could bond virtuous men and people of integrity. On the broader perspectives, these great men brought benefits to all under Heaven, while to a certain extent they brought great benefits to a polity. Hence, the sage lords retained these men with rich emoluments and conferred prestigious positions to honour them. To retain one such worthy person was more than adequate to bring much bounty to ten thousand civilians. That was the true meaning of retaining worthy scholars. Nevertheless, Lord Mengchang indiscriminately solicited both the erudite and the ignoramus, without paying due considerations for the worthy or otherwise. He arrogated his ruler's coffers to create his own clique, striving for personal fame and recognition. He deceived his overlord above him and exploited the civilians under him. He was a scheming scoundrel and was not even commendable. The *Book* says,

---

204 Lord Mengchang 孟嘗君 Tian Wen 田文.

205 The original phase is *yangshi* 養士 meaning 'to retain a group of scholars at one's household.'

"Shou of Shang was the master of felons of All under Heaven, he created a cesspool sheltering corrupted villains." It is a fitting description of Tian Wen.[206]

IV. Chu retained Lord Mengchang as a consultant. The king of Chu presented him with a prized ivory-bedstead. He ordered his attendant Deng Tuzhi to courier the bedstead to return to Qi.[207] Deng Tuzhi did not want to take on the task; he said to Gongsun Xu, [208] a guest of Lord Mengchang, "The ivory bedstead is worth one thousand units of gold. If there is the slightest mishap with the bed, even if I were to sell my wife and children into slavery I could not repay the loss. Sir, if you can come up with a plan so that I do not have to take on the task, I will present you with a prized sword that is handed down from my ancestor." Gongsun Xu agreed to take on the consignment. He went to see Lord Mengchang and said, "Many small states have presented you with their chancellor seals, imploring Your Highness to take on the responsibility as their chancellor. They hold high regard for you as you empathized with the poor and depraved, believing that you could help revive the vanquished states and bring continuation to service their ancestral shrines. People have great admiration for your righteousness and great respect for your integrity. On your initial mission to Chu you have already been presented with a prized ivory-bedstead; I wonder what other valuable gifts the other states have installed for you when you visit them." Lord Mengchang said, "You are right." He decided to decline the present. Gongsun Xu took leave briskly, barely reaching the threshold leading into the front courtyard; Lord Meng asked him to return. He asked, "Sir. Why are you so jubilant, striding forward with vitality?" Gongsun Xu told him the truth. Lord Mengchang subsequently penned a note pinned onto the entrance of his manor; it read, "I welcome people who perceive my mistakes and failings to come forth to reprimand me, allowing me to uphold my integrity; even if enticements are used to induce the person for personals gains. Please enter without hesitation."

Sima Guang remarks:

Lord Mengchang was receptive to admonishments and opinions from others. He heartened himself by encompassing opinions of other's. He accepted their better judgements notwithstanding the hidden agenda; he embraced them as such, not to mention the unadulterated and sincere advice. The *Odes* says, 'When harvesting radish and turnip, the roots may not be edible at times, the tubers as a whole are not to be discarded.' Lord Mengchang did accomplish such outstanding decorum.[209]

---

206 Shou 受 - King Zhou of Shang, Zi Shouxin 商王 紂 子受辛, 31st and last King of Shang, (~ 1075-1046 BCE).

207 Deng Tuzhi 登徒直 retainer at Lord Mengchang's 孟嘗君 manor.

208 Gongsun Xu 公孫戌 was a guest of Lord Menchang.

209 The *Odes,* 詩, "邶風 谷風, "采葑采菲, 無以下體." The *Siku quanshu* 四庫全書, The *Odes,* 詩, p. 395.

Feng 葑 is turnip, the leaves, roots, and stem are edible; however, the stem may be bitter when it is not ripe. The analogy is that an object may have some defects they are not to be discarded.

V. King Xuanhui of Hann considered assigning his court to Gong Zhong and Gong Shu, he solicited the opinion of Miao Liu.[210] Miao Liu responded, "Impossible, don't even think about it. When Jin appointed the six ministers the state was apportioned. [211] Duke Jian of Qi employed the services of Chen Chengzi and Que Zhi he ended up being murdered.[212] When Wei used Xi Shou and Zhang Yi, it lost its territories west of the River *Xihe*.[213] Now Your Highness intends to employ the two men; the outcome will be obvious. As soon as one of them becomes powerful, he will build his power base; the weaker one may even call on the support of foreign powers. Senior ministers at court will form factions competing for personal interests, humiliating the overlord; some may even collaborate with foreigners to cede land for greed. Your kingdom will be in great peril.

---

210 Gong Zhong 公仲, Gong Chi 公侈, Zhong Peng 仲朋 was a notable minister at the Hann court.
Gong Shu 公叔.
Miao Liu 繆留.

211 Six powerful families initially controlled the state of Jin 晉. Fan 范, Zhonghang 中行, Zhi 智, Zhao 趙, Wei 魏 and Hann 韓; later it was reduced to four. See Volume 1- 403-1.

212 Duke Jian of Qi 齊簡公 Jiang Ren 姜壬 (r. 484-481 BCE).
Tian Huan 田恒; Kan Zhi 闞止.

213 Wei Wang 魏.
Xi Shou 犀首 and Zhang Yi 張儀 had both taken on the chancellery position in Wei 魏; however, they were paid by Qin 秦.
Xihe 西河 the west bank of Huanghe River, the eastern part of Shaanxi 陝西.

Volume III. 資治通鑒 卷第三 周紀三 320-298 BCE

The narratives of this volume begin in the first year of King Shenjing of Zhou (320 BCE) and end in the 17th year of King Nan of Zhou (298 BCE).[1]

318 BCE - Chu, Zhao, Wei, Hann and Yan formed an Alliance against Qin; it was defeated.

317 BCE - Qin defeated Hann at Youyu; [2] eighty thousand men were beheaded.

A Qi minister assassinated Su Qin.[3]

316 BCE - King Hui of Qin accepted Sima Cuo's advice and sent an army against Shu.[4] Qin took over the land, and it became powerful.

Ji Guai, the king of Yan, abdicated his throne to Chancellor Zi Zhi.[5]

314 BCE - Zi Zhi sat on the Yan throne and ruled for three years, Yan fell into chaos. General Shi Bei and the former Heir Apparent Ji Ping conspired against Zi Zhi; [6] the kingdom fell into internecine warfare that lasted for several months, several tens of thousands of civilians and soldiers died. Qi took advantage of the chaos sent in their army and executed Zi Zhi and King Ji Guai.

313 BCE - Zhang Yi petitioned at Chu on behalf of Qin, offering six hundred *li* of land to Chu to break up the Alliance with Qi.[7]

312 BCE - Chu, humiliated by the land offer deceit, sent an army against Qin and lost.

King Zhao of Yan was placed on the Yan throne; [8] he shared the trials and tribulations with his people.

311 BCE - Zhang Yi lobbied the fief lords to form a Coalition with Qin. Zhang Yi was enfeoffed.

310 BCE - Zhang Yi left Qin and died in Wei.

307 BCE - Ying Si, the king of Qin, died lifting a tripod.[9]

King Wuling of Zhao introduced foreign clothing and archery on horseback.[10]

---

1 King Shenjing of Zhou 周慎靚王.
King Nan of Zhou 周赧王.

2 Youyu 脩魚.

3 Su Qin 蘇秦.

4 King Hui of Qin 秦惠王; Sima Cuo 司馬錯; Shu 蜀.

5 King Ji Guai of Yan 燕 姬噲; Yan, Zi Zhi 燕 子之.

6 Shi Bei 市被; Yan, Ji Ping 燕 姬平.

7 Zhang Yi 張儀.

8 King Zhao of Yan 燕昭王.

9 Ying Si 嬴駟.

305 BCE - King Wuling of Zhao defeated Zhongshan kingdom. Wei Ran assumed power at the Qin court, placed his nephew Ying Ji on the throne, [11] and he followed up by exterminating the remnants of the Qin nobles.

299 BCE - King Wuling of Zhao abdicated his throne to his youngest son, and gave himself a title of *zhufu* – the Supreme Lord.

299 BCE - Qin lured King Huai of Chu to go to the capital of Qin and held him hostage.

Sir Mengchang was made the chancellor of Qin.[12]

Sir Mengchang escaped from Qin.

Sir Pingyuan played host to several thousand guests at his manor. His guest Gongsun Long advanced a philosophical debate, "A White Horse is Not a Horse."[13]

Volume III. Zhou Records 周紀三

---

320 BCE *Xinchou* 辛丑 Warring States 戰國

King Shenjing of Zhou	周慎靚王	1st year[14]
Duke Jing of Lu	魯景公	26th year
King Hui of Qin	秦惠王	5th year
King Kang of Song	宋康王	9th year
King Huai of Chu	楚懷王	9th year
King Wei of Qi	齊威王	39th year
King Hui of Wei	魏惠王	*Houyuan* 後元 15th year
King Xuanhui of Hann	韓宣惠王	13th year
King Wuling of Zhao	趙武靈王	6th year
King Yan, Ji Guai	燕王姬噲	1st year[15]
Sir Wey Si	衛嗣君	5th year

---

10 King Wuling of Zhao 趙 武靈王.
Foreign or barbarian clothing - *hufu* 胡服.
Archery on horseback - *qishe* 騎射.

11 Zhongshan Kingdom 中山.
Wei Ran 魏冉; Ying Ji 嬴稷.

12 King Huai of Chu 楚懷王.
Lord Mengchang 孟嘗君.

13 Lord Pingyuan 平原君.
Gongsun Long 公孫龍 - 'A White Horse is Not a Horse' 白馬非馬論.

14 King Shenjing of Zhou 周慎靚王 (r. 320-315 BCE).

15 King of Yan 燕王 Ji Guai 姬噲 (r. 320-312 BCE) or (r. 320-316 BCE).

I. The head of state of Wey demoted himself again, now taking on a title as a Lord - *jun*.[16]

II. See footnotes.[17]

---

319 BCE *Renyin* 壬寅 Warring States 戰國

King Shenjing of Zhou	周慎靚王	2nd year
Duke Jing of Lu	魯景公	27th year
King Hui of Qin	秦惠王	6th year
King Kang of Song	宋康王	10th year
King Huai of Chu	楚懷王	10th year
King Xuan of Qi	齊宣王	1st year
King Hui of Wei	魏惠王	Houyuan 後元 16th year[18]
King Xuanhui of Hann	韓宣惠王	14th year
King Wuling of Zhao	趙武靈王	7th year
King Yan, Ji Guai	燕王姬噲	2nd year
Sir Wey Si	衛嗣君	6th year

I. Qin attacked Hann and annexed Yan.[19]

II. King Hui of Wei died (Wei Ying); his son known posthumously as King Xiang (Wei Si), succeeded him. (However, this is incorrect see notes.)[20]

---

16 In 364 BCE the sovereign of Wey 衛 demoted himself to the status of marquis, Marquis Si of Wey demoted himself again as a 'lord' or 'sir' – *jun* 君. Some dictionary defines *jun* as sovereign. However the word *jun* is also used as a respectful title for gentlemen, sir. The head of state of Wey dropped his marquis title; hence, he could not be regarded as a sovereign, merely a ruler of a small polity or head of state.

17 This year Tian Yinqi 田因齊 King Wei of Qi 齊威王 died (r. 358-320 BCE) (r. 356-321) or (r. 356-320) 1st died; his son Tian Pijiang 田辟彊 King Xuan of Qi (r. 319-301 BCE) or (r. 320-302 BCE) 2nd succeeded to the throne.

19 Later regnal year, i.e. the year King Hui 魏惠王 changed his title to king, see below.

19 Yan 鄢 – Yanling 鄢陵 - Yanlingxian Henan 河南 鄢陵縣.

20 King Hui of Wei 魏惠王 Wei Ying 魏罃.
King Xiang of Wei 魏襄王 Wei Si 魏嗣 (318-296 BCE).
King Hui of Wei did not die in 318 BCE, according to Yang Kuan 楊寬; he changed his regnal year to post-regnal *houyuan* 後元 in 318 BCE. For details, see the translation of Yang Kuan's articles. (See appendix 3).
King Xiang of Wei 襄王, "惠王薨, 子襄王立" – *ZZTJ* based its accounts of the Warring States on the *SJ* 史記 whereas the account here of the crowning of King Xiang was based on the *Guben Zhushu jinian* 古本竹書紀年. Hence according to *SJ*, King Hui died during the 35th year (334 BCE) of King Xian of Zhou 周顯王, and by the time when King Xiang

Mengzi paid a visit to the king and departed.[21] He told his friends, "The king has no semblance of a sovereign; one cannot summon up any admiration or respect for the man. He abruptly asked me, 'Is peace possible for all under Heaven?' I answered, 'When all under Heaven is unified.' He asked, 'Who can unify all under Heaven?' 'Someone who repudiates bloodshed and warfare will unify it.' He asked, 'Who would allow him to unify?' I answered, 'Everyone under Heaven aspires to that. Your Highness, do you know about the sprouting crops? When there is a drought during the seventh or eighth month of the year, all the sprouting crops will have withered; however when rain clouds appear followed by torrential rain, the sprouting shoots soon turn green, teeming with life and brimming with vitality. When it happens, who can avert it?'"

318 BCE *Guimao* 癸卯 Warring States 戰國

King Shenjing of Zhou	周慎靚王	3rd year
Duke Jing of Lu	魯景公	28th year
King Hui of Qin	秦惠王	7th year
King Kang of Song	宋康王	11th year
King Huai of Chu	楚懷王	11th year
King Xuan of Qi	齊宣王	2nd year
King Xiang of Wei	魏襄王	1st year
King Xuan hui of Hann	韓宣惠王	15th year
King Wuling of Zhao	趙武靈王	8th year
King of Yan Ji Guai	燕王姬噲	3rd year
Sir Wey Si	衛嗣君	7th year

1. Chu, Zhao, Wei, Hann and Yan combined their forces and attacked Qin; the armies marched as far as the Hangu Pass; Qin responded by opening up the pass to meet the invading armies head on, the allied armies lost and retreated.[22]

became king, it would have been 16 years later during the 2nd year of King Shenjing. *ZZTJ JZ*, vol 1, p. 90.

The *SJ* 史記, 卷 114, 'Wei shijia 魏世家' 第 14, p. 1687.

21 Mengzi, Mencius - 孟子 his polite name was Meng Ke 孟軻.

22 Hangu - Hanguguan Pass 函谷關 – southwest of Lingbaoxian Henan 河南 靈寶縣.

The south-north Alliance proposed by Su Qin 蘇秦 broke up in 332 BCE. Under continuous threats from Qin, the allied forces revived the Alliance. This expedition was proposed by King Huai of Chu 楚懷王 Mi Huai 羋槐; he invited Zhao 趙, Wei 魏, Hann 韓, Yan 燕 and Qi 齊 to make an expedition against Qin 秦. The king of Qi adopted Tian Wen's 田文 strategy, by commanding the army to trail at the rear. Hence, while the five kingdoms were marching against Qin, in reality, they were not unified in their common goal, each trying to preserve its own strength, or had the courage to take the initiative. A few days later, the Qin general, Ying Ji 嬴疾 sent a contingent of soldiers to charge out of the Pass and make a sudden raid against the supply route of the Chu army, which ran out of supplies and retreated first; the armies from the other four kingdoms quickly followed. While the South-north Alliance had broken up some time before, the renewed unification of the other kingdoms did cause considerable concern to Qin. *ZZTJ BY Edition*, vol 1, p. 196-197.

II. The sovereign of Song proclaimed king.[23]

---

317 BCE *Jiachen* 甲辰 Warring States 戰國

King Shenjing of Zhou	周慎靚王	4th year
Duke Jing of Lu	魯景公	29th year
King Hui of Qin	秦惠王	8th year
King Kang of Song	宋康王	12th year
King Huai of Chu	楚懷王	12th year
King Xuan of Qi	齊宣王	3rd year
King Xiang of Wei	魏襄王	2nd year
King Xuanhui of Hann	韓宣惠王	16th year
King Wuling of Zhao	趙武靈王	9th year
King of Yan, Ji Guai	燕王姬噲	4th year
Sir Wey Si	衛嗣君	8th year

I. Qin defeated Hann at Youyu; [24] the army cut off eighty thousand heads. The Qin army captured Hann generals Sou and Shen Cha near Lake Guanze.[25] All the fief lords were greatly alarmed.

II. A Qi minister was vying for power with Su Qin; he sent an assassin to kill him; Su Qin died.[26]

III. Zhang Yi proposed to King Xiang of Wei,[27] "The realm of Liang is no more than one thousand *li*. [28] You have less than three hundred thousand armed soldiers. The terrain at Liang is flat and level; it lacks lofty mountains and large rivers to make your domain unassailable. Your Highness has less than one hundred thousand men to take up defence

---

24 King Kang of Song 宋康王 Song Yan 宋偃.

24 Youyu 脩魚 – east of Yuanwuxian Henan 河南 原武縣.

25 Guanze Lake 觀澤. Qingfengxian Hebei 河北 清豐縣.
The Hann General 韓將 Wei Sou 魏鯫.
The Hann General 韓將 Shen Cha 申差.
The *ZZTJ* named the place as Zhuoze 濁澤, which is in Linyingxian Henan 河南 臨穎縣, it was some 140 km as the crow flies from the battlefield, separated by the Huanghe River 黄河, hence it was probably mistaken. The *SJ* 史記 records the place as Guanze 觀澤, which was more likely. *ZZTJ BY Edition*, vol 1, p. 198.

26 According to the *SJ* 史記 Su Qin did not die from the assassination, he was wounded, and he told the Qi king to put him through the chastisement of five-horse drawn carriages – *julie* 車裂 for treason to flush out the assassin. *SJ* 史記, 卷 39, 'Su Qin liezhuan 蘇秦列傳' 第 9, p. 460.
Su Qin died in 284 BCE while Zhang Yi died in 310 BCE.

27 Zhang Yi 張儀 at this stage was the Chancellor of Wei, and was covertly operating as a Qin infiltrator.

28 Liang 梁 - The capital city of Wei 魏 was Liang 梁, Wei came to be known as Liang.

against Chu, Hann, Qi and Zhao at the borders and passes. Consequently, the land of Liang has become a battlefield for the other states. The fief lords have formed an alliance at the Huanshui River pledging as brotherly states, reinforcing each other. Nevertheless, even blood brothers from the same parents resort to arms and bloodshed when it comes to personal interests over money and wealth. The states are rehashing the strategy advanced by Su Qin before his passing; it is abundantly clear that the Alliance will fail. The way I perceive it, if Your Highness refuses to submit to Qin, its army will advance against *Hewai* - the outer parts of Huanghe River, [29] taking over Juan, Yan and Suanzao regions. It will continue to invade Wey and take control of Yangjin.[30] By then the Zhao army will be obstructed from moving south while Liang (Wei) will be thwarted from marching north; the passage between the south and the north will hence be blocked.[31] Subsequently, Your Highness's state will face a perilous situation. I hence implore you to reconsider the situation. Please spare me my skeletal remains, allow me to resign from my post."[32] The king of Wei then withdrew from the Alliance and appointed Zhang Yi as his emissary to negotiate a peace accord with Qin. Zhang Yi then returned to Qin and resumed his position as the chancellor of Qin.

IV. Duke Jing of Lu died; his son, Lu, succeeded him; he was known posthumously as Duke Ping of Lu.[33]

---

316 BCE *Yisi* 乙巳 Warring States 戰國

King Shenjing of Zhou	周慎靚王	5th year
Duke Ping of Lu	魯平公	1st year
King Hui of Qin	秦惠王	9th year
King Kang of Song	宋康王	13th year
King Huai of Chu	楚懷王	13th year
King Xuan of Qi	齊宣王	4th year
King Xiang of Wei	魏襄王	3rd year

---

29 *Hewai* 河外 - Wei 魏 found its capital initially at Anyi 安邑, the areas west of Huanghe 黄河 (south of present day Hanncheng Shaanxi 韓城縣), and the areas north of Huaxian 華縣 was called *Hewai*. Later Wei moved its capital to Liang 梁, the area north of Huanghe was renamed *Hewai*. *ZZTJ JZ*, Vol 1, p. 92-93.

30 Juan 卷 and Yan 衍 - north of Yuanwuxian Henan 河南 原武縣北.
Suanzao 酸棗 - Yanjinxian Henan 河南 延津縣.
Wey 衛 - Puyangxian Hebei 河北 濮陽縣.
Yangjin 陽晉 - Yunchengxian Shandong 山東 鄆城縣.

31 When Wei 魏 could not march north, the passage would hence be terminated; by then All under Heaven will be divided into two separate portions. The Longitudinal Alliance (south-north) would break down completely.

32 The phrase for resignation - spare me my skeletal remains' is *cihaigu* 賜骸骨.

33 Duke Jing of Lu 魯景公 Ji Yan 姬偃. 34th. Jing means scene or condition.
Duke Ping of Lu 魯平公 Ji Lu 姬旅 (r. 316-297 BCE) or (r. 314-296 BCE) or (r. 322-303 BCE), 35th. Ping means calm or peaceful.

King Xuanhui of Hann	韓宣惠王	17th year
King Wuling of Zhao	趙武靈王	10th year
King of Yan, Ji Guai	燕王姬噲	5th year
Sir Wey Si	衛嗣君	9th year

1. Ba and Shu kingdoms were engaged in a severe conflict; they appealed to Qin for help.[34] King Hui of Qin was considering invading Shu.[35] He was concerned that the expedition would be difficult as the passage was hazardous with narrow passes and defiles. Besides, the state of Hann might launch an attack; hence, he hesitated.[36] Sima Cuo suggested that they should invade Shu; however, Zhang Yi said,[37] "Why don't we attack Hann instead?" The king said, "Please explain." Zhang Yi replied, "Our policy is to befriend with Wei and maintain an affable relationship with Chu. If we attack the areas of the Three Rivers *Sanchuan*, after taking control of the cities of Xincheng and Yiyang we could enter into the suburbs of the two Zhou kingdoms.[38] Following that, we could take possession of the Nine-tripods, [39] and procure the world map and registers of all the people under Heaven. Your Highness could hold the Son of Heaven hostage to command all under Heaven; no one would even dare to object. It is a grand exploit of a mighty king. Your subject has heard if one pursues eminence, he makes a bid at a court; if one is after minor gains, he labours at the market bazaar. The Three-River region *Sanchuan* and the

---

34 Ba 巴 - Zhongqing City Sichuan - 四川 重慶市. The Kingdom of Ba at that stage controlled the southern part of Sichuan. N.B. Ba 巴, and Shu 蜀 were two separate kingdoms controlling groups of foreign ethnic tribes to the southwest and south of the Central Plains - *zhongyuan* 中原.

Shu 蜀 - Chengdu city Sichuan 四川 成都市. The Shu Kingdom controlled the northern part of Sichuan, its area extended to the southernmost part of Shaanxi 陝西, to the foothills of Qinling Mountains 秦嶺.

35 King Hui of Qin 秦惠王 Ying Si 嬴駟.

36 The king of Qin was concerned that Hann might take advantage to attack when the capital was left unguarded while the army was away on a protracted expedition.

37 Sima Cuo 司馬錯.

Zhang Yi 張儀.

38 Three-Rivers region - *Sanchuan* 三川 - The area where the three rivers merge, the Yishui River 伊水, the Luohe River 洛水 and the Huanghe River 黄河, is known as *Sanchuan* - i.e. greater Luoyang 洛陽 areas.

Xincheng 新城 - South of Luoyangxian Henan 河南 洛陽縣.

Yiyang 宜陽 - Yiyangxian Henan 河南 宜陽縣.

Zhou Kingdom was divided into two separate states at this stage; hence, the text refers to it as Er-Zhou 二周.

39 The Nine-tripods - *jinding* 九鼎. Legend has it that when King Yu 禹 founded the kingdom of Xia 夏; he forged nine huge bronze tripods, a time when a tripod was a utensil for cooking. As for Yu, the Nine-tripods were used as a symbol of kingship; each tripod denoted one of the nine provinces – *jiuzhou* 九州 he presided over. Later, it was held that whoever took possession of the Nine-tripods would become the legitimate Son of Heaven. It was then used as a symbol of kingdom and kingship during the Xia 夏, Shang 商 and Zhou 周 dynasties. Huang Z.Y 黄中業, *Sandai jishi benwei* 三代紀事本末 (大禹功績) 遼寧人民出版社. China, 1999, pp. 21-26.

Huang Aimei 黄愛梅 and Yu Kai 于凱, *Qizhizang* 器之藏, Shanghai jiaoyu chubanshe 上海教育出版社, China, 2005, pp 156-158.

Zhou royal house are both the court and market bazaar under Heaven. Your Highness, you are not pursuing after the prominence at court, neither are you going after the market bazaar, instead choosing an expedition against the Rong-Di barbarians, it is far too removed from achieving a grand exploit." Sima Cuo said, "Your subject disagrees. He has heard if a sovereign intends to make his kingdom formidable and prosperous; his priority is to expand his territories; while intending to improve the quality of his armed forces he has to enrich the livelihood his commoners. Moreover, if he intends to be a king he has to inaugurate virtue and morality. When these three prerequisites are met, great exploit will follow. The area of our kingdom is small, and our people are needy. Hence, your subject thinks we ought to embark upon an easy undertaking. The Shu kingdom is a remote barbarian tribe to our southwest, the head of the Rong-Di tribes. The situation there is in turmoil, no different from the reigns of King Jie of Xia and King Zhou of Shang.[40] Marching against them, Qin will be like a pack of wolves descending on a flock of sheep. With a successful campaign, we could expand our territories substantially. Furthermore, taking possession of the riches will enrich our people. We can easily subjugate them without bringing much harm to our people. Besides, no one under Heaven will consider conquering the kingdom an act of callous transgression, while acquiring all the benefits and no one under Heaven would deem us being covetous and avaricious. Whether in name or substance, this campaign is construed as benevolent and righteous - an honourable act to quash violence and end anarchy. On the other hand, if we invade Hann, follow by holding the Son of Heaven hostage, our act will be seen as abhorrent and our deed treasonous, yielding little benefit. Furthermore, we will be branded as an iniquitous state for infringing and violating an area no one dare to tread. It is extremely dangerous. Please allow your subject to clarify the reasons further. All the kingdoms under Heaven are invariably related to the Zhou imperial clan and the ties between Qi, Hann and Zhou are particularly close. If the king of Zhou realizes that he is about to lose his Nine-tripods, and Hann realizes that it is about to lose its Three-River regions *Sanchuan*; the two kingdoms will be encouraged to contrive together. They may even appeal to Qi and Zhao for help, and reach an agreement to resolve the age-old antipathies with Chu and Wei. The king of Zhou might even concede the Nine-tripods to Chu while Hann might cede its Three-River regions to Wei. Your Highness simply cannot prevent it from happening, and it is the perilous situation your subject was referring. The proposal is hardly as comprehensive as making an expedition against Shu." Ying Si accepted Sima Cuo's proposal and raised an army to march against Shu.

It took Qin ten months to quell Shu. The king of Shu was reduced to the status of a marquis. Chen Zhuang was made the chancellor of Shu.[41] Ever since the annexing of Shu, Qin became even more powerful, it became wealthy and treated the other fief states with increasing arrogance.

---

40 King Jie of Xia, Si Lugui 夏桀 姒履癸 (~1600 BCE); King Jie was the last king of Xia.
King Zhou of Shang, Zi Shouxin 商紂 子受辛 (1075-1046 BCE) was the last king of Shang.

41 Chen Zhuang 陳莊 - details of this person are unknown.

11. After the death of Su Qin, his younger brothers Su Dai and Su Li continued to canvass political strategies among the fief lords, and their political manoeuvring was reaping recognition among the fief states.[42]

The son of Zi Zhi, the chancellor of Yan, had a marriage relationship with Su Dai.[43] The chancellor was conspiring to usurp the Yan throne. Su Dai returned from Qi after an emissary mission, Guai the king of Yan asked him,[44] "Do you think the king of Qi will become the new hegemon?" Su Dai responded, "Impossible." Ji Guai asked, "Why?" Su Dai responded, "He does not trust his subjects." The king of Yan then placed all responsibilities on Zi Zhi. Minister Lu Maoshou suggested to the king, "People exalt King Yao, revering him as a sage because he abdicated his throne to his worthy assistant.[45] If Your Highness transfers your power to Zi Zhi, you will attain the eminence of King Yao." The king of Yan conferred all his authority and power upon Zi Zhi. The status and authority of the chancellor escalated. Someone at court suggested, "King Yu of Xia commended Yi but he appointed his son Qi to take on the official duties at court.[46] When he grew old, he realized that Qi lacked the faculties to govern all under Heaven and transferred the authority to Yi; Qi and his clique attacked Yi and took over the regime. People under Heaven maintained that King Yu nominally abdicated his throne to Yi; however, he might have furtively encouraged his son to seize the throne. Now, Your Highness, you have ostensibly assigned the authority to Zi Zhi. However, all the ministers are the prince's followers. Hence, Zi Zhi is merely titular in name, in reality, the prince is presiding at court." The king recalled all the official seals from ministers earning enrolments of three-hundred *dan* or more per year, and they were then transferred to Zi Zhi. Zi Zhi ascended to the throne, sat in state faced south to preside over the kingdom. Ji Guai being quite advanced in years did not attend to the court affairs, he, in essence, was reduced to the status as a subject; Zi Zhi consequently decided all the state affairs.

---

315 BCE *Bingwu* 丙午 Warring States 戰國

---

42 Su Dai 蘇代 and Su Li 蘇厲 were the brothers of Su Qin 蘇秦.

43 It was probably a daughter of Su Dai. The text does not relate who was married to whom, and we have to assume that the Chancellor Zi Zhi 子之 and Su Dai were plotting a revolt against the state.

44 King of Yan 燕王 Ji Guai 姬噲 (r. 320-316 BCE) or (r. 320-312 BCE).
King Xuan of Qi 齊宣王 Tian Pijiang 田辟彊.

45 Lu Maoshou 鹿毛壽 was a minister at the Yan court, details of him are lacking. He is mentioned in the *SJ* 史記, 卷 104, 'Yan Zhaogong shijia 燕召公世家' 第 4, p. 1459.
King Yao 堯帝 Yiqi Fangxun 伊祁放勳 was a legendary king, also known as Tangyao 唐堯, ~ 22nd century BCE.

46 King Yu of Xia 夏禹 Si Wenming 姒文命 (~ before 2070 BCE).
Yi 益. See below.
Qi 啓 Xia Qi 夏啓 Si Qi 姒啓 was the son of King Yu 禹.
Qi 啓 was the second king of the Xia dynasty 夏 (2070-1600 BCE).
According to legend, King Yu 禹, the founder of the Xia Dynasty, had intended to abdicate his throne to Gaotao 皋陶, except Gaotao died before Yu; the throne was passed to Yi 益. However, the fief lords did not pay homage to him but to Qi 啓, the son of Yu, instead. Qi became the successor to the kingdom of Xia; it was supposed to be the beginning of hereditary inheritance in ancient China. Another version of the legend claims that Qi was the founder of Xia and not King Yu.

King Shenjing of Zhou	周慎靚王	6th year
Duke Ping of Lu	魯平公	2nd year
King Hui of Qin	秦惠王	10th year
King Kang of Song	宋康王	14th year
King Huai of Chu	楚懷王	14th year
King Xuan of Qi	齊宣王	5th year
King Xiang of Wei	魏襄王	4th year
King Xuanhui of Hann	韓宣惠王	18th year
King Wuling of Zhao	趙武靈王	11th year
King of Yan, Zi Zhi	燕王子之	1st year
Sir Wey Si	衛嗣君	10th year

1. The king of Zhou died, his son Ji Yan succeeded him; he was known posthumously as King Nan.[47]

---

314 BCE *Dingwei* 丁未 Warring States 戰國

King Nan of Zhou	周赧王	1st year
Duke Ping of Lu	魯平公	3rd year
King Hui of Qin	秦惠王	11th year
King Kang of Song	宋康王	15th year
King Huai of Chu	楚懷王	15th year
King Xuan of Qi	齊宣王	6th year
King Xiang of Wei	魏襄王	5th year
King Xuanhui of Hann	韓宣惠王	19th year
King Wuling of Zhao	趙武靈王	12th year
King of Yan, Zi Zhi	燕王子之	2nd year
Sir Wey Si	衛嗣君	11th year

1. Qin invaded Yiqu and annexed twenty-five cities.[48]

---

47 King Shenliang of Zhou 周 慎靚王 Ji Ding 姬定 (r. 320-315 BCE), 42nd.
King Nan of Zhou 周赧王 Ji Yan 姬延 (r. 314-256 BCE), 43rd was the last king of Zhou.

48 N.B. Yiqu was previously defeated by Qin and became part of Qin in 327 BCE.
Yiqu 義渠 was a barbarian tribe that settled in the area near Ningxian Gansu 甘肅 寧縣.
The text uses the word *qin* 侵, which means invade or intrude. According to the *Zuozhuan* 左傳, Yili 義例 an unconcealed military expedition was called *fu* 伐 or attack, which was accompanied by war-drums and war-gongs; while a stealthy attack or invasion was known as *qin* 侵, unaccompanied by the war-drums and war-gongs.

II. The Wei civilians, who remained in the Qin occupied territories revolted; Qin reacted by invading Wei again, occupying Quwo;[49] they then forcefully repatriated all the Wei civilians from the occupied territories to Quwo.

III. Qin defeated Hann at Anmen; Hann sued for peace by sending Crown Prince Hann Cang to Qin as a hostage.[50]

IV. Zi Zhi was the king of Yan for three years; the state fell into complete chaos.[51] General Shi Bei conspired with Prince Ping to rise against Zi Zhi. The king of Qi sent an emissary to meet the prince with a message,[52] "I am told that you intend to restore the proper status between a sovereign and his subject, and to clarify the appropriate succession between a father and his son. My Kingdom is behind you; we will comply with your instructions." The prince then rallied a group of supporters led by Shi Bei and attacked Zi Zhi, but the uprising failed. Shi Bei turned against the prince; [53] internal strife followed lasting for some months; several tens of thousands of people perished in the ensuing conflict, and the civilians in the kingdom fell into panic and fright.

The king of Qi commanded Zhangzi to lead armies from five cities and the garrisons from the north of his kingdom to attack Yan.[54] The Yan warriors made no attempt to defend their positions, left all its city gates open. The Qi army captured Zi Zhi, chopped him into mincemeat, and pickled his remains.[55] The king of Yan, Guai was also executed.[56]

The king of Qi sought the opinion of Mengzi, "Somebody advised me against annexing Yan while others think otherwise. As a kingdom of ten thousand chariots, it only took me fifty days to vanquish another ten-thousand-chariot kingdom; it was not done through sheer military might. If I do not annex Yan, there will be calamity from Heaven. What if I annex it?" Mengzi answered, "If the people of Yan are pleased and contented with your

---

49 The Wei civilians who remained in the Qin occupied territories.
Quwo 曲沃 - 20 km southwest of Shaanxian Henan 河南 陝縣.

50 Anmen 岸門 - Hejinxian Shanxi 山西 河津縣. Anmen was the border garrison of Hann.
Hann, Hann Heir 韓太子 Hann Cang 韓倉.

51 Zi Zhi 子之 was the minister who usurped the Yan throne.

52 General Shi Bei 市被.
Former Heir Apparent 太子 Ji Ping 姬平.
King Xuan of Qi 齊宣王 Tian Pijiang 田辟彊.

53. For some inexplicable reason, General Shi Bei had a complete about-face.

54 Zhang Zi 章子. His real name was Kuang Zhang 匡章 (he served Qi between ~335-295 BCE). He was a powerful general that served under King Wei of Qi 齊威王, and King Xuan 宣王. Zhang Yi 張儀 tried to frame the general; however, King Wei trusted Zhang Zi impeccably, and he successfully defeated the Qin army at Sangqiu 桑丘. An intensely loyal subject of Qi, he was also successfully in making expeditions to Yan 燕 in the north, he also assaulted Chu 楚 in the south and attacked Hanguguan 函谷關 of Qin. The *ZGC* 戰國策 'Qice 1 - 齊策一', pp. 97-98.

55 The *ZZTJ's* account was based on the *Bamboo annals Guben zhushu jinian* 古本竹書紀年, which is different from the accounts in the *ZGC* 戰國策 and the *SJ* 史記, *ZZTJ JZ*, Vol 1, p. 98. The *Zhanguoce* mentions that Zi Zhi died when the Qi army overwhelmed the Yan capital while the *SJ* provides no details as to when or how he died.

56 The capital of Yan - Jicheng 燕 薊城 – present day Beijing 北京.
King of Yan, Guai, Ji Guai 姬噲.

taking over, you should annex it; King Wu of Zhou was a prime example.[57] On the other hand, if the people of Yan are resentful of your occupation then you should not; King Wen of Zhou did exactly that.[58] When a kingdom with ten thousand chariots defeats another kingdom with comparable strength and the people welcome the victorious army with baskets of food and flasks of wine, there is no other explanation than they have hoped that the invaders would bring deliverance from their misery. If the liberators are worse than the previous regime, people will bring their food and wine to welcome armies from other states."

The other fief lords were planning to go to the aid of Yan. The king of Qi again sought the opinion of Mengzi, "Most of the fief lords are rallying against me. How should I handle this?" Mengzi answered, "Your subject has heard of a small state with merely seventy *li* of land was potent enough to unify all under Heaven; King Tang of Shang did just that.[59] I have yet to hear of a kingdom with one thousand *li* of land being intimidated by the others. The *Book of Documents* says, 'I earnestly await the arrival of my Lord; our people will revive from the liberation.'[60] The king of Yan was a despot; Your Highness sent an army to liberate the people; they were grateful that you had delivered them from the repressive ruler. They brought food in baskets and wine in flasks to welcome your imperial army. However, your army had brought carnage to their parents and brothers, razed their shrines to the ground, and have stolen their national treasures, how would it work? All the kingdoms under Heaven were daunted by the might and power of Qi; now, you have increased your territories by one fold. Your army did not dispense benevolence, and it worsen the situation. You are in essence inviting the other kingdoms to mobilize their armies against you. Your Highness, you should order the release of all the old and young captives, and stop pilfering their national treasures; then consult the people in Yan to elect a new king; thereafter your army should withdraw. With these measures, I believe you could avert a joint expedition against you." The king of Qi refused to listen.

Shortly after, the Yan people revolted. The king said, "I am too ashamed to face Mengzi." Chen Jia responded,[61] "Your Highness, please don't feel uneasy about it." Chen Jia paid a visit to Mengzi and asked, "Who was the Duke of Zhou?" [62] Mengzi said, "A sage of great antiquity." Chen Jia continued, "The Duke of Zhou ordered his elder brother Guanshu (Ji Xian) to keep a close supervision on the vanquished Shang people; [63] however,

---

57 King Wu of Zhou 周武王 Ji Fa 姬發 was the 1st King of Zhou (1046-1043 BCE).

58 King Wen of Zhou 周文王 was the pre-dynastic King of Zhou.

59 King Tang of Shang 商湯 Zi Tianyi 子天乙 (~1600 BCE) was the 1st king of Shang.

60 The *Shujing, Shangshu* 尚書 'zhonghui zhigao 仲虺之誥', "徯我后, 后來其蘇." The stanza refers to the despotic King Jie of Xia 夏桀 (~1600 BCE), and that the people of Xia were waiting for deliverance from King Tang 商湯 from the tyrannical king.

61 Chen Jia 陳賈 was a senior officer at the Qi 齊 court.

62 Duke Dan of Zhou 周公旦 Ji Dan 姬旦 was the younger brother of King Wu of Zhou 周武王, the 4th son in the family.

63 Wu Geng of Shang 商武庚. The *SJ* 史記 refers to him as Lufu 祿父; he was the son of the last king of Shang King Zhou 商紂王. Wu Geng was enfeoffed at Yin 殷 by King Wu of Zhou 周武王; later he revolted.

Ji Xian 姬鮮 was a younger brother of King Wu 周武王. He was enfeoffed at Guan 管 (Zhengzhou Henan 河南 鄭州縣); hence, he also came to be known as Guanshu 管叔. King Wu died when his

Guanshu collaborated with the Shang people to revolt against the state. Did Duke of Zhou have prescience that his elder brother might revolt and had appointed him by design?" Mengzi said, "He did not." Chen Jia responded, "So, even a sage makes mistakes." Mengzi said, "Duke of Zhou was the younger sibling when his elder brother Guanshu made a mistake the negligence on the part of the Duke was understandable.[64] When honourable people in ancient times made mistakes, they tried to make amends for their failings, whereas kings of today, whenever they err, they allow the situation to persist without making atonements for their errors. Honourable people in ancient times did not try to conceal their mistakes; when they erred, it was like a solar or lunar eclipse, everyone could see it. When they made amends and restitution for their errors, people admired them, holding their moral character in high regard. The problem with sovereigns of today is whenever they err; they not only allow their mistake to persist they even make fabrications to justify their deed."

V. King Xuan of Qi passed away this year; his son known posthumously as King Min succeeded him.[65]

---

313 BCE *Wushen* 戊申 Warring States 戰國

King Nan of Zhou	周赧王	2nd year
Duke Ping of Lu	魯平公	4th year
King Hui of Qin	秦惠王	12th year
King Kang of Song	宋康王	16th year
King Huai of Chu	楚懷王	16th year
King Xuan of Qi	齊宣王	7th year
King Xiang of Wei	魏襄王	6th year
King Xuanhui of Hann	韓宣惠王	20th year
King Wuling of Zhao	趙武靈王	13th year
Sir Wey Si	衛嗣君	12th year

---

son King Cheng 周成王 was still very young. Guanshu became one of three regents, acting in conjunction with Caishu 蔡叔 and Duke Dan of Zhou 周公旦. Caishu and Ji Xian were disenchanted with the power of the court being entirely vested in Zhou Dan, and they spread rumours that the Duke schemed to usurp the throne. Together with Wu Geng of Shang 商武庚 they revolted, intending to bring down the duke. The Duke made an expedition to the east, the power base of the former Shang; it took him three years to quell the rebellion. Ji Xian, Caishu and Wu Geng were executed. *SJ* 史記, 卷 22, 'Zhou benji 周本紀' 第 4, pp. 123-124. Duke Dan returned the throne to King Cheng 周成王 after 7 years as regent.

64 The implication was Duke Zhou being a junior in the family was in no position to reprimand his elder brother. Hence, he could not be held accountable for not reprimanding his brother.

65 King Xuan of Qi 齊宣王 Tian Pijiang 田辟彊.
King Min of Qi 齊湣王 Tian Di 田地.
N.B. The text is incorrect; King Xuan of Qi 齊宣王 Tian Pijiang 田辟彊 died twelve years later.

I. Ji, an army colonel *yougeng* of Qin, led an army attacked Zhao, the city of Lin was taken, and General Zhuang Bao was captured.[66]

II. Qin was deliberating an invasion of Qi; however, it was concerned that Qi and Chu had a standing treaty to defend against any potential invaders. The king of Qin sent Zhang Yi to Chu to relate to the king of Chu,[67] "If Your Highness listens to your subject's advice to sever your ties and close your passes with Qi. He will appeal to the king of Qin to present you with six hundred *li* of land at Shangyu for breaking the tie.[68] Furthermore, he will ask the Qin king to present you with maidens from Qin to serve Your Highness as your concubines and ladies-in-waiting. The two kingdoms will pledge a pact of everlasting peace through marriage, coexisting as brotherly states."

The king of Chu was delighted and agreed. The ministers at the Chu court were all congratulating the king for the new accord; Chen Zhen was the only one who was sombre and gloomy.[69] The king was infuriated and said, "I don't even have to raise an army, and I will take possession of six hundred *li* of land. Why are you so gloomy?" Chen Zhen answered, "Your subject does not think it is that simple. From his observation, the territories at Shangyu will never be conceded as pledged; besides, it will prompt Qi to form an alliance with Qin. When the alliance is formed calamities will descend upon us." The king said, "Please explain." Chen Zhen said, "The only reason Qin is treating Chu with respect is because we have Qi as an ally; if we break the pledged tie and shut our passes with Qi we will be completely isolated. What affection does Qin hold for Chu to cede six hundred *li* of land to us at Shangyu? No sooner has Zhang Yi returned to Qin he will renounce his pledge made to Your Highness. After that, to the north, Your Highness will lose the alliance with Qi while, to the west, Qin will harass you. The armies of both kingdoms will be heading in our direction. For the benefit of our kingdom, Your Highness, our best strategy is to profess that we have broken our tie with Qi openly while clandestinely retain our alliance. In the meantime, dispatch an envoy to accompany Zhang Yi to claim the land as promised. It will not be too late to break our tie with Qi if the land is not conceded as pledged." The king said, "I wish you would shut up and speak no more, Master Chen. Just wait, I will get my land." He bestowed the chancellor seal upon Zhang Yi, showering him with elaborate gifts and riches. He issued an edict to bolt the gates and close the passes adjoining with Qi, breaking off the alliance. He commanded a general to escort Zhang Yi to return to Qin. Upon arriving at Qin, Zhang Yi feigned falling from his carriage; he did not show up at the Qin court to pay homage for three months.

When the king of Chu heard of what had happened, he asked, "Does Zhang Yi consider our break with Qi inadequate?" He followed up by sending Song Wei, a valiant man, bringing with him a Song permit for entry into the state of Qi.[70] Song Wei arrived at Qi in the north and

---

66 Ji 疾 Qin army colonel *yougeng*, Ying Ji 秦右更 嬴疾.
Ji was also known as Chulizi 樗里子, alias Chuli Ji 樗里疾.
Yougeng – was the 14th out of the 20 grades in the Qin enfeoffment.
Lin 藺 - Lishixian Shanxi 山西 離石縣.
Zhao, General Zhuang Bao 趙將 莊豹.

67 Zhang Yi 張儀.
King Huai of Chu 楚懷王 Mi Huai 羋槐.

68 Shangyu 商於 - Zhechuanxian Henan 河南 淅川縣.

69 Chen Zhen 陳軫 was at one stage a strategist of Qin 秦. Later he went over to Chu; he was a south-north Alliance proponent. The *ZGC* 戰國策 'Qince 1 秦策一', p. 35-36.

70 Song Wei 宋遺 was a vociferous orator of Chu, an expert at hurling insults against people.

began to shout repulsive insults at the Qi king. The king of Qi was enraged; [71] he promptly broke the tally that denoted the tie with Chu and agreed to enter into an alliance with Qin.

Zhang Yi then went to the Qin court and met the Chu envoy. He asked, "Sir? Why haven't you proceeded to claim the land we agreed upon, from the south to the north and east to west some six *li* in total?" The Chu envoy, in great anger, returned to Chu to report to the king of Chu. The king of Chu was in a towering rage, intending to raise an army against Qin immediately. Chen Zhen asked, "Your Highness, can your subject open his mouth now? It might be a better idea to cede one of our larger cities to Qin, pledging a joint effort with Qin to attack Qi. While we may lose a city to Qin, we still can regain some of the losses by invading Qi. Your Highness, you have broken our ties with Qi, and now we are reproaching Qin for deceiving us. We are prompting Qi and Qin to rally all the armed forces under Heaven to form an alliance against us. Our kingdom will sustain even greater losses." The king of Chu refused to listen. He commanded General Qu Gai as the commanding general to make an expedition against Qin.[72]

Qin responded by appointing Zhang, a colonel *shuzhang*, as commanding general to meet the approaching Chu army.[73]

---

312 BCE *Jiyou* 己酉 Warring State 戰國

King Nan of Zhou	周赧王	3rd year
King Ping of Lu	魯平公	5th year
King Hui of Qin	秦惠王	13th year
King Kang of Song	宋康王	17th year
King Huai of Chu	楚懷王	17th year
King Xuan of Qi	齊宣王	8th year
King Xiang of Wei	魏襄王	7th year
King Xuanhui of Hann	韓宣惠王	21st year
King Wuling of Zhao	趙武靈王	14th year
King Zhao of Yan	燕昭王	1st year
Sir Wey Si	衛嗣君	13th year

1. Spring. Qin and Chu joined battle at Danyang.[74] The Chu army was completely overwhelmed; some eighty thousand warriors were beheaded. Commanding General Qu

---

Song 宋國.

71 King Xuan of Qi 齊宣王 Tian Pijiang 田辟彊.

72 Qu Gai 屈匄 was also known as Qu Gai 屈丐 (?- ~312 BCE) or Qu Gai 屈蓋; he was one of the three ministers dispatched by King Huai of Chu 楚懷王 to recover Quwo 曲沃. *SJ* 史記, 卷 23, 'Qin benji 秦本紀' 第 5, p. 164.

73 The Qin lieutenant colonel, *shuzhang* 秦 庶長 Zhang 章 Wei Zhang 魏章.
左庶長 *zuo shuzhang* was the 10th of the 20 grades of enfeoffment of Qin; *you shuzhang* 右庶長 was the 11th.

74 Danyang 丹陽 - Zhechuanxian Henan 河南 浙川縣 - north of Danshui River 丹水.

Gai together with over seventy senior officers and royal family members were captured.[75] The Qin army annexed the Hanzhong Prefecture.[76] King Chu raised all the available armed forces in his kingdom for a counteroffensive against Qin. The battle was joined at Nantian.[77] The Chu army suffered another appalling defeat. When Hann and Wei heard news of Chu's predicament, they marched south into Chu territories in the Deng County for a surprise attack.[78] Upon hearing news of the invasion, Chu recalled its troops from the front and ceded two walled cities to Qin to sue for peace.

II. The royal family members at Yan placed Prince Ping on the throne; he was known posthumously as King Zhao.[79] After the conquest of Yan, King Zhao mourned the dead, consoled the families of the deceased and cared for the widows and orphans; he shared the joy and sufferings with the civilians. He humbly invited worthy individuals by offering high remunerations for engagement at his court. He said to Chancellor Guo Wei,[80] "Qi took advantage of our internal strife and invaded Yan, defeated us. I know Yan is a small state, and our manpower is limited, and we cannot easily make revenge. However, if I could acquire one most worthy person under Heaven, I will share my reign with him. One day, I will purge the humiliation our former king underwent. It is my aspiration. Sir if you come across a suitable person, please let me know, I will serve under him."

Guo Wei answered, "There was a king in ancient times. He gave his attendant one thousand units of gold to go in search of a horse that could gallop one thousand *li*. When the attendant found the horse it had died, he returned with the dead horse for five hundred units of gold. The king was enraged; the attendant said, 'You bought a dead horse for five hundred units of gold. How much is a live one worth then? Do not worry; a splendid horse will appear soon.' Within one year, the king acquired three one-thousand *li* horses. Now, if Your Highness is resolved in acquiring the most capable person under Heaven, please commence with Wei, use your subject as a 'dead horse'; people more capable than Wei will flock to our kingdom from one thousand *li* away." King Zhao ordered to reconstruct the chancellor's manor, turning it into a palace and honoured him as his tutor. Following this, capable people from other kingdoms flocked to Yan in droves. Yue Yi from Wei and Ju Xin from Zhao arrived at Yan.[81] King Zhao made Yue Yi the deputy chancellor *yaqing* of his kingdom to preside at his court.[82]

---

75 Qu Gai 屈匄. He was executed after being captured.

76 Hanzhongjun Prefecture 漢中郡 - the prefecture extended from Nanzhengxian Shaanxi 陝西 南鄭縣 in the west, and Yunxian and Junxian Hubei 湖北 鄖縣 均縣 to the east.

77 Lantian 藍田 - Lantianxian Shaanxi 陝西 藍田縣.

78 Deng county 鄧 - southeast of Yanchengxian Henan 河南 偃城縣.

79 King Zhao of Yan 燕昭王 Ji Ping 姬平 (r. 312-279 BCE) or (r. 311-279 BCE) or (r. 313-279 BCE). Zhao means luminous and illustrious.

80 Guo Wei 郭隗 was the Chancellor of Yan. The *SJ* 卷 104, 'Yan Zhaogong shijia 燕召公世家' 第 4, pp. 1459-1460.

81 Yue Yi 樂毅 was from Wei 魏. He was a descendant of General Yue Yang 樂羊. Yue Yi was a man with exceptional military skills. He left Zhao 趙 after the Shaqiu incident 沙丘之變 (299 BCE) and went over to Yan 燕, where he assumed the position as Deputy Chancellor, *aqing* 亞卿. In 284 BCE, he led the forces of Zhao 趙, Qin 秦, Hann 韓, Wei 魏 and Yan 燕 to go against Qi 齊, defeated the armed forces of Qi at Jixi 濟西. He is mentioned in the

III. King Xuanhui of Hann died, his son succeeded to the throne; he was known posthumously as King Xiang.[83]

---

311 BCE *Gengxu* 庚戌 Warring States 戰國

King Nan of Zhou	赧王	4th year
King Ping of Lu	魯平公	6th year
King Hui of Qin	秦惠王	14th year
King Kang of Song	宋康王	18th year
King Huai of Chu	楚懷王	18th year
King Xuan of Qi	齊宣王	9th year
King Xiang of Wei	魏襄王	8th year
King Xiang of Hann	韓襄王	1st year
King Wuling of Zhao	趙武靈王	15th year
King Zhao of Yan	燕昭王	2nd year
Sir Wey Si	衛嗣君	14th year

I. The chancellor of Shu killed the marquis of Shu.[84]

II. King Hui of Qin sent his emissary to see King Huai of Chu.[85] The emissary related that the Qin king wished to concede the territories beyond the Wu Pass to Chu in exchange for the land at Qianzhong.[86] The Chu king said, "I don't want to exchange land. Please delivery Zhang Yi to me, and I will present you with Qianzhong." When Zhang Yi heard of this, he volunteered to go forth. The king of Qin said, "The king of Chu will not be pacified until he had you executed. Why are you going?" Zhang Yi said, "Qin is powerful, and Chu is enfeebled. So long as Your Highness is around, they will not have the

---

Lushi chunqiu 吕氏春秋 and the *ZGC* 戰國策 'Weice 魏策'. Also, see the translations of Yang Kuan's 楊寬 articles on the historical authenticity of Yue Yi's conquest of Qi 齊 in his *ZGS* 戰國史. Appendix 3.

Ju Xin 劇辛 was from Zhao 趙. (See 242-II footnotes on this person.)

82 Deputy Chancellor, *yaqing* 亞卿.

83 King Xuanhui of Hann 韓 宣惠王 was the 1st king of Hann, while King Xiang, Hann Cang 韓襄王 韓倉 was the 2nd.

84 The fiefdom of Shu 蜀, now a protectorate of Qin 秦; Chancellor Chen Zhuang revolted; the Marquis of Shu Ying Tongguo 嬴通國 was killed.

Shu Chancellor, Chen Zhuang 蜀相 陳莊 was a chancellor appointed by Qin.

Marquis of Shu, Ying Tongguo 蜀侯 嬴通國 (r. 314-311 BCE).

85 King Hui of Qin 秦惠王 Ying Si 嬴駟.

King Huai of Chu 楚懷王 Mi Huai 芈槐.

86 Wuguan Pass 武關 - 90 km southwest of Shangxian Shaanxi 陝西 商縣 the area included Shangyu 商於.

Qianzhong 黔中 were areas in the western part of Hunan 湖南 and the northern part of Guizhou 桂州.

audacity to touch your subject. Besides, I have befriended Lei Shang, a trusted minion of the king of Chu. Lei Shang has earned the trust of Lady Zheng Xiu, the favourite concubine of the king.[87] He will do anything she says." Zhang Yi set forth.

The king of Chu had Zhang Yi imprisoned, awaiting execution. Lei Shang said to Lady Zheng Xiu, "Zhang Yi is the favourite minister of the king of Qin. He has offered six counties in Shangrong and beautiful women in exchange for his life.[88] His Highness values the land greatly, besides he has great respect for Qin. The women from Qin will be greatly cherished; whereas my Lady, you will be distanced." Lady Zhang Xiu wept day and night and complained to the king, "A subject of a state serves his master to perform his duties. If you execute Zhang Yi, the king of Qin will be greatly enraged. Please allow me to take my son with me to retreat to the south of the River.[89] I do not want to be humiliated and defiled by the encroaching Qin soldiers." The king of Chu pardoned and released Zhang Yi, and made him a guest of honour.

Zhang Yi proposed to the king of Chu, "The creation of the Alliance is like herding a flock of sheep against a ferocious tiger; it is not even a fair match. Your Highness has no intention to submit to Qin; however, if Qin forces Hann and coerces Liang to attack Chu, your kingdom will be in serious peril. Qin now controls Ba and Shu to its west, [90] if it decides to invade your kingdom; all it has to do is to make preparations for ships, loading food and fodder to cruise down the Minjiang River.[91] The ships can easily sail three hundred *li* a day. Within less than ten days, the army will arrive at the Hanguan Pass. [92] As soon as the pass is under siege, you might as well turn all the walled cities east to make defences. Your subject is afraid, regions within the Qianzhong and Wujun prefectures will no longer be yours, Your Highness.[93] If the Qin army marches north passing through the Wuguan Pass, the northern parts of your kingdom will also fall. If Qin decides to attack Chu, it will merely take three months to annihilate your kingdom, whereas it will take at least half a year or more for your allied fief lords to come to your rescue. While you are waiting for the weakling states to come to your aid, you have forgotten the mighty Qin is waiting to pounce on you. Your subject is very concerned for the safety of your kingdom. If Your Highness accepts his suggestion, he will try to make Qin and Chu to exist as brotherly state everlastingly; never resorting to conflict and hostilities." Having acquired Zhang Yi as he had wished for, and with no inclination of relinquishing the territories at Qianzhong the king agreed to Zhang Yi's proposal.

---

87 Lei Shang 勒尚 was the mole planted by Zhang Yi; there is no further information on this person.
Zheng Xiu 鄭袖 was the favourite concubine of Mi Huai 芈槐.

88 Shangyong 上庸 - Zhushanxian Hebei 湖北 竹山縣.

89 Jiangnan 江南 – south of the Changjiang River 長江.

90 Ba 巴 - Chongqing City Sichuan 四川 重慶市.
Shu 蜀 - Chengdu City Sichuan 四川 成都市.

91 Minjiang River 泯江, the river runs in Sichuan, it is a tributary of Changjiang 長江, which it drains.

92 Hanguan Pass 扞關 - Fengjiexian Sichuan 四川 奉節縣.

93 Qianzhong 黔中 – see above.
Wujun Prefecture 巫郡 - Wushanxian Sichuan 四川 巫山縣.

Following this, Zhang Yi travelled to Hann. He said to the king of Hann,[94] "The terrain at Hann is rugged and hazardous, and most of the land is mountainous. The five grains produced here are mostly beans and not wheat. Your kingdom has hardly more than two years of food reserve. You have less than two hundred thousand regular soldiers, compared with Qin, who has over one million armed forces. When the warriors of the various kingdoms east of the Mountains enter into battle, they wear heavy armour, donning helmets, whereas when the Qin warriors enter into battle, they shed their armour, baring their shoulders and chests to face their enemies. They carry decapitated heads with their left hand, grasping hold of seized enemy with their right. Meng Ben and Wu Huo are valiant and ferocious warriors, [95] engaging these gallant warriors to attack small and enfeebled kingdoms is liken to using a one-thousand *jin* sledgehammer to smash fragile bird eggs, no one can escape. If Your Highness resists and does not subjugate, the Qin army will send in its armed forces to take Yiyang; moving east it will make a blockade of Chenggao; [96] your kingdom will be separated into two halves. The Hongtai Palace and the Sanglin Park will no longer be yours.[97] For the benefit of Your Highness, your best option is to subjugate to Qin and make an attack against Chu. It will avert an impending calamity about to descend upon you, besides it will win much grace from Qin. There is no better plan than this." The king of Hann accepted the proposal.[98]

Zhang Yi returned to Qin and reported his feats to the Qin king; the king bestowed six counties as his fief and enfeoffed him as Lord Wuxin.[99]

The king of Qin sent Lord Wuxin as an emissary to travel east to Qi. He said to the king of Qi,[100] "The Alliance advocators no doubt suggested to you that, 'Qi is shielded by

---

94 The text merely mentioned the kingdoms Zhang Yi visited without specifying the names of the kings, (except the first king mentioned in this paragraph, King Huai of Chu 楚懷王). The Hann King was probably King Xiang of Hann, Hann Cang 韓襄王 韓倉.

95 Meng Ben 孟賁 and Wu Huo 烏獲 were men of great physical strengths. See 307-II.

96 Yiyang 宜陽 - Yiyangxian Henan 河南 宜陽縣.
Chenggao 成皋 - Fanshuixian Henan 河南 汜水縣.

97 Hongtai Palace 鴻臺之宮.
Sanglin Park 桑林之苑.

98 According to the *ZGC* 戰國策, the Hann King said, "I am most grateful to you for enlightening me. Please incorporate Hann as a prefecture or county, His Highness is welcome to construct his palace in our territories. I will pay tributes during spring and autumn, and my kingdom will hence be known as Dongfan 東藩 (Eastern Protectorate of Qin). I now present Yiyang 宜陽 to the king of Qin as a tribute." The *ZGC* 戰國策, Hannce 1 韓策 1, p. 296.

99 Lord Wuxin 武信君. Enfeoffment at the time of the Warring States - *Zhanguo* was principally divided into five categories or grades; *gong* 公 – a duke or grand duke; *hou* 侯 – marquis; *bo* 伯 - count, *zi* 子 - viscount; *nan* 男 – baron, although *zi* and *nan* were rarely used. The title of *jun* 君 was also used to address someone below the status of the sovereign or even at times the sovereign of a state. When the Warring States began to elevate their status as kingdoms, the enfeoffment system was kept, the title of *jun* somehow remained, it could also be translated as a lord or duke. At the time of Han 漢 the usage of *gong, hou, bo, zi, nan* titles resumed, only women from the royal families were addressed as *jun* 君. *Jun* was also used to refer a gentry. (Also, see Appendix 2b - Titles).

100 The text does not state which Qi king, mostly likely to be King Xuan of Qi 齊宣王 Tian Pijiang 田辟彊.

San-Jin - Zhao, Wei and Hann. It is a vast region, teeming with many valiant warriors. Even if there were one hundred Qin kingdoms they could do little to unsettle the status of Qi.' Your Highness undoubtedly agrees with their observations; however, you have miscalculated the realities. You see Chu and Qin are now brotherly states; the two royal families have entered into betrothal arrangements. In the meantime, Hann has presented Yiyang to Qin, while Liang followed by ceding the areas beyond the River *Hewai*. The king of Zhao has travelled to Qin to pay homage and ceded the areas between the Rivers *Hejian* as a tribute.[101] If Your Highness is adamant about your stance against Qin, Qin can coerce Hann and Liang to raid the southern part of Qi. It can also command the Zhao army to cross the Qinghe River to lay siege to the Bo Pass; and by that stage, Linzi and Jimo will no longer be part of your kingdom.[102] As soon as war breaks out, even if you try to make peace with Qin, it will be too late." The king of Qi yielded to Zhang Yi's proposal. Zhang Yi departed.[103]

Zhang Yi travelled west and arrived at Zhao.[104] He said to the king of Zhao, "Your Highness, you championed the rest of the fief lords under Heaven to go against Qin. For fifteen years, the Qin army did not have the mettle to march beyond the Hangu Pass.[105] Your valour and power have indeed inspired all the kingdoms east of the Mountains.[106] Pressed by fear and apprehension Qin closed its gates, not daring to relax its vigilance. Nevertheless, Qin has made improvements to its armoury and military, increased and refined its agrarian activities, and stored up grains for the inevitable conflict, lest one day Your Highness might raise an army to chastise Qin for its failings. Inspired by Your Highness's valour the king of Qin conquered Ba and Shu and has taken possession of Hanzhong; he laid siege to the partitioned Zhou kingdom, and his forces have captured the Baimajin Crossing.[107] While the Qin kingdom is located in the westernmost wilderness, [108]

---

101 Yiyang 宜陽 - Yiyangxian Henan 河南 宜陽縣.
Wei 魏 ceded *Hewai* 河外. (The original text uses Liang 梁 the capital city of Wei to denote Wei.)
Xianyang 咸陽 - was the Qin capital near present-day Xi'an City Shaanxi 陝西 西安市.
Hejian 河間 - the areas between Huanghe 黃河 and Zhanghe Rivers 漳河.

102 Qinghe River 清河 – literally means Clear River - The river is in the northern part of Shandong 山東.
Boguan Pass 博關 - Boxingxian Shandong 山東 博興縣.
Linzi 臨淄 - Linzixian Shandong 山東 臨淄縣 was the capital of Qi 齊.
Jimo 即墨 - Pingduxian Shandong 山東 平度縣.

103 The *ZGC* 戰國策 relates, "The Qi 齊 King said, 'My Kingdom, far away in the remote region (of the Middle-plain - *zhongyuan* 中原), is situated near the Eastern Sea. I have never heard of any lasting strategies that are beneficial to my Kingdom; I am privileged to have you to shed light on our ignorance. I pledge my holy shrine to serve under *Qin*.' He then ceded three hundred *li* of land that was bountiful with supplies of fish and salt." *ZGC* 戰國策, 'Qice 1 齊策一', p. 102.

104 The text does not stipulate which Zhao King, it was probably Zhao Yong 趙雍 6th.

105 Hanguguan Pass 函谷關 - Ningbaoxian Henan 河南 靈寶縣.

106 Taihengshan 太行山 is the mountain range that divides Shanxi 山西 and Hebei 河北.

107 Ba 巴, Shu 蜀.
See 316-1.
Hanzhong 漢中 - Southern part of Shaanxi and Northwest of Hubei 陝西南部 湖北西北部 see 312-1.

the pent-up disgruntlement has long been suppressed; Qin has to find relief from this frustration. Now, Qin has a poorly equipped and emaciated army garrisoned near Mianci Lake waiting to cross the Huanghe River; it intends to cross the Zhangshui River to take possession of Bowu.[109] Outside Handan, the Qin army will make camp. On the day of *jiazi* the Qin army will invite your army to a battle, [110] a repeat of the historic event when King Wu of Zhou made an expedition against King Zhou of Yin (Shang).[111] The king of Qin sent me to offer your attendants at Your Highness's court some advice. Chu and Qin are now brotherly states; Hann and Liang have already submitted to Qin as protectorate states in the east. Besides, Qi has presented their most bountiful territories teeming with fish and littering with numerous salt pans to Qin. All these events are like cutting off one's right arm to engage in a fight. How can one survive unaided by one's clansmen? How could one evade danger? Qin can make assaults on three fronts: the first offensive will be the taking of the Wudao Passage; in the meantime, Qin will command the Qi army to cross the Qinghe River by advancing against Handan in the east.[112] Another regiment will lay siege against Chenggao, at the same time, commanding the Hann and Liang armies to march towards the areas beyond the River *Hewai*. Finally, another regiment will march against the Mianchi Lake.[113] What chance does Zhao hold against a concerted onslaught by four kingdoms? Upon capitulation, Zhao will be partitioned into four parts. Your subject is of the opinion that it is a better choice to face the king of Qin personally to settle for a peaceful accord and become brotherly states everlastingly." The king of Zhao acceded to the proposal.[114] Zhang Yi continued with his passage north to Yan.[115] He said to the king of

---

Baimajin 白馬津 – Huaxian Henan 河南 滑縣.

108 Qin was situated to the westernmost of the Middle-plain – *zhongyuan* 中原.

109 Mianchi 澠池 – Mianchixian Henan 河南 澠池縣.

Huanghe River 黄河.

Zhangshui River 漳水.

Bowu 番吾 – Handan 邯鄲 - Pingshanxian Hebei 河北 平山縣. 'Bo' was the archaic pronunciation for *fan* 番; also pronounced as *pan* as a place name.

110 *Jiazi* 甲子. The date could not be traced.

111 Handan 邯鄲 - Pingshanxian Hebei 河北 平山縣. Zhou King 周王.

King Zhou of Shang, Zi Shouxin 商王紂 子受辛. N.B. Shang was also known as Yin, as Shang founded it capital at the place Yin 殷 towards the latter part of the dynasty.

112 Wudao Passage 午道, the place is obscured; it should be a frontier city or passage of Zhao 趙.

Qi 齊. Qinghe River 清河.

Handan 邯鄲.

113 Chenggao 成皋 - Fanshuixian Henan 河南 氾水縣.

Hewai 河外 - South of Zhangshui River 漳水.

Mianchi 澠池 - Mianchixian Henan 河南 澠池縣.

114 The *ZGC* 戰國策 relates, "The king of Zhao (Zhao Yong 趙雍) said, 'When my father (Marquis Su 趙肅侯) was alive, Lord Yang (Li Dui 李兑) was the chancellor. He had total control of the marquisate; he deceived my father and was excessively autocratic. I was studying at the inner palace and could not intervene in court affairs. When my father died, I was still very young and later I took over the kingdom. I was bewildered, and I was thinking to myself that it would be against the enduring interest of our kingdom to form an alliance with the other fief lords, instead of serving Qin. I was making preparations to travel forth to the kingdom of Qin to apologize for our indiscretion; you happen to come by at an opportune moment, and I thank you for giving me some factual

Yan, "The king of Zhao is now paying homage to the king of Qin; he has presented the areas between the rivers *Hejian* to Qin. Your Highness, your kingdom has yet to submit to Qin. When the Qin army lays siege to Yunzhong and Jiuyuan; while commanding Zhao to assault against Yan; Your Highness will lose the Long-Wall along the Yishui River.[116] Qi and Zhao are now merely prefectures or counties of Qin. Without the king's consent, they do not have the audacity to raise an army. If you submit to Qin, the menacing threats from Qi and Zhao will dissipate." The king of Yan presented five cities at the tail end of Chengshan Mountain to sue for peace.[117]

Zhang Yi set forth to return to Qin to report on his achievements; before he reached Xianyang King Hui died. King Wu succeeded to the throne.[118] When King Wu was the crown prince, he was not partial towards Zhang Yi. Upon his accession to the throne, the ministers at court laid unfavourable remarks against Zhang Yi. When the fief lords heard news of the friction between Zhang Yi and the Qin king, they quickly disavowed their earlier pledges; the Coalition with Qin broke up, and the Alliance resumed.

310 BCE Gengxu 庚戌 Warring States 戰國

King Nan of Zhou	周赧王	5th year
Duke Ping of Lu	魯平公	7th year
King Wu of Qin	秦武王	1st year
King Kang of Song	宋康王	19th year
King Huai of Chu	楚懷王	19th year

advice.' He decreed to despatch three hundred war chariots to Mianche 澠池 to pay homage to the king of Qin, and ceded *Hejian* 河間 to Qin 秦." The *ZGC*, 'Zhaoce 2 趙策二', pp. 203-204. (N.B. The text here suggests that Zhao Yong might have travelled forth to Qin. While, later the account in 299 BCE relates that Zhao Yong appeared in Qin incognito, and no one could recognize him; it does not appear to be credible.)

115 King of Yan, the text does not stipulate who he was, it was probably King Zhao of Yan 燕昭王 Ji Ping 姬平.

116 Yunzhong 雲中 - Tuoketuo Neimeng 内蒙 托克托.
Jiuyuan 九原 - Baotou Neimeng 内蒙 包頭.
Yishui River 易水 - the river flows through Yixian Hebei 河北 易縣, it was the boundary of Yan to its southwest.
Yan Long-Walls.

117 Changshan zhiwei 常山之尾 (恆山) 五城 - Five-walled-cities at the tail end of Changshan - Datongxian Shanxi 山西 大同縣.
According to the *ZGC* 戰國策, "Ji Ping 燕 姬平 said, 'Our kingdom is located in the barbaric wilderness, it appears to be a huge kingdom like a strong man, yet its strength is no more than a newborn infant. The other fief lords do not accept our words, and our strategies cannot resolve issues. It is fortunate that I have you, Sir, who came here to shed light on my errors. My people and I intend to face west to accept the leadership of the king of Qin, and I now cede five cities at Changshan zhiwei 常山之尾 to Qin as tributes." The *ZGC* 戰國策, 'Yance 齊策 一', pp. 330-331.

118 Xianyang 咸陽.
Ying Si 嬴駟.
King Wu of Qin 秦武王 Ying Tang 嬴蕩 (r. 310-307 BCE).

King Xuan of Qi	齊宣王	10th year
King Xiang of Wei	魏襄王	9th year
King Xiang of Hann	韓襄王	2nd year
King Wuling of Zhao	趙武靈王	16th year
King Zhao of Yan	燕昭王	3rd year
Sir Wey Si	衛嗣君	15th year

1. Zhang Yi said to King Wu of Qin, "For the benefit of Qin, Your Highness has to contrive some turbulence in the east to procure more territories. Your subject has heard that the king of Qi loathes your subject intensely; hence, whichever kingdom he enters into, it will be attacked. Your Highness, please allow him to travel to Liang; Qi will attack Liang. When the two kingdoms are engaged in an unresolved and protracted war, Your Highness can send your army against Hann, taking over areas around the Three Rivers *Sanchuan*,[119] then follow up by holding the Son of Heaven hostage, appropriating the maps and household registries under Heaven. It is one way to achieve a grand exploit." The king of Qin acceded to it.

Just as Zhang Yi anticipated, Qi invaded Liang, and the king was in a terrible panic. Zhang Yi said to the king, "Do not be overly concerned, I will convince Qi to cease attacking us." He sent his retainer to Chu and hired a Chu local as an emissary to pay homage to the king of Qi.[120] The emissary said to the king, "The approach Your Highness uses is one grand strategy to enhance the King of Qin's trust of Zhang Yi!" The king of Qi asked, "Why did you say that?" The Chu emissary said, "Zhang Yi's departure from Qin was a premeditated subterfuge. Qin had hoped that Qi and Liang would be engaged in a bitter struggle; it would allow them an opportunity to annex the Three River *Sanchuan* district. Now, Your Highness is attacking Liang, you have compromised the internal safety of your state, and externally you have also created adversary by attacking your ally. This is why I believe you have reinforced Qin king's trust of Zhang Yi." The king of Qi ordered his army to withdraw.

Zhang Yi was the chancellor of Wei for one year and died.

Zhang Yi and Su Qin roamed among the fief states and advocated their Horizontal and Vertical political strategies among the fief lords; they acquired immense wealth and attained prestigious positions. The intellects under Heaven zealously emulated their skills; among them was Gongsun Yan from Wei, alias Xishou, who gained international recognition for his discourses. Others included Su Dai, Su Li, Zhou Zui and Lou Huan.[121]

---

119 The Three Rivers *Sanchuan* 三川 – The conference of the three rivers - Yishui River 伊水, Luoshui River 洛水, and Huanghe River 黄河.

120 Retainer - *sheren* 舍人.
Tian Pijiang 田辟彊.

121 Gongsun Yan 公孫衍 alias Xishou 犀首. At one stage Gongsun Yan was a Wei 魏 officer at a place called Xishou 犀首 hence he came to be known as Xishou. He was an advocate of the south-north alliance. In 333 BCE he was appointed the commander general of Qin – *daliangzao* 秦 大良造. According to the *SJ* 史記, Zhang Yi 張儀 was canvassing at Wei at that stage; he proposed an alliance between Qin and Wei to go against Hann 韓. The pact

These men travelled extensively throughout the kingdoms under Heaven, drawing on their crafty and swindling skills to persuade the fief lords to adopt their devious schemes. There had been so many of them that they cannot be recounted individually. Zhang Yi, Su Qin and Gongsun Yan were the most notable among them.

Mengzi comments:

Someone asked, "Are Gongsun Yan and Zhang Yi not outstanding individuals? Whenever they conjured up certain wrathful plans all the fief lords under Heaven were in dire trepidation; when they subsided all under Heaven was serene and peaceful." Mengzi responded, "How could one consider them outstanding? An honourable person sits solemnly according to proper etiquettes, behaving righteously. When he attains success he shares the rewards with the commoners; upon losing power, he cultivates himself; neither riches nor fame can corrupt him, being deprived he does not renounce his values nor does he yield under duress. That is what I call a truly outstanding person."

Yang Xiong in Fayan states:[122]

Someone asked, "Zhang Yi and Su Qin studied political strategy of Horizontal and Vertical tactics under Guigu;[123] they applied what they

---

reached was that Qin would annex the areas in the Three Rivers - *Sanchuan* 三川 while Wei would take possession of Nanyang 南陽 upon the defeat of Hann. The king of Wei acceded to it; Zhang Yi then assumed the position as the chancellor of Wei. On the other hand, Gongsun Yan (Xishou) was canvassing at Hann, the king of Hann agreed to his proposal of ceding Nanyang to Wei 魏, spoiling Zhang Yi's proposed alliance. Later Zhang Yi became the chancellor of Qin; Gongsun Yan left Qin and became the commanding general of Wei, however, at this stage the kingdom was already on the decline. Gongsun Yan successfully brokered an alliance between Wei and Qi and defeated Zhao. In 325 BCE Gongsun Yan orchestrated another alliance between Wei, Zhao 趙, Yan 燕 and Zhongshan 中山 to go against the east-west Coalition of Qin and Chu under Zhang Yi. The allied forces lost to the Chu 楚 army; Gongsun Yan was banished. In 319 BCE, the king of Wei banished Zhang Yi to return to Qin; Wei reinstated Gongsun Yan, the South-north Alliance was rekindled. In 318 BCE the allied forces of Wei, Zhao, Hann, Yan and Chu aided by the barbaric Yiqu tribes 義渠 soundly defeated the Qin army at Libo 李伯. While, later the allied forces sustained a crushing defeat at Hanguguan Pass 函谷關 when they marched towards the Pass, but retreated, see 318 BCE. Gonsun Yan gained repute almost equal to that of Zhang Yi; however, accounts of him are sketchy. The accounts of Gongsun Yan is appended in 'Zhuan Yi zhuan 張儀傳' in the *SJ* 史記, and there are several references to him in the *ZGC* 戰國策. The *SJ,* 卷 40, 'Zhang Yi liezhuan 張儀列傳' 第 10, pp. 492-493.

Yang K., *ZGS* 戰國史, pp. 347, 350-354.

Su Dai 蘇代, Su Li 蘇厲, Zhou Zui 周最 and Lou Huan 樓緩.

122 Fayan 法言, Yangzi 楊子, Yang Xiong 楊雄. This passage is from *Yangzi fayan* 楊子法言, 第 11, 'Yuanqian juan 淵騫卷 (6)'.

123 Guigu - Guiguzi 鬼谷子.

learned and separately contributed over ten years of peace in *zhongguo*. Is it true?" Yang Xiong answered, "They were scoundrels and swindlers. Sages detest and despise them." The person asked, "What if a person studies the erudition of Kongzi while advances the deeds of Zhang Yi and Su Qin?" Yang Xiong responded, "Appalling it would be! It sounds like the sweetest chirpings coming from a phoenix cloaked in the feather of a ferocious bird." The person then asked, "Was Zigong not doing exactly that?"[124] Yang Xiong answered, "Whenever there were chaos and unrest, Zigong was most indignant if they were left unsolved; whereas, Zhang Yi and Su Qin were humiliated for not acquiring fame and glory with their rhetoric." The person continued, "Zhang Yi and Su Qi were intellects. They discarded conventional reasoning, and advanced new and revolutionary thesis of their own." Yang Xiong responded, "In times of antiquity, King Yao disregarded the minions.[125] Did he not believe in engaging capable people? These men might be exceptionally gifted; however, their abilities and aptitudes are not worthy men of our like."[126]

II. The king of Qin sent Gan Mao to Shu, where he executed Zhuang the Shu chancellor.[127]

III. The king of Qin and the king of Wei met at Linjin.[128]

IV. King Wuling of Zhao took Meng Yao, Wu Guang's daughter as wife. The king was exceptionally fond of this woman and named her Queen Hui. She gave birth to a son Zhao He.[129]

---

124 Zigong 子貢. Duanmu Ci 端木賜 (520-446 BCE) was the real name of Zigong. He was a student of Confucius. He was famous for his eloquence. In 484 BCE, the fiefdom of Qi 齊 invaded Lu 魯. Confucius 孔子 sent him to the kingdom of Wu 吳 to appeal for help. The Wu-Lu alliance defeated the encroaching army. The *SJ* 史記 comments, 'No sooner has Duanmu Ci appeared, the Qi army fell into disarray. The Wu Kingdom was undermined; Jin 晉 rose to power while the kingdom of Yue 越 attained hegemony."

125 King - *di* 帝堯 Di Yao.

126 "昔在任人, 帝而難之," This two phases are from the *Book of Documents Shangshu* Yaodian. 尚書堯典. '而難任人'. Di was Di Yao 帝堯. *ZZTJ JZ*, Vol 1, p. 113.

127 King Wu of Qin 秦武王 Ying Tang 嬴蕩.
Gan Mao 甘茂.
Shu Chancellor – *xiang* 蜀相, Chen Zhuang 陳莊 was made chancellor of Shu in 311 BCE.

128 King Xiang of Wei 魏襄王 Wei Si 魏嗣.
Linjin 臨晉 - Daneixian Shaanxi 陝西 大荔縣.

129 King Wuling of Zhao 趙武靈王 Zhao Yong 趙雍.
Wu Guang 吳廣 was a minister at the Zhao court.
Queen Hui 惠后 Wu Mengyao 吳孟姚 alias Wuwa 吳娃.
Zhao He 趙何, later King Huiwen of Zhao 趙 惠文王.

309 BCE *Rengzi* 壬子 Warring States 戰國

King Nan of Zhou	周赧王	6th year
Duke Ping of Lu	魯平公	8th year
King Wu of Qin	秦武王	2nd year
King Kang of Song	宋康王	20th year
King Huai of Chu	楚懷王	20th year
King Xuan of Qi	齊宣王	11th year
King Xiang of Wei	魏襄王	10th year
King Xiang of Hann	韓襄王	3rd year
King Wuling of Zhao	趙武靈王	17th year
King Zhao of Yan	燕昭王	4th year
Sir Wey Si	衛嗣君	16th year

1. Qin created the position of chancellor *chengxiang*; Chuli Ji (Ying Ji) was appointed as the right chancellor.[130]

308 BCE Guichou 癸丑 Warring States 戰國

King Nan of Zhou	周赧王	7th year
Duke Ping of Lu	魯平公	9th year
King Wu of Qin	秦武王	3rd year
King Kang of Song	宋康王	21st year
King Huai of Chu	楚懷王	21st year
King Xuan of Qi	齊宣王	12th year
King Xiang of Wei	魏襄王	11th year
King Xiang of Hann	韓襄王	4th year
King Wuling of Zhao	趙武靈王	18th year
King Zhao of Yan	燕昭王	5th year
Sir Wey Si	衛嗣君	17th year

1. The kings of Qin and Wei met at Ying.[131]

---

130 Chancellor - *chengxiang* 丞相. Right Chancellor *you chengxiang* 右丞相, Ying Ji 嬴疾. (Chulizi 樗里子, his proper name was Chuli Ji 樗里疾). The chancellor position was already in use at Qin; however, the Qin king gave it a new appellation.
Chuli Ji 樗里疾 - The *SJ* 史記, 卷 41, 'Chulizi, Gan Mao liezhuan 樗里子甘茂列傳' 第 11, pp. 511-512.

II. The king of Qin commanded Gan Mao to form an alliance with Wei to attack Hann; the king also commanded Xiang Shou as his assistant.[132] Gan Mao ordered Xiang Shou to return with a message to the king, "Wei has agreed to your subject's proposal; nevertheless, it is hoped that Your Highness will not proceed with the expedition." The king met Gan Mao at Xirang and enquired the reason.[133] Gan Mao answered, "Yiyang appears to be a county, [134] yet, in reality, it is more like a prefecture. With many odds against us, Your Highness raised an army to attack a city; it is a hazardous undertaking. Our army has to march for one thousand *li*, [135] making it even more perilous. In past times, there was a Lu man bearing the same name as Zeng Can committed murder.[136] Someone related the incident to Zeng Can's mother; she ignored it and carried on with her weaving as if nothing had happened. A second and a third person also came to relate to her; she hastily dropped her weaving spindle, scrambling over the wall of her house and ran for her life. Your subject is nowhere as capable as Zeng Can is; Your Highness's trust in him is nowhere comparable to Zeng Can's mother. More than three individuals at your court are suspicion of your subject, once they start spreading dubious rumours, he is afraid, Your Highness will drop your spindle hurriedly! When Marquis Wen of Wei commanded Yue Yang to attack Zhongshan, [137] and the siege took three years. The merits of the general were appraised upon his return to the capital. Marquis Wen handed the general a chest of missives that labelled and denigrated him. Yue Yang was intensely mortified; he backed off and repeatedly apologized by *kowtow*. He said, 'The success was hardly due to your subject, it was entirely Your Highness's effort.' Now, Your Highness, your subject is a visiting consultant having wandered away from his homeland. If Chulizi and Gongsun Shi are to use the Hann kingdom as a deception to libel against him, [138] Your Highness will

---

131 Ying 應 – Yingcheng 應城 - Lushanxian Henan 河南 魯山縣.

132 The king of Qin 秦王 Ying Tang 嬴蕩.
Gan Mao 甘茂, a Xiacai 下蔡 native, was an accomplished Qin general. He studied the hundred schools of thoughts under a certain Shi Ju 史擧 and was introduced to King Huiwen of Qin 秦 惠文王 by Zhang Yi 張儀 and Chuli Ji 樗里疾. In 312 BCE, he assisted Senior Counsellor *zuoshuzhang* Wei Zhang 左庶長 魏章 in annexing the areas in Hanzhong 漢中. Later he was framed by Xiang Shou 向壽 and Gongsun Shi 公孫奭. He defected to Qi 齊 while laying siege to Puban at Wei 魏 蒲阪 and took on a position as a senior counsellor. In 305 BCE he travelled to Chu 楚 as a Qi envoy. The king of Qin wanted Chu to repatriate Gan Mao, but the request was declined. He later died in Wei. The *SJ* 史記,卷 41, 'Chulizi, Gan Mao liezhuan 樗里子甘茂列傳' 第 11, pp. 512-515.
Xiang Shou 尚壽.

133 Xirang 息壤. A town in Jianglingxian 江陵縣. (Chiang-ling-hsien), according to *le Grand dsctionnaire Ricci de la langue chinoise*. Vol.II, p. 911.

134 Yiyang 宜陽 - Yiyangxian Henan 河南 宜陽縣.

135 One thousand *li* – it is a hyperbole.

136 Zeng Can 曾參 505-435 BCE, alias Zengzi 曾子 was a student of Confucius. The incident relates that one should be wary of gossips.

137 Marquis Wen of Wei 魏文侯 Wei Si 魏斯 (r. 446-397 BCE). N.B. Details see Appendix – Warring States – Sovereigns, Heads-of-States, and Marquises.
Yue Yang 樂羊 was the forebear of Yue Yi 樂毅.
Yue Yang attacked and annihilated Zhongshan 中山 in 408-406 BCE.
The kingdom of Zhongshan 中山國 – Dingxian Hebei 河北 定縣.

138 Ying Ji 嬴疾.

undoubtedly listen to their advice. If it happens Your Highness will have betrayed the king of Wei; whereas Gongzhong Chi will abhor your subject." [139] The king said, "I will not listen to any rumour directed against you; Sir, we will swear an oath." An oath was sworn at Xirang.

Autumn. Gan Mao was appointed as commander and Feng as lieutenant colonel *shuzhang* to lead an army to attack Yiyang.[140]

---

307 BCE Jiayin 甲寅 Warring States 戰國

King Nan of Zhou	周赧王	8th year
Duke Ping of Lu	魯平公	10th year
King Wu of Qin	秦武王	4th year
King Kang of Song	宋康王	22nd year
King Huai of Chu	楚懷王	22nd year
King Xuan of Qi	齊宣王	13th year
King Xiang of Wei	魏襄王	12th year
King Xiang of Hann	韓襄王	5th year
King Wuling of Zhao	趙武靈王	19th year
King Zhao of Yan	燕昭王	6th year
Sir Wey Si	衛嗣君	18th year

I. Gan Mao attacked Yiyang; the city remained standing after five months. Just as expected, Chulizi and Gongsun Shi censured him on numerous occasions.[141] The king of Qin summoned Gan Mao to return to the capital and considered withdrawing the troops. Gan Mao said, "Xirang is thither." The king said, "Yes, of course." He raised another army in support of Gan Mao's assault. The Qin army decapitated sixty thousand men; Yiyang fell. Gongzhong Chi of Hann went to the Qin court to offer an apology and pleaded for peace.

II. King Wu of Qin enjoyed strength contest.[142] He appointed strongmen Ren Bi, Wu Huo and Meng Yue as senior officers at court.[143] In the eighth month, the king was having a contest with

---

Gongsun Shi 公孫奭.

139 "If you command me to withdraw from the front."
Gongzhong Chi 公仲侈 was the chancellor of Hann, he and Gan Mao 甘茂 were close friends. Hence, Gan Mao suggested that he might be branded as treasonous.

140 Lieutenant Colonel, *shuzhang* 庶長, Feng 封 Ying Feng 嬴封.

141 Chulizi 樗里子 Ying Ji 嬴疾, alias Chuli Ji 樗里疾. See footnotes in 309 BCE.
Gongsun Shi 公孫奭.

142 King Wu of Qin 秦武王.

143 Ren Bi 任鄙, Wu Huo 烏獲 and Meng Yue 孟説 were strongmen from Qin with exceptional strength. Meng Yue 孟説 alias was Meng Ben 孟賁.

Meng Yue lifting a bronze tripod; he ruptured his veins and died.[144] The Qin court executed the entire family clan of Meng Yue. King Wu did not leave an heir; his younger brother by a different mother Ji was held hostage at Yan; the Qin court sent attendants to escort Ji to return to Qin and placed him on the throne. He was known posthumously as King Zhaoxiang.[145] The mother of King Zhaoxiang was Mi *bazi*, a woman from Chu; she was known as Queen Dowager Xuan.[146]

II. King Wuling of Zhao invaded and annexed territories of the Zhongshan kingdom in the north.[147] The Zhao forces marched past Fangzi and Dai; it then turned north to arrive at Wuqiong and finally reached the River in the west. The Zhao army ascended to the summit of Huanghua Mountain.[148]

King Zhao conferred with Fei Yi the issue of adopting barbarian attire *hufu* and training his civilians with archery skill on horseback.[149] He said, "Obstinate inferiors may ridicule me while the informed understand my decision. Even if the entire world derides and scorns my decision, I am resolved to take possession of the Hu territories and Zhongshan kingdom." The king decreed his civilians to adopt *hufu* clothes; the people opposed his decision. Prince Cheng claimed that his was indisposed and could not attend to court.[150]

The king sent his personal aide to see the prince, and related to him, "When one is at home one takes heed of his elders, but when at court he abides by his overlord. Now I am trying to educate my people to adopt the *hufu* attire; Uncle, only you do not embrace it. I am fretful that the people under Heaven may accuse me of being partial. When presiding over a state it has to be

---

144 The *SJ* -史記 mentions that he broke his knee and died 絕臏而死. *SJ* 史記, 卷 23, 'Qin benji 秦本紀' 第 5, pp. 164-165.

145 Ying Ji 嬴稷 was held hostage at Yan 燕.
King Zhaoxiang of Qin 秦 昭襄王 (306-251 BCE).

146 Dowager Xuan, *taihou*, Mi Bazi 宣太后 羋八子. *Bazi* was not the name of the Dowager; it was a grade of the king's consort.

147 Zhao Zhao Yong - 趙 趙雍.
Kingdom of Zhongshan 中山國 - Ding Xian Hebei 河北 定縣. The kingdom was annihilated in 406 BCE; it was resumed by Duke Huan of Zhongshan 中山桓公 in 380 BCE when Wei was engaged in wars with other fief lords. Yang K. 楊寬, *ZGS* 戰國史, p. 365.
Lingshou 靈壽 - Pingshanxian Hebei 河北 平山縣.
Zhongshan is translated as the Middle Mountain Kingdom, an enclave among the more powerful warring states. It was founded in 414 BCE by a northern nomadic tribe of Rong 戎 or Di 狄 origin and was annihilated in either 296 or 295 BCE. There is only one chapter about Zhongshan in the *ZGC* 戰國策, yet it played a most interesting part in the Warring States political arena. It is worth noting that it was the only nomadic tribe to found a notable polity within Zhongyuan (Central Plain) during this period. Although the people of Zhongshan merged and assimilated with the people of the Central Plain, they retained numerous unique heritage of their nomadic past. Yap J.P., *Wars With the Xiongnu*, pp. 13-14.

148 Huanghua 黃華 – the location of the mountain is obscured.
Fangzi 房子 - Linchengxian Hebei 河北 臨城縣.
Daijun Prefecture 代郡 - Weixian Hebei 河北 蔚縣.
Wuqiong 無窮 the place is obscured.

149 Foreign clothes - *hufu* 胡服, pants, and sleeveless shirt more suitable for mounted archers.
Fei Yi 肥義 the Minister.

150 Zhao Cheng 趙成, Prince Cheng was Zhao Yong's uncle.

conducted with discipline, and the interest of the people is of the essence. When it comes to dispensing edicts, there are conventions and the execution of which must take priority over everything else. To disseminate virtue one commences with the lowly and humble, when it comes to the execution of new policies it commences with the elites. I had hoped to take advantage of my uncle's rectitude to realize my task of introducing *hufu*."

Prince Cheng *kowtow* and responded,[151] "Your subject has heard that Zhongguo is a place cultivated by the sages, and a land that fosters proper rites *li* and music *yue*; kingdoms and barbaric tribes from near and afar aspire and yearn to emulate us. Now, His Highness wishes to abandon our established custom to adopt the barbaric custom by wearing their clothes; changing our traditional way of life; this is against the wish of the people. His subject implores him to reconsider his decision with much prudence."

The envoy duly reported the conversation. The king visited his uncle personally; he said, "To our east we have Qi and Zhongshan; to our north we have Yan and the Dong-Hu tribes; to our west we have the Loufan tribes, and we share our border with Qin and Hann.[152] If we do not adopt archery skill from horseback in preparedness, how can we defend ourselves? Harking back to the time when Zhongshan assisted by the powerful Qi forces successfully ravished our land, they captured and enslaved our people, and they attempted to flood our city of Hao by breaking the dam.[153] Had it not been for the Divine intervention of our holy shrine we would have lost the city. Our ancestors were greatly humiliated by the incident. My decision to adopt barbarian clothes *hufu* and archery skill on horseback is in essence to meet the threats from the four quarters of our state, an attempt to avenge our humiliation brought on by Zhongshan. My uncle's insistence on holding fast to Zhongguo traditions, rejecting my decision to change into barbarian attires, while forgetting the shame of Hao is not exactly what I had hoped for." Prince Cheng had a complete about-face and accepted the king's command. The king presented him with *hufu*. The next day, Zhao Cheng appeared at the court fully attired in *hufu*. The king decreed that henceforth the entire kingdom would adopt the *hufu* attire, and began to train his warriors to shoot arrows on horseback.[154]

---

151 *Kowtow* 叩頭 is also spelled as *koutou*, a ceremony of deep bows or prostrations for solemn occasions at the times of Zhou 周 and Han 漢 when people were kneeling (seated) on mats or slightly raised sitting platforms called *ta* 榻.

152 Zhongshan 中山, *Dong-Hu* 東胡, Loufan 樓煩.

Dong-Hu 東胡 was the collective name of nomadic tribes that settled in the northern parts of present-day Shanxi 山西 and the mid-section and eastern parts of Inner Mongolia 内蒙中部及東部.

Loufan 樓煩 – some texts claimed that the people at Loufan were descendants of Loufanzi 樓煩子, who was a count at the time of King Cheng of Zhou 周成王. As the clan lived among the nomadic tribes of Hu they acquired their habits and were mistaken as barbarian tribes. The name of Loufanxian County 樓煩縣 continues to be in use to this day.

153 Hao 鄗 - Haocheng 鄗城 - Baixiangxian Hebei 河北 柏鄉縣.

154 People in *Zhongyuan* 中原 at this time wore ankle-length tunics; it was suicidal when soldiers were wearing such clumsy tunics to do battle with the infinitely more mobile and agile nomads on horseback. The principle war weapon of the Chinese warriors at the time of the Warring States was still the horse drawn chariot. By the 4th century BCE, the nomads in the north began to conduct battles on horseback. Yap J., *Wars With the Xiongnu*, pp. 15-16.

306 BCE *Yimao* 乙卯 Warring States 戰國

King Nan of Zhou	周赧王	9th year
Duke Ping of Lu	魯平公	11th year
King Zhaoxiang of Qin	秦昭襄王	1st year
King Kang of Song	宋康王	23rd year
King Huai of Chu	楚懷王	23rd year
King Xuan of Qi	齊宣王	14th year
King Xiang of Wei	魏襄王	13th year
King Xiang of Hann	韓襄王	6th year
King Wuling of Zhao	趙武靈王	20th year
King Zhao of Yan	燕昭王	7th year
Sir Wey Si	衛嗣君	19th year

I. King Zhao of Qin sent Shang Shou to bring appeasement at Yiyang.[155] At the same time, the king commanded Chulizi and Gan Mao to attack Wei.[156] Gan Mao suggested to the king that the city of Wusui should be returned to Hann.[157] Shang Shou and Gongsun Shi objected to the suggestion but failed to convince the king.[158] Since then the two men loathed Gan Mao and maligned against him. Gan Mao was in great apprehension, when the army arrived at Puban of Wei he abandoned the siege and absconded.[159] Chulizi reached an agreement with Wei and retreated. Gan Mao escaped to Qi.

II. The king of Zhao annexed the territories of Zhongshan. The army marched as far as Ningduan, turning west he and his army penetrated deep into the Hu territories, annexing the areas; he finally reached Yuzhong.[160] The king of Lin-Hu presented tribute of horses to the king of Zhao.[161] Upon his return to his capital, the king sent emissary Lou Huan to Qin, Chou Ye to Hann, Wang Ben to Chu, Fu Ding to Wei and Zhao Jue to Qi.[162] He then commanded Zhao Gu the assistant magistrate of the Dai Prefecture to preside over the Hu tribes, and Zhao began to enlist the Hu tribesmen.[163]

---

155 Yiyang 宜陽 - Yiyangxian Henan 河南 宜陽縣. It was annexed the previous year.

156 Ying Ji 嬴疾 Chulizi 樗里 子 Ying Ji 嬴疾, alias Chuli Ji 樗里疾.
Gan Mao 甘茂.

157 Wusui 武遂 - Linfenxian Shanxi 山西 臨汾縣.

158 Shang Shou 尚壽 was previously the assistant of Gan Mao. See 308 BCE.
Gongsun Shi 公孫奭.

159 Puban 蒲阪 - Yongjixian Shanxi 山西 永濟縣.

160 Ningduan 寧葮 - Xuanhuaxian Hebei 河北 宣化縣.
Yuzhong 楡中 - Dongshengxian Neimeng 內蒙 東勝縣.

161 Lin-Hu 林胡.

162 Zhao Yong 趙雍 embarked upon a series of diplomatic repositioning.
Lou Huan 樓緩 was the emissary sent to Qin 秦.
Chou Ye 仇液 to Hann 韓.

III. The kings of Chu, Qi and Hann revived the former Alliance treaty.

305 BCE *Bingchen* 丙辰 Warring States 戰國

King Nan of Zhou	周赧王	10th year
Duke Ping of Lu	魯平公	12th year
King Zhaoxiang of Qin	秦昭襄王	2nd year
King Kang of Song	宋康王	24th year
King Huai of Chu	楚懷王	24th year
King Xuan of Qi	齊宣王	15th year
King Xiang of Wei	魏襄王	14th year
King Xiang of Hann	韓襄王	7th year
King Wuling of Zhao	趙武靈王	21st year
King Zhao of Yan	燕昭王	8th year
Sir Wey Si	衛嗣君	20th year

I. A comet was visible.

II. The king of Zhao invaded Zhongshan, and the army annexed areas in Danqiu, Shuangyanghong *zhisai* Pass, following which it took Hao, Shiyi, Fenglong and Dongyuan.[164] Zhongshan sued for peace by presenting four counties to Zhao.

III. Wei Ran, the younger brother of the Dowager Xuan of Qin from a different father, was enfeoffed as Marquis of Rang, while, Mi Rong another younger brother from the same father was enfeoffed as Lord Huayang.[165] Two younger brothers of the king by the same mother were honoured

---

Wang Ben 王賁 to Chu 楚.
Fu Ding 富丁 to Wei 魏.
Zhao Jue 趙爵 to Qi 齊.

163 Dai Chancellor 代相 Zhao Gu 趙固. The text says he was the Chancellor of Dai. However, this was unlikely, as Dai was only a prefecture and he was more likely to be a magistrate.
Dai 代 - Daijun 代郡 - Weixian Hebei 河北 蔚縣.

164 Danqiu 丹丘 – Quyangxian Hebei 河北 曲陽縣.
Shuangyanghong zhisai Pass 爽陽鴻之塞 - *SJ* 史記 relates it as Huayangchi zhisai 華陽鴟之塞 - West of Dingxian Hebei 河北 定縣.
Hao 鄗 - Haocheng 鄗城 there are no records as to when the city was lost to Zhongshan 中山.
Shiyi 石邑 - north of Huoluxian Hebei 河北 獲鹿縣.
Fenglongshan Mountain 封龍山 - south of Huoluxian Hebei.
Dongyuan 東垣 - Zhengdingxian Hebei 河北 正定縣.

165 Qin Dowager 秦太后 Mi Bazi 芈八子.
Marquis Rang 穰侯 Wei Ran 魏冉 was the younger brother of Queen Dowager Mi Bazi by a different father.
Lord Huayang 華陽君 Mi Rong 芈戎 was a younger brother of the Dowager Mi Bazi by the same father.

as Lord Gaoling and Lord Jingyang.[166] Wei Ran was the most capable; from the time of King Hui to King Wu he took on responsible positions at the Qin Court.[167] When King Wu died, the younger brothers of the king vied for the throne; Wei Ran secured the throne for King Zhao.[168] Upon ascending the throne, the king honoured Wei Ran as the commander of Xianyang the capital city.[169] Sometime during this year, Zhuang, a lieutenant colonel *shuzhang* of the Qin army rallied the princes, [170] ministers, and their supporters to stage a revolt. Wei Ran executed all the mutineers, even Queen Huiwen and other imperial members met their premature deaths.[171] Queen Daowu, the wife of King Wu, was banished to return to Wei.[172] Wei Ran summarily deposed all the older and younger brothers of the king who held the slightest ambition. The king was still young; Dowager Xuan attended to the court affairs personally. She transferred the power to Wei Ran, whose authority was awe-inspiring for everybody in Qin.

---

304 BCE *Dingsi* 丁巳 Warring States 戰國

King Nan of Zhou	周赧王	11th year
Duke Ping of Lu	魯平公	13th year
King Zhaoxiang of Qin	秦昭襄王	3rd year
King Kang of Song	宋康王	25th year
King Huai of Chu	楚懷王	25th year
King Xuan of Qi	齊宣王	16th year
King Xiang of Wei	魏襄王	15th year
King Xiang of Hann	韓襄王	8th year
King Wuling of Zhao	趙武靈王	22nd year
King Zhao of Yan	燕昭王	9th year
Sir Wey Si	衛嗣君	21st year

1. The king of Qin and of the king of Chu met at Huangji for a coalition conference. Qin returned Shangyong to Chu.[173]

---

166 Lord Gaoling 高陵君 Ying Xian 嬴顯 was the younger brother of King Zhaoxiang by the same mother. Lord Jingyang 涇陽君 Ying Kui 嬴悝 was another younger brother of King Zhaoxiang by the same mother.

167 King Hui of Qin 秦惠王.
King Wu of Qin 秦武王.

168 King Zhaoxiang was Wei Ran's nephew.

169 Commander of the capital city of Xianyang, *xianyang wei* 咸陽衛 Wei Ran 魏冉.

170 The Lieutenant Colonel, *shuzhang* 庶長 Ying Zhuang 嬴壯.

171 Queen Huiwen 惠文后 (?-306 BCE) was the Queen of King Hui 秦惠王 (or Huiwen), the mother of King Daowu 悼武王. The text states that she died an unnatural death.

172 Queen Daowu 秦悼武 王后 – wife of King Daowu 秦武王.

173 King Zhao of Qin 秦昭王 Ying Ji 嬴稷.
King Huai of Chu 楚懷王 Mi Huai 芈槐.
Huangji 黃棘 - Xinyexian Henan 河南 新野縣.
Shangyong 上庸 - Zhushanxian Hubei 湖北 竹山縣.

303 BCE Wuwu 戊午 Warring States 戰國

King Nan of Zhou	周赧王	12th year
Duke Ping of Lu	魯平公	14th year
King Zhaoxiang of Qin	秦昭襄王	4th year
King Kang of Song	宋康王	26th year
King Huai of Chu	楚懷王	26th year
King Xuan of Qi	齊宣王	17th year
King Xiang of Wei	魏襄王	16th year
King Xiang of Hann	韓襄王	9th year
King Wuling of Zhao	趙武靈王	23rd year
King Zhao of Yan	燕昭王	10th year
Sir Wey Si	衛嗣君	22nd year

I. A comet appeared.

II. Qin invaded Wei and annexed Puban, Yangjin and Fengdu.[174] The Qin army then followed up by annexing Wusui of Hann.[175]

III. Qi, Hann and Wei raised an army to castigate Chu for breaching the Alliance treaty.[176] The king of Chu sent Heir Apparent Heng to Qin as hostage, pleading for help. Qin sent a guest consultant *keqing* Tong leading an army to bring relief to Chu,[177] and the three allied forces retreated.

302 BCE *Jiwei* 己未 Warring States 戰國

King Nan of Zhou	周赧王	13th year
Duke Ping of Lu	魯平公	15th year
King Zhaoxiang of Qin	秦昭襄王	5th year
King Kang of Song	宋康王	27th year
King Huai of Chu	楚懷王	27th year
King Xuan of Qi	齊宣王	18th year
King Xiang of Wei	魏襄王	17th year

174 Puban 蒲阪 - Yongjixian Shanxi 山西 永濟縣.
Yangjin 陽晉 - Jinchengxian Shanxi 山西 晉城縣.
Fengdu 封渡 - Fenglingdu Crossing at Yongjixian Shanxi 山西 永濟縣 風陵渡.

175 Wusui 武遂 - Linfenxian Shanxi 山西 臨汾縣, it was returned to Hann in 306 BCE, now recaptured by Qin.

176 Chu revoked the alliance with the other fief lords, now pledged its allegiance to Qin instead.

177 Guest Consultant *keqing* Tong 客卿 通.

King Xiang of Hann	韓襄王	10th year
King Wuling of Zhao	趙武靈王	24th year
King Zhao of Yan	燕昭王	11th year
Sir Wey Si	衛嗣君	23rd year

I. The kings of Qin and Wei and Prince Ying of Hann met at Linjin. After the meeting, the Hann prince travelled to Xianyang before returning. Qin returned the occupied Puban to Wei.[178]

II. A minister at the Qin court had an altercation with the crown prince of Chu. The Chu prince killed the minister and escaped to return home.[179]

---

301 BCE *Gengshen* 庚申 Warring States 戰國

King Nan of Zhou	周赧王	14th year
Duke Ping of Lu	魯平公	16th year
King Zhaoxiang of Qin	秦昭襄王	6th year
King Kang of Song	宋康王	28th year
King Huai of Chu	楚懷王	28th year
King Xuan of Qi	齊宣王	19th year
King Xiang of Wei	魏襄王	18th year
King Xiang of Hann	韓襄王	11th year
King Wuling of Zhao	趙武靈王	25th year
King Zhao of Yan	燕昭王	12th year
Sir Wey Si	衛嗣君	24th year

I. A total solar eclipse was observed.

II. Qin invaded Hann and annexed Rang of Hann.[180]

III. Hui the magistrate of Shu revolted; the Qin authority sent Sima Cuo to Shu and had him executed.[181]

---

178 King Zhaoxiang of Qin 秦 昭襄王 Ying Ji 嬴稷.
King Xiang of Wei 魏襄王 Wei Si 魏嗣.
The Crown Prince of Hann *taizi* 韓太子 Hann Ying 韓嬰.
Linjin 臨晋 - Dalixian Shaanxi 陜西 大荔縣.

179 The Crown Prince of Chu, *taizi* 楚太子 Mi Heng 芈横.

180 Rang 穰 - Dengxian Henan 河南 鄧縣.

181 Qin General 秦將 Sima Cuo 司馬錯.
Ying Hui 嬴煇 was a son of Ying Ji 嬴稷. According to the *Huayang guozhi* 華陽國志 the incident was quite different. The king of Qin, Ying Ji enfeoffed his son Ying Hui at Shu as the king of Shu 蜀. At an important sacrificial rite, Ying Hui by tradition presented the sacrificial meat to his father; unknown to him the meat was laced with a poison administered by his stepmother. The queen asked the king's

IV. Lieutenant Colonel *shuzhang* Huan of Qin joined forces with Hann, Wei and Qi to attack Chu.[182] The Chu army was routed at Chongqiu; the commanding general Tang Mei died in battle, and the city was annexed.[183]

V. The king of Zhao invaded Zhongshan; the king of Zhongshan escaped to Qi.[184]

VI. See notes.[185]

---

300 BCE Xinyou 辛酉 Warring States 戰國

King Nan of Zhou	周赧王	15th year
Duke Ping of Lu	魯平公	17th year
King Zhaoxiang of Qin	秦昭襄王	7th year
King Kang of Song	宋康王	29th year
King Huai of Chu	楚懷王	29th year
King Min of Qi	齊湣王	1st year
King Xiang of Wei	魏襄王	19th year
King Xiang of Hann	韓襄王	12th year
King Wuling of Zhao	趙武靈王	26th year
King Zhao of Yan	燕昭王	13th year
Sir Wey Si	衛嗣君	25th year

I. Qin sent Lord Jinyang to Qi as hostage.[186]

II. Lord Huayang,[187] made an expedition against Chu. The Chu army was routed; some thirty thousand men were beheaded. Jing Que the Chu commander general was killed in action. Qin went on to annex Xiangcheng. The king of Chu was in desperate straits; he sent his crown prince to Qi as hostage pleading for help.[188]

---

personal attendant to sample the food, killing the attendant. The king was in a rage and ordered Sima Cuo to execute Ying Hui. The *Huayang guozhi* 華陽國志, 卷 3, 'Shuji 蜀志', p. 313.

182 Huan - 奐 Ying Huan 嬴奐, Lieutenant Colonel, *shuzhuang* 庶長.
This campaign was to avenge the death of Qin's minister killed by Mi Heng.

183 Chongqiu 重丘 – northeast of Hezexian Shangdong – 山東 荷澤縣 東北. Another source claims that it was in Renpingxian Shandong 山東 茌平縣 near Liaochengxian 聊城縣.
The Chu Commander 楚將 Tang Mei 唐昧.

184 Zhongshan 中山國 - Dingxian Hebei 河北 定縣.

185 Tian Pijiang, King Xuan of Qi died; and his son Tian Di succeeded to the throne; he was known posthumously as King Min. N.B. The original text has made an error here.
King Xuan of Qi, Tian Pijiang 齊宣王 田辟彊.
King Min of Qi, Tian Di 齊湣王 田地 (r. 300-284 BCE).

186 Lord Jingyang 秦 涇陽君 Ying Kui 嬴悝. Ying Kui was the younger brother of the king.

187 Lord Huayang 華陽君 Mi Rong 芈戎, the uncle of the king of Qin.

188 Mi Rong 芈戎 the uncle of the Qin King.

III. Chuli Ji of Qin died.[189] Lou Huan, a Zhao national, took over the position as chancellor.[190]

IV. King Wuling of Zhao loved of his youngest son Zhao He dearly; he was planning to abdicate the throne to him while he was still alive.[191]

---

299 BCE *Renxu* 壬戌 Warring States 戰國

King Nan of Zhou	周赧王	16th year
Duke Ping of Lu	魯平公	18th year
King Zhaoxiang of Qin	秦昭襄王	8th year
King Kang of Song	宋康王	30th year
King Huai of Chu	楚懷王	30th year
King Min of Qi	齊湣王	2nd year
King Xiang of Wei	魏襄王	20th year
King Xiang of Hann	韓襄王	13th year
King Wuling of Zhao	趙武靈王	27th year
King Zhao of Yan	燕昭王	14th year
Sir Wey Si	衛嗣君	26th year

I. 5th month. *wushen* day.[192] A grand assembly was held at the East Palace *Donggong* of Zhao; the king was to abdicate his throne to Zhao He. The new king, having paid homage at the ancestral shrine, sat on his throne in state. The ministers of the former king were duly appointed as the king's officers. Fei Yi was now the chancellor and the tutor of the king. King Wuling conferred a new title upon himself: the Supreme Lord - the king's father, *Zhufu*.[193] *Zhufu* dedicated the governance of the kingdom to his son. He dressed in barbarian clothes *hufu* and led his generals, officers and troops to make expeditions against the barbarian Hu in the northwest. The army marched out through Yunzhong, Jiuyuan, and turned south to make a surprise visit at Xianyang.[194] *Zhufu*, disguising himself as an emissary, entered Qin to study the environs and terrain of Qin, and to familiarize himself with the personality of the Qin king. Oblivious to the stranger's identity, the king was impressed by the stately man, who did not bear the demeanour of a commoner. The king ordered his staff to give chase

---

Commander General of Chu 楚將 Jing Que 景缺.
Xiangcheng 襄城 - Xiangchengxian Henan 河南 襄城縣.
King of Chu 楚王 Mi Huai 芈槐.
Chu, Crown Prince 楚太子 Mi Heng 芈横.

189 Chulizi 樗里 子 Ying Ji 嬴疾 his proper name was Chuli Ji 樗里疾.

190 Zhao national 趙人 Lou Huan 樓緩.

191 Zhao Yong 趙雍; Zhao He 趙何.

192 It is probably a mistake as there was not a *wushen* 戊申 day during the 5th month of this year.

193 Supreme Lord, *zhufu* 主父 - In later days the title was changed to *taishangwang* 太上皇 meaning - the king's father - Zhao Yong 趙雍.

194 Yunzhong 雲中 - Tuoketuo Neimeng 內蒙 托克托.
Jiuyuan 九原 - Baotouxian Neimeng 內蒙 包頭縣.
Xianyang 咸陽 - Xian Shaanxi 陝西 西安.

after him; however, *Zhufu* had already departed through the Qin Pass. After an inquiry, it turned out to be *Zhufu*. The people of Qin were stunned by his audacity.

II. The king of Qi and the king of Wei met at Hann.[195]

III. Qin invaded Chu and annexing eight cities. The king of Qin sent a missive to the king of Chu, "When Your Highness and I swore a vow as brotherly states at Huangji; you sent your crown prince to my kingdom as a hostage, and our people were jubilant.[196] Prince Ling murdered one of my senior ministers, [197] exhibiting no remorse for his act, and he even took flight. I am incensed by what has transpired; I have thus despatched my army to march against your border. Little did I realize that you would send your crown prince to Qi to seek peace.[198] Your Kingdom and mine are contiguous to each other, besides we have marriage ties. Now that there are disagreements between Qin and Chu, we will be powerless to make the other fief lords to abide by our commands. I propose a personal meeting with Your Highness at the Wuguan Pass to resolve our differences, [199] and try to rekindle our alliance. It is my greatest yearning." The king of Chu was troubled. He was uneasy lest he might be deceived if he proceeded; on the other hand, he was also troubled that he might further aggravate the king of Qin for not proceeding. Zhao Sui, the chancellor, said,[200] "Your Highness, please do not proceed. All we have to do is to strengthen our border defences. The Qin people are like tigers and wolves, besides they are determined to annihilate all the fief lords. They cannot be trusted." Whereas, Lan the son-in-law of King Huai urged him to go. [201] In the end, he decided to set forth. The king of Qin ordered a general to disguise as himself to trick the Chu king to proceed into the Wuguan Pass, where armed guards were hiding for an ambuscade. When the Chu king arrived, the gates of the city were clamped shut. The armed guards took the king captive and had him taken to the west. In Xianyang at the Zhangtai hall in the imperial palace, [202] the king of Qin sat in state receiving homage from his guests, ministers and subjects. The king demanded the king of Chu to surrender Wu and the area in Qianzhong prefectures.[203] The king of Chu held that he would comply if they entered into a pledge of alliance, whereas the king of Qin insisted the ceding of land before further discussions. The king of Chu was enraged, "Qin has tricked me, and now you are demanding land from me by force!" The king refused to yield and the king of Chu was held.

The ministers at the Chu court were greatly alarmed and held a meeting to find a solution to the crisis. They deliberated, "Our king is held for ransom by Qin, and our crown prince is also held hostage in Qi. If Qi and Qin collaborate, Chu will no longer be a state." Some ministers

---

195 King Min of Qi 齊湣王 Tian Di 田地.
King Xiang of Wei 魏襄王 Wei Si 魏嗣.
Xinzheng 新鄭 - Xinzhengxian Henan 河南 新鄭縣.

196 Huangji 黄棘 – Xinyexian Henan 河南 新野縣. (204 BCE).
'Jubilant - for having reached a peaceful accord.'

202 Prince Ling, *taizi* 太子陵 Mi Heng 芈横.

198 'Rather than pursuing a peaceful solution between us.'

199 Wuguan Pass 武關 - Shangxian Shaanxi 陝西 商縣.

200 The Chancellor of Chu 楚相 Zhao Sui 昭睢.

201 Mi Lan 芈蘭 was the son of Mi Huai 芈槐; his wife was a Qin Princess.

202 Zhangtaidian Hall 章臺殿.

203 Wujun Prefecture 巫郡 - Wushanxian Sichuan 四川 巫山縣.
Qianzhongdi 黔中地 - Yuanlingxian Hunan 湖南 沅陵縣.

proposed that perhaps they could place one of the princes at Chu on the throne. The Zhao Sui said, "The king and the crown prince are held hostage in different fief states. If we go against the wish of the king to nominate one of his sons by a concubine, I don't think it is appropriate." In the end, the ministers issued a eulogy notice to Qi. [204] King Min of Qi summoned his ministers for a court conference. Someone suggested, "The prince should be used in exchange for territories north of the Huaihe River at Chu."[205] The Qi chancellor said, "It will not work. If the people at Ying decide to nominate another prince to succeed to the throne, [206] we will end up with a useless hostage. Besides, we will earn a reprehensible reputation for being immoral under Heaven." The person again suggested, "Not really, if the people at Ying place another prince on the throne, we can strike a deal with the new king. 'Cede us the areas in Xiadongguo and we will execute the crown prince on your behalf; [207] if you refuse, we with the help of Qin and Hann (three kingdoms) will place the crown prince on the throne.'"[208] The king of Qi adopted the suggestion of the chancellor. He sent the crown prince to return to Chu; the Chu people made him the new king.[209]

IV. The king of Qin heard that Lord Mengchang was a worthy man, he sent Lord Jingyang to Qi as a hostage in exchange for Lord Mengchang. [210] When the lord arrived at Qin, the king of Qin made him the chancellor.

---

298 BCE *Guihai* 癸亥 Warring States 戰國

King Nan of Zhou	周赧王	17th year
Duke Ping of Lu	魯平公	19th year
King Zhaoxiang of Qin	秦昭襄王	9th year
King Kang of Song	宋康王	31st year
King Qiangxiang of Chu	楚頃襄王	1st year
King Min of Qi	齊湣王	3rd year
King Xiang of Wei	魏襄王	21st year
King Xiang of Hann	韓襄王	14th year
King Wuling of Zhao	趙惠文王	1st year
King Zhao of Yan	燕昭王	15th year
Sir Wey Si	衛嗣君	27th year

---

204 '.. to seek permission from Qi to escort the heir apparent to return to Chu to ascend to the throne.'

205 Huaihe River 淮河.

206 Yingdu 郢都 was the capital of Chu 楚都 - Jianglingxian Hubei 湖北 江陵縣.

207 Xiadongguo 下東國 - territories north of the Huaishui River 淮水 that belonged to Chu 楚.

208 Three kingdoms *San-guo* 三國 - the states of Qi 齊, Qin 秦, and Hann 韓. To translate it as three states would be quite obscured.

209 He was known posthumously as King Qianxiang of Chu 楚 頃襄王 Mi-Xiong Heng 芈熊横 22nd (r. 298-263 or 264 BCE).

210 Qi Prince 齊王子 Lord Mengchang 孟嘗君 Tian Wen 田文.
Lord Jingyang 涇陽君 Ying Kui 嬴悝.

I. Someone counselled the king of Qin, "While Lord Mengchang is our new chancellor; however, without a shadow of a doubt, he will place his national interest before ours. We may see calamities falling upon Qin soon."[211] The king reappointed Lou Huan as chancellor and had Lord Mengchang imprisoned, awaiting execution.[212] Lord Mengchang sent his retainer to appeal to a favourite concubine of the king for help. The woman said, "I want Lord Mengchang's white fox cloak." The cloak was presented to Qin king earlier; hence, her request could not be satisfied. There was a skilled burglar among the guests of Lord Mengchang. He broke into the vault of the Qin palace, stole the cloak and presented it to the woman. The concubine worked on the king of Qin, who finally had Lord Mengchang released for repatriation. Shortly after, he regretted his decision. He sent his guards to go after him, who had already arrived at the border pass. The Qin law stipulated that the city gates closed until the cock crowed at dawn. The time was early when the fugitive and his guests arrived at the gate, and their pursuers were approaching fast. An imitator among the guests was skilled at mimicking cockcrows; when he crowed all the cocks in the wild followed. Lord Mengchang escaped unscathed.

II. Chu sent a missive to Qin, "The Divine of our holy shrine has been most compassionate; our kingdom has a new king." The king of Qin was in a terrible rage; he commanded his army to march out of the Wuguan Pass to attack Chu. The Qin army cut down fifty thousand men and annexed sixteen cities.

III. King of Zhao enfeoffed his younger brother as Lord Pingyuan.[213] Lord Pingyuan was partial to making acquaintance with scholars and intellectuals; several thousand guests were entertained at his manor. Among his guests, there was a Gongsun Long; his treatise of, 'Debates on the Similarities and Dissimilarities of Firmness and Whiteness' had earned him a high reputation.[214] Lord Pingyuan treated him as an honoured guest. At this stage, Kong Chuan (Zigao) travelled from his native land of Lu to Zhao.[215] He met Gongsun Long and held a debate on, "A Slave Has Three Ears".[216] Gongsun Long came up with subtle and profound arguments; Zigao could not repudiate his proposition and was lost for words. He bade him farewell after a short stay.

The next day he visited Lord Pingyuan, who asked, "I believe Master Gongsun put forth a decent debate previously on his argument. Sir, what do you think?" Zi Gao answered, "He virtually convinced me that a slave can have three ears; the only problem is everyone knows it is improbable. This is why your subject wishes to ask Your Highness; a slave has three ears according to his argument, but in reality, it is false, whereas to prove that a slave has two ears is far easier, which is real. My Lord, which one would you choose - the difficult one that is false or the easy one that is real?" Lord Pingyuan could not answer the question. The next day, Lord

---

211 "...if he is not removed."

212 Lou Huan 樓緩 substituted Tian Wen 田文 as Chancellor of Qin.

213 King Hui of Zhao 趙 惠文王 Zhao He 趙何.
Lord Pingyuan 平原君 Zhao Sheng 趙勝.

214 Gongsun Long 公孫龍 was an authority in the philosophy of logic.
Jianbailun 堅白論 – 'A Treatise on Firmness and Whiteness.'
Baimalun 白馬論 – 'A Treatise on White Horse Notion.'
Yitonglun 異同論 – 'A Treatise on Similarity and Dissimilarity.'

215 Kong Chuan 孔穿 Zigao 子高 was a descendant of Confucius.

216 臧三耳 - 'A Slave Has Three Ears'.

Pingyuan said to Gongsun Long, "Sir, please do not debate with Master Kongzi; [217] his reasoning is better than his expression, whereas your expression is better than your reasoning. I am afraid you will lose eventually."

Zou Yan travelled through Zhao.[218] Lord Pingyuan invited him to debate with Gongsun Long on the topic of, "A White Horse is Not a Horse." Zouzi politely declined, he said, "It is not a good idea. You see, the purpose of a debate is to classify matters into exclusive categories hence as not to infringe upon one another and to put forth a prefaced notion unravelling the different extremities to avoid confusion and misconception. It serves to express one's opinion and his general concept, making one's attitude known, allowing people to grasp his viewpoints instead of creating perplexing notions and befuddlements. Hence, the winner of the debate is not to lose his stance, while the loser can appreciate the truth. A debate should be conducted under such a premise. Whereas, if a discussion is expedited on euphuisms, laden with false notions, beautifully crafted phrases and semantics, drawing on the semblance of reality to forcefully make a case, leading people into a quandary of futility - the meaning and objective of the debate is lost. It merely impairs the higher principle of learning. You see when one tries incessantly to wrangle with overwhelming arguments, desiring to mute his opponent into silence, is an ill-conceived notion of debate. It simply damages the moral stature of a worthy man. Zuo Yan does not intend to participate." Everyone at the meeting agreed with the opinion of Zuo Yan. Ever since this incident, Gongsun Long lost his favoured position in the manor.

---

217 Kong Chuan 孔穿, Zigao 子高 and Kongzi 孔子 were all one person.

218 Zou Yan 鄒衍 (305-240 BCE?), Zouzi 鄒子, a Qi 齊 national, was a philosopher at the times of later *zhanguo* 戰國. He was an exceptionally learned man, a *yin-yang* 陰陽 School proponent, and had at one stage taught at the Royal Academy of Qi 齊稷下學宮. He was given the nickname of 'the Colloquist of Yan' - Tantian Yan 談天衍. (Yan – the scholar who makes discourses on anything under the sun – is probably a more appropriate translation.) Based on earlier theses of *Yin-Yang* 陰陽 and Five Phases (Elements) *wuheng* 五行, he proposed, "Wood gives rise to fire 木生火, fire gives rise to earth 火生土, the earth that of gold 土生金, gold that of water 金生水 and water gives rise to wood 水生木," the so-called "Five-mutually-materializations" *wuheng shengsheng* 五行相生." Also, another Treatise of, "Mutually-annihilating of the Five-virtues – *wude xiangsheng* 五德相勝 - Virtue of fire overwhelms water 火勝水, the virtue of water overpowers earth 水勝土, the virtue of earth overpowers gold 土勝金, the virtue of gold overpowers water 金勝水 and the virtue of water annihilates wood 水勝木." He used his Treatise to elucidate that the evolutionary of nature and that the advancement of society was a natural process based on the cyclical succession of mutual materialization and annihilation of *yin* 陰 and *yang* 陽. Further, claiming that ever since the time of Huangdi 黃帝 (who was of earth virtue 土德) the cycle had been recurring; Huangdi was replaced by Xia 夏 (of water virtue 水德), which in turn was replaced by Shang 商 (of gold 金德) and Zhou 周 (of fire 火德). Based on his thesis he went on to predict that a dynasty, employing water as its insignia, would eventually replace fire (Zhou) "代火者必將水." The 49 chapters of the *Yanzi* 衍子 and 56 chapters of the 'Yanzi on Investiture and Cessation - Yanzi shizhong 衍子始終' are lost, merely known through allusions in the *Hanshu* 漢書 Yiwenzhi 藝文志.
The *SJ* 史記, 卷 44 'Mengzi, Xunqing liezhuan 孟子荀卿列傳' 第 14, p. 543. Yang K., *ZGS* 戰國史, pp. 591-592.

Volume IV. 資治通鑒 卷第四 周紀四 297-273 BCE

The narratives of this volume commence during the 18th year (297 BCE) of the reign of King Nan of Zhou and end in his 42nd year (273 BCE).[1]

296 BCE - King Huai of Chu died in Qin.[2]

295 BCE - King Wuling of Zhao, the supreme lord of Zhao, *Zhufu* (Zhao Yong), assisted by Qi and Yan annihilated Zhongshan.[3]

There was internal strife at Zhao; *Zhufu* died of starvation in Shaqiu.[4]

293 BCE - Qin general, Bai Qi defeated Wei and Hann armies at Yique, [5] and decapitated two hundred and forty thousand men. King of Qin nominated Bai Qi as its security commander.

288 BCE - The sovereigns of Qin and Qi proclaimed themselves as monarchs.

286 BCE - King Kang of Song raised an army against Teng and annihilated it; the army then attacked Xue and continued to defeat Qi to its east, Chu to its south and west at Wei. People called him Jie of Song (Despot-Song). King Min of Qi raised an army against Song, annihilating it.[6]

284 BCE - Yan general, Yue Yi defeated Qi; [7] seventy cities fell in six months.

283 BCE - Lin Xiangru returned the piece of priceless jade known as *heshibi* to Zhao.[8]

279 BCE - Lin Xiangyu and Lian Po became fast friends.[9]

Tian Dan used a strategy, King Hui of Yan replaced Yue Yi with Qi Jie; Tian Dan recovered seventy walled-cities lost to Yan. King Xiang of Qi enfeoffed Tian Dan as Lord Anping.[10]

---

1 King Nan of Zhou 周赧王.

2 King Huai of Chu Huaiwang 楚懷王.

3 Supreme Lord, Zhao *Zhufu* 趙主父 Zhao Yong 趙雍.
Zhongshan 中山.

4 Shaqiu 沙丘.

5 Qin General 秦將軍 Bai Qi 白起.
Yique 伊闕.

6 King Kang of Song 宋康王.
Teng 滕; Xue 薛.
Jie of Song 桀宋.
King Min of Qi 齊湣王.

7 Yan General 燕上將軍 Yue Yi 樂毅.

8 Lin Xiangru 藺相如; *heshibi* 和氏璧.

9 Lian Po 廉頗.

10 Tian Dan 田單.
King Hui of Yan 燕惠王. Qi Jie 騎劫.

278 BCE - Qin general, Bai Qi attacked Chu, took capital Ying, and razed Yiling Mound to the ground. Chu moved its capital to Chen; Qin changed Ying into a Southern Prefecture. Bai Qi was honoured as Sir Wuan.[11]

Volume IV. Zhou Records周紀四

---

297 BCE *Jiazi* 甲子 Warring States 戰國

King Nan of Zhou	周赧王	18th year
Duke Ping of Lu	魯平公	20th year
King Zhaoxiang of Qin	秦昭襄王	10th year
King Kang of Song	宋康王	32nd year
King Qingxiang of Chu	楚頃襄王	2nd year
King Min of Qi	齊湣王	4th year
King Xiang of Wei	魏襄王	22nd year
King Xiang of Hann	韓襄王	15th year
King Huiwen of Zhao	趙惠文王	2nd year
King Zhao of Yan	燕昭王	16th year
Sir Wey Si	衛嗣君	28th year

I. King Huai of Chu tried to escape from Qin.[12] The Qin authority discovered his intent and ordered a blockade of the Chu passages. King Huai took a remote path escaped to Zhao. At this time, the Supreme Lord of Zhao *Zhufu* was in Dai; [13] the Zhao people dared not accept his entry. King Huai was about to escape to Wei, but the Qin guards caught up with him and was taken back to the capital.

II. Duke Ping of Lu died, his son Jia , Duke Min succeeded.[14]

King Xiang of Qi 齊襄王. Lord Anping 安平君.

11 Qin General 秦將 Bai Qi 白起.
Chu capital 楚都 Ying 郢 - Yingdu 郢都.
Yiling 夷陵. Chenqiu 陳丘. Lord Wuan 武安君.

12 King Huai of Chu 楚懷王 Mi Huai 芈槐. The king had been held hostage at Xianyang 咸陽 the Qin capital since 299 BCE.

13 Supreme Lord of Zhao, *Zhufu* 趙主父 Zhao Yong 趙雍.
Dai 代.

14 Duke Ping of Lu 魯平公 Ji Lu 姬旅 36th (r. 316-297 BCE) or (r. 314-296 BCE) or (r. 322-303 BCE).
Duke Min of Lu 魯湣 (緡) 公 Ji Jia 姬賈 (r. 296-274 BCE) or (r. 295-273 BCE) or (r. 302-280 BCE). The *Hanshu* 漢書 records him as Duke Min 愍公; while the *Lulizhi* 律曆志 calls him Duke Min 緡公; nevertheless the four words, slightly different in meaning, have the same pronunciation and were used interchangeably.
Yang Kuan 楊寬 (1914-2005 CE) maintained that Duke Min of Lu reigned between 302-280 BCE. (N.B. See the author's translation of Yang Kuan's, 'Reassessing and Verification of Important Chronological Dates of the Warring States.' See Appendix 3.

296 BCE Jiazi 甲子 Warring States 戰國

King Nan of Zhou	周赧王	19th year
Duke Ming of Lu	魯湣公	1st year
King Zhaoxiang of Qin	秦昭襄王	11th year
King Kang of Song	宋康王	33rd year
King Qingxiang of Chu	楚頃襄王	3rd year
King Min of Qi	齊湣王	5th year
King Xiang of Wei	魏襄王	23rd year
King Xiang of Hann	韓襄王	16th year
King Huiwen of Zhao	趙惠文王	3rd year
King Zhao of Yan	燕昭王	17th year
Sir Wey Si	衛嗣君	29th year

I. King Huai of Chu held hostage at Qin took ill and died. The Qin court returned his remains to Chu for burial. The people of Chu lamented over the loss of their king; they wept and mourned as if they had lost a loved-one; [15] all the fief lords were appalled by Qin's inequity.

II. Qi, Hann, Wei, Zhao, and Song formed an alliance to launch an attack against Qin. The armies marched as far as Yanshi then withdrew.[16] Qin returned Wusui to Hann and Fengling to Wei in a bid for peace.[17]

III. The Supreme Lord of Zhao went on a tour in the newly occupied land. He then travelled beyond the west of Dai and met the king of Loufan west of the River *Xihe*; he recruited soldiers from the tribes.[18]

IV. King Xiang of Wei died; his son King Zhao succeeded him.[19]

The word 緡 was changed to 緍 at the time of Tang 唐. It was taboo to use the same personal name of an emperor in a text. The personal name of Emperor Taizong of Tang 唐太宗 (r. 626-649 CE) was Min 緡. *ZZTJ JZ*, Vol 1, p. 128.

15 The posthumous title of Mi Huai 羋槐 was King Huai 懷王.

16 Qin 秦 Yanshi 鹽氏 - Anyi Shanxi 山西 安邑縣.

17 Wusui 武遂 (隧) – southwest of Linfenxian Shanxi 山西 臨汾縣西南.
Fengling 封陵 - Fenglingdu Crossing south of Yongjixian Shanxi 山西 永濟縣南 風陵渡.

18 Zhao Supreme Lord, *Zhufu* 趙太上王 主父 Zhao Yong 趙雍.
Dai 代 - Weixian Hebei 河北 蔚縣.
Xihe 西河 - *Hetao* 河套 was the areas enclosed by the Huanghe loop, Neimeng 内蒙 and northern part of Shaanxi 陝西.
Loufan Tribes 樓煩 - the tribes settled at the present-day Jinglexian Shanxi 山西 静樂縣.

V. The king of Hann died; Jiu, his son, King Xi succeeded.[20]

---

295 BCE *Bing-yin* 丙寅 Warring States 戰國

King Nan of Zhou	周赧王	20th year
Duke Min of Lu	魯湣公	2nd year
King Zhaoxiang of Qin	秦昭襄王	12th year
King Kang of Song	宋康王	34th year
King Qingxiang of Chu	楚頃襄王	4th year
King Min of Qi	齊湣王	6th year
King Zhao of Wei	魏昭王	1st year
King Xi of Hann	韓釐王	1st year
King Huiwen of Zhao	趙惠文王	4th year
King Zhao of Yan	燕昭王	18th year
Sir Wey Si	衛嗣君	30th year

I. Cuo, the security commander *wei* of Qin, attacked Xiangcheng of Wei.[21]

II. The Supreme Lord of Zhao joined forces with Qi and Yan; the armies annihilated Zhongshan; the king was banished to Fushi.[22] *Zhufu* returned to his capital; [23] he rewarded his armed forces and proclaiming an amnesty for the convicts on death row. He further entertained the civilians to a five-day feast of food and wine.

III. The Supreme Lord of Zhao *Zhufu* enfeoffed his eldest son Zhang at Dai, knighting him as Lord Anyang.[24]

---

19 King Xiang of Wei 魏襄王 Wei Si 魏嗣 2nd (r. 318-296 BCE). N.B. This dates according to Yang Kuan 楊寬 are incorrect. For more detail of later textual research on the dates of his reign see the author's translation of Yang Kuan's 'Reassessments and Verifications of Important Chronological Dates of the Warring States' in Appendix III.
King Zhao of Wei 魏昭王 Wei Su 魏遬 3rd (r. 295-277 BCE).

20 King Xiang of Hann 韓襄王 Hann Cang 韓倉 2nd (r. 311-296 BCE).
King Xi of Hann 韓釐王 Hann Jiu 韓咎 3rd (r. 295-273 BCE).

21 Qin Security Commander *wei* 秦尉 Sima Cuo 司馬錯.
Wei 魏 Xiangcheng 襄城 - Xiangchengxian Henan 河南 襄城縣.

22 King of Zhao, *Zhufu* 主父 Zhao Yong 趙雍.
Zhongshan Kingdom – Kingdom in the Mountains 中山國 - Dingxian Hebei 河北 定縣.
Fushi 膚施 - Yananxian Shaanxi 陝西 延安縣. Fushi was the place of origin of the Xianyu 鮮虞 tribe, at this time; it was incorporated into the Zhao domain.

23 Capital of Zhao - Handan 邯鄲 - Handanxian Hebei 河北 邯鄲縣.

24 Dai 代 - The state was annihilated in 475 BCE. However, the name was preserved as a prefecture.
Lord Anyang 安陽君 Zhao Zhang 趙章. Anyang 安陽 was a place name; it was situated at the present day Dingxian Shanxi 山西 定襄縣.

Lord Anyang was degenerate and debauched. He was resentful that the throne was bestowed on his younger brother, and held a grudge. *Zhufu* appointed Tian Buli as his chancellor *xiang*.[25] Li Dui said to Fei Yi,[26] "Prince Zhang is forceful and is conceited; he has gathered many clique members around him, intending to expand his influence. Tian Buli is callously atrocious and haughty at heart. When two malicious individuals are brought together, it ferments conspiracy. You see, when a person of humble origin has certain aspiration, he castoffs all cautions and inhibitions, merely heeding to his immediate gains, without due consideration for devastating consequences. I am afraid catastrophic event will happen soon. Sir, you hold an important position at court; as soon as there are some changes, you will be in the midst of chaos and all the calamities will impinge upon you. Why don't you consider making an excuse for having taken ill and resign from your post, and transfer your responsibilities to Prince Cheng? Do not make yourself a stepping-stone for the looming calamity. It might be better." Fei Yi answered, "Previously when *Zhufu* entrusted me with the position, he said to me, 'Sir please serve with utmost loyalty; do not deviate from your gaol; do not consider recoiling from your objective, and be firm with your pledge until death.' I respectfully thanked His Highness and accepted his instructions, and I inscribed his directives on bamboo slips. I cannot forgo my pledge for possible turbulences. Had I changed my stance it would be an abandonment of my pledge. There is an adage, 'Even had the deceased risen from the dead I would not be ashamed to face him.'[27] If I am to live up to my words, how could I be concerned about my safety? Sir, I appreciate your concern and thank you for being loyal to me as a friend. Nevertheless, I have made my pledge, and I will never renounce my words." Li Dui said, "Aye. Please try your utmost; Sir, I doubt I will see you again after this year." Li Dui departed in tears. Li Dui then paid several visits to Prince Cheng and warned him to take precautionary measures against Tian Buli.[28]

Fei Yi instructed Xin Qi, his personal attendant,[29] "While Prince Zhang and Tian Buli are cultivating their admirable reputation openly the two men are in fact stealthily scheming malicious activities. The prince takes advantage of his father's affection towards him and is carrying out malevolent deeds. It is conceivable that he might even fabricate a decree in the name of *Zhufu* to marshal an uprising; it would not be difficult on his part. I am extremely concerned with the state of affairs. I cannot sleep at night, and I can hardly take my meals. When there are villains milling around, one has to be vigilant. Starting from now, when someone seeks an audience with our king, you are to consult me without fail. I will proceed to ensure there is nothing sinister at stake. The king can proceed if there are no intrigues." Xin Qi said, "Yes, sir."

---

25 Tian Buli 田不禮 - the chancellor, *xiang* 相 of Zhao Zhang. *Xiang* 相 - used here means personal aide.

26 Li Dui 李兑 was the former chancellor of Zhao when Zhao Yong was king.

Fei Yi 肥義 (?-295 BCE), the chancellor of Zhao, the person who supported the military reform of Zhao.

27 "死者復生, 生者不愧." The remark was made by a Jin 晉 minister, Xun Xi 荀息 (?-651 BCE), it appears in the *Spring and Autumn Annals, Chunqiu* 春秋公羊傳 僖公十年. The meaning of the two phrases is, when a person was entrusted with an orphan, it was his responsibility to see that the orphan was protected and cared for; even had the deceased arisen from the dead, the person would not be ashamed to face the arisen. *ZZTJ JZ*, Vol 1, p. 132.

28 Prince Cheng 公子成 Zhao Cheng 趙成 was Zhao Yong's uncle, who supported the king in adopting the barbaric attire *hufu* and archery on horseback.

29 Xin Qi 信期 Fei Yi's attendant.

The Supreme Lord *Zhufu* instructed King Huiwen to sit in state to accept homage from his ministers at court.[30] *Zhufu* was observing on the side; he noticed that his eldest son was acting most nonchalantly, facing north he made a cursory submission to his younger brother. An empathetic feeling overwhelmed *Zhufu*. He considered partitioning Zhao, with Prince Zhang being enfeoffed at Dai.[31] His plan was still under deliberation when it was deferred.

Zhufu and the king made a tour to Shaqiu; [32] they were staying in two separate palaces. Prince Zhang, Tian Buli and their clique members schemed an uprising. They forged a decree that the Supreme Lord had summoned the king for an audience. Fei Yi went to the appointment and was murdered. Gao Xin and the king faced the rebels and entered into battle.[33] Prince Cheng and Li Dui arrived with re-enforcements from the capital and rallied the militias from four local counties to put up staunch resistance. Prince Zhang and Tian Buli were killed, with all their supporters eradicated. Subsequently, Prince Cheng was made the chancellor of Zhao, appended with a title of Lord Anpin while Li Dui was made the security commander of the kingdom *sikou*. [34] King Huiwen being quite young, [35] Prince Cheng and Li Dui assumed control of the state.

Previously, when Prince Zhang lost the fight against the government forces, he made a run for his life and sought refuge in the walled city where *Zhufu* was residing. *Zhufu* ordered the gate opened to give him shelter in the palace. Prince Cheng and Li Dui besieged *Zhufu's* walled-city. When Prince Zhang died, Prince Cheng and Li Dui conspired, "We laid siege to *Zhufu* by going after Zhang. Even if we were to withdraw our forces, our family members and we are finished." They ordered to continue to besiege the city and declared that people who continued to defend the city would be executed. All the palace attendants and guards dispersed without a trace. *Zhufu* also attempted to run for his life but was prevented from leaving; he was left in the palace without food. He searched for newly hatched chicks to satisfy his hunger. He died of hunger after more than three months in the Shaqiu Palace. When people at the Zhao court were certain of his death, then they issued a eulogy to the other fief lords proclaiming his death.

Zhufu had previously designated his eldest son Zhang as the crown prince; later he was presented with a woman called Wu Wa and the king was infatuated with her.[36] He kept the woman company and did not leave his palace for several years. Later she gave birth to a son Zhao He, at which stage *Zhufu* revoked Prince Zhang's inherence right and made his younger son the crown prince. Later Wu Wa died, his love for He had waned somewhat. He felt pity for the former crown

---

30 King Huiwen of Zhao 趙惠文王 Zhao He 趙何.

31 Dai 代 - Weixian Hebei 河北 蔚縣.

32 Shaqiu 沙丘 - Pingxiangxian Hebei 河北 平鄉縣, it is 50 km northeast of the Zhao capital Handan 邯鄲 as the crow flies. It was the same place where Emperor Shi Huangdi 秦始皇帝 died eighty-five years later.
Shaqiu, literally means Sandy Mound. The palace was built on a sandy hill, hence named.

33 Gao Xin 高信, Sima Zhen 司馬貞 maintained that he was Xin Qi 信期; however it cannot be verified. *JJTJ JZ*, Vol, p. 133.

34 Lord Anping 安平君 Zhao Cheng 趙成.
Anping was not a place name, as he brought peace 安 to the kingdom and subjugated 平 the rebels; he was enfeoffed as Lord Anping.
Li Dui 李兑, Zhao Security Commander, *sikou* 司寇.

35 Zhao He 趙何 was around sixteen years old at this stage.

36 Lady Wu Wa 吳娃, Zhao Yong's concubine. See 310 BCE.

prince, and he was considering to make him a king; but while hesitating over the issue, a mutiny broke out causing the internal strife.

IV. Qin relieved the chancery duty of Lou Huan; Wei Ran took his place.[37]

---

294 BCE *Dingmao* 丁卯 Warring States 戰國

King Nan of Zhou	周赧王	21st year
Duke Min of Lu	魯湣公	3rd year
King Zhaoxiang of Qin	秦昭襄王	13th year
King Kang of Song	宋康王	35th year
King Qingxiang of Chu	楚頃襄王	5th year
King Min of Qi	齊湣王	7th year
King Zhao of Wei	魏昭王	2nd year
King Xi of Hann	韓釐王	2nd year
King Huiwen of Zhao	趙惠文王	5th year
King Zhao of Yan	燕昭王	19th year
Sir Wey Si	衛嗣君	31st year

I. Qin defeated Wei at Hai.[38]

---

293 BCE *Wuchen* 戊辰 Warring States 戰國

King Nan of Zhou	周赧王	22nd year
Duke Min of Lu	魯湣公	4th year
King Zhaoxiang of Qin	秦昭襄王	14th year
King Kang of Song	宋康王	36th year
King Qingxiang of Chu	楚頃襄王	6th year
King Min of Qi	齊湣王	8th year
King Zhao of Wei	魏昭王	3rd year
King Xi of Hann	韓釐王	3rd year
King Huiwen of Zhao	趙惠文王	6th year
King Zhao of Yan	燕昭王	20th year
Sir Wey Si	衛嗣君	32nd year

I. Gongsun Xi of Hann accompanied by a junior commander and a small task force from Wei attacked Qin.[39] Marquis Rang (Wei Ran) recommended an army Major *zuogeng* Bai Qi to the Qin

37 Qin 秦, Chancellor Lou Huan 樓緩; Wei Ran 魏冉.

38 Wei 魏, Hai 解 - Jiexian Shanxi 山西 解縣. (N.B. Hai 解 was the archaic pronunciation.)

king, replacing Shang Shou to take command of the army.[40] The Qin army defeated the allied forces of Wei and Hann at the Yique Pass.[41] Some two hundred and forty thousand Hann and Wei soldiers were beheaded; Gongsun Xi was captured, and five cities were also lost in the process. The king of Qin raised Bai Qi to the rank of security commander *guowei*.[42]

II. The king of Qin sent a missive to the king of Chu,[43] "Chu has betrayed us. We are raising a coalesced fief lord force against Chu; please reorganize your armed-men, meet us in battle and fight to our contentment." The king of Chu was full of trepidation; he then sought to resolve the confrontation through a matrimonial union with Qin.

---

292 BCE *Jisi* 己巳 Warring States 戰國

King Nan of Zhou	周赧王	23rd year
Duke Min of Lu	魯湣公	5th year
King Zhaoxiang of Qin	秦昭襄王	15th year
King Kang of Song	宋康王	37th year
King Qingxiang of Chu	楚頃襄王	7th year
King Min of Qi	齊湣王	9th year
King Zhao of Wei	魏昭王	4th year
King Xi of Hann	韓釐王	4th year
King Huiwen of Zhao	趙惠文王	7th year
King Zhao of Yan	燕昭王	21st year
Sir Wey Si	衛嗣君	33rd year

I. King Xiang of Chu took a woman from Qin as a wife.

Sima Guang annotates:

The peremptory and callous deeds of Qin were utterly insufferable. They caused the death of the father and intimidated the son by force. On the other hand, the king of Chu (King Qingxiang) was pathetic and wanting in assertiveness. He bored no resentment against Qin for the death of his father; he even resorted to marrying a woman chosen by his adversary. Alas! Had the king of Chu mastered better statecraft, employing capable administrators to serve at his court even the powerful Qin state could not possibly abuse the

---

39 Hann Officer 韓 Gongsun Xi 公孫喜.

40 Qin, Marquis Rang 秦穰侯 Wei Ran 魏冉.
Wei Ran was enfeoffed at Rang 穰 – Dengxian Henan 河南 鄧縣.
Qin army major, *zuogeng* 左更 Bai Qi 白起. *Zuogeng* was the 12th of the 20 grades of enfeoffed nobles in Qin.
Qin major - Shang Shou 尚壽.

41 Yique 伊闕 - Longmen Pass, 20 km south of Luoyangxian, Henan 河南 洛陽縣南 龍門.

42 State Security Commander *guowei* 國尉. *guowei* was one grade lower that a Qin general.

43 The king of Qin was King Zhaoxiang 秦 昭襄王 and the Chu King was King Qingxiang 楚 頃襄王.

sovereignty of Chu. Xun Qing comments fittingly,[44] "When the power of a state is properly utilized, a small state of one hundred square *li* can achieve independence; while Chu possessing six thousand *li* of terrain it succumbed to the status of a subservient state." Hence, if the sovereign of a state does not apply his authority aptly, merely indulging in the superficial panache and flamboyance of his power, lurking behind it poses an imminent danger of obliteration for his kingdom.

II. Wei Ran of Qin resigned from his post due to illness, a guest consultant *keqing* Zhu Shou took his position.[45]

---

291 BCE *Gengwu* 庚午 Warring States 戰國

King Nan of Zhou	周赧王	24th year
Duke Min of Lu	魯湣公	6th year
King Zhaoxiang of Qin	秦昭襄王	16th year
King Kang of Song	宋康王	38th year
King Qingxiang of Chu	楚頃襄王	8th year
King Min of Qi	齊湣王	10th year
King Zhao of Wei	魏昭王	5th year
King Xi of Hann	韓釐王	5th year
King Huaiwen of Zhao	趙惠文王	8th year
King Zhao of Yan	燕昭王	22nd year
Sir Wey Si	衛嗣君	34th year

I. Qin invaded Hann, and the city of Wan was annexed.[46]

II. The chancellor of Qin, Zhu Shou was relieved of his duties; Wei Ran was reinstated. He was enfeoffed with the counties of Rang and Tao, and was honoured as Marquis Rang.[47] The king moreover enfeoffed Prince Fu at Wan and Prince Kui at Deng.[48]

---

44 Xun Qing 荀卿 Kuang 荀况 Xunzi 荀子 (313-238 BCE) was a Zhao 趙 national, he was a philosopher, educator and literati; he promoted the concept that humans were born maliciously inclined,* versus Mengzi's proposition that humans were born charitable. *SJ* 史記, 卷 44, 'Mengzi Xun Qing liezhuan 孟子荀卿列傳' 第 14, p. 544.
* 荀卿論 - 荀卿獨曰, "人性悪. 桀, 紂, 性也. 堯, 舜, 偽也."

45 Qin Chancellor, *xiang* 秦相 Wei Ran 魏冉.
Guest Consultant, *keqing* 客卿 Zhu Shou 燭壽.

46 Wan 宛 - Nanyangxian Henan 河南 南陽縣.

47 Zhu Shou 燭壽.
Wei Ran 魏冉.
Rang 穰 - Rangyi County 穰邑 - Dengxian Henan 河南 鄧縣.
Tao 陶 - Taoyi 陶邑 - Taoyi Village, north of Yongjixian Shanxi 山西 永濟縣北 陶邑鄉.

48 Ying Fu 嬴市.
Wan 宛.

290 BCE *Xinwei* 辛未 Warring States 戰國

King Nan of Zhou	周赧王	25th year
Duke Min of Lu	魯湣公	7th year
King Zhaoxiang of Qin	秦昭襄王	17th year
King Kang of Song	宋康王	39th year
King Qingxiang of Chu	楚頃襄王	9th year
King Min of Qi	齊湣王	11th year
King Zhao of Wei	魏昭王	6th year
King Xi of Hann	韓釐王	6th year
King Huiwen of Zhao	趙惠文王	9th year
King Zhao of Yan	燕昭王	23rd year
Sir Wey Si	衛嗣君	35th year

I. Wei ceded four hundred *li* of its territories at the east of the river *Hedong* to Qin.[49]

II. Hann ceded two hundred *li* of territories at Wusui to Qin.[50]

III. Mang Mao of Wei, a charlatan, had gained much respect.[51]

289 BCE *Renshen* 壬申 Warring States 戰國

King Nan of Zhou	周赧王	26th year
Duke Min of Lu	魯湣公	8th year
King Zhaoxiang of Qin	秦昭襄王	18th year

Prince Kui 秦公子悝 Ying Kui 嬴悝.
Deng 鄧 - Dengyi 鄧邑 – southwest of Mengxian Henan 河南 孟縣西南.

49 East of the River - *Hedong* 河東地- Southern part of Shanxi 山西南部.

50 Hann 韓 Wusui 武遂 - Linfenxian Shanxi 山西 臨汾縣.

51 Mang Mao 芒卯 was a Wei national 魏人. He served at the state of Wei; and through deceit, he saved the kingdom during several minor crises. He was mentioned in the *ZGC* 戰國策. In 273 BCE, King Zhao of Qin 秦昭王 dispatched Bai Qi 白起 to attack Wei 魏. Lord Mengchang 孟嘗君 Tian Wen 田文 recommended Mang Mao as commander to lead an army to go against Qin. At Huayang 華陽 the Wei army lost a most bloodletting battle. Some 130,000 Wei soldiers lost their lives; Meng Mao escaped. Tian Wen 田文 was relieved of his duties as chancellor of Wei by King Anxi of Wei 魏安釐王. (See 273 BCE). *SJ* 史記, 卷 114, 'Wei shijia 魏世家' 第 14, p. 14.
SJ 史記, 卷 43, 'Bai Qi, Wang Jian liezhuan 白起王翦列傳' 第 13, p. 532.
ZGC 戰國策 'Weice 魏策' 卷 24, 芒卯謂秦王, p. 269.

King Kang of Song	宋康王	40th year
King Qingxiang of Chu	楚頃襄王	10th year
King Min of Qi	齊湣王	12th year
King Zhao of Wei	魏昭王	7th year
King Xi of Hann	韓釐王	7th year
King Huiwen of Zhao	趙惠文王	10th year
King Zhao of Yan	燕昭王	24th year
Sir Wey Si	衛嗣君	36th year

1. Bai Qi the major general *daliangzao* of Qin and Cuo a guest consultant *keqing* led an army against Wei; the army marched as far as Zhi and in this campaign, Qin annexed sixty-one cities.[52]

---

288 BCE *Guiyou* 癸酉 Warring States 戰國

King Nan of Zhou	周赧王	27th year
Duke Min of Lu	魯湣公	9th year
King Zhaoxiang of Qin	秦昭襄王	19th year
King Kang of Song	宋康王	41st year
King Qingxiang of Chu	楚頃襄王	11th year
King Min of Qi	齊湣王	13th year
King Zhao of Wei	魏昭王	8th year
King Xi of Hann	韓釐王	8th year
King Huiwen of Zhao	趙惠文王	11th year
King Zhao of Yan	燕昭王	25th year
Sir Wey Si	衛嗣君	37th year

1. Winter. 10th month. The king of Qin proclaimed as the Western Monarch *xidi*.[53] He dispatched his emissaries to confer the title of the Eastern Monarch *dongdi* to the king of Qi. He further proposed to form an alliance for an attack against Zhao.[54] At this time; Su Dai had just

---

52 Qin, Major General, *daliangzao* 秦 大良造 Bai Qi 白起. *Daliangzao* was the 16th grade of the 20 of Qin's enfeoffment.
Guest Consultant, *keqing* 客卿 Gongsun Cuo 公孫錯.
Zhi 軹 - Jiyuanxian Henan 河南 濟源縣.

53 *Xidi* 西帝.

54 The king of Qin 嬴 Ying Ji 稷.
The terms proposed by Ying Ji were Western Monarch, *Xidi* 西帝 and Eastern Monarch, *Dongdi* 東帝. The term *di* 帝 should be translated as emperor; however, we have to reserve the emperor title for the First Emperor, Qin Shi Huangdi 秦始皇帝. There is no equivalent for the term *di* in English, some scholars translate it as thearch; however, the term is not commonly used as the meaning of which is obscured to most people.
King of Qi 齊王 Tian Di 田地.

arrived from Yan.[55] The king of Qi asked him, "The king of Qin sent Wei Ran to see me and presented me with the title of the Eastern Monarch *dongdi*. Sir, what is your opinion?" Su Dai answered, "I think Your Highness should accept his proposal, however, do not assume the title overtly. If the king of Qin makes a proclamation and no one under Heaven opposes, Your Highness can follow his lead, it will not be too late. Whereas if everyone All under Heaven opposes it, as you did not adopt the title in the first place, you will garner much respect from the other kingdoms for not proclaiming yourself monarch and the approach will be a great asset to your kingdom. As to an allied campaign against Zhao, it depends on whether it is a more viable proposition to go after Zhao or Jie-Song (despotic Song).[56] My opinion is that you should not proclaim yourself as the Eastern Monarch to earn the deference from all under Heaven. You should raise an army against the despotic and reprehensible Song. After conquering Song, Chu, Zhao and Wei kingdoms will be in awe of your prowess. With this move, you are honouring the king of Qin in name; however rendering him a common antipathy among the other states. It is an unassuming and humble approach to retain your dignity and integrity." The king of Qi accepted Su Dai's suggestion; he proclaimed himself the Eastern Monarch for two days and returned the title to Qin.

12th month. Lu Li returned to Qin from Qi.[57] The king of Qin also renounced the Western Monarch title, resuming his former title as king.

II. Qin attacked Zhao, and occupied Duyang.[58]

---

287 BCE *Jiaxu* 甲戌 Warring States 戰國

King Nan of Zhou	周赧王	28th year
Duke Min of Lu	魯湣公	10th year
King Zhaoxiang of Qin	秦昭襄王	20th year
King Kang of Song	宋康王	42nd year
King Qingxiang of Chu	楚頃襄王	12th year
King Min of Qi	齊湣王	14th year
King Zhao of Wei	魏昭王	9th year
King Xi of Hann	韓釐王	9th year

Linzi 臨淄 - Linzixian Shandong 山東 臨淄縣.

55 Su Dai 蘇代.

56 Jie-Song 桀宋.

57 Lu Li 呂禮. Lu Li was a minister *wudafu* 五大夫 at the Qin court when King Zhaoxiang of Qin 秦昭襄王 was king. In 294 BCE Wei Ran 魏冉 wanted to kill him, he escaped to Wei, later he went to Qi. King Min of Qi 齊湣王 wanted to ally with Qin, he banished the Qi minister Zhou Zui 周最 and made Lu Li as chancellor. Lu Li advocated to ally with Qin, Lord Mengchang 孟嘗君 objected; Lord Mengchang then collaborated with Wei Rang, spoiling the proposed Qin-Qi alliance. *SJ* 史記, 卷 23, 'Qinn benji 秦本紀' 第 5, p. 165.
SJ 史記, 卷 42, 'Ranghou liezhuan 穰侯列傳' 第 12, p. 525.
ZGC 戰國策, 'Dongzhouce 東周策 卷 1' 周最謂石禮, p. 5.

58 Duyang 杜陽 - Qingyuanxian Shanxi 山西 清源縣.

King Huiwen of Zhao	趙惠文王	12th year
King Zhao of Yan	燕昭王	26th year
Sir Wey Si	衛嗣君	38th year

I. Qin attacked Wei, and annexed Xinyuan and Quyang.[59]

---

286 BCE *Yihai* 乙亥 Warring States Zhango 戰國

King Nan of Zhou	周赧王	29th year
Duke Min of Lu	魯湣公	11th year
King Zhao of Qin	秦昭襄王	21st year
King Kang of Song	宋康王	43rd year
King Qingxiang of Chu	楚頃襄王	13th year
King Min of Qi	齊湣王	15th year
King Zhao of Wei	魏昭王	10th year
King Xi of Hann	韓釐王	10th year
King Huiwen of Zhao	趙惠文王	13th year
King Zhao of Yan	燕昭王	27th year
Sir Wey Si	衛嗣君	39th year

I. Sima Cuo of Qin attacked Wei in the region within the River *Henei*.[60] Wei sued for peace by ceding Anyi (former capital of Wei).[61] The Qin army expelled all the Wei civilians residing within the city to Wei.

II. Qin defeated Hann at Xiashan Mountain.[62]

III. A swallow hatched a vulture chick at the corner of a city-wall in Song.[63] The grand historian conducted a divination.[64] The divination slip read, 'Auspicious! A small bird that gives birth to a large vulture is a most auspicious sign. (Our Kingdom) will attain hegemony." King Kang of Song was most delighted; he raised an army to attack Teng, annihilated it, he then invaded Xue.[65] In the

---

59 Xinyuan 新垣 - Yuanquxian Shanxi 山西 垣曲縣.
Quyang 曲陽 - Jiyuanxian Henan 河南 濟源縣.

60 Qin general 秦. Sima Cuo 司馬錯.
Wei 魏, *Henei* 河内 was the areas north of Huanghe River 黄河 in Henan 河南.

61 Anyi 安邑 - Xiaxian Shanxi 山西 夏縣.

62 Xiashan Mountain 夏山, place unknown.

63 雀生鷂 (鸇). According to the *Shuoyuan* 説苑 by Liu Xiang 劉向 (77-6 BCE), in his, the word 鷂 used was zhan 鸇, which was a species of hawk. *ZZTJ JZ*, Vol 1, p. 139.

64 Song capital 宋都 – Suiyang 睢陽 - Shangqiuxian Henan 河南 商丘縣.
Divination – the word used in the text is *zhan* 占 – i.e. using the Eight-Trigrams – *bagua* 八卦 as divination. The grand historian used divination by the Eight-Trigrams – *baqua* to determine the tidings of such an extraordinary, paranormal spectacle.

65 King Kang of Song 宋康王 Song Yan 宋偃.

east, he defeated Qi and captured five cities. Turning south, he attacked Chu and seized three hundred *li* of territory; he then defeated the Wei army in the west. The kingdom having made enemies with Qi and Wei, the king conceitedly believed that he could attain hegemony under Heaven. To expedite his aspiration as a hegemon, he shot arrows at Heaven and lashed at Earth with whips.[66] He ordered to burn and dismantle the ancestral shrines for making sacrifices and offerings, scornfully maintaining that he would not submit to ghosts and divine.[67] He drank throughout the night in his palace chamber, commanding his retainers and aides in his inner chamber to chant ceaselessly, "Long Live the King." The retinues at the inner chamber, the attendants in the palace, and people in the street followed the chorus. No one in the kingdom dared to defy the decree. All the people under Heaven labelled him as King Jie of Song.[68] King Min of Qi raised an army and attacked Song; the civilians quickly dispersed, the city was breached. The king of Song made a run for his life and died in the city of Wen.[69]

285 BCE *Bingzi* 丙子 Warring States 戰國

King Nan of Zhou	周赧王	30th year
Duke Min of Lu	魯湣公	12th year
King Zhaoxiang of Qin	秦昭襄王	22nd year
King Qingxiang of Chu	楚頃襄王	14th year
King Min of Qi	齊湣王	16th year
King Zhao of Wei	魏昭王	11th year

Teng 滕 - Tengxian Shandong 山東 滕縣. Teng was a minor fief state. The 14th son of King Wen of Zhou 周文王, Cuo Shuxiu 錯叔繡 was enfeoffed at Teng; the family name was Ji 姬. The sovereign of the state had a duke title.

Xue 薛 - was situated at the southeast of Tengxian Shandong 山東 滕縣; it was a minor city-state.

66 The Song King 宋康王 insolently believed that he could challenge the Divine in Heaven and the Deity on Earth.

67 The holy shrine of a state *she-ji* 社稷; *She* 社 was the earth deity while *ji* 稷 was the grain deity. The two words used together represent the holy shrine of a state. The *Liji* 禮記, 'Tangong xia 檀弓下' says, '能執干戈以衛社稷.' It means a person who was capable of taking up arms to defend one's state.

68 Jie of Song 桀宋. King Kang 宋康王 died away from his state; he did not have a posthumous title. The last king of Xia 夏 was Jie 桀, Si Fugui 姒履癸, who was infamous for being a despot. The Song King was also known for his hideous behaviour; people called him Jie of Song.

69 Wen 温 - Wencheng 温城 - Wenchengxian Henan 河南 温城縣.

King Kang of Song 宋康王 was over 80 years old when he lost his kingdom. It was the end of the state of Song. As a kingdom, it lasted for 44 years, while as a fiefdom and a state it lasted for a total of almost 800 years ending in 286 BCE. The Song fiefdom clan had a family name of Zi 子; they were the descendants of the Shang 商 royal household. When King Wu of Zhou 周武王 founded Zhou in 1046 BCE, according to established tradition he did not demolish the holy shrine of the defeated enemy state; he enfeoffed Wu Geng 武庚, the son of King Zhou of Shang 商紂王 at Yin 殷 to attend to the holy shrine of the Shang royal household. Wu Geng revolted and was executed by the Duke of Zhou 周公. The duke then enfeoffed Wu Geng's brother Wei Zi Qi 微子啓 at Shangqiu 商丘 as a fiefdom – naming it Song 宋 to continue with the shrine offering duties. *SJ* 史記, 卷 108, 'Song Weizi shijia 宋微子世家' 第八, pp. 1500-1506.

King Xi of Hann	韓釐王	11th year
King Huiwen of Zhao	趙惠文王	14th year
King of Yan	燕昭王	28th year
Sir Wey Si	衛嗣君	40th year

I. The king of Qin met the king of Chu at Wan; later at Zhongyang the Qin king met with the king of Zhao.[70]

II. General Meng Wu of Qin attacked Qi and took nine cities.[71]

III. Ever since taking down Song, King Min of Qi had become insufferably arrogant; he invaded Chu to be followed by a campaign against San-Jin - Zhao, Wei and Hann kingdoms in the west.[72] He had intended to take down the two Zhou states to become the Son of Heaven of the entire world.[73] Hu Xuan, admonished him for his iniquity, [74] the king had him executed in the market bazaar.[75] Another minister Chen Ju continued to reprimand him by voicing his opinion; King Zhao also had him bound and executed at the east city gate.[76]

IV. King Zhao of Yan pacified his civilians, bestowing riches and titles on capable people while preparing with Yue Yi for a war against Qi.[77] Yue Yi said, "The kingdom of Qi is the remnant of a hegemonic state and has a large domain, besides the population is also numerous; it cannot be taken easily with our resources. If Your Highness is determined to attack it, we should solicit help from the Zhao, Chu and Wei kingdoms." The king sent Yue Yi to travel to the Zhao state to negotiate an alliance while other envoys were dispatched to Chu and Wei. Through Zhao, the intermediary, the king sought the help from Qin pledging certain rewards for its participation. All the kingdoms despised the arrogance and tyranny of the king of Qi, the proposed alliance against Qi by Yan was eagerly accepted.

---

70 King Zhaoxiang of Qin 秦昭襄王 Ying Ji 嬴稷, 3rd.
King Qingxiang of Chu 楚頃襄王 Mi Heng 芈横 22nd.
Wancheng 宛城 - Nanyanxian Henan 河南 南陽縣.
King Huiwen of Zhao 趙惠文王 Zhao He 趙何.
Zhongyang 中陽 - Zhongyangxian Shanxi 山西 中陽縣.

71 Qin 秦, Meng Wu 蒙武.

72 King Min of Qi 齊湣王 Tian Di 田地. Song 宋.

73 The kingdom of Zhou was partitioned into two separate entities.

74 Hu Xuan 狐咺 was a senior minister at the Qi court. The *Hanshu* 漢書 chronicles him as Hu Yuan 狐爰. *ZZTJ JZ*, Vol 1, p. 140.
In the *ZGC* 戰國策 Volume 13, Qi 齊策 6, p. 136. He was mentioned as Gu Huyuan 孤狐咺; his name should be read as Hu Xuan 狐咺 according to the Tang scholar Yan Shigu 唐 顏師古 (581-645 CE).

75 The term used in the text is - *tanqu* 檀衢 - the term, or phase is improperly understood, as some maintain the word *tan* mean passage or thoroughfare while others maintain it was a Qi city. However, this author maintains the world *qu* 衢 means crisscross or thoroughfare; hence, it probably meant marketplace.

76 Chen Ju 陳舉 was executed at Donglu 東閭, the east city gate of Qi at Linzi 齊 臨淄 - Linzixian Shandong 山東 臨淄縣.

77 King Zhao of Yan 燕昭王 Ji Ping 姬平 4th.
Yue Yi 樂毅.

284 BCE *Dingchou* 丁丑 Warring States 戰國

King Nan of Zhou	周赧王	31st year
Duke Min of Lu	魯湣公	13th year
King Zhaoxiang of Qin	秦昭襄王	23rd year
King Qingxiang of Chu	楚頃襄王	15th year
King Min of Qi	齊湣王	17th year
King Zhao of Wei	魏昭王	12th year
King Xi of Hann	韓釐王	12th year
King Huiwen of Zhao	趙惠文王	15th year
King Zhao of Yan	燕昭王	29th year
Sir Wey Si	衛嗣君	41st year

1. The king of Yan rallied all his military forces in his kingdom and nominated Yue Yi as the commanding general.[78] The Qin Military Colonel *wei* Si Li led a contingent of Qin troops to join forces from San-Jin for a joint expedition.[79] The king of Zhao also presented the state chancery seal to Yue Yi. Yue Yi as the commanding general of the combined forces of Qin, Wei, Hann and Zhao headed against Qi. Meanwhile, King Min of Qi responded by summoning up all his military forces to meet the invading armies at the west of Jishui River; [80] the Qi army suffered a resounding defeat. Yue Yi requested the Qin and Hann forces to withdraw. He invited the Wei army to occupy the territories that previously belonged to Song; [81] he allowed the Zhao army to take possession of the territories between the rivers *Hejian*. [82] Yue Yi, as the commander of his Yan forces, marched north pursuing after the retreating Qi army.[83]

---

78 Yan Commanding General, *shangjiangjun* 燕上將軍 Yue Yi 樂毅.

79 Qin Military Officer, *wei* 秦尉 Si Li 斯離.

80 West of Ji – *Jixi* 濟西. The Ji River 濟水 is now obliterated. The river referred here was in the flood plain of Shandong near Yangxinxian 山東 陽信縣.

81 Song territory 宋地 – The Song territory was centred around Shangqiu 商邱, it extended to Huaxian Henan 河南滑縣 to the northwest; Hezexian Shandong 山東 荷澤縣 to the north, Jinxiangxian Shangdong 山東 金鄉縣 to the northeast. To the east it extended as far as Xuzhoushi Jiangsu 江蘇 徐州市, Yixian in Shandong 山東嶧縣; and southeast to Xuqianxian Jiangsu 江蘇 宿遷縣. In the south its domain covered Taihexian Anhui 安徽太和縣; southwest to Huaiyangxian Henan 河南淮陽縣, and west it extended to Lanfengxian Henan 蘭封縣. The Song domain was located in the present-day Yu – Henan 豫 河南, Lu – Shandong 魯 山東, Su – Jiangsu 蘇 江蘇 and Wan 皖 安徽. *ZZTJ JZ*, Vol 1, p. 144.

82 *Hejian* 河間 - the area was between Jihe 濟河 and Huanghe 黄河, present day Gaotangxian 高唐縣 and Tangyi 堂邑 in Shandong 山東. *JJTJ JZ*, Vol 1, p. 144.

83 N.B. The campaign of Yue Yi 樂毅 against Qi 齊 - see the author's translation of Yang Kuan's 楊寬 textual research on the authenticity of this event, "Reassessments and Verifications of Important Chronological Dates of the Warring States" in the Appendix 3.

Ju Xin advised,[84] "Qi is a formidable state, whereas Yan is small and feeble. With the help of other fief lords, we defeated the Qi army. I think we should take advantage of our victory to occupy the border cities to expand our territories - a sound and long-term approach. Whereas we are circumventing the strategic cities to penetrate deep into the hinterland of Qi, it is unlikely to inflict any long-lasting damage to Qi; besides, it yields little advantage to Yan. Moreover, we are fuelling hatred among the people; it will create a lasting animosity for us to regret in the future." Yue Yi responded, "The king of Qi flaunts his exploits and capabilities, he clings obstinately to his course disregarding the opinions of his subordinates. He banishes and executes all the worthy ministers in his court; merely trusting the toadies and sycophants around him. His decrees and mandates are wantonly despotic and tyrannical. The Qi civilians are resentful with his reign. Now that the Qi army has been routed, if we continue to pursue the retreating forces the people will indubitably revolt against him; when internal strife and chaos ensue Qi will be taken. If we do not take advantage of our success, the king might wake up from his failings and repent of his misdeeds; perhaps he might even try to console his people. By then it would be difficult to anticipate the outcome." The Yan army continued to penetrate deeper into Qi territories. Qi, as anticipated, fell into complete chaos, and the people lost all resolve to defend their kingdom. King Min of Qi ran for his life. Yue Yi entered Linzi; [85] there the army appropriated all the treasures and transported the spoils and the paraphernalia for sacrificial offerings to Yan.

The king of Yan travelled to Jishang, and he rewarded his armies with rich gifts and money followed by banquets. He enfeoffed Yue Yi as Lord Changguo; [86] he then enjoined him to continue to exert pressure on the Qi cities that had remained standing.

II. King Min of Qi escaped to Wey. Lord Si of Wey vacated his palace to allow the king to take up residence, [87] proclaiming himself a subject of the Qi king and provided him with supplies as demanded. Nonetheless, the king of Qi was insolent and impertinent, the court officers at Wey responded by humiliating him. The king left Wey and headed towards Zuo and later Lu.[88] Behaving with such brazen arrogance the two fiefdoms refused him entry; he finally settled at Ju.[89]

The king of Chu dispatched General Nao Chi heading an army to bring relief to Qi;[90] the king of Qi made the general chancellor of Qi. Nao Chi had intended to partition Qi with Yan; he

---

84 Ju Xin 劇辛, Yan military consultant, was a Zhao 趙 national; later he went to Yan 燕, responding to the call of King Zhao of Yan 燕昭王. He died in 242 BCE at the time King Xi of Yan 燕喜王 in a battle against his old acquaintance Pang Xuan 龐煖 also from Zhao 趙. Details see 242 BCE II.

85 Linzi 臨淄 - Linzixian Shandong 山東 臨淄縣.

86 Jishang 濟上 - Yangxinxian Shandong 山東 陽信縣.
Lord Changguo 昌國君, it is translated as 'the Lord who brought prosperity to a kingdom'.

87 Wey 衛. Lord Si of Wey 衛嗣君.

88 Zou 鄒 - Zouxian Shandong 山東 鄒縣.
Lu 魯 - Qufuxian Shandong 山東 曲阜縣.

89 Ju 莒 - Juxian Shandong 山東 莒縣.

90 Chu General - Nao Chi 楚 淖齒. King Qing of Chu 楚頃王 sent Nao Chi to the aid of Qi; King Min of Qi 齊湣王 appointed him as his chancellor. Later the general conspired with Yan 燕 in an attempt to annex Qi. Having captured King Min of Qi, the general hung him from the ceiling of a temple, where he tortured the king by pulling out his tendons and ligaments while he was still alive. A Qi national Wang Sunjia 王孫賈 led four hundred strong men from Jucheng 莒城 to rise in arms and had the general executed. (See below).

imprisoned King Min. The general recounted the atrocious deeds of the king, "Your Highness, do you happen to know the vast area of several hundred *li* between Qiancheng and Bochang rained blood from Heaven, staining the clothes people wore?"[91] The king responded, "I did." The general continued, "Were you aware that between Ying and Bo the ground collapsed exposing underground streams?"[92] The king responded, "I was." Nao Chi continued, "People were weeping and wailing outside your palace to plea for help, yet their wishes were not granted; when they left one could hear their voice in the distance. Were you aware of it?" Tian Di answered, "I knew." Nao Chi continued, "When Heaven rained blood staining clothes people wore, it was a warning from Heaven. When the earth abruptly collapsed exposing the underground spring, it was a warning from Earth. When people were weeping and wailing outside your palace, they were also warning you. Heaven, Earth, and people were all warning you to be cautious, and yet you did not even seem to care. How could I not put you to death for your arrogance?" The king was executed at the Guli Alley.[93]

Xunzi comments:[94]

A sovereign state is a synthesis of the common interest and the influence of its people. A sovereign who embraces the righteous path for governance finds peace and tranquillity for his state, and his people bask in splendorous bliss; in reality, it is a source of happiness. A state under an incompetent leader lacking moral attributes faces menacing hazard and hindrance. A state without a sovereign as such is preferable to

---

91 Qiancheng 千乘 - Gaoyuanxian Shandong 山東 高苑縣.
Bochang 博昌 - Boxingxian Shandong 山東 博興縣.

92 Ying 嬴 - Yingyi 嬴邑 - Laiwuxian Shandong 山東 萊蕪縣.
Boyi 博邑 - Taianxian Shandong 山東 泰安縣.

93 Guli Alley 鼓里 was in the neighbourhood of Juxian 莒縣.
The death of the king of Qi, Tian Di 田地 was glossed over by the *ZZTJ*. When the Chu general arrived at Ju 莒, he realized that the king was deranged; he invited King Tian Di to inspect a military parade and had him arrested. He bound and hung the king from the ceiling of a temple. He was put through the most excruciating tortures imaginable; with his tendons and ligaments ripped out and his skin stripped. The torture lasted for two days and two nights before the king died. We cannot explain why the general had to employ such horrendous abuses on the king; nevertheless, it is believed that he had found the king's arrogance insufferable. In the *ZGC* 戰國策, the responses by the king to the general's questionings were negative statements, whereas in *ZZTJ* they were made affirmative. *ZGC* 戰國策, 卷 13, Qice 齊策 6, p. 136-137.
ZZTJ BY Edition, Vol 2, pp. 293-294.

94 Xunzi 荀子 or Xun Kuang 荀況 (313-238 BCE) was also known as or Sun Qing 孫卿. He was a Zhao 趙 national living towards the late period of the Warring States. He was one of the most outstanding literati of all time and had made many contributions to the literati philosophy. He believed that humans were born malevolent and immorally inclined; and through that, learning and education people started to socialize and become moral and virtuous. Hann Fei 韓非 and Li Si 李斯 were his students. *SJ* 史記, 卷 44, 'Mengzi, Xun Qing liezhuan 孟子荀卿列傳' 第 14, p. 544.
This annotation in the *ZZTJ* is an abbreviated insert from *Xunzi's* 荀子 第 11, 'Wangba pian 王霸篇' 第 11, *Siku quanshu* '*Xunzi* 荀子'pp. 5076-5081.
As Hann Fei 韓非 and Li Si 李斯 were two of the most outstanding Legalists, historians have questioned whether Xunzi was a typical Literati, particularly Li Si who helped Qin to unify All under Heaven, and some scholars have criticized his teachings. Yang K 楊寬, *ZGS* 戰國史, pp. 510-519.

having one. Having reached the extremity, even if a failing sovereign wishes to relegate himself as commoner finds it improbable. King Min of Qi and Duke Xian of Song were exemplary examples.[95]

Consequently, a sovereign who dispenses righteousness and virtue becomes king; one who abides scrupulously by integrity and veracity becomes a hegemon, and one who shepherds a state through power and machination - it is only a matter of time before he meets his end.

No one can bring harm to a state when a sovereign takes the lead to hearten his people in adopting rites and righteousness. A righteous ruler would never lower himself to commit an iniquitous act, or to kill an innocent to procure all the power under Heaven. With resolve as firm as a stone, he rules with his heart dispensing good governance to his state. Hence, his aides are honourable and just individuals; and the judiciary administrators in his court function within the confines of morality, dispensing just and righteousness adjudication. A sovereign who leads his ministers with resolve cultivates an ethos of rites and righteousness; accordingly, his subjects and commoners hold great deference for his righteous path. A state built on such solid foundation is destined to be an enduring nation, it is stable and secure, and there is peace and tranquillity for all under Heaven. Hence, it is said, when a nation is unified under morality and justice, it merely takes one day for people to discern its prominence. King Tang and King Wu were prime examples; by way of promoting righteousness, they became kings.[96]

While a state might not have attained the pinnacle of perfection, albeit the ethics and justice may be less than perfect, nevertheless the essential matters under Heaven are evidently within its grasp. The matters pertaining to penalty, reward, and pledge are unanimously accepted with credibility by the subjects and are wholly convinced of the necessity of such measures. A dispensed decree might be beneficial or detrimental to the interest of the state; however, a worthy leader chooses not to repeal his decree to deceive his subjects. When treaties with neighbouring states are signed and sealed, it might be to the disadvantage of his state, the leader chooses to honour his pledge, never renouncing it to impair his credibility. As such, the military power of a nation strengthens under these circumstances; the national security becomes impeccable, leaving his enemy states in awe. When a state is unified as one with a clear and unblemished foundation, the allies have great faith in the state. Even if it is located in obscure and remote places,

---

95 King Min of Qi 齊湣王 Tian Di 田地.
Duke Xiang of Song 宋献公, Song Yan 宋偃, alias Jie of Song 桀宋. (r. 328-286 BCE) He was also known as King Kang 康王 or King Yan of Song, 35th. His name was Dai Yan 戴偃, he was either the younger brother or son of Song Techeng 宋剔成.

96 King Tang of Shang 商湯 (r. ~ 1600 BCE).
King Wu of Zhou 周武王 (r. 1046-1043 BCE).

its might and potency will command the respect of the most powerful states under Heaven. The Five Hegemons were such entities.[97] It is what I mean when I said the head of state who promotes credibility and integrity attains the status as hegemon.

A head of state takes the lead by promoting material gains and benefits, pays no due considerations to justice and morality, he disregards credibility, places emphasis on profits and gains, swindles his civilians on trivial benefits, deceives his allies for major gains, and neglects to prize the land and treasures he owns while incessantly pilfering resources from other states. Unquestionably, his subjects and civilians will likewise use deceit and trickery to attend to the sovereign. The elites cheat on their subordinates, while the subordinates swindle their superiors, causing dissension and discord between the elites and the commoners. The enemy states naturally disdain and repulse against it while his allies are wary and distrustful. The populous live in a state of relentless conspiracy, scheming and plotting against each other. A state as such weakens and faces peril, once it reaches a point of no return it is destined for annihilation. King Min of Qi and Lord Mengchang were glaring examples. Instead of using his powerful Qi state to promote rites and righteousness, instead of educating civility, and instead of attempting to use his powerful state to unify All under Heaven, King Min was constantly travelling in his carriage to other states arranging complicities; and he took on the venture as his mission. When it was powerful, Qi was formidable enough to defeat Chu in the south, and to the west, it defeated Qin; to its north, it overwhelmed Yan and in the central realm, it annihilated Song. Whence the people at Yan and Zhao rose up against it, it broke off like putrid branches from a tree. When it fell, King Min died with his state annihilated; it was followed by one great genocide under Heaven. King Min was a vile and nefarious example people made reference. It is for no other reason, except individuals like him did not abide by rites and righteousness; instead, they engaged in power manipulation, scheming and machinating conspiracies. A sage lord should properly choose one of the three options carefully. They are also the guiding principles of people who pay attention to virtues. The ones who choose with wisdom will pacify others while those choose erroneously are encumbered by others.

III. Yue Yi heard that there was a worthy man by the name of Wang Zhu from the County of Huayi.[98] He ordered his army not to proceed closer than thirty *li* from the county. He sent an envoy to invite the man to take on administrative duties for Yan, but Wang Zhu respectfully declined. The Yan messenger warned him, "If you decline our offer, we will bring massacre to

97 Duke Heng of Qi 齊恒公 Jiang Xiaobai 姜小白 16th (r. 685-643 BCE).
Duke Wen of Jin 姬重耳 Ji Zhonger 晋文公 24th (r. 636-628 BCE).
Duke Min of Qin 秦穆公 Ying Renhao 嬴任好 9th (r. 659-621 BCE).
King Zhuang of Chu 楚莊王 Mi Lu 芈侣 6th (r. 613-591 BCE).
King Helu of Wu 吳王闔閭 Ji Guang 姬光 6th (r. 514-496 BCE).

98 Huayi 晝邑 - Linzi 臨淄 - Linzixian Shandong 山東 臨淄.
Wang Zhu 王燭.

Huayi." Wang Zhu responded, "A loyal subject does not serve two masters; a chaste woman does not have two husbands. Our kingdom is conquered, and our sovereign is dead, I cannot live alone, and now you are intimidating me by using force. To be alive without rectitude, I am better off dead." He placed a noose around his neck and secured the other end to a branch of a tree; he threw himself down and broke his neck.

IV. Following the victory, the Yan forces penetrated deep into the heartland of Qi, the defenders in the Qi walled-cities dispersed swiftly like the wind as the enemy forces approached. Yue Yi rearranged his army and strictly prohibited his men to loot and raid. He sought capable people among the Qi recluses for engagement, treating them as guests of honour. He reduced the exorbitant taxes, revoking the harsh and perverse policies, and restored the former governance of Qi. The Qi people were overjoyed with the new ruler. Yue Yi then sent his left-army to cross the Jiaoshui River to the Donglai areas.[99] The vanguard force was commanded to march along the east of Taishan Mountain to reach the Sea and occupied Langya. While the right-flank trekked along the Jishui River and Huanghe River to reach the cities of A and Juan to take up the garrison, and to rendezvous with the Wei forces.[100] The rear unit marched close to Beihai Sea, where they pacified the locals at Qiancheng. The centre regiment (Yue Yi) took over the control of Linzi, the capital of Qi. At the outskirt of the capital city, Yue Yi offered sacrifices to Duke Huan of Qi (the former hegemon) and Chancellor Guan Zhong.[101] He hailed and celebrated the scholars and worthy people living in the small villages and the cities. He then ordered his men to give Wang Zhu a solemn and decent burial.[102] Over twenty Qi men were awarded fief estates in Yan, and over one

---

99 Jiaoshui River 膠水.
Donglai 東萊- Yexian Shandong 山東 掖縣.

100 Taishan Mountain 泰山 - in Shandong 山東.
The Sea - Bohai Sea 渤海.
Langya 琅琊 - Zhuchengxian Shandong 山東 諸城縣.
Jishui River 濟水. Huanghe River 黄河.
A 阿 – A'cheng 阿城 - Dongaxian Shandong 山東 東阿縣.
Juan 鄄 - Juancheng 鄄城 - Puxian Shandong 山東 濮縣.

101 Beihai Sea 北海.
Qiancheng 千乘 – Gaoyuanxian Shandong 山東 高苑縣.
Linzi 臨淄 - Linzixian Shandong 山東 臨淄.
Duke Huan of Qi 齊桓公 Jiang Xiaobai 姜小白 (r. 685-643 BCE) was the 15th duke of Qi. Jiang Xiaobai won the power struggle at the Qi court after the death of Duke Xiang of Qi 齊襄公, and he made reforms to the kingdom by merging the military power with government administration and made his civilians warriors. He successfully made Qi one of the five hegemons and the most powerful hegemon at his time. He was instrumental in defeating the encroaching Rong 戎 and Di 狄 tribes and won commendations from the Zhou Son of Heaven 周天子. When he grew old, he became demented and trusted sycophants Yi Ya 易牙 and Shu Diao 豎刁 at his court; he died of hunger during an internal turmoil at Qi.
Chancellor Guan Yiwu 管夷吾 alias Guan Zhong 管仲 (? -645 BCE) was a most capable chancellor of Jiang Xiaobai 姜小白; he died shortly before the duke.
SJ 史記, 卷 102, 'Qi Taigong shijia 齊太公世家' 第 2, pp. 1410-1413.

102 The text used the word 封; it was a posthumous enfeoffment after burial.

hundred individuals were enfeoffed with noble titles. Within a period of six months, over seventy Qi cities were annexed and incorporated into the Yan domain. (N.B.)[103]

V. The king of Qin, the king of Wei, and, the king of Hann met at the capital of Zhou (Luoyang).[104]

---

283 BCE *Wuyin* 戊寅 Warring States 戰國

King Nan of Zhou	周赧王	32nd year
Duke Min of Lu	魯湣公	14th year
King Zhaoxiang of Qin	秦昭襄王	24th year
King Qingxiang of Chu	楚頃襄王	16th year
King Xiang of Qi	齊襄王	1st year
King Zhao of Wei	魏昭王	13th year
King Xi of Hann	韓釐王	13th year
King Huiwen of Zhao	趙惠文王	16th year
King Zhao of Yan	燕昭王	30th year
Sir Wey Si	衛嗣君	42nd year

I. Qin and Zhao met at Rang.[105]

II. Qin attacked Wei; Ancheng was annexed; the army penetrated as far as Daliang before retreating.[106]

III. During the upheaval of Nao Chi at Qi,[107] Tian Fazhang the son of King Min changed his given and family name, eked out a living as a domestic worker at a Jiao household, a former grand historian of the Ju state.[108] The daughter of the grand historian observed that this man was not an ordinary person, with his exceptional bearing and stature. She took pity on him, surreptitiously gave him food and clothes, and an illicit liaison developed between them.

Wang Sunjia was an attendant of King Min. He lost the whereabouts of the king. His mother asked him, "You leave home early in the morning and return late at night; I was waiting for you at

---

103 See the author's translation of Yang Kuan's 楊寬 textual research of the Warring States in the Appendix.

104 The King of Qin 秦王 Ying Ji 嬴稷.
The King of Wei 魏王 Wei Su 魏遬.
The King of Hann 韓王 Hann Jiu 韓咎.
Zhou capital - Luoyang 周都 洛陽.

105 Rangcheng 穰城 - Dengxian Henan 河南 鄧縣.

106 Wei 魏 - Ancheng 安城 - Yuanwuxian Henan 河南 原武縣.
Daliang 大梁 - Kaifengxian Henan 河南 開封縣.

107 The chaos caused by Nao Chi 楚 淖齒之亂

108 Qi Crown Prince 齊太子 Tian Fazhang 田法章.
King Min of Qi 齊湣王 Tian Di 田地.
Ju Grand Historian, *taishi* 莒太史 Jiao 敫.

the door. Now you are leaving home late at night and do not return; I then waited for you at the entrance of the village. You were serving the king, and he has fled and you don't even know his whereabouts. Who are you going to serve now?" Wang Sunjia then returned to the market and proclaimed to the crowd, "Nao Chi has brought devastation to Qi and murdered King Min. People who wish to join me to kill him bare your right arm." Four hundred men responded to his call, they rallied and attacked Nao Chi, killing him. The Qi ministers and chancellor then went in search of the son of King Min, intending to place him on the throne. Concerned that he might be killed Tian Fazhang hesitated and did not respond to the appeal. It took him a long time to decide, and he finally identified himself. The ministers in the Qi court made him the new Qi king.[109] The king and his men established their garrison at the city of Ju and began their struggle against the Yan invaders. They made a proclamation to the people of Qi, "Our new king has ascended to the throne at Ju."

IV. The king of Zhao acquired a piece of priceless jade known as *Heshibi* from Chu.[110] King Zhao of Qin wanted to take possession of the jade and offered him fifteen walled cities in exchange.[111]

---

109 He was known posthumously as King Xiang 齊襄王.

110 King Huiwen of Zhao 趙惠文王 Zhao He 趙何.

Heshibi jade 和氏璧. At around 8th century BCE, Bian He 卞和 a jeweller from the kingdom of Chu discovered a piece of stone; he knew from experience that it was a piece of priceless jade. He presented the piece of stone to King Li of Chu 楚厲王 Mi-Xiong Xuan 羋熊眴 (r. 757-741 BCE). The king thought the jeweller was trying to deceive him and had his left foot chopped off as a punishment. When the next king, King Wu 楚武王 Mi-Xiong Tong 羋熊通 (r. 740-691 BCE) ascended to the throne, Bian He again presented the piece of stone to the new king; this time, the king had his right foot chopped off as he also maintained that the jeweller was trying to deceive him. Bian He embracing his piece of stone cried for three days and three nights at the foothills of Jingshan Mountain 荆山. Much later, when King Wen of Chu 楚文王 Mi-Xiong Zi 羋熊貲 (r. 690-675 BCE) ascended the throne the king sent someone to ask the jeweller why he was so adamant about his belief. He answered, "This is a piece of priceless jade, and the two former kings regarded it as a useless piece of stone. I am not saddened by the loss of my feet, but I am distressed by the fact that a patriot is misconstrued as being wicked and evil." Mi-Xiong Zi then asked a jade expert to cut open the stone, and it transpired that it was indeed a piece of priceless jade. Legend has it that it was pure white and flawless. The king of Chu named it *Heshibi*, Master He's Jade. The *Siku quanshu* 四庫全書, '*Hann Feizi* 韓非子' 'Heshi 和氏', pp. 52, 53.

The *ZGC* 戰國策 relates that the piece of jade was a national treasure of Chu. At the time of King Wei of Chu 楚威王 (r. 339-329 BCE) the priceless piece was bestowed upon a certain Zhao Yang *lingyin* (a chancellor in charge of administration and military) 昭陽令尹, who was meritorious in defeating the Yue kingdom 越. On one occasion, Zhao Yang gave a banquet; the jade was on display for inspection by his guests, someone caused a commotion, and in the midst of confusion, the jade piece was stolen. Someone accused Zhang Yi 張儀 as the culprit. Zhao Yang had Zhang Yi tortured and questioned before he was released. Later Zhang Yi took revenge by raiding the kingdom of Chu. After this incident, the whereabouts of the jade was lost until it resurfaced at Zhao 趙, at this stage it was owned by King Huiwen of Zhao 趙 惠文王 (r. 311-266 BCE). *SJ* 史記 does relate the history and background of the jade stone. *SJ* 史記, 卷 51, 'Lian Po, Lin Xiangru liezhuan 廉頗藺相如列傳' 第 21, p. 642-643.

In 228 BCE, Qin annihilated the kingdom of Zhao and in 221 BCE all the six warring states succumbed to Qin. It is said the *Heshibi* 和氏璧 was carved into a jade seal by the Emperor of Qin and was to become a national treasure of Qin. Carvings on it read in a Seal script *zhuanwen* 篆文, "Mandate from Heaven, forever and ever." "受命於天, 即壽永昌." Since then the jade became a symbol of the mandate from Heaven, and it was passed on to later dynastic emperors to signify the right to govern all under Heaven; it is also said that it was passed on for over one thousand years

The king of Zhao had no intention of giving up the piece of jade. However, he was wary of the powerful Qin. On the other hand, he sensed that he might be swindled in the exchange if he agreed to it. He sought the opinion of Lin Xiangru, [112] who said, "Qin seeks the exchange of the jade piece with cities if Your Highness refuses the deal you have a weak case. If you present the piece of jade to Qin and Qin does not fulfil its pledge, then Qin has a weak case. Of the two options, your subject believes our best choice is that we should accede to the deal and make him bear the consequences of his devious avarice. Your subject will bring the piece of jade with him to travel to Qin. If the king disavows his pledge, your subject will be responsible for its return." The king of Zhao dispatched Lin Xiangru as his emissary to travel to Qin. Arriving at Qin, Lin Xiangru realized that the Qin king had no intention to honour the pledge; he successfully recovered the jade piece by deception. He then arranged his retainers to smuggle it by taking an off the beaten track to return to Zhao. He remained behind waiting for the consequences from the king of Qin. The king of Qin nevertheless thought he was a worthy man and did not execute him, treating him with great honour and returned him to Zhao.

The king of Zhao made Lin Xiangru senior minister at his court.[113]

V. Lord Si of Wey (Wey Si) died, his son Lord Huai succeeded to the fiefdom.[114] Lord Huai had a predilection of probing into people's intimate personal affairs. Someone saw a county magistrate uncovered his padded beddings exposing the tattered mat underneath. When Lord Si learned of it, he presented the magistrate with a new mat. The magistrate was astounded, maintaining that sovereign was predicting things like a divine. There was another occasion when he sent his retainer to go through a border pass; the retainer bribed the customs officer. He then summoned the customs officer for questioning, if travellers had bribed him for free passages and went on to demand the return of the bribe; the officer was stunned out of his wits. Lord Si was extremely fond of a concubine Xie Ji and favoured a minister Ru Er. To avoid being deceived by the persons, he purposefully paid more respect and attention to his rightful wife Wei Fei; raising another minister, Bo Yi in opposition to Ru Er.[115] He explained, "They are my checks and balances."

Xunzi comments:

Marquis Cheng of Wey and Lord Si of Wey were petty minded and calculating sovereigns; [116] having appropriated a vast fortune from their subjects, they did not earn the admiration of their people. Zichan, the minister of Zheng, won popularity among the people through dispensing favours; however, he lacked sagacity in

---

after the Qin dynasty. Another version of the legend claims that it was interred in the burial crypt of the First Emperor of Qin Shi Huangdi 秦 始皇帝 and the piece of jade seal which was passed on for over one thousand years was another piece from Lantian 藍田.

111 King Zhao of Qin 秦昭王.

112 Lin Xiangru 藺相如 (329-259 BCE). It was the incident that relates the common adage of '完璧歸趙', it means to return something to the owner in perfect condition.

113 Senior Minister, *shang dafu* 上大夫.

114 Lord Si of Wey 衛嗣君, 45th; Lord Wey Huai 衛懷君 46th, the names of both marquises are unknown.

115 Xie Ji 泄姬. Ru Er 如耳. Wei Fei 魏妃. Bo Yi 薄疑.

116 Marquis Cheng of Wey 衛成侯 Wey Chi 衛遬 43rd.
Lord Ji of Wey 衛嗣君 45th.

administering a nation. Guan Zhong, on the other hand, was accomplished as administer;[117] nevertheless, he fell short of instituting proper rites and righteousness. Hence, if one employs rites and righteousness to govern a nation with proficiency he becomes king; and if he successfully wins popularity among the people, he attains peace and prosperity for his state. As for those who extort and expropriate they are destined to meet their untimely demise.

---

282 BCE *Jimao*己卯 Warring States 戰國

King Nan of Zhou	周赧王	33rd year
Duke Min of Lu	魯湣公	15th year
King Zhaoxiang of Qin	秦昭襄王	25th year
King Qingxiang of Chu	楚頃襄王	17th year
King Xiang of Qi	齊襄王	2nd year
King Zhao of Wei	魏昭王	14th year
King Xi of Hann	韓釐王	14th year
King Huiwen of Zhao	趙惠文王	17th year
King Zhao of Yan	燕昭王	31st year
Sir Wey Huai	衛懷君	1st year

1. Qin invaded Zhao and annexed two cities.

---

281 BCE *Gengchen* 庚辰 Warring States 戰國

King Nan of Zhou	周赧王	34th year
Duke Min of Lu	魯湣公	16th year
King Zhaoxiang of Qin	秦昭襄王	26th year
King Qingxiang of Chu	楚頃襄王	18th year
King Xiang of Qi	齊襄王	3rd year
King Zhao of Wei	魏昭王	15th year
King Xi of Hann	韓釐王	15th year
King Huiwen of Zhao	趙惠文王	18th year
King Zhao of Yan	燕昭王	32nd year
Sir Wey Huai	衛懷君	2nd year

---

117 Guan Zhong 管仲, see above Guan Yiwu 管夷吾.

I. Qin attacked Zhao and annexed the City of Shicheng.[118]

II. Qin reappointed Marquis Rang as chancellor.[119]

III. Chu, Qi and Hann agreed to form an Alliance to attack Qin.[120] Their conspired scheme was to annihilate the kingdom of Zhou. King Nan of Zhou sent Duke Wu of Eastern Zhou to have an audience with the chancellor of Chu, Zhaozi;[121] he said, "Zhou cannot be taken." Zhaozi responded, "To take Zhou? There is no such plan. Even had it been the case, please enlighten me as to why Zhou cannot be taken?" Duke Wu answered, "The entire domain of Western Zhou is no larger than one hundred square *li*. The king of Zhou is still held as the Son of Heaven. When you partition the kingdom, you will add little land to enhance your territories, and when you vanquish its people, you will add few soldiers to augment your forces. The states that make such an attack will bear the stigma for committing regicide and yet there are people who want to attack the royal Zhou house. The only reason people are salivating over the conquest of Zhou is that - it still possesses the sacrificial apparatus.[122] People know that the flesh of a tiger is flat, in fact rancid, and sharp claws and powerful teeth protect it. Nevertheless, people still go after the animal. If an elk in the swamp donned on a tiger skin, I am afraid ten thousand times more people will be going after it. If Chu is conquered, it will vastly increase the territories of an invader while the subjugation of Chu will be construed as paying reverence to the Son of Heaven.[123] Now, Sir, you intend to annihilate the acclaimed overlord of all under Heaven and take possession of the national treasures left by the three dynasties (Xia, Shang and Zhou).[124] I am afraid no soon had you moved your spoils south to your capital; huge armies will be following your footsteps to march against your kingdom." The king of Chu decided to hold the plan in abeyance.

---

280 BCE *Xinsi* 辛巳 Warring States 戰國

King Nan of Zhou	周赧王	35th year
Duke Min of Lu	魯湣公	17th year
King Zhaoxiang of Qin	秦昭襄王	27th year
King Qingxiang of Chu	楚頃襄王	19th year
King Xiang of Qi	齊襄王	4th year
King Zhao of Wei	魏昭王	16th year

---

118 Zhao 趙 Shicheng 石城 – southwest of Linxian Henan 河南 林縣.

119 Qin Chancellor, *chengxiang* 秦丞相 Wei Ran 魏冉.

120 It was unlikely that Qi 齊 had decided to participate in this event, as Yan 燕 had already occupied nearly the entire kingdom; or perhaps this incident might have taken place before or after the fall of Qi.

121 King Nan of Zhou 周赧王 Ji Yan 姬延 43rd.
Duke Wu of Dongzhou (Eastern Zhou) 東周 武公.
Chu Chancellor, *lingyin* 楚令尹 Zhaozi 昭子.

122 The apparatus for offerings were known as the Nine–Tripods *jiuding* 九鼎.

123 The meaning is - it would be a legitimate excuse for the other fief lords to go against Chu if it attacked Zhou.

124 The Three Dynasties *Sandai* 三代 - Xia 夏, Shang 商, Zhou 周.

King Xi of Hann	韓釐王	16th year
King Huiwen of Zhao	趙惠文王	19th year
King Zhao of Yan	燕昭王	33rd year
Sir Huai of Wey	衛懷君	3rd year

1. General Bai Qi of Qin roundly defeated Zhao. Twenty thousand men were decapitated. Dai and Guanglangcheng were annexed.[125] The king of Qin dispatched General Sima Cuo to rally the garrisoned troops and militia at Longxi to march forth, guided by the Shu scouts to attack Qianzhongdi at the Chu kingdom; [126] the entire area was annexed. Chu presented the area north of Hanshui River and Shangyong to sue for peace.[127]

---

279 BCE *Renwu* 壬午 Warring States 戰國

King Nan of Zhou	周赧王	36th year
Duke Min of Lu	魯湣公	18th year
King Zhaoxiang of Qin	秦昭襄王	28th year
King Qingxiang of Chu	楚頃襄王	20th year
King Xiang of Qi	齊襄王	5th year
King Zhao of Wei	魏昭王	17th year
King Xi of Hann	韓釐王	17th year
King Huiwen of Zhao	趙惠文王	20th year
King Zhao of Yan	燕昭王	34rd year
Sir Huai of Wey	衛懷君	4th year

---

125 Qin General 秦 Bai Qi 白起.
Dai 代 - Weixian Hebei 河北 蔚縣. The city of Guanglangcheng 光狼城 - the place is unknown. According to the *ZZTJ JZ*, the word Dai is superfluous, which created certain confusion, as there is not a city called Guanglangcheng in the Dai Prefecture. *ZZTJ JZ*, Vol 1, p. 151.

126 Sima Cuo 司馬錯.
Longxi 隴西 - Lintaoxian Gansu 甘肅 臨洮縣.
Shu 蜀國 – Chengdushi Sichuan 四川 成都市.
Qianzhong 黔中 - Yuanlingxian Hunan 湖南 沅陵縣.

127 Hanshui River 漢水.
Shangyong 上庸 - Zhushanxian Hubei 湖北 竹山縣.
Bo Yang 柏楊 comments: "The campaign was an arduous and audacious undertaking by the Qin army. From the capital of Qin at Xianyang 咸陽 to Longxi 隴西, the distance was 300 km as the crow flies. From Longxi to Shu 蜀國 it was 550 km and from Shuzhong 蜀中 to Qianzhong 黔中 it was 650 km. The passage was most treacherous, with numerous mountains, rapids, defiles and rivers including the almost impassable Minshan Mountain Range 泯山山脈; Motianling Mountain Range 摩天嶺山脈, Changjiang River 長江, the Yungui Plateau 雲貴高原 and the Wuling Mountain Range 武陵山脈." *ZZTJ BY Edition*, Vol 2, p. 308.

I. Bai Qi of Qin attacked Chu and annexed Yancheng, Dengxian and Xiling.[128]

II. The king of Qin (Ying Ji) sent an emissary to see the king of Zhao, [129] advising him that he intended to make amends to their relationship, and he requested the king to meet him at Mianchi beyond the River - *Hewai.* The Zhao king considered declining the invitation. Lian Po and Lin Xiangru discussed the issue; [130] they said, "If Your Highness does not proceed to the proposed invitation; it will be construed as a sign of weakness and cowardice on our part." Zhao He proceeded to the meeting, accompanied by Lin Xiangru. Lian Po saw the king off at the state border. He bid farewell to the king and said, "The proposed trip should not exceed thirty days. If Your Highness does not return within thirty days, we will place the crown prince on the throne, so as to thwart the Qin king's vile intention of holding you hostage." The king agreed to it.

The two kings met at Mianchi. The Qin king and the Zhao king were having a drinking session, and the kings were enlivened by the toasting and were drinking to satiety. The king of Qin asked the king of Zhao to play a tune on a *se* (zither).[131] The king of Zhao played. Having finished Lin Xiangru requested the king of Qin to play music using a wine jar called *fou.* The king of Qin refused.[132] Lin Xiangru said, "Within these five paces; my Lord, your subject has no hesitation of smearing his blood from his throat on your clothes." The Qin attendants drew their swords attempting to kill Xiangru, who scowled, eyes rolled back ablaze with anger. The attendants withered away. The king was fuming with a restrained anger; he struck the *fou* perfunctorily once. Until the banquet ended, the Qin king was unable to gain the initiative in the confrontation, while the guards from Zhao took great care to ensure their king stayed out of harm's way. The king of Qin did not provoke him further.

Upon returning to Zhao, the king raised Lin Xiangru to the position of the excellence of the state - *shangqing,* [133] a position to the right of General Lian Po. The general said, "I am a mighty general of Zhao; I successfully besieged many cities and won numerous battles, and I have been meritorious. Lin Xiangru is of the most humble origin, because of his smooth-talking ad his eloquence he is raised to a position above me. I am ashamed to be his subordinate." He swore,

---

128 Chu 楚 Yan 鄢 - Yancheng 鄢城 - Yichengxian Hubei 湖北 宜城縣.
Deng 鄧 - Dengxian 鄧縣 - northeast of Xiangyangxian Hubei 湖北 襄陽縣.
Xiling 西陵 - Xiling Gorge, Yichangxian Hubei 湖北 宜昌縣 西陵峽.

129 King of Qin 秦王 Ying Ji 嬴稷.
King of Zhao 趙王 Zhao He 趙何.
Hewai 河外 - south of the Huanghe River, from Shaanzhou 陝州 to the west of Luoyang 洛陽.
(*Henei* 河内 – North of Huanghe from Jiyuan 濟源 to Xiuwu 修武.) *ZZTJ JZ,* Vol 1, p. 161.
Mianchi 澠池 - Mianchixian Henan 河南 澠池縣.

130 Lian Po 廉頗 the General.
Lin Xiangru 藺相如 the court Minister.

131 Zither - *se* 瑟 was a horizontal zither-like stringed instrument, about 2 metres long, originally with 50, but later changed to 25 strings.

132 *Fou* 缶 - was a wine vessel, shaped like a flower vase with a globular base, it was used as a musical instrument by the Xi-Rong 西戎 barbarians. *ZZTJ JZ,* Vol 1, p. 161.

133 Excellence – *shangqing* 上卿.
The seating of Lin Xiangru 藺相如 at the court was to the right of Lian Po 廉頗. *You* 右 - the right minister – i.e. more senior than the left *zuo* 左. It was known as *chaolie* 朝列 – court-seating arrangement.

"When I meet Xiangru next, I will humiliate him." Xiangru was told what the general had said and tried to avoid running into Lian Po. He found excuses not to attend the morning sessions at court by claiming that he was ill; thus dispensing with the inconvenience of vying for seating placements. When Lin Xiangru went into the street, upon seeing the general in the distance, he would make detours avoiding him. The retainers of Lin Xiangru were greatly humiliated by their master. Xiangru asked them, "How do you compare General Lian Po with the king of Qin?" The attendants said, "There is no comparison." Lin Xiangru said, "For all the might and stature of the king of Qin, I yelled and affronted him in his court, and humiliated his subjects. I might be useless; but do you think I am intimidated by the general? The only consideration I have is that the king of Qin does not have the audacity to invade our kingdom for one very simple reason - the presence of the general and myself. You see; when two tigers are engaged in a fight, one is bound to lose. I have been avoiding him, hence as to place the interest of our kingdom above my personal importance. I have relegated my personal interests, my likes and dislikes to the secondary place." When Lian Po was told of the comments, he stripped off his clothes exposing his back and carried a thistle stick on his back as he proceeded to the manor of Lin Xiangru. At the threshold, he humbly knelt, begging for forgiveness. The two men became fast friends and pledged an oath that that they would die for each other.

III. Previously, when the Yan army was laying siege to Anping in Qi, Tian Dan a junior functionary at the marketplace of Linzi was living in the city.[134] He instructed his family members to use wrought iron cages to shield the spoke-caps of their carriages. When Anping fell, throngs of people rushed through the city-gates. In the mayhem, carriages with exposed spoke-caps broke down. Many civilians were held captive by the Yan army. Tian Dan and his family members managed to escape to the city of Jimo as the wheels of their carriages, protected by the iron cages, held out.[135] At this stage, the kingdom of Qi had almost entirely fallen to the Yan forces, only Jimo and Jucheng remained standing.[136] Yue Yi redeployed his army, rallied the forces from the right regiment and the vanguard regiment to besiege Ju; while the left and the rear regiments were diverted to encircle Jimo. The officer at Jimo ventured out to join battle with the assailants and died. The locals at Jimo reasoned, "When Anping was besieged by Yan, Tian Dan and his family clan used iron cages to protect their carriage wheels, he and his family members managed to escape; the man is a talented military strategist." The people in the city elected Tian Dan as their military commander to resist the Yan forces.

Yue Yi laid siege to the two cities and did not make any progress for one year. He ordered his army to lift the siege, and retreated to a distance of nine *li* from the cities and set up barricades and ramparts. He gave strict orders, "The people from the cities who wish to leave are not to be apprehended; and those in privation are to be looked after. People are allowed to return to their former professions to placate those who have surrendered."

Three years elapsed and the two cities held out. Someone at the Yan court made defamatory comments against the general, "Yue Yi is a most resourceful and brilliant general; in one breath he took down over seventy walled-cities; only two remained standing. He does not lack the capacity to take the cities; the reason he does not even attempt to take down the cities in three years is

---

134 Linzi 臨淄 city functionary *shiyuan* 市掾 - Linzixian Shandong 山東 臨淄縣.
Anping 安平 - east of Linzixian 臨淄縣. Tian Dan 田單.

135 Qi 齊 - Jimo 即墨 - Pingduxian Shandong 山東 平度縣.

136 Qi 齊 - Jucheng 莒城 - Juchengxian Shandong 山東 莒城縣.

perhaps he intends to employ the might of our forces to win over the Qi people and then face south as their king. Now that the people at Qi have already submitted to the general, the only reason he is not making a move is that his wife and children are still residing in Yan. There are many beautiful women at Qi; very soon, the general might totally forget his wife. Please give it some considerations, Your Highness."

King Zhao of Yan (Ji Ping) held a splendid banquet and asked the officers who made suggestions previously to attend, berating them, "Our former king fostered capable and virtuous scholars to preside over our kingdom.[137] He did it not for avaricious reasons, and not for expanding his domain for his descendants. Upon his abdication, Zi Zhi the person he chose proved to be lacking in moral character, [138] and he failed to cultivate the responsibility bestowed upon him. The people in our kingdom did not accede to him. The king of Qi was most repressive; he took advantage of our internal strife and murdered our former king. Upon my ascending to the throne, with deep odium and resentment, I resolved to take revenge against Qi for the pain and humiliation they inflicted upon us. Within my kingdom, I treat our ministers with great honour, while from without I invited capable and virtuous guests to come to serve at my court. I have only one concern in mind - to avenge the torment and misery that were brought against us. I pledged that were we successful in our quest, I would share my kingdom with the person who could avenge our humiliation. Now Lord Yue Yi is commanding our army, taking on a perilous quest, going against and defeated Qi, razing their holy shrines to the ground, and successfully avenged the death of our former king. Qi belongs to Lord Yue, besides it has never been part of Yan. If Lord Yue could preside over Qi successfully, and maintain a peaceful coexistence with my kingdom, make a committed pledge against the common foe of all the fief lords, and that would be most auspicious and fortunate for Yan. It is my wish. Why do some of you have to obstruct and hamper?" He ordered to have the defamers executed. He presented the official trappings of his queen to the wife of Yue Yi, the trappings of his crown prince to his son, and carriages for elites and fine stallions to be presented to Yue Li as gifts. Employing a four-horse drawn carriage *luju* accompanied by one hundred carriages *houshu*, [139] he sent his chancellor to Qi to enfeoff Yue Yi as the king of Qi. Yue Yi was greatly alarmed by the king's intended enfeoffment. He resolutely refused to take on the honour and submitted a memorial, and swore an oath of death, articulating his fealty. Ever since, the people of Qi began to respect the honour and virtues of Yue Yi, the people in the other kingdoms came to admire the man, derogatory comments against him ceased.

Shortly after, King Zhao died, his son King Hui ascended to the throne.[140] When King Hui was the crown prince, he was displeased with the general. Tian Dan heard of what had happened, he sowed seeds of discord at Yan, "The king of Qi is dead, only two Qi cities remain standing. Yue Yi and the new King of Yan have had differences between them; hence, the general dares not return to Yan for fear of being ostracised. He uses the excuse of laying a protracted siege of the two cities, whereas his real intention is to assume the throne of Qi. As the people of Qi have not entirely submitted to him, he has not acted steadfastly and resolutely. He has kept deferring an

---

137 Ji Guai 姬噲. This was hardly true as Ji Guai was a befuddled old man.

138 Zi Zhi 子之. See 316 BCE and 314 BCE, Zi Zhi usurped the Yan throne 燕.

139 When a fief lord exited from his residence, he rode on a four-horse drawn carriage called *luju* 輅車, the carriages followed his carriage were called *houshu* 後屬 and was one hundred in number. *ZZTJ JZ*, p. 162.

140 King Zhao of Yan 燕昭王 Ji Ping 姬平 (r. 311 or 313- 279 BCE).
King Hui of Yan 燕惠王 Ji Yuezi 姬樂資 6th (r. 278-272 BCE).

all-out assault against the walled-city of Jimo to accomplish his scheme. What the Qi people fear most is if another general assumes command of the Yan army, Jimo will fall." The king of Yan had all along been suspicious of Yue Yi, and now with Qi's slandering rumours, he sent General Qi Jie to take over the command of the expeditionary forces and summoned Yue Yi to return to Yan.[141] Yue Yi realized that the king would not treat him fairly; he escaped to Zhao. The Yan generals and soldiers were indignant and saddened by the removal of their commander, and they became restive.

Tian Dan instructed the civilians in the city to make sacrificial offerings to their ancestors in their courtyards before every meal. Flocks of birds flew into the city to feed. The Yan besiegers were most curious. Tian Dan made a proclamation, "Heaven will send a Divine Tutor to enlighten me to defend this city." A foot soldier asked, "Can your subject be your tutor?" Having said that the solder arose and bolted. Tian Dan rose, chasing after the fleeing soldier and placed him on a seat facing east and honoured him as his tutor. The soldier begged, "Your subject has insulted you, sir. Please forgive him." Tian Dan said, "Sir, be quiet." He made the man his tutor; henceforth, with every command, he claimed that his divine tutor had inspired him.

Tian Dan announced, "When Yan captures the surrendered Qi soldiers, what they fear most is the punishment of having their noses cut off, and have them lined up on display outside the city. The people in Jimo will be traumatised into submission." When the Yan army heard of this, the general promptly ordered his men to carry out such punishments. The defenders were utterly horrified when they saw their surrendered men having their noses cut off, and they were even more resolved than ever to defend their city. The only fear they held was being captured. Tian Dan continued to spread deceits, "The people of Jimo are apprehensive lest the burial mounds of their ancestors outside the city are disinterred and despoiled; it will send a chill up their spines." The Yan army dug up all the tombs and burned the remains. The Qi defenders in the city watched helplessly from the city-wall in horror, they wailed and wept in despair. The defenders pledged to fight the besiegers immediately; their anger multiplied by ten folds. Tian Dan knew his men were ready for action. He carried wooden planks and shovels to construct rampart preparing for battle working alongside his soldiers; his wife and concubines were also enlisted into the labouring force. The entire family fortune was spent on rewarding and feeding the warriors. He then told his crack armoured warriors to conceal out of sight, while deploying the women, old and infirm men to stand guard on top of the city-wall.

Tain Dan sent an envoy to seek an audience with the Yan generals to negotiate terms of capitulation. The Yan army was joyous, chanting, "Long Live the King!"

Tian Dan then collected one thousand *yi* of gold from the civilians.[142] He instructed a wealthy Jimo resident to present the gold to the Yan generals, saying, "The city is about to fall. Please spare the lives of my family members and don't pillage my fortune." The Yan generals were overjoyed and agreed. With victory in sight, they slackened their defence and watchfulness.

Tian Dan gathered all the oxen within the city, numbering over one thousand heads; crimson red embroidered silk drapes were placed on their backs, each painted with polychrome dragon motifs, razor-sharp daggers were affixed to their horns, and finished off with conga grass soaked

141 Qi Jie 騎劫.

142 *Qian-yi* 千鎰 - Twenty four thousand *liang* 两 of gold.

in oil bound on the tails of the animals. When ready, the tails of the oxen were set alight. It was midnight; the animals were driven out through several scores of holes at the base of the city-wall dug out previously. Five thousand crack troops followed the animals charging into the Yan army camps. The oxen with burning tails, stampeded in pain, charged against the Yan army camps. The Yan troops were stunned out of their wits seeing monstrous oxen with dragon motifs charging towards them. Many were either killed or maimed upon contact; confusion and stampede ensued. The old and feeble defenders bellowed and yelled as they watched; they struck up bronze gongs and rattles causing a tumultuous commotion. The Yan army stunned, dispersed with great trepidation. The Qi soldiers killed General Qi Jie and pursued the retreating forces to the north. The cities previously held by Yan rebelled against their occupiers and became Qi territories again. The army of Tian Dan grew by the day as he pursued after the dwindling retreating army. When the Yan army finally arrived at the area near the River *Heshang*,[143] all the seventy lost cities of Qi were recovered.

Tian Dan escorted King Xiang of Qi (Tian Fazhang) from Ju to return to the capital city of Linzi. The king enfeoffed Tian Dan as Lord Anping.[144]

The king of Qi made the daughter of the grand historian Jiao his queen, and she later gave birth to a son Jian.[145] The grand historian said, "A woman who married a man without going through the proper conventions by a matchmaker is most disgraceful and humiliating for my family. She is not fit to be my offspring, and she has defiled our family name." He refused to see the king and the queen for the rest of his life, and yet the king and the queen continued to honour her father with proper etiquette and with due respect.

IV. The king of Zhao enfeoffed Yue Yi at Guanjin,[146] conferring upon him with prodigious respect and honour to caution Qi and Yan. King Hui of Yan dispatched an emissary to see Yue Yi expressing regret, "General, you over reacted to the seeds of discord being sown, believing that there were differences between us. You have forsaken Yan and settled in Zhao; your future is thus secured, but how can you repay the kindness of our former king bestowed upon you, general?" Yue Yi responded in a missive, "Years ago, when Wu Zixu was engaged by He Lu (the king of Wu), who trusted him unreservedly, the kingdom expanded to encompass Ying.[147] Wu Fucha did not

---

143 *Heshang* 河上, place unknown.

144 King Xiang of Qi 齊襄王 Tian Fazhang 田法章.
Linzi 臨淄 - Linzixian Shandong 山東 臨淄縣.
Lord Anping 安平君. The title means An 安 peace and 平 calm – the combination of the two words means tranquility.

145 Grand Historian, *taishi* 太史 Jiao 敫.
Tian Jian 田建.

146 Guanjin 觀津 - Guanchengxian Shandong 山東 觀城縣.

147 King of Wu 吳王 Helu 闔閭 Ji Guang 姬光 (r. 514-496 BCE).
Wu Zixu 伍子胥.
Ying 郢 – Yingdu 郢都 - Jianglingxian Hubei 湖北 江陵縣, the capital of Chu.
King of Wu 吳王 Fucha 夫差 (r. 495-473 BCE). Changjiang River 長江.
The original text was, "賜之鴟夷而浮之江." The meaning of the term *chiyi* 鴟夷 is obscured. However, the South Dynasty 南朝 historian Pei Yin 裴駰 (372-451 CE) quoting from the Eastern Han, Ying Shao 應劭 (active during the waning years of Eastern Han), "Use horse leather to prepare a *chiyi*, it is shaped like a water vessel called *ke* 榼." It was probably a vessel or bag with a bulging

trust the man; and he bestowed Wu Zixu with a bag, stowed him in the bag and threw it into the Changjiang River. The king of Wu did not appreciate that the admonition of the former sovereign by Zixu was a form of loyalty - the very essence that made the king successful. King Wu had Wu Zixu thrown into the river, feeling no remorse for his deed. On the other hand, Wu Zixu failed to appreciate that the two kings were of dissimilar capacities, and his judgement was at variance with the new king; he thus was thrown into the river for not changing his stance. Your subject, on the other hand, having escaped death upheld His Highness's reputation, allowing his achievements to stay unblemished. In reality, it is a manifestation of the grand exploits of our former king, and as far as your subject is concerned, it was the most favourable option. To blight the much-revered name of our former king would have caused your subjects utmost distress. Faced with obscured indictments that were about to level against me, hoping to escape unscathed was not a favourable option a respectable man would choose; hence, your subject could not remain behind. Your subject has heard, when people with noble character of bygone eras ceased to be friends they would never dishonour or disavow their former acquaintances; nor would loyal subjects cleanse their own names by causing harm to the kingdoms they left behind.[148] Your subject is a ne'er-do-well, lacking in eloquence and wanting in knowledge; nevertheless, he lucubrates the teachings of the sages and feebly attempts to emulate them. Your Highness, your subject is sure you understand his predicament."[149] The Yan king decreed to enfeoff Yue Xian the son of Yue Yi as Lord Changguo.[150] Yue Yi reciprocated by rekindling the former relationship with the king and visited Yan on numerous occasions. Later, he died in Zhao and was honoured with the posthumous title of Lord Wangzhu.[151]

V. Tian Dan was made the chancellor of Qi. He chanced to pass by the Zishui River; he saw an old man wading across the river.[152] The weather was frigidly cold; the old man could barely walk upon reaching the shore. Tian Dan removed his leather cloak and gave it to him. King Xiang was appalled. He muttered to himself, "Tian Dan is most generous to the people. Is he going after my kingdom? I might as well take the initiative of doing something before anything dreadful transpires." At this time, there were no other attendants or court officers around, except a worker busily stringing pearls underneath an awning. King Xiang summoned the man to come forth, "Did you hear what I was muttering?" The pearl artisan answered, "Yes, I heard it." Tian Fazhang asked, "What do you think?" The worker answered, "Your Highness might as well make good use of the circumstances and embrace his deed as your own. Your Highness should issue a decree to make acclamation of Dan's act, saying 'I am concerned that my people might go hungry, Tian Dan provides them with food. I am concerned that our people will get cold; Tian Dan gives his cloak to an old man. I understand the sufferings of our people; the chancellor does not forget the sufferings of our people. I am immensely pleased with Tian Dan as he appreciates my sentiment

---

midsection. *ZZTJ JZ* suspects that the phase was a local dialect of Wu 吳語. *ZZTJ JZ,* Vol 1, p.163. The *Pei Yin jijie* 裴駰 集解 引應劭曰："取馬革為鴟夷. 鴟夷，榼形." *Handian* 漢典 - explanation on 鴟夷.

148 Cleanse one's name means clear one's reputation.

149 It is an abridged version of the letter from 樂毅 to King Hui of Yan 燕惠王 that appears in *ZGC* 戰國策, 'Yance 燕策 2', p. 349 and *SJ* 史記, 卷 50, 'Yue Yi liezhuan 樂毅列傳' 第 20, p. 635.

150 Lord Changguo 昌國君 Yue Xian 樂閒. Changguo 昌國 means 'bringing prosperity' to a state.

151 Lord Wangzhu 望諸君. Wangzhu was a lake in China, one of the nine most notable lakes in ancient China. The wordings had a double meaning, it meant 'looking around at various' and had an implication that Yue Yi was worthy above others.

152 Zishui River 淄水.

completely.' When Tian Dan was kind to our people, and Your Highness commends him, his kindness is Your Highness's." The king said, "Excellent." He bestowed a gift of oxen and wine to Tian Dan. A few days later, the pearl artisan saw the king and said, "At your next court session, it would be a good idea for Your Highness to summon Tian Dan to court and thank him officially. Following that, Your Highness should issue a decree to seek out the people who are depraved in hunger and suffer from cold. Then you offer them relief." Later the king sent his aides to assess the situation in the streets and alleys. They came back with accounts that officers and people in the kingdom were singing his praises, "Now we know why Tian Dan has been so kind and generous with the people; it has been His Highness's idea all along."

VI. Tian Dan recommended Diao Bo to the king.[153] The king had nine favoured ministers, who schemed to depose of Lord Anping (Tian Dan). They suggested to the king, "When Yan was attacking us the king of Chu dispatched a task force of ten thousand men under Nao Chi to come to our aid.[154] Now that our kingdom is peaceful again, and our holy shrine is secured; it is an opportune time to express our gratitude for what the Chu king did." The king asked, "Who is the most suitable person to go?" The answer was unanimous, "Diao Bo is." Diao Bo travelled forth as an envoy. Upon arriving at the kingdom of Chu, the king of Chu gave banquets to entertain the envoy.[155] For several months, he was kept at the Chu court. The nine officers again suggested to the king of Qi, "The only explanation why a ten-thousand-chariot kingdom gives an emissary exceptional reception is because he has a benefactor. Whereas there is no difference in status between Lord Anping and Your Highness, Lord Anping thinks he has complete control of our kingdom. Proper etiquette does not exist between him and Your Highness. Tian Dan is ambitious; he pacifies the civilians within our kingdom while outwardly he is appeasing the Yi and Di foreigners. Furthermore, he recruits capable and intelligent people under Heaven to serve under him. Perhaps he might have higher aspirations. Your Highness, please be careful." One day, the king told his retainer, "Summon Chancellor Dan to come forth." Tian Dan removed his hat gear, bared his feet, exposing his back as he entered to pay homage to the king. For five consecutive days, he pleaded guilty to charges laid against him punishable by death upon departure from court. Finally, the king said, "You are not guilty of any crime, I just want you to carry out your duties as my subject, and I do fancy the protocols due to me as a king."

Shortly after, Diao Bo returned from Chu, and the king gave him a reception banquet. Upon drinking three rounds of toasts, the king said to his attendants, "Summon Chancellor Dan to come forth." Diao Bo hastily moved away from where he was seated, making the solemn etiquette of *kowtow* and said, "Your Highness, are you as sagacious as the sage King Wen of Zhou?[156] " The king answered, "No, I am not." Diao Bo said, "Your subject surely knows that you are not. Are you as wise as Duke Huan of Qi?"[157] "No, I am not either." Diao Bo said, "Your subject also happens to know that you are not. When King Wen chanced to come across the sage Lu Shang, he honoured him as his Grand Duke. When Duke Huan of Qi came across Guan Yiwu he addressed him respectfully as his espoused-father. Now, Your Highness, you are most fortunate that you have

153 Diao Bo 貂勃 was a Qi national, a renowned intellect at Qi, a middle-grade minister. He held off the Yan armies at the walled-city of Jucheng 莒城 for six years. *ZGC* 戰國策, 卷 13, 'Qice 齊策' 6, p. 41.

154 Nao Chi 淖齒 see 284 BCE.

155 King of Chu 楚王 Mi Heng 芈橫.

156 King Wen of Zhou 周文王 Ji Chang 姬昌.

157 Duke Huan of Qi 齊桓公 Jiang Xiaobai 姜小白; see 284-IV footnotes.

Lord Anping and you are addressing him by his name, Dan. Where have you learned such conducts of bringing extinction to your kingdom? Ever since time immemorial, there has not been a man who has made more contributions to a kingdom than Lord Anping. When Yan was laying siege to our kingdom, you made no attempt to save our holy shrine, you escaped to the Chengyang Mountains.[158] Lord Anping, in great trepidation, held out at Jimo. The inner city was no more than three *li*, and the outer wall less than five *li* in circumference; he had less than seven thousand old and feeble men under him, and yet he managed to execute the Yan commanding general, recovering over one thousand *li* of Qi territories. All these were the undertakings of Lord Anping. If he had, at that juncture, decided to forsake Your Highness and proclaimed himself as king, no one under Heaven would have objected to it. For the sake of our kingdom and his moral integrity, he did not. He constructed a plank road and wooden pavilions along the way to the Chengyang Mountains to escort Your Highness and Queen to return to the capital, placing you on the throne.[159] Now that peace and tranquillity have returned to our kingdom, and our people are enjoying prosperity and happiness, but you Your Highness is addressing him by his given name – Dan! It is utterly preposterous; not even an infant child would do that. My suggestion is that you should execute the nine ministers in court promptly. It is the only deed possible to repay for Lord Anping's loyalty unless you want to see our kingdom at stake." The king decreed to have the nine ministers executed, and their family members banished. Ten thousand households at Yeyi County were added to Lord Anping's provision fief.[160]

VII. Tian Dan was about to launch an expedition against the Di tribe; he paid a visit to Lu Zhonglian.[161] Lu remarked, "I am of the opinion that you, general, cannot subjugate the Di." Tian Dan replied, "Your subject defeated the ten thousand chariots Yan army with my weak and feeble soldiers at Jimo and I successfully recovered the Qi markets.[162] How can a petty tribe like Di endure my onslaught?" Gravely slighted by such a remark Tian Dan clambered onto his chariot and departed without bidding farewell. The battles with the Di tribesmen took three months, and the general could make no headway. The children of Qi sang a ballad,

> "His hefty helmet is like a dustpan, more like a sieve. His sword is so long he could use it to prop up his chin. He attacks the Di but to no avail. The only things piling up are the colossal mounds of parched bones of the dead."

Tian Dan, greatly exasperated and in fear, paid a visit to Luo Zhonglian and asked, "Sir, you previously said that I could not defeat the Di, so pray enlighten me." Luo answered, "General when you were fighting at Jimo,[163] you sat on a coarse hemp mat; when you stood you held onto your

---

158 Chengyangshan Mountain 城陽山. Jucheng 莒城 was at the foothills of Chengyangshan.

159 The pavilions were constructed as resting place during the passage.

160 Yeyi County 夜邑 - Yexian Shandong 山東 掖縣.

161 Di 狄 – Towards the waning years of Spring and Autumn, the Di tribes in Zhongyaun 中原 were mostly annihilated. This particular Di tribe was the only one left in the east, present day, Gaoyuanxian Shandong 高苑縣 山東. *ZZTJ JZ*, Vol 1, p. 164.

Lu Zhonglian 魯仲連 (~305-245 BCE) was a brilliant strategist and a celebrated mediator. The name of this person is retained as a person who is apt at making arbitration and mediation until this day. Lu Zhonglian was a Qi nation, a person who disdained fame and wealth.

162 Jimo 即墨 - Jimoxian Shandong 山東 即墨縣.

Qi Xu 齊墟 – Xu 墟, the word means market or alternatively a city or territory that had become a necropolis.

163 Jimo 即墨 - one of the two Qi cities that was left standing.

plough. You encouraged your soldiers and warriors by singing in chorus, 'Where forth can we go? Our holy shrine is on the brink of annihilation. Our salvation depends on today; we have to persevere lest we end up with no place to call home.' At that time, general, you and your warriors had the resolve to die and did not harbour any illusion that you might survive the war against Yan. When your men heard your speech, they quietly wiped away their tears, raising their arms, ready to engage in battles with your enemies anew. That was how you ousted Yan. Now, to the east, the people of Yeyi County are providing payments for your needs and to the west people of Linzi are entertaining you.[164] You wear a gold girdle; riding on a stallion, you galloped between Zishui and Shengshui rivers.[165] You are savouring all the pleasurable things in life, but you carry no desire to perish in combat - and that is the very reason you could not possibly win the war." Tian Dan responded, "Tian Dan is determined and shall persevere. I owe you my appreciation, sir, for inspiring me." The next day, he mustered up his courage and made an inspection of the city in close range. He stood close to the besieged fortress, within the range of enemy arrows and flying projectiles, he beat the war-drums with his sticks and commanded his army. The Di city was breached.

VIII. Previously when King Min (Tian Di) of Qi defeated Song, the king had intended to banish Lord Mengchang (Tian Wen).[166] Lord Mengchang escaped to Wei; King Zhao of Wei appointed him as his chancellor.[167] After that Wei formed an alliance with other fief lords to make a joint assault against Qi. Later King Min was killed, his son King Xiang succeeded to the throne. Lord Mengchang returned (to the fiefdom of Xue,) and he shed all connections with other kingdoms. When King Xiang ascended to the throne of Qi, he was troubled by the lasting influence of Lord Mengchang; the king then made peace with the former minister. Shortly after, Lord Mengchang died. The sons of the Lord vied for the title. Qi and Wei jointly attacked the Xue fiefdom, which was annihilated.[168] None of Lord Mengchang offspring survived.

---

278 BCE *Guiwei* 癸未 Warring States 戰國

King Nan of Zhou	周赧王	37th year
Duke Min of Lu	魯湣公	19th year
King Zhaoxiang of Qin	秦昭襄王	29th year
King Qingxiang of Chu	楚頃襄王	21st year
King Xiang of Qi	齊襄王	6th year
King Zhao of Wei	魏昭王	18th year

---

164 Linzi 臨淄 - Shandong 山東.

165 Zishui 淄水 and Shengshui 繩水, the rivers originate at Linzi 臨淄.

166 Lord Mengchang 孟嘗君 Tian Wen 田文.

167 King Zhao of Wei 魏昭王 Wei Su 魏遫.

168 Sima Qian 司馬遷 comments on the people at Xue 薛: "I paid a visit to the County of Xueyi once. The people there preserve their former local customs; there are many unbridled and unkempt youths. The local customs are entirely different from the former kingdoms of Zou 鄒 and Lu 魯, tracing to the root cause, the locals said, "Lord Mengchang 孟嘗君 solicited and recruited all the chivalrous men under Heaven to expedite his courageous and heroic deeds; crafty and unbridled individuals were similarly recruited, many of them came to the Xue County. There were some sixty thousand families." *SJ* 史記, 卷 45, 'Lord Mengchang liezhuan 孟嘗君列傳' 第 15, p. 554.

King Xi of Hann	韓釐王	18th year
King Huiwen of Zhao	趙惠文王	21st year
King Hui of Yan	燕惠王	1st year
Sir Huai of Wey	衛懷君	5th year

I. Bai Qi, the lieutenant general *daliangzao* of Qin, attacked Chu, the capital city Ying fell. At Yiling, the mausoleums of the imperial household were razed to the ground.[169] The Chu army was completely decimated. The king of Chu moved his capital to Chen.[170] Qin took over Ying and re-established it as the Nanjun Prefecture.[171] Bai Qi was honoured as Lord Wuan.[172]

---

277 BCE Jiashen 甲申 Warring States 戰國

King Nan of Zhou	周赧王	38th year
Duke Min of Lu	魯湣公	20th year
King Zhaoxiang of Qin	秦昭襄王	30th year
King Qingxiang of Chu	楚頃襄王	22nd year
King Xiang of Qi	齊襄王	7th year
King Zhao of Wei	魏昭王	19th year
King Xi of Hann	韓釐王	19th year
King Huiwen of Zhao	趙惠文王	22nd year
King Hui of Yan	燕惠王	2nd year
Sir Huai of Wey	衛懷君	6th year

I. Lord Wuan of Qin pacified the Wu Prefecture and Qianzhong and renamed the two districts as Qianzhong Prefecture.[173]

II. King Zhao of Wei died, and his son King Anxi succeeded him.[174]

---

276 BCE *Yiyou* 乙酉 Warring States 戰國

King Nan of Zhou	周赧王	39th year

---

169 Ying 郢 - Yingdu 郢都 - Jianglingxian Hubei 湖北 江陵縣.
Yiling Mound 夷陵 - Yichangxian Hubei 湖北 宜昌縣.

170 Chen 陳 - Chenqiu 陳丘 - Huaiyangxian Henan 河南 淮陽縣 was to the northeast of the kingdom.

171 Ying 郢 was renamed as Nanjun Prefecture 南郡.

172 Lord Wuan 武安君 *daliangzao* 大良造 Bai Qi 白起. The title of Bai Qi was 'Martial-peace' Marquis. *Daliangzao* was the 16th grade of the 20 grades noble at the Qin court.

173 Wu 巫 - Wujun Prefecture 巫郡 - Wushanxian Sichuan 四川 巫山縣.
Qianzhong 黔中 - Qianzhongdi 黔中地 - Yuanlingxian Hunan 湖南 沅陵縣.

174 King Zhao of Wei 魏昭王 Wei Su 魏遬 (r. 295-277 BCE).
King Anxi of Wei 魏 安釐王 Wei Yu 魏圉.

Duke Min of Lu	魯湣公	21st year
King Zhaoxiang of Qin	秦昭襄王	31st year
King Qingxiang of Chu	楚頃襄王	23rd year
King Xiang of Qi	齊襄王	8th year
King Anxi of Wei	魏安釐王	1st year
King Xi of Hann	韓釐王	20th year
King Huiwen of Zhao	趙惠文王	23rd year
King Hui of Yan	燕惠王	3rd year
Sir Huai of Wey	衛懷君	7th year

I. Lord Wuan of Qin attacked Wei; two cities were annexed.

II. The king of Chu gathered his armies from the eastern sectors, which numbered over a hundred thousand men to push west and managed to recover fifteen counties at Jiangnan - south of the Changjiang River.[175]

III. King Anli of Wei enfeoffed his younger brother Wei Wuji as Lord Xinling.[176]

---

275 BCE Bingxu 丙戌 Warring States 戰國

King Nan of Zhou	周赧王	40th year
Duke Min of Lu	魯湣公	22nd year
King Zhaoxiang of Qin	秦昭襄王	32nd year
King Qingxiang of Chu	楚頃襄王	24th year
King Xiang of Qi	齊襄王	9th year
King Anxi of Wei	魏安釐王	2nd year
King Xi of Hann	韓釐王	21st year
King Huiwen of Zhao	趙惠文王	24th year
King Hui of Yan	燕惠王	4th year
Sir Huai of Wey	衛懷君	8th year

I. Marquis Rang (Wei Ran), the chancellor of Qin, led an army and attacked Wei; [177] Hann sent General Bao Yuan to lead an army to the rescue. The Marquis of Rang faced the Hann army killing some forty thousand men; Bao Yuan escaped to Kaifeng (Daliang the capital of Wei).[178] Wei ceded eight walled-cities to sue for peace. Marquis Rang nevertheless continued his attack against

175 King of Chu, Mi Heng 芈横. At one stage, Chu had one million troops.

176 Lord Xinling 信陵君 Wei Wuji 魏無忌. Xinling 信陵 was a county in Wei, in present-day Ninglingxian Henan 河南 寧陵縣.

177 Qin chancellor, *xiang* Marquis Rang 秦相 穰侯 Wei Ran 魏冉.
Hann general 韓將 Bao Yuan 暴鳶.

178 Daliang 大梁 - Kaifengxian Henan 河南 開封縣.

Wei, General Mang Mao of Wei was driven to Beizhai,[179] and finally, Marquis Rang had Daliang the capital of Wei completely encircled. Wei ceded the City of Wen to settle for peace.[180]

---

274 BCE *Dinghai* 丁亥 Warring States 戰國

King Nan of Zhou	周赧王	41st year
Duke Min of Lu	魯湣公	23rd year
King Zhao of Qin	秦昭襄王	33rd year
King Qingxiang of Chu	楚頃襄王	25th year
King Xiang of Qi	齊襄王	10th year
King Anxi of Wei	魏安釐王	3rd year
King Xi of Hann	韓釐王	22nd year
King Huiwen of Zhao	趙惠文王	25th year
King Hui of Yan	燕惠王	5th year
Sir Huai of Wey	衛懷君	9th year

I. Wei reached an Alliance with Qi. Marquis Rang of Qin attacked Wei again; his army captured four cities beheading some forty thousand men.

II. Duke Min of Lu died; his son, Chou, Duke Qing succeeded him.[181]

---

273 BCE *Wuzi* 戊子 Warring States 戰國

King Nan of Zhou	周赧王	42nd year
Duke Qing of Lu	魯頃公	1st year
King Zhaoxiang of Qin	秦昭襄王	34th year
King Qingxiang of Chu	楚頃襄王	26th year
King Xiang of Qi	齊襄王	11th year
King Anxi of Wei	魏安釐王	4th year
King Xi of Hann	韓釐王	23rd year
King Huiwen of Zhao	趙惠文王	26th year
King Hui of Yan	燕惠王	6th year
Sir Huai of Wey	衛懷君	10th year

---

179 Wei General 魏將 Mang Mao 芒卯.
Beizhai 北宅 - east of Yingyangxian 滎陽縣.

180 Wen 溫 - Wenxian Henan 河南 溫縣.

181 Duke Min of Lu 魯湣公 Ji Jia 姬賈.
Duke Qing of Lu 魯頃公 Ji Chou 姬讎 (Ji Chou 姬仇) (r. 272-249 BCE) or (r. 272-249 BCE) or (r. 279-256 BCE).

I. Zhao and Wei made a concerted attack against Huayang of Hann.[182] Hann appealed to Qin for help, but the king of Qin refused to help. The chancellor of Hann spoke to Chen Shi,[183] "The situation is becoming desperate. Sir, even though you are ill, it would be advisable for you to go to Qin to plead for help. The journey will only take you one night to get there." Upon arriving at Qin, Chen Shi made an appointment to have an audience with the Marquis of Rang. The Marquis said, "The situation at the front must be getting critical, little wonder they send you here." Chen Shi answered, "Not really." Marquis Rang was incensed, "Why?" Chen Shi said, "Had the situation become desperate, Hann would have turned to others for help. I am here because the situation has not reached a critical stage yet, hence seeking help from Qin." The Marquis said, "We will send our army." Marquis Rang accompanied by Lord Wuan (Bai Qi) and the foreign consultant *keqing* Wu Yang led a huge army to Hann's rescue.[184] The army marched for eight days and arrived at the battlefield. At Huayang the Qin army defeated the Wei army resoundingly, pursuing the Wei army headed by Mang Mao.[185] Three Wei generals were captured; some one hundred and thirty thousand men were beheaded. Lord Wuan then attacked the Zhao army under the command of Jia Yan, twenty thousand Zhao men were driven into the Huanghe River, [186] where they drowned.

Duanganzi of Wei recommended the king to cede Nanyang to Qin in a bid for peace.[187] Su Dai said to the king of Wei, "What Duanganzi craves is an official seal from you, and the people yearning your land is Qin. Had the people yearning your land assumed control over a person craving for your official seal, and the person who holds a minister's position has control of your land; very soon all your land will be lost. To continue to make concessions for peace with Qin is like dousing a flame by throwing more firewood onto a blazing fire. When the supply of firewood does not run out, the fire will never be put out." Wei Yu answered, "You are right. However the decision has already been made, nothing can change the course." Su Dai sighed, "This is like playing the game of *xiao* – the owl piece is supposed to be the trump when the opportunity arises one uses it to win over an opponent.[188] However, there are times when it is used to cut losses.

---

182 Huayang 華陽 - Weichuanxian Henan 河南 洧川縣.

183 Chancellor of Hann 韓相, his name is unknown.
Chen Shi 陳筮. Very little is known about this individual.

184 Wei Ran 魏冉.
Marquis Wuan 武安候 Bai Qi 白起.
Foreign consultant, *keqing* 客卿 Wu Yang 胡陽.

185 Mang Mao 芒卯 see 290 BCE III. Some other texts relate him as Meng Mao 孟卯. According to *SJ*, there was no mention of Mang Mao '走芒卯' in 290 BCE III, it is suspected that the statement of '走芒卯' in 290 BCE in *ZZTJ* was a duplication. *ZZTJ JZ*, Vol 1, p. 171.

186 Bai Qi 白起.
Zhao 趙 Jia Yan 賈偃.
Huanghe River 黄河.

187 Duanganzi 段干子, also known as Duangan Chong 段干崇, was a Wei General or Minister.
Nanyang 南陽 - Xiuwuxian Henan 河南 修武縣.
Xiuwu 修武 - Huojiaxian Henan 河南 獲嘉縣.
The Nanyangxian in Henan was founded in 272 BCE, one year later.

188 *Xiao* - owl 梟 was a dice gambling game, also known as *liupo* 六博. The chessboard was marked with tracks for movement of the chess pieces; on two ends of the chessboard, six chess pieces were placed. One of them was called *xiao* owl 梟 - the trump piece, the other five were called *san* 散. Before throwing the dices, of which there were six, the stakes were placed; at each throw, additional

Your Highness is handling the situation with wisdom; you might as well use your trump piece of *xiao*. (N.B. See footnotes to appreciate this statement)." The king of Wei refused to listen. He proceeded to cede Nanyang to settle for peace. Nanyang, in fact, was Xiuwu.[189]

II. King Xi of Hann (Hann Jiu) died; his son King Huanhui acceded to the throne.[190]

III. Hann and Wei having submitted to Qin, the king of Qin (Ying Ji) commanded Lord Wuan to lead an army bolstered by the forces of Hann and Wei to attack Chu. Before the army departed, the Chu emissary Huang Jie arrived at Xianyang.[191] When he heard of the intended attack, he reasoned that Qin having had several military successes could continue to give Chu a crushing blow, annihilating it. He wrote a missive to the king, "Your subject has heard things negate themselves when they reach their ultimate extremes; just like summer that is followed by winter. When things are stacked too high, they collapse and tumble, like a stack of chess pieces.[192] Qin is the almighty kingdom under Heaven; from the east to the west, Qin has control of the land. Ever since time immemorial there has yet to be a kingdom of ten thousand chariots whose domain is as vast as Qin. Our Chu kings, for three generations, have not forgotten that our domain borders with Qi. Nevertheless, our kings did not form an alliance with Qi. The alliance of which would have broken the waist of the south-north Coalition of Wei and Hann in opposition to Qin.[193] You Highness, you assigned Sheng Qiao to serve at the Hann court, he recommended to the king of Hann to cede his territories to Qin.[194] You did not even have to start a war or flex your muscles, and you acquired one hundred *li* of land. It is an indication of Your Highness's exceptional capabilities. Later, Your Highness raised your army to attack Wei, setting up a blockade at Daliang the Wei capital, your army occupied the area of within the River *Henei* and entered into the Xing County to annex Yan, Suanji, Xu and Tao.[195] The Wei army was overwhelmed, milling around like

---

stakes might be added and were cumulative. The one side who made six consecutive owls won the game and all the stakes. When one of the sides had three-cumulative owl throws while the other side had none, the latter was the losing side; the losing side had two choices, he could either increase the stakes and continue playing or concede a loss. On conceding, the stakes on the table would go to the side with three owl throws. The game became fashionable during the latter part of Chunqiu 春秋. Yang K., *ZGS* 戰國史, p. 640.

Whether one could get the owl piece was a random probability, i.e. chance or providence. When one chose to relinquish a game to reduce losses is something one could decide rather than by providence. Su Dai was advising the king to cut his losses.

189 Nanyang 南陽 was, in fact, Xiuwu 修武 - Huojiaxian Henan 河南 獲嘉縣.

190 King Xi of Hann 韓釐王 Hann Jiu 韓咎, 3rd (r. 295-273 BCE).
King Huanhui of Hann 韓 桓惠王 4th (r. 272-239 BCE).

191 Chu envoy 楚使者 Lord Chunxin 春申君 Huang Xie 黄歇 (314-238 BCE).

192 Chinese chess pieces are round.

193 Wei 魏 and Hann 韓 were situated in the heartland of Zhongyuan 中原, Qi 齊 was situated to the east, and it shared its southern border with Chu's northeastern border. The western territories of Qi and Chu circumvented the eastern borders of Wei and Hann. If Qi and Chu were to form an alliance, they would post impending threats to Wei and Hann.

194 Sheng Qiao 盛橋.

195 Wei capital, Daliang 大梁 - Kaifengxian Henan 河南 開封縣.
Henei 河内 - Qinyangxian Henan 河南 沁陽縣.
Yan 燕 - Huaxian Henan 河南 滑縣.
Suanji 酸棘 - Yanjinxian Henan 河南 延津縣.
Xu 虚 - Xuyi 虚邑, both Xuyi and Tao 桃 - Taoyi 桃邑 were within the Yanjinxian County in Henan 河南 延津縣.

drifting clouds, not daring to bring relief to their occupied cities. They were great exploits of Your Highness. You then allowed your army to take a respite for two years and launched another assault. Your army occupied Pu, Yan, Shou and Yuan; continuing it pressed on as far as Ren, Pingqiu, Huang, Jiyang, and Yingcheng; [196] and the kingdom of Wei finally capitulated. Your Highness then occupied the area north of the Pu River and the northern part of the Mo County, [197] cutting off the link between Qi and Qin, while severing the passage between Chu and Zhao. The kingdoms under Heaven strived to rekindle the south-north Alliance on five separate occasions; even after six conferences, all was to no avail; they simply did not have the audacity to raise an army to go to the relief. Again, this proves that Your Highness's might is incomparable. If, however, Your Highness could restrain and conserve some of your strength, applying some constraints on your aspiration to occupy more land by force; promote a little benevolence and righteousness in the occupied land, you may be spared from endless trouble forthcoming. It might even earn Your Highness a reputation that excels the Three Legendary Kings *Sanwang* in virtue, crowning you like the Fourth King, and retitling you as the Sixth Hegemon in addition to the Five Hegemons *Wuba*.[198] You have just overwhelmed Wei. Should Your Highness decide to use your powerful and innumerable forces, and effective weapons to unify all under Heaven, making all the kings under Heaven to submit to Qin, your subject is afraid that the problems will be endless in the future. The *Odes* says,[199] "Without a good beginning a satisfactory end is rare." The Book of Changes *Yijing* also says,[200] "When a fox wades across a river it unfailingly gets its tail wet." The meaning of both analogies is abundantly clear; things are easy at the beginning while picking up the broken pieces is extremely difficult. Many years ago, King Wu had great faith in the Yue kingdom, and he sent his army against Qi, he won a resounding victory at the Ailing Mound.[201] However, upon his return from the front, the king of Yue (Gou Jian) defeated and captured him at the bank of the Three Rivers *Sanjiang*.[202] Zhishi (Zhi Yao) trusted the Hann and Wei family

---

Xing 邢 - Xingyi 邢邑 - Wenxian Henan 河南 溫縣.

The text should read, "舉河內, 入邢, 拔燕, 酸棘, 虛, 桃." Instead of "舉河內, 拔燕, 酸棘, 虛, 桃, 入邢." *JJTJ JZ*, Vol 1, pp. 171-172.

196 Pu 蒲, Yan 衍, Shouyuan 首垣, Ren 仁, Pingqiu 平丘, Huang 黄, Jiyang Shandong 濟陽 all were north of Zhengxian Henan 河南 鄭縣北.

Pu 蒲 - Puyi County 蒲邑 and Shouyuan 首垣 - were all in the county of Changyuanxian Hebei 河北 長垣縣.

Pingqiu 平丘 - was to the southeast of Changhuanxian 長垣縣.

Jiyang 濟陽 – northeast of Lanfengxian Henan 河南 蘭豐縣.

Yan 衍 - north of Zhengxian Henan 河南 鄭縣北.

Ren 仁 - the place is unknown.

Huang 黄 - Waihuang 外黄 – 60 km east of Qixian Henan 河南 杞縣.

Yingcheng 嬰城 – place unknown.

197 Pu 濮 - Pushui River 濮水 between present day Yanjin 延津 and Huaxian 滑縣 Henan 河南.

Mo 磨 - Moyi County 磨邑, the place is obscured.

198 *Sanwang wuba* 三王五霸 – The Three Kings and Five Hegemons.

199 The *Shijing, The Odes* 詩經, "靡不有初, 鮮克有終." *Shijing* 詩經, 'Daya 大雅 Dang 蕩'.

200 The *Book of Changes, Yijing* 易經, '狐涉水, 濡其尾.' *Yijing* 易經, 第 64 卦, 'Weijigua 未即卦'.

201 King of Wu 吳王 Fucha 夫差. The kingdom of Yue 越王國.

Ailing Mound 艾陵 - Taianxian Shandong 山東 泰安縣.

202 The King of Yue 越王 Gou Jian 勾踐.

clans, allied with them against Zhao, and invested a siege at Jinyang; when victory was in sight Hann and Wei revolted and executed him at the Zuotai Terrace.[203] Now Your Highness is incensed as Chu has yet to be annihilated. Perhaps you have overlooked one small aspect - had it fallen, Hann and Wei would gain strength. Your Highness, your subject is of the opinion that your strategy is ill-conceived, and he is concerned for you. You have to remember the kingdom of Chu is your friend while Hann and Wei are your archenemies. You might have fallaciously been led to believe that Hann and Wei are unequivocally submitted to your kingdom. It would be the same mistake made by the king of Wu. Your subject is very concerned that Hann and Wei are merely cajoling and flattering you to deflect their pressing danger while scheming secretly against you. Why is this so? Your Highness has not dispensed any compassion or benevolence to their people, whereas, your kingdom has accrued generations of hatred with their people. There are at least ten generations of fathers, sons, and brothers of Hann and Wei that have succumbed to the forces of Qin. Hence, unless Hann and Wei are annihilated they will remain to be the everlasting concerns of the holy shrine of Qin, whereas as of now, you are aiding your enemies, collaborating with them to assault against Chu. Is this not a mistake? Besides, what route will your army take? Will it march through the territories of your archenemies of Hann and Wei to go against Chu? Once your army is inside their realms, you will have a major concern on hand as it might not have a chance to leave at all. On the other hand, if Your Highness decides not to march through Hann and Wei, your army will have to march farther to the west along the right bank of the Suishui River. There are numerous wide rivers, where flooding is frequent, dense forests line the banks, steep with deep gorges and defiles, and the entire area is a forbidding barren land. Your Highness might earn a reputation for bringing Chu to its knees, but actually, you could not possibly gain any new territories. Furthermore, the day your army marches forward, four kingdoms (Hann, Wei, Qi and Chu) will most definitely rally their forces in response. When Qin and Chu are engaged in the conflict, Wei could lay siege to Liu.[204] Fangyu, Zhi, Huling Mound, Dang, Xiao and Xiang, the former territories of Song will all be annexed.[205] Qi could take advantage of the circumstances and make a sudden raid south against Chu near the Sishui River. These are centrally located, rich, and fertile plains, once fallen into the hands of Wei and Qi; they will become the mightiest kingdoms under Heaven. Your subject is worried for Your Highness. Your best proposition is none other than to befriend Chu. If an alliance between Qin and Chu is struck, you can invade Hann; it will incontestably concede defeat and submit to Your Highness. Having control of the precipitous passes of the Dongshan Mountain range, coupled with the advantage of the bend of the Huanghe River, Hann will relegate itself as a fief of Qin within the Pass. If Your Highness dispatches one

---

Three Rivers *Sanjiang* 三江 - Songjiang River 松江, Loujiang River 婁江, Dongjiang River 東江, the three rivers were all situated between Songjianxian Jiangsu 江蘇 松江縣 and Shanghai city 上海市.

203 Zhi Yao 智瑶.

Jinyang 晉陽.

Zuotai Terrace 鑿臺. Details of the incident see 403-II.

204 Liu 留 - Liucheng 留城 - 25 km southeast of Peixian Jiangsu 江蘇 沛縣.

205 Fangyu 方與 - Yutaixian Shandong 山東 魚臺縣.

Zhi 銍 - Zhicheng 銍城 - 20 km south of Suxian Anhui 安徽 宿縣.

Huling Mound 湖陵 - 25 km north of Peixian Jiangsu 江蘇 沛縣.

Dang 碭 - Dangshanxian Jiangsu 江蘇 碭山縣.

Xiao 蕭 - Xiaoyi County 蕭邑 - Xiaoxian Jiangsu 江蘇 蕭縣.

Xiang 相 - 45 km southwest of Suxian 宿縣.

hundred thousand troops to garrison at Zheng, the kingdom of Liang (Wei) will be in great apprehension; [206] confusion ensues; having occupied Xu, Yanling Mound and Yingcheng the passage between Shangcai and Zhaoling Mound will be cut off.[207] At this juncture, Wei will also capitulate to become a marquis of Guannei of Qin.[208] If Your Highness handles the situation suitably by befriending Chu, you can easily make two kingdoms boasting with ten thousand chariots to submit as your fiefdoms. It will then be time to demand land from Qi, and it will bow humbly to accede its western regions. When Your Highness has achieved that, your domain will straddle across two seas.[209] Your Highness will be presiding from up high, making decrees to all under Heaven. By then, Yan and Zhao could no longer secure help from Qi and Chu, nor could Qi and Chu get help from Yan and Zhao. All you have to do, then, is to coerce Yan and Zhao to go against Qi and Chu. The four kingdoms will capitulate without waiting for a painful thrashing."

The king of Qin acceded to the advice. He instructed Lord Wuan to put the operation on hold and expressed gratitude to Hann and Wei for their intention to help. He returned Huang Xie to Chu and signed a new alliance with the kingdom.

---

206 Zheng 鄭 - Xinzheng 新鄭 - Xinzhengxian Henan 河南 新鄭縣.

207 Xu 許 - Xuchangxian Henan 河南 許昌縣.
Yan 鄢 - Yanling Mound 鄢陵 - Yanlingxian Henan 河南 鄢陵縣.
Shangcai 上蔡 - Shangcaixian Henan 河南 上蔡縣.
Zhaoling Mound 召陵 - Yanchengxian Henan 河南 偃城縣.

208 Marquis of Guannei – Inner Pass Marquis 關內侯.

209 "Your domain will range east from the sea, and west to the Western Sea (Qinghaihu 青海湖)."

Volume V. 資治通鑒 卷第五 周紀五 272-256 BCE

The narratives of this volume begin in the 43rd year of King Nan of Zhou (272 BCE) and end in his 59th year (256 BCE).[1]

270 BCE – Wei national Fan Ju suggested to the king of Qin a strategy of making an alliance with distant states while attacking neighbouring states.[2] The king made him a foreign guest - *keqing*.

266 BCE – King Zhaoxiang of Qin deposed of the Queen Dowager, banished Wei Ran, Mi Rong, Ying Kui and Yin Xian at court; [3] Fan Ju was made the chancellor of Qin.

265 BCE – Qin invaded Zhao and annexed three cities. The king of Zhao appealed to Qi for help; the grand tutor, Chu Long convinced the Queen Dowager to send her youngest son to Qi to be held hostage in exchange for military help.[4]

262 BCE – Qin raided Hann, driving a wedge into the middle section of the kingdom, the northern part of Shangdang was separated from the Hann capital. Feng Ting, the magistrate of Shangdang surrendered the prefecture to Zhao.[5]

260 BCE – Lian Po led the Zhao army to take a stand at Changping; he refused to engage the Qin forces in battles and assumed a defensive strategy. King Xiaocheng of Zhao fell for a Qin ruse by replacing Lian Po with Zhao Kuo, a brilliant theoretical military strategist. Qin sent in Bai Qi. The battle was fought at Changping, Zhao Kuo died in a hail of arrows; four hundred thousand Zhao soldiers were led into an ambush and were summarily buried.[6]

258 BCE – Qin advanced against Handan. The king of Zhao sent Lord Pingyuan to appeal to Chu for help. Mao Sui volunteered himself as a member of the entourage; his sharp wit forced the king of Chu to go to the aid of Zhao.[7]

Lord Xinling, Wei Wuji stole Wei king's military tally to go to the aid of Zhao.[8]

257 BCE – The king of Qin forced Bai Qi to commit suicide.[9]

---

1 King Nan of Zhou 周 赧王.

2 Fan Ju 范雎 Wei 魏人.

3 King Zhaoxiang of Qin 秦 昭襄王.
Wei Ran 魏冉, Mi Rong 芈戎, Ying Kui 嬴悝, Ying Xian 嬴顯.

4 Tutor, Chu Long 觸龍.

5 Shangdang 上黨. Feng Ting 馮亭.

6 Lian Po 廉頗.
Changping 長平.
King Xiaocheng of Zhao 趙 孝成王.
Zhao Kuo 趙括.
Bai Qi 白起.

7 Handan 邯鄲.
Lord Pingyuan 平原君.
Mao Sui 毛遂.

8 Lord Xinling 信陵君 Wei Wuji 魏無忌.

Zhao merchant, Lu Buwei, helped Qin Prince Ying Yiren held hostage in Zhao to escape.[10]

256 BCE – King Nan of Zhou secretly revived the south-north alliance, he failed and was captured and died in Luoyang.[11] This year marked the end of the Zhou kingdom.

Volume V. Zhou Records 5 周紀五

---

272 BCE *Jichou* 己丑 Warring States 戰國

King Nan of Zhou	周赧王	43rd year
Duke Qing of Lu	魯頃公	2nd year
King Zhaoxiang of Qin	秦昭襄王	35th year
King Qingxiang of Chu	楚頃襄王	27th year
King Xiang of Qi	齊襄王	12th year
King Anxi of Wei	魏安釐王	5th year
King Huanhui of Hann	韓桓惠王	1st year
King Huiwen of Zhao	趙惠文王	27th year
King Hui of Yan	燕惠王	7th year
Sir Huai of Wey	衛懷君	11th year

I. The king of Chu appointed Huang Xie as deputy minister *zuotu* and as the personal attendant of Crown Prince Mi Wan; they were sent to Qin as hostages.[12]

II. Qin established the Nanyangjun Prefecture.[13]

III. Qin, Wei and Chu attacked Yan.

IV. King Hui of Yan (Ji Le) died; his son King Wucheng succeeded him.[14]

---

9 King Zhaoxiang of Qin 秦 昭襄王.

10 Lu Buwei 呂不韋.
Qin Prince 秦太子 Ying Yiren 嬴異人.

11 King Nan of Zhou 周 赧王.
Luoyang 洛陽.

12 King Qingxiang of Chu 楚 頃襄王.
Vice Minister, *zuotu* 左徒 Huang Xie 黄歇.
Zuotu was an administrative title unique to Chu 楚; some scholars suggest that the position was only subordinate to the chancellor.
The Tan scholar, Zhang Shoujie 唐張守節 (~700 CE) suggested that it was similar to the position of *zuoyou shiwei* 左右拾遺 responsible for reprimanding at court at the time of Tang. *ZZTJ JZ*, Vol 1, p. 174.
Chu Crown Prince 楚太子 Mi Wan 芈完.

13 Nanyangjun Prefecture 南陽郡 - Nanyangxian Henan 河南 南陽縣.

14 King Hui of Yan 燕 惠王 Ji Lezi 姬樂資 5th (r. 278-272 BCE) or (r. 278-271 BCE).

271 BCE *Gengyin* 庚寅 Warring States 戰國

King Nan of Zhou	周赧王	44th year
Duke Qing of Lu	魯頃公	3rd year
King Zhaoxiang of Qin	秦昭襄王	36th year
King Qingxiang of Chu	楚頃襄王	28th year
King Xiang of Qi	齊襄王	13th year
King Anxi of Wei	魏安釐王	6th year
King Huanhui of Hann	韓桓惠王	2nd year
King Huiwen of Zhao	趙惠文王	28th year
King Wucheng of Yan	燕武成王	1st year
Sir Huai of Wey	衛懷君	12th year

I. Lin Xiangru of Zhao attacked Qi; the army penetrated as far as Pingyi County.[15]

II. Zhao She, a functionary at the agriculture branch of Zhao, was responsible for tax collection. Nine attendants in the household of Lord Pingyuan (Zhao Sheng) refused to pay their taxes; Zhao She had the men executed according to law.[16] Lord Pingyuan was in a towering rage and was about to execute Zhao She. The man said, "Sir, you are an elite member of the Zhao royal household. If you allow your attendants to indulge themselves by not abiding by the law of the state, it will break down; when the law of the state is compromised our kingdom will be in decline. When our kingdom weakens the other fief lords will send in their armies, by then Zhao will cease to exist. What will all your wealth and riches be worth then? A man of your high stature and position should abide by our established law; it will bring harmony at the court and among the civilians. With harmony at court, the people and our kingdom will achieve supremacy; subsequently we will see political stability at Zhao. Sir, you are an elite relative of the king; if you abide by the established directives who under Heaven dares to disparage you?" Lord Pingyuan thought that Zhao She was a worthy person; he recommended him to the king. The king commissioned him to make improvements to the tariff system.[17] Due to his efforts, tax collection was conducted effectively; the people became prosperous, and the national coffers became abundant.

270 BCE *Xinmao* 辛卯 Warring States 戰國

King Wucheng of Yan 燕 武成王 6th (r. 271-258 BCE) or (r. 270-258 BCE).

15 Lin Xiangru 藺相如.

Pingyi 平邑 - Nanlexian Hebei 河北 南樂縣.

16 Agriculture Officer, *tianbuli* 田部吏 Zhao She 趙奢.

Lord Pingyuan 平原君 Zhao Sheng 趙勝.

17 The king was King Huiwen of Zhao 趙 惠文王 Zhao He 趙何 2nd.

King Nan of Zhou	周赧王	45th year
Duke Qing of Lu	魯頃公	4th year
King Zhaoxiang of Qin	秦昭襄王	37th year
King Qingxiang of Chu	楚頃襄王	29th year
King Xiang of Qi	齊襄王	14th year
King Anxi of Wei	魏安釐王	7th year
King Huanhui of Hann	韓桓惠王	3rd year
King Huiwen of Zhao	趙惠文王	29th year
King Wucheng of Yan	燕武成王	2nd year
Sir Huai of Wey	衛懷君	13th year

1. Qin attacked Zhao; the army besieged the city of Yuyu. The king of Zhao summoned Lian Po and Yue Cheng for an audience and asked,[18] "Can we save the city?" Both responded, "The passage is remote, and the route is narrow and treacherous. It will be very difficult." The king asked Zhao She, who responded, "The passage is indeed dangerous and perilous, but when two armies face off in a battle like two mice meeting head-on in a narrow passage, the courageous one wins." The king ordered Zhao She to lead an army to bring relief to the city.

Zhao She left with his army; when it was thirty *li* from Handan, he stopped proceeding. He gave order to his men, "If anyone tries to make any military remonstrations he will be executed."

The Qin army arrived at the west of Wuan and began to beat war drums to launch assaults against the city.[19] The commotion created such tumultuous reverberations that the roof tiles of homes rattled in resonance. An army corporal suggested to Zhao She that they should attack and bring relief to Wuan immediately; Zhao She executed the man. He then held fast to his position at his camp for twenty-eight days, not budging one-step; taking the time to construct new ramparts. A Qin spy slipped into the camp; Zhao She

---

18 Yuyu 閼與 – There is a Yuyushan Mountain 閼與山, which is 25km southwest of Wuanxian Henan 河南 武安縣. However, according to *ZZTJ JZ*, the place might have been Yuyuju 閼與聚, Heshuxian Shanxi 山西 和順縣. *ZZTJ JZ*, Vol 1, p. 179.
Lian Po 廉頗.
Yue Cheng 樂乘 was a clan-kin of Yue Yi 樂毅. (Yue Yi - see 231 and 245 BCE.) Yue Cheng was a Yan general 燕將. In 251 BCE Yan attacked Zhao 趙; Zhao general, Lian Po 廉頗 gave the Yan army a resounding defeat, Li Fu 栗服 the chancellor of Yan and Yue Cheng were captured; Yue Cheng surrendered to Zhao. Zhao enfeoffed him as Lord Wuxiang 武襄君. The following year Yue Cheng and Lian Po laid siege to Yan, which responded by presenting rich gifts to sue for peace. Five years later (245 BCE), King Cheng of Zhao 趙成王 died. King Daoxiang of Zhao 趙 悼襄王 replaced Lian Po with Yue Cheng; Liao Po was furious; he attacked Yue Cheng, who abandoned his post; Lian Po could not stay in Zhao any longer he escaped and found refuge at Wei 魏. 16 years later, in 228 BCE, Qin annihilated Zhao. *SJ* 史記, 卷 50, 'Yue Yi liezhuan 樂毅列傳' 第 20, pp. 635-636.

19 Handan 邯鄲 – Handanxian Hebei 河北 邯鄲縣. Handan was the capital of Zhao.
Wuancheng 武安城 - Wuanxian Henan 河南 武安縣.

entertained him by giving him a superb meal. The spy returned to report to the Qin general, who was jubilant on hearing the news, "They marched for thirty *li* from their capital and ceased to proceed, and they are now making defensive ramparts; Yuyu is no longer a part of Zhao."

After sending off the Qin spy, Zhao She immediately ordered his troops to break camp and hastened to march off; [20] within a day and night, they arrived at the front.[21] When the army was some fifty *li* from Yuyu he ordered his men to make camp, and constructed ramparts for defence. Upon hearing news of the move, the Qin army rallied all their forces to advance towards the Zhao position. An army officer, Xu Li, [22] asked to make a comment on the situation; Zhao She agreed to it. Xu Li said, "The army of Qin would never have guessed that the Zhao army could march here so swiftly. However, they are riding high on their arrogance. General, you have to commit all your troops in readiness, or else we will lose the ensuing battle." Zhao She, "Please show me your tactics." Xu Li reminded the general that he would be put to death for violating the command. Zhao She answered, "Wait. The order was issued at Handan." Xu Li then asked permission to present his opinion; he said, "Whichever side secures control of the Beishan Mountain will win the day." [23] Zhao She promptly dispatched ten thousand men to rush to the Baishan Mountain. The Qin army arrived later and attempted to rush to take the mountain but to no avail. Zhao She took advantage of his position and launched a powerful offensive against Qin, giving the Qin forces a devastating blow, and the siege on Yuyu was finally lifted. Zhao She and his men returned.

The king of Zhao enfeoffed Zhao She as Lord Mafu; his ranking and position were comparable with Lian Po and Lin Xiangru; Xu Li was appointed as an army commander.[24]

11. Marquis Rang recommended Zao a foreign guest *keqing* to the king of Qin. The chancellor then commanded him to attack the Qi state; Gengshou was successfully annexed; Wei Ran added the occupied area to his fief in Taoyi County.[25]

---

20 The distance between Handan and Yuyu 閼與 was 60 km as the crow flies.

21 'One day and one night' – According to *SJ* 史記 *Zhao She zhuan* 趙奢傳 it was 'two days and one-night' march. Sima Qian was of the opinion that the distance between Yuyu and where Zhao She garrisoned was about 200 *li* (about 80 km) in distance, and it would take at least 2 days and one night to arrive at the battlefront. Whereas Sima Guang being influenced by the Tang scholars maintained that, the distance was much closer and that one day and one night would be adequate to cover the march. *ZZTJ* reproduced this entire passage from *SJ*; the only deviation was the 'two days' and 'one day'. *ZZTJ JZ*, Vol 1, p. 179.

22 Sergeant, *junshi* 軍士 Xu Li 許歷.

23 Beishan Mountain 北山.

24 Lord Mafu 馬服君 Zhao She 趙奢.
Lian Po 廉頗. Lin Xiangru 藺相如.
Xu Li 許歷 Army Commander, *guowei* 國尉.

25 Qin Chancellor, Wei Ran 魏冉.
Zao 竈 (灶) a Guest Consultant, *keqing* 客卿; his surname is obscured.
Gangshou 剛壽 - Dongpingxian Shandong 山東 東平縣.
Taoyi 陶邑 - Yongjixian Shanxi 山西 永濟縣.

Before this, Fan Ju a Wei man accompanied Xu Jia, a middle-grade Wei minister *zhongdafu*, to Qi as emissaries.[26] King Xiang of Qi heard that Fan Ju was with exceptional eloquence; [27] he privately bestowed gifts of gold, food and wine upon him. Xu Jia was suspicious that Fan Ju might have divulged the state secrets of Wei to the king of Qi. Xu Jia reported his suspicion to Wei Qi the chancellor upon returning to Wei.[28] The chancellor, seething with a terrible rage, ordered to have the man beaten by clubbing. Fan Ju ended up with broken ribs, his teeth cracked and was at his last gasp as he feigned death. The attendants wrapped him up in reed mats and threw him into the latrine; the chancellor then invited his drunken guests to take turns to urinate on the man, setting it as an example for traitors to give away state secrets. Fan Ju said to the man guarding him, "If I could escape from this, I will reward you with great riches." The guard agreed and asked permission to dispose of the corpse wrapped in the mat. Wei Qi, roaring drunk, answered, "Approved." Fan Ju escaped. Later, Wei Qi regretted his decision; he immediately issued a warrant for the arrest of Fan Ju.

Zheng Anping, a Wei commoner, gave shelter to the fugitive Fan Ju, who changed his name to Zhang Lu.[29] Fan Ju took advantage of the cover of night to meet the Qin imperial usher Wang Ji, [30] who chanced to be in Wei as an envoy. Wang Ji had him transferred to Qin in secret and recommended him to the king, and it was arranged that the king of Qin would meet Fan Ju at the provisional palace.

When Fan Ju was walking in the long corridors in the palace, he pretended that he was not aware he was in the palace complex. The eunuchs in the inner palace bellowed at him angrily and shoved him away, "His Highness arrives." Fan Ju responded by uttering something preposterous, "Is there a king in Qin? Qin is ruled by a Dowager and Marquis Rang."[31] As the king entered, he vaguely picked up parts of the conversation and ordered his attendants to leave them in private. Kneeling most humbly, the king said solemnly,[32] "Sir, please enlighten me and instruct me." Fan Ju responded, "Aye! Aye!" The king made the same request three times; Fan Ju repeated himself three times. The king finally asked,

---

Gangshou and Taoyi counties were separated by a distance of 600 km; it does not appear likely that the occupation of Gangshou could expand Wei Ran's fief. Some scholars maintain that the Taoyi was more likely to be Taoqiu 陶丘, present day Dingtaoxian 定陶縣 in Shandong 山東; which was in the Qi 齊 territories. *ZZTJ BY Edition*, Vol 2, p. 343.

26 Fan Ju 范雎 of Wei 魏 (?-255 BCE); alias Fanshu 范叔.
Mid-grade Minister, *zhongdafu* 中大夫 Xu Jia 須賈.

27 King Xiang of Qi 齊襄王 Tian Fazhang 田法章.

28 Wei Chancellor, *xiang* 魏相 Wei Qi 魏齊.

29 Wei commoner 魏人 Zheng Anping 鄭安平.
Fan Ju changed his name to Zhang Lu 張祿.

30 Qin Imperial Usher, *yizhe* 秦謁者 Wang Ji 王稽.

31 Dowager, Xuan *taihou* 宣太后.

32 Kneeling – The word used for kneeling in the text was 跽 *ji*, a kneeling position.
At that time, chairs and desks had not come into use in China, people sat with the thighs touching the shanks – called *jizuo* kneeling-sit 跽坐; and people sat on a mat or a *ta* 榻, a slightly raised platform or couch. To perform the *kowtow* etiquette, the person bowed without raising himself up from the sitting position. *Ji* 跽- was a kneeling position with the upper torso being held straight and with both knees to the ground. To show respect for someone more senior the person took on a *ji* posture, and he raised himself from the sitting position to do obeisance.

"Sir, you do not intend to instruct me." Fan Ju answered, "Dare he do so? Your subject is but a vagrant in exile. He hardly knows you and we have had no acquaintance in the past. He does have some suggestions for Your Highness to make ratification; nevertheless, the issues he intends to raise are concerned with helping Your Highness and they are wedges between the relationship of you and your family members. While your humble subject has the intention to be of service to you, however, he could not determine what you have in mind. That was why he refused to respond to your request three times. While your subject is giving you some advice today, he might be executed tomorrow. Your subject has no intention of dodging death, as every person will face the inevitable one day, however if he could accomplish something for Qin, he would die without the slightest regret. Besides, his greatest concern is if he should die all the wise men under Heaven will shut their mouths and cease to come to Qin." The king resumed his kneeling posture, "Sir, why did you say that? I am profoundly pleased to meet you; it is a blessing from Heaven to send you to help me to preserve our holy shrine. From now on, everything, significant or trivial, from the dowager down to all the ministers at court will take on your instructions; please do not doubt my sincerity." Fan Ju *kowtowed* and thanked the king, who reciprocated. Fan Ju said, "For all the power of the Qin kingdom, for all the valour of your warriors, when it comes to facing the fief lords under Heaven, it is comparable to *Hannlu* the fierce hounding dogs from Hann chasing after puny hobbling rabbits.[33] The gates at Hanguguan Pass have been kept shut for fifteen years.[34] Qin people do not even have the audacity to steal a glimpse of the mountains in the east. The reason is simple, Marquis Rang, being perfidious to Qin is not even slightly committed to the kingdom; and the strategy Your Highness adopted is also flawed." Ying Ji again raised himself from his sitting position to a kneeling posture said, "Please shed light on my mistakes."

Many attendants around were eavesdropping on the conversations; Fan Ju refrained from discussing sensitive matters. He changed the subject to unrelated issues, in the meantime made an assessment of the earnestness of the king. He leaned forward and spoke, "Marquis Rang circumvented Xue and Wei to attack Qi at Gangshou.[35] It was a serious strategic error. When King Min of Qi launched a successful campaign against Chu to its south, [36] killing thousands of Chu troops and generals; it opened up over a thousand

---

33 The text read, '走韓盧而博蹇兔'. Hann Lu or Hannzilu 韓盧 or 韓子獹 was a hunting dog from the state of Hann, with a dark coat. *ZZTJ JZ*, Vol 1, pp. 180-181.
The *ZGC*, 'Qice 齊策 三' relates, "Hannzilu, the fastest hound under Heaven." "韓子盧者, 天下之疾犬也." *ZGC* 戰國策, 'Qice 齊策 三', p. 118.

34 Hanguguan Pass 函谷關 was 15 km north of Lingbaoshi City 靈寶市. The passages from Luoyang 洛陽 to Xian 西安 was made almost impassable by the stretch of precipitous river valleys in this area; in ancient times, it was called Hangu 函谷 - the Valley of Han 函. At the times of Chunqiu 春秋, Duke Xiao of Qin 秦孝公 annexed the area, then called the area Xiaohan 崤函, he went on to establish Hanguguan. The passage was 7.5 km in length from the east to the west; the valley was so narrow that it only allowed one carriage to pass through. Hence, it is said, "... one man can defend against one thousand." Zhou J. 周儉 et al., *Sichou zhilu* 絲綢之路, Jiangsu Renmin chubanshe 江蘇人民出版社, China, 2012, pp. 40-42.

35 Wei Ran 魏冉.
Xue State 薛國 – Tengxian Shandong 山東 滕縣.
Gangshou 剛壽 - Dongpingxian Shandong 山東 東平縣.

36 King Min of Qi 齊 湣王 Tian Di 田地.

li of new territories, but Qi did not gain a single foot or inch of land. Naturally, the intention was to acquire more territories; circumstances, however, would not allow the king to take possession of the land. When the other fief lords realized that Qi was exhausted after the campaign, they rallied and made a joint assault against it; the kingdom was on the verge of annihilation. In the end, the campaign against Chu benefited Wei and Hann instead. Your Highness why not considers befriending the far-off states while making assaults against those nearby. You see, whenever you gain one inch of land your kingdom gets to retain it when you acquire one foot of land, you will also retain it forever. Hann and Wei are in the heartland of *Zhongguo*, at the very hub of all under Heaven.[37] If Your Highness intends to be the hegemon under Heaven, you should consider befriending with *Zhongguo* (Hann and Wei), having had the control of the hub under Heaven you could then apply pressure on Chu and Zhao. When Chu becomes powerful, you give assistance to Zhao; on the other hand, when Zhao becomes powerful then you offer aid to Chu. Upon the capitulation of those two kingdoms Qi will be in a dire and desperate situation; by then the kingdoms of Wei and Hann could be subjugated easily." The king said, "Excellent." He appointed Fan Ju as a guest consultant *keqing* to counsel the kingdom on military affairs.[38]

---

269 BCE *Renchen* 壬辰 Warring States 戰國

King Nan of Zhou	周赧王	46th year
Duke Qing of Lu	魯頃公	5rd year
King Zhaoxiang of Qin	秦昭襄王	38th year
King Qingxiang of Chu	楚頃襄王	30th year
King Xiang of Qi	齊襄王	15th year
King Anxi of Wei	魏安釐王	8th year
King Huanhui of Hann	韓桓惠王	4th year
King Huiwen of Zhao	趙惠文王	30th year
King Wucheng of Yan	燕武成王	3rd year
Sir Huai of Wey	衛懷君	14th year

1. Qin Colonel *zhonggeng* Hu Shang led an army attacked Zhao at Yuyu.[39] However, he lost the ensuing campaign.

---

268 BCE *Guisi* 癸巳 Warring States 戰國

King Nan of Zhou	周赧王	47th year

37 Zhongguo 中國 see notes on Zhongguo and Zhongyuan 中原.

38 Foreign Guest Consultant, *keqing* 客卿 were foreign nationals serving in another fiefdom.

39 Qin Army Colonel, *zhonggeng* 秦 中更 Hu Shang 胡傷.
Yuyu 閼與 - Wuanxian Henan 河南 武安縣.

Duke Qing of Lu	魯頃公	6rd year
King Zhaoxiang of Qin	秦昭襄王	39th year
King Qingxiang of Chu	楚頃襄王	31st year
King Xiang of Qi	齊襄王	16th year
King Anxi of Wei	魏安釐王	9th year
King Huanhui of Hann	韓桓惠王	5th year
King Huiwen of Zhao	趙惠文王	31st year
King Wucheng of Yan	燕武成王	4th year
Sir Wey Huai	衛懷君	15th year

1. The king of Qin adopted the military strategy proposed by Fan Ju and sent Major *wudafu* Guan to attack Wei and annexed Huai.[40]

---

267 BCE *Jiawu* 甲午 Warring States 戰國

King Nan of Zhou	周赧王	48th year
Duke Qing of Lu	魯頃公	7th year
King Zhaoxiang of Qin	秦昭襄王	40th year
King Qingxiang of Chu	楚頃襄王	32nd year
King Xiang of Qi	齊襄王	17th year
King Anxi of Wei	魏安釐王	10th year
King Huanhui of Hann	韓桓惠王	6th year
King Huiwen of Zhao	趙惠文王	32nd year
King Wucheng of Yan	燕武成王	5th year
Sir Huai of Wey	衛懷君	16th year

1. Dao, the crown prince of Qin, held hostage at Wei died.[41]

---

266 BCE *Yiwei* 乙未 Warring States 戰國

King Nan of Zhou	周赧王	49th year
Duke Qing of Lu	魯頃公	8th year
King Zhaoxiang of Qin	秦昭襄王	41st year
King Qingxiang of Chu	楚頃襄王	33rd year
King Xiang of Qi	齊襄王	18th year

---

40 Major, *wudafu* 五大夫 Wan 綰. *Wudafu* the 9th grade of 20 enfeoffment in Qin.
Huai 懷 - Huaiyi County 懷邑 – west of Wuzhixian Henan 河南 武陟縣 西.

41 Qin *taizi* 秦太子 Dao 悼.

King Anxi of Wei	魏安釐王	11th year
King Huanhui of Hann	韓桓惠王	7th year
King Huiwen of Zhao	趙惠文王	33rd year
King Wucheng of Yan	燕武成王	6th year
Sir Huai of Wey	衛懷君	17th year

I. Qin attacked Wei at Gengqiu.[42]

II. Fan Ju gained increasing trust by the king of Qin took an opportunity to suggest, "When your subject was living east of the Mountains *Shandong*, he heard that there was a Lord Mengchang (Tian Wen), [43] but he had never heard that there was a king in the state of Qi. he only heard that there was a Dowager and Marquis Rang in Qin, he was not even aware that there was a Qin king. Only a person holding the power of a state can be addressed as a king, a person who dispenses the welfare of the state is a king and a person who holds the authority to dispense execution is a king. Nevertheless, the dowager ignores Your Highness, issuing commands on behalf of the state; Marquis Rang does not even have the courtesy of reporting the outcomes of his assignments when he returns from his foreign emissary missions. Lords Huayang (Mi Rong) and Jingyang (Ying Kui) are unduly domineering and unrestrained, holding no regard for Your Highness. Lord Gaoling (Ying Xian) comes and goes as he pleases, [44] not even showing the slightest courtesy or respect for Your Highness. There has never been a kingdom that could evade adversity with four privileged elites conferred with such extraordinary power. Under these four powerful elites, one can say there is not a king in Qin. Marquis Rang is employing the power vested in him, summarily uses it to suppress the other fief lords. He is breaking the military tallies on Your Highness's behalf to make wars and military expeditions extensively; [45] none of the fief lords dares to defy him. Upon winning a war, he sent all the spoils to his fiefdom at Tao County.[46] Whenever our armed forces lost a battle, the enmities created were conveniently discharged upon the Qin people, fermenting latent calamities to destroy the holy shrine of Qin. Your subject is told that when a tree bears too many fruits, they cause the branches to sag and break, damaging the trunk. When the capital of a state becomes outsized, it brings destruction to the central government. When the subjects of a state are given too much power and privileges, the king becomes lowly and humble. When Nao Chi acquired control of Qi, he hang the king from a crossbeam of a temple, he shot the king's thigh with an arrow, pulled out his tendons and tortured him

42 Gengqiu 刑丘 - Wenxian Henan 河南 温縣. Xing 刑 was a very ancient polity, and its history could be traced to the time of King Cheng Tang of Shang 商成湯 ~1600 BCE.

43 Shandong 山東 – east of the mountains – Xiaoshan 崤山.
Qi, Lord Mengchang 齊 孟嘗君 Tian Wen 田文.

44 Dowager Xuan 宣太后.
Marquis of Rang 穰侯 Wei Ran 魏冉, Ying Ji's 嬴稷 uncle.
Lord Huayang 華陽君 Mi Rong 芈戎, Ying Ji's uncle.
Lord Jingyang 涇陽君 Ying Kui 嬴悝, Ying Ji's younger brother.
Lord Gaoling 高陵君 Ying Xian 嬴顯, another younger brother of Ying Ji.

45 Breaking the tally or splitting the military tally - 剖符, only the king of a state was allowed to break a military tally to command a general for a military campaign.

46 Taoyi 陶邑 - Yongjixian Shanxi 山西 永濟縣.

for a whole day and night before the king expired.[47] When Li Dui assumed control of Zhao, he held *Zhufu* in captivity at Shaqiu;[48] the king was without food for a hundred days and died of starvation. The way your subject sees it, the four privileged elites at the Qin court are no different from Nao Chi and Li Dui. One recollects the reasons for the demise of the three dynasties (San-Dai - Xia, Shang and Zhou); it was because the kings had endorsed their trusted subjects and ministers with absolute authority while they carried on with their wonton drinking bouts and hunting sprees. The men they entrusted were suspicious and wary of the capable ministers at court. They purged their superiors and oppressed their subordinates; their only concern was to satisfy their personal avaricious greed, never for a moment did they give any concern for the kings. The kings, on the other hand, were completely oblivious to what was happening; it was not surprising they lost their kingdoms. As of now, from the lowest ranking bureaucrats to the most senior ministers at court including your personal attendants they are all members of the chancellor's clique; and Your Highness is completely isolated. Your subject is extremely apprehensive for Your Highness. If Your Highness passes away one day, he is sure the person succeeding to the throne will not be one of your offsprings." The king agreed with his assessment; he immediately decreed to depose the dowager. Marquis Rang, lords Gaoling, Huayang and Jingyang were all banished to return to beyond the Pass. He appointed Fan Ju as the new chancellor, enfeoffing him as Marquis Ying.[49]

III. The king of Wei sent its minister *zhongdafu* Xu Jia to Qin as an emissary.[50] Marquis Ying (Fan Ju) dressed in his worn and tattered clothes went on foot to greet him. Xu Jia was astounded that Fan Ju was still alive; he said, "Fanshu, how have you been since we parted?"[51] He then invited Fan Ju to stay for a meal and drinks; he presented him with a silk cloak. Fan Ju volunteered to be the emissary's coach driver to head for the Qin chancellor's manor; Fan Ju said to Xu Jia, "Sir, I will go ahead to announce your arrival to the chancellor." Xu Jia found it strange that he was kept waiting for a long time. He asked the attendant, the man answered, "There is no such person called Fanshu here. The person who came in with you is our chancellor; his name is Master Zhang." Xu Jia realized that he was caught up in a deception; lowering himself on his knees, he inched forward towards the approaching Qin chancellor.

Marquis Ying seated as he berated Xu Jia severely, "The only reason you are still alive is that you presented me with the silk cloak, it shows you have not forgotten our past acquaintance entirely." He then ordered his retainers to prepare an elaborate banquet; the nobles and honoured guests were invited; Xu Jia was seated at the lower vestibule. A platter of horse fodder mixed with ground grass and black beans was placed in front of

---

47 Chu general 楚將 Nao Chi 淖齒.
King of Qi 齊王 Tain Di 田地. See 284-II.

48 Li Dui 李兑. Zhao Yong 趙雍.
The Shaqiu incident 沙丘 - Pingxiangxian Hebei 河北 平鄉縣, see 295-III.

49 Dowager, *taihou* 太后.
Wei Ran 魏冉. Mi Rong 芈戎. Ying Kui 嬴悝.Ying Xian 嬴顯.
Chancellor, *chengxiang*, Marquis Ying 丞相 應侯 Fan Ju 范雎.

50 Mid-grade minister, *zhongdafu* 中大夫 Xu Jia 須賈.

51 Fanshu 范叔, a respectful way of addressing an elder or senior.

him, and he was forced to consume the concoction. Fan Ju gave strict instructions to Xu Jia to communicate to the Wei king, "Chop off the head of Wei Qi as soon as possible and send it here; if your king refuses I will cause the capital of Daliang to be awash with blood."[52] Xu Jia duly reported what he was told when he returned to Qi. Wei Qi escaped to Zhao, seeking refuge in Lord Pingyuan's (Zhao Sheng) manor.[53]

IV. King Huiwen of Zhao (Zhao He) died; his son Zhao Dan acceded to the throne, he was known posthumously as King Xiaocheng.[54] Lord Pingyang was made the chancellor.

---

265 BCE *Bingshen* 丙申 Warring States 戰國

King Nan of Zhou	周赧王	50th year
Duke Qing of Lu	魯頃公	9th year
King Zhaoxiang of Qin	秦昭襄王	42nd year
King Qingxiang of Chu	楚頃襄王	34th year
King Xiang of Qi	齊襄王	19th year
King Anxi of Wei	魏安釐王	12th year
King Huanhui of Hann	韓桓惠王	8th year
King Xiaocheng of Zhao	趙孝成王	1st year
King Wucheng of Yan	燕武成王	7th year
Sir Wey Huai	衛懷君	18th year

I. Dowager Xuan of Qin (Mi *Bazi*) died.[55] In the 9th month, Marquis Rang was relieved of all his duties at the Qin court, and he moved to his fiefdom at the Tao County.[56]

Sima Guang annotates:

Marquis Rang was instrumental in helping King Zhao to ascend to the throne; he removed all the hidden hazards and disasters for the king. He recommended Bai Qi to head the Qin army, which annexed Yan and Ying to the south;[57] to the east, the general expanded the Qin territories into the realms of Qi. Marquis Rang brought all the fief lords under Heaven to bow and submit to Qin. Qin became formidable and powerful; it was all due to the indefatigable efforts of the marquis. While he was flawed for being tyrannical, and being depraved and greedy; these faults could easily bring him great misfortune; nonetheless, he was not as heinous as Fan Ju had suggested. As for Fan Ju, he was far from being loyal to the Qin court; neither was he

---

52 Daliang 大梁 - Kaifengxian Henan 河南 開封縣.

53 Chancellor of Wei 魏相 Wei Qi 魏齊.
Wei Qi abandoned his position and escaped to Zhao.
Zhao, Lord Pingyuan 趙平原君 Zhao Sheng 趙勝.

54 King Huiwen of Zhao 趙惠文王 Zhao He 趙何.
King Xiaocheng 孝成王 Zhao Dan 趙丹 (r. 265-245 BCE).

dispensing judicious policies for the benefits of the state. He was after the position held by the marquis, and he went for his throat as soon as a chance arose. Hence, he ruined the king's affectionate relationship with his mother; he upset the genial and caring bond between the uncle and the nephew. Taken as a whole, Fan Ju was a perfidious individual who could bring on the calamitous disaster to a kingdom.

II. The king of Qin nominated his son Lord Anguo (Ying Zhu) as his lawful successor.[58]

III. Qin attacked Zhao and annexed three cities. The king of Zhao (Zhao Dan) having just succeeded to the throne the court power was completely vested in the Queen Dowager, who decided to appeal to Qi for help.[59] The king of Qi responded, "Send Lord Changan to our kingdom as a hostage in exchange for our help."[60] The queen dowager refused, and the Qi army did not march forward. The ministers at the Zhao court remonstrated with the dowager. She said to her attendants, "If anyone dares to raise the issue of sending Lord Changan as a hostage again, this old lady will spit in his face." The left tutor *zhushi* Chu Long volunteered to see the queen dowager.[61] Still fuming with rage the old lady waited as the tutor lumbered his way into the audience hall. The tutor sat down very slowly and said most apologetically, "Your subject has difficulties with these legs. He has not seen Your Highness for a while, and your subject is most apologetic for not attending to Your Highness. He is told you are poorly. Hence, he is here to see you." The Dowager answered, "I have to ride in a palanquin wherever I go."[62] Chu Long asked, "How is your appetite?" The Dowager answered, "I can only eat congee." The dowager's raging anger subsided somewhat. The left tutor said, "Among your subject's useless sons, there is a Shu Qi, [63] he is my youngest, and he is most inadequate and worthless. Nonetheless, he is my favourite. The reason for your subject seeking an audience with Your Highness is to ask a personal favour. He is hoping that you might grant his son a position as a palace attendant, [64] taking on a post, donning a black cloak, to protect the royal palace. He risks death to ask for this favour." The Queen Dowager answered, "Granted. How old is he?" Chu Long said, "Fifteen. He is still very young; your subject hopes he can be assigned to Your Highness before he is discarded in a ditch." The Dowager asked, "Do men also have a soft spot and special affections for your youngest son?" Chu Long answered, "Much more so than women." The Dowager laughed, "No, women dote on their youngest son more." The tutor responded, "According to your subject's observation, you overwhelmingly love your youngest daughter, the queen of Yan, more than Lord Changan." The

---

55 Dowager, Xuan *taihou* 宣太后 Mi *Bazi* 芈八子.

56 Wei Ran 魏冉; Taoyi County 陶邑 - Yongjixian Shanxi 山西 永濟縣.

57 Bai Qi 白起.
Yan 鄢 - Yancheng 鄢城 – Yichengxian Hubei 湖北 宜城縣. See 279-I.
Ying 郢 - Yingdu 郢都 - Jianglingxian Hubei 湖北 江陵縣. See 278-I.

58 The Crown Prince of Qin, *Taizi*, Marquis of Anguo 太子 安國侯 Ying Zhu 嬴柱.

59 The king of Zhao 趙王 Zhao Dan 趙丹.

60 Lord Changan 長安君 was the younger brother of Zhao Dan, the youngest son of King Huiwen of Zhao 趙惠文王.

61 Senior Tutor, *zuoshi* 左師 Chu Long 觸龍.

62 *Nian* 輦, the palanquin referred here is a *nian* 輦." As the pictograph of the word suggests, it is a carriage hauled by two men. 說文, "輦輓車也."

63 Shu Qi 舒祺.

64 Imperial Attendant, *heiyi weishi* 黑衣衛士.

Dowager answered, "Sir. Your observation is wrong; I love Lord Changan most." The Left Tutor retorted, "Your subject does not think so; when parents love their offspring they make provisions for their future. When your daughter was betrothed to the kingdom of Yan, you wept bitterly hugging tightly onto her legs not letting go. Upon her departure, you pined for her, and yet you make sacrifices, praying, 'Pray, do not allow her to return.'[65] From the distance you are constantly offering prayers that her offspring will remain as kings of Yan forever; is it not making long-term plans for her?" The queen dowager said, "You are right." The tutor asked, "Commencing from the present generation, counting backwards by three, who among the Zhao princes' offspring are still around as marquises?" The queen dowager answered, "None." Chu Long said, "A person is affected by a calamity that occurs close at hand; nevertheless it is more likely to bring on lasting consequences upon his descendants. That is not to say the sons and descendants of kings are useless and that all the dukes and nobles enfeoffed are inept and incompetent; rather it means when they are placed in their prestigious positions with rich provision-fiefs and benefits they should make certain contributions to the state. Apparently, you love Lord Changan dearly; you enfeoffed him with the richest land in the kingdom, besides bestowing on him the most valuable jewellery and treasures; yet you are depriving him of a chance to serve our kingdom. Your subject wants to know, in case Your Highness passes on one day how will Lord Changan sustain in our kingdom?" The Queen Dowager answered, "Yes. You are right. Sir, please post him as you consider appropriate."[66]

Lord Changan, heading a huge entourage of attendants with over one hundred carriages, set off to Qi as hostage. Qi responded by sending its army to the aid of Zhao. Qin army retreated.

IV. Lord Anping of Qi (Tian Dan) allied with the forces of Zhao to attack Yan; the army annexed Zhongyang.[67] It then attacked Hann, taking down Zhuren.[68]

V. King Xiang of Qi (Tian Fazhang) died; his son Tian Jian succeeded to the throne; the king was still very young, the Queen Dowager presided at court as regent.[69]

---

264 BCE *Dingyou* 丁酉 Warring States 戰國

King Nan of Zhou	周赧王	51st year
Duke Qing of Lu	魯頃公	10th year
King Zhaoxiang of Qin	秦昭襄王	43rd year
King Qingxiang of Chu	楚頃襄王	35th year

---

65 Women married to the other kingdoms would be returned to their home state if the marriage did not work out.

66 The incident appears in *ZGC* 'Dowager Zhao' 戰國策 '趙太后新用事'. *ZGC* 戰國策, 'Zhaoce 趙策' pp. 239-241.

67 Qi, Lord Anping 齊 安平君 Tian Dan 田單.
Zhongyang 中陽 - Tangxian Hebei 河北 唐縣. It was a Yan county 燕邑.

68 Zhuren 注人 – northwest of Linruxian Henan 河南 臨汝縣 西北.

69 King Xiang of Qi 齊襄王 Tian Fazhang 田法章.
The king of Qi 齊王 Tian Jian 田建 (r. 264-221 BCE). Tian Jian was the last king of Qi; hence, he did not have a posthumous title.

Qi Tian Jian	齊田建	1st year
King Anxi of Wei	魏安釐王	13th year
King Huanhui of Hann	韓桓惠王	9th year
King Xiaocheng of Zhao	趙孝成王	2nd year
King Wucheng of Yan	燕武成王	8th year
Sir Huai of Wey	衛懷君	19th year

I. Lord Wuan of Qin (Bai Qi) attacked Hann; his army annexed nine cities and beheaded fifty thousand men.[70]

II. Tian Dan was appointed as chancellor of Zhao.[71]

---

263 BCE *Wuxu* 戊戌 Warring States 戰國

King Nan of Zhou	周赧王	52nd year
Duke Qing of Lu	魯頃公	11th year
King Zhaoxiang of Qin	秦昭襄王	44th year
King Xiaolie of Chu	楚孝烈王	1st year
Qi Tian Jian	齊田建	2nd year
King Anxi of Wei	魏安釐王	14th year
King Huanhui of Hann	韓桓惠王	10th year
King Xiaocheng of Zhao	趙孝成王	3rd year
King Wucheng of Yan	燕武成王	9th year
Sir Huai of Wey	衛懷君	20th year

I. Lord Wuan of Qin (Bai Qi) attacked Hann and captured Nanyang; the army marched as far as the foothills of the Taihangshan Mountains, where they constructed defensive barricades to impede the mountain passes.[72]

II. King Qingxiang of Chu (Mi Heng) became seriously ill.[73] Huang Xie suggested to Marquis Ying,[74] "The king of Chu is ailing fast; some say he will not recover. It would be a good idea to repatriate the Chu crown prince (Mi Wan);[75] if he succeeds to the throne, he will serve Qin well, complying with your demands, feeling grateful to you for releasing him. It is no different from befriending a state with ten thousand chariots. Being detained here, he is merely a commoner in

70 Lord Wuan of Qin 秦 武安君 Bai Qi 白起.

71 Tian Dan 田單.

72 Nanyang 南陽 – Xiuwuxian Henan 河南 修武縣.
Taihangshan Mountains 太行山 is the mountain range that separates Shanxi 山西 and Hebei 河北.

73 King Qingxiang of Chu 楚 頃襄王 Mi Heng 芈横.

74 Huang Xie 黄歇 was the tutor of the Chu Crown Prince held as hostages at Qin. Fan Ju 范雎.

75 Chu Crown Prince 楚太子 Mi Wan 芈完 was sent to Qin as a hostage in 272 BCE, see 272-I.

cotton garb in Xianyang.[76] Besides, Chu might have a change of heart in making another prince the new king, and you stand to lose the friendship of a nation with ten thousand chariots. It is not a good proposition." Marquis Ying related the suggestion to the king (Ying Ji); [77] the king responded, "Perhaps we should first despatch the prince's tutor to return to Chu bearing our good intentions to the sick king before we release the prince."

Huang Xie conspired with the prince, "Qin is keeping Your Highness here as a hostage for political gains; nevertheless, you with your limited influence have not done anything beneficial to Qin. Now, the two sons of Lord Yangwen are in Chu; [78] if the king passes away unexpectedly, with you being away from the state, the throne is likely to be passed to a son of Lord Yangwen. Your Highness will be deprived of the right to make sacrifices to your ancestors. You might as well take flight with our Chu envoy to return to our kingdom. Your subject will remain behind; his worst fate is they might kill him." The crown prince changed into carriage-driver clothes, took on the position as the envoy's carriage driver, stealthily heading towards the Pass to return to Chu. Huang Xie remained behind taking care of the manor for the crown prince; claiming that the prince had taken ill and was indisposed to meet visiting guests. When he was certain that the prince had travelled for a safe distance, Huang Xie reported to the Qin king, "The crown prince of Chu has returned to Chu. Please grant your subject the gift of death." The king was fuming with anger and was about to comply with his wish. Marquis Ying said, "Huang Xie is a subject of the Chu state; he makes sacrifices for the master he serves. If the crown prince successfully succeeds to the throne, he will nominate Huang Xie as his chancellor. Allow him to leave; a friendly relationship with Chu is ensured." The king agreed to it.

Huang Xie returned to Chu. Three months later, in autumn, King Qingxiang of Chu (Mi Heng) died. King Xiaolie (Mi Wan) succeeded to the throne. He made Huang Xie his chancellor, enfeoffed him with territories north of the Huaihe River as his fief, bestowing upon him with the title of Lord Chunshen.[79]

---

262 BCE *Jihai* 己亥 Warring States 戰國

King Nan of Zhou	周赧王	53rd year
Duke Qing of Lu	魯頃公	12th year
King Zhaoxiang of Qin	秦昭襄王	45th year
King Xiaolie of Chu	楚孝烈王	2nd year
Qi Tian Jian	齊田建	3rd year
King Anxi of Wei	魏安釐王	15th year
King Huanhui of Hann	韓桓惠王	11th year

76 Xianyang 咸陽 – Xi'an city Shaanxi 陝西 西安市.

77 King Zhaoxiang of Qin 秦 昭襄王 Ying Ji 嬴稷.

78 Chu, Lord Yangwen 楚 陽文君, was a son of King Huai of Chu 楚懷王, Mi Wan's uncle.

79 Mi Heng 芈横.
King Xiaolie of Chu 楚 孝烈王 Mi Wan 芈完 (r. 264-238 BCE).
Huaihe River 淮河.
Lord Chunshen of Chu 楚 春申君 Huang Xie 黄歇.

King Xiaocheng of Zhao	趙孝成王	4th year
King Wucheng of Yan	燕武成王	10th year
Sir Huai of Wey	衛懷君	21st year

I. Chu ceded the Zhou County to Qin, [80] pledging a peaceful accord.

II. Lord Wuan of Qin (Bai Qi) made an expedition against Hann and annexed the County of Yewang. The passage to Shangdang was severed (from the rest of the kingdom).[81] Feng Ting, the prefecture magistrate of Shangdang, held a session with the civilians of the prefecture.[82] He reasoned, "The passage to our capital of Zheng has been cut; the Qin army is approaching fast, our Hann government is in no position to come to our aid. It might be a better option for us to surrender to Zhao if they agree to our plight. As the military activities of Qin escalate, Zhao might also be under attack by Qin; it will leave them with no choice but to form an alliance with Hann. When Hann and Zhao are in an alliance, we stand a chance of fending off the invasion of Qin." The magistrate sent his emissary to Zhao. The emissary said to the king, "Hann cannot protect its Shangdang Prefecture. We had intended to surrender it to the encroaching Qin army; however, our officers and people would rather be Zhao's subjects than to be under the yoke of Qin. We are here to present to you, Your Highness, the seventeen walled cities and counties in the prefecture." The king of Zhao sought the opinion of Bao, Lord Pingyang, [83] who said, "A sage is troubled when a trophy is won without any justification. It is likely to be a calamity." The king said, "The civilians at Shangdang are pleased with our worth, why is it unjustified?" Zhao Bao answered, "Qin is like silkworm masticating mulberry leaves, they invaded Hann, and the land is severed into halves, and the two parts could no longer communicate with each other. Qin assumed they could wait it out for Shangdang to surrender, reckoning that the prefecture will fall with this move. As to why the people of Hann do not wish to surrender to Qin - it is a premeditated attempt on their part to shift the disasters onto us. The Qin army is fighting with great exertion, and we are sitting here enjoying the windfalls, augmenting our land without the slightest effort. My concern is - even a formidable state has difficulties arrogating land from the feeble states, and how could we, an enfeebled state, appropriate land from the powerful Qin? We could not possibly ward off the onslaught of the Qin army. It is a flawed notion to accept the capitulation as a justified cause. I think we should refuse the offer." Zhao Dan then sought the opinion of Lord Pingyuan (Zhao Sheng), who said that they should accept the capitulation.

The king of Zhao dispatched Lord Pingyuan to accept the capitulation. He brought with him a decree to enfeoff the magistrate of Shangdang with three fiefs of ten thousand households each, naming him Lord Huayang; [84] while the county prefects were enfeoffed as marquises each with

---

80 Zhouyi County 州邑 - Zhoulingcheng Jianlixian Hubei 湖北 監利縣 州陵城.

81 Qin, Lord Wuan 秦 武安君 Bai Qi 白起.

Communication between the capital of Hann, Xinzheng 新鄭 and Shangdangjun 上黨郡 the northern part of the kingdom was completely blocked as the area was cut in two by the Qin army.

Yewang 野王 - Qinyangxian Henan 河南 沁陽縣.

The capital of Hann - Xinzheng 新鄭 - Xinzhengxian Henan 河南 新鄭縣.

Shangdang 上黨 - Changzixian Shanxi 山西 長子縣.

82 The Prefecture Magistrate of Shangdang, *Shangdang shou* 上黨守 Feng Ting 馮亭.

83 Zhao, Lord Pingyang 趙 平陽君 Zhao Bao 趙豹.

84 Zhao Sheng 趙勝.

three one-thousand household fiefs. All the senior ministers and commoners at Shangdang were augmented by three grades. Feng Ting was inconsolably saddened, in tears he refused to meet the envoy from Zhao, saying, "How could I possibly accept the gift of land I had just capitulated on behalf of my king to be conferred upon myself?"

---

261 BCE *Gengzi* 庚子 Warring States 戰國

King Nan of Zhou	周赧王	54th year
Duke Qing of Lu	魯頃公	13th year
King Zhaoxiang of Qin	秦昭襄王	46th year
King Xiaolie of Chu	楚孝烈王	3rd year
Qi Tian Jian	齊田建	4th year
King Anxi of Wei	魏安釐王	16th year
King Huanhui of Hann	韓桓惠王	12th year
King Xiaocheng of Zhao	趙孝成王	5th year
King Wucheng of Yan	燕武成王	11th year
Sir Wey Huai	衛懷君	22nd year

There was no record this year.

---

260 BCE *Xinchou* 辛丑 Warring States 戰國

King Nan of Zhou	周赧王	55th year
Duke Qing of Lu	魯頃公	14th year
King Zhaoxiang of Qin	秦昭襄王	47th year
King Xiaolie of Chu	楚孝烈王	4th year
Qi Tian Jian	齊田建	5th year
King Anxi of Wei	魏安釐王	17th year
King Huanhui of Hann	韓桓惠王	13th year
King Xiaocheng of Zhao	趙孝成王	6th year
King Wucheng of Yan	燕武成王	12th year
Sir Huai of Wey	衛懷君	23rd year

1. Qin army major *zuoshuzhang* Wang He captured the city of Shangdang.[85] The people escaped to Zhao. Lian Po, the army commander of Zhao, led an army to garrison at Changping, where he took in all the refugees, settling them.[86]

Lord Huayang 華陽君.

85 Qin, army major, *zuoshuzhang* 左庶長 Wang He 王齕. *Zuoshuzhang* was the 18th grade of the 20 Qin enfeoffment.

Wang He turned to attack Zhao. The latter could not hold onto their positions and lose repeatedly; an assistant commander and four army superintendents were killed.

The king of Zhao (Zhao Dan) held a session with Lou Chang and Yu Qing to deliberate how to respond to the threat.[87] Lou Chang suggested that they should send a senior envoy to seek a peaceful settlement. Yu Qing said, "The prerogative of peace or warfare is in the hands of Qin. It is clear by now that Qin is resolved in wiping out all our armed forces; hence, even if we were to send someone of importance to negotiate a peaceful settlement it would be futile. We might as well send our envoy to Chu and Qi, presenting them with rich gifts to come to our aid. If they are agreeable to come to our aid Qin might suspect that we have revived the south-north Alliance; perhaps we still hold a chance for a peaceful settlement."

The king of Zhao refused to listen; he dispatched Zheng Zhu to travel to Qin.[88] Qin bid him welcome. The king of Zhao said to Yu Qing, "You see! The Qin King has accepted him." Yu Qing responded, "Your Highness, a peaceful settlement is now out of the question; our armies will sustain even more severe assaults and attacks. Why? The emissaries from the various kingdoms under Heaven have already arrived at Qin offering congratulations to Qin for its impending victory against us. Zheng Zhu is an eminent and renowned individual among the various states; it is not surprising the king of Qin and Marquis Ying are treating him with great reverence to show the people all under Heaven. When the people under Heaven realize that Your Highness has sought peace with Qin, no one will contemplate raising an army to our aid. When Qin knows that no one under Heaven will come to Your Highness's aid, peace is an improbability."

Just as Yu Qing had predicted, Qin treated Zheng Zhu with great honour. However, it refused to negotiate peace with Zhao. At the front, Qin repeatedly defeated Zhao. Lian Po held his ground in his fortified ramparts refusing to engage the Qin in battle. The king of Zhao was troubled by the commander's many losses and berated him in anger for his cowardice for not engaging the enemy in battle. Marquis Ying used one thousand units of gold to bribe the Zhao people to spread rumours,

---

Shangdang 上黨 - Changzixian Shanxi 山西 長子縣.

86 Commander of Zhao 趙將, Lian Po 廉頗.

Changping 長平 – 10 km west of Gaopingxian Shanxi 山西 高平縣.

87 King Xiaocheng of Zhao 趙 孝成王 Zhao Dan 趙丹.

Zhao ministers: Lou Chang 樓昌 and Yu Qing 虞卿.

Yu Qing 虞卿 was a celebrated roaming canvasser, a Handan 邯鄲 local. He was an expert at making strategic assessment. In 260 BCE, before the great battle of Changping 長平, he had suggested the best way forward was to ally with Chu 楚 and Wei 魏, which would force Qin to settle for a peace treaty. After lifting the siege of Handan, he admonished Zhao Hao 趙郝 and Lou Huan 樓緩 for grovelling before Qin 秦, insisting that Zhao should form an alliance with Qi 齊 and Wei to go against Qin. Later he relinquished his senior position at Zhao to help the chancellor of Wei, Wei Qi 魏齊 (259-IV) and was stranded at Liang 梁, where he composed the *Yushi zhengzhuan* 虞氏征傳 and the *Yushi chunqiu* 虞氏春秋 in 15 volumes. *SJ* 史記, 卷 46, 'Pingyuanjun, Yu Qing liezhuan 平原君虞卿列傳' 第 16, pp. 566-569.

88 Zheng Zhu 鄭朱 wasa senior minister at the Zhao court.

"The army of Qin is only intimidated by Zhao Kuo, the son of Lord Mafu (Zhao She).[89] If he were appointed the commander, the Qin army would disperse. Lian Po is easy to handle, and he will soon surrender." The king of Zhao immediately issued a decree to replace Lian Po by Zhao Kuo. Lin Xiangru warned the king, "Your Highness appoints Zhao Kuo as he has acquired a titular reputation for himself; nonetheless, it is like using glue to fix a broken drum or affixing the strings of a musical instrument (sita). Grant it, the man has read a lot of military texts left by his father on the arts of making war, but he lacks tangible experience in the face of crisis." The king refused to listen.

Before this, when Zhao Kuo was younger, he studied military strategies under his father; he believed he was invincible in all under Heaven. He debated with his father on military deployments and tactics at length; his father could not come up with counter strategies; nonetheless, he did not subscribe to his son's thesis. The mother asked him why, Zhao She said, "War is concerned with killing, which is a serious and sombre matter; whereas my son speaks of it most apathetically. If my son was to be the commander of the Zhao army he would bring the entire Zhao army into extinction." When Zhao Kuo was about to depart to command the Zhao army, his mother presented a memorial to the king stating that Zhao Kuo was in no position to command an army. The king saw her and asked, "How do you know?" The mother answered, "When your humble subject married his father, he was serving as a commanding general. Your subject used to serve food to the senior officers when they met for military discussions. There was more than a score of those seniors; including friends and associates, there were perhaps almost one hundred men. When the former king and the royal families bestowed rich gifts upon my husband, they were distributed among the officers and advisers. When he received a command to go into battle, he immersed himself completely in preparations for war, not ever caring for the well-being of his family members. Now, your subject's son is made a commanding general; he behaves contrarily. He is seated up high, facing east; the officers and attendants dare not even look up to him. All the gold and silk embroideries Your Highness bestowed upon him are kept at home. He makes surveys of where he could seize more prized estates and properties for sale and buys them. Your Highness maintains that he is like his father, but he is not. Your Highness, please do not make him take command of the army." The king answered, "Enough said, I have made up my mind." The mother then pleaded, "Your Highness, if something untoward should go dreadfully wrong, please spare this humble woman and our family members, and please do not allow them to be implicated in his failings." The king agreed.

When the king of Qin heard news of the appointment of Zhao Kuo he appointed Lord Wuan (Bai Qi) as the commanding general in secret; Wang He was relegated to the position as assistant commander.[90] He then decreed that whoever disclosed that Lord Wuan had taken command would be promptly executed. Zhao Kuo arrived at the front; he immediately countermanded the orders issued previously, replacing the officers and assistants appointed by Lian Po. He commanded his men to advance against the Qin position. Lord Wuan enjoined his men to feign defeat and retreated while secretly he ordered two detachments of forces to sally out from both flanks to the rear of their enemy. Zhao Kuo misguidedly perceived that his enemy was retreating and losing ground ordered his men to make a charge; his army penetrated as far as the Qin defence barricades, where the Qin army put up a staunch resistance. By this time, the twenty-five thousand Qin men who had

89 Lord Mafu 馬服君 Zhao She 趙奢.
Zhao Kuo 趙括 was the son of Zhao She.

90 Commanding General, *shangjiang*, Lord Wuan 上將 武安君 Bai Qi 白起.
Assistant Commander, *bijiang* 裨將 Wang He 王齕.

stealthily marched out earlier were approaching at the rear of the Zhao forces. Meanwhile, another five thousand crack cavalrymen were also deployed cutting off the retreating route of the Zhao army to return to the Zhao camp. The Qin forces had by now cut off the Zhao attacking forces and the detachments that remained to defend the camp-battlements. The Zhao supply and reinforcement route was severed. Zhao Kuo continued to dispatch small units of lightly armed soldiers to charge out of his detachment to assault the Qin army, however with little success. Left with no other choice the general ordered his troops to construct makeshift barricades and battlements, settling down to defend their position and to wait for reinforcements.

When the king of Qin heard that the food supply route of the Zhao army had been cut off; he hastened to within the River *Henei*, where he decreed to conscript men fifteen years or older to march to Changping.[91] All the roads leading to the area were cordoned off to ensure that reinforcements, food supplies from Zhao could not slip through. In the meantime, the armies of Qi and Chu were also marching off to the rescue of Zhao. Zhao ran out of food supplies and appealed to Qi for help, pleading for the supply of grains. The king of Qi refused to help.[92] Zhouzi warned,[93] "Zhao is an innate barrier of Qi and Chu; we are closely connected. It is similar to the relationship between one's lips and teeth; when the lips are cut off, one's teeth feels the chill. If Zhao is annihilated now, tomorrow it will be Qi and Chu. To save Zhao is as critical as carrying leaking bowls to douse out a flaming cooking-cauldron. Besides, if we could take down the Qin army and save the Zhao forces, it would bring the highest glory and the title of righteousness to our kingdom. Now, we are even parsimonious with food aids. Is is an inappropriate strategy for our kingdom." The king refused to listen.[94]

9th month. By this stage, the Zhao forces were without food for forty-six days; the men within the besieged barricades resorted to killing others for food in secret. The Qin army applied pressure on the besiegement. Zhao Kuo deployed his crack troops, divided into four units to sally out from the camp. The men fought desperately, making four or five repeated charges at the enemy lines, but failed to break out. In the end, Zhao Kuo led his crack forces and attempted to break out from the encirclement. The Qin army responded by raining arrows at the charging troops; Zhao Kuo died.

Zhao army lost all their resolve to continue fighting; four hundred thousand troops surrendered to Qin.

Lord Wuan said, "Our army had previously occupied Shangdang, and yet the people there are irrepressible and had rather surrender to Zhao. The Zhao warriors are known for their capriciousness. I am afraid they might cause chaos; it is a better arrangement to execute all of them." He deceived the Zhao men and had them buried alive. Two hundred and forty young men were spared and were allowed to return to Zhao. During the series of major battles, the Qin army

---

91 King Zhaoxiang of Qin 秦 昭襄王 Ying Ji 嬴稷.
Henei 河内 - Qinyangxian Henan 河南 沁陽縣.
Changping 長平 - Gaopingxian Shanxi 山西 高平縣.

92 Qi, Tian Jian 齊田建. It seems like a contradiction. On the one hand, Qi was marching off to the rescue and on the other; it refused to help Zhao with food supplies.

93 Zhouzi 周子 was a senior minister at the Qi court.

94 Du Mu 杜牧 (803-852 CE), the Tang poet, remarked, "Qin was not the kingdom that annihilated the six states." "滅六國者, 非秦也."

decapitated some four hundred and fifty thousand Zhao men in total; everyone in Zhao was traumatized by what had transpired.[95]

---

259 BCE *Renyin* 壬寅 Warring States 戰國

King Nan of Zhou	周赧王	56th year
Duke Qing of Lu	魯頃公	15th year
King Zhaoxiang of Qin	秦昭襄王	48th year
King Xiaolie of Chu	楚孝烈王	5th year
Qi Tian Jian	齊田建	6th year
King Anxi of Wei	魏安釐王	18th year
King Huanhui of Hann	韓桓惠王	14th year
King Xiaocheng of Zhao	趙孝成王	7th year
King Wucheng of Yan	燕武成王	13th year
Sir Wey Huai	衛懷君	24th year

---

95 The Battle of Changping 長平之役 was one of the goriest battles during the Warring States period or perhaps in the entire Chinese history. However, to bury such a large number of people alive would certainly not have been an easy undertaking. Many scholars have raised doubts about the four hundred thousand men that were killed in a single wholesale slaughter; nevertheless, the number of people killed appears to be quite probable. It was chronicled that Zhao warriors were capricious, and the Qin soldiers contrived a trick to have the Zhao warriors buried. Only two hundred and forty weak and enfeebled soldiers were returned to Zhao. Some scholars have suggested that the defeated warriors might have been driven off a precipice, a more likely method of mass genocide. Whether it was four hundred thousand or even forty thousand, it would have been a huge number at any rate. Qin adopted this tactic of genocide as a psychological warfare against the other Warring States, and it was proven to be most effective as the other kingdoms simply lost their will to continue fighting. The entire campaign at Changping lasted for three years; it exerted tremendous economic strains on both Zhao and Qin. Yang K., *ZGS*, pp. 412-416. *SJ* 史記, 卷 43 'Bai Qi, Wang Jian liezhuan 白起王翦列傳' 第 13, pp. 533-534. *ZGC* 戰國策 'Qince 秦策', p. 63.

There is a temple called Kuloumiao 骷髏廟, 2.5 km west of Gaoping City Shanxi 山西 高平市; it was constructed at the time of Tang Dynasty. Emperor Xuanzong of Tang 唐玄宗 Li Longji 李隆基 (r. 712-756 CE) paid a visit to the site in 723 CE and saw the entire valley was littered with skeletal remains. He decreed that a temple was to be constructed to pacify the spirits and souls that died there. According to the *Gaopingxian zhi* Gazette 高平縣誌, "Zhao Kuo 趙括 pursued the retreating Qin forces to as far as Qinbi 秦壁, which is the present-day Shengyuangu Valley 省冤谷. The valley is completely surrounded by high mountains on all sides, there is only one passage, wide enough for carriages and horses to enter the basin; the terrain is similar to a sack. The Zhao forces marched in. However, the tide was against them; hence, they constructed ramparts to make defences. Later, Zhao Kuo attempted to break out of the siege; the Qin army shot him with a hail of arrows. The four hundred thousand Zhao soldiers surrendered to Lord Wuan 武安君, who lured them into the valley and had them buried." The local people called the place Shagu 殺谷 – Killing Valley. After the construction of the temple, the mountain to the south of the village was renamed Toulushan Mountain (Skull Mountain) 頭顱山, and Shagu was renamed Shangyuangu 省冤谷, (translated as 'Reflection on Grievances' Valley).

http://baike.baidu.com/view/1855599.htm, 2015, Baidu.

I. 10th month. Lord Wuan divided his army into three parts, one under the command of Wang He attacked Wuan and Pilao of Zhao, which were annexed. The second unit was headed by Sima Geng to march north to pacify Taiyuan; the entire district of Shangdang was annexed.[96]

Hann and Wei sent Su Dai bearing with him rich gifts to arrange an audience with Marquis Ying.[97] He asked the chancellor, "Is Lord Wuan going to lay siege to Handan?" Marquis Ying answered, "Yes." Su Dai said, "As soon as Zhao falls, Qin will be the mightiest King of all under Heaven; Lord Wuan will be raised to the position as one of the Three Excellences *Sangong*.[98] Sir, can you bear the thought of being his subordinate? On the other hand, even if you wished to be his subordinate he might not even agree to it. The Qin army has already attacked Hann, laid siege to Gengqiu and surrounded Shangdang; [99] the people at Shangdang nevertheless would rather be under the rule of Zhao. Furthermore, the hostile sentiments of people under Heaven against Qin's regime have been brewing for long; once Zhao is annihilated, the civilians from the north will find their way into Yan. The people in the East will escape to Qi and the civilians in the south will escape to Hann and Wei; there might not be many men for Your Highness to gain in expanding Qin's military might. It is perhaps a better plan to cede more territories from Zhao, rather than allowing Lord Wuan to steal all of the splendours and honours?" Marquis Ying suggested to the king of Qin, "Our armed men are exhausted. Please accede to Hann and Zhao's plead of ceding territories to settle for peace. It will allow our troops to take a respite." The king agreed to the suggestion. Hann ceded the area in Yuanyong while Zhao surrendered six walled-cities to settle for a peaceful accord.[100]
1st month. The Qin army was ordered to return to the capital. Ever since then, a deep rift developed between Lord Wuan and Marquis Ying.[101]

---

96 Wang He 王齕.
Wuan 武安 - Wuanxian Henan 河南 武安縣.
Pilao 皮牢 – 30 km east of Yichengxian Shanxi, now called Laozhaicun 山西 翼城縣 牢寨村.
Sima Geng 司馬梗.
Taiyuan 太原 – Taiyuanxian Shanxi 山西 太原縣.
Shangdang 上黨 - Southeast of Changzixian Shanxi 山西 長子縣 東南部.
Handan 邯鄲 - Handanxian Hebei 河北 邯鄲縣.

97 King Huanhui of Hann 韓 桓惠王.
King Xiaocheng of Zhao 趙 孝成王.
Su Dai 蘇代.
Qin, Chancellor, Marquis Ying 秦相 應侯 Fan Ju 范睢.

98 Three Excellences = *sangong* 三公. Those were the most senior positions at court, positioned between the king and the chancellor, at times one of the three excellences would assume responsibility as chancellor. During Western Zhou 西周 the Three Excellences were the *taishi* 太師 (Grand Tutor), *taifu* 太傅 (Grand Instructor), and *taibao* 太保 (Grand Marshal); at the time of Han Dynasty, they were known as *dasima* 大司馬 (Grand Marshal), *dasitu* 大司徒 (Chancellor), and *dasikong* 大司空 (Imperial Counsellor). Note - the titles changed over time during the Han dynasty. Yang K., 楊寬, *Xizhoushi* 西周史, Shanghai Renmin chubanshe 上海人民出版社, 2003 China, p. 316-317.

99 Gengqiu 邢丘 - Wenxian Henan 河南 溫縣.

100 Yuanyong 垣雍 – 3 km northwest of Yuanwuxian Henan 河南 原武縣.

101 Bai Qi was not too pleased with the decree, as he saw his chance of annihilating Zhao dashed.

II. The king of Zhao appointed Zhao Hao to take on the responsibility of ceding the six counties to Qin.[102] Yu Qing asked the king of Zhao,[103] "Are the Qin forces tired and exhausted hence they retreated or do you think they are still capable of advancing whereas they chose to retreat to show affection towards Your Highness?" Zhao Dan answered, "The Qin forces have tried their utmost, and naturally it is because they are exhausted." Yu Qing said, "Just as you said, the Qin army retreated as they do not have the resources to conquer us; but now Your Highness, you are making a concession to Qin by offering land they do not have the strength to conquer - this is giving aid to our enemies. Come next year, when they launch another assault against Your Highness, we will be in destitute." Zhao Dan was dithering with uncertainty. At this time, Lou Huan arrived at Zhao.[104] The king of Zhao sought his opinion. Lou Huan said, "Yu Qing makes a superficial assessment of the present circumstances, he fails to see the broader perspectives and implications of the issues at stake. While Qin and Zhao are engaged in continuing warfare, the other kingdoms under Heaven are delighted. Why? They are saying, 'We will take advantage of the powerful Qin to further weaken Zhao.' Your best choice is to cede more land to Qin to settle for peace; on the one hand, it will pacify Qin while on the other hand it will make the other fief lords suspicious that Zhao and Qin might have reached an understanding between them. Otherwise, the fief lords might take advantage of the wrath of Qin and the weakened state of Zhao to partition Zhao. When Zhao is annihilated, what is the use of scheming strategies against Qin?"

When Yu Qing heard of the exchange, he made an appointment to see the king again and said, "The plan proposed by Louzi (Lou Huan) is extremely forbidding. It will make people under Heaven even more suspicious. How could the proposed concession placate the insatiable greed of Qin? Your subject wonders why he did not even mention it would only expose Zhao's cowardice to all under Heaven. Besides, when your subject suggested that we should not cede land to Qin, he did not mean that we should not cede at all. Qin demanded the ceding of six cities from Your Highness, whereas Your Highness should present them to Qi as an enticement. You see Qin and Qi are archenemies, harbouring a spiteful hatred against each other. I don't think Qi would wait until the departure of your envoy to raise an army to come to your assistance. While Your Highness might lose six cities to Qi, you will receive some compensation from Qin, besides you will be able to demonstrate to all under Heaven that you are capable of handling this crisis effectively. Your subject advice is that you should make a proclamation of your intention to all the other kingdoms. I am sure even before Qi takes possession of the six cities, the emissaries from Qin will be bringing rich gifts to negotiate a peace accord at your court. Consequently, Hann and Wei will assess Zhao with a different light. It is one move that will earn you the friendship with three kingdoms, forming an alliance in opposition to the path of Qin." The king of Zhao said, "Excellent." He dispatched Yu Qing to travel to Qi, and with the Qi king, he mapped out a strategy against Qin. Even before Yu Qing had time to return to Zhao, emissaries from Qin arrived at Zhao. Lou Huan heard news of the change of events, slipped out of Zhao quietly and escaped. The king of Zhao enfeoffed Yu Qing with a walled-city for his efforts.

III. Previously when Qin was launching assaults against Zhao, the king of Wei (Wei Yu) asked his ministers their opinions on the state of affairs.[105] Almost all of them maintained that Wei stood to

---

102 Zhao Hao 趙郝.

103 Yu Qing 虞卿, also see 260-I and 259-IV.

104 Lou Huan 樓緩 Louzi 樓子, see 310-I.

105 King Anli of Wei 魏 安釐王 Wei Yu 魏圉.

gain. Kong Bin asked,[106] "Why?" The ministers replied, "If Qin overwhelms Zhao we could submit to Qin; if Qin loses the battle we could take advantage of its exhausted state by launching an attack against it." Zishun (Kong Bin) said, "It is an erroneous notion. Qin has not lost a major campaign since the reign of Duke Xiao (Ying Quliang), [107] and now they have in their rank mighty generals. How could we take advantage of their exhausted state?" The ministers argued, "Even had they won the war against Zhao what do we stand to lose? The humiliation of defeat by our neighbour is our blessing." Zishun said, "Qin is wantonly voracious, and their lust for power is insatiable. If they were victorious against Zhao, they would continue with their expansion. I regret to say the next kingdom to face their army could well be Wei. Our ancestors told us a fable, 'A flock of swallows was nesting under the roof of a house. The mother swallow was most caring, she fed her chicks; when she became old, her offspring reciprocated. The flock was happy and jovial, feeling quite secure at their roosting place. Unexpectedly, the kitchen of the mansion caught fire, and the house was about to be burnt to the ground. The swallows, being black, was not affected by the smoke and they were still quite comfortable in the face of the impending disaster, sadly not even realizing that a great calamity was about to fall upon them.' Now you, sirs, you do not hold the slightest concern that no sooner than Zhao meets its demise, we will be next. I do not understand why some people are as shallow as the swallows."

Zishun was the sixth generation grandson of Kongzi (Confucius). Before this, the king of Wei heard that Zishun was a wise and worthy man; he sent his envoy bearing great gifts of gold and embroideries to invite the scholar to take on the position as chancellor. Zishun said, "If His Highness accepts and adopts my suggestions they could best be used for virtuous governance of a state; even if His Highness were to ask me to drink cold water and consume modest vegetarian food I would be more than willing to comply. If it is because I have a modest reputation that His Highness is bestowing rich gifts and high emoluments for my employment, I have to stress, I am merely an ordinary civilian. Please convey to the king that his court is not lacking with one man short." The emissary insistently beseeched him; Zishun finally yielded and travelled forth to Wei. The king of Wei personally went to the outskirts of the capital city to greet the scholar and appointed him as the chancellor of Wei. Zishun dismissed the minions who won their positions through nepotism or favouritism, replacing them with capable and worthy officers. He directed the funds saved from the superfluous officers disposed to reward the meritorious. The disposed officers were distraught and began to spread spiteful rumours. Wen Zi cautioned Zishun, who responded,[108] "It is difficult to reason with commoners to make reforms, and it has always been that way. Hence, whenever a judicious officer of yesteryear tried to make reforms he invariably met with defamation and resistance in the beginning. When Zichan (Gongsun Qiao) was appointed the chancellor of Zheng, [109] he worked assiduously for three years before the people ceased to criticize him. When my ancestor

---

106 Kong Bin 孔斌 alias Zishun 子順.

107 Duke Xiao of Qin 秦孝公 Ying Quliang 嬴渠梁 25th (r. 363-338 BCE).
It was almost eighty years ago.

108 Wen Zi 文咨 was a minister at the Wei court 魏.

109 Chancellor of Zheng 鄭國相 Gongsun Qiao 公孫橋 Ji Qiao 姬橋 Zichan 子產 (?-522 BCE) was a politician, philosopher and reformist towards the closing era of Spring and Autumn 春秋. During his tenure as the Chancellor of Zheng, he made reforms to Zheng and was highly popular with the commoners. Historians have considered him an archetype of a virtuous and proficient chancellor. *SJ* 史記, 卷 112, 'Zheng shijia 鄭世家' 第 13, p. 1625-1626.

(Kongzi) was the chancellor of Lu, [110] it was a good three months before the people ended their slanders against him. I am trying to make reforms now while I am nowhere as worthy as the sages before me. Nevertheless, the slandering directed against me is the least of my concern." Wen Zi said, "What were the defamations made against your ancestor? Why?" Zishun said, "When my ancestor was the chancellor of Lu, the people chanted, 'The officers in their deerskin cloaks and leather kneepads are deposed; they are recalcitrant, but they committed no offence. The officers wearing their leather kneepads and donning their deer cloaks are ousted, and for no reason.' Three months later, the reform bore fruits, and people were chanting, 'The person wearing a big hat dressed in his leather jacket is the very person who satisfies our needs, he is a fair and an unbiased individual that meet our needs.'" Wen Zi said jubilantly, "I now realize that you are no different from a sage."

Zishun was the chancellor of Wei for nine months; none of his many ambitious suggestions was adopted. He sighed in frustration, "The suggestions I proposed have not been adopted, there must be something seriously flawed with my ideas. They apparently do not meet the expectations of the king, while I am taking pleasure in enjoying rich emolument, relishing a living without accomplishing anything; living like a zombie devouring food in front of him for doing nothing.[111] I am guilty of my idleness." He resigned from his post, making an excuse that he had taken ill. Someone asked him, "The king has lost his trust in you, where do you intend to go, sir?" Zishun answered, "Where can I go? Qin will soon annex the kingdoms east of the Mountains, Qin is iniquitous; [112] I will never head in that direction." He returned home and led a life of leisure. Xinyuan Gu visited Kong Bin and sought his opinion,[113] "When a sage officer presides at court, he undertakes to promote civility and edification; Sir, when you were the chancellor of Wei, I am told that you did not accomplish anything distinctive. Now that you have served notice to the court, were you unsuccessful? Why are you departing so hastily?" Zishun responded, "It was exactly that. Indeed, I did not make any distinctive contributions. Besides the situation is like a person who is affected by a terminal disease, when no outstanding physician can cure him. Qin is determined to conquer all under Heaven. In this state of affairs, a nation could find no security or peace with benevolence and righteousness administration. One is too busy trying to save a state from extinction, what are the use of glibly talks of civility and edification? In days of old, Yi Nie was serving at the Xia court; while Lu Wang (Jiangzi Ya) was serving at the Shang court, [114] despite these sages the dynasties finally fell

---

110 Kongzi 孔子 as the Chancellor of Lu 鲁相.

111 The phase used in the text is '*shili sucan* 尸利素餐', also written as '尸位素餐'. *Shi* 尸 - the original meaning of the word *shi* meant a living person, usually the eldest son or a senior subject at the court of a deceased fief lord. The person took on the task of consuming food offerings made to the deceased; he would be dressed in funeral garbs consuming the sacrificial food on behalf of the dead. From Yap J., unpublished translation of the *Passage of Mountains and Seas* 山海經.

112 East of the Mountains – *Shandong* 山東 – east of Xiaoshan 崤山.

113 Xinyuan Gu 新垣固 – the identity of this person is obscured.

114 Xia dynasty 夏, Yi Nie 伊摯 was Yi Yin 伊尹, a minister at the Xia court. King Tijia of Shang 商太甲 (~1500 BCE), the 4th king of the Shang dynasty, appointed Yi Yin as chancellor.
Lu Wang 吕望 Jiangzi Ya 姜子牙 (?–1025 BCE), was serving at the Shang court 商 at one stage, later King Wen of Zhou 周文王 (r. ? -1046 BCE) made him the tutor. He was also known as Jiang Taigong 姜太公, Jiangzi Ya 姜子牙, Jianggong Wang 姜公望, Lu Wang 吕望, Shangfu 尚父, Shi Shangfu 師尚父 and was the founding father of Jiang Qi 姜齊, the Qi state 齊 during the time of Western Zhou 西周, Spring and Autumn 春秋 and the early Warring States 戰國. The Tian family clan 田齊 usurped the throne of the Jiang clan in 386 BCE. *SJ*, 卷 102, 'Qi Taigong shijia 齊太公世家', 第 2, pp. 1408-1409 and 1418-1419.

and met their end. Did the two sages not attempt to save the kingdoms? Of course, they did; the circumstances and situations prevented them from doing so. The kingdoms east of the Mountains have reached their final impasse, and they are listless. The San-Jin states (Hann, Zhao and Wei) are perennially ceding land to purchase fleeting moments of transitory peace. The partitioned Zhou states are already completely annexed by Qin; while the kingdoms of Yan, Qi and Chu have already capitulated. I can safely predict that within a matter of twenty years, Qin will have complete control of the entire realms under Heaven."

IV. The king of Qin (Ying Ji) was resolved to help Marquis Ying to revenge against his former foes.[115] The news came that Wei Qi, the former Wei Chancellor, was in hiding at Lord Pingyuan's manor, [116] the king invited the Lord for a state visit to Qin through deceit. When he arrived, he was promptly held captive. A missive was sent via an envoy to the king of Zhao (Zhao Dan) demanding, "Unless you send us the head of Wei Qi, Your Highness's brother will never have a chance of leaving the Pass alive."[117] Wei Qi was in a panic; he left and sought shelter under Yu Qing, who relinquished his chancellor seal. Together with Wei Qi the two men escaped to Wei, hoping to seek help from Lord Xinling (Wei Wuji) before escaping to Chu.[118] Lord Xinling refused to give an audience to Wei Qi, lest he placed his kingdom in jeopardy. Wei Qi was angry; out of desperation, he committed suicide. The king of Zhao ordered his head decapitated and presented it to Qin, which finally released Lord Pingyuan.

V. 9th month. Wang Ling, Qin army colonel *wudafu* led an army against Zhao; Lord Wuan came down with an illness and could not accompany the expedition.[119]

---

258 BCE *Guimao* 癸卯 Warring States 戰國

King Nan of Zhou	周赧王	57th year
Duke Qing of Lu	魯頃公	16th year
King Zhaoxiang of Qin	秦昭襄王	49th year
King Xiaolie of Chu	楚孝烈王	6th year
Qi Tian Jian	齊田建	7th year
King Anxi of Wei	魏安釐王	19th year
King Huanhui of Hann	韓桓惠王	15th year

115 King Zhaoxiang of Qin 秦 昭襄王 Ying Ji 嬴稷.
Marquis Ying 應侯 Fan Ju 范雎.

116 Wei Chancellor 魏相 Wei Qi 魏齊.
Zhao, Lord Pingyuan 平原君 Zhao Sheng 趙勝.

117 Pass - Hanguguan Pass 函谷關.

118 Chancellor, Yu Qing 虞卿. Yu Qing was held up at the city of Liang 梁 (Wei 魏), this was where he composed his works, the *Yushi annuals* 虞氏春秋.
Wei Wuji 魏無忌.

119 Qin Army Colonel, *wudafu* 五大夫 Wang Ling 王陵. *Wudafu* was the 5th grade of 20 of Qin enfeoffment.
Bai Qi 白起.

King Xiaocheng of Zhao	趙孝成王	8th year
King Wucheng of Yan	燕武成王	14th year
Sir Huai of Wey	衛懷君	25th year

I. 1st month. Wang Ling attacked Handan, but he failed in the attempt. The Qin government sent a large contingent of reinforcements to Wang Ling's aid. However, it did not improve the situation; Ling lost five army majors *xiao* in battle.[120] At this stage, Lord Wuan (Bai Qi) had recovered from his ailment. The king (Ying Ji) ordered him to take charge to replace Wang Ling. Lord Wuan excused himself, "Handan is strongly fortified and it cannot be taken easily, besides all the reinforcements from other fief lords will be arriving soon. They have been holding bitter hatred against Qin for long; while we had won a victory at Changping; however, in the process we also lost more than half of our men, and our coffers were almost drained empty. To attack the capital of another kingdom in a far-flung land, separated by rivers and mountains is never an easy undertaking. When Zhao attacks our forces within their kingdom, and the reinforcements from other kingdoms attack our forces at the perimeter; our army will lose the ensuing battle." The king realized that he could not coerce the general to move, he ordered Marquis Ying to try to convince him. Lord Wuan excused himself by claiming his old ailment was affecting him again and refused to go forth. With no other alternatives, the king sent Wang He to replace Wang Ling.[121]

II. The king of Zhao dispatched Lord Pingyuan to appeal to Chu for help.[122] Lord Pingyuan had intended to choose twenty of his most reliable martially skilled and literate guests to accompany him; however, he merely came up with nineteen, failing to find a suitable twentieth. A guest by the name of Mao Sui volunteered, requesting to accompany the entourage.[123] Lord Pingyuan said, "A virtuous and worthy person is like a sharp and pointed iron drill; as soon as one places it in his tool pouch its sharp end protrudes and pierces through. Sir, you have been in my manor for three years, no one has even made a mention of your name, besides I do not know you. It goes to prove that your capability is wanting. Sir, you are incapable of going forth. Please stay." Mao Sui responded, "Your subject waited until today before he requests to place this drill in your tool bag. Had you done so earlier, it would have dropped out of the bag long ago; not merely exposing the pointed tip." Lord Pingyuan reluctantly agreed to let him accompany the entourage. The nineteen men were eyeing each other, sniggering with contempt.

Having arrived at Chu, [124] Lord Pingyuan held a meeting with the king of Chu (Mi Wan) to discuss the significances of forming an Alliance. It lasted from sunrise until noon, but a decision could not be reached. Mao Sui held onto his sword and moved swiftly up the stairs to the raised podium where Lord Pingyuan and the king were seated. He said to Lord Pingyuan, "The issue could be decided on the two simple words of 'gain' and 'loss', the revival of the Alliance is beyond critical, and it can be resolved easily. The discussion has lasted since sunrise, and a decision is still pending

---

120 *Xiao* 校 – was a contingent of eight hundred men. It also meant major.

121 Wang He 王齕; Wang Ling 王陵.

122 The king of Zhao 趙王 Zhao Dan 趙丹.
Lord Pingyuan 平原君 Zhao Sheng 趙勝.

123 Mao Sui 毛遂.

124 The capital of Chu 楚, Chenqiu 陳丘 - Huaiyangxian Henan 湖南 淮陽縣, the capital of Chu had since been moved to Chenqiu 陳丘.
King Xiaolie of Chu 楚 孝烈王 Mi Wan 芈完.

by noon. Why is this so?" The king of Chu was in a terrible rage; he bellowed, "Return to your seat! I am having a conversation with your master. Who are you? There is no place for you here." Mao Sui tightened his grip on his sword, moving towards the king, facing him squarely and said, "Your Highness shouts at me, all because you believe you possess a myriad number of troops at Chu. However, within these ten paces your numerous warriors are useless to you. Your Highness, your life is in my hands. You shouted at me in front of my master, what is your intent? King Tang of Shang controlled a measly seventy *li* of land at one stage, and yet he became the Son of Heaven while King Wen of Zhou had no more than one hundred *li* of land and all the fief lords submitted to him.[125] Did they submit to them because of their numerous military forces? No, rather they took advantage of the situation and circumstances and exploited them to the full. Now, Chu has five thousand *li* of land with over one million men bearing halberds; the very assets that could make you hegemon and Chu is so powerful that no other kingdom under Heaven is comparable. Bai Qi is a nonentity; he led several tens of thousands of men to launch attacks against Chu, captured your Yan and Ying counties; and he razed your forebears' holy shrines and mausoleums at Yiling to the ground.[126] The three battles brought excruciating humiliation to your ancestors.[127] The shame and mortification of Chu will endure for a hundred generations to come, even the people at Zhao are affected by the disgrace your kingdom underwent, and yet Your Highness does not seem to care at all. The proposal of an Alliance is for the benefit of Chu, rather than for Zhao. My Lord is here, why did you yell at me in front of him?" The king of Chu apologized, "Aye! Aye! Thank you for your enlightenment, sir. I pledge my holy shrine to follow Zhao in its lead." Mao Sui asked, "Is it affirmed?" The king of Chu answered, "Yes, it is." Mao Sui said to the attendants of the Chu king, "Bring us the blood of a chicken, a dog and a horse for swearing a blood oath."[128] Mao Sui carrying the blood in a bronze basin, very respectfully he kneeled in front of the king of Chu proffering the bowl to the king, and said, "Your Highness, please *shaxue* (performed by wiping a small quantity of blood on one's lips to represent drinking of blood) to express earnestness in your pledge to form the Alliance. It will be followed by his Lordship and then your subject." At the imperial hall, the ceremony of the Alliance was solemnly pledged. Mao Sui clasping onto the bowl with his left hand and with his right hand he beckoned the nineteen guests to come forth, "You sirs, should also participate in this ceremony of blood oath at the lower atrium. You, Sirs, follow our Lord hither and thither, but you are merely good at attaining your means through others."[129] Having accomplished his mission of forming the Alliance, Lord Pingyuan returned to Zhao. He said to his guests, "From now on, I do not think I could make an appraisal of the intellectuals from their appearance." He honoured Mao Sui as his most esteemed guest, seating him above all others in his manor.

---

125 King Tang of Shang 商湯 Zi Taiyi 子太乙 the first king of Shang.
King Wen of Zhou 文王 Ji Chang 姬昌 was a pre-dynastic king of Zhou.

126 Bai Qi 白起, Lord Wuan 武安君.
Yan 鄢 - Yancheng 鄢城 - Yichengxian Hubei 湖北 宜城縣.
Ying 郢 - Yingdu 郢都 - Jianglingxian Hubei 湖北 江陵縣.
Yiling 夷陵 - Yichangxian Hubei 湖北 宜昌縣.

127 Bai Qi destroyed the holy shrines of Chu in 278 and 279 BCE see 279-1 and 278-1.

128 Blood from animals for swearing an oath of an alliance. *Shaxue* 歃血 - was a ceremonial gesture by wiping a small amount of blood on one's lip to represent drinking blood to swear a bloody oath.

129 The statement is, 'Attaining your means through others' – '因人成事'.

The king of Chu responded by sending Lord Chunshen (Huang Xie) to lead an army to give aid to Zhao.[130]

III. The king of Wei also sent General Jin Bi to take command of one hundred thousand men to march to the aid of Zhao.[131] The king of Qin sent an emissary to warn the king of Wei, "It is only a matter of days before I crush Zhao, and whosoever dares to go to its aid will be the next on my list, as soon as I take down Zhao." The king of Wei was greatly shaken; he sent an envoy to order Jin Bi to cease proceeding. The commander ordered his men to pitch camp near Ye; [132] ostensibly giving aid to Zhao, but in reality the army assumed a wait and see approach. The king of Wei then sent General Xin Yuanyan to enter into Handan in secret.[133] Through Lord Pingyuan the general proposed to the king of Zhao that the kingdoms of Zhao and Wei should submit to Qin, honouring the king of Qin as a *Di* – the sovereign for all the kings under Heaven - an attempt to make Qin withdraw. Lu Zhonglian, the Qi man, [134] was staying at Handan at this time. He heard of what was proposed and paid a visit to Xin Yuanyan. He said, "Qin is a brutal state that banishes virtues and righteousness; they promote war by rewarding their soldiers who decapitate their enemies. Should the king of Qin avowedly declare himself as *Di*, I would rather end my own life by jumping into the Eastern Sea than submitting to him as his subject. Besides the king of Liang is not fully aware of the disastrous consequences should the Qin king become the *Di*. I can assure you that I could make the king of Qin chop king of Liang (Wei) into mincemeat and stewed him as bisque." Xin Yuanyan was most annoyed and incensed, "Sir. How can you make the king of Qin chop the king of Liang into mincemeat?" Lu Zhonglian answered, "Of course I can. I am about to tell you why. In ancient times, when Marquis Jiu, Marquis E and King Wen were the Three Excellences presiding at the court of King Zhou of Shang; [135] Marquis Jiu had a beautiful daughter, and he betrothed her to King Zhou. Nevertheless, the king found her repugnant; he chopped the marquis into mincemeat. Marquis E tried desperately to defend Marquis Jiu; the king pickled him as cured meat. When King Wen heard of what had happened, he let off a sigh, and for that, he was incarcerated at the Youli granary for a hundred days, [136] attempting to starve him to death by the confinement. Qin is a kingdom of ten thousand chariots while Liang (Wei) also has ten thousand chariots; the forces and power of both kingdoms are comparable, each with its own king. Having witnessed Qin winning a great battle, you people are completely traumatized and scared out of your wits, intending to make the king of Qin a monarch *Di*, relegating yourselves to the lowly status of being chopped to mincemeat or pickled meat. If the king of Qin were allowed to become the *Di*, he would indubitably establish new legal parameters, dispensing new decrees to all under Heaven. He would irrefutably proceed to replace all the ministers in the various kingdoms, supplanting the ones he found displeasing, replacing them

130 General Huang Xie 黄歇.

131 King Anxi of Wei 魏 安釐王 Wei Yu 魏圉.
Wei commander, *dajiang*, 魏大將 Jin Bi 晋鄙.

132 Yecheng 鄴城 - Linzhangxian Henan 河南 臨漳縣.

133 General Xin Yuanyan 新垣衍.

134 Qi 齊人, Lu Zhonglian 魯仲連.
Zhao Sheng 趙勝.
The king of Qin was to be honoured as a *Di* 帝 - a Son-of-Heaven, or Monarch.

135 Marquis of Jiu 九侯; Marquis of E 鄂侯; King Wen of Zhou 周文王 Ji Chang 姬昌 (Pre-dynastic king of Zhou).
King Zhou of Shang, Zi Shouxin 商紂王 子受辛, the last King of the Shang dynasty (r. ~1075-1046 BCE).

136 Youli 羑里 - Tangyinxian Henan 河南 湯陰縣.

with his so-called 'sagacious' ministers. He would depose of the ones he disliked, replacing with his favourites. He might even give his malicious daughters and concubines from Qin as the queens and concubines of the fief lords. With all these women residing at the Liang (Wei) Palace, how could the king of Liang be restful and at ease? Moreover, you general, what makes you think the king of Qin will trust you and make you a favourite at his court?" Xin Yuanyan rose from where he was seated; he thanked Lu Zhonglian profoundly for three times, "Sir, now I realize that you are an intellect under Heaven. I will return to my kingdom and never raising the subject of honouring the king of Qin as a *Di* again."

IV. King Wucheng of Yan died; his son King Xiao succeeded to the throne.[137]

V. Previous to this Prince Wuji of Wei, with great courtesy and respect, treated the learned and scholars with immense reverence.[138] He made them welcome at his residence; as a result, he had three thousand guests staying at his manor. There was a recluse at Wei by the name of Hou Ying, who had already reached the age of seventy; he came from a deprived background and made a living as a city gatekeeper at the northern gate of Daliang.[139] The prince was hosting a most extravagant banquet at his manor when all the guests had arrived and seated; he ordered his attendants to prepare his carriage. He kept the most privileges left seat in his carriage vacant to drive and escort Hou Sheng to the banquet. Hou Sheng wearing his ragged clothes and shaggy hat-gear alighted in the carriage, without making the proper civility of declining. The prince was even more humble, holding the rein and whip as he steered the carriage forward. Hou Sheng said to the prince, "Your subject would like to pay a visit to a butcher friend of his at the market. Will you please drive by the market on the way to your manor?" The Prince drove the carriage to the marketplace; Hou Sheng alighted to visit his friend by the name of Zhu Hai;[140] he deliberately spending an excruciating length of time over a conversation, while eyeing the reaction of the prince. The prince remained calm and composed; after that Hou Sheng bid his friend farewell and clambered back onto the carriage. Upon arrival at the manor, the prince invited Hou Sheng to be seated at the head-seat reserved for the most honoured guest, introducing him to all the guests at the banquet, everyone at the gathering was aghast by the presence of this humble individual.

Later, the Qin army laid siege to Zhao. The wife of Lord Pingyuan (Zhao Sheng) was the elder sister of Prince Wuji. Lord Pingyuan, under the pressure of the Qin siege, ceaselessly dispatched his envoys to Wei to appeal for help. He reprimanded the prince, "The reason I decided to enter into a marriage arrangement with your family was because I have all along had great admiration for your high moral character, as you always answer to people who are in need of help. Handan is in a most precarious position under siege by the Qin army, and is about to fall at any moment; and yet Wei has not responded to our repeated appeals. While you might consider me lowly and despise me, but, have you no heart for your elder sister?" This much disquieted the prince; he repeatedly appealed to

---

137 King Wucheng of Yan 燕 武成王, his name is obscured.
King Xiao of Yan 燕 孝王 (r. 257-255 BCE), his name is obscured.

138 Prince of Wei 魏公子 Lord Xinling 信陵君 Wei Wuji 魏無忌.

139 Daliang 大梁 - Kaifengxian Henan 河南 開封縣.
City gatekeeper, *yimenjian* 夷門監 Hou Ying 侯嬴 alias Hou Sheng 侯生. Hou Ying (Hou Sheng) committed suicide about the time when Lord Xinling was meeting Jin Bi, as he felt he had committed an act of treason against the king of Wei. *SJ* 史記, 卷 47, 'Wei gongzi liezhuan 魏公子列傳' 第 17, p. 580.

140 Zhu Hai 朱亥 was a butcher and strong man.

the king of Wei for help, hoping he would command Jin Bi to march forth to aid Zhao. Then, through the ministers at court and his guests, and eloquent guests, he tried to persuade the king to reconsider. However, the king refused to listen. Left with no other options, the prince instructed all his guests to gather one hundred or more chariots to march to Zhao to go against Qin, making a last ditch to die fighting.

When the prince and his guests rode past the north gate *yimen*, [141] they came across Hou Sheng. The gatekeeper said, "Try your very best, prince. Your humble subject is old and cannot accompany you." The prince and his entourage rode on for several *li*. Feeling rather disenchanted by the remark, he doubled back and saw Hou Sheng. The gatekeeper laughed and said, "Your subject knew his prince would double back. Sir, you are in a most awkward predicament and you are left with no other options. When you march forth to face the Qin army, you are no more than a piece of meat thrown in front of a starving tiger. What purpose will it serve?" The prince made a humble bow and asked how he could help. Hou Sheng asked the prince to dismiss his retinues and guests to be left alone; and he said, "Your subject has been told that Jin Bi's military tally is kept in the king's bedchamber.[142] His favourite concubine is Lady Ru Ji.[143] Your subject believes she is capable of stealing it. He is also told that you avenged the death of the Lady's father; it is likely she will die to try to help you. If you beseech her, your subject is sure that she will help you. As soon as you get hold of the military tiger-tally, you could take control of Jin Bi's army and head north to the aid Zhao, fighting off the Qin army from the west. It will be a grand exploit, no less significant than the achievements of the Five Hegemons *wubo*."

The prince followed Hou Sheng's instructions; everything turned out as planned, and at length, he took possession of the military tally. Before he departed with the tally, Hou Sheng reminded him, "When a general is engaged at the battlefront, a new decree from a sovereign is not accepted casually. Even with this military tally, Jin Bi might refuse to surrender his command; he could decide to make verification before releasing his army, and if that should happen, you will be in dire straits. Zhu Hai, your subject's friend, is a strongman; renowned for his exceptional strength and he will accompany you. If Jin Bi complies with the command, it will be great if he refuses to surrender his command signal Zhu Hai to kill him on the spot." The prince then invited Zhu Hai to accompany him. When they arrived at Ye, the tally was presented to Jin Bi, [144] the two halves of the tally matched and the prince demanded the surrender of his command. The general was suspicious, he raised his hands and looked into the eyes of the prince and said, "I command one hundred thousand troops garrisoned at the border; and you, sir, coming from nowhere with a tally in a single carriage, demands to take over my commission. Isn't it a little frivolous?" Zhu Hai, upon instruction, produced a forty-catty iron mallet hidden in his sleeves, smashing as hard as he could at Jin Bi, killing him. The prince then took over the command of the army, redeploying and restructuring the armed forces. He ordered, "If a father and a son of a family are both serving in the army, the father is allowed to return; if there are brothers serving in the army, the elder brother is allowed to take leave and go home. Those of you who are the only son of a family, you will also be allowed to leave to serve your parents."

---

141 Yimen – 夷門 – the north gate of a city.

142 Wei Commanding General 晉鄙 Jin Bi.

143 Lady Ruji 如姬 was a favourite concubine of the king of Wei 魏王.

144 Ye 鄴 - Yecheng 鄴城 – Linzhangxian Henan 河南 臨漳縣.

The prince finally selected eighty thousand men to march forward.[145] Wang He had been attacking Handan for a considerable period without success, and as the reinforcements from various kingdoms began to arrive to give aid to Zhao, the Qin army lost several battles. When Lord Wuan (Bai Qi) heard news of the failure, he said, "His Highness would not listen to my advice. So what now?" When the king heard of his remark, he was in a fearsome tantrum; he forced Lord Wuan to resume the commanding position; Bai Qi claimed that he was indisposed, as his ailment had worsened.

---

257 BCE *Jiachen* 甲辰 Warring States 戰國

King Nan of Zhou	周赧王	58th year
Duke Qing of Lu	魯頃公	17th year
King Zhaoxiang of Qin	秦昭襄王	50th year
King Xiaolie of Chu	楚孝烈王	7th year
Qi Tian Jian	齊田建	8th year
King Anxi of Wei	魏安釐王	20th year
King Huanhui of Hann	韓桓惠王	16th year
King Xiaocheng of Zhao	趙孝成王	9th year
King Xiao of Yan	燕孝王	1st year
Sir Huai Wey	衛懷君	26th year

1. 10th month. The king of Qin decreed to revoke the dukedom and all the duties of Lord Wuan, reducing him to the status of a soldier and to be banished to Yinmi.[146]

12th month. Qin again mobilized its forces, the vanguard forces arrived at the City of Fen; [147] Bai Qi having taken ill could not accompany the forces. At this stage, the reinforcements from the various fief lords joined in the attack against Wang He. The Qin general could not endure the continuous onslaughts of the combined forces sought help by sending his envoys to the capital appealing for reinforcements.[148] The king of Qin sent an order to Lord Wuan through an attendant to march off immediately, barring him from staying at Xianyang. Lord Wuan had no choice except to march off. He arrived at Duyou, ten *li* from the west city gate of Xianyang.[149] The king consulted with Marquis Ying, and other senior ministers at court, they said, "Bai Qi had expressed displeasure against the chastisement inflicted upon him before his departure, and repeatedly spoke of his discontent." The king sent an attendant to present Lord Wuan with a sword. Lord Wuan committed suicide. The people in Qin felt sorry for him and lamented his death; people at various counties and villages built shrines to make sacrifices to his spirit.

---

145 By this stage, the Zhao capital had already been under siege by Qin 秦 for over one year.

146 King Zhaoxiang of Qin 秦 昭襄王 Ying Ji 嬴稷.
Lord Wuan 武安君 Bai Qi 白起.
Yinmi 陰密 - Lingtaixian Gansu 甘肅 靈台縣.

147 Fencheng 汾城 - Linfenxian Shanxi 山西 臨汾縣.

148 Wang He 王齕.

149 Duyou 杜郵 is a small village northwest of Xi'an Shaanxi 陝西 西安.

11. Prince Wuji of Wei soundly defeated the forces of Qin at Handan, [150] General Wang He managed to break out from the encirclement, and the siege was lifted. Zheng Anping failed to break out; he with twenty thousand men surrendered to Zhao.[151] Ever since this loss, Marquis Ying was under constant censure by the king of Qin.

Having saved Zhao from the impending fall, Prince Wuji nevertheless did not have the nerve to return to Wei. He and his guests settled in Zhao; he ordered someone to lead the huge army to return to Wei. The king of Zhao held a discussion with Lord Pingyuan with the intent of enfeoffing the prince with five walled-cities. The king of Zhao personally attended to the cleansing of his audience hall proper, while employing the highest etiquettes invited Wei Wuji to proceed to the palace, and he greeted the prince at the palace-gate. He then invited the prince to ascend from the western stairways to be seated at the most prominent position at the imperial hall at the west end. The prince humbly sidestepped and ascended at the eastern stairways, declining to be treated as a national guest; pronouncing that he was but a traitor for having betrayed his kingdom, besides he had not contributed notably to the aid of Zhao. The king and the prince drank until dusk. The king did not have the courage to raise the issue of enfeoffing the prince with five walled cities, as the prince was most modest and humble. Finally, the king presented the prince with the city of Hao as his provision fief instead.[152]

While back at Wei, the king of Wei restored his title of Lord Xinling (to Wei Wuji).

The prince heard that there was a Master Mao, who lived as a recluse among the gamblers in Zhao and another Master Xue, who made a living in a sweet wine shop.[153] The prince aspired to befriend with the two individuals; nonetheless, they avoided becoming acquainted. The prince then took off one day on foot, unaccompanied; he met them and went for a stroll. Later, Lord Pingyuan heard of the incident, reprimanded him. The prince responded, "Sir, I have long held Lord Pingyuan in high esteem. You are recognized for your virtues; that was the very reason I betrayed Wei and came to Zhao's rescue. Now I realize you merely choose the rich and elites to befriend, not the virtuous and learned. I tried to make friends with those two individuals, and I was wary lest they might not accept me; while Lord Pingyuan has considered it mortification." The prince gathered his belongings and was about to leave. Lord Pingyuan removed his headgear formally, offering apologies for the offence. The prince stayed.

Lord Pingyuan was planning to enfeoff Lu Zhonglian for his effort, [154] and he dispatched his retainers to see Lu on three separate occasions, but Lu declined. He then presented Lu with a gift

---

150 Prince of Wei 魏公子 Wei Wuji 魏無忌.
Zhao capital 趙首都 - Handan 邯鄲 - Handanxian Hebei 河北 邯鄲縣.

151 Zheng Anping 鄭安平. Zheng Anping was the person who gave shelter to Fan Ju 范雎 (see 270-11). This battle was the first major loss for Qin since the middle of 4th century; the loss of this battle purchased some time, of nearly two decades for the other warring states. Marquis Ying 應侯, Fan Ju was under censure, as he recommended Zheng Anping to the king of Qin.

152 Hao 鄗.
Tangmuyi 湯沐邑 was similar to *shiyi* 食邑. During the earlier period of Zhou 周 dynasty, *tangmuyi* were enfeoffed land for fief lords to observe fasting and bathing upon making homage to the Son of Heaven. Later it became a territory or land bestowed upon fief lords for levying taxes, but the fief lords did not hold the title for the land.

153 Master Mao 毛公; Master Xue 薛公.

154 Lu Zhonglian 魯仲連.

of one thousand units of gold as a birthday present. Lu Zhonglian laughed and declined, "The most honourable deed of a gentleman is to help others to avoid calamities, solving their problems, not seeking any rewards of any form. If I accepted any form of rewards, it would be considered a business transaction." He bid farewell to Lord Pingyuan and they never met again for the rest of their lives.

III. The spouse of the crown prince of Qin (Ying Zhu), Lady Huayang, [155] was barren. Lady Xia Ji had a son by the name of Ying Yiren, [156] who was sent to Zhao as hostage previously. Qin had made numerous attacks against Zhao at this stage. The Zhao court did not treat Yiren with due etiquettes, maintaining that he was merely the grandson of a lowly concubine of the crown prince, trivial as a hostage held at another fiefdom at best. The carriages and daily supplies made available to Yiren by Zhao were severely inadequate, the prince was not particularly comfortable with his predicament, and his future appeared to be bleak.

Lu Buwei, a wealthy merchant from Yangzhai, [157] chanced to be in Handan. When he uncovered the identity of Yiren, he said, "This is a piece of rare merchandise." He went and met the prince and said, "I can enhance the width of your manor's front entrance and bring glory to your household, Sir." Ying Yiren laughed and responded, "Save the widening for yourself." Lu responded, "Obviously I intend to bring glory to my own household; however, it can only be achieved by making yours first." The Qin prince realized Lu Buwei had something in mind; he invited him to be seated for a lengthy discussion. Buwei said, "The king of Qin is advancing in years. The crown prince loves Lady Huayang dearly; nevertheless, she is barren. Among the twenty or so brothers of yours, Zixi (Ying Xi) is accepted as the legitimate successor; [158] besides, he is aided by Shi Cang.[159] Whereas you are a middle son among your siblings, and you have never been particularly favoured by the royal family. You have been held here for long as a hostage. Once the crown prince ascends the throne, you stand a remote chance of becoming the heir apparent." Ying Yiren asked, "What can I do?" Lu Buwei said, "The only person who can determine the succession to the throne is Lady Huayang. While I might be poor, I would like to use one thousand units of my gold to make a petition on your behalf in the west, securing your succession." Ying Yiren said, "If your plan works, I will share the kingdom of Qin with you. We will jointly preside over it."

Lu Buwei presented Yiren with five hundred units of gold, coaching him to make friends with elites to extend his social circle at Handan. While Lu Buwei used five hundred units of gold to purchase rare treasures and gifts, bearing the gifts he headed west towards the capital of Qin. He made acquaintance with the elder sister of Lady Huayang, through her the gifts and treasures were presented to Lady Huayang. Messages were relayed to the Lady that Yiren was an

---

Xin Huanyan 新桓衍

Lu Zhonglian 魯仲連 convinced Xin Huanyan to relinquish the proposal of making the king of Qin as Monarch *Di* 帝.

155 Ying Zhu 嬴柱; Lady Huayang 華陽夫人.

156 Xiaji 夏姬 was one of the concubines of Ying Zhu 嬴柱.

157 Yangzhai 陽翟 - Yuxian Henan 河南 禹縣.

Lu Buwei 呂不韋 was the sponsor of the *Annals of Lu Buwei, Lushi Chunqiu* 呂氏春秋 or *Lushi Annals*.

158 Ying Xi - Zixi 嬴傒 was an elder brother of Ying Yiren 嬴異人, most likely from a different mother (another concubine.)

159 Shi Cang 士倉.

exceptional worthy and capable man and that he made friends with many wise guests under Heaven. He always sobbed at night ruminating and missing the crown prince and the Lady; adding that, "The Lady is Yiren's Heaven." Lady Huayang was extremely pleased. Later Lu Buwei passed a message to the Lady through her elder sister, "A woman wins the attention and love from her husband through her youthful beauty. Once her beauty wanes, the love and attention also recedes. The love for Lady Huayang by His Highness is overwhelming; however, the Lady is barren without a son. It would be an opportune time for Lady Huayang while she is still young and attractive, to adopt a worthy son among the many sons of the concubines to be designated as Heir, lest one day she might lose the favour of the crown prince, ending up without a chance to air her opinion. Among the many sons by the concubines, Yiren is the most capable and worthy; he knows his position that he has many elder and younger brothers. He is not even close to taking on the heir apparent position, however if Lady Huayang is particularly fond of him, she could give him a kingdom he does not have, and he could be a son that the Lady does not have. The Lady could retain the favour of the crown prince forever."

Lady Huayang thought the proposition made sense; she spoke to the prince at an opportune moment, "Among your sons there is one called Yiren; he is exceptionally capable and worthy. People are always singing his praises." Shedding a few tears, she added, "It is ordained that I could not bear you a son; I wish to adopt Yiren as my son; a son I can depend on for the rest of my life." The prince agreed to it; he presented her with a carved jade tally as a token of the pledge. The prince and Lady Huayang bestowed much riches and treasures onto Ying Yiren, appointing Lu Buwei as his tutor; after that, the fame of Ying Yiren began to spread among all the fief lords.

Lu Buwei married a most attractive woman in the city of Handan; he knew the young woman had become pregnant. There was an occasion when Yiren and Buwei were having a drinking session, whence the prince set eyes on the woman, he asked Lu Buwei to allow him to keep her. Buwei feigned a tantrum, nevertheless presented the woman to him after a while. The girl was pregnant for one year and gave birth to a son, Zheng (Ying Zheng).[160] Yiren made the

---

160 According to the *SJ* 史記, Qin Shi Huang benji 秦始皇本紀 Qin Ying Zheng 嬴政 was the son of Zichu 子楚 Yiren 異人, who in turn was the son of the Qin King Zhuangxiang 楚 秦莊襄王. However, according to the *SJ* 史記, 'Lu Buwei zhuan 呂不韋傳' it relates, "Lu Buwei had taken a most beautiful woman from Handan, a great dancer, as wife; and they had lived together for some time. He knew the woman was pregnant. When Zichu and Buwei were having a drink one day, he saw the woman and was taken in by the woman. Zichu 子楚 rose and drank to offer longevity to Buwei and asked Buwei to give him the woman. Lu was angry; however, when he thought that he had already pledged his entire fortune on Zichu, besides he was after something more substantial, he presented Zhaoji to him. The woman kept her pregnancy a secret. When the time of labour arrived, she gave birth to Zheng 政, Zichu made Zhaoji 趙姬 as his wife.' The *Cambridge History of Qin and Han*, page 95 under the heading of 'Bastardy of the 1st Emperor' suggests that the text was tampered. A similar event that happened at Chu 楚 about this time might have proffered the chronicler an inspiration that Qin, Ying Zheng was the son of Lu Buwei (see below). Later, when Qin laid siege to the Zhao kingdom again, the Zhao king was about to kill Yiren as a retribution. Lu spent six hundred *jin* of gold to bribe the guards to allow Yizen to escape with the retreating Qin forces. Upon his return to his homeland, Yiren changed his clothes into Chu attire and paid homage to Lady Huayang, his foster mother. The Lady was a Chu national, when she saw Yiren she could not hold back her tears by this affectionate gesture; she said, "I am a Chu, you are of course my son." In the meantime, the prince's spouse Zhaoji and her son Ying Zheng, the future Emperor of Qin, were kept as hostages in the kingdom of Zhao. Young Ying Zheng was to spend ten years of his youth in Zhao. Most historians are of the opinion that Ying Zheng was the legitimate son of Yiren, however, as the future Emperor of Qin had committed a hideous crime by burying four hundred and sixty scholars;

woman his wife. Not much later, the army of Qin was besieging Handan; the Zhao people had intended to kill Yiren. Yiren and Buwei spent six hundred catties of gold to pay off the guards saving his life. Yiren escaped to the Qin army encampment and returned home. Yiren donned on Chu attire to pay homage to Lady Huayang.[161] The lady said, "I am a Chu, of course, you are my son." She changed his name to Chu (Ying Chu).

---

256 BCE *Yisi* 乙巳 Warring States 戰國

King Nan of Zhou	周赧王	59th year
Duke Qing of Lu	魯頃公	18th year
King Zhaoxiang of Qin	秦昭襄王	51st year
King Xiaolie of Chu	楚孝烈王	8th year
Qi Tian Jian	齊田建	9th year
King Anxi of Wei	魏安釐王	21st year
King Huanhui of Hann	韓桓惠王	17th year
King Xiaocheng of Zhao	趙孝成王	10th year
King Xiao of Yan	燕孝王	2nd year
Sir Huai of Wey	衛懷君	27th year

---

it was probable that latter day literati took their form of revenge by disparaging him as the illicit son of Lu. Thus, the text read, '....she was pregnant for (one) year and gave birth to Zheng.' Sima Qian in his *SJ* was always discrete with his treatment of historical accounts; he merely made an implication. Sima Guang 司馬光, using the *SJ* as one of his principal sources of reference, merely suggested that Ying Zhang's mother was pregnant before she was given to Ying Yiren and did not mention that Zhaoji hid the secret of being pregnant. *SJ* 史記, 卷 55, 'Lu Buwei liezhuan 吕不韋列傳' 第 25, p. 698.

The *Cambridge History of Qin and Han*, p. 95.

Yap, J., Wars with the Xiongnu, 2009, p.21.

The translators of the *Lushi chunqiu* 吕氏春秋; John Knoblock and Jeffrey Riegel (2001) expresses doubt on Sima Qian's account on this passage, maintaining that it was fabricated to slander Qin Huangdi and Lu Buwei.

The contemporary scholar, Guo Moruo 郭沫若 (1892-1978 CE) in his *Shipipan shu* 十批判書 raised three issues of doubt, 1. The incident is only mentioned in the *SJ* 史記, whereas the *ZGC* 戰國策 makes no mention of it. 2. The incident of, 'Lord Chunshen 春申君 (died in 238 BCE) presented Li Yuan's 李園 sister, who was pregnant, to King Xiaolie of Chu 楚 孝烈王 without a son', was unlikely to be a coincidence with the legitimacy of Ying Zheng 嬴政. It meant that the latter incident was a fabrication based on Lord Chunshen's incident. 3. The *SJ* 史記 'Lu buwei zhuan 吕不韋列傳' mentions, "The woman of Zichu was from an elite family of Zhao." '子楚夫人趙豪家女'. This statement apparently contradicts with another account earlier that, "Lady Zhaoji was the most brilliant among the dancers at Handan." '趙姬乃邯鄲諸姬絶好善舞者.' (N.B. Songsters and dancers were from the lowly caste of court courtesans.) Note the inconsistencies in 吕不韋列傳, in the earlier passage it mentions that the woman Zichu married was a songster and dancer and a few sentences later, it relates that the wife of Zichu ".. was from an elite family of Zhao.")

161 Now his foster mother.

I. Qin general Jiu attacked Hann; the army occupied Yangcheng and Fushu decapitating some forty thousand warriors.[162] Following this, the army made another expedition against Zhao, annexing over twenty counties, enslaving and decapitating ninety thousand enemies.

II. King Nan of Zhou (Ji Yan the 43rd and last king of Zhou) was in a state of terrible panic.[163] He surreptitiously summoned the sovereigns of the other kingdoms to form an Alliance against Qin; the allied army was to strike at Yique, intending to block the Qin army from marching against Yangcheng.[164] Qin sent General Jiu to lay siege to Xizhou (Luoyang). He captured King Nan of Zhou and sent him to Qin. The Son-of-Heaven humbled himself by making the *kowtow* etiquette to the king of Qin and surrendered his thirty-six counties together with thirty thousand civilians as indemnities. The king of Qin accepted his offers and allowed him to return to Zhou. The same year the king of Zhou died.[165]

---

162 Qin General 秦大將 Jiu 摎.
Yangcheng 陽城 – Southeast of Dengfengxian Henan 河南 登封縣.
Fushu 負黍 - Southwest of Dengfengxian 河南 登封縣 西南.

163 The Zhou dynasty was by this time reduced to a small vassal state and in a way, it was still holding its own with its capital at Luoyang 洛陽.
King Nan of Zhou 周 赧王. According to the *Bamboo annals, Zhushu jinian* 竹書紀年 he was King Yin of Zhou 周隱王 Ji Yan 姬延; the last king of Zhou (r. 314-256 BCE).

164 Yique 伊闕 - Luoyang Xian Henan 河南 洛陽縣; Yangcheng 陽城.

165 The date of the founding of Zhou varies with different sources. It is generally accepted as 1046 BCE; nevertheless, it is still doubted by some scholars including D. Nivison, who asserts that it was 1045 BCE, later he changed it to 1040 BCE. Taking the accepted year as 1046 BCE; it lasted for some 790 years and ruled by 43 successive emperors. Whereas, according to Huang Fumi 黄甫謐 (215-282 CE) in his *Diwang shiji* 帝王世紀 he maintains that it was 867 years. (If his assumption were correct, the founding of Zhao would be 1123 BCE). *ZZTJ JZ*, Vol 1, p. 218.

Volume VI. 資治通鑑 卷第六 秦紀一 255-228 BCE

The narratives of this volume begin in the 52nd year of King Zhaoxiang of Qin (255 BCE) and end in the 19th year of the First Emperor of Qin (228 BCE).[1]

255 BCE – Xun Kuang discussed military strategies with King Cheng of Zhao; [2] the virtuous path of a sovereign, and the honourable path of a general.

249 BCE – Qin annihilated the Eastern Zhou Kingdom.[3]

Lu Buwei was enfeoffed as Marquis of Wenxin with one hundred thousand households; [4] Qin annihilated Lu.

247 BCE – Ying Zheng succeeded to the throne at an age of thirteen. Lu Buwei was the regent; Ying Zheng addressed him as Uncle *zhongfu*.[5]

246 BCE – The state of Hann planned construction works to weaken the Qin economy; [6] the result was exactly opposite, it became richer and more prosperous.

244 BCE – Li Mu took on the Xiongnu, who lost a hundred thousand cavalrymen; for more than ten years, the Xiongnu did not encroach upon the Zhao border.[7]

Qin and Yan constructed Long-Walls to defend against the Xiongnu; the nomadic tribes rose.

241 BCE – Armies of Chu, Zhao, Wei, Hann and Wey form an alliance against Qin. Qin opened its gate at Huguguan Pass; [8] the allied forces dispersed.

238 BCE – The Qin King's mother doted on Lao Ai, he was made Marquis Changxin, and he interfered with court affairs.[9]

Lao Ai tried to take on Qiniangong Palace; [10] the insurrection failed; Lao Ai was dismembered by the five-chariot chastisement, his entire family clan was annihilated.

237 BCE – Li Si, the foreign guest, being banished from Qin, made a last-minute submission to Ying Zheng,[11] who asked him to return and adopted his strategies.

---

1 King Zhaoxiang of Qin 秦昭襄王.
Qin Shi Huang 秦始皇帝.

2 Xun Kuang 荀況; King Cheng of Zhao 趙成王.

3 East Zhou 東周.

4 Marquis Wenxin 文信侯 Lu Buwei 呂不韋.

5 Ying Zheng 嬴政.
Zhongfu 仲父 Lu Buwei 呂不韋.

6 Hann 韓 (Zheng 鄭).

7 Li Mu 李牧, Xiongnu 匈奴.

8 Qin 秦, Huguguan Pass 函谷關.

9 Marquis of Changxin 長信侯 Lao Ai 嫪毐.

10 Qiniangong Palace 蘄年宮.

11 Li Si 李斯.

236 BCE – Lu Buwei was relieved of all his duties.

235 BCE – Lu Buwei killed himself.

233 BCE – Hann Fei was sent to Qin as an envoy,[12] he made a submission to the king of Qin. Li Si envious of the ability of Hann Fei forced him to commit suicide.

230 BCE – Qin annihilated Hann, king of Hann, Hann An was captured; the kingdom was renamed the Yingchuanjun Prefecture.[13]

228 BCE – Qin annihilated Zhao, the king of Zhao was captured. Prince Jia of Zhao escaped to Dai proclaiming himself the king of Dai.[14]

Prince Dan of Yan, Ji Dan, plotted with Jing Ke to assassinate Ying Zheng.[15]

Qin Chronicle I 秦紀一 255-228 BCE

---

255 BCE *Pingwu* 丙午 Warring States 戰國

Duke Qing of Lu	魯頃公	19th year
King Zhaoxiang of Qin	秦昭襄王	52nd year
King Xiaolie of Chu	楚孝烈王	9th year
Qi Tian Jian	齊田建	10th year
King Anxi of Wei	魏安釐王	22nd year
King Huanhui of Hann	韓桓惠王	18th year
King Xiaocheng of Zhao	趙孝成王	11th year
King Xiao of Yan	燕孝王	3nd year
Sir Wey Huai	衛懷君	28th year

1. Wang Ji, the magistrate of Hedong Prefecture, was found guilty of collaborating with other fief lords and was executed at the marketplace. Marquis Ying was depressed.[16] During a court

---

12 Hann Fei 韓非.

13 Hann An 韓安, Yingchunjun Prefecture 潁川郡.

14 Zhao Prince 趙公子 Zhao Jia 趙嘉.
King of Dai 代王.

15 Yan Prince 燕太子 Ji Dan 姬丹.
Jing Ke 荆軻.
King of Qin 秦王 Ying Zheng 嬴政.

16 Hedong Prefecture Magistrate 河東郡守 Wang Ji 王稽.
Hedong 河東 - Xiaxian Shanxi 山西 夏縣. The area belonged to Wei previously; Qin annexed it. As the area was situated east of the Huanghe River, it came to be known as *Hedong*, East of the River.
Wang Ji 王稽 recommended Fan Ju 范雎 to the king of Qin. Fan Ju later recommended Zheng Anping 鄭安平 to the Qin court, in 257 BCE Zheng Anping surrendered to Zhao 趙. Fan Ju was in

session, the king of Qin sighed heavily; the marquis enquired the reason he was depressed, the king answered, "Lord Wuan is dead, Zheng Anping defected and Wang Ji was treasonous.[17] I do not have any capable generals who are close-at-hand, whereas there are so many enemy states externally. I am extremely worried." The Marquis was aghast, not knowing how to respond.

Cai Ze, a Yan guest, heard of what had happened, travelled west to Qin.[18] Through his friends, he spread rumours to convey to Marquis Ying, "Cai Ze is an exceptional orator under Heaven; he intends to meet the king of Qin, conspiring to corner and replace the marquis." The Marquis of Ying was fuming with rage; he summoned the man to see him. When Cai Ze met the marquis, he was most arrogant, and the marquis found his attitude most aggravating. The marquis berated him, "Sir, you said you want to take my place as the chancellor, please enlighten me?" Cai Ze answered, "Alas! Sir, why are you so belated in your awakening? The law of nature commands the change of seasons; the serviceability of ministers at any royal court is no different, having accomplished their intended purposes, they are deposed. Are you not aware of what happened to Lord Shang at Qin; Wu Qi at Chu and Wen Zhong the minister of Yue?[19] Do you intend to follow their fates?" Fan Ju refuted by saying, "Why not? Those men achieved the height of righteousness, respect and died honourably. An upright man with noble character should die preserving his admirable name without the slightest regret." Cai Ze responded, "The definitive aspiration of a person pursues at court is that he attains both fame and glory through meritorious service. When one attained fame and retired in honour, and it is considered the greatest achievement. When one secures his reputation and honour, nevertheless dies in the process it is

---

a most precarious position as Qin law stipulated when a person recommended to the Qin court committed certain offences, the referrer would also be punished. While King Zhao of Qin did not chastise him, Fan Ju was apprehensive. (See 270–II and 266-II.)

Marquis Ying 應侯 Fan Ju 范雎.

17 King Zhaoxiang of Qin 秦 昭襄王 Ying Ji 嬴稷.

Lord Wuan 武安君 Bai Qi 白起.

Zheng Anping 鄭安平; Wang Ji 王稽.

18 Cai Ze 蔡澤 was a Yan national 燕人, a learned orator and an expert in horizontal coalition strategy. He travelled extensively throughout the Warring States; however, his talent was not recognized. He finally ended his quest for recognition at the Qin court replacing Fan Ju as the chancellor. After a few months, he claimed that he had taken ill and retired. Later he served under King Xiaowen of Qin 秦 孝文王 and King Zhuangxiang of Qin 秦 莊襄王. He died during the time of Qin Shi Huang 秦 始皇帝. The *SJ* 史記, 卷 49, 'Fan Ju, Cai Ze liezhuan 范雎, 蔡澤列傳' 第 19, pp. 609-613.

19 Gongsun Yang 公孫鞅 of Qin, alias Shang Yang 商鞅.

Duke Xiao of Qin, Ying Quliang 秦孝公 嬴渠梁 (r. 361-338 BCE) appointed Gongsun Yang 公孫鞅 to make reforms to Qin. (See 361-I, 359-I, 350-I, 348-I, 340-I).

Wu Qi 吳起 of Chu 楚 (See 403-381 BCE). King Dao of Chu 楚悼王 Mi Yi 芈疑 (r. 401-381 BCE) appointed Wu Qi 吳起 to make reforms to Chu. (See 387-II, 381-I.)

Wen Zhong 文種 of Yue 越 (?-472 BCE). Wen Zhong was a brilliant strategist at the kingdom of Yue 越 during the period of late Spring and Autumn period 春秋. He and Fan Li 范蠡 served under King of Yue, Si Goujian 越王 姒勾踐 (r. 448-412 BCE). With the help of the two men, the king defeated his archenemy King of Wu, Fu Chai 吳王 夫差. Fan Li retired from his position after the defeat of King Wu, he wrote to Wen Zhong and warned him, "Birds are soaring and dispersing in all directions; fine bows are being stowed away; shrewd hares are taking flights, and the flunky dogs are being cooked as stew." "高鳥散, 良弓藏, 狡兔盡, 走狗烹." Wen Zhong was extremely conceited and arrogant; he continued to serve at court, maintaining he had made notable and meritorious contributions to the state. Someone accused him of treason; the king bestowed on him with a sword to take his own life. The *SJ* 史記, 卷 111, 'Yuewang Goujian 越王 勾踐' 第 11, p. 1607.

considered as an inferior standing. Whereas when a person loses all his standing and reputation and yet still clings on to stay alive, he is considered the most inadequate. Lord Shang, Wu Qi and Minister Zhong were loyal subjects, they were unreservedly dedicated to their overlords, they accomplished what they desired, in the end, and they were commendable. The question is, 'Were Hong Yao and Duke Dan of Zhou not sages and were they not staunchly loyal to their kingdoms?'[20] How are the former three compared with the latter two?" Marquis Ying answered, "Good point." Cai Ze continued, "Duke Xiao, the king of Chu and the king of Yue did not lessen their affection towards their former subjects, and they did not turn their backs against their meritorious subjects. How is your Lord compared with them?" Marquis Ying answered, "I do not know how to compare." Cai Ze asked, "How are your merits compared with the three gentlemen I just mentioned?" "I am not comparable." Cai Ze said, "That being the case, why have you not retired from the Qin court? The calamities awaiting you could be far more severe than the three men faced. There is a common saying, 'When the sun reaches its zenith it goes into decline; and when the moon is full, it starts to wane.' The notion of waxing and waning, of expansion and contraction changes with time, they are forever evolving and shifting; this is an unalterable path propounded by the sage.' As for you, Sir, the reprisals against the people who maltreated you have been fully realized; the favours you owed to the men who saved your life have also been settled.[21] You should be quite satisfied by now. However, you are not preparing for changes. Sir, I am concerned for your safety." Marquis of Ying honoured Cai Ze as his most revered guest and recommended him to the king of Qin. The king summoned him for an audience; he was delighted and appointed him as a foreign guest - *keqing*. Marquis Ying made the excuse that he had taken ill and resigned his post. The king was impressed with the schemes Cai Ze proposed and made him the new chancellor. Several months later, he was relieved of his duties.

II. Lord Chunshen of Chu appointed Xun Kuang as the county magistrate of Lanling.[22]

---

[20] Hong Yao 閎夭 was one of the founding members of the Zhou dynasty. He served under Xibo, King Wen of Zhou 西伯 周文王 Ji Chang 姬昌 (~1152-1056 BCE), who was imprisoned by King Zhou of Shang 商王紂 (r. 1075-1046 BCE). Hong Yao, San Yisheng 散宜生 and Tai Dian 太顛 presented King Zhou with beautiful women and treasures and had King Wen released from his imprisonment. Later Hong Yao went on to help King Wu of Zhou 周武王 to annihilate Shang. The *SJ* 史記, 卷 21 'Yin benji 殷本紀' 第 3, p. 112. The *SJ* 史記, 卷 22, 'Zhou benji 周本紀' 第 4, p. 121.

Duke Dan of Zhou (Duke of Zhou), Ji Dan 周公旦 姬旦 was the fourth son of King Wen of Zhou, Ji Chang 周文王 姬昌 (see above), the younger brother of King Wu of Zhou 周武王 (1046-1043 BCE). After the death of King Wu, the successor King Cheng 周成王 (r. 1042-1021 BCE) was still very young; Duke Dan of Zhou took over as Regent at the Zhou court. The other brothers of King Wu, Guanshu 管叔, Caishu 蔡叔 and Huoshu 霍叔 collaborated with Wu Geng 武庚, the son of Shang Zhou 商紂, together with the Xu 許 and Yan 奄 barbaric tribes from the east revolted; the incident is known as the Rebels of the Three Overseers, *sanjian zhiran* 三監之亂. The duke led an army against the rebels and successfully suppressed the insurrection in three years. During the 7th year of his regency, he returned the throne to King Cheng of Zhou 周成王. The *SJ* 史記, 卷四, 'Zhou benji 周本紀' 第四, p. 124.

[21] He was referring to Zheng Anping 鄭安平 the man who saved Fan Ju's 范睢 life and Wang Ji 王稽 who recommended him to the king of Qin.

[22] Lord Chunshen of Chu 楚春申君 Huang Xie 黄歇.

Xun Kuang 荀況 Xun Qing 荀卿 - magistrate of Lanlingxian Yixian Shandong 蘭陵令 山東嶧縣.

Xun Kuang, also known as Xunzi 荀子 (~325-235 BCE), was a Zhao 趙 national and was one of the most learned scholars towards the closing era of the Warring States. The philosophy of Xunzi was

Xun Kuang was a Zhao national; he once held a discussion with Lord Linwu and King Xiaocheng of Zhao on military affairs.[23] The king asked, "What are the most crucial issues of military matters?"

Lord Linwu answered, "Favourable weather conditions and geographical expediencies are most essential for a successful military campaign, besides keeping a close surveillance on the movements of the enemies. Make certain that one march forth to the battlefield later than one's enemies while arriving earlier; these are all the essential issues pertaining to military deployment." Xun Kuang responded, "Not so, really. Your subject has heard in ancient times when one deployed a military detachment, the leader and his men worked in unison and harmony as one single entity. You see, when an arrow and a bow are misaligned even Yi the legendary archer could not find his mark; when six stallions drawing a chariot racing in disunity even Zaofu the legendary charioteer could not cover any distance.[24] If the officers and his men fail to collaborate closely, even King

---

based on materialism 唯物論, the philosophical monism that matter is the fundamental substance in nature. Li Si 李斯 and Hann Fei 韓非 studied under him for some time. Xun Kuang was one of those wandering scholars. However, he could not be labelled as a mundane canvasser after fame and glory; rather he was more interested in spreading scholarly learning. He travelled extensively during his lifetime and for some time was teaching at the Jixia Academy in Qi 齊 稷下學宫 (山東 臨淄), where he discussed and conferred with scholars on teachings from various scholastic schools, and on three occasions presided over the ceremony of wine offering at the Academy 學宫祭酒 – i.e. as the dean of the Academy. As a man, Xunzi was erudite, extensively well read, and educated. Based on earlier literati doctrines, he selected and condensed the essence of various schools and came up with his personal propositions; expanding the theory of materialism at the time. The *Xunzi* 荀子 in 32 chapters was principally his writing. The texts covered extensive areas of philosophy, logic, politics, and moral. He was against determinism, ghosts, and gods, and affirmed that the laws of nature could not be controlled or moved by human will. As to human nature, he maintained that the innate nature of human was malevolent, opposing the thesis propounded by Mencius 孟子 that human nature was born benign. During the Han era, there were over three hundred chapters of his writings. However, only 32 survive to this day; the others were lost through time.

The *SJ* 史記, 卷四十四, 'Mengzi, Xun Qing liezhuan 孟子 荀卿列傳', 第十四, p. 544.

Yang K. 楊寬 *Zhanguoshi*, pp. 510-514.

Bai S. Y. 白壽彝 *Zhongguo tongshi gangyou* 中國通史綱要, Shanghai Remin chubanshe 上海人民出版社, China, 2001, pp. 107-109.

Wang, S. L. (edit), 王士立, *Zhongguo gudaishi* 中國古代史, Beijing shifan daxue chubanshe 北京師范大學出版社, China, 2001, pp. 160-161.

23 Lord Linwu 臨武君 was a Chu general and a military strategist; he appears in the *ZGC* 戰國策, 'Chuce 4 楚策四' and the 'Xunzi yibingpian 荀子 議兵篇'. Lord Linwu's name is lost.

King Xiaocheng of Zhao 趙孝成王 Zhao Dan 趙丹.

This discourse appears in the *Xunzi* 荀子 'Yibing pian 議兵篇,' which is at slight variance with the accounts here; the account in the *ZZTJ* is abridged. The *Siku quanshu* 四庫全書, *Xunzi* 荀子 'Yibing pian 議兵篇' 第十五 北京藝術與科學電子出版社 pp. 5091.

24 Yi 羿 was a minister at the Xia court 夏代 from the clan of Youqiongshi Dong-Yi 東夷 有窮氏 ~ 19th century BCE. After the death of the founder of Xia Qi 夏啓, his son Taikang 太康 took over the throne and ruled for 29 years; however, he was despotic and debauched, he lost the throne to Yi, who ruled for some time before it was recovered by Shaokang 少康 (the 6th king of Xia). (Information on Yi are based on the *SJ* 史記, the *Dihuang shiji* 帝王世紀, the *Bamboo annals, Zhushu jinian* 竹書紀年 and the *Zuozhuan* 左傳). Huang Z.Y. 黄中業 *Sandai jishi benmo* 三代紀事本末, Liaoning Renmin chubanshe 遼寧人民出版社, 1999, China, pp. 33-35.

Tang of Shang and King Wu of Zhou would fail to make conquest.[25] A person who is adept at winning the loyalty and devotion of his people is an exemplary military leader. Hence, one has to secure unyielding loyalty of his people when commanding a military operation." Lord Linwu contested, "Not so, Sir, the most essential entity with any military operation is to take advantage of favourable conditions, and employ deceptive and unpredictable tactics. You see, all the illustrious generals in the past were elusively unpredictable; they appeared in the least probable places. Sunzi and General Wu used these tactics and were invincible all under Heaven;[26] they did not rely on the loyalty and devotion of their men." Xun Kuang said, "This is not what your subject is addressing here. The benevolent army he is expounding is the ultimate aspiration of a virtuous ruler, whereas you, Sir, are making emphasis on authority, tactic, circumstance, and circumspection. An army under a virtuous leader is not easily deceived by deceptions, whereas those being tricked into ruses are the ones that do not pay due attention to the subtleties of strategy; they are negligent, endangering themselves with indolent indifference; the sovereign and his subordinates are invariably in disunity and discord. One might win the day through luck using the tactics of King Jie to go against another sovereign with comparable capabilities.[27] Whereas employing the tactics of Jie to go against the sage King Yao is like smashing an egg against a rock or dipping one's fingers into boiling water, or diving into water or jumping into a fire; the end is quite obvious, either one gets drowned or burned alive.[28] The army under a virtuous leader is entirely different, the leader and his men are of one mind and function as one single entity. The three brigades of armed forces are completely committed to their common cause. They are closely kneaded like sons serving their fathers, or younger siblings having great respect for their elder brothers; it is comparable to using one's arms to protect one's head, eyes, and torso. Utilizing deception to assault one's enemies is no different than alerting them, allowing them to take precautionary measures. You see, a virtuous leader presiding over a domain of ten *li* has an earshot that extends for a hundred *li*; with one hundred *li* of land, his earshot expands to a thousand *li*; with a realm of one thousand *li*, his perception extends to all within the Four Seas. The people under him are intensely attentive at the outposts watching with vigilance, aided by sharp perception and clear earshot. The army he summons forth are great warriors in action, when discharged they fall into organized rows. When the army strikes out, it is like the priceless Mo Ye swords; [29] things are cut in halves effortlessly upon contact. Upon making contact in battle,

---

According to legend, there were ten suns in the sky; Hou Yi 后羿 shot down nine; he is mentioned in the *Shanhaijing* 山海經. Yi 羿 mentioned above was a descendant of Hou Yi.

Zaofu 造父 was a legendary charioteer of King Mu of Zhou 周穆王 (~976-922 BCE). Zaofu constructed a chariot drawn by six horses to take the king on a passage in the west. He was enfeoffed at Zhao 趙, his descendants adopted Zhao as their family name, so Zaofu was the forebear of the Zhao kingdom. The *SJ* 史記, 卷 113 'Zhao shijia 趙世家' 第 13, p. 1639.

25 King Tang of Shang 商湯王 Zi Lu 子履, after ~1600 BCE.

King Wu of Zhou 周武王 Ji Fa 姬發 (r. 1046-1043 BCE).

26 Sun 孫 Sunzi 孫子 - Sun Wu 孫武.

Wu 吳 – General Wu Qi 吳起.

27 Xia Jie 夏桀 Si Lugui 姒履癸 was the last King of Xia, before ~ 1600 BCE.

28 King Yao 堯帝 Yiqi Fangxun 伊祁放勲 ~ 22nd century BCE.

29 Mo Ye 莫邪 and Gan Jiang 干將 were the names of a pair of prized swords forged during the time of late Chunqiu 春秋. Mo Ye 莫邪 was a Wu 吳 woman, and Gan Jiang 干將 was her husband. The king of Wu 吳王 Helu 闔閭 (r. 514-496 BCE) instructed Gan Jiang to forge a pair of sharp swords. In the process of forging Gan Jiang could not make the metal flow in the furnace; Mo Ye

they are razor sharp like the Mo Ye swords, whoever try to thwart them are totally routed. When the army make camps, they are steady as a foundation rock, when an enemy tries to make contact they will break and retreat. Whereas, what of a despot of a state? Whom could he depend on? Naturally, he depends on his people. The civilians under a despotic leader look longingly up to a virtuous ruler as if he was their own parents, desiring to be under him as if they are yearning for the sweetest fragrance of spices and orchids. Whereas, raising their heads to look up at their own despotic ruler, they are like inmates about to face the scorching facial-tattoo chastisement, or face their deadly adversaries.[30] It is only human nature. Even despotic rulers like Jie or the malicious criminal like Zhi (Liu Zhi) would not bring harm to their own kin and the people they loved.[31] It is

---

asked her husband what could be done. He said, "In times of antiquity when Master Ou Zhizi 歐治子 was forging a sword he used a woman as the furnace deity, and he succeeded." Upon hearing what she was told, Mo Ye leaped into the fire of the furnace; after that, molten steel started to flow smoothly. (According to *Wuyue chunqiu* 吳越春秋 Gan Jiang cut off his wife's hair and nails to throw into the furnace to make the metal flow.) Gan Jiang forged one pair of prized swords called Mo Ye and Gan Jiang. It is said, that it took Gan Jiang three years to forge them. The account is in the *Wuyue chunqiu* and the *Jinshu* 晉書 'Zhanghua zhuan 張華傳'. Gan Jiang kept one of the swords, and when King Helu of Wu found out, he executed him. Before Gan Jiang died he hid the Gan Jiang sword and the secret was passed onto Chi 赤, his unborn son. When Chi grew up and attempted to seek revenge. The king dreamed that a youth was after his life, he decreed a bounty on Chi. An assassin found Chi, who told him the story. The assassin decided to help Chi with his quest. He killed Chi and severed his head to be presented to the king. The king ordered the head to be boiled in a cauldron; while inspecting the decomposing head, the assassin cut off the head of the king, which fell into the cauldron. The assassin also cut off his own head, which also dropped into the cauldron, the imperial guards could not identify which head was whose, and the court buried the three heads at Yichuan County 伊川, a grave known as, 'Tombs of the Three Kings.' However, this account is erroneous, as it is recorded that King Helu died from an arrow wound from his big toe according to the *SJ*. The part about Mo Ye leaping into the furnace was made mythological by the account in *Soushen ji* 搜神記 卷 11, *Sanwang mu* 亩三王墓. There has not been any archaeological evidence to affirm the existence of the pair of swords, which according to texts were steel swords. Nevertheless, there were most likely two swords called Mo Ye and Gan Jiang; whereas the stories and mythical accounts are probably fables written by latter-day scholars.

The *Wuyue chunqiu* 吳越春秋, 'Helu neizhuan 闔閭内傳' 第四 闔閭元年.

Gan Bao 干寶 (translated by Huang D.M. 黄涤明), *Shoushenji quanyi* 搜神記全譯, Guizhou Renmin chubanshe 貴州人民出版社, 1996, China, pp. 296-297.

In 1965, a sword that belonged to the King of Yue, Gou Jian 越王 勾踐 (r. 496-465 BCE), contemporary with the King of Wu, Helu 吳王 闔閭 (r. 514-496 BCE), was unearthed in almost pristine condition at a Chu 楚 tomb in Jiangling Hubei 湖北 江陵. From the bird-script inscriptions carved on the sword, we come to know that it belonged to Gou Jian. The composition of this sword is 80-83% copper, 16-17% tin, and with traces of lead and iron, as compared with Mo Ye and Gan Jiang, which were supposed to be steel swords. The sword of Gou Jian was put to the test; it was still razor sharp and is now kept at the National Museum of China in Beijing. Hence despite the mythical account of Mo Ye and Gan Jiang, the technology of sword forging had already reached a high level of sophistication at the times of late Chunqiu 春秋. It is highly probable that steel swords were also forged during this period as iron became popular during late Chunqiu and the early Warring States period, as evidenced by some recent archaeological finds.

Also, see http://tc.wangchao.net.cn/junshi/detail 23508.html - 2015 王朝网络.

30 *Qingxing* 黥刑 – tattooed to face.

31 Zhi 跖 - Liu Zhi 柳跖 was the younger brother of Liu Xiahui 柳下惠 (~720-621 BCE), a minister of Lu 魯. Liu Zhi was reputed to be the originator of organized gangsters, thieves and bandits. It is said that he had nine thousand followers; with these men, he carried out all sorts of law-breaking activities of stealing, raping, pilfering and killing; hence he is also known as Taozhi 盜跖. Many

no different from asking one's offspring to kill his parents. He will, without fail, divulge what he was ordered. What is the use of trickery then? Hence, a state headed by a virtuous sovereign gets stronger by the day; the fief states who submit to it enjoy peace and tranquillity, the ones that are late in submitting are in peril. The ones who oppose him face collapse, and the ones that betray him are annihilated. The *Odes* say, 'King Wu raises the banner of righteousness, respectfully bearing his hatchet and halberd; radiating like a burning, scorching torch, who dares to stand in his way?'[32] That is a fitting description of what your subject means."

King Xiaocheng and Lord Linwu exclaimed, "Great, what tactical path should a virtuous sovereign assume to advance his military principle?" Xun Qing answered, "When a sagacious lord presides over a state, it basks in good governance; whereas with an inept sovereign, his kingdom falls into disarray. A state enjoys wellbeing when a sovereign expends righteousness and rites in tendering his authority, while on the other hand a despotic ruler snubbing etiquettes and rites, his state is in ruin and turmoil. Stability underpins strength; strength augments power; whereas chaos brings on anarchy and decline, these are the quintessential entities of strength and weakness. A worthy sovereign is committed to promoting virtuous deeds, and his people willingly pledge to his reign; a reprehensible sovereign shuns virtue and rite edification, his people might accept him grudgingly however they cannot be regimented. A state becomes formidable when its people are in compliance with the sovereign; when the people are in defiance against the state, it becomes debilitated. These are the essential conventions of strength and frailty of a state. Qi promotes martial achievements; the government rewards a warrior cutting off the head of an enemy with eight *liang* of gold, even when a battle was lost.[33] An army as such is adequate facing a weaker opponent in battle; it will indubitably scatter and disperse facing tougher opponents, like a flock of birds taking flight in all directions. The Qi warriors are capricious and unreliable, and they can bring on the annihilation of a state. There is no weaker army than this, as these men are essentially the ruffian mercenaries recruited from the market bazaar. Compared with the warriors from Wei, the men are recruits according to stringent criterions. Hefty armours for torso, thighs and shins guards weigh down the Wei soldiers.[34] They are toughened - to draw a twelve *dan* catapult, carry fifty arrows, placing a weighty halberd with the arrows, don a helmet, strap a sword at the waist, lug three days of ration; and are compelled to sprint one hundred *li* at noon.[35] They are relieved of all their tax duties after passing these stringent tests, and are awarded with good agrarian farmlands and comfortable homes. After a lapse of a few years the physical strength of these warriors will wane, the tax exemptions granted cannot be annulled, and the lands and homes granted to them cannot be withdrawn. Even if the state decides to reverse the process, it is impossible to substitute with a more comprehensive one. While Wei has a large domain, owing to reduced tax dues the national treasury is thus inadequate. The Wei army is one that endangers a

---

scholars maintain that he was a fictitious person; nevertheless, there is such an entity mentioned in the *Zhuangzi* 莊子 'Taozhi 盜跖'. *Siku quanshu* 四庫全書 *Zhuangzi* volume 29 莊子 Taozhi 盜跖 第二十九篇, pp. 5220-5221.

32 The *Odes* 詩經, 'Shangsong changfa 商頌 長髮', "武王戴髮, 有虔秉鉞, 如火烈烈, 則莫我敢遏." *Siku quanshu* 四庫全書, The *Odes* 詩經, pp. 495-496.

33 *Liang - zi* 錙 was eight *liang* 两 of gold.

34 三屬之甲 – According to Ru Chun 如淳, "The three armours are the body armour for the torso *shangshen* 上身, thigh-armour *bikun* 髀褌, and shin-guard *jingjiao* 脛繳." The *ZZTJ JZ*, Vol 1, p.230.

35 Twelve *dan* 石 bow – John Hill suggests that it might have been a catapult for launching projectiles. I believe he is correct in his assumption, as no one could draw a 12 *dan* bow. One *dan* was roughly equivalent to 31 kg.

state. The people at Qin are pressed to make a modest subsistence in an impoverished land. The authority is especially merciless and callous. Taking advantage of the supremacy of the authority, the king forces his people to go to war, hiding them in the perilous terrain. Upon winning a war the government dispense handsome rewards to the warriors while exacting severe punishments for losing. If civilian wishes to obtain benefits from the authority, his only choice is to pitch himself against the enemies. The rewards are proportional to his merits in battle; if he decapitates five enemy heads, he is rewarded with a five-family unit as a prize. That is how Qin attained its enduring powerful status. It has taken four consecutive generations to achieve this; [36] it is neither through luck nor chance. Hence, the martially oriented forces of Qi are no match for the well-trained warriors of Wei, while the latter is no match for the crack troops of Qin. Nevertheless, I have to emphasise that the Qin crack troops could hardly withstand the onslaught of the disciplined armies of Duke Huan of Qi and Duke Wen of Jin.[37] Alas, even these disciplined armies could not endure the attacks of the righteous and benevolent armies of King Tang of Shang and King Wu of Zhou. Confronting such righteous armies is likened to tossing a wedge of rice crisp under a huge boulder, being crushed to smatterings. Taking the states above as a whole, they all employ incentives to coerce or motivate their warriors, who merely pursue after personal gains and benefits; they are no different from mercenaries who make a living by selling their military service. These warriors, not paying reverence to the instituted rites of the state, lacking deference to their sovereign, shirking away to perish honourably for their overlord, are wanting in their integrity of fealty and righteousness. There is little doubt that if a fief lord who understands the subtleties of employing integrity, justice and high moral standards to nurture his army, he could annex all the others effortlessly. It is apparent then whether the armed forces are recruited through stringent criterions, through forceful exertion and extortion, through reward and benefits; they are invariably varying forms of deceit. Only through the cultivation of rites and ethics could a leader and his subordinates attain the ultimate goal of cohesion, merging into unanimity with one common goal. When a devious state uses deception against another devious state, there may be some subtle differences between the more astute and the maladroit; whereas when deception is used against a people wholly committed to one common cause it is like using a small dagger hacking away at the colossal Taishan Mountain. When King Tang of Shang marched against King Jie of Xia, and King Wu of Zhou executed King Zhou of Shang, [38] these righteousness kings marched forth leisurely and unassumingly. The people under the two despotic rulers rose up in arms to rally to the cause of the two sage kings; taking down their despots, no different from executing two ruffians at the marketplace. Hence, the 'Tai Manifesto' says, 'King Zhou of Shang

---

36 The four consecutive sovereigns of the Qin 秦: Duke Xiao 秦孝公 Ying Quliang 嬴渠梁 (r. 361-338 BCE), King Hui 秦惠王 Ying Si 嬴駟 (r. 337-311 BCE), King Wu 秦武王 Ying Tang 嬴蕩 (r. 310-307 BCE) and King Zhaoxiang 昭襄王 Ying Ji 嬴稷 (r. 306-251 BCE).

37 Duke Huan of Qi 齊桓公 Jiang Xiaobai 姜小白 (r. 685-643 BCE) was the 16th sovereign of the fiefdom of the Qi 齊 at the period of Chunqiu 春秋. He appointed Guan Zhong 管仲 to make reforms to his fiefdom, which became one of the five hegemonies at the time. *SJ* 史記, 卷 102, 'Qi Taigong shijia 齊太公世家' 第 2, pp. 1410-1413.

Duke Wen of Jin 晉文公 Ji Zhonger 姬重耳 (r. 636-628 BCE) was the sovereign of the Jin state 晉, one of the five hegemons at the period of Chunqiu 春秋, he was known for his capable governance of Jin that transformed his state into hegemony. *Shiji*, 卷 109, 晉世家 *Jin shijia* 第 9, pp. 1524-1529.

King Tang of Shang 商湯 子天乙 marched against King Jie of Xia 夏桀 Si Lugui 姒履癸 (~1600 BCE) while King Wu of Zhou 周武王 Ji Fa 姬發 executed King Zhou of Shang 商紂王 Zi Shouxin 子受辛 (r. 1075-1046 BCE).

was a lone despot.'[39] That is exactly the meaning. It is thus said when the people of a state are properly cultivated by benevolence and integrity the state will lead all under Heaven; a state with lesser edification can easily overwhelm a hostile neighbouring state.[40] As to the warriors that are recruited through stringent criterions, through forceful coercion, through reward and benefits, they face impermanence and uncertainties. They win some and lose others, expand and contract with uncertainties, survive at times while facing annihilation at others. They are riddled with vagaries, rising and falling like tides; hence, they are called *daobing* - an embezzling army - created to pillage, kill and steal.[41] A worthy sovereign with honourable character does not place much emphasis on these warriors."

King Xiaocheng and Lord Linwu agreed, "Excellent. Allow us to ask, how do you select a military commander?" Xun Kuang answered, "There is no greater wisdom than renouncing hesitation and indecisiveness; making an effort is infinitely better than not incurring an error, and there is nothing grander than deciding on an issue without rue. When one reaches the status of making decisions with no regret, he has attained the penultimate, albeit success might not be guaranteed. Hence, the formulated commands, regulations and orders should be strict and stern, and are to be treated with august solemnity. Rewards and punishments are to be expedited with integrity. The army barracks and living quarters are to be maintained and protected with meretricious care and firmness. When the army is advancing or retreating, safety of the soldiers are of paramount importance and the actions are to be executed with agility and swiftness. Make surveillance of one's enemy's position; observe the constant changes, and take cover to penetrate deep into the midst of the enemy. Send in spies to mingle with the enemy. When facing the enemy for a decisive battle, one must be certain that he knows his position, not acting on suspicions or uncertainties. These are called the Six Tactics - *liushu*."[42]

"A commanding general should never be chosen based on the partiality of a sovereign, nor excluding one who is not a favourite at court. A general should neither become negligent or relaxed upon winning a victory, nor be forgetful that one might fail and lose a battle. He should never maintain that he is invincible and loathe his enemy. He should not merely look at the beneficial side of things while ignoring the shortcomings. When evaluating critical issues a general must treat them with circumspection and with meticulous care; and when it comes to dispensing rewards, he has to be generous and munificent. These are the Five Authorities - *wuquan*."[43]

"There are three situations when a general does not take new orders from his lord upon receiving an initial decree. A general would rather be executed than be impelled to march his army into a dire and despondent situation. A commander would rather face execution than marching against an enemy he could not defeat. Moreover, a general would rather be executed

---

39 'The Tai Manifesto, Taishi 泰誓,' "獨夫紂." Dufu was Zhou 紂. The meaning of the statement is - 'King Zhou was deserted and forsaken by his men.' King Wu of Zhou 周武王 called King Zhou *dufu* in his Taishi, 泰誓 (Tiashi 太誓 in the *Shiji*) proclamation, when he raised an army against King Zhou of Shang 商紂王 (r. 1075-1046 BCE). *Siku quanshu* 四庫全書, The *Shangshu* 尚書, p. 317.

40 The text relates, "故兵大齊則制天下, 小齊則治鄰敵."
Daqi 大齊 – the state that had successfully used benevolence and integrity to edify one's people is known as daqi 大齊. 荀子 樂論, "故樂者, 天下之大齊也."

41 *Daobing* 盜兵 - meaning an embezzling army.

42 *Liushu* 六術 - the Six Tactics or Techniques.

43 *Wuquan* 五權 - the Five Establishments or Authorities.

than being commanded to kill or abuse the defeated civilians. These are the so-called the Three Attainments – *sanzhi*."[44]

"Upon receiving an order from the head of the three-armies *sanjun*, with the ranking officers and soldier taking on their respective positions, everything being in good order, his lord could not make a general more blissful, his enemy could not enrage him - this general is branded as the perfect commanding officer. When attending to all matters about military affairs, a competent general is most cautious, treating them with strictest discipline and earnestness; and a general striving for total success in every undertaking he must be fully dedicated to his quest. As for the ones who failed, there is no other reason than they had slackened and become inattentive to their assignments, treating them with indifference. One who attends to his work with dedication far exceeds the inattentive one; a commander while being negligent and careless can bring obliteration to the state he serves. When the national interest is placed before his personal desires, everything will be orderly, everything falls into their respective places; conversely, if the personal interest exceeds that of the common interest of a nation, the outcome is most portentous. When an illustrious general goes into battle, he protects his position as if he was defending a fortress; when he is leading the march, he marches as if he is engaged in a battle. When he is meritorious, he does not flaunt his success, merely assuming his success was due to luck, a result of good fortune. A commanding general respects the planned strategy and executes it without the slightest neglect. He respects his assistants and fellow officers without glossing over the nonessential details; he respects and cares for his men in the rank without abandonment; he respect his enemies without disregard; these are the so-called the Five Attentiveness (or Considerations) *xiedai*.[45] A commander, who has total command of the Six Tactics, Five Establishments, Three Attainments and now topping off with Five Attentiveness, is the kind of military chief a sovereign should be looking for; and the one who practices it is esteemed as a sacrosanct."

Lord Linwu responded, "It makes sense. May I ask how can an imperial army maintain discipline and adhere to command at all times?" Xun Kuang answered, "A devoted commander would rather perish beside the war drum than abandoning it; [46] a steadfast chariot driver would rather die holding onto the reins than releasing them, and dedicated non-combatant clerical officers choose to die amongst his ranks rather than forsaking his fellow men. When warriors hear the war drum they advance or retreat on hearing the sounding of bronze-gong, they abide by their commands in an orderly fashion. The essential issue is discipline, being meritorious is of secondary importance. When an army advances haphazardly or retreats not adhering to order it should be punished with equal chastisements. A victorious army should not summarily execute the weak and enfeebled enemies; fields and farmsteads should be left untouched; surrendered soldiers are not to be incarcerated. The people who continue to resist should indeed be put to the sword without mercy while the ones who manage to escape should be allowed to go free. Capital punishment is reserved for the oppressors, not the soldiers or civilians serving under them; while the subjects who are carrying out duties for the oppressors should likewise be treated like the offenders. Hence, those who submit will be allowed to live, while those who resist shall perish, and escapees will be allowed to leave. Weizi was enfeoffed at the state of Song; he executed the

---

44 *Sanzhi* 三至 - Three Attainments or Realization.

45 *Xiedai* 懈怠 - Five Attentiveness or Considerations.

46 The commanding general was in charge of beating the drum for attack or advancement and sounding the gold – bronze-gong to order a retreat.

treacherous sycophant Cao Chulong in the army camp;[47] the vanquished people of Shang were allowed to recommence their former livelihoods, and the treatments they received were no different from the Zhou civilians. Hence, People nearby were singing praise and accolades, and people from afar flocked to submit to Zhou. The king attended to the welfare of the people from near and far, even people in desolate areas, far-flung from the capital were cared for. Within the realms of the Four Seas, the people were treated as members of one family, and the people from the most remote parts of the kingdom were submissive and subservient; the sovereign was indeed a rightful leader of the people.[48] The *Odes* relates, 'From west to east, from south to north, everyone was won over.'[49] An army under the command of a sage fight to kill, but it does not make gratuitous wars. It does not invest in towns and cities; it does not make assaults; the enemies are jubilant for being allowed to escape, and there are no massacres, no sudden assaults, and least of all enslavements. The time for a military campaign should not exceed the non-farming seasons.[50] The people living under a despot would be envious of such a righteous army, they hate and abhor their own ruler; longing for the righteous army to come forth to liberate them hurriedly." Lord Linwu agreed, "What you said makes sense."

A certain Chen Xiao asked,[51] "Sir when you are addressing military activities, you continually maintained that being benevolent and righteous are of the essence; the problem is - a benevolent person is full of compassion, whereas a righteous person is engrossed in sensible reasoning. How could one reconcile a virtuous sovereign raising an army, as all military activities are for conquest and annexation? Xun Kuang answered, "The purpose of raising an army is not exactly how you characterized it. A benevolent person is indeed full of compassion for people; hence, he abhors those who are ridden with malevolence. A righteous person is also full of reasoning and brims with sensible judgements; hence, he despises those who are despotic and perverse. The objective of a military campaign for a sage lord as such is to quell the despots so as to appease the innocents; it is not for conquest and annexation."

IV. King Xiao of Yan died; his son Xi ascended to the throne.[52]

V. The civilians of the former Zhou kingdom escaped to the east. Qin transported all the national treasuries of Zhou to Qin. Duke Wen of Zhou (Ji Jiu) was banished to the *Danhu zhiju* Bazaar.[53]

---

47 Weizi Qi 微子啓 was enfeoffed at Song 宋 Shangqiuxian Henan 河南 商邱縣.
Cao Chulong 曹觸龍 斷於軍, Cao Chulong was executed at the army camp. Cao Chulong was a eunuch that served at King Zhou of Shang's 商紂王 palace. There is no other information on this incident.

48 The original text describes the person as a *renshi* 人師 - the tutor of the people, it is more appropriate to translate it as - the leader of the people, or an exemplary person.

49 The *Odes, Shijing,* 詩經, 文王有聲, "自西自東, 自南自北, 無思不服." The *Siku quanshu* 四庫全書, the *Odes* 詩經, p. 470.

50 Non-farming seasons. The soldiers at the time of the Warring States were mostly drawn from peasant and civilians; the soldiers were allowed to return home to carry out their farming activities after a military campaign. The adoption of this policy was not to disrupt the farming activities of a state.

51 Chen Xiao 陳囂 was a student of Xunzi 荀子.

52 King Xiao of Yan 燕孝王 7th (r. 257-255 BCE).
Ji Xi 姬喜 8th (r. 254-222 BCE).

VI. Chu invaded Lu; the king of Chu banished the people of Lu to Ju, and annexed its land.[54]

---

254 BCE *Dingwei* 丁未 Warring States 戰國

Duke Qing of Lu	魯頃公	20th year
King Zhaoxiang of Qin	秦昭襄王	53rd year
King Xiaolie of Chu	楚孝烈王	10th year
Qi Tian Jian	齊田建	11th year
King Anxi of Wei	魏安釐王	23rd year
King Huanhui of Hann	韓桓惠王	19th year
King Xiaocheng of Zhao	趙孝成王	12th year
Yan Ji Xi	燕姬喜	1st year
Sir Huai ofWey	衛懷君	29th year

I. Jiu (Qin general) led an army against Wei and annexed the City of Wucheng.[55] The king of Hann travelled to the capital of Qin to pay homage to the king; in the meantime, Wei also submitted to Qin.

---

253 BCE *Wushen* 戊申 Warring States 戰國

Duke Qing of Lu	魯頃公	21st year
King Zhaoxiang of Qin	秦昭襄王	54th year
King Xiaolie of Chu	楚孝烈王	11th year
Qi Tian Jian	齊田建	12th year
King Anxi of Wei	魏安釐王	24th year
King Huanhui of Hann	韓桓惠王	20th year
King Xiaocheng of Zhao	趙孝成王	13th year
Yan Ji Xi	燕姬喜	2nd year
Sir Huai of Wey	衛懷君	30th year

I. The king (King Zhaoxiang of Qin) made a sacrifice to Heaven at the outskirts of Yong.[56]

---

53 Duke Wen of West Zhou 西周文公 Ji Jiu 姬咎.
Danhu zhiju Bazaar 憚狐之聚 - 20 km northwest of Linruxian Henan 河南 臨汝縣 西北二十公里.

54 Lu 魯.
Duke Qing of Lu 魯頃公 Ji Chou 姬讎.
Ju 莒 - Jucheng 莒城 - Juxian Shandong 山東 莒縣.

55 General Jiu 摎. Wei 魏.
Wucheng 吳城 - Pingluxian Shanxi 山西 平陸縣.

11. Chu moved its capital to Juyang.[57]

---

252 BCE *Jiyou* 己酉 Warring States 戰國

Duke Qing of Lu	魯頃公	22nd year
King Zhaoxiang of Qin	秦昭襄王	55th year
King Xiaolie of Chu	楚孝烈王	12th year
Qi Tian Jian	齊田建	13th year
King Anxi of Wei	魏安釐王	25th year
King Huanhui of Hann	韓桓惠王	21st year
King Xiaocheng of Zhao	趙孝成王	14th year
Yan Ji Xi	燕姬喜	3rd year
Sir Huai of Wey	衛懷君	31st year

1. Lord Huai of Wey travelled to Wei to pay homage to the king of Wei; the king executed him, and placed his younger brother on the marquisate throne.[58] He was known as Lord Yuan of Wey, who was the son-in-law of King Wei (Wei Yu).[59]

---

251 BCE *Gengxu* 庚戌 Warring States 戰國

Duke Qing of Lu	魯頃公	23rd year
King Zhaoxiang of Qin	秦昭襄王	56th year
King Xiaolie of Chu	楚孝烈王	13th year
Qi Tian Jian	齊田建	14th year
King Anxi of Wei	魏安釐王	26th year
King Huanhui of Hann	韓桓惠王	22nd year
King Xiaocheng of Zhao	趙孝成王	15th year
Yan Ji Xi	燕姬喜	4th year
Lord Yuan of Wey	衛元君	1st year

1. Autumn. The king died (King Zhaoxiang of Qin); King Xiaowen (Ying Zhu) succeeded him.[60] The king honoured his mother, Tang *Bazi*, as Dowager Tang, and made his son Chu

---

56 King Zhaoxiang of Qin 秦 昭襄王 Ying Ji 嬴稷.
Yongyi Country 雍邑 - Fengxiangxian Shaanxi 陝西 鳳翔縣.

57 Chu 楚 moved its capital to Juyang 鉅陽 - Taihexian Anhui 安徽太和縣. It appeared that it might have moved back to Chenqiu 陳丘 shortly after.

58 Lord Huai of Wey 衛懷君.
The capital of Wei 魏 - Daliang 大梁.

59 Lord Yuan of Wey 衛元君.
King Anli of Wei 魏 安釐王 Wei Yu 魏圉.

(Ying Yiren) his lawful successor. Zhao sent the wife of Chu and children to return to Qin.[61] The king of Hann wearing the most solemn funeral attire went to the sacrificial temple to mourn the deceased Qin king.[62]

II. The king of Yan (Ji Xi) sent Li Fu (a senior minister at court) to pay homage to the king of Zhao and presented the king with five hundred units of gold to host banquets as a gift.[63] Upon returning Li Fu recounted to the king of Yan, "Almost all the young men in their prime had perished at the battle of Changping; [64] the youths of the kingdom have yet to grow up; it can be taken easily." The king summoned Yue Xian, Lord Changguo, for an audience and asked his opinion.[65] The lord said, "Hostile enemies surround the kingdom at its four borders; besides, the Zhao people are skilled and tested warriors. It is not a good idea." The king said, "I will raise an army five times their number." Yue Xian adamantly objected, "It will not work." Ji Xi was beside himself with a ferocious rage; all the ministers at court maintained that it could be taken. The king of Yan then decreed to mobilize two thousand war chariots under Li Fu's command to go against Hao of Zhao.[66] The other unit under the command of Qing Qin was to attack Dai.[67] Jiang Qu, a senior minister at court, counselled against it,[68] "We have just reached a peaceful accord to open up our pass-gates with Zhao, pledging a peaceful alliance; besides we have just presented the king with a gift of five hundred units of gold for banquets. However, no sooner has our envoy returned there is a complete *volte-face,* and now we are advancing to attack them; this is most inauspicious, I do not think our army can win this war." The king refused to listen; he led a detachment of reinforcements to march at the rear of the attacking army. When the king

---

60 King Zhaoxiang of Qin 秦 昭襄王 Ying Ji 嬴稷 (r. 306-251 BCE).
Ying Zhu 嬴柱, known posthumously as King Xiaowen 孝文王, was king for three days – in 250 BCE.

61 Wife of Ying Yiren 嬴異人.
Lady Zhaoji 趙姬, mother of Qin Shi Huang.

62 King Huanhui of Hann 韓 桓惠王.

63 King of Yan 燕王 Ji Xi 姬喜 8th.
Li Fu 栗腹 was a Yan 燕 national. He was the chancellor of Yan 燕相. During the 10th year of King Wuchang of Yan 燕 武成王 (262 BCE) the king made him a general to go against the Hu barbarian 胡, he captured over one thousand *li* of land from the Hu. He then constructed a Long-Wall from Zaoyang 造陽 to Xiangping 襄平 and set up Shanggujun 上谷郡, Yuyangjun 漁陽郡, Youbeipingjun 右北平郡, Liaoxijun 遼西郡 and Liaodongjun 遼東郡 prefectures as defences against the Hu barbarian. During the campaign against Zhao, he and Qing Qin 卿秦 were captured by Zhao and were imprisoned. However, in *SJ*, he died in the campaign against Zhao.
ZGC 戰國策, 卷 31, 'Yance 燕策三' pp. 354-355.
SJ 史記, 卷 104, 'Yan Zhaogong shijia 燕召公世家' 第 4, p. 1460.
SJ 史記, 卷 113, 'Zhao shijia 趙世家' 第 13, p. 1655.
SJ 史記, 卷 51, 'Lian Po, Lan Xiangru liezhuan 廉頗藺相如列傳' 第 21, p. 646.

64 Battle of Changping 長平之役 (260 BCE).

65 Lord Changguo 昌國君 Yue Xian 樂閒 was the son of Yue Yi 樂毅 (accounts of Yue Yi see 284-I).

66 Haocheng 鄗城 - Boxiangxian Hebei 河北 柏鄉縣.

67 Qing Qin 卿秦.
Daijun 代郡 - Weixian Hebei 河北 蔚縣.

68 Jiang Qu 將渠 – a senior minister at the Yan 燕 court.

was marching off, Jiang Qu tried to grasp hold of the embroidered ribbon attached to the tally pouch to prevent the king from proceeding. The king raised his foot and kicked the minister aside. Jiang Qu wept, "Your subject is not making plans for himself; I am doing it for Your Highness."

The Yan army arrived at Songzi; General Lian Po of Zhao took on the position to defend and marched against the invading armies.[69] At the walled-city of Hao, Li Fu was defeated. Yue Cheng defeated Qing Qin at Dai, [70] the victorious Zhao army pursued the retreating army by five hundred *li* to the north. The Zhao army then besieged the Yan capital.[71]

The king of Yan sued for peace. The kingdom of Zhao demanded, "We will only negotiate peace with Jiang Qu." The king of Yan made Jiang Qu his new chancellor to negotiate on behalf of Yan; the Zhao army retreated.

III. Lord Pingyuan of Zhao (Zhao Sheng) died.[72]

---

250 BCE *Xinhai* 辛亥 Warring States 戰國

Duke Qing of Lu	魯頃公	24th year
King Xiaowen of Qin	秦孝文王	1st year
King Xiaolie of Chu	楚孝烈王	14th year
Qi Tian Jian	齊田建	15th year
King Anxi of Wei	魏安釐王	27th year
King Huanhui of Hann	韓桓惠王	23rd year
King Xiaocheng of Zhao	趙孝成王	16th year
Yan Ji Xi	燕姬喜	5th year
Lord Yuan of Wey	衛元君	2nd year

I. Winter, 10th month. The king (King Xiaowen of Qin) ascended to the throne; he died three days later.[73] His son, the heir apparent, Chu (Ying Yiren) succeeded to the throne.

---

69 Songzi 宋子 - Zhaoxian Hebei 河北 趙縣.
Zhao General 趙 Lian Po 廉頗. (see 279-II).

70 Yue Cheng 樂乘.
Qing Qin 卿秦.
Daijun 代郡 - Weixian Hebei 河北 蔚縣.

71 Yan capital was at Jicheng 燕都 薊城 - Beijing 北京.

72 Lord Pingyuan 平原君 Zhao Sheng 趙勝.

73 King Xiaowen of Qin 秦孝文王 Ying Zhu 嬴柱 4th (r. 250 BCE).
History is silent about the true cause of his death; he died at the age of 52.
King Zhuangxiang of Qin 秦莊襄王 Ying Yiren 嬴異人 Ying Chu 嬴楚 (r. 249-247 BCE).

The new king honoured Lady Huayang as Dowager Huayang (his adopted mother) and Xiaji as Dowager, (his mother by birth).[74]

II. A Yan general laid siege to the city of Liaocheng and occupied it.[75] Some officers at the Yan court slandered him for treason; hence, the general did not dare to return to his kingdom and remained in the occupied city. Tian Dan, (the chancellor of Qi), [76] launched a series of offensives against the walled-city, for over a year the situation remained an impasse. Lu Zhonglian wrote a missive on a silk scroll, attached it to an arrow and shot it into the walled city. He related the circumstances the Yan general faced in the missive, "General, for your considerations; if you do not intend to return to Yan, you are better off surrendering to Qi. The Yan kingdom you serve apparently is not coming to your aid while our troops are increasing by the day. What are you waiting for?" After reading the letter, the Yan general was in tears for three days, as he vacillated with uncertainty. If he were to return to Yan he would fall in the ploy of those who were trying to machinate against him; however to surrender to Qi was not a viable option either, as he had slaughtered a myriad number of Qi soldiers; and would be greatly humiliated had he surrendered. In the end, he sighed and said, "To be killed by others, I might as well kill myself." He killed himself. Liaocheng fell into chaos; Tian Dan broke through, recaptured the city and returned to the capital (Linzi).[77] Tian Dan spoke to the king of Lu Zhonglian's merit, the king of Qi was contemplating on enfeoffing him. [78] Lu Zhonglian departed Qi to set sail across the ocean. He told his acquaintances, "For the sake of riches I have to yield to others; I will be better off being poor to enjoy my freedom to my heart's content rather than being encumbered by a few material possessions."

III. King Anxi of Wei asked Zishun (Kong Bin) whom he would consider an exceptional and perfect person under Heaven.[79] Zishun answered, "There is no such person in this world; however if you insist I would say Lu Zhonglian is a person close to such portrayal." The king said, "Lu Zhonglian is too articulate, he is not even natural." Zishun said, "Everybody tries to be eloquent, however when a person tirelessly tries to cultivate his moral character he is a gentleman; whereas a person who speaks unpretentiously in that it becomes part of him, and everything he does is spontaneous, now that is what I call a natural."

---

74 Lady Huayang, *furen* 華陽夫人 Huayang *taihou*, Dowager Huayang 華陽太后.
Dowager Xia, *taihou* 夏太后 Xiaji 夏姬.

75 Yan General, the name of the general, is lost. The *SJ* 史記 mentions that this incident happened twenty years after Tian Dan 田單 recovered Qi. This might have been a new occupation by Yan. See 278-III.
Liaocheng 聊城 - Liaochengxian Shandong 山東 聊城縣.

76 Tian Dan 田單.

77 Linzi 臨淄 - Linzixian Shandong 山東 臨淄縣.

78 Lu Zhonglian 魯仲連.

79 King Anxi of Wei 魏 安釐王 Wei Yu 魏圉.
Kong Bin 孔斌 Zishun 子順 was the 6th generation descendant of Confucius 孔子; some maintain he was the 7th.

249 BCE *Renzi* 壬子 Warring States 戰國

Duke Qing of Lu	魯頃公	25th year
King Zhuangxiang of Qin	秦莊襄王	1st year
King Xiaolie of Chu	楚孝烈王	15th year
Qi Tian Jian	齊田建	16th year
King Anxi of Wei	魏安釐王	28th year
King Huanhui of Hann	韓桓惠王	24th year
King Xiaocheng of Zhao	趙孝成王	17th year
Yan Ji Xi	燕姬喜	6th year
Lord Wey Yuan	衛元君	3rd year

I. Qin engaged Lu Buwei as chancellor.[80]

II. Lord of Dongzhou (Eastern Zhou) conspired with some fief lords to attack Qin. The king ordered the chancellor (Lu Buwei) to march against it (Luoyang). Having been defeated the Lord of Dongzhou was banished to the *Yangrenju* Bazaar; [81] the holy shrine of Zhou ceased to exist, the Zhou kingdom was no more. At the time of its fall, it possessed seven counties, those of Henan (the king's city), Luoyang, Gucheng, Pingyin, Yanshi, Gong and Houshi.[82]

III. The king of Qin enfeoffed Lu Buwei as Marquis Wenxin; [83] he was bestowed with a hundred thousand households as his fief.

IV. Meng Ao attacked Hann and annexed Chenggao and Yingyang; the Sanchuan Prefecture was established.[84]

---

80 Lu Buwei 呂不韋.

81 Duke of East Zhou 東周公.
Yangrenju Bazaar 陽人聚 - west of Linruxian Henan 河南 臨汝縣西.

82 Henan 河南 - the King's City - Wangcheng 王城 = Jiaru 郟鄏 - Jinguwei - northwest of Luoyangxian Henan 河南 洛陽縣西北 金谷圍.
Luoyang 洛陽 - Zhou capital 成周 - Luoyangxian Henan 河南 洛陽縣.
Gucheng 穀城 - Xinanxian Henan 河南 新安縣.
Pingyin 平陰 - Mengjinxian Henan 河南 孟津縣.
Yanshi 偃師 - Yanshixian Henan 河南 偃師縣.
Gong 鞏 - Gongxian 鞏縣 - The fief of the Duke of East Zhou 東周公 封邑 - Gongxian Henan 河南 鞏縣.
Goushi 緱氏 - Goushizhen Yanshixian Henan 緱氏鎮 偃師縣 河南.
Huangfu Mi 皇甫謐 (215-282 CE) remarked, "The Zhou Kingdom was reigned by 37 kings, it lasted for 867 years." Sima Zhen 司馬貞 (Tang scholar around 700 CE) said, "It was the end of the line." *ZZTJ JZ*, Vol 1, p. 236.

83 Marquis Wenxin 文信侯 Lu Buwei 呂不韋.

84 Meng Ao 蒙驁.

V. Chu annihilated the state of Lu, the sovereign Duke Qing of Lu (Ji Chou) was sent into exile in the City of Bian, with his status reduced to that of a commoner.[85]

---

248 BCE *Guichou* 癸丑 Warring States 戰國

King Zhuangxiang of Qin	秦莊襄王	2nd year
King Xiaolie of Chu	楚孝烈王	16th year
Qi Tian Jian	齊田建	17th year
King Anxi of Wei	魏安釐王	29th year
King Huanhui of Hann	韓桓惠王	25th year
King Xiaocheng of Zhao	趙孝成王	18th year
Yan Ji Xi	燕姬喜	7th year
Lord Yuan of Wey	衛元君	4th year

I. A solar eclipse was observed.

II. Meng Ao, the Qin general, attacked Zhao, annexing Yuci, Langmeng, totally thirty-seven walled-cities.[86]

III. Lord Chunshen (Huang Xie) suggested to the king of Chu (Mi Wan), "It will be difficult to defend the area north of the Huaishui River in a state of crisis as it borders with Qi; [87] please bestow your subject a prefecture east of the River - *Jiangdong*." The king of Chu approved the

---

Chenggao 成皋 - Hulaoguan Pass at Fanshuixian Henan - 河南 氾水縣 虎牢關.
Yingyang 滎陽 - Yingyangxian Henan 河南 滎陽縣.
Sanchuan Prefecture 三川 - three major rivers watered the prefecture: Huanghe 黄河, Yishui 伊水 and Luoshui 洛水.

85 Duke Qing of Lu 魯頃公 Ji Chou 姬讎.
Bian 卞 - Biancheng 卞城 - Sishuixian Shandong 山東 泗水縣.
Duke Qing of Lu was previously banished to the city of Jucheng 莒城 in 255 BCE; this was the second occasion when he was sent into exile. The Lu state 魯國 lasted for about 860 years. *ZZTJ BY Edition*, p. 425.
The dukedom was founded at the time of late Shang, the reign of the royal family lasted for 25 generations with 36 sovereigns, the capital city was Qufu 曲阜. *SJ* 史記, 卷 103, 'Lu Zhougong shijia 魯周公世家' 第 3, pp. 1435-1444.
The territories of Lu covered areas south of Taishan Mountain 泰山 in the southern sector of Shandong province 山東, with small sections in Henan 河南, Jiangsu 江蘇 and Anhui 安徽. Lu was the birthplace of Confucius 孔子.

86 Qin General, *shuai* 秦帥 Meng Ao 蒙驁.
Yuci 榆次 - Yucixian Shanxi 山西 榆次縣.
Langmeng 狼孟 - Taiyuanxian Shanxi 山西 太原縣.

87 Lord Chunshen 春申君 Huang Xie 黄歇.
King Xiaolie of Chu 孝烈王 Mi Wan 芈完.
Jiangdong 江東 - East of the Changjiang River.

request. At the former capital of the kingdom of Wu (the Gusu necropolis), Lord Chunshen raised a new walled city; [88] the palace he built was stupendously luxurious and elaborate.

---

247 BCE *Jiayin* 甲寅 Warring States 戰國

King Zhuangxiang of Qin	秦莊襄王	3rd year
King Xiaolie of Chu	楚孝烈王	17th year
Qi Tian Jian	齊田建	18th year
King Anxi of Wei	魏安釐王	30th year
King Huanhui of Hann	韓桓惠王	26th year
King Xiaocheng of Zhao	趙孝成王	19th year
Yan Ji Xi	燕姬喜	8th year
Lord Yuan Wey	衛元君	5th year

I. General Wang He (of Qin) attacked the various cities at the prefecture of Shangdang, annexing the cities; the Qin government renamed it Taiyuan Prefecture.[89]

II. Meng Ao, the Qin general, led an army attacked Wei, occupying Gaodu and Ji.[90] The Wei army lost several battles; the king of Wei (Wei Yu) was intensely troubled, and he dispatched an envoy to Zhao to plead with Lord Xinling (Wei Wuji) to return to Wei.[91] The prince had misgivings that he might be indicted and declined. He gave strict orders to his attendants, "If one of you tries to make arrangements for the Wei envoy to meet me, I will have him executed." The guests at the manor household dared not utter a word of remonstration. Masters Mao and Xue went to see Lord Xinling; [92] they said, "My Prince, the reason you are greatly honoured and respected by all the fief lords is for one simple reason – Wei, your homeland is still standing. The situation at Wei has become desperate, and you are not even slightly disconcerted by the dire circumstances Wei faces. Once the Qin armies capture Daliang, [93] your ancestral shrine will be razed to the ground, how will you face the people under Heaven?" Even before those words were spoken, Lord Xinling had a complete change of heart; he hurriedly returned to Wei in his carriage. The king of Wei hugged and held onto Lord Xinling and broke into tears. He made him the supreme commander of his armies.

---

88 Kingdom of Wu 吳, the Gusu necropolis 姑蘇 - Wuxian Jiangsu 江蘇 吳縣.

89 Qin General 秦 Wang He 王齕.
Shangdangjun Prefecture 上黨郡 - Changzixian Shanxi 山西 長子縣.
Taiyuanjun Prefecture 太原郡.

90 Qin General 秦師 Meng Ao 蒙驁.
Gaodu 高都 – northeast of Jinchengxian Shanxi 山西 晉城縣 東北.
Ji 汲 - Jicheng 汲城 – southwest of Jixian Henan 河南 汲縣 西南.

91 Lord Xinling 信陵君 Wei Wuji 魏無忌. In 258 BCE Wei Wuji stole the tiger military-tally from the kingdom of Wei, he had stayed in Zhao since, as he did not have the courage to return home.

92 Master Mao 毛公 found refuge among the gamblers. (See 257-II). The *ZZTJ JZ*, Vol I, p. 240.
Master Xue 薛公 concealed himself in a sweet wine shop. The *ZZTJ JZ*, Vol I, p. 240.

93 Daliang 大梁 - Kaifengxian Henan 河南 開封縣.

Lord Xinling dispatched envoys to the other fief lords appealing for help when the kings realized that the prince was made Wei commander they to march to Wei to give aid. Lord Xinling led the forces of five kingdoms to go against the Qin forces. The allied forces soundly defeated Meng Ao beyond the River *Hewai*,[94] and the general fled the field with his army. Lord Xinling and his forces pursued the Qin army to the Hangu Pass before retreating.[95]

III. Su Gao, a Wei man from the County of Anling, had a son serving as an officer at the City of Guan of Qin.[96] Lord Xinling repeatedly laid siege to the city but failed. He sent an envoy to see Lord Anling to relate, "Sir, please bring Su Gao here. I intend to make him an army colonel *wudafu*; he will be in charge of my military judiciary."[97] Lord Anjing responded, "Anling is a negligible polity. I do not think I could make my man comply. Please send your envoy to communicate with him directly." Lord Xinling sent his retainer to meet Su Gao at his home and conveyed Lord Xinling's message. Su Gao said, "The Lord thinks highly of me; however he intends to use me as a ploy against the City of Guan. If I comply, people under Heaven will ridicule me as a father assailing a city held by his son. If my son surrenders because of me, he will betray his overlord. As a father trying to induce my son to be treasonous; I am sure the Lord would find such a person most detestable, I cannot comply with his wish, and I respectfully decline by proffering the proper obeisance." The envoy reported the message accordingly; Lord Xinling was fuming with a rage; he sent another envoy to see Lord Anling at his manor, telling him, "Anling is a fief territory of Wei. If I fail to capture Guan, the Qin army will use this strategic post to launch an attack against us, once taken our holy shrine will be in great jeopardy.[98] Please bind and bring Su Gao to my camp; if you do not comply, I will raise an army of one hundred thousand strong to lay siege to your city." Lord Anling responded, "My father, Marquis Cheng, abiding by the directives of King Xiang, took command of the garrison of this city.[99] The king personally handed him the charter of a fief-city taken from the grand archive *taifu*,[100] it read, 'If a subject commits regicide or a son commits patricide, he could never be exonerated even if there is a general amnesty. The same applies to defenders who surrender a city, or soldiers who abscond in the face of the enemies.' Su Gao has declined the senior position His Highness offered him to uphold the rectitude between a father and a son. Whereas His Highness says, 'Bind Su Gao and bring him to my camp alive.' This clearly contravenes with the decree made by King Xiang, and it will refute all the constitutions kept at the grand archive *taifu*. I would rather die than comply with his Lordship's instruction." When Su Gao heard news of the exchanges, he said, "Lord Xinling is ferocious besides being a resolute person; he is intractable. If the message of Lord Anling is conveyed to His Highness, I am afraid calamities

---

94 Hewai 河外 - South of Huanghe River.

95 Hanguguan Pass 函谷關.

96 Wei national 魏人 Su Gao 縮高.
County of Anling 安陵 - Yanlingxian Henan 河南 鄢陵縣.
Guan 管 - Guancheng 管城 - Zhengzhoushi Henan 河南 鄭州市.

97 Lord Anling 安陵君, there is no record of his name. He was a younger brother of King Xiang of Wei 魏襄王.
Army Colonel, *wudafu* 五大夫.
Military Judiciary, *zhijiewei* 執節尉.

98 Anling 安陵 was 70 km from Daliang 大梁, the capital of Wei 魏.

99 His grandfather was 2nd King of Wei Xiangwang 魏襄王 Wei Si 魏嗣.

100 Taifu 太府 – was where the important documents of a state were archived.

are about to befall upon our polity. I have upheld my honour, and I did not violate the righteousness between a subject and his overlord. However, how I could I betray my overlord by allowing the Wei army to bring destruction to our city?" He proceeded to the lodge where the envoy was staying; he slit his own throat. When Lord Xinjing heard of what had happened; he donned on plain funeral garbs and retreated into a side vestibule in his manor to lament over his reprehensible deed. He then sent an envoy to Lord Anling, apologizing most respectfully, "Wuji is a mediocrity; my thoughts were muddled, and my remarks were most inappropriate. Your Highness, please accept my solemn *kowtow* to atone for my indiscretion."

IV. The king (Qin, Ying Yiren) offered ten thousand units of gold as a bribe to spread rumours in Wei against Lord Xinling. Through a guest of Jin Bi disparaging messages were related to the king of Wei,[101] "The prince was in exile in a foreign land for ten years. Upon taking command of the army, all the other fief lords under Heaven are now conforming to Lord Xinling's directives, instead of taking orders from Your Highness." In the meanwhile, the king (of Qin) kept sending envoys to offer greetings to Lord Xinling enquiring as to when he would assume the Wei throne. The king of Wei faced with mounting rumours believed that it might be true; he appointed someone to take over the position as the commander of the army. Lord Xinling realized he was maliciously slandered again; he made an excuse that he had taken ill and that he could no longer attend court sessions. He retired to his manor and spent all his time drinking and frolicking with women. Four years later, he passed away.

King of Hann (Huanhui) expressed his intent to travel forth to Wei to condole with the lord's family and to pay his last respect.[102] Lord Xinling's son thought it was the highest honour conferred on his father; he sought the opinion of Zishun (Kong Bin).[103] Zishun said, "You have to decline with proper etiquettes. When the sovereign of a neighbour state comes forth to mourn the passing of a subject, only the sovereign could entertain him as the head of state. However, now the king of Wei has yet to issue a decree for you to represent him to honour the visiting king; what status will you assume to entertain the king?" The son of Lord Xinling declined the proposed visit.

V. 5th month, 23rd day. The king of Qin died. Crown Prince Zheng (Ying Zheng) acceded to the throne; he was thirteen years of age, because of his young age the court affairs were taken care of by Marquis Wenxin (Lu Buwei); the king addressed him as uncle *zhongfu*.[104]

VI. The people of Jinyang (now under the control of Qin) revolted. [105]

---

101 Jin Bi 晉鄙 was killed by Zhu Hai 朱亥 in 258 BCE; this person was a guest of Jin Bi. (See 258-V).

102 King Huanhui of Hann 韓 恒惠王.

103 Zishun 子順 Kong Bin 孔斌.

104 King Zhuangxiang of Qin 莊襄王 Ying Yiren 嬴異人 (r. 249-247 BCE).
Ying Zheng 嬴政, later Qin Shi Huang 秦始皇帝 (born in 260 BCE; as the king of the Qin Empire. 246-210 BCE.)
Marquis Wenxin 文信侯 Lu Buwei 吕不韋 Uncle *zhongfu* 仲父.
Zhongfu 仲父 was also a respectable way of addressing an important minister at court. The original meaning of the word *zhong* meant younger brother of one's father. Guanzhong 管仲 was also referred to as *zhongfu* 仲父.

105 Jinyang 晉陽 - Taiyuanxian Shanxi 山西 太原縣.

246 BCE *Yimao* 乙卯 Warring States 戰國

King of Qin	秦始王	1st year
King Xiaolie of Chu	楚孝烈王	18th year
Qi Tian Jian	齊田建	19th year
King Anxi of Wei	魏安釐王	31st year
King Huanhui of Hann	韓桓惠王	27th year
King Xiaocheng of Zhao	趙孝成王	20th year
Yan Ji Xi	燕姬喜	9th year
Lord Yuan of Wey	衛元君	6th year

I. Meng Ao (the Qin general) crushed the revolt at Jinyang.[106]

II. The people at Hann came up with a scheme to weaken Qin to impede its drive to the east. Zheng Guo, a waterworks engineer, was sent as a spy to slip into Qin.[107] Having been employed, he began the supervision of excavation and construction of waterways. A canal was constructed from the Mount of Zhongshan to link with the Jingshui River; it was to flow along the foothills of North Mountain to drain into the Luo River.[108] While the works were underway, the conspiracy was uncovered; the Qin authority had intended to execute Zheng Guo. The engineer defended himself by saying, "Yes, your subject's task is to prolong the survival of Hann for some years. However, when the waterworks and canals are finally completed Qin will enjoy the benefits for ten thousand generations to come." The Qin court thought his defence made sense and ordered him to continue with the constructions. The top soil and earth excavated were used as landfills to level low-lying saline areas. As a result, over forty thousand *qing* of arid land were rehabilitated into fertile farmlands; the productivity of a *mu* (acre) was raised to a *zhong* (six *hu* and four *sheng*) in volume; [109] resulting from this, the land within the passes *guanzhong* became even more prosperous.

245 BCE *Bingchen* 丙辰 Warring States 戰國

King of Qin	秦始王	2nd year
King Xiaolie of Chu	楚孝烈王	19th year
Qi Tian Jian	齊田建	20th year

106 Meng Ao 蒙驁.

107 Zheng Guo 鄭國. The project came to be known as Zhengguo Canal 鄭國渠.

108 Zhongshan Mountain 仲山 - Northeast of Liquanxian Shaanxi 陜西 醴泉縣東北.
Jingshui River 涇水.
Beishan Mountain 北山 (referring to the mountains to the north, not a specific mountain).
Luohe River 洛河.

109 *Qing* 頃, *mu* 畝 (acre); *hu* 斛 = 1 *dan* = 120 catties, *sheng* 升 = 202 ml, (however metric measurements varied in different states.)

King Anxi of Wei	魏安釐王	32nd year
King Huanhui of Hann	韓桓惠王	28th year
King Xiaocheng of Zhao	趙孝成王	21st year
Yan Ji Xi	燕姬喜	10th year
Lord Yuan of Wey	衛元君	7th year

I. Duke Biao (of Qin) led an army to attack the City of Juan (in Wei); [110] some thirty thousand soldiers were decapitated.

II. Zhao appointed Lian Po as deputy chancellor to lead an army against Wei, and he successfully occupied Fanyang.[111] At this time, King Xiaocheng died; his son, King Daoxiang, succeeded him.[112] The king sent Lord Wuxiang, Yue Cheng, to replace Lian Po. Lian Po was greatly enraged by this; he attacked Lord Wuxiang, [113] who ran for his life. Lian Po absconded to Wei. After a long stay at Wei, the king of Wei did not trust him and did not employ him.

The army of Zhao suffered a series of defeats by Qin; the king of Zhao was considering re-appointing Lian Po while the ex-general was also eagerly waiting to be of service to his kingdom again. The king of Zhao dispatched an emissary to meet Lian Po to assess if the general could still be of service. Guo Kai, [114] the adversary of Lian Po, bribed the emissary to ruin the plan to retain the old general. When Lian Po met the emissary he consumed one *dou* of rice and ten catties of meat, he then mounted on his warhorse in full panoply, indicating that he was still as vigorous as ever. The emissary returned to the Zhao court and reported, "General Lian Po has aged, nevertheless, he still has an enormous appetite, and while we had our meals he excused himself to go to the latrine on three separate occasions." Zhao Yan thought the old general had passed his prime and decided not summon him to return.

Chu secretly dispatched an emissary to escort Lian Po to Chu and made him a general. Lian Po was not meritorious at Chu. He said, "How I missed my warriors at Zhao." Later he passed away at Shouchun.[115]

---

244 BCE *Dingsi* 丁巳 Warring States 戰國

King of Qin	秦始王	3rd year
King Xiaolie of Chu	楚孝烈王	20th year

110 Duke Biao 麃公 (also pronounced as Pao), the name of this general is lost.
Juan 卷 - Juancheng 卷城 – northwest of Yuanwuxian Henan 河南 原武縣 西北.

111 Lian Po 廉頗 was as deputy chancellor, *jia xiangguo* 假相國.
Fanyang 繁陽 - Neihuangxian Henan 河南 内黄縣.

112 King Xiaocheng of Zhao 趙孝成王 Zhao Dan 趙丹 (r. 265-245 BCE).
Zhao Yan 趙偃, known posthumously as King Daoxiang 悼襄王 (r. 244-236 BCE).

113 Lord Wuxiang 武襄君 Yue Cheng 樂乘 was the son of Yue Yi 樂毅.

114 Guo Kai 郭開 later slandered Li Mu 李牧 and brought on the downfall of the great warrior, and sped up the demise of Zhao 趙. (Also, see 244-III, 232-I, 229-I)

115 The capital of Chu 楚 - Shouchun 壽春 - Shouxian Anhui 安徽 壽縣.

Qi Tian Jian	齊田建	21st year
King Anxi of Wei	魏安釐王	33rd year
King Huanhui of Hann	韓桓惠王	29th year
King Daoxiang of Zhao	趙悼襄王	1st year
Yan Ji Xi	燕姬喜	11th year
Lord Yuan of Wey	衛元君	8th year

I. There was a famine in Qin.

II. Meng Ao, Qin general, attacked Hann; twelve cities were annexed.

III. The king of Zhao made Li Mu the commanding general of his army. The general attacked Yan taking the Wusui County and the City of Fangcheng.[116] Li Mu was an accomplished soldier defending the northern border of Zhao; he had previously resided at Dai and Yanmen, and at that time, he was defending the prefectures against the Xiongnu.[117]

---

116 King Daoxiang of Zhao 趙悼襄王 Zhao Yan 趙偃 4th King.
Li Mu 李牧.
Wusui 武遂 - Xushuixian Hebei 河北 徐水縣.
Fangcheng 方城 - Guanxian Hebei 河北 固安縣.

117 Daijun Prefecture 代郡 - Weixian Hebei 河北 蔚縣.
Yanmen 雁門 - Youyuxian Shanxi 山西 右玉縣.
Xiongnu 匈奴.
It is the first mention of Xiongnu in Chinese annals and chronicles. We do not have a record of the exact date when Li Mu 李牧 was sent to defend the border; judging from the text it must have been at least 15 years before 244 BCE. While this year might have been the first ever mention of Xiongnu in Chinese chronicles, there nevertheless are rather curious passages in the *Hanshu* 漢書 and the *ZZTJ*, missing in the *SJ* 史記; as Chapter 52 of the *Hanshu*, Section 22 relates .... , "The Grand Usher, Hui (Wang Hui 王恢) responded, 'While Your Highness has not spoken; however your humble subject would like to be of service to you. He has heard at the time of the kingdom of Dai; the people had the barbaric Hu to their north; to their south they fought wars with Zhongguo 中國; nevertheless, they managed to provide for their elders and raised their young. They planted trees and ploughed their fields, and their granaries were always bountiful. Xiongnu did not have the courage to provoke and make infliction upon them."' The passage in the *ZZTJ* is in a similar vein, "Your subject has heard that at the time of the Dai, the polity had savage Hu as their northern neighbour, from within they made incessant wars against Zhongguo. Nevertheless, they managed to provide for their elders and raised their young. They planted trees and ploughed their fields; their granaries were always bountiful. The Xiongnu did not have the courage to provoke the people at Dai." The curious aspect of those two passages is the mention of Xiongnu. Dai was one of the minor vassal kingdoms that existed towards the end of the Chunqiu era 春秋 (~700–476 BCE); Zhao finally annihilated it in 475 (458) BCE. If the Xiongnu as a kingdom existed in name at this early date, this account antedates the first account in 244 BCE by at least 230 years. Note that the passages from both accounts are quite specific with their choice of words; in the first instance, it stipulates that there were barbarians - Hu to the north. It is taken to mean that many barbaric Hu tribes that settled to the north of the kingdom of Dai. Then, when we come to the last part, it is quite unambiguous that it was Xiongnu who did not have the courage to provoke them. It is thus reasoned that unless the *Hanshu* 漢書 and the *ZZTJ* are both wrong with the inclusion of Xiongnu; that might have been the case as the *ZZTJ* consistently drew on the *Hanshu* religiously. However, we are baffled by the curious omission of this incident by Sima Qian 司馬遷, who chose to leave out

At Dai and Yanmen, Li Mu was empowered to appoint his staff. The rental proceeds from the local areas were retained at the garrison for border defence expenses. Every day he ordered his retainers to slaughter a few oxen to feed his warriors. The warriors were trained to ride and shoot arrows. They were ordered to keep a vigilant watch out for the beacon signals of approaching enemies, and he sent many scouts to spy on the enemies. Li Mu sternly ordered, "When the Xiongnu raiders enter our territories, all civilians and military staff are to retreat into the forts with their cattle and herds post haste. Those who flout this order by fighting the enemy shall be executed." The Xiongnu warriors repeatedly intruded into the territories; the army sentinels diligently torched the beacons, the cattle and herds were safely herded into the forts, and his army refused to engage in battle. A few years lapsed and the kingdom suffered insignificant losses at the border. The Xiongnu warriors taunted Li Mu for being a weakling; even the defending Zhao warriors were starting to doubt if their general was a coward. Finally, the king of Zhao reprimanded him for his inactivity; [118] however, Li Mu adhered diligently to his plan. The king was so infuriated that he sent another commanding general to replace him. For over just one year, many battles were lost, a large number of civilians and soldiers were killed or enslaved; people at the border could not cultivate their land and herd their cattle. The king eventually ordered Li Mu to resume his command at the border; Li Mu bolted his door and refused to meet the king's attendants, making an excuse that he was poorly. The king resorted to forcing the general to resume his post. Li Mu said, "If Your Highness insists on appointing your subject as your commander, please allows him to do things his way as before; otherwise, he dares not comply." The king agreed.

Li Mu returned to the border defence post, and as envisaged, he resumed the defensive stance he employed before. A few years went by; the Xiongnu tribes made very little headway and assumed that they had intimidated the general. Meanwhile at the encampments, Li Mu nourished and rewarded his men well; his troops, brimming with vitality, were eagerly waiting to engage their enemy. Li Mu selected one thousand and three hundred charioteers, thirteen thousand cavalrymen, fifty thousand warriors who were awarded one hundred units of gold and one hundred thousand skilled archers and had these men put through the most rigorous training. He then allowed a large number of herders to lead herds and cattle to graze in the fields. Xiongnu horsemen came in small marauding groups initially; Li Mi ordered his men to feign defeat and would allow a few scores of men to be captured.

---

the mention of Xiongnu altogether. Furthermore, it is also worth noting that the passages in the *SJ* 史記 immediately prior to the missing passage on the – 'Xiongnu' and after are the same with the other two texts. It has led some to speculate that the year of around 475 (458) BCE or earlier when Dai was still an independent state, might have been the earliest mention of Xiongnu, but the curious aspect remains: as it was the only reference mentioned before 244 BCE in chronicles prepared after 100 BCE. Whether Sima Qian found it uncomfortable to include a statement of Xiongnu two centuries before Li Mu or it was an interpolation made by the *Hanshu*, and subsequently the *ZZTJ* duplicated the same mistake; we can only guess. We probably will never know unless we chance to come across new discoveries of ancient texts or new archaeological finds to further our knowledge to substantiate this point. N.B. Most scholars have passed this off as a scriptural interpolation, as it is established that we can find no compelling evidence from texts earlier than the *ZGC* 戰國策, most likely compiled during the late Zhanguo Warring States or Qin that the phrase was ever used prior than late Zhanguo. Yap J., *Wars with the Xiongnu*, pp. 23-24.

118 We do not know which Zhao King; hence, we could not fix a date for this event; however, it is most likely to be Zhao Xiaocheng (r. 265-244 BCE).

When the Xiongnu Chanyu heard about this, he led a large contingent of cavalrymen to make an incursion into Li's territories.[119] In this encounter, Li Mu laid down an unorthodox battle plan, he ordered two battalions of cavalrymen to sally stealthily out from the right and left flanks circumventing to the rear of the enemy and assaulted them on two separate fronts. The Xiongnu was completely routed; over a hundred thousand Xiongnu cavalry warriors were killed. The Chanyu took flight. Li Mu followed in hot pursuit, and on his way, he laid waste to the Dankan, Dong-Hu tribes and brought the Lin-Hu tribe to its knees.[120] For the next ten or more years the Xiongnu did not have the courage to venture near the border of Zhao.[121]

IV. Previous to this, there were seven kingdoms with people wearing caps and girdles.[122] Of the seven, three (Qin, Zhao and Yan) shared their borders with the Rong and Di barbaric tribes. To the west of the County of Long in Qin, there were the Mainzhu, Gun-Rong, Di and Yuan-zhi-Rong

---

119 There are no records as to which Chanyu.

120 Dankan 檐襤 - north of Weixian Hebei 河北 蔚縣.
Dong-Hu 東胡 – The Dong-Hu settled in the eastern part of Neimeng 內蒙東部.
Lin-Hu 林胡 - northern part of Shanxi 山西.

121 King Daoxiang of Zhao 趙 悼襄王 (r. 244-236 BCE).
Li Mu 李牧 was one of the four greatest commanding generals (Bai Qi 白起, Lian Po 廉頗 and Wang Jian 王翦) during the latter part of the Warring States period. He was made commander of the Zhao army in 244 BCE, the year King Daoxiang of Zhao 趙悼襄王 acceded to the throne. We have no way to establish when the battle with the Xiongnu took place or when they invaded Zhao in the first place. The event raised some interesting points. (a) The Xiongnu appeared from nowhere; they just entered into the Chinese political arena in or around 244 BCE. (N.B.) (b) The kingdom of Zhao was situated north of Huanghe, east of the Ordos plateau and in the western part of Hebei 河北 roughly corresponding to the Shanxi province 山西 of today; hence, the Xiongnu must have come from somewhere north of Shanxi; beyond the Long-Walls. Li Mu was garrisoned at Dai 代 and Yanmen 雁門, this was the area slightly west of where Dong-Hu 東胡 used to settle. It is confirmed later when the text mentions that Dong-Hu settled to the north of Yan, present day northern part of Hebei. (c) A Chanyu was mentioned, but we have no way of establishing who he was, however we know this happened some 40 to 50 years before Maodun Chanyu 冒頓單于 came into power. Maodun died in 174 BCE, at which stage he was the Xiongnu Chanyu for at least twenty-five years, commencing from 201 or 200 to 174 BCE. The exact date of the beginning of his reign could not be established. Li Mu was executed in 229 BCE; given the lapse of years, it is most unlikely that Maodun's father was the first Chanyu. However, we can safely conclude that Xiongnu was already attacking at the Chinese border by around 250 BCE, although there are no records earlier than 244 BCE. (Apart from the possible erroneous inclusion mentioned earlier). (d) Li Mu appeared to be quite experienced in his battle tactics against the Xiongnu; hence, we can conclude that the Chinese at late Zhanguo were already quite knowledgeable when fighting against the nomadic tribes. Li Mu was possibly a native of Zhao, he was from present day Xingtai 邢台, an area situated close to the northern frontier. Li Mu had a given name of Mu, which means pasture, cattle herder or shepherd; it provides suggestion that he might have been a nomadic herder himself. It probably also explains why Li Mu was quite conversant with the Xiongnu battle tactics. Of course, these are purely speculations on the part of the author. It is also interesting to note that Li Mu after defeating the Xiongnu went on to engage the Yankan, Dong-Hu and Lin-Hu tribes. Yap J., *Wars with the Xiongnu*, pp. 25-26.
N.B. Wang Guowei 王國維 (1877-1927 CE) in his '*Guifang Kun-Yi Xian-Yun kao* 鬼方昆夷玁狁考' maintains that Xiongnu was the Guifang 鬼方 tribes mentioned during the time of Shang. *ZZTJ JZ*, Vol 1, p. 245.

122 People wearing caps and girdles - people who practiced *li* or social etiquettes: the seven warring states.

tribes.[123] North of the Qi Mountain, Liang Mountain and around the Jing and Qi rivers (catchment areas within the Qin territories) the Yiqu, Dali, Wuzhi and Quyan tribes settled.[124] To the north of Zhao there were the Lin-Hu and Loufan-zhi-Rong tribes and to the north of Yan, there were Dong-Hu and Shan-Rong.[125] These nomadic tribes settled in the mountainous valleys, rivers and streams; each had its respective chieftain and was to each its own. At times, over one hundred Rong tribes coalesced, but they did not have a single leader to lead them. Later, the Yiqu tribes constructed walled cities and fortifications to defend themselves. The Qin state began to devour their territories like silkworms munching mulberry leaves. At the time of King Hui of Qin, the king annexed twenty-four cities from Yiqu.[126] At the time of King Zhao, Dowager Xuan beguiled the king of Yiqu to Ganquan and had him executed; subsequently, she sent in the Qin forces, which obliterated the Yiqu.[127] From then on, Qin began to build a Long-Walls starting at Longxi, passing through Beidi and ending at the Shang Prefecture; [128] the fortifications were built to curb the incursion of the barbaric Hu.

Earlier, King Wuling of Zhao defeated the Lin-Hu and Loufan tribes to the north; he ordered the construction of Long-Walls from Dai Prefecture, passing through the foothills of Yinshan Mountains to Gaoque; and he established three prefectures – Yunzhong, Yanmen and Dai.[129]

---

123 Long 隴 - Longxixian Gansu 甘肅 隴西縣.
Mianzhu 綿諸 - Tongweixian Gansu 甘肅 通渭縣.
Gun-Rong 緄戎 (Quan-Rong 犬戎) - southern part of Shaanxi 陜西 南部.
Di 翟 - Lintaoxian Gansu 甘肅 臨洮縣.
Yuan-zhi-Rong 獂之戎 - Longxixian Gansu 甘肅 隴西縣.

124 Qishan Mountain 岐山.
Liangshan Mountain 梁山.
Jingshui River 涇水.
Qishui River 漆水.
Yiqu 義渠 - Ningxian Gansu 甘肅 寧縣.
Dali 大荔 - Chaoyi County Shaanxi 陜西 朝邑.
Wushi 烏氏 - Pingliangxian Gansu 甘肅 平涼縣.
Quyan 朐衍 - Baowuxian Ningxia 寧夏 寶武縣.

125 Liu-Hu 林胡; Loufan-Rong 樓煩戎; Dong-Hu 東胡; Shan-Rong 山戎.

126 King Hui of Qin 秦 惠王 - King Huiwen of Qin 秦 惠文王 Ying Si 嬴駟 1st Qin King (r. 337-311 BCE).

127 Queen Dowager Xuan *taihou* 宣太后 was the mother of King Zhaoxiang 昭襄王 Ying Ji 嬴稷.
Ganquan 甘泉 - Chunhuaxian Shaanxi 陜西 淳化縣.

128 Beidi 北地 - Ningxian Gansu 甘肅 寧縣.
Shangjun 上郡 - Suidexian Shaanxi 陜西 綏德縣.

129 King Wuling of Zhao 趙 武靈王 (see 299 BCE-I).
Lin-Hu 林胡 - Northern part of Shanxi 山西北部.
Loufan 樓煩 - Lanxian Shanxi 山西 嵐縣.
Long-Walls from Daijun Prefecture 代郡 - Weixian Hebei 河北 蔚縣.
Yinshan Mountains 陰山 - Inner Mongolia 内蒙.
Gaoque 高闕 - Yinshan Mountain Range 陰山山脈.
Yunzhongjun 雲中郡 - Yulinxian Shanxi 山西 榆林縣.
Yanmenjun 雁門郡 - Youyuxian Shanxi 山西 右玉縣.
Daijun 代郡 - Weixian Hebei 河北 蔚縣.

Later, the Yan general Qin Kai was held hostage by the Dong-Hu tribe, [130] the tribesmen trusted him completely.[131] Upon his return to Yan, he led an army against the Dong-Hu, who retreated by over one thousand *li* to the north.[132] Meanwhile, Yan also constructed new sections of the Long-Walls stretching from Zaoyang to Xiangping; while Shanggu, Yuyang, You Beiping and Liaodong prefectures were established to arrest the incursion of the Hu. [133] Towards the waning years of the Warring States, Xiongnu began to gather strength.

---

243 BCE *Wuwu* 戊午 Warring States 戰國

King of Qin	秦始王	4th year
King Xiaolie of Chu	楚孝烈王	21st year
Qi Tian Jian	齊田建	22nd year
King Anxi of Wei	魏安釐王	34th year
King Huanhui of Hann	韓桓惠王	30th year
King Daoxiang of Zhao	趙悼襄王	2nd year
Yan Ji Xi	燕姬喜	12th year
Lord Yuan of Wey	衛元君	9th year

I. Spring. Meng Ao attacked Wei, capturing Chang and Yougui; the army did not withdraw until the 3rd month.[134]

II. Qin repatriated one of its princes from Zhao (where he was held hostage). The Zhao crown prince (Zhao Chu) was also returned, (he was held at Qin).[135]

III. 7th month. There was a locust infestation at Qin, followed by an outbreak of plague. The government decreed that civilians who donated one thousand *dan* of grain to the state would be knighted as an entry grade marquis.

IV. King Anli of Wei (Wei Yu) died, his son King Jingmin (Wei Zeng) succeeded to the throne.[136]

---

130 Qin Kai 秦開.
Dong-Hu 東胡.

131 The general took advantage of his hostage to study the mountains, valleys and terrains where the nomadic tribes settled.

132 1000 *li* ~ 400 km.

133 Zaoyang 造陽 - Huailaiixian Hebei 河北 懷來縣.
Xiangping 襄平 - Liaoyangxian Liaoning 遼寧 遼陽縣.
Shanggujun Prefecture 上谷郡 - Huailaixian Hebei 河北 懷來縣.
Yuyangjun Prefecture 漁陽郡 - Miyunxian Hebei 河北 密雲縣.
Youbeipingjun Prefecture 右北平郡 - Pingquanxian Hebei 河北 平泉縣.
Liaodongjun Prefecture 遼東郡 - Liaoyangxian Liaoning 遼寧 遼陽縣.

134 Chang 暘 Changcheng 暘城, Yougui 有詭 neither place is known today.

135 Zhao Chu 趙出.

136 King Anxi of Wei 魏安釐王 Wei Yu 魏圉 4th (r. 276-243 BCE).
Known posthumously as King Jingmin 魏 景湣王 Wei Zeng 魏增, 5th (r. 242-228 BCE).

242 BCE *Jiwei* 己未 Warring States 戰國

King of Qin	秦始王	5th year
King Xiaolie of Chu	楚孝烈王	22nd year
Qi Tian Jian	齊田建	23rd year
King Jingmin of Wei	魏景湣王	1st year
King Huanhui of Hann	韓桓惠王	31st year
King Daoxiang of Zhao	趙悼襄王	3rd year
Yan Ji Xi	燕姬喜	13th year
Lord Yuan of Wey	衛元君	10th year

I. Meng Ao attacked Wei; his army annexed Suanji, Yan, Xu, Changping, Yongqiu, and Shanyang totalling over twenty cities; the Dongjun Prefecture was established.[137]

II. When Ju Xin was residing at Zhao, he and Pang Xuan were fast friends; later Ju Xin served at the kingdom of Yan.[138] The king of Yan (Ji Xi) perceived that the power of Zhao was waning rapidly after a series of defeats by Qin; [139] besides General Lian Po had left his native state and the position was taken over by Pang Xuan. The Yan king thought it would be an opportune time to assault against the exhausted state; he sought the opinion of Ju Xin, who said, "Pang Xuan can be defeated easily." The king of Yan appointed Ju Xin as his commanding general to make an expedition against Zhao. Pang Xuan led his forces to battle against the invaders; Ju Xin was killed in action; some twenty thousand Yan soldiers also lost their lives.

III. The fief lords among the various states were greatly troubled by the incessant and relentless military activities launched by Qin.

---

137 Qin general 秦 Meng Ao 蒙驁.
Suanji 酸棘 - Yanjinxian Henan 河南 延津縣.
Yan 燕 - Nanyan 南燕 - East of Yanjinxian 延津縣東.
Xu 虛 - Xuxian County 虛縣 - within the county of Yanjin 延津縣.
Changping 長平 - Xihuaxian Henan 河南 西華縣.
Yongqiu 雍丘 - Qixian Henan 河南 杞縣.
Shanyang 山陽 - Xiuwuxian Henan 河南 修武縣.
Dongjun Prefecture 東郡 - the capital was at Puyangxian 河南 濮陽縣.

138 Ju Xin 劇辛; Pang Xuan 龐煖.
Ju Xin 劇辛 see 312-II. (N.B. It is most unlikely to be the same Ju Xin, or the text made a mistake. As Ju Xin entered Yan 燕 in 312 BCE, and that was 70 years before the event in 242 BCE.)
Liang Yusheng 梁玉繩 in his *Shiji zhiyi* 史記質疑 and Qian Mu 錢穆 in his *Xianqin zhuzi xinian kapbian 144* 先秦諸子系年考辨 144, 'Zou Yan kao 鄒衍考' both maintain that Ju Xin did not enter Yan at this stage (312 BCE). Hence, the *SJ* 史記, 卷 104, 'Yan Zhaogong shijia 燕昭公世家' 第 4; the *SJ* 史記, 卷 113, 'Zhao shijia 趙世家' 第 13 and the *ZZTJ* 資治通鑒 are erroneous. (The information is from the web.)
http://www.guoxue123.com/new/0001/xqzz/158.htm 國學導航 龐煖劇辛考.

139 Yan 燕 Ji Xi 姬喜.

241 BCE *Gengshen* 庚申 Warring States 戰國

King of Qin	秦始王	6th year
King Xiaolie of Chu	楚孝烈王	23rd year
Qi Tian Jian	齊田建	24th year
King Jingmin of Wei	魏景湣王	2nd year
King Huanhui of Hann	韓桓惠王	32nd year
King Daoxiang of Zhao	趙悼襄王	4th year
Yan Ji Xi	燕姬喜	14th year
Lord Yuan of Wey	衛元君	11th year

1. Chu, Zhao, Wei, Hann and Wey formed an Alliance to go against Qin. The king of Chu was nominated the Chief of the Alliance; Lord Chunshen (Huang Xie) was the executive commander.[140] The allied forces went against Qin and successfully captured the Shouling Mound; then it marched as far as the Hangu Pass.[141] The Qin defenders opened their gates to meet the besiegers; the allied forces disintegrated and dispersed.

The king of Chu maintained that Lord Chunshen was responsible for the failure, and began to shun him. A certain Zhu Ying from Guanjin advised Lord Chunshen,[142] "All the people in the world maintain that the Chu was a powerful state; however, under you, the kingdom has become enfeebled. Nevertheless, I do not think you should bear the burden of the failure. When our former king was presiding over the kingdom, [143] Qin was friendly with Chu, and for twenty years, it did not attack Chu. Why? It was perilous for their army to march through the Minesai Pass to attack Chu - an inconvenient option. Alternatively, had they decided to march through the partitioned Zhou states (two Zhou) they would have Hann and Wei menacing at their rear as they made attacks against Chu; [144] it was a perilous alternative. However, the situation is entirely different now; Wei is in great peril and is about to fall at any moment, it can no longer protect the cities of Xu and Yanling, [145] and they will eventually cede those two cities to Qin. By then, the

---

140 King Xiaolie of Chu 楚孝烈王 Mi Wan 芈完 as the Supreme Commander of the Alliance, *zongzhang* 縱長.
Sir Chunshen 春申君 Huang Xie 黄歇 Executive Commander *yongshi* 用事.

141 Shouling Mound 壽陵 - near Luoningxian Henan 河南 洛寧縣.
Hanguguan Pass 函谷關 - Lingbaoxian Henan 河南 靈寶縣.

142 Guanjin local 觀津人 Zhu Ying 朱英. Zhu Ying was a guest staying at Lord Chunshen's 春申君 manor.
Wuyixian Hebei 河北 武邑縣.

143 King Qingxiang of Chu 楚頃襄王 Mi Heng 芈横 (r. 298-263 BCE).

144 Minesai Pass 黽阨塞 – Mine zhisai 黽阨之塞 - Pingjingguan Pass - southeast of Xinyangxian Henan 河南 信陽縣 東南平靖關.
The Two Zhou states 两周.

145 Xu 許 - Xucheng 許城 - Xuchangxian Henan 河南 許昌縣.
Yanling 鄢陵 - Yanlingxian Henan 河南 鄢陵縣.

Qin army will be merely sixty *li* from Chen (Chenqiu the capital of Chu); [146] if that is the case, your subject believes that wars between Qin and Chu will be incessant." Chu then decided to move its capital to Shouchun, renaming it Ying.[147] Lord Chunshen was enfeoffed at Wu, [148] still holding onto his position as the chancellor of Chu.

II. Qin invaded Wei and annexed Chaoge; the army continued with its push and occupied Puyang the capital of Wey. The sovereign of Wey, Lord Yuan, led his subordinates and relocated his capital to Yewang, at this mountainous terrain he offered protection to the Wei territories north of the Huanghe River *Henei*.[149]

---

240 BCE *Xinyin*辛寅 Warring States 戰國

King of Qin	秦始王	7th year
King Xiaolie of Chu	楚孝烈王	24th year
Qi Tian Jian	齊田建	25th year
King Jingmin of Wei	魏景湣王	3rd year
King Huanhui of Hann	韓桓惠王	33rd year
King Daoxiang of Zhao	趙悼襄王	5th year
Yan Ji Xi	燕姬喜	15th year
Lord Yuan of Wey	衛元君	12th year

I. Qin attacked Wei and captured the Ji County.[150]

II. Dowager Xia of Qin (Lady Xia) died.[151] Meng Ao, the Qin general, also passed on.[152]

---

239 BCE *Renxu* 壬戌 Warring States 戰國

King of Qin Shiwang	秦始王	8th year
King Xiaolie of Chu	楚孝烈王	25th year
Qi Tian Jian	齊田建	26th year
King Jingmin of Wei	魏景湣王	4th year

---

146 60 *li* ~ 24km. Chen 陳 - Chenqiu 陳丘 - Huaiyangxian Henan 河南 淮陽縣 - the capital of Chu 楚.

147 Shouchun 壽春 - Shouxian Anhui 安徽 壽縣, renamed as Ying 郢.

148 Wu 吳 was the areas near Taihu Lake 太湖 - Wuxian Jiangsu 江蘇 吳縣.

149 Chaoge 朝歌 - Qixian Henan 河南 淇縣.
Wey 衛 - capital Puyang 濮陽 - Puyangxian Hebei 河北 濮陽縣.
Lord Yuan of Wey 衛元君 47th (r. 252-230 BCE).
Yewang 野王 - Qinyangxian Henan 河南 沁陽縣. Huanghe River 黄河.

150 Jixian 汲縣 - Jixian Henan 河南 汲縣.

151 Dowager Xia 夏太后 - the mother of Ying Yiren 嬴異人 by birth.

152 Qin General 秦將 Meng Ao 蒙驁.

King Huanhui of Hann	韓桓惠王	34th year
King Daoxiang of Zhao	趙悼襄王	6th year
Yan Ji Xi	燕姬喜	16th year
Lord Yuan of Wey	衛元君	13th year

I. Wei ceded the city of Ye to Zhao.[153]

II. King Huanhui of Hann died; his son An (Hann An) succeeded to the throne.[154]

---

238 BCE *Guihai* 癸亥 Warring States 戰國

King of Qin Shiwang	秦始王	9th year
King Xiaolie of Chu	楚孝烈王	26th year
Qi Tian Jian	齊田建	27th year
King Jingmin of Wei	魏景湣王	5th year
Hann Hann An	韓韓安	1st year
King Daoxiang of Zhao	趙悼襄王	7th year
Yan Ji Xi	燕姬喜	17th year
Lord Yuan of Wey	衛元君	14th year

I. Qin attacked Wei and occupied the cities of Yuan and Pu.[155]

II. Summer. 4th month. It was a cold summer; some commoners died from the cold spell.

III. The king of Qin (Ying Zheng) resided at Yong.[156]

IV. 17th day. The king of Qin (Ying Zheng) was initiated as an adult, at the age of twenty; he wore a crown and carried a sword.

V. Yang Duanhe of Qin attacked Wei and occupied the City of Yanshi.[157]

VI. Previously, before the Qin king ascended to the throne, he was still very young. The queen dowager, Lady Zhaoji, continued her illicit affair with Marquis Wenxin (Lu Buwei).[158] When the king grew a little older, Marquis Wenxin for fear of the secret might be exposed, he schemed by

---

153 Yecheng 鄴城 - Linzhangxian Henan 河南 臨漳縣.

154 King Huanhui of Hann 韓 桓惠王.
Hann An 韓安 5th.

155 Yuancheng 垣城 - Yuanquxian Shanxi 山西 垣曲縣.
Pucheng 蒲城 - Puxian Shanxi 山西 蒲縣.

156 Yongcheng 雍城 - Fengxiangxian Shaanxi 陜西 鳳翔縣.

157 Qin General Yang Duanhe 楊端和.
Yanshicheng 衍氏城 - 15 km north of Zhengzhoushi Henan 河南 鄭州市.

158 Zhaoji 趙姬.
Lu Buwei 呂不韋 Marquis Wenxin 文信侯.

presenting his retainer Lao Ai to the queen dowager as a chamberlain, [159] asserting that the man was a eunuch. The queen dowager doted the man, and in due course, she gave birth to two sons.[160] Lao Ai was enfeoffed as Marquis of Changxin and was bestowed the Taiyuan Prefecture as his fief; all the state affairs were taken care of by him;[161] innumerable people aspired to be his guest at his manor because of his prominent position. Finally, one of the king's attendants who had fallen out with him divulged that Lao Ai was not a eunuch. The king decreed to send Lao Ai for trial. Lao Ai was in a dreadful panic and took the initiative by revolting; he used the royal seal to forge a decree and mustered up an army to attack the Qinnian Palace.[162] The king ordered his chancellors Lord Changping and Lord Changwen to lead the palace guards to fight against the rebels.[163] At Xianyang pitched street battles followed, several hundred people died in the ensuing fights. Eventually, Lao Ai's and his army lost, the eunuch tried to escape, but he was captured. Autumn. During the 9th month, Lao Ai, his three immediate family clans (father's, mother's, and wife's), his close associates were dismembered by five-horse drawn chariots - the chastisement of *julie*.[164] The entire family clan of Lao was annihilated. The retainers with lesser charges were banished to Shu, [165] over four thousand families were implicated.

The king then decreed that the queen dowager to be relocated to Fuyang Palace in Yong to be incarcerated.[166] He executed her two sons, further decreeing, "If someone dares to utter a single word criticizing the matter about the Queen Dowager I will have him executed, cutting off his limbs and have his remains littered at the palace-gate." Twenty-seven people died for daring to utter a remark.

Mao Jiao, a guest orator from Qi, sent a memorial to the king pleading for an audience.[167]

The king sent a retainer to meet Mao Jiao and asked, "Have you not seen the corpses mounting in increasing numbers outside the palace gate?" Mao Jiao responded, "Your subject has heard that there are twenty-eight star-chambers in the sky, however as of now only twenty-seven people have been executed. Your subject would like to round off the number. He does not fear death." The messenger reported this to the king dutifully. When the friends and compatriots staying with Mao Zao heard of what he had done, they swiftly gathered up all their belongings and dispersed in great haste. At the Qin court the king was raging with ferocity, he bellowed, "This man is trying to insult me. Have the giant cauldron ready; I will have him stewed alive; I will not spare him the comfort of being dismembered for display." The king was seated at state in his imperial hall, clutching his sword, foaming at his mouth. Mao Jiao was summoned to the

159. Lao Ai 嫪毐.

160 As to who sired the sons we do not know.

161 Marquis Changxin 長信侯.
Taiyuan 太原 - Taiyuanxian Shanxi 山西 太原縣.

162. Qinnian *or* Qinian Palace 鄿年宮.
Yongcheng 雍城 - Fengxiangxian Shaanxi 陝西 鳳翔縣.

163. Two lords at the court, their names are unknown. Lord Changping 昌平君 and Lord Changwen 昌文君.

164. *Julie* 車裂 quartered by five chariots.

165. Shu 蜀 - Sichuan 四川.

166. Fuyang palace 萯陽宮.
Yongcheng 雍城 - Fengxiangxian Shaanxi 陝西 鳳翔縣.

167 Mao Jiao 茅焦.

audience hall; he calmly and unhurriedly proceeded towards the king and saluted him with the most solemn propriety twice. He rose and said, "Your humble subject has heard that people who are alive refrain from discussing death. People who have a country shun from talking about annihilation. However, a person who does not speak of death cannot prevent him from dying, and a person who refrains from talking about the annihilation of his kingdom cannot make it last any longer. It is the quintessential principle of life and death; the state of being and obliteration is what all sages and rulers strive to comprehend. Does Your Highness wish to listen?"

Ying Zheng responded, "What are you referring to."

Mao Jiao continued, "The deeds of Your Highness are fanatical and absurd to boot. Do you not realize it yourself? You dismembered your stepfather; [168] you ordered the bagging of your two stepbrothers and had them battered to death while relocating your mother to Yong. You summarily executed your loyal attendants who dared to speak their minds. Even the infamous King Jie and King Zhou of Shang, [169] notorious for their abominable brutality, were not remotely comparable with Your Highness. When news of your ferocity spreads to All under Heaven, people who had previously intended to submit to you would have second thoughts. No one will dare come near Qin again. Your subject worries for you, Your Highness. Here his speech comes to a close." He doffed off his coat, prostrating himself on the implement for execution. The king descended from his throne, using his hand to raise Mao Jiao to his feet and said, "Sir, please don your clothes. I will listen to your counselling." Mao Jiao was appointed as a senior minister at the Qin court. The king personally drove his imperial carriage, leaving the left-seat vacant to go forth to escort the queen dowager to return to Xianyang; the bond between the mother and son was mended.

VII. King Xiaolie of Chu (Mi Wan) did not have a son. Lord Chunshen (Huang Xie) was troubled by this.[170] He searched for many women with procreative physiques to be presented to the king as concubines; after many attempts, the king still did not have a son. A certain Li Yuan from Zhao had intended to present his younger sister to the Chu king, [171] however when he heard that the king was infertile, he vacillated as he was concerned that she might not win the favour of the king had she been kept at the palace for a long time without bearing a son. Instead, he schemed to present his sister to Lord Chunshen as a concubine. Shortly after, Li Yuan requested a leave of absence from the chancellor to return home; he purposely delayed his return. Lord Chunshen enquired about his delay in returning to duty. Li Yuan said, "The king of Qi (Tian Jian) sent an envoy to our household intending to take your subject's younger sister in marriage. He entertained the envoy for a few days, thus delaying his return to duty." Lord Chunshen asked, "Has the king make a formal proposal yet?" "Not yet." Lord Chunshen then took Li Yuan's younger sister into his manor as a concubine. Shortly after, the woman became pregnant. Li Yuan persuaded his sister to suggest to the chancellor, "The king of Chu pledges his faith in you; even blood brothers are not comparable. Your Highness has been a chancellor of Chu for over twenty years if the king should pass on without leaving an heir, the person who succeeds to the throne is likely to be one of his brothers. Each person has his favoured and trusted ministers; how can you

---

168 Stepfather, the text uses the phrase *jiafu* 假父.

169 Jie 桀 was the last king of Xia 夏 ~ 1600 BCE.
Zhou 紂 was the last king of Shang 商 before 1046 BCE.

170 Huang Xie 黄歇 the chancellor of Chu, Lord Chunshen 春申君.

171 Zhao national 趙人 Li Yuan 李園.

guarantee you will retain your supreme position as the chancellor of the state? Worse still, Your Highness has presided over a senior position for too long; chances are you might have inadvertently been discourteous to some of the royal members at court; calamity ensues as soon as one of the brothers ascends to the throne. I am pregnant since no one happens to know, if you present me to the king, given your importance at court, he will most likely make me a favourite. Ten months later if I were blessed by Heaven to give birth to a son, Your Highness's son could be the future king of Chu; the kingdom could be yours. Is it not a better prospect than facing uncertain calamities?" Lord Chunshen was overjoyed with the suggestion, he sent the woman back to the Li Yuan's household and kept the woman under close surveillance; he then made a recommendation to the king of Chu. The king duly summoned the woman to his palace and made her a favourite. The woman gave birth to a son later, and the boy was made the heir apparent.

Li Yuan's sister was made the queen of Chu, and Li Yuan was given important responsibilities at court. He was uneasy lest Lord Chunshen might divulge the secret; hence, he clandestinely kept a few assassins at his manor intending to have the chancellor murdered. Many people in the kingdom knew about the happening and began to gossip. Later, the king of Chu took ill. Zhu Ying said to Lord Chunshen,[172] "In this world, there are vicissitudes to one's good fortune as well as calamity; one simply cannot predict with certainty. Sir, you are living in a world with infinite permutations of uncertainties, serving a king who is totally capricious; how can you possibly get by without a friend who is willing to lend you a hand in time of uncertainties?" Lord Chunshen asked, "What do you mean by sudden change of good fortune?" Zhu Ying answered, "Your Highness, you have been the chancellor of Chu for over twenty years; while being addressed as a chancellor you are in truth the king. Now the king is ill, and he is about to expire at any moment, upon his death you will be the regent, giving aid to the young king. When the young king grows up you will return the power to him. Why don't you simply assume power, sit in state facing south and proclaim yourself as the king of Chu? It is what I meant by an unexpected change of good fortune." "What do you mean by unexpected calamity?" Zhu Ying answered, "Li Yuan does not attend to the state fares. He is your enemy. He does not preside over the military affairs of the state; nevertheless, he has been grooming some deadly strongmen at his manor for a while. No soon as the king passes on; Li Yuan will be the first person to be summoned to court, assuming total control of the state, and will execute Your Highness to prevent the divulgence of the secret, this is what I meant by unexpected calamity." "What do you mean when you said – an unexpected friend who is willing to give a hand?" Zhu Ying answered, "Consider making your subject a palace attendant; as soon as the king passes on, and as Li Yuan arrives at court, he will have him executed for Your Highness. So, your subject is your unexpected friend who is willing to lend you a hand." Lord Chunshen said, "You need not concern yourself with these matters, it could not happen. Li Yuan is a weakling, besides I have treated him well. How could the situation reduce to such a state?" Having been refused Zhu Ying realized that his dire warnings fell on deaf ears; in great fear, he ran for his life.

Seventeen days later, the king of Chu passed away. Li Yuan was indeed the first person summoned to court. At the palace, his assassins were waiting for the arrival of Lord Chunshen at the Jimen gate.[173] As the Lord unsuspectingly arrived at the palace, the assassins rushed forth and cut him down; they threw his head outside the Jimen Palace gate. Li Yuan sent his retainers to the

---

172 Zhu Ying 朱英 was a guest at Huang Xie's 黃歇 household, also see 241-1.

173 Jimen gate 棘門.

deceased chancellor's household; the entire family clan was executed to the last person. The crown prince, Mi Han, ascended to the throne and was known posthumously as King You.[174]

Yang Xiong annotates:

> Someone raised the question, "Did any of those men Lord Xinling (Wei Wuji), Lord Pingyuan (Zhao Sheng), Lord Mengchang (Tian Wen) and Lord Chunshen (Huang Xie) ever make any constructive contributions to their states?"[175] The answer is, "The sovereigns presiding over their states failed to rule their kingdoms appropriately; these sycophants and crafty charlatans assumed power to reign on their behalf. So, what contributions did they make?"[176]

VIII.The king (Ying Zheng) maintained that Marquis Wenxin was meritorious in serving the former king of Qin; he could not bear to execute him.[177]

---

237 BCE *Jiazi* 甲子 Warring States 戰國

King of Qin	秦始王	10th year
King You of Chu	楚幽王	1st year
Qi Tian Jian	齊田建	28th year
King Jingmin of Wei	魏景湣王	6th year
Hann Hann An	韓韓安	2nd year
King Daoxiang of Zhao	趙悼襄王	8th year
Yan Ji Xi	燕姬喜	18th year
Lord Yuan of Wey	衛元君	15th year

1. Winter. 10th Month. Marquis Wenxin was relieved of his duty as the chancellor of Qin and commanded to return to his fief. The ministers at the Qin imperial household and the ministers at court decided, "The guest officers from the various fief states are merely canvassers swaying opinion on behalf of their fief lords; these men sow seeds of discord among our court officers, please banish them." The Qin government arrested and expelled foreign guests in the kingdom; Li

---

174 Chu Crown Prince 楚太子 Mi Han 羋悍 later King You of Chu 楚幽王 (r. 237-223 BCE).

175 The four princes were collectively known as the Four Gentlemen of Zhanguo 戰國四君子 or Four Princes of Zhanguo 戰國四公子.
Lord Xinling 信陵君 Wei Wuji 魏無忌.
Lord Pingyuan 平原君 Zhao Sheng 趙勝.
Lord Mengchang 孟嘗君 Tian Wen 田文.
Lord Chunshen 春申君 Huang Xie 黃歇.

176 Yangzi's 揚子 perspective of the four lords was in variance with people of later days, as people name them as the *sijunzi* 四君子 the four worthy gentlemen.

177 Ying Zheng found out through investigations that Lu Buwei was involved in conspiring in the palace intrigue; however, Lu Buwei was instrumental in making his father the former king in his ascension to the throne, hence he hesitated.

Si, a guest *keqing* from Chu, was among the ones being purged.[178] Upon leaving, he submitted a memorial to the king. It read, "In ancient times, when Duke Mu of Qin appealed to accomplished intellects to go to his court as officers.[179] From the realms of Xi-Rong in the west, he acquired You Yu; from the east at Wan he acquired Baili Xi; he welcomed Jianshu at Song and escorted him to court, and from Jin, he beseeched Pi Bao and Gongsun Zhi to come forth.[180] With these men, he successfully annexed twenty polities; he became the hegemon among the Western Xi-Rong barbarians.[181] Duke Xiao of Qin adopted the reforms initiated by Shang Yang (Gongsun Yang); [182] as a result, all the fief lords subjugated to Qin; the kingdom became powerful and has since been enjoying splendid governance. King Hui employed the schemes advanced by Zhang Yi effectively disengaged the Vertical Alliance instigated by the six kingdoms, [183] obliging them to serve Qin. Then King Zhao acquired Fan Ju, [184] who was instrumental in weakening the power of the distaff

178 Li Si 李斯.

179 Duke Mu of Qin 秦穆公 Ying Renhao 嬴任好 (r. 659-621 BCE).

180 Xi-Rong 西戎; You Yu 由余. You Yu was a minister from Mianzhu state 綿諸 among the Xi-Rong tribes. He was instrumental in helping Duke Mu to handle the Rong situation.

Wancheng 宛城 - Nanyangxian Henan 河南 南陽縣.

Baili Xi 百里奚, Xizi Ming 奚子明. Baili Xi, a Chu 楚 national, came from an impoverished family. Having served at Song 宋 and Qi 齊 for some time, later he was recommended to serve in the Yu state 虞 as minister. In 655 BCE, Duke Xian of Jin 晉献公 annihilated Yu, Baili Xi refused to serve in the Jin court and was reduced to the status of a slave. Later he escaped to return to Chu to work as a shepherd. Duke Mu of Qin 秦穆公 (r. 659-621 BCE) heard that Xi was a most capable individual; he sent his retainers to purchase Baili Xi for five sheets of black ram-fleece and made him a senior minister at the Qin court. He came to be known as the Five Fleece Minister 五公羊大夫. He was instrumental in making Qin the hegemon in the Xi-Rong 西戎 realms.

Jianshu 蹇叔 of Song 宋. Jianshu was a Song national that served at Qin about the same time as Baili Xi. He was living as a recluse attending to his farms. On two separate occasions, he gave Baili Xi sound advice not to take up appointments in Qi (when Prince Wuzhi 無知 committed regicide and was later killed) and Yu 虞 (which it was annihilated by Jin). Later Baili Xi recommended him to Qin, and the Qin court made him the right chancellor 右相. As a man, Jianshu was totally indifferent to fame and wealth, however, when Baili Xi insisted that he need help from his friend, Jianshu gave up all the gifts that were bestowed on him by the Qin Duke, and travelled forth to lend his close friend a hand. The *SJ* 史記, 卷 23, 'Qin benji 秦本紀' 第 5, pp. 157-160.

Pi Bao 丕豹 of Jin 晉 was the son of Bi Zheng 丕鄭 a minister at the Jin court. In 650 BCE, Bi Zheng was executed by Duke Hui of Jin 晉惠公 while working as an emissary in Qin. Ji Bao escaped to serve under Qin.

Gongsun Zhi 公孫支 was serving under Duke Mu of Qin 秦穆公 at the Qin court as chancellor. When the Qin Duke retained Baili Xi, he realized that he was not comparable to the man; he relinquished his position to the latter and took on the position as deputy chancellor. The *Spring and Autumn annals* 春秋左氏傳 'Xigong 僖公'.

The three men Baili Xi, Jianshu and Gongsun Zhi came to epitomize the ideal of, "Selecting the virtuous, employing the able, promote the capable, develop sharp eyes to identify the talented, mutually dependent, and to work in harmony," '舉賢任能, 謙恭讓賢, 慧眼識人, 相互依存, 相互配合.' A motto propounded by later day scholars.

181 Qin 秦, "...遂霸西戎."

182 Duke Xiao of Qin 秦孝公 (r. 361-338 BCE).

Gongsun Yang 公孫鞅.

183 King Hui of Qin 秦惠王.

Zhang Yi 張儀 (also see 333 BCE to 310 BCE.)

184 King Zhao of Qin 秦昭王.

clique while greatly augmenting the power of the royal household. The four dukes and kings made good use of the foreign guests to achieve their grand deeds. From what we have gathered, one asks – 'where have the foreign guests failed in serving Qin?' Qin is not a land that produces attractive women, nor a land with fine music composers, not even a land that produces fine pearls and exquisite jade pieces. Your Highness, you have made a large collection of those above. When selecting your officers, you do so aberrantly; you do not even have any qualms as to whether they are capable or otherwise, not questioning the rights from the wrongs; all of them, who are not of Qin origin are dismissed, and all alien guests are banished. You are placing more emphasis on women, music pearls and jade pieces than your consideration for the skilled and talented people. Your subject has heard that Mount Tai does not reject dust to enhance its growth. Hence, it becomes a colossal mound; a river or sea do not reject trickles of water from streams to increase its depth; while a king does not spurn intellectuals hence as to manifest his virtues. For those reasons, the legendary Three Kings - *Sanhuang* and Five Lords - *Wudi* were invincible. Now, Your Highness, you are banishing non-Qin intellects to assist your enemies. You are sending these alien guests to serve the other fief lords; it is no different from assigning your army to the bandits or yielding your fodder and supplies to thieves."

The king summoned Li Si to see him and restored his former position while revoking the decree to banish foreign guests. At that juncture, Li Si had arrived in the County of Liyi; [185] and was recalled to return to the Capital. The king adopted Li Si's proposed strategies. Qin sent clandestine speakers and emissaries to other fiefdoms bringing with them rich gifts of gold and jade pieces for canvassing activities. Fief lords and influential people who could be bribed were bought by rich enticements while assassins removed those obstinate loyalists refusing to collaborate. The clandestine activities drove wedges between the royal elites and their subjects; the illustrious generals then followed up the *coup-de-grace*; within a matter of a few years, Qin unified all under Heaven.[186]

236 BCE *Yichou* 乙丑 Warring States 戰國

King of Qin	秦始王	11th year
King You of Chu	楚幽王	2th year
Qi Tian Jian	齊田建	29th year
King Jingmin of Wei	魏景湣王	7th year
Hann Hann An	韓韓安	3rd year
King Daoxiang of Zhao	趙悼襄王	9th year
Yan Ji Xi	燕姬喜	19th year
Lord Yuan of Wey	衛元君	16th year

Fan Ju 范雎.

185 Liyi County 驪邑 - Lintongxian Shaanxi 陝西 臨潼縣.

186 The six kingdoms collapsed between 225 - 220 BCE. It is estimated that the Qin armies killed, executed and massacred 1,668,000 soldiers during the twenty major battles between 346 and 234 BCE; the figure does not include the minor battles and civilian causalities.

I. Zhao attacked Yan and annexed Liyang.[187] Before the siege was concluded, generals Wang Jian, Huan Yi and Yang Duanhe made an expedition against the Zhao city of Ye, and in the ensuing battles, nine cities fell.[188] Wang Jian continued his attack against Yuyu and Laoyang; while Huan Yi annexed Ye and Anyang.[189]

II. King Daoxiang of Zhao (Zhao Yan) died, his son King Youmu (Zhao Qian) succeeded to the throne.[190] The mother of Zhao Qian was a courtesan; nevertheless, King Daoxiang was so infatuated with the woman that he disposed of Zhao Jia (Zhao Jia) the crown prince, replacing him with Zhao Qian.[191] Zhao Qian was notorious for his repulsive behaviour in the kingdom.

III. It had been over a year since Marquis Wenxin retired to his fief state; fief lords, guests and envoys were milling and gathering in the avenue where he was residing to pay him respect. The king found this most disquieting and was apprehensive lest he might eventually revolt; he wrote a letter to the Marquis, "Sir, what contributions have you made to Qin to deserve a remuneration of ten thousand fief-households at south of the River *Henan*?[192] What relationship do you hold with Qin for being honoured as my Uncle *Zhongfu*? You should take your entire family with you and journey to Shu."[193] Marquis Wenxin knew he was being oppressed; he feared for his life.

---

235 BCE *Bingyin* 丙寅 Warring States 戰國

King of Qin	秦始王	12th year
King You of Chu	楚幽王	3rd year
Qi Tian Jian	齊田建	30th year
King Jingmin of Wei	魏景湣王	8th year
Hann Hann An	韓韓安	4rd year
King Youmou of Zhao	趙幽繆王	1st year
Yan Ji Xi	燕姬喜	20th year
Lord Yuan of Wey	衛元君	17th year

---

187 Liyang 貍陽 - Miyunxian Beijing 北京 密雲縣.

188 Qin generals: Wang Jian 王翦, Huan Yi 桓齮, Yang Duanhe 楊端和.
Ye 鄴 - Linzhangxian Henan 河南 臨漳縣.

189 Yuyu 閼與 - Wuanxian Henan 河南 武安縣.
Laoyang 轑陽 - Liaoxian Shanxi 山西 遼縣.
Ye 鄴 - Linzhangxian Henan 河南 臨漳縣.
Anyang 安陽 - Anyangxian Henan 河南 安陽縣.

190 King Daoxiang of Zhao 趙 悼襄王 Zhao Yan 趙偃.
King Youmu of Zhao 趙 幽穆王 Zhao Qian 趙遷 (r. 235-228 BCE) 5th.

191 Zhao Jia 趙嘉.

192 *Henan* 河南 - south of the River.

193 Shu Prefecture 蜀郡.

I. Marquis Wenxin committed suicide by drinking a *zhen* wine; his family buried him clandestinely.[194] When his former retainers and associates came to mourn his passing they were turned away. The king decreed, "Henceforth, ministers who behave like Lao Ai or Lu Buwei will have their fortunes confiscated, and their family members apprehended, setting this as an example for all."[195]

Yangzi Fayan Annotates:[196]

Someone asks, "Lu Buwei used people as merchandise, trading them for goods. Is he not a wise and resourceful individual?" Yang Xiong says, "Who could say he was wise and resourceful? He exchanged his family clan with a fief state. He was one of the most audacious thieves. I have seen with my own eyes that petty thieves could make off with one *dan* of grain; [197] I have yet to come across one like him, one who attempted to steal Luoyang."

II. Summer. From the 6th to the 8th month it did not rain in Qin.

III. Qin rallied its armed forces from four countries to help Wei to attack Chu.

---

234 BCE *Dingmao* 丁卯 Warring States 戰國

King of Qin	秦始王	13th year
King You of Chu	楚幽王	4th year
Qi Tian Jian	齊田建	31st year
King Jingmin of Wei	魏景湣王	9th year
Hann Hann An	韓韓安	5th year
King Youmou of Zhao	趙幽繆王	2nd year
Yan Ji Xi	燕姬喜	21st year
Lord Yuan of Wey	衛元君	18th year

I. Huan Yi, the Qin general, attacked Zhao; he defeated Hu Zhe the Zhao commanding general at Pingyang.[198] More than one hundred thousand men were decapitated, and Hu Zhe was killed. The king of Zhao (Zhao Qing) made Li Mu the commander-in-chief; the battles were

---

194 *Zhen* wine 酖. According to 胡三省 (1230-1302 CE), "*Zhen* is a bird from the south. It eats a poisonous snake called *fu* 蝮蛇 (a species of viper). The feather of the bird is soaked in wine, when consumed, he dies instantly." The *ZZTJ JZ*, Vol 1, p. 259.

195 Lao Ai 嫪毐.
Lu Buwei 呂不韋.

196 The *Fayan* 法言 was compiled by Yang Xiong 揚雄 (53 BCE -18 CE).

197 *Dan* 石 = 10 *dou* 斗.

198 Qin General 秦將 Huan Yi 桓齮.
Pingyang 平陽 - Linzhangxian Henan 河南 臨漳縣.
Zhao General 趙將 Hu Zhe 扈輒.

re-joined at Yian and Feixia.[199] The Qin invaders suffered a resounding defeat; Huan Yi escaped to return to Qin. The king of Zhao enfeoffed Li Mu as Lord Wuan.[200]

---

233 BCE *Wuchen* 戊辰 Warring States 戰國

King of Qin Shiwang	秦始王	14th year
King You of Chu	楚幽王	5th year
Qi Tian Jian	齊田建	32nd year
King Jingmin of Wei	魏景湣王	10th year
Hann Hann An	韓韓安	6th year
King Youmou of Zhao	趙幽繆王	3rd year
Yan Ji Xi	燕姬喜	22nd year
Lord Wey Yuan	衛元君	19th year

1. Huan Yi made another expedition against Zhao; the army successfully took Yian, Pingyang and Wucheng.[201]

The king of Hann (Hann An) ceded land to sue for peace; he gave up his imperial seal of the kingdom, pleading to relegate his kingdom to be a protectorate of Qin. He summoned Hann Fei to court and appointed him as a state envoy *pin*.[202]

Hann Fei was a Hann prince. He was a learned scholar in Legalism *Fashu*.[203] When he saw his kingdom was weakening progressively, on several occasions, he made submissions to the king, who did not adopt his ideas. It detested him to see the court for failing to source capable officers for administrative duties; in their stead, they embraced frivolous and incompetent individuals as lowly as useless insects as their aides, placing these men in positions far above their capabilities.[204] When the kingdom was at peace, illusory scholars

---

199 King Youmu of Zhao 趙幽穆王 Zhao Qian 趙遷.
Yian 宜安 - Goachengxian Hebei 河北 藁城縣.
Feixia 肥下 - southwest of Feigaocheng 河北 肥藁城西南.

200 Lord Wuan 武安君 Li Mu 李牧.

201 Qin General Huan Yi 秦 桓齮.
Yian 宜安 - Goachengxian Hebei 河北 藁城縣.
Pingyang 平陽 - south of Linzhangxian Henan 河南 臨漳縣.
Wucheng 武城 - within the county of Linzhangxian Henan 河南 臨漳縣.

202 Hann An 韓安. Hann Fei 韓非.
Pin 聘 – when a fief lord sent a minister to visit another state, the emissary was called *pin*.

203 Legalism - *Fushu* 灋術 - 灋 was the archaic word for *fu* 法.

204 According to Hann Fei these men were like the five-destructive insects gnawing at the core of the kingdom.
The *Wudu* 五蠹 the phrase means the 'Five-destructive species of insects', it was used as a metaphor to symbolize the inept and useless sycophants at court, the useless and non-productive subjects in one's kingdom. The five destructive species of insects were - the intellects that pervert the system with their brush; politicians who carried out seditious and treasonous activities; the chivalrous heroes and strongmen (gangsters); the personal attendants of the sovereign and senior

were greatly favoured, while, in times of national crisis, armoured generals and helmet wearing warriors took their place. The people cultivated by the court were not put into good use; while the ones engaged were wrongly cultivated. Hann Fei sadly observed what was transpiring, the righteous and straightforward officers were ostracized and disparaged by the crafty and malicious ministers in power. He made assessments of the merits and failings of the past and composed his observations in five texts: the *Gufen*, the *Wudu*; the *Neichu*; the *Waichu*, the *Shuolin* and the *Shuonan* (see notes for explanation and translation) in fifty-six volumes, with over one hundred thousand words.[205]

The king of Qin had heard that Hann Fei was a worthy man and had intended to meet him. At this stage, Hann Fei was an envoy at Qin representing Hann, and he submitted a memorial to the king. It read, "Qin has a vast terrain of several thousand *li*. It boasts of having a million armed men; no other state under Heaven is comparable with Qin's military command, and its reward and punishment system. Your subject risks his life to plead for an audience with Your Highness. He intends to present to you with a stratagem to break the Vertical Alliance under Heaven. My Lord, please allow your subject to relate to you his plan. If it proves to be ineffective, that Zhao does not surrender, Hann is not annihilated, Chu and Wei do not submit; and Qi and Yan are not subjugated; furthermore if the hegemon of Qin is not fully established, with all the fiefdoms coming forth to pay homage; then, My Lord, please execute your subject – setting it as an example for those who are disloyal to Your Highness." The king was pleased with the submission and was about to give Hann Fei a reception. Li Shi resentful of the submission said to the king, "Hann Fei is one of the many Hann princes. While Your Highness wishes to make a conquest of all the fief lords, please do not forget Hann Fei will pledge his ultimate loyalty to Hann, not to Qin; it is only human nature. Now that Your Highness does not intend to use him, it is not a sensible idea to detain him here for long; we might end up with dire consequences in the future. It is a better option to use a legal pretext to indict him and have him executed." The king agreed; he ordered the prince to stand trial. Li Si clandestinely sent someone to visit the prince and gave him some poison, coercing him to take his life. Hann Fei made another attempt to have an audience with the king but failed. Shortly after, the king recanted, he dispatched his attendants to pardon and release the prince, but he had died.

Yangzi Fayan Annotates:

Someone asked, "Hann Fei composed, 'On Calamities and the Difficulties of Canvassing *Shuonan*.' He met his demise when canvassing his ideal in a foreign land. Dare I ask you why he behaved contrary to what he advocated?" Yangzi

---

ministers who deceived their superiors while suppressing their subordinates; and the artisans and merchants who were perennially after material gains and luxuries. *ZZTJ BY Edition*, 1986, 6th edition, Taiwan, pp. 468-469.

205 The *Gufen* 孤憤 - *On Disillusionment with the World* (*On Being Lonely and Indignation.*)

The *Wudu* 五蠹 - *The Five-destructive Insects*. See above.

The *Neichu* 内儲 - *Inner Parables.*

The *Waichu* 外儲 - *External Parables.*

The *Shuolin* 說林 - *On Numerous Issues, Numerous like Trees in a Forest.*

The *Shuonan* 說難 - *On the Difficulties of Lobbying and Canvassing. ZZTJ JZ*, Vol 1, p. 262.

said, "It was the text that brought his demise." "Why?" "You see, a worthy man behaves according to reputable rites and is regulated by morality and justice. He proceeds if what he advocates is recognized; otherwise, he takes leave. One should be the least concerned if what he propounds is not met with approval. Trying to canvass others while being fretful that he might be met with censure, thence all infelicitous measures could be taken. The person again asked, "That was the concern that Hann Fei had - that his principle might not meet with approval. Was it not?" Yangzi maintains, "Canvassing one's ideal that is not based on ethical premises and the moral path is a very serious concern. Whereas if the ethical path one preaches does not meet his objective, he should be his least concern."

Sima Guang annotates:

Your subject has heard a man of noble character loves his kin; he also loves people's kin. His love extends to his country, and it extends to the people of other states. Hence, a man of noble character can achieve great exploits, with his name radiating prominently throughout the whole world enjoying great fame; whereas Hann Fei schemed for Qin, attempting to depose his kingdom, and he did it for no other purpose than peddling his ideal. His crime is so hideous that even death could not absolve him. Why should anyone pity such a person?[206]

---

232 BCE *Jisi* 己巳 Warring States 戰國

King of Qin Shiwang	秦始王	15th year
King You of Chu	楚幽王	6th year
Qi Tian Jian	齊田建	33rd year
King Jingmin of Wei	魏景湣王	11th year
Hann Hann An	韓韓安	7th year

206 The submission of Hann Fei to the king of Qin to betray his own kingdom does not make sense, whereas in the earlier passage it was stated quite categorically that he was extremely apprehensive about the declining state of his own kingdom. One of the other works by Hann Fei is the *Hann Feizi* 韓非子, which demonstrates he was with great wisdom, the entire text was based on most logical and sensible writings. Bo Yang 柏楊 maintains that the *SJ* 史記 and the *ZGC* 戰國策 do not include this passage and that there is another incident that is mentioned in the latter; Hann Fei was framed by Tao Jia 桃賈, not Li Si 李斯. Hence, according to Po Yang this part of the narratives was internationally censored by Sima Guang 司馬光; as Hann Fei was a Legalist; whereas Sima Guang's opponent at the Song court 宋朝廷 was Wang Anshi 王安石 who was a Legalist disguised as a literati. It was perhaps under those circumstances that Sima Guang attempted to demonize his political opponent at court branding Hann Fei subtly as treasonous.
ZZTJ BY Edition, 1986, 6th edition, Taiwan, p. 471.

King Youmou of Zhao	趙幽繆王	4th year
Yan Ji Xi	燕姬喜	23rd year
Lord Yuan of Wey	衛元君	20th year

I. The king of Qin raised another army against Zhao, one of Qin's army columns penetrated as far as Ye, another reached Taiyuan and annexed Langmeng and Fanwu. When Li Mu confronted the Qin army, it withdrew and returned.[207]

II. Previously, Dan the crown prince of Yan (Ji Dan) was held hostage at Zhao, [208] where he befriended the king of Qin. When the king acceded to the Qin throne, Dan was sent to Qin as a hostage. The king did not regard him with due etiquettes. Greatly infuriated, Ji Dan absconded to return to his homeland.

---

231 BCE *Gengwu* 庚午 Warring States 戰國

King of Qin	秦始王	16th year
King You of Chu	楚幽王	7th year
Qi Tian Jian	齊田建	34th year
King Jingmin of Wei	魏景湣王	12th year
Hann Hann An	韓韓安	8th year
King Youmou of Zhao	趙幽繆王	5th year
Yan Ji Xi	燕姬喜	24th year
Lord Yuan of Wey	衛元君	21st year

I. Hann presented the territories at Nanyang to Qin.[209] 9th month, Qin sent its army to take control of the ceded territories.

II. Wei ceded land to sue for peace.[210]

III. An earthquake occurred at (the Zhao Prefecture of) Dai. From the west of Lexu to the north of Pingyin more than half of the towers, houses and walls collapsed in ruin;[211] the quake caused a huge fissure of one hundred and thirty *bu*.

---

207 Ye 鄴 - Linzhangxian Hebei 河南 臨漳縣.
Taiyuan 太原 - Taiyuanxian Shanxi 山西 太原縣.
Langmeng 狼孟 – was within Taiyuanxian 太原縣.
Fanwu 番吾 - Pingshanxian Hebei 河北 平山縣.
Li Mu 李牧.

208 Yan Prince 燕太子 Ji Dan 姬丹.

209 Nanyang 南陽 - Nanyangxian Henan 河南 南陽縣.

210 The text does not specify what area.

211 Dai Prefecture 代郡 – Weixian Hebei 河北 蔚縣.
Lexu 樂徐 place unknown.
Pingyin 平陰 - southwest of Jinanshi Shandong 山東 濟南市.

230 BCE *Xinwei* 辛未 Warring States 戰國

King of Qin Shiwang	秦始王	17th year
King You of Chu	楚幽王	8th year
Qi Tian Jian	齊田建	35rd year
King Jingmin of Wei	魏景湣王	13th year
Hann Hann An	韓韓安	9th year
King Youmou of Zhao	趙幽繆王	6th year
Yan Ji Xi	燕姬喜	25th year
Lord Yuan of Wey	衛元君	22nd year

I. Sheng, the capital mayor *neishi* of Qin led an army against Hann; Hann An, the king of Hann was captured, the kingdom was annihilated; the Qin government set up the Yingchuan Prefecture at the territories of the former kingdom.[212]

II. Dowager Huayang *taihou* of Qin died.[213]

III. There was a severe famine in Zhao.

IV. Lord Weyyuan (the sovereign of Wey) died, his son Wey Jue succeeded to the state.[214]

229 BCE *Renshen* 壬申 Warring States 戰國

King of Qin	秦始王	18th year
King You of Chu	楚幽王	9th year
Qi Tian Jian	齊田建	36rd year
King Jingmin of Wei	魏景湣王	14th year
King Youmou of Zhao	趙幽繆王	7th year
Yan Ji Xi	燕姬喜	26th year
Lord Jue of Wei	衛衛角	1st year

212 Capital Mayor of Qin *neishi* 秦内史 Sheng 勝.
Xinzheng 新鄭 - the capital of Hann.
The Sovereign of Hann 韓 Hann An 韓安.
Yingchuanjun Prefecture - Yuxian Henan 潁川郡 河南 禹縣.
Hann 韓 - 333-230 BCE the kingdom lasted for 104 years. Hann was the first state to fall.

213 Lady Huayang, *taihou* 秦太后 華陽夫人 she was the grandmother of Qin Shi Huang.

214 Lord Weyyuan 衛元君 (r. 252-230 BCE)
Sovereign of Wey 衛君 Wey Jue 衛角 (r. 229-209 BCE).

1. Wang Jian, the Qin general, led the forces at Shangdi (Shangjun Prefecture) to attack Jingjing; while Duanhe (Yang Duanhe) led the forces from Henei to make a joint attack against Zhao.[215] Li Mu and Sima Shang,[216] (the Zhao generals) put up resistance against the Qin forces. Meanwhile, Qin agents bribed Guo Kai the favourite minister of the king of Zhao (Qian) with a large quantity of gold; [217] through the minion, they calumniated that Li Mu and Sima Shang were scheming a mutiny. The king of Zhao ordered Zhao Cong and a Qi general, Yan Ju to take over their commands.[218] Li Mu refused to relinquish his command; he was arrested and executed, and Sima Shang was dismissed.

---

228 BCE *Guiyou* 癸酉 Warring States 戰國

King of Qin Shiwang	秦始王	19th year
King You of Chu You	楚幽王	10th year
Qi Tian Jian	齊田建	37th year
King Jingmin of Wei	魏景湣王	15th year
King Youmou of Zhao	趙幽繆王	8th year
Yan Ji Xi	燕姬喜	27th year
Lord Jue of Wei	衛衛角	2nd year

1. Wang Jian completely overwhelmed the Zhao forces, killing Zhao Cong, and Yan Ju fled the field. The Qin forces stormed Handan; the king (Zhao Qian) was captured.[219] The king of Qin (Ying Zheng) rode out to Handan, where he ordered the execution of all the enemies of his mother's family (Dowager Zhao Ji). The king then returned to the capital via Taiyuan and Shangjun Prefecture.[220]

---

215 Qin General 秦將 Wang Jian 王翦.
Shangdi 上地 (Shangjun Prefecture 上郡) – Suidexian Shaanxi 陝西 綏德縣.
Jingjing 井陘 – 河北 井陘縣 Jingjingxian Hebei.
Duanhe 端和 Qin General, Yang Duanhe 秦將 楊端和.
Henei 河内 – Qinyangxian Henan 河南 沁陽縣.

216 Li Mu 李牧.
Sima Shang 司馬尚.

217 Guo Kai 郭開.

218 Zhao Cong 趙葱.
Qi General 齊將 Yan Ju 顔聚.

219 Qin General 秦將 Wang Jian 王翦.
General, Zhao Cong 趙葱.
General, Yan Ju 顔聚.
Handan Zhao capital 趙都 邯鄲.
King of Zhao 趙王 Zhao Qian 趙遷.

220 Taiyuan 太原 - Taiyuanxian Shanxi 山西 太原縣.
Shangjun Prefecture 上郡 - Suidexian Shaanxi 陝西 綏德縣.
Xianyang 咸陽 - Xian City Shaanxi 陝西 西安市.

II. The Dowager (Lady Zhaoji) died.[221]

III. Wang Jian garrisoned his army at Zhongshan to continue to exert pressure on Yan.[222] Prince Jia (Zhao Jia) gathered several hundreds of the Zhao nobles and escaped to Dai;[223] there he crowned himself the king of Dai. The former Zhao officers and administrators who managed to escape showed up steadily to pledge fealty to the new king. The remnants of the Zhao army rallied with the Yan army and garrisoned at Shanggu.[224]

IV. King You of Chu (Mi Han) died, his younger brother Hao (Mi Hao) succeeded to the throne.[225] 3rd month. An elder brother of Hao by a concubine, Fuchu (Mi Fuchu) assassinated the king and made himself the new ruler.[226]

V. King Jingmin of Wei (Wei Zeng) died; his son Jia (Wei Jia) assumed the throne.[227]

VI. The crown prince of Yan, Dan (Ji Dan) resentful of the king of Qin, (Ying Zheng) vowed to take revenge. He sought the opinion of his tutor Ju Wu.[228] The prince's tutor told him that he had to seek the support of the San-Jin of Zhao, Wei and Hann in the west, to the south he needed to join forces with Qi and Chu, and to the north, he had to make peace with the Xiongnu to go against Qin. The prince responded, "My Tutor's strategy will take too much time to secure all the supports, I am in anguish, and I am fretful, I do not have the time to wait."

Shortly after, Fan Yuqi, a Qin general,[229] having perpetrated an offence at the Qin court absconded to Yan. The prince offered him asylum and accommodated in a guest lodge. Ju Wu

---

221 Queen Dowager of Qin 秦太后 Zhaoji 趙姬.

222 Wang Jian 王翦.
Zhongshan 中山 - Dingxian Hebei 河北 定縣.

223 Zhao Jia 趙嘉.

224 Shanggu 上谷 – Huailaixian Hebei 河北 懷來縣.

225 King You of Chu 楚幽王 Mi Han 芈悍.
King Ai of Chu 楚哀王 Mi Hao 芈郝.
According to the *SJ* 史記, King Xiaolei 楚 孝烈王 had three sons. During the 10th year, King You 幽王 died, he was succeeded by his younger brother, Mi You 芈猶 by the same mother; he was known as King Ai 哀王. King Ai was king for slightly more than two months, the followers of King Ai's elder brother Fuchu 負芻 attacked and killed King Ai, placing Fuchu on the throne.' *SJ*, 卷 110, 'Chu shijia 楚世家 第' 10, p. 1580.
Both the *SJ* and The *Shiji suoyin* 史記索隱 maintain that King Xiaolei had three sons, and Fuchu was a son by a concubine of King Xiaolei 哀王之庶兄.
While according to the *ZGC* 戰國策, King Xiaolei 楚孝烈王 was infertile and did not leave a son, the son who succeeded him was by Lord Chunshen 春申君. Apparently, *ZZTJ* based its account on *ZGC* that King You was an illegitimate son of Lord Chunshen. *ZGC*, 卷 17, Chu 楚四, pp.179-182.

226 Mi Fuchu 芈負芻 26th.

227 King Jingmin of Wei 魏 景湣王 Wei Zeng 魏增.
Wei Jia 魏假 6th.

228 Ji Dan 姬丹 Yan Zidan 燕子丹.
Taifu 太傅 Ju Wu 鞠武.

229 Fan Yuqi 范於期, also pronounced as Fan Wuji. Yang Kuan 楊寬 maintains that this general might have been Huan Yi 桓齮, partly because his name phonetically resembled that of Fan Yiqi. Huan Yi

remonstrated with the prince, "The spiteful and ferocious temperament of the Qin king is more than adequate to bring on the chill of an unsettling terror, not even considering the baleful hatred he holds against Yan. As if it is not enough, should he find out that you are giving shelter to General Fan, our predicament is like leaving a piece of meat on a well-trodden path of a hungry tiger. Your Highness, please send General Fan Yuqi to the Xiongnu territories without delay."

Ji Dan said, "General Fan is in a destitute state, and he is cornered. He has nowhere to run under Heaven, and he came to me for help. I will risk my life to protect him. Sir, please come up with another option." Ju Wu responded, "It is impossible to take on a perilous venture hoping to emerge unscathed and is equally absurd to create a hazardous dilemma for oneself while considering it a blessing. Poorly circumspect plans and ill-conceived deeds invariably lead to even more dire consequences. For the sake of making a friend without considerations for the devastating peril our kingdom might endure, it is tantamount to amassing additional enmities upon ourselves." Ji Dan refused to heed.

The prince heard that Jing Ke, a Wey national, was a worthy man.[230] He prepared a most humble invitation supplemented by rich gifts to request for an appointment. The prince said to Jing Ke, "Qin has captured the king of Hann, it has also continued to its drive south to attack Chu. Its army has arrived at Zhao in the north, and Zhao is unlikely to withstand the assault of Qin, after that calamity will descend on Yan.[231] Yan is a small state, we have lost several battles, and we simply could not defend ourselves against the onslaught of Qin. The power of Qin daunts all the other fief lords; no one dares to form an alliance against Qin. My plan is to find a most valiant man under Heaven, who could hold the king of Qin hostage, force him to relinquish the lands he has arrogated from other fief lords. It would be a deed reminiscent of Cao Mo holding Duke Huan of Qi hostage,[232] a repeat of the prodigious episode. If the attempt failed, he should be killed forthwith. All the Qin generals are away from the capital, once a crisis as such occurs there will be chaos among the ministers at court, creating misgiving and confusion. The fief lords could take advantage of the chaos to realign the Alliance against Qin, and it will break. Master Jing, please give this matter with due considerations." Jing Ke accepted the proposal. The prince made Jing Ke his guest of honour residing at a premium lodge. The prince visited Jing Ke daily while providing him with every conceivable thing he needed. Later, when Wang Jian annihilated Zhao,[233] The Prince

---

joined battle with Li Mu 李牧 at Feixia 肥下 and was defeated. (See 234-1). He escaped to Yan 燕 according to the *ZGC* 戰國策 and was killed because he lost the battle; whereas the *ZZTJ* 資治通鑒 chronicles that after the defeat he escaped to return, thereafter there were no more records of his whereabouts. Yang K, 楊寬 戰國史 *Zhanguoshi*, p. 431.

230 Jing Ke 荊軻.

231 This visitation to Jing Ke was before the fall of Zhao earlier that year.

232 Cao Mo 曹末; Lu 魯.

In 681 BCE, Duke Huan of Qi, Jiang Xiaobai 姜小白 held a conference with Duke Zhuang of Lu 魯莊公 Ji Tong 姬同 at the Keyi County 柯邑. A Lu general, Cao Mo 曹沫 held Jiang Xiaobai hostage at knifepoint. Reluctantly the Duke of Qi relinquished all the territories he had previously captured from the kingdom of Lu.

Duke Huan of Qi 齊桓公 Jiang Xiaobai 姜小白.

Duke Zhuang of Lu 魯莊公 Ji Tong 姬同.

Keyi 柯邑 - Dongaxian Shandong 山東 東阿縣.

233 Wang Jian 王翦.

Zhao's throne was passed on to a former Prince, Zhao Jia 趙嘉, see 228-1.

became disturbingly alarmed and was about to dispatch Jing Ke on his assignment immediately. Jing Ke reminded him, "If your subject goes forth now, he does not possess a means to ensure that the Qin king would grant him an audience in person. However, if your subject could have General Fan's head, enhanced with a map of Dukang of Yan to be presented to the king, [234] he is sure the king will be most delighted and grant your subject an audience." The prince said, "General Fan in dire despondency sought shelter under me; I do not have the heart to betray him." Jing Ke secretly paid Fan Yuqi a visit and said, "It is beyond belief how maliciously the Qin court treated you and your family members. The king executed all your parents' clansmen to the last person. It is said that he places a price of one thousand catty *jin* of gold and ten thousand households as fief on your head. What do you have in mind?" Fan Yuqi released a long sigh with tears streaming down his face said, "What can I do?" Jing Ke answered, "I would like to have the general's head. When I announce that I will present your head to the king of Qin, the king will be beside himself with glee and will undoubtedly grant me an audience. I intend to grasp hold of the king by his sleeve with my left hand, with the dagger in my right; it will be thrust against his chest. General, your vengeance will hence be vindicated, and the ignominious shame upon the prince of Yan will also be erased." Fan Yuqi said, "I have been gnashing my teeth with bitter odium, loathing day and night, hoping to make avenge for my family. This is it." He slit his won throat. The prince heard of Jing Ke's visit to the general, and rushed to his rescue but no avail; he wept over the body of the general. He then ordered to place the decapitated head in a wooden gift container. Before this, the prince had procured the sharpest dagger under Heaven, and it was infused with a deadly poison by the artisans. The dagger was tried on a person, no sooner had blood seeped through the garment of the victim, and he died. The prince then instructed his attendants to prepare Jing Ke to journey forth. Jing Ke took up the position as the head of the Yan envoy assisted by Qin Wuyang, a valiant man from Yan; the two proceeded to travel to Qin.[235]

---

234 Dukang map 督亢之地圖, Dukang was the most fertile area of Yan, it was situated in the present day Dingxing 定興, Xincheng 新城 and Guan 固安 in Hebei 河北.

235 Qin Wuyang 秦舞陽.
The following passage is not in the *ZZTJ*: Before Jing Ke departed from Yan, his friends donned on white headdresses and garbs; bidding him farewell beyond the city gate of the Yan Capital. As he departed, he chanted, "The chilly wind wails, the water of Yishui River 易水 is frigidly cold. This valiant man ventures to the fore, never to return." '風蕭蕭兮易水寒, 壯士一去兮不復反.' Without even looking back, he went forth. This poem has been one of the most poignant verses in Chinese literary history. *SJ* 史記 卷 56, Cike liezhuan 刺客列傳 第 26, p. 711. It provides us with a hint of the frame of mind of the ancient people: whether Jing Ke was a fool beyond redemption or a hero who felt he could single-handedly change the course of history we have no way of telling. However, it does give us an insight as to why ancient people made sacrifices to save their kingdom, avenge their family clans among other brave exploits, all these rationales to us modern men seem beyond comprehension. Jing Ke was not even a Yan citizen. He might have been an opportunist, taking advantage of a situation. The outcome of which could bring him fame and glory, or perhaps he genuinely believed in his cause, or he was profoundly conscious of the impending collapse of all the six states that he had tried to take on a mission to revert the course of history. History is silent about his motive to undertake such a suicidal mission. The *Yan Dan Zi* 燕丹子 a histological novel composed at the time of Qin or Han does not provide us with any insight into the event either. Qin Wuyang, the valiant young man who accompanied Jing Ke to Qin, was the grandson of Qin Kai 秦開, the general who was held hostage by the Dong-Hu 東胡 (see 244-IV).

Volume VII. 資治通鑒 卷第七 秦紀二 227-209 BCE

The narratives of this volume commence from the 20th year of the king of Qin, Ying Zheng in 227 BCE and end in the 1st year of the Second Emperor of Qin, *Ershi huangdi* (209 BCE).[1]

227 BCE – Jing Ke made an unsuccessful attempt to assassinate the king of Qin, Ying Zheng.[2]

226 BCE – Wang Jian attacked Yan, defeating the Yan army; Prince Ji Dan escaped to Liaodong. The king of Yan sent an assassin to cut off the head of the crown prince to sue for peace.

225 BCE – General Wang Ben of Qin annihilated Wei, the king of Wei, Jia was executed.[3]

224-223 BCE – General Wang Jian of Qin invaded Chu, Mi Fuchu, [4] the king of Chu was captured; Chu was annihilated.

222 BCE – Wang Ben led an army against Liaodong, Ji Xi, the king of Yan was captured. Yan met its end.

Wang Ben continued with his success and defeated the Zhao kingdom at Dai; the king of Dai, Zhao Jia was captured.

222-221 BCE - Wang Ben attacked Qi, the king of Qi, Tian Jian surrendered.

221 BCE - Qin unified the entire world. Qin Shi Huang maintained that his virtues exceeded the Three Emperors, and his exploits were beyond the Five Kings; he changed his title to Huangdi – the August Emperor. He divided his kingdom into thirty-six prefectures. He unified measurements and weighing system. He repatriated one hundred and twenty thousand heroes and elite households to Xianyang by decree and then ordered the construction of expressways throughout his kingdom.

220-219 BCE - The Emperor made expeditions and tours throughout his kingdom. At the tops of the Yishan, Langya, Zhifu mountains he erected stone steles in praise of his successful exploits.

219 BCE - The Emperor ascended to the summit of Taishan Mountain, where he made sacrifices to Heaven, and at the foothills, he made sacrifices to the Earth deities.

The Emperor travelled to the shore of the Eastern Sea, where he sent off the Qi occultist Xu Fu to lead thousands of virgin boys and girls to set sail; Xu Fu went in search of the immortals and the elixir of life.

---

1 Qin Shi Huang 秦始皇帝.

2 Jing Ke 荆軻.

3 Qin general 秦將軍 Wang Ben 王賁.
King of Wei 魏王 Wei Jia 魏假.

4 King of Chu 楚王 Mi Fuchu 芈負芻.

215 BCE – The Emperor sent Meng Tian to head up three hundred thousand troops to attack the Xiongnu and to construct the Long-Wall to prevent the encroachment by the nomadic tribes.[5]

214 BCE – Five hundred thousand convicts and civilians were relocated at Wuling in the far south of the kingdom.[6]

213 BCE – The Emperor buried scholars and burned books. 212 BCE – Meng Tian was ordered to construct expressways from Yunyang to Jiuyuan, the task was never completed. The Emperor conscripted seven hundred thousand convicts to construct the Epang (Afeng) Palace and his burial mound at Lishan.

210 BCE – The Emperor died at Shaqiu. Zhao Gao and Li Si fabricated the imperial decree made Ying Huhai the successor to the throne; then decreed that Ying Fusu the crown prince, take his own life. The Emperor was buried at Lishan Mound. Meng Tian and Meng Yi were executed.

209 BCE – Ying Huhai meted out a bloodbath, executed his brothers, sisters and nobles. Chen Sheng and Wu Guang took up arms and revolted. Liu Bang raised an army at the county of Pei. Xiang Liang and Xiang Yu rebelled at Kuaiji. The former nobles of various kingdoms during the times of the Warring States rose up in rebellion.

Qin Chronicle II 秦紀二

227 BCE *Jiaxu* 甲戌 Warring States 戰國

King of Qin	秦始王	20th year
Chu Fuchu	楚負芻	1st year
Qi Tian Jian	齊田建	38th year
Wei Weijia	魏魏假	1st year
King Dai of Zhao	趙代王	1st year
Yan Ji Xi	燕姬喜	28th year
Wey, Wey Jue	衛衛角	3rd year

5 Meng Tian 蒙恬.

6 Wuling 五嶺 now known as Nanling 南嶺 is a mountain range that separates the southern part of Zhongyaun 中原 from Guangdong 廣東 and Guangxi 廣西 the two provinces to the south. The mountain range situated in Hunan 湖南, Jiangxi 江西, Guangdong and Guangxi 廣西 provinces commences from the north-western part of Guangxi stretching towards the east, ends in the southern parts of Min 閩 – Fujian 福建. It is roughly 600 km from east to west, and about 200 km from the north to the south. The mountain range is made up of five principal mountains – Yuechengling 越城嶺, Dupangling 都龐嶺, Mengzhuling 萌渚嶺, Qitianling 騎田嶺, and Dagengling 大庚嶺. Han Dian 漢典 and *Zhonghua renmin gongheguo fensheng dituji* 中華人民共和國分省地圖集 Ditu chubanshe 地圖出版社, China, 1974, p. 83

I. Jing Ke arrived at Xianyang. Through Meng Jia, a favourite minion of the king of Qin, he prepared a humble letter pleading to seek an audience with the king.[7] The king was ecstatic; he promptly granted him an audience. The king donned his regal garments and diadem fitting for formal court occasions, also ordered the nine grade elites and officers to attend the reception.[8]

Jing Ke advanced towards the king clutching the map of Yan with both hands. He unfurled the map as he reached the end of the scroll, and the dagger emerged.[9] With his left hand clutching hold of the king's sleeve, with his right Jing Ke wielded his dagger and thrust at the king. Before he could reach him, the king stunned, abruptly rose to his feet ripping off his sleeve and broke free, with the assailant pursuing after him. The king scuttled aimlessly encircling the pillars in the audience hall. The officers at court were awestruck and dumbfounded; everyone lost their composure. According to Qin law, senior officers and attendants attending court were prohibited from carrying arms; all the attendants could do was to dash forward fighting off the assassin with bare hands and yelled, "Your Highness, draw your sword, draw your sword." The king drew his sword and with one strike, he lopped off Jing Ke's left leg from the thigh down. Jing Ke incapacitated, with his dagger he hurled at the king, but missed, striking a bronze pillar. Jing Ke knew he had missed his chance; he berated the king, "I failed as I had intended to keep you alive holding you hostage to sign a treaty to repay my prince." The imperial guards quartered Jing Ke; his body parts were hoisted over the city gate for public display. The king threw a ferocious tantrum and his anger was far too fearful to behold. He decreed to increase the forces to march forth to Zhao and ordered Wang Jian to lead the combined armed forces to attack Yan. The battle was joined on the west bank of the Yishui River against the joined forces of Yan and Dai, [10] which were completely overwhelmed.

---

226 BCE *Yihai* 乙亥 Warring States 戰國

---

7 The capital of Qin - Xianyang 秦 咸陽.
Meng Jia 蒙嘉. Meng Jia was a junior attendant 中庶子 *zhongshuzi* at the Qin court. The *SJ* 史記, 卷 56, 'Cike liezhuan 刺客列傳' 第 26, p. 711.
Some suspect that Meng Jia might not have had the influence to persuade the Qin king to meet Jing Ke in person; or as some maintain, Ying Zheng genuinely believed that Yan was about to submit to Qin.
Fan Yuqi 樊於期 see 228 BCE.
The map of Dukang of Yan 燕督亢之地圖. See 228-VI.

8 The nine grades of elites and officers or dignitaries *jiubin* 九賓. These were the duke 公 *gong*, marquis 侯 *hou*, count 伯 *bo*, viscount 子 *zi*, baron 男 *nan*, junior enfeoffed lord (?) 孤 *gu*, minister 卿 *qing*, counsellor 大夫 *dafu*, scholar 士 *shi*. The phrase of *jiubin* 九賓 originates from Zhouli 周禮; however, its meaning and designation changed over time. According to Liu Bozhuang 唐 劉伯莊 (627-649 CE), he claimed that it was not critically important to draw on ancient texts to verify who the nine grades of dignitaries were, and that the phrase meant an important state function. The *ZZTJ JZ*, p. 271.

9 Details of this section vary considerably from that of the *SJ*, which tells us that, the valiant young Qin Wuyang's 秦武開 expression had by then turned into a deadly parlour, quivering with fright. Jing Ke, with nerves of steel, laughed and explained to the king that the lowly peasant from the barbaric north had never had a chance of meeting a real king. The *SJ* 史記, 卷 56, 'Cike liezhuan 刺客列傳' 第 26, p. 712.

10 Yishui River 易水.

King of Qin	秦始王	21st year
Chu Fuchu	楚負芻	2nd year
Qi Tian Jian	齊田建	39th year
Wei Weijia	魏魏假	2nd year
King Dai of Zhao	趙代王	2nd year
Yan Ji Xi	燕姬喜	29th year
Wey, Wey Jue	衛衛角	4th year

I. Winter, 10th month. Wang Jian captured Ji (the capital of Yan), the king of Yan (Ji Xi) and the crown prince (Ji Dan) led the kingdom's elite troops retreated to Liaodong.[11] The Qin general, Li Xin, was hot on the heels of the retreating army.[12] The king of Dai, Jia (Zhao Jia) wrote a missive to the king of Yan demanding the head of Prince Dan.[13] The prince escaped and went into hiding near the Yanshui River.[14] The king of Yan sent an emissary to visit the prince and had him assassinated, and was planning to present his head to the king of Qin. However, the king continued the attack against Yan.

II. Wang Ben, the Qin general, attacked Chu, [15] he annexed more than ten cities. The king of Qin asked Li Xin, "I intend to conquer Jing (Chu).[16] General, according to your estimate, how many men do you think will be adequate?" Li Xin answered, "No more than two hundred thousand." The king then asked Wang Jian, [17] the general answered, "Nothing short of six hundred thousand." The king said, "General, you have passed your prime, and you have lost you nerve." The king nominated Li Xin and Meng Tian to lead two hundred thousand troops to make an expedition against Chu. Wang Jian claimed that he had taken ill, resigned from his post, and retired to his hometown at Pinyang.[18]

---

225 BCE *Bingzi* 丙子 Warring States 戰國

King of Qin	秦始王	22nd year
Chu Fuchu	楚負芻	3rd year

---

11 Wang Jian 王翦.
Ji 薊 - Jicheng 薊城 - near present-day Beijing 北京.
Ji Xi 姬喜.
Liaodong 遼東 - Liaoyangxian Liaoning 遼寧 遼陽縣.

12 Qin general 秦將 Li Xin 李信.

13 King of Zhao 趙王 Zhao Jia 趙嘉.

14 Yanshui 衍水 - now known as Taizihe 太子河 (Crown Prince River) naming after Ji Dan 姬丹, one of the longest rivers in Liaoning 遼寧.

15 Qin general 秦將 Wang Ben 王賁.

16 Qin general 秦將 Li Xin 李信.
Jing 荆 – the capital of Chu 楚 was Jing, so the statement '吾欲取荆,' meant, 'I intend to conquer Chu.'

17 Qin general 秦將 Wang Jian 王翦.

18 Li Xin 李信 and Meng Tian 蒙恬.
Pinyang 頻陽 - Fupingxian Shaanxi 陕西 富平縣.

Qi Tian Jian	齊田建	40th year
Wei Weijia	魏魏假	3rd year
King Dai of Zhao Dai	趙代王	3rd year
Yan Ji Xi	燕姬喜	30th year
Wey, Wey Jue	衛衛角	5th year

I. Wang Ben, the Qin general, attacked Wei; the army diverted the water from the River to inundate Daliang.[19] During the 3rd month, the walls of the city collapsed; Jia (Wei Jia) the king of Wei surrendered; he was duly executed. The Wei Kingdom came to an end.[20]

The king sent his attendant to see Lord Anling of Wei; the envoy related the message, "I intend to exchange your city of Anling for five hundred *li* of land."[21] Lord Anling responded, "Your subject is greatly honoured by the generosity of His Highness, especially when he intends to exchange a large territory for a small city. He is most grateful for the offer; nevertheless, your subject dares not comply, as the former king of Wei bestowed the city upon him. He will defend the city to the very end, and he dares not comply with the exchange." The king was moved by the virtue of the man, and he did not force the issue.

II. Li Xin attacked Pingyu of Chu while Meng Tian invested his army against the City of Qin, [22] the Chu army was completely routed. Li Xin followed up by attacking Yanying, [23] which was breached. The army continued to march west, intending to meet up with Meng Tian's forces at Chengfu; [24] however, the Chu army hotly pursued Li Xin's forces; for three days and nights, the Qin army was afforded no rest. Li Xin was sounding defeated; two fortified ramparts were breached; seven commander-grade officers *duwei* were killed.[25] Li Xin escaped to return to the Qin capital. When the king heard of the defeat, he threw a towering tantrum. He then personally went to Puyang to visit Wang Jian. He said apologetically, "General, I did not adopt your proposal. Li Xin has brought great shame and dishonour to our Qin army. While you have taken ill, how heartless you are to leave me to my own devices?" Wang Jian excused himself, claiming that he was unwell and indisposed to lead an army. The king said, "Whatever happened came to pass, enough said." Wang Jian said, "If Your Highness insist on using your subject to take command, he insists that he need six hundred thousand men." Ying Zheng responded, "I will comply with your scheme."

---

19 Wang Ben 王賁.
Wei 魏 - Daliang 大梁 - Kaifengxian Henan 河南 開封縣.

20 Wei 魏 as a kingdom lasted for 145 year, from 369 to 225 BCE.

21 Wei, Lord Anling 魏 安陵君; Anling 安陵 – Yanlingxian Henan 河南 鄢陵縣. (See 247 BCE).
Ji Xi 姬喜.
Liaodong 遼東 - Liaoyangxian Liaoning 遼寧 遼陽縣.

22 Qin general 秦將 Li Xin 李信.
Li Xin Pingyu 平輿 – Runanxian Henan 河南 汝南縣.
Meng Tian 蒙恬 attacked Qin 寢 - Shenqiuxian Henan 河南 沈邱縣.

23 Yanying 鄢郢 - Huainanxian Henan 河南 淮陽縣.

24 Chengfu 城父 - southeast of Boxian Anhuai 安徽 亳縣 東南.

25 Commander grade *duwei* 都尉.

Wang Jian took command of six hundred thousand men to march against Chu. The king personally sent off the army at Bashang.[26]Before marching off, Wang Jian requested the bestowment of large plots of fine farmland. The king said, "All you have to do is to march off, general. Why are you troubled for being poor?" Wang Jian said, "No matter how meritorious your generals have been in the past, Your Highness has never bestowed them with any enfeoffment. While Your Highness still needs the service of your subject, he thinks it is an opportune moment to ask for some bestowments; he is only doing it for his descendants." The king burst out laughing. When the army arrived at the Pass, [27] Wang Jian had by then dispatched five more envoys to ask for further land bestowments from the king. Someone asked, "General, are you not getting too persistent begging for more bestowment?" Wang Jian answered, "Not really. You see, His Highness is most suspicious of the people around him, never trusting anyone serving under him. He has entrusted me with the entire armed forces of the kingdom; if I do not make a request for more bestowments for my descendants to show my fealty he might become most suspicious, doubting that I might revolt."

---

224 BCE *Dingchou* 丁丑 Warring States 戰國

King of Qin	秦始王	23rd year
Chu Fuchu	楚負芻	4th year
Qi Tian Jian	齊田建	41st year
King Dai of Zhao	趙代王	4th year
Yan Ji Xi	燕姬喜	31st year
Wey, Wey Jue	衛衛角	6th year

1. Wang Jian took the route south of Chen (Chenqiu) and arrived at Pingyu.[28] When Chu heard that Wang Jian had returned with an enlarged force, they hurriedly rallied all the combat capable men within the kingdom to go into defence. Wang Jian commanded his men to stay within the ramparted barracks, refusing to engage in battle. The Chu army challenged the Qin forces several times but failed to draw out the enemy. Wang Jian ordered his men to rest in the camps, allowing the soldiers to bathe and wash every day, and he ordered to prepare good food and drinks to console his men; and shared his meals with his soldiers. After a considerable length of time, Wang Jian sent his attendant to pry on his men on the games they were playing to entertain themselves. The attendant reported, "The army officers are playing games of tossing stones and leaping." Wang Jian said, "It is time." The Chu forces failing to provoke a battle decided to march east; Wang Jian followed in hot pursuit. He then ordered his crack troops to attack; the Chu army was given a resounding defeat. The Chu army retreated to the south of Qi County, where

---

26 Bashang 霸上 - East of the Xi'an City on the shore of Bashui River 西安市東 霸水之畔.

27 Wuguan Pass 武關 - Shangxian Shaanxi 陝西 商縣 武關.

28 Chenqiu 陳丘 - Huaiyangxian Henan 河南 淮陽縣.
Pingyu 平輿 - Runanxian Henan 河南 汝南縣.

General Xiang Yan of Chu died in action, [29] and the Chu forces dispersed. Wang Jian followed up his victory by assuming controls of numerous cities and counties.

---

223 BCE *Wuyin* 戊寅 Warring States 戰國

King of Qin	秦始王	24th year
Chu Fuchu	楚負芻	5th year
Qi Tian Jian	齊田建	42nd year
King Dai of Zhao	趙代王	5th year
Yan Ji Xi	燕姬喜	32nd year
Wey, Wey Jue	衛衛角	7th year

1. Wang Jian and Meng Wu captured the king of Chu, Mi Fuchu. The kingdom fell; it was renamed the Chu Prefecture.[30]

---

222 BCE *Jimao* 己卯 Warring States 戰國

King of Qin	秦始王	25th year
Qi Tian Jian	齊田建	43rd year
King Dai of Zhao	趙代王	6th year
Yan Ji Xi	燕姬喜	33rd year
Wey, Wey Jue	衛衛角	8th year

1. Qin launched another major military campaign. Wang Ben attacked Liaodong (Yan) and captured the king of Yan, Xi (Ji Xi).[31]

Sima Guang annotates:

Yan Dan, failing to contain his ephemeral wrath, made affront against Qin - a kingdom as ferocious as a tiger and as vicious as a wolf. His plan was insubstantial and shallow, and he acted injudiciously. It incited further animosity, quickening the demise of his state. His failed attempt made the

---

29 Qinan 蘄南- Suxian Anhui 安徽 宿縣.
Chu Commanding General 楚將軍 Xiang Yan 項燕. (Xiang Liang 項梁 was the son of General Xiang Yan, and Xiang Yu 項羽 was the grandson.)

30 King of Chu 楚王 Mi Fuchu 羋負芻.
Chu as a kingdom lasted for 519 years, 741-223 BCE. N.B. There was not a Chu Prefecture 楚郡; it was probably a temporary measure; Chu was later divided into three prefectures - Jiujiang 九江, Zhang 鄣 and Kuaiji 會稽. *ZZTJ JZ*, Vol 1, pp. 275-276.

31 As a kingdom, Yan 燕 lasted for 111 years 333-222 BCE. It was founded by Zhaogong 召公 and as a state, it lasted from roughly 1045 BCE to 222 BCE, details see below.

proffering of sacrifices to the Holy Shrine of Yan came to an abrupt end.[32] What a grave transgression against his ancestors! Some maintain that he was an honourable man. It is preposterous! The mandate of a sovereign is to designate capable individuals to take charge of administrative duties, to uphold the political practice within established rites and etiquettes, to dispense benevolent rules to preside over his subjects, and to employ credible and honourable policies to deal with his neighbouring states. Through these prudent measures, a sovereign acquires judicious officers to advance righteous policies for his state, while his subjects embrace his munificence and his neighbouring states are affable for his rectitude. When a sovereign attains such a position, the institution of his kingdom is as substantial as foundation stones; the supremacy of the state burns and shine so bright, that whoever dares to make contact breaks into smatterings; and one who tries to antagonize is completely scorched. Even if there are more formidable, more ferocious adversaries, what are the causes for concern? Dan (Ji Dan), an heir of a kingdom boasted of having ten thousand chariots, did not choose the suitable path. Instead, he chose the deprived practice of an ignoramus individual and indulged in a thievery act to avenge his personal rancour and humiliation. He failed and met his demise, with his ancestral holy shrine leveled to a necropolis. Was it not sad? To lower oneself proceeding on all fours, inching forward on one's knees, grovelling in front of a more commanding person is not a sign of respect. Abiding by one's personal pledges is not an entity of integrity. Dispensing people with riches and jewellery is not a gesture of benefaction. Lopping off one's head and spilling one's guts is not a deed of bravery. In a word, a person as such is the likes of Baigong Sheng of Chu, merely being mindful of the short-term nuisance while not caring for the enduring moral consequences (see notes).[33] Jing Ke, for returning the generous

---

32 The holy shrine of Yan 燕社稷. Duke Zhao of Yan 燕召公 Ji Shi 姬奭, 11th century BC, was the first duke of Yan. The duke was a personal aide - *taibao* 太保 to the king. King Wu of Zhou 周武王 (r. 1046-1043 BCE) enfeoffed him at Zhao 召, southwest of Qishanxian Shaanxi 陕西 岐山縣西南, hence he came to be known as Duke Zhao. Ji Ke 姬克 the eldest son of Duke Zhao was enfeoffed at Yan 燕. As a fiefdom, Yan lasted for over 800 years. The *SJ* 史記, 卷 104, 'Yan Zhaogong shijia 燕召公世家' 第 4, p. 1457.

33 Mi Sheng 芈勝 was also known as Bai Sheng 白勝, or Baigong Sheng 白公勝 (?-479 BCE). He was the grandson of King Ping of Chu 楚平王 Mi Qiji 芈棄疾 (r. 528-516 BCE). The newly wedded wife of Crown Prince Mi Jian's 芈建 was a ravishing beauty, and the old king attempted to kill his son to take possession of the woman. Mi Jian escaped to the fiefdom of Zheng 鄭, where he was embroiled in the state politics and intrigue and was killed. Mi Sheng (Bai Sheng), the son of Mi Jian was still being swaddled when this happened in 527 BCE. Later when he grew up he returned to the kingdom of Chu and attempted to persuade his elders to take revenge for his deceased father; he rebelled against the kingdom; nevertheless, he failed and committed suicide. The *SJ* 史記, 卷 110, 'Chu shijia 楚世家' 第 10, pp. 1570 & 1573.

gifts and favours bestowed upon him by the prince took little heed of the wellbeing of his seven family clans, attempted to strengthen Yan while weakening Qin with a dagger.[34] Is it not foolhardy? Hence, when Yang Xiong made commentaries on the assassins, he maintained that You Li was a trivial entity, he die like a spider being squashed; Nie Zheng died like a strong man at best; while Jing Ke died like an assassin.[35] None of them should even be considered virtuous or worthy. He added, "From the perspective of a gentleman, Jing Ke is no more than a bandit or thief." Well said! [36]

II. Wang Ben (Qin general) attacked Dai (Zhao); the king of Dai (Zhao Jia) was captured.[37]

---

34 尺八匕首 - one *che* eight *cun* bishou – one-foot eight-inch dagger.

35 Yao Li 要離 (?-513 BCE) was an assassin at the time of King Helu of Wu 吳王 闔閭 (r. 514-496 BCE), he assassinated Qingji 慶忌 for the king of Wu and died in the process. There are conflicting accounts of the background of this assassin. The incident of the assassination of Qingji 慶忌 appears in the *Wuyue chunqiu* 吳越春秋, 'Helu neizhuan 闔閭内傳' 卷四, 闔閭二年; whereas in the *Zuozhuan* 左傳, Qingji 慶忌 died in 475 BCE and the incident was entirely different from the accounts of the *Wuyue chunqiu*. The *SJ* has no mention of this incident. Many scholars consider the account in *Wuyue chunqiu* as fictitious. The incident - *ZZTJ JZ*, Vol 1, p. 278.

Nie Zheng 聶政 see 397-I.

36 Sima Qian 司馬遷 makes an annotation on Jing Ke 荆軻: "When people deliberate over Jing Ke, they invariably relate the fate of Prince Dan, that he inspired - 'the Heaven to rain millet' and 'a horse to grow horns.'* It is rather absurd. They also mention that Jing Ke in his assassination attempt had wounded the king of Qin; none of these incidents was true. Previously, when Gongsun Jigong 公孫季功 and Dong Sheng 董生 befriended with Xia Wuqie 夏無且,** they told me what had transpired. Commencing from the times of Cao Mo 曹沫 to Jing Ke; there were five illustrious men;*** their accomplishments, their failures and their stances were open-minded and sincere, they did not hide their personal mandates; their reputations outlived them by ages. Such is the truth." The *SJ* 史記, 卷 56, 'Ceke liezhuan 刺客列傳' 第 26, p. 713.

* When Ji Dan 姬丹 was held as a hostage at Qin 秦, he requested to return to his own kingdom. Ying Zheng 嬴政 refused, he said, "Unless the crest of crows turned white, and horses grew horns, I would not allow you to leave." The prince raised his head to face Heaven and heaved a long sigh, and as it transpired, the crest of a crow turned white, and a horse also grew horns. The *Yan Danzi*, Volume 1 燕丹子卷上. The work was anonymous and was not listed in the *Hanshu* 漢書, 'Yiwenzhi 藝文志', it was considered as a novel more so than a historical account, scholars have been debating the time when it was composed for centuries.

** We only know those three men by their names; the details of their lives are obscured.

*** The five assassins were: Cao Mo 曹沫. In 681 BCE Cao Mo held the Duke Huan of Qi 齊桓公 Jiang Xiaobai 姜小白 hostage for ransom. (See 228–VI footnotes).

Zhuan Zhu 專諸. In 515 BCE, Zhuan Zhu hid a dagger in a dish of cooked fish and successfully assassinated the king of Wu, Liao 吳王僚. The *SJ* 史記, 卷 56, 'Cike liezhuan 刺客列傳' 第 26, p. 705.

Yu Rang 豫讓 was the assassin who attempted to kill Zhao Wuxu 趙無恤; the incident happened in 453 BCE. (See 403-III).

Nie Zheng 聶政 (See 397-I).

Jing Ke 荆軻 (See 228-VI).

37 Zhao 趙 fell the next year. Zhao as a kingdom lasted for 105 years, 326-221 BCE.

III. Qin general, Wang Jian, pacified Jing the territories in Jiangnan (the former kingdom of Chu, south of the Changjiang River). He continued to defeat the numerous tribes of Bai-Yue; he then established the Prefecture of Kuaijijun.[38]

IV. 5th month. The Qin government authorized civilians to celebrate by holding banquets.

V. Before this, the Dowager of Qi, [39] a virtuous and capable woman handled Qin with diplomacy; moreover, she successfully established affable relationships with other fief states. The Qi kingdom was located at the remote seashore to the far east. When Qin was preoccupied with attacking and invading the San-Jin kingdoms of Wei, Hann, Zhao, Yan and Chu, and these states were busily defending themselves, Qi was spared from being mired in the incessant turmoil. For over forty years since the ascension of the king, Tian Jian, [40] Qi did not sustain any military attacks. At her deathbed, the dowager instructed the king, Jian, "There are some officers who are worthy for appointment." The king said, "Wait; I will have their names written down." The dowager said, "Good." When the king returned with his brush and writing slips, the dowager said, "This old woman has forgotten what she was saying." After the passing of the dowager, Hou Sheng was appointed as chancellor.[41] A large amount of bribes from Qin drained into his coffer while similar generous treatments also entertained the Qi envoys and guests who visited the Qin court. The guests working against the interest of Qi advised the king that the best diplomatic policy was to submit and serve Qin; and that there was no need to make improvements to the military equipment or to make repairs to the deference installations. When the other kingdoms appealed to Qi for help, the ministers invariably advised against it. It afforded Qin to annihilate the five kingdoms with ease. The king of Qi was about to depart to Qin to pay homage to the king of Qin when he arrived at the city gate (of Linzi). A gate commander asked him,[42] "Our kingdom has a king, is it for our holy shrine, or is it for Your Highness?" Tian Jian responded, "Naturally it is for our holy shrine." The commander asked, "That being the case, why is Your Highness leaving our holy shrine to go to Qin?" The king asked his carriage driver to double back and returned to his palace. The magistrate of Jimo, [43] heard of what had happened, made an appointment to see the king, and suggested, "Qi has several thousand *li* of land, and we boast of having several million armed men. Now, there are several hundred former ministers of San-Jin who

---

Qin General 秦將 Wang Ben 王賁.

Dai 代 - Weixian Hebei 河北 蔚縣.

King Dai of Zhao 趙代王 Zhao Jia 趙嘉. Zhao Jia escaped to Dai in 228 BCE.

38 Yue Kingdom 越 was annihilated by the combined forces of Chu and Qi in 306 BCE. The *ZZTJ* does not chronicle this event. (See 334-III footnotes.)

Changjiang River 長江.

Bai-Yue 百越. There were scores of minor tribal states after the Yue Kingdom broke up in 306 BCE.

Prefecture of Kuaijijun 會稽郡 – Wuxian Jiangsu 江蘇 吳縣.

39 The daughter of the grand historian, *Taishi* Ao 太史敖. (See 279-III)

40 Tian Jian 田建.

41 Hou Sheng 后勝 was from the Dowager's family clan.

42 Linzi 臨淄 - Linzixian Shandong 山東 臨淄縣.

City-gate commander, *yongmen sima* 雍門司馬.

43 Jimo 即墨 - Pingduxian Shandong 山東 平度縣.

refused to submit to Qin and are staying in the areas of A and Zhen.[44] If Your Highness rallies these men and assigns them with one million of our armed men, commands them to go against Qin, it is believed the Linjin Pass could be taken.[45] At Yanying (the former Chu capital), there are also several hundred officers who refused to surrender to Qin; and they find refuge in the city of Chengnan.[46] Your Highness should also consider rallying them, providing them with one million armed men; command them to restore their former kingdom; the Wu Pass could also be taken.[47] With these measures the prestige of Qi could be established; the kingdom of Qin could also be annihilated; it is not merely for the security of our kingdom." The king of Qi refused to listen.

---

221 BCE *Gengchen* 庚辰 Warring States 戰國

King of Qin Shiwang	秦始王	25th year
Qi, Tian Jian	齊田建	44th year
Wey, Wey Jue	衛衛角	9th year

1. Qin general, Wang Ben, attacked Qi from the south of the former Yan; the army marched swiftly into Linzi; no civilian put up a resistance. Qin sent someone to persuade the king of Qi with a pledge of five hundred *li* of land for his surrender; the king agreed to it.[48]

Qin banished the king to the County of Gong in a pine and cypress forest; the king finally succumbed to starvation.[49] The people of Qi reproached their king for not participating in the Alliance and that he only heeded the advice of the sycophants and guests at court, bringing on the demise of the kingdom; they wrote an ode to lament the loss of their homeland:

> Was it a pine or cypress forest? The banishment of Jian to Gong was the grinds and drudgeries of the guest canvassers.

The people of Qi chastised Jian for not retaining foreign guests wisely.

Sima Guang annotates:

The Vertical Alliance and the Horizontal Coalition were ceaselessly volatile with impermanence; nevertheless, it was, in essence, the most favourable disposition for the six kingdoms. When the former kings (the founding fathers of Zhou) founded the

---

44 A 阿- A'jing and Zhenyi 阿井 甄邑.

45 Linjinguan Pass 臨晉關 - Chaoyixian Shanxi 山西 朝邑縣.

46 Yanying 鄢郢 - Shouxian Anhui 安徽 壽縣 former Chu capital.
Chengnan 城南 – Nanpoxian Jiangxi 江西 南坡縣.

47 Wu Pass 武關 – Wuguan - east of Shangxian Shaanxi 陝西 商縣東.

48 Qi 齊 as a kingdom lasted for 128 years, 359-221 BCE.

49 Gong 共 - Gongyi county 共邑 - Huixian Henan 河南 煇縣. Gong was an ancient polity.

kingdom, they enfeoffed ten thousand fiefdoms; they held that the fief lords would be benign to one another and cherish each other,[50] through formal visitations they could develop affable relationships, promoting their blissful affiliation through banquets, forming alliances to sponsor solidarity. The notion was forthright; the kings of Zhou needed their concerted corporation and unanimous support to safeguard the state they founded. Had the six kingdoms held one another with honest intentions and confided in each other, thence no matter how ruthless, and brutal Qin was - it could not be a threat to their existence. The composite of San-Jin (Zhao, Hann and Wei) was an innate topographical barrier for Qi and Chu; while Qi and Chu were also the root and foundation of the San-Jin; strategically and politically they were inseparable and indivisible. When Wei, Zhao and Hann attacked Qi and Chu, they were digging away and dismantling their foundations; while when Qi and Chu invaded the San-Jin, they, in fact, were eliminating their innate barricades; how imprudent and irrational were these fiefdoms; it was no different from ingratiating oneself to thieves. It is like saying, "The thieves and bandits are devoted to me they will never attack me." It was preposterous to the extreme.

11. The king (of Qin) finally united all under Heaven; he maintained that his virtues were above that of the Three Kings *Sanhuang* and his exploits surpassed that of Five Lords *Wudi*. He changed his title to Emperor *Huangdi*.[51] The state proclamations would henceforth be known as *zhi*, his decrees known as *zhao* and he would address himself as *Zhen*.[52] He honoured King Zhuangxiang (his deceased father Ying Yiren) as the Supreme Emperor *Taishanghuang*.[53] Finally, he decreed, "The posthumous title, based on the deeds and exploits of a king when he was alive, appended to a deceased Emperor is no more than the deliberations on the parts of his sons and subjects; they are ineffectual and futile, riddled with overindulgence. Posthumous titles will hence be abrogated. *Zhen* (I am) *Shi Huangdi*, the First Emperor of Qin; my descendants who follow me will be related

50 Ten thousand - was a hyperbole.

51 *Sanhuang Wudi* 三皇五帝 - The Three Kings and Five August Lords. Those were the legendary kings of prehistoric China. As to whom the Three Huang and Five Di were, there have been many scholastic debates. Generally speaking - *Sanhuang* were Tianhuang 天皇, Dihuang 地皇 and Taihuang 泰皇; and the *Wudi* were Huangdi 黄帝, Zhuanxu 顓頊, Diku 帝嚳, Yao 堯 and Shun 舜. The *ZZTJ JZ*, Vol 1, p.282.

Qin Shi Huangdi 秦始皇帝 - Huangdi is roughly translated as the August Lord or Emperor. By the time of Warring States, the titles of kings and sovereigns had completely lost their meanings, every vassal lord was a king, and hence Ying Zheng made himself - Shi Huangdi 始皇帝, the First August Lord or the commencement of the lord king. This term was adopted and had been in use for over two thousand years until the end of the Qing dynasty 清 when the Republic of China toppled it in 1912.

Ying Zheng 嬴政 came to be known as Qin Shi Huangdi 秦始皇帝 - the First Emperor of Qin.

52 State proclamations were known as *zhi* 制, the Emperor's decrees were known as *zhao* 昭, and he addressed himself as *zhen* 朕, instead of 'I or me' used by his subjects and commoners.

53 Ying Yiren 嬴異人, the Supreme Emperor, *Taishanghuang* 太上皇.

to as *Ershi* - Second Generation,[54] *Sanshi* - Third Generation and so forth for ten thousand generations, and until eternity."

III. Many years before this, during the time of kings Wei and Xuan of Qi; Zou Yan advanced a scholastic thesis: "On the Relations of the Five Virtues".[55] When Shi Huangdi finally unified All under Heaven, Qi scholars made a submission of the thesis to the Emperor. The Emperor accepted the notion, maintaining that the virtue of the Zhou Kingdom was fire based; Qin replaced Zhou, and based on the inference that fire overwhelmed water; hence, the Qin Empire was water based. He changed the calendar and made the tenth month of every year be the commencement of each new year. All the court homages and celebrations were rescheduled to concur with the first day of the tenth month. The colour chosen for the official trappings, military banners and imperial tallies was black.[56] The number six (and its multiples) was chosen as the auspicious number for the state.

IV. Chancellor Wan (Wang Wan) wrote to the Emperor that Yan, Qi and Jing (Chu) territories were remotely located from the capital and suggested that he should enfeoff his princes at these locations to maintain control of the state.[57] The Emperor disseminated the proposal to his ministers to assess its feasibility. The minister of the judiciary, Li Si remarked, "Kings Wen and Wu of Zhou enfeoffed many sons and brothers with the same family names.[58] After a few generations, their descendants became estranged; they attacked and assaulted against each other like archenemies. The Sons of Heaven of Zhou could do little to thwart these activities. Now, with Your Majesty's spiritual inspiration you have unified the entire world within the Seas. The kingdom is now divided into prefectures and counties. It is far easier to take care of your meritorious subjects and your princes with handsome payments drawn from taxes. Besides, it is a far better approach for tranquillity if there are no divergence of opinion under Heaven. Hence, enfeoffment is not a sensible idea." The First Emperor said, "The perennial wars and battles under Heaven were attributed to the marquises and kings. I am grateful for the spirits of my ancestors to help me bring some peace and tranquility to all under Heaven. To establish new states is to promote potential military activities in the future, and it will be difficult for the kingdom to find serenity and respite. The judiciary minister's is thus right with his assessment."

---

54 Second Generation Emperor, *Ershi* 二世.

55 King Wei of Qi 齊 威王 and King Xuan of Qi 齊 宣王.
Zhongshi wudi zhiyun 終始五德之運. Zou Yan 鄒衍 (~305-240 BCE) composed the *Wudi xiangyun* 終始五德相運; in which he relates that the five virtues are - gold, wood, water, fire and earth. He expounded on the interrelationship of the five elements (phases), earth is superior to water, water over fire, fire over gold, gold over wood; while wood is above earth. Zou Yan maintains that the kingdom of Zhou 周 held the virtue of fire, using fire as the symbol of the dynasty. Zou Yan was a *Yin-Yang* school 陰陽 proponent, a Qi 齊 national. His works include the *Wudi zhongshishuo* 五德終始說 and the *Da Jiuzhoushuo* 大九州說. His alias was Zouzi, Master Zou 鄒子. *ZZTJ JZ*, Vol 1, p. 283.

56 Black is considered as a colour by the Chinese.

57 Chancellor, *chengxiang* 丞相 Wang Wan 王綰.
Qin's capital was at Xianyang 咸陽 - Xianshi Shaanxi 陕西 西安市.

58 Judiciary Minister, *yanwei* 延尉 Li Si 李斯.
King Wen of Zhou 文王, father of King Wu, the pre-dynastic King of Zhou.
King Wu of Zhou 周武王 (r. 1046-1043 BCE).

Hence, the Emperor decreed to install thirty-six prefectures in his kingdom;[59] a magistrate *shou* was installed in each prefecture, aided by a military commander *wei* and a prefecture inspector *jian*. The Emperor then decreed the confiscation all the weapons under Heaven and had them transferred to Xianyang. Huge bells and holding frames were forged out of the metal collected; the rest of the metal was used to forge twelve bronze men, weighing one thousand *dan* each, and these statues were displayed within the imperial palace enclosure. He decreed the unification of laws and ordinances, weights and measurements throughout the kingdom.[60] In the meantime, one hundred and twenty thousand wealthy and elite families were relocated at Xianyang. The holy shrines of the former Qin kings at Zhangtai Terraces and Shanglin Park were all constructed on the south bank of the Wei River.[61] Previously, when a fief kingdom was annihilated, a replica of the kingdom's palace was reconstructed at Beibang (northwest of) Xianyang.[62] At the south bank of the Weishui River, the string of palaces stretched from Yongmen towards the east until the last of them reached (the conference of) Jing and Wei rivers.[63] Numerous terraces and towers were constructed along the stretch, with dual-decked expressways connecting the palaces. Women that belonged to the fief lords and musical instruments appropriated were kept in their respective palaces.

---

220 BCE *Xinsi* 辛巳 Qin Empire 秦帝國

Emperor of Qin, Shi Huangdi	秦始皇帝	27th year
Wey, Wey Jue	衛衛角	10th year

I. The First Emperor made an inspection tour at Longxi, Beidi and Jitoushan Mountain; on the return trip he passed through the Huizhong Palace.[64]

II. The government constructed the Xingong Palace on the south bank of the Wei River; upon completion, it was renamed the Jimiao Palace.[65] From this palace, an expressway extended all the way to Lishan Mound.[66] An entrance gate was constructed at Ganqian Palace, connecting the capital city of Xianyang via a walled passageway for pedestrians and

---

59 The thirty-six prefectures of Qin – see Appendix 2a.

60 Unification of law and ordinance *fa* 法; *du* 度 – weights and measurements; *heng* 衡, *dan* 石, *zhang-chi* 丈尺.

61 Zhangtaigong Palace 章臺宮; Shanglin Garden 上林; Weishui River 渭水.

62 Beiban 北阪 was at the northwest of Xi'an 西安.

63 Yongmen 雍門 - Goalingxian Shanxi 陕西 高陵縣.
Weishui River 渭水.
Jing 涇.

64 Longxi 隴西 - Lintaoxian Gansu 甘肅 臨洮縣.
Beidi 北地 - Ningxian Gansu 甘肅 寧縣.
Jitoushan 雞頭山 - Gaopingxian Shaanxi 陕西 高平縣.
Huizhong Palace 回中宮 - Guyuanxian Gansu 甘肅 固原縣.

65 Weishui River 渭水.
Xin Palace 信宮 was the Changxin Palace 長信宮 at the time of Han. Jimiaogong Palace 極廟宮.

66 Lishan Mound 驪山.

cargo carts.[67] From the capital city expressways radiated out in different directions throughout the entire kingdom.

---

219 BCE *Renwu* 壬午 Qin Empire 秦帝國

Emperor of Qin, Shi Huangdi	秦始皇帝	28th year
Wey, Wey Jue	衛衛角	11th year

1. The First Emperor made an inspection tour of the eastern prefectures and counties. He ascended the summit of Yishan Mountain, where he ordered a stone stele erected, and he then made tributes to his incomparable exploits.[68] He assembled sixty literati from Lu at the foothills of Mount Taishan, where they discussed the ceremonial offerings to Heaven of *feng* and Earth of *shan*.[69] Some maintained, "In times of antiquity when people made sacrificial offerings of *fengshan* they used cattail grass to swathe the carriage wheels to avoid damaging the rocks and stones, woods and plants in the surrounding habitat. They swept the floor clean to offer sacrifice and sat on grass mats to offer prayers." The scholars held varying opinions; the Emperor thought the practices proposed were impractical and difficult to implement; henceforth he dismissed the literati.

The Emperor decreed the construction of a new carriageway from the southern foothills to the summit of Taishan Mountain. At the peak, he erected another stone stele adorned with praises of his virtues and achievements. From the northern slope, he

---

67 Ganquangong Palace 甘泉宮 - Jingyangxian Shaanxi 陝西 涇陽縣.
Xianyang 咸陽 – Xi'an City 西安市.
Zouyishan Mountain 鄒嶧山 – Yishan 嶧山- southeast of Zouxian Shandong 山東 鄒縣東南. During the reign of Qin Shi Huang, he erected seven steles throughout his kingdom; the *SJ* 史記 has records of six; missing this one in Yishan. The *Taiping huanyuji* 太平寰宇記 (Northern Song 北宋) says, 'The stone carving on a cliff wall by Li Si 李斯 was called Shumen 書門. The First Emperor rode on a carriage drawn by goats ascended to the site, and the path is still there. The original stone carving was destroyed; the one in existence was a copy carved during later days." The *ZZTJ JZ*, Vol 1, p. 290.

69 The literati from Lu 魯 儒生.
Taishan Mountain 泰山.
Feng-shan 封禪. *Feng-shan* was sacrificial ceremonies to Heaven and Earth. Taishan is the highest peak in Eastern China; it is also known as the Eastern Peak Dongyue 東岳 (嶽). At the apex of the mountain, a sacrificial altar was constructed to make sacrifices to Heaven; a ritual practice called *feng*; while at a lower peak off Taishan, Liangfushan Mountain 梁父山 sacrificial offerings were made to Earth, called *shan*. The real significance and procedures of the ceremonies were lost in great antiquity; nevertheless, they had continued to be employed to manifest the power of emperors with exemplary achievements and exploits. Tang Guiren 湯貴仁 – The *Taishan Feng-shan yu jisi* 泰山封禪與祭祀, Qilu shushe 齊魯書社, China, 2003.
To raise an altar for making sacrifices to Heaven was called *feng* 封. While to widen clearings to make sacrifices to Earth was called *shan* 墠, later the word was changed to *shan* 禪. Jin *Tiakang diji* 晉 太康地記 (Jin Geographical Chronicle) states, 'Erecting an altar at Taishan to make sacrifice to Heaven denotes elevating height; while widening clearings *shan* 墠 at Liangfu 梁父 to make sacrifice to Earth signifies broadening.' The *ZZTJ JZ*, Vol 1, p. 290.

descended to proceed to Liangfu Mountain,[70] where he made sacrifices of *shen* to the Earth Deity. The ceremonies were based essentially on the sacrificial practices to the Heavenly Divine used by the grand prayer master *taizhu* at Yongcheng (the former capital of Qin);[71] the secret documents were archived, and the details were not divulged to the commoners. Following that, the Emperor travelled to the shore of the Eastern Sea, where he made offerings and sacrifices to mountains and rivers as well as to the eight deities.[72] From the southern slope of Langya Mountain he ascended; being delighted with the surrounding he stayed in the area for three months. At Langya, he ordered the construction of Langya Terrace,[73] where another stone stele, inscribed with accolades of his virtues and expression of fulfillment, was erected.

Before this, Song Wuji, Xianmen Zigao and a few other Yan nationals claimed that they had mastered the practice of metaphysical transformation - morphing the mortals into immortals.[74] The mystics and occultists at Qi and Yan all strived to coach and practise the techniques. The former kings of Qi, King Wei, King Xuan and King Zhao of Yan entirely believed their words and had dispatched their attendants to set sail into the Ocean in search of Penglai, Fangzhang and Yingzhou mountains.[75] It was said that the three mythical mountains were in the Bohai Sea not far removed from the mortals; however, when mortals tried to approach the islands, a strong wind would blow the ship off course. Some claimed that a few mortals had landed and found the elixir of life and the immortals on the islands. When the First Emperor arrived at the seashore, several occultists including Xu Shi from Qi rivalled to submit numerous memorials on the subject.[76] They implored the Emperor to observe abstinence and fasting, and to dispatch virgin boys and girls to set sail into the Ocean in search of the mountains. The Emperor decreed Xu Shi to gather several thousand virgin boys and girls to accompany him to set

---

70 Liangfushan Mountain 梁父山.

71 Grand prayer master, *taizhu* 太祝.

72 The eight deities 八神 according to the *Fengshan shu* 封禪書 were:
Celestial Deity, *Tianshen* at Yuanshui River 天神 (天主) 淵水.
Earth Deity, *Dishen* at Liangfushan Mountain 地神 梁父山.
Warrior Deity, *Bingshen* 兵神 Chiyou 蚩尤.
Gloomy Deity, *Yinsheng* 陰神 Sanshan 三山.
Positive Deity, *Yangshen* 陽神 Zhifushan Mountain 芝罘山.
Moon Deity, *Yueshen* 月神 Laishan Mountain 萊山.
Solar Deity, *Reshen* 日神 Chengshan Mountain 成山.
Time (Season) Deity, *Shishen* 時神 Langya Mountain 琅琊山.
The *ZZTJ JZ*, Vol 1, p. 290.

73 Langya Terrace 琅琊臺.

74 "....while the corporal body might disintegrate, the spiritual entity was transmuted into an immortal being to ascend into Heaven."

75 Yan 燕人 - Song Wuji 宋毋忌; Xianmen Zigao 羨門子高.
Qi King 齊王 Tian Yinqi 田因其 (r. 358-320 BCE).
King Xuan of Qi 齊宣王 Tian Bijiang 田辟疆 (r. 319-301 BCE).
King Zhao of Yan 燕昭王 Ji Ping 姬平(r. 312-279 BCE)
Bohai Sea 渤海 - Penglai 蓬萊, Fangzhang 方丈, and Yingzhou 瀛州 were the three mythical islands where the immortals were claimed to live.

76 Xu Fu 徐市 Xu Shi 徐福.

sail. The ships set sailed and returned; the occultist made an excuse that the wind was blowing in the wrong direction, and he added, "We failed to get any closer; however, we saw the islands in the distance."

The Emperor returned to the city of Pengcheng, where he fasted, observed abstinence, said prayers, made offerings and preparing to recover the Zhou tripod that was lost at Sishui River.[77] He ordered one thousand men to dive into the river searching for the bronze tripod but failed to find it. He then headed southwest by crossing the Huaishui River to arrive at Hengshan Mountain in the Nanjun Prefecture. Sailing along the River (Changjiang) the entourage arrived at Xiangshan Mountain, where the Emperor made offerings to Lady Xiangjun.[78] A storm blew up; the entourage barely managed to make the crossing. The Emperor asked his erudite academician, "Who was Lady Xiangjun?" The academician answered, "It is said that she was the daughter of King Yao, the wife of King Shun; [79] she was buried here." The First Emperor lost his temper; he ordered three thousand convicts to denude the entire mountainside leaving the topsoil totally exposed; he then returned from Nan Prefecture via the Wuguan Pass to the capital.[80]

11. The forebears, of Zhang Liang a Hann national, had for five generations served as chancellors at Hann;[81] later when the kingdom was annihilated, Zhang Liang expended his belongings and properties, worth one thousand units of gold, to seek revenge for the demise of his state.

---

218 BCE *Guiwei* 癸未 Qin Empire 秦帝國

---

77 Pengcheng 彭城 - Tongshanxian Jiangsu 江蘇 銅山縣.
Sishui 泗水 River.
The 'Nine Bronze Tripods' - *jiuding* 九鼎 were handed down to the Zhou dynasty. According to legend, King Yu of Xia 夏禹 forged the nine bronze tripods when he became king. It was a symbol of kingship, and it was said, whosoever took possession of the nine tripods would become the Son of Heaven. It was further claimed that when the Qin government was transporting the prized possession to the capital, one of them tumbled overboard and sank into the Sishui River. In fact, the nine tripods had long disappeared by the time of Qin, besides their existence could not be substantiated. Furthermore, there is no compelling archaeological evidence to suggest that the people of China had mastered the technique of forging large bronze cauldrons as early as circa 2000 BCE, whereas minor bronze objects were most likely to be in use. The nine tripods might have been forged during Zhou. The *ZZTJ BY Edition*, Taiwan, 1986, p. 512; and *ZZTJ JZ,* Vol 1, p. 291.

78 Huaishui River 淮水.
Hengshan Mountain 衡山 north of Dangtuxian Anhui 安徽 當塗縣.
Nanjun Prefecture 南郡 - Jianglingxian Hubei 湖北 江陵縣; Changjiang River 長江.
Xiangshan 湘山 - Xiangtanxian Hunan 湖南 湘潭縣.
Lady Xiangjun 湘君 – see below.

79 Lady Xiangjun 湘君 was the daughter of King Yao 堯帝; she was the wife of King Shun 舜帝.

80 Nanjun 南郡 - Jianglingxian Hubei 湖北 江陵縣.
Wuguan Pass 武關 - Shangxian Shaanxi 陝西 商縣.

81 Zhang Liang 張良.

Emperor of Qin, Shi Huangdi 秦始皇帝 29th year
Wey, Wey Jue 衛衛角 12th year

I. The First Emperor made a tour at the eastern prefectures and arrived at the Sands of Bolangsha at Yangwu.[82] Zhang Liang hired a strongman to wield a huge iron mallet to strike at the Emperor riding in a carriage; the assassin mistakenly struck the carriage rode by his attendant. The Emperor was stunned, he ordered the arrest of the assassin, but failed. The Emperor then decreed a search for the assassin across the kingdom; the search lasted for ten days.

II. The First Emperor ascended the Zhifushan Mountain; there he carved another stone stele commending his virtues; on the return trip, the entourage passed through Langya to return to the capital via Shangdang.[83]

---

217 BCE *Jiashen* 甲申 Qin Empire 秦帝國

Emperor of Qin, Shi Huangdi 秦始皇帝 30th year
Wey, Wey Jue 衛衛角 13th year

There was no record this year.

---

216 BCE *Yiyou* 乙酉 Qin Empire 秦帝國

Emperor of Qin, Shi Huangdi 秦始皇帝 31st year
Wey, Wey Jue 衛衛角 14th year

I. Qin decreed that the black-headed people (civilians) were to make registration of ownership of land.[84]

---

215 BCE *Bingxu* 丙戌 Qin Empire 秦帝國

Emperor of Qin, Shi Huangdi 秦始皇帝 32nd year
Wey, Wey Jue 衛衛角 15th year

---

82 Sands of Bolangsha at Yangwu Henan 博浪沙 - Yangwuxian Henan 河南 陽武縣.

83 Zhifushan Mountain 芝罘山.
Langya 琅琊 - Zhuchengxian Shandong 山東 諸城縣.
Shangdang 上黨 - Changzixian Shanxi 山西 長子縣.

84 Qianshou 黔首 - Black-headed people. According to the *SJ* 史記, Qin Shihuang benji, 26th year, 'When the Emperor first unified all under Heaven, he changed the name of his people (Qin) to *qianshou*.' The *SJ* 史記, 卷 24, 'Qin Shihuang benji 秦始皇本紀' 第 6, p. 190.

I. The Emperor travelled to Jieshi.[85] He ordered a Mister Lu from Yan to search for the immortal Xianmen.[86] He then ordered his attendants to carve accolades at the stone gate. The walls of the city were dismantled, and the embankments to prevent inundation were also razed to the ground.

II. The Emperor made a trip to the north to make an inspection tour; he took the Shangjun Prefecture route.[87]

III. Mister Lu returned from overseas, he presented a facsimile of an occult text *Lutushu* to the emperor.[88] It read, "Hu will bring demise to Qin."[89] The Emperor commanded General Meng Tian to lead an army of three hundred thousand men to make expeditions against the Xiongnu (Hu) in the north.

---

214 BCE *Dinghai* 丁亥 Qin Empire 秦帝國

Emperor of Qin, Shi Huangdi	秦始皇帝	33rd year
Wey, Wey Jue	衛衛角	16th year

I. The Qin court conscripted former fugitives, idlers that were married into rich families, and merchants as soldiers to occupied areas in Nanyue and Luliang. Three new prefectures Guilin, Nanhai and Xiang were inaugurated, and some five hundred thousand civilians and convicts were relocated to the Wuling mountainous regions to settle among the people of Yue (Guangdong).[90]

---

85 Jieshi 碣石 - Changlixian Hebei 河北 昌黎縣. There have been many debates on the exact location of Jieshi.

86 Yan national 燕人 Mister Lu 魯生.
Xianmen 羨門 see 219-I.

87 Shangjun Prefecture 上郡 - Suidexian Shaanxi 陝西 綏德縣.

88 *Lutushu* 錄圖書, a divination text.

89 The *Cambridge History of Qin and Han,* suggests that this statement was dubious at best and was probably tampered by later chroniclers. Page 97.
The original meaning of the word *Hu* 胡 was a derivative of the phase *huzi* 胡子 meaning dewlap or beard; it was used to describe the people from Central Asia with a beard (which looked like an ox's dewlap). The original usage of the term did not carry any derogatory connotations but was evolved later to mean the barbarians from the north of China exclusively.
Hu - barbarians. Alternatively, the statement could be translated to read, 'Hu will bring the final demise of Qin.' It is noted that the Emperor's youngest son was Ying Huhai 嬴胡亥, bearing the same character of Hu, who was to bring down the Empire. Hence later day chroniclers suggested that the occult text meant the son Huhai and not the barbaric Hu that caused the fall of the Empire. Yap, J., *Wars With the Xiongnu*, 2009, p. 40.

90 Nanyue 南越 - present day Guangdong 廣東 and Guangxi 廣西.
Luliang 陸梁 were areas north and south of Wulingshan Mountain Range 五嶺 (Nanling 南嶺) in the northern part of Guangdong 廣東, the locals were known for their viciousness and banditry activities, hence known as Luliang. *Handian* 漢典 and the *Zhonghua renmin gongheguo fensheng dituji* 中華人民共和國分省地圖集 地圖出版社, 1974, China, p. 83.
Guilinjun Prefecture 桂林郡 - Guilinxian Guangxi 廣西 桂林縣.
Nanhaijun Prefecture 南海郡 - Guangzhou City Guangdong 廣東 廣州市.
Xiangjun 象郡 - present day northern part of Vietnam.

II. Meng Tian expelled the Xiongnu tribes and recovered the territories south of the River *Henan*;[91] he hence established forty-four counties *xian* in the region. He ordered his men to construct Long-Walls and build fortresses at strategic locations in compliance with the terrain, commencing from Lintao to Liaodong the wall stretched for more than ten thousand *li*.[92] Meng Tian then led his army crossed the Huanghe River and occupied the mountainous region north of the river;[93] from there his army penetrated further north. The troops were exposed to the elements for more than ten years. Meng Tian normally garrisoned his command at the Shangjun Prefecture, and he held sway in the land of the Xiongnu.

---

213 BCE *Wuzi* 戊子 Qin Empire 秦帝國

Emperor of Qin, Shi Huangdi	秦始皇帝	34th year
Wey, Wey Jue	衛衛角	17th year

I. The Qin government decreed that magistrates or law enforcers who falsely indicted innocents or exacted spurious confessions through duress, allowing criminals to go free or passing wrong convictions were to be banished to the frontier as convicts to construct the Long-Walls or to the far off land of Nanyue.

II. Chancellor Li Si submitted a memorial to the Emperor, "Previously at the time of the fief lords; the former states used to vie for intellects and canvassers to serve at their courts. Whereas all under the Heaven is now peaceful, the state law has been unified; the civilians are to turn their attention to farming and artisanship activities while the scholars should learn the new state laws. Nevertheless, many of the scholars instead of adhering to the developments of the time are emulating things ancient and antiquated. Some have gone as far as condemning our current practices, spreading misinformation among the Black-headed, and are causing confusion and consternation, instilling unlawful teachings among the civilians. Whenever a new decree is proclaimed everyone refutes it with his personal perspective, debating and arguing incessantly. In their official capacities at court, they express consent while harbouring hidden dissension; no sooner have they left court than they are publically criticising the government's policies in the side streets and alleys. Some flaunt their perverse opinions against the state for recognition; others propose opinions contrary to the establishment to heighten their stance, and some go as far as heading groups of followers to defame law of the state. If the diffusion of twisted reasoning is not proscribed and contained, there is a concern that the authority of Your Majesty will be seriously compromised. These men are likely to form cliques and clans among the commoners. If such activities are prohibited, it would be more expedient for the state. Your subject implores that history texts that are not related to Qin be burned by the historian ministers, whereas erudite academicians are exempted to possess them.[94] People under Heaven, who have collections of the

---

91 Meng Tian 蒙恬.
Henan 河南 - areas south of He, Huanghe 黄河.

92 Lintao 臨洮 - Minxian Gansu 甘肅 岷縣. 10,000 *li* = 4,158 km. (However this was probably a hyperbole.)
Liaodong 遼東 - Liaoyangxian Liaoning 遼寧 遼陽縣.

93 It was along the Yinshan Mountain Range - Yinshan Mountain Range 陰山 - Neimeng 内蒙.

94 Erudite Academician, *boshi* 博士.

Book of Odes, the *Venerated Documents* and the writings of the hundred schools of philosophy, are to surrender their books to the prefecture magistrate and local military commander for burning.[95] People who defiantly discuss the *Odes* and the *Shujing* are to be punished by decapitation at the marketplace. People who pledge allegiance to antiquated values while denouncing present ones are to be executed along with their family members. Law enforcers who are aware of such stated transgressions but failed to report them will also face the same castigation as the lawbreakers. Within thirty days upon the proclamation of this law, people who refuse to surrender their books for burning will have their face tattooed and face four years of hard labour *chengdan*.[96] Texts on medication, divination and agrarian skills are not included in this prohibition. People who intend to learn legalism can approach the legal officers to apply for apprenticeship under proper guidance." The Emperor decreed, "Approved."

Chen Yu from Wei said to Kong Fu,[97] "The authority intends to destroy the texts owned by our former kings. Sir, you being the custodian of these texts, I am afraid a major calamity is about to befall on you." Zi Yu answered, "I spend my time studying what appear to be useless scholastic works. People who understand me are my friends; Qin is certainly no friend of mine. What calamity is there for me? I will have the texts securely stowed away, and wait for the day when people are allowed to solicit them freely; by then, there will be no calamity."

---

212 BCE *Jichou* 己丑 Qin Empire 秦帝國

Qin Emperor, Shi Huangdi	秦始皇帝	35th year
Wey, Wey Jue	衛衛角	18th year

1. Meng Tian was commanded to construct an expressway to extend from Yunyang to Jiuyuan.[98] It was to be a thoroughfare of one thousand and eight hundred *li*, [99] it required levelling mountains and filling up valleys; it took many years, but it was never completed.

---

95 The *Book of Odes, Shijing* 詩經.
The *Shujing* 書經 also known as *Shangshu*, the *Venerated Document, Book of Document* 尚書.

96 Tattoo on the face, *qingxing* 黥刑.
Chengdan 城旦 - hard labour for four years.

97 Wei national 魏人 Chen Yu 陳餘. Chen Yu was the fast friend of Zhang Er 張耳. (See 209-IV). Chen Yu studied literati and was quite learned.
Kong Fu 孔鮒 was the ninth generation grandson of Confucius. The First Emperor of Qin enfeoffed him as Lord Wentong 文通君 of Lu 魯 and appointed him as a tutor, *shaofu* 少傅. The *SJ* 史記, 卷 117, 'Kongzi shijia 孔子世家' 第 17, p. 1748.
When the Qin Emperor persecuted the literati and burned books, Kong Fu had the works of the literati and ancient texts hidden in the wall panels of the former manor of Confucius. The books were recovered at the time of Emperor Jing of Han 漢景帝 (r. 156-141 BCE) when King Gong of Lu 魯恭王 Liu Yu 劉余 dismantled the old home of the Kong family to extend his palace.
When Chen Sheng 陳勝 revolted against the Qin government; he appointed Kong Fu as his erudite academician and grand tutor. *Shanghu* 尚書, by Xu K.T (translated by), *Shangshu*, Guangzhou chubanshe 廣州出版社, 2004, p.1.

98 Yunyang 雲陽 - Chunhuaxian Shaanxi 陝西 淳華縣.
Jiuyuan 九原 - Baotou city Neimeng 內蒙 包頭縣.

II. The First Emperor maintained that Xianyang was far too populous, and the palace built by the former kings was inadequately small; he ordered a new imperial hall to be constructed in the Shanglin Park, south of the Weishui River.[100] Workers began construction of the audience hall of the Epang Palace at the park; it was to be five hundred *bu* in the east to west orientation and fifty *zhang* from the south to the north; [101] ten thousand people could be seated comfortably in the upper hall. At the lower hall, flagpoles of five *zhang* in length could be hoisted.[102] An elevated boulevard linked the new palace hall with the Nanshan Mountain, the summit of which served as the gateway to the palace.[103] From Epang Palace, a dual-decked expressway was constructed, it straddled across the Weishui River running directly into Xianyang; the structural design was taken after the *gedao* celestial path – 'From the Polaris across the Milky Way to the Royal Chamber Star'.[104] The Emperor ordered seven hundred thousand castrated workers to construct his new palace at Epang Palace; some were directed to construct his grave mound and mausoleum at Lishan Mountain.[105] Stone blocks and large boulders were quarried and transported from the Beishan Mountain while timber logs were brought in from Shu and Jing.[106] There were three hundred palaces within the Pass *Guanzhong* and four hundred more beyond.[107]

The Emperor ordered a boulder to be erected within the Gou County (in the Donghaijun Prefecture), [108] which was designated as the eastern gate of the Qin Empire.

The government then relocated thirty thousand households to the County of Liyi and fifty thousand to Yunyang; [109] these families were exempted from tax levies and corvee duties for ten years.

---

99 700 km as the crow flies.

100 Shanglinyuan Imperial Park 上林苑; Weishui River 渭水.

101 Epangshan *or* Afangshan 阿房山, *Afanggong* 阿房宮. The pronunciation of *Epang* is based on reconstructed ancient pronunciation, modern pronunciation is Afanggong.
1 *bu* = 1.38 metre; 500 *bu* = 700 metres; fifty *zhang* = 115 metre.
It was five hundred *bu*, 700 metres in the east to west orientation.
And it was fifty *zhang*, 115 metre from the south to the north.

102 The flag poles were five *zhang* in length, 11.5 metres.

103 The distance between Zhongnan Mountain 終南山 and Epang Palace was 40 km as the crow flies.

104 *Gedao* 閣道 was a raised road path with battlements.
The orientation of the path was taken after the direction of the Polar Star *Beidou* 北斗 crossing the Milkyway to end in *Yingxing* 營星 and *Shixing* 室星 – the Royal star-chamber.

105 Lishan 驪山 - is 25 km north of Xi'an City 西安市.

106 Beishan Mountain 北山, the place is unknown; it can be interpreted simply as mountains in the north.
Jing 荊 - Jing was previously part of Chu 楚 territories, it was located in parts of Hubei 湖北 and Hunan 湖南.
Shu 蜀 - Chongqing City Sichuan 四川 重慶市.

107 The palaces were called *xinggong* 行宮 - the provincial palaces for the emperor's abode while he was on tour. These were probably the palaces built by the former fief lords; the text does not explain who built them.
Guanzhong 關中 was the area surrounding Xi'an Shaanxi 陜西 西安, and there were four passes:
East - *Hangu* 函谷; West - San 散關; North - Xiao 蕭關 and West - Wu 武關.
Guanwai 關外 - were areas beyond Ganguguan 函谷關 東.

108 Quxian County 朐縣 - Donghaijun Prefecture 東海郡 - Donghaixian Jiangsu 江蘇 東海縣.

109 Liyi 驪邑 - Lishan Mound, Lintongxian Shaanxi 陜西 臨潼縣 驪山.

III. A Master Lu suggested to the First Emperor, "According to esoteric practice, it is advisable for a sovereign to make regular covert tours and expeditions to avoid the encroachment of spirits and poltergeists. When the evil spirits and poltergeists are exorcized, the fortuitous immortals *zhenren* will duly appear.[110] Your Majesty should not allow your subjects to know which palace you are staying; with these measures, you could acquire the elixir of immortality." The Emperor said, "I truly admire the immortals." Henceforth, dropping his earlier appellation of *zhen*, he addressed himself as *zhenren*. He then directed the two hundred and seventy provisional palaces within two hundred *li* from the capital to be connected by dual-decked passageway and bridges.[111] At each palace, curtains and drapes, musical instruments of drums and bells were installed, and beautiful courtesans were repositioned; the women assigned to their respective palaces were not allowed to move freely. After that, the Emperor moved from palace to palace; when someone disclosed his whereabouts he was duly put to death.

At the Liangshan Palace, the First Emperor watched from the hilltop that the Chancellor Li Si had employed a large contingent of carriages and cavalry guards; [112] he was irritated by what he saw. One of the eunuchs quietly informed Li Si, who promptly reduced the number of his carriages and guards. The Emperor was in a terrible rage, he said, "One the eunuchs must have divulged my remarks." He ordered an investigation; when no one came forth, he ordered all the eunuchs who were serving him at the time executed. Ever since then, no one knew the whereabouts of the Emperor; when senior ministers and officers needed the approval of certain decisions, they gathered at the Xianyang palace waiting for the Emperor to appear.

Masters Hou and Lu held numerous discussions on the Emperor and made derogatory remarks covertly; [113] later the two men ran for their lives. When the Emperor heard of what had happened he was greatly infuriated, he said, "I respected Master Lu and others greatly, and I have bestowed upon them with handsome gifts, but they talked behind my back and slandered against me. I will investigate into these men who are spreading malevolent thoughts among the Black-headed." He ordered the judiciary officer to arrest the scholars.[114] These men tried desperately to save their own skin by implicating others; in the end, some four hundred and sixty or more men were buried alive at Xianyang. The executions were made known to all under Heaven, serving as warnings to others.

The First Emperor decided to increase the number of people to be banished to the frontier and border regions. Fusu, the eldest son of the emperor, reprimanded him,[115] "The scholars study Confucius teachings, applying their learnings as law; Your Majesty is now using the harsh law to make changes, your subject is uneasy that there might be turbulence under Heaven." The Emperor lost his temper; he sent Fusu to the Shangjun Prefecture, [116] where he was to supervise the activities of Meng Tian.

Yunyang 雲陽 - Chunhuaxian Shaanxi 陝西 淳化縣.

110 Immortals, *zhenren* 真人.

111 To allow him to travel clandestinely.

112 Liangshan Palace 梁山宮 - Ganxian Shaanxi 陝西 乾縣. Chancellor, Li Si 李斯.

113 Master Hou 侯生 and Master Lu 盧生.

114 It is not sure if we could translate the people he arrested as literati or scholars, as the text relates them as *zhusheng* 諸生, later day scholars interpret them as scholars or students.

115 Crown Prince, *Ying Fusu* 嬴扶蘇.

116 Shangjun Prefecture 上郡 - Suidexian Shaanxi 陝西 綏德縣.

211 BCE *Gengyin* 庚寅 Qin Empire 秦帝國

Emperor of Qin, Shi Huangdi	秦始皇帝	36th year
Wey, Wey Jue	衛衛角	19th year

I. A piece of meteorite fell and landed in the Dongjun Prefecture.[117] Someone carved words on it, which read, "When the First Emperor dies, the land will be quartered." The Emperor dispatched his judiciary officers to make investigates; no one admitted to the act; the Emperor decreed all the people living nearby executed; the meteorite was burned.

II. Thirty thousand households were relocated to north of the River - *Hebei* and Yuzhong;[118] each person was enfeoffed with one grade of noble ranking.

210 BCE *Xinmao* 辛卯 Qin Empire 秦帝國

Emperor of Qin, Shi Huangdi	秦始皇帝	37th year
Wey, Wey Jue	衛衛角	20th year

I. Winter. 10th month, 7th day. The First Emperor went on another expedition. Left Chancellor Li Si accompanied him while Right Chancellor Feng Quji remained at the capital.[119] The Emperor had over twenty sons; Ying Huhai, the youngest was his favourite.[120] When he asked to accompany the entourage, it was duly granted.

11th month. The Emperor and his entourage arrived at Yunmeng, where he paid sacrificial homage from a distance to King Yu, Shun, who was buried at Jiuyi Mountain.[121] The Emperor and his entourage then embarked on ships and sailed downstream along the Changjiang River; the entourage made explorations at Jike, crossing the great river again at Haizhu.[122] Sailing past Danyang County the entourage arrived at the Qiantang Lake.[123] When it arrived at Zhejiang, the

117 Dongjun Prefecture 東郡 - Puyangxian Hebei 河北 濮陽縣.

118 Hebei 河北 - North of Hetao 河套 and south of the Yinshan Mountain Range 陰山.
Yuzhong 榆中 - Yulinxian Shaanxi 陝西 榆林縣.

119 Left Chancellor, *zuo chengxiang* 左丞相 Li Si 李斯.
Right Chancellor, *you chengxiang* 右丞相 Feng Quji 馮去疾.

120 Ying Huhai 嬴胡亥.
It was Shi Huangdi's fourth and last expedition.

121 Yunmeng 雲夢 - Anluxian Hubei 湖北 安陸縣.
King Shun 舜帝 Yao Zhonghua 姚重華, 7th legendary king after *Huangdi* 黄帝.
King Yao 堯帝 died at Jiuyishan 九疑山 - Ningyuanxian Hunan 湖南 寧遠縣 when he was making an expedition against the Miao 苗 tribes to the south of Zhongyuan 中原.

122 Jike 藉柯 - unknown.
Haizhu 海渚 - unknown.

123 Dangyang 當陽 - Dangtuxian Anhui 安徽 當塗縣.
Qiantang 錢唐 - Qiantangjiang Lake Hangzhou Zhejiang 浙江 杭州 錢塘江.

river swelled and became unexpectedly choppy. The entourage then travelled further west by one hundred and twenty *li*, and at the narrowest point of Xiazhong, it crossed the river.[124] Later, at the summit of Kuaiji Mountain the Emperor paid homage to Da Yu (King Yu).[125] He gazed out towards the South Sea - Nanhai; at the summit, he erected another stone stele extolling his virtues. On the return journey, the entourage passed through Wu crossing the river again at Jiangcheng; sailing north along the eastern seacoast to Langya and arrived at Zhifu.[126] The entourage came across a colossal fish; the retainers shot it with arrows, killing it. The entourage then continued with its excursion and arrived at the Pingyuanjin Crossing; [127] by this time, the Emperor had taken ill.

The First Emperor detested the utterance of death; hence, none of his officers and ministers at court had the nerve to inquire the arrangements for succession after his passing. When he became seriously ill he ordered the director of the Imperial carriage, also holding the custody of the imperial seal and insignia, Zhao Gao,[128] (a eunuch) to prepare an edict to be presented to the Heir Apparent Fusu. The edict read, "You are to return to Xianyang to make arrangements for the funeral service and burial." The imperial edict was sealed and kept by Zhao Gao; however, the dispatch was not delivered as decreed.

Autumn, 7th month, 20th day. The First Emperor expired at the Pingtai Palace in Shaqiu. [129]

Chancellor Li Si was of the opinion that the Emperor having passed away from the capital, there were concerns that the princes and the civilians might take advantage of the confusion and revolt. He decided to keep it a secret and not to issue an obituary proclamation. The coffin was

---

124 Xiazhong 狹中 - Fuyangxian Zhejiang 浙江 富陽縣.

125 Kuaijishan 會稽山 - Shaoxingxian Zhejiang 浙江 紹興縣.
Xia Yu 夏禹 Si Wenming 姒文命 was the legendary founder of the Xia dynasty ~ 2070 BC.

126 Wujun 吳郡 - Wuxian Jiangsu 江蘇 吳縣.
Jiangcheng 江乘 - Jurongxian Jiangsu 江蘇 句容縣.
Langya 瑯琊 - Zhuchengxian Shandong 山東 諸城縣.
Zhifu 之罘 - north of Yantai Shandong 山東 煙臺.

127 Pingyuanjin 平原津 - Pingyuanjie Shandong 山東 平原街. Ying Zheng 嬴政 believed that there were immortals living on the Penglai Island 蓬萊 in the Donghai Sea 東海, a mythical island off the coast of the Eastern Sea where the immortals were alleged to live. On this particular occasion, he was in search of Xu Fu 徐福 the occultist who led him to believe that there was an elixir, which could give mortals immortality. Xu Fu having convinced the Emperor was allowed to set sailed with three thousand virgin young boys and girls for Penglai and was never seen again. The *SJ* 史記, 卷 24, 'Qin Shihuang benji 秦始皇本紀' 第 6, pp. 192, 196. Some people believe that Xu Fu ended up in Japan, where shrines bearing his name are still in existence.
It was the palace where King Wuling of Zhao 趙武靈王 Zhao Yong 趙雍 starved to death in 295 BCE see 295-III.
It was the 12th year of his reign as the Emperor of Qin and 37th year as the king of Qin; he was fifty years old. Qin Shihuang, an indefatigable worker and a megalomaniac, was plagued by superstition; he became a victim of spiritual mediums – the occultists: people who claimed that they could offer him immortality. Occultists and men well versed in esoteric rites claimed that they could commune with the immortals of the Eastern Sea, and proffer potions that would offer him immortality, and he believed them totally.

128 Zhongju fuling 中車府令 hangfu xishi 行符璽事 Zhao Gao 趙高.

129 Pingtaigong Palace Shaqiu 平太宮 沙丘 - Pingxiangxian Hebei 河北 平鄉縣.

kept at the Emperor's bedchamber coach *wenliangju.*[130] Only the most trusted palace attendants (eunuchs) seated at the coach steering it; when it came to mealtimes, food was presented to the imperial coach as normal. The court officers and ministers who accompanied the entourage presented their memorials and missives as usual. The eunuchs approved the submissions from the carriage. Apart from Huhai, Zhao Gao and a few trusted court eunuchs, perhaps no more than five or six people knew of the passing of the Emperor.[131]

Previously, when the Emperor was alive, he trusted and favoured the Meng family clan. General Meng Tian was commanding an army at the front while Meng Yi, the brother of Meng Tian, was serving at the Qin court attending to the civic affairs; [132] the two brothers were honoured as the most loyal and trusted officers at court. Senior officers at court, even the generals and chancellors did not have the courage to challenge the brothers. Zhao Gao, the eunuch, was born with a congenital defective reproductive organ.[133] The First Emperor learned that the man had great physical strength and was exceptionally educated in prison proceedings and judiciary matters he made him the director of the imperial carriage *zhongjufu ling.*[134] The Emperor then ordered his youngest son Ying Huhai to learn legal proceedings under the eunuch; the young prince confided in him completely. There was an occasion when Zhao Gao perpetrated a serious offence; the Emperor had Meng Yi presided over the trial; Meng Yi found him guilty and sentenced him to death. The Emperor nevertheless maintained that he was exceptional capable and decreed that he would be absolved of the conviction with his status restored. Having earned the trust and favour of Huhai, besides he loathed the Meng brothers bitterly, he proposed to Huhai to forge an edict by the First Emperor to execute Fusu, after which make Huhai the Crown Prince. Ying Huhai readily agreed to the proposal. Zhao Gao added, "This is a critical undertaking, without the cooperation of the chancellor it might not be accomplished." They saw Li Si. Zhao Gao said, "His Majesty's edict to his eldest son, the tally and the royal seal are in the custody of Ying Huhai. Sir, it is up to you and me to decide who will be the rightful successor to the throne. What do you say?" Li Si said, "How dare you utter words that could bring on the annihilation of a kingdom? We as subjects of a state are in no position to discuss these matters." Zhao Gao asked Li Si, "Allow me to ask you, of your abilities, your strategic skills, your meritorious awards, your perseverance and your trust by the crown prince, is there one entity that matches that of Meng Tian?" Li Si answered, "None." Zhao Goa said, "Right you are! No sooner had the eldest son acceded to the throne, the new chancellor would be Meng Tian, while Your Highness, bearing your seal as Marquis of Tong, will be sent packing to return to your hometown.[135] It is a commendable idea if you pledge your fealty with Huhai. He is benevolent and trustworthy and has all the virtues and qualifications to be a great emperor. Please give it due consideration." Li Si thought the proposition made sense, finally decided to acquiesce with the intrigue. The conspirators forged an edict from the First Emperor to make Ying Huhai the crown prince, thence forged another edict to remonstrate Fusu for failing to expand the realms of the

---

130 *Wenliangju* 轀涼車 – the term was initially used to mean bed-chamber carriage, the carriage had panels that could be opened for cool air or closed to keep warm; later the term was used to mean hearse.

131 Ying Huhai 嬴胡亥. Zhao Gao 趙高.

132 Meng Tian 蒙恬; Meng Yi 蒙毅.

133 *Yingong* 隱宮 was possibly a condition called *cryptorchidism*. N.B. Other authors have interpreted *yingong* as castration.

134 The Director of Imperial Carriage - *zhongju fuling* 中車府令.

135 Marquis Tong 通侯.

kingdom, and accused him for having caused inordinate losses at the front. The edict went on to reproach him for making derogatory remarks in his memorial submissions, unremittingly rankling that he should be at the capital to assume his position as the rightful heir. In the same edict it also decreed that General Tian was guilty of failing to instruct Ying Fusu properly for his transgressions; it went on to decree that the two men were bestowed with the gift of death; in closing it ordered the general to hand over the military command to Deputy Commander Wang Li.[136]

Upon receiving the edict, Fusu wept as he returned to his apartment and was about to take his own life. Meng Tian said, "His Majesty is still away from the capital, and he has yet to elect a crown prince to succeed to the throne. He commanded your subject to lead three hundred thousand troops to defend the border at the front, with Your Highness as the Army Protector; these are momentous responsibilities for all under Heaven. Now, an envoy appears from nowhere demanding we take our own lives, how are we to know if there is nothing sinister behind this? Perhaps we should seek further clarifications before we take our lives." The envoy repeatedly urged them to take their own lives. Fusu said to Meng Tian, "If my father bestows upon me with death what other clarifications do I need?" He killed himself. Meng Tian refused to take his own life; the envoy handed him over to the legal department and had him imprisoned at Yangzhou,[137] while assigning one of Li Si's retainers to take over the military command. The envoy return to report what had happened. When Huhai heard that Fusu had died, he was about to release Meng Tian. At this stage, Meng Yi returned after making sacrifices to the mountains and rivers on behalf of the Emperor. Zhao Gao said to Huhai, "Our former Emperor had all along thought of Your Highness as sagacious and had considered to make you the crown prince. Meng Yi had always reprimanded against it. You should have him executed." Meng Yi was transferred to the Dai Prefecture to be incarcerated.

The imperial entourage started from Jingjin arrived at Jiuyuan.[138] It was the middle of summer and the corpse in the carriage gave off a repulsive stench. Li Si ordered his attendants to load one *dan* of slated-fish on one of the carriages to mask the stench.[139] The entourage used sections of the expressway and travelled back towards Xianyang;[140] upon arrival, an obituary proclamation was released on the passing of the First Emperor. Prince Huhai acceded to the throne.

---

136 Wang Li 王離.

137 Yangzhou 陽周 - Andingxian Shaanxi 陝西 安定縣.

138 Jiuyuan 九原 - Baotouxian Neimeng 內蒙 包頭縣.

139 The text uses the word *bayou* abalone; however at the time of Zhanguo it also meant salted-fish. Han 漢 Liu Xiang 劉向 mentions in his *Shuiyan* 說苑 Zayan 雜言, '鮑魚之肆 – a store that sells salted-fish', and the *baoyu* mention is not abalone. As salted-fish gives off a dreadful stench, it was used to mask the smell of the decomposing corpse.

140 The route taken by the procession was extremely convoluted; they were probably using the extensive expressway built by Qin Shi Huang in 212 BCE (see 212-1). It was also likely that the entourage was trying to confuse the civilians by taking a protracted route. However, it was equally likely that Zhao Gao 趙高 and Li Si 李斯 were biding their time for Meng Tian 蒙恬 to commit suicide, who with 300,000 troops under the general's command could easily hold sway over the fortune of the empire.

9th month. The First Emperor was interred at Lishan Mound.[141] The grave-pit was extraordinarily deep; molten copper was poured into the openings to prevent underground water seepage.[142] A vast quantity of rare treasures, full to the brim, was interred with the burial. Artisans installed mechanical trap-devices with strong crossbows that could be triggered by the slightest touch by the unsuspecting intruders. In the core of the grave atrium, mercury was used to simulate running water of rivers, lakes and seas, and mechanical apparatuses were installed to create movements. The arched cupola of the burial crypt was painted with the celestial bodies in Heaven. On the pavement below, the realms of the First Emperor's kingdom were depicted. The women from his seraglio who did not give birth to any children were interred. When the funeral ceremonies were finally completed someone suggested that perhaps, the artisans and workers who installed the mechanisms might divulge how the contraptions worked and revealed the secrets to grave robbers; as a result, all the workers were interred in the grave.[143]

II. The Second Emperor had intended to execute Meng Tian and his brother immediately. Ziying, [144] the son of Huhai's brother, [145] said, "When the king of Zhao executed Li Mu and retained Yan Ju and when the king of Qi killed the generational loyalist and engaged Hou Sheng the two kingdoms met their demise.[146] The Meng family members are the most trustworthy ministers of Qin; they are irreplaceable strategists of our kingdom. Your Majesty's decision to depose of them and place your trust on devious sycophants will lead to ministers at court to lose confidence in our court while the military staff at the front will lose their morale." Ying Huhai refused to listen and decreed the execution of Meng Yi and the state secretary Tian.[147] Meng Tian exclaimed before he died, "My family and forebears have served Qin for three generations. I was the commanding general of three hundred thousand troops, garrisoned at the front. Notwithstanding the fact that I am imprisoned here I could easily rally my forces to turn against the state; however, I would rather die honourably upholding my firm conviction of righteousness; I dare not violate the teachings of my ancestors nor can I forget the benevolence of the former Emperor." He took a poison and died.

---

141 Lishan 驪山 is 20 km east of Xi'an 西安 - The entire mausoleum site was 203 million sq. metres, it was completely enclosed by three consecutive revetments. The outermost enclosure had a circumference of 6,210 metres, 17.5 metres in height; the stamped-earth rampart was 7 metres in thickness, the enclosure boasted of four tall towers to each of the four cardinal corners. The innermost enclosure was 2,050 metres in circumference. All told there were ten entrance gates each boasting a massive gate of 9 - 12 metres in width. In the innermost enclosure, there were multi-storied buildings, and soldiers were garrisoned within the enclosed areas; none of these structures survived. Yap. J., *Wars With the Xiongnu,* 2009, p. 47.

142 Water seepage into the surrounding area of the coffin.

143 Burton Watson's the *Translation of the Records of the Grand Historian* has a detailed account of the First Emperor and Second Emperor of Qin. The *Zizhi tongjian's* account is quite short and abbreviated. Watson, B. *Records of the Grand Historian, Qin,* The Chinese University of Hong Kong, 1993, pp. 35-83.

144 Ying Ying later the 3rd king of Qin.

145 Ziying 子嬰 Ying Ying 嬴嬰.

146 Yan Ju 顏聚 (see 229-I).
King of Qi 齊王 Tian Jian 田建.
Hou Sheng 后勝 (222-V).

147 Second Emperor, Er Shi Huangdi 二世皇帝, Ying Huhai 嬴胡亥. He was 20 years old this year (208 BCE).
Neishi 内史 – State Secretary. One is under the impression that Meng Tian was the Grand Commander of the Qin forces; we have no idea as to why the text gives him a title of *neishi* – Secretary or Governor of Capital.

Fayan Annotates:

Someone asks, "Meng Tian was staunchly loyal and yet he was sentenced to death. What purpose does loyalty serve?" Yang Xiong responded, "From the west at Lintao to the east at Liaoshui River he opened up mountains and filled up valleys; the deaths and wounded resulting from such activities were incalculable; his loyalty could not exonerate his crimes."[148]

Sima Guang annotates:

The First Emperor of Qin inflicted severe torments and sufferings on the people all under Heaven; Meng Tian was instrumental in implementing the deeds, the extent of his repressiveness is more than evident. Nevertheless, Meng Tian understood his duty as a subject, he might have died a wrongful death for a crime he was not responsible, he remained loyal to his end; his fealty is commendable.

---

209 BCE *Renchen* 壬辰 Qin Empire 秦帝國

Qin Second Emperor	秦二世	1st year
Wey, Wey Jue	衛衛角	21st year
King of Chu, Chen Sheng	楚王 陳勝	1st year Xiangjiang 襄疆元年
King of Zhao, Wu Cheng	趙王 武臣	1st year
King of Qi, Tian Dan	齊王 田儋	1st year
King of Yan, Hann Guang	燕王 韓廣	1st year
King of Wei, Wei Jiu	魏王 魏咎	1st year

I. Winter. 10th month, 10th day. A general amnesty was proclaimed.

II. Spring. The Second Emperor of Qin made a trip to the prefectures and counties in the east accompanied by Li Si. The entourage travelled first to Jieshi, then headed south along the coast and arrived at Kuaiji.[149] The unmarked stone steles erected by the First Emperor were finally appended with inscriptions; the Second Emperor ordered the names of the ministers who

148 Yang Xiong 揚雄 (53 BCE-18 CE).
The Long-Wall, built by Qin commenced at Lintao skirted through Gaoque and extended all the way to Liaodong, was an extraordinary and stupendous feat of engineering. Nevertheless, it was not entirely built by Qin; it was extensions of those Long-Walls built by Zhao and Yan kingdoms over a couple of centuries. Meng Tian was assigned to make repairs and build new sections to link the breaks left by Zhao and Yan. According to some estimates, the sections built by Meng Tian were probably no more than three to four hundred km. Yap. J., *Wars With the Xiongnu*, 2009, p. 48.
Lintao 臨洮 - Lintaoxian Gansu 甘肅 臨洮縣.
Gaoque 高闕 - Yinshan Mountain Range Neimeng 內蒙 陰山.
Liaodong 遼東 - Liaoyangxian Liaodong 遼東 遼陽縣.

149 Jieshi 碣石 - Changlixian Hebei 河北 昌黎縣.
Kuaiji 會稽 - Shaoxingxian Zhejiang 浙江 紹興縣.

accompanied him to be included. The inscriptions made tributes to the successful exploits and virtues of the former emperor. Thereafter the entourage returned.

Summer. 4th month. The Second Emperor returned to Xianyang. He asked Zhao Gao, "Being alive in this corporeal world is like charging in a six-horse carriage through a narrow crevice.[150] I have assumed total control of all under Heaven, with absolute power is in my hand. I can do whatever I want, listen to what pleases me, watch what delights me; I will enjoy life to the full until the day I die. What say you?" Zhao Gao answered, "Your Majesty, only a sage emperor could have such profound aspiration; this was proscribed by the inept and befuddled kings of bygone eras. However, while your thinking is accurate, it cannot be put into practice yet. Please allow your subject to explain to you. The conspiracy at Shaqiu was conducted in utmost secrecy; [151] however, some princes and ministers are becoming suspicious. The princes are your elder siblings while the ministers at court were the subjects your father appointed. Your Majesty now sits in state; these men are disgruntled and dissatisfied. Your subject is afraid that there might be unpredictable consequences. Your subject lives in great trepidation day and night for fear of dying an untimely and violent death. How can Your Majesty commit yourself to blissful celebrations as it stands?" The Second Emperor asked, "What should we do?" Zhao Gao responded, "Your Majesty should introduce even harsher laws and implement more severe chastisements; people found guilty of certain transgressions should be coerced to make them implicate others who are related to them; this will dispose of the ministers and royal member cliques. Your Majesty should then gather the poor and depraved; enrich the poor, while ennobling the depraved; and eliminate all the ministers installed by the former Emperor while placing your trusted retainers in their places. Your Majesty's benevolence on these people will be greatly appreciated. Subterfuge and machination will cease when these scourges are removed. When the ministers at court are anointed by your munificence, all relishing the generous bestowments of Your Majesty, you could then sit back and relax and enjoy the pleasurable things in life to your heart's content. There is not a better plan than this." The Second Emperor readily acceded to it.

The Second Emperor decreed to amend the standing laws and ordinances with even more ruthless and austere measures. When ministers and princes committed certain offences, they were promptly arrested and sent to Zhao Gao for trial. Twelve princes were executed in the public market of Xianyang; ten princesses were dismembered at Du, [152] and the victims had their family properties and fortunes confiscated. People arrested from confessions extracted from the victims were so numerous that they could not be tallied. Prince Jianglu and two of his younger brothers were imprisoned in the inner palace awaiting sentence.[153] The Second Emperor sent an usher to inform the prince, "You have committed a crime of insolence as a subject, punishable by death. You are hereby sentenced to be executed by the prison warden according to law." Jianglu defending himself said, "At court I have always abided by instructions of the ushers, never breaching the etiquettes; and at the holy shrine, I always abided by my mandatory obligations,

---

150 Meaning the lifespan of a human is short.

151 Shaqiu 沙丘 - Pingxiangxian Hebei 河北 平鄉縣. Zhao Gao 趙高 was referring to the conspiracy in 210 BCE (see 210-1).

152 Duyou 杜郵 - a small town west of Xi'an Shaanxi 陝西 西安市. General Bai Qi 白起 committed suicide at Duyou in 257 BCE. (257-1). The princesses were executed by *zhe* 矺 = *zhe* 磔 - the chastisement of dismemberment by five-horse or oxen drawn carriages running off in different directions.

153 Ying Jianglu 嬴將閭.

never losing my integrity. When certain decrees are dispensed, I did not acted incorrectly, nor had I said anything out of place. How could it be a crime of insolence, pray enlighten me with evidence so to allow me to die without remorse." The attendant replied, "Your subject does not intend to conduct a discussion on the subject; he is merely executing the decree." Jianglu was grief-stricken; he raised his head to face skywards bellowing out three times, "I am innocent." The three siblings wept bitterly, they drew their swords and ran themselves through. The entire royal family clan was in a state of horror.

Prince Gao, one of the princes, was planning to run for his life; however, he feared the worst for his family members. He wrote a memorial to the Second Emperor, "Your subject visited the former Emperor frequently when he was alive; His Majesty bestowed fine food and excellent wine upon him when he was in the palace. When your subject took leave, he allowed him to use his imperial rickshaw. He bestowed imperial trappings upon your subject, besides he used to present him with prized horses from the royal stable. Now that His Majesty has departed before your subject, by right, he should accompany him, but he did not. As a son, he is unfilial; as a subject, he is disloyal. Your subject, being unfilial and disloyal, does not deserve to be alive in this world. Your Majesty, please take pity upon your subject and allow him to be interred at the foothills of the Lishan Mound." Upon receiving the memorial, the Second Emperor was immensely pleased. He summoned for Zhao Gao and showed him the memorial, "Have I pressed them too hard?" Zhao Gao answered, "When your subjects are in constant fear of death; how could they find time to contemplate revolt?" The Second Emperor promptly approved the request; he bestowed his brother with one hundred thousand units of money for his funeral.

The Second Emperor ordered to resume the construction of Epang Palace.[154] Fifty thousand men of outstanding physical strength were conscripted to garrison at Xianyang and were taught archery skills. The abundant number of dogs, horses and animals kept at the royal zoo needed a large quantity of food, when the supplies became inadequate, the Second Emperor ordered the transport of bean, millet, fodder and straw to the capital for his animals, and the hauling labourers were ordered to provide their own food. He then decreed that people, living within three hundred *li* from Xianyang, were forbidden to consume their own crops.

III. Autumn. 7th month. Chen Sheng from the city of Yangcheng and Wu Guang from Yangxia County led a mob of peasants in rebellion at the Qi County [155] and started an insurrection against the kingdom. At that time, people living in the left side of a village were conscripted for corvée service.[156] Chen Sheng and Wu Guang were troop leaders *tunzhang*, who were commanded to lead nine hundred conscripts to garrison at Yuyang.[157] En route to their destination at Daze hamlet they came upon a torrential rainstorm, [158] the passage became impeded. Realizing that they had

---

154 Epang Palace 阿房宮.

155 Chen Sheng 陳勝. Yangcheng 陽城 - Dengfengxian Henan 河南 登封縣.
Wu Guang 吳廣. Yangxia 陽夏 - Taikangxian Henan 河南 太康縣.
Qi 蘄 - Suxian Anhui 安徽 宿縣.

156 This was reminiscent of the legal system introduced by Gongsun Yang 公孫鞅 in 359 BCE. When the government ran out of convicts for conscription, they conscripted their relatives; next came the neighbours living to the right and following that the left door neighbours of the convicts. (See 359-I).

157 The two men were troop leaders, *tunzhang* 屯長.
Yuyang 漁陽 - Miyunxian Hebei 河北 密雲縣.

158 Dazexiang Hamlet 大澤鄉 - Suxian Anhui 安徽 宿縣.

failed to reach the garrison on time, and the penalty mandated that they would be executed for missing the appointed time, they revolted.

Chen Sheng and Wu Guang, spurred on by the hatred and abhorrence of the people against Qin, cut down the army commander leading the group. They rallied their men together and gave a speech, "You have missed the deadline to reach your destination, and all of you will face certain execution; even if you somehow escaped execution, it is known six or seven out of ten of you would die serving at the garrisons. If you brave men are to face death, you might as well die honourably in the cause of a great exploit. The lords and kings are made; they are neither born nor preordained by Heaven." All the conscripts agreed to it. The two men deceitfully claimed that they were Prince Fusu and Xiang Yan, [159] and an altar was duly constructed for all to swear an oath of allegiance. They called their new state the Mighty Chu – Da Chu; Cheng Sheng proclaimed himself the general while Wu Guang took on the position as the military commander.[160] The rebels attacked and took Dazexiang Hamlet; they then followed up by laying siege to Qi Prefecture, which was taken.[161] Chen Sheng then dispatched Ge Ying, a native of Fuli, to lead an attachment to march east; the army took the cities of Zhi, Zan, Ku, Zhe and Qiao.[162] When the rebels were on the march, they gathered new recruits. Upon arriving at Chen, there were some six or seven hundred war chariots, with over one thousand cavalrymen and several tens of thousands of foot soldiers. The army besieged Chen; the magistrate and the military commander were away at that juncture, and it was defended by a county secretary. He led the armed forces against the besiegers, as the battle broke out at the Qiaomen Gate the secretary lost and died.[163] Chen Sheng marched into Chen.

IV. Previous to this, Zhang Er and Chen Yu from the Daliang County were fast friends.[164] When Qin annihilated Wei, the Qin authority heard of the reputation of the two men and posted generous rewards for their capture. The two changed their names and took on lowly positions as village gatekeepers in Chen, irking out a living. On one occasion Chen Yu made a minor transgression and was physically thrashed by a local functionary; he was about to rise to resist when Zhang Er warned him by treading on his foot, warning him to continue to sustain the caning. When the functionary departed, Zhang Er took Chen Yu to the shades of a mulberry grove,

---

159 Ying Fusu 嬴扶蘇.
General Xiang Yan of Chu 項燕 died in 224 BCE fighting against the Qin invaders under the command of Qin Commander Wang Jian 秦 王翦. (See 224 BCE-I).

160 Mighty Chu Kingdom, *Da Chuguo* 大楚國.
General, *jiangjun*, Chen Sheng 將軍 陳勝.
Military Commander, *duwei*, Wu Guang 都尉 吳廣.

161 Dazexiang Hamlet 大澤鄉 - Suxian Anhui 安徽 宿縣.
Qi 蕲 - Qijun Prefecture 蕲郡 - Suxian Anhui 安徽 宿縣.

162 Ge Ying 葛嬰 a native of Fuli 符離人 - Suxian Anhui 安徽 宿縣.
Zhi 銍 - Zhicheng 銍城 - Suxian Anhui 安徽 宿縣.
Zan 酇 - Zancheng 酇城 - Yongchengxian Henan 河南 永城縣.
Ku 苦 - Kuxian County 苦縣 - Luyixian Henan 河南 鹿邑縣.
Zhe 柘 - Zhecheng 柘城 - Zhechengxian Henan 河南 柘城縣.
Qiao 譙 - Qiaocheng 譙城 - Boxian Anhui 安徽 亳縣.

163 Qiaomen 譙門, the City-gate of Chen – Chenqiu 陳丘.

164 Zhang Er 張耳 and Chen Yu 陳餘.
Daliang 大梁 – Kaifengxian Henan 河南 開封縣.

where he admonished him, "What did I tell you previously? For the sake of a minor insult, you risked your life with a junior law enforcer." Chen Yu thanked him for saving him. When Chen She (Chen Sheng) and his men arrived at the City of Chen, Chen Yu and Zhang Er presented their names and made an appointment to meet the general. Chen She was aware of the reputation of the two men, and he was extremely delighted.[165] The local heroes, strongmen and elders at Chen greeted Chen She amiably and implored the general to proclaim as the king of Chu. Chen She sought the opinion of Zhang Er and Chen Yu; the two men responded, "Qin is repugnantly despotic; it has conquered and annihilated all the kingdoms under Heaven and is now abusing the people with great treachery. General, you risk ten thousand deaths to revolt because you believe you could save the people in all under Heaven by disposing of the despotic Qin government. You have just assumed control of Chen, and now you intend to make yourself a king; aren't you too hasty to divulge your hidden agenda? We believe you should not proclaim king; you should lead your army to march swiftly west; instruct your attendants to search the remnants of the royal family clans from the six former kingdoms, and help them restore their states; creating as many enemies for Qin as possible. With many enemies, the strength of Qin will be weakened, while making many allies will strengthen your position. You do not even have to be engaged in major battles in the wilderness, nor make defences at the counties and prefectures you captured; you could bring down the despotic Qin rule. When it finally falls, you could march into Xianyang, and as you preside at court, you could command the formerly deposed fief lords to come forth to honour you as the new king. The fief lords would be most grateful to you for reinstating their kingdoms, and you would have won them over with your virtue. The grand cause of founding a new kingdom will be within your reach. As of now, you have just taken a small County of Chen, and you intend to proclaim king, we believe people under Heaven might lose their desire to be more exertive in their fight against Qin." Chen She refused to accept their proposal; he made himself the king of Chu, naming his kingdom - Zhang Chu.[166]

At that stage, the civilians at various counties and prefectures agonized under the oppressive laws of Qin strived to kill the local officers in response to the call of Chen She.

The *Qin* government ushers returned from the east to give the Second Emperor factual assessments of the revolts;[167] he lost his temper and had the ushers imprisoned. Henceforth, when he asked the ushers who returned, they invariably replied, "The so-called rebels are groups of petty thieves, pilfers and robbers; the local magistrates and militia officers are having them arrested and apprehended, and they have been completely eradicated. They are of no serious concern." The Second Emperor was delighted.

Chen She enfeoffed Wu Shu (Wu Guang) as the deputy king. Wu Shu led an army aided by numerous generals pushed west to attack Yingyang.[168]

Zhang Er and Chen Yu proposed to the king of Chen (Chen Sheng) that he should consider sending a special task force to attack and occupy the former territories of the Zhao kingdom. The

---

165 Chen Sheng 陳勝 was also known as Chen She 陳涉, also, as the king of Chen 陳王 when he proclaimed king at the City of Chen.

166 King of Chu 楚王, Zhang Chu 張楚 means Da Chu 大楚, Great Chu. As he proclaimed king at Chen, he was also known as the king of Chen 陳王.

167 Grand Ushers - *yezhe* 謁者.

168 Yingyang 滎陽 – Xi'an City Shaanxi 陝西 西安市.

king of Chen accepted the proposal; he made his old acquaintance Wu Chen, a Chen local, as commander, with Shao Sao as the military-judiciary officer; Zhang Er and Chen Yu as the left and right commanders; [169] the leaders led three thousand men north and marched towards Zhao. The king of Chen (Chen Sheng) also ordered Deng Zong, a native of Ruyin, to attack the Jiujiangjun Prefecture.[170] At this stage, the army of Chu was made up of several thousand men to each fighting unit, and there were an innumerable number of those units.

Ge Ying arrived at the City of Dongcheng; he made Xiang Jiang the king of Chu; however as soon as he heard that Chen She had previously proclaimed himself as king, he executed Xiang Jiang; [171] thereafter he returned to Chen to make a report; Chen She had Ge Ying executed.

The king of Chen sent Zhou Shi to lead an army to march into the territories of the former Wei kingdom and occupied the land. He then appointed Sir Fang, a Shangcai local, Cai Ci as commander *shangzhuguo*.[172] In the meantime, he heard that a Chen local Zhou Wen was most capable and worthy, besides having some military knowledge. Hence, he issued him with a general's seal, [173] enjoining him to march west against the Qin government.

Wu Chen heading off with his armed forces crossed the (Weihe) River at Baima. (He was now in the territories of the former Zhao Kingdom). [174] The general then dispatched his retainers to go to the counties in the area to rally the local strongmen and valiant individuals, who responded to the call enthusiastically. On his march, the general recruited several tens of thousands of men joining the insurgent army. They affectionately called Wu Chen, Sir Wuxin.[175] The army subjugated over ten walled cities as it marched while some others chose to defend their positions; Wu Chen then headed northeast and was preparing to lay siege to Fanyang. A Fanyang local by the name of Kuai Che gave Sir Wuxin some advice,[176] "Sir, it appears you have to engage in new battles to gain new territories, and you have to storm cities before you could occupy them.

---

169 Chenqiu local, Commander, *jiangjun* 陳丘人 將軍 Wu Chen 武臣.
Military Judiciary Officer, *hujun* 護軍 Shao Sao 邵騷.
Left Commander, *zuo xiaowei* 左校尉 Zhang Er 張耳.
Right Commander, *you xiaowei* 右校尉 Chen Yu 陳餘.

170 Deng Zong 鄧宗 Ruyin local 汝陰人 - Fuyangxian Anhui 安徽 阜陽縣.
Jiujiangjun Prefecture 九江郡 - Shouxian Anhui 安徽 壽縣.

171 Dongcheng 東城 - Dingyuanxian Anhui 安徽 定遠縣.
Ge Ying 葛嬰.
King of Chu 楚王 Xiang Jiang 襄彊.

172 Zhou Shi 周市 took Wei 魏.
Sir Fang 房君 Cai Ci 蔡賜 from Shangcai 上蔡 - Shangcaixian Henan 河南 上蔡縣. *Shangzhuguo* 上柱國.
Throughout this translation, the author has translated *jun* 君 as Lord, however in this instance and some others it is translated as Sir, as it is believed the title of Lord was enfeoffed, while the Sir title was used by commoners to honour someone they respected at times.

173 Zhou Wen 周文.

174 Wu Chen 武臣.
Weyhe River 衛河 at Baimajin Crossing 白馬津 - Huaxian Henan 河南 滑縣.
The Zhao Kingdom 趙國.

175 Sir Wuxin 武信君 Wu Chen 武臣.

176 Kuai Che 蒯徹 - Fanyang 范陽人- Dingxian Hebei local 河北 定縣.

Your subject thinks it is a wrong strategy. If you heed his advice, you do not have to do battle to occupy new territories, and you do not have to storm walled-cities to annex them. He believes a piece of written missive will easily pacify one thousand *li* of land. What do you think?" Sir Wuxin asked, "What are the details?" Kuai Che answered, "Master Xugong, the magistrate of Fanyang is venal to boots, besides he is spineless; [177] he will surrender ahead of the other magistrates. Sir, if you consider him as one of Qin's magistrates, you might as well continue with your strategy of slaughtering the ten cities you brought down previously. I am afraid the rest of the walled cities and counties will shut their city gates like a clam, and they will not be easy to be taken down. Whereas, if you hand me the marquis seal for enfeoffment, I will present it to the magistrate, allow him to ride on an ornate carriage adorned with crimson wheels and spokes to travel to all parts of the former territories of Yan and Zhao as your courier; I am sure all the walled cities in the surrounding areas will surrender." Wu Chen said, "Brilliant." He dispatched one hundred luxurious carriages, [178] accompanies by two hundred cavalrymen, with Kuai Che bearing the marquisate seal to go forth to bid Master Xugong the magistrate to surrender. As soon as the news spread, over thirty cities and counties in Yan and Zhao surrendered.

The king of Chen (Chen She) having despatched Zhou Zhang (Zhou Wen), and believing that the situation at Qin was in chaos, [179] he nevertheless, underestimated Qin and took it lightly, and he did not take any precautionary measures in defending his garrisons. Kong Fu, the erudite academician, warned the king, [180] "Your subject has read from the military texts, 'Do not assume that the enemy could no longer make assaults; one must make full preparations to be attacked.' Your Highness is asserting that the enemy cannot attack us, while not preparing for one. If we were to lose a single battle, it would be too late to regret." The king of Chen responded, "You, Sir, do not have to be overly concerned with my military decisions."

Zhou Wen arrived at the Pass, on his way he gathered new recruits.[181] At this stage, he boasted of having a thousand war-chariots, with several hundred thousand foot soldiers. The army then garrisoned at the city of Xi.[182] The Second Emperor was in great shock; he called a session to consult his ministers, "What do we do?" The minister of lesser treasury Zhang Han said, "The thieves and bandits have arrived at our city gates, besides the number is huge. [183] To recall our regulars from the nearby counties would be too late. We have a large number of convicts working at the Lishan Mound; [184] please grant these men a general amnesty, give them weapons and order them to fight against the rebels." The Second Emperor duly granted a general amnesty for all under Heaven. He sent Zhang Han to gather all the convicts at the Lishan Mound as well as all the sons born to slaves to face the Chu army. The Chu army sustained a major defeat; Zhou Wen fled.

---

177 The Magistrate of Fanyang, Master Xu 范陽令 Xu Gong 徐公. The word gong 公 used here does not denote a Duke; it was an appellation given to someone the commoners respected as a senior, an officer or an elder, and hence, in this case, it is translated it as master.

178 *Anju* carriage 安車 - carriage with a canopy.

179 Zhou Wen 周文.

180 The erudite academician, *boshi* 博士 Kong Fu 孔鮒. (See 213-II and footnotes.)

181 Pass 關 - Hanguguan Pass 函谷關 was within Lingbaoxian Henan 河南 靈寶縣.

182 Xi 戲 - Xicheng 戲城 - East of Lintongxian Shaanxi 陝西 臨潼縣東.

183 Minister of Lesser Treasury, *shaofu* 少府 Zhang Han 章邯. *Shaofu* was the treasury of the palace, not the state.

184 Lishan Mound 驪山, the burial mound of the First Emperor of Qin.

Zhang Er and Chen Yu arrived at Handan.[185] When they heard of the retreat of Zhou Wen, and that King Chen (Chen She) had executed many of his generals who were vilified and slandered by others. They proposed to Sir Wuxin (Wu Chen) that he should proclaim king. 8th month. Wu Chen proclaimed as the king of Zhao; he made Chen Yu the supreme commander, while Zhang Er was nominated as the right chancellor and Shao Sao as the left chancellor.[186] He then dispatched his envoys to notify the king of Chen, who became violently enraged and was about to execute all the clan members of Sir Wuxin, to follow an attack against the newly established Zhao kingdom. Fang Jun, the state minister *zhuguo* reprimanded against it,[187] "Qin has yet to be annihilated, and now you intend to execute Sir Wuxin's and his followers' family members, you are creating another Qin. Your best option is to ride with the tide, send him a message of felicitations, and advise him to move west to attack the Qin kingdom." The king of Chen (Chen She) accepted the proposal, he settled Sir Wuxin (Wu Chen) family members at the palace as hostages, enfeoffed Zhang Ao the son of Zhang Er as Sir Chengdu; [188] and sent an envoy to honour the accession of the new Zhao king. The envoy prompted the new king to make haste to march towards the Pass (Hangu the vital Qin Pass). Zhang Er and Chen Yu nevertheless said to the king, "Your enthronement is not an idea of Chu (Chen She); hence, the envoy who came here to offer felicitations is but a matter of expediency. Once Qin is toppled, we are certain Chu will come after Zhao. A better alternative is to march north to take control of the territories previously under the Yan and Dai kingdoms; thereafter you could head south to recover areas within the River *Henei* to expand your domain.[189] At that stage, the kingdom of Zhao would have a realm reaching as far south as the River (Huanghe River); to the north, you will possess Yan and Dai. Even if Chu would annihilate Qin, [190] it could do little to compromise Zhao. If, however, Chu could not defeat Qin, our strength in Zhao would increase as a result. You could then sit in wait for Qin and Chu to weaken; we believe Your Highness could then make a bid for complete control of all under Heaven." The king of Zhao (Wu Chen) thought the approach was sound; he decided not to march west; he dispatched Hann Guang to the former domain of Yan, with Li Liang marching off to Changshan Mountain and Zhang Ye to Shangdang, [191] where they attempted to assume control of the respective territories 9th month. Liu Bang (the future Emperor of Han), a man from Pei, started an insurrection in Pei.[192] At about the same time, a Xiashang local, Xiang

---

185 Handan 邯鄲 - Handanxian Hebei 河北 邯鄲縣.

186 King of Zhao 趙王 Wu Chen 武臣, he was also known as Sir Wuxin 武信君 before he proclaimed King.
Supreme Commander, *dajiangjun* 大將軍 Chen Yu 陳餘.
Right Chancellor, *you zaixiang* 右宰相 Zhang Er 張耳.
Left Chancellor, *zuo zaixiang* 左宰相 Shao Sao 邵騷.

187 State Minister, *zhuguo* 柱國 Fang Jun 房君.

188 Sir Chengdu 成都君 Zhang Ao 張敖.

189 Yan 燕 - Beijing City 北京市.
Dai 代 - Weixian Hebei 河北 蔚縣.
Henei 河内 the areas north of Huanghe River 黄河 at Qinyangxian Henan 河南 沁陽縣.

190 Chu 楚. Chen Sheng 陳勝.

191 Hann Guang 韓廣.
Li Liang 李良. Changshan Mountain 常山 - Yuanshixian Hebei 河北 元氏縣.
Zhang Ye 張黶.
Shangdang 上黨 – Changzixian Shanxi 山西 長子縣.

192 Liu Bang 劉邦, alias Liu Ji 劉季.

Liang gathered a group of men and took on another revolt at the Wu.[193] Tian Dan, a native of the Di County, also raised a revolutionary army at Qi.[194]

Liu Bang alias Liu Ji, carried a most regal aura and a stately countenance, had a high nose bridge; it was said that he had seventy-two black moles on his left thigh. He was gregarious, keen on making friends, a most generous soul, broadminded at heart and had high aspiration; however, he was not given to demanding physical activities. Previously, when he was a commune constable *tengzhang* at Sishang Village, [195] a Danfu local by the name of Master Lugong, who dabbled in physiognomy, was amazed by his splendid stature; upon setting eyes on him, he betrothed his daughter (Lu Zhi) to him in marriage.[196] Later Liu Ji took on the post as the commune constable to lead a group of conscripts to march to Lishan Mound. En route, many of the men took flight and when Liu Ji arrived at Fengxi Hamlet the group stopped for water and rested, [197] he realized that, by the time he arrived at Lishan, all the convicts under his custody would have all absconded. By nightfall, he quietly unfastened the ropes binding the remaining conscripts and said, "You, Sirs, run for your life, this is also where I will run for mine." Among the young men, a score or more decided to remain with him as his followers. There was an occasion when in the middle of the night Liu Ji, roaring drunk, was staggering through a marshland; he came across a huge snake obstructing the footpath. He wielded his sword hacking the snake into halves. An old woman appeared cried bitterly, "My son was the son of the White Lord *Baidi*; he morphed into a snake, he was lying here on the footpath, and he was killed by the son of the Crimson Lord *Chidi*," [198] having said that she vanished.

Liu Ji and his followers found hideouts between the Mangshan and Dangshan mountains and river regions.[199] After that, many strange and extraordinary occurrences took place, when young men from the Pei County heard of what had happened they aspired to rally to Liu Ji's ranks. When Chen She rose up in rebellion, the county magistrate of Pei was considering to respond to

---

Pei 沛 - Peixian Jiangsu 江蘇 沛縣.
Later he was Han *Gaodi* 漢高帝, Han *Gaozu* (posthumously) 漢高祖.

193 Xiaxiang 下相 - Suqianxian Jiangsu 江蘇 宿遷縣.
Xiang Liang 項梁 was from Wujun Prefecture 吳郡 - Wuxian Jiangsu 江蘇 吳縣.
Xiang Yu 項羽 alias Ji 籍.

194 Diyi County 狄邑 - Gaoyuanxian Shandong 山東 高苑縣.
Tian Dan 田儋. Qi 齊 - Shandong 山東.

195 Village Chief, *tingzhang* 亭長; Sishangcun Village 泗上村.

196 Danfu 單父 - Danxian Shandong 山東 單縣.
Lu Wen 呂文.
Lu Zhi 呂鴙. The text does not mention her name at this stage.

197 Fengxi 豐西 - Fengxian Jiangsu 江蘇 豐縣.

198 White Lord, *Baidi* 白帝; Red Lord, *Chidi* 赤帝. There were Five August Lords, or deities according to the *Zhouli* 周禮 'Tianguan zhongzai dazai 天官冢宰大宰' – 'Si wudi 祀五帝' that says, "Make sacrifices to the Five Lords." The Tang scholar Jia Gongyan 唐 賈公彥 annotates, "There were Five Lords. The Green Lord in the east; the Crimson Lord in the south; the Yellow Lord in the centre; the White Lord in the west and the Black Lord in the north."
唐賈公彥疏, "五帝者, 東方青帝靈威仰, 南方赤帝赤熛怒, 中央黃帝含樞紐, 西方白帝白招拒, 北方黑帝汁光紀."

199 Mang 芒 - A mountain near Yongchengxian Henan 河南 永城縣.
Dang 碭 - Dangshanxian Jiangsu 江蘇 碭山縣.

the call.[200] The bureau clerk *yuan* Xiao He and the judiciary clerk *zhuli* Cao Can advised the magistrate,[201] "You are a Qin officer and you plan to revolt; if the people in Pei oppose your decision, you will fail. We believe your best option is to look for other outlaws who have escaped; there are several hundred of them; being intimidated by these men, we are sure the others would be coerced into compliance." The magistrate then ordered Fan Guai to make contact with Liu Ji.[202] At this stage, Liu Ji had acquired several scores of men, perhaps even close to a hundred. The magistrate had a sudden change of heart as he realized if this group of outlaws were allowed to enter his county, he might not be able to contain them; he had a complete about-face and ordered the city gate be closed, commanding the local militia to make preparations for defence. He then planned to have Xiao He and Cao Can executed; when the two men realized his intent, they scaled off the walls of the city and escaped into Liu Ji's army camp. Liu Ji prepared a missive written on a silk scroll; [203] attached to an arrow, it was delivered by shooting into the city. In the letter, Liu Ji gave an account of the state of affairs. When the elders in the walled-city read the letter, they led their young people to go against the Pei magistrate, killing him. They opened the gate of the city to welcome Liu Ji and his men and honoured him as Master Pei (Pei Gong).[204] Xiao He and Cao Can took charge of recruiting young men of Pei to join the ranks; three thousand men assembled, the group began their quest of rallying to the call of the other fief lords.

Xiang Liang (another rebel leader) was the son of the former Chu general, Xiang Yan.[205] Having committed the crime of murder, he was hiding from the authorities at Wu with his nephew Ji (Xiang Yu). Many of the learned scholars at Wuzhong were Xiang Liang's students.[206] When Ji (Xiang Yu) was younger, his uncle taught him to recite scholarly texts but he failed miserably, he then took up swordsmanship, in which he did not excel. Xiang Liang was most infuriated with the nephew of his; Ji said to him, "Learning how to read and write is merely for remembering names. A sword is an effective weapon against one person in combat. Both are not worth learning. I would rather devote my time learning tactics to wage battles against ten thousand." Xiang Liang hence taught him military tactics from texts; Ji was elated, except he barely managed to grasp the essentials, and he did not attempt to delve into the finer details.

Ji, over eight *chi* tall, had the strength to lift a bronze tripod, and his physical attributes were beyond any ordinary person. [207] Yan Tong, the prefecture magistrate of Kuaiji, heard of the uprising of Chen She, assessed the prospect of participating; he had intended to assign Xiang

---

200 Chen Sheng 陳勝.

201 County Magistrate of Peixian 沛縣守.
Judiciary Clerk *yuan* 掾, Cao Can 曹參.
Bureau Clerk, *zhuli* 主吏 = *gongcao* 功曹 - Xiao He 蕭何. According to the *Hanshu* 漢書, 'Cao Can zhaun 曹參傳,' 'Can 參 was a *yuyuan* 獄掾 and Xiao He was a *zhuli* 主吏.' According to *Shiji suyin* 史記索隱, "*Zhuli* 主吏 is *gongcao* 功曹." *ZZTJ JZ*, Vol 1, p.321.

202 Fan Guai 樊噲.

203 Silk scroll - *bo* 帛.

204 Master Pei, Peigong 沛公.

205 Xiang Liang 項梁 was the son of Xiang Yan 項燕 the Chu general that died in 224 BCE (224-1).
Xiang Yu 項羽 *Ji* 藉 was the grandson of Xiang Yan; Xiang Liang was Ji's uncle.

206 Xiang Liang was an accomplished scholar.
Wuzhong 吳中 - Wuxian Jiangsu 江蘇 吳縣.

207 Bache 八尺 – was about 1.70 or 1.88 metre.

Liang and Huan Chu as his military commanders.[208] At that stage, Huan Chu was in hiding as a fugitive in the marshes of a wasteland. Xiang Liang said, "Huan Chu has absconded into hiding. No one knows his hideouts except Ji." He ordered his nephew to bear his sword to wait at the reception hall while he entered the audience hall to speak with the magistrate. He seated with the magistrate, "Please summon Ji, instruct him to go in search of Huan Chu." The magistrate answered, "Yes." Xiang Liang summoned Ji to enter. Shortly after, Xiang Liang glanced at Ji and said, "Now." Ji drew his sword and lobbed off the head of the magistrate. Xiang Liang holding the head of the magistrate hastily removed the official magistrate seal and wore it on his side. The abrupt change of events caused great alarm to the attendants and guards, and they fell into chaos. Ji killed several scores of men, perhaps as many as a hundred, and all the people submitted, falling onto the ground not daring to rise from their positions. Xiang Liang then summoned forth his former acquaintances, the valiant and strongmen in the county for a gathering. He announced the incident was contrived to raise a righteous army against the Qin government. He then recruited the regulars serving in the Wu Prefecture to be enlisted, as well as incorporating the civilians living in the region; overall, he managed to conscript eight thousand men. Xiang Liang took over the magistrate position of the Kuaiji Prefecture, with Ji as his assistant general. After that, they led their army to lay siege to counties that had not surrendered in the surrounding areas. This year Ji (Xiang Yu) was twenty-four years of age.

Tian Dan was from the royal house of Qi, his younger cousins Rong and Heng were influential and powerful men,[209] and had won the supports of the locals. In the meantime, General Zhou Shi of the Chu kingdom continued with his expedition, finally arrived at Di;[210] the city defended itself by closing all its city gates. Tian Dan had one of his slaves bound and sent to the magistrate followed by a group of youths; he asked permission to execute the man. The magistrate of Di sat in his office, summoned Tian Dan to come forth; Tian Dan wielded his sword and killed the magistrate, he then rallied the young men and sons and brothers of the influential officers in the county. He reasoned with them, "All the fief lords under Heaven are rising in unison against Qin; proclaiming themselves as kings. Qi was an ancient state established long ago, I am Dan, and my surname is Tian, and I should be the rightful king of Qi." He proclaimed himself as the king of Qi; he raised his army from his city to go against Zhou Shi (the Chu general); the latter could not defend his position and retreated. Tian Dan then led his forces to march east and recovered areas that were formerly Qi territories.

Meanwhile, General Hann Guang (abiding by the directives of the king of Zhao, Wu Chen), marched north and recovered the former Yan territories.[211] The prominent local people and valiant men proposed to make Hann Guang the king of Yan; however, he said, "My mother is at Zhao, I cannot comply." The Yan people said, "The kingdom of Zhao faces the threats of Qin to its west, to the south they have to worry about Chu; they do not have the strength to go against us. Furthermore, even with the present strength of Chu, they do not have the audacity to afflict harm

---

208 Prefecture Magistrate of Kuaijijun 會稽守 Yin Tong 殷通.
Xiang Liang 項梁 and Huan Chu 桓楚.

209 Tian Dan 田儋 was from the House of Qi 齊; Tian Rong 田榮 and Tian Heng 田横 were his younger brothers.

210 Chu General 楚將 Zhou Shi 周市. Di 狄 - Diyi 狄邑 - Gaoyuanxian Shandong 山東 高苑縣.

211 Zhao General 趙將 Hann Guang 韓廣.
King of Zhao 趙王 Wu Chen 武臣.
Yan territory 燕地.

on the family members of Zhao. Do you think the king of Zhao has the nerve to bring harm to your family members?" Hann Guang was finally convinced and proclaimed himself the king of Yan. A few months later, Zhao sent Hann Guang's mother and family members to return to Yan.

The king of Zhao (Wu Chen), Zhang Er and Chen Yu made raids along the northern border with Yan, occupying its territories. The king of Zhao managed to find some leisure time ventured out alone on one occasion and was captured by the Yan army. Yan held him hostage and demanded the ceding of land for his release. Zhao kingdom dispatched envoys to negotiate his release several times; the Yan army executed all the envoys. A lowly cook from the Zhao kingdom went to call on the Yan commander, and asked, "Sir, do you know what Zhang Er and Chen Yu desire most?" The Yan commander answered, "The return of their king." The Zhao cook laughed aloud and said, "Sir, you have no idea what these two men desire. Wu Chen, Zhang Er and Chen Yu holding on their horse whips expended great efforts to retake several scores of Zhao cities. The two men have a hidden agenda to face south calling themselves kings. Who in his right mind would want to be a mere chancellor or general for the rest of his life? As the state is still in turmoil and unsettled, they do not dare to split the occupied land into three parts; hence, according to seniority by age, they nominated Wu Chen, the most senior among them, as king to pacify the Zhao people. Now, the situation at Zhao has settled down somewhat; these two men are planning to partition the kingdom, waiting to make themselves kings, except it is not the right time yet. Sir, you are holding the king of Zhao (Wu Chen) here as a hostage. They have repeatedly sent envoys to negotiate his release, however, in reality, they had hoped that you might have him executed; no sooner is he out of the way they will partition Zhao into two parts making themselves kings. Yan can be subjugated easily as far as the kingdom of Zhao is concerned; if however it ends up as two separate states, under two capable kings, and when they decide to make a combined attack to chastise Yan for the death of their king, Yan could be taken down easily." The Yan commander immediately ordered the release of the king of Zhao (Wu Chen); the cook steered the carriage to escort the king to return.

V. Zhou Shi (the Chu general) returned from the County of Di, en route, he passed through the former domain of Wei. He planned to reinstate a former prince of Wei, Lord Ningling (Wei Jiu) as the king of Wei.[212] Jiu was held in Chen and could not travel to Wei.[213] When all the former land of Wei had been taken, the subordinates of the Chu general had wanted Zhou Shi to take over the position as the king of Wei. Zhou Shi said, "When all under Heaven is in turmoil, only then loyal subjects will emerge. The whole world is against the despotic Qin government, the right and proper path is to nominate a descendant of the former Wei kingdom as king." His subordinates continued to argue that he should take on the position as king. Nevertheless, Zhou Shi resolutely declined. He sent his retainers to travel to Chen to escort Wei Jiu to Wei; it took him five separate occasions to convince the king of Chen (Chen She) to allow Wei Jiu to leave. Wei Jiu was made the king of Wei; Zhou Shi assumed the position as his chancellor.

VI. This year, the Second Emperor decreed to relegate the Lord of Wey (Jie, the sovereign of Wey) to the status as a commoner; the state of Wey finally fell.[214]

---

212 Sir Ningling 甯陵君 Wei Jiu 魏咎 made King of Wei 魏王.

213 Chen 陳 - Chenqiu 陳丘 - Huaiyangxian Henan 河南 淮陽縣.

214 Wey Jue 衛角 was the 42nd sovereign of Wey. The fiefdom lasted for 904 years from 1112 to 209 BCE.

Volume VIII. 資治通鑒 卷第八 秦紀三 208-207 BCE

The narrations of this volume commence from the 2nd year of the Second Emperor of Qin *Ershi Huangdi* (208 BCE) and ended in the 3rd year of his reign (207 BCE).[1]

208 BCE. – The king of Chen (Chen She) led his army against the Qin government; General Zhang Han overwhelmed the rebels.[2]

- Chu generals murdered Wu Guang.
- Zhuang Jia, the coachman, murdered the king of Chen (Chen She).[3]
- Xiang Liang learning of the death of Chen She adopted strategy proposed by Fan Zhen, placed Mi Xin, the grandson of King Huai of Chu on the throne, the capital was established at Xuyi.[4]
- The Second Emperor of Qin was fatuous and despotic, trusting only the eunuch Zhao Gao, [5] and assigned all national affairs to his care. Zhao Gao forced the death of Right Chancellor Feng Quji, Commander Feng Jie; and executed Left Chancellor Li Si; [6] all their family clan members were executed.
- Zhao Gao was made chancellor; he decided on everything at court.
- Xiang Liang defeated the Qin armies on numerous occasions, and became arrogant; Zhang Han of Qin soundly defeated the Chu general at Dingtao, [7] Xiang Liang died in battle.
- King Huai of Chu pledged, "Whoever enters the Inner Pass *guannei* first will be enfeoffed as king."
- The king of Chu ordered Liu Bang to march west against the Qin government while Xiang Yu was to march north to bring relief to Julu.[8]
-

207 BCE. Xiang Yu executed Song Yi, the Chu supreme commander; [9] he then marched north to give bring relief to Julu; he commanded his men to wreck all the vessels for the river crossing, bringing with them only three days of rations to show resolve. The Qin army was soundly defeated at Julu.

---

1 Emperor of Qin, *Ershi Huangdi* 秦二世皇帝.

2 King of Chen 陳王 Chen Sheng 陳勝, Chen She 陳涉.
Qin General 秦將 Zhang Han 章邯.

3 Coachman - Zhuang Jia 莊賈.

4 Xiang Liang 項梁; Fan Zeng 范增.
King of Chu 楚王 Mi Xin 芈心 (r. 208-206 BCE) was the grandson of King Huai of Chu 楚懷王. He was initially known as Latter King Huai of Chu 後 楚懷王; later Xiang Yu 項羽 made him King Yi of Chu 楚義王.
King Huai of Chu 楚懷王 Mi Huai 芈槐 (328-296 BCE), was the Chu King that was held hostage by Qin in 299 BCE and died in 296 BCE.
Xuyi 盱眙.

5 Zhao Gao 趙高.

6 Right Chancellor, *xiang*, Feng Quji 馮去疾. General, *jiangjun* 將軍 Feng Jie 馮劫.
Left Chancellor 左相 Li Si 李斯.

7 Xiang Liang 項梁. Dingtao 定陶.

8 Master Pei (Peigong) Liu Bang 劉邦. Xiang Yu 項羽. Julu 鉅鹿.

9 Chu Supreme Commander, *qingzi guanjun* 卿子冠軍 Song Yi 宋義.

- General Zhang Han capitulated to Chu; Xiang Yu made him the king of Yong.[10]
- Zhao Gao assumed total control of the Qin court, ministers and officers at court dared not challenge him.
- Zhao Gao murdered the Second Emperor and tried to place Ying Ying (Zi Ying) on the throne as Qin king.[11]
- Zi Ying stabbed Zhao Gao to death and annihilated his three family clans.

Qin Chronicle III 秦紀三

208 BCE *Guisi* 癸巳 Qin Empire 秦帝國

Qin Second Emperor	二世皇帝	2nd year
King of Chu, Chen Sheng	楚王 陳勝	2nd year
Chu Jingju	景駒	1st year
Chu Huaiwang - Mi Xin	楚懷王 芈心	1st year
King of Zhao, Wu Chen	趙王 武臣	2nd year
Zhao Xie	趙歇	1st year
King of Qi, Tian Dan	田儋	2nd year
Tian Jia	田假	1st year
Tian Shi	田市	1st year
King of Yan, Hann Guang	燕王 韓廣	2nd year
King of Wei, Wei Jiu	魏王 魏咎	2nd year
Wei Bao	魏豹	1st year
King of Hann, Hann Cheng	韓王 韓成	1st year

1. Winter. 10th month. Ping, a Qin inspector-officer *jian* from the Sichuan Prefecture, led an army encircled the forces of Master Pei (Liu Bang) at Feng.[12] Master Pei led his men to meet the attackers, and the government forces were defeated. Following this, he ordered Yong Chi to remain in Feng to defend the city.[13]

---

10 King of Yong 雍王.

11 King of Qin 秦王 Ying Ying 嬴嬰 Zi Ying (子嬰).

12 Ping 平 - Qin Inspector Officer *jian* at Sichuan 泗川 - Sishuijun Prefecture 泗水郡監. (N.B. Sichuan 泗川 should be Sishui 泗水, the text made a mistake.) *ZZTJ JZ*, Vol 1, p. 338.
Master Pei - Pei Gong 沛公- Liu Bang 劉邦 Liu Ji 劉季.
Feng 豐 - Fengyi County 豐邑 - Fengxian Jiangsu 江蘇 豐縣.

13 Yong Chi 雍齒. Yong Chi was one of the early followers of Liu Bang 劉邦. The second year of Liu Bang's uprising was one of the most difficult times for him. Yong Chi, at Fengyi 豐邑, surrendered to Wei 魏 (Zhou Shi 周市). Liu Bang was fuming with rage and tried to retake Fengyi on numerous occasions, but failed. Liu Bang, then surrendered to Xiang Liang 項梁 at Xuecheng 薛城. *SJ* 史記, 卷 26, 'Gaozu benji 高祖本紀' 第 8, p. 271.

11th month. Master Pei with his forces arrived at the City of Xue and besieged it. Zhuang, the magistrate of Sishui Prefecture, battled with the invading forces, lost and escaped to Qi; Master Pei sent his left commander after him and had him executed.[14]

II. Zhou Zhang (Chu general) led his men retreated to the east to beyond the (Hangu) Pass; at Caoyang the army ceased advancing and made garrison.[15] More than two months later, Zhang Han (Qin general) marched out of the Pass and attacked the Chu army; Zhou Zhang lost the ensuing battle, retreated again, this time to Mianchi Lake.[16] Ten or so days later Zhang Han attacked again; the Chu army sustained a severe onslaught. Zhou Wen (Zhou Zhang) committed suicide by cutting his neck, the soldiers under him dispersed.

III. The deputy king of Chu, Wu Shu (Wu Guang) besieged Yingyang.[17] Li You, the magistrate of Sanchuan Prefecture, defended the city, and the besiegers did not make any headway.[18] General Tian Zang of Chu and others schemed,[19] "Zhou Zhang's forces have been defeated, and the Qin army will arrive in a matter of days. We are besieging Yingyang and could not make any headway; when the Qin army arrives, we will face certain defeat. It will serve us better to leave a small force to garrison at Yingyang while deploying all our crack troops to meet the Qin army head-on. The deputy king is conceited and unfamiliar with military tactics, it is not worth our time to reason with him, and all our efforts might come to nothing." The commanders then forged a decree from the king of Chen (Chen She) to have Wu Shu executed.[20] His head was presented to the king of Chen. The king sent his attendants bearing the Chu chancellor seal to present to Tian Zang and appointed him as the supreme commander.[21] Tian Zang then ordered Li Gui and a few other officers to garrison outside the city of Yingyang.[22] He then led his crack troops to march west against the approaching Qin army. At the Aocang Granary the battle was joined, Tian Zang died, and the Chu army was completely routed.[23] The Qin general, Zhang Han, followed up by attacking

---

14 Xue 薛 - Xuecheng 薛城 - Tengxian Shandong 山東 滕縣.
Magistrate of Sishui Prefecture, Zhuang 泗水郡 長 壯.
Qi 戚 - Qixian 戚縣 - Jiaxiangxian Shandong 山東 嘉祥縣.
Left Commander, *zuosima* 左司馬, was in charge of punishment and execution *xinglu* 刑戮 in the army.

15 Chu General, Zhou Zhang 楚將 周章. The text simply refers to the Pass, which was the Hangu Pass 函谷關.
Caoyang 曹陽 - south of Lingbaoxian Henan 河南 靈寶縣南.

16 Qin General, Zhang Han 秦將 章邯.
Mianchi Lake 澠池 - Mianchixian Henan 河南 澠池縣.

17 Deputy King of Chu, *jiawang*, Wu Guang 假王 吳廣. The polite name of Wu Guang was Shu 叔.
Yingyang 滎陽 - Yingyangxian Henan 河南 滎陽縣.

18 Li You 李由 was the Magistrate of Sanchuanjun Prefecture – *shou* 三川郡守. Li You was the son of Li Si 李斯.
Sanchuan 三川 - Sanchuanjun Prefecture 三川郡 - Luoyangxian Henan 河南 洛陽縣.

19 Chu General, *jiangjun*, Tian Zang 楚將軍 田臧.

20 King of Chen 楚王 - Chen Sheng 陳勝 Chen She 陳涉.

21 Chancellor of Chu - *lingyin* 令尹.
Commanding General – *shangjiang* 上將.

22 Li Gui 李歸, one of the Chu generals.

23 Aocang Granary 敖倉 - Northwest of Yingyangxian Henan near the Huanghe River 河南 滎陽縣西北 臨黃河.

Li Gui garrisoned outside Yingyang, again defeated the Chu forces, Li Gui and several commanders died.[24]

Deng Yue, a Yangcheng local and his forces were garrisoned at the city of Jia, one of the generals under the command of Zhang Han defeated him. While a Zhi local, Wu Feng was garrisoned at Xu.[25] Zhang Han defeated him as well. The Chu forces from the two defeated cities escaped to City of Chen.[26] The king of Chen (Chen She) executed Deng Yue.

IV. The Second Emperor kept reproaching Li Si, who held a three-excellence *sangong* position, had allowed the bandits to run rampant.[27] Li Si was in a panic and not knowing how to respond; nevertheless, his rapaciousness for power kept him from giving up his post. He submitted a memorial to appease the emperor, "A sage sovereign is one who understands the full implications of judicious supervision and chastisement. Hence, Shenzi (Shen Buhai) said,[28] 'A sovereign, who reigns all under Heaven and not being able to indulge himself, enjoying life to the full, is no more than a prisoner in shackles bounded by his people. Very simply put a sovereign who fails to supervise and administer his subjects effectively ends up attending to everything personally. He is no different from King Yao and King Yu, [29] both of whom were fettered and shackled by their subjects.' Hence, if the brilliant legalist practices advanced by Shenzi and Hann Fei are not expedited skillfully by a sovereign Lord, [30] attempting to embrace all the responsibilities under Heaven to satisfy his wellbeing, toiling with his body and mind, making sacrifice for the hundred surnames by taking on their trials and tribulations, he is no different from working as hard labour for the black-headed. He is not a sovereign who presides all under Heaven. What glory and grandeur does he hold for being addressed as an Emperor? It is said a wise lord makes expedient decisions, implementing judicious rules, acting in *ad arbitrium*. Consequently, the power is vested in the hands of the Emperor, not his subjects; only then could those idle speculators of virtue, benevolence, and righteous path be eradicated. Your Majesty should prohibit the submission of reprimanding memorials, putting an end to admonishers wantonly indulgent with their unconstrained comments. When these measures are implemented, your subjects and civilians will be busily making amends with their flaws and will be running scared, and not afforded time to contemplate revolts." The Second Emperor was extremely delighted. He decreed even more stringent and austerity measures to be imposed on his ministers and subjects. The measure of

---

24 Qin General 秦將軍 Zhang Han 章邯.

25 Deng Yue 鄧說 - Yangcheng local 陽城人- Dengfengxian Henan 河南 登封縣.
The word Yan 郯 should be Jia 郟 - The text made a mistake, the city was recorded as Yan 郯, it should be Jia 郟 - Jiacheng 郟城 - Jiaxian Henan 河南 郟縣. *ZZTJ JZ*, Vol 1, p. 339.
Wu Feng 伍逢 Zhicheng local 銍城人- Suxian Anhui 安徽宿縣.
Xu 許 - Xucheng 許城 - Xuchangxian Henan 河南 許昌縣.

26 Chen 陳 - Chenqiu 陳丘 – Huaiyangxian Henan 河南 淮陽縣.

27 Second Emperor, Ying Huhai 二世皇帝 嬴胡亥.
Three-Excellences, *sangong*, Li Si 三公 李斯.

28 Shen Buhai 申不害 (385-337 BCE). See 351 BCE; Shen Buhai was appointed the Chancellor of Hann 韓國 in 351 BCE and held the position for fifteen years. He was also known as Shenzi 申子; he was renowned for his legalism and his *shu* 術 – 'techniques (tactics) thesis' and was a proponent of the *Yin* 陰 and *Yang* 陽 school of thought.

29 Yao 堯 - King Yao, Yiqi Fangxun 堯帝 伊祁放勳.
Yu 禹 - King Yu, Si Wenming 夏禹 姒文命.

30 Hann Fei 韓非 (~280-233 BCE) see 233 BCE.

merits and loyalty was based on the abilities of officers who could exact the most taxes or execute the most people. Henceforth, half of the people in the streets were convicted facing condemnation, and the markets were littered with body remains from the executions. The people in the kingdom were in such dire terror and repulsion that they yearned for a major upheaval to end their miseries.

V. General Li Liang of Zhao had at this stage taken Changshan and returned to Handan to report his mission to the king of Zhao.[31] The king of Zhao (Wu Chen) again commanded him to take Taiyuan.[32] By the time he arrived at Shiyi County, the Qin army had already set up a blockade at Jingjing in wait;[33] the Zhao army was impeded from advancing. The Qin generals forged a letter from the Second Emperor to summon the rebels to surrender. Upon receiving the letter, Li Liang was suspicious; he decided to return to Handan to seek reinforcements. When about to enter Handan he came across the elder sister of the king of Zhao returning from a banquet with an entourage of retainers. The general thought it was the king of Zhao; he speedily descended from his warhorse and knelt most humbly at the wayside to pay respect. The king's elder sister was in a drunken stupor and had no inkling that it was General Li Liang; she sent a cavalryman to reciprocate the protocol. Li Liang had all along held a prestigious position, faced with such lowly exchange he looked most embarrassingly at his followers as he rose from his position. An army attendant said, "All the able people under Heaven are rising in arms, and the most capable ones have become kings. The king of Zhao had all the while been your underling. General, his elder sister, is so insolent that she did not even have the slightest courtesy to alight from her carriage to reciprocate your civility. Please execute her." When Li Liang first received the letter from Qin inviting him to surrender, he was already vacillating with uncertainty; and now with the insufferable humiliation his anger was fuming with infinity; he ordered his attendants to have the woman executed. He then led his army to launch a sudden raid against Handan, which was ill prepared for this sudden change of events. Li Liang killed the king of Zhao (Wu Chen) and Shao Sao (the left chancellor).[34] Zhang Er and Chen Yu being well connected to a web of friends in the kingdom were forewarned of the impending perils, escaped unscathed.[35]

VI. Qin Jia, a man from Chen, a certain Zhu Jishi from Fuli and some followers also raised an army at the Donghai Prefecture and went on to besiege the magistrate of Donghai at the city of Tan.[36] When the king of Chen (Chen She) heard of their move, he named Pan, Sir Wuping, as

---

31 Zhao General, Li Liang 趙將 李良.
Changshan 常山 - Yuanshixian Hebei 河北 元氏縣.
Zhao capital - Handan 趙首府 邯鄲.

32 King of Zhao, Wu Chen 趙王 武臣.
Taiyuan 太原 - mid-section of Shanxi 山西 中部.

33 Shiyi 石邑 - Huoluxian Hebei 河北 獲鹿縣.
Jingjing 井陘 - Jingjingguan Pass, Jingjingxian Hebei 河北 井陘縣 井陘關.

34 Left Chancellor, Shao Sao 邵騷.

35 Zhang Er 張耳. Chen Yu 陳餘.

36 Qin Jia 秦嘉 - Chen local 陳人. The place name of Chen is wrong; it should be Ling 淩, according to Hu Sansheng 胡三省. *ZZTJ JZ*, Vol 1, p. 340.
Ling 淩 - County of Lingyi 淩邑 - Suqianxian Jiangsu 江蘇 宿遷縣南.
Zhu Jishi 朱雞石- Fuli local 符離人, Peixian Jiangsu 江蘇 沛縣.
Donghaijun Prefecture 東海郡 - this is probably an error, as Donghaijun Prefecture did not exist at the time of Qin.

general to supervise the army besieging Tan.[37] Qin Jia refused to comply; he made himself the commander general *dasima*, and told his subordinates, "Sir Wuping is an unfledged youth; he knows nothing about military strategy. Don't listen to him." He claimed he had received a decree from the king of Chen and had Sir Wuping executed.

VII. The Second Emperor sent army secretary *changshi* Sima Xin and Dong Yi to provide additional supports to Zhang Han to fight against the bandits and insurgents.[38] At this stage, Zhang Han had successfully defeated Wu Feng (at the city of Xu); he then attacked the Chen (Chu) commander *zhuguo* Feng Jun, killing him.[39] Continuing, Zhang Han attacked the western part of Chen (Chu) under the command of Zhang He.[40] The king of Chen went out to supervise the battle.[41] Zhang He died in the ensuing battle.

12th month. The king of Chen (Chen She) rode to Yuyin; on his passage back he passed through the City of Lower Chengfu; the carriage driver Zhuang Jia murdered the king and surrendered to Qin.[42]

Previously when Chen She (Chen Sheng) assumed the title of king, his former acquaintances came in droves to seek patronage from him. His father-in-law also came to his court; the king of Chen treated him with indifference, no different from his ordinary guests, merely performing the minimal protocol of bowing instead of the formal etiquette of prostration due to an elder. The father-in-law was enraged, he said, "One who takes advantage of dissension to proclaim himself as king, besides being insolent to his elders, is not likely to endure." He rose to leave without bidding farewell. The king of Chen kneeled in front of his father-in-law to beg for forgiveness, he ignored him and departed. Later, more friends and relatives came to gather at his palace, and they reminisced about things and events in the past. Someone suggested, "Your Highness, your guest is so ill-bred and boorish, incessantly babbling nonsense, he is going to weigh down on your

---

Tan 郯 - Tancheng 郯城 - Tanchengxian Shandong 山東 郯城縣.

37 King of Chen 陳王 i.e. the King of Chu 楚王, Chen Sheng 陳勝, Chen She 陳涉. The *SJ* 史記 has a detailed account of Chen Sheng. *SJ* 史記, 卷 118, 'Chen She shijia 陳涉世家' 第 18, pp. 1769-1773.
Army Supervisor, *jian* 監 Sir Wuping 武平君 Pan 畔.

38 The Second Emperor of Qin 秦二世皇帝 Ying Huhai 嬴胡亥.
Secretary, *changshi* 長史 Sima Xin 司馬欣. The *SJ* and the *Hanshu* refer to Dong Yu 董翳, Zhang Han 章邯 and Sima Xin 司馬欣 collectively as the San-Qin 三秦 when the Qin generals later surrendered to Chu 楚 and were enfeoffed at the territories of Qin 秦, mostly in the Shaanxi province 陝西.
Militia Commander, *duwei* 都尉 Dong Yi 董翳.
Qin General, Zhang Han 章邯.

39 Wu Feng 伍逢.
Xu 許 - Xucheng 許城 - Xuchangxian Henan 河南 許昌縣.
Chu Commander, *zhuguo* 楚 柱國 Feng Jun 房君.

40 Chu General 楚將 Zhang He 張賀.

41 The king of Chu 楚王 Chen Sheng 陳勝.
The capital of Chu 楚首府 – Chenqiu 陳丘 - Huaiyangxian Henan 河南 淮陽縣.

42 Yuyin 汝陰 - Fuyangxian Anhui 安徽 阜陽縣.
Chengfu 城父 - Boxian Anhui 安徽 亳縣.
Carriage Driver of Chen Sheng, Zhuang Jia 莊賈.
Details of Chen Sheng's demise are lacking. He was king for six months.

reputation." [43] The king of Chen had his acquaintance executed. As a result, his friends began to take leave, and he ended up with no one close to him. The king of Chen had appointed Zhu Fang as the minister of imperial affairs *zhongzheng* and Hu Wu as inspector *siguo* in charge of intelligence to preside over the generals and ministers.[44] When the military commanders returned to the capital with the newly conquered land, the two men were always critical of their performances, finding faults for not adhering strictly to the decrees and orders from the king. Some of the generals were even accused of violating the edict and were castigated. The ones who austerely observed the king's order were considered loyal, the generals and commanders they disliked were sent to the judiciary for trial and were summarily sentenced. The military commanders under the king had no emotional attachment to him; in the end, he failed.

Lu Chen, a former attendant responsible for household cleaning for the king of Chen, was the commander of the Green Turban and was garrisoned at Xinyang. After the death of the king, he attacked the city of Chen, recaptured it, and declared it as the Chu capital. He then executed Zhuang Jia and had the remains of the king of Chen (Chen She) buried in the Dang County with a posthumous title of the King of Yin – Melancholy King.[45]

Earlier than this, the king of Chen had dispatched a Zhi local Song Liu to lead an army to take Nanyang and to attack the Wuguan Pass.[46] Song Liu successfully took Nanyang and settled in the city. When news arrived that the king of Chen had died, the army under him became restive; Song Liu and his men surrendered to the Qin government. The Second Emperor ordered to have Song Liu to be dismembered, setting it as an example to the public.

VIII. The chancellor of Wei, Zhou Shi, led an army to lay siege to Feng and Pei; he sent his attendants to persuade Yong Chi to surrender.[47] Yong Chi loathed Master Pei (Liu Bang) and was

---

43 According to the *SJ*, it was an old friend of Chen Sheng; *JJTJ* is unclear if it was one friend or many. *SJ* 史記, 卷 118, 'Chen She shijia 陳涉世家' 第 18, p. 1772.

44 Minister of Imperial Affairs, *zhongzheng* 中正 Zhu Fang 朱防, the *SJ* 史記 refers to him as Zhu Fang 朱房.

Inspector in charge of Intelligence, *siguo* 司過 Hu Wu 胡武.

45 Personal Attendant, *juanren*, Lu Chen 涓人 呂臣.

Lu Chen 呂臣 became the Green Turban Commander 蒼頭軍. The foot soldiers in those days wore a green head turban; hence, they came to be known as Green Turbans.

Xinyang 新陽 - Taihexian Anhui 安徽 太和縣.

Chenqiu 陳丘 - Huaiyangxian Henan 河南 淮陽縣.

Zhuang Jia 莊賈.

The posthumous title of Chen Sheng - Yinwang 隱王 – Melancholy King.

Dangyi County 碭邑 - Dangshanxian Jiangsu 江蘇 碭山縣.

46 Zhiyi local, Song Liu 銍邑人 宋留. Zhiyi 銍邑 - Suxian Anhui 安徽 宿縣.

Nanyang 南陽 - Nanyangxian Henan 河南 南陽縣.

Wuguan Pass 武關 - Shangxian Shanxi 陝西 商縣.

47 Wei (Wei Jiu 魏咎).

Chancellor, Zhou Shi 魏相 周市.

Feng 豐- Fengxian Jiangsu 江蘇 豐縣 was the base area of Liu Bang.

Pei 沛 – Peixian *Jiangsu* 江蘇 沛縣.

Yong Chi 雍齒 (?-192 BCE) came from the same county as Liu Bang. He was later enfeoffed by Liu Bang and was given a posthumous title of Marquis of Su 肅侯. (Also see F.N. 13).

not inclined to be his underling; hence, he surrendered to Wei instead. Master Pei ordered his army to attack Feng but failed to retake the county.

IX. (After the death the king of Zhao,) Zhang Er and Chen Yu gathered the remnants of the Zhao forces, the number despite everything came to several tens of thousands; the generals then attacked Li Liang.[48] Li Liang lost the ensuing battle and surrendered to Zhang Han (the Qin general). Someone among the guests suggested to Zhang Er and Chen Yu, "I am afraid you gentlemen cannot secure a foothold in this kingdom as you are mere sojourners in Zhao. However, there is one possible way for you to gain prominence; perhaps you should consider electing a descendent from the Zhao royal house as king while you two gentlemen take on subsidiary positions as aides." Zhang Er and Chen Yu found a certain Zhao Xie (from the remnants of the former Zhao royal household), and during the first month in spring, they elected him as the king of Zhao; the capital was established at Xindu.[49]

X. When Dongyang locals Ning Jun and Qin Jia heard news of the recurring defeats of the king of Chen (Chu) they elected Jing Ju as the new Chu king.[50] They sent an army to march towards Fangyu County preparing to go against the Qin position at Dingtao.[51] Gongsun Qing was dispatched as an emissary to go to the Qi kingdom, [52] seeking to form an alliance to attack Qin. The king of Qi, Tian Dan said,[53] "The king of Chen (Chen She) has suffered repeated losses, we do not even know if he is still alive. Why did you Chu people elect a new king without consulting us?" Gongsun Qing responded, "Qi (Tian Dan) did not confer with the kingdom of Chu, and you proclaimed yourself as king, so why should Chu (Jing Ju) solicit your opinion? Besides, it was Chu which began the insurrection; Chu has the right to command all under Heaven." Tian Dan executed Gongsun Qing.

The left, and right commanders of Qin regiment resumed attacks against the City of Chen (the capital of Chu) and captured it.[54] General Lu Chen escaped; he then assembled the remnants of his army to meet up with Qingbu the leader of a band of bandits from Pan; the two armies joined force and soundly defeated the Qin army at Qingbo, the city of Chen was recaptured by Chu.[55]

---

48 The King of Zhao 趙 Wu Chen 武臣.
Zhang Er 張耳, Chen Yu 陳餘.
Li Liang 李良 was the Zhao general who revolted against Wu Chen.

49 Zhao Xie, the King of Zhao 趙歇 (?-205 BCE). Zhao Xie was from the royal house of Zhao.
Xindu 信都 - Jixian Hebei 河北 冀縣.

50 Ning Jun 寧君 and Qin Jia 秦嘉 - Dongyang local 東陽人, Tianchangxian Anhui - 安徽 天長縣.
SJ 史記, 卷 18, 'Chen shijia 陳涉世家' 第 18, pp. 1769-1772.
King of Chu 楚王 Jing Ju 景駒.

51 Fangyu 方與 - Yutaixian Shandong 山東 魚台縣.
Dingtao 定陶 - Dingtaoxian Shandong 山東 定陶縣.

52 Gongsun Qing 公孫慶. *SJ* 史記, 卷 18, 'Chen She shijia 陳涉世家' 第 18, pp. 1769-1772.

53 King of Qi 齊王 Tian Dan 田儋.

54 Qin Left and Right Commander, *zuo you xiaowei* 秦左右校尉.
The Chu capital 楚都 - Chenqiu 陳丘, Huaiyangxian Henan 河南 淮陽縣.

55 Chu general, *jiangjun* 楚將軍 Lu Chen 呂臣.
Qingbo 青波 - the area between Xixian and Xincaixian Henan 河南 息縣 新蔡縣 交界.

Qingbu was from the Liu County, his family name was Ying, he had committed an offense against the Qin state and was sentenced to have his face tattooed, and by established decree, he was dispatched to the Lishan Mound to serve hard labour.[56] At that stage, there were several hundred thousand convicts labouring at the site; Ying Bu befriended some of the most influential leaders and heroes among the convicts. He with a group of these men escaped to the area of Changjiang River, irking out a living as bandits and thieves. Wu Rui, the magistrate of Panyang County, was a popular officer, well liked and supported by the locals and heroes of the underworld; they fondly addressed him as Sir Pan.[57] Ying Bu, by then had gathered several thousand men, went to meet the magistrate. Wu Rui gave his daughter to Qingbu in wedlock and made him the leader of his troops, instructing him to go against the Qin army.

XI. Jing Ju, the king of Chu, pitched camp at the Liu County; Master Pei (Liu Bang) with his men went to submit to the king.[58] In the meantime, Zhang Liang, leading a group of one hundred or more youths, was also heading towards the direction of Jing Ju.[59] On their way, the two groups met, having made some exchanges Zhang Liang decided to concede to Master Pei. Master Pei made Zhang Liang his stable officer.[60] En route, Zhang Liang on many occasions instructed Liu Bang on an ancient text - the *Arts of War - Taigong bingfa.* [61] Master Pei, extremely gifted, was

---

Qingbu 黥布 real's name was Ying Bu 英布, a man from the County of Liu 六縣. See below.

Pan 番 – Panyang 番陽 - Poyangxian Jiangxi 江西 鄱陽縣. (*'Pan'* is also pronounced as *'fan'*番, as a place name it is pronounced as 'pan').

56 Qingbu 黥布, Ying Bu 英布 was his real name, is chronicled as Qingbu 黥布 in the *SJ* 史記. The word – *qing* 黥 means tattoo. The general was tattooed for transgressing a crime against the Qin state and came to be known as Qingbu. As the magistrate of Panyang gave his daughter to Qingbu as wife, Qingbu also came to be known as Pandao 番盜 – the Thief of Pan. For more details about Qingbu see *SJ* 史記, 卷 61, 'Qingbu liezhuan 黥布列傳' 第 31, pp. 791-795. In addition, Sima Qian, Records of the Grand Historian, translated by Watson B., The Biography of Qing Bu, The Chinese University of Hong Kong 1993, pp. 153-162.

Lishan 驪山 was the burial mound of Qin First Emperor.

57 Panyang County Prefect 番陽縣令 Wu Rui 吳芮 Sir Pan 番君. (The word *'pan'* is also pronounced as *'po'*.

58 The king of Chu 楚王 Jing Ju 景駒.

Liu 留 - Liuxian County 留縣 - Peixian Jiangsu 江蘇 沛縣東南.

59 Zhang Liang 張良, the Hann 韓 man who attempted to assassinate the First Emperor, see 218-I.

60 Stable officer, *jiujiang* 厩將.

61 The *Art of War*, 'Taigong bingfa 太公兵法'. The book was also known as the *Liutao* 六韜, the *Taigong liutao* 太公六韜 or the *Sushu* 素書. Duke of Jiang, Taigong 姜太公 was the title given to the founding sovereign of the fiefdom of Qi 齊, Jiang Ziya 姜子牙. It is assumed that Jiang Tiagong composed the *Taigong bingfa*. However, it is most unlikely. The text took the form of a conversation between Taigong, King Wen 文王 and King Wu 武王. The book is not listed in the *Hanshu* 漢書 Yiwenzhi 藝文志 under the heading of military texts by various masters. However, it appears under the heading of Daojia 道家 under 'Taigong 太公'. The *Hanshu* 漢書 relates that it has a total of 237 volumes, which were composed of 81 volumes on Stratagems – 'Mou 謀' in 81 volumes; Discourse – 'Yan 言' 71 volumes and Military – 'Bing 兵' 85 volumes. The text was unlikely to have been composed by Taigong, as to the real author, history is silent; most scholars believe it was composed at the time of the Warring States. Ever since the time of Southern Song Dynasty 宋 (1127-1279 CE), and particularly during the Qing Dynasty 清 (1616 or 1644-1912 CE), scholars had suspected the authenticity of the text, maintaining that it was a fabrication after the Han period 漢 (202 BCE- 220 CE). Among a large quantity of bamboo slips that were uncovered in the Western

able to follow it with ease, and he began to place the tactics into good use. Zhang Liang tried to instruct the other generals on the *Arts of War*; however, no one could comprehend him. He said, "Master Pei is a God-given talent." Hence, he decided to stay with Master Pei. Master Pei and Zhang Liang eventually met up with Jing Ju; they sought reinforcement from the king to make a counteroffensive against the Feng County.[62]

At that stage, Zhang Han and Sima Yi commanded their armies to pacify the territories that were under Chu in the north. They ordered wholesale slaughter between the County of Xiang and the City of Dang.[63] Ning Jun from Dongyang joined forces with Master Pei and pushed west to the west of Xiao, where the battle was joined; they were defeated and had to retreat to the Liu County.[64]

2nd month. The combined forces under Master Pei laid siege to the Dang County, which was taken in three days; the army incorporated the six thousand armed forces at the county into their ranks, together with their existing forces the army had increased to nine thousand strong. During the 3rd month, the army took the Xiayi County; Master Pei then returned to lay siege to Feng but failed in the attempt. [65]

XII. Zhao Ping, a Guangling man, acted according to the instructions by the king of Chen (Chen She) laid siege to Guangling, and the city held. When he heard news that the king of Chen had been defeated and escaped, and the Qin army under the command of Zhang Han was approaching, he sailed across the Changjiang River to the south.[66] He came up with a fabricated decree saying that he was instructed by the king of Chen to appoint Xiang Liang as the army commander *shangzhuguo*.[67] He said to him, "The areas east of the River *Jiangdong* are now under the control of Chu.[68] You are to head west post haste to go against the Qin forces." Xiang Liang led eight thousand men to sail across the River (Changjiang) and marched west. He heard that Chen Ying

---

Han Tomb at Yinqiao Mountain Linyi Shandong 山東 臨沂 銀雀山 in 1972, more than fifty slips were on the *Liutao*; which proved that the text was already in wide circulation at the time of Western Han 西漢. Also, see Appendix - Literature on the Warring States, #16, translation from Yang Kuan's *ZGS* 戰國史. p. 25.
古詩文網 六韜 - http://www.gushiwen.org/guwen/liutao.aspx

62 Feng 豐 - Fengyi 豐邑 - Fengxian Jiangsu 江蘇 豐縣.

63 Zhang Han, Qin Commander 章邯.
Qin General, Sima Yi 秦 司馬夷.
Xiang 相 - Xiangxian 相縣 - Suxian Anhui 安徽 宿縣.
Dang 碭 - Dangyi 碭邑 - Dangshanxian Jiangsu 江蘇 碭山縣.

64 Ning Jun 寧君 - Dongyang local 東陽人 - Tianchangxian Anhui 安徽 天長縣.

65 Xiayi County 下邑 - east of Dangshanxian Jiangsu 江蘇 碭山縣東.
Feng 豐 - Fengyi 豐邑 - Fengxian Jiangsu 江蘇 豐縣.

66 Zhao Ping 召平 - Guangling local 廣陵人 - Jiangduxian Jiangsu 江蘇 江都縣.
King of Chen (Chu), Chen Sheng, Chen She 楚王 陳勝 陳涉.
Qin General, Zhang Han 秦 章邯.
Changjiang River 長江.

67 Chu Supreme Commander, *shangzhuguo*, Xiang Liang 楚 上柱國 項梁.

68 Jiangdong 江東 – the area in southern parts of Jiangsu, in the Taihu Lake District - 江蘇南部 太湖流域.

had occupied Dongyang, [69] he sent an envoy to meet up with him, seeking to form an alliance to march west.

Chen Ying, the former county secretary *lingli* of Dongyang resided in the county, [70] was a cautious person and a man with rectitude; people addressed him as an elder and paid him with great respect. When rebellion set in, the young people in the county killed the county magistrate, after that they gathered twenty thousand men and appealed to Chen Ying that he proclaim king. The mother of Chen Ying said to him, "Ever since I married your father, I have never heard that any one of your ancestors had held a senior government position. Now that your reputation has preceded you, this is not propitious. It is a better option to seek shelter under a capable leader, if the quest is successful it may even land you with a title of marquis; if you fail, you can easily make a getaway, don't create a name for yourself to be censured by people under Heaven." Chen Ying hence declined to be king; he told his men, "The Xiang family clan has for many generations been the army commanders of the Chu kingdom; if we are to achieve something illustrious, we need their reputation. If we build upon their illustrious name, Qin will be annihilated." His followers agreed to the arrangement; Chen Ying submitted his army to Xiang Liang.

Ying Bu (Qingbu) having defeated the Qin army in battle continued with his march east; when he heard that Xiang Liang and his men had sailed across the Changjiang River, he and a General Pu went forth and submitted together.[71]

The number of followers of Xiang Liang had increased to sixty or seventy thousand men at this stage; he ordered his men to pitch camp at Xiapi.[72] Jing Ju (the king of Chu) accompanied by Qin Jia, were at the east of Pengcheng City preparing for the onslaught against Xiang Laing.[73] Xiang Liang in front of his men declared, "The king of Chen (Chen She) was instrumental in raising arms against the Qin government; he lost a few battles, and his whereabouts is unknown. Qin Jia has betrayed our king by electing Jing Ju as the king of Chu; this is grand impiety." He commanded his men to march against Qin Jia, who lost appallingly and escaped to Huling, hotly pursued by Xiang Liang forces.[74] Qin Jia tried to fight back for one whole day but died in the battle, his forces all submitted to Xiang Liang. The king of Chu, Jing Ju, ran for his life and later died in Liang (Wei).[75]

---

69 Chen Ying 陳嬰. Chan Ying served under Xiang Yu, later when Xiang Yu died he surrendered to Han 漢. *SJ* 史記, 卷 25 'Xiang Yu benji 項羽本紀' 第 7, p. 237.
Dongyang 東陽 - Tianchangxian Anhui 安徽 天長縣.

70 County Secretary of Dongyang - Dongyang *lingli* 東陽令吏.

71 Ying Bu, Qingbu 英布.
Changjiang River 長江.
General Pu 蒲將軍.

72 Xiapi 下邳 – Pixian Jiangsu 江蘇 邳縣.

73 King of Chu, Jing Ju 楚王 景駒.
Qin Jia 秦嘉.
Pengcheng 彭城 - Tongshanxian Jiangsu 江蘇 銅山縣.

74 Huling 胡陵 - Yutaixian Shandong 山東 魚臺縣.

75 Wei 魏 (Wei Jiu 魏咎).

Having taken in the armed men of Qin Jia, Xiang Liang led his men through Huling and was about to march west. At this time, Zhang Han arrived at the Li County; [76] Xiang Liang sent two commanders Zhu Jishi and Yu Fanjun to battle against the Qin forces.[77] Yu Fanjun died in the battle; Zhu Jishi was given a sound thrashing and escaped to return to Huling. Xiang Liang led his army to garrison in the City of Xue and had Zhu Jishi executed.[78]

Master Pei led several hundred men to meet Xiang Liang. Xiang Liang allotted him with five thousand men and ten middle-grade colonels *wudafu*. With this force, Liu Bang renewed his assault against the Feng County; he finally succeeded in recapturing the county; Yong Chi escaped to Wei.[79]

Xiang Liang commanded Xiang Yu to besiege the walled-city of Xiangcheng; [80] the city put up a staunch resistance. It fell eventually. Xiang Yu ordered all the soldiers and civilians in the city buried alive. After that, he returned to report to Xiang Liang.

Xiang Liang finally received confirmation that the king of Chen (Chen Sheng) had died; he summoned all the generals to meet at the Xue County to discuss plans to move forward, Master Pei also attended.[81] Fan Zeng, a Juchao local, had reached the age of seventy years old and usually spent his time at home; [82] he was known for his brilliant military tactics. He went and said to Xiang Liang, "It did not surprise me the slightest that Chen Sheng (Chen She) failed. When Qin annihilated the six kingdoms, Chu was perhaps the most innocuous victim. Ever since King Huai of Chu (see notes) was deceived to enter into the Qin territories, being held hostage with no prospect of returning home, [83] the people nevertheless still cherished the memory of their king to this day. It prompted Master Nangong to remark, 'Even if only three households remain of the Chu kingdom, it will be the Chu that finally vanquished Qin.'[84] Chen Sheng was the first person to start the insurrection, instead of placing a descendant of the Chu royalist on the throne, he made himself king; he lacked stature and credibility, and he was bound to fail. You, Sir, raised an army to the east of the Changjiang River; the former commanders of the Chu kingdom have all submitted to you, besides for several generations your family members had been Chu generals; you are truly qualified to nominate a descendant of the Chu royal family as the king of Chu."

---

76 Li 栗 - Lixian County 栗縣 - Xiayixian Henan 河南 夏邑縣.

77 Zhu Jishi 朱雞石.
Yu Fanjun 餘樊君.

78 Xue 薛 - Xuecheng 薛城 - Tengxian Shandong 山東 滕縣.

79 Yong Chi 雍齒.
Fengyi 豐邑 - Fengxian Jiangsu 江蘇 豐縣.
Kingdom of Wei, Wei Jiu 魏咎.

80 Xiang Yu 項羽.
Xiangcheng 襄城 - Xiangchengxian Henan 河南 襄城縣.

81 Xuecheng 薛城 - Tengxian Shandong 山東 滕縣.
Liu Bang 劉邦.

82 Fan Zeng 范增 - Juchao local 居鄛人 - Chaoxian Anhui 安徽 巢縣.

83 King Huai of Chu 楚懷王 Mi Huai 芈槐. (See 299-III)

84 Master Nangong of Chu 楚南公, "楚雖三戶, 亡秦必楚." Chu Nangong was a *Yin-Yang* scholar at the time of late Zhanguo 戰國.

Xiang Liang agreed with what he had related, and he went in search of Mi Xin a grandson of Mi Huai alleged to be herding goats, living among peasants.[85]

Summer. 6th month. Xiang Liang elected Mi Xin as King Huai of Chu in compliance with the aspiration of the Chu people.[86] Chen Ying was nominated as the supreme general *shangzhuguo*, enfeoffed with five counties.[87] The capital was located at the Xuyi County; Xiang Liang proclaimed himself Sir Wuxin.[88]

Zhang Liang suggested to Xiang Liang,[89] "Now that you have placed a descendant of Chu on the throne, it is perhaps a sensible idea for you to consider placing one of the former Hann princes, Lord Hengyang (Hann Cheng) on the throne. [90] He is the most worthy among the princes to be elected as king. With such a move, you will spread your influence by forming additional cliques." Xiang Liang instructed Zhang Liang to locate Hann Cheng, who was later made the king of Hann while Zhang Liang was made the chancellor *situ* of Hann.[91] Zhang Liang and the king of Hann heading an entourage of over a thousand men marched west to recover the former territory of Hann. However, no sooner had they successfully taken over several cities than the Qin government forces managed to recover them; finally, the group of men resorted to carrying out guerrilla activities in the vicinity of Yingchuan River.[92]

XIII. The Qin general, Zhang Han, having defeated the king of Chen (Chen She) decisively, continued his march against the king of Wei at Linji.[93] The king of Wei sent Zhou Shi to go to Qi and Chu to appeal for help.[94] The king of Qi, Tian Dan, led an army to answer to the call; while Chu General Xiang Ta also marched with Zhou Shi to bring relief to Wei.[95] In the midst of night, Zhang Han ordered his men to wear mouth-gags *xianmei* to give the combined forces of Qi and Chu a surprise attack at the city of Linji; [96] the king of Qi and General Zhou Shi died in the battle. The king of Wei, Wei Jiu, representing his people, negotiated a deal for the surrendering of the city; he then committed suicide by setting himself on fire. The younger brother of the king Wei

---

85 Mi Xin 芈心; Mi Huai 芈槐.

86 King Huai of Chu 楚懷王 Mi Xin 芈心.

87 Chu Supreme Commander, *shangzhuguo* 上柱國 Chen Ying 陳嬰.

88 Xuyi 盱眙 - Xuyixian Anhui 安徽 盱眙縣.
Sir Wuxin 武信君 Xiang Liang 項梁.

89 Zhang Liang 張良.

90 Hann Prince 韓王子 Lord Hengyang 横陽君 Hann Cheng 韓成.

91 Zhang Liang 張良 - *situ* 司徒. *Situ* was in charge of the land of a state and the edification of the people.

92 Yingchuan 潁川 - Yingchuanjun Prefecture 潁川郡 - Yuxian Henan 河南 禹縣.

93 Qin General 秦將軍 Zhang Han 章邯.
Chu King 楚王 Chen Sheng 陳勝.
Linji 臨濟 was 25 km northwest of Chenliuxian Henan 河南 陳留縣 西北 二十五公里. Linji was the capital of Wei.

94 King of Wei 魏王 Wei Jiu 魏咎. Zhou Shi 周市.
King of Qi 齊王 Tian Dan 田儋 and King of Chu 楚王 Mi Xin 芈心.

95 Chu General 楚將 Xiang Ta 項它.

96 *Xianmei* 銜枚 - Mouth-gag – soldiers were issued with wooden sticks about the size of chopsticks and were ordered to bite on the gag, which was to prevent making noise or teeth cluttering due to cold when conducting a surprise nocturnal operation.

Bao escaped to Chu to seek refuge.[97] The king of Chu issued Wei Bao with several thousand fighting men and ordered him to recover his former kingdom. In the meantime, Tian Rong, the younger cousin of the king of Qi, gathered the remnants of generals and soldiers of his cousins to retreat to the east and garrisoned at Donga; [98] Zhang Han pursued after him unrelentingly and had the city besieged. When the ministers of Qi heard news of the death of Tian Dan they placed Tian Jia, a younger brother of the former Qi king, on the throne; [99] Tian Jue was made the chancellor, and Tian Jue's younger brother Tian Jian was made the army general. [100]

Autumn. 7th month. There was incessant rain for days. Sir Wuxin (Xiang Liang) led his army to attack the city of Kangfu.[101] When he heard the news that Tian Rong was besieged at Donga, he hastily marched towards the city. Below the city-wall he gave the Qin army a thrashing; Zhang Han could not defend his position retreated to the west. Tian Rong then led his army to return to the kingdom of Qi in the east. In the meantime, Sir Wuxin was alone hot on the trail of the Qin army; he dispatched Xiang Yu and Master Pei to besiege the city of Chengyang; [102] having taken the city it was slaughtered to the last person. The Chu army followed up by marching to the east of Puyang; [103] it attacked Zhang Han, defeating the Qin army again. Zhang Han summoned up the tenacity of his men and marched briskly into Puyang, where they put up a staunch resistance. Then they broke the banks of the river, flooding the perimeters of the city to stall the advances of the Chu forces.

Meanwhile, Master Pei and Xiang Yu marched off to attack Dingtao.[104]

8th month. Tian Rong (the cousin of the deceased Tian Dan) led his army broke out from the siege to attack the king of Qi (Tian Jia); the king could not sustain the onslaught and escaped to the kingdom of Chu (Mi Xin).[105] General Tian Jian led his forces to go to the aid of the Zhao kingdom (Zhao Jie), [106] when he heard news of his king's defeat he lost his nerve and did not proceed. Tian Rong then elected Tian Fu, the son of Tian Dan, as the king of Qi; Tian Rong was made the chancellor, and Tian Heng as the army general, the former territory of Qi was reinstated.[107]

---

97 Wei Bao 魏豹.

98 Tian Rong 田榮.
Donga 東阿 - Yangguxian Shandong 山東 陽穀縣.

99 Tian Jia 田假.
King of former Qi 齊王 Tian Jian 田建 (r. 264-221 BCE).

100 Chancellor - *Xiang* 齊相 Tian Jue 田角.
Qi General 齊將 Tian Jian 田間.

101 Sir Wuxin 武信君 Xiang Liang 項梁.
Kangfu 亢父 - Jiningxian Shandong 山東 濟寧縣.

102 Chengyang 城陽 - Puxian Shandong 山東 濮縣.

103 Puyang 濮陽 - Puyangxian Hebei 河北 濮陽縣.

104 Dingtao 定陶 - Dingtaoxian Shandong 山東 定陶縣.

105 Tian Rong 田榮 was the cousin of the deceased Tian Dan 田儋.
King of Qi 齊王 Tian Jia 田假.
Chu, Mi Xin 楚 羋心.

106 General, Tian Jian 田間. Zhao 趙 Zhao Xie 趙歇.

107 King of Qi 齊王 Tian Fu 田福 was the son of Tian Dan 田儋.

The Qin army under the command of Zhang Han had by now regained its strength. Xiang Liang sent envoys to Qi (Tian Fu) and Zhao (Zhao Xie) to seek reinforcements for a combined attack against Zhang Han. Tian Rong said, "If Chu executes Tian Jia while Zhao executes Tian Jue and Tian Jian, we will march forth to the rescue." Both Chu and Zhao refused, Tian Rong was in a terrible rage; he refused to help in the end.

XIV. Zhao Gao, the superintendent of the Qin imperial household *langzhongling* took advantage of the Second Emperor's partiality towards him exploited his power with ferociousness and brutality;[108] avenging the people he loathed or offending him with vicious abandonment, many as a result died. He was apprehensive lest someone might divulge his malicious deeds. Hence, he suggested to the Second Emperor, "The Son-of-Heaven of a mighty kingdom reigns supreme, and his subjects should merely be aware of his utterances while not meeting him in person. Your Majesty is young; you are ill informed on matters that are brought before you. You sit in court every day, and you meet your subjects. When you reproach them or express praises for their work, there is a chance Your Majesty might make a misjudgement, and you might not have the opportunity to make amends. It is not a prudent measure to manifest the virtues and sagaciousness of the Son-of-Heaven. It is better for Your Majesty to retire in seclusion in the forbidden palace; decree to appoint your subject and some senior attendants well versed with the legal system to administer on your behalf, reviewing the submitted missives and memorials. The ministers and officers at court will no longer be able to pose thorny issues to challenge and contest your dispositions and pronouncements. Everyone under Heaven will maintain that Your Majesty is a sage emperor." The Second Emperor agreed to it and adopted the arrangement. After that, he did not attend the imperial court sessions or preside over meetings and ceased to meet all the senior ministers in person; he then spent all his time in the inner palace. The superintendent of the Qin imperial household and the senior attendants presided at court, everything pertaining to the kingdom was decided by Zhao Gao.

Zhao Gao was informed that Chancellor Li Si opposed to the arrangement and had reproached against it.[109] He met him and said to the chancellor, "The criminal activities east of the pass are worsening and are getting rampant by the day. His Majesty nevertheless is conscripting more hard labourers to construct the Epang Palace,[110] besides he is keeping a large number of useless hunting dogs and horses for his pleasure at the palace. Your subject honestly wants to reprimand against it; nevertheless, I am holding a humble position at court. Now, I believe it is your responsibility as the chancellor of the state to remonstrate His Majesty. You should make expostulates against His Majesty's actions and decisions." Li Si said, "Of course, I have intended to voice out my concern for long. However, His Majesty does not appear in court and has spent all his time in the inner palace. Besides, the admonitions I intend to raise cannot be communicated through someone else. I do not even know if he has time to spare?" Zhao Gao responded, "Sir, you should make admonitions indeed, I will try my best to make arrangements for you." Zhao Gao waited until the Second Emperor was zealously preoccupied with his feasting and music, with beautiful women lining in front of him. He then sent for the chancellor, "His Majesty has some

---

Chancellor, *xiang* 相 Tian Rong 田榮.

General, *jiang* 將 Tian Heng 田橫.

108 Superintendent of the Qin Imperial Household, *langzhongling* 秦郎中令 Zhao Gao 趙高.

109 Qin Chancellor 秦丞相 Li Si 李斯.

110 Epang 阿房宮 palace.

spare time to see you." The chancellor proceeded to the inner palace gate to make a submission, but on the third occasion, the Second Emperor lost his temper, "When I was free the chancellor did not come; why does he have to show up when my personal affairs preoccupy me? Does he think I am young and look down on me?" Zhao Gao responded accordingly, "Your Majesty is aware that Li Si was complicit with the Shaqiu conspiracy; [111] while Your Majesty is now our Emperor presiding over our kingdom, whereas Li Si is merely a chancellor; his aspiration is abundantly clear, he wishes to be enfeoffed as a king. Had Your Majesty not raised the issue with your subject, he would not have the audacity to discuss the subject; but since you asked, he might as well relate all the circumstances to you. Li You, the eldest son of the chancellor, is the magistrate of Sanchuan Prefecture; [112] where the Chu rebels like Chen She and others rose up in rebellion. Li You did not raise his army against them even when those rebels marched through Sanchuan. Your subject is informed that Li You and the rebels have made frequent missive exchanges. Nevertheless, your subject did not have the nerve to raise this issue with Your Majesty as he did not have tangible evidence; particularly when the chancellor is now presiding over the imperial court, his power is more encompassing than Your Majesty." Ying Huhai thought what Zhao Gao said made sense; he decided to make an investigation and deal with the chancellor; however he reasoned that it might come to nothing. Hence, he ordered his retainers to conduct a clandestine investigation on the alleged collaboration between the magistrate and the rebels.

When Li Si heard of the emperor's intention, he promptly prepared a memorial recounting the countless indiscretions of the eunuch, "Zhao Gao has usurped and exploited the imperial court, now holding absolute power over it, and is dispensing rewards and punishments no different from Your Majesty. Years ago, when Tian Chang (Tian Huan) was the chancellor of Qi under Duke Jian, he took advantage of the kindness of his king and courted popularity with his subordinates and purchased the supports of the ministers at court. In the end, he committed regicide, he put Duke Jian to death and assumed control of Qi.[113] It is a proverbial historical incident. Now, Zhao Gao harbouring malevolent intent is behaving most treacherously. Everyone knows that his personal wealth exceeds that of Tian Shi; besides his greed is insatiable while still pursuing more wealth and fortune.[114] His power at court is only second to Your Majesty; he, in fact, is holding you hostage. He is no different from Hann Qi, the chancellor of the former sovereign of Hann, Hann An.[115] Your Majesty, please resume full control of your authority; if my words are not heeded, your subject is afraid that he might rise in revolt." The Second Emperor responded, "What nonsense! Zhao Gao is a eunuch. He never indulges himself while he could live in comfort, and he has never

---

111 Conspiracy at Shaqiu 沙丘. See 210-1.

112 Magistrate of the Sanchuanjun Prefecture, *Sanchuanjun shou* 三川郡守 Li You 李由.

113 Chancellor Tian Huan 田桓, alias Tian Chang 田常.
Duke Jian of Qi 齊簡公 Jiang Ren 姜壬, 29th (r. 484-481 BCE). *SJ* 史記, 卷 102, 'Qi Taigong shijia 齊太公世家' 第 2, p. 1418.
SJ 史記, 卷 116, 'Tian Jing Zhongwan shijia 田敬仲完世家' 第 16, pp 1716-1717; and *SJ* 史記, 卷 57, 'Li Si liezhuan 李斯列傳' 第 27, p. 727.

114 Tian Chang 田常, Tian Huan 桓. Tianshi 田氏 the Tian family clan.

115 King of Hann, Hann An 韓安 was the last king of Hann; however, there is no mention of a chancellor named Hann Qi 韓玘 in *SJ* 史記. Hann An - see 203–1.
Hu Sansheng 胡三省 comments, "In Li Si's 李斯 memorial to Ying Huhai 嬴胡亥, he stressed that Qin was about to meet its final demise; hence, he emphasised the incident of Hann Qi 韓玘. When Hann was about to meet its final annihilation, there was a certain Hann Qi, acting as the chancellor, it was used by Li Si to forewarn the impending danger that Qin faced..." *ZZTJ JZ*, Vol 1, p. 344.

broken his loyalty in the face of danger. His conduct is uncontaminated by iniquities around him, he is honest and cautious and has worked so hard to be raised to the position he holds today. He pledges his loyalty; he keeps his position by pledging his honour. I think he is a worthy subject, and you, Sir, have your misgivings. Why? Besides, if I do not trust Zhao Gao, who can I trust? Allow me to tell you; Zhao Goa is an incorruptible person; he is capable, experienced, and full of vigour. He has won the hearts of his subordinates, meeting all my requirements. Now, Sir, please do not try to slander him." The Second Emperor was so besotted by Zhao Gao and that he feared Li Si might have him executed. Hence, he related to him the contents of the memorial in private. Zhao Goa responded, "The chancellor is only wary of me; if I die, he will become the Tian Chang he mentioned in his memorial."

By this time, there were increasing banditry and thieving activities; the government unremittingly sent armed forces to march east from the Guanzhong Pass to suppress the rebellions. Right Chancellor Feng Quji, Left Chancellor Li Si and Military Commander Feng Jie jointly presented a memorial to remonstrate the Emperor.[116] The memorial read, "The outlaws and bandits beyond the Guandong Pass in the east are ceaselessly causing trouble; [117] the government forces have repeatedly suppressed those activities, killing many; however these bandits and mutineers greatly out-number our armed forces. Tracing the root causes of the problem are the many corvées deployed at the frontier border, and our civilians are being weighed down by heavy taxes and levies. We propose Your Majesty to cease the construction of the Epang Palace, [118] as well as to reduce the number of conscripts at the frontier." The Second Emperor responded, "Being the sovereign of a state he has the privilege to do whatever he pleases and as he deems appropriate. He has all the power in his hand to exercise strict laws; when these measures are properly enforced his subjects within the Four Seas will be contained. In times of antiquity, when kings Yu and Xia, prestigious and worthy as they were, expended their efforts by attending to the welfare of the civilians, they did not have the slightest inkling that law and legal establishments could bring peace and prosperity.[119] Our former Emperor unified all under Heaven by obliterating all the fiefdoms and marquisates, and our kingdom enjoyed peace and prosperity; he suppressed the barbaric tribes at the four quarters of our kingdom; even now within our realms, there is peace and tranquility. To construct a new palace in honour of our deceased Emperor is merely a manifestation of his mighty exploit, every one of you is fully aware of his achievements. I have only been on the throne for two years and within this very brief span of time, bandits and thieves have risen, causing unnecessary trouble and problems to my kingdom. You, Sirs, my trusted subjects, are doing little to end our problems, and now you are asking me to revoke the policies lay down by my father. You have not repaid the virtues that were bequeathed upon you by our former Emperor, besides you are disloyal to me. Why are you allowed to be seated amid the most senior members of my court?" He ordered the arrest of the three men to stand trial. Feng Quji and Feng Jie committed suicide; Li Si refused to take his own life and surrendered to the prison

116 Right Chancellor, Feng Quji 馮去疾; Left Chancellor, Li Si 李斯; National Military Commander, Feng Jie 馮刼. Feng Jie was the son of Feng Quji.

117 Guandong 關東 – meaning east of the Pass – i.e. east of Hanguguan Pass 函谷關.

118 Epang Palace 阿房宮.

119 Yu 虞 King Shun 舜帝, Yao Zhonghua 姚重華. Chinese historians had the habit of referring to the name of a state as a reference to a king. In this instance, the text merely refers to Yu 虞 and Xia 夏, which was supposed to mean King Shun and King Yu 夏禹.
King of Xia 夏, Xia Yu 夏禹.

ward. The Second Emperor ordered Zhao Gao to preside over the trial of the chancellor; employing a charge that Li Si and his son Li You were implicated in insurgent activities and had all his relatives and guests arrested.

Zhao Gao presided over the trials of Li Si, and the ex-chancellor was thrashed and beaten over a thousand strokes. He could not tolerate the excruciating pain and punishments inflicted upon him, and confessed under duress that he was guilty of all the charges.

Li Si did not take his own life because he was confident of his eloquent oratory; also believing that he had made immense meritorious contributions to the kingdom, and in the end, he could defend his innocence, hoping that the Second Emperor would eventually realize the underlying truth and grant him special dispensation. He made another submission to the Second Emperor from his prison cell. He wrote, "Your subject has been the chancellor of Qin, presiding over the civilians for over thirty years. When he began his tenure, the kingdom occupied a small domain, no more than one thousand *li* of territory; and we had several hundred thousand warriors at best. Your subject, poorly gifted, sponsored and trained a large number of spies and emissaries; bearing large quantities of gold and precious jade pieces to travel to all the kingdoms canvassing and lobbying. Meanwhile, we sped up the training of our armed forces and updated our military equipment in secret. He made reforms to the political edification of the Kingdom; he raised and promoted brave and meritorious warriors and commanders, and he was instrumental in getting the kingdom to honour and respect meritorious people. Finally, Qin held Hann hostage; we weakened Wei; we defeated Yan and Zhao and, in the end, we annihilated Qi and Chu; ultimately, Qin brought down the six kingdoms, annexing their lands, and captured their kings and lords. Above all, your subject aided the former Emperor to elevate to the position as the Son of Heaven. Later, our army marched north to push the Hu and Mo barbaric tribes menacing our frontier to move north;[120] to the south, our army pacified the hundred Yue tribes. All these grand exploits were manifestations of the strength and prowess of mighty Qin. Your subject further unified the measurements, weights and writing system of our kingdom, these measures make Qin whole, further consolidating the mighty Qin Empire. Nevertheless, had all those efforts been construed as transgressions and felonies against the state, your subject would have been executed long ago. Your subject is most fortunate that Your Majesty has allowed him to continue to serve at your court. It is his earnest hope that Your Majesty will make a thorough investigation into the matter." The memorial was passed onto Zhao Gao, who ordered his retainers to discard the document, he remarked, "How could a convict submit a memorial?"

Zhao Gao sent ten or so of his guests disguised as imperial counsellors *yushi*, ushers *yuzhe* and imperial attendants *daizhong* to take turns to visit the ex-chancellor, claiming that the emperor had decreed to investigate into the detention. Li Si related to them the truth and that he had never harboured any intent to revolt; the wardens continued to beat him for changing his admissions. In the end, the Second Emperor did send some of his personal attendants to investigate into the matter; Li Si by then dared not venture to make changes to his earlier admissions. The adjudication was presented to the Second Emperor, who was immensely pleased. "Had it not been Zhao Gao," he said, "The chancellor would have deceived me." The Second Emperor had previously dispatched attendants to the Sanchuan Prefecture to make an investigation of Li You; when they arrived, the Chu army had already killed the magistrate. Upon their return to the capital, it was when Li Si was being jailed and placed on trial; they reported to

[120] Hu 胡; Mo 貉 nomadic tribes.

Zhao Gao that Li You did not collaborate in the uprising; however Zhao Gao fabricated that he complicit, and the charge was also levelled against him. Consequently, Li Si was sentenced to be punished by the five penalties *wuxing*, and to be executed by hacking into halves at the waist in the market of Xianyang.[121] As Li Si was led to his execution from the prison, his middle son was also taken to the market to meet a similar fate. The ex-chancellor looked back at his son and said, "How I wished that you and I could bring our yellow hounds to hunt beyond the East-gate of Shangcai, chasing after those crafty rabbits. I am afraid we will never be able to do that again." The father and son faced each other cried and wept bitterly. All the members of the three family clans related to Li Si were executed. The Second Emperor then made Zhao Gao the chancellor; everything trivial or significant was hence taken care of by the eunuch.

XV. Having crushed the Qin army at Donga, Xiang Liang (the Chu general) led his forces northwest and arrived at Dingtao, [122] where they gave the Qin army another trashing. In the meantime, Xiang Yu and Master Pei (Liu Bang) also won a great battle against the Qin forces at Yongqiu, and cut down the magistrate of Sanchuan Prefecture, Li You.[123] A series of great victories overwhelmed Xiang Liang as he began to slight the Qin army, and was becoming increasingly arrogant and conceited. The former Chu chancellor Song Yi reprimanded him,[124] "Having won a victory when the general becomes conceited and the soldiers become slackened with negligence, the army is bound to fail. Now our forces have shown signs of slackening off while the Qin forces are gathering strength; your subject finds it unsettling and he fears for your safety." Xiang Liang did not take heed. He dispatched Song Yi as an envoy to the Qi kingdom (Tian Shi). En route, Song Yi met the Qi envoy Sir Gaoling, Xian.[125] Song Yi asked him, "Are you going to meet up with Sir Wuxin?" Gaoling answered, "Yes." Song Yi said, "Your subject is of the opinion that Sir Wuxin is about to meet his downfall. My lord, you should perhaps proceed slowly to avoid death, whereas if you try to make haste you might face calamity." At this stage, reinforcements from the Second Emperor were arriving large numbers to give aid to Zhang Han of Qin. Without losing any time, the general attacked Dingtao, the Chu army lost and dispersed, Xiang Liang died in the battle.

During the seventh to the ninth month of this year, there were continuous torrential downpours. Xiang Yu and Master Pei were besieging Waihuang, but they failed in the attempt. They turned towards Chenliu instead.[126] Then they heard the news that Sir Wuxin had died. The officers and soldiers were greatly shaken by the loss of their commander; the generals decided to retreat to the east. They met up with General Lu Chen, en route, and together they escorted King Huai of Chu (Mi Xin) from Xuyi to the City of Pengcheng.[127] Lu Chen pitched camps at the

---

121 The five penalties – *wuxing* 五刑 – normally were 1. Tattooing to the face; 2. cutting off one's nose; 3. chopping off both legs; 4, whipping until death and 5. cutting off one's head and chopped to mincemeat. (Li Si was cut in halves at the waist.)

122 Donga 東阿 - Yangguxian Shandong 山東 陽穀縣.
Dingtao 定陶 - Dingtaoxian Shandong 山東 定陶縣.

123 Yongqiu 雍丘 – Qixian Henan 河南 杞縣.
Sanchuanjun Prefecture Magistrate, Li You 三川郡守 李由. (The son of Li Si.)

124 Chu Chancellor, Song Yi 楚相 宋義.

125 Sir Gaoling, Xian 高陵君 顯.

126 Waihuang 外黃 - east of Qixian Henan 河南 杞縣東.
Chenliu 陳留 - Chenliuxian Henan 河南 陳留縣.

127 General Lu Chen 呂臣.

eastern outskirt of Pengcheng; Xiang Yu took the west; while Master Pei set up his camps near Dang.[128]

XVI. Wei Bao recovered twenty cities that were the former territory of the Wei kingdom; King Huai of Chu (Mi Xin) enfeoffed Wei Bao as the king of Wei.[129]

XVII. 9th month - intercalary month. King Huai of Chu merged the forces of Lu Chen and Xiang Yu and made himself the commander-in-chief. He appointed Master Pei the prefecture magistrate of Dang, enfeoffed him as Marquis Wuan, [130] and commanded him to take charge of the militia of the prefecture. Xiang Yu was enfeoffed as Marquis Changan and as the Duke of Lu.[131] He made Lu Chen take charge of the armed forces of his kingdom, with the title of *situ*, while the father of Lu Chen, Lu Qing was made the chancellor *lingyin*.[132]

XVIII. Zhang Han, having overwhelmed Xiang Liang, assumed that Chu was no longer a threat led his army across the Huanghe River to the north shore to march against the kingdom of Zhao (Zhao Xie).[133] En route, he was unstoppable, until he finally arrived at Handan, where he forcefully relocated all the residents to *Henei*.[134] He then proceeded to dismantle the walls and ramparts of the city, razing the entire city to its very foundations. Zhang Er and Chen Yu managed to escape with the king of Zhao (Zhao Xie) to the walled-city of Julu.[135] The Qin general, Wang Li followed and had the city surrounded.[136] Chen Yu rode to Changshan where he recruited several tens of thousands of warriors; he then returned with the men and pitched camp at the northern outskirt of the walled-city of Julu.[137] Meanwhile, Zhang Han and his Qin forces pitched camp at the south of the city, on the plain of Jiyuan. Zhao repeatedly appealed to Chu (Mi Xin) for help. The Qi (Tian Shi) envoy Sir Gaoling, Xian, was staying at the city of Pengcheng at this stage. He arranged

---

King Huai of Chu 楚懷王 Mi Xin 羋心.
Xuyi 盱眙 - Xuyixian Anhui 安徽 盱眙縣.
Pengcheng 彭城 - Tongshanxian Jiangsu 江蘇 銅山縣.

128 Dangyi County 碭邑 - Dangshanxian Jiangsu 江蘇 碭山縣.

129 Wei Bao 魏豹.
King Huai of Chu 楚懷王 Mi Xin 羋心.

130 Marquis Wuan 武安侯 Liu Bang 劉邦.

131 Marquis Changan 長安侯 Duke of Lu 魯公 Xiang Yu 項羽. Lu was the former Lu Kingdom 魯國, capital Qufu 曲阜; it became the provision fief of Xiang Yu.

132 *Situ* 司徒 Lu Chen 呂臣. *Situ* was defined earlier as a minister in charge of the land of a state and the edification of the people. Lu Chen started the Green Turban Army *cangtoujun* 蒼頭軍. When King Huai of Chu 楚懷王 combined the forces of Lu Chen and Xiang Yu, he was given a title of *situ*, which meant his military power was stripped. The title he held *situ* was probably a titular designation, which prompted him to submit to Liu Bang later.
Chancellor, *lingyin* 令尹 Lu Qing 呂青.

133 Kingdom of Zhao 趙王 Zhao Xie 趙歇.

134 Handan 邯鄲 - Handanxian Hebei 河北 邯鄲縣.
Henei 河内 the areas on the north bank of Huanghe River in Henan 河南.

135 Zhang Er 張耳, Chen Yu 陳餘.
King of Zhao 趙王 Zhao Xie 趙歇.
Julu 鉅鹿 - Pingxiangxian Hebei 河北 平鄉縣.

136 Qin General 秦將 Wang Li 王離.

137 Changshan 常山- Yuanshixian Hebei 河北 元氏縣.

an audience with the king of Chu, [138] and said, "Song Yi is from your kingdom, he had accurately predicted that Sir Wuxin (Xiang Liang) would fail; and only a few days later the commander met his end. A man who can predict the outcome of a battle is undoubtedly a military genius." The king (Mi Xin) summoned Song Yi to see him. Upon detailed discussions, he was greatly pleased with the capability of the man. He made him the supreme commander *shangjiangjun*; with Xiang Yu as the second-in-command *cijiang*; while, Fan Zeng took on a position as junior commander *weijiang*.[139] The other generals were all listed under Song Yi, and the commander was given an honorific title – 'The Champion of Generals *qingzi guanjun*.'[140]

Previously, King Huai of Chu issued a pledge with his commanders and generals that whoever was first to enter into the Inner Pass *Guanzhong* would be enfeoffed as king.[141] At that stage, the combating power of the Qin army was still quite formidable; when it was on the move, the rebel forces would run for their lives and were least inclined to engage the Qin forces in battle; attempting to lay siege to government walled cities within the Pass was not an enticing proposition. Xiang Yu bitterly hated the Qin army for killing Xiang Liang, his uncle; he volunteered to march forth with Master Pei. King Huai of Chu deliberated the issue with several old generals and commanders, they all maintained, "Xiang Yu is callously brutal; at the Xiangcheng campaign he buried all the innocent civilians alive, not a single soul was spared.[142] All the cities he laid siege to were razed to the ground. Furthermore, the several offensive campaigns undertaken by Chu have been unsuccessful, including the ones commanded by the king of Chen (Chen She) and Xiang Liang. It would be rash to continue to take risks. It is perhaps a sensible idea to solicit a commander who is virtuous, employing benevolence, and righteousness as a motto to invite the Qin population in the west to join our fold. The despotic Qin government have ravaged and wreaked havoc on the Qin people for too long; it will take little effort for a benevolent and caring leader to win over the hearts of the people, sparing the lives of people, leaving their properties untouched, and allow them to enjoy their freedom. Xiang Yu is hardly a suitable candidate; on the other hand, Master Pei is a forgiving soul and being more matured; he can be dispatched." King Huai hence rejected Xiang Yu's proposition to march west towards the Qin capital; he sent Master Pei to march west to siege land and territories. Master Pei gathered the remnants of King Chen (Chen Sheng) and Xiang Liang troops, marched from Dang County to Chengyang and Gangli; [143] there he successfully broke into two Qin held army barracks.

---

207 BCE *Jiawu* 甲午

---

138 Qi (Tian Shi) 齊 田市.
Sir Gaoling 高陵君 Xian 顯.
Pengcheng 彭城 - Tongshanxian Jiangsu 江蘇 銅山縣.

139 Supreme Commander, *shangjiangjun* 上將軍 Song Yi 宋義.
Second in Command, *cijiang* 次將 Xiang Yu 項羽.
Junior Commander, *weijiang* 末將 Fan Zeng 范增.

140 Supreme Commander 上將軍 *shangjiangjun, qingzi guanjun* 卿子冠軍 Song Yi 宋義.

141 Inner Pass – *Guanzhong* 關中 - southern part of Shaanxi 陝西南部.

142 Xiangcheng 襄城 - Xiangchengxian Henan 河南 襄城縣.

143 Dang 碭 - Dangyi County 碭邑 - Dangshanxian Jiangsu 江蘇 碭山縣.
Chengyang 成陽 – Puxian Shandong 山東 濮縣.
Gangli 杠里 – Wuchengxian Shandong 山東 武城縣.

Qin Second Emperor	秦二世皇帝	3rd year
King Huai of Chu, Mi Xin	楚懷王 芈心	2nd year
King of Zhao, Zhao Xie	趙王 趙歇	2nd year
King of Qi, Tian Shi	齊 田市	2nd year
King of Yan, Hann Guang	燕王 韓廣	3rd year
Zhang Tu	臧荼	1st year
King of Wei, Wei Bao	魏王 魏豹	2nd year
King of Hann, Hann Cheng	韓王 韓成	2nd year

I. Winter. 10th month. Tian Du, the Qi (Tian Fu) general acting in defiance of the instruction of Chancellor Tian Rong led his troops to join force with Chu to give aid to Zhao.[144]

II. At Chengwu Master Pei defeated the local armed forces garrisoned at Chengwu in the Dong Prefecture.[145]

III. The supreme commander of Chu, Song Yi, arrived at Anyang; [146] he held his men back for forty-six days without making a move. Xiang Yu said to the commander, "The situation at Zhao is getting desperate under the siege of Qin. We should cross the River immediately commanding our forces to attack the Qin forces at the outer perimeters, while letting Zhao forces make assaults from within the walled city, coordinating a frontal and rear assault. I believe the Qin army will break." Song Yi responded, "Not so. One can kill a gadfly on an ox with one strike, but it will not cause any damage to the eggs of a flea. If Qin attacks Zhao and wins, their forces will become exhausted; we can then take advantage of their fatigue. If it loses, we can beat our war drums to pursue it all the way to the west; I am sure we will win a great victory. It is a superior strategy to allow Qin and Zhao to fight it out between them, and we can avoid a confrontation with Qin. When making charges and going into battles in full armours and weapons, I am hardly your match; whereas when it comes to devising military tactics; Sir, you are not my equal." He then instructed, "Military personnel who behave ferociously like tigers, fiercely like sheep, ravenously like wolves; and people who are intractable and refuse to comply with my military commands will have their heads cut off." He then dispatched his son Song Xiang to travel to the kingdom of Qi (Tian Fu) to take up the post as chancellor, [147] and he accompanied his son to Wuyan,[148] where a lavish banquet was laid on for his son and the officers.

By that time, the weather had turned extremely cold and started to rain heavily; the soldiers were suffering from cold and hunger. Xiang Yu told his attendants, "We should be making concerted efforts to attack the Qin forces instead of waiting frivolously here, not making any

144 General, Tian Du 田都.
Qi, Tian Fu 齊 田福.
Chancellor, Tian Rong 田榮.

145 Chengwu 成武 - Chengwuxian Shandong 山東 城武縣.
Dong Prefecture 東郡 - Puyangxian Hepei 河北 濮陽縣.

146 Supreme Commander of Chu 上將軍 Song Yi 宋義.
Anyang 安陽 – Caoxian Shandong 山東 曹縣.

147 Song Xiang 宋襄.

148 Wuyan 無鹽 - Dongpinxian Shandong 山東 東平縣.

advancement. We have a failed harvest this year, and people are suffering from famine. Our soldiers are rationed mostly with beans and vegetables; worse still, we do not have any reserve in the army. In the face of such dire circumstances, the commander is hosting an elaborate banquet, drinking and entertaining the senior officers. Instead of crossing the river to the north to secure the food reserves from Zhao, then make a joint assault against the Qin forces, we are held up here with this mindless claim of, 'Wait, we will take advantage of their weakened state.' The newly created Zhao kingdom (Zhao Xie) stands a very slim chance against the strong Qin army; it will fall, which will make Qin even more formidable; what sort of nonsense 'they will exhaust themselves' is being addressed here. How can we take advantage of their weakened state when they are gathering strength? Besides, we have just sustained a series of devastating losses; our king is extremely uneasy. Having assigned all the troops to the hands of our supreme commander the security and safety of our kingdom hinge ever so precariously with this one move; our commander has no concern whatsoever with our military affairs. Instead, he is expending unnecessary effort taking care of his personal affairs. He cannot be the ridgepole and pillar of our holy shrine."

11th month. In the morning, at the military camp, Xiang Yu paid respect to the Supreme Commander Song Yi. In the tiger tent, Xiang Yu cut off the head of Song Yi. The general exited the tent, showing the head to the soldiers and announced, "Song Yi collaborated with Qi, intending to revolt against Chu. The king of Chu secretly instructed me to execute him." The generals and commanding officers thoroughly shocked and yielded, not daring to protest. All remarked, "It was your family that placed our King Huai on the throne in the first place, and now general, you have made another significant contribution to our kingdom by quelling an internal dissension." The officers and generals pledged support to Xiang Yu and made him the deputy supreme commander. They then dispatched attendants to pursue after the son of Song Yi (Song Xiang) and hunted him down when he was about to enter the Qi state (Tian Fu), where they had him executed. Xiang Yu sent Huan Chu to report to King Huai on what had happened; the king decided to allow the situation to take its course and made Xiang Yu his supreme commander.

IV. 11th month, 12th day. Master Pei (the Chu general) heading his detachment of armed men marched towards the County of Li.[149] While, on the march, he came across Marquis Gangwu (possibly a Wei general);[150] he attacked and took in the four thousand troops under the marquis. He then continued his march, and met up with Wei generals Huang Xin and Wu Man;[151] the combined forces gave the Qin army a severe beating.

V. Tian An the grandson of Tian Jian (the last king of the former kingdom of Qi), occupied areas north of the Ji region; he led his forces to rendezvous with Xiang Yu to bring relief to Zhao (Zhao Xie).[152]

---

149 Liyi 栗邑 - Xiayi Henan 河南 夏邑.

150 Marquis Gangwu 剛武侯, (Wei 魏將?) it is not certain who this Marquis Gangwu was.

151 Under the Wei King 魏王 Wei Bao 魏豹.
Wei General 魏將 Huang Xin 皇欣.
Wei General 魏將 Wu Man 武滿.

152 Tian An 田安.
Tian Jian 田建 was the last King of the former kingdom of Qi 齊 5th.
Jibei regions 濟北 – Gaotangxian Shandong 山東 高唐縣.

VI. Qin General Zhang Han ordered his troops to construct a walled passage from the river (Fuyanghe River to the city of Julu) to transport food supplies to General Wang Li, [153] who was investing fierce attacks against Julu. Inside the walled city, the defenders were far fewer, and food supplies were dwindling. Zhang Er being holed up appealed to Chen Yu for help several times; however, Chen Yu was of the opinion that his forces were far too meagre to take on the much more formidable Qin forces, so he decided not to venture forward. The impasse lasted for several months; Zhang Er was furious and blamed Chen for not taking any action. He dispatched Zhang Ye and Chen Ze to reprimand Chen Yu, "You and I are tested friends; we did not have any qualms to die for each other. Now, the king and I are on the verge of death; you with several tens of thousands of troops are sitting there idly in wait, doing nothing and not coming to our rescue. Why kind of friendship is that? If the pledge we made still holds, then let us go against the Qin army jointly and die together. We might even stand one or two chances out of ten to come out alive." Chen Yu responded to the envoys, "I fully understand the situation. I cannot possibly go against the Qin forces at this stage, to do so is tantamount to sacrificing my entire army for nothing. I want to remain alive to avenge His Highness and Zhang Er. To perish together in a battle makes no sense whatsoever; it is no different from tossing a piece of meat at a starving tiger. What purpose would it serve?" Zhang Ye and Chen Ze appealed persistently, [154] asserting that they would die trying. In the end, Chen Yu issued them with five thousand crack troops to assault the Qin forces. In the ensuing battle, not one man survived. At this stage, the Qi and Yan armies had also arrived to come to the aid of Zhao. While Zhang Ao (Zhang Er's son) also gathered troops from the region of Dai, [155] he rallied over ten thousand men and garrisoned next to Chen Yu's camps; realizing that the Qin forces were far too formidable, no one dared to make a move.

Xiang Yu had created quite a stupendous reputation for himself at Chu after executing *qingzi guanjun* (Song Yi). He followed up by dispatching Sir Dangyang and General Pu to lead twenty thousand men to cross the River, heading straight at Julu in an attempt to bring relief to the besieged city.[156] The operations went as planned; the army managed to cut off the walled-expressway built by Zhang Han. The Qin general, Wang Li was thus left with depleted food supplies. Chen Yu, in the meantime, sent his retainers to appeal to Xiang Yu for help. At length, Xiang Yu decided to lead his entire force north by crossing the river. Having sailed across the (Zhanghe) River, the general ordered his men to sink all the crossing vessels, shattering all the cooking utensils, and burned all the army tents; each fighter was issued with three days of rations; a resolute act to show that every man would die fighting. When they arrived, the Chu armies had Wang Li's forces completely encircled; the soldiers from both sides then entered into pitched

---

Zhao, Zhao Xie 趙歇.

153 Qin General 秦將 Zhang Han 章邯.
Fuyanghe River Crossing 滏陽 河渡口.
Julu 鉅鹿 - Pingxiangxian Hebei 河北 平鄉縣.
Qin General 秦將 Wang Li 王離.

154 Zhang Ye 張 黶; Chen Ze 陳澤.

155 Qi 齊; Yan 燕 Zhao 趙.
Zhang Er's son Zhang Ao 張敖.
Dai 代 - Weixian Hebei 河北 蔚縣.

156 Sir Dangyang 當陽君 and General Pu 蒲將軍, names of both individuals are lost.
Zhangshui River 漳河. Julu 鉅鹿.

mortal combat at close quarters, the armies joined battles for nine rounds. Finally, the Qin army was driven back and defeated. Zhang Han retreated, hotly pursued by the armies of other fief lords gathered near the walled city. The armies of the other fief lords only then dared to strike out; they cut down General Su Jue of Qin and captured Wang Li.[157] General She Xian of Qin defiantly refused to surrender; he set himself alight.[158] When the battle was joined, the Chu army was valiant and ferocious beyond other armies. At that stage, over ten battalions of allied armies from various kingdoms had gathered beyond the walled city, yet no one had the courage to go to Chu's aid. When Xiang Yu ordered his men to charge, the troops from the other fiefdoms were watching from their ramparts. The Chu men fiercely and ferociously charged into the Qin barracks, pitching one against ten; the cries of battle and killing were deafening; the soldiers hiding in their ramparted barracks were utterly horrified by what they witnessed.

When the Qin army was finally defeated, Xiang Yu proceeded to meet the generals from the various fiefdoms. The warriors from other kingdoms had such great admiration and respect for the man that as he entered the barrack gate, all the generals kneeled down, inching forward on their knees, not daring to look up to him. Xiang Yu became the supreme commander of all the kingdoms, all submitted to his instructions.

The king of Zhao and Zhang Er came out of the besieged city of Julu to meet the generals, expressing gratitude to the armies that came to their aid. When Zhang Er saw Chen Yu, he reprimanded him severely for not going to Zhao's aid, and he asked the whereabouts of Zhang Ye and Chen Ze.[159] When told that they had perished, he refused to believe, distrustfully suspected that Chen Yu might have had them executed, and he pressed his query for several times. Chen Yu, insulted by the allegation, could not contain his anger, "Sir, I have no idea that you hate your subject this much. Do you think he prizes this general seal?" He removed his official commander seal attached to the silk sachet from his girdle and handed it over to Zhang Er, taken aback by such a move, but he refused to take it back. Chen Yu then excused himself to go to the latrine. A guest of Zhang Er said to him, "When Heaven grants you something if you do not take it you will be chastised. Now General Chen has returned the commander seal to you; and you refuse to retrieve it, this is against the wish of Heaven, it will be a calamity if you do not take it back. Take it back quickly." Zhang Er retrieved the seal and wore it on his girdle, taking away the command of Chen Yu's men. Upon his return from the latrine, Chen Yu realized that Zhang Er did not politely decline his resignation. Bitterly disappointed, he stormed out of the imperial hall, followed by several hundred of his devoted warriors. He and his men took up fishing activities along the river valleys and swamps in the neighbouring areas.[160]

After that, the king of Zhao returned to Xindu.[161]

---

157 Qin General, Su Jue 蘇角. Wang Li 王離.

158 Qin General, She Xian 涉閒.

159 Zhang Ye 張黶; Chen Ze 陳澤, both men appeared in the *SJ* and the *ZZTJ* in the incident related here, there are no other details.

160 Fuyanghe River 滏陽河.

161 Sima Qian 司馬遷 annotates: Zhang Er 張耳 and Chen Yu 陳餘 were two exceptionally talented individuals and were known extensively throughout the world. The guests and retainers who followed them were also outstanding individuals; they were either chancellor or minister in their respective states, (this was before the six kingdoms fell to Qin). When Chang Er and Chen Yu were impoverished, (the Qin government had placed bounties on their heads), they swore an oath to die

VII. Spring. 2nd month. Master Pei (Liu Bang) attacked the County of Changyi; [162] he came across Peng Yue, who decided to submit to him with his troops.

Peng Yue, a local of the Changyi County, was making a living by fishing in the lake at Juye;[163] later he became an outlaw. When Chen Sheng and Xiang Liang began their insurrections, one hundred or more youths in the nearby lake districts paid Peng Yue a visit; they beseeched him, "Master Zhong, please be our leader."[164] He declined and said, "Your subject cannot concur." The youths were insistent. Finally, Peng Yue agreed. The group of men pledged that they would assemble the next day at daybreak, and agreed that people late for the gathering would be executed by having their heads cut off. The next morning at daybreak, some ten or more youths arrived late, and the latest did not even show up until noon. Peng Yue said to the youths most apologetically, "Your subject is getting old. All of you, Sirs, intend to make him your leader; he was left without a choice. How can he instil some discipline into you? We had agreed to meet at daybreak; many did not show up as pledged. He cannot execute all who were late; in which case, he will execute the one who showed up the latest." He ordered the judiciary officer to prepare to execute the youth. The young men were laughing and joking, "Why do we have to get to this? We will never be late again." Peng Yue unbending with his decision, commanded to have the youth executed. He then ordered his men to raise a sacrificial terrace to swear to an oath of commitment. The youths were shocked out of their wits not daring to raise their heads to look up at the altar. The group of insurgents began to roam in the local areas seizing control of land,

---

for each other, and their sentiment was truly genuine. Nevertheless, when they rose to high positions, they vied for power and became rivals; in the end, both men suffered the consequences. How could two men who respected and cherished each other so dearly had a complete *volte face* to loathe and scorn each other so bitterly? Were they not supercilious and mundane individuals? While they bred most reputable names for themselves and entertained a large number of guests at their households; nevertheless, their deeds and behaviours were far inferior to the likes of Wu Taibo 吳太伯 and Wu Jizha 吳季札. The *SJ* 史記, 卷 59, 'Zhang Er, Chen Yu liezhuan 張耳 陳餘列傳' 第 29, p. 773.

The founding father of the Zhou clan, Ji Danfu 古公亶夫 姬亶夫* had three sons, Wu Taibo 吳太伯, Ji Zhongyong 姬仲雍 and Ji Jili 姬季歷. Danfu had intended to give the tribal chief title to Ji Jili. Wu Taibo and Ji Zhongyong were concerned that their father might feel guilty to bequeath the leadership position to the youngest son; the two elder brothers took leave and broke away to settle in the wilderness, they became the founding fathers of the Wu Kingdom 吳國 in the south of Zhongyuan 中原. Wu Mengshou 吳夢壽 (~586 BCE) the first king of Wu had four sons, Wu Zhufan 吳諸樊, Wu Yuzhi 吳餘祭, Wu Yimei 吳夷昧, and Wu Jizha 吳季札. The king was of the opinion that Wu Jizha was the most worthy, hence he instructed that the throne would first go to the eldest, followed by Wu Yuzhi and then to the youngest. However, Wu Jizha declined the arrangement.* Ji Danfu was the grandfather of King Wen of Zhou 周文王, and great grandfather of King Wu of Zhou 周武王, the dates of this historical account could not be ascertained. *SJ* 史記, 卷 101, 'Wu Taibo shijia 吳太伯世家' 第 1, pp. 1393-1394.

162 Changyi 昌邑 - Jinxiangxian Shandong 山東 金鄉縣.

Changyi local, Peng Yue 昌邑人 彭越. Changyi 昌邑 - Juye 鉅野 - Juyexian Shandong 山東 鉅野縣. Peng Yue was one of the earlier followers of Liu Bang. In 196 BCE he offended Liu Bang for not responding to the Han Emperor's request to attack *Chen Xi* 陳豨. In 196 BCE, he was arrested for alleged treason; he was banished to Shu 蜀 as a commoner. On the way, he met Empress Lv 呂后 and he appealed to her claiming that he was innocent. The Empress pretended that she sympathized with him and brought him back to Xian. He was chopped into mincemeat. *SJ* 史記, 卷 60, 'Wei Bao, Peng Yue liezhuan 魏豹彭越列傳' 第 30, pp. 785-787.

163 Changyi local 昌邑 Jinxiangxian Shandong 山東 金鄉縣.

164 Zhong 仲 was Peng Yue's alias.

recruiting vagrant soldiers and stragglers into their fold. In the end, they gathered over a thousand men, they then rallied with the troops under Master Pei and helped him to lay siege to the Changyi County.[165] The city was difficult to break, Master Pei reconsidered his options and decided to continue west with his troops, bypassing Gaoyang.[166]

Li Yiqi was a Gaoyang local; [167] he came from a poverty-stricken family, and he took up employment as an alley watchman. A cavalryman under Master Pei happened to be living in the alley where Li Yiqi was working. Yiqi said to the cavalryman, "Scores of fief generals have passed through Gaoyang; when one tries to strike a conversation with these so-called military leaders, one finds them to be intolerant to the excess, bigoted to say the least, and they incessantly accentuate on trivial and pretentious etiquettes. They are thoroughly complacent with themselves, believing they are above others, and not willing to accept people with aspiring ambitions. I have heard that while Master Pei might be arrogant, he is very approachable, and he is fond of discussing grand exploits; he is the kind of man I intend to follow. Unfortunately, no one has made an introduction on my behalf. If you chance to see him, please convey to him, 'In the alley of my hometown, there is a certain person bearing a family name of Li; he is over sixty years old, and his is eight *chi* in height. Everyone who comes across him thinks he is crazy, but he resolutely believes that he is not.'" The cavalryman responded, "Master Pei is not partial to literati and scholars. Whenever a literati guest wearing a scholar's hat-gear comes to visit him, he promptly removes his hat, urinating into it. He swears and uses the most profane languages. One simply cannot approach him and reason with him on scholarly ideals." Li Yiqi said, "Let us give it a try." The cavalryman did as he was beseeched.

Master Pei arrived at Gaoyang and was staying at the post-station lodge; [168] he sent his retainers to summon Li Yiqi to come forth for an interview. When Li Yiqi arrived, Liu Bang had his legs sprawled wide on the divan; two young maidservants were washing his feet. As the watchman entered, he made a perfunctory greeting instead of the most proper etiquette due to an elder. Li Yiqi said, "You, Sir, do you intend to help the Qin government to attack all the nobles or do you intend to lead them to go against Qin?" Liu Bang was fuming, and broke into profanities, "You lowly depraved literati; people from all under Heaven are suffering intolerably under the despotic rule of Qin; that is why all the people are rising in arms. What 'helping Qin to attack the nobles' are you babbling about?" Li Yiqi said, "If you intend to unite all the righteous lords under Heaven to dispose of the despotic rulers; this is no way to bid your elder welcome." Master Pei swiftly ceased what he was doing, rising from his divan, straightening his trappings appropriately; he then solemnly invited the watchman to be seated on the seat reserved for the guest of honour, proffering apologise as he did. Li Yiqi then gave him a lecture on the Horizontal and Vertical Alliances during the time of the six kingdoms. Master Pei was overjoyed, and he invited Li Yiqi to share a meal with him. He asked, "So what should we do?" Li Yiqi said, "You have a motley mob, a rowdy crowd and unruly stragglers; you have less than ten thousand men, and you intend to march against the heartland of the powerful Qin. It is what people refer to as 'testing a tiger with one's head between its jaws.' The County of Chenliu is strategically located; it is the hub of the four quarters of all under Heaven; besides the city has a lot of food reserves. Your subject is well

165 Changyi 昌邑 - Jinxiangxian Shandong 山東 金鄉縣.

166 Gaoyang 高陽 - Qixian Henan 河南 杞縣.

167 Li Yiqi 酈食其 - Gaoyang local, 高陽人. Li Yiqi was a well-read individual.

168 Gaoyang 高陽 – Qixian Henan 河南 杞縣.

acquainted with the magistrate. It is worthwhile to send your subject as an emissary to convince him to surrender; I am confident I can accomplish the task with ease; even if he does not yield, I could be your coordinator from within the walled city." Li Yiqi was thus dispatched to go to the city. Master Pei with his army followed closely behind. It took little effort for Li Yiqi to convince the magistrate to submit. Master Pei enfeoffed Li as Sir Guangye.[169] Li Yiqi then spoke to Master Pei about his younger brother, Li Yishang. Li Yishang had previously gathered some four thousand men under him; [170] they came to submit to Master Pei, who made Yishang a commanding general. Master Pei then led the garrisoned troops at Chenliu to march off; [171] Li Yiqi took on the duty as a canvasser, he travelled to various fiefdoms representing Master Pei as his emissary.

VIII. 3rd month. Master Pei attacked Kaifeng, but he failed to bring it down.[172] Without much ado, he continued to push west; at Baima, he met the Qin General Yang Xiong in battle.[173] Later, east of Quyu another battle was joined, the Qin army was defeated, Yang Xiong retreated to Yingyang.[174] The Second Emperor sent his attendants to have Yang Xiong executed for having lost the battle.

Summer. 4th month. Master Pei marched south and attacked Yangchuan; the entire population of the city was massacred.[175] He followed up by sending Zhang Liang to secure the territory that previously belonged to the kingdom of Hann. At that stage, a Zhao general Sima Yan was preparing to cross the Huanghe River to march against the Pass.[176] Master Pei attacked Pingyin to the north, cutting off the Huanghe River crossing; followed by an assault south against the eastern part of Luoyang; [177] however he lost the battles. He then headed south, passing through Huanyuan.[178] Zhang Liang led his troops and joined forces with Master Pei. He then instructed the king of Hann, Hann Cheng to garrison at the city of Yangzhai; [179] while he and Zhang Liang continued with their march south.

6th month. Master Pei and his forces joined battle with the Qin army under the command of a certain Yi, the magistrate of Nanyang Prefecture, and the battle was fought in the County of

---

169 Marquis Guangye 廣野君 Li Yiqi 酈食其.

170 General, *jiang* 將 Li Yishang 酈食商.

171 Chenliu 陳留 - Chenliuxian Henan 河南 陳留縣.

172 Kaifeng 開封 - Kaifengxian Henan 河南 開封縣.

173 Baima 白馬 - Huaxian Henan 河南 滑縣.
Qin General 秦將 Yang Xiong 楊熊.

174 Quyu 曲遇 – Zhongmouxian Henan 河南 中牟縣.
Yingyang 滎陽 - *Yingyangxian Henan* 河南 滎陽縣.

175 Yingchuan 潁川 - Yuxian Henan 河南 禹縣.
The text does not explain why he massacred the entire city; the civilians here were probably Qin people. It was likely that Liu Bang was from the east, and he hated the Qin people so intensely that he ordered a massacre.

176 Zhao General (under Zhao Xie 趙歇), Sima Yan 司馬卬.
Huanghe River 黃河.

177 Pingyin 平陰 - Mengjinxian Henan 河南 孟津縣.
Luoyang 洛陽.

178 Huanyuan 轘轅 - Southwest of Yanshixian Henan 河南 偃師縣西南.

179 Hann King 韓王 Hann Cheng 韓成.
Yangzhai 陽翟 - Yuxian Henan 河南 禹縣, the former capital of Hann.

Chou.[180] The Qin army was resoundingly defeated. The Chu army subsequently marched into the Nanyang Prefecture; while Magistrate Yi retreated with his forces into the City of Wan, (the capital city of the prefecture).[181]

Master Pei then decided to circumvent the City of Wan in the west. Zhang Liang counselled him, "I know you are most eager to advance towards the Pass; [182] nevertheless, the Qin army is still numerous, besides they still have control of the most strategic passes. If the City of Wan is not taken now, it will pose as a formidable force menacing at your rear. It will then be a perilous situation to handle, with a powerful Qin army to face and Wan menacing at your rear." Master Pei thought it made sense; he changed his mind. In the midst of night, he led his army to march back to Wan via a sidetrack, with his banners hidden out of sight. Before daybreak, he had the entire walled city of Wan surrounded by three layers. The magistrate of Nanyang Prefecture (Yi) was stricken with fear, and he was about to commit suicide. His attendant Chen Hui said,[183] "Wait, sir. You can die later." Chen Hui scaled off the city wall and saw Master Pei. He said, "Your subject has been told that King Huai of Chu had pledged that whoever made it first to Xianyang, [184] he would be enfeoffed as king. Now, Sir, you are besieging the Prefecture of Wan, which is a large area with several scores of walled cities.[185] The officers and civilians are of the opinion that even if they surrendered they will face certain death; hence, the people at Wan climb to the top of the city-wall and are staunchly guarding the city refusing to surrender. Sir, you are held up here besieging the city, I am sure there will be many causalities. If you withdraw, the soldiers of Wan will be trailing behind you. If this happens, you will miss the opportunity to enter Xianyang first, besides you will have Wan forces lurking at your rear, obstructing you from reaching the capital. If I were you, I would invite the Qin officers and generals to surrender. Enfeoff the magistrate with the title of marquis and make him garrison at the city, bring the armed forces in the city with you to march west. After that, the walled cities you march through will willingly unbolt their city gates to welcome you. Your passage will be unimpeded." Master Pei was greatly pleased, he said, "Excellent."

Autumn. 7th month. Magistrate Yi of Nanyang Prefecture surrendered. Master Pei enfeoffed him as Marquis Yin while bestowing one thousand households to Chen Hui as his fief. As Master Pei and his army continued their march, all the cities they came across opened their city gates surrendering to them. At Danshui River, Marquis Gaowu, Sai, and Marquis Xiang, Wang Ling, also surrendered.[186] Master Pei then doubled back to attack Huyang; the army met General Mei Juan, under Sir Fan (Wu Rui the magistrate of Fanyu County); the armies joined forces to laid siege to

---

180 Magistrate of Nanyang Prefecture 南陽郡守, Yi 齮.
Chouyi 犨邑 - Lushanxian Henan 河南 魯山縣.

181 Wan 宛 - Wancheng 宛城 – Nanyangjun Prefecture 南陽郡 capital city - Nanyangxian Henan 河南 南陽縣.

182 Guan 關 - Wuguan Pass 武關 - Shangxian Shaanxi 陝西 商縣.

183 Chen Hui 陳恢.

184 Xianyang 咸陽 – Xi'an City Shaanxi 陝西 西安市.

185 Chen Hui 陳恢 referred Wan as a prefecture 宛城; however, there is no record of a Wan Prefecture, it was probably a large county, and Wancheng was the capital city of the county.

186 Danshui River 丹水 - Zhechuanxian Henan 河南 淅川縣.
Sai 鰓 - Qin, Marquis Gaowu 秦 高武侯.
Wang Ling 王陵 Marquis Xiang 襄侯.

Xi and Li;[187] both counties submitted. Master Pei gave strict orders that the troops were strictly prohibited from looting and pilfering; the civilians at Qin were overjoyed (by the discipline of the marching army).

IX. (In the meantime, to the north,) after the collapse of the Qin army under Wang Li; General Zhang Han retreated to Jiyuan and garrisoned.[188] Xiang Yu in the meantime pitched camp on the south bank of Zhang River.[189] The two forces faced each other on the opposite banks of the river, and the front became quiet.

The Qin army having sustained defeat on several occasions, the Second Emperor sent his attendants to reprimand Zhang Han for the losses. The Qin general was in fear; he dispatched his secretary Sima Xin to return to the capital city of Xianyang,[190] to seek further instructions from the Emperor. Sima Xin waited at the palace gate for three days for an audience with Zhao Gao; the chancellor refused to meet him, indicating that he had reservations. The secretary beat a hasty retreat to return to the front, taking an alternate route as he came. As expected, Zhao Gao sent his men after him. However, the secretary managed to return to the barracks safely. He reported to Zhang Han, "Zhao Gao is now holding the supreme power at court. No one is willing to make a decision or even trying to make an effort. If we overwhelm the rebels, Zhao Gao will be most envious of our achievements; whereas if we fail, we will also face death. General, please give it some thought as to what we should do next."

Chen Yu, in the meantime, also wrote a letter to Zhang Han, "Bai Qi was a mighty general of Qin.[191] He conquered Yingdu in the south; in the north, he buried Lord Mafu (see notes and see 260-I).[192] The number of walled cities and territories he vanquished was innumerable; in the end, he was bestowed with a gift of death.[193] Meng Tian was a valiant general of Qin; to the north, he expelled the barbaric *Rong* tribes; he opened up several thousand *li* of new territory in Yuzhong; nonetheless, he was executed at Yangzhou.[194] Why did these mighty generals meet their premature deaths? It is very simple - they were so meritorious that the Qin court could not find ways and means of rewarding them; they had them executed. General, you have been the Qin commander for three years now; one hundred thousand or more of your enemies have died under your

---

187 Huyang 胡陽 - Tanghexian Henan 河南 唐河縣.
Prefect of Panyang County 番陽守 Wu Rui 吳芮.
General Mei Juan 梅鋗.
Panyang 番陽 - Poyangxian Jiangxi 江西 鄱陽縣.
Xi 析 - Xiyi 析邑 - northwest of Neixiangxian Henan 河南 內鄉縣 西北.
Li 酈 - Liyi 酈邑 - northeast of Neixiangxian 內鄉縣 東北.

188 Jiyuan 棘原 - Pingxiangxian Hebei 河北 平鄉縣.

189 Zhang 漳南 – south of Pingxiangxian Hebei 河北 平鄉縣.

190 Sima Xin 司馬欣.

191 Chen Yu 陳餘; Zhang Han 章邯.
Qin General, Bai Qi 白起 (See 257-I).

192 Yingdu 郢都 - Jianglingxian Hubei 湖北 江陵縣 - the former capital of Chu 楚. (See 278-I).
Changping 長平之役 – The Battle of Changping - Changzixian Shanxi 山西 長子縣. (See 260-I).

193 See 257-I.

194 Meng Tian 蒙恬. He was forced to take his own life. (See 210-II).
Yuzhong 榆中 - Dongshengxian Neimeng 內蒙 東勝縣.
Yangzhou 陽周 - Andingxian Shaanxi 陝西 安定縣.

command. In the meantime, the fief lords are still rising in arms, and the number is increasing by the day. Zhao Gao worked his way up in court through fawning and groveling; once he realizes that he can no longer contain the situation and is about to be chastised by the Emperor he will shift the blame onto you; he may even send someone to relieve you of your duties, absolving himself from all responsibilities. General, you have been away from the capital for too long, there are much enmities and hostilities lurking everywhere in the palace and court. It can be summed up: one is executed for being meritorious, also executed for his failures. Heaven above intends to end the kingdom of Qin, a fact even the mindless and ignorant knows. General, you are facing a profound dilemma; at the imperial court, you cannot voice your opinion, while at the war-front you are heading an army of a dying empire. You are alone and helpless in your quest, there is no one you can turn to or rely on, and yet you are still harbouring a glimmer of hope that you will be fine in the end. What a tragedy! General, it is better for you to consider defecting, take part in the allied forces; march against the despotic government; then appropriate a region of your own, then face south to proclaim yourself as king. Is it not a more appealing proposition than facing the prospect of being trussed onto the chopping block to be hacked into halves accompanied by your wife and children?"

Zhang Han was vacillating with uncertainty; he dispatched an emissary Shi Cheng to meet Xiang Yu in secret to discuss conditions of his surrender. While negotiation was still under way, Xiang Yu sent General Pu employing *coup de main*, [195] the army marched briskly through Sanhu and arrived at the south bank of Zhang (Fuyang) River; [196] it then attacked, breaking the Qin forces. Xiang Yu led his main forces pursued the retreating army all the way to Wushui River, [197] defeating the Qin forces again. Zhang Han again sent a retainer to see Xiang Yu in secret, intending to submit. The Chu general held a military conference with his men, and he concluded, "We do not have sufficient food supplies to continue fighting, we might as well accept Zhang Han's surrender." The generals and officers present all acceded to it, said, "Excellent." On the south bank of the Huanshui River, near the South Shang ruins, [198] Xiang Yu made preparations for a pledge ceremony. After pledging the alliance, Zhang Han advanced to meet Xiang Yu; he cried tears of mixed feelings, relating to the Chu general the oppression he had received from Zhao Gao. Xiang Yu enfeoffed him as King Yong.[199] He was asked to remain at the command headquarters. The Qin army secretary *changshi*, Sima Xin was promoted to the position as supreme commander *shang jiangjun* to lead the surrendered Qin army.[200]

X. Shen Yang, a Xiaqiu local, led his forces took Henan and submitted to Xiang Yu.[201]

---

195 General Pu, *jiangjun* 蒲將軍.

196 Sanhu 三戶 - Cixian Hebei 河北 磁縣.
Fuyanghe River 滏陽河.

197 Wushui River 汙水.

198 Huanshui River 洹水, Anyanghe River 安陽河 the river originates at Lichengxian Shanxi 山西 黎城縣, it drains into Weyhe River 衛河.
Shangqiu Ruin 商丘 - West of Anyangxian Henan 河南 安陽縣西.

199 King of Yong 雍王 Zhang Han 章邯.

200 Qin Army Secretary, *changshi* 秦長史 Sima Xin 司馬欣 as Supreme Commander 上將軍.

201 Shen Yang 申陽 - Xiaqiu local 瑕丘人 – Shandong Cixian 山東 磁縣.
Henan 河南 - South of the Huanghe River 黄河.

XI. Zhao Gao, the chancellor *zhongchengxiang* of Qin, schemed to usurp the power of Qin; [202] he was nevertheless hesitant that the ministers might not acquiesce to his deceit; hence, he decided to test the waters. He presented a stag to the Second Emperor, pointing at it he said, "This is a horse."[203] The Emperor laughed, "The chancellor has mistaken a stag for a horse." Zhao Gao turned and asked the ministers, some remained silent; he pressed for an answer, some responded that it was a horse while others said it was a stag. Zhao Gao committed to memory the ministers who challenged him and had them persecuted subsequently. Ever since then, the ministers at the court feared him and dared not expose his transgressions and offences to the Second Emperor. Before this event, Zhao Gao had repeatedly assured the Emperor that the bandits and thieves causing trouble east of the Pass were petty thieves and local riffraff, irritating nuisances at best. Later, when Xiang Yu captured Wang Li and other generals while Zhang Han lost a series of battles, urgent dispatches of military failures were arriving at court with unceasing frequency pleading for reinforcements. Almost all the cities and areas east of the Hangu Pass had revolted; [204] the kings and generals leading their men from various states were marching west towards the heartland of the Qin kingdom.

8th month. Master Pei led several tens of thousands troops attacked the Wuguan Pass, [205] having breached the walled city, a wholesale slaughter followed. Fear completely consumed Zhao Goa; for fear that, the Second Emperor might execute him. He made an excuse that he had taken ill and stayed away from the morning court sessions. The Second Emperor had a dream; he dreamed that a white tiger attacked and mauled the left horse drawing his carriage, [206] the horse died. When he woke, he was miserable and depressed. He asked the court occultist to make an interpretation of his dream. The diviner replied, "Jingshui River is the cause of the problem."[207] The Second Emperor then made observations of fasting and offering prayers at Wangyi Palace.[208] He was preparing to go to the river to drown four white horses as sacrificial offerings; in the meantime, he asked his attendants to see Zhao Gao reprimanding him for the unrest and banditry activities. Zhao Gao was stricken with fear. He conspired with his son-in-law, Ju Yue the capital mayor of Xianyang, and his younger brother Zhao Cheng, hatching a plot.[209] He told them, "His Majesty is totally oblivious to all reprimands and counseling; now the situation of the kingdom has become desperate, and he is making me bear all the dire consequences. We should banish him and place Ziying on the throne. The prince is known for his benevolence and frugalness; people have great respect for the man." The conspirators secured some palace attendants *langzhongling*

---

202 *Zhong chengxiang* 中丞相 Zhao Gao 趙高. Normally the chancellor was not permitted to enter the inner palace. Nevertheless, Zhao Hao was a eunuch, and he thus carried a title of *zhong chengxaing*, Chancellor of the Inner Palace.

203 According to the *SJ* 史記, there were two stags. *ZZTJ* is unclear if there were two or one.

204 Hanguguan Pass 函谷關.

205 Wuguan Pass 武關 - Shangxian Shaanxi 陕西 商縣.

206 *Caoma* 驂馬. Four horses drew the carriages for the nobles, the pair of horses in the middle was called *fuma* 服馬, while the two on the outer were called *caoma*, the left, and right *caoma*.

207 Jingshui River 涇水 originates at Gansu 甘肅; it passes through Guanzhong 關中 to drain into the Weishui River 渭水.

208 Wangyigong Palace 望夷宮 – West of Jingyangxian Shaanxi 陕西 涇陽縣西.

209 The Capital Mayor of Xianyang, Xiangyang, *ling* 咸陽令 Yan Yue 閻樂. He was probably a son-in-law of an adopted daughter, as Zhao Gao was a eunuch. It was common for eunuchs to adopt children as their sons and daughters.
Zhao Cheng 趙成.

as their planted agents within the palace. The insurgents claimed that a gang of thieves had kidnapped the mother of the mayor of Xianyang while they secretly whisked the old woman away to the manor of Zhao Gao. Ju Yue was ordered to mobilize his law-enforcers to go against the transgressors; he led a thousand or perhaps more elite troops and arrived at the Wangyi Palace entranceway. As they entered, they bound the imperial guard commander and bellowed, "Thieves and bandits have entered into the palace proper, why have you not stopped them?" The commander responded, "The security in and around the palace is extremely tight and austere, how could this be possible?" Ju Yue cut the commander down. The group of conspirators then rushed into the inner palace; they came upon imperial guards and eunuchs; forthwith, they were all duly cut down. The imperial guards and eunuchs stricken by this sudden change of event took flight, only a few remained to fight to the end; several scores of imperial guards perished. Some of the attendants became turncoats, accompanying Ju Yue and scurried into the inner palace. The dissident archers shot arrows at the canopies and throne curtains in the audience hall. The Second Emperor was in an overpowering rage; he summoned for his attendants. By this time, all had dispersed or refused to engage in combat, except for one eunuch, who stayed, as he dared not take leave. The Second Emperor escaped to his inner chamber; he asked the eunuch, "Why didn't you warn me?" The eunuch answered, "Your subject dared not warn you, which is the reason why he is still alive. Had he warned you, Your Majesty would have executed him long ago." Ju Yue and his men approached the Second Emperor, facing him and recounted his failings, "Sir, you have been arrogant and conceited all your life; executing and slaughtering innocents; now all under the Heaven is rebelling against you. What do you plan to do?" The Second Emperor asked, "Can I see the chancellor?" Ju Yue answered, "No." The Second Emperor continued, "Please make me a king of a prefecture." Ju Yue declined. The Second Emperor implored, "Make me a marquis of ten thousand households." Ju Yue declined. The Second Emperor finally begged, "Make my wife and me as black-heads, similar to the fate of failed fief lords."[210] Ju Yue said, "Your subject is taking orders from the chancellor, he asked him to eliminate a despotic Emperor on behalf of the people under Heaven. You have spoken many words; your subject dares not relate your message to the chancellor." He bellowed to his armed men to move forward. The Second Emperor committed suicide.

Ju Yue reported what had transpired to Zhao Gao. The eunuch gathered all the Qin ministers and the royal princes to a meeting at court and gave an account of the death of the Second Emperor. He said, "Previously, the kingdom of Qin was but a paltry and insignificant state, our former Emperor made great exploits and unified all under Heaven; he honoured himself as *Di* – the Grand First Emperor. The six former kingdoms by now have resumed their former territories; the realms of Qin are shrinking by the day, the use of the title of *Huangdi* is merely nominal in name. The title is thus to be revised and reverted to its former status." The court officers and ministers nominated Ziying (Ying Ying) as the new king of Qin. The deceased Second Emperor was summarily buried as a commoner at Yichun Park in Dunan.[211]

---

210 Black-heads – 黔首 commoners.

211 Qin Second Emperor, Ying Huhai 二世皇帝 嬴胡亥.
Yichun Park 宜春苑; Dunan 杜南 - the southeast outskirt of the City of Xi'an in Shaanxi 陕西 西安市 東南郊.

9th month. Zhao Gao instructed Ziying to bathe and observe the practice of fasting and abstinence; [212] an auspicious date was chosen to present the imperial jade seal for the new king at the holy temple of Qin ancestors. The fasting lasted for five consecutive days. In the meantime, Ziying conspired with his two sons, "Zhao Gao murdered the Second Emperor at Wangyi Palace; for fear of being impeached by the ministers and generals at court, in the pretence of righteousness he places me on the throne. I have heard through speculation that he has made arrangements with the kingdom of Chu (Mi Xin) that as soon as the royal house of Qin is out of the way, he will proclaim himself as king in the Inner Pass – Guanzhong. He has instructed me to bathe and observe fasting; it is very likely that he will assassinate me at the holy shrine. I will pretend to be ill, claiming that I am indisposed to go to the shrine; I am sure the chancellor will come to urge me to go alone. When he arrives, we will dispose of him."

On the appointed date, Zhao Gao sent his attendants several times to urge Ziying to make haste to go to the scheduled ceremony; the prince did not respond and waited. As expected, Zhao Gao appeared at the palace where Ziying was fasting, and said, "The ceremony scheduled is a grand ritual for our kingdom. Why is Your Highness not proceeding?" Ziying stabbed and killed Zhao Gao at the fasting palace; the prince then ordered the three family clan members related to Zhao Gao to be executed.

Ziying sent reinforcements to the Yaoguan Pass, [213] reinforcing the defences. Master Pei and his army, having just arrived, intended to launch attacks against the Pass immediately. Zhang Liang said, "The Qin forces are still quite formidable, we have to be careful. We should send some soldiers to plant Chu flags and banners in the surrounding hillocks, giving the defenders the impression that the entire area is completely swarming with our troops. Then we will send Li Yiqi and Lu Jia to go to the Qin camp to persuade the defending generals to surrender, bribing them with rich rewards." [214] The invading army proceeded as planned, and as expected the Qin generals agreed to surrender. Master Pei was going to accept the surrender, when Zhang Liang said, "It is quite obvious that the Qin generals are about to surrender and rebel against their government. However, their subordinates and soldiers might not comply. I think we should take advantage of their slackened state to make a forceful attack." Master Pei, leading his army, skirted past the Yaoguan Pass and ascended the Kuishan Peak nearby.[215] There the army launched an unexpected and swift assault against the Qin forces at the south of Lantian; the Qin forces sustained a brutal thrashing, and the victorious Chu forces pursued the retreating army all the way to the north of Lantian, where the Qin forces sustained another trouncing.

---

212 Ying Ying 嬴嬰.

213 Yaoguan Pass 嶢關 - Lantianxian Shaanxi 陝西 藍田縣 東南.

214 Li Yiqi 酈食其.
Lu Jia 陸賈.

215 Kuishan Peak 蕢山 - near Yaoguan Pass 嶢關.

Appendix 1a

Warring States kings and lords – dates of reign from different sources

Legend - B = Po Yang 柏楊

Z = Zhongguo lishi niandai jianbiao 中國歷史年代簡表

L = Liuguo jinian 六國紀年 Chen Mengjia 陳夢家

Zhou 周 - family name Ji 姬

Zhou, King Weilie 威烈王 Wu 午 38th	(425-402 BCE)B	(425-402 BCE)Z	(425-402 BCE)L
Zhou, King An 安王 Jiao 驕 39th	(401-376 BCE)B	(401-376 BCE)Z	(401-376 BCE)L
Zhou, King Lie 烈王 Xi 喜 40th	(375-369 BCE)B	(375-369 BCE)Z	(375-369 BCE)L
Zhou, King Xian 顯王 Bian 扁 41st	(368-321 BCE)B	(368-321 BCE)Z	(368-321 BCE)L
Zhou, King Shenjing 慎靚王 Ding 定 42nd	(320-315 BCE)B	(320-315 BCE)Z	(320-315 BCE)L
Zhou, King Nan 赧王 Yan 延 43rd	(314-256 BCE)B	(314-256 BCE)Z	(314-BCE)L

Chu 楚 - family name Mi-Xiong 芈熊

Chu, King Sheng Shengheng 聲王 Dang 當 16th	(407-402 BCE)B	(407-402 BCE)Z	(407-402 BCE)L
Chu, King Dao 悼王 Yi 疑 17th	(401-381 BCE)B.	(401-381 BCE)Z	(401-381 BCE)L
Chu, King Su 肅王 Zang 臧 18th	(380-370 BCE)B	(380-370 BCE)Z	(381-370 BCE)L
Chu, King Xuan 宣王 Liangfu 良夫 19th	(369-340 BCE)B	(369-340 BCE)Z	(369-340 BCE)L
Chu, King Wei 威王 Shang 商 20th	(339-329 BCE)B	(339-329 BCE)Z	(339-329 BCE)L
Chu, King Huai 懷王 Huai 槐 21st	(328-299 BCE)B	(328-299 BCE)Z	(328-299 BCE)L
Chu, King Qianxiang 頃襄王 Heng 橫, 22nd	(298-264 BCE)B	(298-263 BCE)Z	(298- BCE)L
Chu, King Xiaolie 孝烈王 Yuan 元 23rd	(263-238 BCE)B	(262-238 BCE)Z	
Chu, King You 幽王 Han 悍 24th	(237-228 BCE)B	(237-229 BCE)Z	
Chu, King Ai 哀王 You 猶 (郝) 25th	(228- BCE)B	(228- BCE)Z	
Chu, King Fu 楚王 負芻 Fuchu 負芻 26th	(227-223 BCE)B	(227-223 BCE)Z	
Chu, Lord Changping 昌平君 Qi 啓 27th	(223- BCE)B	(223- BCE)Z	

Hann 韓 - family name Ji 姬

Hann, Marquis Jing 景子 Qian 虔	(408-400 BCE)B	(409-401 BCE)Z	(408-400 BCE)L
Hann, Marquis Lie 烈侯 Qu 取	(399-387 BCE)B	(400-378 BCE)Z	(399-377 BCE)L
Hann, Marquis Wen 文侯	(386-377 BCE)B	(Hann Liehou)Z	
Hann, Marquis Ai 哀侯	(376-371 BCE)B	(377-375 BCE)Z	(376-374 BCE)L
Hann, Marquis Gong 共侯[1]	(374-363 BCE)B	(374-363 BCE)Z	(373-362 BCE)L
Hann, Marquis Yihou 懿侯 Ruoshan 若山	(370-359 BCE)B	(374-363 BCE)Z	
Hann, Marquis Zhaoxi 昭釐侯 Wu 武	(358-333 BCE)B	(362-333 BCE)Z	(361-333 BCE)L
Hann, Marquis Wei, King Xuanhui 威侯[2] 宣惠王 1st			

1 Hann Gonghou 韓共侯 the *SJ* 史記, 'House of Hann 韓世家' refers to him as Marquis Yi of Hann 韓懿侯, whereas in the *SJ* 史記, 'Sequence of the Six States 六國年表' he is referred to as Marquis of Zhuang 莊侯, named Ruoshan 若山. Marquis Gong of Hann 韓共侯 and Marquis Yi of Hann 韓懿侯 was one person.

2 In 325 BCE Marquis Wei of Hann 韓威侯 proclaimed as King Xuanhui of Hann 韓宣惠王.

	(332-312 BCE)[B]	(332-312 BCE)[Z]	(332-312 BCE)[L]
Hann, King Xiang 襄王 Cang 倉 2nd	(311-296 BCE)[B]	(311-296 BCE)[Z]	(311- BCE)[L]
Hann, King Xi 釐王 Jiu 咎 3rd	(295-273 BCE)[B]	(295-273 BCE)[Z]	
Hann, King Huanhui 桓惠 4th	(272-239 BCE)[B]	(272-239 BCE)[Z]	
Hann, Hann An 韓安 5th	(238-230 BCE)[B]	(238-230 BCE)[Z]	
Jin 晉 - family name Ji 姬			
Jin, Duke Lie 晉烈公 Ji Zhi 止	(422-393 BCE)[B]	(419-393 BCE)[Z]	(415-389 BCE)[L]
Jin, Duke Xiao 晉孝公 Ji Qi 頎	(392-378 BCE)[B]	(392-378 BCE)[Z]	(388-369 BCE)[L]
Jin, Duke Jing Duke of 晉静公[3] Ji Jujiu 俱酒	(377-376 BCE)[B]	(377- BCE)[Z]	
Lu 魯 - family name Ji 姬			
Lu, Duke Mu 魯穆公 Ji Xian 顯	(410-377 BCE)[B]	(407-376 BCE)[Z]	
Lu, Duke Gong 魯共公 Ji Fen 奮	(376-355 BCE)[B]	(375-353 BCE)[Z]	
Lu, Duke Kang 魯康公 Ji Mao, 毛	(354-346 BCE)[B]	(352-344 BCE)[Z]	
Lu, Duke Jing 魯景公 Ji Yan 偃	(345-317 BCE)[B]	(343-315 BCE)[Z]	
Lu, Duke Ping 魯平公 Ji Lu 旅	(316-297 BCE)[B]	(314-296 BCE)[Z]	
Lu, Duke Min 湣公 (Wen 文公) Ji Jia 賈魯	(296-274 BCE)[B]	(295-273 BCE)[Z]	
Lu, Qing Duke Qing 魯頃公[4] Ji Chou 仇 (讎)	(273-249 BCE)[B]	(272-249 BCE)[Z]	
Qi 齊 - family name Lu 呂			
Qi, Duke Kang 齊康公 Jiang Dai 姜貸	(404-379 BCE)[B]	(404-385 BCE)[Z]	(404-386 BCE)[L]
Qi 齊 family name Tian 田			
Qi, Grand Duke Tiagong 齊太公 He 和	(413-388 BCE)[B]	(404-385 BCE)[Z]	(385-384 BCE)[L]
Qi, Marquis, Yan 齊 剡	(387-378 BCE)[B]	(384-376 BCE)[Z]	(383-375 BCE)[L]
Qi, Duke Huan 齊桓公 Wu 齊午	(377-359 BCE)[B]	(375-357 BCE)[Z]	(374-357 BCE)[L]
Qi, King Wei 齊威王 Yinqi 因齊 1st	(358-320 BCE)[B]	(356-321 BCE)[Z]	(356-319 BCE)[L] [5]
Qi, King Xuan 齊宣王 Pijiang 辟彊 2nd	(319-301 BCE)[B]	(320-302 BCE)[Z]	(318-301 BCE)[L] [6]
Qi, King Min 齊湣王 Tian Di 地 3rd	(300-284 BCE)[B]	(301-284 BCE)[Z] [7]	
Qi, King Xiang 齊襄王 Tian Fazhang 法章 4th	(283-265 BCE)[B]	(283-265 BCE)[Z]	
Qi, King Jian 齊王建 Tian Jian 建 5th	(264-221 BCE)[B]	(264-221 BCE)[Z]	
Qin 秦 - family name Ying 嬴			
Qin, Duke Jian 簡公 Ying Daozi 悼子	(414-400 BCE)[B]	(414-400 BCE)[Z]	(414-406 BCE)[L]
Qin Duke Jing 敬公	(405-394 BCE)[L]		
Qin, Duke Hui 惠公	(399-387 BCE)[B]	(399-387 BCE)[Z]	(393-387 BCE)[L]
Qin, Duke Chu 出公	(386-385 BCE)[B]	(386-385 BCE)[Z]	(386-385 BCE)[L]

3 Duke Jing was the last ruler of Jin. *ZZTJ* relates that he was reduced to the status as a civilian in 376 BCE.

4 Lu Qing, Duke of 魯頃公 was banished to Jucheng 莒城 by Chu 楚 in 255 BCE according to *ZZTJ*.

5 Yang Kuan's researched date – 356 BCE

6 Yang Kuan's researched date – 319 BCE.

7 Yang Kuan's researched date – 300 BCE.

Qin, Duke Xian 獻公 Ying Shixi 師隰	(384-362 BCE)[B]	(384-362 BCE)[Z]	(384-362 BCE)[L]
Qin, Duke Xiao 孝公 Ying Quliang 渠梁	(361-338 BCE)[B]	(361-338 BCE)[Z]	(361-338 BCE)[L]
Qin, King Hui, 惠王 Ying Si 駟 1st [8]	(337-311 BCE)[B]	(337-311 BCE)[Z]	(337-311 BCE)[L]
Qin, King Wu, 武王 Ying Dang 蕩 2nd	(310-307 BCE)[B]	(310-307 BCE)[Z]	(310-307 BCE)[L]
Qin, King Zhaoxiang 昭襄 Ying Ji 稷 3rd	(306-251 BCE)[B]	(306-251 BCE)[Z]	(306- BCE)[L]
Qin, King Xiaowen 孝文王 Ying Zhu 柱 4th	(250- BCE)[B]	(250- BCE)[Z]	
Qin, King Zhuangxiang 莊襄王 Yiren 異人 5th	(249-247 BCE)[B]	(249-247 BCE)[Z]	
Qin, Shihuangdi, Emperor 始皇 Zheng 政 1st [9]	(246-210 BCE)[B]	(246-210 BCE)[Z]	
Qin, Ershi Emperor 二世皇帝 Huhai 胡亥 2nd	(209-207 BCE)[B]	(209-207 BCE)[Z]	
Qin, Ziying 子嬰 3rd	(207 BCE)[B]	(207 BCE)[Z]	

Song 宋 - family name Zi 子

Song, Duke Dao 悼公 Zi Gouyou 購由	(403-396 BCE)[B]	(403-396 BCE)[Z]
Song, Duke Xiu 休公	(396-373 BCE)[B]	(395-?)[Z]
Song, Pibing 辟兵	(372-370 BCE)[B]	(?)[Z]
Song, Ticheng 剔成	(369-329 BCE)[B]	(369-329 BCE)[Z]
Song, King Kang 康王 Song Yan 宋偃	(328-286 BCE)[B]	(328-286 BCE)[Z]

Song 宋 was annihilated by Qi 齊 in 286 BCE.

Wei 魏 - family name Ji 姬

Wei, Marquis Wen 文侯 Wei S 斯	(446-397 BCE)[B]	(446-397 BCE)[Z]	(445-396 BCE)[L]
Wei, Marquis W 武侯 Jisi 擊嗣	(396-371 BCE)[B]	(396-371 BCE)[Z]	(395-370 BCE)[L] [10]
Wei, King Hui, Liang Huiwang, 梁惠王[11G]	(370-319 BCE)[B]	(370-319 BCE)[Z]	(369-318 BCE)[L] [12]
Wei, King Xiang 襄王 Si 嗣	(318-296 BCE)[B]	(318-296 BCE)[Z]	(317- BCE)[L] [13]
Wei, King Zhao 昭王 Wei Su 遫	(295-277 BCE)[B]	(295-277 BCE)[Z]	
Wei, King Anxi 安釐王 Wei Yu 圉	(276-243 BCE)[B]	(276-243 BCE)[Z]	
Wei, King Jingmin 景湣王 Wei Zeng 增	(242-228 BCE)[B]	(242-228 BCE)[Z]	
Wei, Wei Jia 假[14]	(226-225 BCE)[B]	(227-225 BCE)[Z]	

Wey 衛 - family name Ji 姬

Wey, Duke Shen, Tui 頹 41st	(414-373 BCE)[B]	(414-373 BCE)[Z]
Wey, Duke Sheng 聲公 Xun 訓 42nd	(372-362 BCE)[B]	(372-362 BCE)[Z]
Wey, Marquis Cheng 成侯 Su 速 43rd	(361-333 BCE)[B]	(361-333 BCE)[Z]
Wey, Marquis Ping 平侯 44th	(332-325 BCE)[B]	(332-325 BCE)[Z]

---

8 King Hui of Qin changed his title to King in 324 BCE.

9 Emperor Qin Shihuangdi, Emperor 秦始皇, from 221 BCE.

10 Yang Kuan's researched date - 395 BCE

11 Wei, King Hui 魏惠王 changed his regnal year to post regnal year *houyuan* 後元 in 335 BCE. The *SJ* 史記 is incorrect with his reigning date of 370-335 BCE according to textual research by Yang Kuan 楊寬.

12 Yang Kuan's researched date – 369 BCE.

13 Yang Kuan's researched date – 318 BCE.

14 Wei Jia 魏假 was executed by Qin 秦 in 225 BCE.

Wey, Sir Sijun 嗣君 45th	(324-283 BCE)[B]	(324-283 BCE)[Z]	
Wey, Sir Huai Sir 懷君 46th	(282-252 BCE)[B]	(282-253 BCE)[Z]	
Wey, Sir Yuan 元君 47th[15]	(251-230 BCE)[B]	(252-230 BCE)[Z]	
Wey, Wey Jue 衛角 48th	(229-209 BCE)[B]	(229-209 BCE)[Z]	
Yan 燕 - family name Ji 姬			
Yan, Duke Min 湣公 aka Min 閔公	(434-403 BCE)[B]	(433-403 BCE)[Z]	(438-415 BCE)[L]
Yan, Duke Xi Ji Dai 僖公 Dai 姬戴 (Kuan 款).[16]	(402-373 BCE)[B]	(402-373 BCE)[Z]	(414-370 BCE)[L]
Yan, Duke Huan 桓公 (372-362 BCE)[B]	(372-362 BCE)[Z]	(369-359 BCE)[L]	
Yan, Duke Wen 文公	(361-333 BCE)[B]	(361-333 BCE)[Z]	(358-330 BCE)[L]
Yan, King Yi 易王, 1st	(332-321 BCE)[B]	(332-321 BCE)[Z]	(329-321 BCE)[L]
Yan, Ji Guai 姬噲 2nd	(320-316 BCE)[B]	(320-312 BCE)[Z]	(320-312 BCE)[L]
Yan, Zi Zhi 子之 3rd	(315-312 BCE)[B]	(316-314 BCE)?	
Yan, King Zhao 昭王 Ping 平 4th.[17]	(312-279 BCE)[B]	(311-279 BCE)[Z]	(311- BCE)[L]
Yan, King Hui 惠王 Yuezi 樂資 5th	(278-272 BCE)[B]	(278-272 BCE)[Z]	
Yan, King Wucheng 武成王 6th	(271-258 BCE)[B]	(271-258 BCE)[Z]	
Yan, King Xiao 孝王 7th	(257-255 BCE)[B]	(257-255 BCE)[Z]	
Yan, Ji Xi 姬喜 8th[18]	(254-222 BCE)[B]	(254-222 BCE)[Z]	
Yue 越 - family name Si 姒			
Yue, King 越王 Yi 翳	(no record)[B]	(411-376 BCE)[Z]	(411-376 BCE)[L]
Yue, King 越王 Zhujiu 諸咎	(no record)[B]	(376-375 BCE)[Z]	(375 -363 BCE)[L]
Yue, King 越王 Cuozhi 錯枝[19]	(no record)[B]	(375 BCE)[Z]	
Zhao 趙 - family name Zhao 趙[20]			
Zhao, Marquis Lie of 烈侯, Zhao Ji 籍 1st	(409-400 BCE)[B]	(409-387 BCE)[Z]	(408-387 BCE)[L]
Zhao, Marquis Wu[21] 武侯 2nd	(399-387 BCE)[B]		

---

15 Yang Kuan's 楊寬 textual research indicated that Lord Yuan of Wey 衛元君 was not a younger brother of Lord Wey Si, 衛嗣君 and was more likely to be a younger brother of Lord Huai 衛懷君. Furthermore, Wey Jue 衛衛角 ascended to the throne in 241 BCE and that he was not a son of Lord Yuan 衛元君.

16 Duke Xi of Yan 燕僖公 was more likely to be Duke Houjian of Yan 燕後簡公, Ji Dai 姬戴 or Ji Kuan or 姬款.

17 *SJ* 史記, 'Sequence of the Six States' and 'House of Yan Biography' maintain that he reigned between 311-279 BCE a total of 33 years.

18 Yan Ji Xi 燕姬喜 was captured by Qin 秦 in 222 BCE.

19 Yue 越 met its demise in 375 BCE.

20 The original xing 姓 (clan's name) of Zhao was Ying 嬴, same as Qin's 秦. The Ying clan was the descendants of Zaofu 造夫, the legendary charioteer of King Mu of Zhou 周穆王.

21 Duke Wu of Zhao 趙武 (?-387 BCE), also known as Marquis Wu of Zhao, was the younger brother of Marquis Lie 趙烈侯. The *ZZTJ* relates during the 2nd year of King An of Zhou 周安王 (400 BCE) Marquis Lie died. People at Zhao made his younger brother Marquis Wu the new sovereign. During the 15th year of King An (387 BCE), Duke Wu died, the Crown Prince Zhang 太子章 of Marquis Lie was placed on the throne. He was known as Marquis Jing 趙敬侯. When Marquis Lie died, Marquis

Zhao, Marquis Jing 敬侯 Zhao Zhang 章 3rd	(386-375 BCE)B	(386-375 BCE)Z	(386-374 BCE)L
Zhao, Marquis Cheng 成侯 Zhao Zhong 種 4th	(374-350 BCE)B	(374-350 BCE)Z	(373-350 BCE)L
Zhao, Marquis Su 肅侯 Zhao Yu 語 5th	(349-326 BCE)B	(349-326 BCE)Z	(349-326 BCE)L
Zhao, King WulingJ 武靈王 Zhao Yong 雍 1st[22]	(325-299 BCE)B	(325-299 BCE)Z	(325-299 BCE)L
Zhao, King Huiwen 惠文王 Zhao He 何 2nd	(298-266 BCE)B	(298-266 BCE)Z	(298- BCE)L
Zhao, King Xiaocheng 孝成王 Zhao Dan 丹 3rd	(265-245 BCE)B	(265-245 BCE)Z	
Zhao, King Daoxiang 悼襄王 Zhao Yan 偃 4th	(244-236 BCE)B	(244-236 BCE)Z	
Zhao, King Youmu 幽穆王 Zhao Qian 遷 5th	(235-228 BCE)B	(235-228 BCE)Z	
Zhao, King Dai 代王 Zhao Jia 嘉 6th[23]	(227-222 BCE)B	(227-222 BCE)Z	

Zheng 鄭 - family name Ji 姬

Zheng, Duke Ru 鄭繻公 Ji Dai 姬駘	(422-396 BCE)B	(422-396 BCE)Z
Zheng, Duke Kang 鄭康公	(395-375 BCE)B	(395-375 BCE)Z

Zheng 鄭 was annihilated by Hann 韓 in 375 BCE

Jing was still very young. Duke Wu, the younger brother of Marquis Lie assumed the position as regent. He probably was concerned about the experience in Zhao when Master Huan 趙桓子, the son of Xiang 趙襄子, was killed by the people of Zhao when he usurped the succession; hence, he retained his lord title without claiming to be a Marquis. It was for this reason when the Zhao nationals prepared the *Shiben* 世本 they did not know how to chronicle this incident and did not relate that Duke Wu succeeded to the throne. When the Wei 魏 historians prepared the *Bamboo annals* 竹書紀年, the chronicler continued to use the reigning title of the deceased Marquis Lie. Shen Changyun 沈長雲 the *Zhaoguo shigao* 趙國史稿, 2000, Zhonghua shuju 中華書局.

22 King Wuling of Zhao 趙武靈王 abdicated to King Huiwen 趙惠文王 in 299 BCE.

23 Zhao was annihilated by Qin in 222 BCE.

Appendix 1b - Major Events - 500-210 BCE

Major Events of the Warring States 戰國 and Qin Dynasty 秦朝 from 500 to 210 BCE
Some scholars have used 475 BCE as the demarcation year between Chunqiu 春秋 and the Warring States 戰國, whereas *ZZTJ* commences its narratives from 403 BCE, a copious amount of information are thus lacking for a period of 72 years. The author has incorporated a brief summary of the events leading up to 403 BCE. (This section is translated from pages in Chunqiushi 春秋史 by Zhu Shunlong and Gu Derong, and *Zhanguoshi* 戰國史 by Yang Kuan).[1]

500 BCE – The fief lords of Qi 齊 and Lu 魯 met at Jiagu Valley 夾谷, Confucius was the Master of Ceremonies, he asserted that the meeting should be conducted with full etiquettes and ceremonies.

Jin 晉 besieged Wey 衛; Qi 齊, Wey 衛 and Zheng 鄭 met at Anfu 安甫, to plan a counterattack against Jin.

499 BCE – Lu 魯 and Zheng 鄭 formed an alliance, revolted against Jin.

498 BCE – Lu and Qi met at Huang 黃 for an alliance.

497 BCE – Qi and Wey attacked Henei 河内 of Jin.

Zhao Yang 趙鞅 executed Wu 午 of Handan 邯鄲, the son of Wu occupied Handan and revolted against Jin. Fanshi 范氏 and Zhonghengshi 中行氏 attacked Zhao Yang, who escaped to Jinyang 晉陽.

Zhi 智, Hann 韓 and Weishi 魏氏 received orders from the Duke of Jin to attack Fanshi and Zhongehngshi; they escaped to Chaoge 朝歌.

Zhao Yang took over the power of Fan Yang 范鞅.

496 BCE – Chu 楚 annihilated Dun 頓.

Wu 吳 and Yue 越 joined battle at Zaili 檇李; Wu lost the battle. The King of Wu Helu 闔廬 wounded in battle died; his son Fu Chai 夫差 succeeded to the throne.

Jin laid siege to Chaoge 朝歌, Lu, Qi and Wey sought out ways to rescue Fan and Zhonghengshi. The armed forces of Jin defeated Fan and Zhonghengshi and continued to defeat Zheng and Fan's combined forces.

495 BCE – Chu 楚 annihilated Hu 胡.

494 BCE – Chu besieged Cai 蔡, which surrendered.

---

1 Zhu Shulong 朱順龍 and Gu Derong 顧德融, *Chunqiushi* 春秋史, pp. 559-564.
Yang Kuan 楊寬, *ZGS* 戰國史, pp. 722-697.

Wu and Yue joined battle at Fujiao 夫椒, Yue lost the battle; Wu entered into Yue; Gou Jian 句踐 surrendered to Wu 吳.

Qi 齊 and Wey 衛 combined forces marched to the rescue of the rebels at Handan 邯鄲 of Jin 晉; laying siege to Wulu 五鹿.

Qi 齊, Lu 魯, Wey 衛 and Xianyu 鮮虞 again attacked Jin, annexed Jipu 棘蒲.

Jin 晉 attacked Chaoge 朝歌.

493 BCE – Qi sent food and fodders to aid Fanshi 范氏, escorted by the Zheng army 鄭. Zhao Yang 趙鞅 raised an army, defeated Zheng at Tie 鐵, capturing one thousand over carriages. Cai 蔡 relocated to Zhoulai 州來.

492 BCE – Zhao Yang 趙鞅 laid siege to Chaoge 朝歌; Fanshi 范氏 and Zhonghengshi 中行氏 escaped to Handan 邯鄲.

491 BCE – Chu 楚 made an expedition against Manshi 蠻氏. Jin captured Manzi 蠻子 and returned him to Chu.

Qi 齊 and Wey 衛 went forth to assist Fanshi by laying siege to Wulu 五鹿.

Zhao Yang 晉 趙鞅 of Jin besieged Handan, which surrendered; Zhonghengshi 中行氏 escaped to Xianyu 鮮虞, Qi offered the clan shelter at Boren 柏人.

490 BCE – Jin 晉 laid siege to Boren 柏人, Fanshi 范氏 and Zhonghengshi 中行氏 escaped to Qi 齊; Jin finally quelled the unrest at Jin.

489 BCE – Jin attacked Xianyu 鮮虞.

Chenshi 陳氏 and Baoshi 鮑氏 of Qi 齊 annihilated Guoshi 國 and Gaoshi 高氏 executed Yan Ruzi 晏孺子, and placed Daogong 悼公 on the throne.

488 BCE – Wu 吳 and Lu 魯 met at Zeng 鄫. Lu 魯 attacked Zhu 邾, which sought help from Wu 吳.

487 BCE – Song 宋 annihilated Cao 曹.

Wu 吳 made an expedition against Lu 魯 on behalf of Zhu 邾, later Lu and Wu signed an alliance.

486 BCE – Wu 吳 constructed the Hangou Conduit 邗沟, which joined Jiang 江 and Huai 淮 rivers to open up the water passages to invade Qi 齊.

485 BCE – Wu 吳 rallied the forces from Lu 魯, Zhu 邾 and Tan 郯 to attack Qi 齊.

Chenshi 陳氏 clan at Qi 齊 murdered Duke Dao of Qi 齊悼公 and placed Duke Jian 簡公 on the throne.

The navy of Wu 吳 attacked Qi from the sea 齊; Qi defeated it, Wu retreated.

484 BCE – Wu 吳 and Lu 魯 attacked Qi 齊; the battle was joined at Ailing 艾陵, Qi lost.
The King of Wu Fu Chai 吳王夫差 executed Wu Yuan 伍員 (Wu Zixu 子胥).

483 BCE – Lu 魯 introduced tillage tax, *yongtianfu* 用田賦.
Wu 吳 met the fief lords of Lu 魯 and Wey 衛.

482 BCE – Wu 吳 constructed deep conduits to connect Yishui 沂水 and Jishai 濟水 rivers. The Wu King headed north to meet the fief lords at Huangchi Lake 黃池; Wu 吳 and Jin vied for hegemony.
Yue took advantage of the void at Wu, attacked Gusu 姑蘇 the capital; Wu 吳 sued for peace.

481 BCE – The *Lu Chunqiu* (*Lu annals*) 魯春秋 concluded this year.
Song 宋 underwent a dissension called the Rebellion of Huanzhui 宋桓魋之亂.
The Left Chancellor of Qi Chen Heng (Tian Chang) 齊左相 陳恒田常 (成子) executed the Right Chancellor Jian Zhi 右相監止; following this he pursued Duke Jian of Qi 齊簡公 (r. 484-481 BCE) to Shuzhou 舒州 where he had him executed; he then placed Qi Pinggong 齊平公 on the throne. The Tian family clan assumed total control of Qi.

480 BCE – The Chancellor of Chu Zixi 楚令尹 子西 and Minister Sima Ziqi 司馬子期 made an expedition against Wu 吳, the army penetrated as far as Tongrei 桐汭.

479 BCE – Confucius died 孔子.
Bai Gongsheng 白公勝 (see 403-1 footnotes), a Minister of Chu 楚, executed Zixi 子西 and Ziqi 子期 and had King of Huai of Chu 楚惠王 (r. 479-432 BCE) imprisoned.[2] Duke Yi 葉公 led an army for a counteroffensive; Bai Gongsheng lost and committed suicide.

478 BCE – Yue 越 attacked Wu 吳, which suffered a great defeat at Lize 笠澤.[3]
The craftsmen at Wey 衛 revolted. The Rong barbarians 戎 killed Duke Zhuang of Wey 衛莊公.
Chu 楚 annihilated Chen 陳.
Gongsun Chao a Minister of Chu 楚 公孫朝 led an army against Chen 陳, it was annihilated.[4]

---

2 Another source claims it was 488 BCE.
3 South of *Suzhou Jiangsu* 江蘇 蘇州南.
4 Another source claims it was 489 BCE.

477 BCE – Ba 巴 attacked Chu 楚, laid siege to You 鄾; Chu made a counteroffensive and managed to beat off the invaders.

476 BCE – Yue 越 attacked Chu 楚.

Zhi Yao 智瑶 minister of Jin 晉 (Zhi Yao 知瑶, Master Zhi Xiangzi 智襄子 died 453 BCE, see 403-11) invaded Zheng 鄭; Qi 齊 went to its rescue.

Shen Zhuliang of Chu 楚 沈諸梁 (Duke of Yegong 葉公) made an expedition against the Dongyi 東夷 in the east. Sanyi 三夷 reached an armistice with Chu.

Master Xiang of Zhao (Xiangzi) 趙襄子 (r. 457-448 BCE) set up a ruse for the king of Dai 代王; the King was executed, and the polity was annihilated. Xiangzi enfeoffed his nephew, Zhao Zhou 趙周 as Lord Daicheng 代成君.[5]

475 BCE – Yue 越 laid siege to the capital city of Wu 吳.

474 BCE – Yue 越 sent emissaries to Lu 魯.

473 BCE – Yue 越 broke into the capital of Wu, King of Wu, Fu Chai 吳王 夫差 (r. 495-473 BCE) committed suicide, Wu was annihilated.

King of Yue 越王 Gou Jian 勾踐 (r. 496-465 BCE) and the Fief Lords from Jin 晉 and Qi 齊 met at Xuzhou 徐州; there they paid tributes to the Zhou court. King Yuan of Zhou 周元王 (r. 475-469 BCE) bestowed a Duke title 伯 (hegemon) upon Gou Jian.[6]

472 BCE – Lu 魯 and Yue 越 made friendly exchanges.

Zhi Yao 晉 智瑶 of Jin made an expedition against Qi 齊; the latter was defeated at Liqiu 犁丘.

471 BCE – Duke Ai of Lu 魯哀公 paid tribute at Yue 越.

470 BCE – The craftsmen at Wey 衛 revolted, Duke Chu of Wey 衛出公 was banished.

469 BCE – Duke Jing of Song 宋景公 died; the three powerful family clans of Huang 黄, Ling 靈 and Yue 樂 took over the court.

468 BCE –Duke Ai of Lu 魯哀公 (r. 494-467 BCE) tried to solicit the help of Yue 越 to go against the San-heng (the three ministers) 三恒; however he was driven off by the latter.[7]

Yue 越 moved its capital to Langya 琅琊.

---

5 This event probably happened much later than 476 BCE.

6 The exact year is uncertain. San-Jin

7 San-heng 三恒 - the three descendants of the Duke of Lu Henggong 魯恒公 (~711-694 BCE) - Jisunshi 季孫氏, Mengsunshi 孟孫氏 and Shusunzhi 叔孫氏 that were controlling the Lu court.

467 BCE – Duke Ai of Lu 魯哀公 died; Duke Dao 魯悼公 succeeded him. Marquis of Lu was submissive to the San-huan ministers 三恒 at court, no different to a junior Marquis.

464 BCE – King of Yue 越王 Gou Jian 勾踐 (or 465?) died; Lu Ying 鹿郢 succeeded to the throne.
Zhi Yao of Jin 晉 智瑶 attacked Zheng 鄭.

463 BCE –Duke of Sheng of Zheng 鄭 聲公 (r. 500-463 BCE) died, his son Duke Ai 哀公 (r. 462-424BCE) succeeded to the sovereignty.

462 BCE – Zhi Yao 智瑶 of 晉 constructed a walled-city at Gaoliang 高粱.

461 BCE – Qin 秦 constructed moats near the Huanghe River 黄河.
Qin attacked Dali 大荔 with 20,000 men and captured its capital.

458 BCE – Zhishi 智氏, Zhaoshi 趙氏, Hannshi 韓氏 and Weishi 魏氏 the four ministers of Jin 晉 partitioned the fief land of Fanshi 范氏 and Zhonghengshi 中行氏, making them their counties.
Zhi Yao 智瑶 annihilated Chouyou 仇由 (a minor fief state situated between Jin 晉 and Zhongshan 中山國, which was founded by nomadic Baidi 白狄.)[8]

457 BCE – Zhi Yao 智瑶 launched an attack against Zhongshan 中山, the Mound of Qiongyu zhiqiu 窮魚之丘 was taken.[9]
Qin 秦 entered into warfare with Mianzhu 綿諸.[10]

456 BCE – Qin made Pinyang 頻陽 a county.
Jin 晉 Hann Pang 韓龐 took the walled-city of Lushicheng 盧氏城. The combined forces of Hann 韓 and Wei 魏 annihilated Yiluo Yin-Rong 伊洛陰戎.[11]

455 BCE – Zhi Yao 智瑶 extorted land from Zhao 趙, which refused; he then raised the combined forces of Zhi 智, Hann 韓 and Wei 魏 and had Zhao besieged at Jinyang 晉陽. (See 403-11)

---

8 Chouyou 仇由 was a minor fief state situated between Jin 晉 and Zhongshan 中山國; it was founded by the nomadic Baidi 白狄.

9 Qiongyu zhiqiu 窮魚之丘 - Yixian Hebei 河北 易縣.

10 Also known as Mianzhu-Rong 綿諸戎 – a nomadic tribe that moved in from the west and settled near Tanshuijun Prefecture of Qin 秦 天水郡 present day Gansu 甘肅; it was later annihilated by Qin.

11 Yiluo Yin-Rong 伊洛陰戎 were the nomadic tribes that settled between Yi and Luo rivers.

453 BCE – Hann 韓, Zhao 趙 and Wei 魏 annihilated the Zhishi 智氏 clan, and appropriated the land. (See 403-11).

The Chancellor of Zhao 趙 Zhang Mengtan 張孟談 introduced agrarian land reforms 田畝制.

452 BCE – Duke Chu of Jin 晉出公 (r. 474-452 BCE) escaped to Chu 楚.[12]

451 BCE – A Left Chancellor *zuoshuzhang* of Qin 秦 左庶長 constructed a walled-city at Nanzheng 南鄭.

448 BCE – The King of Yue 越王 Bushou 不壽 was murdered, Zhu Ju 朱句 succeeded to the throne.

447 BCE – Chu 楚 annihilated Cai 蔡.[13]

446 BCE – The founding year of Marquis Wen of Wei 魏文侯.

445 BCE – Chu 楚 annihilated Qi 杞, it continued to expand to the east until it reached Sishui River 泗水.

444 BCE – Qin made an expedition against Yiqu 義渠 and captured the leader of the tribe.[14]

441 BCE – Nanzheng 南鄭 revolted against Qin 秦.

440 BCE – King Kao of Zhou 周考王 (r. 440-426 BCE) enfeoffed his younger brother at South of the River- *Henan* 河南, he was known as Duke Huan of Western Zhou 西周 桓公 (r. 440-415 BCE).[15]

434 BCE – The Sovereign of Jin 晉 had Jiang 絳 and Quwo 曲沃 regions as his fief. However he had to pay tributes to Hann 韓, Wei 魏 and Zhao 趙.

433 BCE – Marquis Zeng, Yi 曾侯乙 died,[16] King Hui of Chu 楚惠王 (r. 488-432 BCE) prepared ceremonial gifts to the Marquis state to pay reverence to the deceased Marquis at Xiyang 西陽.

---

12 Another version states that this event did not happen until 457BCE.

13 It was founded by the 5th younger brother of King Wu of Zhou 周武王 Ji Du 姬度 at Cai 蔡.

14 Yiqu 義渠 was an ancient nomadic tribe that settled at the north of Jingshui River 涇水 and the Ordos Plateau 陝西北部, and it was mentioned at the time of Wuyi 武乙 -1147-1113 BCE in late Shang 商.

15 The Zhou Kingdom was split into two parts, Western Zhou 西周 and Eastern Zhou 東周.

431 BCE – Chu 楚 annihilated Ju 莒.[17]

430 BCE – Yiqu 義渠 made an expedition against Qin 秦, its army approached the north bank of Weishui River 渭水.

429 BCE – Duke Zao of Qin 秦躁公 (r. 442-429 BCE) died; his younger brother returned from Jin 晉 to assume the throne of the sovereign state. His was known posthumously as Duke Huai of Qin 秦懷公 (r. 428-425 BCE).

425 BCE – The Chancellor of Qin 秦, Huang 庶長 晁 and others forced Duke Huai of Qin 秦懷公 to commit suicide.

424 BCE – Zhao 趙 moved its capital to Zhongmou 中牟.

423 BCE – Hann 韓 made an expedition against Zheng 鄭, Duke You of Zheng 鄭幽公 was killed.

422 BCE – Qin 秦 constructed Shang-xia-zhi shrines (Upper and Lower) 上下畤, [18] to make sacrifices to Huangdi 黄帝 and Yandi 炎帝.

419 BCE – Wei 魏 constructed a walled-city at Shaoliang 少梁, Qin 秦 laid siege to it.

418 BCE – Wei 魏 and Qin 秦 joined battle at Shaoliang 少梁.

417 BCE – Qin constructed defence ramparts at the banks of Huanghe River 黄河.
Wei 魏 again constructed a walled-city at Shaoliang 少梁, Qin 秦 laid siege to it.

416 BCE – Duke You of Jin 晉幽公 (r. 437-420 BCE) was murdered by the Marquis Wen of Wei 魏文侯. Wei sent its army to quell the unrest at Jin, and made the son of Yougong – Zhi 止 as the new sovereign, he was known posthumously as Duke Lie of Jin 晉烈公 (r. 419-393 BCE).

---

16 The tomb of Marquis Zeng Yi 曾侯乙 was discovered in 1978 in Suizhoushi Hubei 湖北 隨州市; 15,000 burial objects were unearthed, including a complete set of bronze chimes called pianzhong 編鐘.

17 Ju 莒 fiefdom was founded around 1046 BCE at the time of the founding of Zhou, all we know is that it was a Yi 夷 state near Lu 魯, the history of this state is very sketchy.

18 Shang-xia-zhi 上下畤 - Upper Temple for making sacrifices to Huangdi 黄帝 and a Lower Temple for making sacrifices to Yandi 炎帝.

415 BCE – Qin 秦 made repairs to the walled-city of Pangcheng 龐城. Then it commenced constructing Jigucheng 籍姑城.

414 BCE – Yue 越 annihilated Teng 縢.[19]

Duke Wu of Zhongshan 中山 武公 (r. 414-497 BCE) took over the sovereign of Zhongshan.[20]

413 BCE – Qi 齊 made an expedition against Wei 魏, Huangcheng 黄城 was in total ruin, and the army followed up by laying siege to Yanggu 陽孤.

Yue 越 annihilated Tan 郯.[21]

Qin 秦 and Wei 魏 joined battle; Qin was defeated at Zheng 鄭.

Chu 楚 attacked Wei 魏; the army reached Shangluo 上洛.

412 BCE – Wei 魏 laid siege to Fanpangcheng 繁龐城 of Qin; the civilians were driven away.

Qi 齊 made an expedition against Lu 魯, successfully took Ju 莒 and Anyang 安陽.

409 BCE – Wei 魏 made an expedition against Qin 秦, and constructed two walled cities – Linjin 臨晉 and Yuanli 元里.

Qin government ordered its hundred surnames (government officers) to carry swords.

408 BCE – Wei 魏 invaded Qin 秦, the land west of the River 河西 *Hexi,* was completely annexed; two walled cities were constructed – Luoyin 洛陰 and Taiyang 郃陽. Qin retreated to Luoshui River 洛水 where they construct defences along the riverbank, a new walled city Zhongquancheng 重泉城 was constructed.

Qin recognized the ownership of land by people living and working on the farmlands 初租禾.

Wei 魏 invaded Zhongshan 中山.

Hann 韓 invaded Zheng 鄭, annexing Yongqiu 雍丘.

Qi 齊 invaded Wey 衛, annexing Cheng 郕.

407 BCE – Zheng 鄭 invaded Hann 韓, the Hann army was attacked at Fushu 負黍.

Qi 齊 invaded Wey 衛, taking Guanqiu 貫丘.

---

19 The *Shijia suoyin* 史記索隱, 'House of Zhao 趙世家' quoting from the *Bamboo annals* 紀年, 'Yue Zhu Ju 越 朱句' 34th year.
Teng 縢 was founded by Cuo Shuxiu 錯叔繡 – the 14th son of King Wen of Zhou 周文王.

20 Zhongshan Duke Wu 中山 武公 was the second Duke of Zhongshan.

21 Tan 郯 was an ancient polity, little is known of its history. It is mentioned in the *Zuozhuan* 左傳 Zhaogong 17th year 左傳昭公 十七年 that Tanzi 郯子 went to the Lu 魯 court in 525 BCE to pay homage, and he mentioned that he was the descendant of Shaohao 少昊, son of Huangdi 黄帝 the 26th century BCE legendary figure and that the tribe used bird as totem.

406 BCE – Wei 魏 annihilated Zhongshan 中山. (This was the first annihilation.)

405 BCE – Qi 齊 fell into complete chaos.[22]

The Minister of Qi Tian Dao 齊田悼 died, the state fell into chaos, Tian Bu 田布 killed Gongsun Sun 公孫孫; Tian Hui 田會 revolted at Linqiu 廩丘 and surrendered to Zhao. Tian Bu besieged Linqiu; Tian Hui sought help from San-Jin; Hann 韓, Zhao 趙 and Wei 魏 sent armed forces to the relief of Linqiu 廩丘. (This was a major battle during the early part of Zhanguo; it lasted for two years.)

Yue 越 annihilated Zeng 繒 (Zeng 鄫).[23]

404 BCE – San-Jin 三晉 made a combined assault against Qi 齊, the armies entered into the areas near the Qi Long-Walls. Marquis Wen of Wei 魏文侯 (r. 446-397 BCE) forced the Marquis Qi 齊侯 to pay a visit to King Weilie of Zhou 周威烈王 (r. 425-402 BCE); he then coerced the King of Zhou 周 to ennoble the three heads of state of Hann 韓, Zhao 趙 and Wei 魏 as fief lords.

403 BCE – King Weilie of Zhou 周威烈王 officially enfeoffed the heads of state of Hann 韓, Zhao 趙 and Wei 魏 as fief lords. (403-I)

402 BCE – Bandits killed King Sheng of Chu 楚聲王 (r. 407-402 BCE). (402-II)

401 BCE – Qin 秦 made an expedition against Wei 魏, the army reached Yanggu 陽孤. (401-I)

400 BCE – Hann 韓, Zhao 趙 and Wei 魏 made a combined assault against Chu 楚, the army reached Sangqiu 桑丘 before retreating. (See 400-I)

Zheng 鄭 laid siege to Yangzhai the capital of Hann 韓 陽翟. (400-II)

399 BCE – Chu 楚 returned Yuguan Pass 榆關 to Zheng 鄭.

398 BCE – The Zheng court 鄭 executed its Chancellor Ziyang 子陽 (Si Ziyang 駟子陽), the followers of Ziyang rebelled against the state. (See 398-I) Chu 楚 laid siege to Zheng.

---

22 Tian Qi Daozi 6th year 田齊 悼子, Daozi died Qi Minister Gongsun Hui 公孫會 (Tian Hui 田會) revolted at Linqiu 廩丘 and surrendered to Zhao 趙. It sparked off a war between the San-Jin 三晉 and Qi. Tian Bu 田布 led his forces to lay siege to Linqiu while the Wei General Zhai Jue 翟角 and Zhao General Kong Xie 孔屑 and the Hann 韓 forces rushed to rescue Gongsun Hui. The Qi army lost the ensuing battle; some thirty thousand men died.

23 The 7th King of Xia Zhu 夏 杼 (Yu 予 around 18th century BCE) - enfeoffed his second son Qulie 曲列 at Zeng 鄫; the fiefdom lasted for over one thousand years.

397 BCE – Nie Zheng 聶政 assassinated the Hann 韓 Chancellor Xia Lei 俠累 (Hann Kui 韓傀). (397-II)

396 BCE – The Ziyang 鄭子陽 faction murdered Duke Ru of Zheng 鄭繻公. (396-I)

395 BCE – Qin 秦 made an expedition against Yaozhu 繇諸 (Mianzhu 綿諸).[24] (According to Yang Kuan, this was the first year of Marquis Wu of Wei 魏武侯.)

394 BCE – Fushu 負黍 under the occupation of Zheng 鄭 revolted; it was returned to Hann 韓. (394-II)

Qi 齊 invaded Lu 魯, the city of Zui 最 was taken. Hann 韓 sent an army to Lu's rescue. (394-I)

393 BCE – Chu 楚 invaded Hann 韓; Fushu 負黍 was annexed.

Wei 魏 invaded Zheng 鄭, at Suanzao 酸枣 a walled city was constructed.

Wei defeated the Qin 秦 forces at Wang 汪 (Previously it was mistaken as Zhu 注).

392 BCE – Qi 齊 sent Duke Kang of Qi 齊康公 (r. 404-392 BCE) into exile on an island. (He died in 379 BCE.) (See 379-II)

391 BCE – Wei 魏, Zhao 趙 and Hann 韓 made a combined expedition against Chu 楚, the Chu army was defeated at Daliang 大梁 and Yuguan 榆關.

Qin 秦 assaulted against Yiyang 宜陽 of Hann 韓; six counties were annexed. (391-I)

390 BCE – Qin 秦 and Wei 魏 joined battle at Wucheng 武城. (390-I)

Qin 秦 reconstructed Shaan 陜 and made it into a county.

Qi 齊 annexed Xiangling 襄陵 of Wei 魏. (390-II)

389 BCE – Qin 秦 laid siege to Yinjin 陰晉 of Wei 魏.

Qi 齊 Tian He 田和 met Marquis Wu of Wei 魏武侯 at the Zhuoze Marsh 濁澤; the Marquis made a request to the king of Zhou 周王 on behalf of Tian He to be enfeoffed. (389-II)

387 BCE – Qin 秦 made an expedition against Shu 蜀; Nanzheng 南鄭 was annexed. (387-I)

386 BCE – Tian He 田和 was enfeoffed. (386-I). (Tian He changed his regnal year to 1st year.)

Zhao 趙 moved its capital to Handan 邯鄲. (386-II)

---

24 Yaozhu 繇諸 (Mianzhu 綿諸) was a nomadic tribe that settled in the areas west of Qin, present day Tianshui Gansu 甘肅天水. The tribe moved into the area towards the end of the Western Zhou 西周 period.

385 BCE – Jun 菌 the Chancellor of Qin 秦 murdered his sovereign Chuzi 出子 and placed Prince Lian 連 as the head of state. (See 385-I).[25] The court abrogated the practice of human sacrifice during interment 止從死.

Hann 韓 invaded Zheng 鄭, annexing Yangcheng 陽城. It followed up with an expedition against Song 宋; Pangcheng 彭城 fell; the Duke of Song Daogong 宋悼公 (r. 403-385 BCE) was captured. (385-III)[26]

384 BCE – Qi 齊 attacked Wei 魏 at Liuqiu 廩丘; Zhao went to the aid of Wei; Qi was given a resounding defeat.

383 BCE – Qin 秦 moved its capital to Yueyang 櫟陽.

Zhao 趙 constructed a new walled city, Gangpingcheng 剛平城, to make preparations for an attack against Wey 衛, which sought help from Wei 魏. Wei defeated the army of Zhao at Tutai 兔台. (See 383-I)

382 BCE – Qi 齊 and Wei 魏 helped Wey 衛 to make an assault against Zhao 趙, Wey 衛 annexed Gangping 剛平, and the army reached as far as Zhongmou 中牟.

381 BCE – Zhao 趙 appealed to Chu 楚 for help; which came to its aid by attacking Wei 魏; the battle was joined at Zhouxi 州西; the Chu army then marched through the capital of Wei 梁門 (Daliang 大梁 Kaifengxian Henan 河南 開封縣); it marched as far as Huanghe 黄河.

Zhao 趙 launched a counter-offensive against Wei, annexing Jipu 棘蒲 and Huangcheng 黄城.

Chu 楚 launched an expedition against Baiyue 百越, annexing areas in Dongting 洞庭 and Cangwu 蒼梧.[27]

King Dao of Chu 楚悼王 (r. 401-381 BCE) died, the nobles at Chu rose up against the reformist Wu Qi 吳起, who was killed next to the remains of the King. (381-I)

380 BCE – Qi 齊 invaded Yan 燕, annexing Sangqiu 桑丘. (380-I) Wei 魏, Zhao 趙 and Hann 韓 went to Yan's rescue. (380-II)

The State of Zhongshan 中山 was restored about this time. (Wei 魏 overran the Fiefdom in 408 BCE.)

379 BCE – Duke Kang of Qi 齊康公 died. (r. 404-392BCE); this was the end of the Jiang 姜 family clan. (379-I)

Qin 秦 converted Pu 蒲, Lantian 藍田, Shan 善 and Mingshi 明氏 to counties.

---

25 Prince Lian 連公子 - alias Shixi 師隰, the Duke of Qin Xiangong 秦献公 (r. 384-362 BCE).

26 Other texts maintain that it was possibly Song Xiugong 宋休公 was the head-of-state when Song fell to Hann 韓 in 385 BCE.

27 It probably happened earlier than this year.

378 BCE – Qin 秦 expanded its commerce activities at the bazaars 初行為市.

Zhai 翟 (Di 狄) defeated Wei 魏 at Kuai 澮.[28] (378-I)

Wei 魏, Zhao 趙 and Hann 韓 forces drove Qi 齊 to as far as Lingqiu 靈丘. (378-II)

Yue 越 moved its capital to Wu 吳.

377 BCE – Shu 蜀 launched a campaign against Chu 楚, annexing Zifang 兹方. (377-I)

Chu 楚 constructed Ganguan Pass 扞關 to prevent further incursions.

Zhao 趙 made an expedition against Zhongshan 中山; the battle was joined at Fangzi 房子.

376 BCE – Zhao 趙 launched another expedition against Zhongshan 中山, the battle was joined at Zhongren 中人.

375 BCE – Qin assigned five families into a Wu unit 伍, it was a means of strengthening the control of registration of its population. "為户籍相伍."

Wei 魏 annexed the Yuguan Pass 榆關 that belonged to Chu 楚.

Hann 韓 annihilated Zheng 鄭; Hann moved its capital to Xinzheng 新鄭. (375-II)

374 BCE – Hann Shanjian 韓山堅 (Hann Yan 韓嚴) murdered Marquis Ai of Hann 韓哀侯 (r. 377-375 BCE). Hann Ruoshan 韓若山 succeeded to the sovereignty, he was known as Marquis Yi of Hann 韓懿侯 (alias Marquis Gong 共侯, r. 374-363 BCE) posthumously. (*ZZTJ* records this in 371 - 371-II)

Tian Wu 田午 murdered his sovereign, Tian Yan 田剡 and his young son Xi 喜; he made himself the new sovereign of Qi; known posthumously as the Duke Huan of Qi 田桓公.[29]

373 BCE – The Yan 燕 army defeated Qi 齊 at Lingu 林孤. (373-I)

Wei 魏 also made an incursion into Qi 齊 and reached as far as Boling 博陵 (See 373-III); while Lu 魯 also invaded Qi and entered into the Yangguan Pass 陽關. (373-II)

372 BCE – Wey 衛 invaded Qi 齊, Xueling 薛陵 was annexed.

Zhao 趙 invaded Wey 衛; some seventy-three counties and villages were taken. (372-I)

Wei 魏 defeated Zhao 趙 at Lin 藺. (372-II)

371 BCE – Wei 魏 invaded Chu 楚, Luyang 魯陽 was taken.[30] (371-I)

---

28 Zhai 翟 as a polity was founded by an ancient Che-Di 赤狄 nomadic tribe; it was annihilated at the times of Chunqiu 春秋 by Jin 晉, probably the remnants of the nomadic tribes that settled to the West of Wei 魏, or the settlers at the foothills of the Eastern part of Taihengshan 太行山. N.B. Northerners pronounce the word 翟 as Di instead of Zhai.

29 The reigning years of Duke Huan 田桓公 varied with different accounts (377-359), (375-357) (374-357) BCE.

Hann 韓 Yan Sui 嚴遂 murdered Marquis Ai of Hann 韓哀侯. (371-II)

370 BCE – Zhao 趙 raided Zhen 甄 a Qi 齊 city. (N.B. In *ZZTJ* it is recorded as Juan 鄄; See 370-II)

Marquis Wu of Wei died, Gongsun Huan 公孫緩 vied for succession with Wei Ying 魏罃. (371-III)

369 BCE – Hann 韓 and Zhao 趙 supported Gongzhong Huan of Wei 魏 公仲緩, his adversary Wei Ying 魏罃 was besieged at Zhuoze Marsh 濁澤. Hann did not agree to Zhao's strategy and retreated. Wei Ying defeated the Zhao 趙 army and Gongzhong Huan; he made himself the sovereign of Wei, known posthumously as King Hui of Wei 魏惠王 (r. 370-319 BCE). (369-III) (According to Yang Kuan, this was the first year of King Hui of Wei 魏惠王.)

Zhongsun 中山 constructed Long-Walls.

368 BCE – Zhao 趙 invaded Qi 齊, the army reached as far as the Long-Walls. (368-II)

Zhao 趙 and Hann 韓 made a combined assault against Zhou 周.

Qi 齊 invaded Wei 魏 and took Guan 觀. (368-I)

367 BCE – Duke Wei of Western Zhou died 西周威公; Prince Gen 根公子 contended the sovereignty in the East; Zhao 趙 and Hann 韓 sent an army to his aid; ever since Western Zhou 西周 broke into two separate kingdoms, the West -Zhou (Xizhou) 西周 and East-Zhou (Dongzhou) 東周.

366 BCE – The heads-of-state of Wei 魏 and Hann 韓 met at Zhaiyang 宅陽. (Also known as Beizhai 北宅 a Wei County, present day Rongyang Hebei 河北 滎陽). (366-I)

Wei 魏 constructed a walled-city at Wudu 武都; Qin 秦 defeated the Wei forces.

Qin 秦 again defeated Hann 韓 and Wei 魏 ally at Luoyin 洛陰.[31] (366-II)

365 BCE – Wei 魏 army invaded Song 宋 (365-I) and annexed Yitai 儀台.

Zhao 趙 annexed Zhen 甄 of Wey 衛.[32]

364 BCE – Qin 秦 defeated Wei 魏 at Shimen 石門,[33] some sixty thousand soldiers were decapitated. (See 364-I) Zhao 趙 went to Wei's rescue.

363 BCE – Qin 秦 raid Wei 魏 at Shaoliang 少梁, Zhao 趙 went to its rescue.

30 Lushanxian Henan 河南 魯山縣

31 Yangquxian Taiyuanshi Shanxi 山西 太原市 陽曲縣.

32 Zhen 甄 is also known as Juan 鄄; present day Juancheng Shandong 山東 鄄城縣.

33 Shimen 石門 – southwest of Yunchengshi Shanxi 山西 運城市.

362 BCE – Wei 魏 defeated the combined forces of Zhao 趙 and Hann 韓 on the north bank of Kuai 澮 River. (362-I) Zhao General Yue Zuo 樂祚 was captured. The Wei army followed up by annexing Pinlao 皮牢, Lieren 列人 and Fei 肥.

Marquis Cheng of Zhao 趙成侯 (r. 374-350 BCE) and Marquis Zhao of Hann 韓昭侯 (alias Marquis Li of Hann 韓釐侯 r. 362-333 BCE) met at Shangdang 上黨.[34]

Qin 秦 attacked Wei at Shaoliang 少梁. (362-II)

361 BCE – On the 3rd day of the 4th month Wei 魏 moved its capital to Daliang 大梁.[35]

King Hui of Wei 魏惠王 (r. 370-319 BCE) and Marquis Zhao of Hann 韓昭侯 (r. 362-333 BCE) met at Wusha 巫沙.

Qin annihilated Huan 貆;[36] the Huan King was executed.

360 BCE – Wei 魏 redirected the flow of Huanghe River into Putianze Marsh 圃田澤 for constructing a canal for transportation.[37]

359 BCE – Wey Yang 衛鞅 (Shang Yang 商陽) lobbied at the Qin 秦 court; he convinced Duke Xiao of Qin 秦孝公 (r. 361-338 BCE) to make reforms. (359-I)

358 BCE – General Long Jia of Wei 魏 龍賈 led his forces to construct Long-Wall at the western border of the fiefdom.

Qin 秦 defeated Hann 韓 forces at Xishan Mountain 西山. (358-I)

Chu rechanneled Heshui 河水 (Huanghe River 黄河) to drain Changyuan 長垣 (northeast of Henan 河南東北) of Hann 韓.[38]

357 BCE – Hann 韓 and Wei 魏 made exchanges of territories; Wei acquired Shouyuan 首垣 (Changyuan 長), Zhenglu 鄭鹿 counties. (357-I)

---

34 Shangdang 上黨 (Changzi Shanxi 山西 長治市.)

35 Daliang 大梁 (Kaifengxian Henan 河南 開封縣).

36 Huan 貆 - Little is known about this minor ethnic tribe to the northwest of ancient China, it was probably a tribe which raised pigs.

37 Putianze Marsh 圃田澤 is in Zhongmouxian Henan 河南中牟縣. The construction of Honggou 鴻溝 was a monumental project; Wei 魏 started the project in 361 BCE to improve its transportation system. At Yuanyangxian Henan 河南 原陽縣 the Huanghe River was opened up to drain into Putianze Marsh, then the water from the lake was redirected to the north of capital city of Daliang 大梁 (present-day Kaifeng Henan 河南開封); skirting round the city the water flow south, passing through Tongxu 通許, and Taikang 太康 to drain into Shashui River 沙水. It continues south to reach southeast of Chen 陳 (Huaiyang Henan 河南 淮陽) to drain into Yingshui River 潁水 a major tributary of Huaishui River, the fourth most important river system in China. The opening up of Honggou connected Huanghe 黄河, Jishui 濟水, Poshui 濮水, Sishui 泗水, Heshui 菏水, Jushui 雎水, Yingshui 潁水, Rushui 汝 水 and Woshui 渦水 rivers.

38 Shouyuan 首垣 Changyuan (長垣 northeast of Henan 河南東北)

Song 宋 made an expedition against Hann 韓 and annexed Huangchi 黄池; while Wei 魏 made a raid against Zhu 朱 of Hann.
Wei 魏 besieged Zhaiyang 宅陽 of Hann. King Hui of Wei 魏惠王 and Marquis Zhao of Hann 韓昭王 reached an agreement at Wusha 巫沙, the siege on Zaiyang was lifted.

356 BCE – Marquis Gong of Lu 魯恭侯 (r. 382? or 375-353 BCE), Marquis Heng of Song 宋桓侯 (r. 362-350 BCE?), Marquis Cheng of Wey 衛成侯 (r. 371-343 BCE) and Marquis Zhao of Hann 韓昭侯 (r. 362-333 BCE) made tributes to King Hui of Wei 魏惠王 (r. 370-319 BCE). Marquis Cheng of Zhao 趙成侯 (r. 374-350 BCE), King Wei of Qi 齊威王 (r. 356-321 BCE) and Marquis Heng of Song 宋桓侯 met at Pinglu 平陸 (the southernmost part of Shanxi 山西); later they met the Duke Wen of Yan 燕文公 (r. 361-333 BCE) at A 阿. (356-I)
Qin 秦 appointed Shang Yang 商鞅 as its Chancellor *shuzhang* 庶長; the reformation was in force.

355 BCE – Zou Ji 鄒忌 used the analogy of the harmony of sitar and drum to earn a chancellor position to make reforms at Qi.
Shen Buhai 申不害 was appointed Chancellor (Xiang 相) of Hann 韓, he employed the techniques of Shu 術 (power or authority) a branch of Legalism 法家 to govern the fiefdom. The *ZZTJ* enters the event in 351 BCE, 351-III)
Zhao Xixu 昭奚恤 was made the Chancellor *lingyin* 令尹 of Chu 楚; he was extremely autocratic. (The *ZZTJ* enters the event in 353 See 353-III)
King Hui of Wei 魏惠王 and Duke Xiao of Qin 秦孝公 (r. 361-338 BCE) met at Duping 杜平. (355-II)[39]
Song Sicheng Zihan 宋 司城子罕 (Daishi 戴氏 or Song Techeng 宋剔成 r. 370?-329 BCE) murdered (according to Bamboo Annals) Marquis Huan of Song 宋桓侯 (r. 373?-370 BCE) and usurped the sovereignty. (According to *ZZTJ* he died. 370-VI)

354 BCE – Zhao 趙 made an expedition against Wey 衛, Qi 漆 and Fuqiu 富丘 were annexed.
Wei 魏 marched to the rescue of Wey 衛 and besieged the Zhao 趙 capital.

353 BCE – Qi 齊 went to the aid of Zhao 趙 by attacking Wei 魏; the Wei army was defeated at Guiling 桂陵. Qi formed an alliance with Song 宋 and Wey 衛 to lay siege to Xiangling 襄陵. Wei 魏 took the capital of Zhao – Handan 邯鄲. (353-I)

352 BCE – Qin 秦 besieged Anyi of Wei 魏安邑, the county surrendered. (See 352-I)
Wei 魏 employed the forces of Hann 韓 to defeat a combined assault by Qi 齊, Song 宋 and Wey 衛 at Xiangling 襄陵. (352-II) Qi sought help from Jing She 景舍 a minister of Chu 楚 to negotiate a peaceful settlement.

---

39 Duping 杜平 - Dengchengxian Shaanxi 陕西 澄城縣

351 BCE – Qin 秦 constructed a pass at Shang 商; then followed up with a siege against Guyang of Wei 魏 固陽; Guyang surrendered. (See 351-I)

Wei 魏 returned Handan 邯鄲 to Zhao 趙; the two fiefdoms signed a peaceful accord at Zhangshui River 漳水. (See 351-II)

350 BCE – Qi 齊 lengthened its stretch of Long-Walls to defend against its invaders.

Qin 秦 moved its capital from Yong 雍 to Xianyang 咸陽; [40] it went on to set up numerous counties. (See 350-I)

Qin 秦 introduced pathways in the fields for passage, instead of wading through the fields 開裂田的千百封疆.

349 BCE – Qin 秦 introduced junior bureaucrats at the counties - *zhishi* 秩史.

348 BCE – Qin 秦 introduced taxing and corvee services according to the size of land held by the peasants - 初為賦. (348-I)

King Hui of Wei 魏惠王 (r. 370-319 BCE) and Marquis Su of Zhao 趙肅侯 (r. 349-326 BCE) met at Yinjin 陰晉 (Huayinxian Shaanxi 陝西 華陰縣).

347 BCE – Prince Fan of Zhao 趙公子 范 attacked Handan 邯鄲, he was unsuccessful and died. (347-I)

344 BCE – King Hui of Wei 魏惠王 (r. 370-319 BCE) proclaimed king; he called a conference at Fengze 逢澤; he then led the fief lords to pay homage to the Son of Heaven at the Zhou court 周.

Qin 秦 sent Prince Shaoguan 少官, heading an army to attend the conference at Fengze Lake. (343-I)

The head-of-state of Qi 齊 brought along his senior ministers to Qin for a state visit.

343 BCE – Zhao 趙 made a raid against Shouyuan of Wei 魏 首垣.

342 BCE – Wei 魏 made a raid against Hann 韓, which was defeated at Liang 梁 and He 赫; Qi 齊 came to the rescue of Hann and attacked Wei.

341 BCE – Qi General Tian Ji 齊 田忌 backed by Sun Bin 孫臏 gave the Wei 魏 army a resounding defeat at Maling 馬陵, Wei General Pang Juan 魏 龐涓 committed suicide, the Crown Prince Shen 太子申 was captured. (341-I)

---

40 Yong 雍 - Fengxiangxian Shaanxi 陝西 鳳翔縣 to Xianyang 咸陽 present day Xian Shaanxi 陝西 西安.

340 BCE – Qi 齊, Qin 秦 and Zhao 趙 made a combined assault against Wei 魏. (*ZZTJ*, Qin did not participate 340-III)

Shang Yang of Qin 秦 商鞅 used trickery and had Wei Prince Gongzi Ang 魏 公子卬 captured; Wei army suffered a major loss. (340-I)

Qin enfeoffed Shang Yang 商鞅 at Shang 商; he was enfeoffed as Lord Shang 商君. (340-II)

339 BCE – Wei 魏 excavated an enormous waterway at Beiguo of Daliang 大梁 北郭 to drain river water into Putian 圃田. (Also see 360 BCE above.)

338 BCE – Duke Xiao of Qin 秦孝公 (r. 361-338 BCE) died; Shang Yang 商鞅 was executed. (338-I)

Qin 秦 defeated the army of Wei 魏 at Anmen 岸門;[41] General Wei Cuo 魏錯 was captured.

337 BCE – The heads-of-state of Chu 楚, Hann 韓, Zhao 趙 and Shu 蜀 went to Qin 秦 to pay homage.

336 BCE – The heads-of–state of Wei 魏 and Hann 韓 went to Donga 東阿 to pay tribute to King Wei of Qi 齊威王 (r. 356-321 BCE).

Qin introduced round bronze money with a square hole in the centre 初行錢.[42]

335 BCE - The heads-of–state of Wei 魏 and Hann 韓 went to Zhen 甄 to pay tribute to King Wei of Qi 齊威王 (r. 356-321 BCE).

Qin 秦 took Hann's Yiyang 韓 宜陽. (335-I)

334 BCE – King Hui of Wei 魏惠王 (r. 370-319 BCE) adopted Hui Shi's 惠施 suggestion, he made a tribute to King Wei of Qi 齊威王 (r. 356-321 BCE) at Xuzhou 徐州, honouring him as King, Qi reciprocated by honouring King Hui as King. (334-I) (According to Yang Kuan, King Hui of Wei changed his regnal year to year 1 魏惠王改元).

333 BCE – Zhao 趙 laid siege to Huang 黄 of Wei 魏, but failed to take the city.

At Zhangshui 漳水 and Fushui 滏水 river banks Zhao 趙 constructed sections of Long-Wall.

Chu 楚 besieged Xuzhou of Qi 齊 徐州 (333-I), the Qi General Shen Zhuan 申縛 was given a thrashing.

332 BCE – Wei 魏 ceded Yinjin 陰晉 to Qin 秦, Qin changed its name to Ningqin 寧秦. (332-II)

---

41 Anmen 岸門 - 山西河津縣 Hejinxian Shanxi.

42 Minted bronze money 初行錢, - the money half a *liang* 两 in weight was round in shape with a square hole in the centre for easier threading with strings, previous to this the hole in the centre was also round.

Qi 齊 and Wei 魏 made a combined assault against Zhao 趙 (332-I); the latter broke the bank of Huanghe River 黄河 to flood the Qi and Wei armies.

331 BCE – The people at Yiqu 義渠 revolted, Qin 秦 sent its Chancellor Cao 操 to quell the revolt.

330 BCE – At Diaoyin 雕陰 Qin 秦 defeated Wei 魏, General Long Jia 龍賈 was captured. (333-III)
Wei ceded the territory west of He – Hexi 河西 to Qin. (330-I)

329 BCE – Qin 秦 raided and annexed Fenyin 汾陰, Pishi 皮氏 and Jiao 焦 west of the River that belonged to Wei 魏.[43] (329-I)
Wei 魏 made a raid into Jingshan Mountain 陘山 in Chu's 楚 territory.

328 BCE – Qin 秦 introduced a new title for chancellor *xiangbang* 相邦, Zhang Yi 張儀 was appointed Chancellor. (328-I)
Wei 魏 again ceded fifteen counties to Qin 秦, including Shaoliang 少梁.[44] (328-I)

327 BCE – Qin 秦 changed the name of Shaoliang 少梁 to Xiayang 夏陽; it returned Jiao 焦 and Quwo 曲沃 it occupied earlier to Wei.[45] (327-II)

326 BCE – Marquis Su of Zhao 趙肅侯 (r. 349-326 BCE) died; Qin 秦, Chu 楚, Yan 燕, Qi 齊 and Wei 魏 each dispatched over ten thousand crack troops to attend to the funeral service. (326-I)
Qin first made sacrifice called *chula* 初腊 to ghosts and spirits during the summer, held at Longmen 龍門.

325 BCE – On the *wuwu* 戊午 day of the 4th month of this year Lord Huiwen of Qin 秦惠君 (r. 337-311 BCE) declared himself as King. (325-I)
King Hui of Wei 魏惠王 (r. 370-319 BCE) met King Xuanhui of Hann 韓 宣惠王 (Marquis Wei of Hann 韓威侯 r. 332-312 BCE) at Wusha 巫沙; he honoured him as King.
Qi 齊 defeated Zhao 趙 at Pingyi 平邑; the Zhao General 趙 Hann Ji 韓舉 was captured.

324 BCE – Qin 秦 Zhang Yi 張儀 took Wei's 魏 Shaan 陝 and Zhushangjunsai Pass 築上郡塞. (324-I)

---

43 Pishi 皮氏 - Hejinshi Shanxi 山西河津市.
Jiao 焦 – Shaanxian Henan 河南 陝縣, Jiao was a walled city.

44 Shaoliang 少梁 today's Hannchengshi Shaanxi 陝西韓城市, was a most important military strategic post.

45 Quwo 曲沃 is a county of Linfenshi Shanxi 山西臨汾氏; it was the capital of the deposed Jin 晉.

King Hui of Wei 魏惠王 (r. 370-319 BCE) and King Wei of Qi 齊威王 (r. 356-321 BCE) met at Donga 東阿.

323 BCE – Chu General 楚柱國 Zhao Yang 昭陽 made a raid against Wei 魏, the army broke into Xiangling 襄陵 and occupied eight counties.
Qin dispatched Zhang Yi 秦 張儀 on a peace mission; he met the senior ministers of Qi 齊 and Chu 楚 at Niesang 齧桑.[46] (323-1)
Gongsun Yan 公孫衍 made a proposal to the heads of state of Yan 燕, Zhao 趙, Zhongsun 中山, Wei 魏 and Hann 韓 to mutually recognize other heads of state as kings.

322 BCE – Wei appointed Zhang Yi 張儀 as Chancellor, Hui Shi 惠施 was discharged. (322-1)
Qin made an expedition against Quwo 曲沃 and Pingzhou 平周 of Wei 魏. (322-1)

321 BCE – Zhang Yi 張儀 was the Chancellor of Qin 秦 and Wei 魏 simultaneously.

320 BCE – Qin 秦 army marched through the territories of Hann 韓 and Wei 魏 to make an expedition against Qi 齊; King Wei of Qi 齊威王 (r. 356-321 BCE) appointed Kuang Zhang 匡章 to put up a defence.
Qin made an expedition against Yiqu 義渠, annexed Yuzhi 郁郅.[47]

319 BCE – Qin besieged Yan 鄢 of Hann.[48] (319-1)
Qi 齊, Chu 楚, Yan 燕, Zhao 趙 and Hann 韓 backed Gongsun Yan 公孫衍 as the Chancellor of Wei 魏.
Hui Shi 惠施 returned to Wei 魏. (According to Yang Kuan, King Hui 魏惠王 died this year.)

318 BCE – King Yan of Song 宋偃王 self-proclaimed as King. (318-11)
The combined forces of Wei 魏, Zhao 趙, Hann 韓, Chu 楚 and Yan 燕 formed an alliance against Qin 秦; the armies did not make any progress and retreated. (318-1)
The King of Yan Guai 燕噲王 abdicated his throne to his Chancellor Zi Zhi 子之. (316-11)

317 BCE – Qin 秦 defeated the combined forces of San-Jin 三晉 (Zhao 趙, Hann 韓 and Wei 魏) at Xiuyu 修魚.[49] (317-1)
Qi 齊 joined force with Song 宋 to invade Wei 魏; the Wei army lost at Guanze 觀澤.

46 Niesang 齧桑 - Peixian Jiangsu 江蘇 沛縣.
47 Yuzhi 郁郅 - Qingchengxian Gansu 甘肅 慶城縣.
48 Yan 鄢 – Yanlingxian Henan 河南 焉陵縣.
49 Xiuyu 修魚 - Yanyangxian Henan 河南 原陽縣?

316 BCE – Qin 秦 sent Sima Cuo 司馬錯 to attack Shu 蜀, Shu was annihilated. (316-I)

Qin 秦 took Zhongdu 中都 and Xiyang 西陽 of Zhao 趙.[50]

315 BCE – Qin 秦 invaded Hann 韓, the battle was joined at Zhuoze Lake 濁澤 (or Shuhuang 蜀潢.)

There was unrest at Yan 燕, General Shi Bei 市被, and Prince *Taizi* Ping 太子平 made an attack against Zi Zhi 子之.

314 BCE – The Qin 秦 army won a great victory against Hann 韓 at Anmen 岸門.[51] (314-III)

Zi Zhi of Yan 燕 子之 made a counterattack killing General Shi Bei 市被 and Prince Ping 太子平. (314-IV)

Qi 齊 sent its General Kuang Zhang 匡章 against Yan 燕; the General took Yan in fifty days. (314-IV)

Zhao 趙 recalled the Prince of Yan *Gongzi* Zhi 公子職 to return to Yan to take on the position as the sovereign; he was known posthumously as King Zhao of Yan 燕昭王. (312-II)

Qin made a raid against Yiqu 義渠, 25 walled cities were annexed. (314-I)

313 BCE – Qin 秦 sent General Chuli Ji 樗里疾 to attack Zhao, the Zhao General Zhao Zhuang 趙莊 was captured, Lin 藺 was annexed. (313-I)

312 BCE – Jing Cui of Chu 楚 景翠 led an army to besiege Yongshi of Hann 韓雍氏; Qin 秦 came to Hann's rescue by making a counter-offensive against Jing Cui.

Wei Zhang of Qin 秦 魏章 defeated Chu's army at Danyang 楚 丹陽, in the process Qu Gai 屈丐 was captured, the area of Hanzhong 漢中 was captured. (312-I)

The combined armies of Qi 齊 and Song 宋 laid siege to Zhuzao 煮棗 山東 曹縣西北;[52]

The Qin 秦, Wei 魏 and Hann 韓 forces forced Qi 齊 to retreat to Pushui River. Shengzi 聲子 (or written as Zhuizi 贅子) was captured.

Qin defeated Chu at Lantian 藍田; the Hann 韓 and Wei 魏 armies penetrated into the territories of Chu to as far as Deng 鄧. (312-I)

311 BCE - Qin 秦 General Chuli Ji 樗里疾 gave aid to Wei 魏 to go against Wey 衛.

Qin raid Chu 楚 and captured Zhaoling 召陵.[53] Luoheshi Henan 河南 漯河氏.

310 BCE – Qin 秦 made another expedition against Yiqu 義渠 and Danli 丹犁.[54]

---

[50] Zhongdu 中都 – near Tiayuanshi Shanxi 山西太原 and Xiyang 西陽 Zhongyangxian Shanxi 山西中陽.

[51] Anmen 岸門 – south of Hejinxian Shanxi 山西 河津縣 南.

[52] Zhuzao 煮棗 山東 曹縣西北.

[53] Zhaoling 召陵. Luoheshi Henan 河南 漯河市.

(Zhang Yi 張儀 died this year.)

309 BCE – Qin 秦 adopted the Chancellor – *chengxian* 丞相 position, Chuli Ji 樗里疾 was appointed as Left Chancellor (309-I), and Gan Mao 甘茂 as the Right Chancellor.

308 BCE – Qin 秦 annexed Yiyang 宜陽 of Hann 韓. (307-I)

307 BCE –King Wuling of Zhao 趙武靈王 introduced Hu attire and archery on horseback reform to his army. (307-III)

Zhao 趙 made an expedition against Zhongshan 中山 and penetrated as far as Fangzi 房子. (307-III)

Qin 秦 introduced the title of General *jiangjun* 將軍; Wei Ran 魏冉 was appointed General.

306 BCE – Zhao 趙 made a raid against Zhongshan 中山, and the army reached as far as Ningjia 寧葭; the army then penetrated into the realms of the barbarians at Yuzhong 榆中. (306-II)

Chu 秦 annihilated Yue 越; a new prefecture was established at Jiangdong 江東.

305 BCE – Zhao 趙 made a raid against Zhongshan 中山, Danqiu 丹邱, Huayang 華陽, Chizhicai 鴟之塞, Hao 鄗, Shiyi 石邑, Fenglong 封龍, Dongyuan 東垣. Zhongshan ceded four counties to sue for peace. (305-II)

304 BCE – Qin 秦 and Chu 楚 met at Huangji 黄棘 for a senior conference; Qin returned Shangyong 上庸 to Chu. (304-I)

303 BCE – Qin 秦 took Wusui 武遂 of Hann 韓. (303-II)

Qin 秦 made raids against Puban 蒲阪, Jinyang 晉陽 and Fengling 封陵 of Wei 魏. (303-II)

Qi 齊, Wei 魏 and Hann 韓 made a combined assault against Chu 楚; Chu sent its Crown Prince to Qin as a hostage; Qin 秦 sent an army to relieve Chu. (303-III)

302 BCE – Zhao 趙 made raids against Hezongshi 河宗氏, Xiu 休, Hun 溷, Zhu 諸 and Mo 貉 the various Rong 戎 and Di 狄 tribes that settled along middle reaches of the Huanghe River 黄河;[55] thence it proceeded to set up Jiuyuan 九原 and Yunzhong 雲中 prefectures.

Zhao 趙 sent its Minister Nu 奴 to garrison at Jiuyuan 九原.

King Xiang of Wei 魏 襄王 and the Crown Prince Ying of Hann 韓嬰 went to the Qin 秦 court to pay homage. (302-I)

---

54 Danliguo 丹犁國 was in Meishanxian Sichuan 四川 眉山縣; it was a very old Dian 滇 branch race that settled in Sichuan.

55 Hezongshi, Xiu, Hun, Zhu and Mo 休, 溷, 諸, 貉 the various Rong and Di tribes that settled along middle reaches of the Huanghe River 黄河.

301 BCE – Qin 秦 army took Rang 穰 a Hann 韓 city. (301-II)

Qi 秦 sent Kuang Zhang 匡章, Wei 魏 dispatched Gongsun Xi 公孫喜 and Hann 韓 sent Bao Yuan 暴 鳶 to lay a siege against Fangcheng 方城 of Chu 楚. The Chu General Tang Mei 唐昧 was killed; Hann and Wei captured areas north of Wan 宛 and Ye 葉. (301-IV)

300 BCE – Qin 秦 invaded Chu 楚, Xincheng 新城 was taken, Chu General Jing Que 景缺 was killed. (300-II)

Zhao 趙 invaded Zhongshan 中山 again.

299 BCE – King Huai of Chu 楚懷王 was deluded to go to Qin 秦, the King of Qin had he incarcerated. (299-III)

King Wuling of Zhao 趙 武靈王 abdicated his throne to his youngest son Zhao He 趙何 (King Hui of Zhao 趙惠王) and honoured himself as the Supreme King – Zhufu 主父. (299-I)

Lord Mengchang Tian Wen 孟嘗君 田文 of Qi 齊 was invited to Qin to take on the position as chancellor. (299-IV)

298 BCE – Qin 秦 successfully annexed ten or more Chu 楚 cities, including Xi 析. (298-II?)

Zhao 趙 sent Lou Huan 樓緩 to Qin as chancellor and Chou Hao 仇郝 to Song as chancellor.

Lord Mengchang 孟嘗君 田文 returned to Qi 齊. (298-I)

The combined forces of Qi 齊, Hann 韓 and Wei 魏, attacked Qin 秦 at Hanguguan Pass 函谷關.

297 BCE – King Wuling of Zhao 趙 武靈王 left for Dai 代; to the west he met the King of Loufanwang 樓煩王 at west of the River *Xihe* 西河, he then decided to recruit the forces into his army. (296-III)

The combined forces of Qi 齊, Hann 韓 and Wei 魏 continued to attack Qin 秦.

296 BCE – The combined forces of Qi 齊, Hann 韓 and Wei 魏 made an inroad into Hanguguan pass 函谷關, which belonged to Qin 秦. Qin sued for peace by returning the areas beyond Hannhe River 韓河, Wusui 武遂, Weihe River 魏河 and Fengling 封陵. (*ZZTJ* says Zhao 趙 and Song 宋 participated 298-II)

Zhao 趙 annihilated Zhongshan 中山, the King of Zhongsun was repatriated to Fushi 膚施. (295-II)

295 BCE – Prince Zhang of Zhao 趙章 vied for the Zhao throne and lost to his younger brother. Having failed in the coup, he escaped into the palace where his father Zhufu 趙 武靈王 was staying. Prince Cheng 公子成 and Li Dui 李兑 had the palace surrounded; Zhufu died from starvation. (295-III)

Qin Lou Huan 樓緩 was relieved of his Chancellor duties, Wei Ran 魏冉 resumed the post. (295-IV)

King Zhao of Yan 燕昭王 sent Su Qin 蘇秦 to Qi 齊, helped Qi to make a raid against Song 宋.

294 BCE – Qi 齊 employed one of Qin's 秦 ministers Lu Li 吕禮 as Chancellor.

Qi Tian Jia 齊 田甲 held the King of Qi hostage, Lord Mengchang 孟嘗君 absconded.

293 BCE – Qin General 秦 Bai Qi 白起 defeated the combined army of Hann 韓 and Wei 魏 at Yique 伊闕, decapitated two hundred and forty thousand men; the Wei General Gongsun Xi 魏將軍 公孫喜 was captured. (293-I)

292 BCE – The Qin General Bai Qi 秦 白起 attacked Wei 魏 and took Yuan 垣.

291 BCE – The Qin General Bai Qi 秦 白起 attacked Hann 韓 and took Wan 宛. (291-I)

Qin Sima Cuo 秦 司馬錯 attacked Wei 魏 and took Zhi 軹; he followed up to attack Hann 韓 and took Deng 鄧.

Qin 秦 enfeoffed Prince Shi 市 at Wan 宛; and Prince Kui 悝 at Deng 鄧. (291-II)

290 BCE – Wei 魏 ceded 400 *li* of land to the east of the River *Hedong* to Qin 秦. (290-I)

Hann 韓 ceded 200 *li* of land at Wusui 武遂 to Qin 秦. (290-II)

289 BCE – Qin 秦 annexed sixty-one Wei 魏 walled-cities. (289-I)

288 BCE – King Zhao of Wei 魏昭王 went to the Zhao court 趙 to pay tribute and presented Yincheng 陰成 and Genie 葛孽 as gifts. He then enfeoffed the son of Li Dui 李兑 at Heyang 河陽 and Gumie 姑密.

10th month, Qin Wei Ran 秦 魏冉 met with the King of Qi 齊, self-proclaimed as Eastern Emperor and Western King. 12th month, Qi employed Su Qin's 蘇秦 strategy, ended the use of the title and formed an alliance against Qin. (According to *ZZTJ* it was Su Dai 蘇代 and not Su Qin 288-I, according to *ZZTJ* Su Qin died in 317, see 317-II) (See 284 BCE below, Su Qin lived until 284 BCE).

287 BCE – Su Qin 蘇秦 rallied the forces of Zhao 趙, Qi 齊, Chu 楚, Wei 魏 and Hann 韓 to go against Qin 秦; the military activity ceased at Chenggao 成皋. Qin returned parts of Zhao and Wei territories in a bid to settle for peace. (See 288 notes)

Qin 秦 attacked Wei 魏 and annexed Xinyuan 新垣 and Quyang 曲陽. (287-I)

286 BCE – Qin 秦 raid *Henei* 河内 of Wei 魏; Wei ceded Anyi 安邑 to Qin 秦. (286-I)

The Zhao General 趙將 Han Xiwei 韓徐為 attacked Qi 齊.

Qin 秦 defeated the Hann 韓 army at Xiashan 夏山. (286-II)

Qi 齊 annihilated Song 宋; the King of Song Yanwang 宋偃王 died in Wen of Wei 魏 温. (286-III)

285 BCE – King Zhao of Qin 秦昭王 and King Qingxiang of Chu 楚頃襄王 met at Wan 宛; he then met King Hui of Zhao 趙惠王 at Zhongyang 中陽; Qin proposed a vertical coalition to go against Qi 齊. (285-I)

Qin General Meng Ao 秦 蒙驁 made a raid against Qi 齊, annexing nine walled-cities. (285-II)

284 BCE – King Zhao of Qin 秦昭王 and King Zhao of Wei 魏昭王 met at Yiyang 宜陽; then at Xincheng he 新城 met with King Xi of Hann 韓釐王. King Zhao of Yan 燕昭王 went to the Zhao court 趙 to pay homage to the King Huiwen of Zhao 趙惠文王.

Five fiefdoms formed a coalition to go against Qi, Yan army under Yue Yi 樂毅 entered into the capital city of Qi, of Linzi 齊 臨淄. Wei 魏 recovered its former territory of Song 宋, while Chu 楚 recovered its former Huai Beidi 淮北地. (284-I) (According to *ZZTJ*, Chu was not mentioned in the alliance against Qi 齊.)

(Su Qin 蘇秦 died this year according to *Changsha Mawangdui Zhangu zonghengjia shu* 長沙馬王堆戰國縱橫家書.)

283 BCE – King Huiwen of Zhao 趙惠文王 met with King Zhao of Yan 燕昭王. Zhao attacked Qi 齊 and took Yangjin 陽晉.

King Zhao of Qin 秦昭王 and King Qingxiang of Chu 楚頃襄王 met at Yan 鄢 and Rang 穰 on two separate occasions.

Qin 秦 made a raid against Wei 魏, the army reached as far as Daliang 大梁; Yan 燕 and Zhao 趙 marched to Wei's 魏 rescue. (283-II)

282 BCE – King Zhao of Qin 秦昭王 and King Xi of Hann 韓釐王 met at Xincheng 新城, following which he met with King Zhao of Wei 魏昭王 at Xinmingyi County 新明邑.

Qin 秦 attacked Zhao 趙, took Lin 藺 and 祁 walled-cities. (282-I?)

Zhao 趙 made a raid against Boyang at Wei 魏 伯陽.

281 BCE – The Qin government enfeoffed Wei Ran 秦 魏冉 with the territories captured from Qi 齊, including Dingtao 定陶.

Zhao 趙 broke the Riverbank, followed up with an expedition against Wei 魏.

280 BCE – Qin 秦 Bai Qi 白起 raided Zhao 趙, annexing Guanglang 光狼. (280-I)

Qin 秦 ordered Sima Cuo 司馬錯 to attack from Shu 蜀 against Chu Qianzhong 楚黔中. Chu sued for peace by ceding Hanbei 漢北 and Shangyong 上庸. (280-I)

Zhao 趙 attacked Qi 齊 at Maiqiu 麥邱.

279 BCE – King Zhao of Yan 燕昭王 died, King Hui 燕惠王 replaced Yue Yi 樂毅 with Qi Jie 騎劫; Qi Tian Dan 齊 田單 made a counter-offensive, recovering all the seventy walled-cities lost to Yan 燕. (279-III)

King Zhao of Qin 秦 昭王 and King Huiwen of Zhao 趙惠文王 met at Mianchi 澠池 for a peace accord. (279-II)

Qin 秦 sent Bai Qi 白起 to made an expedition against Chu 楚; Yan 鄢, Deng 鄧 and Xiling 西陵 were annexed. (279-I)

The Chu General Zhuang Qiao 莊蹻 marched through the Qianzhong Prefecture 黔中 to raid at Dianchi Lake 滇池.

278 BCE – Qin 秦 Bai Qi 白起 captured Chu's capital city of Yanying 楚 鄢郢. The general torched and razed Yiling 夷陵 to the ground, the mausoleums of the ancestors of Chu; he then proceeded to Jingling 竟陵 and Anlu 安陸, there he established a new prefecture – Nanjun 南郡; the army continued south, capturing Dongting Wuzhu 洞庭五渚, and Jiangnan 江南. Chu was forced to move its capital to Chen 陳.(278-I)

Qu Yuan 屈原, the great Chu 楚 poet and patriot, sensing his state was the road of moribund, killed himself by jumping into the Miluo River 汨羅江.

277 BCE – Qin 秦 sent the Magistrate of Shu Zhang Ruo 蜀守 張若 to make an expedition against the prefectures of Wujun 巫郡 and Qianzhongjun 黔中郡. (According to *ZZTJ*, it was Bai Qi 白起 277-I)

276 BCE – Chu 楚 recovered fifteen counties in Qianzhong 黔中; it then proceeded to establish new prefectures as defence and offence against Qin. (276-II)

Zhao sent its General Lian Po 趙將 廉頗 to made a raid against Ji 幾 of Wei 魏.

Qin annexed two Wei walled-cities. (276-I)

275 BCE – Zhao sent Lian Po 趙將 廉頗 raid Wei's Fengling 魏 防陵 and Anyang 安陽.

Qin 秦 invaded Wei 魏; the army reached as far as Daliang 大梁. Hann 韓 dispatched Bao Yuan 暴鳶 to the rescue, he was defeated by the Qin army and retreated to Qifeng 啓封.

Wei ceded Wen 温 to Qin to settle for peace. (275-I)

274 BCE – Zhao sent Yan Zhou 趙 燕周 attacked the walled cities of Changcheng 昌城 and Gaotang 高唐, in Qi's 齊 territories.

Qin 秦 annexed Wei's 魏 Cai 蔡 and Zhongyang 中陽 four cities altogether. (274-I)

273 BCE – Zhao 趙 and Wei 魏 made a combined attack against Hann 韓, the armies reached as far as Huayang 華陽. Qin 秦 sent Bai Qi 白起 and Hu Yang 胡陽 to Hann's relief. The battle was joined at Huayang 華陽; it was a one-sided victory for Qin; Wei General Meng Mao 魏將 孟卯 ran for his life. It then took down Juan 卷, Caiyang 蔡陽 among other minor cities. It then joined battle with the Zhao General Jia Yan 趙 賈偃. Qin followed up by laying siege to Daliang 大梁, the capital of Wei; Zhao and Yan 燕 came to Wei's rescue. Wei ceded Nanyang 南陽 to Qin for a peaceful settlement. (273-I)

272 BCE – The Chancellor of Yan Gongsun Cao 公孫操 murdered King Hui of Yan 燕惠王 and placed King Wucheng 武成王 on the throne. (*ZZTJ* merely mentions King Hui died.)
Qin 秦 finally annihilated Yiqu 義渠.
Qin 秦 and Chu 楚 gave aids to Hann 韓 and Wei 魏 to attack Yan 燕. (272-III)

271 BCE – Lin Xiangru of Zhao 趙 藺相如 made an expedition against Qi 齊, his army reached as far as Pingyi 平邑. (271-I)

270 BCE – Qin 秦 sent its Guest Minister Zao 灶 (also written as 造) to lead an army against Gang 剛 and Shou 壽, two cities of Qi. (270-II)

269 BCE – Qin General Hu Yang 秦 胡陽 marched pass Shangdang 上黨, the territory of Hann 韓 to invest a siege at Zhao's Yuyu 閼與. (269-I) Zhao General Zhao 趙將 趙奢 Zhao She proceeded to the rescue and gave the Qin army a resounding defeat. (270-I)

268 BCE – Qin Minister Wan 秦 綰 to invest a siege against Huai 懷 of Wei 魏. (268-I)

266 BCE – Qin 秦 captured Xingqiu 邢丘 of Wei 魏. (266-I)

265 BCE – Qin 秦 annexed three walled cities of Zhao 趙. (265-III)
Qin 秦 captured Shaoqu 少曲 and Gaoping 高平 of Hann 韓.

264 BCE – Bai Qi of Qin 秦 白起 took Jingcheng in Hann 韓 涇城, near Fenshui River 汾水.

263BCE – Qin 秦 captured Nanyang 南陽, south of Taihengshan in Hann 韓 太行山. (264-I)

262 BCE – Qin 秦 captured Yewang 野王 of Hann 韓, severing the passage between Shangdang 上黨 and Hann capital of Xinzheng 新鄭. The magistrate of Shangdang surrendered to Zhao 趙. (262-II)

261 BCE – Qin *Zuoshuzhang* 秦左庶長 Wang He 王齕 laid a siege against Shangdang. Lian Po 廉頗 defended against the Qin invaders at Changping 長平. (260-I)

Qin 秦 occupied Goushi 緱氏 and Lun 綸 of Hann.
Chu occupied Xuzhou 徐州 of Lu 魯.

260 BCE – Zhao 趙 replaced Lian Po 廉頗 with Zhao Kuo 趙括; Bai Qi the Qin General 秦 白起 gave Zhao a resounding defeat at Changping 長平, over 400,000 surrendered soldiers were buried alive. (260-I)

259 BCE – Wang He of Qin 秦 王齕 made a raid against Wuan of Zhao 趙 武安; while Sima Geng 司馬梗 attacked Taiyuan of Zhao 趙 太原. (259-I)
Wang Ling of Qin 秦 王陵 laid siege against the capital of Zhao – Handan 趙 邯鄲. (259-V)

258 BCE – Wang He of Qin 秦 王齕 replaced Wang Ling 王陵 to lay siege to Handan 趙 邯鄲. (258-I)
The Chancellor of Qin Fan Sui 秦 范睢 appointed Wang Ji 王稽 as the Magistrate of Hedong 河東守, and Zheng Anping 鄭安平 as General.

257 BCE – Lord Xinling of Wei 魏 信陵君 Wei Wuji 魏無忌 and Lord Chunxinjun of Chu 楚春申君 led forces to go to Zhao's 趙 rescue. Qin General Zheng Anping 秦將 鄭安平 surrendered to Zhao; the Qin army met a resounding defeat at Hedong 河東 – East of the River. (257-II)

256 BCE – Chu 楚 annihilated Lu 魯; the Sovereign of Lu was relocated to Ju 莒. (255-V and 249-V)
Qin 秦 annihilated Xizhou 西周, the Sovereign of Xizhou was relocated to Danhu 𢡆狐.
Zhou Nanwang 周赧王 died. (256-II)
Qin 秦 occupied Hann's Yangcheng 韓 陽城 and Fushu 負黍. (256-I)

255 BCE – The Prefecture of Hedong Wang Ji 王稽 committed a transgression against the state and was executed. (255-I)
The Chancellor of Qin Fan Ju 秦 范睢 died.

254 BCE – Qin 秦 made a counter-offensive against Wei 魏 at *Hedong* 河東, it proceeded to occupy Wu 吳. (254-I)
Wei 魏 attacked an isolated Qin territory to the east, Taojun Prefecture 秦 陶郡; it went on to annihilate Wey 衛. (N.B. It was not the total annihilation of Wey. Wey met its final demise in 209 BCE.)

253 BCE – Chu 楚 moved its capital to Juyang 巨陽 as a temporary measure. (253-II)

251 BCE – Yan Generals under Li Fu and Qing Qin 燕將 栗腹 慶秦 led six hundred thousand men to make an attack against Zhao 趙; Lian Po 廉頗 and Yue Cheng 樂乘 gave the invaders a decisive defeat, the Zhao army made a counteroffensive and had the Yan capital surrounded. (251-II)

250 BCE – Zhao 趙 returned to besiege the Yan 燕 capital.

249 BCE – Zhao 趙 returned to besiege the Yan 燕 capital.

Qin 秦 appointed Lu Buwei 吕不韋 as Chancellor. (249-I)

Qin annihilated Dongzhou 東周 (249-II); it followed up by attacking Hann 韓 annexed Chenggao 成皋 and Ronyang 榮陽; then it proceeded to establish the Sanchuanjun 三川郡 Prefecture. (249-II)

247 BCE – Qin 秦 occupied Gaodu 高都 and Bo 波 of Wei 魏. (247-II)

Qin 秦 made a raid against Yuci 榆次, Xincheng 新城, Langmeng 狼孟 of Zhao 趙, altogether 37 cities fell. (248-II)

Sir Xinlingjun of Wei 魏 信陵君 rallied the forces of five States to made a raid against Qin 秦; General Meng Ao 蒙驁 was defeated beyond the River *Hewei* 河外. (247-II)

246 BCE – Qin 秦 had total control of Shangdang 上黨, Hann 韓 territory.

General Meng Ao 蒙驁 quelled the unrest at Jinyang 晉陽, the Prefecture of Taiyuan 太原 was established. (246-I)

245 BCE – Zhao General Lian Po 趙將 廉頗 took Fanyang of Wei 魏 繁陽. (245-II)

Qin 秦 retook Juan of Wei 魏 卷. (245-I)

244 BCE – Meng Ao 蒙驁 took 13 Hann 韓 walled-cities. (*ZZTJ* said it was 12 cities, 244-II)

Qin 秦 took Chang 暘 and Yougui 有詭 of Wei 魏. (243-I)

243 BCE – Zhao 趙 sent its General Li Mu 李牧 to lay a siege against Yan's Wusui 燕 武遂 and Fangcheng 方城. (244-III)

242 BCE – Yan 燕 sent its General Ju Xin 劇辛 to go against Zhao 趙, Pang Xuan 龐煖 made a counter-offensive, Ju Xin was killed. (242-II)

Qin General Meng Ao 秦將 蒙驁 captured Hann 韓 cities of Suanzao 酸棗, Yan 燕, Xu 虛 and Taoren 桃人, altogether twenty or more walled cities were taken. The Dongjun 東郡 Prefecture was established. (242-I)

241 BCE – Chu 楚 moved its capital to Shouchun 壽春. (241-I)

Qin 秦 captured Chaoge 朝歌 that belonged to Wei 魏. (241-II)

Qin repatriated the Sovereign of Wey Jue 衛角 to Yewang 野王; it was made a vassal of Qin. (241-II)

General Pang Xuan of Zhao 趙將 龐煖 led the armed forces of five States – Chu 楚, Wei 魏, Yan 燕 and Hann 韓 against Qin 秦; the army penetrated as far as Zui 蕞. (According to *ZZTJ*, it was the Chu, Zhao, Wei, Hann and Wey armies under Huang Xie 黄歇. 241-I)

240 BCE – Qin 秦 took Long 龍, Gu 孤 and Qingdu 慶都 of Zhao 趙.

Qin captured Ji of Wei 魏 汲. (240-I)

239 BCE – Qin 秦 sent Lord Changan, Cheng Jiao 長安君 成蟜 (Cheng Qiao 盛橋) to lay siege against Shangdang of Zhao 趙 上黨. Cheng Jiao surrendered to Zhao at Tunliu 屯留; Zhao enfeoffed him at Rao 饒.

238 BCE – Qin 秦 sent Yang Duanhe 楊端和 to lay siege to Shouyuan 首垣, Pu 蒲 and Yanshi 衍氏 of Wei 魏. (238-V)

Marquis of Changxin Lao Ai 長信侯 嫪毐 rebelled against the state; the King of Qin quelled the internal unrest. (238-VI)

237 BCE – Qin 秦 relieved of all the duties of Lu Buwei 吕不韋 as the Chancellor. (237-I)

236 BCE – Zhao General Pang Xuan 趙將 龐煖 attacked Yan 燕 and took Li 狸 and Yangcheng 陽城. Qin 秦 Generals Wang Jian 王翦, Huan Yi 桓齮 and Yang Duanhe 楊端和 made assaults against Zhao, and took Yuyu 閼與, Laoyang 橑陽, Ye 鄴, Anyang 安陽, altogether nine walled cities were taken. (236-I)

235 BCE – Qin 秦 rallied warriors from four prefectures to help Wei 魏 to go against Chu 楚. (235-III)

234 BCE – Qin 秦 General Huan Yi 桓齮 attacked Pingyang 平陽 and Wucheng 武城 of Zhao 趙; Zhao General Hu Zhe 扈輒 was killed. (234-I)

233 BCE – Qin General Huan Yi 秦將 桓齮 continued with his attack against Zhao 趙 at Chili 赤麗 and Yian 宜安; at Fei 肥 Li Mu 李牧 gave the invaders a resounding defeat; Huan Yi fled the field and ran for his life. (234-I and 233-I)

Hann sent its emissary Hann Fei 韓非 to Qin 秦; trying to make a case that Qin should take on Zhao 趙 first; shortly after Hann Fei was forced to take his own life. (233-I)

232 BCE – Qin 秦 made a major expedition against Zhao 趙, one army unit attacked at Ye 鄴; another marched from Taiyuan 太原 to Fanwu 番吾. The defending General Li Mu 李牧 fought off the invaders. (232-I)

231 BCE – Teng 騰 the Deputy Magistrate of Nanyang of Hann 韓 南陽 surrendered to Qin 秦, Qin made him a Minister at court. (According to *ZZTJ* it was Sheng 勝.)

230 BCE – Qin 秦 sent Teng 騰 to raid against Hann 韓; the King of Hann An 韓安 was captured. Hann was annihilated and converted into a Prefecture, Yingchuanjun 潁川郡. (230-I)

229 BCE – Qin General Wang Jian 秦將 王翦 led the armed forces from Shangdang 上黨 to march against Jingjing 井陘. Yang Duanhe 楊端和 led the armies from Between the Rivers *Hejian* 河間 to march against Handan 邯鄲 (229-I); they were supported by the nomadic Jianglei 羌瘣 forces.

Zhao Qian 趙遷 replaced Li Mu 李牧 with Zhao Cong 趙葱 and Yan Ju 顏聚. (229-I)

228 BCE – Qin 秦 annihilated the Zhao 趙 forces, the King of Zhao Qian 趙遷 was captured at Dongyang 東陽. (228-I)

Prince Jia of Zhao Jia 趙嘉 made a run for his life and found refuge at Dai 代; he proclaimed as the King of Dai 代王. (228-III)

227 BCE – Qin 秦 generals Wang Jian 秦將 王翦 and Xin Sheng 辛勝 attacked Yan 燕 and Dai 代, at the west bank of Yishui River 易水 they defeated the combined forces of Yan and Dai. (228-III) The Prince of Yan Dan 燕丹 sent Jing Ke 荊軻 to assassinate the King of Qin, but the attempt failed. (227-I)

226 BCE – Qin 秦 took the capital of Yan Ji 燕 薊; the King of Yan moved his capital to Liaodong 遼東. (226-I)

Qin General Wang Ben 秦將 王賁 attacked Chu 楚, over ten walled cities were taken. (226-II)

Xinzheng 新鄭 rebelled against Qin 秦; King An of Hann 韓安王 died.

225 BCE – Qin General Wang Ben 秦將 王賁 laid siege to the capital of Wei Daliang 魏 大梁; the banks of Huanghe 黄河 and Dagou 大溝 were breached, flooding the city. Daliang fell, the King Jia 假 surrendered, Wei 魏 was annihilated. (225-I)

Qin 秦 generals Li Xin 李信 and Meng Wu 蒙武 made assaults against Chu 楚; Li Xin failed and returned. (225-II)

224 BCE – Qin 秦 generals Wang Jian 王翦 and Meng Wu 蒙武 defeated the Chu 楚 forces; Chu General Xiang Yan 項燕 committed suicide. (224-I)

Qin 秦 set up Shanggujun 上谷郡 and Guangyangjun 廣陽郡 prefectures.

223 BCE – Qin 秦 armies entered into the capital of Chu of Shouchun 楚 壽春; the King of Chu Fu Chu 負初 was captured; Chu was annihilated. (223-I); Qin established the Chu Prefecture. (223-I)

222 BCE – Qin 秦 quelled the areas that were formerly under Chu in Jiangnan 楚 江南, and established Kuaijijun 會稽郡 Prefecture. (222-III)

Qin General Wang Ben 秦將 王賁 made attacks against Liaodong 遼東, the King of Yan Xiwang 燕喜王 was captured; Yan was annihilated (222-I); he then followed with an invasion of Dai, the King of Dai Jia 代王假 was captured; Zhao 趙 was annihilated. (222-II)

221 BCE – Wang Ben 秦將 王賁 attacked Qi 齊 from the southern part of Yan 燕; the King of Qi Jian 齊王 建 was captured, Qi was annihilated. (221-I)

Qin 秦 finally conquered and vanquished all the territories in Zhongyuan 中原 and achieved grand unification. It was the commencement of the Qin dynasty. Ying Zheng gave himself a new title Huangdi 皇帝. His command was known as *zhi* 制 and his decrees known as *zhao* 詔; he addressed himself as *zhen* 朕. The Emperor abrogated posthumous titles shifa 謚法. He decreed that the dynasty was founded on the virtue of water *shuide* 水德, the colour chosen for the court was 'black'; and six was the auspicious number of the state. He then decreed to divide his kingdom into 36 prefectures, where a magistrate, a militia commander and a superintendent were installed. The weapons were all confiscated to be forged into 12 bronze statues. He decreed to standardize writing scripts; measures, weights, and carriage ruts were to have the same width throughout the kingdom. He relocated 120,000 households to Xiangyang, the capital. (221-II and 221-III)

219 BCE - The Qin Emperor made expeditionary tours to the east of his kingdom, he erected stone steles to manifest his exploits. Xu Fu 徐福, the occultist, led several thousand boys and girls to sail across the sea in search of the immortals. (219-I)

218 BCE – The Emperor took on his second expedition to the east; as Bolangsha beach 博浪沙, an attempt was made on his life. (218-I)

216 BCE - The Emperor decreed to all the civilians to buy farming lands. (216-I)

215 BCE – The Emperor commanded Meng Tian 蒙恬 to lead 300,000 troops to attack Xiongnu. (215-III)

214-BCE - The Qin army recovered 44 counties south of the River, *Henan*. Meng Tian constructed new sections of the Long-Walls. The Long-Walls commenced from Liaodong 遼東 in the east to Lintao 臨洮 in the west, stretching for over 10,000 *li*. The Emperor conscripted convicts; useless sons-in-law married into wealthy families and merchants as soldiers to attack Nanyue 南越 and Luliangdi (south of Qinling 秦嶺南) 陸梁地; and established Nanhaijun 南海郡, Guilinjun 桂林郡 and Xiangjun 象郡 prefectures. (214-I and 214-II)

213 BCE – Li Si submitted a memorial to burn all the scholarly and literati books. The Emperor decreed to ban all the books apart from the *Qinji* 秦紀. People who learned and discussed *shi* 詩, *shu* 書 and books of the 'Hundred Schools' would be executed in the marketplace. (213-II)

212 BCE – The Emperor conscripted 700,000 men to construct the Afanggong palace 阿房宮 and his mausoleum at Lishan Mound 驪山. He commanded to erect a giant stone block at the Eastern Sea as the Eastern Gate of Qin. Masters Hou and Lu 侯生, 盧生 taunted the Emperor, greatly inflamed by their remarks, he ordered to bury 460 literati and occultists alive. (212-I and 212-II)

211 BCE – Someone at Dongjun Prefecture carved, "When the Emperor dies, the land would be divided" on a piece of meteorite stone. The Emperor executed all the civilians living in the area. (211-I)

210 BCE – The Emperor made his 4th and last expedition to the east, accompanies by the chancellor Li Si 李斯, Ying Huhai 嬴胡亥. Zhao Gao 趙高 conspired with Ying Huhai and Li Si not to dispatch obituary; they then forged a decree to the Crown Prince Ying Fusu and General Meng Tian to commit suicide. When the hearse arrived at Xianyang, Ying Huhai succeeded to the throne. During the 9th month, the Emperor was interred at Lishan 驪山. (210-I)

Appendix 2a

36 Prefectures of Qin

Neishibu 内史部 – capital.

Sanchuanjun 三川郡 - Luoyangxian Henan 河南 洛陽縣. Founded by Qin, King Zhuangxiang 秦莊襄王 9th year, former Hann territories.

Hedongjun 河東郡 - Xiaxian Shanxi 山西 夏縣. Established by Qin, King Zhuangxiang 秦莊襄王, 21st year, former Wei capital.

Nanyangjun 南陽郡 - Nanyangxian Henan 河南 南陽縣. Established by Qin, King Zhuangxiang 秦莊襄王, 35th year, Chu territory.

Nanjun 南郡 - Jianglingxian Hubei 湖北 江陵縣. Established by Qin, King Zhuangxiang 秦莊襄王, 29th year, former Chu capital.

Jiujiangjun 九江郡 - Shouxian Anhui 安徽 壽縣. Established by Qin, King of Qin, Zheng 秦王 政, 24th year, Chu territory.

Zhangjun 鄣郡 - Changxingxian Zhejiang 浙江長興縣.

Kuaijijun 會稽郡 - Wuxian Jiangsu 江蘇 吳縣. Established by Qin, Chu territory, annexed by King of Qin, Zheng 秦王 政 25th year.

Yingchuanjun 潁川郡 - Yuxian Henan 河南 禹縣. Established by Qin, King of Qin, Zheng 秦王 政, 17th year, Hann capital.

Dangjun 碭郡 - Dangshanxian Jiangsu 江蘇 碭山縣. Established by Qin, Wei territory, annexed by Qin King of Qin, Zheng 秦王 政, 22nd year.

Sishuijun 泗水郡 - Peixian Jiangsu 江蘇 沛縣. Established by Qin, King of Qin, Zheng 秦王 政, 24th year, Chu territories.

Xuejun 薛郡 - Tengxian Shandong 山東 滕縣. Established by Qin, King of Qin, Zheng 秦王 政, 24th year, Chu territory.

Dongjun 東郡 - Poyangxian Hebei 河北 濮陽縣. Established by Qin, King of Qin, Zheng 秦王 政, 5th year, Wei territory.

Langyajun 琅琊郡 - Zhuchengxian Shandong 山東 諸城縣. Established by Qin, King of Qin, Zheng 秦王 政, 26th year, Qi territory.

Qijun 齊郡 - Linzixian Shandong 山東 臨淄縣. Established by Qin, King of Qin, Zheng 秦王 政, 26th year, Qi territory.

Shanggujun 上谷郡 - Huailaixian Hebei 河北 懷來縣. Established by Yan, Yan territory, annexed by King of Qin, Zheng 秦王 政, 21st year.

Yuyangjun 漁陽郡 - Miyunxian Hebei 河北 密雲縣. Established by Yan, Yan territory, annexed by King of Qin, Zheng 秦王 政, 21st year.

Youbeipingjun 右北平郡 - Pingquanxian 河北 平泉縣. Established by Yan, Yan territory, annexed by King of Qin, Zheng 秦王 政, 25th year.

Liaoxijun 遼西郡 - Lulongxian Hebei 河北 盧龍縣. Established by Yan, Yan territory, annexed by King of Qin, Zheng 秦王 政, 25th year.

Liaodongjun 遼東郡 - Liaoyangxian Liaoning 遼寧 遼陽縣. Established by Yan, Yan territory, annexed by King of Qin, Zheng 秦王 政, 25th year.

Daijun 代郡 - Weixian Hebei 河北 蔚縣. Established by Zhao, former Dai territory, later taken over by Zhao, annexed by King of Qin, Zheng 25th year.

Julujun 鉅鹿郡 - Pingxiangxian Hebei 河北 平鄉縣. Established by Qin, Zhao territory, annexed by King of Qin Zheng 23rd year.

Handanjun 邯鄲郡 - Handanxian Hebei 河北 邯鄲縣. Established by Qin, Zhao capital, annexed by King of Qin Zheng 19th year.

Shangdangjun 上黨郡 - Changzixian Shanxi 山西 長子縣. Established by Hann, later surrendered to Zhao, annexed by King Zhuangxiang of Qin 3rd year.

Taiyuanjun 太原郡 - Taiyuanxian Shanxi 山西 太原縣. Established by Qin, former capital of Zhao, King Zhuangxiang of Qin 3rd year.

Yunzhongjun 雲中郡 - Tuoketuoxian Neimeng 內蒙 托克托縣. Established by Zhao, Zhao territory, Annexed by King of Qin, Zheng 秦王 政, 13th year.

Jiuyuanjun 九原郡 - Baotoushi Neimeng 內蒙 包頭市. Established by Qin, Zhao territory.

Yanmenjun 雁門郡 - Youyuxian Shanxi 山西 右玉縣. Established by Zhao, Zhao territory, annexed by King of Qin Zheng 19th year.

Shangjun 上郡 - Suidexian Shaanxi 陝西 綏德縣. Established by Wei, Wei territory, annexed by Huiwang of Qin 10th year.

Longxijun 隴西郡 - Lintaoxian Gansu 甘肅 臨洮縣. Established by Qin, original enfeoffed land.

Beidijun 北地郡 - Ningxian Gansu 甘肅 寧縣. Established by King Zhaoxiang of Qin, former Rong territory.

Hanzhongjun 漢中郡 - Nanzhengxian Shaanxi 陝西 南鄭縣. Established by Chu, annexed by Qin during King Hui of Qin 秦惠王 latter 13th year.

Bajun 巴郡 - Chongqingshi 重慶市. Established by Qin, former Shu Kingdom, annexed by Qin King Hui 秦惠王 of Qin 後元 latter 14th year.

Shujun 蜀郡 - Chengdushi 成都市. Established by Chu, former Shu territory, annexed by Qin during King Hui 秦惠王 of Qin 後元 latter 14th year.

Qianzhongjun 黔中郡 - Yuanlingxian Hunan 湖南 沅陵縣. Established by Chu, Chu territory, annexed by King Zhaoxiang of Qin 30th year.

Changshajun 長沙郡 - Changshaxian Hunan 湖南 長沙縣. Established by Qin, Chu territory, annexed by King of Qin Zheng 25th year.

Appendix 2b - Titles and Enfeoffment [1]

Listings –
1. Imperial Household
2. Enfeoffment of Titles
3. Chancellor
4. Central Administration
5. Qin Enfeoffment
6. *Sanjin* 三晉, Qi 齊 and Yan 燕 Enfeoffment
7. The Enfeoffment System at Chu 楚
8. Official Titles and Institution Terms

1. Imperial Household

The sovereign was the head of state; he was the highest ruler of a kingdom or a state. Before the Warring States - *Zhanguo* 戰國 epoch, at the times of Xia 夏, Shang 商 and Zhou 周 the king was known as *hou* 后 or *wang* 王. *Wang* held a supreme position, and it was believed that his engagement was a mandate from Heaven, hence he was also known as the Son of Heaven - *tianzi* 天子 or *tianwang* 天王 and he addressed himself as *yuyiren* - 予一人.[2] After *Chunqiu* saw the great demise of the power of *Zhou* kings, some of the hegemons began to address themselves as *wang*, some of them even called themselves *huang* 皇 or *di* 帝. The meaning of *di* before the time of *Zhanguo* was *shangshen* the Deity Above 上神 and the word - *huang* was used to address the sovereign. The legends of the *sanhuang* 三皇 and *wudi* 五帝 were probably idealized by the literati during the time of the Warring States or later as we find no compelling evidence from older records or archaeological evidence that the terms were used before this period. When the First Emperor of Qin 秦始皇帝 finally quelled the six states, he decided that a title of *wang* was simply far too modest for his mighty exploit. Hence, he addressed himself as *huangdi*; this was a term for the kings and sovereigns of China for the next twenty-one centuries, i.e. until the final demise of Qing 清 (from 221 BCE to CE 1911). The Emperor called himself as *zhen* 朕. His subject addressed him as *bixia* 陛下 - equivalent to Your Majesty. A chronicler addressed him as *shang* 上 – the lord above - equivalent to His Majesty (the only exceptions is Wang Mang 王莽 in the *Hanshu* 漢書 and the *Hou Hanshu* 後漢書; he is simply addressed as Mang 莽. The edict or decrees issued by an emperor was known as *zhao* 昭 or *chi* 敕 - imperial order or decree; later it was also known as *yuzhi* 諭旨 or *shengzhi* 聖旨.

The Heir Apparent was known as *huangtaizi* 皇太子, at the time of the Warring States *Zhanguo,* it was known simply as *taizi* 太子 and at times *gongzi* 公子.

The spouse of the emperor was *huanghou* 皇后 - Empress.

The emperor's mother was addressed as *taihou* 皇太后 - Empress Dowager.

---

1 The author wishes to emphasize that the interpretations of the terms is a subject by itself and the various renderings are generalizations, besides the usages of the titles and terms changed with time.

2 *Shu* 書 Tanggao – 湯誥, 王曰, '嗟! 爾萬方有衆, 明聽于一人誥.'

A princess was known as *gongzhu* 公主.

2. Enfeoffment of Titles

Enfeoffment at the time of the Warring States was principally divided into five categories or grades; *gong* 公 - duke or grand duke; *hou* 侯 – marquis; *bo* 伯 - count, *zi* 子 - viscount; *nan* 男 – baron, although *zi* and *nan* were rarely used. The title of *jun* 君 was also used to address someone below the status of the sovereign. When the Warring State fiefdoms began to elevate their status as kingdoms, the enfeoffment system was kept, the title of *jun* somehow remained, it could also be translated as a lord or duke; however, to avoid confusion, the author has translated it as 'lord' or 'sir' at times. At the time of Han 漢 the *gong, hou, bo, zi, nan* titles resumed, only women from the royal families were addressed as *jun* 君. *Jun* was also used to refer to a gentry. *Jue* 爵 – *jue* was a feudal title or rank bestowed by the head-of-state or the king. See footnotes on the five grades of feudal ranking 五等爵.[3]

Gong 公, roughly translated as duke.

Hou 侯, roughly translated as marquis.

Bo 伯, roughly translated as viscount.

Zi 子, roughly translated as count.

Nan 男, roughly translated as baron.

The seven Warring States, through a series of reform and modifications, had gradually transformed their administrative function by appointing *shi* 仕 - scholars or educated men as government officials, as local prefecture magistrates. They were measures to consolidate political power in the central courts and the introduction of which principally displaced the conventional power-base held by the enfeoffed nobles. Enfeoffment of fief lords was still in use to a limited degree, the extent of enfeoffment of fief land varied considerably. Some of the lords were simply

3 The translations of the titles into English are very rough equivalents.

The thorny issue on the five grades of feudal ranking 五等爵 in ancient China has long been an unresolved and disputed subject. Li Feng 李峰 made studies of the bronze scripts materials 金文 from the time of Western Zhou 西周 (1046-771 BCE) and Eastern Zhou 東周 (770-476 BCE) and used the information to make comparisons with other scriptural materials. He maintains the usage of the titles of *gong* 公, *hou* 侯, *bo* 伯, *zi* 子 and *nan* 男 was already in place at the time of Western Zhou. They were applied in various fief states at the time. However, the social order and status of these states varied considerably; the titles conferred did not adhere to strict conformity or consistent sequence in terms of ranking. He, hence, concludes that the ranking system was not methodical and organized. The politicians of the Spring and Autumn epoch probably created and introduced the differentiation of status and ranking. The introduction of which led to the creation of the hegemons during the time - they were used as specifications of rankings and to harmonize the relationships between the various states. It was probably also used as measures for making tributes to the hegemons. The system was further merged with the allocation of land and other etiquettes to become a complicated and idealized system. The system was well regarded by literati of the Warring States and was promoted as an idealized paradigm.

Li Feng 李峰 on 'The Origin of the Five Grades of Dukedom 論五等爵稱的起源', in Li Zongkun 李宗焜 ed; the *Guwenzi yu gudaishi* 古文字與古代史, Third Volume 第三輯, Zhongyang yanjiuyuan lishi yuyan yanjiusuo, 中央研究院歷史語言研究所, Taiwan, 2012. p. 159.

enfeoffed with the right to tax certain counties; in other instances, the lords might be bestowed with limited ownership of land or fiefs. The enfeoffed fief lord had to preside at the bestowed territories and ruled in compliance with prescribed mandates by the state. At times, the sovereign of a state might send a chancellor or magistrate to aid the fief state. In most instances, the lords were enfeoffed after satisfying their assigned duties (Shang Yang see 340-II and Lord Chunshen 黄歇 see 263-II were some of the exceptions.) The enfeoffed fief lord was allowed to construct his own walled cities, palaces and a number of guards and soldiers. Similar to the prefectures, the military power of the fief state was centralized in the state, only the central government, the king of the state had the power to mobilize an army.

3. Chancellor

At the time of *Xia* and *Shang*, the chancellor was a *wu* 巫 or *wushi* 巫史 a shaman in charge of divination for the court. It was called a *gongqing* 公卿 at the times of *Zhou* 周 and Spring and Autumn epoch or simply as *qing* 卿 at the time of the Warring States.

The term *zaixiang* 宰相 – chancellor suggests that he was in charge of sacrifice for the state, as the word *zai* - means to slaughter later to mean preside over. However, *zaixiang* was only one of the many terms given to the chancellor of a state, he was also called *xiang* 相, *chengxiang* (Han) 丞相 (Han), *xiangguo* 相國, *lingyin* 令尹 (Chu 楚). At the time of Qin, there were two chancellors, *zuo* 左 - Left and *you chengxiang* 右丞相 - Right Chancellor.

4. Central Administration

Departmentalized administration probably commenced during the time of *Zhou* 周. There were six major departments: *situ* 司徒 Minister of Education and Cultural Affairs, *sima* 司馬 - Minister of War, *sikong* 司空 - Minister of Public Works, *sikou* 司寇 - Minister of Justice, *dahangren* 大行人 - Minister of Vassal Affairs and *zongbo* 宗伯 - Minister of Shrine and Clan.

5. Qin Enfeoffment

The enfeoffment in Qin was basically introduced by Shang Yang; [4] the reward of enfeoffment was based on the number of enemies a soldier killed; hence, the Qin soldier had to decapitate the heads of enemies to return to the army camp as proof. The twenty rankings are listed as below:

1. *Gongshi* 公士 – was the first grade of enfeoffment, a ranking of nobility called *jue* 爵. Shang Yang's reform stipulated when a Qin soldier decapitated the head of an officer rank

---

4 The 20 grades of noble enfeoffment 秦爵二十等 was introduced by Shang Yang 商鞅 when he made reforms to Qin, the ranks of nobles were changed to reflect military achievements, and not based on social status or parentage. Nobles who were not meritorious during battles and wars were debarred from being listed in genealogical archives and were disallowed to own noble ranking titles. (See 359-I and 338-I). Yang Kuan 楊寬, The *Hanshu* 漢書 'Baiguanbiao 百官表'. *Zhanguoshi* 戰國史, pp. 253-259. The *Shangjunshu* 商君書, Jingnei Volume 19 境内 第 19.

of its enemy (甲士); he would be rewarded with a rank of *gongshi*, with one *qing* 頃 of land, a homestead and one retainer. The rank of *gongshi* earned an annual emolument of 50 *dan* 石 of millet.[5]

II. *Shangzao* 上造 – the *shangzao* was one grade higher than the *gongshi*. The holder of this rank had to continue to serve in the army. The annual emolument was 100 *dan* of millet.

III. *Zanniao* 簪裊 – the *zanniao* one grade higher than *shangzao*. The holder of this rank had to continue to serve in the army. During active duty, in the army camp, the holder was entitled to one *dou* 斗 of fine rice, half a *sheng* 升 of fermented sauce *jiang* 醬, a tray of vegetable 菜羹, half of *dan* of dry hay *gancao* 干草 (for sleeping on).[6] The annual emolument was 150 *dan* of millet.

IV. *Bugeng* 不更 – the *bugeng* was a ranking of nobility. After attaining this title, the holder was relieved from serving active duties. The annual emolument was 200 *dan* of millet.

V. *Dafu* 大夫 – *dafu* was an administrative ranking noble.[7] It was a ranking below the ministers, see footnotes. The annual emolument was 250 *dan* of millet.

VI. *Guandafu* 官大夫 - *guandafu* was an administrative ranking noble, the 6th rank. The annual emolument was 300 *dan* of millet.

VII. *Gongdafu* 公大夫 – the *gongdafu* was one grade senior to *guandafu*. It was also known as Seventh-grade Minister, *qidafu* 七大夫. At the time of Qin, a *gongdafu* did not have to observe the *kowtow* etiquettes when he met the local county prefects, merely performing greetings with clasped hands. The annual emolument was 350 *dan* of millet.

VIII. *Gongcheng* 公乘 - the *gongdafu* was one grade more senior to *gonddafu*. The rank holder was allowed to use a state carriage, hence the term *gongcheng*. At the time of Qin, all enfeoffment higher than the 7th grade were considered senior ranking nobles. The annual emolument was 400 *dan* of millet.

IX. *Wudafu* 五大夫 – holder of this rank was entitled to tax revenues from a county *shiyi* 食邑 as emolument. The holder earned an annual emolument of 450 *dan* of millet.

X. *Zuoshuzhang* 左庶長 – *zuoshuzhang* was the 10th grade of noble ranking.[8] The holder earned an annual emolument of 500 *dan* of millet.

---

5 1 *dan* 石 = 30.75 kg.
If a soldier cut off the heads of two enemies, and if his parents were bonded servants they would be released immediately, and had his wife been a contract slave, she would resume the status as an ordinary civilian.
When a soldier killed five officer-ranked enemies, he would be bestowed with five-household members as his retainers. On winning a battle, junior officers were raised by one grade and the senior officers by three grades.

6 Recent excavated bamboo slips indicate that the meals taken by different ranking officers and soldiers varied in accordance to their ranking.

7 During the Zhou and Warring States times, the ranking administrators were divided into minister *qing* 卿, officer *dafu* 大夫 and junior officer *shi* 士.

8 Before the reformation by Shang Yang 商鞅, there were four grades of *shuzhang* 庶長: *dashuzhang* 大庶長, *youshuzhang* 右庶長, *zuoshuzhang* 左庶長 and *sijushuzhang* 駟車庶長. The four grades of *shuzhang* were both ranking nobles as well as administrative duty officers. *Dashuzhang* was the

XI. *Youshuzhang* 右庶長 - The holder earned an annual emolument of 550 *dan* of millet.

XII. *Zuogeng* 左更 - The holder earned an annual emolument of 600 *dan* of millet.

XIII. *Zhonggeng* 中更 - The holder earned an annual emolument of 650 *dan* of millet.

XIV. *Yougeng* 右更- The holder earned an annual emolument of 700 *dan* of millet.

XV. *Shaoshangzao* 少上造 - The holder earned an annual emolument of 750 *dan* of millet.

XVI. *Shangdazao* 大上造 - The holder earned an annual emolument of 800 *dan* of millet.

XVII. *Siju shuzhang* 駟車庶長 - The holder earned an annual emolument of 850 *dan* of millet.

XVIII. *Dashuzhang* 大庶長 - *dashuzhang* was the 18th grade of noble ranking. This rank was only junior to *guanenihou* and *chehou.*[9] The holder earned an annual emolument of 900 *dan* of millet.

XIX. *Guanneihou* 關内侯 – The title was awarded to military commanders who were meritorious. The holder of the title was not bestowed with a fief estate. However, he was entitled to the tax revenues from a number of counties and rental incomes from lease of land. The holder earned an annual emolument of 950 *dan* of millet.

XX. *Chehou* 彻侯 – *chehou* was the highest ranking of the enfeoffed nobles. The holder earned an annual emolument of 1000 *dan* of millet.

Chehou 彻侯 was also known as *liehou* 列侯, below the rank of *chehou* there was another rank of *lunhou* 倫侯. The stone stele erected by Qin Shi Huang during his 28th year, Langyatai keshi 琊琊台刻石 lists the names of enfeoffed lords and ministers in accordance to their rankings. They were the *liehou* 列侯 (*chehou*), followed by the *lunhou*, the *qing* 卿 and lastly *wudafu* 五大夫.

6. San-Jin 三晉, Qi 齊 and Yan 燕 enfeoffment

The enfeoffment of San-Jin (Zhao, Wei and Hann), Qi and Yan were principally divided into two major grades, that of *qing* 卿 and *dafu* 大夫.

a. *Qing* was divided into Senior Minister *shangqing* 上卿 and Junior Minister *yaqing* 亞卿. For example, Lin Xiangru 藺相如 and Yu Qing 虞卿 were both appointed as *shangqing* (*SJ* 史記 Lin Xiangru liezhuan 藺相如 列傳) and (*SJ* 史記 Yuqing liezhuan 虞卿列傳).[10] Mengzi 孟子 was at one time a *qing* at Qi 齊 (*Mengzi*, Gongsun Chou volume 1 孟子公孫丑上篇, Gaozi, Volume 2, 告子下篇). Yue Yi 樂毅 was at one time the

attendant of the king, and the position was equivalent to chancellor of the state. *Youshuzhang* were retinues of members of the royal family while *zuoshuzhang* were retinues of non-royal family nobles. The *sijushuzhang* attended to royal family affairs. With the exception of *zuoshuzhang*, royal family members held the other three positions.

9 This position was already in use during the time of Duke Xian of Qin 秦憲公 (r. 716-704 BCE) (*SJ* 史記 has mistaken his name as Duke Ning of Qin 秦寧公.)

10 Yang Kuan 楊寬, *Zhanguoshi* 戰國史 p. 252.

yaqing of Yan (*Shiji* 史記, Yue Yi liezhuan 樂毅列傳). Jing Ke 荊軻 was also honoured as *shangqing* at Yan (*Zhanguoce* 戰國策, Yance 3 燕策 3).[11]

b. The *dafu* rank was divided into Head Officer, *changdafu* 長大夫; Senior Officer *shangdafu* 上大夫; and Middle-grade Officer *zhongdafu* 中大夫. When Wu Qi 吳起 was serving at Wei 魏 as the Magistrate of Xihe 西河守, he rewarded his meritorious followers with the title of *changdafu* (*Lushi chunqiu* 呂氏春秋 Shenxiaopian 慎小篇) alternative he used the title of State Officer *guodafu* 國大夫 (*Hannfeizi* 韓非子, Neichushuo Volume 1 内儲說上篇). Xu Jia 須賈 (270-II and 266-II) was at one stage the *zhongdafu* of Wei (*SJ* 史記, Fan Ju liezhuan 范雎列傳). Lin Xiangru was also served as a *shangdafu* (*SJ* 史記, Lin Xiangru liezhuan 藺相如 列傳). Chun Yukun 淳于髡, Tian Pian 田駢, Jiezi 接子, Shen Dao 慎到, and Huai Yuan 環淵 were listed as *shangdafu* in Qi at one stage or the other.[12] (*SJ* 史記, Mengzi Xunqing liezhuan 孟子荀卿列傳). Besides these officers and ministers, Wei and Zhao also had a grading called *wudafu* 五大夫, which was equivalent to the 9th grade of Qin's enfeoffment. (*ZGC* 戰國策, Weice 4 魏策, Zhaoce 3 趙策; *Lushi chunqiu* 呂氏春秋, Wuyipian 無義篇).

Besides the above, Zhao had another set of enfeoffments. In 262 BCE when Qin attacked Yewang 野王 of Hann 韓, Hann had intended to present Shangdang Prefecture to Qin to sue for peace, when Feng Ting 馮亭, the Magistrate of Shangdang presented the seventeen counties in Shangdang to Zhao. (See 262-II) Zhao sent Zhao Sheng 趙勝 to relate to Feng Ting, 'The King of Zhao instructs Sheng to relate to you. The magistrate will hence be enfeoffed with 10,000 households; the county prefects are enfeoffed with 1,000 households. The title of marquis is hereditary. All the officers and civilians in the prefecture will be advanced by three grades in their entitlements - 益爵三級. To ensure there will be peace among the officers and civilians, they are hence bestowed with six units of gold.' (*SJ* 史記, Zhaoshijia 趙世家).

7. The Enfeoffment System at Chu 楚

During the time of the Warring States, the rankings of enfeoffment in Chu and Qin 秦 were unique. The highest-ranking enfeoffment in Chu was known as *zhigui* 執珪.[13] According to *Lushi chunqiu*, when Chu issued a warrant against Wu Yuan 伍員, [14] the government placed a bounty, '... whosoever could capture Wu Yuan; he would be enfeoffed with the title of *zhigui*, an emolument of 100 *dan* (of millet), and one thousand *yi* 鎰 (each 20 or 24 *liang* 两) of gold.'

---

11 These appointments are mentioned in *ZZTJ*.

12 None of these names appeared in *ZZTJ*.

13 Gui 珪 (圭) was a tubular-shaped piece of carved jade, the top, signifying Heaven, is rounded whereas the bottom is square, signifying earth. The tradition could be traced all the way back to the days of King Yu. In the *Book of Documents*, Yugong 書 禹貢, 'Yu bestowed *gui*, 禹錫 (賜) 圭 (珪).' The nobles enfeoffed had to hold onto their jade piece when they made homage to the king at court hence the term *zhigui* 執珪.

14 Wu Yuan 伍員 was a notorious bandit who was associated with Liu Zhi 柳跖. Liu Zhi see footnotes 255-II.

(*Lushi chunqiu* 呂氏春秋, Yibaopian 異寶篇.) Zhao Yang 昭陽 had at one stage held an official title of *shangzhuguo* and enfeoffed as *shangjiegui*, '官為上柱國, 爵為上執珪.' (*ZGC* 戰國策, 'Qice 齊策' 2). Jing Cui 景翠 was also, '爵為執珪, 官為柱國'[15] (*ZGC* 戰國策, 'Dongzhouce 東周策'). During the battle of Hanzhong 漢中 (312-1), 'Over 70 marquises of Tong - *tonghou* 通侯 and *zhigui* nobles died.' (*ZGC* 戰國策 'Chuce 楚策 1'). Zhuang Xin 莊辛 was enfeoffed as Lord Yangling 陽陵君,[16] and he held a title of *zhigui* (*ZGC* 戰國策, 'Chuce 楚策 4'). Besides the above, Chu also had the official title of *wudafu* 五大夫 (*ZGC* 戰國策, 'Chuce 楚策 1') and *sanlu dafu* 三閭大夫 (*Chuci* 楚辭, 'Yufu 漁夫').

8. Official Titles and Institutional Terms

The list of titles translated as following is based on Cambridge History of China, Crisis in *Han* China, *Bo Yang's Zizhi tongjian* and the author's interpretation.[17] The title system in used by the *Han* court was principally based on *Qin* tradition, which in turn was based on earlier traditions developed during the latter *Zhou* Dynasty. The author wishes to stress that the translations of the titles are by no means perfect, and many of them are subjected to debate.

Bichen 嬖臣 – minion. (This is not a title).

Bijiang 裨將 - Assistant Commander.

Boshi 博士 - Erudite Academician.

bowenshi 博聞師 - Senior Consultant.

Canjun 參軍 – *canjun* was the Military Consultant of the Chancellor.

Changshi 長史 – Personal Aid or Secretary of a Chancellor, Li Si 李斯 was a *changshi* at one stage.

Cheng 丞 – Secretary.

Chengxiang 丞相 or *xiang* – the term was introduced by Duke Wu of Qin 秦武王 (r. 310-307 BCE) before this it was known as *xiangguo* 相國. It was used in *SJ* 史記, Lian Po, Lin Xiangru liezhuan 廉頗藺相如列傳, '且庸人尚羞之, 況于將相乎.'

Cishi 刺史 - originally was the title of an Inspection Officer, it was also known as *taishou* 太守 at times.

Dafu 大夫 – the term changed with time. In general, it meant the ministers at court; it was also a ranking title in Qin's enfeoffment. See Qin enfeoffment.

Daliangzao 大良造 - Army Commander, 16th grade of the Qin enfeoffment.

Dajiangjun 大將軍 – Grand Commander or Command-in-chief, it was the highest military rank at the time of Warring States and Han.

Duwei 都尉 – Military Commander, later as district superintendent.

Guowei 國尉 - Army Commander.

Jiangjun 將軍 – General.

15 Jing Cui 景翠 was a Chu officer, also known as Jing Cuo 景痤.

16 Zhuang Xin 莊辛 was a minister of King Qingxiang of Chu 楚頃襄王 (r. 298-264 BCE).

17 Reference – Yap, J., The *Wars with the Xiongnu*.

Keqing 客卿 – Guest Consultant.

Langzhong 郎中 – Attendant or Guard of the imperial household or palace.

Lingyin 令尹 - was an administrative and military commander rank at Chu 楚, the position was equivalent to chancellor in other states.

Lixu 里胥 – Hamlet Constable.

Lizheng 里正 – Hamlet Officer.

Neishi 内史 - Capital Mayor.

Pin 聘 – when a fief lord sent a minister to visit another state, the emissary was called *pin*.

Qing 卿 – Ministers. At the time of Zhou, Spring and Autumn and Warring States, the king and his fief lords all had *qing* – ministers as their aides. They were divided into three grades; the most senior was Senior *shangqing* 上卿, followed by Middle *zhongqing* 中卿 and Junior *xiaqing* 下卿. *Shiji* 史記, 'Lian Po, Lin Xiangru liezhuan 廉頗藺相如列傳', '廉頗為趙將... 拜 (相如) 為上卿.'

Sangong 三公 - Three Excellences. Those were the most senior positions at court; they were positioned between the king and the chancellor, at times one of the three excellences would assume the responsibility as chancellor. During Western Zhou 西周 the Three Excellences were the *taishi* 太師 (Grand Master or Teacher), *taifu* 太傅 (Grand Tutor), and *taibao* 太保 (Grand Marshal); at the time of Han Dynasty, they were known as *dasima* 大司馬 (Grand Marshal), *dasitu* 大司徒 (Chancellor), and *dasikong* 大司空 (Imperial Counsellor). Note - the titles changed over time during the Han dynasty. Yang K., 楊寬, *Xizhoushi* 西周史, Shanghai Renmin chubanshe 上海人民出版社, 2003 China, p. 316-317.

Shangdafu 上大夫 – was a minister at court. It was junior to *qing* 卿. *SJ* 史記, Lian Po, Lin Xiangru liezhuan 廉頗藺相如列傳, '... appointed Xiangru as *shangdafu,* 拜相如為上大夫.' At that stage, Lin Xiangru 藺相如 held a lower position to Lian Po 廉頗, who was a *shangqing* 上卿.

Shangjiang 上將 – Senior Commander.

Shangjiangjun 上將軍 - Supreme Commander.

Shiyuan 市掾 – City Functionary.

Sima 司馬 – at the time of *Zhou* and the Warring states, *sima* was in charge of military affairs.

Taishou 太守 – Prefecture Magistrate *taishou* was also known as *junshou* 郡守 or *cisshi* 刺史. It was the highest ranking officer in a prefecture.

Taizi 太子 - Prince, in most instance it was used to mean Heir Apparent.

Taifu 太傅 - Grand tutor. See *taishi*; it was also the title of the tutor of the Crown Prince.

Taishi 太師 - Grand Master or Teacher. The Three Excellences was made up of *taishi* 太師, *taifu* 太傅 and *taibao* 太保. (The term *taibao* was rarely used at the time of the Warring States.) *Taifu* also meant the teacher of the Crown Prince. Three Excellences see *sangong* 三公.

Tashi 太史 – Grand Historian. At the time of Western Zhou and Chunqiu 春秋, it was a senior position at court, and the holder was responsible for supervising scribes and memorials, issuance of commands to fief lords and to chronicle state events. The holder was also responsible for keeping the court calendar and sacrificial offerings as well as being the Liberian of the court archive.

Wudafu 五大夫 - see Qin enfeoffment.

Xiang 相 – see Chancellor.

Xiangguo 相國 – see Chancellor.

Xianling 縣令 – County Prefect. (Some have translated the title as County Magistrate. However, it tends to be confused with Prefecture Magistrate.)

Xianzhang 縣長 - County Head.

Xiao 校 – was a contingent of eight hundred military men. It also meant Major.

Yin 尹 – see *lingyin* 令尹, it was divided into *zuoyin* 左 and *youyin* 右, they were assistants to *lingyin* 令尹.

Yongshi 用事 - Executive Commander.

Youshiguo 右司過 - Right Inspector.

Yueguan 樂官 - Music Officer.

Yuren 虞人- Minister of Agriculture.

Yushi 御史 – *yushi* was originally the Historian Officers, later it became the Imperial Counsellor. The counsellor was responsible for making impeachments as well as to keep the ministers and officers in check.

Zhong chengxiang 中丞相 – Palace Chancellor, usually a eunuch, hence he was allowed to serve in the inner palace.

Zhongshuzi 中庶子 - Junior Assistant.

Zongzhang 縱長 - Supreme Commander.

Zuoshiguo 左司過 - Left Inspector

Zuoshuzhang 左庶長 - Left Colonel. See Qin enfeoffment.

Zuotu 左徒 – was a ministerial grade unique to Chu 楚. The holder was responsible for reprimanding the king, and to recommending capable people to serve the state. *SJ* 史記, Qu Yuan liezhuan 屈原列傳, 'Qu Yuan, whose polite name was Ping, had a family name as the State of Chu. He was the *zuotu* of King Huai of Chu. 屈原者, 名平, 楚之同姓也, 為楚懷王左徒.' (Qu Yuan 屈原 did not appear in *ZZTJ*).

Appendix 2c

Posthumous titles 謚號 [1]

The Duke of Zhou and the Grand Duke Wang were meritorious at the Battle of Muye; they helped to lay down the foundation of the kingdom. When they were finally laid to rest, they were honoured with posthumous titles. [2] To confer a posthumous title - *shi* 謚 is a eulogy of a person's lifetime comportment. *Hao* 號 is a manifestation of the merits and deeds of the individual when he was alive. The quantity of horses, chariots and the trappings bestowed (for interment) is an expression of the ranking position he held. Hence, a person who had high moral character is conferred with a prestigious and panegyrical title, while one deficient with moral character is conferred with an inferior designation. The moral comportment of an individual stems from oneself; other people confer his posthumous title.

Shen - 一人無名曰神 - a person who could not be conferred a title by others is known as *shen* 神 – deity or god.

Sheng - 稱善口簡曰聖 [3] - A sovereign who was astute in selecting worthy individuals to serve under him is called a *sheng* - sage.

Sheng - 敬賓厚禮曰聖 - A sovereign who honoured his guests with humility and generous gifts is a *sheng* - sagacious.

Di - 德象天地曰帝 - A sovereign with virtues as lofty as heaven and deep as earth is called a *di* – sovereign.

Huang - 静民則法曰皇 - A sovereign who instituted laws and statutes to allow his subjects to live in peace is called a *huang* - emperor.

Wang - 仁義所在曰王 - a sovereign who had the attributes of benevolence and righteousness is called a *wang* - king.

Jun - 賞慶刑威曰君 [4] - a sovereign who was fair, equitable with award and punishment is known as *jun* – lord.

---

1 Posthumous titles 謚號. Chinese historical texts rarely make references of the characters and comportments of the sovereign lords; however, one could glean at their personal characters by making a study of their posthumous titles. As there are many different interpretations to a title, it is generally difficult to append a specific posthumous title to a sovereign lord mentioned; hence, I have left out the translations of posthumous titles in the footnotes.

2 *Yizhoushu* 逸周書, 卷 6, 'Yifajie 謚法解' 第 54, *Yizhoushu huijiao jizhu* 逸周書彙校集注, Huang Huaixin 黄懷信, Zhang Maorong 張懋鎔 Tian Xudong 田旭東 et al ed., Shanghai guji chubanshe 上海古籍出版社, China, 2008. pp. 618-707. (N.B. This edition is in slight variance with another edition, which commences by stating, 'The date was the third month of the year, during the first quarter moon...')

"維周公旦, 太公望開嗣王業, 攻于牧野之中; 終葬, 乃制謚叙法. 謚者, 行之迹也, 號者, 功之表也; 車服,位之章也, 是以大行受大名, 細行受小名, 行出於己, 名生於人."

Muye 牧野之役 – The Battle of Muye (1045 BCE) was the battle when King Wu of Zhou 周武王 defeated the forces of King Zhou of Shang 商紂王.

3 口 – the word is missing. According to *Zhengyi zhengyi* 逸周書正義, the word is *fu* 賦. The interpretation of the statement is based on 賦簡, *Yizhoushu huijiao jizhu* 逸周書彙校集注, p. 628.

4 Those two entries are not from the version of the *Yizhoushu* 逸周書 the author used.

Jun - 從之成群曰君 - a sovereign lord supported and upheld by many is known as a *jun* – lord.[5]

Gong - 立制及衆曰公 - a sovereign lord or head-of-state who established institutions for others is called a *gong* - duke.

Hou - 執應八方曰侯 - a head-of-state whose behaviour was acclaimed by all people from all over is a *hou* – marquis.

Posthumous title in *Zizhi tongjian*

The author has selected a number of the posthumous titles listed in the *Yizhoushu* 逸周書; these titles were commonly used during the times of the Zhou dynasty and the Warring States era. The posthumous titles are listed as they appear in the *Yizhoushu*.

Jian - 壹德不解曰蕑 (簡) - A sovereign lord who relentlessly promoted moral behaviour is given a posthumous title of *jian*.

Jian - 平易不疵曰蕑 - A sovereign lord who was modest, unassuming, and averted criticizing others is given a posthumous title of *jian*.

Wen - 經緯天地曰文 - A sovereign lord who complied with the harmony of Heaven and Earth is given a posthumous title of *wen*.

Wen - 道德博厚曰文 - A sovereign lord whose moral character was extensive and profound is given a posthumous title of *wen*.

Wen - 學勤好問曰文 - A sovereign lord who was committed to learning and knowledge is given a posthumous title of *wen*.

Wen - 慈惠愛民曰文 - A sovereign lord who was benevolent in providing and caring to his subjects is given a posthumous title of *wen*.

Wen - 愍民惠禮曰文 - A sovereign lord who had compassion and was sympathetic towards his subjects, and behaved with proper comportment with his people is given a posthumous title of *wen*.

Wen - 錫民爵位曰文 - A sovereign lord who bestowed enfeoffment to his subjects has a posthumous title of *wen*.

Wu - 剛彊直理曰武 - A sovereign lord who was firm, unyielding, and truthful is given a posthumous title of *wu*.

Wu - 威彊叡德曰武 - A sovereign lord who was assertive, powerful, and astute with morality is given a posthumous title of *wu*.

Wu - 克定禍亂曰武 - A sovereign lord who overcame plagues and calamities, quelled disturbances is given a posthumous title of *wu*.

Wu - 刑民克服曰武 - A sovereign who ruled equitably by law is given a posthumous title of *wu*.

Wu - 大志多窮曰武 - A sovereign who was ambitious and militarist inclined is given a posthumous title of *wu*.

---

5 Lord, posthumous titles were usually applied to sovereign lords and heads of state. Some ordinary civilians were also given posthumous titles.

Gong - 敬事供上曰恭 - A sovereign lord who was dedicated to his task and honoured his seniors is given a posthumous title of *gong*.[6]

Gong - 尊賢貴義曰恭 - A sovereign lord who respected the sagacious and esteemed the righteous is given a posthumous title of *gong*.

Gong - 尊賢敬讓曰恭 - A sovereign lord who respected the sagacious, and behaved with proper etiquettes is given a posthumous title of *gong*.

Gong - 既過能改曰恭 - A sovereign lord who made amends to his failings is given a posthumous title of *gong*.

Gong - 執事堅固曰恭 - A sovereign lord who worked with resolve and determination is given a posthumous title of *gong*.

Gong - 安民長娣曰恭 - A sovereign lord who cared for his subjects, seniors, and siblings is given a posthumous title of *gong*.

Gong - 執禮敬賓曰恭 - A sovereign lord who greeted his guests with proper comportment and etiquette is given a posthumous title of *gong*.

Gong - 芘親之門曰恭 [7] - A sovereign lord who defended and protected his parents and kin is given a posthumous title of *gong*.

Gong - 尊長讓善曰恭 - A sovereign lord who respected seniors and complied with comity is given a posthumous title of *gong*.

Gong - 淵源流通曰恭 - A sovereign lord who promoted his lineage is given a posthumous title of *gong*.

Ding - 大慮静民曰定 - A sovereign lord who was thoughtful and astute, and brought peace and tranquility to his people is given a posthumous title of *ding*.

Ding - 安民法古曰定 - A sovereign lord who brought appeasement to his people by emulating the past is given a posthumous title of *ding*.

Ding - 純行不傷曰定 - A sovereign lord who had an impeccable behaviour and comportment is given a posthumous title of *ding*.

Xian - 博聞多能曰獻 - A sovereign lord who was knowledgeable and accomplished is given a posthumous title of *xian*.

Xian - 聰明叡哲曰獻 - A sovereign lord was who intelligent, visionary and sagacious is given a posthumous title of *xian*.

Yi - 温柔聖善曰懿 – A sovereign lord who was affable, reasonable, and sensible is given a posthumous title of *yi*.

Xiao - 五宗安之曰孝 - A sovereign lord who brought peace and harmony to his five-generation progenitors and offspring is given a posthumous title of *xiao*.

Xiao - 協時肇享曰孝 - A sovereign lord who initiated fulfilment to his subjects is given a posthumous title of *xiao*.

Xiao - 秉德不回曰孝 - A sovereign lord who upheld virtues and moral principles laid down by his progenitors is given a posthumous title of *xiao*.

---

6 Senior, the word shang 上 can be taken to mean senior – his overlord, or elders.

7 The word *pi* 芘 was synonymous with the word *bi* 庇.

Xiao (*kao*) - 大慮行節曰孝 (考) [8] - A sovereign lord who performed sacrificial offerings with reverence is given a posthumous title of *kao*.

Kang - 温年好樂曰康 - A sovereign lord who brought peace and bliss to his people is given a posthumous title of *kang*.

Kang - 安樂撫民曰康 - A sovereign lord who appeased his subjects by reigning with peace is given a posthumous title of *kang*.

Kang - 令民安樂曰康 - A sovereign lord who allowed his subject to settle in peace and happiness is given a posthumous title of *kang*.

Cheng - 安民立政曰成 - A sovereign lord who instituted wise directives and rules is given a posthumous title of *cheng*.

Mu - 布德執義曰穆 - A sovereign lord who upheld morality and righteousness is given a posthumous title of *mu*.

Mu - 中情見貌曰穆 - A sovereign lord who spontaneously expressed his personal sentiments is given a posthumous title of *mu*.

Qing - 敏以敬順曰傾 - A sovereign lord who was adroit and cautious, caring and compromising with his subjects is given a posthumous title of *qing*.

Zhao - 昭德有勞曰昭 - A sovereign lord who remunerated the virtuous and honourable people is given a posthumous title of *zhao*.

Zhao - 聖文周達曰昭 - A sovereign lord who acquired a virtuous reputation is given a posthumous title of *zhao*.

Ping - 治而清省曰平 - A sovereign lord who attended to his state affairs without failings is given a posthumous title of *ping*.

Ping - 執事有制曰平 - A sovereign lord who attended to his state affairs according to established institution is given a posthumous title of *ping*.

Ping - 布綱治紀曰平 - A sovereign lord who instituted principled regulations for his state is given a posthumous title of *ping*.

Jing - 由義而濟曰景 - A sovereign lord who employed righteous governance to attain his ends is given a posthumous title of *jing*.

Jing - 布義行綱曰景 - A sovereign lord who promoted righteousness with decisiveness is given a posthumous title of *jing*.

Wei - 彊以剛果曰威 - A sovereign lord who was bold, stalwart with resolve is given a posthumous title of *wei*.

Wei - 猛以彊果曰威 - A sovereign lord who was formidable, acted with decisiveness is given a posthumous title of *wei*.

Wei - 彊毅信正曰威 - A sovereign lord who acted with decisiveness and promoted integrity is given a posthumous title of *wei*.

Huan - 辟土服遠曰桓 - A sovereign lord who expanded and augmented his territories, while heartening his subjects is given a posthumous title of *huan*.

Hui - 柔質受課曰惠 - A sovereign lord who was mellow and broadminded; and was affectionate to his people is given a posthumous title of *hui*.

---

[8] It is assumed that the word *xiao* here is a mis-script of *kao* 考.

Zhuang - 兵甲亟作曰莊 – A sovereign lord who was bellicose is given a posthumous title of *zhuang*.

Zhuang - 叡通克服曰莊 - A sovereign lord who was farsighted with astuteness and made his people embrace his rule is given a posthumous title of *zhuang*.

Zhuang - 死於原野曰莊 - A sovereign lord who died in the wilderness is given a posthumous title of *zhuang*.

Zhuang - 屢征囗伐曰莊 - A sovereign lord who repeatedly made expeditions is given a posthumous title of *zhuang*.

Zhuang - 武而不遂曰莊 - A sovereign lord who failed in his military exploit is given a posthumous title of *zhuang*.

Huai - 幸義揚善曰懷 - A sovereign lord who chose righteousness and promoted kindness is given a posthumous title of *huai*.

Huai - 慈義短折曰懷 - A sovereign lord who was caring, virtuous, and died young is given a posthumous title of *huai*.

Jing - 夙夜警戒曰敬 - A sovereign lord who constantly (day and night) made admonition of himself is given a posthumous title of *jing*.

Jing - 夙夜恭事曰敬 - A sovereign lord who was absorbed in his task day and night with diligence is given a posthumous title of *jing*.

Jing - 象方益平曰敬 [9] - A sovereign lord who employed lawful governance to promote peace is given a posthumous title of *jing*.

Jing - 合善法典曰敬 - A sovereign lord acts according to established regulations is given a posthumous title of *jing*.

Lie - 有功安民曰烈 - A sovereign lord who was meritorious with military exploit to bring peace to his people is given a posthumous title of *lie*.

Lie - 秉德遵業曰烈 - A sovereign lord who applied virtuous rule, acted in compliance with the directives laid down by his progenitors is given a posthumous title of *lie*.

Su - 剛德克就曰肅 - A sovereign lord who was unyielding, acted with morality for accomplishment is given a posthumous title of *su*.

Su - 執心決斷曰肅 - A sovereign lord who was decisive and self-assured is given a posthumous title of *su*.

Ling - 死而志成曰靈 - A sovereign lord who attained his aspiration after death is given a posthumous title of *ling*.

Ling - 極知鬼事曰靈 - A sovereign lord who was familiar with ghost and divine matters is given a posthumous title of *ling*.

Ling - 亂而不損曰靈 - A sovereign lord who abused law and regulation with abandonment is given a posthumous title of *ling*.[10]

---

9 According to Pan Zhen 潘振, "The word *xing* 象 has the same meaning of *fa* 法 – law, and *fang* 方 means the path 道." *Yizhoushu huijiao jizhu* 逸周書彙校集注, p. 671.

10 The face value of '亂而不損' appears to contradict with the accepted interpretation of the title. It also means that a sovereign lord should pay due diligence to his state at the time of crisis, but failing to do so. King Wuling 趙武靈王 was given such a title, as he abdicated his throne to his son, Zhao He 趙何.

Ling - 不勤成名曰靈 - A sovereign lord who attained fame without putting in any effort is given a posthumous title of *ling.*

Ling - 死見鬼能曰靈 - A sovereign lord who appeared as apparition after death is given a posthumous title of *ling.*

Shang - 短折不成曰殤 – A sovereign lord with a short lifespan and died before attaining adulthood is given a posthumous title of *shang.*

Shang - 未家短折曰殤 - A sovereign lord with a short lifespan and died before entering into wedlock is given a posthumous title of *shang.*

Dao - 年中早夭曰悼 - A sovereign lord who died during his middle age is given a posthumous title of *Dao.*

Dao - 肆行勞祀曰悼 – A sovereign lord who indulged in excess behaviour and wantonly wasteful in making sacrificial ceremonies is given a posthumous title of *Dao.*

Dao - 恐懼從處曰悼 – a sovereign lord who reigned in apprehension is given a posthumous title of *Dao.*

Min - 在國逢難曰愍 - A sovereign lord who faced foreign aggression during his reign is given a posthumous title of *min.*

Min - 在國連憂曰愍 - A sovereign lord who faced natural calamities during his reign is given a posthumous title of *min.*

Min - 禍亂方作曰愍 - A sovereign lord who faced natural calamities and sedition is given a posthumous title of *min.*

Ai - 蚤孤短折曰哀 - A sovereign lord being forlorn during youth and died young is given a posthumous title of *ai.*

Ai - 恭仁短折曰哀- A sovereign lord who was polite, modest, benevolent, and died young is given a posthumous title of *Ai.*

You - 蚤孤有位曰幽 - A sovereign lord being forlorn during youth and lost his throne is given a posthumous title of *you.*

You - 壅遏不通曰幽 - A sovereign lord who was befuddled is given a posthumous title of *you.*

You - 動祭亂常曰幽 - A sovereign lord who did not comply with the proper etiquettes of the seasons is given a posthumous title of *you.*

Xuan - 聖善周聞曰宣 - A sovereign lord, whose sagaciousness was known by all, is given a posthumous title of *you.*

An - 好和不爭曰安 - A sovereign lord who was congenial and refrained from wrangling is given a posthumous title of *an.*

Sheng - 不生其國曰聲 - A sovereign lord who born in foreign land is given a posthumous title of *sheng.*

Li - 致戮無辜曰厲 - A sovereign lord who wantonly slaughtered the innocents is given a posthumous title of *li.*

Yi - 好更改舊曰易 - A sovereign lord who was fond of making changes is given a posthumous title of *yi.*

Kuang - 貞心大度曰匡 – A sovereign lord who was chaste at heart and broadminded is given a posthumous title of *kuang.*

Xuan - 施而不成曰宣 - A sovereign lord who had intended to bequeath, however failed is given a posthumous title of *xuan*.

Xian - 惠無内德曰献 - A sovereign lord who made bequeath, however lacking innate morality is given a posthumous title of *xian*.

Other Definitions

辟地為襄 – the word *xiang* has an implication of expanding territories.

視遠為恒 – the word *heng* has a meaning of being far-sighted or visionary.

柔克為懿 – *yi* has a meaning of being gentle and moderate while able to accomplish great deeds.

有過為僖 – *xi* has a meaning of a sovereign lord who had erred.

Two posthumous titles not found in *Yizhoushu*.

Xi 釐 - has the same meaning as *xi* 僖.

Rue 繻 - means fine silk fabric.

Appendix 2d

Weights and Measurements

1 *cun* 寸 = 2.31 cm

10 *cun* = 1 *che* 尺

10 *che* = 1 *zhang* 丈

10 *zhang* = 1 *yin* 引

Yue 龠 = 10.5 cc

2 *yue* = 1 *he* 合

10 *he* = 1 *sheng* 升

10 *sheng* = 1 *dou* 斗

10 *dou* 斗 = 1 *tong* 桶 (*hu* 斛)

24 *zhu* 銖 = 1 *liang* 两

16 两 *liang* = 1 *jin* 斤

30 *jin* = 1 *jun* 鈞

4 *Jun* 鈞 = 1 *dan* 石

1 *dan* 石 = 30.75 kg.

1 *qing* 頃 = 100 *mu* 畝= 1000 fen 分 = 10,000 *li* 釐 = 66,666 $^{2}/_{3}$ m^2.

Source - Zhao Yifeng 趙軼峰 Zhao Yi 趙毅 *Zhongguo gudaishi* 中國古代史, 5th edition, Gaodeng jiaoyu chubanshe 高等教育出版社, China, 2005, p.233

Appendix 3 – Yang Kuan's textual research – translated by Joseph P. Yap

Textual Research on the Warring States Historiography Materials [1]

This is a translation of parts of the introductory chapter of Yang Kuan's *History of The Warring States Zhanguoshi.*[2]

Part 1

Unique Attributes of Warring States Historiography

The historical materials on the Warring States that are available for textual research have presented us with daunting difficulties; they are fragmented or incomplete narratives due to different reasons, and they need to be reorganized through thorough investigations. The accessible materials are scattered in various historical texts with unreliable date entries, blended with facts and in many instances, fictitious contents fabricated or composed by latter-day scholars. Different from the chronicles of the Spring and Autumn period when there are more reliable chronological annals, such as the *Commentary of Zuo, Zuozhuan.* [3] Moreover, the Warring States historical materials were at variance with the dynastic historiographies after Qin and Han, when each dynasty had a comprehensive and detailed historical chronicle. There is an even more compelling reason why the historical account of the period was so incomplete and fragmentary; it was in essence due to the burning of books by Qin Shi Huang. The First Emperor decreed to burn all the *Shijing, Shangshu,* and chronicles related to the fief states, [4] "...as they contained disparaging and scornful accounts (of Qin)." ('Sequence of the Six Warring States', in the *SJ*). [5] We know that the *Book of Odes* (the *Shijing*); the *Book of Documents* (the *Shangshu*) compositions, and the texts compiled by the various classic authors at the Spring and Autumn era were already in wide circulation during the Warring States epoch when even the commoners had access to the texts. Civilians and scholars had the texts secretly concealed when the 'burning' decree went into effect.

---

1 Yang Kuan 楊寬, *ZGS* 戰國史, 2003, pp. 10-20.

2 Yang Kuan 楊寬, *The History of Warring States, Zhanguoshi* 戰國史 - Shanghai remin chubanshe 上海人民出版社, 2003, Pages 10-41 and Pages 723-731. (The articles that appeared in the book were probably written during the 1980's. However, the dates could not be verified.) *Zhanguoshi* 戰國史 is abbreviated as *ZGS* 戰國史.
Yang Kuan (1914-2005 CE), was an authority on ancient Chinese history. He was a history professor in numerous Chinese universities and ended his career as the Professor of History in Fudan University 復旦大學; he migrated to the US in 1984 and lived out his life in Miami. He was one of the most influential Warring States scholars during the 20th century. He published over 230 articles and publications during his lifetime. He participated in the compilation of *The Chinese Phase Encyclopedia, The Cihai* 辭海; his works include *The Historical Atlas of China* 中國歷代地圖集; *The History of Western Zhou* 西周史, etc.

3 Annals - *Biannianti* 編年體, The *Commentary of Zuo, Zuozhuan* 左傳.
Chunqiu - Spring and Autumn has three connotations. First it has the meaning of Spring and Autumn epoch, a period between 770-476 BCE. Secondly, the phase *chunqiu* means one year in ancient texts. Thirdly, *Chunqiu* was a text compiled and edited by Confucius and is usually referred to as *the Annals.*

4 The *Book of Odes, Shijing,* 詩經.
The *Book of Documents, Shangshu* 尚書.

5 The *SJ* 史記 卷三, 'Sequence of the Six Warring States, Liuguo nianbiaoxu 六國年表序' relates, "... 燒天下 '詩', '書', '尚書', 諸侯史記尤甚, 為其有所刺譏也..."

Destruction of these texts was not universal; [6] after the reign of Qin, many lost texts resurfaced from civilian collections. On the other hand, the texts about the warring states prepared as official chronicles were typically kept in the state archives, and they met a different fate when the decree was proclaimed. When the Grand Historian Sima Qin was composing his *Taishigong shu,* [7] the other name for *Shiji*, he asserted, "The remnants of writings and events of antiquity are entirely collected in this work by the Grand Historian." [8] Nonetheless, the primary textual sources of the Warring States that appear in *Shiji* were essentially based on the *Records of Qin* - *Qinji* and the texts written by the political strategists. [9] Qin, during the period of the Warring States, was cultural unfledged compared with the most progressive states situated in the heartland of *Zhongyuan* (Central Realm). The historical accounts and chronicles in *Qinji* compiled by the Qin official chroniclers tended to be more rudimentary, in most instances 'they did not include dates of events and the contents tended to be sketchy'. As a result, the sections of the Warring States in the *Shiji* are beset by many inaccuracies and errors, the historical events of the six fiefdoms are particularly inadequate; besides being fragmentary, there are omissions and, in many cases, events are disorderly arranged. Gu Yanwu, (the late Ming scholar) pointed out that the Spring and Autumn Chunqiu and Warring States eras were periods of extreme political turmoil in (Chinese) history, that, "... the texts and chronicles are deficient, and much of the historical materials were lost. Historiographers are often bewildered by the obscured contents." (The *Rizhilu*, under the title of, 'The Cultures and Customs of Late Zhou.') [10]

The compilation of the *Shiji* was predominantly based on the materials available to Sima Qian during his time. Besides the *Qinji*, there were the writings of the political strategists that Sima Qian drew on; as he remarked, "The political realignments and power shifted during the time of the Warring States (chronicled by the Qin historians) were more than adequate ...." (See notes). [11] It is noted that, during Qin and early Han, the practice of political canvassing and tendering of political strategies to the ruling elites continued. The various political doctrines evolved during the Warring States were still being propagated by Kuai Tong (pre and early Han), Zhufu Yan (died 126 BCE), and other political strategists; [12] hence, it appears that Qin did not

---

6 The decree to burn book was issued in 213 BCE, which was only 11 years before the founding of Han.

7 *The Records of the Grand Historian, Taishigong shu*, 太史公書, *SJ* 史記.

8 *SJ* 史記, 卷 100, 'Taishi gong zixu 太史公自自序', "天下遺文古事, 靡不畢集于太史公."

9 The *Records of Qin, Qinji*, 秦記.

Zonghengjia 縱横家 – Political Strategists, South-north Coalition (Vertical) and West-east Alliance (Horizontal).

10 "史文闕軼, 考古者為之茫昧."

Scholars honoured Gu Yanwu 顧炎武 (1613-1682 CE) as Master Tinglin 亭林先生; he was a Chinese philologist and geographer. The quote is from his *Rizhilu* 日知録, Volume 13 卷十三, 'The Cultures and Customs of Late Zhou - Zhoumo fengsu 周末風俗.'

11 This statement needs clarification as it continues " ...然戰國之權變亦頗有可採者, 何必上古, 秦取天下多暴, 然世異變, 成功大.. " – The meaning is, "The political realignments and power shifts during the time of the Warring States 'chronicled by the Qin historians' were more than adequate; one does not have to reiterate other ancient events. Qin quelled All under Heaven with force and made great exploit...." *SJ* 史記, 'Sequence of the Six States 六國年表'.

12 Kuai Tong 蒯通 was a strategist of the King of Qi, Hann Xin 齊王 韓信. (See 209-IV.)

Zhufu Yan 主父偃 (?-126 BCE), was an imperial counsellor at the Han court during the time of Emperor Wu of Han 漢武帝. He studied the school of Long-short and Vertical-horizontal; later he

successfully torch all of the Warring States political-strategy texts. At the commencement of Western Han, the imperial libraries and commoners had copies of those texts. The *Zhanguoce - The Warring States Strategies* compiled by Liu Xiang towards the waning years of Western Han was based on the collections of political strategist texts kept at the imperial library. Six different editions were available to him; named *Guoce, Guoshi, Duanchang, Shiyu, Changshu,* and *Xiushu* (see translations in the footnotes). [13] In 1973, a silk scroll was excavated from a Han tomb at Changsha Mawangdui; [14] researchers named it, the *Book of Warring States Political Strategists, Zhanguo zonghengjia shu* in 27 chapters, [15] it is believed to be one of the editions in circulation among the civilians at the time of Han. Besides the above, chapters from the *Political Strategists of Strengths and Weaknesses* by Kuai Tong and others were also in wide circulation among the civilians. The *Hanshu* 'Kuai Tong Biography' states, "Kuai Tong discussed the political changes and power shifts during the Warring States era, and he writes essays on his thesis; it has eighty-one chapters. He named it *Meaningful Things - Junyong*."[16]

During the turbulent years of the Warring States when the fief states were frantically engaged in perennial wars and battles, each vying for supremacy or survival, the political strategists were perhaps the most admired scholars among the different scholastic schools to earn approval as ministers by the state sovereigns. [17] These men became influential ministers at the more powerful Qin and Qi courts, where their strategies being implemented held sway the political standing of the state they were employed. It was commonplace for a major strategic decision to influence the outcome of the political standing of a state and the intricate interlinking relationship with others. These political strategists, in reality, were the foreign diplomats, canvassers, and tacticians employed by the powerful fief lords for their national political strategies.

---

studied the *Zhouyi* 周易, and the *Annals* (*The Chinese Classics*), 春秋 when he realized that Emperor Wu subscribed to literati studies. N.B. Zhufu Yan came much later.

In fact, the political thoughts also endured in the memories of the surviving scholars. (For example, Li Yiqi 酈食其 (268-204 BCE) was able to recount to Liu Bang 劉邦 the political alliances during the Warring States period. 207-VII.)

13 The title of *The Warring States Strategies, The Zhanguoce* 戰國策 (abbreviated as *ZGC* 戰國策) was appended by Liu Xiu 劉秀 (劉歆 ~50 BCE-23 CE). The texts available in the Han libraries for Liu Xiu's research were the *State Strategies, Guoce* 國策, the *State Matters, Guoshi* 國事, *Strengths and Weaknesses, Duanchang* 短長, *On Matter of Things, Shiyu* 事語, the *Book of Strengths, Changshu* 長書, and the *Xiushu* 修書.

The word *ce* 策 was derived from a term for horsewhip. *Ce* was a whip with a pointed end to thrash the horse to make it race faster; hence, the word has the meaning of steering. (N.B The word *ce* also mean scripting on bamboo slips.)

14 The Changsha Mawangdui Hanmu 長沙馬王堆 漢墓, Hunan Changshashi 長沙市 湖南. It was a group of three Han tombs that belonged to the Chancellor of Changsha, Li Cang 長沙丞相 利蒼, his wife Xin Zhui 辛追, and Li Xi 利狶 (either the son or brother of Li Cang).

15 *The Book of Warring States Strategists,* the *Zhanguo zonghengjia shu* 戰國縱橫家書. Published in 1983.

16 The *Hanshu* 漢書, 'Juan Tong Biography, Juan Tong zhuan 蒯通傳'. The birth and death dates of Kuai Tong 蒯通 (Kuai Che 蒯徹) are obscured, he was a strategist of the King of Qi, Hann Xin, 齊王韓信 and lived about the time of Liu Bang 漢 劉邦 (256-195 BCE), the first emperor of Han. The *Meaningful Things, Junyong,* 雋永. The date of the composition could not be established.

17 Political Strategist *Zonghengjia* 縱橫家 is often described as orator; however, the author believes the modern terms of 'lobbyist' or 'canvasser' are probably quite appropriate. These were wandering canvassers that roamed from state to state with little national fidelity.

Liu Xiang named the text he compiled 'Warring States Strategies', *Zhanguoce* (Liu Xiang – *Editing the Warring States Strategies Index Journal, Jiao Zhangguoce shulu*). [18] The text is a compilation of records of the strategies employed by the roaming canvassers (or lobbying/orators) during the Warring States, and the strategies propounded by them were the so-called 'The Horizontal-Vertical or Long-Short Strategies.'[19] The *SJ* 'Sequence of the Six States' [20] relates, "When the three-family clans partitioned Jin and the Tian clan displaced the Jiang of Qi, it was when the six states came into power. [21] The states entered into an exhaustive and devastating period vying for supremacy through diplomacy and warfare; the Political Strategy School became prevalent." The term Vertical and Horizontal *zong-heng* means the use of political diplomacy in conjunction with

---

18 Liu Xiang 劉向 (77-6 BCE) was the father of Liu Xiu 劉秀, the father and son worked together as a team in the compilation and editing ancient texts to be included in the *Editing the Warring States Strategies Index Journal,* the *Jiao Zhangguoce shulu* 校戰國策書錄.

(Yang Kuan's footnotes) - Wang Guowei 王國維 (1877-1927 CE) in his *The Bamboo Slips Examination and Assessment, the Jiandu jianshukao* 簡牘檢署考 he says, "I suspect the roaming canvassers from the time of Zhou and Qin placed much emphasis on this text, hence naming it, 'writing the text on slips – *ce* 策.' The bundles were either long or short. Hence, it was also named *duan-chang,* 短長. The *Changshu* were particularly long. Hence, it came to be known as *Length or the Long Book, Changshu,* 長書; or *Length or Long Book,* or *the Xiushu* 修書. It is believed that the character *ce* used by Liu Xiang 劉向 bore the meaning of 'strategy', and the book was not named after its original meaning of *ce* (horse whip)." This particular interpretation appears to be supported by some evidence; however, in reality, it is a false premise. In the *State Strategies,* the *Guoce,* 國策 the word *ce* originally meant strategy - *maoce* 謀策; while *duan-chang* also meant the short or long of strategies, hence named *duan-chang.* This particular term *duan-chang* was often used with *zong-heng* 縱橫, generally referred to as the 'School of *Zong-heng duan-chang zhishuo*' '縱衡短長之説' or 'The Practises of Long and Short, Vertical and Horizontal techniques', '*Changduan zongheng zhishu*', '長短縱橫之術.'

Liu Xiang 劉向 in his *Editing the Warring States Strategies Index Journal, Jiao Zhanguoce shulu* 校戰國策書錄 states, "...(these) were the political strategies employed by the roaming canvassers during the time of the Warring States." "戰國時游士輔用國為之策謀."

N.B. Shorter texts were written on slips of two *chi* 尺 and four *cun* 寸 long (~25 cm); while the longer *Jian* 簡 was reserved for classics; i.e. written in longer slips.)

19 The Horizontal-Vertical, Long-Short Strategies - *Zhongheng Changduan zhishu* - 縱橫長短之術.

Hezong lianheng 合縱連橫 – The definition offered by Hann Fei (~281-233 BCE) in *Hannfeizi* 韓非子 is, "*Zong* 縱, to ally the weak states to go against one strong state or allied states. *Heng* 横 – is to serve under a strong state to go against the weaker states."

To explain the *zong-heng* terminology, according to another school of thought – 'It was based on the topology of the Warring States. Qin was situated to the western extremity of China while the other states were situated to the east. Traditionally the explanation of *zong-heng* was thus based on the fact that the direction of South-North was known as *zong*-vertical, whereas the East-West orientation was known as *heng*-horizontal. Qin being situated to the west, and the other six States were to the east. When the six states formed an alliance against Qin, it was defined as South-North alliance hence also known as *he-zong* 合縱. While, when the various states at one stage or other forming an ally with Qin it was thus a – East-West orientation, hence it was defined as *lian-heng* 連横.'

SJ 史記 'Sequence of the Six Warring States 六國年表'.

21 Jiang of Qi 姜齊. The Qi Fiefdom under the Jiang clan was founded by the Grand Duke of Jiang, Taigong 姜太公 (~1156-1017 BCE) who was enfeoffed at Qi, present-day Shandong 山東 at around 1046 BCE.

Actually, it should be seven states; historians often neglected Qin, which conquered the other states.

war to form alliances between different states. The so-called *duan-chang* was a term used to denote the alliance of the weaker states in opposition to the stronger ones, claiming that the strategy one propounded was the longest (most potent or preferred). [22] It was for this reason that the texts archived at the imperial libraries of early Han named the texts the *State Strategy - Guoce, Weak and Strength - Duan-chang*; some were named as *Changshu*, or *Xiushu*, both meaning the *Books of Strength* (potency). [23] Whereas the text named *Juanyong* edited by Zhai Tong, the meaning of which is more obscured; according to *Zhu* by Yan Shigu, "... the word *Juan* means fatty meat and *yong* means strength." [24] When the words are placed together, the title of the text can be interpreted as, 'Meaningful and Strength.'

Justifiably, the Political Strategists placed much emphasis on the consequences of the strategy employed, maintaining, "The act of implementing a strategy is quintessential of all decisions, and it is to be imparted upon the hearer (adherent) for survival or annihilation. (*Zhanguoce* 'Qin Strategy 2.') [25] Alternatively, it is said, "A person, who accepts felicitous advice, has knowledge of insight; while a person, good at making thorough and profound thinking, is capable of seizing an opportunity for survival or annihilation." (Kuai Tong's dialogue in *SJ* 'Marquis Huaiyin Biography') [26] Hence, these strategists maintained that if a sovereign accepted sound advice from others (strategists), he could attain kingship. It was almost a cliché in those days when the strategists said, "If you listen to my advice, providing you with the prescience of vicissitudes, you could be king; and it is entirely up to Your Highness." (*Zhanguo zonghengjia shu* Chapter 24; and *ZGC* 'Qin Strategies 2'). [27] The Political Strategists believed, "A major foreign policy decision makes one king, whereas a minor one brings peace to one's kingdom." (*Hann Feizi* 'Wudu pian') [28] Moreover, "Vertical Coalition will eventually bring hegemony while with *Heng*

---

22 These are only a couple of definitions of *zong-heng*; however, the author believes that none of them is satisfactory. N.B. The Strengths (Long) and Weaknesses (Short) is one of the theories of the explanation of *chang-duan*, propounded by Hann Feizi.

23 The *State Strategies, Guoce*, 國策, *Duan-chang* 短長 or 'Strength and Weakness' 長短.
Changshu 長書 or *Xiushu* 修書.

24 The *Juanyong* 雋永. The word *juan* 雋 means the succulent meat of birds, and is used to describe the subtle and profound meanings of poems. To translate it simply as meaningful lacks the subtlety of what the word is intended to convey.

Yan Shigu 顏師古 (581-645 CE) Tang historian, in his *Annotations, Zhu* 注.

25 The *ZGC* 戰國策 'Qin Strategies, Qince 2 秦策二', relates, "計者事之本也, 聽者存亡之機也."

26 The *SJ* 史記, 'Marquis Huaiyin Biography, Huaiyinhou liezhuan 淮陰侯列傳', Kuai Tong 蒯通 says, "夫聽者事之候也, 計者事之機也."

27 The *Zhanguo zonghengjia shu* Chapter 24, 戰國縱橫家書 第 24 章, relates, "計聽知順逆, 雖王可也."

The contents in the *Zhanguo zonghengjia shu* Chapter 24, and the *ZGC* 戰國策 'Qin Strategy 秦策二' are the same except the word '順', meaning to follow or obey is replaced by the word '覆', meaning to cover.

The statement, "計聽知順逆, 雖王可也," was made by Chen Zhen 陳軫 in 'Qin Strategy 2 秦策二'. Chen Zhen 陳軫, served at Qi 齊, Qin 秦 and Chu 楚, was one of the more outstanding strategists during the time of the Warring States, he was active about the same time as Zhang Yi 張儀. (*ZZTJ* 313-11).

28 The *Hann Feizi*, 韓非子 'The Five Destructive Pests, Wudupian 五蠹篇', "外事, 大可以王, 小可以安."

Alliance one becomes king of the grand unification." (*Hann Feizi* 'Zhongxiao pian'). [29] The so-called *wang* – king, means to unify and to attain a grand unification.

The Vertical and Horizontal political strategists at the time of the Warring States placed much emphasis on strategies, schemes, and power shifts. The texts by these individuals collected and collated extensive historical incidents and experience, not merely limited to their political thoughts, their canvassing orations, and strategies; they also included advise to kings and lords regarding their suggestions to seek help from other states, on political maneuvering, and on forming alliances for winning battles. For instance, in the '*ZGC*, Zhao Strategy 3' there is an extensive passage on King Wuling of Zhao, who made reforms and adopted the nomadic attire of *hufu* and the equestrian skill of shooting arrows from horseback; [30] these were more relevant accounts of military reforms by legalists than political strategies. The other instance is the last chapter of the *Current Edition of ZGC*, (Yao Hong's compilation was based on Su Che's *Gushi*), and it records a lengthy passage on Bai Qi responses to King Zhao of Qin's inquiries. [31] The passage records the reasons why Bai Qi thought he could successful lay siege to the capital of Chu at Yanying, then continued to defeat Hann and Wei allied armies at Yique. [32] He stated, "It all depends on the situations and circumstances, (and by taking advantage of) natural environ, and divine interventions do not predicate the outcome." It was militaristic and strategically oriented. From these inclusions, we realize that the *ZGC* does conserve some essential historical information on the Warring States.

The *ZGC* is an important work of historiography being compiled and composed by the political strategists; the canvassing-roaming orators probably used it as an indispensable text to study and fathom the intricacies of political strategies and intrigues. It is believed that many canvassers employed the established terminologies and incorporated the jargons for writing their memorial submissions. The submitted missives to the fief lords on strategies were also widely copied and emulated. Towards the final years of the Warring States, at the time of Qin and the beginning of Han, some of the political strategists did indeed embellish the incidents of political strategies; they fabricated events of some of the celebrated strategists and generals, incorporating them into their lobbying and oration tools. Some of them went as far as fabricating fictitious events and stories of political strategies. It is an area of concern for historiographers, and the contents should be authenticated and verified with due diligence.

The *Bamboo Annals* as a Tool to Verify the Dates of the Sequence of Six States in the *Shiji*

The 'Sequence of the Six States' in the *SJ* is littered with numerous erroneous entries of the succession sequence and reigning dates of the sovereigns during the Warring States period, particularly the six fief lords to the East. The *Bamboo Annuals* that was discovered in a Wei tomb during the early years of the Western Jin Dynasty (281 CE) in Jixian County was invaluable in

29 From The *Hannfeizi* 韓非子, 'On Fealty and Piety, Hanfeizi zhongxiao pian 忠孝篇', "縱成必霸, 橫成必王."

30 The *ZGC* 戰國策, 'Zhao Strategy 3, Zhaoce 3 趙策 三'.
King Wuling of Zhao 趙武靈王, *hufu* 胡服.

31 Yao Hong 姚宏 (Song 宋?), Current Edition of *Zhanguoce, Jinben Zhanguoce* 今本戰國策.
Su Che 蘇徹 (1039-1112 CE), *Ancient History*, the *Gushi*, 古史.
Qin General 秦將 Bai Qi 白起, King Zhao of Qin 秦昭王.

32 Chu Yanying 楚鄢郢, Hann 韓 and Wei 魏. Yique 伊闕.

filling some of the gaps as well as supplementing the inadequacies in the *SJ*.[33] The text, written on bamboo slips, had an extensive coverage of the historical events during the Xia, Shang, Western Zhou, the Spring and Autumn periods of the Jin State, as well as chronicles of Wei during the Warring States period.[34] The Chronicle ended in the 20th year of King Xiang of Wei (299 BCE).[35] The compilers at the time of Western Jin named it the *Bamboo Annals - Zhushu jinian*. The text was valuable in that it filled in some of the gaps in the *SJ*; furthermore, it was used to correct errors and erroneous entries. Unfortunately, the original text was lost again during the Song Dynasty. The Current Edition of the *Zhushu jinian* is a reconstructed compilation by later historians, and there are numerous mistakes. Scholars since the time of Qing Dynasty have used the *Old Edition of Bamboo Annals* (*Guben Zhushu jinian*), which scholars before the *Song* Dynasty were using as textual references to compile an up-to-date edition; however, it is still, regrettably, not without errors and omissions. More recently, scholars have used the accounts and records in the *Old Edition of Bamboo Annals* to rectify and make amendments to the errors on the Warring States in the *SJ*; outstanding results have been accomplished; notwithstanding all the efforts and remarkable discoveries, the results are far from being satisfactory. An up-to-date historiographic analysis and re-compilation is probably due.

Using the dates chronicled in the *Bamboo Annals* to rectify the errors in *SJ* is a pivotal issue for determining the reigning years of King Xiang of Wei. *SJ* states that King Hui of Wei died during the 36th year of his reign; his son King Xiang of Wei died after 16 years of reign and the grandson King Ai died during his 23rd year. Historians, based on the records in the *Bamboo Annals* noted that King Hui did not die during the 36th year of his reign. He merely changed his

---

33 The *Bamboo Annals, Zhushu jinian* 竹書紀年 (abbreviated as *Bamboo Annals* 竹書紀年) has also come to be known as the *Ji Tomb Annals, Jizhong jinian,* 汲冢紀年. In 281 CE,* a cache of bamboo slips was discovered by an illegal gravedigger *Bu Zhun* 不准 (*Fou Biao* – the ancient pronunciation), at the time of Western Jin 西晉. The text in the form of bamboo slips were interred with the remains of the King Anxi of Wei, 魏安釐王 (another version claims that it was King Xiang of Wei 魏襄王); the text thus escaped the fate of being burned by Qin Shi Huangdi. In the same tomb, other texts, including the *Discourses of the States, Guoyu* 國語; the *Book of Changes Yijing* 易經 and the *Mu Tianzi zhuan,* 穆天子傳 were discovered. The records of the *Bamboo Annals* commenced from the legendary period of Xia Dynasty 夏 (2070-1600 BCE) to King Xiang of Wei 魏襄王 20th year (299 BCE). The Jin court 晉 decreed the court scholars to have the texts deciphered from the tadpole script - *kedouwen* 蝌蚪文 to the chancery script. Unfortunately, the original text was lost during the Song dynasty; only fragmentary copies, quotations and references survived in other texts. Before the closing of the 19th century and the beginning of 20th century, scholars including Zhu Youzeng 朱右曾 (1838 CE *Jinshi* 進士 – a presented scholar in the imperial examination for civil servants) and Wang Guowei 王國維 (1877-1927 CE) undertook the task of restoring the text. It was conducted through collating and compiling the fragmentary copies, the references, and quotations that were available. The contents of the book were revitalized and have since been used extensively for textual research on the early history of China and Warring State. Although there is an edition in circulation that was published during the 14th century, however, many scholars believe it is a fabricated work.

Zhu Yuanqing 朱淵清, *Zaixian di wenming* 再現的文明, China, 2001. Chapter 3, Huadong shifan daxui chuban 華東師範大學出版.

Zhang Yuchun 張玉春, *Zhushu jinian yizhu* 竹書紀年譯注, China 2003. pp 1-3.
(* Another source claims that the discovery of the slips was in 279 CE).

34 Xia 夏, Shang 商, Xizhou 西周, Spring and Autumn 春秋 period of Jin 晉 and chronicles at Wei 魏.

35 King Xiang of Wei 魏襄王.

36th regnal year to his 1st year (when he proclaimed king), [36] and that he reigned for 16 more years. It was argued that if the assumption was correct, then the dates of the reign of King Xiang was changed to the 1st (Post-regnal) year of King Hui and the years of the reign of King Ai was changed to King Xiang; the problems could easily be resolved. Nevertheless, it did not solve the problem. In that, if a comparison of the dates of major events during the reign of Marquis Wu of Wei and King Hui of Wei in *the Bamboo Annals* and *SJ* were made, we find there are discrepancies of one or perhaps two years between them. However, none of the major events recorded fall within the same year. Furthermore, the discrepancies of two years were mostly related to war. While we appreciate war could last for more than one year; major events such as Qin's enfeoffment of Lord Shang (Shang Yang), and the occasion when the Lu, Wey, Song and Zheng fief lords travelled to Wei to pay homage, were unlikely to have taken place over two consecutive years. One particular incident of importance is mentioned in *SJ's* 'Sequence of the Six States' during the 16th year of the Duke Xian of Qin (369 BCE) when an eclipse was observed; according to *SJ*, it was the 2nd year of King Hui of Wei. Whereas, in the *Bamboo Annals* (*Kaiyuan zhanjing* vol. 101 quoting from *Bamboo Annals*), [37] chronicles, ". during the 1st year of King Hui of Wei, the day became dark." The phase of "day became dark" was another expression for an eclipse. [38] A check on astronomical records, there indeed was an annular eclipse on the 11th day of April 369 BCE, according to the Julian calendar. Hence, the record of King Hui of Wei by *SJ* was out by one year. If that was the case, during the 36th year of the king's reign he must have changed his regnal year; his 36th year became his 1st year. [39] Hence, in reality, the king had only ruled for 35 years by then, and he changed his regnal year to 1st year during his 36th year. This is in contrast with the *SJ*, which records that during his 36th year of reign, King Hui of Wei died; resulting from which mistake, the subsequent reigning years for both Marquis Wen of Wei, and Marquis Weiwu deviated by one year. Although the error was merely one year, it caused considerable difficulties in identifying the reigning years of six other fief lords in the east in the *SJ*.

---

36 Regnal year is also known as eponymous dating – or reigning year; i.e. taking the year of the accession of the ruler as year one; known as *jiyuan* 紀元, the year after as two, and so forth. The first modification to the reigning period came during the Warring States when two rulers (one was King Hui of Wei 魏惠王) recommenced the cycle from the 1st year *yuannian* 元年 to *gaiyuan* 改元. (The author translates it as 'post-regnal year' – it means changing the sovereign regnal year to year one again by giving it a new designation. It was supposed to be for luck or auspicious reasons or for observing an auspicious event; history is silent about his intent; it was true for the later emperors). It is also known as *gengyuan* 更元. It became a common practice after Emperor Wen of Han 漢文帝 (r. 180-157 BCE) during the Han dynasty. *ZGS* 戰國史, p. 271.

37 The *Kaiyuan* Divination Book, *Kaiyuan zhanjing*, 開元占經 volume 101.

Kaiyuan zhanjing 開元占經 was composed by the Indian astrologist Qutan Xida (Gautama Siddha) 昙瞿悉達 around 718-726 CE, the book was lost towards the end of Tang 唐, and recovered during the Ming Dynasty 明.

Qutan Xida was born in Changan and attained the position of Historian 太史監 at the Tang court 唐. Bai Shouyi 白壽彝 ed., *Zhongguo tongshi* 中國通史 Vol 6 B, 第 6 卷 下册, 第 48 章, 第 7 節, '中外天文學交流', China, 1991.

38 The day became dark – *zhouhui* 晝晦 – eclipse.

39 The first regnal year of a new ruler commenced one year after the death of the former ruler, as the successor, either the son or brother had to observe 'one year' of mourning. Hence, traditionally the 36th would be the last year while the 37th was to be 1st year. It was where the mistake arose; instead of using the 37th year he used 36th as year 1st, as the marquis did not die during that year, he did not wait for the next year to make it the 1st year of his continuing reign as a king. (The ascension year of a king or fief lord was also known as *gaiyuan* 改元.)

There are also numerous mistakes in the sequencing and reigning years of the Tian clan of Qi sovereigns according to *SJ*. We could use the quotes of *Shiji suoyin* 'House of Tian Biography', *Shiji suoyin* 'House of Wei Biography' and *Shiji suoyin* 'Lord Mengchang Biography' from *Bamboo Annals* to compare with the records in *SJ* to make rectifications. [40] *Zhuangzi* 'Quqie pian' says, [41] "Tian Chengzi (Tian Chang) committed regicide, [42] he assassinated the sovereign of Qi; after twelve successful generations, the Tian family clan usurped the throne." However according to *SJ*, ".... Tian Chang's reign was followed by Xiangzi Pan, Zhuangzi Bai, Duke Tai He, Duke Huan Wu, King Wei Yinqi, King Xuan Pijiang, King Min Di, King Xiang Fazhang and Wang Jian. [43] The Qi (Jiang clan) then met its demise." Only ten Tian generations are mentioned. Comparing the *Bamboo Annals* with *SJ*, we realize that Daozi is missing after the reign of Zhuangzi Bai; and again after the reign of Duke Tai of Qi (Taigong), Houyan is missing. *SJ* mentions Duke Huan of Qi died during his 6th year; whereas *Shiji suoyin* 'House of Tian Biography' says, "King Hui of Liang (Wei) reigned for 13 years; after 18 years of King Huan of Qi before we saw the reign of King Wei." [44] Hence, the 6 years of Duke Huan of Qi in *SJ* was an erroneous entry; as it had mistaken a '6' for '18', (translator's note - as 6 in Chinese has the semblance of 18 in the Chinese script when it is written vertically.) [45] As a result, the *SJ*, having missed out the reign of Tian Houyan of 9 years, then later making another error of missing 12 years it pushed the reign of King Wei of Qi forward by 21 years. As a consequence, the reigns of King Xuan and King Min were all pushed forward by 21 years. Hereafter, the dates of the reign of kings Wei, Xuan and Min of Qi in *SJ* are all erroneous.

---

40 The *Shiji suoyin* 史記 索隱 'Hereditary House of Tian Biography Obscured Passage, 田世家索隱. (Note abbreviated as *Shiji suoyin,* 'House of Tian Biography 田世家.')

Shiji suoyin 史記 索隱 'House of Wei Biography 魏世家'.

Shiji suoyin 史記 索隱 'Lord Mengchang Biography 孟嘗君列傳'.

The *Historical Records Obscured Passage Elucidation, Shiji suoyin,* 史記索隱 was composed by the Tang 唐 historian Sima Zhen 司馬貞 (679-732 CE), the book has referred to numerous lost texts. By the time of *Jin* 晉 (265-420 CE) the *SJ* 史記 had been copied for many generations, different versions varied considerably, it prompted the *Jin* scholar Xu Guang 徐廣 to compose the *Historical Records by Pronunciation and Meaning*, the *Shiji yinyi,* 史記音義. Later, at the time of Sima Zhen the text was even more complicated with additives, changes, and mistakes; to overcome the problem with his research he sourced from over 400 texts to elucidate and illustrate his work. Sima Zhen based some of his datings on the *Bamboo Annals,* which was still in existence.

N.B. The *Shiji suoyin* 史記索隱; The House of Tian Biography obscured passage elucidation. In this translation, we will use the notion of the *Shiji suoyin* 史記索隱, 'House of Tian Biography, 田世家'. Etc.

41 The *Zhuangzi* 莊子, 'Open-chest, Quqie pian 胠篋篇'. (Zhuangzi 莊子 ~ 369-286 BCE).

42 Tian Chengzi 田成子 (Tian Chang 田常) (Approx. 480 BCE).

43 Tian Chang 田常 → Xiangzi Pan 襄子盤 →Zhuangzi Bai 莊子白 →(Daozi 悼子) →Taigong He 太公和 →(Houyan 侯剡) →Duke Huan Wu 桓公 午 →King Wei Yinqi 威王 因齊 →King Xuan Pijiang 宣王 辟彊 (疆) →King Min Di 湣王 地 →King Xiang Fazhang 襄王 法章 →Wang Jian 王建. The Qi Jiang 姜 family clan ended in 391 BCE.

Daozi 悼子 and Houyan 侯剡 are the two omitted by *SJ* 史記.

44 The *Shiji suoyin* 史記 索隱.

The *Shiji suoyin* 史記索隱 'House of Tian Biography, 田世家,' Duke Hui of Liang (Wei) 梁 (魏) 惠公.

The capital of Wei 魏 was Liang 梁; hence, it also came to be known as Liang 梁.

The *Shiji suoyin* 史記 索隱.

45 The bamboo scripts were written vertically; the format is still in use with some of the books published in Taiwan and Hong Kong.

An example is that both *Mengzi* and *ZGC* relate that King Xuan of Qi took advantage of the confusion in Yan to invade the state. [46] It was when King Guai of Yan abdicated his throne to Chancellor Zi Zhi, after that the kingdom fell into complete anarchy; the king of Qi sent General Kuang Zhang to attack Yan, [47] defeating it. *SJ* 'Sequence of the Six States' dates this event during the 1st year of King Nan of Zhou, and as the 10th year of King Min of Qi. Hence, the chronicle of the reigning year of kings Xuan and Min of Qi in *SJ* are erroneous. According to *Shiji suoyin* 'Lord Mengchang Biography' quoting from the *Bamboo Annals*, 'During the latter 15th post-regnal year (*houyuan*) of King Hui of Liang (Wei), King Wei of Qi died.' Hence, King Xuan of Qi's 1st year should be the 2nd year of King Shenjing of Zhou (319 BCE)'. [48] During the reign of King Nan of Zhou 1st year (314 BCE), Qi made an expedition against Yan defeating it; so it was the 6th year of King Xuan of Qi, and these dates correspond with the accounts in the *Mengzi* and *ZGC*.

Removing Fabricated History of Political Strategies

It is accepted that the authors of political strategists placed much emphasis on the values and significances of political strategies and inter-state diplomacies; and in most instances, they attempted to inflate the outcomes or aftermaths of the strategies or schemes introduced. Su Qin and Zhang Yi were two successful political strategists and were greatly admired by the political strategists of the time; [49] their works had long been studied; their orations and letters on strategies were learned and revered as scriptural manuals by their adherents. Under these circumstances, it is believed, that many counterfeit texts were created to meet the needs of the scholars studying political strategy. The scholars fictitiously made the two men as adversaries in two different camps, active at the same time, one being the Horizontal Alliance (East-west) proponent and the other Vertical Coalition (South-north) advocate. However, in reality, Su Qin and Zhang Yi lived in different times. Zhang Yi was the chancellor of King Hui of Qin (r. 337-311 BCE) while Su Qin was the Chancellor of King Min of Qi (r. 300-284 BCE); [50] they were not and could not be in opposition to each other. It was Gongsun Yan (*Hezong*), who was operating in opposition to Zhang Yi (*Lianheng*). [51]

---

46 Mengzi 孟子 (372-289 BCE).

47 *Mengzi*, 孟子; *ZGC* 戰國策.
King of Yan 燕王 Guai 噲 abdicated his throne to Yan Zi Zhi 燕子之.
King Xuan of Qi 齊宣王.
Qi General 齊將 Kuang Zhang 匡章.

48 The *Shiji suoyin* 史記索隱, 'Lord Mengchang Biography,孟嘗君列傳.'
15th post-regnal year (*houyuan*) of King Hui of Liang (Wei), 梁 (魏) 惠王後元 15th year.
King Wei of Qi 齊威王 die during the 15th (post-regnal year) of King Hui of Liang (Wei) 梁 (魏) 惠王後元.
King Xuan of Qi 齊宣王 1st year should be the 2nd year of King Shenjing of Zhou 周慎靚王 (319 BCE).

49 Su Qin 蘇秦, Zhang Yi 張儀.

50 Zhang Yi 張儀 was the Chancellor of King Hui of Qin 秦惠王 (r. 337-311 BCE).
Su Qin was the Chancellor of King Min of Qi 齊湣王 (r. 301-284 BCE).

51 Gongsun Yan 公孫衍 (*hezong* 合縱) (~360-300 BCE).
Zhang Yi 張儀 (*lianheng* 連横).

The *Hanshu* 'Yiwenzhi' has 31 chapters on Su Qin 'Suzi' and ten chapters on Zhang Yi 'Zhangzi';[52] more chapters were devoted to Su Qin than Zhang Yi. In *ZGC*, there are more chapters on Su Qin; the reason as most scholars assume is that there were more fabricated chapters written on Su Qin.[53] Sima Qian was aware of the situation. It prompted him to remark in *SJ* 'Su Qin Biography' "People often comment that many of the events relating to Su Qin are fictitious. Moreover, fabricated events are often attributed to Su Qin...," nevertheless; Sima Qian did not go further, he made no attempt to identify the fictitious elements from the factual. Hence, in his 'Su Qin Biography' he had inadvertently incorporated a copious amount of fictitious materials, and went on to claim that, "Su Qin was the frontrunner of the *Hezong* alliance, and he was the chancellor of the six kingdoms." Adding, "As a result of his political maneuvering, the state of Qin did not have the courage to steal a peep of the East beyond the Hanguguan Pass for 15 years."[54] The Song scholar, Huang Zhen points out in his *Huangshi rechao,*[55] "... it was an inflated claim by the roaming-canvassing orators; it was entirely fictitious."[56]

The French Sinologist Henri Maspero (1882-1945 CE) published an article in Asian Studies; he maintains that 'Su Qin Biography' was a romanticized fictitious novel."[57] However, in reality, we know Su Qin was a real individual, and it was a case of anachronistic entries into historical account; the political strategists probably fabricated some of his deeds late in the Warring States era. Naturally, the strategies employed by Su Qin were greatly amplified and exaggerated. It is well established and accepted that accounts of Su Qin and Zhang Yi in the current version of *ZGC* is probably a combination of facts and fabrications. The 1973 discovery of the silk-script at the Han Tomb in *Mawangduai,*[58] named the *Book of Warring States Strategists*, is invaluable in verifying and authenticating some of the accounts of Su Qin,[59] who spread rumours of discord on behalf

---

52 *Hanshu* 漢書 'Classification of Books and Literature, Yiwenzhi 藝文志.' (abbreviated as *Hanshu* 漢書 'Yiwenzhi 藝文志'.

31 chapters on Su Qin, Suzi, 蘇子.

10 chapters on Zhang Yi, Zhangzi, 張子.

Su Qin 蘇秦 has been considered by scholars as the more 'righteous' entity* as against Zhang Yi, who served under the despotic Qin. *Throughout Chinese history, Qin has been conceived as the despotic hegemon, which through deceit and military might overwhelmed the weaker states. Su Qin operating to aid the underlings probably earned more respect from these scholars than Zhang Yi who was aiding the most predominant state.

54 Meaning, 'Qin dared not venture east of the Pass'.

55 Song 宋 Huang Zhen 黄震 (1213-1281 CE). The *Huangshi Copy, Huangshi rechao*, 黄氏日鈔.

56 The statement means, 'Qin dared not venture east of the Pass' in 'Su Qin Biography' was contrived.

57 French Sinologist Henri Maspero (1883-1945 CE) – *Le romande Sou Ts'in*, 蘇秦的小說 was published in *Asian Studies*, - the 25th Anniversary Commendatory Memorial Publication of French Fareast Institute in Henei Vietnam. (Paris 1925). Translated by Peng Chengjun 馮承鈞 which appeared in *Beiping tushuguan kan* 北平圖書館刊, Volume 7, Issue 6.

58 *The Book of Warring States Strategists*, the *Zhanguo zonghengjia shu* 戰國縱橫家書.

59 (Yang Kuan's footnotes) In *ZGC* 戰國策, 'Qince 1, 秦策'. Su Qin said to King Hui of Qin 秦惠王 (r. 337-312 BCE), "Your Highness has the advantage of procuring produce from Ba 巴, Shu 蜀 and Hanzhong 漢中 in the west; to your north you have the Hu-He 胡貉 tribes to supplement you with horses. You have the Wushan Mountain 巫山 and Qianzhong 黔中 to demarcate your southern border, and to the east, you have the unassailable Xiao River 淆 (水 河南 陽城縣東北) and Han Pass (Hangu Pass 函谷関 河南靈寶縣) for your defence." The fact is Qin did not capture Wujun 巫郡 and Qianzhong 黔中 until the 30th year of King Zhao of Qin 秦昭王 (280 BCE); apparently this statement is incorrect. In 'Yance 燕策' Su Qin said to Marquis Wen of Yan 燕文侯 (r. 361-333

of Yan, and through his counterespionage formed an alliance against Qin. It is accepted that the text has shed much light on the authenticity and fallacy of the accounts related in *SJ* and *ZGC*.

Authenticating Yue Yi's Defeat of Qi

Zhao annihilated the Zhongshan Kingdom and went on to annex a large region from the kingdom founded by the nomads to its northwest. [60] Qi, Qin, and Zhao became the three most formidable states during the middle Warring State period. The years between the 19th to the 23rd (288-284 BCE) year of King Zhao of Qin, was the most hotly contested interlude between the three kingdoms, [61] all vying to take control of the Song domain. In the 19th year of King Zhao of Qin, the chancellor of Qin, Wei Ran paid homage to the king of Qi; [62] he suggested to the king that he and Qin should proclaim as *Di* - as emperors of the east and the west respectively. [63] They then would follow up by rallying the armed forces from the five kingdoms to go against Zhao, with the objective of partitioning its territories. Two months later, King Min of Qi, abiding by the suggestion of Su Qin, [64] gave up the idea to proclaim emperor; turning to ally with Zhao instead; then, rallied the five kingdoms to go against Qin. Resulting from the campaign, Qin also relinquished the shortly held title of emperor, besides returning some previously occupied cities to Zhao and Wei. Qi took advantage of the confusion by invading Song and annihilated it. The act aroused strong discontent from Wei and Zhao. Qin then took on the initiative of forming an alliance *Hezong*, raising an army against Qi; it followed by allying with Zhao, besides calling on the support of Yan. The combined forces of five armies appointed Yue Yi, the Yan chancellor, as Zhao chancellor, [65] also assuming the position as the Supreme Commander of the Allied forces to march against Qi. During the 22nd year of King Zhao of Qin reign, the Qin General Meng Ao

---

BCE), "To the east of Yan you have Chaoxian 朝鮮 and Liaodong 遼東. To your north, you have the Lin-Hu 林胡 and Liufan 樓煩 nomadic tribes, and to your west, you have Yunzhong 雲中 and Jiuyuan 九原." However, it was very unlikely Yan had such a vast territories in northeast Zhongyuan, as it was not until the Qin Empire defeated the *Lin-Hu* before Zhongguo 中國 (ancient China) assumed control of this vast region. As for Yunzhong 雲中 and Jiuyuan 九原, they were Zhao 趙 territories. 'Qice 1, 齊策' relates, 'Su Qin lobbied at Qi, he said to King Xuan of Qi 齊宣王 (r. 320-302 BCE) that Qi had intended to serve under Qin in the west.' It does not quite coincide with the situation of the political environment, as Qi had not weakened to the point where it had to serve under Qin. (Besides Qi was situated from the far-flung east of Zhongyuan 中原, as geographically it was far too remote for Qin to exert any influence over it at that stage.)

The Song 宋 scholar Wang Zhen 黄震 (1213-1281 CE) says in his *Huangshi Richao* 黄氏日鈔, "Scholars before us said, 'Su Qin created an alliance. For fifteen years, the Qin forces did not venture to march beyond the Pass to the east.' I believe it was fabricated by later strategists, it did not happen." Recent scholars are even more skeptical about the authenticity of the many events related to Su Qin. The recently unearthed silk scroll of *the Book of Warring States Strategists* (1973) from a Han tomb at Mawangdui 馬王堆 漢墓帛書 further confirms that many of the textual references to Su Qin's canvassing in *SJ* 史記 – 'Su Qin Biography 蘇秦列傳' were fabricated, while the accounts in *ZGC* 戰國策 are a mixture of fictions based on some historical truths.

60 Zhao invaded Zhongshan 中山國 on three separate occasions. (307, 305 and 301 BCE)

61 King Zhao of Qin 秦昭王.

62 Chancellor of Qin, Wei Ran 魏冉.

63 *Di* – 帝.

64 In *ZZTJ*, it was Su Dai who made the recommendation. (See 288-1)

65 Yan Chancellor 燕相 Yue Yi 樂毅 as Zhao chancellor 趙相. (See 284-1)

successfully captured nine walled-cities east of the River *Hedong* at Qi; [66] it was the initial success of the combined forces of *Hezong*. The combined forces under the leadership of the Zhao chancellor, Yue Yi, led the allied forces from the eastern border of Zhao to attack Qi, annexing Lingqiu west of River Ji in Qi. [67]

The next year, Yue Yi led the allied forces overwhelmed the Qi forces at Jixi; General Zhuzi of Qi made a run for his life. [68] Yue Yi, as the Yan chancellor, led the Yan army penetrated deep into the realms of Qi; the Qi defenders were defeated at Qinzhou (West of Yongmen, Ximen at the capital city of Linzi). [69] Qi General Dazi died in battle, [70] the capital Linzi was lost, and King Min of Qi made a run for his life. For five years, Yue Yi remained in Qi; and in the process, he captured over 70 walled-cities. The fact that Yue Yi was able to defeat Qi with much ease was due to his appointment as the chancellor by two kingdoms, that of Zhao and Yan. He used the title of Zhao chancellor to lead the forces against the main force of Qi, besides he was using the title of Yan chancellor to pursue the initial victory. Furthermore, he was assisted by Su Qin, who was sowing seeds of discord at the court of King Min of Qi, and the king fell for the ruse. Su Qin was a spy sent to the Qi State by Yan, having earned the trust of King Min and was made Qi chancellor. Su Qin contrived a scheme in Qi to rally the five states to go against Qin, which offered Qi an opportunity to annihilate Song; it was also a trick to weaken Qi by being engaged in years of war against Song. Furthermore, it was a move to weaken the relationship between Qi and Zhao; hence, as to allow Yan to employ the power of Qin and Zhao to go against Qi.

The employment of military backings of other states by the weaker state of (Yan) to go against the once-powerful state of Qi was perhaps one of the most successful examples of *Hezong*; resulting from which, Yue Yi was held with reverence by the political strategists as one of the most celebrated tacticians. Shortly after, Yue Yi's sponsor, King Zhao of Yan died; King Hui of Yan succeeded him. [71] The new king was troubled by the power and the reputation of Yue Yi; he ordered Qi Jie to replace the general; [72] Yue Qi escaped to Zhao. Consequently, Yue Yi became a forlorn champion held in reverence by the political strategists. For this reason, there were numerous false accounts on Yue Yi employing the *Hezong* strategy, of which the 'Replying to the letter from the King of Yan - Bao Yanhuiwang shu' [73] is indisputably one of the fabricated texts.

ZGC 'Yan Strategy I' and *SJ* 'House of Yan Biography' relate, "As soon as King Zhao of Yan assumed to the throne, he promptly invited sages to serve at his court. He honoured Guo Kui as his Tutor. Yue Yi travelled to Yan from Wei; Zou Yan left from Qi and Ju Xin went to Yan from Zhao. [74] After 28 years the kingdom became prosperous and powerful, the soldiers were all willing

---

66 Qin General, Meng Ao 蒙驁 (290-240 BCE).

67 Lingqiu 靈丘, present day south of Gaotang Shandong 山東 高唐南. *Jixi* 濟西 – west of River Ji 濟, the river had become obliterated.

68 Qi General Zhuzi 齊將觸子.

69 Qinzhou 秦周 - West of Yongmen 雍門之西, Ximen 西門 was at the capital Linzi 臨淄.

70 Qi General, Dazi 達子.

71 King Zhao of Yan 燕昭王. King Hui of Yan 燕惠王.

72 Qi Jie 騎劫. (See 279-III)

73 'Replying to the Letter of King Hui of Yan, *Bao Yan Huiwang shu.*' 報燕惠王書. This letter appears in *ZGC* 戰國策, 'Yan Strategy 燕策 2', p. 348. The letter is reproduced in parts in *ZZTJ* (See 279-IV).

74 The *ZGC* 戰國策, 'Yan Strategy 燕策 1', p. 335

to fight. Hence, Yue Yi allied, " ... with Qin, Chu and the San-Jin (Wei, Hann, and Zhao) to lay siege to Qi, defeating it." The claim that King Zhao (r. 313-279 BCE) assumed the Yan throne and honoured Guo Kui as his Tutor is likely to be a historical fact. However, where the part of the text that relates Yue Yi, Zhou Yan, and Ju Xin went to Yan when the king was inviting sages to go forward was most likely to have been fabricated by later wandering political canvassers. Ju Xin was a Yan general towards the latter part of the Warring States and was a colleague of Zhou Yan; both men could not possibly enter Yan at the time of King Zhao of Yan. Yue Yi went to serve Yan after the death of King Wuling of Zhao, (the king who succumbed to hunger); which was well after the 17th year of King Zhao of Yan. Furthermore, Yue Yi was not an orthodox canvasser. He was a descendant of the renowned Wei general, Yue Yang, and had for some time served at Zhao as a senior minister. Previous to this, he, at the time of King Xuan of Qi (r. 320-302 BCE), had proposed to King Wuling of Zhao to form an alliance with Chu and Wei to attack Qi to save Yan when it was in turmoil (*ZGC* 'Zhao Strategy 3'). The King of Zhao ordered Yue Yi to escort the then Yan crown prince in exile at Hann to return to Yan to ascend the throne; known posthumously as King Zhao of Yan. Later, upon the death of King Wuling of Zhao, Yue Yi left Zhao for Wei. Appointed as an emissary of Wei, he went to Yan; the Yan king appreciated his talents and retained him.

The account of King Zhao of Yan's attempt to solicit capable ministers to his court, after ascending to the throne is undoubtedly a falsified account, even the article on, 'Replying to the letter of King Hui of Yan' was also falsified, mostly likely created by the wandering canvassers. In the letter, Yue Yi suggests to King Zhao, that the four states of Yan, Zhao, Chu, and Wei should align against Qi, and that it could be taken easily. He then took on an emissary mission to Zhao, upon his return, the allied army attacked Qi. However, the truth is, when Yue Yi led the five allied forces of Qin, Zhao, Hann, Wei, and Yan against Qi; Chu was not among the allies. (*SJ,* 'Qin Basic annals' and 'House of Zhao Biography.') Before the launch of the campaign, the Qin and Zhao sovereigns met. General Meng Ao of Qin began the attack and defeated nine walled cities of Qi at the east of the River *Hedong*; it was the initial phase of the *Hezong* campaign. Qin engineered the Five-allies of *Hezong,* and it was based on the scheme proposed by Su Qin, who presented a memorial to the King of Zhao, in which he stated, "Using Qi as bait, hence, to make it known to all under Heaven." [75] (The *SJ* and Zhao Strategy 1'.) The text has a description of the battle, "Under the divine providence of Heaven, the spirit of the former kings, the armies of Zhao, Wei and other kingdoms situated north of the River rallied to the call of our former kings and penetrated as far as Jishang River. The huge army garrisoned at Jishang was ordered to attack Qi, and gave it a resounding defeat. The light brigade and elite troops penetrated into the capital city of Qi." The text suggests that Yue Yi initially annexed the area joining Qi and Yan at *Hebei*; he followed up by occupying Jishang, and from Jishang penetrated into the capital city of Qi. However, the Yan army did not march south to invade and capture the west of the River area *Hebei* of Qi; rather it marched south along the eastern border of Zhao with the Zhao forces, and then the armies from the five states defeated the main force of Qi west of Ji. Following this, Yue Yi led the lone Yan forces to pursue the Qi forces retreating to the east. At Qinzhou, another

---

Guo Kui 郭隗 as his Tutor 師. (See 312-11)
Yue Yi 樂毅 from Wei 魏.
Zou Yan 鄒衍 from Qi 齊.
Ju Xin 劇辛 from Zhao 趙.

75 蘇秦獻書趙王, "以齊為餌, 先出聲于天下."

battle was won, finally penetrating deep into the capital city of Linzi. Yue Yi won two decisive battles in the war against Qi. First he defeated the Qi General Chuzi; then, the second decisive battle was won when he defeated and killed Dazi at Qinzhou. The details of which are related in *Lushi chunqiu* 'Guanxun pian' and *ZGC* 'Qice 6.' [76] *Lushi Annals* 'Guizhi pian' relates the failure of the King Min of Qi, [77] adding, "It was a result of the departure of Chuzi and the death of General Dazi." From the above we can get an idea that the letter of Yue Yi's 'Replying to the Letter of King Hui of Yan' was most certainly a grandly exaggerated account of Yue Yi's single-handed exploit by rallying the other states to go against Qi. The letter was written with much poise, laden with poignant sentiments, and had moved generations of readers. It prompted Sima Qian to note, "When the Qi national Kuai Tong and Zhufu Yan read the letter they had to put down the text to wipe away tears." [78] Nonetheless, the letter was a later day fabrication, and the events did not tally with historical facts.

Authenticating Yue Yi's Vanquish of Qi in the *Zizhi tongjian*

The *Zizhi tongjian* (*ZZTJ*) has a lengthy description of Yue Yi's defeat of Qi; however, not all the entries are in the *SJ*, *ZGC* and other pre-Qin literature. It is now considered that latter-day scholars fabricated most of the accounts. *Tongjian* commenced with the account when King Zhao of Yan assumed to the throne, Yue Yi and Ju Xin went from Zhao to serve Yan, [79] which is recorded during the 3rd year of King Nan of Zhou (321 BCE). Then twenty-eight years later during the 31st year of King Nan, Yue Yi led the Yan army to march north (against Qi). Ju Xin and Yue Yi had a difference of opinion. Ju Xin maintained, "It is an opportune time to cede the border cities to expand Yan's territories...." and that it was not a good idea to penetrate far too deep into the heartland of Qi. Nevertheless, Yue Yi maintained that they should continue their drive into Qi, "The people of Qi will rise in revolt, and dissension will ensue from within. Qi can be taken." Following that, Yue Yi marched into Qi, "...the kingdom fell into utter chaos; King Min of Qi made a run for his life." Yue Yi entered Linzi. Apparently, this part of the text was to embellish the prescience of Yue Yi as he had the astuteness to predict that Qi would fall with his campaign. However, in reality, the disagreement between Yue Yi and Ju Xin was entirely fabricated as the two men lived in different times. *ZZTJ* further relates that Ju Xin was killed by the Zhao General Pang Xuan during the 5th year of Qin Shihuang, which was the 3rd year of King Daoxiang of Zhao (242 BCE) according to *SJ* 'House of Zhao Biography.' [80] If that indeed was the case, then according to *ZZTJ*, Ju Xin was a Yan general for over 70 years, which appears to be improbable.

ZZTJ further relates that "Yue Yi prohibited his army to loot the land of Qi; he reduced the corvee and repealed the harsh rules of the country." Latter-day scholars were of the opinion that the episode was based on the teachings of Mengzi, who presented the notion to the king of Qi. The king did not use it on his people, whereas Yue Yi used it to rule the occupied Qi. (*Dashiji*

---

76 The *Lushi Annals* 吕氏春秋, 'Guanxun pian 權勛篇'.
The *ZGC* 戰國策 'Qi Strategy 6 齊策'.

77 The *Lushi Annals* 吕氏春秋, 'Guizhi pian 貴直篇'.

78 Qi Kuai Tong 齊 蒯通 and Zhufu Yan 主父偃.

79 Ju Xin 劇辛.

80 Zhao General, Pang Xuan 龎煖, killed Ju Xin during the 5th year of the king of Qin Ying Zheng 秦王嬴政, and it was the 3rd year of King Daoxiang of Zhao 趙悼襄王 (242 BCE) according to *SJ* 史記, 'House of Zhao Biography, 趙世家'.

quoting *Chenshi* from *Yanping*.) [81] Apparently, the text attempted to portray Yue Yi as a 'righteous and chivalrous knight.' *ZZTJ* further relates, as soon as Yue Yi entered into Linzi, he divided his armies into four regiments. "The left column crossed the Jiaodong and Donglai rivers. [82] The vanguards advanced along the east of Taishan Mountains reaching the sea to take Langya. [83] The right column marched along the River (Huanghe), Ji River, Tuna River and Juan to join the forces of Wei. [84] The rear detachment was commanded to garrison at Beihai to placate the civilians at Qiancheng." [85] Then, "In a matter of six months, he annexed over seventy walled-cities; these were all prefectures and counties." This account does not tally with the records in *SJ* Yue Yi Biography', [86] which states, "Yue Yi stayed in Qi for five years, and captured over 70 Qi walled-cities." Huang Shisan in his *A Brief Chronicle of Late Zhou* comments, "According to the *Investigation of Ancient Events - Jigulu*, during the 35th year of King Nan of Zhou, [87] Yue Yi stayed in the Qi territories; during the next few years, he annexed over 70 walled-cities. Sima Guang, the author of *ZZTJ*, later realized that it was a mistake, but he could not make changes to his '*Tongjian*.'" In reality, the account of Yue Yi dividing his armies into four battalions is an entirely fabricated narrative. *Tongjian* states, during the 36th year of King Nan of Zhou, "Yue Yi ordered his Right Army and his Vanguards to combine to lay siege to Ju; while he commanded the Left and Rear Armies to besiege Jimo." [88] This account lacks credence, in that the four battalions were already dispatched to rather remote areas, and it made no sense to recall them to lay siege to Ju and Jimo. As to the narratives of Yue Yi at Qi that, "He made sacrificial offerings to Duke Huan of Qi and Guan Zhong in the outskirts, he exalted the outstanding individuals in the villages; and enfeoffed Wang Shu posthumously by raising his tomb. Twenty or more Qi people were enfeoffed at Yan while over one hundred individuals were enfeoffed at Ji." [89] It was a highly improbable account, as only a few fief lords can be verified during the entire history of Yan at the time of the Warring States; hence, it was most unlikely that there were over twenty enfeoffed Qi lords at Yan. All these extravagant accounts were probably created to epitomize Yue Yi as a 'righteous and chivalrous knight.'

---

81 Lu Zulian 呂祖謙 (1137-1181 CE), *Major Events, Dashiji* 大事記.
Chenshi from Yanping 陳氏延平, details are obscured.

82 Left column 左軍 - Jiaodong 膠東 and Donglai 東萊.

83 Vanguard 前軍 - Taishan Mountain 泰山, Langya 琅琊.

84 Right column 右軍 – He 河, Ji 濟, Tuna 屯阿, Juan 鄄.

85 Rear - Beihai 北海 to pacify the civilians at Qiancheng 千乘.

86 The *Shiji* 史記, 'Yue Yi Biography, Yue Yi liezhuan 樂毅列傳'.

87 Huang Shisan 黄式三 (1789-1862 CE), *A Brief Chronicle of Late Zhou, Zhouji bianlue* 周季編略.
Sima Guang 司馬光 (1019-1086 CE), *Investigation of Ancient Events, Jigulu* 稽古錄.
King Nan of Zhou 周赧王.
(See 284-1. The 35th year of King Nan 周赧王 should be 280 BCE. However *ZZTJ* appended this event to the 31st year of King Nan (284-1), the author has no means of verifying this discrepancy. However, given the fact that Yue Yi stayed in Qi for five years, it was quite probable.)

88 Ju 莒; Jimo 即墨.

89 Duke Huan of Qi 齊桓公 (r. ?-643 BCE) one of the five hegemons during the times of Spring and Autumn 春秋.
Guan Zhong was the Chancellor of Qi 齊相 管仲 (725-645 BCE).
Wang Shu 王蠋 was a worthy minister at Qi. Yue Yi intended to appoint him as Minister after the defeat of Qi, Wang Shu remained loyal to Qi and refused to serve under Yue Yi; he committed suicide.
Ji 薊.

Legend has it that when King Wu of Zhou vanquished Shang. "(He) released Jizi, and enfeoffed him at the tomb of Bigan, and he made recognition of the Musical Minister of Shang, Rong, who retired to live among the civilians, and enfeoffed the son of King Zhou, Wugeng Lufu." (*SJ*, 'Yin Basic annals - Yin benji.') [90] It is thought that the scholars who inflated the great exploits of Yue Yi had tried to compare him with King Wu of Zhou; perhaps the story invented met the mandates of the composer of *ZZTJ*, 'governance with the righteous path – *zhidao*, [91] hence the story was incorporated.

ZZTJ relates that Yue Yi laid siege to Ju and Jimo for one year and could not subjugate the two walled cities; he ordered the siege lifted and instructed, "Civilians leaving the cities are allowed to go free. People who are suffering are to be provided for. Civilians are allowed to take up their former professions, allowing them to settle down." In the end, after three years, Yue Yi still could not conquer the walled cities. Someone at the Yan court slandered against him; the slanderer said to King Zhao, "...Yue Yi is fighting a protracted war, so as to claim kingship in the south." The king executed the slanderer, and proclaimed, "The state of Qi belonged to Yue Yi." He sent his chancellor to Qi to enfeoff the general as the king of Qi. Yue Yi swore he would not take on the position, henceforth the people of Yan began to appreciate the righteousness of the general, and his fealty inspired the other fief lords. The incident is not recounted in *SJ*, *ZGC*, and other Pre-*Qin* literatures; hence, it is very likely to have been fabricated by latter-day scholars. The eight-volume of the *Tongjian* on the Warring States and Qin, submitted to the Emperor Yingzong of Song (r. 1063-1067 CE) by Sima Guang was a draft submission; [92] it is supposed that this passage met the mandate of the author on the thesis he wished to expound in his work. Hence, he included it.

Compilation of Warring States Historic Information and Chronology [93]

The historical materials on the Warring States had over the centuries dispersed and scattered; besides, most of the writings are fragmented and incomplete. The materials available to us are littered with chronological errors, and historical facts are intermingled with fabrications composed by latter-day scholars. A serious re-examination on the historiography and compilation of Warring States information and chronology is pressingly required. The first seven volumes of the *ZZTJ* was the first attempt at making compilations by affixing and revising the chronological dates of the Warring States events. Some of the compilations are accurate. For instance, it did not adopt *SJ's* 'House of Wei Biography' account of, "Marquis Wu of Wei died, his son Wei Ying ascended to the throne, and he was known posthumously as King Hui of Wei." [94] Instead, it opted for, "Wei Ying

---

90 "釋箕子之囚, 封比干之墓, 表商容之閭, 封紂子武庚路祿父."
SJ 史記, '*Yin benji*, 殷本紀'. Jizi 箕子 was the uncle of King Zhou of Shang 商紂王; he was incarcerated by the King when he reprimanded him.
Bi Gan 比干 was another uncle of the King; he was executed for reprimanding the despotic King.
Shang Rong 商容 was the Musical Minister at the Shang court; he retired to live among the civilians.
Wu Geng 武庚, Lufu 祿夫 was the son of King Zhou of Shang, his posthumous title was Wu Geng; his name was Lufu.

91 *Zhidao* 治道.

92 Song Yingzong 宋英宗 (r. 1063-1067 CE).

93 Yang Kuan 楊寬, *ZGS* 戰國史, Pages 30-41.

94 *SJ* 史記, 'House of Wei Biography, Wei shijia 魏世家'. Marquis Wu of Wei 魏武侯.
Wei Ying 魏罃, known posthumously as King Hui of Wei 魏惠王.

contested with Gongzhong Huan for the throne,[95] and the latter was killed in the process." The latter account is credible. [96]

Later, during the time of Southern Song, Lu Zulian compiled *Dashiji*; still later, Qing scholar Lin Chunpu compiled *Zhanguo jinian* and Huang Shisan came up with the *Zhouji bianlue*;[97] these scholars continued the work began by *ZZTJ*. *Dashiji* commences its narratives from the 39th year of King Jing of Zhou, which was the 14th year of Duke Ai of Lu (481 BCE), it was intended to be a continuation of the annals tradition, and the chronological compilation ended in the 2nd year of *Zhenghe* of Emperor Wu of Han. [98] The so-called major events, as the title suggests, are nevertheless sketchy. However, the book does offer some textual research and clarifications, which are appended in the explanations – 'Jieti'. [99] *Zhanguo jinian* commences its narratives from the 1st year of King Zhen of Zhou (468 BCE); [100] the author merely made some comparisons of major events between different texts, with partial textual research. *Zhouji bianlue* also commences from the 1st year of King Zhen of Zhou; it makes a compilation of *SJ*, *ZGC*, and

---

95 Gongzhong Huan 公中緩 (公子公) was the younger brother of Wei Ying. (See 371-111)

96 (Yang Kuan's footnotes): *SJ* 史記, 'House of Wei Biography' states, "Marquis Wu of Wei died, his son Ying 罃 ascended to the throne, he was known posthumously as King Hui 惠王. During the 1st year of King Hui. Prior to this, Marquis Wu 武侯 died. Ying, the son of the Marquis and Gongzhong Huan 公中緩, vied for succession (as Crown Prince *Taizi*). The forces of Hann 韓 and Zhao 趙 attacked Wei 魏. The battle was joined at Zhuoze Lake 濁澤; Wei forces lost completely; the sovereign of Wei was surrounded. Later Hann and Zhao had a difference of opinion; Hann retreated. The Grand Historian remarked, "When a sovereign died, and he did not have a suitable son for succession, the kingdom could be conquered easily." The *ZZTJ* has a slightly different rendering, "Marquis Wu of Wei died, he did not designate a Crown Prince. His son Ying and Gongzhong Huan vied for succession. The kingdom fell into chaos." Later, Hann withdrew its troops, and it continues, "Ying killed Gongzhong Huan and succeeded to the throne, he was known posthumously as King Hui of Wei." The account in *ZZTJ* appears to be more complete. *SJ* 'House of Wei Biography' shows some contradiction with its passage, "Marquis Wu died, his son ascended to the throne; he was known posthumously as King Hui." The passage does not correspond with the passage that follows. *Shuijing* 水經 'Zhuozhangshui zhu 濁漳水注' quoting a reference from *Bamboo Annals* 紀年, "During the 1st year of King Huicheng of Liang 梁惠成王 (King Hui of Wei), the Ye 鄴 army (Wei Ying's army) defeated the Handan 邯鄲 army (Zhao 趙) at Pingyang 平陽. *SJ* 史記, 'House of Wei Biography 魏世家' relates, "Gongsun Qi 公孫頎 said, "Wei Ying 魏罃 has acquired Wang Cuo 王錯, having had control of Shangdang 上黨, he now has control of half of the Kingdom." Ye was close in proximity with Shangdang; hence, when Wei Ying had control of Ye and vied for the throne with Gongsun Huan, and he had control of Shangdang. In the meantime, Hann had withdrawn, the army of Ye defeated the Zhao forces. As a result, Wei Ying defeated Gongsun Huan, killing him and ascended to the throne; before the year-end, the regnal year was changed to the 1st year. The *ZZTJ* account of, 'Wei Ying killed Gongzhong Huan and ascended to the throne' is accurate.

97 Southern Song 南宋 Lu Zulian 呂祖謙 (1137-1181 CE), The *Major Events, Dashiji*, 大事記.
Qing 清 Lin Chunpu 林春溥 (1755-1862 CE). The *Warring States Chronicles, Zhanguo jinian* 戰國紀年.
Huang Shisan 黄式三 (1789-1862 CE), *A Brief Chronicle of Late Zhou, Zhouji bianlue* 周季編略.

98 The *Dashiji* 大事記 chronicles commence during King Jing of Zhou 周敬王 39th year, Duke Ai of Lu 魯哀公 14th year (481 BCE); and end in 2nd year of *Zhenghe* 征和二年 (90 BCE) Emperor Wu of Emperor Wu of Han 漢武帝 (157-87 BCE).

99 'Jieti 解題' – explanations.

100 The *Zhanguo jinian* 戰國紀年.
King Zhen of Zhou 周貞王 (r. 468-441 BCE).

other Pre-Qin historiographic works; which were listed and compared, completed with appendices of sources; it is a more comprehensive and encompassing work. Huang Shisan spent most of his life working on the compilation of this work. Huang Yizhou, [101] his son, then made a through re-editing of the work. He wrote an article ('The House of Yue Addendum and Differentiation, Shi Yue shijiabu bingbian'), which was published in *Jingji zazhu* under the category of 'History - Shishuo.' [102] His investigation indicated that Chu vanquished the kingdom of Yue during the 22nd year (307 BCE) of King Huai of Chu, [103] and the result was incorporated into *Zhouji bianlue*. The account presented is quite credible.

The books above compiled during the period were restricted and limited by their knowledge and information available at their time, and they suffered from three fundamental flaws.

1. These works did not make comprehensive revisions to the wrongly appended dates. The dates of reigns by kings Hui and Xiang of Wei that appeared in *ZZTJ* and other older books were rectified according to the *Bamboo Annuals - Guben Zhushu jinian*; however, the dates of the reign of kings Wei, Xuan and Min of Qi in *ZZTJ* and other manuscripts did not make corrections according to *Bamboo Annuals*. *ZZTJ* merely added 10 years to the reign of King Wei, followed by pushing back the reign of King Xuan by 10 years. Whereas, *Dashiji* further extended the reign of King Xuan by 10 years and shortened the reign of King Min by 10 years. (*A Brief Chronicle of Late Zhou - Zhouji bianlue* follows *Dashiji*.) The aim of making the modifications by these books was to find conformity with the dates mentioned in the *Mengzi* and other texts, as well the year when King Xuan of Qi defeated the state of Yan. [104] The fact that the dates corresponded was purely coincidental and was hardly based on any verifiable facts. Furthermore, the wrong dates appended to the other states were likewise left unchanged.
2. The books mentioned did not try to separate the fictitious inventions from historical facts. *ZZTJ*, *Dashiji* and other manuscripts based their accounts in *SJ*, which chronicled Su Qin's wandering and canvassing activities with his *Hezong* proposition at the six states; between the 35th to 36th year of King Xian of Zhou (334-333 BCE). [105] The event of Zhang Yi trying to convince the five kingdoms to form *Lianheng* with Qin was appended to the 4th year of King Nan of Zhou (311 BCE). [106] The contents of the oration and did not correspond with the political status at that particular juncture. King Hui of Wei and King Wei of Qi met at Xuzhou to confer with each other as kings during the 35th or 36th year of King Xian of Zhou;[107] it incited the King of Chu to attack Qi at Xuzhou, defeating it. Under such circumstances, it was very unlikely that the six states could form an alliance to go against

---

101 Huang Yizhou 黄以周 was the son of Huang Shisan 黄式三.

102 'Supplements to the Yue Household and Discussions, Shi Yue shijiabu bingbian,' '史越世家補 并辨', published in *Jingji's Collection of Miscellaneous Works, Jingji zazhu*, 儆季雜著 under the heading of 'History, *Shishuo* 史說'.

103 22nd year (307 BCE) of King Huai of Chu 楚懷王.

104 The *Mengzi*, 孟子. King Xuan of Qi 齊宣王 defeated the Kingdom of Yan 燕.

105 Su Qin 蘇秦 was active during the 35th to 36th year of the King Xian of Zhou 周顯王 (334-333 BCE). (N.B. This is a wrong assumption; Su Qin died in 284 BCE.)

106 Zhang Yi 張儀 was active during 4th year of King Nan of Zhou 周赧王 (311 BCE). NB. Zhang Yi died in 310 BCE.

107 Xuzhou 徐州.

Qin. The truth is, Su Qin was the chancellor of Qi, he and Li Dui conspired to ally the five kingdoms (*Hezong*) to attack Qin, but that was the 14th year of King Min of Qi Min (287 BCE). [108] Zhang Yi while trying to petition Chu and Zhao, for an alliance mentioned that Su Qin was executed by the king of Qi, 'by the five-chariot chastisement at the market bazaar,' [109] which was during the 17th year of King Min of Qi. Zhang Yi could not have known that Su Qin was to be executed 20 years later. (Author's note - Apparently, recent studies of the texts uncovered at Mawangdui shed further light on the dates of the deaths of Su Qin and Zhang Yi.) [110] There is little doubt now that the rivalry between Su Qin and Zhang Yi as the Vertical and Horizontal strategists was created and fabricated by later political strategists. *ZZTJ* not only included the deceptions created by these political strategists recorded in *SJ*, but it also incorporated fabrications created by later scholars. The incident of Yue Yi's conquest of Qi, mentioned earlier, was a prime example. The inclusion of such fabricated and false materials has devastatingly tarnished the reputation of Warring States historiography.

3. The manuscripts did not make a comprehensive search of all available materials for re-editing and compilation. *A Brief Chronicle of Late Zhou - Zhouji bianlue*, while more encompassing and inclusive than others, still lacks a fully comprehensive coverage, particularly about historical events; and it does not attempt to cover the many reforms in the various kingdoms during this particular era in detail. Some scholars suggested that the manuscripts placed much emphasis on historic experience and lessons to be learned, and the accumulation of historic materials had not been thorough; the inclusion of all available materials were thus incomplete, and these manuscripts are probably less valuable in making historiography research and the studies of reforms than they should have been.

More recently, scholars have used the *Bamboo Annals - Guben jinain* to correct the mistakes in the *SJ* 'the Sequence of the Six States'. The works included Lei Xueqi's '*An Investigation of Bamboo Annals* and *Verification of Bamboo Annals*; Zhu Youzeng's '*In Search of Truth in Jizhong Annals*; Wang Guowei's '*A Compilation of Old Edition of Bamboo Annals*; Qian Mu's '*Chronicles of Pre-Qin Masters* and Chen Mengjia's '*Chronicles of the Six States*.' [111] Lei Xueqi,

---

108 Su Qin was the Chancellor of Qi.
Li Dui 李兑.
14th year of King Min of Qi 齊湣王 (287 BCE).

109 The five-chariots chastisement at the market bazaar 五馬分屍.

110 The *ZZTJ* states that an assassin murdered him. (See 317-11).
The silk scroll manuscript discovered in the Han tomb at Mawangdui Hanmu in Changsha in 1973 長沙 馬王堆 漢墓帛書 was coined by researchers as the *Book of Warring States Strategists, The Zhangou zonghengjia shu* 戰國縱横家書. The manuscript has 27 chapters divided into three parts. The first part has 14 chapters; these are the letters of Su Qin 蘇秦 and records of his conversations. Zhang Yi died in 310 BCE; Su Qin died in 284 BCE; Su Qin was active after the death of Zhang Yi 張儀. When Zhang Yi was the Chancellor of Qin, Su Qin had not entered into politics. From this silk manuscript, we are able to determine the authenticity of The *ZGC* as well as to rectify the errors in the *SJ's* 史記, 'Su Qin Biography.'

111 Originally published in 1949 Yinjing University Publication, Volumes 34, 36 and 37. The combined edition was published by Xuexi shenghuo chubanshe 1955. 原刊一九四九年燕京學報 34, 36, 37 期, 合訂本于一九五五年由學習生活出版社出版.
Lei Xueqi 雷學淇, *An Investigation of Bamboo Annals, Kaoding Zhushu jinian* 考定竹書紀年; the *Verification of Bamboo Annals, Zhushu jinian yizheng*, 竹書紀年義証.

a Qing scholar, was most notable for his outstanding work on his research and annotations of the *Bamboo Annals*; he went on to make numerous amendments to the incorrect dates that appear in *SJ*. His original work of *Verification of Bamboo Annals* was a hand-written manuscript in circulation, and it was not until the 1940's before the Xiugengtang Printing Press made a Linotype edition of his work. [112] Qian Mu's manuscript on *Chronicles of Pre-Qin Masters* is an outstanding piece of research in identifying the active dates of the various Pre-Qin scholars and masters. To verify the dates of the masters, he used the *Old Edition of the Bamboo Annals* to authenticate the dates of 'Sequence of the Six States.' He then conducted numerous research 'Kaobian' and listed his findings in the *Tongbiao*. [113] His 'Kaobian' has shed much light on the dates of the major wars and events during the Warring States, which offer us a clearer glimpse of the political state of affairs as well as the interconnected changes that transpired. He further authenticated some of the important historical facts, for instance, his theses on 'Verification of Pengcheng being the capital of Song during the Zhanguo period', and 'Verification of Chun Yukun being a Contract-Slave' are highly regarded. [114] His manuscript of the *Chronicles of the Pre-Qin Masters* has made invaluable contributions to our understanding of the Warring States period, and his compilation of the Warring States has a profound influence on the study of history among scholars.

Between 1946 and 1949, I (Yang Kuan) published some 30 manuscripts of a series of articles on *Research on the Historic Events of the Warring States.* [115] In the article on, 'The Reigning Years of King Hui of Liang', I pointed out that there were one or two years of discrepancies between the accounts in the *Old Edition of Bamboo Annals* and *SJ* on the major events that happened during the reign of Marquis Wu of Wei and King Hui of Wei, and that the discrepancies of two years were war related. [116] I concluded that *SJ's* accounts on the regnal commencement years of the Marquis Wen of Wei, Marquis Wu of Wei and King Hui of Wei all missed out by one year. [117] King Hui of Wei changed his 36th regnal year to his 1st year *gaiyuan*. Before he changed his regnal year, he only reigned for 35 years. Hence, when *SJ* erroneously entered his death during the 36th year of his reign, the 'one year' was the discrepancy. Qian Mu

---

Zhu Youzeng 朱右曾, *In Search of Truth in Jizhong Annals, Jizhong jinian cunzhen* 汲冢紀年存真. Zhu Youzeng was a 進士 *jinshi* - presented scholar during the Daoguang 18th year (1838) civic entrance examination.

Wang Guowei 王國維, *A Compilation of Old Edition of Bamboo Annals, Guben Zhushu jinian jijiao* 古本竹書紀年輯校.

Qian Mu 錢穆 (1895-1990), *Chronicles of Pre-Qin Masters, Xianqin Zhuzi xinian* 先秦諸子系年; and

Chen Mengjia 陳夢家 (1911-1966), *Chronicles of the Six States, Liuguo jinian*, 六國紀年.

112 Xiugengtang Printing Press 修綆堂.

113 'Kaobian 考辨'; General Listings, *Tongbiao* 通表.

114 Qian Mu 錢穆, 'Verification of Pengcheng being the Capital of Song during Zhanguo Period, Zhanguoshi Songdu Pengcheng zheng 戰國時宋都彭城証' and 'Verification of Chun Yukun was a Contract-Slave, Chun Yukun wei rennu kao 淳于髡為人奴考.'

115 Yang Kuan's 楊寬, *Research on the Historic Events of Zhanguo, Zhanguo shishi congkao* 戰國史事叢考.

116 'The Reigning Years of King Hui of Liang, *Liang Huiwang di nianshi*, 梁惠王的年世.'
The *Old Edition of Bamboo Annals, Guben Zhushu jinan* 古本竹書紀年, and the *SJ* 史記.
King Wu of Wei 魏武侯.

117 First Regnal year 紀元. Marquis Wen of Wei 魏文侯, Marquis Wu of Wei 魏武侯 and King Hui of Wei 魏惠王 (King Hui of Liang 梁惠王).

raised doubts about this observation in his 'On Affirming the Years of Reign by King Hui of Liang.'[118] He went on to clarify the reasons for the discrepancies by pointing out that some scholars maintained that it was *SJ* that made the mistake in the first place; others had erroneously used the dates of the *Bamboo Annals* as a reference. Hence, it would be an incorrect approach. He added, "...mistakes as such are strewn throughout all ancient texts. It will be difficult for further in-depth discussions." I followed up with another article on, 'A Further Discussion on the Reigning Years of King Hui of Liang.'[119] In the article I illuminated with further evidences that there indeed was a discrepancy of one year between the two texts; and, I pointed out that 'the dates of the total solar eclipse between the two texts were out by 'one year' that was a clear proof to support my thesis.[120]

Between 1948 and 1949, Chen Mengjia published his *Sequence of the Six States - Liuguo jinian* and concentrated his research on verifying the dates of *SJ* based on the dates extracted from *Old Edition of the Bamboo Annals.*[121] He came to the same conclusion as I did that the dates of Marquis Wen of Wei, Marquis Wu, and King Hui quoted in *SJ* were all out by one year; nevertheless, he maintained that before King Hui changed his regnal year, there were 36 years. He concluded by moving back the reigns of kings Hui and Xiang by one year. On the other hand, I was of the opinion that the observation he made was unfounded and could not be substantiated. If a comparison of the *Bamboo Annals* and *SJ* is made on events pertaining to King Hui of Wei, there were five separate events that had one year of discrepancy; while two events were out by two years, which were all war related. We know wars can persist for more than one year whereas there was no event that corresponded to the same year. Besides, the important entry of the total eclipse was also out by one year, and the enfeoffment of Lord Shang (Shang Yang) by Qin was also out by one year. It became apparent that the *SJ's* account of King Hui's regnal year was mistaken. If we were to make a comparison of the two texts, by changing the regnal year of King Hui (the so-called *gaiyuan*, i.e. changing the 36th year to the 1st year of his post regnal date);[122] we found that the dates of events between kings Hui and Xiang match perfectly. The evidence on the three discrepancies Chen Mengjia produced was thus inaccurate, as *SJ* was erroneous in the chronicles of the three events in the first place. He had chosen partially incorrect entries of *SJ* to

---

118 Qian Mu 錢穆, 'On Affirming the Years of Reign by King Hui of Liang, Guanyu Liang Huiwang zaiwei niansui zhi shangque', '關于梁惠王在位年歲之商榷'.

119 Yang Kuan 楊寬, 'A Further Discussion on the Reigning Years of King Hui of Liang, Zailun Liang Huiwang di nianshi, 再論梁惠王的年世'.

120 (Yang Kuan's footnotes.)
Yang Kuan 楊寬, 'Liang Huiwang di nianshi 梁惠王的年世' was published in *Dongnan ribao wenshi zhoukan* Vol 6. August 8, 1946; 東南日報 文史周刊 第六期 1946 年 8 月 8 日.
Qian Mu 錢穆, 'Guanyu Liang Huiwang zaiwei nianshi zhi shangque 關于梁惠王在位年歲之商榷' was published in *Weshi zhoukan*, Vol 10. September 5, 1946 刊于文史周刊第十期 9 月 5 日.
Yang Kuan 楊寬 'A Further Discussion on the Reigning Years of Liang Huiwang 再論梁惠王的年世', Published in *Wenshi zhoukan* Vol 14. October 3, 1946. 刊于文史周刊第十四期 10 月 3 日.

121 Chen Mengjia 陳夢家, '*Sequence of the Six States, Liuguo jinian*, 六國紀年'. This book has the same name as *SJ's* chapter of 'Sequence of the Six States.'

122 *Gaiyuan* 改元 was also known as *gengyuan* 更元 – changing the regnal year. Xin Deyong 辛德勇 (1959-), 'A further discussion on the commencement of using *jinian* in ancient China, 重談中國古代以年號紀年的啓用時間', 2008 年 7 月 3 日. The article appeared in *Wenshi* 文史, 2009 年第 1 輯, 2008. The article also appears in Xin Deyong's book Jianyuan yu Gaiyuan 建元與改元, Zhonghua shuju, 中華書局, China, 2013.

compare with the *Bamboo Annals*, thus, the outcome was suspect at best. [123] According to the *Bamboo Annals,* King Hui of Qi died during the 15th year of post-regnal *houyuan* of King Hui of

---

[123] (Yang Kuan's footnotes): *SJ* 史記 'House of Wei Biography 魏世家' relates, during the 8th year of King Ai of Wei 魏哀王 the kingdom attacked Wey 伐衛, (whereas in *SJ* 史記 'Sequence of the Six States 六國年表' it uses the word besieged Wey 圍衛 instead of attack.) *Shiji suoyin* 史記索隱, *Shiji Obscured Passage* quotes from *Bamboo Annals*, "8th year, Zhai Zhang 翟章伐衛 attacked Wey." *SJ* 'House of Wei Biography' records during the 16th year of King Ai of Wei, "Qin 秦 took our Pufan 蒲反, Yangjin 陽晉, and Fengling 封陵." (*SJ* 史記, 'Sequence of the Six States 六國年表' has the same quote.) While *Shiji suoyin* 索隱 quoting *the Bamboo Annals* 紀年 it is, "....Jinyang 晉陽 and Fenggu 封谷." From this, we can deduce that the regnal year - *jiyuan* 紀元 of King Xiang of Wei 魏襄王 in *SJ* and *Bamboo Annals* are the same. Chu 楚 made two sieges against Yongshi 雍氏; the first one was during the 3rd year of King Nan of Zhou 周赧王, which was the 7th year of King Xiang of Wei. According to *Shiji jijie* 史記集解, 'House of Hann Biography' 韓世家 quoting Xu Guang 徐廣 (351 or 352-425 CE), the accounts in *the Bamboo Annals* 紀年 and *SJ* 史記, 'Qin basic Annals 秦本紀' and *SJ* 史記, 'House of Tian Biography 田世家' are identical. The second incident was during the 15th year of King Nan of Zhou, that was the 19th year of King Xiang of Wei; then according to *Shiji jijie* 史記集解, 'House of Hann Biography' quoting Xu Guangyue, the dates of *the Bamboo Annals* and *Shiji jijie* 史記集解 'House of Hann Biography' * correspond.

As to the three pieces of evidence produced by Chen Mengjia 陳夢家 in the *Bamboo Annals* and *SJ* 史記 that King Hui of Liang *houyuan* (後元 later regnal year), and King Xiang of Wei's 1st year were one year off; the result was that he had taken partial information from *SJ* to compare with the data from *the Bamboo Annals*. The result of which was thus not credible. The examples are listed below: 1. The *Bamboo Annals* states that during the 4th month, 13th year of King Hui of Liang's 梁惠王 reign, King Wei of Qi 齊威王 enfeoffed Tian Ying 田嬰 at Xue 薛." (Quoting from *Shiji suoyin* 史記索隱 'Lord Mengchang Biography 孟嘗君列傳'), Chen Mengjia points out that using *SJ* 'Sequence of the Six States' 六國年表 King Min of Qi 3rd year 齊湣王 (equivalent to King Hui of Liang *Houyuan* 14th year), ".... Enfeoffed Tian Ying at Xue." However, according to *SJ* 'Lord Mengchang Biography', "King Min ... was on the throne for three years and he enfeoffed Tian Ying at Xue." Of the so-called three years, one has to deduct the first year of reign, counting from the changing of regnal year (*gaiyuan*), it should be the 2nd year King Min of Qi 齊湣王, which tallied with the accounts in the *Bamboo Annals*. 2. The *Bamboo Annals* records that Zhang Yi 張儀 died during the 5th month of the 9th year of the reign of the King Xiang of Liang 梁襄王. (Quoting from *Shiji suoyin* 史記索隱 'Zhang Yi Biography'), Chen Mengjia pointed out that in *SJ* 史記, 'Sequence of the Six States 六國年表, Zhang Yi died during the 10th year of King Ai of Wei as a comparison. However, in *SJ* 史記 'Sequence of the Six States', under the heading of Qin-listing (Qin-biao) 秦表, it relates that during the 1st year of the reign of King Wu of Qin 秦武王, "Both Zhang Yi and Wei Zhang 魏章 died at Wei." King Wu of Qin 1st year was the 9th year of King Xiang of Wei; again, this tallied with the records of the *Bamboo Annals*. 3. *Bamboo Annals* records during the 12th year of King Xiang of Wei, "Qin General Gongsun Huan 公孫緩 led an army to attack our Kingdom, the city of Pishi 皮氏 was besieged." (Quoting from Commentary on Rivers and Waters *Shuijing* 水經 'Fenshuizhu 汾水注'). Chen Mengjia uses the passage in *SJ* 史記, 'Sequence of the Six States 六國年表' King Ai of Wei 13th year, "Qin attacked Pishi, the city held out, Qin departed." for comparison. However, *SJ* 史記, 'House of Wei Biography' appended this incident, as the 12th year of King Ai of Wei, and the wordings are the same; this tallied with the accounts of the *Bamboo Annals*. The interpretation of this is the war continued for two years, hence the discrepancy. Since the three examples pointed out by Chen Mengjia were based on partial evidence and records, the proposal of pushing back the dates of the regnal 1st year of King Hui of Wei and King Xiang of Wei by one year proposed in Chen Mengjia's *Sequence of the Six States* 六國紀年, as against the dates of *SJ* 史記 cannot hold.

Wei, Chen Mengjia having moved the dates of kings Wei and Xuan of Qi back by one year; they were also incorrect.

Categorization of Institutions and Regulations of the Warring States

The period from the Chunqiu epoch to the Warring States was a time of major economic, political and culture reforms. After this period, the Qin and Han dynasties essentially adopted the court systems instituted during this time. Hence, the categorization and research on institutions and regulations of the Warring States are of great importance. At that time, the economic development and subsequent reforms to the allotment of farmlands, taxes and corvée, monetary systems, and registry of household systems went through considerable transformations. Following the political and military changes, it led to the concentration of power at the sovereign courts; further leading to the introduction of military and administrative bureaucracies.[124] Layers upon layers of bureaucrats were overseeing the prefectures and counties; in the process, decrees and regulations, and measurements of volume and weight made by the central courts were applied uniformly throughout the individual fief states. All the states also essentially adopted the system of enfeoffment, while new systems were also introduced for the newly enfeoffed lords. During the time of the Warring States, the seven states all went through a series of reforms at different times, these reforms did not happen simultaneously, rather they were staggered, and the results from these transformations varied considerably. The seven states each had their unique attributes while their political systems and institutions were largely similar; their efforts gave rise to different results. It is thus believed that their institutions and regulations require categorization and research for further elucidation.

The Ming-Qing scholar Dong Yue published, '*A Study of the Seven States - Qiguo kao*', [125] in the book he collected all the available historical information on the institutional systems of the seven states and categorized them in a coherent order; regrettably, the text was an incomplete draft and was never published. The 14 categories he used were extremely complicated and convoluted, the events about 'Spring and Autumn – Chunqiu' took up about three-tenths of the entries. Some of the information he used were extracted from fictitious history and fictions published by later scholars. The 'Catalogue of the Imperial Library *Siku Quanshu* Zongmu tiyao' points out. [126] "The imaginary and bizarre entries are similar to the works of Liu Xiang's '*Biography of the Immortal Deities - Liexian zhuan*'; Zhang Hua's '*Sensory Interaction and Miscellaneous Essays - Ganyinglei congzhi*', *Zihuazi, Fuzi,* and Wang Jia's '*Historical Remnants – Shiweiji*' (see footnotes). [127] Perhaps, more appropriately, the fables of literary scholars; possibly

* (*Shiji Collective Elucidations, Shiji jijie* 史記集解 in 80 chapters. It was compiled by the South Dynasty 南朝 (420-479 CE) scholar Pei Yin 裴駰 based on various available texts and materials at his time, it is considered as one of the three most important annotations works on *SJ*, the other two being *Shiji suoyin* 史記索隱 and *Shiji zhengyi* 史記正義).

124 Author's note – one can make out that initially the military and administration titles were merged during the beginning of the Warring States.

125 Dong Yue 董説 (1620-1682 CE), *A Study of the Seven States, Qiguo kao*, 七國考.

126 The *Catalogue of the Imperial Library, Siku quanshu* 四庫全書, 'Zongmu tiyao 總目提要'.

127 The *Biography of the Immortal Deities, Liexian zhuan*, 列仙傳.
Zhang Hua 張華, the Jin scholar 晉, (232-300 BCE), the *Sensory Interaction and Miscellaneous Essays, Ganyinglei congzhi* 感應類叢志.

fictions and miscellaneous entities are all listed as significant references." Furthermore, some of the ancient texts cited were in fact fabricated by Dong Yue. For instance, in Volume 12, in 'The Penal System of Wei - *Wei xingfa*' there is a passage on *Fajing*,[128] which was quoted from Huan Tan's '*New Notion – Xinlun*'; it was a fabricated piece by Dong Yue.[129] The more recent publication of '*A Study of the Appended Information on the Seven States - Qiguo kaoding bu*' by

---

Zihuazi, 子華子 was a very ancient book, composed at the time of pre-Qin 先秦, the text was lost during the time of Han Liu Xiang 漢 劉向, and the current copy appeared during the time of Southern Song 南宋. Studies of the text show that the contents were based on the philosophy of Huang and Lao (Huangdi 黄帝 and Laozi 老子), the benevolent governance of Huangdi and the 'in a tranquil state of inactivity' philosophy by Laozi.

The *Fuzi* 符子. Fu Lang 符琅, was the nephew of Fu Jian 符堅, a Di 氐 ethnic tribesman, a Qian-Qin General 前秦 and a philosopher at the time of Jin 晉 at around 380 CE. He was a bizarre and eccentric person, who was passionate about the teachings of Zaozi 老子 and Zhuangzi 莊子; he composed several score of articles listed under *Fuzi*.

Wang Jia 王嘉 (?-390 CE), *Historical Remnants, Shiweiji*, 拾遺記. The text was composed by Wang Jia at the time of Jin. He recorded all the legendary events, ranging from mythical Paoxishi 庖牺氏 down to the time of Eastern-Jin 東晉, encompassing bizarre and fictitious events that conventional history would not incorporate.

128 *Fajing* 法經.

129 (Yang Kuan's footnotes): The Czechoslovak Sinologist Timoteus Pokora (1928-1985) published an article in the *Archiv Orientalni* (1959), volume 27, 'The problem of *Fajing* 法經 by Li Kui being Dual Fabrication, 李悝法經的一個雙重偽做問題'. He maintains that the text of *Xinlun* 新論 by Huan Tan 桓譚 was lost in antiquity. The quotations and references made by Dong Yue in his *A Study of the Seven States* 七國考 were entirely fabricated. Before the article was published, Pokora sent the article to me (Yang Kuan) for verification. I supported his interpretation. *A Study of the Seven States* 七國考 listed articles in *Fajing*, 法經 under the headings of *Zhenglu* 正律 Principle Regulations, Miscellaneous Regulations *zalu* 雜律, Reduction Regulations *Jianlu* 減律; these entities did not tally with *Jinshu xingfazhi* 晉書刑法志. The Miscellaneous Regulations quoted were: Prohibition on Adulatory Behaviour; Prohibition on Trickery *Jiaotong* 狡童 (N.B. There is probably an error here, the word 童 should be 禁), *Chengjin* 城禁 Prohibition on Leaving Walled-cities Illegally; *Xijin* 嬉禁 Prohibition on Gambling; *Tujin* 徒禁 Prohibition on Illegal Gathering in Public and *Jinjin* 金禁 Prohibition on Bribery; this again was in variance with *Jinshu Xingfazhi* 晉書刑法志. The *Tujin* 徒禁 said, "When a group of people gather for more than one day, their activities should be questioned. As for 3, 4 or 5 days, they should be executed." Execution should not be implemented if the explanations they proffered are valid. The Prohibition on Bribery, said, "If a chancellor 丞相 accepts bribery, his subordinates should be executed. If a general or officer 犀首 or a person of lower grade than a general accepts a bribe, he is to be executed; not all bribery cases should be executed, a certain level of bribery is reached, before the punishment is enforceable." Textual studies revealed that during the time of Marquis Wen of Wei 魏文侯, the term *chengxiang* 丞相 was not in use; the term was introduced by Duke Wu of Qin 秦武王; before this, it was known as *xiangguo* 相國. Xishou 犀首 was actually an alias of Gongsun Yan 公孫衍. Hence, the interpretation of general or officer was erroneous. The fact that the *A Study of the Seven States, Qiguokao* 七國考 Volume One, had mistakenly used the titles of *Chengxiang* and *Xishou* in defining the titles at the Wei court, proved that the quotes from *Fajing* 法經 in 七國考 were fabricated by Dong Yue. In the preface, Dong Yue annotated, "I have studied the *Qinshu* 秦書 and the Legalism on the Ten Tribes 十族之法, as well as Wei 魏 Li Kui's 李悝 *Fajing* 法經 (Wei 魏 Canon of Laws), they send a chill up my spine. I thus composed *Xingfa* 12 刑法第十二." The book (*A Study of the Seven States*) was entirely fabricated by *Dong Yue*.

Mu Wenyuan identified many of the inaccuracies; [130] he then proceeded to append and restore the institutional system based on the original entries; the result was helpful for readers and researchers. Regrettably, the original texts on the institutions and regulations of Warring States are in disarray, presented in an unorderly fashion; he failed to make a comprehensive categorization, and the research fell short of the current textual research requirements. It is thus proposed that an up-to-date version of 'A Compilation of the Law, Political, Economic Systems of the Warring States' [131] is warranted.

Geography of Warring States, Textual Research, and Map Compilation

During the turbulent years of the Warring States, the states went through incessant wars, territorial attrition, and annexation. Due to the political strategy of Vertical Coalition (integration) and Horizontal Alliance, changing topology and terrain of the states were frequent. When it comes to discussing topology of the status of wars, a comprehensive compilation of textual research on the geography and compilation of new maps is also warranted.

Qing scholars conducted extensive research into the place names of the Warring States. The notable ones include: Zhang Qi's 'Warring States Geography Explained', (which was incorporated in the *Historiography Series*); Cheng Enze and Di Ziqi, 'A Research on the Geography of State Strategies' (incorporated in *Yueyatang congshu* book series) and Gu Guanguang's '*The Geography of the Seven States.*' [132] The compilation by Gu Guanguang was the most comprehensive; while the textual research by Cheng and Di were in more detail though both works were still inadequate in many aspects. Cheng and Di did a thorough textual study of the place of origin of the fief lords and their ministers, by using their surnames as place names. (For example, it was based on the premise that a place named Su could be where Su Qin was supposed to have come from.) [133] Apparently, this was an erroneous approach. The *Warring States Territorial Maps* compiled by Yang Shoujing (incorporated in '*Successive Dynasty Maps and Atlas*' [134] was predominantly based on the works of Cheng and Di. In reality, the work used only the place names in the *Warring States Strategies ZGC*, and he made the same mistakes as Cheng and Di, by using surnames and family names for identification of geographical locations.'[135] The more contemporary work by Zhong Fengnian, 'A Study of Changes of Territory of the Various States

130 *A Study of the Appended Information on the Seven States, Qiguokao dingbu* 七國考訂補 by Mu Wenyuan 穆文遠 (1930-2012).

131 *A Compilation of the Law, Political, Economic System of the Warring States, Zhanguo Huiyao* 戰國會要.

132 Zhang Qi 張琦 (contemporary) – 'Warring States Geography Explained, Zhanguoce shidi 戰國策釋地' (published 1990), (it was incorporated in the *Historiography Series, Shishu congshu,* 史學叢書.)

Cheng Enze 程恩澤 (1785-1837 CE) and Di Ziqi 狄子奇 (?) – A Research of the Geography of State Strategies, *Guoce diming kao* 國策地命考 (incorporated in *Yueyatang congshu* 粵雅堂叢書 book series) and Gu Guanguang 顧觀光 (1799-1862 CE) - *The Geography of the Seven States, Qiguo dilikao* 七國地理考.

133 True in some instances.

134 The Warring States Territorial Maps, Zhanguo jiangyu tu', compiled by Yang Shoujing 楊守敬 (1839-1915) (incorporated in *Successive Dynastic Maps and Atlas, Lidai yu ditu,* 歷代輿地圖).

135 The *Surname and Family Name Places, Zhuguo xingshi di* (?) 諸國姓氏地.

During the Warring States' was published in *Yugong* the bimonthly publication; [136] but it was not published in a combined edition. Between 1970 and 1971, I (Yang Kuan) was seconded to the Geography-History Department at Fudan University. Qian Linshu and I collaborated to produce the first volume of the *Chinese History Atlas*; [137] it was published in 1982. In the work, the Warring States maps were based on the verifiable works of the Qing scholars, appended with amendments and corrections, and the maps were entirely redrawn. The locations of the Fief States, Prefectures, Counties of Middle Epoch of the Warring States (350 BCE); *The Map of the Locations of Fief Lords* was principally based on the first edition of my book, *A History of the Warring States, ZGS.* [138]

Archaeological Discoveries and New Textual Information

Archaeological discoveries with new textual information have made invaluable contributions in restoring the scattered historical records, as well as making amendments to the anachronistic errors in the historical texts. Recent discoveries have been of great help in correcting the dates and entries; furthermore, they have been most useful for determining the authenticity of inserted materials. We have previously raised the importance of the discovery of the *Bamboo Annals* during the Western Jin Dynasty. Later, during the Northern Song period, the study of the bronze script became widespread, scholars began to place emphasis on the study of stone scriptures and bronze inscriptions on bronze utensils; it created an interest to collect, research and publish these findings. The trend started when a 'stone-drum with carved calligraphies' was discovered during the early years of the Tang dynasty at *Fengxiang*; it was later transferred to the capital city (Xi'an). Further discoveries of these stone drums were also made at the time of the regnal years of Jiayou (1056-1063 CE), and Zhiping (1064-1067 CE) in Fengxiang and Chaonachiu; [139] three slabs of stone carving with scripts of, 'Qin curses Chu script.' [140] The then-contemporary scholars Su Shi and Ouyang Xiu; [141] placed great emphasis on the discoveries, they compiled records and conducted philological studies of the texts. The original stone slabs and stone rubbing were lost during the Southern Song era; facsimiles exist in the *'Jiangtie'* and *'Rutie'* and were published in the *Yuan Zhizheng Zhongwu kanben* publication.[142] More recently Rong Geng researched into the ancient scripts, using the materials in *'Jiangtie'* and *'Rutie'*, and incorporated them into his work of,

136 Zhong Fengnian 鐘鳳念, 'A Study of the Changes of Territory of the Various States during the Warring States – Zhanguo geguo jiangyu bianqiankao 戰國各國疆域 變遷考' in *Yugong* 禹貢. (*Yugong* was a biweekly publication that was introduced in March 1934. The publication ceased publication in July 1937. It was an important publication that included ethnicity, geography, and history of China.)

137 Between 1970 and 1971 (Yang Kuan) from the Geographic History Department at the University of Fudan 復旦大學歷史系 歷史地理研究室 and Qian Linshu 錢林書 collaborated to produce the first volume of '*Chinese Historic Atlas*', 中國歷史地圖集.

138 *ZGS* 戰國史.

139 Fengxiang 鳳翔 – was the old capital of Qin 秦 – Yong 雍.

Jiayou 嘉祐 (1056-1063 CE), the 9th regnal period of Emperor Ren of Song 宋仁宗. Emperor Ying of Song 宋英宗, Zhiping 治平 (1064-1067 CE) in Fengxiang 鳳翔 and Chaonachiu 朝那湫.

Chaonaqiu 朝那湫 – this was the place where sacrificial offerings were made to 湫淵 the water deity.

140 'Qin zu Chu wen, 秦詛楚文'.

141 Su Shi 蘇軾 (1039-1112 CE), Ouyang Xiu 歐陽修 (1007-1072 CE).

142 *Jiangtie* 絳帖 and *Rutie* 汝帖 were facsimiles of the scripts, and *Yuan zhizheng zhongwu kanben* 元至正中吳刊本.

Ancient Stone Carving Piecemeal.' [143] Guo Moruo employed the *Yuan Zhizheng Zhongwu kanben* publication to edit another version of 'Qin Scourge Chu script.' [144] It was the incident when the king of Qin ordered the imperial diviner to utter a curse against the king of Chu, calling forth the Deities of Wuxian and Dashen Jueqiu to crush the Chu army. [145] Imperial Diviner Zongzhu was the official shaman at the holy shrine; [146] these diviners supposedly possessed the mystical power of the shaman. The legendary Wuxian was the original master of shamanism, and these men were capable of communicating with the Divines and acted as intermediaries between the corporals and the Divines. [147] Dashen Jueqiu was the Deity at the Qiuyuan Lake. [148] It was said that he was comparable in power to Hebo, the Lord of the River, [149] who was the Master of the Underworld of the Abyss. This information provided us with some details that, like the Song state people, the Qin people also employed shamans or priests to utter curses against its enemies before a battle. Rong Geng, [150] the contemporary Chinese scholar, asserted that it was at the time of King Hui of Qin Gengyaun 12th year (313 BCE). The incident happened when Zhang Yi deceived the King of Chu that Qin would cede six hundred *li* of land to Chu if the latter were to break its pledged alliance with Qi. Having been tricked, Chu retaliated by sending a huge army against Qin. The king of Qin commanded his imperial diviner to utter curses against the encroaching Chu army. The stone slabs were where the curses were carved. [151] These stone slabs have yielded important historical information. (See *ZZTJ* translated text 313-11).

---

143 Rong Geng 容庚 (1894-1983 CE), *Ancient Stone Carving Piecemeal, Gu shike lingshi* 古石刻零拾.

144 Guo Moruo 郭沫若 (1892-1978 CE) *Zu Chuwen kaoshi* 詛楚文考釋 was published in *Guo Moruo quanji* 郭末若全集, Vol 9 under the heading of 'Kaogubian 考古編'.

145 Deities of *Wuxian* 巫咸 and *Dashen Jueqiu* 大沈厥湫.

146 Imperial Diviner, *zongzhu* 宗祝.

147 Xuxian 巫咸 is mentioned in the *Shanhaijing* 山海經 and mention is made of a Wuxian Polity 巫咸國.

148 Qiuyuan Lake 湫淵 was a lake at the time of Qin in Pengyangxian 彭陽縣; it has since dried up.

149 Hebo 河伯 the River Lord. The River deity, some say he was the Deity of Huanghe 黄河, others say it was the Deity of all rivers in Zhongguo 中國. It is said he rode on a white tortoise, preceded by multi-coloured fish and went on his inspection tours of the rivers. People prayed to him and made offerings ensuring that there was no flooding or inundations.

150 Rong Geng 容庚 (1894-1983 CE).

151 (Yang Kuan's footnotes): - Guo Moruo 郭沫若 (1892-1978 CE) is of the opinion that the other piece of 'Yatuo Wen 亞駝文' from *Zu Chuwen* 詛楚文 was a fabricated work of the time of Song 宋, which is quite probable. 'Yatuo Wen 亞駝文' is not appended in '*Jiangti* 絳帖' or '*Rutie* 汝帖'.

(Author's note – There are three pieces of *Zu Chuwen* 詛楚文 stone inscriptions, *Gao Wuxian wen* 告巫咸文, *Gao Da ShenJueqiu wen* 告大沈厥湫文, *Gao Yatuo wen* 告亞駝文; the three scripts are basically similar, except the deities are different.)

(Yang Kuan's footnotes): Chen Weizhan 陳煒湛 (1938-) published an article on, 'Presenting Doubts on the Curses on Chu.' 詛楚文献疑, in *Studies of Ancient Texts*, 古文字研究 volume 14. The author, failing to grasp the meanings of those shamanistic curses, maintains that the three stone inscriptions were fabrications from the time of the Tang 唐 and Song 宋 dynasties, and he does not come up with any constructive evidence. He maintains that the script-type was suspicious and that it was a variant form of Small-seal *xiaozhuan* 小篆 that belonged to the Qin dynasty rather than that of the Warring States. In reality, at the time of the Warring States, there already were two forms of calligraphy. The bronze scripts and stone carvings belonged to the neat script 工整一體, which was the origin of *xiaozhuan*; whereas the scripts used on bronze utensils, bamboo and silk scrolls belonged to the cursive script *caoshutai* 草率體 (meaning hasty brush stroke), which was the

Part II. Verification of Important Chronological Dates of the Warring States [152]

The chronicles of historical events of each of the fief states were based on the years of the reign of the different fief lords during the Warring States. For histography research, to ensure that the dates of entry were properly chronicled, besides using the years of reign, historians have also converted the dates to the Julian calendar for easy reference. However, many of the dates and sequences of succession chronicled in the *SJ* 'Sequence of the Six States' are inaccurate. [153] Scholars have used the *Bamboo Annals* for textual research to verify the dates and sequence of succession; numerous errors have since been validated and corrected. [154] Nevertheless, not all the revisions are completely satisfactory. Hence, it is felt that some of the major events needed further reassessment and verification.

1. The Reigning Dates of marquises Wen of Wei, Wu of Wei, kings Hui and Xiang of Wei. [155]

SJ 'Sequence of the Six States', records that the 1st year of the Marquis Wen of Wei was the 2nd year of the King Weilie of Zhou, [156] which was 424 BCE. The 1st year of Marquis Wu of Wei is recorded as the 16th year of King An of Zhou, [157] which was 386 BCE. The 1st year of King Hui of Wei was the 6th year of King Lie of Zhou, which was 370 BCE. The 1st year of King Xiang of Wei was the 35th year of King Xian of Zhou, which was 334 BCE. Besides, the 1st year of the King Ai of Wei was the 3rd year of King Shenjing of Zhou,

---

precursor of *lishu* 隸書 clerical Script. The script used on 詛楚文 was the neat script, for instance, the word *wu* 巫 was written as 𠀁, which corresponded with the oracle bone script 甲古文 and bronze script 金文. Contemporary researchers have employed the '*Zu Chuwen* 詛楚文' to decipher the word '𠀁 as *wu* 巫' used on oracle bones and bronze scripts. Chen Weizhang further suspects that the context did not make sense, and the historical incident was equally doubtful. The fact is, the scripts were scourge chants used by the shamans, and they did not make sense at any rate. The shamans uttered a curse on the enemy, "...for breaching a pledge, and a curse is thus warranted. 倍(背)盟犯詛." Meanwhile, all the crimes of the former emperors and kings that brought on the annihilation of their kingdoms were appended onto the king of the enemy state as curses. Chen Weizhan further mentions that the texts and phases appeared to have been copied from earlier texts. All these were the incantations of the shamans; the scholars at the time of Tang and Song could not possibly fabricate these scripts, as they had no knowledge of the practice then. Su Shi 蘇軾 (1037-1101 CE) composed a poem,[NB] "....Hollowing out the fetus is an innocent act; the kinsfolk are being surrounded and harassed. Tallying all the allegations, they are far worse than the unrest during the time of King Jie and King Zhou...." and "......刳胎殺無罪, 親族遭圍绊, 計其所稱訴, 何啻桀 紂亂." It goes to demonstrate that Su Shi did not understand the nature of the 詛楚文. Details see my article (Yang Kuan) 'Qin zu Chu wen suobianying di zudi wushu', '秦詛楚文所表演的詛的巫術' that was published in *Wenxue weichan* 文學遺產. 1995 年 6 期.

[NB] Su Shi 蘇軾 (Song), '鳳翔八觀，并叙其二' 詛楚文.

152 Translated from *Yang Kuan* 楊寬 – *ZGS* 戰國史, Pages 723-731. N.B. Some parts of this article have already appeared in the previous pages; however, this is different article.

153 *SJ* 史記 – 'Sequence of the Six States, Liuguo nianbiao 六國年表'.

154 The *Bamboo Annals - Old Edition Bamboo Annals, Guben zhushu jinian* 古本竹書紀年.

155 Marquis Wen of Wei 魏文侯, Marquis Wu of Wei 魏武侯, King Hui of Wei 魏惠王 and King Xiang of Wei 魏襄王.

156 King Weilie of Zhou 周威烈王.

157 King Xiang of Wei 魏襄王.
King Xian of Zhou 周顯王.

which was 318 BCE. [158] The dates of the reigns of marquises Wen, and Wu of Wei, and kings of Hui, and Xiang of in the 'Sequence of the Six States' are seriously flawed.

There is a passage in the *Mengzi*, which relates that King Hui of Liang (Wei) said to Mengzi, "There is no state under Heaven that was more formidable than the State of Jin;[159] something, you, Old Sir, are fully aware. However, when I ascended the throne, we lost a battle to Qi in the east, and my eldest son died. [160] To the west, I lost seven hundred *li* of land to Qin. To the south, I was humiliated by Chu. The disgrace and humiliations mortify me; I intend to seek revenge for the dead by making sacrifices. How can I accomplish it?" (This is from *Mengzi* – 'Liang Huiwang Part I.') [161] The passage is also narrated in *SJ* in 'The House of Wei Biography', in which it states that it was during the 30th year of King Hui of Wei when Prince Shen died at the Battle of Maling. Whereas, 'the loss of seven hundred *li* of land to Qin in the West,' was the incident when Wei ceded the areas west of the River *Xihe* and Shangjun Prefecture to Qin. The humiliation by Chu was the battle of Xiangling when Chu General Zhao Yang defeated the Wei army. [162] However, according to *SJ*, the ceding of Xihe to Qin was during the 5th year of King

---

158 The following dates are from the *SJ* 史記 – 'Sequence of the Six States 六國年表'. (The dates are flaw according to Yang Kuan.)

1st year Marquis Wen of Wei 魏文侯 = 2nd year King Lie of Zhou 周烈王 - 424 BCE.

1st year Marquis Wu of Wei Wuhou 魏武侯 = 16th year King An of Zhou 周安王 - 386 BCE.

1st year King Hui of Wei 魏惠王 = 6th year King Lie of Zhou 周烈王 - 370 BCE.

1st year King Xiang of Wei 魏襄王 = 35th year King Xian of Zhou 周顯王 - 334 BCE.

1st year King Ai of Wei 魏哀王 = 3rd year King Shenjing of Zhou 周慎靚王 - 318 BCE.

159 The *Mengzi*, Mengzi visited King Hui of Liang (Wei) 孟子見梁 (魏) 惠王.

State of Jin 晉. The Wei 魏 family clan was ministers of Jin prior to 403 BCE. After 403 BCE, the three family clans of Wei, Zhao 趙 and Hann 韓 partitioned Jin. The King of Liang 梁 (Wei) still referred to Wei as Jin.

SJ 史記 – 'House of Chu Biography 楚世家' relates, "King Xuan of Chu 6th year 楚宣王六年. The San-Jin 三晉 (Three-Jins) became powerful, Wei was particularly commanding." Hence, he said, "There is no state more formidable than Jin."

160 According to *ZZTJ*, his son was captured.

161 Mencius –The *Mengzi* 孟子, 'King Hui of Liang Part I, Liang Huiwang shangpian 梁惠王上篇'.

This visitation is not related in *ZZTJ*.

一洒之 – After winning a battle, one made sacrifice to honour the dead; in this case it meant 'avenge the dead'.

162 The *SJ* 史記, 'House of Wei Biography 魏世家'.

"長子死焉" - 30th year of King Hui of Wei 魏惠王, according to the *SJ* the Crown Prince *Shen* 太子申 died in the Battle of Maling 馬陵. (However, from recent archaeological finds, the prince was captured and did not die, see below.)

"西喪地于秦七百里" - Loss of 700 *li* of land to Qin in the West of Wei, by ceding areas west of the River - *Xihe* 西河 and Shangjun Prefecture 上郡.

"南辱于楚" - Humiliation by Chu was the Battle of Xiangling, when Wei was defeated by the Chu General Zhao Yang 楚柱國 昭陽 at Xiangling 襄陵.

A cache of bamboo strips was unearthed from a Han Tomb at Yinqueshan Mound 銀雀山 漢墓竹簡 in 1972. The script has a detailed account of the battle of Guiling 桂陵, where no mention is made of Pang Juan 龐涓; however, during the second Battle of Maling 馬陵 (13 years later), it mentions Pang Juan committed suicide and Shen the Crown Prince of Wei 太子申 was captured.

Xiang of Wei, the ceding of Shangjun Prefecture was the 7th year of King Xiang, and the defeat by Chu at Xiangling happened during the 12th year of King Xiang. How could King Hui possibly know what happened after his death and related his humiliations to Mengzi? Apparently, *SJ* must be incorrect with its sequencing.

The *SJ* 'House of Wei Biography' relates,' [163] "King Hui of Wei died during his 36th year, his son King Xiang ascended to the throne; King Xiang died during his 16th year, his son King Ai succeeded to the throne. King Ai reigned for 23 years and then died. However, the *Bamboo Annals* has a different account, [164] it says, "During the 36th year of King Hui, the king changed his regnal year *gaiyuan*, recommencing from the 1st year, he changed his title to King Huicheng of Wei and died in the 16th year." (Du Yu's *Clarifications on Collections of Chunqiu Books and Biographies Postscripts*) and *Generational Records - Shiben* also relate, [165] "King Hui gave birth to King Xiang, and he fathered King Zhao." (This is a quote from *Shiji suoyin*, 'House of Wei Biography'.) There was not a King Ai. [166] The truth is during the 36th year of King Hui of Wei; the king did not die, he merely changed his regnal year to 1st year – (a practice called *gaiyuan*); [167] he continued to reign for 16 more years before he died. *SJ* had mistakenly used the *gaiyuan* regnal 1st year of King Hui as the 1st year of King Xiang of Wei, assigning the reign of King Xiang to the reign of King Ai. Ever since the discovery of the *Bamboo Annals* (during the time of *Jin* in 281 CE), the text has been used to correct the mistakes of the *SJ* in the chronicles of Warring States; it was a correct assumption. The mistakes in *SJ* can also be inferred by studying the text thoroughly. The *SJ* 'House of Zhao Biography' says, [168] "During the 1st year of King Wuling of Zhao ... King Hui of Liang (Wei), accompanied by his Crown Prince Si, King Xuan of Hann and his Crown Prince Cang, went forth to the Xingong Palace to pay homage." According to the *SJ* 'Sequence of the Six States' it was the 10th year of King Xiang of Wei. However, Si was the name of King Xiang. (*Shiji suoyin* 'House of Wei Biography' quoting from *Generational Records*; and *Shiji suoyin* 'Su Qin's Biography' quoting from *Generational Records* that both texts matched, "King Xiang of Wei's name was indeed Si".) If the year was indeed the 10th year of King Xiang of Wei, the Crown Prince could not possibly be Si; in other words, it was King Hui of Wei who led

---

The 'Sun Bin Bingfa Captured Pang Juan 簡本, 孫臏兵法 禽龐涓 Edition, mentions that Sun Bin captured Pang Juan at Guiling 桂陵, apparently contradicts with the accounts in the *SJ* 史記.

163 *SJ* 史記, 'House of Wei Biography 魏世家.'

164 The *Bamboo Annals* 竹書紀年.

165 *Du Yu* 杜預 (222-285 BC), West Jin 西晉 – The *Clarifications on Collections of Chunqiu Texts and Biographies Postscripts*, The *Chunqiu jingzhuan jijie houxu* 春秋經傳 集解後序.
The Generational Records, the *Shiben* 世本, also known as *Xiben* 系本 or *Diaben* 代本, is a record of dynastic history of sovereigns from the time of the legendary Huangdi 黄帝 to the time of the Warring States, and the inheritance centres on Jin 晉, it was composed during the time of the Warring States. The book was probably composed by a Zhao 趙 national and has been estimated to be compiled between 234-228 BCE.
杜預春秋經傳 集解后序 and 世本 relate, "惠王生襄王, 襄王生昭王."

166 The *Shiji suoyin* 史記索隱, 'House of Wei Biography, 魏世家.'

167 *Gaiyuan* 改元 was also known as *gengyuan* 更元 – changing the regnal year.

168 The *SJ* 史記, 'House of Zhao Biography 趙世家', 1st year of King Wuling of Zhao 武靈王.
King Hui of Liang 梁惠王 and Prince Si 太子嗣.
King Xuan of Hann 韓宣王 and Prince Cang 太子倉 went to Xin palace 信宮 to pay homage.

Crown Prince Si to the Zhao Court to pay homage. Then when we base the account on the *Bamboo Annals*, the year of homage was the latter-regnal year, *houyuan* 10th year, of King Hui of Wei. In which case, the Crown Prince was Si (King Xiang). From this, we are able to verify the accuracy of the *Bamboo Annals*.

The next question to raise is, "Does one solve the problem if we were to change the regnal date of King Xiang of Wei in *SJ* to King Hui's *houyuan* - regnal year; and to change the reign of King Ai in *SJ* to the reign of King Xiang? The answer is negative, as when we try to compare the events that transpired during King Hui of Wei in both texts; the years chronicled in the two texts do not match entirely, and some of the events were out by two years and others by one year. Why was it so?

Events related to King Hui of Wei with one-year variance between the *Bamboo Annals* and *Shiji*:

a. The *Commentary on Rivers and Waters* on 'Heshuizhu'[169] and *Lushi* 'Guoming ji Part 4' quote from the *Bamboo Annals*,[170] "During the 2nd year of King Huicheng of Liang (Wei), Tian Shou of Qi led an army to attack Zhao, the city of Guan, was besieged,[171] and Guan surrendered." Whereas, the *SJ* 'House of Wei Biography' states, "During the 3rd year of King Hui, the Qi army defeated our army at Guan."
b. The *Shiji suoyin* 'House of Wei Biography' quoting from the *Bamboo Annals*, "Marquises Gong of Lu, Huan of Song, Cheng of Wey, and Xi of Zheng came to court to pay homage, the incidents all happened during the 14th year (of King Hui of Liang). Whereas in *SJ* 'House of Wei Biography' and *SJ* 'Sequence of the Six States' read, "During the 15th year of King Hui, Lu, Wey, Song and Zheng lords came to court."[172]
c. The *Shiji suoyin* – 'Sunzi, Wu Qi Biography', relates Wang Shao's quotes from *Bamboo Annals*, which said,[173] "King Hui of Liang 17th year, Qi Tian Ji defeated Liang at Guiling." *Commentary on Rivers and Waters Shuijing* – on 'Jishui River, Jishuizhu' also quoting from the *Bamboo Annals* says, "King Hui of Liang (Wei) 17th year, Tian Qi (Tian Ji) made an expedition against my Dongbi, the battle was joined at

169 *Shuijingzhu* 水經注 - The *Commentary on Rivers and Waters* – Huanghe 黄河, the Heshuizhu 河水注 (N.B. Some translators have appended a 'classic' to the title, I have chosen to leave it out, as the word – *Jing* 經 used here bears no notion as a classic.)

170 The *Lushi, the Major History or State History* 路史, 'Guomingji, part 4 國名紀丁', the name of the book implies 'Major History', it was composed by the Song scholar Luo Bi 宋羅泌 (1131-1189 CE), in 47 volumes. The text includes history, geography, customs and genealogy from the most ancient times; even before the legendary *Huangdi* 黄帝, tracing back as far as the mythical San-Huang 三皇, Wu-Di 五帝. (Luo Bi, an experienced and well-travelled scholar, probably based his writings on oral traditions gathered from various parts of China in his days; unfortunately, he did not append records of his sources.)

171 Tian Shou of Qi 齊田壽 attacked Zhao 趙, the city of Guan 觀.

172 The *Shiji suoyin* 史記索隱, 'House of Wei Biography' 魏世家.
The *Bamboo Annals* 紀年.
The *Shiji suoyin* 史記索隱, 'House of Wei Biography 魏世家'.
The *SJ* 史記, 'Sequence of the Six States 六國年表.'

173 The *Shiji suoyin* 史記索隱, 'Sunzi, Wu Qi Biography, 孫子吳起列傳', Wang Shao 王劭 quoting from the *Bamboo Annals*.

Guiyang.[174] (The *Commentary on Rivers and Waters* says, "Guiyang is, in fact, Guiling," as the word 'yang' was mistaken for 'ling.') Our army was defeated, and it dispersed." Whereas, in *SJ* 'House of Wei Biography' it says, "During the 18th year of King Hui of Wei, the army laid siege to Handan (of Zhao); Zhao appealed to Qi; Qi commanded Tian Ji and Sun Bin to the rescue of Zhao. [175] The army defeated Wei at Guiling." The account in *SJ* 'Sequence of the Six States' is similar. (See 353-1)

The *SJ* 'House of Wei Biography' says, "The *Bamboo Annals* relates, 28th year, ...joined battle with Qi's Tian Ban at Maling. [176] Two years prior, Wei defeated the army of Hann at Maling. [177] 18th year, Zhao (it should be Qi) again defeated Wei at Guiling. Guiling and Maling are different places." The above statement was a quote from the *Bamboo Annals*. The 'two years prior' and '18th year' were based on *SJ* 'House of Wei Biography' to relate that Guiling and Maling were different places. Former scholars have often mistaken *Suoyin's* 'two years prior' and '18th year' as the actual accounts of the *Bamboo Annals*. Hence, we could not use this piece of evidence to claim that the *Bamboo Annals* and *SJ* match in these dates.

d. The *Commentary on Rivers and Waters* on 'Huaishui River' quotes from the *Bamboo Annals*, "King Hui of Liang (Wei) 17th year. Song Jing Gu, Wey Gongsun Cang allied with the army of Qi to besiege my Xiangling." [178] 18th year, the King allied with Hann and defeated the combined armies of the fief lords at Xiangling." The account in *SJ* 'House of Wei Biography, relates it as King Hui, '19th year the fief lords besieged my Xiangling.' *SJ* 'Sequence of the Six States' has the same account.

e. The *Commentary on Rivers and Waters* on 'Zhuoshui and Zhangshui Rivers' and *Lushi* 'Guomingji' quoting from the *Bamboo Annals* say, [179] "During the 30th year of King Huicheng of Liang (Wei), Qin enfeoffed Wey Yang (Shang Yang) at Wu, [180] the place is renamed Shang." The *SJ* 'Lord Shang Biography' also says, [181] "The *Bamboo Annals* relates, 'Qin enfeoffed Shang Yang during the 30th year of King Hui." Whereas, according to *SJ* 'Sequence of the Six States' it relates, "Qin enfeoffed Shang Yang,

---

174 *The Commentary on Rivers and Waters, Shuijing* 水經 on 'Jishui River, 濟水注', quoting from *Bamboo Annals*.
SJ 史記, 'House of Wei 魏世家'.
King Huicheng of Liang 梁惠成王.
Qi Tian Qi 齊田期 (Tian Ji 田忌).
Dongbi 東鄙. Guiyang 桂陽 陵.

175 King Hui of Wei, 惠王. Handan (of Zhao) 趙 邯鄲. Qi Tianji 齊田忌. Sun Bin 孫臏.

176 Qi Tian Ban 齊田肦 battled with Wei at Maling 馬陵.
Shiji suoyin 史記索隱, 'House of Wei 魏世家', "Quoting from *Bamboo Annals* 紀年'.

178 Song, Jing Gu 宋景敾 Wey, Gongsun Cang 衛公孫倉.
Xiangling 襄陵.
The Commentary on Rivers and Waters 水經注 on 'Huaishui River 淮水注', quoting from *Bamboo Annals* 紀年.

179 *The Commentary on Rivers and Waters* 水經注 on 'Zhuoshui and Zhangshui Rivers 濁漳水注.'
Lushi 路史, 'Guomingji 國名紀, Part 6 己.'

180 Wu 鄔 changed to Shang 商.

181 *Shiji suoyin* 史記索隱, 'Lord Shangjun Biography 商君列傳'.
'Bamboo Annals 紀年.'

the military commander, with the title of *daliangzao*;"[182] during the 22nd year of Duke Xiao of Qin, i.e. 31st year of King Hui of Wei, the 30th year of King Xuan of Chu. *SJ* 'Qin Basic Annals' also states, "Duke Xiao of Qin 22nd year, Shang Yang was enfeoffed as a fief lord, appending him with the title of Lord Shang." Finally, *SJ* 'House of Chu Biography' also relates, "King Xuan 30th year, Qin enfeoffed Wey Yang at Shang."

Events with Variance of Two Years between the *Bamboo Annals* and *Shiji*

(I) *SJ* 'Sunzi, Wu Qi Biographies' records Wang Shao quoting from the *Bamboo Annals*, "(King Hui of Liang) 27th year, 12th month, Tian Ban of Qi defeated Liang at Maling." *Shiji suoyin* 'House of Wei Biography'[183] quotes from the *Bamboo Annals*, "(King Hui of Liang) 28th year joined battle with Tian Ban of Qi at Maling." *Shiji suoyin* 'Lord Mengchang Biography' states, [184] "The army was defeated at Maling." Moreover, under *Shiji suoyin*, it also adds, "According to the *Bamboo Annals* it was the 28th year of King Hui of Liang." However, in *SJ* 'House of Wei Biography' it is entered as, "(King Hui) 30th year.... In the end the crown prince joined battle with Qi; the battle was lost in Maling." It is similar to *SJ's* 'Sequence of the Six States'.

(II) The *Shiji suoyin* 'The House of Wei Biography' quoting from the *Bamboo Annals* says, "(King Hui) 29th year 5th month, Qi Tian Ban attacked our Dongbi. [185] 9th month, Wey Yang of Qin attacked our Xibi.[186] 10th month, Handan (Zhao) attacked our Beibi. [187] The King counterattacked against Wey Yang, our army lost." The *Commentary on Rivers and Waters* 'Sishui River' quoting from the *Bamboo Annals* relates, [188] "King Hui of Liang 29th year 5th month, Tian Ban of Qi and the Song people attacked our Dongbi, besieging Pingyang."[189] *Shiji suoyin* 'Lord Shang Biography' also quoting from the *Bamboo Annals* says, [190] "King Hui of Liang 29th year, Wey Yang of Qin assaulted Liang at Xibi." While, 'House of Wei Biography' relates it as, "King Hui 31st year, Qin, Zhao and Qi made a combined assault on my kingdom." *SJ* 'Sequence of the Six States' also relates it as, "King Hui of Wei 31st year, Lord Shang of Qin attacked my kingdom; our Crown Prince Ang was captured." [191] Adding that it was during this year - "Qi and Zhao combined their forces against Wei."

---

182 Qin enfeoffed Shang Yang 商鞅 the Military Commander, *daliangzao* 大良造.
SJ 史記, 'Sequence of the Six States 六國年表.'

183 The *Shiji suoyin* 史記索隱, 'Sunzi and Wu Qi Biographies 孫子吳起列傳' relates Wang Shao's 王劭 quote from *Bamboo Annals* 紀年.
The *Shiji suoyin* 史記索隱, 'House of Wei 魏世家' quoting from *Bamboo Annals* 紀年.

184 The *Shiji suoyin* 史記索隱, 'Lord Mengchang Biography 孟嘗君列傳'.

185 Qi Tian Ban 齊田朌 attacked our Dongbi 東鄙.

186 Qin Wey Yang 秦衛鞅 attacked Liang (at) Wei Xibi 梁魏西鄙.

187 Handan (Zhao) 邯鄲 (趙) attacked our Beibi 北鄙.

188 The *Commentary on Rivers and Waters* 水經注 on 'Sishui River, Sishuizhu 泗水注'.

189 Pingyang 平陽.

190 The *Shiji suoyin* 史記索隱, 'Lord Shang Biography 商君列傳.'

191 Crown Prince Ang 卬.

Making a comparison of the events on King Hui of Wei chronicled in the *Bamboo Annals* and *SJ*, there are five instances where the discrepancy was one year, two with a divergence of two years, whereas none of the instances corresponded in the same year. Textual researchers were aware of these discrepancies. (For instance, *Lei Xueqi's* work on '*Bamboo Annals Meaning Substantiation*' *Zhushu jinian yizheng* and other works.) [192] Some of the scholars speculated that it might have caused by the fact that the chronicles in *SJ* were based on Zhou calendar *zhouzheng*, [193] whereas the calendar system used by the *Bamboo Annals* was Xia calendar *xiazheng*. [194] It was further argued that all the cited events fell within mid-winter or the second month of winter *zhongdong* or the last month of Winter *jidong*; [195] hence by using the Zhou calendar *zhouzheng*, these events would fall into the first month or second month of the next year. However, the question remains; why did all the events regarding King Hui of Liang mentioned in the *Bamboo Annals* inadvertently happened during the mid-winter *zhongdong* or late-winter *jidong* time? Further, why did none of the events recounted in the *Bamboo Annals* and *SJ* correspond? It is accepted that a war could last for more than one year; whereas instances such as the enfeoffment of Lord Shang (Shang Yang) by Qin could not possibly spread over two years. Furthermore, the incident of Lu, Wey, Song and Zheng lords paying homage to King Hui at the Wei court could not last for two years. We know that the composition of the *SJ* was based on the '*Qin Annals*' (*Qinji*), the dates of the major events should be fairly accurate. The *Bamboo Annals*, being a Wei court chronicle, should also be quite precise with its historical dates. Hence, the question of the discrepancy between the *Bamboo Annals* and *SJ* remains unsolved. Why is there a discrepancy of one or two years on the chronicles of the events on King Hui of Wei between the two texts? If the problem were not solved the use of the *Bamboo Annals* to authenticate the dates in *SJ* would never be accurate. It is a key issue that required attention for verification and authentication of the chronologies of the Warring States.

There are other discrepancies besides King Hui of Wei in the *Bamboo Annals* and *SJ*; the years of reigns of marquises Wen and Wu of Wei are also in variance. Both *SJ* 'House of Wei Biography' and *SJ* 'Sequence of the Six States' record that Marquis Wen of Wei was on the throne for 38 years and Marquis Wu reigned for 16 years. Whereas *Shiji suoyin* 'House of Wei Biography' says under the heading of, "Marquis Wen died" that, "The *Bamboo Annals* relates, (Marquis Wu of Wei) died during his 50th year." Then upon "Marquis Wu's death," it adds, "The *Bamboo Annals* related, 'Marquis Wu died in his 26th year.'" Both Lei Xueqi in his *Zhushu jinian yizheng* and Wang Guowei in his *Guben Zhushu jinian jixiao* maintain that the *Bamboo Annals* was correct and that based on *SJ*'s account of Marquis Wu's

---

192 Lei Xueqi 雷學淇 *Bamboo Annals Meaning Substantiation, The Zhushu jinian yizheng* 竹書紀年義証.

193 *Zhouzheng* 周正 – the Zhou dynasty used the 11th month of each year as the first month of the next new year.

194 *Xiazheng* 夏正 – the Xia Dynasty used the first month of the new year as the first month of the year.

195 *Zhongdong* 仲冬 – mid winter month; *Jidong* 季冬 is last month of winter.

year of death, one could deduce the dates of the reign of marquises Wen and Wu. As a result, it was established that Marquis Wen's 1st year was the 23rd year of King Ding of Zhou (446 BCE), and Marquis Wu's 1st year was King An of Zhou 6th year (396 BCE). However, *Shiji suoyin* 'House of Wei Biography' quoting from the *Bamboo Annals* says, "The first year of Marquis Wu of Wei was the 14th year of Marquis Lie of Zhao." Marquis Lie of Zhao 1st year fell on the 18th year of King Weilie of Zhou. (*SJ* 'House of Zhao Biography' and 'Sequence of the Six States' made an error by affixing an extra Duke Wu after Marquis Liu.) Marquis Lie 14th year should be the 7th year of King An of Zhou. Why is there a difference of one year between Lei Xueqi's and Wang Guowei's computations of the above? Had the record of Marquis Wu of Wei in *SJ* been ten years shorter than the *Bamboo Annals* then the discrepancies between *SJ* and the *Bamboo Annals* should be ten years. However, the compilations show that there were only nine years. For instance:

(a). The *SJ* 'House of Wei Biography' says, "Marquis Wu 2nd year, ... the Marquis constructed the walled cities of Anyi and Wangyuan," Whereas '*Shiji suoyin* quoting from the *Bamboo Annals* says, "11th year.... The Marquis constructed the walled cities of Luoyang, Anyi and Wangyuan."

(b). The *SJ* 'House of Hann Biography' says, "Marquis Ai of Hann 2nd year, he annihilated Zheng. Hence, the state moved its capital to Zheng." The 2nd year of Marquis Ai of Hann in the *SJ* should be the 12th year of Marquis Wu of Wei; whereas *Shiji suoyin* quoting the *Bamboo Annals* says, "During the 21st year of Marquis Wu, Hann annihilated Zheng, Marquis Ai entered into Zheng."

Again, why is there a one-year discrepancy of Marquis Wu of Wei's reign based the textual research of Lei Xueqi and Wang Guowei and the quote of *Shiji suoyin* from the *Bamboo Annals*? This apparently is related to the one-year discrepancy between the *Bamboo Annals* and *SJ* accounts of King Hui of Wei's reign that was mentioned earlier.

SJ 'House of Wei Biography' says, "During the 1st year, King Xiang met the other fief lords at the Xuzhou province, recognizing each other as kings." '*Qin Basic Annals - Qin benji*' also chronicles that this was the year, "...when Qi and Wei sovereigns proclaimed kings." [196] (The accounts in *SJ* 'House of Tian Qi Biography' and Lord Mengchang Biography' are similar.) Since *SJ* had mistaken King Hui's change of regnal year to the 1st year of King Xiang; we can establish that it was a result of when the sovereigns of Qi and Wei began to honour each other as kings. It was similar when Duke Huiwen of Qin changed his title to king, he also changing his regnal year. [197] The *Bamboo Annals* states that during the 36th year King Hui of Wei changed his regnal year to 1st year; he did not wait until the following year to change his regnal year to 1st; Tian He of Qi did the same thing when he proclaimed himself as Marquis. Hence, the 36th year of King Hui of Wei's reign was the 1st year of his regnal year - *guaiyuan* year, thus before the change there were only 35 years. Due to the mistake made by Sima Qian, 'King Wei changed his regnal year during the 36th year' replacing it with, 'The King died during the 36th year.' Resulting from

196 *SJ* 史記, 'Qin benji 秦本紀'
SJ 史記, 'House of Tian Qi 田齊世家.'

197 King Huiwen of Qin 秦惠文王 (337-311 BCE). It was the year when the Duke of Qin Bosi 秦伯駟 proclaimed as king, known as King Huiwen of Qin.

this error, the reign of King Hui of Wei before he changed his regnal year; in the *SJ* Sima Qian had appended one extra year to King Hui of Wei; subsequently, Marquis Wu of Wei's reign was also pushed forward by one year. The discrepancy of one-year chronicled in the *Bamboo Annals* and *SJ* on King Hui of Wei and; the discrepancy of one-year, between the textual research by Lei Xueqi and Wang Guowei and the dates provided by *Shiji suoyin* quoting from the *Bamboo Annals*, were all the consequence of the error made by Sima Qian. Whereas the discrepancy of two-years on events about King Hui in the *Bamboo Annals* and *SJ* were related to wars, as wars could extend for more than one year. Since *SJ* based its records on '*Qin Annals Qin ji*',[198] which being a state chronicle of Qin; it was interested in the outcome of the battles of other states. Hence, the records of the wars were all appended to the year after the wars.

There are scientific evidence that could substantiate the claim that the *SJ* made an error by one-year on the regnal year of King Hui of Wei. *SJ* 'Sequence of the Six States' chronicles, "During the 16th year of Duke Xian of Qin, there was a severe epidemic raging among its people. A solar eclipse was observed." According to *SJ* 'Sequence of the Six States' it was the 2nd year of King Wei of Wei. [199] However, in *Kaiyuan zhanjing* Volume 101 quoting from the *Bamboo Annals* it says, [200] "King Hui of Liang 1st year, a day became dark *zhouhui*." [201] The phase *zhouhui* means eclipse. To verify this, there is a reference of *zhouhui* in conjunction with the term eclipse *rishi* in *SJ* 'Sequence of the Six States,' [202] "During the 34th year of Duke Li of Qin there was an eclipse *rishi* and the day darkened *zhouhui*." Moreover, "During the 3rd year of Duke Xian of Qin there was an eclipse - *zhouhui*," the above accounts prove that 'eclipse - *rishi* and '*zhouhui*' were used synonymously to mean solar eclipse. A search of astronomical records showed that there indeed was an annular solar eclipse during the 13th hour and 9th minute on the 11th day of April 369 BCE. (Zhu Wenxin –'Investigations of the Eclipses during the Warring States and Qin in the *Investigation of Eclipses throughout the Dynasties*.). [203] Since the *Bamboo Annals* relates that during the 1st year of King Hui that there was an eclipse - hence the 1st year of King Hui was 369 BCE. Whereas *SJ* 'Sequence of the Six States' mentioned that the 1st year of King Hui of Wei was the 7th year of King Lie of Zhou, which was 370 BCE; hence the record of King Hui by *SJ* was off by one year.

Shiji jijie states under the heading of 'House of Wei Biography,' [204] "King Xiang died, his son King Ai ascended to the throne.", "Xun Xu quoting He Qiao said, [205] '...

---

198 The Qin Ji 秦紀 – the court history of Qin.

199 *SJ* 史記 'Sequence of the Six States 六國年表.'

200 *Kaiyuan zhanjing*, 開元占經 Volume 101 quoting from *Bamboo Annals* 竹書紀年. (See footnotes above)

201 *Zhouhui* 晝晦. The phase *zhouhui* means a solar eclipse.

202 *Rishi* 日蝕.

203 Zhu Wenxin 朱文鑫 (1883-1939) - 'Investigations of the Eclipses during the Warring States and Qin, Zhanguo ji Qin rishekao, 戰國及秦日食考', in *The Investigations of Eclipses throughout the Dynasties, Lidai rishe kao*, 歷代日食考.

204 *Shiji jijie* 史記集解 was composed by Pei Yin 裴駰 (year of birth and death unknown) the Nan-Chao 南朝 Liu Song 劉宋 (420-479 CE) scholar.

205 From *Shiji jijie* 史記集解.

based on ancient texts, King Huicheng having sat on the throne for 36 years and (during which year) changed his regnal year to 1st year. After changing his *guaiyuan,* he died during the 17th year of his latter regnal date." *Shiji suoyin* also relates, "The *Bamboo Annals* said, 'King Huicheng 36th year was also known as the 1st latter regnal year; during the 17th year he died." "House of Wei Biography' under the entry of 'King Hui died' *Shiji suoyin* adds, "The *Bamboo Annals* related, 'King Huicheng 36th year was changed to 1st year after the regnal era change. He did not die." Under 'House of Tian Biography', 'King Hui of Wei died' entry, *Shiji suoyin* also said, "At this time, King Hui of Liang changed his regnal era to 1st year; he did not die." All the above verified that King Hui of Wei changed his regnal year during his 36th year and that the *Bamboo Annals* is accurate. Lei Xueqi's assumption that King Hui only reigned for 35 years before he changed his regnal year was an accurate assessment. However, using this to assume that there were 17 years during the *houyuan* – latter regnal era years was a wrong assumption. *Shiji jijie* and *Shiji suoyin* account of 17 years should be an error of 16 years. Du Yu in his *Chunqiu jingzhuan jijie huoxu* quoted from the *Bamboo Annals* and maintained that it was 16th years. [206] From this, we could conclude that King Hui of Wei changed his regnal era year when 'Qi and Wei' recognized each other as kings. Hence, he changed his regnal year; after the change, he only reigned for 16 years. *SJ* had mistaken the latter regnal era years as the reign of King Xiang of Wei. Nevertheless, the 16 years post-era-reign is a certainty.

Overall, *Sima Qian* shortened Marquis Wen of Wei's reign by 12 years, also shortening the reign of Marquis Wu of Wei by ten years; and mistook the changing of regnal year as the year of death of King Hui during th 36th year. Finally, he added one extra year to the reign of King Hui of Wei and Marquis Wu of Wei. Later he erroneously assigned the reign of 'Latter Regnal era Year of King Hui of Wei' to King Xiang of Wei; resulting from which there was an added King Ai of Wei; and mistakenly assigned King Xiang Wei's reign to King Ai. With this series of mistakes, I believe we could use the information in the *Bamboo Annals* to make adjustments and corrections.

Based on the textual research from the above we can conclude - (1) the 1st year of Marquis Wen of Wei should be the 24th year of King Ding of Zhou, i.e. 445 BCE. (2) Marquis Wu of Wei 1st year should fall on the 7th year of King An of Zhou, which was 395 BCE. (3) King Hui of Wei 1st year should be the 7th year of King Lie of Zhou, which was 369 BCE. Then during his 36th year, i.e. 334 BCE, he changed his regnal Year (latter regnal era year) to 1st year; the 1st year of King Hui, *houyuan.* (4) The 1st year of King Xiang of Wei should be the 3rd year of King Shenjing of Zhou, which was 318 BCE. [207]

Xun Xu 荀勖 (?-289 CE) the Western Jin 西晉 scholar quoting from He Qiao 和嶠, another Western Jin 西晉 scholar (?-292 CE).

206 Du Yu 杜預 – The *Chunqiu jingzhuan jijie houxu* 春秋經傳 集解后序.

207 These are the researched dates presented by Yang Kuan:
Marquis Wen of Wei 1st year 魏文侯 元年 = King Ding of Zhou 周定王 24th year - 445 BCE. (*SJ* 史記 424 BCE)
Marquis Wu of Wei 1st year 魏武侯 元年 = King An of Zhou 周安王 7th year - 395 BCE. (*SJ* 史記 386 BCE)

2. The Reigning Years of Kings of Wei, Xuan and Min of Qi

SJ 'Sequence of the Six States' records that the 1st year of King Wei of Qi as the 24th year of King An of Zhou, which was 378 BCE. Further, the 1st year of King Xuan of Qi is recorded as the 27th year of King Xian of Zhou, i.e. 342 BCE; and records King Min of Qi's 1st year as the 46th year of King Xian of Zhou, i.e. 322 BCE. The arrangements of the dates of these kings in *SJ* are also seriously flawed.

If we study *ZGC* 'Yan Strategy 1', [208] it says, "The 3rd year of Zi Zhi. Yan fell into complete chaos. .... Chuzi said to King Xuan of Qi, 'This is time to enslave Yan.'. ... The King ordered Zhangzi (Kuang Zhang) to lead the armies from five capitals and deployed the troops from the north (of Qi) to attack Yan. [209] (This account is similar to that in the *SJ* 'House of Yan Biography'.) The account related in *ZGC*, it was King Xuan of Qi who attacked Yan Zi Zhi; however, according to *SJ* 'Sequence of the Six States' the account is recorded during the 1st year of King Nan of Zhou, and according to *SJ* 'Sequence of the Six States', it should be the 10th year of King Min of Qi. So, who was it then? Was it King Xuan of Qi or King Min? According to the *Mengzi*, Shen Tong, a minister at the *Qi* court, had asked Mengzi in private, [210] "Is it fitting to take Yan?" Mengzi answered, "Yes, Zi Guai should not abdicate his throne to Zi Zhi while Zi Zhi should not take over the throne from Zi Guai." (*Mengzi* 'Gongsun Chou xiapian'), [211] continues, "Qi invaded Yan," and "it was conquered in fifty days." King Xuan of Qi asked Mengzi, ".. should I annex the land?" Later, "Qi people attacked Yan, and it was taken; the other fief lords were deliberating as to how to save Yan." King Xuan of Qi again asked Mengzi, "How should I handle the situation?" (*Mengzi* 'King Hui of Liang Part 2'). [212] Later the people of Yan revolted. The king said, "I am too ashamed to face Mengzi." (*Mengzi* 'Gongsun Chou xiapian.') [213] So, in both instances, the king was King Xuan of Qi and not King Min. It is thus quite apparent that *SJ* made a wrong entry on the reigning years of Qi. Former textual researchers had also noticed this problem and attempted to amend the year dates of Qi in *SJ*. For instances, *ZZTJ* added ten years to the reign of King Wei of Qi and pushed back the reign of King Xuan of Qi by ten years. *Dashiji* shortened the reign of King Min of Qi by ten years, extending the reign of King Xuan by ten years; their objective was to make the year of the expedition against Yan to corresponding with the accounts of the *Mengzi* and the *ZGC*. However, the way it was treated and that they corresponded was purely coincidental and was without any base.

Marquis Hui of Wei 1st year 魏惠王 元年 = King Lie of Zhou 周烈王 7th year - 369 BCE. (*SJ* 史記 370 BCE)

Marquis Xiang of Wei 1st year 魏襄王 元年 = King Shenjing of Zhou 周 慎靚王 3rd year - 318 BCE. (*SJ* 史記 334 BCE)

208 The account in *ZGC*, 戰國策 'Yan Strategy 1' 燕策 1 and *SJ* 史記, 'House of Yan 燕世家' are the same.

209 Chuzi 儲子, Qi general.

Zhangzi 章子 (Kuang Zhang 匡章).

210 Mengzi 孟子.

Qi minister 齊臣 沈同 Shen Tong.

211 King of Yan 燕王 Zi Guai 子噲; Zi Zhi 子之.

212 *Mengzi* 孟子, 'Liang Huiwang Part 2', 梁惠王下篇.

213 *Mengzi* 孟子, 'Gongsun Chou Part 2', 公孫丑 下篇.

If we were to correct the erroneous dates of Qi that appear in *SJ* we have to depend on the *Bamboo Annals* just as we did with the Wei dates. The *Shiji suoyin* quoting from the *Bamboo Annals* says, "During the 5th year of Duke Kang of Qi, Marquis Tian, Wu, was born; during the 22nd year Marquis Tian Tan was enfeoffed. [214] Ten years later Tian Wu of Qi committed regicide, and killed the child, Ruzi Xi; he made himself a duke." (*Shiji suoyin* 'House of Tian Biography' quoting from *Bamboo Annals*), [215] "King Hui of Liang 12th year, which was the 18th year of Duke Huan of Qi; only later did King Wei first appear; hence, Duke Huan was on the throne for 19 years and died." (*Shiji suoyin* 'House of Tian Biography' quoting from the *Bamboo Annals*.) While 'House of Wei Biography' says, "According to the *Bamboo Annals*, during the 18th year of Duke You of Qi, King Wei was enfeoffed." (Duke You was mistaken for Duke Huan.)[216] "King Wei 14th year, Tian Ban made an expedition against Liang (Wei); the battle was joined at Maling." (*Shiji suoyin* 'House of Tian Biography quoting from the *Bamboo Annals*.) [217] *Shiji suoyin* 'Sunzi, Wu Qi Biographies' also quoting from the *Bamboo Annals* says, "(King Hui of Liang) 27th year, 12th month, Tian Ban of Qi defeated the army of Liang at Maling.) "During the 15th year of the latter regnal era of King Hui of Liang (*houyuan*), King Wei of Qi expired." (*Shiji suoyin* 'Lord Mengchang Biography' quoted from the *Bamboo Annals*). Based on these accounts, we come to realize that *SJ* had omitted Marquis Tian, Tan, who reigned between the Tian Duke *Taigong* (Tian He) and Tian Duke Tian. The recorded reign of 6 years for Duke Huan and 36 years for King Wei were erroneous.

Tian Marquis Tan was enefoffed during the 22nd year of Duke Kang of Qi; which was the 19th year of the King An of Zhou. The 1st year should be during the 20th year of the King An of Zhou, which was 382 BCE. The 1st year of Duke Huan was the 2nd year of the King Lie of Zhou, i.e. 374 BCE.

The 18th year of Tian Duke Huan was the 13th year of King Hui of Wei, or the 12th year King Xian of Zhou; this was the year King Wei of Qi ascended to the throne. Hence, the 1st year of King Wei of Qi should fall in the 13th year of King Xian of Zhou, i.e. 356 BCE. The Battle of Maling happened during the 14th year of King Wei of Qi, which was the 27th year of King Hui of Wei or the 26th year of King Xian of Zhou, i.e. 343 BCE. [218] Later during the latter regnal era 15th year of King Hui of Wei, it was the 1st year of King Shenjing of Zhou, King Wei of Qi died; King Xuan of Qi succeeded him. In which case the 1st year of King Xuan of Qi should be the 2nd year of Shenjing

---

214 Duke Kang of Qi 5th year 齊康公, Marquis Tian Wu 田侯午 was born; (on the) 22nd year Tianhou Tan 田侯剡.

215 "Later Qi Tian Wu committed regicide, and killed the child, Ruzi Xi 孺子喜; he made himself the Duke of Qi." This passage is not mentioned in *SJ* 史記.
Shiji suoyin 史記索隱, 'House of Tian 田世家 索隱' quoting from *Bamboo Annals* 紀年説:
"梁惠王十二年當齊桓公十八年, 後威王始見, 則桓公立十九年而卒." The phase of '始見' is rather ambiguous; it should mean King Wei 威王 appeared or succeeded after the death of Duke Huan of Qi 齊桓公.

216 Duke You 幽公 was mistaken for Duke Huan 齊桓公.

217 *Shiji* 史記, 'House of Tian Biography suoyin 田世家 索隱' quoting from *Bamboo Annals* 紀年.
Shiji 史記, 'Sunzi Wu Qi Biography suoyin 孫子 吳起列傳 索隱' quoting from *Bamboo Annals* 紀年.
田侯剡一代 was missing.

218 The Battle of Maling 馬陵 happened during the 14th year of King Wei of Qi 齊威王, which was the 27th year of King Hui of Wei 魏惠王 or the 26th year of King Xian of Zhou 周顯王.

of Zhou; [219] i.e., 319 BCE. Tallying the total: Tian Marquis Tan reigned for ten years (from the beginning to the end), [220] Tian Duke Huan reigned for 19 years, and King Wei of Qi reigned for 38 years. *SJ* missed out 9 years for Tian Marquis Tan, 12 years for Tian Duke Huan and one year for King Wei of Qi; subsequently, the reigning years of kings Wei, Xuan, and Min of Qi were all misaligned. As a result, all the dates did not correspond with that of the *Mengzi* and the *ZGC*.

According to the *Bamboo Annals,* the 1st year of King Xuan of Qi was the 2nd year King Shenjing of Zhou, i.e. 319 BCE. Hence, during the 1st year of King Nan of Zhou (314 BCE) when Qi attacked Yan, it should be the 6th year of King Xuan of Qi. Now, according to this account, this corresponds with all the accounts in *Mengzi* and the *ZGC*. According to the *ZGC,* 'Qi Strategy 2', [221] "Hann and Qi formed an alliance; Zhang Yi allied with Qin and Wei to attack Hann. The King of Qi said, '.... I intend to go to its rescue.' Tian Chensi (Tian Ji) said, '.... Zi Guai gave his kingdom to Zi Zhi, the civilians do not support him, and the fief lords do not subscribe to it. If Qin attacks Hann; Chu and Zhao will go to its rescue, this is divine providence, and Heaven has bestowed Yan onto me.' The King (Qi) said, 'Excellent.' He agreed to go to the rescue of Hann and sent the Hann emissary to return. The Hann people, having been assured by Qi's pledge, continued their struggle against Qin. Chu and Zhao, as expected raised armies to the rescue of Hann, Qi taking advantage of the void raided Yan. It brought Yan down in thirty days." It apparently was a mistake made by Sima Qian; he mistakenly merged another incident of, "Qi made an expedition against Yan and annexed Sangqiu." [222] It happened during the 22nd year of King An of Zhou. Furthermore, he mistook Tian Duke Huan's 1st year to be during the 18th year of King An of Zhou; mixing it up with the incident that happened during the 5th year of Duke Huan of Qi. [223]

Shiji suiyin did not make a comparison with the *Bamboo Annals* on the year of death of King Xuan of Qi. According to *SJ* 'House of Tian Biography', King Xuan of Qi was on the throne for 19 years. Based on the year of death of King Wei of Qi, according to the accounts in the *Bamboo Annals,* we can deduce that the year of death of King Xuan, and the year of King Min's ascension to the throne should fall in the 14th year of King Nan of Zhou. [224] i.e. 301 BCE. It was the year when the chancellor of Qi, Tian Wen sent Kuang Zhang to ally with Hann and Wei to lay siege to the walled city of Fangcheng of Chu, and killed General Tang Mie of Chu at Chuisha near Pishui River. [225] According to *Xunzi* 'Wangba pian', "The defeat of Chu was at the time of King

---

219 King Hui of Wei 魏惠王.
King Shenjing of Zhou 周 慎靚王.
King Wei of Qi 齊威王.
King Xuan of Qi 齊宣王.

220 The text uses - 'from the beginning to end' 首尾. It means that if a sovereign reigned for say ten years, it does not literally mean he was on the throne for a full ten years, he might die on the ninth year but would have it counted as ten years; the succeeding sovereign would take up the following, year 11th as his 1st regnal year.

221 Tian Chensi 田臣思 (Tian Ji 田忌) said, '.... Zi Guai 子噲 gives his Kingdom to Zi Zhi 子之.

222 Sangqiu 桑丘.

223 Duke Huan of Tian's 1st year 田桓公 元年 should be during the 18th year of King An of Zhou 周安王; this incident was mixed up with the incident of Duke Huan of Qi (Tian) 5th year 田桓公 五年.

224 The *SJ* 史記, 'House of Tian Biography 田世家.'
King Huan of Qi 齊宣王.
King Wei of Qi 齊威王.
King Min of Qi 齊湣王.

225 Chancellor of Qi, Tian Wen 齊相田文.
Kuang Zhang 匡章.

Min of Qi;[226] hence, we can affirm that by this year, King Min of Qi was already on the throne. Based on the above we can deduce that the 1st year of King Min was the 15th year of King Nan of Zhou,[227] i.e. 300 BCE.

From the above textual research, we can affirm that, 1. King Wei of Qi's 1st year was the 13th year of King Xian of Zhou, i.e. 356 BCE. 2. The 1st year King Xuan of Qi was the 2nd year of King Shenjing of Zhou, 319 BCE, and 3. The 1st year of King Min of Qi was the 15th year of King Nan of Zhou,[228] 300 BCE.

It has to be pointed out specifically that some scholars have attempted to merge the three Qi kings of Wei, Xuan, and Min into two kings as Wei and Xuanmin by changing the *SJ* 'Sequence of the Six States', claiming it is a new listing. This, I have to emphasis is purely imaginary, the attempt is groundless and does not correspond with any historical facts. (Please see details in Chapter 6, Section 8 of this book *Zhanguoshi*, "On the use of the rites of posthumous titles." (N.B. by the translator – the chapter is not translated.)

3. The Reigning Years of Master Xiang of Zhao and Marquis Lie of Zhao

There are errors with the reigning years of masters Xiang and Huan of Zhao, as well as Marquis Lie of Zhao in *SJ* 'Sequence of the Six States'.[229] *SJ* lists Master Jian of Zhao's death to be during the 17th year of Duke Chu of Jin, 458 BCE;[230] this is erroneous. On the one hand, *SJ* 'House of Zhao Biography' says, "Duke Chu of Jin 17th year, Master Jian died. The Prince *Wuxu* (replaced his brother) to assume the position; he was Master Xiang", while, on the other hand, it says, "During the 1st year of Master Xiang of Zhao, Yue besieged Wu. Master Xiang reduced his observance of fasting during the period of mourning; and sent his retainer Chu Long to see the King of Wu, extending his condolences." Checking the *Zuozhuan*, reveals that the incident of Yue besieging Wu transpired during the 20th year of Duke Ai of Lu, or 37th year of Duke Ding of Jin, which was 475 BCE. This year Master Xiang of Zhao was still observing the obligatory mourning of his father Master Jian, affirming that Master Jian had already died. Hence, the 1st year of Master Xiang of Zhao should be 474 BCE.[231]

Walled-city of Fangcheng of Chu 楚方城.
Chu 楚 General Tang Mie 唐蔑 was killed at Chuisha 垂沙 near the Pishui 沘水 River.

226 King Min of Qi 齊閔王 = Minwang 湣王.

227 According to the *Xunzi* 荀子 'Wangba pian 王霸篇.'

228 Based on the above textual research we can affirm that, 1. The 1st year of King Wei of Qi 齊威王 was the 13th year of King Xian of Zhou 周顯王, 356 BCE; 2. The 1st year of King Xuan of Qi 齊宣王 year was the 2nd year of King Shenjing of Zhou 周慎靚王, 319 BCE, and 3. King Min of Qi's 1st year 齊湣王 was the 15th year of King Nan of Zhou 周赧王, 300 BCE.

229 Master Xiang of Zhao (Xiangzi) 趙襄子.
Master Huan of Zhao (Huanzi) 趙桓子.
Marquis Lie of Zhao 趙烈侯.
The *SJ* 史記, 'Sequence of the Six States 六國年表'.

230 *SJ* 史記, 'House of Zhao Biography 趙世家.'
Duke Chu of Jin 晉出公.
The Crown Prince Wuxu 無恤, Xiangzi 襄子.
Yue 越 besieged Wu 吳.
Chu Long 楚隆.

231 The *Zuozhuan*, 左傳.

SJ 'House of Zhao Biography' relates, "(Marquis Lie) 9th year Marquis Lie died. His younger brother Duke Wu ascended to the throne; Duke Wu died during the 13th year. [232] Zhao re-elected Marquis Lie's Crown Prince Zhang to succeed; he was Marquis Jing." [233] The *Shiji suoyin* says, "Qiao Zhou said, '*Shiben* and others who spoke of Zhao Yu; [234] there was no such evidence, based on other evidence." Going through *Shiji suoyin* 'House of Wei Biography,' [235] quoting from the *Bamboo Annals*, it says, "Marquis Wu of Wei 1st year should be the 14th year of Marquis Lie of Zhao." Hence, it is known that Marquis Lie did not die in his 9th year. The account in the *SJ* that, "... his younger brother acceded to the throne lacks credibility." *SJ* 'House of Zhao Biography' says that the given name of Marquis Lie was Ji and Marquis Jing of Zhao's given name was Zhang. However, Duke Wu, the younger brother of Marquis Lie, did not have a given name; besides Marquis Lie of Zhao and Marquis Jing were both marquises, why was there a Duke, (a more senior enfeoffment), that was lodged between two marquises? [236] It is quite evident that the *SJ* had created a generation of Duke Wu; then allocated 13 years from the reign of Marquis Lie to Duke Wu. Hence, in our textual research we have decided to eliminate Duke Wu mentioned in *SJ* 'Sequence of the Six States' and returned the 13 years to Marquis Lie.

Furthermore, *Shiji suoyin* 'House of Jin Biography' quoting from the *Bamboo Annals* says, "Marquis Ai of Hann and Marquis Jing of Zhao died during the 15th year of Duke Huan." [237] Duke Huan of Jin 15th year was the 22nd year of Marquis Wu of Wei, i.e. 374 BCE; it was one year later than the account of the death of Marquis Jing of Zhao in *SJ* Sequence of the Six States'. [238] Since we do not have other additional information to go by, we will adopt the dates used *SJ's* Sequence of the Six States'.

4. The Years of Reign of Marquises Ai, Yi, and Zhao of Hann

Yue besieging Wu 越圍吳.
Duke Ai of Lu 魯哀公.
Duke Ding of Jin 晉定公.
Master Xian of Zhao 趙襄子.
Master Jian 趙簡子.

232 The *SJ* 史記, 'House of Zhao 趙世家'.
Marquis Lie 烈侯 .
Duke Wu 武公.

233 Crown Prince Zhang 章 - Marquis Jing 敬侯.

234 The *Suoyin* 索隱.
Qiao Zhou 譙周 (201-270 CE), Shu-Han scholar 蜀漢.
The *Shiben* 世本.

235 The *Shiji suoyin* 史記索隱, 'House of Wei 魏世家' quoting the *Bamboo Annals* 紀年.

236 The SJ 史記, 'House of Zhao Biography 趙世家'.
Zhao Liehou 趙烈侯 had a given name of Ji 籍.
Zhao Jinghou 趙敬侯 given name was Zhang 章.
Duke Wu 武公.

237 *Shiji suoyin* 史記索隱, 'House of Jin Biography 晉世家 索隱' quoting from the *Bamboo Annals* 紀年.

238 Marquis Ai of Hann 韓哀侯.
Marquis Jing of Zhao 趙敬侯.
Duke Huan 桓公.
The *SJ* 史記, 'The Sequence of the Six States 六國年表.'

SJ Sequence of the Six States' records that Marquis Ai of Hann was on the throne for six years and died during the 5th year of King Lie of Zhou, which was 371 BCE. Furthermore, Marquis Zhuang of Hann reigned for 12 years and died in the 10th year of King Xian of Zhou, that is 359 BCE, whereas Marquis Zhao of Hann 1st year was the year after. The chronological arrangements of the years reign of the Hann sovereigns in the 'Sequence of the Six States' are also erroneous. [239]

SJ 'House of Hann Biography' records Marquis Ai 6th year, "Hann Yan committed regicide, he killed the sovereign Marquis Ai, placing his son the Marquis of Yi on the throne." [240] *Shiji suoyin* says, "The *Bamboo Annals* Marquis Yi was, in fact, mistaken for Marquis Zhuang.' Further, *Bamboo Annals* says, 'Duke Huan of Jin enfeoffed Marquis Ai at Zheng. Hann Shanjian deceived his lord Marquis Ai, and placed Hann Ruoshan on the throne.' Ruoshan was Marquis Yi, and Hann Yan was Hann Shanjian." Adding, "*Bamboo Annals*, Marquis Wu of Wei 21st year, Hann annihilated Zheng; Marquis Ai entered Zheng. 22nd year, Duke Huan of Jin enfeoffed Marquis Ai at Zheng." *Shiji suoyin* 'House of Jin Biography' says, "*Bamboo Annals* related, 'Marquis Wu of Wei died during the 19th year of Duke Huan, Marquis Ai of Hann and Marquis Jing of Zhao died in the 15th years of Duke Huan." Thus, it can be established that Marquis Ai of Hann died during the 22nd year of Marquis Wu of Wei. Duke Huan of Jin 15th year was the 2nd year of King Lie of Zhou, i.e. 374 BCE.

Marquis Yi of Hann is referred to as Marquis Yi, Ruo, in the *Commentary of Rivers and Waters* on 'Qinshui.' *Shiji suoyin* 'House of Jin', and the *Commentary of Rivers and Waters* on 'Zuzhang River' also refer to him as Marquis Gong of Hann. [241] Marquis Yi of Hann killed Marquis Ai in 374 BCE and made himself the new sovereign. It is believed that he did not wait until the next year before changing his regnal year.

Commentary of Rivers and Waters 'Jishuizhu' quotes from the *Bamboo Annals* says, "(King Hui of Liang 9th year) the King met Marquis Xi of Zheng at Wusha." [242] Marquis Xi of Zheng was,

---

239 Marquis Ai of Hann 韓哀侯.
King Lie of Zhou 周烈王.
Marquis Zhuang of Hann 韓莊侯.
King Xian of Zhou 周顯王.
Marquis Zhao of Hann 韓昭侯.

240 The *SJ* 史記 'House of *Hann* 韓世家'.
Hann Yan 韓嚴.
Marquis Yi 懿侯.
The *SJ* 史記, 'House of Hann 韓世家.'
Shiji suoyin 史記索隱 quoting from *SJ* 史記, 'The Sequence of the Six States 六國年表.'
Bamboo Annals 紀年 - Duke Huan of Jin 晉桓公.
Marquis enfeoffed at Zheng 哀侯于鄭; Hann Shanjian 韓山堅; Maruis Ai 哀侯; Hann Rushan 韓若山.
Rushan was Marquis Yi – '若山即懿侯也'; Hann Yan was Han Shanjian – '則韓嚴為韓山堅也.'

241 The *Shuijing* 水經 'Qinshuizhu 沁水注'.
The *SJ* 史記, 'House of Jin 晉世家'.
The *Shuijing* 水經, 'Zuzhangshui Zhu 濁漳水注'.
Marquis Gong of Hann 韓共侯.

242 King Hui of Liang 梁惠成王.
Marquis Xi of Zheng 鄭釐侯.
Wusha 巫沙.
The *Shuijing* 水經, 'Jishui 濟水注', quoting from the *Bamboo Annals* 紀年.

in fact, Marquis Zhao of Hann. King Hui of Liang 9th year was 361 BCE. *SJ* "House of Zhao Biography' says, "Marquis Cheng of Zhao 13th year, 'Marquis Cheng and Marquis Zhao of Hann met at Shangdang." [243] Marquis Cheng of Zhao 13th year was 362 BCE. We can conclude that 1st year of Marquis Zhao of Hann as 358 BCE arranged by 'House of Hann Biography' was erroneous. However, since we do not have further information to base on, we will use 362 BCE as his 1st year.

5. Identifying the Reigns of Dukes Jian and Hui of Qin

SJ 'Sequence of the Six States' records that Marquis Jiang of Qin reigned for 15 years; after him was Duke Hui of Qin, [244] who was on the throne for 13 years. The accounts in the *Bamboo Annals* are in variance. *Shiji suoyin* 'Qin Basic Annals' says, "Quoting from the *Bamboo Annals*, Duke Jian died during the 9th year, Duke Jing succeeded him, after 12 years; Duke Hui ascended to the throne." *Shiji suoyin* 'Qin Shihuang basic Annals' says, "Wang Shao based on the *Bamboo Annals* said, "After Duke Jian, it was Duke Jing, Duke Jing was on the throne for 13 years, before it was passed onto Duke Hui." [245] Wang Shao based his calculation by including the first regnal year, the year of ascension; whereas Sima Zhen (author of *Shiji suoyin*) only counted the years of the post-regnal era year of Duke Jing. [246] It explains why both two authors were quoting from the same source of *Bamboo Annals*, however, they came up with different conclusions for Duke Jing. *SJ* 'Sequence of the Six States' chronicles that Duke Jian and Duke Hui were on the throne for a total of 28 years; whereas according to *Bamboo Annals* Duke Jian only reigned for 9, adding Duke Jing's 13 years, Duke Hui was thus left with 7 years. Since there are insufficient materials to substantiate our textual research, we have to rely on the information provided by *SJ* 'Sequence of the Six States'.

6. Identifying the Reigns of the Yan Sovereigns

SJ 'Sequence of the Six States' chronicles that Duke Xian of Yan was on the throne for 28 years; Duke Xiao of Yan reigned for 15 years, Duke Cheng of Yan was on the throne for 16 years, Duke Min of Yan with 31 years, Duke Xi of Yan reigned for 30, Duke Huan of Yan reigned for 11 and Duke Wen of Yan was on the throne for 21 years. [247] Whereas the *Bamboo Annals's* accounts vary

---

The *SJ* 史記, 'House of Zhao 趙世家.' The kings met at Shangdang 上黨."

243 Marquis Cheng of Zhao 趙成侯.
Marquis Zhao of Hann 韓昭侯.
Shangdang 上黨.

244 Duke Jian of Qin 秦 簡公.
Duke Hui of Qin 秦惠公.

245 Wang Shao 王劭.
The *Bamboo Annals* 紀年.

246 Sima Zhen 司馬貞- only included the post-regnal years of Duke Jing of Qin 秦敬公.

247 The *SJ* 史記, 'Sequence of the Six States 六國年表'.
Duke Xian of Yan Xian 燕献公.
Duke Xiao of Yan 燕孝公.
Duke Cheng of Yan 燕成公.
Duke Min of Yan 燕湣公.
Duke Xi of Yan 燕釐公.
Duke Huan of Yan 燕桓公.

with the above accounts. [248] *Shiji suoyin* 'House of Yan Biography' says, "Wang Shao quoting from the *Bamboo Annals*, his results was: Duke Xiao followed Duke Jian, there was no Duke Xian." [249] "According to *Bamboo Annals* Master Zhibo was killed during the 2nd year of Duke Cheng." [250] "According to *Bamboo Annals*, Duke Weng died in his 24th year, Duke Jian ascended to the throne for 13 years, when the Three-Jin Ministers (San-Jin) became enfeoffed as fief lords." [251] "*Bamboo Annals* relates that Duke Jian died in his 45th year." From all these information, we could establish that the dates of the reign of the Yan sovereigns were something like this: 1. Duke of Xian did not exist in Yan. 2. Duke Cheng 1st year was the year before the Three-Jin's annihilation of Master Zhibo, which was the 15th year of King Ding of Zhou, 454 BC. 3. In *Bamboo Annals* Duke Min of Yan is written as Duke Wen of Yan, he was on the throne for 24 years; following him was Duke Jian, who reigned for 45 years. 4. The year Duke Jian of Yan ascended to the throne was 13 years before, "San-Jin were enfeoffed as fief lords. The regnal years should be during the 12th year of King Weilie of Zhou, 414 BCE. [252] From the above we deduce that the 1st year of Duke Wen of Yan was during the 3rd year of King Xiao of Zhou, i.e. 438 BCE. As to the dates of reign after Duke Jian of Yan, we do not have any information to conduct any further textual research. We thus have to rely on the information provided by *SJ* Sequence of the Six States'. According to *Bamboo Annals*, Duke Jian of Yan died in 370 BCE, which was the 3rd year of Duke Huan of Yan, according to *SJ* 'Sequence of the Six States' hence, we could only shorten the reign of Duke Huan of Yan by three years.

Duke Wen of Yan 燕文公.

248 The *Bamboo Annals, Guben Zhushu jiniain*, 古本竹書紀年.

249 The *Shiji suoyin* 史記索隱, 'House of Yan 燕世家.'

Wang Shao 王劭.

250 Zhibo 智伯.

251 The *Bamboo Annals* 紀年.

Duke Wen 燕文公.

Duke Jian 燕簡公.

The Three-Jin ministers (San-Jin) enfeoffed as Fief Lords 三晉命邑為諸侯.

252 Duke Xian 献公.

Duke Cheng of Yan 燕成公.

King Ding of Zhou 周定王.

The Jinian 紀年.

Duke Min of Yan 燕湣公 = Duke Wen of Yan 燕文公.

Duke Jian of Yan 燕簡公.

King Weilie of Zhou 周威烈王.

Part III

Archaeological Discoveries and New Textual Information [1]

In September of 1942, tomb robbers unearthed a piece of silk scroll in a Chu tomb at Zidanku at the outskirt of Changsha Hunan. [2] The scroll came to be known as the *Chu Silk Manuscript - Chu boshu* (also known as *Chu zengshu*). The scroll is now on display at the Arthur M. Sackler Gallery in Washington DC. The earliest facsimile of the scroll appeared in a book called the *Late Zhou Silk Manuscript Textual Research* by Cai Jixiang published in 1944. [3] In 1966, the Metropolitan Museum in New York, using an infrared camera and films for aerial photography, took pictures of the scroll, and restored several faded characters due to discolouration that had become illegible. Scholars around the global have since made extensive studies of the text. The silk scroll is rectangular in shape; to the four sides of the scroll, each representing one season, the twelve deities of the twelve months of a year are illustrated in colour, with three deities to each side. Beside each deity, there is a name, appending alongside the appropriate and tabooed things to do during each month. To the four cardinal corners of the scroll, there are four trees bearing green, red, white and black leaves. It leaves us with little to speculate that it was a simplified calendar, advocating what the '*Yin-yang Five Phases School*' of philosophy on the thought of 'Heaven-Human Induction Ideology' to decide how to deal with corporal matters. [4] When this is compared with the 'Twelve Monthly Depictions in *Lushi Annals* (*Lushi chunqiu* 'Shierji' - *Liji* 'Yueling bian'), [5] the contents are remarkably similar; both are rich in mythical contents. Depicted in the centre of the scroll there are two paragraphs of characters; one of the paragraphs has eight lines while the other has thirteen. The first eight relates that the Lord Baoxi (Fuxi) ordered the deities of the four seasons to preside over the year in succession; known as *sishi* or *siji* - the four seasons. [6] The Flaming Lord - Yandi then commanded Zhurong, the Fire Deity, to direct the four deities to

---

1 Yang Kuan 楊寬, *ZGS* 戰國史, pp. 37-41

2 The *Chu Silk Manuscript, Chu boshu*, 楚帛書, also known as the *Chu zengshu* 楚繒書, was found at Zidanku in a Chu tomb at the eastern outskirt of Changsha Hunan 湖南 長沙東郊 子彈庫 楚墓.

See - Chang, Kwang-Chih, *The Archaeology of Ancient China*, Yale University Press, US, 1977. Early Civilizations in South China, pp. 432-440.

3 The *Late Zhou Silk Manuscript Textual Research, Wanzhou zengshu kaozheng* 晚周繒書考証 by Cai Jixiang 蔡季襄 (1898-1979 CE).

4 'Ying-yang – the Five Phases (Elements)', Yingyang wuheng 陰陽五行.

The origin of 'Heaven-Human induction ideology' 天人感應 was from the *Hongfan* 洪范, "肅時 寒若." "乂時暘若." The statements imply that the governance by a sovereign could affect the changes in the weather. Dong Zhongshu 董仲舒 (179-104 CE), the Han scholar, went a step further, he anthropomorphized Heaven maintaining that it had consciousness and could master over all natural phenomena.

5 The *Lushi Annals* 呂氏春秋 'Shierji 十二紀' and the *Liji* 禮記 'Yueling bian 月令篇'.

6 Baoxi 雹壹 (Fuxi 伏戲) or Fuxi 伏羲 was one of the three mythical deity-kings, 'Three Sovereigns' San-Huang 三皇. It is said that he created the eight–trigram, *Bagua* 八卦 and taught people how to fish and hunt providing games for the kitchen; he was also known as Paoxi 庖犧.

Sishi 四時 *siji* 四季 the four seasons.

Fuxi 伏羲 - see Yuan Ke 袁珂, Zhongguo gudai shengua 中國古代神話, Huaxia chubanshe 華夏出版社, China, 2004. pp. 26-31.

descend (to earth), [7] to create Heaven and Earth; commanding them to preside over the alterations of the four seasons, setting the sun and moon, day and night in motion - more specifically, it is the creation myth. The thirteen-line paragraph relates that when the motion of the sun and moon was in disarray, the four seasons would be out of phase, creating catastrophic disasters; and it was due to disrespect by human while making sacrificial offerings to the hundred deities for not conducting them in earnestness. The Divine would command the four seasons to disrupt its motions. One can glean at the twelve deities at the four borders (four seasons) correspond with the two passages. It was probably written by the Chu *Yin-yang Wuheng* philosophers; the thesis principally corresponds with Marquis Lu on Punishments in the Book of Documents (*Shanshu Luxing*) and the Great Western Passage in the Passage of the Mountains and Seas (*Shanhaijing* 'Great Western Passage'). [8] It states, '(the Deity) Zhong Li (Zhurong) received commands from the Divine to create Heaven and Earth and to preside over the precise motion of the sun and moon myth.'

In 1948, one piece of 'Qin enfeoffed its Right Chancellor (deputy) Chu at Zongyi clay rooftile script' was discovered in Huxian County Shaanxi. These type of roof tiles was prepared by pressing clay into a mould with embossed scripts; [9] the script characters were then brushed with crimson paint, they were then transferred to a kiln for treatment with high heat. The resulting tile called *wa* has a highly glossy sheen. Duan Shaojia kept the original find in Xian, [10] but now it has been transferred to the Museum at Shaanxi Normal University (Teacher's University). Chen Zhi briefly examined the scripts on the tile, and the findings were published in the *Xibei daxue xuepao* 1957 Volume 1. [11] The scripts indicate that the tile was prepared during the 4th year of King Hui of Qin (334 BCE), the king decreed to enfeoff Zhongyi; the tile was presented at his residence by the imperial usher, after due ceremonies, it was then buried in the ground. The ceremony was similar to later day's proof of land ownership. The tile states, "4th year. The Son of Heaven (King of Zhou) sent his senior minister Chen to bestow wine used for making offering to (Kings) Wen and Wu."

---

7 Yandi – The Flaming Lord 炎帝. Yandi was a legendary tribal leader of ancient China; it is said that he invented farming and taught people how to farm. Later he went into war with Huangdi 黄帝 another legendary tribal king. Yandi lost the battle. Thereafter, the two clans merged. Chinese people have identified themselves as the descendants of Yan and Huang 炎黄子孫.

Zhurong 祝融 was another entity of the three mythical 'Three Sovereigns' *San-Huang* 三皇, his name was Zhongli 重黎. He became the Fire Deity that settled in the extreme south. Legend has it that he was able to preserve 'fire' for people or create fire for the ancient people.

8 The *Book of Documents, Shangshu* 尚書, Luxing 呂刑 Marquis Lu on Punishments.

The Passages of Mountains and Seas, *Shanhaijing* 山海經 'Great Western Passage Dahuang xijing 大荒西經'. (N.B. the title is usually translated by scholars as the *Classic of the Mountains and Seas*, the author has translated it as the *Passages of Mountains and Seas*, as the word *jing* 經 used in the title bears no notion of a classic. From notes of an unpublished translation of the text by Joseph P. Yap.)

9 *The Qin enfeoffed its Right Chancellor Chu at Zongyi clay tile script; Qin feng youshuzhang Chu zongyi washu* 秦 封右庶長歜宗邑 瓦書 roof tile.

Huxian County Shaanxi 陜西 鄠縣.

10 Duan Shaojia of Xian 西安, 段紹嘉 (1899—1981 CE) was a bronze script and archaeology researcher.

11 Chen Zhi 陳直 (1901-1980) was the Professor of History at Xibei University.

The *Xibei daxue xuepao* 西北大學學報 1957 Volume 1.

[12] This was the same passage recorded in the *SJ* 'Qin Basic Annals', and *SJ* 'Sequence of the Six States' that King Huiwen of Qin, "During the 4th year of the Son of Heaven prepared sacrificial wine offerings to (kings) Wen and Wu."

In 1980, a set of wood slips was excavated from a Warring States tomb, at Qingchuan Sichuan. [13] They belonged to the period of King Wu of Qin, 2nd year (309 BCE) when the Qin King commanded Chancellor Gan Mao and Capital Magistrate Yan to make reforms to the laws on farmland. [14] The strips chronicle that on the day of winter solstice 2nd year, the 11th month the King commanded Chancellor Wu, [15] and magistrate of the capital city Yan 口口 to make changes to the laws on farmland." [16] (口 - two characters missing). Wu was Gan Mao, as Wu and Mao - the two words were synonymous. *Hannce* 1 and *Yueyuan* 'Zayan pian' both recorded Gan Mao as Gan Wu. Then according to *SJ* 'Qin Basic annals', [17] "This year, the (Qin) State introduced the position of chancellor - *chengxiang*." Gan Mao was the right chancellor, which correspond with the information on the wood slips. Hence, the wood slips provided us with valuable information on the farmland laws of Qin.

During recent years, there have been numerous discoveries of bamboo slips in Warring States tombs in Hubei and Hunan provinces, (these are funeral objects.) From these funeral objects, scholars have uncovered the names of several fief lords that were not chronicled in historical records. For instances, a batch of bamboo slips from two tombs at Leigudun Mound and Jiangling Pama Mound Tomb #1; the names of 11 fief lords were deciphered, [18] they were enfeoffed at the time of King Hui of Chu. Another batch of bamboo slips at Cangshan Mound Jingmen, [19] names of twenty-three fief lords were deciphered. It could be gleaned at that enfeoffment at Chu was particular common.

The Historical Value of Bronze Scripts

The majority of the bronze inscriptions from the time of the Warring States are with short engravings; for historical verification they are not as significant as the Zhou and Chunqiu bronze scripts; nevertheless, there have been some important finds and are helpful in filling in the

---

12 Minister Qing 卿 - Chen 辰.
Scripts on the tile, "四年周天子使卿大夫辰來致文武之酢." Wen and Wu 文武 were King Wen of Zhou 周文王 and King Wu of Zhou 周武王 (1046-1043 BCE). The statement means – 'wine offerings were made to Kings Wen and Wu.' It signified the official fief status of a fief lord.
The *SJ* 史記 'Qin Basic Annals, Qin benji 秦本紀', "秦惠文君, "四年天子致文武胙."
The *SJ* 史記 'Sequence of the Six States 六國年表'.
Zuo 酢 - toasting one's host with wine.

13 Sichuan Qingchuan mudu 四川青川 木牘.

14 King Wu of Qin 2nd year (309 BCE) 秦武王.
Gan Mao 甘茂 and Capital Magistrate Yan 匽. "更修為田律."

15 *Jiyoushuo* 己酉朔 (Winter solstice).

16 Chancellor Wu 戊 was Gan Mao 甘茂 and Neishi Yan 内史匽口口 two words are missing, and the name is obscured.

17 The *ZGC* 戰國策, *'Hannce* 1, 韓策一' and the *Yueyuan* 說苑, 'Zayan pian 雜言篇'.

18 Leigudun Mound 擂鼓墩 and Jiangling Pama Mound 江陵 拍馬山.

19 Cangshan Mound Jingmen number 2 grave mound 荊門倉山二号墓.

historical voids, where chronicled accounts are lacking. The followings are some of the more notable finds:

1. The Chu Xiongzhang Bo (bronze bell). [20] One bronze bell was unearthed during the time of Northern Song at Anlu Hubei. [21] The inscription texts were published in Xue Shanggong's publication *An Treatise on the Identification of Bronze Bells, Tripods, and Ceremonial Vessels from Various Dynasties.* [22] In 1978, at the tomb of Marquis Zheng at Leigudun in Suixian Hubei, another piece was excavated. The bronze script chronicles, '...during the 56th year of King Hui of Chu (433 BCE), the bronze bell was forged for use at the ancestral shrine of the Marquis of Zheng; it was transported to Xiyang (Southwest of Guangshan Henan) for memorial ceremonies and offerings.' From this information, we are able to deduce that the capital city of the Zheng state was located at Xiyang and that according to the established rite; the holy shrine of the sovereigns was located in the capital city.
2. Biaoshi, Bronze Chime Bells *bianzhong.* [23] During the 1930's a set of 14 pieces of ceremonial bronze bells was unearthed in Jincun Village, Luoyang in Henan. [24] They are now on display at the Royal Canadian Ontario Museum, and *Sen-oku Hakuka kan* Museum, Japan. [25] The script chronicles during the 22nd year (404 BCE) of the King Weilie of Zhou, the Hann General Biao Jiang, "... made an expedition against Qin, and pressed against Qi, he entered into the realms of the Long-Walls. The vanguards met at Pingyin." [26] It is the passage that appears in the *Bamboo Annals* (*Guben zhushu jinian*) that relates, "During the 13th year of Duke Lie of Jin, he ordered Master Jing of Hann, Master Lie of Zhao and Zhai Yuan to make an expedition against Qi, and entered into the areas near the Long-Wall." It is the same passage as in the *Lushi Annals* 'Xiaxian pian', [27] "Marquis Wen of Wei won a battle against Qi at the east of the Long-Walls; he captured the Marquis of Qi and presented him to the Son of Heaven. The Son-of-Heaven conferred upon the Marquis a new title of Shangwen." [28] It was the year when the Three-Jin (San-Jin) made an expedition against Qi and entered

---

20 Chu – Xiongzhang *bo* 楚熊章鎛 (bronze bell). A *bo* is different from a *zhong* 鐘, which has concave bottom; the *bo* has a flat bottom.

21 Northern Song 北宋 (960-1127 CE) at Anlu Hubei 安陸 - 湖北安陸.

22 Xue Shanggong 薛尚功 (?), *An Treatise on the Identification of Bronze Bells Tripods and Ceremonial Vessels from Various Dynasties, Lidai zhongding yiqi kuanshi fatie* 歷代鐘鼎彝器款識法帖. (The book was published in 1144 CE).

23 Biaoshi Bronze Chime Bells, *Biaoshi bianzhong* 驫氏編鐘.

24 Jincun Village, Luoyang Henan 河南 洛陽 金村.

25 Royal Ontario Museum, Canada.
Sen-oku Hakuka kan Museum, Japan 日本泉屋博物館.

26 22nd year of King of Zhou, Weileiwang 周威烈王.
Hann general, Biao Qiang 韓將驫羌. Pingyin 平陰.

27 The *Bamboo Annals, Guben zhushu jinian* 古本竹書紀年.
Duke Lie of of Jin 晉烈公.
Master Jing of Hann (Jingzi) 韓景子, Master Lie of Zhao (Liezi) 趙烈子 and Zhai Yuan 翟員.
The *Lushi Annals* 呂氏春秋 'xiaxian pian 下賢篇'.

28 "魏文侯東勝齊于長城, 虜齊侯献諸天子, 天子賞文侯以上聞."

into the areas near Long-Wall; [29] the three fief lords coerced the Marquis of Qi to go to the Zhou Court to pay homage to the Son of Heaven - King Weilie of Zhou. The next year, they made petitions to the Son of Heaven to enfeoffed the Three-Jin ministers as marquises. [30] (See *ZZTJ* 403-1).

3. Marquis Chen, Wu, Bronze Vessel *dun.* [31] There were two pieces of bronze vessels *dun* from the Marquis of Chen Wu; one was from the 10th year of the Marquis. It was initially a collection of Rong Geng and is now on display at Huanan Normal Academy. The write-ups on the vessel was published in *The Lost Bronze Scripts of Shang and Zhou.*[32] The second piece was from the 14th year of the Marquis of Chen, and the script was published in the *Identification of Ancient Recorded Bronze Script*; [33] the bronze vessels are now on display at the Chinese History Museum. *SJ* "House of Tian Biography' relates that Duke Huan of Qi, Wu died during the 6th year of his reign; [34] whereas the *Bamboo Annals* says it was the 18th. Based on the above two pieces of bronze, we have been able to determine that the *Bamboo Annals* is correct, as the *SJ* had mistaken the number '6' for '18'. [35]
4. Three Pieces of Qi Measurements Cauldrons - the Zi Hezi *fu*, Chen Chun *fu* and Zuo Guan *he.* [36] The three pieces of cauldrons were unearthed in 1856 in Lingshanwey Jiaoxian Shandong. Wu Dacheng recorded the scripts in his *Kezhai jigulu.* [37] Shanghai Museum produced a volume called the *Qi Volume Measurements, Qi liang*. Zi Hezi *fu* is now kept at the Chinese History Museum, Chen Chun *fu* and Zuo Guan *he* are kept at the Shanghai Museum. Master Zi Hezi was Master Tian Hezi of Qi (the Grand Duke of Qi). [38] From the inscriptions, we have an understanding of the volume measurement used by the kingdom of Qi and the system implemented. From the *fu* we have been able to deduce the equivalents of *hu* in other states. [39] Tian Qi's *he* was equivalent to the *dou* unit measure used in other states.
5. Volume Measure of Shang Yang, the 'Square Sheng' *fang-sheng*. (It is also known as Shang Yang's Measure.)[40] Gong Xinming of Hefei originally owned the volume

---

29 San-Jin 三晉 – Zhao 趙, Wei 魏 and Hann 韓. The Qi Long-Wall was built to impede the encroachments of the San-Jin. The text literally states that San-Jin*'s* armies entered into the Long-Wall, which does not make sense.

30 (403 BCE was the year when *ZZTJ* commences its narratives.)

31 Marquis of Chen Wu *dun* 陳侯午敦. *dun* is a spherical cauldron, with three supporting legs. Marquis Chen was Duke Huan of Qi, Tain Wu 齊桓公 田午. (See 403-1)

32 *The Lost Bronze Scripts of Shang and Zhou, Shang Zhou jinwen luwei* 商周金文錄遺.

33 The *Identification of Ancient Recorded Bronze Script, Jun gulu jinwen* 攈古錄金文.

34 The *SJ* 史記 'House of Tian Biography 田世家'. Duke Huan of Qi, Wu 齊 桓公午.

35 Chinese text was written vertically, with a (10) 十 followed by an (8) 八, and it looked like a (6) 六.

36 *Zi Hezi fu* 子禾子釜; *Chen Zhun fu* 陳純釜; and *Zuo Guan he* 左關鉌.

Tian Qi's *He* 鉌 = *dou* 斗 measure in other fief states.

Lingshanwey Jiaoxian Shandong 山東膠縣 靈山衛.

37 Wu Dacheng 吳大澂 recorded the scripts in his *Kezhai jigulu* 愙齋集古録.

38 Zi Hezi 子禾子 was Tian Hezi of Qi 齊 田和子, i.e. Grand Duke of Qi, Qi Taigong 齊太公.

39 *Hu* 斛 was equal to 10 *dou* 斗, about 100 litres.

40 The Square Sheng unit of Shang Yang, *fang-sheng* 商鞅方升. The measure is a rectangular shaped tray, with a handle on one of the long-side. Strictly speaking, it should not be called a square measure 方升. The volume is 202.15 cc. The tray was forged in 344 BCE, the 18th year of King Xiao

measure;[41] later, Gong moved to Tangquan at Pukou, where he composed the *Pukou Tangquan xiaozhi*. Later the scripts of the measure were recorded in 'Qin Bronze and Stone Carving Lexicon.' [42] The bronze measure is now on display at the Shanghai Museum. On the inner left side of the tray measure, the inscription read, 'Duke Xiao of Qin 18th year.'[43] The inner face opposite to the handle reads 'Zhongquan' (Puchengxian Shaanxi), as it was designated for use by the City of Zhongquan. [44] At the bottom of the tray, it reads, "The decree of Qin Shi Huang 26th year. [45] On the opposite face of the tray facing Duke Xiao of Qin, 18th year is a single word – *Lin* (a place name and it has not been identified.) [46]

6. Marquis of Zheng Yi, Bronze Chime Bells *bianzhong*. [47] In 1978, a complete set of sixty-four pieces of bronze chime bells was excavated from the tomb of Marquis of Zheng Yi's Tomb, at the Leigudun Mound Suixian. [48] The bells are now on display at the Hubei Provincial Museum. [49] Each of the bells has markings for two harmonic tones, which means each bell can produce two separate tones for musical orchestration. The inscriptions also record the twelve different tonal pitches and solmization used by the states of Zeng, Chu, Zhou, Qi, and Jin.
7. Lord E Qi, Tally *jie*. [50] In 1957, four pieces of bronze tallies were uncovered in a garden that belonged to a Qiu family in Shouxian Anhui, [51] while another piece was discovered in 1960. They are now kept at the Chinese History Museum and Anhui Provincial Museum. Among the pieces are the 'Carriage Tally *ju-jie*' and 'Vessel Tally *zhou-jie*',

---

of Qin 秦孝王. The engraving of Qin Shi Huang on the bottom of the tray indicated that he adopted measurement Shang Yang introduced in 344 BCE.

41 Gong Xinming 龔心銘 (1865-? alias Jingzhang 字景張) of Tangquan Pukao Hefei Anhui 安徽 合肥, 浦口 湯泉; *Pukao Tangquan xiaozhi* 浦口 湯泉小志.

42 The *Qin Bronze and Stone Carving Lexicon, Qin jinwen keci* 秦金石刻辭.

43 Duke Xiao of Qin, 18th year - 秦孝公十八年.

44 Zhongquan 重泉 - Pucheng Shaanxi 陝西 蒲城.

45 The decree of Qin Shihuangdi 26th year 秦始皇二十六年詔 (221 BCE). It was the first year of Ying Zheng 嬴政 as the Emperor of Qin.

46 Lin 臨.

47 'The Marquis of Zeng Yi Bianzhong Bronze Chime Bells 曾侯乙編鐘.' Marquis of Zenghou Yi 曾侯乙 (r. 477-433 BCE). Zeng was a minor fief state in Suixian Hubei 湖北隨縣; the sovereign had a family name of Si 姒.

48 Leigudun Mound Suixian 湖北 隨縣 擂鼓墩. The 64 bells were arranged in three rows, supposedly suspended from three bell-racks.

49 Hubei Provincial Museum 湖北省博物館.

50 Lord E, Qi 鄂君 啓 Tally *jie* 節. The bronze tallies were shaped like split-bamboo segments, with a slightly concave cylindrical surface, between 29.6 to 31cm in length; and it appears that the set of five separate segments probably made up a cylindrical whole; scripts were curved on the converse-surface of the tallies. It was an important find that provide us with valuable information on how the Chu people managed taxes at the passes. The scripts stipulate the number of carriages and boats allowed, the waterways, land passages and the counties the merchandise were allowed to pass through; the distance travelled and the goods sanctioned. Tolls on waterways and road - see Bernbolz, Peter., and Vaubel, Roland; Explaining Monetary and Financial Innovation: A Historical Analysis, Springer 2014. The book is available at the internet.
Also, see - *Zhanguoshe* 戰國史 pp. 114-115.

51 Qiu family in Shouxian Anhui 丘家 安徽壽縣.

these tallies were bestowed upon Lord Ejun Qi (in 323 BCE) by King Huai of Chu, [52] the text decree that the Lord was exempted from paying taxes for transporting goods and merchandise through certain land and river passages.

8. King Cuo of Zhongshan, Tripod *ding* and Square Pot *fang-hu*. [53] The two bronze vessels were discovered in the tomb of King Cuo of Zhongshan in Sanji, Pingshan Hebei. [54] They are now stored at Hebei Historical Relic Department in Hebei. The scripts relate when King Xuan of Qi defeated Yan (314 BCE), Chancellor Bang of Zhongshan and General Zhou took advantage of the situation and attacked Yan, annexing several hundred *li* of land and several scores of walled-city. [55] The bronze pot has scripts of the genealogy of the kings of Zhongshan. [56] In *SJ* 'House of Zhao Biography', Marquis Xian of Zhao states, "Duke Wu of Zhongshan was first enfeoffed."[57] *Shiji suoyin* (*Shiji Obscured Passage*) quoting from the *Bamboo annals* relates, "Duke Wu of Zhongshan settled at Gu (Hebei Dingxian), [58] Duke Huan relocated to Lingshou, King Wuling of Zhao annihilated the Kingdom." Duke Wu of Zhongshan was the sovereign annihilated by Duke Wen of Wei, [59] at which stage Duke Wu settled at Gu. Duke Huan was the sovereign who restored the Zhongshan kingdom and relocated the capital to Lingshou. [60]
9. Carvings and Inscriptions on Warring States Weapons *ke-ci*. [61] It was fashionable during the time of Warring States to inscribe names of officers, designers, insignias of artisans, and the place where the weapons were manufactured or used. This information is valuable to help us identify the place of origin; the manufacturing systems employ as well as the political situation of the Warring States. For instance, in 1983, a Qin halberd was unearthed at the tomb of King Yuenan at Xianggang Mound Guangzhou. [62] The inscriptions read, "During the 4th year of the king, he appointed

52 Carriage Tally - *jujie* 車節 and Vessel Tally - *zhoujie* 舟節.
Lord E, Qi 鄂君啓 (in 323 BCE) by Chu Huaiwang 楚懷王.

53 King Cuo of Zhongshan 中山王 嚳, tripod, *ding* 鼎.
King Cuo of Zhongshan 中山王 嚳, square pot, *fang-hu* 方壺.

54 The King of Zhongshan Tomb in Sanji, Pingshan Hebei 河北平山三汲中山王墓. (Lingshou Zhongshan Capital-city 中山都城 靈壽).

55 King Xuan of Qi 齊宣王 (r.320-302 BCE) (N.B. *ZZTJ* has different dates of his reign; it relates that he died in the same year).
Chancellor Bang 邦 and General Zhou 賙. "中山相邦, 司馬賙". The word Zhou 賙 (賙) was probably a word unique to Zhongshan, as with the king's name of Cuo 嚳, which was also unique to Zhongshan.

56 "皇祖文, 武, 桓祖成考." ... are the posthumous titles of the Zhongshan kings.

57 The *SJ* 史記 'House of Zhao 趙世家'.
Marquis Xian of Zhao 趙献侯.
Duke Wu of Zhongshan 中山武公.

58 Gu 顧 - Dingxian Hebei 河北 定縣.

59 Duke Wen of Wei 魏文侯.

60 Duke Huan 桓公. Lingshou 靈壽.
There is some information on the restoration of Zhongshan Kingdom. However, details are lacking. The bronze pot provides us with additional information about the duke's involvement with the transformation.

61 *Ke-ci* 刻辭.

62 Qin halberd 秦戟.

Zhang Yi as chancellor, (this halberd) is crafted by the Military Commander 口 Cao."[63] The 4th year of the king was King Hui of Qin *Gengyuan* 4th year (321 BCE). Zhang Yi was the same Zhang Yi that appears in historical texts; (however the character Yi is written differently.) [64] The Military Commander Cao was the same person who quelled the internal strife at Yiqi during the 6th year of King Hui; this is according to *SJ* 'Sequence of the Six States'. [65] Textual reference relates that Zhang Yi was the chancellor of Qin, and during the 3rd year of King Hui of Qin he was appointed as the chancellor of Wei, and his post at Qin was retracted. From this, we gather that Zhang Yi was appointed the chancellor of Wei as he successfully deployed his *lian-heng* Horizontal Coalition strategy, whereas in reality he was still the chancellor of *Qin*; in a convenient position to further his plan. The halberd carries a place name Yang, which is east of Baihe Shaanxi, northeast of Nanzheng. [66] Nanzheng was a violently contested territory between Qin and Shu at the time of Zhang Yi; Qin had already annexed the area. The Qin commander garrisoned his troops at Yang, making preparations to invade Hanzhong that was Chu's territory.

Zhao Hu 趙眜 (137-122 BCE) was the grandson of Zhao Tu 1st King of Nanyue 南越國王趙佗 (r. 203-137 BCE).

King Nanyue Zhao Tuo at Xianggang Mound Guangzhou 廣州象崗.

63 "During the 4th year of the king, the king appointed Zhang Yi as chancellor, (this halberd) crafted by Ministry Commander 口 Cao." "王四年相邦張義 庶長口操之造," *SIC*. The word 口 is missing. (N.B. There appears to be mistake with the second statement; other texts show the sentence reads, "..... 庶長口操戈.")

64 King Hui of Qin Gengyuan 秦惠王 4th year (321 BCE).
Zhang Yi 張義 = Zhang Yi 張儀

65 Yiqi 義渠 during the 6th year of the King Hui of Qin 秦惠王 - this was according to the *SJ* 史記, 'Sequence of the Six States 六國年表'.

66 Yang 鍚 was east of Baihe Shaanxi 陝西 白河東; northeast Nanzheng 南鄭 東北, present day Hanzhong 漢中.

Part IV.

Literature on the Warring States

The textual materials concerning the Warring States have dispersed and scattered over the centuries; besides most of the scripts available to us are partial or fragmented. Errors, unfortunately, plague the information that has come down to us; historical facts are intermingled with fabricated history composed by latter-day scholars. There are forty-two manuscripts that contain references to the Warring States, and they require careful compilation, collation, and authentication for better rendering of the historical events:

1. The *Shiji,* the *Records of the Grand Historian* or *Historical Records,* 史記.[1] The book was composed by Sima Qian 司馬遷 at around 90-85 BCE. It was the first historical text in China to use the historiography technique of dividing chapters of accounts into basic annual – *benji* 本記 or *ji* 記. The *benji* and *shijia* 世家 are the annalistic chronicles of the kings and fief lords while the *liezhuan* 列傳 or biographies are the historical accounts of the ministers, subjects and other personnel who served at court. *Shu* 書 are documents and memorials that chronicle institutions, decrees, regulations and systems; and *nianbiao,* 年表 are the date annals. The historic accounts on the Warring States are – "Qin benji 秦本紀; Qin Shihuang benji 秦始皇 本紀; Liuguo nianbiao 六國年表; Tianguanshu 天官書; Hequshu 河渠書; Qi shijia, 齊世家; Lu shijia 魯世家; Yan shijia 燕世家; Wey shijia 衛世家; Song shijia 宋世家; Jin shijia 晉世家; Chu shijia 楚世家; Yue shijia 越世家; Zheng shijia 鄭世家; Zhao shijia 趙世家; Wei shijia 魏世家; Hann shijia 韓世家; Tian shijia 田世家; Laozi, Zhuangzi, Shen Buhai, Hann Fei liezhuan 老子 莊子 申不害 韓非列傳; Wu Qi liezhuan 吳起列傳; Zhongni dizi liezhuan 仲尼弟子列傳; Shangjun liezhuan 商君列傳; Su Qin liezhuan 蘇秦列傳; Zhang Yi, Chen Zhen, Xi Shou liezhuan 張儀 陳軫 犀首列傳; Chulizi, Gan Mao, Gan Luo liezhuan 樗里子, 甘茂, 甘羅列傳; Ranghou liezhuan, 穰侯列傳; Bai Qi, Wang Jian liezhuan 白起 王翦列傳; Mengke, Chun Yukun, Shen Dao, Zou Shi, Xun Qian liezhuan 孟軻 淳于髡 慎到 騶奭 荀卿 列傳; Mengchangjun liezhuan 孟嘗君列傳; Pingyuanjun, Yu Qing liezhuan 平原君 虞卿列傳; Xinlingjun liezhuan 信陵君列傳; Chunshenjun liezhuan 春申君列傳; Fan Ju, Cai Ze liezhuan 范雎 蔡澤列傳; Yue Yi liezhuan 樂毅列傳; Lian Po, Lin Xiangru, Zhao She, Li Mu liezhuan 廉頗 藺相如 趙奢 李牧列傳; Tian Dan liezhuan 田單列傳; Lu Zhonglian liezhuan 魯仲連列傳; Qu Yuan liezhuan 屈原列傳; Lu Buwei liezhuan 呂不韋列傳; Cike liezhuan, 刺客列傳; Li Si liezhuan 李斯列傳; Meng Tian liezhuan 蒙恬列傳, Bian Que liezhuan 扁鵲列傳; Xiongnu liezhuan 匈奴列傳; Xi-Nan-Yi liezhuan 西南夷列傳; Huaji liezhuan 滑稽列傳, and Huozhi liezhuan 貨殖列傳.

   The Qing scholars Liang Yusheng 清 梁玉繩 in his *Shiji zhiyi* 史記志疑, and *Zhang Wenhu* 張文虎 in the *Jiaokan Shiji jijie suoyin zhengyi zhaji* 校刊史記集解索隱正義札

[1] The *SJ* 史記, 'Sequence of the Six States, Liuguo nianbiao 六國年表'.

記 make detailed corrections and collations to the text.[2] More recently, the Japanese scholar Takigawa Kametaro 瀧川龜太郎 in the *Shiji huizhu kaozheng* 史記會注考証 made a complete compilation of collations and corrections gathered by previous scholars. [3]

2. The *Hanshu, Book of Han* or the *History of the Former Han Dynasty* 漢書 was compiled by the Eastern Han scholar Ban Gu 東漢 班固. [4] It is the official historiography text on the former Han Dynasty. Accounts of the Warring States, include: 'Tables of nobles from families of the imperial consorts, Baiguan gongqingbiao 百官公卿表'; 'Treatise on punishment and law, Xingfazhi, 刑法志; 'Treatise on food and commodities Shihuozhi 食貨志'; Treatise on astronomy, Tianwenzhi 天文志'; 'Treatise on geography, Dilizhi 地理志; Treatise on rivers and canals, Gousuzhi 沟洫志; 'Treatise on literature, Yiwenzhi 藝文志'; and 'Traditions of Xinan Yi, Xi-Nan-Yi liezhuan 西南夷列傳; these passages fill many of the voids in the *SJ*. The Qing scholar Wang Xianlian 清 王先謙 compiled the *Addendum to Hanshu, Hanshu buzhu*, 漢書補註.

3. The *Houhan Shu*, the *Book of the Later Han* or the *History of the Later Han Dynasty* 後漢書 was compiled by the South Dynasty scholar Song Fanye 南朝 宋范曄. [5] It is a chronicle of the Eastern Han. There are passages concerning the Warring States; for instance, Xiqianzhuan 西羌傳 and Nan-Man Zhuan, 南蠻傳 record the minor ethnic tribes during the Warring States. It also fills some historical events left out by the *SJ*. The Qing scholar Wang Xianlian 清 王先謙 compiled the *Collective Clarification of Houhan shu*, the *Hou Hanshu jijie* 後漢書集解.

4. The *Zhanguoce, The Warring States Strategies*, 戰國策. [6] The book was compiled by Liu Xiang 漢 劉向 of Western Han and was based on the writings and essays of the political strategists of the Warring States. [7] Gao You 高誘 of Eastern Han made annotations to the texts. [8] However, by the time of the Song Dynasty, the original text was lost; Zeng Gong of Song 宋曾鞏 appended and recompiled some of the texts. [9] The current version is a

---

2 Qing scholar 清 Liang Yusheng 梁玉繩 (1744?-1819?); *Shiji zhiyi* 史記志疑
Qing scholar 清 Zhang Wenhu 張文虎 1808-1885 CE.

3 Japanese scholar Takigawa Kametarō, 瀧川龜太郎 (たきがわ かめたろう 1865-1946 CE).
The *Shiji huizhu kaozheng* 史記會注考証 published in 1934.

4 Eastern *Han* 東漢 *Ban Gu* 班固 (32-92 CE).

5 South Dynasty Liu Song 南朝 劉宋 scholar, Song Fanye 范曄 (398-445 CE).

6 Author - There are numerous other texts related to *ZGC*; however, only the ones referred to by Yang Kuan are included.

7 Han scholar 漢 Liu Xiang 劉向 (77-6 BCE).

8 Gao You 高誘 was in charge of military finance, chariots, and horses 司空掾 in 205 CE towards the waning years of East Han 東漢, his dates of birth and death are obscure.)

9 Song scholar 宋 Zeng Gong 曾鞏 (1019-1083 CE)

compilation by Yao Hong 南宋 姚宏 a Southern Song scholar.[10] It is said that he based his compilation on the works of Kong Yan 孔衍 a Jin 晉 scholar, who compiled *Chunqiu houyu,* 春秋後語; and that he obtained the reference of *Chunqiu houyu* written by the Jin 晉 scholar Kong Yan 孔衍.[11] Bao Biao of Southern Song dynasty 南宋 鮑彪 re-edited the text and made new annotations to the work.[12] Wu Shidao of Yuan dynasty 元 吳師道 then made amendments and corrections;[13] it was to become another edition of the text. The Qing scholar Yu Chang 清 于鬯 compiled an edition of the text but was not published;[14] while the Japanese scholar Guan Xiuling 關修齡 appended addendums to the text in the *Zhanguoce gaozhuzhu buzheng* 戰國策高注補正 and 橫田惟孝 wrote the *Zhanguce zhengjie* 戰國策正解.[15] *Jin Zhengwei* 金正煒, the more recent scholar, composed the *Zhanguoce bushi* 戰國策補釋. The *Zhanguoce Jizhu Huikao,* 戰國策集注滙考 was penned by Zhu Zugeng 諸祖耿,[16] in recent years. All the works aforementioned are useful references. The publication by He Jianzhang 何建章,[17] the *Zhanguoce zhushi* 戰國策注釋, includes the annotations from Yu Chang, Guan Xiuling 關修齡 and Hengtian Weixiao 橫田惟孝.

5. The *Book of the Warring States Strategists,* the *Zhanguo zonghengjia shu* 戰國縱橫家書. It was one of the silk-script scrolls 帛書 excavated from the Han Tomb at Mawangdui Changsha in 1973, 長沙馬王堆漢墓. The text contains 27 chapters, of which 16 chapters are lost texts, and had never been seen before the discovery. The book is divided into three parts; part 1 has 14 chapters, (only 2 had been seen previously); they are the letters and dialogs of Su Qin 蘇秦. The chapters provide us with reliable historical information; from which we can determine the authenticity of *ZGC,* shedding much light on the errors in the *SJ* 史記 'Su Qin Biography 蘇秦列傳'.

6. The *Bamboo Annals,* the *Old Edition of Bamboo Annals, Guben zhushu jinian* 古本竹書紀年. The text was an annual compilation of the warring states by the Wei 魏 court historians. The chronicle ended during the 20th year of King Xiang of Wei 魏襄王 (299 BCE).[18] The accounts related are invaluable for correcting the errors in the *SJ*; it has been used to revise

---

10 South Song scholar 南宋 *Yao Hong* 姚宏 lived around 1100 CE.

11 Jin scholar 晉 Kong Yan 孔衍 (258-320 CE); he was the 22nd descendant of Kongzi.

12 Southern-Song scholar 南宋 Bao Biao 鮑彪 (?) was an 1128 CE presented scholar 進士.

13 Yuan scholar 元 Wu Shidao 吳師道 (1283-1344 CE).

14 Qing scholar 清 Yu Chang 于鬯 (~1862-1919 CE).

15 Guan Xiuling 關修齡 (1283-1344 CE) appended addendums to *Zhanguoce gaozhuzhu buzheng* 戰國策高注補正 composed by Han Gao You 漢 高誘.
Hengtian Weixiao 橫田惟孝 (1774-1829 CE) the *Zhanguce zhengjie* 戰國策正解.

16 Qing scholar 清 Zhu Zugeng 諸祖耿 (1899-1989 CE).

17 He Jianzhang 何建章 (1925-) contemporary scholar. 戰國策注釋 (written between 1964 and 1982).

18 King Xiang of Wei 魏襄王 (r. 318-296 BCE).

the year errors in 'Sequence of the Six States, Liuguo nianbiao', particularly the reigning dates of the Wei and Qi rulers. The original text was lost at the time of Song 宋. *The New Edition Jinben Zhushu Jininan*, 今本竹書紀年 (or *Current Edition*) is a re-compilation by later scholars; and many mistakes are noted. The Qing scholar Zhu Youzeng 朱右曾 compiled the '*Authenticating the Zi Tomb Annals, Jizhong jinian cunzhen*, 汲冢紀年存真' by extracting quotations and references from the *Shiji Obscured Passages, Shiji suoyin*, 史記索隐; *Jijie jijie*, 史集記解 as well as the *Commentary on Rivers and Waters*, the *Shuijingzhu*,水經注. Wang Guowei 王國維 (20th-century scholar) complied, [19] the *Current Edition Bamboo Annals Textual Critique and Research*, the *Jinben zhushu jinian shuzheng* 今本竹書紀年疏証 and the '*Old Version of Bamboo Annals Recompilation and Reediting, Guben zhushu jinian jijiao* 古本竹書紀年輯校. The genera of compilations from references and quotations from the old version are referred to as "Guben – Old version" and the existing versions are referred to as "Jinben – New Version." More recently, Fan Xiangyong 范祥雍 made an edited compilation of Wang Guowei's work. [20] Fang Shiming 方詩銘 and Wang Xiuling 王修齡 recompiled all the lost texts and came up with another version of the *Old Edition Bamboo Annals Recompilation and Reediting, Guben Zhushu jinian jizheng*, 古本竹書紀年輯証. [21] However, all the publications since the *Jizhong Jinian cunzhen* 汲冢紀年存真 by *Zhu Youzeng* 朱右曾 include varying mistakes and errors in some form or other. [22]

---

19 Wang Guowei 王國維 (1877-1927 CE).

20 Fan Xiangyong 范祥雍 (1913-1993 CE).

21 Fang Shiming 方詩銘 (1919-2000 CE).
Wang Xiuling 王修齡 (1880-1963 CE).

22 (Yang Kuan's footnotes) - For Instance in 334 BCE (the 35th year of King Xian of Zhou, 周顯王), King Hui of Wei 魏惠王, and King Wei of Qi 齊威王 met at 'Xuzhou 徐州 recognizing each other as kings.' As a result of the event, King Wei of Chu 楚威王, 'defeated Qi at Xuzhou' the next year. The *SJ* 史記 'House of Yue Biography 越世家' records that King Wei of Chu gave 'the Yue a major defeat', killing King Wujiang of Yue 越王 無彊, while at the same time 'defeated Qi to the north at Xuzhou.' This is compared with the *Shiji suoyin* 史記索慲, quoting from the *Bamboo Annals* 紀年, which says, "According to *Bamboo Annals* 紀年, 10 years after the death of Yuezi Wuzhuan 粵子無顓, Chu attacked Xuzhou, there is not a statement that states, 'Chu defeated Yue and killed Wujiang.'" The statement referred to the *Bamboo Annals* by *Suoyin* that 'Chu attacked Xuzhou' should be the same as when King Wei of Chu defeated Qi at Xuzhou. *Suoyin* goes on to relate, "There is not such a statement that Chu defeated Yue and killed Wujiang." That is to say the *Bamboo Annals* did not chronicle the event of Chu annihilating Yue by killing Wujiang and Chu defeated Xuzhou in the same instance. The *Bamboo Annals, Jinben jinian* 今本紀年 relates that during the 22nd year of King Xian of Zhou, 'Chu attacked Xuzhou.' It is based on the reference of the reigns of Yue kings from the *Bamboo Annals* quoted by *Shiji suoyin* 'House of Yue Biography', and it was established that 10 years after the death of *Wuzhuan* was exactly the 22nd year of King Xian of Zhou. The *Current Edition of Bamboo Annals* records during the 36th year of King Xian of Zhou that, 'Chu laid sieged to Qi at Xuzhou, following which it attacked Yue, killing Wujiang.' Further using *SJ* 史記, 'Sequence of the Six States 六國年表' accounts on the year of siege of Xuzhou 徐州 by Chu and the accounts in the House of Yue; the situation in Current Edition of Jinian 今本紀年 ended up with King Wei of Chu made an expedition against Xuzhou, as well as making another incident when King Xuan of Chu attacked Qi, twelve years prior to this. Zhu Youzeng 朱右曾 also based his

7. *The Chronology Annals, Biannianji* 编年記. It is an excavated bamboo script text that was unearthed at a Qin Tomb at Shuihudi in Yunmeng Hebei 湖北雲夢睡虎地秦墓 in 1976. The deciphered text appeared in Volume 6, 1976 *Wenwu* 文物. The records started during the 1st year of King Zhao of Qin 秦昭王 (306 BCE), ending in the 30th year of Qin Shi Huang 秦始皇帝 (217 BCE), a total of 90 years. The script carries a chronology of the tomb owner Xi 喜. It narrates the important events related to the owner, his relatives, their dates of birth and death; however, most of the important events included in the annals were related to the wars, leading to the grand unification of the six states by Qin. It is invaluable in offering us details of the final years of the Warring States. It can fill in some of the blanks lacking in the *SJ*, as well as making corrections to the errors and confusion.

8. The *Yunmeng Qin's Legalism, Yunmeng Qinlu* 雲夢秦律. Numerous bamboo slips were unearthed in 1976 in the Qin tomb in Suihudi Yunmeng Hebei 湖北雲夢睡虎地秦墓. There are five categories of *Qinlu – Qin Legal System*. One of the texts uses a 'question and answer' approach between Qin 秦 and Xia 夏. The subject dealt with issues of, "...intending to be a *Xia*.", on "...intending to be a Qin subject," [23] on "When the fief lords come to Qin to pay homage, they should bear gifts of jade to present to the king," and so on. The text was composed just before the grand unification of China by Qin. It is an important document for researching into the legal system of Qin, beside an invaluable piece of work for analysing the Qin society. The five articles of deciphered *Qinlu* appeared in Volume 7 and Volume 9 of the 1976 Edition of *Wenwu* 文物.

9. *The Generational Records of the Fief Lords, the Shiben* 世本 is also known as *Xiben* 系本 or *Diaben* 代本. [24] The text is the genealogical chronicle of the different royal fief families of the Pre-Qin epoch, complete with the reigning dates of the Sons of Heaven and fief lords. At the time of Song, the original text was lost. During the Qing Dynasty, scholars using references and quotes from various sources and edited numerous versions of the text. In

---

reference of the years of reign of King of Yue from the quote from the *Bamboo Annals* from the *Shiji suoyin* 'House of Yue'. He concluded that the year that Chu attacked Xuzhou was during the 24th year of King Hui of Wei, which was the 22nd year of King Xian of Zhou, he also concluded that the 'Chu attacked Qi' incident were two separate incidents. Later, the *Old Edition Bamboo Annals* also adhered to this error. Hence, the *Bamboo Annals* only records the incident when King Xuan attacked Xuzhou 徐州 and does not make a reference to the incident of 'King Wei 楚威王 attacked Xuzhou 徐州'. In reality, the quote of the years of reign by the Yue King from the *Bamboo Annals* by *Shiji suoyin* 'House of Yue' was erroneous possibly due to lost segments of the text. Hence, it could not be used to affirm the year when the expedition was made.

23 This was the law introduced by King Zhao of Qin when he annihilated the Yiqu 義渠. "可(何) 謂真? 臣邦父母產子及產地而是謂真. 可(何) 謂夏子? 臣邦父秦母謂殹 (也)." It was an assimilation policy introduced by Qin to integrate and assimilate the Yiqu tribes. The question relating to the issue is, 'How do you define a Qin or to become a Xia?' The answer to the question was if either one of the parents of the infant was a Qin national, he or she became a Xia – i.e. Qin national.

24 *The Shiben* 世本, is also known as *Xiben* 系本 or *Diaben* 代本. Contemporary scholars maintain that there is a mention of King Qian of Zhao 趙遷, the then king of Zhao; it leads them to conclude that the *Shiben* was compiled towards the waning years of the Warring States, between Shi Huangdi 13th to 19th year (234-228 BCE). It was thus compiled 60-70 years after closing of the *Bamboo Annals*.

1957, Shangwu Printing Press 商務 published a collection of eight separate versions, *Shiben bazhong,* 世本八種. The versions by Lei Xueqi 雷學淇 and Mao Panlin 茆泮林 are more comprehensive than the others.

10. *The Chronology of Huayangguo, Huayang guozhi,* 華陽國志. [25] Chang Qu 常璩 composed the text during the Jin 晉 dynasty. It recounts the history of the kingdoms and tribes in the southwest of (Zhongyuan 中原) from most ancient time to Eastern Jin; some of the accounts touched on the Warring States period, the text has been helpful in providing some of the missing accounts in the *SJ*. [26]

11. *The Lost History of Zhou, Yizhoushu,* 逸周書. [27] The military specialists probably composed the text during the time of the Warring States. Some of the contents are indeed the missing chapters of the *Zhoushu* 周書. The text makes accolades and praises of the military exploits by King Wu of Zhou 周武王 and the munificence of the Duke of Zhou's 周公 governance. It is believed that the Warring States scholars composed most of the chapters in the text; they attempted to emulate the writing style of the Zhou period. There appear to be many fabricated events, for instance, it says the minor ethnic tribes from the four corners of the world came to the Zhou court to pay homage to King Cheng of Zhou 周成王. However, the contents do provide genuine conditions and situations of the minor ethnic tribes that settled beyond the realms of Zhongyuan 中原. The Qing scholars Zhu Youzeng 朱右曾 composed the *Yizhoushu jixun jiaoshi,* 逸周書集訓校釋; Tang Dapei 唐大沛 composed *Yizhoushu fenbian jushi,* 逸周書分編句; and He Qiutao 何秋濤 composed the *Wanghuipian jianshi,* 王會篇箋釋. More recently Huang Huaixin 黄懷信 and others compiled and edited an edition called the *Yizhoushu huaixiao jizhu* 逸周書滙校集注. [28]

12. *The Comprehensive Mirror in Aid of for Good Governance, Zizhi tongjian* 資治通鑿. [29] The book was compiled and edited by Sima Guang 司馬光 of the Song dynasty 宋. The records commence from the 23rd year of King Weilie of Zhou 周威烈王 (403 BCE) when the Son of Heaven enfeoffed the three ministers of Jin 晉 - Wei 魏, Zhao 趙 and Hann 韓 as fief lords, it includes a brief description of the partitioning of the state of Jin. Volume 1 through Volume 7 of the book chronicle the events of the Warring States. It was a first attempt to record the history of the Warring States in chronological order. [30] Some of the textual and chronological research are accurate. A few of the historical events included were fabrications

---

25 Huayang guo 華陽國 – was the area southwest of Zhongyuan 中原, a general term for the area.

26 See 301-111, the revolt at Shu 蜀.

27 Yi 逸 means omitted.

28 Zhu Youzeng 朱右曾 (?)清 Qing scholar, the *Yizhoushu jixun jiaoshi,* 逸周書集訓校釋.
Tang Dapei 唐大沛 (?) 清 Qing scholar, *Yizhoushu fenbian jushi,* 逸周書分編句.
He Qiutao 何秋濤 (1824-1862 CE) the *Wanghuipian jianshi,* 王會篇箋釋.
Huang Huaixin 黄懷信 (1951 -) the *Yizhoushu huaixiao jizhu* 逸周書滙校集注.

29 Comprehensive Mirror to Aid in Government.

30 Biannianti 編年體.

by later scholars. For instance, parts of Yue Yi's 樂毅 defeat of Qi 齊 are not entirely credible accounts. (While the event did happen, the details were fabricated. For details, see the translation of Yang Kuan's article 'Authenticating Yue Yi's Defeat of Qi'. The incident in *ZZTJ*, see 284-I, III, IV and 279-III, IV.) There are also other places when the treatment of historical events was distorted or unclear, for example, the account of King Xian of Zhou 20th year says 周顯王, "Qin Shang Yang 秦商鞅 made reforms to corvée and taxes at Qin." [31]

13. *The Mozi, Mohist,* 墨子. [32] The text is a compendium of Mohist thesis, words and deeds of Mozi. Chapters on "Shangxian 尚賢, Shangtong 尚同, Jianai 兼愛, Feigong 非攻, Jieyong 節用, Jiezang 節葬, Tianzhi 天志, Minggui 明鬼, Feile 非樂 and Feiming 非命," were probably earlier compositions, written down during the time between Chunqiu and the early Warring States. The chapters on "Gengzhu 耕柱, Guiyi 貴義, Gongmeng Luwen 公孟魯問 and Luwen 魯問" record the words, deeds and philosophy of Mozi; while, "Fayi 法儀, Qihuan 七患, and Ciguo 辭過." record his comments and remarks and were earlier compositions. The chapters on Jingshang 經上, Jingshuo shang 經説上, Jing xia 經下, Jingshuo xia 經説下, Daqu 大取, and Xiaoqu 小取 are more concise and the topics have broader coverage; these pieces were compiled by latter-day Mohists. 'Beichengmen 備城門' is a chapter on military defence tactics for walled cities; it was probably composed by Qin Guxi 禽滑釐, a student of Mozi. [33]

14. *The Art of War, Sunzi bingfa* 孫子兵法 was composed by Sun Wu 孫武 during the final years of Chunqiu 春秋. The *Sunzi bingfa* in the form of bamboo slips was discovered in a Han tomb in Yinque Shan Linyi Shandong 山東臨沂銀雀山 in 1972. Some the chapters are

---

[31] Yang Kuan's annotations:
SJ 史記, '*Qin benji* 秦本紀' chronicles, 'Duke Xian of Qin 14th year (348 BCE), Qin introduced taxes 初為賦.' *Shiji suoyin* 史記索隱 quoting from Qiao 譙周, '... First introduced military taxes *junfu* 軍賦.' Dong Yue 董説 in his *Qiguokao* 七國考 Volume 2 explains that it was a '*koufu* 口賦 (mouth tax, i.e. per person)' which is correct. The *Qinlu* 秦律 (Qin Law) bamboo slips excavated from Yunmeng 雲夢 refer to it as *hufu* 户賦, household tax; it was a taxation based on the number of people in each household to exact the military taxes *junfu* 軍賦. It was a new taxation introduced by Shang Yang 商鞅; the *ZZTJ* states that Shang Yang made changes to the taxation, which is a wrong interpretation. (see 348-I)

[32] Shangxian 尚賢 respecting the worthy.
Shangtong 尚同 identifying with the superior.
Jianai 兼愛 universal love.
Feigong 非攻 against war.
Jieyong 節用 being fugral.
Jiezang 節葬 thrifty on funeral.
Tianzhi 天志 Failing to understand the broder perspectives of thing.
Minggui 明鬼 understanding ghosts and spirits.
Feile 非樂 repudiating *yue* – the ritual of Music.
Feiming 非命 not providence.

[33] Qin Guxi 禽滑釐.

not in the current versions of the book, namely 'Wuwen pian 吳問篇', 'Dixing 2 地形', and 'Huangdi attacked Chidi 黃帝伐赤帝'. 'Wuwen pian' discusses the land and tax reforms at Jin by the six ministers. 'Yongjian pian, 用間篇, how to spy effectively' a discussion on, "when Zhou dynasty rose in power, Lu Ya 呂牙 was serving at Yin 殷 (Shang 商)." [34] It probably inspired some scholars - at the later time of the Warring States to write, 'When Yan 燕 rose in power, Su Qin 蘇秦 was serving at Qi 齊.'

15. *The Art of War by Sun Bin, Sun Bin bingfa*, 孫臏兵法. The original manuscript, well known to the scholastic world, had long been lost. A copy was discovered in a Han tomb in Yinque Shan Linyi in Shandong 山東 臨沂 銀雀山 in 1972. The text was deciphered by a special group and compiled the *Sun Bin bingfa*. In the text, the Battle of Maling is chronicled, when Sun Bin was the strategist. The text also has passages of the questions and answers between Sun Bin and King Wei of Qi 齊威王, and Chen Ji 陳忌 (Tian Ji 田忌); and elaborations on Sun's military strategies.

16. *The Six Sheath, Liutao* 六韜 was an early Warring States composition by military strategists, [35] the author was supposed to be Taigong Wang 太公望 of early Western Zhou. The text was included in the Song compilation of the *Seven Volumes of Military Strategies, Wujing qishu* 武經七書. From the Han tomb in Yinque Shan Linyi in Shandong 山東 臨沂 銀雀山 in 1972, fragments of *Liutao* were discovered along with *Sunzi bingfa, Sun Bin bingfa* and *Wei Lioazi* 尉繚子. From the finds, we have been able to establish that the text was not a latter-day fabrication. [36] We learn from the contents that the crossbow *qiangnu* 强弩 and *bashi-nu* 八石弩 were already in use at that stage; [37] and the text emphasises the use of chariots for charging into enemy's rank. It was likely to be composed during the earlier years of the Warring States. *Liutao* is not listed in *Hanshu* 漢書 'Yiwenji 藝文志'; however listed under other texts of Taigong 太公. (The text has 237 chapters and is listed under the Doaist 道家 classification.) *Liutao* should be one of the versions of Tiagong. The text records King Wen of Zhou 周文王 was searching for a sage to be his aide; he visited Taigong Wang 太公望 who was fishing on the bank of a river. Taigong (Jiang Taigong 姜

---

34 Lu Ya 呂牙, or Lu Shang 呂尚. His family name was Jiang 姜, alias Ziya 子牙. As he was enfeoffed at Lu he came to be known as Lu Shang he was also honoured as Taigong Wang 太公望. He was the earliest military strategist in Chinese history. When he was young, he attempted to obtain employment at Chaoge 朝歌 the capital city of Yin 殷 (Shang 商) but was unsuccessful. He then moved to Shaanxi 陝西, at River Weishui 渭水, he made a living by fishing. At around 1060 BCE, when he was eighty years old, he met Xibo Ji Chang 西伯姬昌 (King Wen 周文王), who maintained that he was a military genius and appointed him as his military commander, honouring him as Grand Duke Wang 太公望. When Ji Chang died, Ji Fa 姬發 (King Wu 周武王) also honoured him as his Military Commander. His son, Duke Ding of Qi 齊丁公 was the founder of the Qi state 齊; the Jiang family line in Qi lasted until 396 BCE.

35 Tao 韜 the word means sheath or scabbard.

36 'The fabrication inferred here' is that it was scripted much later than the Warring states.

37 John Hill suggests that it was the nine-stone catapult.

太公) presented him with strategies to topple the enemy states. The book propounded that before a military expedition by force *wufa* 武伐, there should be an expedition to win over the civilians by civil approach *wenfa* 文伐. It also means one does not have to resort to arms to collapse the enemy state, *wenfa* coupled with strategies to corrupt the sovereign will be more than adequate; hence, one must pledge support to the expansionism intent of the enemy state. "Nourish it so that it becomes powerful; give support for its expansion; when it becomes too strong, it will invariably break. When it over-extends itself, it will collapse." The text of *Tiagong yinfu zhimou* 太公陰符之謀 studied by Su Qin 蘇秦 probably was the text of *Taigong*. When Su Qin became an agent of Yan 燕 to infiltrate into Qi 齊 causing it to collapse, he used this strategy. *Liutao* composes of 6 volume and 60 chapters; they are divided into 'Literary Sheath, Wentao 文韜; Military Sheath, Wutao 武韜; Dragon Sheath, Longtao 龍韜; Tiger Sheath, Hutao 虎韜; Leopard Sheath, Baotao 豹韜; and Canine Sheath, Quantao 犬韜.' The essence of the chapters do not correspond well with the titles; it is believed that it was caused by later day scholars attempting to append passages to the original texts.

17. The *Laozi* 老子. The text is traditionally believed to have been composed by Laozi at the time of Chunqiu; however based on textual research, it should be the work of early Warring State scholars. The text had a profound influence on the Doaist 道家 and Legalism 法家 movements during the middle and latter era of the Warring States.

18. The *Liezi* 列子 was composed by the Doaist Liezi and his students during the Warring States.[38] There were originally eight chapters, but only two survived after the Upheaval of Rongjia 永嘉之亂 (311 CE), only *Yangzhu* 楊朱 and *Shuofu* 說符 are passed down. Zhang Zham's 張湛 father and his colleagues worked together to restore the text from references and quotations; Zhang Zham 張湛 was responsible for the annotations. The text has some fabricated insertions; however, not entirely; it preserves some of the original thesis of Liezi.

19. The *Yin Wenzi* 尹文子 was composed by the Daoist Yin Wen 尹文.[39] There is only one chapter listed in *Hanshu* 漢書 'Yiwenzhi 藝文志' under Mingjia 名家. The edition that survives today is divided into two chapters, 'Dadao 大道 part 1 and 2'.

20. The *Mengzi* 孟子, Mencius. The text records the sayings and deeds of the literati Mencius. Mencius visited King Yan of Song 宋王偃 when the king was on the throne. He then travelled to Zou 鄒, Teng 滕, Lu 魯 and other fief states. During his final years, he visited Wei 魏, Zeng 曾 and met with King Hui of (Wei) Liang (魏) 梁惠王, and carried out a series of discussions and conversations. At one stage, he was appointed as a guest minister

---

38 Zheng national 鄭人 *Ziezi* 列子.
The *Lie Yukou* 列禦寇. The text is also known as *Zhongxue jing* 仲虛經, *Zhongxu zhenjing* 仲虛真經. Each of the chapters was based on some parables to elucidate the Daoist philosophy.

39 Yin Wen 尹文 (360-280 BCE?).

of Qi, King Xuan of Qi 齊宣王; it was when Qi invaded and defeated Yan 燕, the latter fell into total disarray. From the conversations, one obtains certain accurate information about the incident.

21. The *Zhuangzi* 莊子 the text is a compendium of the thesis of the Doaist Zhuangzi.[40] The seven chapters on, "Xiaoyaoyou 逍遥游; Qiwulun 齊物論; Yangshengzhu 養生主; Renshijian 人世間; Dechongfu 德充符; Dazongshi 大宗師; and Yingdiwang 應帝王", are traditionally attributed to Zhaungzi; while later adherents composed the other chapters. The last chapter Tianxia pian 天下篇 makes a collective discussion on the genesis of ancient literary schools; it is an influential piece of work.

22. The *Jingfa* 經法 and *Shidajing* 十大經 and some other works on silk scrolls were discovered in a Han tomb in Mawangdui; Changsha 長沙 馬王堆 漢墓 in 1973. *Jingfa* and *Shidajing* were composed before *Laozi Yiben juan* 老子乙本卷. They were the lost texts that belonged to the Middle-Warring States era by the Huang-Lao School 黄老學 of scholars.

23. The *Xunzi* 荀子 was composed by the literati Xunzi and his followers.[41] During the reign of King Min of Qi 齊湣王, Xunzi suggested to the king that he should appoint Lord Mengchang 孟嘗君 as his Chancellor, the incident appeared in 'Qiangguo pian 强國篇.' Later he went to Qin, he met Qin King Zhao of Qin 秦昭王 and the Qin Chancellor Fan Ju 范雎 and made a lengthy speech, which is recorded in 'Ruxiao pian 儒效篇' and 'Qiangguo pian 强國篇'. Following which he discussed military strategies with Lord Linwu 臨武君 and King Xiaocheng of Zhao 趙孝成王 (the lengthy conversation appears in the *ZZTJ* see 255-II) and *Yibing pian* 議兵篇. Li Si 李斯 emulated Xunzi's thesis and composed the *Xue diwang shishu* 學帝王之術. Xunzi responded to Li Si's write up in a lengthy article, which appears in 'Yibing pian 議兵篇' (255-II).

24. The *Hannfeizi* 韩非子 is a compendium of the thesis prepared by the Legalist 法家 Hann Fei and his followers.[42] In the text, there are records of his deeds and a few articles purportedly composed by him; including 'Cun Hann 存韓', 'Wentian 問田'. It appears that that some of the works by the political strategists also find their way into the compilation;

---

40 The *Zhuangzi* 莊子, Zhuangzi's family name was Zhou 周 (369-286 BCE).

41 The *Xunzi* 荀子 (313-238 BCE). Xun Kuang 荀况 also known as Xun Qing 荀卿. (See 255-II.)

42 The *Hann Feizi* 韩非子 (280?-233 BCE). (See 233-I.)
'Gufen 孤憤 - On Disillusionment with the World (On Being Lonely and Indignate.')
'Wudu 五蠹 - The Five-destructive Insects.' See above.
Neichu 内儲 - *Inner Parables.*
Waichu 外儲 - *External Parables.*
Shuolin 說林 - *On Numerous Issues, Numerous like Trees in a Forest.*
Shuonan 說難 - *On the Difficulties of Lobbying and Canvassing.*

such as 'Chujian Qin pian 初見秦篇'. Other works include 'Shuolin 説林' part 1 and part 2; 'Neichu shuo 内儲説 part 1 and part 2'; 'Waichushuo 外儲説, Left part 1 and 2, Right part 1 and 2 (4 chapters)'; and 'Shiguo 十過', etc. The work provides us with imperial evidence on the incidents and events that transpired during the Chunqiu epoch and the Warring States and is used for textual research on numerous historical events. (Hann Feizi, see 233-I)

25. The *Lushi chunqiu* or *Lushi Annals* 呂氏春秋 by Lu Buwei 呂不韋. Lu Buwei was the Chancellor of Qin Shi Huang 秦始皇帝. [43] He invited the guests staying in his manor to compose the *Lushi chunqiu*. It is a compendium of all the schools of thought at the time of the Warring States. It was prepared with an objective to provide the Qin kingdom a paradigm shift after the unification. The text includes an extensive array of different schools of thought: *Yin-yangjia wuheng* 陰陽家五行; Legalism *fajia* 法家; Agriculturalist *nongjia* 農家; Daosim 道家; Militarism *bingjia* 兵家, schools. The text drew on incidents at the time of the Warring States and is an invaluable piece in studying the history of the period.

26. The *Gongsun Longzi* 公孫龍子. The text was composed by Gongsun Long 公孫龍 a scholar during late Warring States period. [44] (See *ZZTJ* 298-III.)

27. The *Shangjun shu* 商君書. [45] The text was compiled by later adherents of Wey Yang 衛鞅 (Lord Shang 商君). It was probably composed during the final years of the Warring States. 'Gengfa pian 更法篇' records the debates between Shang Yang and the royal family members. Some of the passages were extracted from King Wuling of Zhao 趙武靈王, who proposed making reforms by adopting *hufu* 胡服 (barbarian attire); his followers probably inserted it. (Lord Shang 商君 see 359-I, 350-I and 348-I. *Hufu* - see 307-III.)

28. The *Guanzi* 管子. The content of this book is extremely mixed, and the dates of compilation varied considerably. Most of the works were probably compiled by Legalists from Qi 齊, making use of Guan Zhong's 管仲 name for the compilation. Hann Feizi 韩非子 relates, "People within our realms are all speaking of peace, the merchants are in hiding; Guan's Legalists have rules about this." (This is a quote from 'Wudu pian 五蠹篇', hence we gather that the *Shangjun shu* 商君書 and *Guanzi* 管子 were already in wide circulation during the time of Hann Fei 韩非. The texts are mixed with writings from Daoism 道家; Military, *bingjia* 兵家; *yin-yangjia* 陰陽家, Agriculturalist, *nongjia* 農加; and Commodity traders *huzhijia* 貨殖, as well as some other works that were composed during the time of Qin and Han.

---

43 Lu Buwei 呂不韋 (292-235 BCE). See translation 257-III; 247-V; 238-IV; VIII; 237-I; 236-III; 235-I.

44 Zhao national 趙人, Gongsun Long 公孫龍 (320-250 BCE). See the passage on his philosophy in the translation in 298-III.

45 Shangjun 商鞅, Gongsun Yang 公孫鞅, Wey Yang 衛鞅.

29. The *Weiliaozi* 尉繚子. There are 31 chapters in *Hanshu* 漢書 'Yiwenzhi 藝文志' on Militarism, *Weliao* 尉繚. Under the heading of *Zajia* 雜家, Yiwenzhi mentions that there were 29 chapters of *Weliao* 尉繚. Song scholars incorporated the *Weiliaozi* 尉繚子 edition that exists today into the *Wujing Qishu* 武經七書. The *Qunshu zhiyao* 群書治要, that was compiled during the Tang dynasty, has four abridged chapters. Fragments of *Weiliaozi* 尉繚子 were discovered at the Han tomb in Yinque Shan Linyi Shandong 山東臨沂銀雀山 in 1972, along with *Sunzi bingfa* 孫子兵法, *Sun Bin bingfa* 孫臏兵法; the contents correspond with the existing edition. We can establish that the current edition of the *Weiliaozi* 尉繚子 is the same text as *Weliao* 尉繚 in the *Hanshu* Yiwenzhi composed by the military strategists.

30. The *Heguanzi* 鶡冠子 was a *Chu* national, he lived towards the final year of the Warring States.[46] He became a recluse, living as a hermit in the mountains; he wore a military headset that was adorned with nightingale feathers. Hence, he came to be known as Heguanzi. *Hanshu* 漢書 'Yiwenzhi 藝文志' records it has a chapter on the *Heguanzi.* When the Tang poet Hann Yu 唐 韓愈 came across the text, it had 16 chapters; the current edition has 3 volume and 19 chapters. In the text, Heguanzi's student Pang Xuan 龐煖 wrote a chapter discussing military strategy;[47] it appears that later scholars appended this work into *Heguanzi. Hanshu* 漢書 'Yiwenzhi 藝文志' records that it had three chapters on Pang Xuan under Military Strategist.

31. The *Yiji cizhuan* 易系辭傳, *Yizhuan* 易傳 was originally a series of lectures given by Confucius 孔子 on the *Book of Changes, Yijing* 易經 to his students, and they compiled the work. *Yiji cizhuan* is one of the most important pieces of the work; it is believed that the work was handed down from the time of early Warring States and committed in writing by Chu 楚 scholars. The scholars, in turn, enriched its contents; the result of which is a synthesis of literati philosophy, merged with Daoist theoretic, with reforms and further developments of the original thesis.

32. The *Dazai liji* 大戴禮記 was composed by Dai De 漢 戴德 of Western Han; he based the works of the *Li* 禮 – Rites and the *Ji* 記 written earlier by the 70 students and followers of Confucius to make a compilation of the work. Within it, there is a piece on 'Zengzi 曾子', based on the thoughts and deeds of Zengzi; it was probably extricated from *Hanshu* 漢書 'Yiwenzhi 藝文志' under the heading of Literati 儒家類 - *Zengzi* 18 chapters. In *Dazai liji* 大載禮記 there is another section that relates the three incidences when Confucius paid homage to Duke Ai of Lu 魯哀公 under the heading of 'Kongzi sanchao ji 孔子三朝記' in seven chapters. It was compiled by his 70 students; it is believed that it was also extricated

46 The name of 鶡冠子 is lost.

47 Pang Xuan 龐煖 was a Zhao General at the time of King Wuling of Zhao 趙武靈王. See *ZZTJ* 242-11.

from *Hanshu* 'Yiwenzhi' and the *Analects*, *Lunyu* 論語, from the seven chapters of 'Kongzi sanchao ji 孔子三朝記'.

33. The *Liji* 禮記 is also known as *Xiao liji* 小禮記. It was composed by the Western Han 漢 scholar, Dai Sheng 戴聖. The work is based principally on the compilations of the *Li* 禮 and *Ji* 記 by the 70 students and followers of Confucius; Dai Sheng collected the works and edited them into this volume. Within the text, the chapter on 'Yueling pian 月令篇' was adopted from the work of 'Yinyang mingtang 陰陽明堂' by the 70 students. The passage of one year is divided into twelve months, each with detailed descriptions of the changes and natural phenomena, and suitability of each month for specific administrative work. The passage was later adopted and incorporated into the introductory chapter of the *Lushi Chunqiu* 呂氏春秋 'Shier ji 十二紀'. In *Liji* there are two chapters of 'Zhongyong 中庸', which are the passages that appear in *SJ* 'Kongzi Household Biography 史記孔子世家' composed by Zisi 子思. There is another chapter of 'Daxue 大學', which carries some of the sayings by Zengzi 曾子, recorded by his later followers.

34. The *Zhouli* 周禮. The work was a political manual prepared by the literati during the Warring States. The text describes the various bureaucratic rankings, their respective positions, institutions, and regulations in the various fief states. It was an idealized archetype for the bureaucrats during the time of Chunqiu 春秋 and Warring States. The text divides Heaven, earth, and the four seasons as the six officers, Liuguan 六官. Towards the beginning of Western Han, the section on 'Dong-guan 冬官 Chapter – Winter Officer' was lost, it was replaced by 'Kaogong ji 考工記', a work, believed to be composed at Qi 齊 towards the beginning of the Warring States years.

35. The *Yugong* 禹貢 is a chapter in *The Book of History,* or *Book of Documents, Shangshu* 尚書.[48] The work is a fabricated piece of work prepared during the middle period of the Warring States. The book assumed the heading of Yu, a hero who quelled the great flooding problem in China during the mythical era. It was a historical atlas of ancient China and to a certain degree, rudimentarily and scientifically based. The text divides China into nine provinces, detailing the topologies, mountains, rivers, forests, swamps, soil categories, produce, transportation, and mandatory tributes by the richness or quality of the soil or land. The text shows that the people during the time of Warring States had a fairly compressive understanding of the topology and geography of China. The edited copy by the Qing 清 scholar Hu Wei 胡渭 the *Yugong zhuizhi* 禹貢錐指 has a fairly comprehensive annotations on the original text.[49]

36. The *Shanhaijing* 山海經 is the earliest compilation and a compendium of ancient Chinese records of mountains, rivers, produce, customs and culture, and geography. The text is

---

[48] Strictly speaking, the Yugong 禹貢 is not a book, merely a chapter.

[49] Qing 清 scholar, Hu Wei 胡渭 (1633 -1714 CE).

divided into Wuzang Shanjing 五藏山經, Haiwaijing 海外經; Haineijing 海内經 and Dahaungjing 大荒經, in four parts. Wuzang shanjing was (probably) written towards the latter part of the Warring States while Dahuangjing was composed towards the closing years of the Warring States; Haineijing was a work that belonged to the early years of Western Han. In the text, many mythical accounts are retained; included are the numerous, customs, minerals, probably one of the earliest documents in the world that belong to this genera. The Qing scholar, Hao Yiheng 清 郝懿行 made extensive textual research of the text, and wrote the *Shanhaijing jianshu* 山海經箋疏. [50]

37. *Suwen* 素問 is the earliest medical text in China, which discusses the physiological principles of pathology. It was predominantly composed during the latter part of the Warring States.

38. The *Chuce* 楚辭 was composed by Qu Yuan 屈原 and his followers and is a literary work. Liu Xiang 劉向 of Western Han 西漢 edited the works into a combined volume. Wang Yi 王逸 of Eastern Han 東漢 also made an analysis of the poems. The text was principally composed by the poet while his adherents might have tried to emulate his style and came up with some of the pieces included in the text. The poems presented the unique literary experience of Chu, the sentiments and the consonant rhymes were unique to Chu's local dialect. The poems describe the customs and culture of Chu, produce, and legendary myths. Among the chapters, "Lisao 離騷, Jiuge 九歌, Tianwen 天問, and Zhaohun 招魂"are the most known pieces.

39. The *Shuoyuan* 説苑 and *Xinxu* 新序 were both compiled by Liu Xiang 劉向 of Western Han 漢. The text is a categorized compilation of historical events and legendary tales from Pre-Qin 先秦 down to the beginning of Han. The text was used to erudite the perspectives of the literati and their ethical standards. The records in the Warring States are of historical values. During the more recent years, Zhao Shanyi 趙善詒 composed the *Shuoyuan shuzheng* 説苑疏証 and the *Xinxu shuzheng* 新序疏証, [51] and he appended references of the texts that have appeared in other literary works.

40. *The Hannshi waizhuan* 韓詩外傳. Hann Ying 韓嬰 composed the book during the time of Han Jingdi 漢景帝. Initially, Hann Ying composed the *Hannshi nei waizhuan* 韓詩内外傳. The *Neizhuan* (inner volume) was lost between the time of two Song dynasties. Each of the articles in *Waizhuan* commences with a story; the *Shijing* is then quoted to verify the account. All the stories that appear in the text have some differences with accounts in other texts; however, it does have a certain value for textual research. Contemporary scholar Xu Weiyu 許維遹 composed the *Hannshi waizhuan jishi* 韓詩外傳集辭. [52]

---

50 Qing 清 Hao Yiheng 郝懿行 (1757-1825 CE).

51 Zhao Shanyi 趙善詒 (1911-1988), *Shuoyuan shuzheng* 説苑疏証 and the *Xinxu shuzheng* 新序疏証 published in 1989.

52 Xu Weiyu 許維遹 (1905-1951 CE).

41. *The Commentary on Rivers and Waters, Shuijingzhu* 水經注 was composed by Li Daoyuan 酈道元 during the Northern Wei 北魏 dynasty.[53] The text was based on another earlier text called *The Shuijing* 水經, it was used to make reference to major rivers and streams and their tributaries, describing the places they flow through; treating the history of the places mentioned in depth. Many of its references are quotes from the *Bamboo Annals, Zhushu jinian* 竹書紀年 and older texts. It describes the places mentioned during the Warring States and the conditions of the places. Mentions are also made of the Chu Fangcheng 楚方城, Wei Changcheng 魏長城, Qi Changcheng 齊長城 and Yan Changcheng 燕長城, as well as the construction of the Zheng Dam in Qin, - the Zhengguo water dike in Qin called 鄭國渠 (see 246-11). The text was based on history texts available to Li at the time. It contains invaluable historical references that fill in some parts lacking in the *SJ*. For instance, in *Mianshui Zhu* 沔水注 it relates that the Qin General Bia Qi made an attack against Chu's other capital Wu 楚 Yan 鄢; he directed the water from the river to inundate the walled-city. Several hundred thousand soldiers and civilians died from drowning. Two illustrated editions of the text that were composed by Yang Shoujing 楊守敬 and Xiong Huizeng 熊會貞,[54] the *Shuijingzhu shu* 水經注疏 and the *Shuijingzhu tu* 水經注圖 are useful references for studying the history of the Warring States.

42. *The Gushi* 古史 was composed by the Song Su Zhe 宋 蘇轍 (poet).[55] He re-edited the biographic texts of the Pre-Qin period in entirety, and it preserves many of the references that were lost after Song. For instance, in the 'Bai Qi zhuan 白起傳', there is a long passage about Bai Qi holding a long conversation with King Zhao of Qin 秦昭王; and a reference to Bai Qi's objection to invade Handan. Previous scholars had treated this subject as a lost text in the *ZGC* 戰國策, to which it was appended.

---

53 Li Daoyuan 酈道元 (466 or 476-527 CE). The original *Bamboo Annals, Zhushu jinian* was lost during the 9th century. Hence, Li Daoyuan probably had a genuine copy of the lost text.

54 Yang Shoujing 楊守敬 (1839-1915 CE), 熊會貞 (1859-1936 CE).

55 Su Zhe 宋 蘇轍 (1039-1112 CE).

Appendix 4

The Dynasties of China

Pre-Qin 先秦 – The Three Dynasties (*Sandai* 三代)

Xia 夏	ca. 21st -1600 BCE.
Shang 商	ca. 1600-1045 BCE
Early Shang	ca. 1600- ~1400 BCE
Yin 殷	~1400-1045 BCE
Zhou 周	1045-256 BCE
Western Zhou 西周	1045-771 BCE
Eastern Zhou 東周	770-256 BCE
Spring and autumn 春秋	770-476 BCE
Warring States 戰國	475-221 BCE
Qin 秦	221-206 BCE
Han 漢	202 BCE -220 CE
Western Han 西漢	202-23 CE
新 Xin	9-23 CE
Eastern Han 東漢	25-220
Wei 魏, Jin 晉, Nan-Bei Chao 南北朝	220-589
Sanguo 三國	220-280
Wei 曹魏	220-265
Han Shu Han 蜀漢	221-263
Wu SunWu 孫吳	220-280
Jin 晉	265-420
Western Jin 西晉	265-420
Eastern Jin 東晉	317-420
Liu Chao 六朝	222-589
Sixteen Kingdoms 十六國	304-439
Nan-Bei Chao 南北朝	420-589
Southern Dynasties 南朝	420-579
Liu Song 劉宋	420-479
Qi 齊	479-502
Liang 梁	502-557
Chen 陳	557-589
Northern Dynasties 北朝	386-581
Northern Wei 北魏	386-534
Eastern Wei 東魏	534-550
Western Wei 西魏	535-556
Northern Qi 北齊	550-577

Northern Zhou 北周	557-581
Sui 隋	581-618
Tang 唐	618-907
Wudai Shiguo 五代十國	902-979
Five Dynasties (North China) 五代	907-960
Ten Kingdoms (South China) 十國	902-979
Song 宋	960-1279
Northern Song 北宋	960-1127
Southern Song 南宋	1127-1279
Liao 遼 (Qidan Khitan 契丹)	916-1125
Jin 金 (Nuzhen 女真 Jurchen)	1115-1234
Xia 夏 (Dangxiang 黨項, Tangut)	1038-1227
Yuan 元 (Mongol 蒙古)	1279-1368
Ming 明	1368-1644
Qing 清 (Manchu 滿洲)	1644-1912
Republic of China 中華民國	1912-1949
People's Republic of China 中華人民共和國	1949

References:

Bai, Shouyi 白壽彝. *Zhongguo tongshi gangyou* 中國通史綱要, Shanghai Remin chubanshe 上海人民出版社, China, 2001. ISBN 7-208-00136-7/K.34

Bai, Shouyi 白壽彝. (Bai, Zhide, 白志德 ed.) *Bai Shouyi jiang lishi – Xian Qin Qin-Han juan* 白壽彝講歷史 先秦 秦漢卷, Zhongguo gongren chubanshe 中國工人出版社, China, 2008. ISBN 978-7-5008-4017-6

Ban, Gu 班固 *Hanshu* 漢書, (proofread by Chen, Huanliang 陳煥良, and Zeng, Xianli 曾憲禮), Yuelu shushe 岳麓書社, China, 1993. ISBN 7-80520-376-8

Chang, Kwang-Chih, *The Archaeology of Ancient China*, Yale University Press, US, 1977. ISBN 0-300-02145-3
- Further Developments of Civilization in North China to 211 BCE.
- Early Civilizations in South China.

Chang Qu 常璩, *Huayang guozhi* 華陽國志 (translated by Tang Chunsheng 唐春生 et al.), Chungqing chubanshe 重慶出版社, China, 2008. ISBN 978-7-5366-9458-3

Chen Mengjia 陳夢家, *Xizhou niandaikao, Liuguo jinian* 西周年代考 六國紀年, Beijing Zhonghua shuju 北京中華書局, China, 2005. ISBN 978-7-101-04382-2

Elisseeff, Danielle and Vadime, (Translated by Larry Lockwood), *New Discoveries in China*, Chartwell Books, Inc., US, 1983. ISBN 0-89009-840-9

Gan, Bao 干寶, *Shoushenji quanyi* 搜神記全譯 (translated by Huang, Diming 黄涤明), Guizhou Renmin chubanshe 貴州人民出版社, China, 1996. ISBN 7-221-04010-9

Gu, Derong 顧德融 and Zhu, Shunlong 朱順龍, *Chunqiushi* 春秋史, Shanghai remin chubanshe 上海人民出版社, China, 2003. ISBN 7-208-04544-5

Guoyu yizhu 國語譯注, Li, Benda 李本達 ed., Xue Anqin 薛安勤 and Wang, Liansheng 王連生, 8th edition, Jilin wenshi chubanshe 吉林文史出版社, China, 1996. ISBN 7-80626-138-9/I.32

Feng, Shi 馮時, Wu Sheng (edit) 胡繩, *Archaeoastronomy in China, Zhongguo tianwen kaoguxue* 中國天文考古學, Shehui kexue wenxian chubanshe 社會科學文獻出版社, China, 2001. ISBN 7-80149-602-7/K.80

Huang Aimei 黄愛梅 and Yu Kai 于凱, Qizhizang 器之藏, Shanghai jiaoyu chubanshe 上海教育出版社, China, 2005. ISBN 7-532-9734-X/I-0058

Huang, Zhongye 黄中業, *Sandai jishi benmo* 三代紀事本末, Liaoning Renmin chubanshe 遼寧人民出版社, China, 1999. ISBN 7-205-04156-2

Ji, Jingfen 嵇景芬 ed., *The Map of China Archaeology* 中國考古大發現, Renlei zhiku gufen youxian gongsi 人類智庫股份有限公司, Taiwan, 2006. ISBN986-7044-25-8

Lei, Haizong 雷海宗, *Guoshi gangyao* 國史綱要, Wuhan chubanshe 武漢出版社, China, 2012. ISBN 978-7-5430-6740-0

Lewis, Edward Mark, *the Early Chinese Empires*, Qin and Han, the Belknap Press of Harvard University Press, UK, 2007. ISBN 978-0-674-02477-9

Li, Zehou李澤厚, *Zhongguo gudai sixiang shilun* 中國古代思想史論, Tianjin shehui kexueyuan chubanshe 天津社會科學院出版社, China, 2003. ISBN 7-80688-001-1

Li, Daoyuan 酈道元, *Shuijingzhu* 水經注, (proofread by Tan Shuchun 譚屬春 and Chen Aiping 陳愛平) Yuelu shushe 岳麓書社, China, 1995. ISBN 7-80520-555-8

Ming Dong Gu with Rainer Schulte, *Translating China for Western Readers, Reflection, Critical and Practical Essays*, State University of New York Press, Albany, US, 2014. ISBN 987-1-4384-5511-2

- Nylan, Michael, Translating Texts in Chinese History and Philosophy.

Li, Feng, *Early China, A Social and Cultural History*, Cambridge University Press, UK, 2013. 978-0-521-89552-1

Li Zongkun 李宗焜 ed., the *Guwenzi yu gudaishi* 古文字與古代史, Third Volume 第三輯, Zhongyang yanjiuyuan lishi yuyan yanjiusuo, 中央研究院歷史語言研究所, Taiwan, 2012. ISBN 13: 978-9-8603-2251-4.

Liu, Xiang 劉向 ed., *Zhanguoce* 戰國策, annotations by He Wei 賀偉, Hou Yangjun 侯仰軍, 點校, 5th edition, Qilu shushe 齊魯書社, China, 2010. ISBN 978-7-5333-1484-2

Liu, Xiang 劉向 ed., *Zhanguoce* 戰國策, Fan Xiangyong 范祥雍 *Zhanguoce jianzheng* 戰國策箋證, Shanghai guji chubanshe 上海古籍出版社, China, 2011. ISBN 978-7-5325-5990-9

Lu, Simian 呂思勉, *Xian Qinshi* 先秦史, Shanghai guji chubanshe 上海古籍出版社, China, 2005. ISBN 7-5325-4029-4

Qian, Cunxun 錢存訓, *Shuyu zhubo* 書于竹帛, 上海世紀出版社, Shanghai shiji chuban jituan 上海世紀出版集團. China, 2006. ISBN 7-80678-471-3.

Qian, Mu 錢穆, *Zhongguo shixue mingzhu* 中國史學名著, Lantai chubanshe 蘭臺出版社, Taiwan, 2001. ISBN 957-0422-25-4

Qi, Liang 啓良, *Zhongguo wenmingshi* 中國文明史, Huacheng chubanshe 花城出版社 China, 2001. ISBN 7-5360-3332-X

Qi, Sihe 齊思和, *Zhongguoshi tanyan* 中國史探研, Hebei jiaoyu chubanshe 河北教育出版社, China, 2003. ISBN 7-5434-3866-6/K.111

Rawson, Jessica, *Ancient China, Art and Archaeology*, Harper & Row Publishers, US, 1980. ISBN 0-06-438435-7

Siku quanshu 四庫全書, Yu Liwen 于立文 ed., Beijing yishu yu kexue dianzi chubanshe 北京藝術與科學電子出版社, 2007, China. ISBN 978-7-900722-95-5
(Includes - *Chunqiu* 春秋, *Hann Feizi* 韓非子, *Hanshu* 漢書, *Kongzi* 孔子, *Laozi* 老子, *Liji* 禮記, *Lunyu* 論語, *Mengzi* 孟子, *Shangshu* 尚書, *Shiji* 史記, *Shijing* 詩經, *Xunzi* 荀子, *Yijin* 易經, *Zizhi tongjian* 資治通鑒, *Zhuangzi* 莊子).

Sima, Guang 司馬光, *Zizhi tongjian* 資治通鑒, *Bo Yang Edition* 柏楊版資治通鑒, Translated by Bo Yang, 6th edition., Yuanliu chuban gongsi 遠流出版公司, Taiwan, 1986.

Sima, Guang 司馬光, *Zizhi tongjian* 資治通鑒, Chen Liankang 陳連康 ed. et al. Xian chubanshe 西安出版社, China, 2002. ISBN 7-80594-877-1

Sima, Guang 司馬光, *Zizhi tongjian* 資治通鑒, *Zizhi tongjian jinzhu* 資治通鑒今註, annotated by Li, Zongdong 李宗侗; Xia, Deyi 夏德儀 et al., Vol 1, Commercial Press 臺灣商務印書局, Taiwan, 2011. ISBN 978-957-05-2652-3

Sima, Guang 司馬光, *Zizhi tongjian* 資治通鑒, Rao Zongyi 饒宗頤 ed., Zhonghua shuju, 中華書局, Hong Kong, 2013. ISBN 978-988-8263-03-5

Sima, Qian 司馬遷, *Shiji* 史記, *Records of the Grand Historian - Qin Dynasty*, Translated by Watson, Burton, The Research Centre for Translation, Chinese University of Hong Kong, Columbia University Press Book, Hong Kong, 1993. ISBN 978-0231-08169-6

Sima, Qian 司馬遷, *Shiji* 史記, Wu, Yun 吳雲 ed. and translated et al. Zhongyang minzu daxue chubanshe 中央民族大學出版社, China, 2002. ISBN 7-81056-624-5

Tang, Guiren 湯貴仁, *Taishan Fengshan yu jisi* 泰山封禪與祭祀, Qilu shushe 齊魯書社, China, 2003. ISBN 7-5333-1148-5

Tang, Xiaofeng 唐曉峰 and Huang, Yijun 黃義軍, *Readings in History, Historical Geography* 歷史地理學讀本, Beijing daxue chubanshe 北京大學出版社, China, 2006. ISBN 7-301-09420-5

Tong, Shuya 童書亞 *Chunqiushi* 春秋史, Shanghai guji chubanshe 上海古籍出版社, China, 2012. ISBN 978-7-5325-5549-9

Wang, Li 王力 ed., *Zhongguo gudai wenhua changshi* 中國古代文化常識, Shiji tushu chubanshe 世界圖書出版社, China, 2008. ISBN 978-7-5062-8689-3/C.18

Wang, Shili 王士立 and Sun, K. Q. 孫開秦 ed., *Zhongguo gudai shi* (Vol 1), 中國古代史 上册, Beijing shifan daxue chubanshe 北京師范大學出版社, China, 2001. ISBN 7-303-01093-9

Wang, Yinglun 王應麟, *Tongji dili tongshi* 通鑒地理通釋, ed. proofread by Fu Linxiang 傅林祥, Zhonghua shuju chubanshe 中華書局出版社, China 2013. ISBN 978-7-101-09464-0.

Wilkinson, Endymion, *Chinese History A Manual*, Harvard University Asia Center for the Harvard-Yenching Institute, US, 2000. ISBN 0-674-00249-0

Xia, Zengyou 夏曾佑, *Zhongguo dudaishi* 中國古代史, Tuanjie chubanshe 團結出版社, China, 2005. ISBN 7-80214-128-1.

Xiong, Yihong 熊依洪 ed. et.al., *Xin Qin wenxue daguan* 先秦文學大觀, Beijing yanshan chubanshe 北京燕山出版社, China, 2008. ISBN 978-7-5402-1930-7

Yang, Fan 楊帆 ed., *Zhongguo lishi niandai jianbiao* 中國歷史年代簡表, Joint Publishing (H.K.) Co. Ltd.,三聯書店, 2nd edition, Hong Kong, 2003. ISBN 962-04-2180-9

Yang, Kuan 楊寬, *Xian Qinshi shijiang* 先秦史十講, Fudan daxue chubanshe 復旦大學出版社, China, 2006. ISBN 7-309-04883-0

Yang, Kuan 楊寬, *Xizhoushi* 西周史, Shanghai renmin chubanshe 上海人民出版社, 2003 China. ISBN 7-208-04538—0/K.998

Yang, Kuan 楊寬, *Zhanguoshi* 戰國史, Shanghai renmin chubanshe 上海人民出版社. 2003. ISBN 7-208-04537-2

Yap, Joseph, *Wars with the Xiongnu, A Translation from Zizhi tongjian*, AuthorHouse, US, 2009. ISBN 879-1-4490-0605-1

Yizhoushu 逸周書, *Yizhoushu huijiao jizhu* 逸周書彙校集注, Huang, Huaixin 黄懷信, Zhang Maorong 張懋鎔 Tian Xudong 田旭東 et al ed., Shanghai guji chubanshe 上海古籍出版社, China, 2008. ISBN 978-75325-4391-5

Yuan Ke 袁珂, Zhongguo gudai shengua 中國古代神話, Huaxia chubanshe 華夏出版社, China, 2004. ISBN 7-5080-3233-0

Zhang, Yinlin 張蔭麟, *Zhongguo shigang* 中國史綱, Shanghai guji chubanshe 上海古籍出版社, China, 2007. ISBN 978-7-5325-4322-9/K.824

Zhang Yuchun 張玉春, *Zhushu jinian yizhu* 竹書紀年譯注, Heilongjiang renmin chubanshe 黑龍江人民出版社, China, 2003. ISBN 7-207-04394-5

Zhao, Yi 趙毅 and Zhao, Yifeng, 趙軼峰, *Zhongguo gudai shi* 中國古代史, (2002), China, Gaodeng jiaoyu chuban she, 高等教育出版社, China, 2002. ISBN 978-7-0401-1502-4

Zhongguo lishi baike quanshu, The, 中國歷史百科全書, Zhongguo dabaike chunshu chubanshe 中國大百科全書出版社, China, 1994. ISBN 7-5000-5190-5

Zhonghua renmin gongheguo fensheng dituji 中華人民共和國分省地圖集, Ditu chubanshe 地圖出版社, China, 1974.

Zhou, Jian 周儉 et al, *Sichou zhilu* 絲綢之路, Jiangsu renmin chubanshe 江蘇人民出版社, China, 2012. ISBN 978-7-214-08404-0

Zhou, Gucheng 周谷城, *Zhongguo tongshi* 中國通史, 22nd edition. Shangmu yinshuguan 商務印書館, China, 2001. ISBN 7-208-00330-0

Zuo, Qiuming 左丘明, Chunqiu, Zuozhuan 春丘左傳, ed. and translated Wu, Zhaoji 吳兆基, Jinghua chubanshe 京華出版社, China, 1999. ISBN 7-80600-446-7/G

References from the web:

The information provided by Wikipedia are suspect at best, however, the author finds them helpful as they provide quick reference guide for further readings and research. Some of the web sites are quite reliable, the followings are the one the author finds helpful:

Zizhi tongjian Hu Sansheng 資治通鑒 胡三省注 Vol 1-8. 國學導航. 卷1-8. Guoxue123.com copyright 2006.

http://www.guoxue123.com/Shibu/0101/01zztjhz/index.htm

Zhang Zhipeng 張志鵬, *Tengguo xinkao* 滕國新考
http://www.gwz.fudan.edu.cn/SrcShow.asp?Src_ID=1428

Xin, Deyong 辛德勇*, Zhongtan zhongguo gudai yi nianhao jinian de qiyong shijian* (An additional discussion on the introduction of nianhao in ancient China), 2014-12-16
重談中國古代以年號紀年的啓用時間 pdf file
http://yun.baidu.com/share/link?uk=3042116754&shareid=1965636062&third=1&adapt=pc&fr=ftw

Liu, Xiang 劉向 ed., *Zhanguoce* 戰國策, He, Jianzhang 何建章, Zhanguoce zhushi 戰國策注釋, Zhonghua shuju 中華書局, China, 1992. ISBN 7-101-00622-1/K.270, pdf file
http://vdisk.weibo.com/s/cXnhAK9kgiz7a

Wu Hui 吳慧*, Chunqiu shiqi de duliangheng* 春秋時期的度量衡, pdf.
http://www.hprc.org.cn/pdf/ZJSY199104013.pdf

Zhongguo shexueshu dianzihua jihua 中國哲學書電子化計劃 http://ctext.org/zh

Zizhi tongjian

(This is an important web-site to conduct textual research, it has amassed practical all the classical and historical texts from the most ancient time to the time of the Qing Dynasty. Furthermore, the texts are available in the simplified and traditional characters.)

Bai Shouyi 白壽彝 ed., *Zhongguo* 中國通史 12 卷, Zaixian yuedu 在線閱讀 http://www.xiexingcun.com/tongshi.asp

Index A – Subjects and Persons Index (in alphabetical order)

Note: Some of the entries are mentioned in passing in the text. Please read the footnotes, as details are expanded.

Index B - Sovereigns and Royalty of the Warring States (arranged in succession chronological order as in *ZZTJ*)

Jin, Duke Xiao 晉孝公 Ji Qing 姬傾 succeeded 393-II
Jin, Duke Xiao 晉孝公 died 378-III

Jin, Duke Jing, Ji Jujiu 晉靖公 姬俱酒 succeeded 378-III
Jin, Duke Jing, Ji Jujiu 晉靖公 banished by Wei 魏, Hann 韓 and Zhao 趙, Jin 晉 ended 376-I

Lu House 魯

Lu, Duke Mu, Ji Xian 魯穆公 姬顯 died 377-III

Lu, Duke Gong, Ji Fen 魯共公 姬奮 succeeded 377-III
Lu, Duke Gong 魯共公 died 355-III

Lu, Duke Kang, Ji Mao 魯康公 姬毛 succeeded 355-III
Lu, Duke Kang, Ji Mao 魯康公 died 346-II

Lu, Duke Jing, Ji Yan 魯景公 姬偃 succeeded 346-II
Lu, Duke Jing 魯景公 姬偃 died 317-IV

Lu, Duke Ping, Ji Lu 魯平公 姬旅 succeeded 317-IV
Lu, Duke Ping, Ji Lu 魯平公 姬旅 died 297-II

Lu, Duke Min, Ji Jia 魯緡公 姬賈 succeeded 297-II
Lu, Duke Min, Ji Jia 魯緡公 died 274-II

Lu, Duke Qing, Ji Chou 魯頃公 姬讎 succeeded 274-II
Lu, Duke Qing of Lu 魯頃公 banished to Ju 莒 255-V
Lu, Duke Qing of Lu 魯頃公 banished by Chu 楚 to Bian 卞 as commoner, end of Lu 249-V

Qi House 齊

Qi, 齊 Tian Chang 田常, (Chen Chengzi 陳成子) mentioned by Sima Guang 司馬光 403-I

Qi, 齊- Tian 田 clan - Tian Chang (Heng) 田恒 (常 成子) - Master Xiang, Tian Pan 田盤 (襄子) Tian Bai 田白 (Master Zhuang 莊子) - Tian He 田和 (Taigong 太公) 391-II

Qi, Tian clan 齊田氏 ousted Duke Kang 齊康公 of Qi 齊姜氏 391-II
Qi, Duke Kang 齊康公 姜貸 banished; Tian clan seized power of Qi 391-II

Qi, Chen Chengzi 陳成子, Tian Chang 田常 mentioned by Miao Liu 繆留 321-V
Qi, Tian Chang 田常 mentioned by Li Si 李斯 208-XIV

Qi, Tian He, Taigong 齊田和 太公 met fief lords 389-II
Qi, Tian He 齊太公 enfeoffed as sovereign of Qi (see footnotes) 386-I
Qi, Tian He 齊太公 died (see footnotes) 385-IV

Zhao King 趙王 Zhao Xie 趙歇 placed on the throne by Chen Yu 陳餘 and Zhang Er 張耳 208-IX
Zhao King 趙王 besieged in Julu 鉅鹿 208-XVIII
Zhao King 趙王 after the lifting of Julu 鉅鹿 returned to his capital Xindu 信都 207-VI

Zhou House 周
Zhou, King Weilie 周威烈王 Ji Wu 姬午 enfeoffed San-Jin minister as fief lords 403-I
Zhou, King Weilie 周威烈王 died 402-I

Zhou, King An 周安王 Ji Jiao 姬驕 succeeded 402-I
Zhou, King An 周安王 agreed to enfeoff Qi Tian He 齊田和 as fief lord 389-II
Zhou, King An 周安王 decreed to enfeoff Qi Tian He 齊田和 as fief lord 386-I
Zhou, King An 周安王 died 376-I

Zhou, King Lie 周烈王 Ji Xi 姬喜 succeeded 376-I
Zhou, King Lie 周烈王 King Wei of Qi 齊威王 paid homage at the Zhou court 370-I
Zhou, King Lie 周烈王 died 369-II

Zhou, King Xian 周顯王 Ji Bian 姬扁 succeeded 369-II
Zhou, King Xian 周顯王 bestowed special trapping to Qin 364-I
Zhou, King Xian 周顯王 died 321-I

Zhou, King Shenjing 周慎靚王 Ji Ding 姬定 succeeded 321-I
Zhou, King Shenjing 周慎靚王 died 315-I

Zhou, King Nan, Ji Yan 周赧王 姬延 succeeded 315-I
Zhou, King Nan 周赧王 revived Alliance, captured by Qin died in Xianyang - End of Zhou 256-II

Zhou Princes
Zhou, Prince Ji Ding 姬定 escaped to Jin 晉 399-I

Zhou, Lord Wu, Eastern Zhou 東周武君 enfeoffed 281-III

Zhou, Qin 秦 banished Duke Wen of Western Zhou 西周文公 255-IV
Zhou, Eastern Zhou 東周君, Lord of Eastern Zhou banished to Yangrenju 陽人聚 249-II

Index C

Major Events by State (arranged in chronological order by state)

Chu 楚, sent Nao Chi 淖齒 to relief Qi 齊 under siege by Yue Yi of Yan 燕 樂毅;
Nao Chi executed Qi King 284-II
Chu 楚 planned with Qi 齊 and Hann 韓 to attack Qin 秦 and annihilate Zhou 周, King of Zhou sent Duke Wu of Dong-Zhou 東周昭公 convinced Zhaozi 昭子 that it was a bad idea,
Chu ceased campaign 281-III
Chu 楚, attacked by Qin Bai Qi 秦 白起, Yan 鄢, Deng 鄧, and Xiling 西陵 occupied 279-I
Chu 楚 attacked by Qin 秦 Bai Qi 白起, took Ying 郢 and Yiling 夷陵, Chu moved capital to Chen 陳 278-I
Chu 楚 lost Wu 巫 and Qianzhong 黔中 to Qin 秦 277-I
Chu 楚 recovered 15 counties in Jiangnan 江南 276-II
Chu 楚, Huang Xie of Chu 楚黃歇 convinced Qin 秦 not to attack Chu (mentioned *Sanwang Wubo* 三王五伯, Zhibo 智伯, King Wu 吳王 and King Yue 越王) 273-III
Chu 楚, Wei 魏 and Qin 秦 attacked Yan 燕 272-III
Chu 楚, King Qingxiang 頃襄王 gravely ill and died, King Xiaolie succeeded 孝烈王 263-II
Chu 楚 ceded Zhou 州 to Qin 秦 262-I
Chu 楚 sent Huang Xie 黃歇 Lord Chunshen 春申君 to Zhao's 趙 aid 258-II
Chu 楚, Huang Xie 黃歇 appointed Xun Kuang 荀況 as Lanling magistrate 蘭陵令 *ling* 255-II
Chu 楚 occupied Lu 魯, banished Lu Qinggong 魯頃公 to Ju 莒 255-IV
Chu 楚 moved capital to Juyang 鉅陽, (moved back to Chenqiu 陳丘 shortly after) 253-II
Chu 楚 annihilated Lu, Duke Qing 魯頃公 banished to Bian 卞 249-V
Chu 楚, Huang Xie 黃歇 (Lord Chunshen 春申君) constructed a new city at Jiangdong 江東 248-III
Chu 楚, Lian Po 廉頗 settled at Chu 245-II
Chu 楚, Zhao 趙, Wei 魏, Hann 韓 and Wey 衛 revived Hezong 241-I
Chu 楚 moved capital to Shouchun 壽春 changed name to Yingdu 郢都 241-I
Chu 楚, King Xiaolie 孝烈王 died, Huang Xie 黃歇 killed by Li Yuan 李園 King You 幽 succeeded 238-VII
Chu 楚 attacked by Qin 秦 and Wei 魏 forces 235-III
Chu, King You 楚幽王 died, King Ai 哀王 succeeded; Mi Fuchu 羋負芻 killed King Ai, proclaimed king 228-IV
Chu 楚 attacked by Li Xin 李信 at Pingyu 平輿, Meng Tian 蒙恬 at 寢, Chu lost, Li Xin broke Chu at Yanying 鄢郢, rallied with Meng Tian at Chengfu 城父, Qin 秦 lost, Chu defeated the retreating Qin forces 225-II
Chu 楚 attacked by Wang Jian 王翦, defeated General Xiang Yan 項燕 died 224-I
Chu 楚, King Mi Fuchu 羋負芻 captured by Wang Jian 王翦, Meng Wu 蒙武, set up Chu 楚郡 Prefecture 223-I

Post Chu

Da-Chu 大楚, Chen Sheng 陳勝 and Wu Guang 吳廣 revolted, called their state Da-Chu 209-III
Da-Chu 大楚, Ge Ying 葛嬰 made Xiang Jiang 襄彊 Chu king, Xiang Jiang killed by Ge Ying Chen Sheng 陳勝 executed Ge Ying 209-IV
Chu 楚, Xiang Liang 項梁 son of Xiang Yan 項梁 and Xiang Yu 項羽 revolted against Qin 秦 209-IV
Da-Chu 大楚 (Chen Sheng 陳勝) Zhou Zhang 周章 killed by Zhang Han 章邯 (Qin 秦) 208-II
Da-Chu 大楚, Wu Guang 吳廣 killed by general, Zhang Han 章邯 won many battles 208-III

Hann 韓 Marquis Yi of Hann 韓懿侯 died, succeeded by Marquis Zhao 昭侯 359-II
Hann 韓 defeated by Qin 秦 at Xishan 西山 358-I
Hann 韓 and Wei 魏 met at Hao 鄗 357-I
Hann 韓 attacked Dong Zhou 東周, occupied Ling Guan and 陵觀, Lingqiu 廪丘 353-II
Hann 韓 appointed Shen Buhai 申不害 chancellor 351-III
Hann 韓 attacked by Wei 魏, Battle of Maling 馬陵之役 341-I
Hann 韓 Shen Buhai 申不害 died 337-I
Hann 韓 attacked by Qin 秦, Yiyang 宜陽 of Hann occupied 335-I
Hann 韓, Marquis Zhao 昭侯 constructed a high tower 334-II
Hann 韓 high gate completed, Marquis Zhao 韓昭侯 died, succeeded by Marquis Wei 威侯 333-II
Hann 韓 according to Su Qin 蘇秦; Hann had an area of 900 *li*, several hundred thousand soldiers, all brave warriors, best weapon manufacturer under Heaven 333-III
Hann 韓 and Yan 燕 sovereigns proclaimed king; Marquis Wei 威侯 changed his title to King Xuanhui 宣惠 323-II
Hann 韓 King Xuanhui intended to assign his court to Gongzhong 公仲 and Gongshu 公叔, Mao Liu 繆留 reprimanded against it 321-I
Hann 韓 attacked by Qin 秦, Yan 鄢 occupied 319-I
Hann 韓, Chu 楚, Zhao 趙, Wei 魏, and Yan 燕 allied against Qin 秦; armies arrived at Hangu Pass 函谷關 318-I
Hann 韓 defeated by Qin 秦 at Youyu 脩魚, lost 80,000 men; generals Wei Sou 魏鯁, Shen Cha 申差 captured at Zhuoze 濁澤 317-I
Hann 韓 defeated by Qin秦 at Anmen 岸門, Prince Hann Cang 韓倉 sent to Qin as hostage 314-III
Hann 韓 and Wei 魏 attacked Chu 楚 at Deng 鄧 while Chu 楚 engaged in war with Qin 秦 312-I
Hann King Xuanhui 韓宣惠王, King Xiang 襄王 (Cang 倉) succeeded 312-III
Hann King Xuanhui 韓宣惠王 visited by Zhang Yi 張儀 311-II
Hann 韓, Gan Mao of Qin 秦 甘茂 and Wei 魏 attacked Hann at Yiyang 宜陽 308-II
Hann 韓, Gongsun Chi 公孫侈 went to Qin 秦 to offer apology 307-I
Hann 韓, Chu楚 and Qi 齊 resumed the Hezong alliance 306-III
Hann 韓, attacked by Qin 秦, Wusui 武遂 occupied 303-II
Hann 韓, Qi 齊, Wei 魏 attacked Chu 楚 for breaking *Hezong* 303-III
Hann 韓 Prince Ying 太子嬰, Wei King 魏王, Qin 秦 King and met at Linjin 臨晉 302-II
Hann 韓 Rang 穰 occupied by Qin 秦 301-II
Hann 韓, Wei 魏 and Qi 齊 commanded by Qin 秦 attack Chu 楚 301-IV
Hann 韓, King of Qi 齊王 and King of Wei 魏王 met at Hann 299-II
Hann 韓, Qi 齊, Wei 魏, Zhao 趙 and Song 宋 attacked Qin 秦; Qin returned Wusui 武遂 to Hann and Fengling 封陵 to Wei for peace 298-II
Hann 韓, King Xiang 韓襄王 died, King Xi 韓釐王 succeded 298-V
Hann 韓 attacked Qin 秦, aided by Wei 魏, Bai Qi 白起 defeated the allies, 240,000 men died, Hann General Gongsun Xi 公孫喜 captured 293-I
Hann 韓 attacked by Qin 秦, Wan 宛 taken 291-I
Hann 韓 ceded 200 *li* of land at Wusui 武遂 to Qin 秦 290-II

Qi 齊, King Xiang 齊襄王 died, Qi, King, Tian Jian 齊田建 succeeded, Queen Dowager as Regent 265-V
Qi 齊, Tian Jian 田建 refused to send supplies to Zhao 趙 army under siege at Changping 長平 260-I
Qi 齊, Queen Dowager died, a capable woman who exercised judiciary diplomacy; Tian Jian 田建 was feeble and indecisive, refused to help escaped ministers and generals from defeated states 222-V
Qi 齊, Tian Jian 田建 surrendered, died of hunger in a pine or cypress forest 221-I

Post Qi
Qi 齊, Tian Dan 田儋 of Diyi 狄邑 revolted at Qi 齊, proclaimed Qi king, recovered Qi territories 209-IV
Qi 齊, Tian Dan 田儋 died fighting against Zhang Han 章邯, Tian Jia 田假 brother of Tian Dan took over, Tian Dan's cousin Tian Rong 田榮 attacked Tia Jia 田假; Tian Jia escaped to Chu 楚, Tian Rong 田榮 made Tian Fu 田福, son of Tian Dan, Qi king, Tian Rong 田榮 as Chancellor, Tian Heng 田横 as general 208-XIII
Qi 齊, Tian Du 田都 general of Tian Fu 田福 marched to Julu 鉅鹿 to go against Qin 秦 207-I
Qi 齊, Tian An 田安 grandson of Tian Jian 田建 marched to Julu 鉅鹿 to go against Qin 秦 207-V

Qin 秦
Qin 秦 attacked Wei 魏 reached as far as Yanggu 陽孤 401-I
Qin 秦, Duke Jian 簡公 died, Duke Hui 惠公 succeeded 400-V
Qin 秦 attacked Hann 韓 at Yiyang 宜陽, occupied 6 villages 391-I
Qin 秦 and Jin 晉 joined battle at Wucheng 武城 (It should be one of the San-Jin) 390-I
Qin 秦 attacked Jin 晉 (?) 389-I
Qin 秦 invaded Shu 蜀, occupied Nanzheng 南鄭 387-I
Qin 秦, Duke Hui 惠公 died, succeeded by Duke Chu 出公 387-III
Qin 秦 major revolted, killed Duke Chu 出公, placed Duke Xian 獻公 on the throne 385-I
Qin 秦 defeated Wei 魏 and Hann 韓 at Luoyang 洛陽 366-II
Qin 秦 defeated San-Jin armies at Shimen 石門, killed 60,000 men 364-I
Qin 秦 defeated Wei 魏 at Xiaoliang 少梁, General Gongsun Cuo 公孫痤 captured 362-II
Qin 秦, Duke Xian 獻公 died, succeeded by Duke Xiao 孝公, who resolved to make reforms 362-V
Qin 秦, Duke Xiao 孝公 invited capable people to Qin, Gongsun Yang 公孫鞅 went forward 361-I
Qin 秦, Gongsun Yang 公孫鞅 made reform 359-I
Qin 秦 defeated Hann 韓 at Xishan 西山 358-I
Qin 秦, Duke Xiao of Qin 秦孝公 met King Hui of Wei 魏惠王 at Duping 杜平 355-II
Qin 秦 defeated Wei 魏 at Yuanli 元里, killed 7000 men and occupied Shaoliang 少梁 354-I
Qin 秦 Gongsun Yang 公孫鞅 attacked Wei 魏 352-I
Qin 秦 Gongsun Yang 公孫鞅 attacked Wei 魏, occupied Guyang 固陽 351-I
Qin 秦 capital - moved from Liyang 櫟陽 to Xianyang 秦遷都咸陽 350-I
Qin 秦 army and Wei 魏 army met at Tong 彤 350-II
Qin 秦 Gongsun Yang 公孫鞅 introduced new tax law, effective immediately 348-I
Qin 秦, King Xian of Zhou 周顯王 enfeoffed King of Qin as Bo 伯; other fief lords offered

Qin 秦, Wei Ran 魏冉 attacked Wei 魏, Wei lost 4 cities, 40,000 men 274-I
Qin 秦 sent Bai Qi 白起 and Hu Shang 胡傷 to Hann's aid 韓 when Zhao 趙 and Wei 魏 attacked Huayang 華陽, Qin defeated Wei, Wei lost 130,000 men, Zhao lost 20,000 men 273-I
Qin 秦, Huang Xie of Chu 楚 黄歇 convinced Qin not to attack Chu 楚 (mentioned *Sanwang Wubo* 三王五伯, Zhibo 智伯, King Wu 吳王 and King Yue 越王) 273-III
Qin 秦 set up Nanyang Prefecture 南陽郡 at Wan 宛 272-II
Qin 秦, Wei 魏, and Chu 楚 attacked Yan 燕 272-III
Qin 秦 attacked Zhao 趙, besieged Yuyu 閼與, Zhao She 趙奢 marched to the rescue 270-I
Qin 秦, Wei ran 魏冉 recommended Du 灶 (竈) to attack Gangzhou of Qi 齊 剛壽 to enrich his fief at Taoyi 陶邑 270-II
Qin 秦, Fan Ju 范雎 met King Zhaoxiang 秦昭襄王 270-II
Qin 秦, Hu Shang 胡傷 *zhonggeng* 中更 attacked Yuyu at Zhao 趙 閼與, lost 269-I
Qin 秦 King used Fan Ju 范雎 strategy, commanded Wan 綰 to attack Wei 魏 occupied Huai 懷 268-I
Qin 秦 attacked Wei at Xingqiu 魏 邢丘 266-I
Qin 秦 King banished Dowager Xuan 宣太后, Wei Ran 魏冉, Lord Gaoling 高陵君, Lord Huayang 華陽君, Lord Jingyang 涇陽君, Fan Ju 范雎 enfeoffed as Marquis of Ying 應侯 266-I
Qin 秦 King made revenge for Fan Ju 范雎 266-III
Qin 秦 King nominated Ying Zhu 嬴柱 as successor 265-II
Qin 秦 attacked Zhao 趙, occupied 3 cities; Zhao appealed to Qi 齊 for help; Qi wanted a Zhao hostage 265-III
Qin 秦 Bai Qi 白起 attacked Hann 韓, took 9 cities, decapitated 50,000 264-I
Qin 秦 Bai Qi 白起 attacked Hann 韓, took Nanyang 南陽 263-I
Qin 秦 took over Zhou 州 from Chu 楚 262-I
Qin 秦 Bai Qi 白起 attacked Hann 韓, took Yewang 野王, cut off passage to Shangang 上黨, Feng Ting 馮亭 magistrate of Shangdang surrendered to Zhao 趙 262-II
Qin 秦, Wang He 王齕 *zuoshuzhang* 左庶長 took Shangdang 上黨; King of Zhao replaced Lian Po 廉頗 with Zhao Kuo 趙括. Bai Qi 白起 秦 defeated Zhao at Changping 長平, buried 400,000 趙 men alive 260-I
Qin 秦, Bai Qi 白起 continue attacks against Zhao 趙 after the fall of Changping 長平; Zhao sent Su Dai 蘇代 to see Fan Ju 范雎, convinced Qin to withdraw 259-I
Qin 秦, Qin King lured Lord Pingyuan 平原君 to Qin, held hostage in exchange for Wei Qi's 魏齊 head 259-IV
Qin 秦, Wang Ling 王陵 attacked Zhao 趙 259-V
Qin 秦, Wang Ling 王陵 lost at Handan 邯鄲, replaced by Wang He 王齕, Bai Qi 白起 refused to command 258-I
Qin 秦, Qin King threatened to go against Wei 魏 after taking down Zhao 趙, Wei hesitated 258-III
Qin 秦 forced Bai Qi 白起 to suicide, step up attack against Zhao 257-I
Qin 秦 lost to allies of Lord Xinling 信陵 of Wei 魏; Wang He 王齕 retreated, Zheng Pingan 鄭平安 surrendered, Fan Ju 范雎 under censure 257-II

Qin 秦 severely cold summer at Qin 238-II

Qin 秦 King Ying Zheng 秦王 嬴政 lived in Yong 雍 238-III

Qin 秦 King Ying Zheng 秦王 嬴政 turned twenty 238-III

Qin 秦 Yang Duanhe 楊端和 attacked Wei 魏 occupied Yanshi 衍氏 238-V

Qin 秦, Lao Ai 嫪毐 revolted, lost and executed, clan members banished 238-VI

Qin 秦 banished all foreign guests, Li Si 李斯 wrote a memorial to King of Qin, recalled 237-I

Qin 秦 attacked while Zhao 趙 attacked Yan 燕; Qin 秦 Wang Jian 王翦, Huan Yi 桓齮, Yang Duanhe 楊端和 attacked Zhao 趙 at Ye 鄴; Wang Jian attacked Yuyu 閼與 Laoyang 轑陽, Huan Yi took Ye 鄴 and 安陽 236-I

Qin 秦, King forced Lu Buwei 呂不韋 to take his own life 235-I

Qin 秦 drought 235-II

Qin 秦 mobilized troops from 4 prefectures to aid Wei 魏 attack Chu 楚 235-III

Qin 秦 General Huan Yi 桓齮 attacked Zhao, killed Zhao General Hu Zhe 趙 扈輒, killed 100,000 men Li Mu 李牧 took command, defeated Huan Yi 桓齮 fled the field 234-I

Qin 秦 General Huan Yi 桓齮 attacked Zhao 趙, took Yian 宜安, Pingyang 平陽 and Wucheng 武城 Hann King 韓王 ceded land and relinquished national seal to Qin 233-I

Qin 秦, Li Si 李斯 forced Hann Fei 韓非 to commit suicide 233-I

Qin 秦, Qin attacked Zhao 趙, reached Ye 鄴, Taiyuan 太原, attacked Langmeng 狼孟 and Fanwu 番吾, Li Mu 李牧 took over defence, Qin army withdrew 232-I

Qin 秦, accepted ceded Nanyang 南陽 from Hann 韓 (N.B. It was already set up in 272-II?) 231-I

Qin 秦 also accepted ceded land from Wei 魏 231-II

Qin 秦, Sheng 勝 *neishi* of Xianyang 咸陽 captured Xinzheng 新鄭 and the King of Hann 韓王 Hann ended, Qin founded the Yongchuan Prefecture 潁川郡 230-I

Qin 秦 attacked Zhao 趙, Wang Jian 王翦 attacked Jingjing 井陘; Yang Duanhe 陽端和 supported; Li Mu 李牧 and Sima Shang 司馬尚 put up resistance; Qin bribed Guo Kai 郭開; Zhao king replaced generals with Zhao Cong 趙葱 and Yan general Yan Ju 燕 顔聚; Li Mu killed, Sima Shang discharged 229-I

Qin 秦, Wang Jian 王翦 attacked Zhao 趙, Zhao Cong 趙葱 killed, Yan Ju 顔聚 died in action, Handan 邯鄲 fell, King Youmu 幽穆王 captured 228-I

Qin 秦, Wang Jian 王翦 garrisoned at Zhongshan 中山 to exert pressure on Yan 燕 228-III

Qin 秦, Yan Ji Dan's 燕姬丹 assassination against Qing King failed, Wang Jian 王翦 attacked Yan 燕, Defeated Yan and Zhao 趙 forces 227-I

Qin 秦, Wang Jian 王翦 attacked Yan, took Ji 薊; King Ji Xi 姬喜 and Prince Dan 丹 escaped to Liaodong 遼東 pursued by Qin Li Xin 李信. Ji Xi killed his son, did not contain the encroaching Qin 226-I

Qin 秦, Wang Ben 王賁 attacked Chu 楚, occupied 10 or more cities; Ying Zheng 嬴政 sent Li Xin 李信, Meng Tian 蒙恬 with 200,000 men to attack Chu, Wang Jian 王翦 retired 226-II

Qin 秦, Wang Ben 王賁 attacked Wei, King of Wei 魏王 surrendered, executed 225-I

Qin 秦, Qin offered 500 *li* of land in exchange of Anling of Wey 衛, Lord of Wey 安陵君 declined 225-I

Qin 秦 attacked Chu 楚, Li Xin 李信 attacked Pingyu 平輿, Meng Tian 蒙恬 attacked 寢,

Zhang Han 章邯 to gather convicts from Lishan 驪山 to make defence, Da-Chu 大楚 army retreated 209-IV
Qin 秦, Zhang Han 章邯 defeated Li Gui 李歸 at Yingyang 滎陽; and Deng Yue 鄧說, Wu Feng 伍逢 208-III
Qin 秦, Second Emperor 二世皇帝 kept berating Li Si 李斯, introduced harsher laws, many died 208-IV
Qin 秦, Zhang Han 章邯 attacked Wei 魏, Killed Qi Tian Dan 齊田儋, King of Wei Jiu 魏咎 suicided 208-XIII
Qin 秦, Zhang Han 章邯 defeated by Xiang Liang 項梁 at Donga 東阿, Zhang Han retreated 208-XIII
Qin 秦, Zhao Gao 趙高 suggested Ying Huhai 嬴胡亥 to stay in the inner palace, Zhao Gao executed Li Si 李斯 forced Feng Quji 馮去疾 chancellor and Feng Jie 馮劫 to suicide, Qin in chaos 208-XIV
Qin 秦, Qin reinforced Zhang Han 章邯, Xiang Liang died at Dingtao 項梁 208-XV
Qin 秦 Zhang Han 章邯 attacked Zhao 趙, camped near Julu 鉅鹿, Wang Li 王離 besieged Julu 208-XVIII
Qin 秦 Zhang Han 章邯 and Wang Li 王離 besieged Julu 鉅鹿, Zhang Han defeated by Xiang Yu 項羽 207-VI
Qin 秦 Zhang Han 章邯 surrendered to Xiang Yu 項羽, enfeoffed as King Yong 雍王 207-IX
Qin 秦, Zhao Gao 趙高 (Qin 秦) controlled the Qin court; Liu Bang 劉邦 took Wuguan 武關; Zhao Gao 趙高 forced Huhai to suicide; Zhao Gao intended to make Ying Ying 嬴嬰 king; Ying Ying killed Zhao Gao 207-XI

Song 宋
Song 宋, Duke Dao 悼公 died, succeeded by Duke Xiu 休公 396-II
Song 宋 attacked by Hann 韓; Duke Xiu 休公 captured 385-III
Song 宋, Duke Xiu, Song Tian 休公 died, Duke Pi 辟公 succeeded 373-V
Song 宋, Duke Pi 辟
公 died, Song Ticheng 宋剔成 370-VI
Song 宋 attacked by Wei 魏 365-I
Song 宋, Zhao 趙 and Qi 齊 met at Pinglu 平陸 356-II
Song 宋, altar at Taiqiu 太丘 collapsed 336-I
Song 宋, Song Yan 宋偃 revolted, Song Ticheng 剔成 escaped to Qi; Yan succeeded 329-III
Song 宋, King Kang 宋康王 Song Yan 宋偃 proclaimed king 318-II
Song 宋, King Kang Jie 宋康桀 annihilated Teng 滕, attacked Xue 薛, Qi 齊, Chu 楚 and Wei 魏, finally defeated by Qi 齊, King Kang escaped to Wei 魏 died at Wen 温; Song 宋 annihilated 286-III

Wei 魏
Wei 魏 annihilated Zhongshan 中山 (mentioned) 403-V
Wei 魏 attacked by Qin 秦; army arrived at Yanggu 陽孤 401-I
Wei 魏, Hann 韓 and Zhao 趙 attacked Chu 楚 armies arrived at Sangqiu 桑丘 400-I
Wei 魏 attacked Zheng 鄭 393-I

Wei 魏 attacked by Qin 秦 Yang Duanhe 楊端和, Yanshi 衍氏 occupied 238-V
Wei 魏 attacked Chu 楚 assisted by Qin 秦 235-III
Wei 魏 ceded land to Qin 秦 231-II
Wei 魏, King Jingmin 景湣 died, Wei Jia 魏假 succeeded 228-V
Wei 魏, King of Wei 魏王 surrendered when Qin 秦 attacked, executed; Wei annihilated 225-I

Post Wei
Wei 魏, Zhou Shi 周市 (Da-Chu 大楚) refused to proclaim king, elected Sir Ningling 寗陵君 Wei Jiu 魏咎 209-V
Wei 魏, Wei Jiu 魏咎 suicided after defeat by Zhang Han 章邯, Wei Bao 魏豹 took over 208-XIII
Wei 魏, Wei Bao 魏豹 recovered 20 Wei cities, King Huai of Chu 楚懷王 made Wei Bao King 208-XVI

Wey 衞
Wey 衞, Duke Shen 愼公 died, Duke Sheng 聲公 succeeded 373-VI
Wey 衞 attacked by Zhao 趙, 73 villages 372-I
Wey changed title from Duke to Marquis, became protectorate of San-Jin 346-III
Wey sovereign relegated title to Lord 320-I
Wey 衞, Wei 魏, Hann 韓, Chu 楚 and Zhao 趙 revived Hezong 241-I
Wey 衞 attacked by Qin occupied capital Puyang 濮陽; Wey King moved capital to Yewang 野王 241-II
Wey 衞, Qin 秦 offered 500 *li* of land in exchange for Anling of Wey 衞, Lord of Wey 安陵君 declined 225-I
Wey annihilated 衞國亡 209-VI

Yan 燕
Yan, Duke Min died 湣公, Duke Xi 僖公 succeeded 403-VI
Yan 燕 defeated Qi 齊 at Linhu 林狐 373-I
Yan 燕, Duke Xi 燕僖公 died, Duke Huan 燕桓公 succeeded 373-IV
Yan 燕 and Zhao 趙 met at A 阿 356-I
Yan 燕 attacked by Qi 齊 occupied 10 counties, later returned 332-III
Yan 燕 sovereigns proclaimed king, 323-II
Yan 燕, Wei 魏, Hann 韓, Chu 楚 and Zhao 趙 allied against Qin 秦; armies arrived at Hangu Pass 函谷關 318-I
Yan 燕 Ji Guai 姬噲 abducated to Zi Zhi 子之 316-II
Yan 燕, Zi Zhi 子之 on throne 3 years, Yan in chaos, Prince Ji Ping 姬平 revolted, Qi 齊 invaded, killed Zi Zhi and Ji Guai 姬噲 314-IV
Yan 燕 installed Prince Ji Ping 姬平 on the throne, known as King Zhao 昭王 312-II
Yan 燕, King Zhao 燕昭王 on the throne, resolved to make revenge against Qi 齊 312-II
Yan 燕, Zhao 趙, and Qi 齊 annihilated Zhongshan 中山 295-II
Yan 燕, King Zhao 燕昭王 prepared to take revenge against Qi 齊 285-IV
Yan 燕, Yue Yi 樂毅 as commander attacked Qi, Qi lost 70 cities 284-I
Yan army penetrated deep into the heartland of Qi Yue Yi 樂毅 (Mentioned Qi Huangong 齊桓公 and Guan Zhong 管仲） 284-IV

Zhao 趙, Wei 魏, and Hann 韓 attacked Qi 齊 the armies arrived at Sangqiu 桑丘 380-II
Zhao 趙 raid against Wey 衛, failed 379-I
Zhao 趙, Wei 魏, and Hann 韓 attacked Qi 齊 reached Lingqiu 靈丘 378-II
Zhao 趙, Hann 韓 and Wei 魏 deposed Duke Jing of Jin 晉靖公 376-II
Zhao, Marquis Jing 敬侯 died, Marquis Cheng 趙成侯 375-III
Zhao 趙 attacked Wey 衛, occupied 73 villages near capital Diqiu 帝丘 372-I
Zhao 趙 defeated by Wei 魏 at Beilin 北藺 372-II
Zhao 趙 attacked Qi 齊, reached Juan 鄄 370-II
Zhao 趙 defeated by Wei 魏 at Huai 懷 370-III
Zhao 趙 and Hann 韓 invaded Wei 魏 when it fell into chaos 369-III
Zhao 趙 invaded Qi 齊, occupied Long-wall (see notes) 368-II
Zhao 趙, Hann 韓 and Wei 魏 allies defeated by Qin 秦 at Shimen 石門 364-I
Zhao 趙 and Hann 韓 defeated by Wei 魏 at Kuai 澮 362-I
Zhao 趙 and Yan 燕 met at A 356-I
Zhao 趙, Qi 齊 and Song 宋 met at Pinglu 平陸 356-II
Zhao 趙, Handan 邯鄲 sieged by Wei 魏, Chu 楚 sent Jing She 景舍 to the rescue 354-II
Zhao 趙, Zhao saved by Qi 齊, Handan 邯鄲 fell to Wei 魏, Battle of Guiling 桂陵之役 353-I
Zhao 趙, Wei 魏 returned Handan 邯鄲 to Zhao, signed treaty at Zhang River 漳水 351-II
Zhao 趙, Marquis Cheng 成侯 died, Zhao Xie 趙緤 vied with Zhao Yu 趙語, Zhao Xie escaped to Hann 韓 350-III
Zhao 趙, Zhao Fan 范 attacked Handan 邯鄲, failed, executed 347-I
Zhao 趙 and Qi 齊 attacked Wei 魏 340-III
Zhao 趙, Su Qin 蘇秦 visited Marquis Su 肅侯 333-III
Zhao 趙 broke river dam to flood the camps of Qi 齊 and Wei 魏; the armies retreated 332-I
Zhao 趙, Marquis Su 肅 died, Zhao Yong 趙雍 succeeded 326-I
Zhao 趙, Zhao Yong 趙雍 refused to proclaim King 323-II
Zhao 趙, Yan 燕, Wei 魏, Hann 韓, and Chu 楚 allied against Qin 秦; armies arrived at Hangu Pass 函谷關 318-I
Zhao 趙 attacked by Qin Ji 秦 疾, Chu Lizi 樗里子 *yougeng* 右更 captured Zhuang Bao 莊豹 and Lin 藺 313-I
Zhao 趙, Zhang Yi 張儀 visited Zhao King, convinced the King to align with Qin 秦 311-II
Zhao 趙, Zhao Yong 趙雍 introduced foreign attire and archery on horseback 307-III
Zhao 趙, Zhao Yong 趙雍 invaded and occupied land to Zhao's north 306-II
Zhao 趙, Zhao Yong 趙雍 invaded Zhongshan 中山, took Danqiu 丹丘, Shuangyanghong 爽陽鴻, Hao 鄗, Shiyi 石邑, Fenglong 封龍 Dongyuan 東垣, Zhongshan ceded 4 counties for peace 305-II
Zhao 趙 attacked Zhongshan 中山, King of Zhongshan escaped to Qi 齊 301-V
Zhao 趙, Zhao Yong 趙雍 intended to abdicate his throne to Zhao He 趙何 300-IV
Zhao 趙, Zhao Yong 趙雍 (King Wuling 武靈王) abdicated to Zhao He 趙何, called himself Zhufu 主父 299-I
Zhao 趙, King Huiwen 惠文王 enfeoffed his brother Lord Pingyuan 平原君 298-III
Zhao 趙, Qi 齊, Hann 韓, Wei 魏 and Song 宋 attacked Qin 秦; the armies arrived at

Index D

Chapter Summary – by year

Volume 1. 資治通鑒 卷第一 周紀一 403-369 BCE

The narratives of this volume commence from the 33rd year (403 BCE) of King Weilie of Zhou 周威烈王, ending in the 7th year of King Lei of Zhou 周烈王 in 369 BCE.

403 BCE - The three principal ministers of Jin 晉 - the family clans of Wei 魏, Zhao 趙 and Hann 韓 were enfeoffed this year. The three ministerial family clans San-Jin had previously annihilated the Zhi 智 clan and divided their land.

Master Xiang of Zhao, Zhao Wuxu, 趙襄子 趙無恤 hated Zhi Yao (Zhibo) 智瑤 智伯 balefully; he used his skull as his drinking goblet.
Yu Rang 豫讓 attempted to assassinate Zhao Wuxu to avenge the death of his master, Zhi Yao.
Marquis Wen of Wei, Wei Si 魏文侯 魏斯 attracted many capable people to his state.
Wu Qi 吳起 killed his wife to earn a general position at Wei 魏. When his mother died, he did not attend her funeral; Marquis Wen of Wei made him a general. Wu Qi was an exemplary army commander.

397 BCE - Xia Lei, the chancellor of Hann 韓相 俠累, was assassinated by Nie Zheng 聶政.

389 BCE - The minister of Qi, Tain He 齊大夫 田和 was enfeoffed as a fief lord, he took over the Qi state.

387 BCE - Wu Qi 吳起 left Wei 魏 and headed off to serve Chu 楚. King Dao of Chu 楚悼王 made him the chancellor. Wu Qi introduced reforms to Chu by instituting new legal systems and strengthening the military power. He pacified the people to the south at Bai-Yue 百越, holding off the encroachments from the San-Jin (Hann, Zhao and Wei); he made expeditions against Qin 秦 to the west. The feudal lords were getting apprehensive about the strengthening of Chu; however, the royal elites and nobles at Chu were resentful of Wu Qi.

381 BCE - King Dao of Chu died; Chu nobles, royalist, and elites killed Wu Qi.

371 BCE - Marquis Wu of Wei, Wei Ji 魏武侯 魏擊 died. He did not leave a will, his son Wei Ying 魏罃 vied for the throne with Gongzhong Huan 公中緩; the state fell into complete chaos.

370 BCE - King Wei of Qi 齊威王 was fair with merits and punishments. He enfeoffed the minister at Jimo 即墨大夫 for his merits and executed the magistrate of Donga 東阿大夫 for deception; the fiefdom entered into a period of resurgence.

Volume II. 資治通鑒 卷第二 周紀二 368-321 BCE

The narratives of this volume commence from the first year of King Xian of Zhou 周顯王 in 368 BCE and ending in his 48th year in 321 BCE.

361-359 BCE - Duke Xiao of Qin 秦孝公 succeeded to the throne, he was humiliated by the treatment of his state by the other fief lords; he decided to make reform by inviting capable people to carry out reforms. Shang Yang aliases Gongsun Yan and Wey Yang 商鞅 公孫鞅 衛鞅 responded to his call and began making critical changes to Qin, which ended up as one of the most powerful states during the latter part of the Warring States era.

355 BCE - King Wei of Qi 齊威王 and King Hui of Wei 魏惠王 discussed their respective perspectives of national treasuries.

353 BCE – Wei 魏 invaded Zhao 趙, the capital city was under siege; the army of Qi 齊 marched off to the rescue of Zhao; Tian Ji 田忌 was made the commanding general, with Sun Bin 孫臏 as the military strategist. Instead of heading towards Zhao, the Qi army laid siege to Wei, forcing it to retreat from Zhao; the retreating forces were given a resounding defeat at Guiling 桂陵.

351 BCE - Shen Buhai 申不害 was made the chancellor of Hann, and he began to make reforms to the state; it started to gather strength.

341 BCE - Wei 魏 attacked Hann 韓; Qi 齊 again sent Sun Bin 孫臏 to march off to the rescue. Sun Bin employed a deception and defeated Pang Juan 龐涓 at the Maling Gorge 馬陵; the crown prince of Wei, Shen 魏太子 魏申 was captured while General Pang Juan committed suicide.

340 BCE - Wey Yang 衛鞅 led the Qin forces 秦 against the Wei army 魏, which was defeated, the king of Wei sued for peace by ceding the areas west of the River *Hexi* 河西.

340 BCE - Wei 魏 moved its capital from Anyi 安邑 to Daliang 大梁 to avoid confrontation with Qin 秦.

340 BCE - Qin 秦 enfeoffed Wei Yang 衛鞅 with fifteen counties, and gave him the title of Marquis of Shang 商君.

338 BCE - Duke Xiao of Qin 秦孝公 died, the nobles and elites at Qin took revenge on Wey Yang 衛鞅, he was dismembered by five charging carriages.

334 BCE - Chu 楚 defeated Yue 越, annexing the territories that previously belonged to the defunct kingdom of Wu 吳, the kingdom of Yue became a protectorate of Chu.

333 BCE - Su Qin 蘇秦 and Zhang Yi 張儀 promoted their concepts of forming the Vertical Alliance 合縱 (South-North) and Horizontal Coalition 連橫 (East-West).

321 BCE - Qi, Sir of Mengchang 齊 孟嘗君, hosted several thousand of guests at his manor.

Volume III. 資治通鑒 卷第三 周紀三 320-298 BCE

The narratives of this volume begin in the first year of King Shenjing of Zhou 周 慎靚王 (320 BCE) and end in the 17th year of King Nan of Zhou 周赧王 (298 BCE).

318 BCE – Chu 楚, Zhao 趙, Wei 魏, Hann 韓 and Yan 燕 formed an alliance against Qin 秦; the alliance was defeated.

317 BCE - Qin 秦 defeated Hann 韓 at Youyu 脩魚; some eighty thousand men were decapitated.
A Qi 齊 minister assassinated Su Qin 蘇秦.

316 BCE - King Hui of Qin 秦惠王 accepted Sima Cuo's 司馬錯 advice sent an army against Shu 蜀. Qin took over the land and became more powerful.
Ji Guai, the king of Yan 燕 姬噲 abdicated his throne to his chancellor, Zi Zhi 燕 子之.

314 BCE - Zi Zhi 燕 子之 sat on the throne of Yan and ruled for three years, Yan fell into chaos. General Shi Bei 市被 and the former heir apparent, Ji Ping 燕 姬平 conspired against Zi Zhi, the kingdom fell into internecine warfare that lasted for several months, several tens of thousands of civilians and soldiers died. Qi 齊 took advantage of the chaos, sent in their army and executed Zi Zhi and King Ji Guai 姬噲.

313 BCE - Zhang Yi 張儀 lobbied at Chu 楚 on behalf of Qin 秦, offering 600 *li* of land to Chu to break up the alliance with Qi 齊.

312 BCE - Chu 楚 humiliated by the land offer deceit sent an army against Qin 秦 and lost. King Zhao of Yan 燕昭王 was placed on the Yan throne; he shared the trials and tribulations with his people.

311 BCE - Zhang Yi 張儀 lobbied the fief lords to form the Horizontal Coalition. Zhang Yi was enfeoffed.

Ying Si, the king of Qin 秦 嬴駟 died lifting a cauldron.

310 BCE - Zhang Yi 張儀 left Qin 秦 and died in Wei 魏.

307 BCE - King Wuling of Zhao 趙 武靈王 introduced foreign clothing 胡服 and archery on horseback 騎射.

305 BCE - King Wuling of Zhao 趙 武靈王 defeated Zhongshan Kingdom 中山.

Wei Ran 魏冉 assumed power at the Qin court 秦, placing his nephew Ying Ji 嬴稷 on the throne and he followed up by exterminating the remnants of the Qin nobles.

299 BCE - King Wuling of Zhao 趙 武靈王 abdicated his throne to his youngest son, and gave himself a title of 'Supreme Lord' *zhufu* 主父.

299 BCE - Qin 秦 lured King Huai of Chu 楚懷王 to go to the capital of Qin and held him hostage.

Lord Mengchang 孟嘗君 was made chancellor of Qin.

Lord Mengchang escaped from Qin.

Lord Pingyuan 平原君 played host to several thousand guests at his manor. His guest Gongsun Long 公孫龍 advanced a philosophical logic debate, "A white horse is not a horse." 白馬非馬論.

Volume IV. 資治通鑒 卷第四 周紀四 297-273 BCE

The narratives of this volume commenced during the 18th year (297 BCE) of the reign of King Nan of Zhou 周赧王 and ended in his 42nd year (273 BCE).

296 BCE - King Huai of Chu 楚懷王 died in Qin 秦.

295 BCE - The supreme lord of Zhao, *Zhufu* (Zhao Yong) 趙 主父 趙雍, assisted by Qi 齊 and Yan 燕 annihilated Zhongshan 中山.

There was internal strife at Zhao 趙; *Zhufu* 主父 died of starvation in Shaqiu 沙丘.

293 BCE - Qin army major, Bai Qi 秦將軍 白起 defeated Wei 魏 and Hann 韓 armies at Yique 伊闕, and decapitated two hundred and forty thousand men. King of Qin nominated Bai Qi as its security commander.

288 BCE - The sovereigns of Qin 秦 and Qi 齊 proclaimed themselves as emperors.

286 BCE - King Kang of Song 宋 康王 raised an army against Teng 滕, annihilating it; the army then attacked Xue 薛 and defeated Qi 齊 to its east, Chu 楚 to its south and west at Wei 魏. People called him Jie of Song 桀宋 (Despot-Song). King Min of Qi 齊湣王 raised an army against Song, annihilating it.

284 BCE - Yan general, Yue Yi 燕上將軍 樂毅 defeated Qi 齊, seventy walled-cities fell in six months.

283 BCE - Lin Xiangru 藺相如 returned the piece of priceless jade known as *heshibi* 和氏璧 to Zhao 趙.

279 BCE - Lin Xiangyu 藺相如 and General Lian Po 廉頗 became tested friends.
Tian Dan 田單 of Qi schemed a strategy, King Hui of Yan 燕惠王 replaced Yue Yi 燕樂毅 with Qi Jie 騎劫. Tian Dan recovered seventy walled-cities lost to Yan. King Xiang of Qi 齊 襄王 enfeoffed Tian Dan as Lord Anping 安平君.

278 BCE - Qin general, Bai Qi 秦將 白起 attacked Chu 楚, took Yingdu 郢都, and razed Yiling 夷陵 to the ground. Chu moved its capital to Chenqiu 陳丘; Qin changed Yingdu into a Southern Prefecture. Bai Qi was honoured as Lord Wuan 武安君.

Volume V. 資治通鑒 卷第五 周紀五 272-256 BCE

The narratives of this volume begin from the 43rd year of King Nan of Zhou 周 赧王 (272 BCE) and end in his 59th year (256 BCE).

270 BCE - Wei national Fan Ju 魏 范雎 submitted a memorial called the, 'Make an alliance with distant states, attack neighbouring states strategy' to the king of Qin. The king made him a foreign guest consultant – *keqing* 客卿.

266 BCE - King Zhaoxiang of Qin 秦 昭襄王 deposed the Queen Dowager, banishing Wei Ran 魏冉, Mi Rong 芈戎, Ying Kui 嬴悝 and Yin Xian 嬴顯; Fan Ju was made the chancellor of Qin.

265 BCE - Qin 秦 invaded Zhao 趙 and annexed three cities. The king of Zhao appealed to Qi 齊 for help; the grand tutor, Chu Long 觸龍 convinced the Queen Dowager to send her son to Qi 齊 as hostage, a prerequisite in exchange for military help.

262 BCE - Qin 秦 raided Hann 韓, driving a wedge into the middle section of the kingdom, the northern part of Shangdang 上黨 was separated from the Hann capital. Feng Ting 馮亭 the magistrate of Shangdang surrendered the prefecture to Zhao 趙.

260 BCE - Lian Po 廉頗 led the Zhao army to take a stand at Changping 長平. He refused to engage in battle with the larger Qin army, assuming a defensive strategy. King Xiaocheng of Zhao 趙 孝成王 fell for a Qin 秦 ruse by replacing Lian Po with Zhao Kuo 趙括, a brilliant theoretical military strategist. Qin sent in Bai Qi 白起. The battle was fought at Changping; Zhao Kuo died in a hail of arrows; four hundred thousand Zhao soldiers were led into an ambush and were summarily buried.

258 BCE - Qin 秦 followed up by advancing against Zhao's capital Handan 趙都 邯鄲. The king of Zhao sent Lord Pingyuan 平原君 to appeal to Chu 楚 for help. Mao Sui 毛遂 volunteered himself as a member of the entourage; his sharp wit forced the king of Chu to go to the aid of Zhao.

Wei Wuji, Lord Xinling 信陵君 魏無忌 stole Wei king's military tally to go to the aid of Zhao.

257 BCE - The king of Qin forced Bai Qi 白起 to commits suicide.

Zhao merchant, Lu Buwei 趙 呂不韋, helped Qin Prince Ying Yiren 秦太子 嬴異人 held hostage in Zhao to escape.

256 BCE - King Nan of Zhou 周 赧王 secretly revived the South-North Alliance, he failed and was captured and died in Luoyang 洛陽. This year marked the end of the Zhou Kingdom.

Volume VI. 資治通鑒 卷第六 秦紀六 255-228 BCE

The narratives of this volume begin in the 52nd year of the King Zhaoxiang of Qin 秦昭襄王 (255 BCE) and ends in the 19th year of Qin Shi Huangdi 秦始皇帝 (228 BCE).

255 BCE - Xun Kuang 荀況 discussed military strategies with King Cheng of Zhao 趙成王; the virtuous path of a sovereign, and the virtuous path of a general.

249 BCE - Qin 秦 annihilated the Eastern Zhou Kingdom 東周.

Lu Buwei was enfeoffed as Marquis Wenxin 文信侯 呂不韋 with one hundred thousand households; Qin 秦 annihilated Lu 魯.

247 BCE - Ying Zheng 嬴政 succeeded to the throne at an age of thirteen. Lu Buwei was the regent; Ying Zheng addressed him as Uncle *zhongfu* 仲父 呂不韋.

246 BCE - The state of Zheng 鄭 planned construction works at Qin 秦 to weaken the Qin economy; the result was exactly opposite; it became richer and more prosperous.

244 BCE - Zhao Li Mu 趙 李牧 took on the Xiongnu 匈奴, who lost a hundred thousand cavalrymen; for more than ten years, the Xiongnu did not encroach upon the Zhao border.

Qin 秦 and Yan 燕 constructed Long-Walls to defend against the Xiongnu; the nomadic tribes rose.

241 BCE - Chu 楚, Zhao 趙, Wei 趙, Hann 韓 and Wey 衛 armies formed a South-North Alliance against Qin 秦. Qin opened its gate at Huguguan Pass 函谷關; the Alliance forces dispersed.

238 BCE - The Qin King's mother doted on Lao Ai 長信侯 嫪毐, he was made Marquis Changxin, and he interfered with court affairs.

Lao Ai tried to take on Qiniangong Palace 蘄年宮; the insurrection failed; the five-chariot chastisement dismembered Lao Ai, his entire family clan was annihilated.

237 BCE - Li Si 李斯 the foreign guest being banished from Qin made a last-minute submission to Ying Zheng 嬴政, who asked him to return and adopted his strategies.

236 BCE - Lu Buwei 呂不韋 was relieved of all his duties.

235 BCE - Lu Buwei took his own life.

233 BCE - Hann Fei 韓非 was sent to Qin as an envoy, he made a submission to the king of Qin. Li Si 李斯, envious of the ability of Hann Fei, forced him to commit suicide.

230 BCE - Qin 秦 annihilated Hann 韓, king of Hann, Hann An 韓安 was captured; the kingdom was renamed the Yingchuanjun Prefecture 穎川郡.

228 BCE - Qin annihilated Zhao 趙, the King of Zhao was captured. Prince of Zhao, Zhao Jia 趙公子 趙嘉 escaped to Dai proclaimed as the king of Dai 代王.

The prince of Yan, Ji Dan 燕太子 姬丹, plotted with Jing Ke 荆軻 to assassinate Ying Zheng 秦王 嬴政.

Volume VII. 資治通鑒 卷第七 秦紀二 227-209 BCE

The narratives of this volume commence from the 20th year of the Emperor Shi Huangdi of Qin, Ying Zheng 秦始皇帝 in 227 BCE and end in the 1st year of the Second Emperor of Qin, Ershi Huangdi 二世皇帝 (209 BCE).

227 BCE - Jing Ke 荆軻 made an unsuccessful attempt to assassinate the King of Qin, Ying Zheng 秦王嬴政.

226 BCE - Qin General Wang Jian 秦將 王翦 attacked Yan 燕, defeating the Yan army; Crown Prince Ji Dan 姬丹 escaped to Liaodong 遼東. The king of Yan sent an assassin to cut off the head of the crown prince to sue for peace.

225 BCE - Qin General, Wang Ben of 秦將軍 王賁 annihilated the Wei Kingdom 魏, the king of Wei, Jia 魏王 魏假 was executed.

224-223 BCE - Qin General, Wang Jian of 秦將 王翦 invaded Chu, Mi Fuchu, King of Chu 楚王 羋負芻 was captured; Chu was annihilated.

222 BCE - Qin General Wang Ben 秦將軍 王賁 led an army against Liaodong 遼東, Ji Xi 燕王 姬喜, the king of Yan was captured. Yan met its end.

Wang Ben continued with his success, and defeated the Zhao Kingdom 趙 at Dai 代; the king of Dai, Zhao Jia 代王 趙嘉 was captured.

222-221 BCE - Qin General Wang Ben 秦將軍 王賁 attacked Qi 齊, the king of Qi, Tian Jian 田建 surrendered.

221 BCE - The Qin Kingdom unified the entire world 秦統一天下. Qin Shi Huangdi 秦始皇帝 maintained that his virtues exceeded the Three Emperors, and his exploits were beyond the Five Kings 三皇五帝; he changed his title to Huangdi 皇帝 – the August Emperor. He divided his kingdom into thirty-six prefectures. He unified measurements and weighing system. He repatriated one hundred and twenty thousand heroes and valiant households to Xianyang 咸陽 by decree, then ordered the construction of expressways throughout his Kingdom.

220-219 BCE - The Emperor made expeditions and tours throughout his kingdom. At the tops of the Yishan 嶧山, Langya 琅琊, Zhifu 之罘 mountains he erected stone steles in praise of his successful exploits.

219 BCE - The emperor ascended to the summit of Taishan Mountain 泰山封禪, where he made sacrifices to Heaven and made sacrifices to the Earth deities.

Ying Zheng 嬴政 travelled to the shore of the Eastern Sea, where he sent off the Qi 齊 occultist Xu Fu 徐福 to lead thousands of virgin boys and girls to set sail, he went in search of the immortals and the elixir of life.

215 BCE - Ying Zheng 嬴政 sent Meng Tian 蒙恬 to head up three hundred thousand troops to attack the Xiongnu 匈奴 and to construct Long-Walls 長城 to prevent the encroachment by the nomadic tribes.

214 BCE - Five hundred thousand convicts and civilians were relocated at Wuling 五嶺 in the far south of the kingdom.

213 BCE - Ying Zheng 嬴政 buried scholars and burned books 焚書坑儒.

212 BCE - Meng Tian 蒙恬 was ordered to construct expressways from Yunyang 雲中 to Jiuyuan 九原, the task was never completed. Ying Zheng conscripted seven hundred thousand convicts to construct the Epang (Afeng) 阿房宫 palace and his burial mound at Lishan 驪山.

210 BCE - Ying Zheng 嬴政 died at Shaqiu 沙丘. Zhao Gao 趙高 and Li Si 李斯 fabricated the imperial decree made Ying Huhai 嬴胡亥 the successor to the throne; then decreed that Ying Fusu 嬴扶蘇, the crown prince, take his own life. Shi Huangdi 秦始皇帝 was buried at Lishan Mound 驪山. Meng Tian and Meng Yi 蒙毅 were executed.

209 BCE - Ying Huhai 二世皇帝 嬴胡亥 meted out a bloodbath executing his brothers, sisters and nobles. Chen Sheng 陳勝 and Wu Guang 吳廣 took up arms and revolted. Liu Bang 劉邦 raised an army at the County of Pei 沛縣. Xiang Liang 項梁 and Xiang Yu 項羽 rebelled at Kuaiji 會稽. The former nobles of various kingdoms during the times of the Warring States also revolted.

Volume VIII. 資治通鑒 卷第八 秦紀三 208-207 BCE

The narrations of this volume commence from the 2nd year of the Second Emperor of Qin Ershi Huangdi 秦二世皇帝 (208 BCE) ending in the 3rd year of his reign (207 BCE).

208 BCE - Chen Sheng 陳勝 led his army against the Qin government forces 秦 in the west; Qin general Zhang Han 秦將 章邯 defeats the rebels.
Chu generals 楚軍 murdered Wu Guang 吳廣.
Chen Sheng 陳勝 was murdered by his coachman, Zhuang Jia 莊賈.
Xiang Liang 項梁 learning of the death of Chen Sheng 陳勝 adopted strategy proposed by Fan Zhen 范增, placed Mi Xin 楚王 芈心, the grandson of King Huai of Chu 楚懷王 on the throne; the capital was established at Xuyi 盱眙.
The Second Emperor, Ershi Huangdi 秦二世皇帝, was fatuous and despotic, trusting only the eunuch Zhao Gao 趙高, assigning all national affairs to his care. Zhao Gao forced the death of Chancellor Feng Quji 馮去疾, Commander Feng Jie 將軍 馮劫; and executed the Left Chancellor Li Si 左相 李斯; all their family clan members were executed.

Zhao Gao was made chancellor; he decided everything important or otherwise.
Xiang Laing 項梁 defeated the Qin army 秦 on numerous occasions became arrogant. Qin general Zhang Han 秦將 章邯 soundly defeated the Chu general at Dingtao 定陶; Xiang Liang died in battle.
King Huai of Chu 楚懷王 pledged, whoever enters the Inner Pass *guannei* 關内 first, would be enfeoffed as King.

The Chu King 楚懷王 ordered Liu Bang 劉邦 to march west against the Qin government, while Xiang Yu 項羽 was to march t the north to bring relief to Julu 鉅鹿.

207 BCE - Xiang Yu 項羽 executed Song Yi, the Chu supreme commander 卿子冠軍 宋義; he followed up by marching north to give aid to Julu 鉅鹿, enjoining his men to wreck all the vassals for the river crossing, bringing with them only three days of rations to show resolve. The Qin army was defeated at Julu.

General Zhang Han 秦將 章邯 capitulated to Chu 楚, Xiang Yu 項羽 made him the king of Yong 雍王.

Zhao Gao 趙高 assumed total control of the Qin court, ministers and officers at court dared not challenge him.

Zhao Gao murdered Ershi Huangdi 秦二世皇帝 and made Ying Ying (Zi Ying) 秦王 嬴嬰 (子嬰) the King of Qin.

Zi Ying executed Zhao Gao and annihilates his three family clans.

THE AUTHOR

Joseph P. Yap is a self-educated historian. Having spent many years in the business community as a corporate executive, he decided to turn his attention to translating ancient Chinese texts into English. He believes that there is certainly no shortage of excellent translators, particularly from the academic world. However the literature we inherit from the ancient Chinese are so vast that numerous books and texts are still left unattended, and he believes that these valuable texts and chronicles should be made available to a wider English readers. He published his first book *The Wars with the Xiongnu* in 2009. He is presently working on Book 2 and Book 3 - Volume 9 to 30 of *Zizhi tongjian* – The Han Empire.

35574383R00389

Printed in Great Britain
by Amazon